MARKETING

MARKETING

AN INTRODUCTORY TEXT SEVENTH EDITION

MICHAEL J. BAKER

WP

First edition 1971, reprinted 1972, 1973
Second edition 1974, reprinted 1976, 1977, 1978
Third edition 1979, reprinted 1980, 1981 (twice), 1982, 1983
Fourth edition 1985, reprinted 1986, 1987, 1988, 1990
Fifth edition 1991, reprinted 1993, 1994
Sixth edition 1996, reprinted 1997
Seventh edition 2006

Westburn Publishers Ltd
23 Millig Street
Helensburgh
G84 9LD
Argyll
Scotland, UK

visit us on the World Wide Web at:
http://www.westburn.co.uk

Designed by Design Deluxe Ltd.

ISBN-13: 978-0-946433-03-2
ISBN-10: 0-946433-03-8

British Library Cataloguing-in-Publication Data
A catalogue record for this book is available from the British Library

10 9 8 7 6 5 4 3 2 1

Printed and bound in the United Kingdom by Bell and Bain Ltd.

CONTENTS

7   The distribution of consumer goods – retailing

8   Consumer behaviour

9   Organisational buying behaviour

10   Market segmentation

Part Three – The Marketing Mix

20 Personal selling and sales promotion

Part Four - Marketing in Practice

21 The company: organising for marketing

22 Planning and implementing marketing

PREFACE TO THE SEVENTH EDITION

The first Edition of *Marketing: An Introductory Text* was published by Macmillan in 1971. It was one of only three general texts by a British author and ran to 287 pages. As the printing history reveals, between then and 1996 it went through five further editions and seventeen reprints; it was the English Language Book Service preferred text for sale in less affluent countries; and was also translated into other languages.

Reviews of the Sixth edition (1996) had the following to say:

"This is a tried and tested text which has already proved its worth to thousands of students." (Norman Waite)

"Michael has an unrivalled claim to being the most influential force in the development of marketing education in Britain during the last twenty years. This book is deservedly recognised as a classic for those coming to the subject for the first time - yet still contains important insights and lessons for those established in the profession. It is a book of substance and quality which has been, and will continue to be, a fundamental building block of marketing education." (Peter Turnbull)

"Michael Baker's Marketing: An Introductory Text has greatly helped to shape marketing education in Britain over the decades." (John Saunders)

So why has a Seventh Edtion been so long in preparation? Essentially because, as a result of mergers and acquisitions in the book publishing industries, many of the major players found themselves with several titles that previously competed with each other were now in the same list. In consequence, and to secure the economies of scale that had prompted the acquisitions, many well established texts were discontinued so that publishers could concentrate on the mass market.

So Macmillan metamorphosed into Palgrave and decided not to invest in a Seventh edition. Inevitably, as time passes a textbook becomes dated and sales fall away. Now, under some contracts, if a book goes out of print, and the publisher does not reprint it, the rights revert to the author who can look for another publisher. And so here is a completely revised version of what used to be the best-selling book of its kind, published by Westburn Publishers which is best known for its academic journals.

While the content and structure of this Seventh Edition has been extensively revised and updated, its positioning remains the same. In my view marketing is an applied social science. Like many other professionally oriented subjects – medicine, architecture, engineering – marketing is a synthetic discipline that seeks to pull together theories, knowledge, and ideas from a variety of more theoretically based 'single disciplines', and integrate them into a holistic approach capable of implementation through practice.

Marketing's foundations are to be found in three major, and much longer established disciplines – economics (and particularly micro economics which deals with the behaviour of individuals and firms in the market place), psychology –

which is concerned with individual behaviour, and sociology – which is concerned with the behaviour of people in social groupings and organisations, both formal and informal.

The discipline of marketing relates essentially to the process of exchange, of the context within which it occurs, which is bounded and constrained by the environment, its institutions and infrastructure, and the managerial activities involved in shaping supply to satisfy demand. To this end the book is divided into Four Parts. The first of these deals with the nature of marketing in theory and practice, and with the market as a mechanism for ensuring that supply matches demand. The second part deals with the theoretical underpinnings derived from the core disciplines, while the third looks at the heart of marketing practice – the management of the marketing mix. Finally, we conclude with a discussion of the application of marketing in practice.

The preparation of this edition benefited greatly from a competitive analysis undertaken by the third year marketing class at Strathclyde University, members of which have read most of the best known textbooks. Their conclusions were that, apart from the obvious need to update the content, the substance of the book and its approach stood up well, especially in relating theory to practice and in offering alternative explanations and arguments rather than a simplified and homogenised description. The design of the book and the absence of support materials were seen as weaknesses, but most students felt that in many cases these were overdone resulting in high prices.

Listening to the voice of the customer is a sound marketing principle. Accordingly, this edition has:

- Been designed in two colours, which enhance navigation of the text, with key terms highlighted and summarised in a comprehensive Glossary
- Avoids the inclusion of pictures that add little to the verbal explanation, but add significantly to the size and cost of a book;
- Passes on the savings made in printing with a competitive price;
- Has an associated website *www.marketing7e.com* on which the student will find a Study Guide; access to the Westburn Dictionary of Marketing ,advice on the Written Analysis of Case Studies, and case studies.
- And for lecturers, a full set of PowerPoint presentations complete with notes.

As for the structure of the text, the chapter sequence has been modified to improve the flow of the material but the main changes may be summarised as:

1 Chapter 9 – Channels of Distribution has been divided into two chapters; Chapter 6 The Business System looks at business channels while Chapter 7 is focused on The Distribution of Consumer Goods – Retailing.

2 A completely new Chapter 14 deals with the subject of Branding and Brand Management.

3 The former Chapter 16 is now Chapter 18 –Mass Communication.

4 Chapter 19 is new and deals with Direct Marketing.

5 The separate chapters on Personal Selling and Sales Promotion have been combined.

I think this is a worthy successor of the sixth edition. I hope you do so too, and would be delighted to receive any feedback that might make the next edition even better.

Michael J. Baker,
University of Strathclyde   January 2006

ACKNOWLEDGEMENTS

The publishers would like to thank the following for their permission to reproduce copyright material in this text.

American Marketing Association
Booz Allen Hamilton Inc.
bradgroup
CACI
Cambridge University Press
Cinema Advertising Association
Controller of HMSO
DMIS
Edward Elgar
Elsevier
GfK NOP
Government Actuary's
Haymarket Business Publications Ltd.
Houghton Mifflin Company
IGD
Indian Institute of Management,
    Ahmedabad, India
ISP
John Wiley & Sons, Ltd.

Keith Crosier
Management Horizons
Riten Bhatia
Nielsen Media Research
Nigel Piercy
NRS Ltd
Palgrave Macmillan
Pearson Education, Inc.
Pira International Ltd.
Pierre Rodocanachi
Royal Mail
Simon and Schuster, Inc.
SRI Consulting Business Intelligence
The Conference Board
The McGraw-Hill Companies, Inc.
The Ogilvy Group Inc.
The University of Chicago Press
Thomson Learning
WARC (World Advertising Research
    Center)

Every effort has been made to trace the owners of copyright material within this text, however, the publisher would be pleased to receive any additional information available.

PART ONE

> "The enigma of marketing is that it is one of mankind's oldest practices, but the most recent of the business disciplines."

While the above comment was made some thirty years ago, it is still true today – everyone thinks that they know what 'marketing' is, but relatively few really do. The purpose of this book is to help correct this situation by providing an overview of what the marketing *discipline* is really all about – what in other disciplines is called the **normative theory**.

Now one of the problems with theory is that most people consider it some kind of airy-fairy thinking that has little, if anything, to do with the real world. Nowhere is this more true than with the subject of marketing where many perceive there to be a huge gap between theory and practice. One explanation for this is that, whatever your age, you have a lifetime's experience of being a consumer and so a lifetime's experience of being on the receiving end of marketing practice. However, being familiar with something does not necessarily mean that you understand it – I am typing this on my PC but haven't the faintest idea how it works.

If you study this book carefully then, by the time you have finished reading it, you should have a sound understanding of the subject. Such an understanding is fundamental to any professional practice be it accounting, architecture, engineering, medicine, marketing or what have you.

So what is this 'normative theory', and how does it relate to practice? The short answer is that normative theory spells out *how* you should do something to achieve the best results. It is prescriptive, and it is based on observation of what works best in practice. However, simple observation alone may not be sufficient to enable us to understand and explain a phenomenon. In order to do so we may need to repeat an observation many times, under many different circumstances, before we can detect a pattern and come up with a plausible explanation. And, when we have, we will have to keep testing the explanation – or knowledge – to check that it is correct.

Some things we can only learn, or confirm, through direct experience – but life is too short to learn much this way. Most things we can learn from other people's experience. Formal study of a body of knowledge, and the normative theory based on it, is a much quicker and cost effective way to learn about most complex subjects. Clearly, you know and believe this or you would not be reading a textbook, or studying for a qualification.

Most of this book is concerned with theoretical explanations of why things are the way they are in the domain of marketing, and the implications of this for buyers and sellers in a market. To begin with though Part One will seek to explain the nature of marketing and some of the distinguishing features of the context in which it occurs.

WHAT IS MARKETING?

> ### Learning Goals *After reading this chapter you should be able to:*
>
> - State the basic principles underlying the concept and practice of marketing.
>
> - Trace the development of the marketing concept and explain why marketing was 're-discovered' in the second half of the twentieth century.
>
> - Review the theoretical foundations on which the practice is based and explain why marketing is a 'synthetic' discipline that underpins a professional practice.
>
> - Offer an opinion on the existence of a genuine theory of marketing in its own right.
>
> - Assess the relevance of theory and its application in practice.

INTRODUCTION

Sixty years ago the verb "marketing" was rarely encountered in everyday English usage. When it was it was almost invariably used in an old-fashioned, if not archaic, way to describe housewives buying everyday goods for household consumption. Indeed, its use was largely restricted to the purchase of fresh produce such as fish, meat and vegetables sold in specialised market places of a kind still to be found in many towns.

Today, the situation is totally different; 'marketing' is a word encountered everywhere, in every imaginable context. In addition to the buying and selling of goods and services, it is applied to people, places, and even causes – it has become ubiquitous. One result of this familiarity is that everyone thinks that they know what marketing is – and so they do in the way that we *understand* other practices like architecture, engineering and medicine. But, the fact that we think we know what these terms mean in a simplified and generalised way does not mean that we understand them in all their complexity – nor does it mean that we would be able to practice the subject professionally.

If you are reading this it is fairly safe to assume that you want to *understand* what marketing is, and that some of you may want to take up a career that involves the practice of marketing. If so, then this book will give you both an overview of the subject, as well as providing a sound foundation for more advanced study. Either way, in order to understand the subject it is necessary to define it, and that is the purpose of this introductory chapter.

To begin with, we summarise the commonplace perception of marketing and contrast it with what we believe is the reality. To explain and justify our belief, we review a wide selection of definitions of marketing and suggest that they can be classified into three major categories. In order to explain why there are different interpretations of the subject it is necessary to be aware of what it is that motivates us to consume, and how these drives, physiological and psychological, have influenced economic development. **Maslow's 'Hierarchy of Human Needs'** and **Rostow's 'Stages of Economic Development'** provide insight into these issues, and a useful foundation to trace the evolution of marketing from pre-history to the present day.

As we shall see, marketing as a professional practice is a management discipline, and **'scientific management'** only emerged at the beginning of the twentieth century with the writings of Henry Taylor. Accordingly, although we will show that many modern marketing practices can be traced back to the Industrial Revolution or earlier, marketing as we know it now is essentially a twentieth century phenomenon. If we are to understand it then it is essential that we are familiar with the changes that have occurred in the immediate past, and we cover these in some detail.

The chapter concludes with a summary of the status of marketing thought and practice today, together with an outline of some of the challenges facing the subject that will be addressed in more detail in later chapters.

THE MYTH AND THE REALITY

If you want to define something the best place to start usually is with a dictionary – the bigger the dictionary, the greater the number of explanations. However, for normal purposes *The Concise Oxford Dictionary* is an excellent place to start and, if we do, then we find the following: **marketed, marketing 1** *tr.* sell. **2** *tr.* offer for sale. **3** *intr.* Buy or sell goods in a market. Now, of course, you know the difference between the transitive and intransitive but, in case it has temporarily slipped your memory, a transitive verb requires a direct object, implicit or explicit, whereas an intransitive verb does not.

However, one is only likely to consult a dictionary if uncertain as to what a word means. But, as we noted in the introduction above, 'marketing' is such a familiar and ordinary word we are unlikely to do so. If you were to undertake a straw poll amongst family and friends not studying marketing, then we predict the majority would define marketing as some form of selling (the transitive use) rather that an activity that encompasses both buying and selling. Thus most customers/consumers regard marketing as something that is done to them, rather that an activity in which they are an active participant. Yet it is the latter that is meant by marketing theorists and practitioners. So, the perception that marketing is some kind of 'selling with knobs on' is a myth and not the reality.

A second myth is that marketing was 'invented ' in the United States, by firms like Coca Cola and McDonalds, and has only recently spread to other countries. In reality, exchange of goods and services was the first step towards civilisation as we know it today, and it is claimed that writing only came into existence several millennia BC when merchants needed to keep a record of their transactions. Further, even so-called modern marketing practices, like celebrity advertising, style obsolescence and direct mail campaigns, can be traced back to the Industrial Revolution.

Third, marketing is often portrayed as being deceptive and misleading using high-pressure sales techniques, promotion and advertising to encourage people to consume more – often of things they don't really need. In turn this leads to a materialistic society, a decline in values and a loss of social consciousness. As we shall see, the proponents of marketing argue that real marketing is based on enlightened self-interest in which both parties gain value from exchange – a win-win situation. This leads to an improvement in human welfare, increases the standard of living, and enhances the quality of life. While we will always try to identify criticisms of marketing – legitimate or not – the reader should be warned that we are in favour of the practice and are likely to present it in a favourable light.

Some definitions

Although the formal study of Marketing in the UK dates to the late 1950s, it had been taught in American universities from the mid-nineteenth century, and the first Professor of Marketing was appointed in the Wharton Business School in the 1880s. As a result there are many definitions of marketing, which reflect the development of the subject, and in Table 1.1 we have collected a selection from a variety of sources covering the period from 1920 to the present day. We have deliberately put these in chronological order as this begins to illustrate how people's perception of (modern) marketing has changed over time.

As we progress through this book many of the ideas encapsulated in these definitions will occur. The problem is that most of the definitions are not particularly memorable – especially those that try to include everything like 10, 11 and 12 - while those that don't are usually too vague to be of much practical use. However, as Keith Crosier observed, after reviewing more than 50 definitions in the 1970s, we can see that they fall into three distinct categories.

First, there are definitions that conceive of marketing as a *process*. Second, there are those that see marketing as a *concept or philosophy of business*. And, third, there are those that emphasise marketing as an *orientation*.

The **marketing as a process school** dominated thinking in the late nineteenth century through to about 1930. It was strongly associated with the land grant universities in the USA, with a concern for the selling and distribution of primary agricultural products, and the new business schools, mainly endowed by wealthy industrialists who had strong interests in industrial products, and what we now call business to business marketing (B2B). Individual consumers were of limited interest and economic concepts of competition and market forces commanded most attention.

The **marketing as a concept school** began to emerge in the 1930s when the experiences of the Great Depression made it clear that producers could not continue

Table 1.1 Marketing definitions

1   The function of marketing is the establishment of contact. (Cherington 1920)

2   Marketing is the process of determining consumer demand for a product or service, motivating its sale and distributing it into ultimate consumption at a profit. (Brech 1953)

3   Marketing is not only much broader than selling, it is not a specialised activity at all. It encompasses the entire business. It is the whole business seen from the point of view of its final result, that is, from the customer's point of view. Concern and responsibility for marketing must therefore permeate all areas of the enterprise.

4   Marketing is the distinguishing the unique function of the business. (Drucker 1954, items 3 and 4)

5   Marketing is the performance of business activities that direct the flow of goods and services from producer to consumer or user.

   ■ Marketing is the creation of time, place and possession utilities.
   ■ Marketing moves goods from place to place, stores them, and effects changes in ownership by buying and selling them.
   ■ Marketing consists of the activities of buying, selling transporting and storing goods.
   ■ Marketing includes those business activities involved in the flow of goods and services between producers and consumers. (Converse, Huegy and Mitchell 1965).

6   Marketing is the process whereby society, to supply its consumption needs, evolves distributive systems composed of participants, who, interacting under constraints – technical (economic) and ethical (social) – create the transactions or flows which resolve market separations and result in exchange and consumption. (Bartels 1968, pp.29-33).

7   Marketing is the set of human activities directed at facilitating and consummating exchanges. (Kotler 1972).

8   Marketing is concerned with the creation and maintenance of mutually satisfying exchange relationships. (Baker 1976).

9   The purpose of a business is to create and keep a customer. (Levitt 1983a).

10 Marketing is the business function that identifies current unfilled needs and wants, defines and measures their magnitude, determines which target markets the organisation can best serve, and decides on appropriate products, services, and programmes to serve these markets. Thus marketing serves as the link between a society's needs and its pattern of industrial response. (Kotler 1988).

11 Marketing is both a set of activities performed by organisations and a social process. In other words, marketing exists at both the micro and macro levels. Micro marketing is the performance of activities which seek to accomplish an organisation's objectives by anticipating customer or client needs and directing a flow of need-satisfying goods and services from producer to customer or client.

   Macro marketing is a social process which directs an economy's flow of goods and services from producers to consumers in a way which effectively matches supply and demand and accomplishes the objectives of society. (McCarthy and Perreault 1994).

12 Today we see the marketing concept as a statement of organisational culture, an agreed-on set of shared values among the employees of a company representing a commitment to put the customer first in all management and operations decision making. It calls for everyone in the organisation to think about their job in terms of how it delivers value to customers. (Webster 1994)

Table 1.1 Marketing definitions continued

13 Marketing is the management process responsible for identifying, anticipating and satisfying consumer's requirements profitably. (Chartered Institute of Marketing).

14 Activities that facilitate and expedite satisfying exchange relationships through the creation, distribution, promotion and pricing of products (goods, services, ideas). (Marketing Association of Australia and New Zealand).

15 "Marketing is an organisational function and a set of processes for creating, communicating and delivering value to customers and for managing customer relationships in ways that benefit the organisation and its stakeholders". (American Marketing Association, 2004)

16 Marketing is selling goods that don't come back to people who do. (Anon)

17 The delivery of a standard of living. (Anon.)

to expect an ever-growing demand to absorb all their output when competing mainly on price and the sale of largely undifferentiated products. Clearly, adopting the assumption that consumers are homogeneous did not reflect the reality. The theory of perfect or monopolistic competition began to give way to the theory of imperfect competition, and an acceptance that consumers are heterogeneous. This being so it is necessary to develop an understanding of consumer needs, and then create products and services to satisfy them – the essence of the marketing concept. In turn, this directed attention towards the behavioural sciences, and particularly psychology and sociology. However, the main emphasis was on demand stimulation through advertising and personal selling.

As we shall see, demand stimulation is a short-term solution to over-supply/ strong competition, and it was not many years before it was appreciated that a more radical approach was called for. Basically, it was recognised that success in the new competitive environment required a radical rethinking of the firm's basic strategy from one focused on production and selling i.e. the firm itself, to one focused on the market and customers. In other words the firm's primary orientation was to be marketing as reflected in Peter Drucker's definitions. Thus, from being a support function, marketing moved to centre stage and became the dominant *managerial* orientation - the marketing management school.

These three dimensions are all involved in modern marketing which is why we consider marketing to be a synthetic discipline.

MARKETING AS A DISCIPLINE

A 'discipline' is defined, inter alia, as: "a branch of instruction or learning", and "mental, moral, or physical training" (*Concise Oxford Dictionary*). In the former sense, students are more likely to think of a discipline as a subject of study like English, Mathematics, Chemistry etc., for these are the building blocks of courses of study in school, colleges and universities. In this sense, as we observed earlier, marketing is one of the most recent if not most recent of the business disciplines. When the first edition of this book appeared in 1971 there were only two Departments of Marketing in British universities and the first Honours degree in Marketing was introduced in 1973 at the University of Strathclyde. As for schools, there was no mention of it in the curriculum at all. Today, this has changed radically, and a straw poll of our first year class at Strathclyde in 2004 suggested that over a third of our new undergraduates had studied marketing before coming to university.

Despite this recognition, there is still a large number of people who are uncertain about the provenance or standing of marketing as an academic discipline. In part this is due to the proliferation of definitions of the subject, discussed earlier, combined with the fact that everyone is involved in marketing and so regards it as an everyday activity that doesn't require any formal study. Of course the same could be said about one's native language – while everyone can speak it, it doesn't mean that they fully understand it or are qualified to instruct others. Nor do you require a formal qualification of any kind to speak a language, and herein lies the problem in convincing some people that marketing is an academic discipline and a professional practice.

While the word '**profession**' embraces a host of meanings, including 'Trade, art, a vocation, business, calling, career, discipline and work' it is usually used in a more restricted sense to describe a practice which is regulated by its practitioners. In turn, this regulation restricts admission to persons who have demonstrated mastery of a defined body of knowledge that covers the philosophy, laws, principles, wisdom and so on, considered necessary for effective practice. The professions of architecture, engineering and medicine among others, have all gone through the process of defining, and redefining what constitutes the appropriate body of knowledge, and what one needs to achieve to be considered qualified.

Marketing, and its sister discipline Procurement, are now firmly established as professional practices as evidenced by their chartered status. Such status is only granted when a body of practitioners can satisfy the Privy Council that there is formal body of knowledge that can be examined, and that admission to the practitioner body is restricted to those who have successfully passed examinations in the subject at an appropriate level. Further, given evidence of experience in practice, and commitment to a programme of continuing professional development to keep their knowledge up-to-date, members of the Chartered Institute of Marketing can earn the designation 'Chartered Marketer' similar to the title Chartered Engineer awarded by the professional engineering bodies. But, what differentiates, Chartered Engineers, medical practitioners, solicitors and so on from Chartered Marketers, is, that like the old Craft Gilds, these other professions limit the practice of the profession to qualified members. While this may occur in marketing in the fullness of time, currently anyone can claim to be a marketing expert and there can be no doubt that the existence of 'quacks' and 'cowboys' does nothing for the reputation of the marketing profession.

Another thing that distinguishes professional qualifications from those in the single or 'core' disciplines is that they are **multi-disciplinary**, and it is this that prompted me to state that marketing is a **synthetic discipline**.

Ordinarily, when people speak of something as being 'synthetic' they mean that it is an artificial substitute for 'the real thing', just as nylon and polyester are man-made substitutes for cotton and wool. However, this is not the original sense of 'synthetic', and if we again consult our dictionary we find the meaning defined as: "the process or result of building up separate elements, especially ideas, into a connected whole, especially into a theory or system". This is the sense we intend when we call marketing a synthetic discipline because it seeks to synthesise knowledge and ideas derived from other disciplines into an integrated and *systematic* way of thinking about exchange processes.

What distinguishes modern marketing from earlier practice is that it has converted from a craft to a profession in exactly the same way as architecture, engineering and medicine, all of which are synthetic disciplines. Now the distinction between a craft and a profession is that crafts are based on directly acquired experience, whereas professions are based on the mastery of a body of knowledge that defines how the practice should be executed to optimum effect. In the case of synthetic disciplines the body of knowledge is derived from a number of other more narrowly defined 'single' disciplines like mathematics, physics, anatomy and physiology etc. One thing which tends to distinguish these subjects from multi-disciplinary subjects like marketing is their level of abstraction. In economics, for example, it is necessary to specify a series of assumptions in order to develop a theory of competition as an abstract concept against which to compare various real-world competitive states as a basis for further analysis and prediction.

Professional practices like marketing tend largely to eschew this kind of formal theorisation, and concentrate their efforts more on seeking to synthesise or integrate the insights and findings from the core disciplines into a holistic explanation of real, rather than abstract, problems. The difficulty with the latter was summarised succinctly in an article entitled *'Decay of the Dismal Science'* by Robert Chote (1995). He wrote:

> The obsession with algebraic elegance has led economists increasingly to interpret real world behaviour in ways that are theoretically defensible but palpably absurd. Some real business cycle theorists argue with straight faces, for example, that unemployment topped three million in the UK during the 1980s because the jobless were voluntarily taking more leisure time in the belief that work would be better paid a couple of years later.

There is, however, a significant difference between the more theoretically based social sciences, such as economics, psychology and sociology, and those based on them like marketing. Comparatively few persons who study the former subjects actually go into jobs as economists, psychologists or sociologists, while the great majority of people who study marketing do go into business, and those who specialise usually intend to practice. This is not to say that marketing lacks theoretical foundations – it does, and many of the these are the subject of chapters in Part II.

In the case of marketing, the core disciplines are mainly other social sciences, and include anthropology, economics, psychology and sociology. Their integration, and the emergence of marketing as a profession rather than a craft or practice, has only taken place within the last sixty years or so. To understand why this should be so – and we think it important that one does understand the origins of the subject – requires some knowledge of the history of exchange behaviour. In turn this calls for an appreciation of human motivation and its implications for economic development, and may be found in two well know theories developed by Abraham Maslow and W. W. Rostow.

First, however, it will help if we define the context within which exchange behaviour occurs which, at the macro level, is an **economy**. Nowadays we think mainly of national economies but, in fact, an economy is any definable community and economics is concerned with its wealth and resources, especially the production and consumption of resources. With regard to resources it is assumed, and so accepted, that these are scarce so that the fundamental problem of an economy may be defined as *maximising satisfaction through the consumption of scarce resources.*

This definition requires us to find answers to three questions which Samuelson (1989) identified as:

1   *What* commodities shall be produced and in what quantities? That is, how much and which of alternative goods and services shall be produced?

2   *How* shall goods be produced? That is, by whom and with what resources and in what technological manner are they to be produced?

3   *For whom* are goods to be produced? That is, who is to enjoy and get the benefit of the goods and services provided? Or, to put it another way, how is the total of the national product to be distributed among different individuals and families?

Clearly, the place to start is with some understanding of what gives the individual satisfaction, and to answer this question we need to understand human motivation.

A THEORY OF HUMAN MOTIVATION

This heading was the title of an article published in the *Psychological Review* by Abraham Maslow in 1943 that has become one of the best known and widely referenced 'theories' in the whole field of business and management studies.

According to Maslow we possess five basic needs that can be placed in a hierarchy such that as lower order needs are satisfied we lose interest in them and concentrate on satisfying the most pressing needs at the next higher level. These five needs are illustrated in Fig. 1.1.

At the bottom of the hierarchy are **physiological needs**. These are basic drives that are essential to survival. Some like hunger and thirst arise mainly from internal stimuli, but others, like the threat of pain, injury or death, may be triggered by external stimuli.

It is generally believed that these needs are dominant and override all other

Figure 1.1 Maslow's 'Hierarchy of Needs'

considerations although, in exceptional circumstances, persons such as suicide bombers seeking to satisfy higher order needs may suppress them.

Safety needs come next in importance and can themselves be ranked in a rough hierarchy - physical security; stable and routine pattern of living, avoiding the risk of the unknown; acquisition of protection against an uncertain future (religion, insurance). While physiological needs are specific to the individual, safety needs are often satisfied through group membership following the adage 'there's safety in numbers'. Individual behaviour is the primary focus of the discipline of Psychology, while group behaviour is the primary focus of the discipline of Sociology – an important reason why marketing needs to synthesise ideas from both.

Love needs include the need for affection and the feeling of belonging to a group - family, social group, work group, and so on. Much marketing activity seeks to cater for these needs, and includes some approaches most criticised by anti-marketers. For example, advertising that suggests that failure to use a product - toothpaste, shampoo etc. - will lead to ostracism or exclusion from a group you aspire to join.

Esteem needs include such things as recognition, status, prestige, reputation, and so forth. In affluent societies achievement of these needs is often reinforced and made public through the acquisition of physical objects which are felt to be appropriate to a person's position in life - clothing, motor cars etc. etc. See the Sunday supplements for a sample of such objects!

Self-actualisation represents the highest level of need to 'do one's own thing'. Relatively few people would seem to aspire to or reach this level, being content to lead a materialistic life keeping up with the Jones'. However, when people are at this level they are usually little interested in or influenced by the market place.

Maslow's need levels are reflected closely in the history of economic development. For an understanding of this we can learn a lot from Rostow's theory.

ECONOMIC DEVELOPMENT AND THE
EVOLUTION OF A THEORY OF CONSUMPTION

If one examines the development of an advanced economy such as our own, one can clearly distinguish a number of phases through which it has passed, each of which represents a step forward as compared with the preceding stages.

Perhaps the best known, and some would argue the most important, discussion of the stages in economic development is to be found in W. W. Rostow's *The Process of Economic Growth* (1962). In his preface to the second edition, Rostow states 'The objective here is to provide a framework of theoretical concepts within which the variety of growth experiences can be systematically arranged, similarities and differences systematically isolated.' The outcome is summarised in the penultimate chapter, 'The Stages of Economic Growth', in which he distinguishes the following:

1 The traditional society.
2 The pre-conditions for take-off.

3   The take-off.

4   The drive to maturity.

5   The age of high mass consumption.

6   Beyond the age of high mass consumption. (subsequently Rostow designated this stage 'The search for quality').

The arguments underlying Rostow's thesis are not amenable to the kind of simplification which is necessary when addressing a sub-issue in an introductory textbook, and merit consideration in full, However, his 'stages' have proved to be a very robust concept, and provides a useful framework for distinguishing between economies at different stages of development and, thereby, for discussing the relevance and application of various marketing principles and practices. For example, consider the salient characteristics of each stage:

Traditional societies are characterised by a lack of systematic understanding of their physical environment and the 'technology and tools necessary to achieve any significant improvements in productivity'. In such societies 75 per cent or more of all activity is focused in the food production necessary to sustain the society and any surplus tends to be controlled by rich landowners who dissipate it rather than invest in new technology.

The initial **pre-conditions for take-off** were created in Western Europe out of two characteristics of the post-medieval world which interacted and reinforced each other: the gradual evolution of modern science and the modern scientific attitude; and the lateral innovation that came with the discovery of new lands and the rediscovery of old, converging with the impulse to create new technology at certain strategic points. The **widening of the market** – both within Europe and overseas – brought not only trade but increased specialisation of production, increased inter-regional and inter-national dependence, enlarged institutions of finance, and **increased market incentives** to create new production functions. (Rostow, *Process of Economic Growth*, my emphasis).

The **take-off** consists, in essence, of the achievement of rapid growth in a limited group of sectors, where modern industrial techniques are applied. Technically, take-off is distinguished as occurring when society is able to sustain an annual rate of net investment of around 10 per cent, and 'usually witnesses a definitive social, political and cultural victory of those who would modernise the economy over those who would either cling to the traditional society or seek other goals'. To achieve this, the 'corps of entrepreneurs and technicians must be enlarged, and sources of capital must be institutionalised' so that it can be deployed into the most promising growth opportunities. It can be seen that emerging economies like India and China are at this stage.

The **drive to maturity** is defined by Rostow as' the period when a society has effectively applied the range of [then] modern technology to the bulk of its resources', and he offers the following symbolic dates:

Great Britain	1850	Sweden	1930
United States	1900	Japan	1940
Germany	1910	Russia	1950
France	1910	Canada	1950

Of maturity, Rostow makes the following trenchant observation:

At maturity, however, the professional managers become more important: the nameless, comfortable, cautious committee men who inherits and manage large sectors of the economy, while the society begins to seek objectives which include but transcend the application of modern technology to resources.

The **age of high mass consumption** is only one of three such objectives that Rostow distinguishes – the other two being increased security, welfare, and, perhaps, leisure to the working force; and enlarged power for the mature nation on the world scene. As he notes, 'A good deal of of the history of the first half of the twentieth century can be told in terms of the pattern and succession of choices made by various mature societies' among these three options.

While commentators like Galbraith (*The New Industrial State*) and others would seem to agree that there is another stage *beyond high mass consumption* the nature of this has yet to be determined. Like the highest stage in Maslow's hierarchy, Self-actualisation', this may consist of a recycling back to the values of a more traditional society. Concerns for the environment, 'Green marketing' 'retromarketing' and similar trends may well foreshadow this, and will be looked at in more detail later on. For now, given that Britain was the first economy to pass through most of the stages, a short review of its economic history will help illustrate how Rostow's Stages and Maslow's Need Hierarchy parallel one another.

The early beginnings

The early stages of economic development may be considered as falling into three distinct phases – **survival, self sufficiency,** and **specialisation.**

While there is no written record of the organisation of early communities, but long before the emergence of 'traditional society', it is clear that humankind very quickly came to understand the benefits of collaboration and exchange. If every individual, or individual family group, has to depend solely on its own resources then it is clear that the variety of things that can be produced and consumed is decidedly limited. Further, if one is a 'Jack of all trades', and keeps switching from one activity to another, then one's productivity will also suffer. Obviously, it would be much better if people concentrated on performing the tasks they perform best and the vestiges of gender stereotyping today still reflect this in casting males in the role of hunter/gatherer and females as homemakers. But this is a very crude and basic level of task specialisation – a subsistence economy in which even minor changes may have major effects.

The first step towards breaking this vicious circle occurred when tribes ceased to be nomadic, domesticated animals, and began to cultivate crops. For this to be possible exchange had to take place, and for this to be efficient there was a need for a known meeting place where those with surpluses to exchange could make contact with one another. This place was the **market**. The great thing about the market was that you could quickly see what was available, and negotiate on a face-to-face basis with the person offering goods for exchange. In the absence of money, barter is not the easiest or quickest way to establish the exchange value of different products and services, so the invention of 'money' as a store of value and medium of exchange, like writing, was created to facilitate exchange. Once an effective market exists, and a medium of exchange, then it is possible to take the first major step towards a stable and more affluent society. This step is task specialisation. When people concentrate on doing what they are best at they become more skilled and proficient, and individual productivity is increased. Further, because of certain natural advantages, people in some areas develop skills and products not available in others, and trade between communities begins to develop, and with it a new merchant class of intermediaries.

From the Norman Conquest to the mid-fourteenth century, England's economy was organised on a feudal basis in which the Manor represented the major economic unit of production and consumption. The Manorial system was based on an ideal of self-sufficiency under which each self contained community endeavoured to meet all its own requirements with regard to production and consumption. Under such a system the variety of goods available for consumption depended directly on the factors of production possessed by the community, and the skills of the people comprising it. The limitations imposed by the size of the unit, coupled with similar limitations with regard to the skill and knowledge of its members, effectively reduced this to a subsistence economy concerned primarily with satisfying the basic needs of life – food, clothing, shelter and safety.

For a variety of reasons the feudal system broke down far earlier in England than in Europe generally. Among the more important reasons was the shortage of labour following the Black Death, and the demand for English wool to trade with Europe for commodities not readily available in the economy. This demand encouraged the Manorial lords to free the serfs from their feudal duties so that they might possess the land and rear sheep on it. This dispossession of the serfs led to a migration of population from the country to the towns in search of employment in the developing craft industries.

Craft industry leads to specialisation in the production of particular goods with the increased productivity noted earlier. However, for many centuries, the practice of crafts was strictly controlled by Craft Gilds – the forerunners of the Trade Unions of the 19th and 20th centuries – to limit the quantity produced and keep prices up. This restraint of competition was partly offset by the Gilds requiring minimum standards of their members – an early case of quality control. In the absence of competition and the creation of surpluses, the population, and therefore the market, grew only slowly. This impasse was broken by a major break through.

The division of labour

The next stage of economic development is usually exemplified by Adam Smith's (1776) account of the pin making industry, where an enormous increase in output followed job simplification. Smith noted that where men were engaged in all processes involved in the manufacture of pins their average output was twenty pins per day; when the manufacture of pins was broken down into separate processes, output for the group rose to over four thousand pins per man per day.

Smith's description of this primitive production line identified at least ten different tasks:

> One man draws out the wire, another straightens it, a third cuts it, a fourth points it, a fifth grinds it at the top for receiving the head; the head requires two or three distinct operations; to put it on is a peculiar business, to whiten the pins is another; it is even a trade by itself to put them into the paper.

Two points are of particular significance in this step forward. First, organisation is required to bring together the men, provide a workplace and source raw materials. Second, the enormous increase in output reduces the price of the product, necessitates the development of channels of distribution to make it available to those with a demand for it, and leads to the exploitation of a much larger market. It also means that the 'factory' tends to produce standardised products and no longer makes to the order of individual customers

The Industrial Revolution – the breakthrough

The period when this change occurred was the time of a major breakthrough in economic development – the Industrial Revolution – which was to give a major impetus to the growth of a factory economy, job specialisation and mass production techniques. The nature of the steam engine as a power unit – large, inefficient and expensive – meant that its installation was only justified if it could be used to drive several smaller machines such as looms. This required the construction of factories in which machines and operatives could be assembled; while the simplification of the process meant that unskilled labour could be readily trained to perform simple operations.

Concurrent with the increase in output of both capital and consumer goods, lines of communication were developed (canals and, later, railways) as were distributive channels to cope with the movement and sale of this massively increased output. By 1800 we had already become 'a nation of shopkeepers', a derisory epithet used by Napoleon who was later to learn to his cost that only a rich and strong economy can support extensive service industries. It is important to remember that at this time Britain was virtually the sole source of supply for a world hungry for manufactured goods. The disposable income of the home consumer was small, but a rapid expansion of population due to advances in medicine and public health created a continually expanding market.

Industrialisation and international trade

Throughout the nineteenth century home industry expended enormously, as did world demand for our products. In 1850 Britain's exports amounted to nearly 40 per cent of all international trade, which, when it is realised that, by definition, the maximum any single nation could achieve is 50 per cent, is an extremely impressive figure. It is a performance that has never been surpassed, but the date also marked a watershed in international economic development. 1850 was to see the United States and, later, other European states emerge as competing industrial powers. At first the trend characteristic of the first half of the century continued – the export of capital goods to help establish basic industries in overseas countries in exchange for raw materials and food, along with a nearly insatiable demand for consumer goods. The development in other countries resulted in a considerable increase in total output so that, although Britain's share declined, its volume and value continued to increase rapidly as the increase in income in these other countries created an evergrowing demand for our products.

Initially, the newly emergent industrial economy must pass through the same stages noted in the case of Britain – namely, the development of basic industries such as iron and steel, which provide the raw materials of manufacturing industry, followed by the development of the latter along with lines of communication, and channels of distribution. However the process, and the drive to maturity, is considerably speeded up for the newcomer as it is able to make use of existing knowledge and skill, and unite all the latest design in plant and equipment pioneered by someone else. As a result the new industrial nations are able to achieve rapid economic growth, creating a growing demand for basic consumer goods which can largely be met by the economy itself. In the meantime, however, the original industrial nations are not standing still but are channelling their skill and knowledge into the production of more sophisticated products which the new industrial nations are eager, and able, to buy.

As a consequence of this economic development an increasing number of people are earning incomes that enable them to translate their latent demand for consumer goods into effective demand. The age of mass consumption, mass marketing and materialism has dawned.

The creation of 'excess supply'

Up until this stage in economic development, supply was constantly chasing an ever-increasing demand, largely fuelled by a rapidly expanding population. But, with increased affluence and better standards of living, there is a natural tendency for population growth to slow down, or even go into decline. Further, there is a physical limit to how much an individual can consume with the result that demand slows down, or even stagnates. Meantime technological and managerial innovation continues to fuel the growth of supply, with the result that in the most advanced economies there is the potential for the creation of excess supply.

Now it is clear that even in the most affluent countries there is an unequal distribution of wealth and, internationally, this is even more the case. So, while industrialisation and globalisation will both increase and help re-distribute wealth, since the middle of the last century there has been an **excess supply** of certain goods and services Today this is certainly true of many world markets and particularly consumer durables like motor cars, electronic products and white goods (washing machines, refrigerators etc.). The result of this change has been dramatic. No longer is demand for a product chasing a limited supply so that sale is an automatic consequence of production. Today large numbers of producers are competing for the privilege of supplying the consumer with their output, while trying to combat the claims of alternative or substitute goods. Under these conditions supply is controlled by demand rather than having to accept that which is supplied. Marketing must replace the narrower concept of selling in the sense of merely distributing one's output.

The situation now is one in which consumer demand dictates what will be produced. In a sense this has always been the case, as producers have always followed the path of least resistance and concentrated on those goods for which there is the strongest demand. When people have limited resources this is concentrated on essential requirements necessary for the maintenance of life, leaving very little for expenditure on desirable but less essential goods and services. This pattern is evident in many underdeveloped and less developed countries where around 90 percent of income is spent on essentials, leaving only 10 per cent for the purchase of medical services, non-essential foodstuffs and so on. In advanced economies the figure is nearer 50 per cent, even allowing for a significant increase in the variety and quality of the 'essentials', leaving an equal amount for the purchase of non-essential goods, services, leisure and saving.

Within the realm of essential purchases the nature and volume of demand are relatively simple to predict, and patterns of group behaviour are notably marked. But, in the case of discretionary demand, forecasting demand for any given good or service is notoriously difficult. It is this difficulty, allied to the increased competition between suppliers, that was to lead to the articulation of the modern marketing concept and acceptance of marketing as the primary orientation of the successful business.

TRADITIONAL MARKETING

This 'potted' history of the stages of economic development does scant justice to the subject but, it is hoped, sufficient to underline that marketing is not a recent innovation. What it shows is that for the great majority of recorded history demand has exceeded supply so that the emphasis in 'classical' economics has been the increase of supply to satisfy this demand. Indeed, this fact was so self-evident that Adam Smith in his *Wealth of Nations* (1776), makes only one reference to consumer demand when he states "Consumption is the sole end and purpose of production". The rest of his book is focused on how to increase production !

What economic history develops, above all else, is a sense of accelerating change. At the turn of the nineteenth century there were no steam locomotives or ships, large-scale steel production had still to be developed, as had the telephone, electricity, the internal combustion engine and innumerable other things that were familiar, although not commonplace, by the end of the century. In the twentieth century the tempo quickened, and within fifty years of the first manned flight, man had a satellite in space orbiting the earth. Table 1.2 indicates the elapsed time between 'invention' and commercial development of a number of familiar products and emphasises this increase in the tempo of technological change.

Two points need stressing here. First, each new development adds momentum to the process in that it increases productivity. This may be immediately discernible when automation is introduced, or less directly so when a more powerful computer enables us to solve problems previously thought insoluble. These, in turn, may provide the key to further technological advance. The second point is that increased wealth results in an overall improvement in the standard of living accompanied by an increase in the population and, thereby, the size of the market.

The 're-discovery' of marketing and the emergence of the modern marketing concept is generally attributed to the United States in the 1950s. As we shall see, several prominent names are associated with this event of whom a key contributor was Robert Keith who followed an historical approach in identifying what has become known as **"Three Era's" conceptualisation** – **Production**, **Sales** and **Marketing**.

Keith identified these three different eras based on the evolution of the Pillsbury Company in the USA. Pillsbury was, and is, a manufacturer of bakery products, a category of what are generically termed **fast moving consumer goods** or 'fmcg'. In the mid-nineteenth century its emphasis was on increasing supply and reducing costs – the primary characteristics of a **production orientation**. As new companies entered the market, and competition intensified, more emphasis was given to selling differentiated products; but this differentiation was based on what the firm could make using its existing technology and assets. So the distinguishing feature of a **sales orientation** is '*selling what we can make*'.

But, as we have seen, with the potential for excess supply, it became clear that selling harder needed to be replaced by selling *smarter*. Selling smarter means that, before committing yourself to the sale of a new product in the hope of maintaining competitiveness, you need first to establish what it is the customer wants. In the days of craft industry this was relatively simple – the potential customer discussed their wants with you, and you produced what they had specified. But, with industrialisation and the concentration of production in factories, a physical separation developed between producer and customer which, in time, became a psychological separation too. As long as demand exceeds supply then customers can't afford to be too choosy and have to buy what is available. But, as variety and choice increase customers will prefer those sellers whose offering most closely matches their needs – usually those who are closest to the customer – and others will go out of business for lack of custom. So, in order to restore and maintain competitiveness, a new strategy is called for which is based on determining what the customer wants and then *making what we can sell*. It is this that we call a **marketing orientation**.

Keith's description of the evolution of Pillsbury and the identification of three eras mirrors our description of overall economic development but is not universally accepted. Gilbert and Barley (1990) dismiss this so-called 'Traditional View' and comment:

> *Such a view infers that a sales orientation did not exist during (or before) the production era but came into being as a result of supply exceeding demand.*
>
> *Similarly, it suggests that marketing practices were not developed until it became apparent that pushing goods on to the market was not as effective as focusing on the provision of satisfaction.*

Table 1.2 Elapsed time, invention to commercial development, of some familiar products

Product	Time from invention to commercial exploitation
Electric motor	65 years
TV	52 years
Vacuum tube	33 years
Zip-fastener	30 years
X-ray tube	18 years
Frozen foods	15 years
Nuclear reactors	10 years
Radar	5 years
Solar batteries	3 years
Doubling of computing capacity	18 months

In order for the two suppositions above to be true, the 'Marketing Era' school of thought makes the following inferences:

- That neither sales nor marketing practices were fully applied in business until towards the end of the production era which lasted until the 1930s.
- That sophisticated marketing practices were not incorporated into business operations until the 1950s.
- There was little or no competition in the market place during the production era when demand exceeded supply.
- Firms gave little thought to marketing before and during the production era.

Clearly, these suppositions are unrealistic – you only have to visit the souk in Cairo or a bazaar in India to realise immediately that merchants have always worked hard to sell their wares. Whether or not this amounts to what we call marketing today is a matter of debate, but does raise the question....

How modern is modern marketing?

This rhetorical question was the title of an article published in the *Journal of Marketing* in 1988 (Fullerton). In this article Fullerton disputes the existence of a 'production era' for the following reasons:

1 *It ignores well established historical facts about business conditions- competition was intense in most businesses, over-production common, and demand frequently uncertain.*

2 *It totally misses the presence and vital importance of conscious demand stimulation in developing the advanced modern economies. Without such stimulation the revolution in production would have been stillborn.*

3 *It does not account for the varied and vigorous marketing efforts made by numerous manufacturers and other producers.*

4 *It ignores that dynamic growth of new marketing institutions outside the manufacturing firm.* (p 111)

A particularly telling point concerns the need for active demand stimulation, and the need for production and marketing to work in tandem. "Some of the famous pioneers of production such as Mathew Boulton and Josiah Wedgwood were also pioneers of modern marketing, cultivating large-scale demand for their revolutionary inexpensive products with techniques usually considered to have been post 1950 American innovations: market segmentation, production differentiation, prestige pricing, style obsolescence, saturation advertising, direct mail campaigns, reference group appeals, and testimonials among others". (p.112)

In Fullerton's view 'demand-enhancing marketing' spread from Britain to Germany and the USA. In the USA it was adopted with enthusiasm and Americans came to be seen as "the supreme masters of aggressive demand stimulation", a fact frequently referred to in contemporary marketing texts of the early 1890s. Numerous examples support Fullerton's contention that producers of the so-called production era made extensive use of marketing tools and techniques as well as integrating forward to ensure their products were brought to the attention of their intended customers in the most effective way.

Fullerton's analysis reflects a growing interest in the history of marketing thought and confirms that "modern marketing has a rich heritage worthy of our attention". (p 123) Whether one should substitute his conceptualisation as contained in his complex flux model for the widely accepted Production - Sales - Marketing Era's model is not seen as an either/or choice. Indeed, Fullerton's emphasis on the origins and evolution of marketing thought and practice reflects the historical research approach and merit attention in its own right. By contrast the 'Era's' model' is seen, at least by me, as serving a different purpose in that it seeks to distinguish between marketing as a practice clearly present in both the Production and Sales Eras, and marketing as a philosophy of business which shifts the emphasis from the producers pursuit of profit as the primary objective, to the achievement of customer satisfaction which, in the long-run, is likely to achieve the same financial reward.

NEO-CLASSICAL MARKETING

The discipline of economics was first articulated by thinkers such as Smith, Malthus and Ricardo, and was concerned primarily with issues of growth and development – hence Smith's *Wealth of Nations*. Over time interest developed in the principles of efficient resource allocation, and the proponents of this school were identified as 'neo-classical' to distinguish them and their ideas from those of the original, 'classical' economists. Although we are unaware that others have made such a distinction when tracing the evolution of marketing thought, we think it might be helpful to describe current ideas about marketing as 'neo-classical' on the grounds that the subject is still concerned with the same issues as the original writers on the subject. However, as we have seen, over time the relationship between supply and demand has changed radically requiring significant changes in the practice of marketing and the normative theory that seeks to explain it.

In the early 1990s an authoritative and widely accepted statement summarising the current status of marketing was given by Fred Webster Jr in an article entitled "The changing role of marketing in the corporation" (*Journal of Marketing*, October 1992). In this article Webster set out "... to outline both the intellectual and pragmatic roots of changes that are occurring in marketing, especially **marketing management**, as a body of knowledge, theory, and practice and to suggest the need for a new paradigm of the marketing function within the firm". (p 1)

In his article Webster dates the early roots of the development of marketing as an area of academic study to around 1910 with a growing interest in the marketing of agricultural products in the Midwestern land grant universities. Three separate schools were identified:

1 Focusing on the *commodities* themselves
2 Focusing on the *institutions* involved.
3 Focusing on the *functions* performed by these institutions.

All three schools tended to be descriptive rather than normative, with the functional being the most analytical and providing the basis for conceptual development.

Relatively little attention was given to managerial factors or orientation, and "marketing was seen as a set of social and economic processes rather than as a set of managerial activities and responsibilities." (p.2) This perspective began to emerge in the late Forties and early Fifties and, in Webster's view "The managerial approach brought relevance and realism to the study of marketing, with an emphasis on problem solving, planning, implementation, and control in a competitive marketplace." (p.2)

The new **Managerial School**, represented by scholars such as Howard (1957), McCarthy (1960) and Kotler (1967), looked upon marketing as a problem solving and decision-making process and drew heavily on analytical frameworks from economics, psychology, sociology and statistics. It was during the 1950s that the marketing concept was articulated, by writers such as Drucker (1954), McKitterick (1957) and Levitt (1960), emphasising customer satisfaction as the primary objective of the organisation with profit being seen as the reward.

Unsurprisingly, proponents of the institutional/functionalist view were not ready lightly to discard the accumulation of 50 years of writing and research, and the managerial approach was not received with universal enthusiasm. However, as calls for greater rigour in approaches to management education gathered momentum in the late Fifties and early Sixties so the Managerial School became dominant, and was to remain so for nearly three decades.

The foundation of the Managerial School was the basic **Micro economic paradigm** emphasising profit maximisation and the nature of transactions between buyer and seller. "Behavioural sciences models were used primarily to structure problem definition, helping the market researcher to define the questions that are worth asking and to identify important variables and the relationships between them." (p 3) To measure and analyse these relationships sophisticated statistical analysis was called for, and the marketing function grew within major organisations as groupings or departments containing individuals with the requisite expertise and professionalism - a development well-suited to the culture of large, divisionalised, bureaucratic and hierarchical organisations. Such organisations were the "engines of economic activity" (Miles and Snow 1984) for more than a century, and were the dominant organisations as the managerial approach to marketing developed in the 1950s and 1960s. Often, marketing departments evolved from sales department as these large organisations moved slowly to adopt the greater rigour and discipline offered by the new managerial orientation.

In the large, divisionalised corporations, where size and economies of scale and experience were seen as leading to competitive success, "The task of the marketing function was first to develop a thorough understanding of the marketplace to ensure that the firm was producing goods and services required and desired by the consumer." (p 4) Having done so, marketing was responsible for creating and sustaining consumer preference through manipulation of the mix variables - product, price, promotion and distribution. Centralised, corporate marketing departments were the order of the day.

During the late 1970s and early 1980s the move towards **decentralisation** began to gather momentum as the concept of the **strategic business unit (SBU)**, with profit and loss responsibility found favour with corporate management. Inevitably, decentralisation led to duplication and excessive numbers of layers of middle management. Faced with increased competition, both domestically and internationally, cost containment became an imperative and "downsizing" the consequence. However, downsizing was only a partial solution and more radical restructuring was clearly required.

The new organisations emphasised partnerships between firms; multiple types of ownership and partnering within the organisation (divisions, wholly-owned subsidiaries, licensees, franchisees, joint ventures, etc); teamwork among members of the organisation, often with the members from two or more co-operating firms; sharing of responsibility for developing converging and overlapping technologies; and often less emphasis on formal contracting and managerial reporting, evaluation and control systems. (p5)

Although Webster perceives no strong consensus in the terminology and typology for describing the new organisation forms, he proposes a continuum running from pure transactions through repeated transactions, long-term relationships, buyer-seller partnerships (mutual, total dependence), strategic alliances (including joint ventures), network organisations, to vertical integration.

As one moves along this continuum the role of the marketing function will change and Webster describes each of these phases in some detail. Based on his analysis of the evolution of exchange relationships Webster states:

The intellectual core of marketing management needs to be expanded beyond the conceptual framework of microeconomics in order to address more fully the set of organisational and strategic issues inherent in relationships and alliances." To do so will require closer consideration of phenomena which, traditionally, have been "the subject of study of psychologists, organisational behaviourists, political economists and sociologists. The focus shifts from products and firms as units of analysis to people, organisations, and the social processes that bind actors together in ongoing relationships. (p 10)

In order to consider the role of marketing in the evolving organisation Webster argues that it is essential to recognise that marketing really operates at 3 strategic levels - corporate, business or SBU, and functional or operation level. He argues further that it is a failure to distinguish clearly these three levels which underlies much of the misdefinition and misunderstanding of the marketing concept over the years. "In addition to the three levels of strategy we can identify three distinct dimensions of marketing - marketing as *culture*, marketing as *strategy*, and marketing as *tactics*" (original emphasis, p 10). Marketing as culture is the responsibility of corporate and SBU levels, marketing as strategy is the emphasis of the SBU level, and marketing as tactics is the focus of the operating level responsible for managing the marketing mix. Webster elaborates on each of these propositions and reiterates his view that "the political economy and organisational behaviour models seem to be more appropriate for a strategic view of the marketing function as distinct from the sales or demand stimulation function, for which the microeconomics paradigm is still more fitting." (p 13)

In conclusion, Webster offers us a definition and an opinion. Marketing is "…. the management function responsible for making sure that every aspect of the business is focused on delivering superior value to customers in the competitive marketplace." (p 14)

Webster's seminal article was to have an almost revolutionary impact on marketing thought in the USA with him being credited as the founder of what is the dominant paradigm of marketing today – relationship marketing. While this view is mistaken, there can be no doubt that Webster was instrumental in popularising relationship marketing as a truer reflection of the marketing concept than the marketing management approach that had preceded it.

THE EMERGENCE OF 'RELATIONSHIP MARKETING'

While the 'three eras' – production, sales, marketing – approach is too simplistic to reflect the complex reality, it did lead to the development of the managerial school described by Webster. As noted, this school of thought dominated the teaching and practice of marketing for around 30 years from 1960 to 1990, and was epitomised by the writings of Eugene McCarthy and Philip Kotler. It was McCarthy who introduced the **4Ps** of marketing – **Product**, **Price**, **Place**, and **Promotion** – which provided structure to most textbooks and courses, and is still evident today. As for Philip Kotler, his *Marketing Management* is probably the best-selling marketing textbook of all time, and is now in its twelfth edition. It was the sub-title of this book - 'Analysis, Planning and Control' – that firmly positioned marketing as a managerial function.

While the marketing management model was undoubtedly dominant, it was not the only interpretation. Indeed, an alternative interpretation of the market economy had existed for well over a century and was widely practised in many countries. This practice emphasised relationships rather than transactions as the essence of the exchange process, and it was this that gave rise to what is now widely recognised as **'relationship marketing'**.

The relationship marketing model can trace its lineage directly from the work of European economists in the 1930s (the Copenhagen School's **'parameter theory'**). In turn this theory evolved as an explanation of the working of several free market economies in Europe which seemed quite different from the dominant UK and USA economies. The existence of two very different interpretations of capitalism – **Anglo-Saxon** which prevailed in the UK and USA, and **Germanic-Alpine** which existed in many European and other economies – was masked by the Cold War between the major capitalistic and communist countries of the world. As a result of this confrontation, interpretation of the two states – capitalism and communism – tended to polarise into extreme versions. In the case of capitalism it tended to be Milton Friedman's version of the free market economy practiced in the USA and, to a lesser extent, the UK, rather than that to be found in many other democratic free market economies.

The collapse of communism in Eastern Europe, prompted a Frenchman, Michel Albert, to write a book entitled *Capitalisme contre capitalisme* in which he pointed out that the elimination of communism had thrown into relief the fact that there is not a single, monolithic model of capitalism, but several. Further, it appears that the Germanic-Alpine model leads to superior economic performance than the alternative Anglo-Saxon model. Dussart (1994) summarised the essential differences between these two models as shown in Table 1.3

As can be seen from this table there are significant differences between the two models of economic organisation, but it was not until the US economy began to falter in the 1980s that anyone seriously questioned the marketing management model. With hindsight, perhaps this model was 'selling with knobs on', but it had certainly proved superior to the sales orientation that had preceded it. Basically, the marketing management model is founded on the idea of manipulating the elements of the marketing mix to achieve superior sales performance. However, its managerial emphasis is on what sellers do *to* buyers not *for* them. In addition marketing mix management and the marketing department become synonymous with the marketing function, which tends to separate them from other functions and alienate them too – especially when marketers claim that the organisation should be organised round, and subservient to them. Understandably, as US firms lost competitiveness marketing was blamed, resulting in what has been termed 'marketing's mid-life crisis'. Another solution was called for, and it was this that prompted Webster to examine 'The Changing Role of Marketing in the Corporation'.

During the 1990s the 'relationship' became firmly established and recognised as a true reflection of the marketing concept in that it emphasises that marketing begins and ends with the customer, and is looking for win-win outcomes in which both buyer and seller gain value through exchange – in other words, a mutually satisfying exchange relationship. (See definition 8, Table 1.1!) As will become clear in later chapters, such 'relationships' do not necessarily mean that every exchange requires personal interaction between buyer and seller – there is still plenty of scope for arms-length **transactions**. However, it is important that such transactions are based on doing things *for* customers rather than doing things *to* them. Table 1.4 provides a useful comparison of the salient differences between transactional and relationship marketing to highlight what this might involve.

MARKETING IS EVERYBODY'S BUSINESS

One consequence of the recognition that adoption of the marketing concept required the whole organisation to be orientated towards the delivery of customer satisfaction was the view that 'marketing is everybody's business'. While this may seem a good thing it may also be a dangerous one. If something is everybody's

Table 1.3 Major differences between the two models

	Anglo-Saxon	Germanic-Alpine
Basic Principle	Free competition	Controlled competition
Power Centres	The Bank Customer (as consumer) Company over customer	The Stock Exchange Management over shareholder
Time Perspective	Short-term The tyranny of the Quarterly Report	Long-term *Development* as opposed to *profit*
Type of Business Relationship	Ad hoc *transaction*	Long-term *relationship*
Social Involvement	Weak	Strong

Source: Based on Dussart, C. in M.J. Baker, *Perspectives on Marketing Management,* (1994) © John Wiley & Sons Limited. Reproduced with permission.

business it may quickly become 'nobody's' business and give rise to three major threats:

1 *Complacency*
2 *Neglect* of the marketing function
3 The *substitution* of technology for people

The threat of complacency is not a new one, and the analysis of failure frequently shows this to be the prime cause. This notion is central to perhaps the most

Table 1.4 Contrasting relationship and transactional marketing

Transactional Marketing	Relationship Marketing
Do the deal and disappear	Negotiate a win-win sale situation and stay around, being a resource for better results
Push price	Promote value
Short term thinking and acting	Longer-term thinking and acting
Build the business on deals	Build the business on relationship
Getting new customers	Keeping all customers and clients
No structure for on-going business	Structure created to support relationship, special club and memberships for frequent users-buyers
Selling focused	Relationship focused for results
Short-term empathy	Long-term empathy and rapport
Incentive for doing the deal	Incentives for long-term relationships and revenue
Foundation of sale telling and selling	Foundation of revenue trust
Race for a sale result	Swift, strong, safe and enduring in results through relationship building
Value of the customer in this sale	Value of the customer seen over 3, 5, 10 years
After-sales support and service poor	After-sales support and service strong - seen as cost investment in the relationship
Product-service focused	People expectations and perception focused
Rewards - incentive for 'doing deals'	Rewards - incentive for maintaining and growing relationship and revenue
'The deal the end'. Pursuit of deal	The sale - just the beginning. Pursuit of long-term relationships and results.

famous and widely read article on the subject of marketing – Ted Levitt's 'Marketing Myopia' (1960).

In 'Marketing Myopia' Levitt begins by pointing out that every declining industry was once a growth industry, and sets out to identify what it is that causes once successful companies to fail. Fundamentally, he argues that a primary cause is a fixation on the product sold by the firm, rather than a concern for the need that the product satisfies. Using the American railroads, which appeared to be in terminal decline in the 1950s, as an example, he points out that at the turn of the twentieth century the railroads were the most sought after blue chip stock on the New York exchange, but that the seeds of their decline had already been sown. The reason for this were the development of the internal combustion engine and its potential for air and road travel. The railroad management were myopic – and complacent – because they did not realise that when someone bought a railroad ticket they wanted *transportation* and that if other more convenient and comfortable substitutes became available they would switch to these new products. Had the railroad management appreciated this they could have diversified and become an integrated transportation business. Instead, they sneered at the imperfections of the early cars and planes, and failed to remember that the early trains had experienced similar failings.

In other words, producers must concentrate on the **need** served rather than the specific means of satisfying it or, as Levitt said "When a man goes into a hardware store to buy a quarter inch drill – he needs a quarter inch hole". The day someone invents a new way of making holes the drill industry will start to decline! Given that new product development is the foundation of competitive strategy and the motivation of entrepreneurs, no-one can afford to ignore its potential impact and be complacent because currently they are a market leader.

As will become clear as you read through this book, marketing is a *complex* subject. The fact that marketing has become recognised as a **synthetic discipline** and a profession is because there is an extensive body of knowledge and normative theory that underpin the practice. It follows that the marketing function needs to be managed by specialists who are familiar with this knowledge. So, while every member of an organisation can subscribe to the marketing concept as a business philosophy, and be marketing oriented, this is not to say that they are able to perform specialist marketing tasks that are the responsibility of the marketing function.

The third threat is that in the pursuit of cost economies and downsizing, management will seek to substitute technology for people and/or outsource basic marketing functions to lower cost suppliers. The dangers of doing this are already apparent in the problems being experienced by many organisations which have lost contact with their customers, and so compromised the relationship they had built up with them. A classic case in point is branch banking. Once you close branches down, customers realise that money is a commodity that you can source from the lowest cost supplier, or save with the organisation offering the best return on your capital on a day-to-day basis. So much for customer loyalty now.

MARKETING'S 'DOMAIN'

Domain, which literally means an area under one rule, is a word that has become popular in the business disciplines to spell out the scope, nature and boundaries of a subject.

As we have seen, while marketing has existed since people first began to live together in communities, the current practice has largely developed in the last century or so. To begin with the emphasis in the production era was on the distribution of primary products. Then as mass production switched the emphasis from primary to secondary, or manufacturing, industry, the emphasis was on selling harder in increasingly more competitive markets. During this sales era, there was a clear distinction between consumer and industrial marketing, and little overlap between them. Then, around the 1950s, we saw the emergence of what we have termed 'neo-classical marketing' and the marketing management school of thought. Initially, the focus of this school was on consumer markets but, as the 1960s progressed, the same ideas began to migrate into industrial markets with notable success, and leading thinkers like Kotler and Levy began to inquire into the 'transferability' of the marketing concept.

In a seminal article published in 1969, Kotler and Levy identified a need to redefine the scope of marketing and asserted: "It is the authors' contention that marketing is a pervasive societal activity that goes considerably beyond the selling of toothpaste, soap and steel". Behind this proposition is the recognition that, with increased wealth and welfare arising from industrialisation, more time and money can be allocated to other forms of social activity with a shift in emphasis from products to services, and from business organisations to all kinds of organisation.

As Kotler and Levy pointed out, all these social organisations – the Church, universities, government departments, hospitals and so forth – perform the classic business functions. Finance is necessary to pay for the organisation's operations, and a personnel function is necessary to ensure that people are available to perform these operations. A production function is necessary to organise the most efficient and effective use of inputs to achieve the desired level of outputs. Purchasing is necessary to acquire these inputs and, presumably, marketing is needed to dispose of the outputs. While such ideas were considered extravagant, if not heretical, at the time, they are now the accepted wisdom and virtually every organisation – profit and not-for-profit – has a marketing function.

If we accept the marketing concept, essentially we are agreeing to a simple proposition that supply should be a function of demand and, therefore, subservient to it. Demand is the controlling factor, and the analysis and understanding of it must underpin all marketing activities. Following Bates and Parkinson (1969) we can distinguish four managerial aspects of demand, namely:

1 *Analysis and forecasting*; that is, marketing research.
2 *Product development and design.*
3 *Influencing of demand* – design, packaging, advertising, selling, promotion and so forth.
4 *Service* – distribution, after-sales service etc.

While much of this book is concerned with the specialised marketing functions that deal with these issues, the first requirement is to look at the wider context within which marketing takes place. Accordingly the remainder of Part I will look at the nature of marketing strategy and management and the interaction of demand and supply. Then, in Part II we look at some of the more important theoretical constructs and ideas that underpin marketing practice. To begin with we look at the environment within which exchange relationships occur. First, the external or macro-environmental, and then the micro-environment in terms of markets and the industries and firms that serve them. Next we look at the business system or value chain which link producers and customers, and finally the factors that influence the buying behaviour of customers.

It is in Part III that we examine the managerial aspects of demand in detail when we consider the **Marketing Mix**. The idea of a mix of marketing functions was conceived by Professor Neil Borden of the Harvard Business School as:

A schematic plan to guide analysis of marketing problems through utilisation of

(a) *a list of the important forces emanating from the market which bear upon the marketing operations of an enterprise;*
(b) *a list of the elements (procedures and policies) of marketing programs.*

The marketing mix refers to the apportionment of effort, the designing, and the integration of the elements of marketing into a program or 'mix' which on the basis of appraisal of the market forces, will best achieve the objectives of an enterprise at a given time.

(1964, pp2-7)

As we shall see, Borden identified twelve distinct functions which McCarthy reduced to his 4Ps of Product, Price, Place and Promotion. Each of these functions is a specialisation in its own right, and many are the basis of a distinct professional body – Market Research, Advertising etc. While it is unlikely that anyone could achieve mastery of all these specialisations, in an introductory course it is important to gain an overview of the more important aspects of each function, and an understanding of how they relate to one another, and may be combined to create a unique marketing mix. Accordingly, we look in some detail at marketing research, product policy, packaging, branding, pricing, distribution, advertising, selling and brand management before seeing how these may be used in practice in Part IV.

In Part IV we first consider how organisations manage the marketing function as a whole before reviewing the preparation of a marketing plan that links the specialisations together in a co-ordinated programme of activity. Next we take a detailed look at the application of marketing principles and techniques to international marketing and the growth area of services. Finally, we identify a number of current issues and trends, such as ethics and green marketing, which give some indication of where marketing is going in future as it continues to evolve. In this chapter we also include a review of the current debate about a new 'paradigm' or model of marketing which may have important implications in the future.

Taken together these topics and issues help define the domain of marketing. To begin our exploration of it we shall look first at the strategic issues facing the marketing function and their implications for its management.

Summary

In this chapter we have provided an overview of the origins, evolution, scope and nature of modern marketing.

An examination of a wide range of definitions indicated that there is a very large number but that in essence, they can be classified into three major categories:

1 Marketing as a **process**
2 Marketing as a **concept** or **philosophy of business**
3 Marketing as a **business orientation**

We then looked at the nature of marketing as a **discipline** and concluded that it may be described as **synthetic** in the sense that it has a multi-disciplinary foundation and integrates concepts and ideas from a number of core disciplines like Economics, Psychology and Sociology.

Next, we examined two basic theories that underpin the nature of marketing – **Maslow's Theory of Motivation** and **Rostow's Theory of Economic Development.** Ultimately, it is human motivation that drives economic development, the basic objective of which is "to maximise satisfaction from the utilisation of scarce resources. In pursuit of this objective we showed how **task specialisation,** the **division of labour** and **industrialisation** greatly increased the volume and variety of **supply.** Initially, however, increased supply resulted in population growth so that the primary focus still remained on increasing **production.**

But, as production and productivity continued to grow as a result of innovation and the growth of international trade, population growth began to slow down in the more affluent, industrialised economies, creating a potential for **excess supply.** This increased competition and an emphasis on a **sales orientation.** This orientation proved only a short-term solution and led, in the 1950s, to the statement of the **modern marketing concept** which stresses that supply must be driven by demand so that producers must determine what customers want before creating outputs.

However, a review of recent economic history revealed that this notion, and the development of new marketing techniques were not as recent as many people appeared to think. What was different was the recognition of marketing as a **professional practice** and a **managerial orientation**. It was soon recognised that these ideas and their application were **transferable** to other contexts like services, and all kinds of organisation.

The modern marketing management school of thought proved to be short-lived with its stress on the manipulation of the **marketing mix** to manage demand and bend it to the will of the supplier. With the collapse of communism in Eastern Europe in the 1980s it became clear that a theory of exchange based on **transactions** was insufficient to sustain long-term competitiveness and interest began to grow in exchange as a **relationship**. One consequence of this, and the emphasis on a **marketing orientation**, was that marketing suddenly became 'everybodies business', which called in question the need for a specialist marketing function in the organisation. The chapter concluded with a review of marketing's **domain** which showed that although marketing may be a universal business philosophy and orientation its **practice** is specialised and calls for knowledge and understanding of the knowledge base that is the foundation of normative theory and its application. It is these that are the subject of the rest of the book.

Review questions and problems

1 Definitions of marketing appear to fall into three different categories that see it as a *process*, a *concept* and an *orientation*. Explain the similarities and differences between these perspectives and develop a definition of your own that integrates them into a single definition.

2 What is normative theory? What relevance has it for professional practice?

3 It is claimed that professional practices are based on synthetic disciplines. What is meant by 'synthetic', and how would you explain this in terms of the engineering, medical and marketing professions?

4 Santayana said: "He who is unaware of history is bound to repeat it". How and why might a knowledge of the history of marketing be important for its modern practice?

5 What is the 'Three Eras' explanation of the evolution of marketing practice? Is it correct; is it useful?

6 "Marketing is everybodies business". Discuss.

7 What is meant by the transferability of the marketing concept? Show how it might be relevant to a charity like the Red Cross.

8 The marketing management concept is the antithesis of the real marketing concept because it focuses on what to do *to* customers rather than what to do *for* them. Explain and discuss.

9 What is the *domain* of marketing? Do you consider that it might become so specialised like law and medicine that only those with formal qualifications will be allowed to practice it? What arguments are there, for and against, allowing this to happen?

10 What is it that distinguishes relationship marketing from earlier approaches to marketing practice?

Key terms

4Ps – product, price, place and promotion
age of high mass consumption
Anglo-Saxon interpretation of capitalism
decentralisation
demand-enhancing marketing
division of labour
domain
drive to maturity
economy
esteem needs
excess supply
fast moving consumer goods (FMCG)

Germanic-Alpine interpretation of capitalism
human motivation
increased market incentives
industrial revolution
love needs
managerial school
market
marketing
marketing as a concept
marketing as a process
marketing management
marketing management school
marketing mix

marketing orientation
Maslow's hierarchy of human needs
micro-economic paradigm
multidisciplinary
need
normative theory
parameter theory
physiological needs
pre-conditions for take off
production orientation
profession
relationship marketing
Rostow's stages of economic development

safety needs	strategic business unit (SBU)	- production, sales and
sales orientation	survival	marketing
scientific management	synthetic discipline	traditional societies
self-actualisation	take off	transactions
self-sufficiency	task specialisation	widening of the market
specialisation	three era's conceptualisation	

Supplementary reading list

Baker, M. J. (Ed.) (2003), *The Marketing Book*, 5th edn, (Oxford: Butterworth-Heinemann).
This book contains 30 chapters contributed by experts covering all the topics likely to be covered in an introductory marketing course. It is revised regularly and should be the first place to look for an authoritative overview of individual topics, and for suggestions for further reading.

Borden, N. (1964), "The Concept of the Marketing Mix", *Journal of Advertising Research*, 4 (June), pp.2-7.

Booms, B.H. and Bitner, M.J. (1981), Marketing strategies and Organisation Structures for Service Firms', in *Marketing of Services* (Chicago: American Marketing Association, pp.47-51.

Copeland, Melvin T. (1923), "Relation of Consumers' Buying Habits to Marketing Methods", *Harvard Business Review* (April).

Fullerton, R. A. (1988), "How Modern is Modern Marketing?", *Journal of Marketing*, Vol. 52 No. 1, January, pp. 108-25.

Kotler, P. and Levy, S. (1969), "Broadening the Concept of Marketing", *Journal of Marketing*, Vol. 33, January, pp. 10-15.

Levitt, T. (1960), "Marketing Myopia", *Harvard Business Review* (July--August 1960) p. 45.

Maslow, A. (1943), "A Theory of Human Motivation", *Psychological Review*, 50.

McKitterick, J. B. (1957), "What is the Marketing Management Concept?", in Frank M. Bass (ed.), *The Frontiers of Marketing Thought and Science*, (Chicago; American Marketing Association), pp. 71-81.

Rostow, W. W. (1962), *The Process of Economic Growth* 2nd edn. (New York: Norton).

Webster, F. E. (1992), "The Changing Role of Marketing in the Corporation", *Journal of Marketing*, Vol. 56, October, pp. 1-17.

MARKETING IN PRACTICE

| Learning Goals | *After reading this chapter you should be able to:* |

- Define the essence of marketing in theory and practice.

- Be able to define strategy and understand the contribution which marketing has to make to the overall direction and management of an organisation.

- Explain the concepts of organisational culture and the product life cycle.

- Understand the concepts of market opportunity and competitive advantage.

- Grasp the nature of the marketing audit.

- Appreciate the need to set out clear objectives.

- Define the marketing mix.

- Recognise the basic strategic alternatives open to an organisation.

INTRODUCTION

In the first chapter we examined the substance of the marketing concept and observed how the process of economic development had tended to 'dehumanise' the nature of the exchange process.

This dehumanisation through the adoption of task specialisation, the division of labour and the application of technology to the production or supply side of consumption was essential to improve productivity and enhance the standard of living. However, as we have seen, a natural consequence of improved standards of living is an increase in the population – more infants survive, people live longer – which results in a concomitant increase in demand. In other words, the size of the market increases and the supply side has to work even harder to keep up.

One consequence of this struggle to keep pace with an ever growing demand was still further specialisation in production and the emphasis upon what Ricardo was to term 'comparative advantage'. While Ricardo was seeking to explain the benefits of international trade, precisely the same benefits existed within nation states and led to the concentration of particular industries in particular localities. Glass manufacturing at St Helens and St Gobain, iron smelting in South Wales and the Saar, textiles in Lancashire and Lille, ceramics in Staffordshire and Sevres and so on. Because of the economies of scale and mass production, such favoured locations were able to serve ever more distant markets more cost-effectively than smaller less well endowed local producers, resulting in a significant physical separation between producer and consumer.

In time this separation was to become psychological too, with producers assuming they knew what consumers wanted and justifying their assumptions by observing that the market was absorbing all their output, and was clamouring for more.

So long as the market continued to expand exponentially through population growth there can be little doubt that the emphasis upon the mass production of undifferentiated products resulted in the maximum overall satisfaction. However, with a slowing down in population growth, and a continued acceleration in supply through technological innovation and change, the potential arose for the creation of an excess supply in certain markets. As soon as this occurs the nature of competition changes from so-called perfect competition, under which the product is assumed to be homogeneous, to imperfect competition under which suppliers recognise that if their output is indistinguishable from other suppliers then consumers will have no reason to prefer them to any other supplier, with the possible result that they will be left with unsold goods. Given this possibility individual suppliers need to devise specific plans in order to compete with and succeed against other suppliers in the same line of business. In other words they need a **strategy**, which may be defined broadly as a statement of purpose and the means of achieving it. Why do we need a strategy? Because strategy is concerned with future action and it is a cliché, but true, that the rest of our lives will be spent in the future.

There are numerous books which are devoted solely to the subject of strategy – its definition, formulation and execution. In this chapter we can only touch on some of the bare essentials but it is felt to be important to introduce them early on as the whole purpose of marketing – both concept and function – is to help structure and improve both the efficiency and effectiveness of exchange relationships, with the ultimate goal of maximising satisfaction from the consumption of scarce resources. Accordingly, in this chapter we shall seek to define the nature of strategy and **strategic planning** as well as the concepts of **organisational culture** and the **product life cycle**, for the latter defines the inevitable pattern of change within which the firm must exist, and the former the way the organisation chooses to approach and deal with its survival and growth. This consideration leads naturally to the concepts of **market opportunity** and **competitive advantage** which underlie all successful strategies.

In order to formulate a strategy it will be argued that one must carry out a **marketing audit** which will take in both the external threats and opportunities which exist in the competitive environment, as well as the firm's own strengths and weaknesses. Based upon such an analysis the firm will wish to articulate clear objectives, both to provide direction for the firm's efforts as well as milestones to record progress and achievement. In developing such objectives it will be shown that the firm has only a small number of **strategic alternatives** available to it, and techniques for identifying and selecting these will be proposed. Once a core strategy has been defined its effective execution will depend upon the optimal selection of the elements of the **marketing mix** – the combination of product, price, place and promotion – and this notion will be introduced for extended development in Part III of the book. In selecting the optimal marketing mix it is vital that the firm have a clear view of how it wishes to position itself against its rivals and the idea of **'positioning'** will be introduced and described.

However, before we address these issues it will be useful to summarise and review what are the distinguishing features of marketing in both theory and practice.

THE NORMATIVE THEORY OF MARKETING

Theorists and teachers of all kinds are familiar with the objection that starts: "It's all very well in theory but, in practice ......". Such objections are often made by persons who are ignorant of the theory; they certainly do not appreciate that in most cases 'best' theory is derived from the observation, confirmation and codification of best **practice**. Indeed, one of the characteristics that distinguishes a profession from a craft is the existence of an agreed body of knowledge that can be communicated through formal learning, thereby avoiding the diseconomies and hit-and-miss nature of "learning by experience". The existence of a profession of marketing, and formal qualifications of graduate and postgraduate standing, mean that there is agreement as to what constitutes effective marketing. It follows that ignorance or neglect of these principles will result in underperfomance, and so could not be construed as "best possible marketing".

As noted in the Chapter 1, modern marketing can be dated to the 1950s and the articulation of the 'marketing concept'. This is encapsulated in the two definitions offered, and may be regarded as the underlying philosophy which underpins both an approach to the conduct of business (a marketing 'orientation'), and its actual practice. Modern marketing has evolved as a response to the recognition that major changes in the global environment call for new approaches to managing production and distribution. The solution proposed is the adoption of a marketing orientation that puts the customer at the beginning of the production-consumption cycle rather than at its end. To do so requires a fundamental shift in attitude away from 'selling what we make' to 'making what we can sell'. Unfortunately, while this concept seems both simple and obvious to those who have adopted it, there is ample evidence that it is widely misunderstood and so misapplied.

While academics and practitioners may quibble over the precise definition, scope and nature of 'marketing', there is widespread, if not universal agreement, that *real* marketing has four essential features:

1 It starts with an understanding of customer needs, and sets out to supply goods and services that meet these as precisely as possible.

2 It takes a long-run perspective, i.e. it seeks to build relationships and encourage repeat purchase (customer loyalty).

3 It seeks to make use of *all* the company's resources, i.e. it is the integrative and coordinating function that ensures these are combined in the most effective way to ensure profitable sales.

4 It recognises *innovation* as the primary source of economic growth and promotes and encourages this to secure the continuing survival and success of the organisation.

Adoption of these principles is fundamental to the efficient and effective performance of the marketing **function** i.e. what marketing managers actually **do**.

Basically, the marketing function is responsible for the management of the marketing mix, a concept conceived by Professor Neil Borden of the Harvard Business School, and we discuss this in some detail later in the chapter.

Unfortunately, while Borden's original conceptualisation contained *twelve* elements, this proved too many for easy memorisation and regurgitation with the result that most novices are familiar only with McCarthy's (1960) grossly simplified **Four Ps** of Product, Price, Place and Promotion. Clearly, this formulation neglects explicit recognition of the analysis of the forces that shape and control the selection of the optimum mix of product, price, place and promotion. It will be recalled, however, that Analysis and Forecasting were one of the four key management functions identified in Chapter 1. In turn, this function is generally agreed to comprise at least *six* steps:

- Diagnosis   *Where is the company now and why?*
- Prognosis   *Where is the company headed?*
- Objectives   *Where should the company be headed?*
- Strategy   *What is the best way to get there?*
- Tactics   *What specific actions should be undertaken, by whom, and when?*
- Control   *What measures should be watched to indicate whether the company is succeeding?*

The importance of these steps is recognised in the content of both introductory and more advanced textbooks on marketing, most of which follow Borden in analysing the external environment in which the firm is to compete before discussing the formulation of a strategy, and a specific action plan detailing the unique marketing mix to be used.

Diagnosis

When addressing a marketing problem most analysts follow a procedure very similar to that followed by practitioners in other disciplines. In essence, this may be thought of as 'successive focusing' in which the problem solver applies increasingly powerful diagnostic techniques in order evaluate the specific issue concerned. Thus, while the principles apply to all problems, their relevance and importance will vary considerably according to the context and the precise nature of the problem to be diagnosed and solved. In the marketing discipline at least three parameters are considered important in deciding how to proceed, namely:

1 *Nature of the end use market;*
2 *Product or service;*
3 *Profit or not-for-profit.*

The main distinction in terms of the nature of the market is between 'Business–to-Business' (B2B) and 'Business-to–Consumer' (B2C), and in Table 2.1 we present a synthesis of factors or characteristics that are generally cited in the literature, both academic and practitioner, as differentiating between B2B and B2C markets, and the implications, or consequences, that these have for the development of an effective marketing strategy. In addition to these ten characteristics other authorities would cite leasing, renting and the extension of credit as also being more important in many business markets.

However the main value of the Table is that it summarises succinctly the significance of these characteristics for marketing practice in the B2B context. As we shall see, other contexts like B2C, marketing of services, marketing for NPOs etc. call for different emphases. In all cases, however, the development of a strategy and plans for its execution, place a premium on sophisticated environmental analysis and long-range economic and technology forecasting. All of these are **critical success factors (CSF)** for any organisation that wants to operate successfully in any industry, so that they may anticipate emerging market opportunities, and be in a position to meet these with appropriate and attractive goods and services. It is for this reason that Chapter 4 is focused explicitly on these issues.

EFFECTIVE MARKETING IN PRACTICE

In competitive markets it is now accepted that it is very difficult to create and sustain a competitive advantage. Technological innovation protected by patents may confer this, but competitors are notorious for breaking or getting round such objective advantages. As a result other factors, such as trust and commitment, are seen as playing an increasingly important role in determining which suppliers will be preferred by prospective buyers. This recognition has given rise to the current emphasis on **relationship marketing** and the practice of **customer relationship management.** Today, it is now accepted that who you know, and who knows you are just as, if not more important to winning business as the traditional elements of the marketing mix. In fact, being able to meet the customers requirements in terms of meeting the product specification, price and delivery terms are necessary conditions in whose absence you will not even be considered qualified to compete, let alone be considered as a supplier. In other words, you will not get beyond Step 4 in the sequence suggested earlier.

This extremely eclectic review provides some basis for identifying what might qualify as best marketing practice. In all markets the first responsibility of the marketer is to identify a market opportunity, and then organise the company's skills, resources and assets to satisfy the need profitably. Once an organisation has committed itself to the creation of a supply it is inevitably constrained by the nature of that supply. In mass markets this means that the seller must know which sub-group, or market segment, has needs that most closely match the precise characteristics of their offering. They must then target this segment and position themselves so that their offering is seen as superior to all those with similar features and performance characteristics. This is achieved through the development of a unique marketing mix with a particular emphasis on branding, advertising, sales promotion, pricing and distribution. In other words, the product

Table 2.1 Distinguishing characteristics of B2B markets

Factor	Principle Consequences for:		
	Marketing Research	*Marketing Management*	*Other Functions*
1 *Small/finite customer numbers*	■ Identifiable targets ■ Focused research ■ Qualitative as well as Quantitative approaches	■ Personal contact ■ Relationship cultivation ■ Potential to react to individual customers' needs	■ Need for close liaison with customers for Product/ Innovation requirements
2 *Fewer but larger orders*	■ Need for comprehensive and continual information and intelligence about customers and competitors	■ Necessity for competitiveness ■ Use of relationships/ knowledge to get in and remain 'in' ■ Customer closeness ■ Predictability of demand	■ Irregular demand for specific products ■ Complexities of plant scheduling and/or inventory carrying ■ Time a critical variable

3 *Heterogeneity of size*	■ Inappropriateness of small percentage and random samples
	■ Focus on stratified/census techniques
	■ Need to secure deep knowledge of major players
		■ Segmentation by size/ importance
		■ Focus of effort on major players/ opinion leaders
		■ Customisation of products for major users
		■ Risk of ignoring requirements of other segments
			■ Request for priority for major customers affecting
			  - production schedules
			  - terms of business
			■ Dependence on oligopolistic customer demand
			■ Potential proliferation of product varieties

4 *Concentration of business*	■ Accessibility of populations	■ Ease of communication ■ Structure of sales function ■ Structure of distribution channels	■ Choice of transportation ■ Use/location of warehouses
5 *Derived Demand*	■ Complexity of downstream research ■ Need to research end markets ■ Familiarity with/use of consumer research techniques	■ Need to identify end markets ■ Multiple product users ■ Contact with customer; derivation of demand pull as well as supply push strategies ■ Establishment of *consumer* preferences/ loyalties	■ NPD/R&D focus on end use applications ■ Delays in implementing new products due to customer redesign requirements ■ Need for sustainable demand for end product
6. *Reciprocity of buyer/seller*	■ 'Captive' research environment	(a) ■ Stable customer relationships ■ Risk of unwanted inertia/'buyer pressure' (b) ■ Mutuality of benefit ■ Repeat business ■ Loyalty/ relationship development	(a) ■ Risk sharing ■ Inertia/brake on corporate R&D development ■ Potential 'offset' deals (b) ■ Experience sharing ■ improved cost effectiveness ■ Relationship development with corresponding customer functions

Table 2.1 Distinguishing characteristics of B2B markets continued

	Principle Consequences for:		
Factor	Marketing Research	Marketing Management	Other Functions
7 Buyer/seller inertia	■ Accessibility/regularity of contact	■ Relationship building opportunities ■ Supply chain development ■ Market stability ■ Risk of competitor outflanking	■ High switching costs ■ Collaboration in NPD ■ Risk of lack of innovation
8 Technical complexity	■ Multiplicity of uses confuses research environment ■ Need for access to user markets	■ Need for familiarity with specification processes ■ Involvement in negotiations pre/during/post transaction ■ Tendency towards technically qualified sales personnel ■ Need for detailed comprehension of user environments	■ Delays in introducing new products (see Derived Demand) ■ Multifunctional 'sales' teams ■ Enhanced importance of process innovation
9 Technological/ economic trends	■ Need for continual monitoring of end markets	■ Understanding of end markets and close relationships with end users and intermediaries ■ Development of more than one operational market ■ Technology forecasting	■ Operational flexibility ■ Ability to reassess forward orders ■ Minimise lead times ■ Maintenance of technological updatedness
10 Rational/ group buying	■ Need to gain access to several elements of DMU ■ Need to employ indirect as well as direct instruments ■ Increased importance of 'intelligence' ■ Increased emphasis on intentions/attitude research	■ Multi level communications strategies ■ Need to identify users and deciders ■ Need to focus on real motivation of each DMU element ■ Relationship building at all levels ■ Development of corporate image of 'customer friendliness'/ 'customer closeness'	■ Need for total corporate market orientation ■ Involvement in major promotional activities, exhibitions etc. ■ Development of TQM/Total Customer Service ■ Integration of Production strategies with Marketing

Source: Bernard, K. (1995) in Baker, M.J. (ed.) *Marketing: Theory and Practice*, 3rd edn, (Basingstoke: Macmillan)

is unchanged and the task is to match demand to the available supply. (Obviously, if this is unattractive or uncompetitive the seller will lack customers, and go out of business!).

Our survey of the normative theory of best marketing practice suggests *eight* requirements that need to be met if a firm is to succeed, namely:

1 That it has a competitive product to offer.

2 That it has undertaken appropriate research and identified potential buyers.

3 That it is known to potential buyers and included in their "bid lists" i.e. for direct invitation to tender, or, for consumer goods, it is part of their "evoked set" or products considered suitable in principle.

4 That it has ensured the organisation meets the basic 'objective' needs of the intending buyer.

5 That it has established the critical success factors looked for by the intending buyer.

6 That it is familiar with the competition so that it can match or better their offering, and take advantage of any weaknesses they may have.

7 That it can develop a stronger value proposition embracing both objective (price, performance etc.) and subjective (quality, value etc.) elements.

8 That it is recognised as a reliable and trustworthy supplier of the desired product or service.

In management terms this requires the seller, or their agent, to perform the *four* key functions spelled out in Chapter 1:

1 *Analysis and Forecasting*.

2 *Product design and development*.

3 *Effective communication* – advertising, promotion, personal selling etc.

4 *Service* – advice, distribution (making the product available), after-sales service etc.

Strategic Marketing Planning (SMP) embraces all these function and calls for the development of unique plans that co-ordinates them to achieve a 'mix' suitable to the particular situation in hand. There is a well documented and clearly articulated normative theory that prescribes how these tasks should be performed most effectively.

STRATEGY AND STRATEGIC PLANNING

All successful businesses owe their existence to the recognition and existence of a market opportunity. This statement is as true of the technologically driven inventor such as Clive Sinclair, or the production orientated Henry Ford, as it is of the marketing orientated Anita Roddick. Each of these entrepreneurs succeeded because they brought to the market place a new product which consumers instantly recognised as fulfilling a felt need. Subsequently, one (Sinclair) was to fail badly and another (Ford) was to falter because their initial intuitive success was not supported by a clearly defined strategy for building upon this. In the case of Sinclair the prospect of low-cost calculators, personal computers and miniature televisions, were enormously attractive to consumers captivated with the marvels of microelectronics. His products proved the markets existed, but poor delivery and, even worse, poor product performance made him an easy victim for those second to the market with more reliable products, guaranteed delivery and after-sales service. Similarly, Henry Ford created the mass automobile market with his Model T but lost out to General Motors because he failed to develop a second generation motor-car to satisfy the increased needs of more sophisticated and demanding buyers.

It was failures of these kinds, but of industries rather than firms, which prompted Ted Levitt (1960) to write his seminal article, 'Marketing Myopia'. Using the American railroad system as his exemplar, Levitt pointed out how the invention of the steam engine revolutionised overland transportation, opened up continents and created an industry which, by 1900, was amongst the richest and most successful in the land. By 1950 this once, all-powerful industry was in ruins surviving only with Federal aid and on a greatly reduced basis. What went wrong? Basically the railroad management lacked a strategy based upon clear understanding of the business they were in defined in terms of the needs served. What the railroad moguls failed to appreciate was that the steam locomotive and the railroad were but one step in the evolution of the transportation business. Railways offered significant benefits in speed, comfort and carrying capacity over the stage-coach, ox-train and river/canal barges they largely displaced. Their downfall lay in not appreciating that further technological progress would result in even more convenient, speedy and comfortable means of transportation with the invention of the internal combustion and jet engines. Consumers owe no loyalty to suppliers, only to themselves. If a superior product or service is made available to meet their needs they will have no hesitation in switching to it. Thus, as inner city congestion increases we are seeing an increased demand for improved public transportation systems and growing investment in mass transit/light railways. The question is, if you are a motor-car manufacturer or a director of National Car Parks what plans have you for coping with the implications of this change?

To answer this question effectively it is widely agreed that one should undertake a formal and structured analysis along the lines proposed earlier, namely:

- Diagnosis   *Where is the company now and why?*
- Prognosis   *Where is the company headed?*
- Objectives   *Where should the company be headed?*
- Strategy   *What is the best way to get there?*
- Tactics   *What specific actions should be undertaken, by whom, and when?*
- Control   *What measures should be watched to indicate whether the company is succeeding?*

The first question 'where is the company now?' is frequently couched as 'what business are we in?' Following Levitt's analysis in 'Marketing Myopia' touched on above, it is now accepted that the answer to this question must be in terms of the need served rather than the specific means of serving it. Thus Levitt argued that if the railroad managers had perceived of themselves as being in the transportation business rather than the railroad business then they would have regarded the invention of the internal combustion engine as opening up a whole new range of transportation opportunities. As it was they ignored it initially as unsophisticated and undeveloped (just as steam engines had been 60 years previously) and then sought to compete with it in markets where railroads had little or no competitive advantage. Of course, 'the transportation business' is far too broad a definition for operational strategic planning, but it is the kind of fundamental assessment necessary to initiate such operational strategic planning.

If one considers an archetypal 'marketing' product, such as detergents, then we might wish to consider the manufacturers as being in the cleanliness business. If this is the case then there are at least three developments which could seriously threaten the industry out of which Procter & Gamble and Unilever make millions of pounds profit every year. First, textile manufacturers have developed and are improving soil-resistant treatments which prevent fabrics from becoming dirty so easily, and so reduce the incidence of cleaning. Second, there is the potential of disposables – napkins, plates, cups, tablecloths and, above all else so far, babies' diapers. (Procter & Gamble saw this coming and market the leading Pampers brand!) Third, there is an ecologically benign technology known as ultrasonics which literally shakes dirt out of fabrics without any need for chemicals which pollute the environment. If you are Electrolux or Hoover making cleaning boxes (rather than washing machines) the change in technology is only a limited threat – if you are Procter & Gamble or Unilever it could be fatal. Perhaps Levitt summed it up best of all, as we have noted, when he observed 'When a man goes into a hardware store to buy a quarter inch drill he needs a quarter inch hole'. As soon as someone like Black & Decker develop a handheld laser gun which can drill holes with infinite accuracy in any material, then the twist-drill business will be dead, but the hole-making business will continue to flourish.

This continuous cycle of innovation and change is described and analysed in one of marketing's central concepts – the **product life-cycle**.

THE PRODUCT LIFE-CYCLE CONCEPT

In Market Development (Baker, 1983) we described the product life-cycle concept as follows:

> *The paradox of the product life cycle (PLC) concept is that it is one of a very small number of original marketing ideas to enjoy a wide currency and yet is largely discredited in terms of practical application and relevance. That it should be discredited reflects a failing on the part of practitioners to understand the role and potential contribution of theory and concepts rather than any intrinsic deficiency in the concept itself – an assertion we will now seek to substantiate.*

The analogy of a product life-cycle is firmly founded in the biological sciences and the observation that living organisms pass through an inevitable cycle from conception, through gestation, to growth leading to maturity. In turn, the mature organism begins to decay progressively until its life is terminated in death. This progression is as familiar to us as life itself, and none would deny the inescapable sequence through which the normal organism will pass. That said, it would be a foolhardy bioscientist who would attempt to generalise about the expectations of a particular organism without first establishing its genus, species and subspecies; and even then they would only speculate about any distinct organism in terms of some form of probabilistic statement concerning expected future outcomes.

The validity of this assertion is easily demonstrated by reference to ourselves – human beings. An inspection of life expectancies quickly reveals major disparities between the inhabitants of advanced, affluent economies and their unfortunate brothers and sisters in the developing countries. Thus, while the average British male can look forward to a life-span of 72 years, an Indian has a life expectancy of only 53 years. However, if we were to compare a Briton and an Indian aged 30 years, the discrepancy in their respective life expectancies would be relatively small. The problem is a familiar one in the field of descriptive statistics; means or averages are largely meaningless unless we also possess some measure of dispersion about the mean. In the case of Indians, infant mortality is very high and the age distribution at death is heavily skewed towards young persons. On the other hand, if you survive the dangers of childhood, the probability of a reasonably long life is quite high. A broadly similar pattern also applies to Britons, in that infants and young children are more susceptible to disease and death by accident or genetic defect than are teenagers and adults. On the other hand, by enabling weak specimens to survive childhood one increases the probability of death in middle life, with the result that life expectancies for mature adults are very similar in advanced as well as in developing countries.

Actuaries understand this perfectly and base life insurance premiums upon average probabilities. The impression that your policy is written specifically for you is illusory, for no actuary would presume to predict your personal life expectancy. The irony is that while all of this is entirely commonplace and acceptable to us as insurance risks, as managers we expect analogous models to possess a level of predictive ability which cannot be achieved with very large populations of essentially homogeneous units. The level of information which we are likely to possess about a product group, such as detergents or industrial fasteners, is minuscule by comparison with the demographic data available upon people in general, or nationalities in particular. But, despite this, we try to make a generalised statement about the sales history of a successful (unspecified) product into a highly specific predictive device. In fact, PLCs can be used as forecasting tools, but only when one has a considerable amount of information about the product, or one analogous to it, and the market into which the product is to be introduced. In the present context, however, the relevance of the PLC is that it is a constant reminder of the inevitability of change and does mirror the stages through which all successful products pass. These stages and the titles given to them are represented in Figure 2.1. As can be observed, the conventional PLC is seen as comprising four basic stages when sales are plotted against elapsed time from introduction. First, there is a period of very slow growth when the new product or idea is introduced to prospective users. This phase is terminated by a transition to a period of very rapid growth which eventually levels off into a period of maturity, followed by a decline culminating in termination of the life cycle.

As noted, this is a conventional representation of a life cycle and must not be taken too literally for, depending upon the product type, the length of the various phases may vary considerably in just the same way as the average length of the mature phase of human beings has a strong correlation with socio-economic status. Similarly, overall life spans will vary enormously, so that fashion goods, like mayflies, are here today and gone tomorrow, while basic materials such as steel have very extended lives analogous to, say, elephants. But, given these caveats, the PLC does contain a number of important messages for us at both a strategic and a tactical level, and we shall return to these frequently in later chapters. At this juncture we merely wish to emphasise the message expressed so eloquently by Ted Levitt (1960) in his seminal article, 'Marketing Myopia', which opens with a sentence which, while tautological, is a requiem for much of UK (and US) industry today: 'Every declining industry was once a growth industry.'

As we have seen earlier, Levitt's thesis is simplicity itself: too many companies and industries are product orientated and so become preoccupied with the manufacture and distribution of a product to the extent that they lose sight of the basic need which the product satisfies. In consequence, such producers become vulnerable to attack by competitors with improved or substitute products, but their myopia usually prevents them from distinguishing this until it is too late to do anything about it. Myopia or complacency is always well to the fore in preventing the managers of declining industries from remembering the inevitable logic of the PLC: none of us is immortal. Furthermore, many entrepreneurs who rise to fame and riches through an intuitive ability to spot a market opportunity and to develop a product able to satisfy that opportunity overlooked what we have claimed is a marketing maxim: 'the act of consumption changes the consumer'. Railways opened up whole new possibilities for cheap, long-distance travel in comfort and at speed, but cars enabled travellers to plan their journeys to suit their own convenience and not be bound by the tyranny of the timetable, while aeroplanes offered such enormous benefits in terms of speed that many services still largely ignore the total satisfaction of their customers.

But the seeds of self-destruction are built into every innovation. General Motors saw that once consumers had become accustomed to the basic benefits of a Model T, many of them aspired to something different and better, just as the Germans saw that economy and reliability would win a significant share of the market, only to be outperformed by the Japanese who added a high level of 'extras' as standard equipment to their own compact cars. Similarly, excess capacity in air transportation has resulted in significant changes in the competitive posture of many airlines.

Levitt's prescription for myopia is that firms think of their business in terms of the basic needs they satisfy, so that railroads, car manufacturers and airlines are

Figure 2.1 The product life cycle

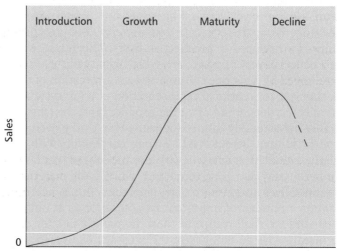

all part of the 'transportation business' and thus are concerned with features such as accessibility, convenience, comfort, reliability, speed, frequency and relative cost. Of course, the railways do recognise this, and do attempt to maximise the attractiveness of their product offering within the limitations imposed by technology and their ability to generate finance for investment. It is conceivable that if they had recognised the incipient threat of the internal combustion engine, they would have diversified into an integrated transportation system and so could have shared in the part new, part substitute market for cars and buses. However, it is by no means certain that such a diversification would have proved successful. What is certain is that there is a finite demand for transportation of all kinds and that with the evolution of new forms, so the railroads were bound to mature then decline in the manner predicted by the PLC concept. Furthermore, within the industry, some products (models, brands) and the firms that make them will grow, prosper and decline so that they, too, exhibit the characteristic phases of the life cycle.

In defining product–market structures the key factor to be taken into account is the degree of differentiation recognised by suppliers in seeking to satisfy a market. At the most basic level there is the generic need of the kind described by Levitt in 'Marketing Myopia' such that 'transportation needs' could be satisfied by a myriad of different means ranging from bicycles to supersonic aeroplanes. Next, there is the industry level need in which suppliers of essentially similar products such as motor-car manufacturers or airlines are seen as competing directly with one another. However, experience shows that, as soon as the industry's capacity matches or exceeds the demand for its undifferentiated output, so individual firms will seek to protect their own market share by catering for a specific segment of demand and developing differentiated products which satisfy that segment of demand better than the undifferentiated product. (The concept of segmentation is a particularly important one in marketing and the subject of Chapter 10.)

In addition to product differentiation markets have traditionally been defined also in terms of geography. But, as we shall see in the discussion of globalisation in Chapter 23, the definition of markets on a local area basis is being rapidly eroded by advances in transportation and communication.

The discussion this far has emphasised the fundamental truth that business activity and exchange is based upon the existence of needs, and that while these needs are enduring the means of satisfying them are subject to continuous change. While the most basic of all business objectives is survival, some organisations succeed while others fail. To a large degree the explanation of this is to be found in another key concept – that of **organisational culture**.

ORGANISATIONAL CULTURE

Irrespective of its stage in the firm's life cycle a major influence, if not the major influence upon an organisation's situation, is its culture. Two authorities on the concept of organisational culture (Deal and Kennedy, 1982) have the following to say:

> *Every business – in fact every organisation – has a culture. Sometimes it is fragmented and difficult to read from the outside – some people are loyal to their bosses, others are loyal to the unions, still others care only about their colleagues who work in the sales territories of*

the Northeast. If you ask employees why they work, they will answer 'because we need the money'. On the other hand, sometimes the culture of an organisation is very strong and cohesive; everyone knows the goals of the corporation, and they are working for them. Whether weak or strong, culture has a powerful influence throughout an organisation; it affects practically everything, from who gets promoted and what decisions are made, to how employees dress and what sports they play. Because of this impact, we think that culture also has a major effect on the success of the business.

Deal and Kennedy's belief received strong support from research by the present author and Prof Susan Hart (1989) in *Marketing and Competitive Success*. During the 1980s there was an upsurge of interest in the nature of critical success factors following the publication of Peters and Waterman's (1982) path-breaking *In Search of Excellence: lessons from America's best run companies*. Based upon a detailed review of practices and performance in a cross-section of eminently successful American companies, the two McKinsey consultants identified eight critical success factors as follows:

1 A bias for action.
2 Close to the customer.
3 Autonomy and entrepreneurship.
4 Productivity through people.
5 Hands-on, value-driven.
6 Stick to the knitting.
7 Simple form, lean staff.
8 Simultaneous loose–tight properties.

Despite the enthusiastic reception and recognition given to Peters and Waterman's analysis and findings, many were critical of the methodology – especially its anecdotal approach, its emphasis solely upon obviously successful companies (although many were experiencing difficulties in the years immediately following the book's publication) without any reference to less-successful companies, many of which claimed to possess at least some of the desired attributes; and the absence of specific advice on how one could operationalise the recommendations for action.

To address these criticisms Baker and Hart (1989) undertook an analysis of a matched sample of both successful and less-successful firms within a cross-section of growth (sunrise) industries and declining (sunset) industries. The findings confirmed that many of the attributes of successful firms were also present in less successful firms, and so could not be used to differentiate between them. Indeed, one initially surprising result was that managers in sunset industries appeared generally to be more able than most of their counterparts in sunrise industries. On reflection it is clear that when the market is growing rapidly managerial mistakes are compensated for by buoyant demand and generous margins. Conversely in a declining market, mistakes or lack of attention to detail lead to loss of market share, pressure on margins and loss of competitive edge.

In the final analysis, very few managerial practices emerged which were present in successful firms but absent in less successful firms such that one could recommend the latter to follow the example of the former (for example to invest in more marketing research). Consequently, we were driven to the conclusion that success is not so much a matter of what you do but of how well you do it.

In other words, culture and commitment are vital to organisational performance. However, this is not to say that professional managerial practices and procedures are unimportant, and the first step in developing successful competitive strategies must be to play to and exploit the firm's strengths while avoiding and/or improving upon its weaknesses.

The identification and listing of a firm's strengths and weaknesses comprises the internal element of the marketing audit or **SWOT analysis** (strengths, weaknesses (internal), opportunities and threats (external)). David W. Cravens (1988) suggests that the following information should be used to summarise the firm's strengths and weaknesses in each target market:

- Business scope and objectives; Market position;
- Market target(s) and customer base;
- Marketing programme positioning strategy;
- Financial, technical, and operating capabilities;
- Management experience and capabilities; and
- Special capabilities (for example, access to resources, patents).

Once identified and listed, the firm's strengths and weaknesses need to be related to the external environment which, as noted above, comprises the product-market, competitive and environmental situations. The external environment represents both the ultimate constraint and opportunity for the organisation's freedom of action. Further, because it is common to all competitors, those who understand it best will be able to use this knowledge as a source of competitive advantage. We will look at environmental analysis in detail in Chapter 4.

DETERMINING COMPETITIVE ADVANTAGE

In a major article, 'Assessing Advantage: A Framework for Diagnosing Competitive Superiority' (April 1988), George S. Day and Robin Wensley observe:

> The notion that superior performance requires a business to gain and hold an advantage over competitors is central to contemporary strategic thinking. Businesses seeking advantage are exhorted to develop distinctive competences and manage for lowered delivered cost or differentiation through superior customer value.
>
> The promised pay-off is market share dominance and profitability above average for the industry. The advice is sound, but usually difficult to follow.

In the authors view, the main difficulty arises from deficiencies in available approaches to diagnosing competitive advantage. They then analyse this with a view to proposing a process which will ensure 'a thorough and balanced assessment of the reasons for the competitive position of a business'.

Two broad approaches to determining competitive advantage may be discerned; one based on customers and the other on competitors. Customer focused assessments best satisfy the marketing concept in that the firm seeks to define precisely the needs of specific market segments and then organise itself to satisfy a segment's needs better than any other supplier. By contrast, competitor assessment emphasises an analysis of the strategy and tactics of those firm(s) which are considered to be the major competitors for the segment or segments which the firm is seeking to dominate. Firms which emphasise competitor assessment '. . . watch costs closely, quickly match the marketing initiatives of competitors, and look to their sustainable edge in technology. Managers keep a close watch on market share and contracts won or lost to detect changes in competitive position'. By contrast, customer-focused firms pay relatively little attention to these criteria and emphasise the quality of customer relationships.

Experience, and the available evidence, indicates that firms tend to one or other of these two perspectives when what is required is a balance between them. However, as Day and Wensley point out, such a balance is difficult to achieve because of the lack of any clear agreement as to just what constitutes competitive advantage. In essence Day and Wensley see competitive advantage (or distinctive competence) arising from either superior skills or superior resources. These give rise to positional advantages in terms of either superior customer value or lower relative costs, with performance outcomes in terms of satisfaction, loyalty, market share and profitability. This is then reinvested to sustain and improve the original source of advantage. These elements are summarised in Figure 2.2.

As Day and Wensley point out, analysing competitive advantage is but a means to an end – how to improve on one's performance and success. Such analysis frequently leads to the listing of so-called critical success factors – the Peters and Waterman listing of eight attributes of successful firms being a classic example (see p. 64). However, as the analysis by Baker and Hart (1989) referred to earlier revealed, critical success factors tend to be highly situation specific; that is, what works in one industry under one set of circumstances may be entirely inappropriate in another industry, or under other circumstances. At best, critical success factors (CSF) of the kind listed in Table 2.2 tend to be *necessary* but hardly ever *sufficient* reasons for success and little, if anything, is usually said as to how CSF may be converted into actual advantage.

Indeed the rank ordering given in Table 2.2 really applies only to the views of the managers participating in the Baker and Hart study. Managers in other industries may have quite different views. For example, in markets such as clothing, household textiles, floor coverings and so on, most managers rank 'Design' first rather than last.

Figure 2.2 The creation and sustenance of competitive advantage

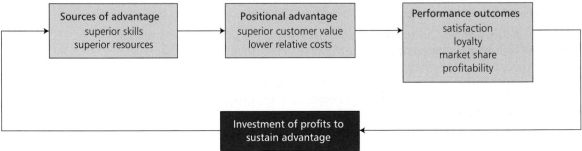

Source: Day, G. S. and Wensley, R. (1988), 'Assessing Advantage: A Framework for Diagnosing Competitive Superiority', *Journal of Marketing*, Vol 52, April, pp. 1-20, American Marketing Association.

In the opening quotation from Day and Wensley, reference was made to lower delivered cost, and differentiation which are two of the three core 'generic' strategies identified by Michael Porter (1980) in his seminal work *Competitive Strategy*. The third core strategy, 'focus', has been rejected by critics of Porter such as Shiv Mathur of the City Business School on the grounds that 'focus' is concerned with the market scope of differentiation and cost leadership. (In passing it should be noted that Porter's analysis follows closely the much earlier distinction of core marketing strategies into undifferentiated (cost leadership), differentiated and concentrated (focus). Implicitly, Day and Wensley follow this view (although they appear to be singularly unaware of the UK and European literature on marketing strategy) when they stress the importance of the 'drivers' or structural determinants which convert superior skills or resources into positional advantages. Day and Wensley's analysis is more suited to an advanced rather than introductory textbook but, essentially, the point they make is that superior skills and resources are not automatically converted into competitive advantage. This transformation is accomplished by management taking strategic choices, and implementing these tactically in accordance with a predetermined timetable. Success will accrue to those organisations most in tune with prevailing customer needs, and the determination of these will be best achieved through a combined analysis of consumers themselves, and of competitive offerings. Eleven methods of assessing advantage are discussed in detail by Day and Wensley and are summarised in Table 2.3.

Table 2.2 Critical success factors - product factors influencing competitiveness *(in rank order)*	
1	Performance in operation
2	Reliability
3	Sale price
4	Efficient delivery
5	Technical sophistication
6	Quality of after-sales service
7	Durability
8	Ease of use
9	Safety in use
10	Ease of maintenance
11	Parts availability and cost
12	Attractive appearance/shape
13	Flexibility and adaptability in use
14	Advertising and promotion
15	Operator comfort
16	Design

Source: Baker, M.J. and Hart, S.J. (1989) *Marketing and Competitive Success* (London: Philip Allan).

THE MARKETING AUDIT

The process of assessing advantage plays a central role in strategic marketing planning and is frequently described as a **marketing audit** or **SWOT analysis**, particularly in texts dealing with corporate strategy as opposed to marketing strategy (the maintenance of this distinction is becoming increasingly difficult as more and more organisations adopt the marketing concept and accept that they should be market led and customer driven). SWOT is an acronym for Strengths and Weaknesses (that is, the firm's internal status), and Opportunities and Threats which define the external environment.

Probably the most definitive statement of the nature of the marketing audit is to be found in an article by Philip Kotler, William Gregor and William Rogers (1977). According to Kotler et al., 'The marketing audit as an idea dates back to

Table 2.3 Methods of assessing advantage	
Competitor-centred	*Customer-focused*

A *Assessing sources*
(*distinctive competences*)
  1 Management judgements of strengths and weaknesses
  2 Comparison of resource commitments and capabilities
  3 Marketing skills audit	

B *Indicators of positional advantage*
  4 Competitive cost and activity comparisons
    (a) Value chain comparisons of relative costs
    (b) Cross-section experience curves
	5 Customer comparisons of attributes of firm versus competitors
	  (a) Choice mode
	  (b) Conjoint analysis
	  (c) Market maps

C *Identifying key success factors*
  6 Comparison of winning versus losing competitors
  7 Identifying high leverage phenomena
    (a) Management estimates of market share elasticities
    (b) Drivers of activities in the value chain	

D *Measure of performance*	**8** Customer satisfaction surveys **9** Loyalty (customer franchise)
10a Market share	**10b** Relative share of end-user segments
11 Relative profitability (return on assets)	

Source: Day, G. S. and Wensley, R. (1988), 'Assessing Advantage: A Framework for Diagnosing Competitive Superiority', *Journal of Marketing*, Vol 52, April, pp. 1-20, American Marketing Association.

the early fifties. Rupert Dallmeyer, a former executive of Booz Allen Hamilton, remembers conducting marketing audits as early as 1952.' As the term suggests, the practice in seen as similar in intention to the accounting audit and Kotler et al. offer the following definition:

A marketing audit is a comprehensive, systematic, independent, and periodic examination of a company's – or business unit's – marketing environment, objectives, strategies and activities with a view of determining problem areas and opportunities and recommending a plan of action to improve the company's marketing performance.

The author's own view is that the marketing audit should not go so far as recommending a plan of action, and prefers to regard it as an activity which will inform and guide the planning process. Indeed, a great deal of a marketing audit can be undertaken by specialist staff (just as an accounting audit is) with the final evaluation and interpretation being left to the company's operating management. The latter is an important part of successful planning.

During the 1960s and 1970s a great deal of planning activity was delegated to specially formed strategic planning departments. Despite the detail and sophistication of the plans developed by such planning units, many formerly successful organisations which could afford them got into serious trouble in the late 1970s and early 1980s. In seeking to determine the reasons for their changed fortunes, many of these organisations recognised that strategic planning is the senior management function, and could not be delegated to staff specialists. Where this was done firms were ignoring the wisdom and experience of the senior management who, consequently, felt no ownership of the resulting plans and so were less committed to their implementation.

In the late 1980s and early 1990s a very similar reaction to formalised marketing departments also became apparent. As more organisations and managers accepted Drucker's (1954) definition of marketing as '. . . the distinguishing, the unique function of the business' and as relationship marketing displaced transactional marketing, so senior managers assumed direct responsibility for marketing and encouraged all employees to become involved with and responsible for marketing practice. The result has been a marked decline in the importance of formal marketing departments.

As stated above, a marketing audit should comprise a comprehensive, systematic and periodic review of all aspects of the organisation's internal operations and external environment.

(The other criterion 'independent' is, naturally, one consultants would recommend but its value is regarded as limited unless a firm has seriously lost its way for the reasons touched on above) The importance of the evaluation of the external environment is the subject of Chapter 4, but aspects of reviewing key elements of the firms' internal operations will be dealt with when discussing the elements of the marketing mix in greater detail in Part III.

THE MARKETING MIX

The concept of the marketing mix and its component elements comprises the content of Part III but, at this juncture, it will be helpful to provide a brief introduction to one of the longest established and most useful concepts in the marketing repertoire.

While the idea of a marketing mix is generally attributed to Neil Borden of the Harvard Business School he freely acknowledges that he picked up the idea from another HBS professor – James Cullinton. Like most ideas that withstand the test of time, the concept of the marketing mix is elegant in its simplicity and merely observes that the marketing manager has a limited number of ingredients at his disposal but, like a master chef, he can combine these into an almost limitless number of recipes.

Identification and listing of the ingredients of the marketing mix ranges from the very simple to the very complex. At one end of the spectrum there is Eugene McCarthy's 4 P's of Product, Price, Place and Promotion while at the other there is the much longer listing of Borden himself which is reproduced as Table 2.4.

While McCarthy's 4 P's still enjoy considerable currency most observers would agree that at the very least they need to be extended to include consideration of People, that is the most basic but probably most complex of the mix ingredients, and to acknowledge the importance of research in determining both the nature of the ingredients to be used and the most appropriate recipe.

Table 2.4 Elements of the marketing mix

1 Merchandising – product planning:
   (a) Determination of product (or service to be sold – qualities, design, etc.) To whom, when, where and in what quantities?
   (b) Determination of new product programme – research and development, merger
   (c) Determination of marketing research programme

2 Pricing:
   (a) Determination of level of prices
   (b) Determination of psychological aspects of price, e.g. odd or even
   (c) Determination of pricing policy; e.g. one price or varying price, use of price maintenance, etc.
   (d) Determination of margins: freedom in setting?

3 Branding:
   (a) Determination of brand policy, e.g. individual brand or family brand

4 Channels of distribution:
   (a) Determination of channels to use, direct sale to user, direct sale to retailers or users' sources of purchase, e.g. supply houses
       Sale through wholesalers
   (b) Determination of degree of selectivity among dealers
   (c) Devising of programmes to secure channel cooperation

5 Personal selling:
   (a) Determination of burden to be placed on personal selling and methods to be employed
       (1) For manufacturer's organisation
       (2) For wholesalers
       (3) For retailers
   (b) Organisation, selection, training and guidance of sales force at various levels of distribution

Table 2.4 Elements of the marketing mix continued

6 Advertising:
   (a)   Determination of appropriate burden to be placed on advertising
   (b)   Determination of copy policy
   (c)   Determination of mix of advertising:
          to trade
          to consumers
   (d)   Determination of media

7 Promotions:
   (a)   Determination of burden to place on special selling plans or devices and formulation of
          promotions:
          (1)   to trade
          (2)   to consumers

8 Packaging:
   (a)   Determination of importance of packaging and formulation of packages

9 Display:
   (a)   Determination of importance and devising of procedures

10 Servicing:
   (a)   Determination of importance of service and devising of procedures to meet consumer needs
          and desires

11 Physical handling – warehousing – transportation – stock policy

12 Fact-finding and analysis – marketing research

Source: N. Borden (1964), 'The Concept of the Marketing Mix', *Journal of Advertising Research,* Cambridge University Press.

LIMITED STRATEGIC ALTERNATIVES

Many years before it became fashionable to draw analogies between military and business strategy the author proposed (Baker, 1975) the view that an organisation has only a limited number of basic strategies available to it. In simple terms these may be listed as:

- *Peaceful co-existence* or 'do nothing'.
- *Direct assault* or price competition.
- *Indirect or flanking attack* using product, place and/or promotion.
- *By-pass or avoidance of competition* through innovation.
- *Withdrawal* – a deliberate and planned decision to disengage.

(A very similar approach was popularised several years later (1981) by Philip Kotler.) An even simpler notion of competitive alternatives is contained in Igor Ansoff's (1968) 'Growth Vector Matrix' which included only two dimensions: 'Mission', which is equivalent to target market, and 'Technology'. Further, in the interests of simplicity, Ansoff only recognises two states – present and new – giving four basic alternatives which he described as market penetration, market development, product development and diversification.

Given the present market and present product the organisation will only be able to grow if it can encourage its existing customers to consume more or attract customers away from other current suppliers (**market penetration**). As we have already seen, if the firm is to win new customers then it must offer some advantage as perceived by potential customers which, if there is no change in the product, must be based upon price (a **cost leadership strategy**) or place and/or promotion (which offers **differentiation**). For reasons which will become clearer in later chapters, most organisations avoid price competition (it reduces margins, is highly visible and may be seen as predatory by regulatory agencies) and prefer to use any cost advantage to differentiate their product through other less obvious and less objective advantages such as reputation, availability, after-sales service, and so forth.

But, given that all consumers may have objective differences drawn to their notice while other, less tangible benefits of the kind listed in the previous sentence often exist largely in the subjective viewpoint of the potential purchasers, and vary widely in nature (that is, the seller cannot control them in the same way as their product specification), most sellers' preferred growth strategy is **product development**. In the case of a product development strategy it is assumed that one already has detailed knowledge of one's customer base, and so is able to utilise this knowledge continuously to update and improve the product (or service) in order to match the increased expectation of one's own customers, and offset the claims of one's competitors. (As a working rule of thumb it has been estimated that it costs five times as much to create or win a new customer as to retain an existing one.) Concentration on product development as the preferred strategy (differentiation) has resulted in an acceleration of technological change, and shorter and shorter product life cycles. Despite this, it is likely to remain a

Figure 2.3 A growth vector matrix

Supply Demand	Current Technology / Products	New Technology / Products
Current Customers	Market Penetration	Product Development
New Customers	Market Development	Diversification

Source: Adapted from an original idea by Ansoff (1968).

preferred strategy as it enables the seller to exploit their knowledge of particular customer groupings or market segments to the full.

The third strategy suggested by the matrix is **market development** which assumes that the firm retains the same technology but finds new customers for it. Basically, it can do this in one of two ways. First, the firm can move into geographically new markets, that is it extends the place dimension; or, second, it can find new uses for the existing product. For example, Dow Chemicals developed what we now call shrink wrap as a packing material to protect weapons during the Second World War. With the end of the war this market was greatly reduced, but Dow saw that the material had considerable potential in the domestic market and, after one or two setbacks, successfully launched it in this new market.

While new uses for existing products offer an opportunity for market development, the greater opportunity is undoubtedly that offered by extending the scope of the physical market by expanding into new areas. For the small or startup company this may simply entail expansion into an adjacent region with no need to modify any of the elements of the marketing mix; that is, the potential customers in the new region are the same in terms of language, culture, social and economic characteristics, etc. as those in the original market. For the large or highly specialised company, however, extension of the physical market may well require it to cross national boundaries and sell to customers with different languages, customs, and so on. Such 'international marketing' is dealt with in greater detail in Chapter 23.

The final option offered by the matrix is that of **diversification**, which is closely analogous to the by-pass or innovation strategy mentioned earlier. Clearly, this option carries the greatest risk for, by definition, the firm has no prior experience of either the market, or the technology, as is the case with all the preceding options. In many cases, indeed the great majority, innovation is introduced to the market by a new entrant, as opposed to an existing player, as the latter has a vested interest in protecting their current investment in the known and proven technology. That said, a characteristic of the long-established multinational corporation is its ability to recognise the inevitable implications of the product life cycle and to switch from old to new technology as the latter begins to take off in the rapidly expanding growth phase of the life cycle. (This is sometimes called 'the strategy of the fast-second' or 'imitative innovation'.) Clearly, Ansoff's model is about as simple as one can get and, in fact, a more complex 3x3 matrix was proposed at virtually the same time, and an example is shown in Figure 2.4. (Ansoff did later update his matrix with an additional dimension (1988)). However, this simplicity is seen as a great virtue as the emphasis in this section has been upon reducing the nature of strategy formulation to the bare essentials. Once this has been done the key strategic variable(s) will be easier to identify and, as the later discussion of the mix elements will make obvious, the decision-maker will still be faced with a very wide ranging selection of tactical alternatives. We will touch on this briefly in the final section on **Positioning**.

POSITIONING

In common with most of the other basic ideas introduced in this chapter the concept of positioning is both a simple and intuitively appealing one. In essence positioning means the achievement of a unique place in a competitive market for a particular product such that some worthwhile sub-group of consumers perceive you to be different in some meaningful and important respect from all other competitors. In order to determine the position of a product – whether one's own or a competitor's – the first step must be to establish what are the key criteria or attributes which consumers use to judge performance and distinguish between the competitive offerings available to them. Once these key attributes have been defined a survey may be undertaken to find out how consumers perceive each of

Figure 2.4 A product development matrix

Market \ Product	Current	Modified	New
Current	Status Quo	Improved	Replacement
Extended	New Uses	Enhanced	Replacement
New	New Customers	Enlarged	Diversification

Source: Adapted from an idea by Johnson and Jones (1957).

Figure 2.5 Product positions in a competitive market

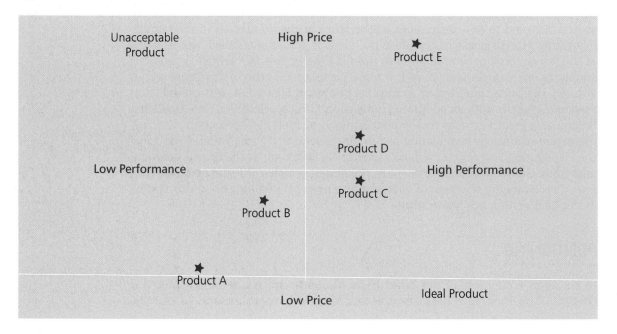

the different brands in terms of the relevant criteria. This information may then be plotted using pairs of dimensions such as price and performance to determine the position of the ideal product (lowest price/highest performance) and the actual position of the products surveyed as shown in Figure 2.5.

While the techniques (cluster analysis and perceptual mapping) used in this type of analysis are beyond the scope of an introductory text – a more extended description is to be found in our discussion of Baker's Box in Chapter 14.

Summary

In this chapter we have explored some of the strategic dimensions of marketing in order to provide a framework and perspective for examining the key areas of marketing in greater detail throughout the rest of the book.

It has been argued that marketing is very much about change on the grounds that consumers in the pursuit of their self-interest will always prefer that product or service which offers them the greatest satisfaction. As producers strive to distinguish themselves one from another they will seek to capitalise on this pursuit of self-interest by defining the particular needs of specific customer groups and seeking to satisfy them better than any of their rivals. In doing so they will tend to prefer the creation of objective differences in the physical product or service as these are more readily communicated and evaluated than are more subjective values which relate to aspects such as reputation or aesthetic qualities. Thus, every product has a life cycle in which new and better ways of serving basic needs continuously displace older and less satisfactory means of serving the same needs.

In order to succeed in a competitive environment great attention and effort is now given to determining what factors are critical to success. However, as our analysis shows, such **critical success factors (CSFs)** are necessary but not sufficient conditions for competitive success. In the real world what distinguishes between more and less successful firms is the quality of management and its implementation of the CSFs – something which may be seen in the organisational culture of a firm. It would also seem that successful firms are those which are skilled in identifying the existence of market opportunities and developing or exploiting those in which they enjoy a comparative advantage vis-á-vis their competitors. This ability to match strengths with opportunities while avoiding threats and making good weaknesses in the firm's performance is greatly enhanced by the conduct of formalised marketing audits and SWOT analyses and the articulation of clear objectives.

In particular, competitive advantage arises from the manipulation of the ingredients of the marketing mix (product, price, place, promotion and people). Such manipulation requires first the selection of one of a very small number of limited strategic alternatives, most of which may be distinguished in terms of the two dimensions of Ansoff's growth vector matrix – mission or markets (people or demand) and technology or product (firms or supply). By definition, for competition to exist two or more suppliers will seek to serve the same market. Their success in doing so will depend very much upon the last concept introduced in this chapter – positioning. Positioning requires the supplier to determine the nature of the attributes which consumers use to judge the performance and satisfaction offered by different product offerings and seek to develop a unique combination which will appeal to a sufficiently large subgroup (or segment) of users to make the differentiation profitable to the supplier

In sum, the selection of a successful marketing strategy depends very much upon the firm's ability to interpret the environment in which it is competing and to organise itself in such a way as to exploit those opportunities most in keeping with its own strengths and competences.

Review questions and problems

1 'The product life cycle (PLC) concept is seriously deficient as a management tool, but continues to receive a great deal of management attention.' Why do you think this is, and how far do you consider that the PLC can play a useful part in shaping companies' new product development and launch strategies?

2 Assess the implications of the product life cycle (PLC) concept for strategic marketing planning.

3 The 'bottom line' of an internal appraisal of a firm's marketing system is to identify strengths and weaknesses; the environmental appraisal yields opportunities and threats.
   (a) How are strengths and weaknesses related to opportunities and threats in devising the marketing strategy for a firm.
   (b) How could you systematically search for strengths and weaknesses in a marketing strategy?

4 Discuss the ways in which a marketing manager might assess the position of a product in its life cycle.

5 Identify the components of the marketing mix and explain the importance of each in strategic planning.

6 Examine the view that the marketing planning function is central to the profitability of the organisation.

7 Discuss the implications of the statement that "Consumers owe no loyalty to suppliers, only to themselves".

8 "Every declining industry was once a growth industry". What explanation did Levitt (1960) offer to support this claim, and what solution(s) did he suggest to stop decline setting in?

9 Why do you think the PLC might be useful when thinking about developing a marketing strategy but of little use as a predictive device?

10 What is 'organisational culture'? How might it influence or effect corporate performance?

11 Explain the notion of 'sustainable competitive advantage' (SCA). What actions might a firm take to develop SCA?

12 Describe and evaluate the four strategies suggested by Ansoff's (1968) 'growth-vector' matrix.

Key terms

4 Ps (product, price, place, promotion)
business to business (B2B)
business to consumer (B2C)
competitive advantage
cost leadership strategy
critical success factors (CSF)
customer relationship management
differentiation

diversification
function
market opportunity
market penetration
marketing audit
marketing development
marketing mix
normative theory
organisational culture
positioning

practice
product development
product life cycle
relationship marketing
strategic alternatives
strategic marketing planning (SMP)
strategy
SWOT analysis

Supplementary reading list

Baker, M. J. (2000), *Marketing Strategy and Management*, 3rd edn, (Basingstoke: Palgrave). *(A new Fourth Edition is to be published in 2006)*

Baker, M. J. (Ed.) (2003), *The Marketing Book*, 5th edn, (Oxford: Butterworth-Heinemann)

Baker, M. J., and Hart, S. J. (1989) *Marketing and Competitive Success* (London: Philip Allen).

Kotler, P., Gregor, W. and Rodgers, W. (1977), "The Marketing Audit Comes of Age", *Sloan Management Review*, Winter, pp. 25-43.

McDonald, M. (1999), 'Developing and implementing a marketing plan', in Baker, M.J. (ed.) *IEBM Encyclopedia of Marketing*, (London: Thomson Learning).

DEMAND AND SUPPLY

| Learning Goals | *After reading this chapter you should be able to:* |

- Define and describe a demand schedule and a demand curve.

- Distinguish between needs and wants.

- List the determinants of demand and distinguish between potential, latent and effective demand.

- Define a product and list its characteristics.

- Define supply and explain the concept of diminishing returns.

- Explain the nature and relevance of Maslow's Hierarchy of Needs.

- Discuss the origins and importance of branding.

- Define the various categories of industrial and consumer goods and the distinguishing characteristics of services.

INTRODUCTION

In Chapter 1 it was stated that the principal objective of economic organisation is to maximise satisfaction from the consumption of scarce resources. It was further proposed that, while suppliers have always concentrated on producing those goods and services in greatest demand, the industrial revolution resulted in both a physical and psychological separation between producer and consumer as the former concentrated on mass production and distribution to cater for the needs of a rapidly expanding market. But, as population growth began to slow down in the industrialised economies, a potential for excess supply to develop led to increased competition between sellers and what we termed the "rediscovery of marketing" – the requirement that producers base their decisions on a careful analysis of the customers requirements, and the tailoring of their output to match these requirements. The implications of this change, and the need to develop strategies for competing with the suppliers of similar or substitute goods and services were reviewed in Chapter 2.

While basic economic theory is concerned largely with price–quantity relationships, and other demand determinants are invariably excluded for more sophisticated treatment, corporate success is very closely related to the manufacturer's ability to predict the strength and nature of demand as a basis for deploying the firm's resources. Consequently, management is deeply concerned with all those variables which condition demand.

In this Chapter we turn out attention to the forces of demand and supply as it is the interaction between these that creates the need for markets where an equilibrium between them may be achieved through the operation of the price mechanism. To begin with we look at **demography** – the study of populations – as this is at the very heart of the marketing process. Populations are made up of people, and it is people who have a demand for different kinds of goods and services. It is their satisfaction that the market mechanism seeks to fulfil. Accordingly, the analysis of a population in terms of its age, gender, ethnic composition, education, income etc. is fundamental to the understanding of consumption behaviour and effective marketing. Next we examine how specific needs may be aggregated to construct **demand schedules** that indicate the existence and nature of market opportunities. In turn this leads to consideration of ways in which producers decide which goods to offer for sale in which markets – the concept of **supply**.

DEMOGRAPHICS

Demographics may be defined as the study and analysis of the size , composition, behaviour and distribution of populations. Knowledge and understanding of these factors is critical to government and the formulation of social policy – i.e macro decisions about the allocation of resources – "what is to be done" – while competition and marketing determine "how" it will be achieved. Because of the importance of population statistics to governments such information is universally available, although its quality varies significantly between nations. Nonetheless, population statistics are the foundation on which market analysis rests.

Given that demographics track the characteristics and behaviour of individuals from cradle to grave they are the most reliable descriptor of current needs and conduct, and the best single predictor of future trends. Extrapolation of population changes enables us to develop scenarios of the future that suggest what actions need to be taken to achieve desired outcomes.

Of course, extrapolation is an inexact science and subject to the occurrence of both random and predictable events such as the devastation caused by the tsunami in the Indian Ocean in 2004. But, in the absence of such events, once a child is born we can predict fairly accurately its life expectancy and basic needs at various stages of its life cycle for education, housing, medical care, leisure and recreation and so on. And, while we cannot predict the precise means by which these needs will be satisfied, we can devise both national and international policies to guard against the dangers of over-population and the destruction of non-renewable resources.

These problems are not new. In 1798 the Rev. Thomas Malthus published his 'Essay on the Principle of Population' in which he challenged the prevailing view that increases in population would result in economic growth and wealth creation. Malthus claimed that while population increased in a geometrical progression – 1, 2, 4, 8 16 etc – production of food only increased following an arithmetic progression – 1, 2, 3, 4, etc. Ultimately, demand for food would exceed the supply and could only be brought into equilibrium through increased deaths arising from disease or war, or fewer births as a result of birth control.

As a result of technical progress, a slowing down of the birth rate in developed countries, and the development of previously unexploited resources, Malthus' negative controls have been avoided in the advanced economies and controlled to a degree in the newly industrialised and emerging economies like India and China. On the other hand 50% of the world's population is malnourished, and millions die every year from famine, disease and war. At the same time the destruction of the world's rain forests to clear land for cultivation, and the rapidly increasing consumption of non-renewable fossil fuels have led to global warming and major long-term climate change.

While modern marketing evolved as a response to the possibility of excess supply in affluent economies, there can be no doubt that the major challenge of the twenty first century will be the stabilisation of global demand to maintain an equilibrium with the supply available from renewable resources without destroying our environment. In parallel, it is essential to bring about a more equitable distribution of the world's wealth among all its people. Failure to do so can only lead inevitably to the Malthusian controls of famine, disease and war. These are heroic tasks, but they are precisely the kinds of problems that professional management and sound marketing practice are equipped to deal with.

Population

People constitute the basic raw material from which markets are made, for, ultimately, the demand for any given product or service depends upon the aggregate demand of individual consumers. One of the major arguments behind our attempts to gain membership of the European Economic Community was that this would open the door to a market with a population which was then five times as great as that of the United Kingdom. Clearly, this represents an enormous potential for increasing sales.

Absolute numbers are only one aspect of population, however, three other important aspects being age and sex distribution, geographical distribution and family size.

In the past decade the age distribution of the population of the UK and many other advanced industrial countries has attracted increasing attention. Essentially this attention has arisen from the realisation that, with declining birth rates and longer life expectancies, the population is 'ageing'. Thus, an increasing proportion of people are to be found in the older age groups and a lesser proportion in the younger and 'working' age groups. The implications of these changes in the composition of the population are profound. Consider, for example, the markets for education and health care.

In the case of education many of the readers of this book will be aware that in the 1980s many primary and secondary schools were being closed down for lack of 'customers'. In their naivety planners in the Department of Education and Science extrapolated this trend and predicted a decline in the need for places in further and higher education and began to cut back on funding. Fortunately, the educationists were able to point out the difference between potential demand (all young people leaving secondary education) and effective demand (the proportion able and wanting to benefit from higher education). In addition to a growing interest in higher education a closer examination of the population statistics, also revealed that although the overall birth rate had declined, in fact it had increased in Social Classes I and II which traditionally have the highest participation rates in higher education. The lesson is clear; while absolute numbers are important in defining market potential it is usage, or effective demand which determines market size. When the government recognised this fact in the early 1990s and proposed a significant increase in higher education, its projections of a 30 per cent participation rate were quickly exceeded by the demand for these additional places. Since then the Government has raised its targets for participation to 50% and is seeking to encourage more young people from Social Classes III and IV to stay on in Higher Education, with a corresponding increase in demand for facilities and teachers.

At the other end of the age spectrum the effect of an ageing or 'greying' population has also had a marked effect on consumption patterns. Nowhere is this more evident than in the demand for health care, and the provision of sheltered housing, nursing homes and geriatric facilities in hospitals. Here again, careful analysis of trends in the population, informed by knowledge of the likely incidence of particular diseases or disabilities such as diabetes or arthritis, can offer considerable insight into future demand and market opportunities. Table 3.1 is based on Government Actuaries projections and indicates how the proportion of those under and over age 30 is expected to change from 37.0%: 63.0% in 2005, to 33.0%: 67.0% by 2031.

As implied in the preceding paragraphs many products are associated with a particular stage of the human life cycle, and recognition of this has led to the adoption of the life-cycle concept as a useful means of distinguishing the effect of age on consumption patterns. Although it is increasingly recognised that

Table 3.1 Projected population by age to 2051 (UK Figures, 2003-based population projections).

	Projected populations at mid-years by age last birthday						
	2005	2010	2015	2021	2031	2041	2051
Ages	Thousands						
0-14	10,793	10,425	10,329	10,447	10,533	10,243	10,208
15-29	11,431	11,968	11,961	11,455	11,130	11,321	11,156
30-44	13,391	12,578	12,052	12,405	12,703	11,995	12,067
45-59	11,636	12,136	12,983	12,952	11,789	12,599	12,110
60-74	8,177	9,204	9,757	10,502	11,871	11,082	11,207
75 & over	4,596	4,856	5,289	6,075	7,675	9,302	10,038
Males	29,382	30,030	30,681	31,432	32,337	32,748	32,893
Females	30,642	31,136	31,689	32,403	33,362	33,795	33,894
Totals	60,024	61,166	62,370	63,835	65,700	66,543	66,787

Source: Government Actuary's Department, NTC. 2005. © Government Actuary's Department

young children influence purchasing decisions, their lack of purchasing power usually excludes them from life-cycle classificatory systems which concentrate on **decision-making units** (**DMU**s). A widely accepted system distinguishes the following eight stages:

1   Young, single.

2   Young, married, no children.

3   Young, married, youngest child under six.

4   Young, married, youngest child over six.

5   Older, married, with children.

6   Older, married, no children under eighteen.

7   Older, single.

8   Other.

Although the distinction between Young and Older is not explicit, and category 8 is a meaningless 'catchall', the concept provides a useful basis for breaking down the total population into sub-groups for more detailed analysis. (A useful exercise is to visualise the variations that one would anticipate in consumption patterns as between the different categories in this system.) Life-style analysis is currently enjoying an enormous wave of popularity amongst marketers and numerous references to its application are to be found in the management literature. An extended review of the application of the family life-cycle concept is given by Rob. W. Lawson (1988), 'The Family Life Cycle: A Demographic Analysis'.

The Office of the Deputy Prime Minister in the UK compiles statistics about UK households (*http://www.odpm.gov.uk*) and provides numerous statistics about household composition.

The physical distribution of the population has a direct bearing upon the marketer's ability to make their products available to potential customers at an economic cost. The concentration of population in Britain, backed by extensive transportation facilities, make this factor less important than in many other parts of the world, for example the United States, Australia and Africa. In the case of bulky materials of low unit value, such as cement, or when considering entry into an export market, it will take on added significance in measuring potential demand. Physical location also has an important bearing upon the existence of regional wants and preferences; porridge, tripe and jellied eels immediately call to mind Scotland, Lancashire and London respectively. Similarly, woollens are in greater demand in the north, and cottons in the south. Overall, however, such differences are less marked than in many larger countries.

For planning and administrative purposes, the marketer will often find it convenient to subdivide the country into areas in some systematic way. An obvious approach is to use the Government Office Regions, namely:

Great Britain		
North East	West Midlands	South West
North West	East	Wales
Yorkshire/Humberside	London	Scotland
East Midlands	South East	Northern Ireland

The great advantage of using this scheme is that the standard regions are widely used in the collection of Government statistics, and are capable of further subdivision into counties, conurbations, boroughs, and so on. On the other hand the standard regions listed above differ from those used prior to the 1971 Census and may be subject to change with further Local Government reorganisation. Several other alternatives are available, including the Nielsen Areas, and 'Geographia's' marketing regions, each of which has its advantages and disadvantages. However, all are to be preferred to a purely arbitrary subdivision which precludes direct use of published data

Households

While population studies are ultimately concerned with the individual, for planning and marketing purposes the household is often used. As can be seen from Table 3.2, households are defined in terms of the number of persons living together in a dwelling unit, viz:

While the above Table does not suggest major changes, over the past decade or so, more detailed analysis confirms that there have been significant and important changes. To begin with in 1992 there were 22,225,000 households in Great Britain; in 2002 it was 24,350,000 – an increase of around 10%. It is this statistic that is important for the marketer because household size has a direct bearing on housing itself, the size of appliances and cars, container size, etc., etc. In conjunction with income, it also has an important effect on household purchasing patterns for, despite certain economies present in large families, it is clear that for a given income such families will spend more on essentials than small families. Digging

Table 3.2 Size of household

Size of household	1991 %	2003 %
1 person	26	27
2 persons	35	36
3 persons	17	17
4 persons	16	13
5 persons	6	4
6 or more persons	2	1

Table 3.3 Marital status by sex

Marital status by sex	1991		2002	
	Male %	Female %	Male %	Female %
Married	62	57	54	50
Cohabiting	6	5	10	9
Single	24	17	26	20
Widowed, divorced etc.	8	21	10	20

deeper still it becomes apparent that a number of social trends lie behind the drift towards smaller households, and understanding these is critical to successful marketing planning. For example, consider Table 3.3 summarising changes in marital status over the same period.

Again it is important to remember that the number of both males and females has increased by around three-quarters of a million over this time so that the actual change is greater than might appear when considering the percentages.

Statistics of these kind are freely available from various Government Departments and a number of Professional, Commercial and Trade sources. Many of those of most use to marketers are collated into the various Pocket Book series published by the World Advertising Research Center (*www.warc.com*). As they are constantly being revised the reader should access the original sources as Tables reproduced in books are almost immediately out of date.

Income

Income is a major demand determinant and is widely used as a measure of potential demand. With the increase in the number of 'working wives', and recognising that the household is the most common decision-making and purchasing unit, it is more useful to think in terms of aggregate household income than to consider the major wage-earner's income alone.

Two concepts are particularly useful in analysing income levels – net disposable income, and discretionary purchasing power. The former consists of income from all sources including wages, interest on savings and investments, health and welfare benefits and so on, less taxes. It is a measure of the amount available for saving and expenditure. Discretionary purchasing power comprises that amount available after all 'essential' expenditures have been met – it is 'uncommitted' income which the consumer may spend, or save, as he or she pleases. As noted in Chapter 1, increasing income levels are invariably paralleled by an upgrading in what is considered essential but, overall, Engels's Laws seem to hold, namely: As

DEMAND

We live in a changing world

In a Report on Packaging's Place in Society produced by the University of Brighton in collaboration with Pira, the following major trends were identified:

- People are living longer
- More of us live alone
- We have more disposable income
- Our time is pressured (and precious)
- We are becoming more health conscious – and greater choice is offered

- Brands have become globalised – but we like to be treated as individuals
- The food we consume and the way we prepare it has changed
  Freezers and microwaves are now standard in most kitchens
  We consume more prepared food products
  So we spend less time cooking
  But we spend more time and money eating out
  In the home, convenience foods require different packaging
  Cultural differences also influence the food we eat and the packaging we use

real income increases the proportion spent on food tends to decline, expenditures on rent, heating, etc., remain constant while the proportion spent on clothing, education, recreation and travel, etc., tends to increase.

Most incomes are earned in payment for services rendered, and so depend upon the demand for the services in question (as modified by restrictive practices that limit entry to a trade or profession). In broad terms, occupation is determined by education, and there exists a strong correlation between the two and income so that, in the absence of income data, many researchers use education/occupation as a surrogate. Incomes vary considerably across occupational categories and the reader should consult the Department for Trade and Industry and Department for Work and Pensions, or the 'New Earnings Survey' from National Statistics *http://www.statistics.gov.uk* for detailed information on wage rates and earnings. One must be careful not to confuse the two, for wage rates do not necessarily bear any resemblance to the actual wages paid in a particular job or area. Further, the incidence of overtime, bonuses and the like has a marked effect on earnings, and it is the latter with which the demand analyst is primarily concerned.

Effective demand (discussed in more detail below) implies that consumption is a function of available income, and this relationship has been the subject of extensive research over a long period. Three separate theories have evolved out of this research in an attempt to explain variations in aggregate consumption functions and may be summarised as:

1. The **absolute income hypothesis**, which holds that expenditures/savings are a function of income.

2. The **relative income hypothesis**, which holds that expenditures/saving patterns depend upon the relative position of the spending unit on the income scale, and not on the absolute income earned. This hypothesis recognises the 'keeping up with the Jones' phenomenon.

3. The **permanent income hypothesis**, which holds that expenditures are based on average income expectations over time. This hypothesis recognises that consumption patterns are relatively stable over time, which suggests that consumers average out their expenditures; that is, under inflation they anticipate that they will make good current dissaving, due to price increases, out of future wage increases.

An additional, and complicating, factor in recent years has been the increased availability of credit. Although the amount of credit an institution is prepared to extend to an individual is usually related to their income, there are now so many separate sources that the relationship between credit and income has become tenuous. Clearly, the ready availability of credit has done much to enable the consumer to translate latent demand into an effective demand, and has become an important demand determinant.

Collectively, the factors reviewed above are socio-economic variables, and form the basis of a broad but useful classificatory system. Until recently differences in ethnic origin and religion have usually been considered too slight to merit inclusion in such a system. But, over the past half century or so there has been a steady and significant increase in the size of the ethnic minorities as can be seen from Table 3.4.

In recent years much of this growth has arisen from the enlargement of the European Union, and as a consequence of political change and unrest in many other countries. Today the activities and behaviour of ethnic minorities have become major political issues, while the growth in the number of persons with different consumption behaviour has created important new market segments in the UK market.

Equally important, immigrants have introduced the native population to new products and services generating a demand for new foods, fashion, restaurants, tourism etc.

PSYCHOLOGICAL FACTORS

When discussing the distinction between needs and wants it was noted that needs are essentially physiological and instinctive, but that such generalised, basic drives are subject to modification by other factors, resulting in specific wants. To a large degree these 'other factors' are psychological. However, people live in social groups, membership of which modifies behavioural response to the extent that it would be more correct to identify these factors as psycho-sociological and/or socio-psychological. Collectively, the study of these influences has created a whole new field of marketing, usually referred to as 'consumer behaviour'. An extended discussion of the more important concepts is the subject of Chapter 8.

Demand

Before proceeding to discuss factors that influence demand it will be useful to distinguish between **needs**, **wants** and the function of **choice**.

A *need* is something fundamental to the maintenance of life, such as food, drink, shelter and clothing. Needs are largely physiological in the sense that they are basic and instinctive drives with which we are born. It is clear, however, that a need may be satisfied by any one of a large number of alternatives; for example thirst may be alleviated by water, tea, coffee, beer, wine and so forth. The availability of alternative means of satisfying a need constitutes *choice*, provision of which is central to the practice of marketing. In the absence of substitute, or alternative, goods there can be no choice, and needs and wants become synonymous. Where there is more than one way of satisfying a basic need, physiological drives will be modified by economic, sociological and psychological factors. Variations in these factors will predispose individuals to prefer a specific alternative and this

Table 3.4 Estimated size of ethnic minorities in Great Britain

Year	000s	% of total population
1951	200	0.4
1961	500	1.0
1971	1200	2.3
1981	2100	3.9
1991	3015	5.5
2003	4659	7.9

preference constitutes a *want*.

By and large, economists tend to be concerned only with what they term **effective demand**, which is defined as demand backed up by purchasing power. However, most managers are also interested in two other types of demand – which we may describe as 'potential' demand and 'latent' demand.

A **latent demand** may be thought of as one which the consumer is unable to satisfy, usually for lack of purchasing power. For example, many housewives may have a latent demand for automatic dishwashers, but, related to their available disposable income, this want is less strong than their demand for other products and so remains unsatisfied. In other words, wants are ranked in order of preference and satisfied to the point where disposable income is exhausted. From the manufacturer's point of view, the problem is to translate latent demand into effective demand by increasing the consumer's preference for their particular product vis-à-vis all other product offerings.

A demand schedule for a specific product may be thought of as expressing effective demand, by which is understood demand backed by the ability to pay a given price.

When deciding to enter a market a critical decision is the price to charge for one's product. Given that the quantity demanded varies with the price asked, what we would like to know is just what is the effective demand for our product at any given price. As a working rule of thumb the more features our product has, and the higher its perceived quality, the higher the price we can ask and vice-versa. In a completely new market we will have to depend on judgement and experience and proceed largely by trial and error. On the other hand, if we are entering an existing market we can research it and estimate how much will be demanded at any given price. This estimate is our demand schedule which we can express graphically as a curve as shown in Figure 3.1

Figure 3.1 Simple demand curve and schedule

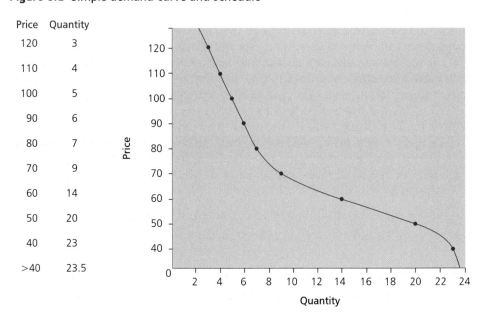

Price	Quantity
120	3
110	4
100	5
90	6
80	7
70	9
60	14
50	20
40	23
>40	23.5

This 'classical' **demand curve** is for an undifferentiated product where every unit on offer for sale is identical to every other so that the amount customers are prepared to pay is a reflection of how important the object is to them, and how much they can afford and are willing to pay to secure a supply. Supposing that the product is petroleum based we can see that for organisations and persons that depend on it their demand is hardly effected by price increases, although they will need to offset this by raising their prices to their customers. Conversely, as price falls, more and more people will be able to afford it and consume it in larger quantities resulting in a rapid growth in demand. We return to this relationship between price and the quantity demanded later in the chapter.

As noted earlier, a latent demand may be thought of as a demand which the consumer is unable to satisfy, usually for lack of purchasing power. Latent demand may also be thought of as a vague want in the sense that the consumer feels a need for a product, or service, to fill a particular function but is unable to locate anything suitable. It is clear that latent demand constitutes an important consideration in management planning. In the case of a demand which is latent due to lack of purchasing power a manufacturer may be able to change a consumer's preference through their marketing and promotional activities. Alternatively, if there is a trend towards increasing disposable income, then the producer may be able to project how such increases in purchasing power will enable consumers to translate their latent demand into an effective demand. Given such a forecast they will be able to plan increased production, distribution and sales to keep pace with rising disposable incomes.

In the case of a demand which is latent because the consumer is unaware of the existence of a product or service which would satisfy an ill-defined want, then clearly if the manufacturer produces a product which they feel should satisfy the need, they will wish to bring it to the attention of those with a latent demand for it. Alternatively, if a manufacturer does not produce a product which should satisfy a known latent demand, but is able to specify what the characteristics of such a product would be, then the latent demand becomes a marketing opportunity which they may wish to exploit.

Potential demand may be said to exist where a consumer possesses purchasing power but is not currently buying. Thus, where a marketer has identified a latent demand and developed a new product to satisfy it, the potential demand consists of all those who can back up their latent want with purchasing power. In another context potential demand may be thought of as that part of the total market or effective demand for an existing product which a firm might anticipate securing through the introduction of a new competitive product.

Once again it must be stressed that while the economists' model serves a useful purpose as a basis for analysing the real world, the assumptions upon which it rests are clearly unrealistic. Thus elementary economic texts usually make assumptions about consumer demand as follows:

1 The consumer's wants remain unchanged throughout.
2 S/he has a fixed amount of money available.
3 S/he is one of many buyers.
4 S/he knows the price of all goods, each of which is homogeneous.
5 S/he can, if s/he wishes, spend their money in very small amounts.
6 S/he acts rationally.

Of these assumptions only 2 and 3 seem likely to be true with any frequency in the real world. For the rest, as managers are only too aware, consumer demand is fickle and changes frequently. Knowledge of the existence of all those goods which the consumer might buy, let alone their prices, seems unlikely. Further, goods are not infinitely divisible and consumers have to pay the price asked for a product, whether it be 10p for a box of matches or £250 for a colour television set. While these differences between the model and the real world are fairly obvious, this is not always true with respect to the correct interpretation of what constitutes rational behaviour.

While the economist talks about rationality in terms of consumers maximising their satisfaction, satisfaction is usually defined in terms of solely objective criteria. Using such an interpretation the price–quantity relationship assumes a distorted level of importance and excludes any concept of subjective satisfaction. That consumers do gain subjective satisfaction is apparent from the existence of brand preference for largely undifferentiated physical products, such as baked beans, coffee, detergents and so on. In fact the creation of subjective differentials in the mind of consumers may be just as important in differentiating a product as the development of real physical differences.

Because consumers take cognisance of subjective values this is not to say that they are behaving irrationally, for clearly it would be irrational to ignore such subjective preferences. It is just because consumers do have different preferences and perceptions that producers have found it necessary to develop differentiated products and sophisticated marketing techniques.

If one traces the development of management thought during the past century, one can distinguish three main phases. First, there was a production orientation which mirrored a condition which dates back from before recorded history – namely an excess of demand over available supply. However, because of the technological revolution of the eighteenth, nineteenth and twentieth centuries a position was reached by the 1920s where the advanced economies of the Western world were producing more basic goods than they were able to consume or sell elsewhere.

Faced with a situation in which one is producing more than the market is absorbing the immediate reaction is to try and stimulate consumption further. Such efforts gave rise to the second major managerial orientation, which has been termed the 'sales management orientation' While it is understandable that producers should increase their efforts to sell what they can currently make, it is also clear that this can be but a short-term remedy if there is a basic imbalance between supply and demand. This, in fact, was the case with the industrialised economies of the West, but the full implications of such a situation were deferred owing to the outbreak of the Second World War. On the conclusion of the war there was a backlog of unsatisfied consumer demand, with the result that most producers found themselves in a sellers' market until the early 1950s. At this time excess supply once again began to develop, and producers began to look for a new managerial philosophy to enable them to earn a satisfactory return on the resources under their control.

The philosophy which emerged, and which was to give rise to the third major 'managerial orientation', was that of marketing. As we have seen, in its simplest terms the marketing philosophy postulates that supply is a function of demand, and therefore must be subservient to it. To this end producers set out to measure the nature of demand in terms of both objective and subjective influences on consumer buying behaviour.

SUPPLY: FIRM AND PRODUCT

Although there are many kinds of 'organisation' or distinct types of formal association which might be responsible for supply creation, our main concern here is with the form of business organisation which we call the firm.

In economic theory certain simplifying assumptions are made about the firm. It is assumed that a single person, the entrepreneur, is the owner of the individual firm and that s/he behaves rationally in that their prime objective is to maximise money profits. Further, it is assumed that entrepreneurs will always minimise costs, that the price of all factor inputs are known and fixed, and that each firm produces only one product. Now, no sane economist really believes in these assumptions. They merely adopt them in order to simplify their analysis and develop explanations of the ways firms will behave given these conditions. In other words the economist is attempting to develop a benchmark model so that s/he can then determine how relaxation of the simplifying assumptions might affect real-world behaviour. Unfortunately many students who have only taken an introductory course in economics never proceed to the stage when real-world considerations are introduced into the model. Accordingly such students find it very difficult to relate observed reality with the simplistic descriptions contained in introductory economic texts.

We have already noted that few, if any, firms regard profit maximisation as their primary goal. The reasons why the unbridled pursuit of profit should not be the sole objective of management is apparent in the role of profit itself. Profit is generally regarded as the reward for the assumption of risk and on the whole it is accepted that the greater the risk, the greater should be the reward. It is also accepted that risk is usually measured in terms of the likelihood of loss. Accordingly professional management tends to try and balance its activities in such a manner so as not to put the whole corporation at risk. Clearly by doing so it forgoes the possibility of maximising profits. It also avoids the possibility of maximising losses!

One area where the firm does make a conscious decision is in terms of its product mix. Fundamentally there is a basic conflict between the relative merits of specialisation and the attractions of diversification. If one pursues a policy of specialisation, one should be able to benefit from the economies of scale in purchasing and production, and so reduce costs to the minimum. At the same time it is clear that any diminution of demand for the single-product firm will result in an immediate loss in earnings and, if continued, this could result in the firm operating at a loss. Diversification offers a firm the opportunity to spread the risk associated with fluctuation in demand for a particular product. At the same time diversification usually requires a firm to duplicate many of the basic business functions, especially in production and marketing, and so increases its cost base. It is clear that if the firm is not operating on a basis of minimum cost, then it will be able to earn less profits than firms which have chosen to specialise in the production of a single product – at least in the short term.

Just as economists make simplifying assumptions about the firm, so too they make simplifying assumptions about the firm's output – its product. The basic assumption which is made is that the output of different firms competing in the same market are viewed as homogeneous by potential consumers. Given this assumption, together with that of a single price, it is clear that users have no rational basis for differentiating between different suppliers of the same product. Accordingly decisions by a consumer to buy a product are perceived as decisions between different categories of products rather than choices between similar products produced by different firms. Thus elementary economic theory proposes that, given a finite disposable income, the consumer will adjust their purchases of different product categories in order to maximise their overall satisfaction. In the sense that all products which the consumer might consider purchasing are competing with one another, they are to some degree substitutes for one another. However, this concept of substitution is too crude to explain the nature of competition between companies like Unilever and Procter & Gamble in the detergent market, Ford and General Motors in the motor-car market, Hoover, Electrolux and Dyson in the vacuum-cleaner market, and so on. For this purpose we need a clearer definition of possible degrees of difference between products. That proposed by J. M. Clark (1961) provides a useful basic distinction.

Essentially Clark proposes three categories of products. 'First there are those which satisfy the same principal want, and in which the producer is free to imitate others as closely as he wishes, using techniques that are not radically different from theirs and differentiating his product only to the extent that it seems advantageous to him to do so, in order to appeal to some subsidiary want more effectively than other variants do, and thus fit into a gap in the array of variant products'. Clark terms this first category 'differentiated competition' and it is clear that different brands of detergent, motor-car and vacuum-cleaner fall into this category.

Clark's second category, which he terms substitution', is defined as including 'products that appeal to the same principal want but which are inherently and inescapably different, due either to different materials or basically different techniques'. Into this category, perhaps, we might put the use of a laundry service in place of the purchase of detergents for home washing; the use of public transport or perhaps bicycle or motor-bicycle in place of a motor-car; or a manual carpet-sweeper, or even a brush, in place of an electric vacuum-cleaner. Clearly, in all these instances the substitute product is competing directly with that for which it is a substitute, and seeks to satisfy the same basic want.

In Clark's words 'the third category embraces products that serve independent wants and are substitutes only in the mathematic sense that spending more for one leaves less to spend on others'. We return to issues of product differentiation later in this book

In the preceding section attention was focused on those factors which determine the precise character of demand for specific goods and services. Here, our objective will be to examine how these demand determinants are reflected in the supply of products designed to satisfy particular wants as identified by the marketer.

THE 'PRODUCT' IN THEORY AND PRACTICE

As a subject, economics is largely concerned with maximising satisfaction through the optimum use of scarce resources. Inherent in this construct is tacit acceptance of the fact that available resources are insufficient to satisfy all conceivable demands of mankind, although it is recognised that conditions of over-supply are perfectly possible in the particular.

In theory, production, or the creation of supply, is a function which expresses the relationship between inputs and outputs. Inputs are referred to generically as 'factors of production', and broadly classified as land, labour, capital and management, while outputs are identified as products. (To avoid endless repetition the term 'products' will be taken to include both physical goods and services, unless stated to the contrary.) Given that there is a finite limit to the availability of factors of production, whereas demand is theoretically infinite, it follows that we need a criterion which will enable us to determine priorities in the use of these factors in order to maximise satisfaction. Such a criterion is provided by the Law of Variable Proportions or, as it is more usually termed, the Law of Diminishing Returns. This law states that incremental units of a given factor of production, other factors being held constant, will yield increasing returns up to a certain point, beyond which diminishing returns will set in. This point is not fixed, and will vary with changes in technology and the other inputs. However, at any given point in time, it is theoretically possible to determine the optimum allocation of inputs which will maximise total output.

In reality, the multi-dimensional complexity of products precludes viable analysis, and economists have found it necessary to suppress such variables in developing theories of competition. Thus, although more sophisticated treatments recognise product differentiation as a competitive variable, in theory the product is usually viewed as a homogeneous entity. In practice, products may be differentiated by any one of a multiplicity of variables as indicated by the following definition:

Those aspects of the good or service exchanged whether arising from materials, or ingredients, mechanical construction, design durability, taste, peculiarity of package or container or service all products beyond the raw material stage are highly variable, for the most part on a continuous scale. (E. Chamberlin, 1957)

To further complicate the issue, product differences are determined by the perception of the individual consumer, from which it follows that Daz, Persil Automatic, Bold and Ariel Automatic are all different products, whereas 'detergent' is a generic name for a group of products possessing similar physical characteristics. In an article entitled 'What is a Product?', C. P. Stephenson (1968) emphasised this point by defining a product as 'everything the purchaser gets in exchange for his money', and listed the following 'extras' associated with the physical product:

- Advisory services
- After-sales service
- Replacements
- Designing and planning services
- Deliveries
- Guarantees
- Credit terms
- Reputation
- Experience

The idea that the product is 'everything the purchaser gets for his money' has been developed considerably in recent years through the writings of marketing gurus like Ted Levitt and Philip Kotler and the emergence of the augmented product or service, as illustrated in Figure 3.2. (The growing interest in the marketing of services is reviewed in Chapter 22 but, at this point, it is worth drawing attention to the convergence in thinking which recognises that physical products possess intangible benefits while intangible services usually require physical inputs in their creation and consumption.)

The idea of the augmented product is probably a direct descendant of Levitt's 'Marketing Myopia' in which he argued that one must define market opportunities in terms of the core benefit desired by the potential consumer. Thus, the hungry man wants 'food' but, within the constraints of disposable income and physical availability, will probably have access to literally hundreds of possible solutions to his need. In selecting a particular type of food he will have regard to a wide range of attributes which distinguish one food from another ranging from physical attributes such as animal or vegetable origin, taste and consistency, through considerations such as its perceived quality, packaging or presentation, as well as the brand name or reputation of the supplier. Finally, the hungry man will have regard for any other benefits associated with different product offerings which will enable him to distinguish between them and select that which most closely meets his needs at the time at which the decision is to be made. For example, is the food prepared or not, can he consume it on the premises or will he have to consume

Figure 3.2 The augmented product

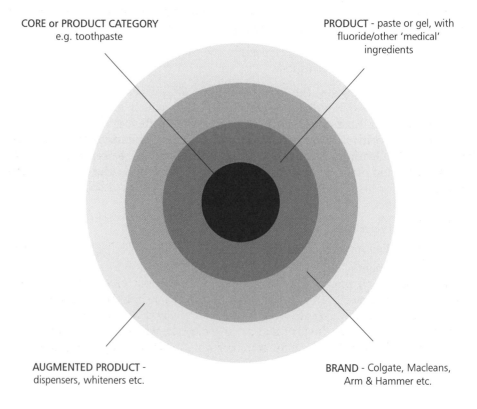

CORE or PRODUCT CATEGORY
e.g. toothpaste

PRODUCT - paste or gel, with
fluoride/other 'medical'
ingredients

AUGMENTED PRODUCT -
dispensers, whiteners etc.

BRAND - Colgate, Macleans,
Arm & Hammer etc.

it elsewhere, is it to be served or self-service, and so on? The use of increasingly specific criteria to discriminate between goods which pure economists would regard as largely homogeneous or 'generic' products like breakfast cereals, soap, detergent, bread, and so on, lies at the very heart of buyer decision making. As a consequence it also lies at the heart of successful product development and the execution of effective marketing strategies. We shall return to this theme many times, especially in the discussions of Consumer Behaviour (Chapter 8), Market Segmentation (Chapter 10) and Product Policy (Chapter 12).

Individually, and collectively, all these factors will lead consumers to distinguish between the product offerings of competing firms in order to best satisfy their particular wants.

Classification of products

Given that products may be differentiated in a multiplicity of ways, some form of classification is desirable to simplify discussion and permit the formulation of general principles. Although several bases for classification have been proposed, the most widely adopted system distinguishes two major categories – industrial or B-2-B goods, and consumer or B-2-C goods – and is based on the purpose for which the goods are purchased. In the case of industrial goods this same criterion is used to further subdivide the category, but in the case of consumer goods a second criterion, method of purchase, has been found more useful. It is the author's opinion that little useful purpose can be served by following the example of many writers who attempt to develop their own definitions. Verbal dexterity is rarely mistaken for originality and, in the case of definitions, usually only serves to confuse what it is intended to clarify. Accordingly the definitions used here are those adopted by the American Marketing Association.

Consumer Goods

> *Goods destined for use by the ultimate household consumer and in such form that they can be used by him without further commercial processing.*

Consumer goods are generally divided into three sub-categories according to the method in which they are purchased following the terminology first proposed by Melvin T. Copeland – convenience goods, shopping goods and specialty goods (Copeland, 1923, 'Relation of Consumers' Buying Habits to Marketing Methods').

Convenience goods

> *Those consumer goods which the customer usually purchases frequently, immediately and with the minimum of effort.*

This category encompasses a wide range of household products of low unit value. It is implicit that products in this category have low brand loyalty, as the user is not prepared to go to any effort to secure a supply and will accept a substitute. From this it follows that the producer must secure the widest possible availability if he is to maximise sales. Price for convenience goods is usually highly elastic.

Shopping goods

Those consumer goods which the customer in the process of selection and purchase characteristically compare on such bases as suitability, quality, price and style.

Products in this group are more complex than convenience goods and exhibit a higher degree of differentiation. Usually they are purchased less frequently and are of higher unit value. Many consumer durables fall into this category. Price for shopping goods is usually elastic.

Specialty goods

Those consumer goods on which a significant group of buyers characteristically insists and for which they are willing to make a special purchasing effort.

Some critics argue that this is a meaningless category as the 'special purchasing effort' required is due to limited availability and that otherwise such goods would fall into one of the other groups. This argument is rejected on the grounds that brand insistence has a very real bearing on the consumer's patronage of different outlets, and therefore on the retailer's stock policy. Thus, although the housewife may be indifferent to the brand of canned peas she buys and will take what is available, she may well change to another store altogether if she cannot find her preferred brand of baby food, shampoo or headache remedy. The price of specialty goods is usually inelastic.

Industrial goods

Goods which are destined for use in producing other goods or rendering services, as contrasted with goods destined to be sold to ultimate consumers.

Certain goods which fall into this category may also be classified as consumer goods; for example paper, typewriters, chairs, fuel oil, and so on. Where such an overlap exists, the purpose for which the product is bought determines its classification.

Industrial goods fall into four main categories:

Raw materials

Those industrial materials which in part or in whole become a portion of the physical product but which have undergone no more processing than is required for convenience, protection, economy in storage, transportation or handling.

Threshed grain, natural rubber and crushed ore fall into this category.

Equipment

Those industrial goods which do not become part of the physical product and which are exhausted only after repeated use, such as major installations or installations equipment, and auxiliary accessories or auxiliary equipment.

Installations equipment includes such items as boilers, presses, power lathes, ATMs, and so on, while auxiliary equipment includes trucks, office furniture, hand tools and the like.

Fabricated materials

> *Those industrial goods which become a part of the finished product and which have undergone processing beyond that required for raw materials but not so much as finished parts.*

Steel, plastic moulding powders, cement and flour fit this description.

Supplies

> *Those industrial goods which do not become a part of the physical product or which are continually exhausted in facilitating the operation of an enterprise.*

Examples of supplies include fuel, stationery and cleaning materials.

Although few producers give much thought to actually classifying their output along the above lines, this is probably due to the fact that their product line falls within a single category, and not because there is no value in developing such a classification. In fact the product category has a fundamental effect on the firm's marketing strategy as a whole, as well as having far-reaching implications for its internal organisation and operation. This point will be examined in greater detail in Chapter 21.

Services

Services are generally distinguished from physical products in terms of their *intangibility*; their *inseparability* - the difficulty of separating the service from the supplier of the service; their *heterogeneity* – or lack of standardisation, and the problems of matching highly *perishable* outputs with *fluctuating demands*. These differences and their implications for marketing are discussed at length in Chapter 22.

PRICE ELASTICITY AND DIFFERENTIATION

Earlier, we discussed briefly different kinds of demand – effective, latent, potential – and introduced the notions of the demand schedule and the demand curve. Now that the idea of product differentiation has been raised it will be useful to revisit the nature of demand.

As shown in Figure 3.1, the normal demand curve slopes downward from left to right indicating that as price falls the quantity demanded will increase. While there are some exceptions to this relationship they are of limited importance. From the producer/sellers point of view the critical issues are what quantity will be demanded at any given prices, and how might this be affected by an increase or decrease in that price. In the real world the only certain way of establishing this is through trial and error by setting a price and seeing how many customers are prepared to pay it. However, repeated observations of price-quantity relationships in many different markets has enabled us to make some useful generalisations about the relationship that can be used both in planning and managing the marketing mix. In theory, these relationships are embodied in the concept of price elasticity.

Price elasticity is of three kinds – **inelastic, elastic** and **infinitely elastic** Inelastic demand is where changes in price have little or no effect on the quantity demanded. This being so, if we plot the relationship graphically the demand 'curve' will appear as a vertical line. Basically, this situation exists where the product or service is so important to the intending buyer that they are prepared to pay as much as they can afford to gain a supply. This is as true of the multi-millionaire bidding for a painting by Van Gogh as it is for the drug addict, or the starving person wanting bread or potatoes. For whatever reason these goods have a special importance for the buyer and so may be thought of as **specialty goods.**

However, demand for most goods is **elastic** by which we mean that an increase or decrease in the asking price will result in a proportionate change in the quantity demanded and may be represented by a diagonal line. Elastic demand reflects both the relative importance of an object to the intending buyer as well as their purchasing power. Obviously, the more money you have the more you can afford to pay, but this ability is tempered by your perception of the satisfaction you might gain from other purchases you may wish to make. In other words there is an opportunity cost as spending more on beer leaves less for books and vice-versa. In economist speak we will optimise our overall satisfaction when the marginal utility of everything we purchase is the same. In practice it means that we will shop around to get the best value for money for any given expenditure on a bundle of goods and services. Accordingly, we may think of these as **shopping goods.**

The third state of demand is said to be **infinitely elastic** in the sense that a marginal reduction in price will result in everyone with a demand for that good buying from the supplier offering this price. In theory, it is this potential that motivates suppliers to pursue economies of scale so that they can undercut the competition and force them out of business – a **cost leadership strategy.** As we shall see a prerequisite for customers buying solely on the basis of price is that they must perceive all the competitive offerings as being identical , or **perfect substitutes** for one another. We will also see that, from the sellers point of view, this is the last thing they want to happen, and that 'marketing' is the way to prevent it. Nonetheless, in the mass market for frequently purchased, low cost goods like bread, cereals, milk and salt where it is difficult to differentiate the basic product, then price will have a stronger influence on the purchase of what we call **convenience goods.** The demand curve for such goods is a near horizontal line. All three demand curves are illustrated in Figure 3.3 and when combined result in the classic 'normal' demand curve.

An example of competition between Ford and General Motors for the emerging US car market at the beginning of the twentieth century illustrates why the notion of elasticity is fundamental to marketing theory and practice.

In the early years of the twentieth century car manufacturing was a 'batch' activity in which individual manufacturers performed most of the tasks involved in making a car. It was labour intensive and enjoyed few economies of scale, and so it was very expensive with the lowest priced car costing around $1250. Demand was essentially inelastic as few could afford this price. For Henry Ford this represented a major marketing opportunity as the normal demand curve predicted that if he could make a car for a lower price it would trigger an increase in demand. Of course, he couldn't predict by how much any given reduction would increase demand but, if he could make a significant reduction he was convinced there was sufficient latent demand to make it profitable. And so he determined to make a car for $500. His imaginary demand curve probably looked something like Figure 3.4.

Ford's major innovation and contribution to management practice was his concept of continuous mass assembly on a production line. While Ford was not the first to see the advantages of a 'flow line', as these had been adopted thirty years earlier in can manufacturing, he was the first to apply it to a complex assembly operation like car manufacturing. While some essential components were made by Ford, such as engine blocks, many others like tyres and electrical

Figure 3.3 Elasticity of demand

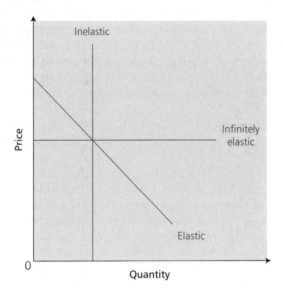

Figure 3.4 Ford's imaginary demand curve for the US auto market 1908

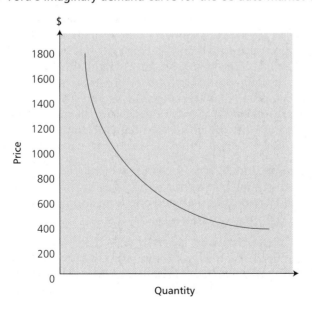

parts were bought in from other specialist suppliers All were put together in a pre-determined sequence with each worker performing only one, or a small number of tasks before the developing car moved on to the next work station. As a result of this division of labour (see Chapter 1) Ford was able to train lower cost unskilled workers in place of the multi-skilled engineers needed for batch assembly.

In a marketing context many people remember Ford for his famous statement "You can have any colour of car you want, so long as it's black". This is often cited as the antithesis of the marketing concept as it appears to pay no heed to the customers desire for a coloured motor car. In reality Ford was highly marketing oriented – in his view a person with only $500 to spend would prefer to have a black car than no car at all. In other words he concentrated on the primary satisfaction, and ignored things that might compromise its achievement.

While coloured cars were available this was an expensive process. Either they were hand painted involving several applications, or they were stove-enamelled in a big 'oven'. To build an oven large enough to accommodate a moving assembly line would have needed a huge investment, and added significantly to the cost. Instead Ford went for the only paint that would dry quickly in the open air – black Japan lacquer.

Ford's single-minded approach paid off. By 1916 the US car market had increased several times over. Ford had a two-thirds market share, and was selling the Model T for $258.

Given the scale of Ford's operations, and his overall market share, none of his rivals could compete with him on price. It was this dilemma that faced the Product Planning committee at General Motors when they sat down in April 1924. (You can find the description of this meeting in Alfred Sloane's *My Years at General Motors*.) It was at this meeting that an alternative to a cost leadership strategy was decided on.

If we look at the demand curve for cars in the US in 1924 it probably looked something like Figure 3.5 with ■ being the price of a Model T.

GMs dilemma was that they could not *make* a car for less than $350, so all the demand to the right of that price point was unavailable to them. But, if we look at the demand curve in another way (and, implicitly, Sloane and his colleagues must have) then we can assert that that every unit of demand to the *left* of Ford's price would be willing to pay more than $250 for a car if it had some added value meaningful to the customer. To do so calls for a strategy of **differentiation** and GM achieved this by developing a **portfolio** of different makes (or brands) of cars from economy to super luxury and emphasising how, over your lifetime, you could progress from an inexpensive entry model to a prestigious luxury car. To highlight this progression, and the differences between models, they did at least three important things:

1 They introduced an annual model change so that each year's new model could be easily distinguished from the previous year. All Model Ts looked alike and so could not be differentiated one from another.

2 They promoted the differences strongly.

3 They conceived of the "trade-in" whereby your older car would be taken as a down payment against a new car. In doing so they created a second-hand car market in which they were able to sell differentiated used GM models for less than the price of a new Model T.

By the time Ford recognised this threat, and the need for a new model, it was too late as the Model A was launched in 1929 at the onset of the Great Depression. By now GM had market leadership and this has only come under serious threat in recent years – not from Ford but Toyota.

Understanding the relationship between price and quantity as represented by demand curves is fundamental to understanding marketing. To begin with we must recognise that price is a surrogate for the individual's needs and wants. As we shall see when discussing buyer behaviour, these are the consequences of complex decisions about many interacting variables. Where the decision is low risk, and so *low involvement*, the economic and psycho-social risks are small. There tend to be limited differences between the products offered by competing suppliers (they are near perfect substitutes) so the emphasis is on price and demand is highly elastic. Originally, marketers designated this an **undifferentiated strategy** due to the lack of differences between products. Nowadays, it is better known as a **cost leadership strategy**.

At the other end of the spectrum some buyers have a very strong interest in a product category (high involvement/high perceived risk) so their demand is price inelastic, often to the point where they are unwilling to accept a substitute good at all. Only those sellers who can match the buyers need precisely will be considered, but their reward is likely to be premium prices and high loyalty. Such specialty markets call for a **concentrated, focus or niche** strategy.

In theory, and by definition, there can only be *one* cost leader in a market, and they would have a **monopoly** – at least in the mass market for the undifferentiated commodity. Because of the fear that sole suppliers might abuse their monopoly power, most democracies with 'free' markets enact legislation to prevent this

Figure 3.5 GM's perceived demand curve 1924

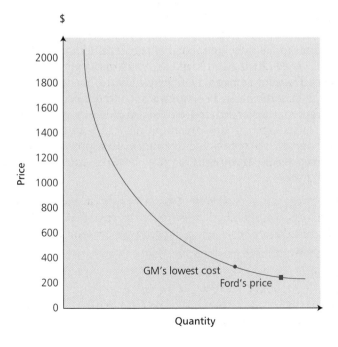

occurring. The result tends to be an **oligopoly** in which 80% of the supply is concentrated in the hands of 20% of the sellers, while the remaining 80% of suppliers account for only 20% of all sales. In such 'imperfect' markets the only way to secure patronage if you cannot offer the lowest price is through **differentiation**. It is this that is reflected in the downward sloping demand curve and is the main driver of marketing practice. If we are to implement the marketing concept we must first determine the precise nature of the customers wants, the strength of which is measured by the price they are prepared to pay over and above the price for a standardised, undifferentiated, homogeneous supply. How to achieve this is what marketing is all about.

COMPETITION AND THE PROVISION OF CHOICE

As noted, the ability to create excess supplies of basic goods is of relatively recent origin and is largely responsible for the current emphasis on marketing, as opposed to production. This change of emphasis recognises that the competitive 'ground rules' appropriate to conditions of excess demand must be modified under the threat of excess supply.

Maslow's concept of a need hierarchy (introduced in Chapter 1 and discussed at greater length in Chapter 8) is reflected in the nature of consumer demand As can be seen from Figure 3.6 Maslow classifies needs as falling into five categories with the most important at the base of the pyramid At the first level, the consumer's prime concern is to satisfy a basic need such as hunger, thirst or shelter, by whatever means are available. Under conditions where there is an insufficiency of supply to satisfy these basic needs, factor inputs are restricted to those alternatives which offer the maximum output consistent with certain minimum levels of satisfaction. In the last century this objective was achieved by product standardisation, which permitted the division of labour and the adoption of mass production techniques. Such conditions prevailed in the United States during the second half of the nineteenth century and, to a lesser degree, in much of Western Europe. Today they are typical of the developing economy.

Once the basic needs have been satisfied, consumers advance to a higher and more sophisticated level of demand. Deficiencies in the 'standard' product become apparent, through possession and consumption, and are expressed in the market place by a preference for differentiated products which more nearly satisfy specific

Figure 3.6 Maslow's hierarchy of needs

wants. Moreover, the economic growth associated with mass production, and its attendant economies of scale, increases discretionary purchasing power to the point where consumers can afford to pay more for improved, and differentiated, products.

Product homogeneity is fundamental to the existence of perfect competition, under which price is determined solely by market forces and so is beyond the producer's control. In these circumstances a firm's profitability is a direct consequence of its cost structure, and the natural emphasis is on production. The realisation that consumers are both willing and able to pay a premium for products with distinctive attributes offers the firm the opportunity to exercise a degree of control over the market, and escape direct competition with its rivals. Such a position is clearly to be preferred, and has led to the present concentration on marketing with its emphasis on the provision of choice to meet varied consumer preferences.

BRANDING

Recognising that homogeneity of product offering precluded identification of a given producer's output at the point of sale, manufacturers 'revived' the practice of branding as a means of distinguishing their product from that of their competitors.

Craftsmen have long been accustomed to identifying their work, either by signature or by the use of a distinctive symbol particular to them. In fact this practice was mandatory under the gild system to protect customers and to ensure that shoddy workmanship could be traced back to its originator. An example of this is the 'hallmark' used on silver as a guarantee of purity and indicator of its origin. Over time, this practice has enabled consumers to form judgements as to the value of given names and symbols as indicators of the quality of the product, and as a guarantee of satisfactory performance.

Clearly, the identification of a product is two-edged in the sense that although it permits satisfied customers to repeat purchase, it also allows them to avoid repetition of an unsatisfactory purchase. None the less, branding is now standard practice for the majority of goods, although it is most frequently associated with products purchased for personal consumption. From both the consumer's and producer's point of view the brand serves as a useful shorthand expression for a whole collection of attributes and properties associated with a given product. In part these associations are built up by advertising; in part they are the result of the consumer's perception and past experience. Whatever their origin, the brand enables the purchaser to obtain products which satisfy highly specific wants, without having to resort to a detailed description of them.

Brand names may be given to individual products, for example Daz, Bold, Persil Automatic and Ariel Automatic, and so on; or a generic, or family, brand may be used for a firm's complete product line, for example Heinz, Black & Decker, St Michael. Individual brand names are expensive to establish, and usually require a large investment in advertising and sales promotion. Their use is usually restricted to situations where:

1   Potential sales of each product are sufficient to justify the necessary expenditures.

2   The products vary in price, quality, etc., and are designed to appeal to different market segments.

3   There is a radical innovation with a high risk of failure and the company does not wish to prejudice the success of existing brands.

As a result of accelerating technological change it is becoming increasingly difficult to sustain a competitive advantage through physical differentiation of the product. In consequence firms depend more and more on branding as a means to build customer recognition and loyalty. This importance is reflected by a separate, new Chapter on the topic (Chapter 14).

Summary

This chapter has introduced and defined some of the basic factors which underpin marketing practice with a particular emphasis on the nature of demand and supply. Many of these ideas and concepts will be developed in greater detail in subsequent chapters. Having established the nature of marketing, and some of the distinguishing features of the context in which it occurs, in Part II we will focus on the marketing environment and its effects on competition and buyer behaviour.

Review questions and problems

1 Explain why demographic data is important for marketing planning.

2 Discuss the implications of an 'aging' population for marketing strategy.

3 In what ways might the growth of ethnic minorities be seen as a marketing opportunity?

4 Clearly explain what you understand by the term 'demand'. In what sense can a knowledge of this economic concept have practical application?

5 How is Maslow's 'hierarchy of needs' reflected in the nature of consumer demand?

6 What factors would you consider most important in forecasting the demand for

- Automatic washing machines
- Cold water detergents
- DVDs
- Fluoride toothpaste
- Frozen dinners

- Mobile phones
- Package tours?

7 Describe the problems confronting the marketing executive when they set out to discover what the consumer wants.

8 How useful is the classification of goods described in the text? Suggest an alternative classificatory system.

9 How, and on what grounds, would you classify the following products:

(a) Branded pain remedies, butter, detergents, frozen peas, matches, petrol, shirts, stockings?

(b) Cement, lathes, lubricants, sulphuric acid, transistors, wood pulp?

10 What is the price elasticity of demand? How is this concept related to the classification of goods?

11 Why has the practice of branding grown in importance with the re-discovery of marketing?

Key terms

absolute income hypothesis	fabricated materials	permanent income hypothesis
choice	focus strategy	population
concentrated strategy	households	portfolio
consumer goods	income	potential demand
convenience goods	industrial goods	price elasticity
convenience goods	inelastic	raw materials
cost leadership strategy	infinitely elastic	relative income hypothesis
demand	latent demand	services
demand schedules	monopoly	shopping goods
demographics	needs	specialty goods
demography	niche strategy	supplies
differentiation	oligopoly	supply
effective demand	opportunity cost	undifferentiated strategy
elastic	perfect substitutes	wants
equipment		

Supplementary reading list

Baker, M. J. (Ed.) (2003), *The Marketing Book*, 5th edn, (Oxford: Butterworth-Heinemann).

Copeland, M. T. (1923), "Relation of Consumers' Buying Habits to Marketing Methods", *Harvard Business Review* (April).

Heeler, R. M., and Chung, E. K. (1999), 'The economics basis of marketing', in Baker, M.J. (ed.) *IEBM Encyclopedia of Marketing*, (London: Thomson Learning).

"In Part II we are concerned with the environment in which sellers have to compete, and the factors that influence and govern their behaviour."

In Part I we looked at some of the foundations of marketing. As we saw, exchange is a source of increased user satisfaction and a major driver of economic growth. Until comparatively recently demand has exceeded supply so that the emphasis has been on increasing supply. Now, however, in the advanced economies population growth has slowed while productivity has accelerated. As a consequence the supply of goods and services potentially exceeds effective demand, and sellers have to compete fiercely with one another for the customers patronage.

In Part II we are concerned with the environment in which sellers have to compete, and the factors that influence and govern their behaviour. To this end we start with a review of the **macro-environment** which is common to all buyers and sellers so that an understanding of it is vital to both strategic and tactical decision-making. For purposes of analysis it is usual to group the myriad factors that make up this environment into **four categories** – **Political**, **Economic**, **Sociological** and **Technological** – hence **PEST** analysis. Some authors offer alternative acronyms e.g. STEP, or more complex frameworks with more factors such as PESTEL. We will stick with PEST because the political factors usually determine the nature of the economic system, e.g. free, regulated or controlled market, which, in turn, influences the distribution of wealth and social organisation, together with the extent of investment in R&D and technological development.

As a working generalisation, the PEST factors are common to all suppliers and so affect them all equally. Accordingly, they should be analysed first. That said, the detailed laws and regulations governing exchange relationships may vary from country to country, and trading bloc to trading bloc. These may modify the terms of trade for sellers from different regions and so will have to be taken into account in establishing what might be called the 'rules of engagement'.

Once these rule have been established the next phase of the analysis must focus on the **micro-environment**. Specifically, we must analyse the structure of markets, the basis of competition between organisations serving the market, and the consequences of this on the individual firm's performance. Such analysis usually focuses on what in Chapter 2 we called **critical success factors** (CSF), and it is these that competing firms will seek to optimise through their marketing strategies and plans. To do so they must establish their strengths and weaknesses through an internal analysis or **marketing audit** which comprises the third element of the environmental analysis.

Unlike many other marketing textbooks we distinguish a fourth element of the environment and call this the **Business System**. Another name for this system is the **value chain** which is closely linked to the notion of the **supply chain**. All three concepts recognise the existence of a complex network of institutions and relationships through which resources or inputs flow until consumed directly or indirectly by the ultimate consumer. It is the buying behaviour of the final consumer that determines the nature and strength of these flows and Chapters 7 and 8 are concerned first with individual, or consumer behaviour, and then with buying behaviour in organisations.

Finally, we take a closer look at the procedures developed by marketers to enable them to put their analysis of the marketing environment and buyer behaviour into practice – the notion of **market segmentation**.

PART TWO

ENVIRONMENTAL ANALYSIS

4

Learning Goals   *After reading this chapter you should :*

- Know why an understanding of the environment of marketing is an essential prerequisite for competitive success.

- Be able to identify some of the long-run secular changes which are shaping the future environment

- Appreciate why organisations need to plan for uncertainty in order to maximise the opportunities open to them while avoiding potential threats to their continuing success.

- Recognise the importance of formulating assumptions and developing contingency plans based upon them.

- Comprehend the importance of environmental analysis and be able to distinguish various methods for monitoring change in the environment.

- Understand the concept of weak signal management.

- Be able to define and execute a QUEST (quick environmental scanning technique) analysis.

- Be aware of the need to establish a formal routine for regular environmental analysis as a key input into the organisation's marketing information system.

- Appreciate the importance of environmental analysis at both the macro (national) and micro (organisational) levels.

INTRODUCTION

In Chapter 1 it was proposed that marketing is concerned essentially with mutually satisfying exchange relationships. It was further proposed that as our ability to increase the supply of goods and services has grown so it has become possible to pay closer attention to the specific needs of more clearly defined sub-groups of consumers, and to cater for these market segments through the provision of differentiated products. In the affluent industrialised economies such as the United States this potential to create an excess supply of any particular good or service led to greatly increased competition between the suppliers of such goods and services and led to what we have termed the rediscovery of marketing. No longer can suppliers be sure that their assumptions about the nature of demand are correct and are unlikely to change. In Table 4.1 are listed a number of cherished assumptions which are now thought to be obsolete. To readers brought up in the 1980s it probably seems incredible that anyone could have ever held such assumptions in the first place, but for many years it was assumptions such as these that underpinned most of the strategic thinking and planning of many of the world's most successful organisations.

In this chapter we shall examine some of the factors which have resulted in the need not only to revise our former cherished assumptions, but to continuously monitor and review those which enjoy currency today. While it has become a cliché to talk of the pace of accelerating change, all the evidence points to the fact that this reflects reality and that, since it is competition which fuels the pace of change, we can look forward to even greater change in the new millennium as international competition intensifies. Accordingly, in this chapter we shall seek to identify some of the major changes which offer both threats and opportunities to the continued existence of an organisation. In order to cope with this change it will be suggested that an organisation must take formal steps to monitor the environment in which it is operating and intends to operate in the future. Four broad approaches will be proposed, namely: **PEST analysis; weak signal management** as developed by Ansoff; **QUEST (Quick Environmental Scanning Technique)** the methodology first proposed by Burt Nanus; and, finally, a formal environmental scanning activity as an element in the marketing information system.

Table 4.1 Cherished assumptions now thought obsolete

- Inflation will never exceed 5 per cent per annum
- Energy will always be cheap and abundant
- The price of oil will never exceed $2 a barrel
- Import penetration of home markets will never exceed 15 per cent
- The primary aim of business is to make money
- Strict financial control is the key to good administration
- Market growth of 10 per cent per annum
- Workers do not have an important impact on productivity or product quality
- The consumerist movement does not represent the concerns of a significant portion of the buying public
- Success comes from having the resources to quickly adopt innovations successfully introduced by others
- Frequent styling changes are more important to customers than product quality

Source: Reprinted from 'Environmental Scanning', Brownlie, D., in Baker, M.J. (ed.) *The Marketing Book*, 4th.edn copyright (1999) with permission from Elsevier.

PLOTTING THE FUTURE

In recent years it has been frequently suggested that one of the major factors which distinguishes the Japanese approach to business compared with that of the United States or Great Britain, is its willingness to take a long-term view of investment. By contrast it is argued that many British and American companies take a very short-term view on future investment and are unlikely to take on projects where the payback is more than three or at most five years. This reluctance to take decisions which will influence the fortunes of an organisation 10 to 15 years into the future is quite understandable given that the further one attempts to plan for the future the greater the uncertainty one is faced with, the less structured and more complex is the information with which one has to deal, the greater the judgement which has to be exercised, and the higher the consequences if one commits an organisation to a course of action which cannot easily be changed once it has been embarked upon. Thus, long-term strategic planning is more like the navigation of a supertanker than a sailing dinghy where decisions to change the course of the former may have to be taken up to an hour ahead of any action, whereas one can change the direction of a sailing dinghy instantaneously. It is because environmental analysis possesses these characteristics that it is generally the preserve of senior managers. A survey of top European chief executive officers undertaken in the 1980s identified eight factors which characterise the environment which they felt faced management up to the millennium. These eight factors were:

1 A demand for quality and advice;
2 A move towards a service culture;
3 An emphasis upon the specialist;
4 Shortening strategic time horizons;
5 Scenario planning replacing forecasting;
6 A reduction in head office functions;
7 A wider international outlook;
8 Tighter legislation.

As we move into the next century it is clear these trends continue alongside those identified by Naisbitt as 'megatrends' referred to later.

The demand for quality and advice is everywhere apparent and closely related towards the move towards a service culture. In advanced industrialised economies service activities now count for almost two thirds of the gross domestic product of countries like the United States and members of the European Union. To a large degree this shift from manufacturing to service industries reflects the application of technology to manufacturing, resulting in a greatly increased output of more sophisticated products with a much lesser labour content than previously. Advances in technology have also meant that any new ideas can quickly be imitated or copied by other suppliers. Indeed, it has been estimated that any new technological innovation will be fully diffused through the world within 18 months of its first appearance. Against such a background producers have found it necessary to add value to their core products by providing additional advice and services.

These two trends give rise to the emphasis upon specialisation as suppliers seek to define particular market segments with greater and greater precision in an attempt to exercise monopoly power over a particular market niche, rather than compete head on with other suppliers of essentially undifferentiated products or commodities in mass markets. However, increased competition and technological change put considerable pressure upon management to plan to recover their investment within a shorter and shorter strategic time horizon. It follows that, in seeking to chart the long-term future of an organisation, less reliance can be placed upon traditional forecasting methods most of which depend upon an extrapolation of current trends into the long-term future. However, experience shows that technological innovations have resulted in a step change in activity, rather than a smooth transition from the current solution to a problem to a new solution. In recognition of this, management now has to plan by developing scenarios which represent their best expectations of what the future or futures facing the organisation may be like. The sixth factor identified in the survey, namely the reduction in head office functions recognises that with increased competition organisations need to remain flexible and responsive to changes in the market place. To do this, authority and responsibility need to be decentralised, and located in the operating divisions which are close to the customers.

The two remaining trends referred to – a wider international outlook and tighter legislation – reflect the enormous increase in world trade which has taken place in recent years and the efforts of sovereign governments both to ensure that the quality of products and services traded meet the needs of their citizens, whilst also seeking to protect domestic producers from unfair competitive practices by third parties wishing to sell into their markets.

Table 4.2 contains a longer listing of what has been termed the '**new international business realities**' that are perceived to be facing companies in recent years. These mirror the **megatrends** identified by John Naisbitt in his book of that name, first published in 1982. In an effort to determine the major trends which were taking place in American society Naisbitt hypothesised that as the relationship between news and advertising in print media remained approximately constant then new news would continuously displace old news. Accordingly, if one undertook a content analysis of the news contained in print media through the United States it should define the issues of most interest and concern to the American public. As a result of his analysis Naisbitt concluded that the United States was in a *state of transition from an industrial society to an information based society*. This megatrend has been confirmed in Western Europe and is a trend which may be anticipated to spread to more and more of the advanced industrial economies. The second major trend which he identified was that *innovations pursue the path of least resistance*. Essentially, this suggests that end users or consumers are more willing to take up major technological innovations than are business or industrial organisations. One explanation of this may be that ultimate customers are concerned with the benefits delivered by high technology and are less concerned how those benefits are delivered. By contrast, people in organisations feel obliged to try and understand the technology before exposing their organisations to the risk which its adoption might expose them to. Given that any new technology must represent significant potential risks it is unsurprising that organisations take longer to make such decisions than do consumers. However, while consumers embrace high technology gladly they have also exhibited a strong wish for greater

Table 4.2 New international business realities

- Continued structural unemployment in the OECD countries
- The end of the age of bureaucratic centralism
- Constant struggles with public spending
- Major shift in demographics
- Politics in democratic countries will increasingly become a matter of choice between hard and soft options
- Debt problems in developing countries will become institutionalised and there will be growth in aid dependency
- Gulf separating world's industrial nations from developing countries will remain wide
- Terrorism will continue as a disruptive force
- Investment will be oriented towards the short term
- Proliferation of small businesses
- Disappearance of 'automatic' growth in all major economies
- Heightened competition especially from the emerging economies of Brazil, Russia, India and China (the BRIC countries)
- Common product values
- Erosion of patent protection
- The change in financial services
- Postal services will continue to deteriorate
- Trend towards dichotomy in many areas of business operation – global or national niche
- Continued shortening of product life cycles
- Decline in manufacturing will continue vis-à-vis services
- Economies of scale are disappearing in some industries
- Transportation will increasingly give way to communication
- Changes in technology have made obsolete some human and corporate assets and created new ones
- Extreme and unpredictable currency variations – inhibiting rational decision making in manufacturing, sourcing, pricing
- Volatility of basic commodity prices – leading to large changes in national purchasing power
- Merger mania
- Privatisation

social involvement with one another, and this has created a burgeoning demand for new forms of leisure and recreational activity.

In a lecture given to the Royal Society of Edinburgh in 2004 Frances Cairncross, Chair of the ESRC, listed 10 trends to be faced in the coming century:

1 *Population growth/reduction*
2 *Aging*
3 *Immigration*
4 *Resource shortage*

5 *Price stability* – high inflation not a normal state of affairs

6 *Technological change* – qv the pill, cell phone, motor car, satellite technology

7 *Shaping ourselves* – drugs, cosmetic surgery, DNA technology = 'designer people'

8 *Religion* – increased interest eg. In USA, Islamic fundamentalism

9 *Smaller government* – a service industry that should have been improved by technology

10 *New superpower* – while USA will remain powerful in the foreseeable future, China and India will match or overtake over the next 50 years.

She also identified five major worries: the growth of terrorism, the occurrence of new diseases, for example SARS, the possibility of deflation, the problem of environmental deterioration, and the failure to reduce the poverty gap.

Improvements in information and communication have resulted in a much greater awareness of global issues, and recognition that national economies are part of a larger, interdependent world economy. Recognition of this global interdependence has pointed to the need for long-term thinking on development by contrast to short term exploitation, such as the destruction of the Amazon rainforests, which has characterised much past decision-making. Four closely related megatrends are the move to **decentralisation** and **diversity** as opposed to **centralisation** and **homogeneity**, from **institutional help** to **self-help**, from **representative** to **participative democracy**, and to **networks** in place of **hierarchies**. All of these trends indicate the wish of individuals to be involved in planning and organising their own lives. In summary, we can see that we are moving towards a **post-industrial information era** with shifts from standardisation to customisation, from centralisation to decentralisation, from dependence to self-help, from transportation to communication, from autocracy to participation, from hierarchies to networks, and from a state of information scarcity to one of information overload.

Numerous other studies confirm the findings reported above and allow us to state a number of basic propositions which most authorities would agree with. First, without any doubt, the pace of change is accelerating. Second, as a consequence, most aspects of the future are characterised by high levels of risk or uncertainty. Thirdly, while some aspects of the future may be extrapolated from current trends most aspects of it are likely to be both dynamic and discontinuous. Confronted with uncertainty the reaction of many organisations is to seek more and better information. However, because of the pace of change, delays in decision-making in the quest for more and better information is more likely to lead to a loss of competitive leadership than an improvement in competitive performance.

Faced with such a scenario it is clear that management must seek to organise its thinking about possible futures in a structured and systematic way. In an analysis undertaken in the 1960s, Francis Aguilar identified four main modes of what he termed **environmental scanning**. These modes are summarised in Figure 4.1 and represent a series of steps which might be termed **successive focusing**. Thus, undirected viewing is a part of the manager's everyday activity through which they seek to ensure that they remain aware of information relevant to their responsibilities, e.g. by reading newspapers and watching CNN News. As a result of this general awareness, s/he is likely to identify particular pieces of information which deserve to be followed up. Initially, this follow up will be of a fairly informal kind which is summarised by the phrase 'keeping an eye on things'. If this informal search throws up events or information which could have a direct influence on the firm's actions, then a formal and deliberate search needs to be initiated. To assist management in organising its thinking three complementary approaches may be recommended – **environmental analysis, weak signal management,** and **QUEST**. However, before reviewing these in more detail it will be helpful to look at the nature of uncertainty and the use of assumptions in helping cope with it.

UNCERTAINTY AND ASSUMPTIONS

In an article entitled 'Planning in a Changing Environment' Dale D. McConkey (1988) offered the following observation:

Effective planning requires managers to plan for uncertainty – not for certainty. In the past planning for certainty made sense. Domestic and world economies were more stable. Change occurred less rapidly. The future could be predicted with a greater degree of accuracy. There were fewer uncontrollable variables. Product life cycles were longer; product development cycles were shorter. Planning was easier. But it is now more and more difficult to predict the future with any degree of accuracy. Thus planning must concentrate on uncertainty – in fact on multiple uncertainties.

In order to cope with such uncertainty McConkey argues that managers will have to subscribe to several practices that may represent dramatic departures from the way they previously planned. Specifically, firms will need to:

1   Place more emphasis on planning for uncertainty.
2   Integrate all planning – strategic, long and short-range – more effectively.

Figure 4.1 Successive focusing

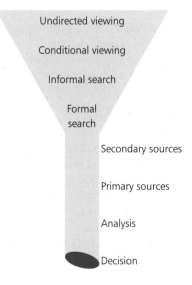

Undirected viewing

Conditional viewing

Informal search

Formal search

Secondary sources

Primary sources

Analysis

Decision

3   Review product performance more rigorously and be prepared to redeploy resources more frequently to optimise total performance.

4   Acquire more and better information.

5   Improve their environmental scanning abilities.

6   Determine their strategy based primarily on external market opportunities, rather than internally perceived strengths.

7   Emphasise marketing rather than selling.

8   Review their plans more frequently.

9   Provide better staff support for operating managers.

Faced with uncertainty it is necessary to try and predict or forecast the nature and direction of future events, and articulate these as assumptions around which one can construct the strategic plan. McConkey (1988) offers a useful definition of assumptions as follows:

> *Assumptions are generally defined as best present estimates of the impact of major external factors, over which the manager has little if any control but which may exert a significant impact on performance or the ability to achieve desired results.*

In the opening paragraph of this chapter, reference was made to **assumptions** and, in Table 4.1, we listed a number of cherished assumptions which had underpinned much of the strategic thinking and planning of firms in the 1950s and 1960s. While these particular assumptions are obsolete, and not held by anyone any longer, one should not underestimate the need for relevant assumptions as an essential element in the strategic planning process. The question is '*What are appropriate and relevant assumptions?*' Most of the answers are to be found in environmental analysis of the kind discussed in this chapter.

Several clues as to the assumptions which should be built into strategic planning have already been reviewed in the first section of the chapter 'Plotting the future'. To develop formal assumptions, however, one must devise highly specific statements which are much more focused than the broad generalisation of the kind proposed by Naisbitt in Megatrends, or derived from surveys of senior executives and the like. For example, one needs to be specific about factors such as interest rates and the rate of inflation, and cannot avoid the issue by making vague statements about increases or decreases. However, it is also important to recognise that one does not have to make assumptions about anything or everything which may occur in the future – only those events or issues which are significant and of direct relevance to the organisation developing the plan. McConkey argues that the formulation of assumptions should proceed in orderly steps and proposes the following sequence:

1   *Isolate* those future events that are most likely to have a significant effect on the company's business, i.e the key issues;

2   *Evaluate* as accurately as possible the probable effects of these events;

3   *Determine* whether an assumption is necessary; if so, formulate the assumption;

4   *Record* all assumptions;

5   Continuously *track* the validity of all assumptions;

6 *Revise* the assumptions and plans and take corrective action when assumptions prove to be incorrect.

From this it is clear that assumptions represent our best guess as to the future state of affairs at the time we are drawing up or revising our strategic plan. With the passage of time these future events become nearer, and the information available to us becomes more certain. It follows, therefore, that we should monitor the accuracy of our assumptions and be prepared to adjust our plans to reflect changes in our original assumptions.

When formulating assumptions it will also be helpful to try and quantify how likely or **probable** it is that a given assumption will materialise. Initially most people are more willing to express the likelihood of an outcome in qualitative or verbal terms such as 'Very likely', 'Likely', 'Unlikely', or 'Very unlikely'. When pressed, however, it is surprising how wide a discrepancy may exist between two different people's expectations of a given outcome when required to quantify this. Thus one person may consider an event 'likely' when it is just better than an evens (50/50) chance, whereas another would only consider it 'likely' if the odds were 3 to 2 on (0.75 or 75 per cent probability). For planning purposes it is vital that all the decision makers share the same scale of values albeit that these values will be subjective, that is particular to each individual decision-maker, rather than objective in which case there would be a known or certain outcome for a given event.

In addition to formulating probability estimates, McConkey also recommends that one should assign a **confidence factor** especially when dealing with highly critical assumptions upon which major investment decisions may be made. In

HOW WRONG CAN YOU BE?

- On 1/1/1962 the group later known as The Beatles auditioned for Decca Records. Decca turned them down as did four other British record companies over the next four months.

- In 1975 Steve Wozniak worked for Hewlett Packard in California. He built a computer in his garage and offered it to H.P. who turned it down. Wozniak and his partner Steve Jobs started Apple Computers.

- Victor Fleming who directed "Gone with the Wind" declined 20% of the profit for a fee. He thought the film would be "the biggest white elephant of all time". Gary Cooper turned down the role of Rhett Butler and said "I'm just glad it'll be Clark Gable who's falling flat on his face, and not Gary Cooper."

- Lord Kelvin, President of the Royal Society, said in 1885 "Heavier than air flying machines are impossible".

- Robert Milliken, who won the Nobel Prize for Physics, said in 1923 "There is no likelihood man can ever tap the power of the atom."

- In 1946 Darryl F. Zanuck, head of 20th Century Fox Studios said; "Video won't be able to hold on to any market it captures after the first six months. People will soon get tired of staring at a plywood box every night."

- Civil War General John Sedgwick's last words about the enemy were "They couldn't hit an elephant at this dist...." An enemy bullet killed him before he could finish.

Source: C. Carf And V. Navasky (1984), *The Experts Speak*, (New York: Pantheon Books)

this context 'Confidence' refers to the amount of confidence the manager has in the data on which their probability estimate was based, so that even though a manager might consider that a given event was very likely (90 per cent chance of occurrence) if they had no facts on which to base this assumption then it would have a low confidence value. Under such circumstances – a strong 'hunch' such and such would happen – the manager would be likely to increase their efforts to secure more and better information to test this belief. As noted earlier, there are several complementary approaches which will help the manager do this, and these will be reviewed in the sections which follow.

ENVIRONMENTAL ANALYSIS

Environmental analysis seeks to provide "information about events and relationships in a company's future environment... which would assist top management in its tasks of charting the company's future course of actions". Environmental analysis or scanning is responsible for three major activities:

1 generation of an up-to-date database of information on the changing business scene;

2 alerting management to what is happening in the market place, the industry and beyond;

3 disseminating important information and analyses to key strategic decision-makers and influencers within the organisation.

In establishing a formal environmental analysis function certain key criteria must be satisfied. First, environmental trends, events and issues must be reviewed on a regular and systematic basis. In order to do this it is important that explicit criteria are established with which one may evaluate the likely impact of the monitored environmental trends. Because it is a formal activity then it should be guided by written procedures, and responsibility for the implementation of these procedures must be clearly assigned. Experience indicates that scanning reports, updates, forecasts and analyses have greater impact when documented in a standardised format, when it is generated on a regular basis, and disseminated to predetermined personnel according to a timetable.

Where environmental scanning is embedded in a corporate strategy-making unit it is likely to be charged with the responsibility of monitoring, forecasting and interpreting issues, trends and events which go far beyond the customer, market and competitive analyses that many firms perform as a matter of routine. It may be expected to provide a broad but penetrating view of possible future changes in the demographic, social, cultural, political, technological and economic elements of the business environment. Its purpose may then be to arm the firm's strategic decision makers with information and analyses and forecasts relevant to the strategies and plans which govern how the firm is to respond to a changing business environment. It should also provide a basis for questioning the assumptions which underpin the firm's strategic thinking, and for generating new assumptions.

It is clearly important to look further afield than the task environment and Table 4.3 gives a framework for the analysis for the wider business environment.

A survey undertaken in the 1980s of American corporations indicated that formal environmental analysis resulted in:

1 Increased general awareness by management of environmental change
2 Better strategic planning and decision-making
3 Greater effectiveness in government matters
4 Better industry and market analysis
5 Better results in foreign businesses
6 Improvement in diversification, acquisitions and resource allocation
7 Better energy planning.

In other words, an all-round improvement in performance.

To make an effective contribution to the commissioning of an environmental scanning system, top management should attempt to establish a procedure by

Table 4.3 A framework for analysing the macro-environment

Cultural	Including the historical background, ideologies, values and norms of the society. Views on authority relationships, leadership patterns, interpersonal relationships, nationalism, science and technology.
Technological	The level of scientific and technological advancement in society. Including the physical base (plant, equipment, facilities) and the knowledge base of technology. Degree to which the scientific and technological community is able to develop new knowledge and reapply it.
Political	The general political climate of society. The degree of concentration of political power. The nature of the political organisation (degrees of decentralisation, diversity of functions, etc.). The political party system.
Legal	Constitutional considerations, nature of the legal system, jurisdictions of various governmental units. Specific laws concerning formation, taxation, and control of organisations.
Natural Resources	The nature, quantity and availability of natural resources, including climatic and other conditions.
Demographic	The nature of human resources available to the society; their number, distribution, age and sex. Concentration of urbanisation of population is a characteristic of industrialised societies.
Sociological	Class structure and mobility. Definition of social roles. Nature of social organisation and development of social institutions.
Economic	General economic framework, including the type of economic organisation -private versus public ownership; the centralisation or decentralisation of economic planning; the banking system; and fiscal policies. The level of investment in physical resources and consumption

Source: Adapted from Kast, F. E. and Rosenweig, J. E. (1974).*Organisation and Management: A System Approach*, 2nd Edition © The McGraw-Hill Companies, Inc.

means of which the following parameters can be defined, and redefined from time to time as circumstances dictate:

- The boundaries of both the task and the wider business environment
- The appropriate time horizon for future studies
- The allocation of responsibility for environmental scanning
- The degree of formality circumscribing environmental scanning

To define the boundaries of the firm's environments in terms of concrete measures is an almost impossible task for all but the smallest of one-product, one-customer firms. Nevertheless, the environmental scanner needs practicable guidelines by means of which he or she is able to separate relevant from irrelevant environmental information. In theory, the clearer the definition of the environment (i.e. the **search domain**), the clearer should be the nature of the information collected.

The importance of **macro-environmental analysis** is that it defines the threats and opportunities facing the firm, both now and in the future. Further, the macro-environment is essentially the same for all firms and all industries and so defines the boundaries and parameters within which competition at the micro level takes place.

PEST ANALYSIS

The framework for undertaking an environmental analysis was suggested in Table 4.3 and comprised eight discrete elements. For most purposes, however, a much simpler approach using four elements is used and easily remembered by the acronym PEST standing for **Political, Economic, Sociological and Technological**. Each of these main elements is capable of wide definition and it is up to the analyst to decide how broadly or narrowly they wish to define them. An obvious factor influencing this decision is the organisation's size and the scope of its activities. For the small organisation operations may be restricted to a Local neighbourhood, and the scope of its environmental analysis will be similarly restricted. Larger organisations may operate at a Regional or National level, with very large organisations operating at the International or Global level. However, it must be remembered that while the extent of the analysis will be affected significantly by organisational size its content will remain essentially the same on the basis that global trends impact on international/national trends which, in turn, have a major bearing on regional or local trends. Below are suggested some of the more important factors which should be considered when undertaking a macro-environmental analysis. It is up to you to decide which to include and what level of detail is appropriate for your organisation.

Political factors

Political factors are usually considered first because they influence and often determine the economic, social and technological factors. Politics control both internal and external relations and determine a country's basic economic policies, the balance between public and private ownership, and the degree of central control exercised over the organisation's actions. Politics also determine social policy and through it education, employment, health, welfare etc. Obviously politics will have a major influence on a firm's strategy. Among the main factors to be considered may be included:

- Ideological beliefs and tensions between them
- Relations between the country where the organisation is based and other countries
- Trade groupings and trade relations
- Policies on immigration, employment and emigration
- National or Local
- Basic ideology and the balance between free enterprise and central control
- Overall political stability
- Trade policy with regard to imports, exports and exchange control
- Fiscal policies
- Education policy
- Employment policy
- Health and welfare policies
- Regional development policy

Economic factors

Economic factors probably have the most direct effect upon the organisation in that they determine the nature and degree of competition, incentives for wealth creation, the prosperity and purchasing power of the population, the availability or otherwise of foreign exchange etc. etc. For purposes of analysis it is usual to distinguish between long-term and short-term factors. At the national level the more important of these are:

Long-term

- The general level of economic activity as indicated by the stage of development reflected by its infrastructure and the proportions of persons employed in primary, secondary and tertiary industries.
- The skills, availability and costs of its labour force.
- Market potential.
- Demographic structure.
- Availability of factors of production - land, labour and capital
- Distribution of wealth and taxation levels.

Short-term

- Phase in the business cycle.
- Inflationary of deflationary tendencies.
- Interest rates.
- Balance of payments.
- Tax levels.

Economic analysis should start with one's own country and then be extended to other countries with which the organisation has dealings as buyer and/or seller.

Social factors

Social factors influence the organisation both externally and internally in that they determine the structure of society and the patterns of behaviour which are acceptable to the people who comprise that society. In turn these values will have a major bearing upon both politics and economics. Among the more important social factors may be numbered:

- Cultural traditions
- Class structure

THE SUNDAY TIMES TOP TEN TECHNOLOGY TRENDS FOR 2005

On January 2nd 2005 the *Sunday Times* (Christoper Price) listed the 10 trends that it considered would dominate technological change in 2005:

1 *Wireless and broadband.* Short range broadband wireless communication will spread rapidly both in public places like hotels, shopping malls etc. and in offices where intranets will offer fast and almost limitless interconnectivity.

   The next development, trials of which started in January 2005, is **wi-max** which gives broad band interconnectivity over a range of 30 miles. This technology would break the monopoly of major telecoms companies like BT who own the copper lines linking exchanges with homes and offices.

2 *More web services.* Movies will be added to music and accelerate the take up of multi-media centres that combine PCs and TVs. Books may also become available through such centres already on offer from Sony and Microsoft.

3 *Hand-helds go hybrid.* Similar combinations of offerings will become available through hand-held devices.

4 *Games without frontiers.* Broadband will also enable real-time interactive game playing and intensify the competition between firms like Nintendo, Microsoft and Sony to develop new products like Sony's Halo 2, that had US Sales of $125 million on its launch day.

5 *Internet telephony.* **VOIP (voice over internet protocol)** will enable voice transmissions to sent as data. As data calls cannot be billed, the established telecom companies will lose revenue and be forced to innovate to hold share. Price predicts they will do this by redefining themselves as 'solutions providers providing all things to all users' in an increasingly complex market place.

6 *Voice recognition.* Still to take off but its adoption for use with mobile phones is likely to achieve widespread adoption.

7 *Feeling secure.* Internet security is a top priority.

8 *More outsourcing.* Many of the developments cited will make the management of IT services increasingly complicated and create an opportunity for online remote service management by third parties.

9 *More offshoring.*

10 *Enter the dragon.* Building on its acquisition of IBMs PC business, China will continue to develop in this market while western IT providers seek to build markets there.

- Family structure
- Attitudes to consumption and patterns of spending
- Attitudes to work and money
- Attitudes to gender
- Racial, language and religious differences
- Ethnocentrism (degree to which people are inward rather than outward looking)

Clearly, each of these factors is capable of considerable sub-division so that it is up to the analyst to decide which are most relevant and what are the most appropriate measures to capture their impact on organisational behaviour.

Technological factors

Technological factors differ from the other three major categories in the sense that technology is of the very essence of the organisation. Manufacturing organisations are set up to exploit particular technologies while other organisations are invariably dependent upon technology to a greater or lesser degree in order to discharge their primary function e.g. the modern service organisation's dependency upon information technology. In turn, **technological innovation** is the major source of economic growth and a necessary if not sufficient condition for overall competitiveness, i.e. technology determines performance levels which means that to compete an organisation must be at the same level of technological development as its major rivals if it is to compete at all. To succeed it should strive to develop a technological advantage over its rivals. Technological innovation may be embodied in the product itself and/or the process by which it is produced, distributed and consumed or used. Its influence is pervasive and the major source of competitive advantage. That said, technology now diffuses very rapidly indeed and needs constant improvement and upgrading if it is to remain a source of sustainable competitive advantage. In reviewing technology the major factors to consider are:

- The nature of the industry and its core technology(ies)
- The products and/or services produced
- The processes and/or equipment involved
- The skills and competences required to manage the technology
- The market(s) served - do the users need education or skills to access the technology, does it depend upon other products or systems for its use?

As stressed, the above listings are only indicative of the factors which the analyst may wish to take into account in developing an overview of the present and future environment, and the threats and opportunities which it may hold for the organisation.

Weak signal management

According to Ansoff most companies depend heavily upon **extrapolative techniques** in order to forecast sales, the economy and the much wider environmental issues which are of concern to them. In his view, such techniques do not have the ability to capture surprises and discontinuities which, as our earlier analysis has indicated, are more likely to be the norm rather than the exception. Accordingly, he suggests that other types of environmental appraisals are called for and proposes that managers should seek to structure their conditional viewing in such a way that they are more likely to pick up the weak signals which may herald future changes in the environment.

In examining why signals related to future change may appear weak to an organisation, Ansoff suggests that this may be due to at least one or other of four reasons. First, while the signal may have originally been strong, it may have become attenuated because the organisation is not tuned in to the right wavelength. The second explanation is that the original signal strength may have been reduced because of the existence of some filter between the organisation and the source of the signal or, possibly, because of 'jamming' between the receiver and the source of the signal. A third explanation is that the discontinuity or trend which is the source of the signal is a long way off and by the inverse square law the greater the distance between source and receiver the weaker the signal. Finally, it may be that at the very start of the discontinuity a signal is inherently very weak and so only likely to be recognised by those with specialist knowledge and/or paying particular attention to it.

Given that all firms face the same external environment, it is obvious that the sooner any given organisation can pick up weak signals that herald future change the more likely it will be able to position itself, either to take advantage of the opportunity which they offer, or to avoid any potential threat contained within them. In order to maximise the likelihood that the organisation will be able to do this, it needs to encourage persons who will act as gatekeepers, amplifiers and filters for weak signals in the environment. **Gatekeepers, amplifiers and filters (GAFs)** are people who are expert in the sector of the environment in which the organisation is scanning for information. In order to accomplish their task they must be positioned on the boundary between the organisation and its circumscribing environment. GAFs are at the forefront of expertise and are defined as gatekeepers because it is through them that the organisation is able to look out into the surrounding environment. They are amplifiers because they are closest to the source of weak signals, and filters because it is through their expertise that they are able to distinguish the signal and screen out the 'noise' surrounding it.

While the concept of weak signal management is clear, and may be likened to the work of an astronomer or radio enthusiast scanning the heavens or airwaves in search of hitherto undetected signals, the operationalisation of the concept is not without difficulty. One approach which offers a means for reviewing and evaluating the weak signals that may be picked up by the firm's management, is the QUEST methodology proposed by Burt Nanus (1982).

QUEST

QUEST is an acronym for **'quick environmental scanning technique'** and offers a broad and comprehensive first approximation to environmental trends and events that are critical to strategic decisions.

Nanus defines QUEST as:

a future research process designed to permit executives and planners in an organisation to share their views about trends and events in future external environments that have critical implications for the organisation's strategies and policies. It is a systematic, intensive, and relatively inexpensive way to develop a shared understanding of high priority issues and to focus management's attention quickly on strategic areas for which more detailed planning and analysis would be beneficial.

Certain key assumptions underline the QUEST technique. First, it is assumed that the individual executives in a firm have a view of the dynamics of the changing environments which face them. It is further assumed that in the aggregate these views represent the organisation's understanding of its environment. However, in the absence of a technique such as QUEST it is unlikely that these separate views (assumptions) are articulated and shared. Thus, while individual executives may programme their future expectations into their decision-making, there is no guarantee that their perceptions and interpretations of the same facts are known to and/or shared by their managerial colleagues. Only if there is a formal mechanism for enabling the firm's executives to share their different perceptions and interpretations will it be possible to identify any mismatch or disagreement between them. However, if any disagreement or mismatch is made explicit it will then become possible for management to negotiate a consensus on the interpretation of the information available to it, and on the desired future towards which the organisation is working. As with most aspects of decision-making, a systematic approach within an agreed framework is likely to yield better results more quickly than would an unstructured approach. Further, given that the outcome is to be achieved through a negotiated consensus between the key managers, then such a process is more likely to instil a sense of ownership in the outcome than would separate independent evaluations. Table 4.4 summarises the steps involved in implementing a QUEST analysis. The purpose of step 1 is to achieve an agreed start point for the scanning exercise. As noted above, the purpose is to help bring out into the open and share the collective wisdom and experience of the participants in terms of their future expectations. The actual methodology for executing a QUEST analysis, is contained in steps 3 to 9 in Table 4.4.

Table 4.4 QUEST: implementation

1 Review current environmental conditions
2 Explain purpose and methodology
3 Review 'futures' literature to stimulate thinking
4 Define scope and boundaries for discussion including stakeholders and performance indicators
5 Identify key issues
6 Select agreed list
7 Assess probability of occurrence
8 Develop a Cross Impact Matrix (CIM)
9 Analyse CIM and develop scenarios

Experience shows that the benefit of a QUEST analysis will be greatly enhanced by a review of other scenarios or projections of likely futures such as those contained in books like *Future Shock* (Toffler, 1971), *Limits to Growth* (Meadows et al., 1972) or the publications of the Brookings Institution or the Government's Foresight Initiative. Such speculations by other futurists are both a source of useful ideas to stimulate thinking and an indication of the scope of the exercise. However, as step 4 in the sequence indicates, for a given organisation operating in a particular industry and markets it is important that some limitations be placed upon the exercise so that its scope and boundaries need to be defined, as do statements as to the perspective from which the analysis is to be undertaken, and what criteria or performance indicators are to be used in assessing the importance and/or relevance of any identified issue. Step 5 is perhaps the most important step in the sequence as it is the one in which the participants are invited to define what they see as the **strategic** or **key issues** facing their organisation. Key issues may be defined as forthcoming developments, either inside or outside the

Figure 4.2 Cross-impact matrix

Event	Probability	1	2	3	4	5
1		■				
2			■			
3				■		
4					■	
5						■

organisation, which are likely to have an important impact on the ability of the organisation to meet its objectives. More simply put, key issues are those which could either make or break the organisation. Issues which, if well handled, will produce disproportionate benefit but which, if badly handled, could prove to be disastrous for the company. Key issues are often characterised by high opportunity costs for an organisation in that they are likely to foreclose other options. Clearly, there needs to be a limit to the number of key issues, and the best way to proceed is to invite each of the participants to construct their own list of say five and then circulate these so that the group may proceed to stage 6, which is the agreement of a select list. Once the agreed list has been prepared the participants should then assess the likelihood of probability of occurrence of each of the events contained in the key-issue analysis.

This, in turn, should be summarised in a **cross impact matrix** of the kind illustrated in Figure 4.2 in which the impact of each of the key issues is examined in the context of the other key-issues. Finally, analysis of the cross-impact matrix should enable the group to develop scenarios which represent their own best expectation and understanding of the futures which face their own organisation.

From the foregoing description it is clear that QUEST is a broad brush and subjective approach. While its value cannot be overestimated, it will be greatly enhanced if it is undertaken within the context of a formal environmental analysis activity. Indeed, it is such a formal environmental analysis activity which should provide the information input for both stages 1 and 3 of the QUEST methodology. However, while QUEST provides a means for structuring the knowledge and ideas of the senior managers responsible for strategic direction, environmental analysis is an integral part of the firm's marketing intelligence and information system and, as such, is a staff function which should be manned by professional researchers.

According to Aguilar, environmental analysis seeks to provide 'information about events and relationships in a company's future environment . . . which would assist top management in its tasks of charting the company's future course of actions'. Environmental analysis or scanning is responsible for three major activities. First, it is responsible for generating an up-to-date database of information on the changing business scene. Second, it is responsible for alerting management to what is happening in the market place, the industry and beyond. And, third, it is responsible for disseminating important information and analyses to key strategic decision-makers and influencers within the organisation.

In establishing a formal environmental analysis function certain key criteria must be satisfied. First, environmental trends, events and issues must be reviewed on a regular and systematic basis. In order to do this it is important that explicit criteria are established with which one may evaluate the likely impact of the monitored environmental trends. Because it is a formal activity then it should be guided by written procedures and responsibility for the implementation of these procedures must be clearly assigned. Experience indicates that scanning reports, updates, forecasts and analyses have greater impact when documented in a standardised format and when such documentation is generated on a regular basis and disseminated to predetermined personnel according to a timetable. Finally, successful environmental analysis and scanning systems depend upon the application of formal techniques such as Delphi studies and writing of multiple scenarios. In other words an all-round improvement in performance.

Tables 4.5 and 4.6 summarise major sources of information on the business environment and their relative importance.

Table 4.5 Sources of information on the business environment

Location	Types	Sources of information on business environment
Inside the company	Written	Internal reports and memos, planning documents, market research, MIS
	Verbal	Researchers, sales force, marketing, purchasing, advisors, planners, Board
	Combination	Formal and informal meetings (e.g. working parties, advisory committees)
Outside the company	Written	Annual reports, investment reports, trade association publications, institute yearbooks, textbooks, scientific journals, professional journals, technical magazines, unpublished reports, government reports, unpublished papers, abstracts, newspapers, espionage
	Verbal	Consultants, librarians, government officials, consumers, suppliers, distributors, competitors, academics, market researchers, industry bodies, journalists, spies, bankers, stockbrokers
	Combination	Formal and informal meetings, membership of government working parties and advisory boards, industry bodies, trade associations

Source: Brownlie, D. (1999) 'Environmental Analysis', in Baker, M.J. (ed.) *IEBM Encyclopedia of Marketing*, (London: Thomson Learning)

Table 4.6 The relative importance of sources of environmental information

1 Verbal sources of information are much more important than written sources; 75 per cent of information cited by executives was in verbal form

2 The higher the executive in the organisation, the more important verbal sources became

3 Of the written sources used, the most important were newspapers (two-thirds), then trade publications, then internal company reports

4 The major sources of verbal information are subordinates, then friends in the industry, and very infrequently superiors

5 Information received from outside an organisation is usually unsolicited

6 Information received from inside the organisation is usually solicited by the executive

7 Information received from outside tends to have a greater impact on the decision-maker than inside information

8 The outside sources used vary according to the job of the manager. Thus, marketing managers talked more to customers

9 The larger the company, the greater the reliance on inside sources of verbal information

Source: Brownlie, D. (1999) 'Environmental Analysis', in Baker, M.J. (ed.) *IEBM Encyclopedia of Marketing*, (London: Thomson Learning)

Summary

In this chapter it has been argued that competition takes place within an environment which is common to all the competing firms. This environment is becoming more complex and changing more rapidly due to accelerating technological change and increased international competition. Given this setting it is top management's responsibility to monitor the environment so that it may both anticipate and plan for the future. Such monitoring should be continuous and comprise both formal environmental analysis as an input into the marketing information system and informal through weak signal management and environmental scanning of the kind proposed by the QUEST technique. Formal environmental analysis needs to be structured to satisfy the needs of the decision-makers, who will use this as an input to their strategic thinking and planning, and has become a specialist function with many professional tools and techniques available.

Finally, we have looked briefly at the application of environmental analysis at the macro or national level and at the micro, organisational or 'task' level. The latter is often referred to as a marketing 'audit' and is returned to later.

Review questions and problems

1 Do most firms have a choice between adapting to or controlling their environment?

2 Using an industry of your choice as an example, explain the role of an environmental analysis, and how it might help a firm within the industry.

3 What is the significance of separating the 'task environment' from the 'wider environment' in an environmental appraisal of the firm? Give practical examples to illustrate your main points.

4 Since the mid-1980s the industrial, political, legal and social environment under which firms and consumers operate has undergone fundamental changes. Identify some of these major changes, and explain how they have affected a marketer's response to the market-place.

5 Describe the means at your disposal to evaluate the possible effects of changes in uncontrollable variables on the consumer market-place.

6 The commercial structure of any country develops, some argue, in stages, and is related to the stages of economic development. Describe these stages, and any action that governments can take to influence the progress of development.

7 How does 'going international' affect the environmental perspective of a firm?

8 Examine the importance of environmental scanning in the development of an international marketing strategy. In your answer, clearly identify the key components of the environment of concern to the international marketer, and their marketing implications.

9 How might the study of the macro-environment influence the thinking of an industrialist in developing a marketing strategy and a government minister in considering competition policy?

10 Identify the main players in a company's external environment. Explain why marketers must monitor the environmental forces outside the firm.

11 Identify the main areas to be considered in a company's macro-environment. Explain why it is important for a company to take these forces into consideration when developing their marketing strategy.

12 Identify the main players in the company's micro-environment. Detail the effect each one has on the firm's effectiveness in serving its target market.

Key terms

assumptions
centralisation
confidence factor
cross impact matrix
decentralisation
diversity
environmental analysis
environmental scanning
extrapolative techniques
gatekeepers, amplifiers and filters
  (GAFs)
hierarchies

homogeneity
institutional help
macro environmental analysis
megatrends
networks
new international business
  realities
participative democracy
PEST (political, economic,
  sociological, technological)
post industrial information era
probability

QUEST (quick environmental
  scanning technique)
representative democracy
search domain
self help
strategic / key issues
successive focusing
technological innovation
VOIP (Voice Over Internet
  Protocol)
weak signal management
wi-max

Supplementary reading list

See general texts.

INDUSTRY, COMPETITOR AND SELF-ANALYSIS

| **Learning Goals** | *After reading this chapter you should be able to:* |

- Explain what is meant by an 'industry'.

- Describe the changes that have taken place in industrial structure, and identify the causes of structural change over the past century.

- Clarify the concept of industrial concentration.

- Describe the nature of competition and explain the effect this will have upon interactions between competitors in the market.

- Undertake an analysis of competitors and customers.

- Evaluate the organisation's strengths and weaknesses by means of a marketing audit.

INTRODUCTION

A review of other major marketing text books, undertaken in preparing revisions for this edition, revealed that only one (*Mastering Marketing* by Foster and Davis), contained any significant discussion of the economic foundations on which the marketing discipline rests. Most other texts summarise the influence of economic factors within a chapter dealing with the External Environment under headings such as 'Economic and Competitive Forces'. Similarly, discussions of competition, demand and supply are generally confined to chapters dealing with pricing or, occasionally, general issues of strategy and competition.

Against this background some may question the continued inclusion of a chapter which looks at the structure of industry, theories of competition and the interaction of demand and supply at the macro level. While some of the detail contained in earlier editions has been removed, the author is firmly convinced of the importance of a chapter of this kind which provides a sound theoretical foundation for the development of our new synthetic discipline of marketing. One of the major problems which besets the social sciences is their proclivity to overlook past research and findings with the inevitable result that later generations continuously re-invent the wisdom of their forefathers. This is quite different from the physical sciences where students are grounded in the agreed knowledge base of their subject or discipline and invited to look forward to see how they may advance from this established base line. But, while students of the physical sciences only need to observe a horizon of 180 from their base line, social scientists, including business studies students, persist in ignoring the existence of a base line and so have to scrutinise a horizon of 360 – a much more difficult and time-consuming task.

While both sets of scientists inevitably criticise the other's approach and methodology, it is important to recognise that the physical scientist's establishment of an agreed base line is not the same as agreeing that the wisdom of the past is not subject to revision or even replacement. Indeed, the whole history of science is one of discovery leading to revision or rejection of previously accepted 'facts'. The point is, if you don't have a point of departure it is difficult to measure your progress – a principle which underlies all strategic planning. Similarly, it is important to recognise that in every field of inquiry we need at least a null hypothesis about the existing state of affairs as a basis for comparisons with reality established through inquiry and research.

Whether marketers like it or not their discipline is centrally concerned with the solution of economic problems in a social and behavioural context. As Chung and Heeler (1999) in the *IEBM Encyclopedia of Marketing* observe:

> *The German Historical School of Economics provides much of the philosophical foundation of the discipline of Marketing. Both Harvard and the University of Wisconsin, considered two of the original centres of influence in the development of marketing thought in the USA, built their marketing departments around German trained economists (Jones and Monieson 1990). This so-called Historical School was concerned with solving real economic problems and its 'practitioner' perspective still exerts major influence on Marketing scholarship today.*   (Chung and Heeler, in Baker 1999)

It has also been claimed (Bartels 1988) that 'economic theory has provided more concepts for the development of marketing thought than has any other social discipline.' It follows that one should give at least some consideration to the discipline of economics in establishing a base line for marketing.

In the first chapter we looked briefly at the stages of economic development which led to the emergence of advanced economies with the potential of creating an excess supply of goods and services. To cope with this change in the traditional balance between supply and demand a new approach to resource allocation became necessary. We termed this the 'marketing concept' because of its emphasis upon the market (demand) as the primary basis for investment and production (supply) decisions.

Of course the marketing concept is not new, for producers have always sought to identify those goods in strongest demand, and then set out to supply them. However, under conditions of chronic supply deficiency it requires little expertise or sophistication to identify beforehand the most salient demands. Successful entrepreneurs have always been those who have intuitively identified such unsatisfied demands. But in complex, modern markets this is rarely possible without a sound understanding of market structure and market forces and it is these factors which comprise the subject-matter of Part II.

In this chapter we look first at the structure of industry before examining the phenomenon of **concentration** in some detail. Attention is then turned to **theories of competition** and the **interaction of supply and demand at the macro level** This is followed by a discussion of **competition and market structure** or **Micro-environmental analysis**. Chapter 6 then explores micro aspects of supply and demand in more detail.

Students of economics may well be familiar with the content of this chapter, while others may consider it peripheral to a marketing textbook (a view that has been put to me often!). My own view, and the reason for the chapter's inclusion, is that marketing is all about securing **competitive advantage** and that competition occurs within markets served by firms which belong to particular industries. As has been argued in the previous two chapters, it follows that the practice of marketing at the level of the individual firm is determined largely by external factors within which the firm has to operate. A knowledge of the structure of markets and competitive behaviour is thus essential to the identification of market opportunity, the development of effective marketing strategies, and their efficient and profitable execution. This view has prevailed since the third edition appeared in 1979, and has been greatly reinforced by the fact that industry analysis of the kind advocated here has been central to the highly influential writings of Michael Porter of the Harvard Business School (*Competitive Strategy: Techniques for Analysing Industries and Competitors* 1989; *Competitive Advantage* 1985; and *The Comparative Advantage of Nations* 1990).

Without in any way wishing to detract from Michael Porter's seminal contribution to competitive analysis and strategic planning at both the national and firm level, he would be the first to acknowledge that his insights developed from his study of the field known as Industrial Economics at Harvard College. It is against this background that this chapter has been developed.

THE STRUCTURE OF INDUSTRY

Any discussion of the role of **industry** should start with some definition of what we understand by the term. In everyday usage we are accustomed to refer to industries such as the motor industry, the chemical industry or the electronics industry without specifying the basis on which a given firm may be judged to be a member of a particular industry. Essentially, *individual firms are categorised as belonging to particular industries by virtue of the nature of their output*. Thus most definitions of an industry tend to rest upon the existence of competition between sellers of similar products. However, as we shall see, changes in the nature of industrial organisation have resulted in many firms becoming members of more than one industry. Similarly, changes in a firm's **product mix** may well lead to a change in its basic industrial classification. We return to some of these distinctions below, but first we must consider a more fundamental distinction between types of industry.

Conventionally all industry is divided into three major groupings, which are frequently referred to as the **primary**, **secondary** and **tertiary** sectors. *Primary* industry is concerned with the *production of raw materials* and includes agriculture, forestry and fishing. *Secondary* industry includes mining and quarrying and incorporates all those firms concerned with *changing the nature and form of raw* *materials through some form of manufacturing process to the point where they are suitable for consumption either by other industrial users or by ultimate consumers*. Finally, the *tertiary* sector embodies all those *organisations which provide services*, such as wholesaling, retailing, transportation, banking, entertainment, tourism, health, education etc. etc.

In the twentieth century, considerable changes have taken place in the relative importance and size of these three sectors. As can be seen from Table 5.1 employment in the primary sector fell from 8.14 per cent in 1911 to 0.08 per cent in 2004. In fact this downward trend has persisted since the industrial revolution, and was apparent even before that. At the time of the industrial revolution alternative employment opportunities in manufacturing industry encouraged a migration from the rural areas to the new factory towns, and allowed farmers to substitute capital for labour through the employment of more efficient farming methods. This trend has continued to the present day with the result that mechanisation, advances in plant and animal breeding, and the development of chemical aids have enabled the primary sector to register a significant improvement in output despite a continually declining workforce.

Table 5.1 also shows that there has also been a decline in numbers employed in the secondary sectors too, counter-balanced by the significant increase in numbers in the tertiary sector. This has accelerated in the past decade or so as more and more women have entered the labour force.

However, the numbers employed in an industry are only one measure of the level of activity. An equally, if not more significant measure is output, and comparative statistics are given in Table 5.2.

Table 5.1 Industrial analysis of occupied population of the United Kingdom, 1911-2004 ('000s)

Year	1911	1951	1973	1982	1988	1994	2004
PRIMARY Agriculture, Forestry & fishing	1494	1149	433	354	696	305	221
SECONDARY Energy & water supply Other mineral & ore extraction Construction Manufacturing	8524	11163	9894	7451	6362	5182	4832
TERTIARY (SERVICES) Transport, storage & communication Banking, Finance, Insurance etc. Public Admin, Education, Health Distribution, Hotels & Restaurants Other	8333	10301	12335	13285	15168	17500	21685
TOTAL	18351	22610	22662	21090	22226	22987	26138

Source: Various National Statistics

Data such as those presented in Tables 5.1 and 5.2 clearly indicate the marked changes which have taken place in industrial structure within a decade. Before examining some of the causes which would seem to account for this change, it is important to stress that precise comparisons are difficult due to changes in the definition of industries, and in the manner in which data have been collected. It is also important to emphasise that broad categories such as those in the two tables disguise marked changes within the categories themselves. Thus in the engineering industry motor-cars and aircraft have come into existence and exhibited marked growth while more traditional industries such as railway locomotives and shipbuilding have exhibited a decline. Similarly, in the textile industry a chemical revolution has led to the substitution of synthetic fibres for their natural counterparts. More than anything else, change in industrial structure in the twentieth century reflects the application of technology which has led to extensive modification of the traditional craft industries, and the birth of completely new industries such as electronics and aviation. The impact of this technological revolution is implicit in the disproportionate increase in productivity vis-à-vis employment and other factor inputs. However, technological discovery

Table 5.2 Gross domestic product by industry groups, current basic prices, UK (£million)

Year	1995	1996	1997	1998
Agriculture, hunting, forestry and fishing	11,714	11,963	10,595	9,731
Mining, quarrying of energy producing materials	2,581	2,470	2,394	2,301
Other mining and quarrying	1,437	1,621	1,609	1,678
Manufacturing	136,747	143,485	148,619	151,197
Electricity, gas and water supply	15,562	16,120	16,230	15,851
Construction	32,948	34,563	36,927	38,945
Wholesale and retail trade (including motor trade)	74,148	78,698	85,865	91,405
Hotels and restaurants	18,409	20,471	22,585	24,246
Transport, storage and communication	52,297	53,994	57,916	62,200
Financial intermediation	42,726	42,730	43,852	46,199
Real estate, renting and business activities	116,348	125,722	140,316	159,348
Public administration and defence	38,859	38,938	38,727	38,722
Education	34,212	36,633	38,865	41,187
Health and social work	42,481	45,254	46,960	49,918
Other services	27,421	30,669	34,786	38,116
(Adjustment for Financial services (FISIM)[a]	-25,499	-25,557	-25,678	-27,732
TOTAL	622,389	657,775	700,567	743,314

[a] Financial intermediation services indirectly measured

Source: National Statistics website: *www.statistics.gov.uk* Crown copyright material is reproduced with the permission of the Controller of HMSO and the Queen's Printer for Scotland.

and advance are only a partial explanation of the radical changes which have taken place in the last century.

CAUSES OF STRUCTURAL CHANGE

As noted in the preceding section, changes in industrial structure are not an invention of the twentieth century and are to be discerned from the industrial revolution onwards. As a very broad generalisation it would seem that the catalyst for change has been on the supply side but that, ultimately, the nature and extent of change has been determined by demand. In simple terms the industrial revolution was the joint outcome of a mechanical and an organisational revolution. The mechanical revolution is generally attributed to the harnessing of steam power, which led to an organisational revolution in the setting up of a factory system to replace the cottage industry which had preceded it. The enormous increase in output which accompanied these changes led to a marked improvement in living standards and set in train widespread changes in demand.

It is difficult to generalise about changes in demand as these arise from a number of different yet inter-related causes. The trend towards greater social equality has led to enormous improvements in education, as well as to a redistribution of income, and it is clear that both education and income have marked effects upon consumption patterns. In turn, the move to greater social equality has had a major impact on the supply side of the economy. In the UK since the end of the Second World War in 1945 we have seen the State take control of many industries and the provision of services such as Healthcare, Gas, Electricity, Water, etc. etc. During the 1980s, under Margaret Thatcher, a Conservative government set about returning many of these industries to private ownership. In 1995, the Labour Party under Tony Blair revised Clause 4 in its Constitution concerning public ownership of industry in recognition that public opinion tended to prefer private to public ownership.

At the same time industry has not been slow to realise the opportunity which is implicit in increased personal disposable incomes. As personal incomes increase the proportion expended upon purchases essential to life diminishes, and even allowing for increased saving the individual is able to increase their consumption. The latent demand represented by unexpended personal incomes is one of the major spurs to new-product development whereby manufacturers compete to translate this latent demand into an effective demand for their own output. In their efforts to communicate the availability of their new and improved products the manufacturer is aided by the evolution and growth of new channels of communication.

Demographic changes, too, have their impact upon demand. With an increased life expectation Britain now has an ageing population with a concomitant increase in the demand for products suited to the older age groups, for increased medical services, and so on.

Further changes in the structure of industry can be attributed to the impact of foreign competition. Until the middle of the nineteenth century Britain had few competitors for manufactured goods. However, since that time many other nations have industrialised, and our dependency on imported food and raw materials has required that we open our markets to these foreign manufacturers. Certainly, the decline of the traditional textile industries owes much to highly competitive imported textiles from countries with lower labour costs than our own.

Collectively, all these changes in demand have resulted in a corresponding change in industrial structure. Some firms will decline and disappear while others will adjust to the changed environment within which they operate and continue their existence. Similarly, new technology will spawn new firms and new industries.

In his book *The Structure of Industry in Britain*, G. C. Allen (1970) advances six reasons to explain how firms are persuaded to take up new lines of manufacture, namely:

> the movement may occur as a by-product of efforts to solve some problems of production and distribution, or as the result of growth which leads to plant imbalance, or as the consequence of some technical discovery which may have a wider application than the original context, or simply because firms see enlarged opportunities in pressing their existing marketing organisation into new uses. The spreading of risk may provide the motive, or the pressure of adversity may impel firms to try new fields as their only chance of survival as substantial producers.

The phraseology used by Allen tends to suggest, albeit unintentionally, that firms only embark upon some new form of activity by chance, or because they are driven to it. As will become clearer later in dealing with product policy, firms tend to adopt a more purposive attitude than that implied in the above extract.

Without dwelling on the causes of industrial change, many of which are dealt with in greater detail later, it is appropriate here to examine an apparent consequence of central interest to any discussion on industrial structure, namely the degree of **industrial concentration**.

Industrial concentration

In addition to the changes that have taken place between and within industries in terms of their overall size measured by numbers employed or value of their output, there have also been marked changes in the nature of the firms which comprise these industries. A frequently remarked trend has been what J. K. Galbraith (1974) in *The New Industrial State* has termed the rise of the '**super corporation**'. In simple terms Galbraith's argument is that an increasing proportion of all output is being concentrated in the hands of a limited number of producers. By virtue of the control which these super corporations exercise over supplies of essential goods and services it is implied that the super corporation may exercise undue influence over the operation of the state. More explicitly it is maintained that supply dominance of this kind eliminates competition to the detriment of the average consumer.

Not all students of industry subscribe to the Galbraithian view, and maintain that the emergence of a limited number of very large firms does not necessarily imply the elimination of competition in the market place. Clearly, if one is to determine the relative merits of the opposing arguments, some form of measure is required which enables us to make a comparative industry analysis over time. A convenient and widely used measure is the concentration ratio.

In fact, economists have two concepts of concentration. At the **macro**, or **national level**, the concept of concentration is used to define the proportion of total industry output accounted for by some predetermined percentage of all firms. At the micro or industry level the concentration ratio expresses the percentage share of total sales of that industry accounted for by a predetermined percentage of all firms in the industry. It will be noted that both descriptions of concentration ratios state that they are computed by calculating the proportion of all output accounted for by a predetermined number of firms, and it should be noted that there is no universally agreed convention to state what this number should be. Accordingly, when one is interpreting concentration ratios it is most important to ascertain the basis of the computation. In the United Kingdom the most widely used concentration ratios are based on the proportion of all sales in a given product group accounted for by the five largest firms.

As indicated earlier, there is disagreement between economists as to the degree of concentration in UK manufacturing industry and to the extent of change in such concentration over time. Writing in 1969, Allen (in the book referred to earlier) took the view that while the available evidence was fragmentary, such calculations as had been attempted seemed to indicate a stabilisation and possibly a slight decline in the overall concentration in industry since 1930. Further, an examination of the identity of the largest companies shows marked changes in this period, reflecting the changing fortunes of the different industries, with the emergence, of new areas of activity such as electronics.

The calculation of concentration ratios in the UK is made difficult by the quality of the data. For example, in 1974 David Elliot ('Concentration in UK Manufacturing Industry'), explained that his data was incomplete because:

(a) *The Business Statistics Office is bound by disclosure rules and does not publish product groups where individual firms may be identified.*

(b) *Product groups where sales are less than £10 million were not generally shown.*

(c) *No product groups had been selected covering work-done activities.*

(d) *Products that could not be identified as being homogeneous were omitted.*

Despite these deficiencies Elliot's analysis contradicted Allen's and showed an increase in concentration. This increase was attributable to two major causes. First, certain firms like IBM and Xerox grew disproportionately in the 1960s and early 1970s due to the superior nature of their products and management. Second, considerable growth was attributable to merger and acquisitions.

A more recent analysis by Roger Clarke (1993) shows that during the 1970s concentration was relatively stable or declining despite high levels of merger activity. During the 1980s, however, concentration fell markedly as can be seen from Figure 5.1 taken from Clarke.

Clarke also expresses reservations about his data but feels the general trend is clear. He observes: 'Part of the fall in concentration was due to the continuing growth in foreign trade and its effects were similar to those found in the 1970s. In addition to this, however, substantial falls in domestic concentration were also observed. These could reflect the effects of government "supply-side" policies in the 1980s or they may be associated with technological changes (for example, in electronic engineering) tending to favour smaller firms' (pp. 13–16). Other explanations are firms moving production offshore and downsizing their operations.

Historically, such changes in industry structure have been accompanied by significant changes in competition and performance, but research is lacking to document this. This lack of research implies a lack of interest in the subject which is confirmed by Michael Waterson (1993) in 'Are Industrial Economists Still Interested in Concentration?' A major reason for this is the shift in emphasis from structure to conduct or behaviour. Waterson's view is that concentration is still a 'big question' in industrial economics and deserves more attention. We concur with this view. Firm size and market share are subject to close scrutiny and regulation in most countries, as indeed they are in the European Union as a

Figure 5.1 Trends in concentration in UK manufacturing, 1980-89

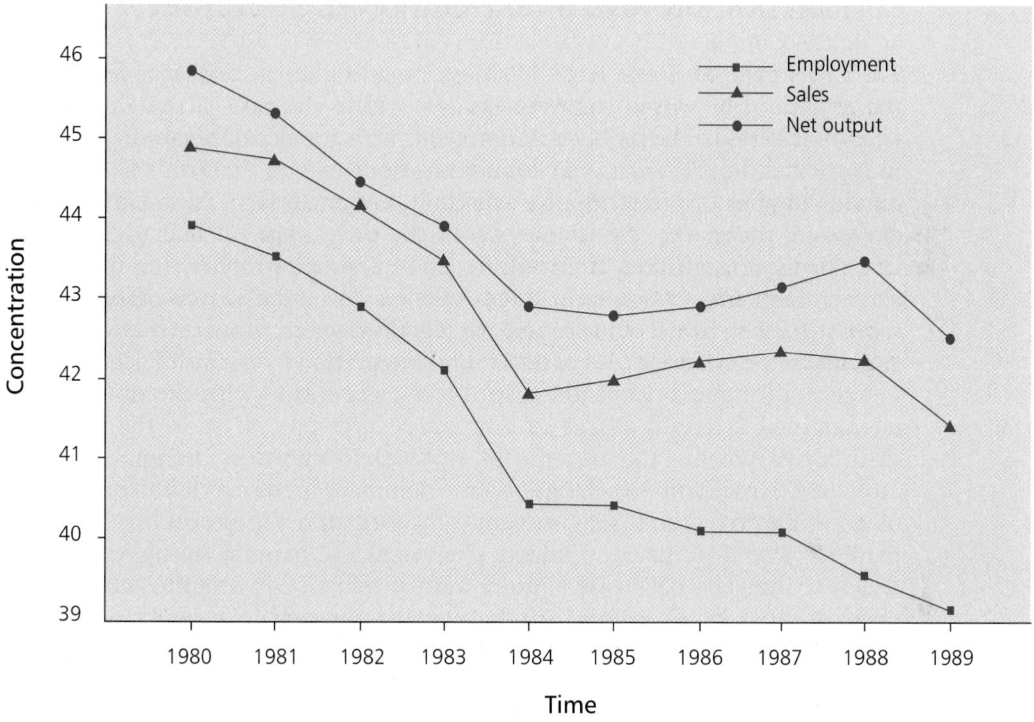

Source: Clarke, R. (1993), 'Trends in Concentration in UK Manufacturing, 1980–89', Ch. 7 in Casson, M. and Creedy, J. (eds), *Industrial Concentration and Economic Inequality* (Aldershot: Edward Elgar Publishing Ltd).

Table 5.3 The structure of the retail grocery trade in Great Britain, Concentration: share of turnover 2002

Top 2% of shops	41.7%
Top 5% of shops	71.4%
Top 10% of shops	85.3%
Top 20% of shops	94.8%

Source: ACNielsen, *The Marketing Pocket Book 2005*, published by WARC (*www.warc.com*).

whole, a fact reflected in mergers and acquisition policy. It should also be noted that with the growth of the service sector there has been a trend towards the dominance of many sectors such as retailing, banking, insurance, final services etc. by a comparatively small number of large organisations. This is illustrated in Table 5.3 which summarises the concentration in share of Turnover in the Retail Grocery Trade:

As we shall see later, this concentration in retailing has had a major impact on the structure of channels of distribution (Chapter 7 The Business System and Chapter 15 Channel Management).

CONCENTRATION AND ORGANISATIONAL STRUCTURE

The development of the large business organisation is closely associated with the growth of improved communications, and in the case of the United States, where most research has been undertaken, with the development of the railroad in particular. Improvements in communications extend the firm's ability both to obtain supplies of factor inputs, especially raw materials, while simultaneously expanding the market for its output. In the early stage of their evolution most large firms concentrated their efforts upon a single product line or functional activity. Similarly, in the early stages of their development the managers of the more successful firms, who are also usually the owners, focus their attention upon expanding though a process of horizontal integration by means of acquisition and merger with other organisations in direct competition with them. Once a firm has attained a certain degree of dominance over one phase in the productive/ distributive process the benefits of **vertical integration** become increasingly attractive. Thus a firm which has become dominant in the extraction or production of a basic raw material may integrate forward into the processing of that raw material into a finished product. Conversely, a manufacturing concern may decide to integrate backwards into primary production in order to achieve control over essential factor inputs. Similarly, firms engaged in primary or secondary industries may perceive advantages through integrating forward into the tertiary sector and achieving control of the distributive function. Clearly, dominant retail and wholesaling organisations may see similar advantages to be gained through integrating backwards into manufacturing and primary production.

With increasing size there developed a need for a more specialised organisational structure, and for the delegation of authority and responsibility to subordinates. In the early stages of their development most large corporations adopted a functional form of organisation with professional managers appointed to head each of the various functions, for example finance, production, sales, and so on.

With the transfer of control from owner-entrepreneurs to professional managers it is possible to discern a change in the primary goal of the firm. Thus, while owner-entrepreneurs tend to pursue a primary objective of profit maximisation, professional managers tend to emphasise survival and a satisfactory level of earnings, to be achieved through sales maximisation rather than profit maximisation.

However, as noted earlier when discussing the six causes of change cited by Allen, this view is essentially a negative one. While it is true that most firms adapt themselves to their environment and react to changes in their market, the really dominant firms in any industry appear to have adopted a more positive approach. In A. C. Chandler's (1966) classic study *Strategy and Structure*, two alternative strategies to integration were identified. In essence these two alternative strategies are growth through geographical expansion or market development, and diversification which is a combination of both new product and market development. However, as firms pursued either or both of these alternatives it soon became apparent that the traditional functional form of organisation was inappropriate for multi-product firms operating in a number of different markets. Thus, in the 1920s, Dupont and General Motors began to develop a divisional structure which has now become the dominant form of organisation. It is not proposed to dwell on such issues here but it is important to point out that since the 1920s there has been an increasing trend towards diversification. As a result of this diversification many of the larger firms operate in several different industries and one must not assume automatically that the very large firms are necessarily dominant in all markets in which they compete.

Interest in the degree of concentration in industry arises largely because of the light which it throws upon market structure and, as Richard Caves (1972) notes, 'market structure is important because the structure determines the behaviour of firms in the industry, and that behaviour in turn determines the quality of the industry's performance'. However, as Caves points out, concentration is but one element of market structure, other main elements of which are product differentiation, barriers to the entry of new firms, the growth rate of market demands, the elasticity of market demand, and the ratio of fixed to variable costs in the short run. Collectively all these determine the nature of competition in the market place and it is to this that we now turn our attention.

THEORIES OF COMPETITION

Current thinking about competition, like many other economic concepts, owes much to the original contribution of Adam Smith, whose *Wealth of Nations* was first published in 1776. As J. M. Clark (1961) points out, Smith lays the foundation of this thought by defining two competition states – **full and free competition**, and **complete monopoly** – and, in a loose fashion, the contrasting outcomes to be expected of each of these states.

Clark offers a useful summary of the evolution of economic thinking about competition from Smith's original and sometimes rather vague specification through to the contributions of Ricardo, Cournot and Marshall, in the course of which he points out how theory has changed to reflect reality. At the time when Smith first proposed the two basic competitive states, monopoly was essentially a local phenomenon which was to be eroded during the nineteenth century with the development of more efficient lines of communication and transportation; while perfect competition mirrored the bargaining power of people engaged in cottage industries such as weaving. Similarly, as we have noted earlier, agriculture was a much more dominant form of economic activity in terms of employment and the markets in agricultural commodities have traditionally approached most nearly to the model of perfect competition.

Just as the impact of the industrial revolution was to lead to improvements in communication and transportation which diminished local monopolies, so the growth of manufacturing industry diminished the importance of agriculture and led to attention being focused upon intermediate competitive states distinguished as being 'imperfect'.

During the nineteenth century the major emphasis of economic activity was upon supply creation or output and its effect upon price. Together these were seen as the crucial **competitive variables**. In Clark's view it was the addition of the chemical revolution to the preceding mechanical and electrical revolutions which was to give rise to product proliferation and lead to a situation in which:

> automatically, the differentiated product has become an economic variable at least as important as price, along with the methods of selling efforts and demand creation that necessarily go with product differentiation.

The addition of product and selling efforts as variables alongside the traditional inputs of price and output demanded a radical restructuring of the economist's original model, and gave rise to the theories of imperfect competition formulated by Edward Chamberlin (1933) and Joan Robinson (1933).

Thus we now recognise that between the polar extremes of monopoly and perfect competition there exists an almost infinite variety of states of imperfect competition. For purposes of analysis, understanding, and prediction it is important that one should be able to distinguish how certain basic elements influence the development of a particular competitive state. It is also important that one should be able to identify the salient facets of each of these states. To this end we are here concerned primarily with the three basic elements of an economic system – supply, demand, and the market – and their interaction, that is the state of competition.

Our discussion of supply will concentrate first upon those organisations responsible for its creation, and will then examine the nature of their output. This consideration will be followed by a summary of some of the more salient factors which go together to make up and influence demand. Next we examine the nature of the mechanism through which supply and demand are brought together – the market – and finally we review the basic competitive states to establish the emergence of product differentiation as a major competitive strategy.

Competition and market structure

In essence the nature of competition and of market structure is the outcome of the interaction between supply and demand. As indicated above, it is normal to define two limiting conditions – monopoly and pure competition – and to categorise intermediate forms of competition as 'imperfect'. What, then, are the salient characteristics of these states? Before addressing this issue it is necessary to remind ourselves of the concept of **demand elasticity**, for it is this factor which is usually used as the basic indicator of the nature of competition.

Under normal conditions most people anticipate that an increase in the price of a good will result in a decline in the amount demanded, while conversely any fall in price should be accompanied by an increase in the quantity demanded. In simple terms elasticity is a measure of the degree to which a change in price will result in a change in demand. Where a very small change in price is accompanied by a major change in demand, we say that that product has a high elasticity of demand.

In the case of pure competition three basic conditions must be satisfied: namely, **large numbers of producers, homogeneous output, and freedom of entry.** In fact, when talking of a large number of firms it would be more accurate to speak of low levels of concentration, for the basic condition which we are seeking to define is one in which decisions by any single firm have little or no effect upon the output of the industry as a whole. As we have noted earlier, homogeneity in a product depends upon the perception of a prospective buyer. Only in the case of commodities and raw materials is it usual to find agreement that the output of two different producers which meets a given specification can in fact be treated as identical products. The third condition for the existence of pure competition is freedom of entry, by which we mean that there are no barriers or artificial restrictions to prevent any individual or firm from setting up in business to produce supplies of the product in question. It should be noted that pure competition is not synonymous with perfect competition, for the former only describes the competitive state between suppliers, while the latter makes further assumptions about conditions in the market. Essentially these assumptions are that all buyers and sellers have perfect knowledge of the activities of one another, that there are no transportation costs and that there is perfect mobility of factors of production between industries. Under these conditions the market determines the price of a product and effectively the firm has no control over its destiny whatsoever. The polar extreme to a situation of perfect competition is one of **pure monopoly**. By definition a **monopolist** is the sole supplier of a particular product or service, with the result that firm and industry are synonymous. In economic theory a pure monopolist has no competition at all. Clearly such a position cannot exist, for it presumes that the monopolist commands all of a consumer's income. For practical purposes we consider that a state of monopoly exists when there is no close substitute for the monopolist's output. Applying the concept of concentration a monopolist would have a concentration ratio of 100 per cent. Because the monopolist does not face direct competition from other suppliers, as is the case under conditions of perfect competition, it is frequently held that he has no incentive to maximise his efficiency. Clearly under conditions of perfect competition producers must maximise their efficiency, for if they do not their costs will rise above those of their rivals, but they will be unable to recoup these higher costs through increased prices. In the long run, therefore, the inefficient producer under conditions of perfect competition will be forced out of business.

From the foregoing descriptions it is clear that conditions of perfect competition and pure monopoly are exceptions rather than the rule. They are the limiting conditions. Under both sets of conditions the seller reacts solely to external environmental forces. However, in intermediate states between the two extremes the factor which really distinguishes imperfect competition is that the firm has to take account not only of the external environment within which it must operate, but also of the action of other suppliers in the market place. The need, under conditions of imperfect competition, for firms to take into account the actions of their immediate competitors makes for a much more complex situation, and one demanding a far higher level of managerial skill. Under conditions of imperfect competition sellers are mutually interdependent, and so must allow for each other's actions when formulating their plans.

As noted earlier when discussing different managerial orientations during the twentieth century, the growth of imperfect competition is of relatively recent origin.

In fact it was not until the early 1930s that Edward Chamberlin and Joan Robinson first put forward their theories of imperfect competition. In time, therefore, the proposal of a theory of imperfect competition coincided with a change from the production to the sales management orientation, and the need for companies to compete with one another along dimensions other than cost and price.

Theories of imperfect competition frequently invite an analogy with games in which choices of courses of action are limited, not only by the rules of the game but also by the actions of one's competitors. Thus we find that the study of competition places increasing emphasis upon the strategic choices made by participating firms, and the impact which these have upon both the fortunes of their competitors and market structure.

In making such choices firms have to operate within the environmental constraints – political, legal and social – common to them all. Thus in order to develop a distinctive and, it is hoped, successful strategy they have found it beneficial to give much closer attention to three aspects of micro-environmental analysis that are critical to successful strategic marketing planning:

1 *Industry/market analysis*

2 *Competitor analysis*

3 *Customer analysis*

We will examine each of these in turn.

Industry/Market analysis

Competition exists where two or more firms seek to serve the same end-use market. Long before the emergence of modern marketing management, economists undertook a detailed analysis of the nature of competition and the basic framework for evaluating competitive behaviour was developed by industrial economists in the 1930s. The industrial economists' model, which provides the foundation for much of Michael Porter's work on competitive strategy, contains three elements – market structure, conduct and performance. Figure 5.2 outlines the key feature of the model which may be summarised as:

- All firms are faced with essentially the same basic conditions.
- As a result of these conditions and competition within the market, every industry develops a particular structure.
- The structure of the industry determines the alternatives open to its members and, through them, their conduct.
- Competition within the market determines the performance of individual firms.
- The model is dynamic.

The model is dynamic because it recognises that markets are open systems subject to external forces (public policy, environmental change, etc.) and to adjustment to internal forces as reflected by the feedback loops.

As we noted earlier, for purposes of analysis economists recognise a number of competitive states which both define and are defined by structure, conduct and performance:

Figure 5.2 The structure-conduct-performance paradigm

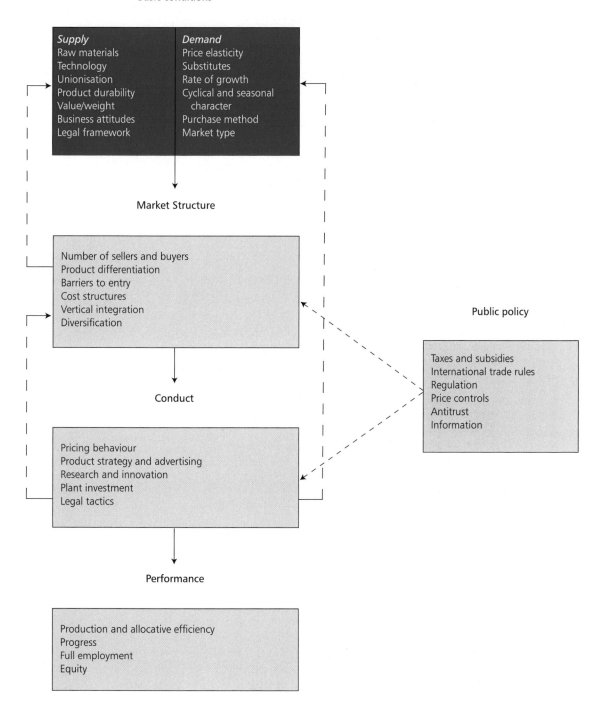

Source: Scherer, F. M. and Ross, D., *Industrial Market Structure and Economic Performance*, Third Edition, Copyright © 1990 by Houghton Mifflin Company. Used with Permission.

- *monopoly*
- *oligopoly*
- *monopolistic or imperfect competition*
- *pure competition*

and this provides a useful first cut for competitive analysis, viz. Figure 5.3.

Monopoly and pure or perfect competition rarely occur in the real world but are useful to define a spectrum of competitive states with oligopoly and imperfect competition lying between them. In practice, competition is defined by rivalry between firms seeking to satisfy the same customer needs, i.e. it is customer needs that define the market and the nature of the firm's business.

Definition of the firm's business (Levitt 1960) is critical to define both the boundaries/parameters of the market, and the identity of competitors. Competitor analysis normally comprises two elements:

Figure 5.3 Competitive analysis

Competitive state ⟍ Factor	Monopoly	Oligopoly	Imperfect	Pure
Number of competitors	None	Several	Many	Very many
Product	Homogeneous	Some differentiation	Much differentiation	Homogeneous
Price	What the market will bear	Very similar	Very different	Determined by demand
Promotion	Limited	Quite extensive	Very extensive but targeted	Very limited
Place	Restricted	Extensive	Selective	Universal
Barriers to entry	Very high	Many	Few	Very few
Examples	Utilities	Cars Strong brands	Clothes	Commodities

Figure 5.4 Value chain analysis

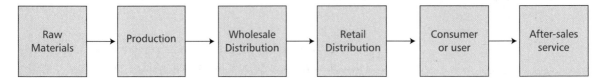

1 *Value chain analysis.*

2 *Individual competitor analysis.*

Value chain analysis was developed by McKinsey & Co. in the 1960s as a tool to evaluate competition based on the view that business is a system which links raw materials (supply) with customers (demand) and comprising six basic elements, as shown in Figure 5.4.

Starting with raw material extraction, the analysis proceeds by examining each major subsystem in turn in order to establish the interrelationship and interdependence between them in terms of:

The degree of competition within and between each subsystem, e.g. raw material extraction might be in the hands of only one or a few producers so that conditions are oligopolistic, while retail distribution could be characterised by thousands of small sellers none of whom could influence the market. Clearly the latter circumstances describe perfect competition, and both sets of conditions apply in the oil industry. Thus in establishing the nature of competition one should measure:

- *The number of competitors;*
- *Their profitability;*
- *Their degree of integration;*
- *Their cost structure;*
- *The existence and nature of any barriers to entry*, e.g. technological, size of investment in production and/or marketing.

Where, in the total system, value is added by the activities of members of the production, distribution, or servicing subsystems. For example a significant proportion of turnover in many consumer-durable industries is accounted for by after-sales servicing and the efficiency of this sector may have a radical influence upon the market shares of individual suppliers, as well as on industry profitability.

The location of *economic leverage* in the system. Does this arise from being a fully integrated producer, or can one exercise leverage by avoiding the extensive fixed investment implicit in vertical integration and concentrating on only one subsystem?

Where is the system's *marketing leverage*? Usually this is associated with control of a scarce resource, which might be an essential raw material, a patent on a process, control of a distribution channel, a brand name ('Sony, Nokia) or some other type of consumer franchise.

Once the analyst has established the major characteristics of the production, distribution and servicing subsystems, the next task must be a thorough documentation of the consumer or user. Such documentation requires answers to the five basic questions which underlie all market research – who, what, where, when and how.

1 *Who* buys in terms of demographic and socio-economic criteria such as age, sex, income, education, occupation, marital status, etc. (for consumers), or status, authority, functional specialisation, etc. (for users)? Who consumes?

(Compare consumption and purchase of breakfast cereals; of hand tools in a factory; etc.)

2 *What* do people buy in terms of variety, design, performance and price characteristics?

3 *Where* do people buy? In specialist outlets, in general purpose outlets, by mail or telephone from a catalogue, in the home or on their premises, via the Internet, i.e. how important is direct selling through representatives versus indirect selling via the media?

4 *When* do people buy? Are purchases seasonal, regular, irregular, associated with another activity, etc?

5 *How* do people buy? Impulsively, after considerable deliberation, in large quantities, from multiple sources or a single source, etc?

A sixth and equally important question is '*Why*?' Unlike our other five questions, a definitive and factual answer cannot usually be supplied. However, when we consider that consumers (or users) do not buy products as such, but rather the satisfactions yielded by the product, then even a partial understanding of the satisfactions looked for will go a long way towards explaining actual behaviour in the marketplace.

At this juncture you should have developed a good understanding of both the company and the environment in which it is operating. It now remains to combine the two threads of the analysis in order to isolate the company's particular strengths and weaknesses in terms of the environmental threats and opportunities. An indication of the sort of questions appropriate to such a comparison is given in Figure 5.5, which is taken from McKinsey's model. This evaluation will be

LISTENING TO THE 'VOICE OF THE MARKET'

A banner headline in the *Sunday Times* of April 16 2005 announced "Australia trounces France". But this wasn't in the Sports Section about a visit by the Wallabies to Paris, this was in a special report on wine. Author John Fredrick reported:

"Little more than a decade ago France sold Britain more than seven times as much wine as Australia did. Now Australian sales to Britain outstrip those of France both in volume and value. It is a reversal of fortune that the French insisted could never happen.

It is a familiar tale of those who enjoy market dominance resting on their laurels and assuming they have a divine right to success. The French believed there was an immutable truth that their wines were best. It has come as a shock to belatedly realise that British consumers no longer agree.

Much market analysis has gone into explaining (excusing?) the success. Australian wines have enjoyed, but the explanation is simple. Australian wine producers gave British drinkers what the wanted, while French producers were still trying to sell what they thought Britons should have.

Australia's success is based on consistently reliable quality and supplying technologically perfected wines endowed with ample, even lavish fruit. Their wines are intelligently labelled with the names of the ingredient grape varieties on the front and helpful, practical information on the back. Above all, these accessible, easily understood wines are sold at prices that make them terrific value."

Put simply, Australian wine producers both understand and practice marketing.

reinforced by the self-analysis discussed later.

Competitor analysis

Once you have completed the industry/market analysis it is possible to identify those firms which are in direct competition with your own organisation and submit these to a detailed review. In this section we look at a number of approaches and

Figure 5.5 Company's measurable strengths and weaknesses

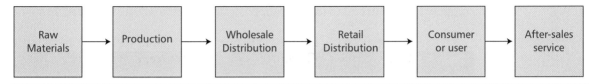

| Raw Materials | Production | Wholesale Distribution | Retail Distribution | Consumer or user | After-sales service |

How does the company compare in raw materials?

- Do they have advantages in supply?
- Degree of integration?

How does the company compare in technology?

- What is their rate of product, process improvement?
- How good is process efficiency?
- Advantages in location of facilities?

How does the company compare in cost and profit?

- Raw material costs?
- Processing costs?
- Profit?
- Return on investment?
- Access to capital?

How does the company compare in channels?

- In which channels are company's sales concentrated?
- Do products reach point of sale faster or more efficiently?

How does the company compare in distributors?

- Have they more, larger, or more effective distributors?
- Share of channels sales?

How does the company compare in economics?

- Compensation of distributors?
- Distribution costs?
- Service costs?

How does the company compare in products?

- Have they greater variety, better design or quality, lower price, superior performance?
- Share of market?

How does the company compare in customers?

- Who are core buyers; core consumers?
- Do these customers buy more frequently in larger quantities, or more consistently?
- How is company's product used?
- Who are core competitors?

How does the company compare in services?

- Does company have a service advantage - type, quality or quantity?

How does the company compare in pricing?

- Do they have price advantage (price/quality relationship)?
- Are they price leader?

How does the company compare in economics?

- Service costs?
- Cost of consumer marketing?

techniques for achieving this. (Note: in addition to direct competitors who are offering products or services which are close substitutes for your own output, it is also useful to consider other firms with whom you may compete indirectly. For example in the market for consumer durables, furniture, floorcoverings, white and brown goods all compete with each other for the consumer's discretionary purchasing power. Such competition is indirect. For the purposes of competitor analysis we are primarily concerned with firms serving the same segment(s) as ourselves, e.g. manufacturers of washing machines, or of TVs, etc.)

Jain (1990, p.85) suggests that in determining the degree of direct or indirect competition it is useful to look at four basic dimensions – customer need, industry

---

Table 5.4 Competitive substitutes

Customer need: liquid for the body

Existing:	Thirst
Latent:	Liquid to reduce weight
Incipient:	Liquid to prevent aging

Industry competition (How can I quench my thirst?)

Existing industries:	Hard liquor
	Beer
	Wine
	Soft drink
	Milk
	Coffee
	Tea
	Water
New industry:	Mineral water

Product line competition (What form of product do I want?)

Me-too product:	Regular cola
	Diet cola
	Lemonade
	Fruit-based drink
Improved product:	Caffeine-free cola
Breakthrough product:	Diet and caffeine-free cola providing full nutrition

Organisational competition (What brand do I want?)

Type of firm:	Coca-Cola
	Pepsi Cola
	Seven-Up
	Dr Pepper
New entrants:	General Foods
	Nestlé

Scope of business

Geographic:	Regional, national, multinational
Product/market:	Single vs. multiproduct industry

competition, product line competition, and organisational competition. Table 5.4 indicates how these sources of competition may be used to identify competitive substitutes.

In undertaking a competitor analysis it is important to strike a balance between essential and desirable information. Theoretically we would like to know as much about our competitors as we know about ourselves but, as we shall see when we consider the recommended scope of the self-analysis, realistically the time and effort involved would rarely justify this

It follows that the competitors chosen for detailed review must be selected with care. It is also important to decide how serious competitors are seen to be in developing your overall strategy. George Day and Robin Wensley (1988) identify two different emphases in developing a competitive strategy, the first of which see this focusing on rivalry with competitors, and the second on concern for the customer. From these two dimensions Day creates a simple two-by-two matrix of perspectives on advantage as shown in Figure 5.6.

The four 'types' of firm may be described as follows:

1 *Self-centred firms* tend to be internally orientated and focus on improvements in efficiency to improve performance. Sales volume is the main external indicator and the emphasis is on market penetration. Self-centred firms survive only where there is an absence of competition, as in mature markets where there is a state of peaceful co-existence or where the firm has some sort of monopoly power.

2 *Competitor-centred firms* tend to predominate in mature markets with little or no growth potential where competition has become a zero sum game. Such markets are often capital-intensive with mature technologies and little opportunity for product innovation. Market penetration strategies dominate.

3 *Customer-orientated firms* are frequently found in fragmented industries which are characterised by high levels of product or service differentiation leading to the existence of many segments. Under these circumstances customer satisfaction is the key indicator of performance and firms pay comparatively little attention to competitors. Product and market development are key strategies.

Figure 5.6 Perspectives on advantage

EMPHASIS ON COMPETITOR COMPARISONS

		Minor	Major
EMPHASIS ON CUSTOMER PERSPECTIVES	Minor	Self-centred	Competitor-centred
	Major	Customer-orientated	Market-driven

4 *Market-driven firms* represent the norm in competitive markets where success depends upon a concern for customer needs, which drive the competitive strategy, taking into account the need to adjust this to position the firm against others which are also seeking to serve the same customer/market segments. Such firms pursue multiple strategies involving market penetration as well as market and/or product development.

Given the need to develop a strategy which takes account of competitors, it follows that any analysis of them should be based upon clear views about the source of competitive advantage. In broad terms, sources of competitive advantage may be divided into two major categories which may be defined as critical success factors and skill and competences. As we saw in Chapter 2, **Critical success factors** (CSF) are basically independent of the firm in the sense that they define those activities or attributes which are necessary conditions for survival in a particular market. For example in markets for fabricated materials such as steel or polymers you must be able to manufacture to agreed industry standards and specifications to be even considered a competitor in the first place. By contrast, skill and competences are particular to the firm and define its ability to satisfy the CSF, and also any comparative advantage it possesses vis-à-vis its major competitors.

Critical success factors

The absolute number of potential CSF is large (Thompson and Strickland 1990, identified over forty) but of these only a few are likely to be truly critical in any given competitive situation. Clearly, a key skill of the strategist is the ability to determine just what these are! Clarkson (1966) cites the work of Rockart (1979) and a group at MIT who identified four major sources of critical success factors as follows:

1 *Structure of the particular industry* Each industry by its very nature has a set of critical success factors that are determined by the characteristics of the industry itself. Each company in the industry must pay attention to these factors. For example for the airline industry, fuel efficiency, load factors, and an excellent reservation system are held to be the most important CSFs.

2 *Competitive strategy, industry position and geographic location* Each company in an industry is in a unique situation that is determined by its history and current competitive strategy. For smaller organisations within an industry dominated by one or two large companies, the actions of the major companies will often produce new and significant problems. A competitive strategy for the smaller firm may mean establishing a new market niche, discontinuing a product line completely, or redistributing resources among various product lines. For example in the personal computer industry, the survival of many smaller firms depends upon the compatibility of their products with IBM. Just as differences in a firm's position within an industry dictate CSFs, differences in geographic location can lead to differing CSFs from one company to another.

3 *Environmental factors* Changes in the gross national product, the economy, political factors, and demographics lead to changes in the critical success factors of various industries and firms. At the beginning of 1973 virtually no

chief executive in the UK or USA would have listed 'energy supply availability' as a critical success factor. Following the oil embargo, however, this factor suddenly became more important. (Note also how defence requirements diminished after 1989 as a consequence of the 'peace dividend' but have since increased again with the fight against terrorism.)

4 *Temporal factors* Internal organisation considerations often become temporal critical success factors. These are areas of activity that are significant for the success of an organisation for a particular period of time because the activities are below the threshold of acceptability. For example if several key executives of a global advertising agency quit to form a competing 'spin-off firm', rebuilding of the executive group would become a critical success factor for the organisation. The case of Saatchi and Saatchi illustrates this.

Skills and competences

The notion of **'distinctive competence'** first came into currency at the Harvard Business School in the business policy course. Selznick (1957) defined it as any factor at which a firm was uniquely good by comparison with its main competitors. Such distinctive competences may exist in any key area, as suggested by Table 5.4.

Identifying distinctive competences should be undertaken in conjunction with the value chain analysis (see Figure 5.4).

The concept of distinctive competences was further developed by Pralahad and Hamel (1990) in their analysis of factors underlying Japanese competitive success in which they identified the acquisition and exploitation of distinctive, or what they called 'core' competences, as a major source of competitive advantage. In Pralahad and Hamel's study a core competence was seen as a unique and difficult to replicate combination of a number of distinctive competences. Thus, while competitors might benchmark and match specific skills and competences, it was the combination of these which conferred the sustainable competitive advantage For example Pralahad and Hamel see Coca-Cola's competitive advantage arising from a combination of brand strength, distribution network and geographic spread. For Benetton it is fast cycle time, computer-aided manufacture and just-in-time dyeing, while for Toyota it is just-in-time manufacturing, fast cycle times and economies of scale.

In some cases core competences evolve or 'emerge' (Mintzberg and Walters 1985); in others they are the outcome of deliberate strategic planning. For example Pralahad and Hamel describe Canon's assault on the copier market as comprising and eight-step plan as follows.

1 Establish the strategic intent to 'beat Xerox'.

2 Identify Canon's existing core competences.

3 Understand Xerox's technology and patents to identify the necessary competences.

4 License the technology to gain market experience and develop the core competences not already possessed.

5 Invest in R&D to improve on the existing technology to acquire and start to exploit core competences, primarily to achieve cost reductions, e.g. by standardisation of components, improving ease of maintenance and replenishment.

6 License out own technology to fund further R&D and thus further consolidate the core competences required to beat Xerox.

7 Open challenge with 'business warfare', first by attacking markets where Xerox is weakest – Japan, then Europe.

8 Finally, an innovative, rather than imitative, attack on markets where Xerox is strongest, e.g. by selling rather than leasing, distributing through office equipment retailers rather than direct, and focusing promotion on end-users rather that on corporate functional heads.

Customer analysis

The essence of customer analysis is the determination of **buyer behaviour.** It lies at the very heart of developing an effective marketing strategy. While there are many common elements in buyer behaviour, it is useful to distinguish between individual, or **consumer behaviour (CB or B2C)**, and **organisational buyer behaviour (OBB or B2B)**, and these are dealt with separately in Chapters 8 and 9.

However, it is important to remember the common elements that underpin all buyer behaviour, and these may be stated as:

1 Consumption is a response to a felt need which may be prompted by in-built stimuli (physiological) or an extrinsic cue which triggers a response based on experience or learning. It follow that awareness of a need is the first step in the buyer decision process. Given the number of cues or stimuli competing for our attention (awareness), we possess an in-built defence mechanism known as selective perception which operates at the subconscious level and only admits information to our conscious awareness when it is felt such information will satisfy a need.

2 On recognising a cue or stimulus we can decide whether to consider it further (interest), or ignore it – at least for the time being. If consideration stimulates genuine interest, then we will evaluate both the need and the information we have about objects which may satisfy the need. Given the strength of the need and the degree of risk we perceive in making a decision, we may search for additional information.

3 In evaluating the information we have gathered, two criteria dominate both individual and organisational buying behaviour – fitness for purpose (will it satisfy the need?) and cost benefit (is it worth it?). Rationality requires that we will prefer the object which offers the highest perceived value. (It is important to remember that in selecting and evaluating this information subjective influences such as attitudes, opinions and emotions will all affect the decision process.)

4 Provided that one object clearly outperforms all the others, the decision maker will have no difficulty in reaching a conclusion. The dilemma we face is that, by definition, competition means that we will have access to closely matched alternatives in terms of both fitness for purpose and cost benefit. It follows that, in discriminating between objectively near-perfect substitutes, we will have to use our subjective preferences – what we term 'behavioural response' in our model of buyer behaviour. (See Chapter 7).

If this simple model of buyer behaviour is correct, then it follows that sellers must define carefully both the objective needs which customers are seeking to satisfy, as well as the subjective factors which may influence or modify the individual's perception of the objective factors.

Self-analysis

Having completed an analysis of the external microenvironment, the penultimate step in the marketing appreciations is to compete a self-analysis or what is sometimes referred to as an internal audit In many respects the internal audit covers the same issues as the competitor analysis in that it is designed to identify and evaluate assets, resources, skill and competences. That said, the internal audit is likely to be much more comprehensive, if for no other reason than that one has open access to much more information. For example in the *IEBM Encyclopedia of Marketing* (Baker 1999), Aubrey Wilson writes:

> The audit commences with the collection and study of the company's documentation. The usually comprises the following, but for the individual organization there may also be specific items:
>
> Organization chart (official and informal).
> Corporate/market/profit plan/budgets.
> Sales analysis.
> Job specifications of marketing and sales personnel including the sales or order office.
> Catalogues and brochures (own and competitors').
> Press releases.
> Sales force costs analysis.
> Media advertising and direct mail material including schedules and appropriations (own and competitors')
> Other marketing costs analysis.
> Sales force reporting formats.
> Customer database formats.
> Enquiry records.
> Pricing forms including discount structure.
> Sales analysis (home and export).
> Sale force's, agents' and distributors' performance assessment forms.
> New product search reports and evaluations.
> List of journals and publications received.
> List of external statistics regularly received.
> Guarantee claim record.
> Credit note analysis.
> Complaints analysis.
> Service record formats.
> Agency contracts.
> Terms of business.
> Costing and pricing formats.
> Training programmes for sales and/or marketing people – content and frequency.
> Details on any market research and customer satisfaction undertaken or bought in during the last one or two years.

While such an audit should provide a good summary of the nature and extent of the company's assets, together with an indication of the relative importance of the major business functions, its value can only be realised by comparison with similar data for companies with which it is competing. To obtain this one must carry out an external audit as described earlier.

The development of effective marketing strategies requires firms to match skills and competences (competitive advantages) with market opportunities.

Conventional wisdom proposes:

- *Structure follows strategy.*
- *Strategy should be marketing oriented, i.e. based on customer needs.*

The reality is that structure usually determines strategy, and almost invariably does so in the short term. It follows that a clear definition and measurement of the firm's strengths and weaknesses is a prerequisite for strategic marketing planning.

The internal marketing audit comprises five main elements:

1 *The marketing strategy audit.*
2 *The marketing organisation audit.*
3 *The marketing systems audit.*
4 *The marketing productivity audit.*
5 *The marketing function audit.*

The marketing strategy audit contains two main elements:

1 *Identification and evaluation of the firm's marketing objectives.*
2 *Identification and evaluation of the firm's marketing strategy and its relationship to the declared objectives.*

The marketing organisation audit contains three main elements:

1 *Evaluation of the formal structure.*
2 *Evaluation of the marketing function.*
3 *Evaluation of the interface efficiency.*

The marketing systems audit is concerned with four major subsystems:

1 *Marketing information.*
2 *Marketing planning.*
3 *Marketing control.*
4 *New Product development.*

The marketing productivity audit measures two major dimensions:

1 *Profitability.*
2 *Cost effectiveness.*

The marketing function audit is focused on the main elements of the marketing mix:

- *Product.*
- *Price.*
- *Distribution.*

- *Personal selling.*
- *Advertising, promotion and publicity.*

In addition to the specific marketing resources, a full self-audit should also define and measure the firm's other major resources in respect of:

- *Physical – land, buildings, etc.*
- *Technology.*
- *Finance.*
- *Procurement.*
- *Personnel.*

Six alternative auditing approaches are:

1 *Self-audit.*
2 *Lateral audit, i.e. persons from different functions audit each other.*
3 *Audit from above.*
4 *Company auditing office.*
5 *Company task-force audit.*
6 *External audit.*

While the intention is to measure internal strengths and weaknesses as objectively as possible, the important thing is to compare the firm with its competitors to form a relative judgement. Factor rating tables should be constructed to assist this process.

In sum, the internal appraisal should provide answers to the following questions:

- *What is the company's present position?*
- *What is the company good at?*
- *What are the major problems faced?*
- *What is the company poor at?*
- *What major resources, expertise exist?*
- *What major resources, expertise deficiencies exist?*

PUTTING IT ALL TOGETHER

By now you should have an excellent understanding of the major macro-environmental trends which influence all firms in all industries; of the micro-environmental forces which shape competition and particularly market structure, conduct and performance (critical success factors); of your customers' needs and expectations and your own and competitors' strengths and weaknesses. It remains to try and synthesise all this information into a single simplified summary statement which will provide the basis for developing your own strategy and marketing plan. The technique for achieving this us usually known as the **SWOT analysis** – SWOT being an acronym for **Strengths, Weaknesses, Opportunities and Threats.**

In discussing self-analysis we stated that developing an effective marketing strategy is essentially a matching process in which the firm seeks to identify marketing opportunities which will allow it to use its resources, skills and competences to optimum effect. While it is true that long-term survival and success depend on the ability to detect and anticipate major trends in the macro-environment, in practice it is probably better to realise that the long term is made up of a series of short terms and, in the short term, it is 'survival' that matters. This perspective enables us to reconcile the main schools of thought about strategic planning. While the majority of theorists and consultants extol the benefits of structured long-term strategic planning, followers of Henry Mintzberg take the view that strategy 'emerges' as the organisation responds to changes in its environment. The hybrid and preferred solution is that we must have a strategy which gives an overall sense of direction and purpose for the long term. Without this, how do we know what corrective actions to take when confronted by an unforeseen or unanticipated event in the short term? In the same way that the sailor must adjust his course to allow for wind and weather beyond his control, so the manager needs to modify the long-term strategy in the light of emerging events. It is the summary or SWOT analysis which provides the basis for deciding where we are today – our strengths and weaknesses – and what future possibilities are available to us – opportunities and threats.

As noted earlier, you should have already identified the key issues and critical success factors which define the opportunities and threats in the external environment as well as your own strengths and weaknesses. What we need to do now is combine these to provide an overview of the current position and likely future events.

The Institute of Management lists the benefits of SWOT analysis as:

- *A framework for identifying and analysing*
- *An impetus to analyse a situation and develop suitable strategies and tactics*
- *A basis for assessing core capabilities and competences*
- *The evidence for, and cultural key to, change*
- *A stimulus to participation in a group experience*

However, some commentators are critical of the technique and IM cites Hill and Westbrook's criticism that SWOT analysis is ineffective because of its tendency to produce:

- *Long lists*
- *Description rather than analysis*
- *Unprioritised lists*

In order to conduct a SWOT analysis the IM Checklist identifies the following stages:

1 *Establish the objectives*
2 *Select appropriate contributors*
3 *Allocate research and information gathering tasks*
4 *Create a workshop environment*
5 *List strengths*

6 *List weaknesses*

7 *List opportunities*

8 *List threats*

9 *Evaluate listed ideas against objectives*

10 *Carry your findings forward.*

Finally, the IM lists the following Do's and Dont's for SWOT analysis:

Do
Be analytical and specific.
Record all thoughts and ideas in stages 5-8.

SWOT

SWOT is a popular and widely used analytical device. In 1993-4 the UK Department of Trade and Industry commissioned a survey into its use as part of its Manufacturing, Planning and Implementation (MPI) scheme. Of the 50 companies reviewed 20 used SWOT involving 14 consulting companies. The survey findings seriously questioned the value of the technique.

Three broad approaches were identified:

1 A single senior manager or consultant undertakes the analysis.

2 Several senior managers undertake individual SWOTs which are then collated. A meeting may be held to agree a communal SWOT.

3 The SWOT is the output of one or more meetings which may be facilitated by a consultant.

Four major weaknesses were identified:

1 Vague, general and non-specific terms such as performance and value-for-money were used to describe factors.

2 No analysis or verification of any point was undertaken.

3 All points were universal, i.e. assumed to apply equally to all products, functions and markets.

4 Consultants created their own lists which differed significantly from company personnel lists without consultation or explanation.

The number of factors identified varied from 11 to 216 with an average of 40. On average more weaknesses than strengths were identified and slightly more opportunities than threats. However, in only one case were factors grouped, prioritised, weighted or sequenced in any way.

Perhaps the major criticisms of SWOT analysis were that it was used largely to create a list of factors around which to structure a discussion but lacking the substantial analysis called for by a strategic analysis. As a result, the output lacked relevance and insight and only 3 companies made further use of it. While Hill and Westbrook's evaluation suggests that SWOT analysis should be rejected we believe that it is a useful technique if used properly. Accordingly, we recommend that:

1 You should avoid ambiguity and clarify/define the terms used.

2 Resolve conflicts of interpretation and meaning, e.g. between internal and external factors or factors seen as both S and W or O and T.

3 Choose an appropriate level of analysis – corporate, SBU or Market.

4 Develop meaningful lists of factors not shopping lists.

5 Prioritise and/or weight the factors.

6 Confirm the accuracy and relevance of all data, especially where opinion based.

7 Incorporate/use the findings into subsequent analysis and implementation.

Reference: Hill, Terry and Westbrook, Roy, "SWOT Analysis: It's Time for a Product Recall", *Long Range Planning*, Vol.30, No 1, 1997, 46-52

Be selective in the final report.
Choose the right people for the exercise.
Choose a suitable SWOT leader or facilitator.

Don't
Try to disguise weaknesses.
Merely list errors and mistakes.
Lose sight of external influences and trends.
Allow the SWOT to become a blame-laying exercise.
Ignore the outcomes at later stages of the planning process.

Summary

In this chapter we have focused on the analysis of competition and began by explaining why an understanding of industry structure is important to the development of an effective marketing strategy. Given that the most extensive and rigorous study of competition has been undertaken by economists then the best place to begin is with a review of their theories.

For purposes of analysis, industries are classified as falling into one of three categories – **primary**, **secondary**, and **tertiary**. Primary industry embraces agriculture, fishing forestry and mining, while secondary industry is concerned with **manufacturing**, and tertiary industry with **services**. In less developed economies the main source of employment and wealth creation is in primary industries; in developed economies it is manufacturing, and in the most advanced economies it is service provision.In pursuit of economic growth (remember Rostow's theory from Chapter 1), countries seek to industrialise and throughout the twentieth century the **newly industrialised countries (NICs)**, and now the 'emerging economies' have emphasised the development of manufacturing. Because of their lower costs these countries have been a major source of competitive manufactured goods in the advanced economies with the result that the emphasis in these countries has increasingly focused on services.

As industries mature there is a tendency towards concentration with a significant proportion of all output being concentrated in the hands of a comparatively small number of dominant firms. Because of their size these firm enjoy major scale economies making it impossible for the very large number of small firms to compete with them on price, and forcing them to differentiate to survive. **Concentration** is apparent in all classes of industry - primary, secondary and tertiary – and the degree of concentration is a major indicator of the nature of competition within an industry, be it manufacturing, retailing, or the provision of financial or other services.

The degree of concentration is a major indicator of industry structure, and industry structure is a major determinant of the ways in which firms compete in an industry (conduct) and of their performance. The study of **structure-conduct-performance** has been the focus of the major sub-field of **industrial economics** since the 1930s and its theories are based on empirical research into the way firms compete with one another in the real world. As a result of their inquiry, industrial economists have pointed out that while monopoly and perfect competition are seen as polar positions anchoring a continuum of competitive states, the great majority of activity lies somewhere between them and may be described as imperfect. Where there is a state of monopoly or perfect competition then markets will behave in the way that theoretical economists predict they will. Most of the time, however, such conditions do not prevail so firms have to develop different kinds of competitive strategies, and they do so by manipulating the elements of the **marketing mix**.

In order to decide what mix to adopt, firms must undertake three kinds of analysis – of the industry and market, their competitors, and of their customers. Industry/market analysis is best addressed by means of the SCP (structure-conduct-performance) model described above. Competitor analysis is usually based on the idea of the value chain proposed by McKinsey in the 1960s which traces the conversion of raw materials into finished goods for consumption, and examines where and how value is added in the process. To understand what represents value it is necessary to understand **buyer behaviour**. Conventionally, such behaviour is classified as **organisational** or **consumer** and these were discussed briefly as an introduction to the two specialised chapters that follow.

Given an understanding, of the industry, the competition, and customer needs, the final part of the analysis is to identify what particular skills and competences the firm has which will enable it to compete successfully with its rivals. This self-analysis is achieved by means of a **marketing audit** that diagnoses the firms strengths and weaknesses that may then be compared with the threats and opportunities detected in the industry/competitor/customer analyses by means of a **SWOT analysis**.

Finally, we would reiterate the point made in the introduction that the highly influential work of Michael Porter is directly derived from his studies of industrial economics at Harvard in the late 1960s as applied to the study of Business Policy at the Harvard Business School where he now teaches. With such a pedigree it would be foolish to underestimate the insights offered by SCP analysis.

Review questions and problems

1 It is said that oligopolies could not be created except by means of heavy consumer advertising. The advertisers maintain that the security created by this relatively stable situation gives protection and time to embark on product development and improvement. Discuss this statement in relation to the detergent market.

2 What are the advantages and disadvantages of industries which are dominated by a few large-scale companies manufacturing similar, but differentiated, products?

3 What does the Government mean when it refers to its 'industrial strategy'? Say whether you think the strategy is viable and describe, using examples, the effect it has had on the structure of UK industry.

4 What relationship is there between oligopoly and the concept of product differentiation?

5 To what extent do you accept the statement that much so-called planned obsolescence is actually the working out of competitive and technological factors, both signifying a dynamic economy?

6 Under what circumstances might a fall in the price of a commodity lead to a decrease in the quantity demanded?

7 Define and distinguish between price elasticity of demand and income elasticity of demand.

8 In an oligopolistic market, why do prices tend to respond slowly to changes in market conditions?

Key terms

buyer behaviour
channels of communication
competition and market structure
competitive advantage
competitive strategy
competitive variables
competitor analysis
competitor centred firms
complete monopoly
concentration
concentration ratio
consumer behaviour
critical success factors
customer analysis
customer orientated firms
degree of competition
demand
demand elasticity
differentiated competition
disposable income
distinctive competence
diversification
economic leverage
effective demand

entrepreneur
environmental factors
foreign competition
freedom of entry
full and free competition
geographic location
homogeneous output
individual competitor analysis
industrial concentration
industry
industry position
industry structure
industry/market analysis
interaction of supply and
   demand
latent demand
macro level
macro-national level
market driven firms
marketing concept
marketing leverage
mechanical revolution
micro/industry level
micro-environmental analysis

monopolist
new product development
   (NPD)
organisational buyer behaviour
organisational revolution
potential demand
primary sector
producers
product
product differentiation
product mix
pure monopoly
secondary sector
self centred firms
self-analysis
substitution
super-corporation
SWOT (strengths, weaknesses,
   opportunities and threats)
temporal factors
tertiary sector
theories of competition
value chain analysis
vertical integration

Supplementary reading list

Porter, M. E. (1980) *Competitive Strategy* (New York: Free Press).
Porter, M. E. (1985) *Competitive Advantage* (New York: Free Press).
Porter, M. E. (1990) *The Competitive Advantage of Nations* (London: Macmillan).
Scherer, F. M. and Ross, D. (1990) *Industrial Market Structure and Economic Performance*, 3rd
   edn (Boston: Houghton-Mifflin).

See also any introductory economics texts or introductory marketing texts.

THE BUSINESS SYSTEM – CHANNELS OF DISTRIBUTION

6

Learning Goals *The objective of this chapter is to introduce the student to the formal systems and structures which have developed over time to facilitate the physical transfer of goods from the raw material stage into ultimate consumption. After reading this chapter you should be able to:*

- Define the nature of and role played by the distribution system.

- List the five essential functions performed by a distribution channel.

- Review the advantages and disadvantages of the three basic alternatives available when selecting a distribution policy:
  - direct sale;
  - sale through an intermediary;
  - a dual policy.

- Define raw materials and the distinction between finite and renewable raw materials.

- List some salient features of extractive industries.

- Account for the development of producer–user agreements.

- Discuss some key aspects of agricultural production and marketing.

- Explain the features underlying the growth of processing.

- Describe the channels used for fresh produce and the role of Marketing Boards.

- Identify the distinguishing characteristics of business to business marketing.

- List the main factors which influence the structure of industrial distribution channels.

- Describe the effect of industry concentration on industrial channels and exemplify this by reference to the distribution of steel.

INTRODUCTION

Every transaction between buyer and seller depends on the existence of a network, or business system, to enable contact to be made and exchange to occur. Even the simplest of exchanges – the purchase of eggs, cheese or vegetables at your local Farmers Market – depends on a multitude of previous exchanges to make it possible. The farmer had to buy tools and equipment, seeds and fertiliser, livestock and feedstuffs, storage and packaging materials, transport to the market and the hire or purchase of a display area before he could make his goods available for you to purchase. And each of the individuals or organisations from whom he purchased supplies or inputs went through a similar process to make something available for sale.

The network or system that supports all these exchanges is usually called the channel of distribution and the process itself simply distribution. Now distribution or Place is one of the major elements of the marketing mix and every marketing textbook has a chapter dealing with the topic. Very few distinguish between the infrastructure of distribution and the managerial implications of this for marketing strategy and planning. (A notable exception is Adrian Palmer (2000) who has separate chapters on Channel Intermediaries and Physical Distribution and Logistics). We consider this to be a weakness as, at any given point in time, the existing channels of distribution, including the means of transportation and communication that support them, are as much a feature of the marketing environment as the other PEST factors. As such the business system represents both a challenge and an opportunity for firms competing for the customers patronage. Innovation in methods of distribution can be just as important as new product development in securing a competitive advantage. Accordingly, in this Chapter we will look at the functions of distribution systems from the extraction/ production of raw materials through to their delivery to retailers for sale into ultimate consumption. Retailing, and the relationship between manufacturers and retailers has changed significantly in recent decades. Accordingly, in this new edition we have taken the opportunity to give a separate chapter to the subject.

To begin with we expand on the concept of the value chain introduced in the last chapter. Then we look at the function of the distributive channel and the salient differences between direct sale and the use of intermediaries. We then follow the logic of the business system by starting with a review of the distribution of raw materials.

Next we look at the distribution of industrial goods; that is, those products and services sold by one producer to another for use in the creation of consumer goods and services. Traditionally this field of activity was known as industrial marketing although, as we shall see, many people now refer to this as 'business to business' or B2B marketing.

VALUE CHAINS

In Chapter 1 we considered briefly some of the issues which define an economy. It will be recalled that the first of these stages was termed 'Traditional society' which is characterised by its lack of a systematic understanding of the environment, and the technology and tools necessary to achieve any significant improvement in productivity. In such societies, and particularly the most primitive ones, the great majority of people's time is taken up with survival and the satisfaction of basic physiological needs. The first real step in the process of civilisation occurred when people began to establish settlements, rather than pursue a nomadic existence in which they moved from place to place seeking food and other essential materials. The point we are seeking to establish is that place and location has played a fundamental role in the evolution of exchange and the development of marketing.

Originally, the market was a physical location where people could exchange surpluses; at first in kind (barter or counter-trading), and subsequently through a medium of exchange such as money. The opportunity to exchange surpluses and thereby increase satisfaction encouraged task specialisation which, in turn, increased productivity and output. However, early settlements were severely limited in their production/consumption opportunities by virtue of the raw materials or factors of production available to them. Over time trade between settlements developed and further specialisation of function occurred based upon the exploitation of natural local advantages. It was observation of this phenomenon which prompted Ricardo to formulate his **theory of comparative advantage** in which he demonstrated that through specialisation and exchange two countries could both gain, even though one country had a natural advantage (that is, was more cost-effective) in producing both the products which were to be exchanged.

More recently, Michael Porter (1990) in his *Competitive Advantage of Nations* has argued that the classical theory based upon the concept of factor endowment 'is at best incomplete and at worst incorrect' as an explanation of the competitive performance of nations. Porter's thesis is that while a natural endowment is important it is the way such endowments are used which is more important, and he points to the fact that in many cases, such as Japan, factor deficiencies have acted as a spur to innovation and superior performance. However, one does not need to develop the argument further to appreciate that the potential to innovate and specialise will only add value and increase satisfaction if the goods produced can be made available to users and consumers who have a demand for them. To achieve this requires the existence of channels of distribution, and of specialists and intermediaries to facilitate the flow of goods from producers to consumers. It is this topic which forms the subject of this chapter.

This chapter is concerned with the infrastructure of distribution and is largely descriptive. Its inclusion and the detail it contains are believed to be important as an understanding of existing channels of distribution, and the factors which underlie or condition their structure and operation, represent external factors over which the individual firm or supplier has limited control. This understanding is essential when making channel decisions and using 'place' as an element in the marketing mix. **Channel Management** is returned to in more detail in Chapter 16 but, in this chapter we first consider the basic functions of **distributive channels** before looking at the distribution of raw materials as the first step in the so-called **value chain** introduced in the previous chapter. As noted, the value chain is the modern equivalent to McKinsey's conceptualisation of the 'business system' which was first introduced at the Harvard Business School in 1970 when the author was teaching the class in Creative Marketing Strategy. A simplified value chain to deliver a can of tuna to a customer is reproduced in Fig. 6.1

Another description of the value chain is the **supply chain**. While there are some differences between these concepts – for example, the supply chain focuses more on **logistics** – both are concerned with study of the linkages between what previously were often treated as separate and discrete activities. Lancioni (2005) observes: "From this perspective, the focus of channel management was on making each firm in the distribution channel more efficient and productive. Each firm operated on its own, seeking to make the highest profits and acting independently to price its products and services. With the advent of supply chain management and the concept of a supply system emerging, the perspective of industrial managers changed from one of an "…..*intrafunctional* vision, where the focus was on the individual firms in the channel, to an interfunctional view where emphasis is now placed on the co-operation that occurs between firms"

Figure 6.1 A simplified value chain to deliver a can of tuna to a customer

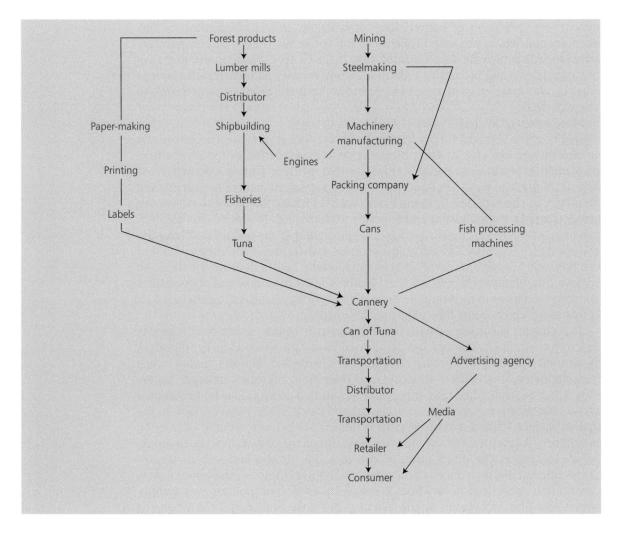

Source: Möller, K. and Wilson, D. (1999) 'Business Marketing' in Baker, M.J. (ed.) *IEBM Encyclopedia of Marketing*, (London: Thomson Learning)

(Lancioni 2000, p.2). In turn, this view has led to the view of value/supply chains as **networks** with an emphasis upon **relationships** between members of the network in place of simple transactions.

Fernie (2003) identifies five trends in both industrial and consumer markets that brought about this integration, namely:

1 The shift from a push to a pull, i.e., a demand, driven supply chain

2 The customer is gaining more power in the marketing channel.

3 The role of information systems to gain better control of the supply chain.

4 The elimination of unnecessary inventory in the supply chain.

5 The focus upon core capabilities and increasing the likelihood of outsourcing non-core activities to specialists.

Taken together these trends underlined the importance of efficiency in the linkages in the value chain and the significance of **time based competition** as a source of competitive advantage in rapidly changing markets.

DISTRIBUTION: A NEGLECTED SUBJECT

It is generally agreed that the modern subject of marketing owes its origin to economists' inquiries into the nature of the distributive process at the end of the nineteenth century.

However, despite this early interest, it is only in recent years that the firm has turned its attention to the role which distribution has to play as an element of competitive strategy.

In a review of the status of distribution in the 1960s, Donald Bowersox (1969) advanced two reasons which he felt accounted for the delay in the development of this area of marketing:

1 the lack of computers and applied analytical tools sufficient to deal with the complexities of the problem; and

2 the absence of adequate **motivation**.

Of these it was felt that the latter was the more important, and two main factors may be distinguished which were to provide the necessary motivation – **technological innovation** and **increased competition**. Writing in the April 1962 issue of *Fortune*, Peter Drucker characterised distribution as the 'Economy's Dark Continent' and noted that whereas the cost of physical distribution accounted for as much as half of the total cost of finished goods, it had received relatively little attention by comparison with managements' cost reduction efforts in other directions. Since the publication of this article there has been an enormous expansion in the literature of physical distribution, but it is significant that little of the research represented by this literature has been concerned with the strategic implications of channel policy. As Bowersox notes, extant concepts assume vertical integration or, alternatively, take the viewpoint that physical distribution operations and responsibilities cease where a transfer of ownership occurs. The latter ignores the fact that many manufacturers sell at least part of their output through intermediaries, and implies that they take no further interest in the sales process once their output has passed into the wholesaler's inventory. Similarly, vertical integration is atypical of present distributive structures.

Given the competitive pressures attributable to escalating costs, increased industrial concentration as the result of acquisition and mergers, and the threat of product obsolescence inherent in accelerating technological innovation, it is clear that distribution policy has become a question of acute importance to the marketer and this is reflected in the systems/ value chain approach described earlier.

The function of the distributive channel

In order to avoid misunderstanding, a **channel of distribution** is here defined as: '*The structure of intra-company organisation units and extra-company agents and dealers, wholesale and retail, through which a commodity, product or service is marketed*'. This definition was designed to be broad enough to include: (a) both a firm's internal marketing organisation units and the outside business units it uses in its marketing work and (b) both the channel structure of the individual firm and the entire complex available to all firms (*Marketing Definitions*, American Marketing Association, 1962). The *Dictionary of Marketing* (*www.westburn.co.uk*) explains further '*a channel consists of all those steps through which a product must pass between its point of production and consumption*'.

As economies develop there is an increasing emphasis on specialisation and the division of labour, as a result of which a 'gap' develops between producer and user. The primary purpose of a distributive channel is to bridge this gap by resolving spatial and temporal discrepancies in supply and demand. Irrespective of the extent of these discrepancies, certain essential functions need to be performed which may be summarised as:

1 Transfer of title to the goods involved.
2 Physical movement from the point of production to the point of consumption.
3 Storage functions.
4 Communication of information concerning the availability, characteristics and price of the goods.
5 The financing of goods in transit, inventory and on purchase.

The importance of these functions varies, depending upon the nature of the goods themselves. Physical movement and storage tend to predominate in the case of bulky raw or part-processed materials such as basic chemicals, petroleum products and steel, where price and specification are standardised and the market is comprised of a limited number of buyers and sellers. As the complexity of the product increases the provision of information and product service becomes predominant. In the case of consumer goods, advertising and sales promotion constitute the major communication channel, but industrial goods depend more on personal selling owing to the more heterogeneous nature of the goods involved and the possibility of modifying them to meet end-user requirements. Some indication of the possible complexity of the distribution channel for a commonplace product like the broiler chicken is shown in Figure 6.2.

Reference to Figure 6.2 makes it clear that it is the transfer of ownership which determines channel structure as no reference is made to service organisations

Figure 6.2 British broiler production flow plan

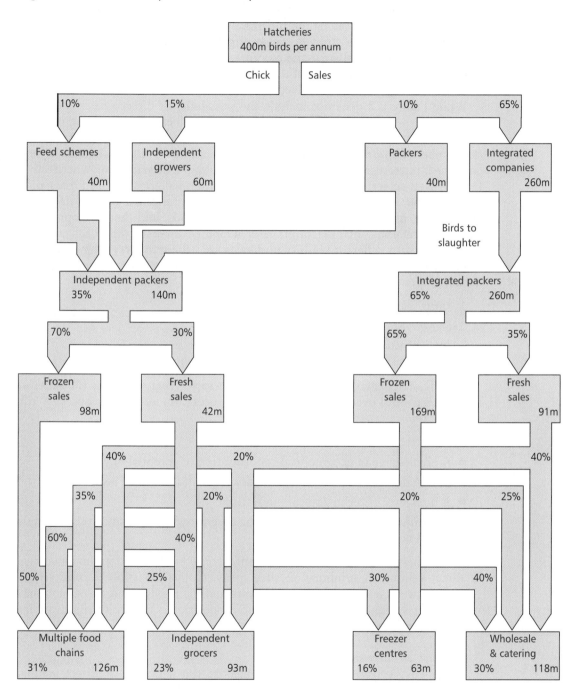

The flow chart is prepared only an as example, the information contained therein is not an accurate analysis of the broiler industry.
Source: Produce Studies Limited, Newbury, England.

that may be involved in the physical movement and/or storage of the product. Rosenbloom (1999, pp. 137–54) emphasises this distinction '. . . because it is the trading relationship involving the functions of buying, selling and transferring of title where most of the strategic marketing issues emerge' (p. 139). According to Rosenbloom, channel structure has three basic dimensions: the length of the channel, the intensity in terms of the number of intermediaries at each level, and the types of intermediaries involved.

While Figure 6.2 does not include the possibility of direct sale by producer to consumer – the shortest channel structure – it does make clear the possible complexity and varying length of the channel. As noted above, intensity refers to the number of intermediaries involved at each level or step in the channel. Where only one intermediary is used this is termed **exclusive distribution**; where only a few are used **selective** and where all possible intermediaries are used **intensive**. The types of intermediary involved are usually determined by the nature of the product, although in the case of consumer goods, and the development of scrambled retailing, manufacturers may adopt an intensive approach and sell through as many different kinds of outlets as are willing to carry their product.

Essentially, however, a manufacturer is faced with three basic alternatives when deciding upon a distribution policy:

1 *Direct sale*;

2 *Sale through an intermediary*;

3 *A 'dual' policy combining direct sale with the use of an intermediary.*

Direct sale

The major advantage associated with direct sale is that it permits the seller to retain full control over the total marketing process. Its usage is favoured by the existence of:

- A limited number of potential buyers;
- A high degree of geographical concentration of potential buyers;
- A high degree of technical complexity requiring extensive service;
- A high level of technological innovation;
- Stable demand conditions; that is the absence of seasonal and cyclical trends which necessitate stockholding.

Any of these factors in itself may be sufficient to predicate adoption of a policy of direct selling; in combination they are virtually irresistible. Conversely, a conflict between, say, the number of buyers and their geographic dispersion may make direct selling a totally uneconomic proposition – the major disadvantage linked with this approach.

Sale through an intermediary

When cost considerations militate against the adoption of direct selling, manufacturers frequently make use of an intermediary who, by acting on behalf of a number of buyers and sellers, is able to perform the necessary functions more economically; that is, the gross margin demanded by the intermediary is less than the on-cost which would be incurred through providing the same services oneself. The advantages and disadvantages of using an intermediary may be summarised as:

Advantages:

1 *Cost advantages*: use of an intermediary,
- minimises the cost of a field sales organisation,
- eliminates warehousing costs,
- minimises inventory financing charges,
- minimises sales costs – invoicing, financing or accounts, etc.,
- minimises the risk of loss through inventory obsolescence,
- minimises loss through bad debts and reduces the cost of credit control,
- eliminates local delivery costs,
- reduces the costs of processing to meet non-standard orders.

2 *Coverage*. The use of intermediaries allows the producer to reach all potential users without having to incur the fixed costs which would arise if direct selling were used.

3 *Provision of service*. Intermediaries can provide immediate availability and necessary pre and after-sales service on a local basis more effectively than many producers.

Disadvantages:

The major disadvantage associated with the use of an intermediary is the loss of direct control over any, or all, of the following:
- Selling effort   – Customer selection;
                   – Call frequency;
                   – Product emphasis;
                   – Promotion and missionary selling effort.
- Pricing.
- Delivery.
- Service – Standard and availability.

Clearly, the importance attached to retaining control over these functions will vary from product to product and manufacturer to manufacturer.

Dual distribution

In order to try and reconcile the conflict between the desirability of direct contact and the economies offered by selling through an intermediary, many manufacturers have adopted a compromise solution, usually referred to as '**dual**' **distribution**. Under this alternative the manufacturer sells part of their output direct but entrusts the balance of their sales effort to an intermediary. As noted elsewhere, this policy is favoured by the existence of the 'heavy half' phenomenon, where a limited number of users constitute the major demand, with the balance fragmented among a large number of small or irregular users.

The major disadvantage associated with dual distribution is the difficulty intrinsic in determining a fair division of the market between producer and intermediary.

Many of these issues will become clear in the following pages where we look at patterns of distribution in more detail.

THE DISTRIBUTION OF RAW MATERIALS

The term 'raw materials' is often used to describe the physical goods used in manufacturing without distinguishing between natural raw materials and semi-manufactured, or fabricated, materials. For example the raw materials used in the packaging industry – paper, plastics, fibre-board and so on – are the finished goods of other manufacturers in the chemical industry. To avoid confusion the term will be used here to describe materials in their natural state such as coal, wool, wheat and rubber, which are often termed 'primary commodities'.

A broad distinction may be made between those raw materials which occur in a natural state and those which are the result of man's efforts in developing particular types of natural products through agriculture. The distinction is a logical one, for whereas man cannot alter the absolute supply of 'natural' raw materials, he can increase the supply of crops, both in absolute amount and in terms of specific varieties. Accordingly they merit separate treatment.

'Natural' raw materials

This category is the one with which the so-called extractive industries are concerned and includes mineral deposits, forest and sea products. It is recognised that it is possible for man to increase the supply of both the latter, just as it may one day be possible to increase the total supply of minerals through deep excavation, or mining them on the moon. In this context, however, they will be treated as being in fixed supply for we have yet to achieve the technological breakthrough which makes such possibilities economically feasible. That this is so is evident in the conservation policies which have been widely adopted.

Another feature which is common to the supply of natural raw materials is that not only is supply fixed in an absolute sense, it is also fixed in the short term if all existing plant is operating at capacity. In other words, supply is not immediately responsive to increases in demand owing to the time-lag between such an increase becoming apparent and resources being diverted to exploit the market opportunity which such excess demand represents. Mines and sawmills cannot be opened overnight, and fishing fleets take time to construct. In the case of minerals the delay is especially protracted as most of the accessible deposits are already being exploited, so that not only do mines have to be opened but road, rail and port facilities also have to be developed. Even reopening disused mines takes time, as is evident from the efforts made in Cornwall during the 1970s and 1980s to cash in on the world shortage of tin, or the efforts to extract oil in hostile environments like the North Sea and Alaska following the energy crisis of the 1970s.

Because supply cannot readily be increased in the short term, prices for raw materials react very quickly to variations in demand in the way in which economic theory predicts they will. In fact commodity markets are usually used as examples when studying supply and demand because these factors can be clearly distinguished in operation, free from the complications which advertising, sales promotion and the like introduce into consumer goods markets. Owing to the tendency for raw material prices to fluctuate widely with variations in both demand and supply, many attempts have been made to stabilise the functioning of commodity markets – usually with little success as will be seen below.

Salient features of the extractive industries

The extraction of raw materials is usually expensive, and involves considerable capital investment, even in the case of the more common materials such as coal, iron ore, basic chemicals and mineral oil. As a result, production of these materials is usually concentrated in the hands of a limited number of firms with the necessary capital and technical resources. From the point of view of the basic industries which process and refine these raw materials, the uncertainties associated with a free market represent a considerable threat to their own security and stability, and predispose them to secure control over a substantial part of their raw material requirements. This is not always possible, however, as many countries limit, or forbid, foreign participation, particularly where they have a monopoly over available supplies. In these circumstances the firm has no option but to buy in the world's commodity markets, the operation of which is very similar to the wheat market described in detail later in this chapter. In an introductory text of this nature it is not possible to consider political interference in the operation of free markets; for example the Arab countries' restriction of oil supplies following the Arab–Israeli conflict in 1973 and the subsequent establishment of OPEC as a producer cartel, or the sanctions imposed on Iraq following its invasion of Kuwait in 1990.

The position with regard to the less common raw materials differs in that although production tends to be concentrated for the reasons outlined above, demand is made up of a large number of consumers with limited individual requirements. To satisfy these demands, specialist markets have been developed wherein the processes of concentration, equalisation and dispersion can take place; for example the London Metal Exchange. In addition to what might he termed the basic raw materials of industry such as oil, chemicals, iron ore and so on, and the rare materials such as gold, silver, tin and diamonds, there is a wide range of materials which occur regularly in nature, and are relatively easy to extract with limited capital equipment. Like many other raw materials they are usually bulky, and the cost of transportation plays a significant role in their marketing. Extraction is closely governed by the proximity of the market to the source of supply and distribution is strictly local, precluding the need for the central markets associated with less common materials. Sand and gravel are examples of such locally distributed materials.

Producer-user agreements

As noted earlier, the inherent instability of commodity markets has stimulated both producers and users to seek some form of agreement to minimise the impact of fluctuations in supply and demand. Under normal conditions the establishment of an agreement is beneficial to both buyer and seller, as it invariably fixes a price bracket for the commodity. Thus, producers can treat the lower limit of the bracket as a guaranteed selling price and plan their output accordingly. Similarly, the buyer can cost his own output in the knowledge that the price of the raw material content cannot exceed the upper limit set by the bracket. However, if supply and demand should get in serious imbalance such agreements are put to a test which few are capable of surviving.

The classic example of the validity of this statement must be the International

Tin Council, which was long quoted as the model for such agreements. For many years the council successfully held prices within the limits agreed on by producers and users, through the maintenance of a buffer stock. As soon as the price of tin fell to the lower limit prescribed by the agreement the Council entered the market, and supported it by buying at that price until sufficient excess supply had been removed for the price to rise above the 'floor'. (These are identical to the tactics of the Bank of England in the foreign exchange market.) Similarly, at the other end of the scale, as soon as excess demand or a decline in supply resulted in the price reaching the agreed ceiling, the Council would release stocks until the price fell within the bracket.

A particularly attractive feature of the scheme was that it was self-financing, as the margin between the upper and lower limits was sufficient to cover the stockholding and administrative costs involved. The Tin Council functioned perfectly on this basis until the early 1960s, when demand began to outstrip supply with the result that the market price was invariably near its upper limit. In order to keep the price within the prescribed limits the Council was increasingly called upon to release its stocks, but was never able to replenish them at the lower price. Eventually the inevitable happened and the stocks were exhausted, leaving a free market in which prices spiralled rapidly before stabilising at a more realistic level some £500 above the old limit. It is possible that the market free-for-all might have been avoided if the Council had had more funds at its disposal with which to build up stocks in time of excess supply, or had appreciated the fundamental disequilibrium earlier and raised the market price sooner. As it was, the Council's operations masked the development of imbalance between supply and demand and gave the market a false appearance of stability.

While the Council survived this crisis it collapsed in 1990 and was disbanded.

Agricultural products

Agricultural products may properly be regarded both as industrial raw materials and as **consumer goods**. In that there are significant differences in distribution, depending upon whether crops are sold direct into consumption, or to manufacturers for processing, it will be convenient to deal separately with these two categories. At the same time there are certain features common to both which deserve consideration prior to a discussion of the salient differences in distribution. Probably the most striking feature of agriculture is the smallness of the average production unit. Although there has been a consistent trend towards larger unit size in nearly every industrialised country as alternative employment opportunities have become available, this is still true today. In the author's opinion there is unlikely to be a significant decline in the number of small farms and, in fact, it seems reasonable to anticipate that their numbers will increase. As the world's population continues to expand geometrically so will the demand for food increase. At present the economists' calculations are based on average income per acre, from which it is argued that farms are too small to enable the average farmer to attain an adequate standard of living. Further, it is true that increased unit size would permit more extensive use of laboursaving equipment and improve the marginal productivity of capital by comparison with investment in a small farm.

These arguments neglect the fact that the small, intensively farmed unit has a significantly higher yield per acre than the large, mechanised unit – a comparison of average wheat yields as between the United States and Holland reveals that the latter are some 400–500 per cent greater than the former. In the future, as demand outstrips supply, prices will rise and thus make intensive farming not only necessary but also more profitable. If the argument is valid, it would seem that the supply of agricultural products will continue to flow from a large number of small producers albeit of a more sophisticated kind. The current 'green revolution' and the associated interest in natural or organic foods has also seen a revival in the fortunes of the small production unit.

Although agricultural products are usually thought of as being homogeneous, in fact there are considerable variations in quality, and some form of grading process is necessary before they can be offered for sale. Further, crops are perishable and need careful handling and storage to prevent deterioration. Neither of these operations can be performed economically on a small scale, nor with the limited resources at the small farmer's disposal, and a complex distributive network has been developed to facilitate the marketing of crops and foodstuffs.

The causes of market disequilibrium

A commonly observed feature of agricultural markets is the erratic fluctuation of price, particularly in the short term. This instability is essentially attributable to variations in supply, as the demand for most agricultural products is fairly stable and predictable in advance. Obviously, climate is a major cause of supply instability, but its effects are compounded by the behaviour of producers in the manner outlined below.

In the case of many products such as wheat, cotton, rubber and livestock, a high proportion of the total supply is accounted for by large, specialist producers. Allowing for the vagaries of climate, their output tends to be fairly constant and calculable in advance, from which it follows that the major variations in supply must be attributed to the output of the small farmers.

Most land may be used to grow a variety of crops, and the major decision facing the small producer is which crop to plant in order to gain the greatest return; a decision that must be made several months before the crop will be ready for sale. In assessing market opportunity it is natural that the farmer should be influenced by current prices, and there is a strong probability that a large number will independently decide to plant those crops which are currently fetching the best prices. The reason certain crops are fetching above average prices is clearly due to the fact that the existing supply is insufficient to satisfy the total demand, and thus the price mechanism is having the desired effect of encouraging an increase in supply. However, it would be purely fortuitous if the separate decision of thousands of producers to increase planting of a specific crop resulted in an exact balancing of supply and demand. It is nearly certain that the increased supply will depress price and fail to meet the farmer's expectations. Further, the decision to switch from, say, wheat to barley will reduce the supply of wheat and its price will go up, thus encouraging the farmer to increase his acreage under wheat and to decrease planting of barley. It is the time-lag between the decision to sow a particular crop and its reaching fruition, the inability to go back on the decision once it is made, and the farmer's imperfect knowledge of others' sowing decisions which create fluctuations in supply that disturb **market equilibrium**.

Given the possible variations in supply, and its diverse origins, it is not surprising that man has developed elaborate marketing systems to permit concentration of output so that it may be made available to those with a demand for it. Such marketing systems possess many features in common and the discussion of the market for a single product will help to clarify these. The wheat market in the United States is particularly well documented and will be used as an example here.

The marketing of wheat

The first stage in the marketing of wheat is concentration at the local elevator by individual farmers. The elevator may be owned by an independent wholesaler, or by the farmers themselves as a cooperative. In either case the elevator will usually offer to purchase the grain outright at central market price, less the cost of freight to the central market and the elevator owner's commission, or, alternatively, to store the grain for a fixed charge. The farmer's decision to sell or store is based on the current price, and expectations as to its future movements, as against the cost of warehousing. (Note: there is an absolute floor to market price determined by Federal Government subsidy. This subsidy is analogous to the guaranteed farm prices offered by the British Government to ensure a minimum level of domestic production prior to entry to the EU when the Common Agricultural Policy came into force.)

Most of the grain in local elevators is resold to manufacturers in the same area, but the balance is sold either to wholesalers in the 'terminal' markets, for example the 'Wheat Pit' in Chicago, or else sent to commission agents in such centres for sale at the best price available. Dealers at the central market frequently combine the functions of merchants, agents and brokers, unlike other markets

THE IMPACT OF THE MARGINAL PRODUCER

A good example of the manner in which the small farmer determines the final level of supply is afforded by the market for natural rubber. Between the two world wars the leading rubber-producing countries agreed to limit supply in order to ensure a fair market price for their output; for example the Stephenson Scheme in South-east Asia. The restriction in supply forced prices up and encouraged the peasant farmers in the Dutch East Indies to clear land, which they would otherwise have been unable to cultivate, to plant rubber trees. These trees were not given the same careful attention as is typical of the commercial plantation, and which accounts for the major production costs, they were simply left to grow for the eight to ten years necessary to achieve maturity. As soon as the trees were big enough to tap, native rubber flooded on to the market, causing prices to plummet and the producer agreements to collapse.

The native product is only slightly inferior in quality to the plantation product, and now accounts for about 30 per cent of total supply.

The commercial grower's position is aggravated by the fact that although they are committed to the high fixed costs of maintaining their plantation, the native grower is not, and only taps their trees when the market price justifies the effort. Thus, whenever the market price becomes favourable from the plantation owner's point of view the marginal producers enter the market and force the price down.

where dealers tend to specialise in only one of these functions.

The merchant is usually in business for himself and buys stocks with the intention of reselling them at a higher price, so that his income is determined both by the size of the margin and by the volume of business transacted. By contrast, agents usually act on behalf of a client for a fixed commission, and so may find it more profitable to achieve a high turnover than to withhold supplies until the price rises; similarly, they lack the merchant's incentive to buy at the lowest price. Brokers occupy an intermediate position between merchants and agents as they buy and sell both for clients and on their own behalf. Unlike merchants, however, they rarely take physical delivery or hold stocks.

In order to bring buyers and sellers into physical contact and facilitate the exchange of title to goods, it is usual to find a place specifically designated for this purpose. Usually the dealers who comprise the 'exchange' or 'market' draw up rules to regulate the transaction of business, and to exclude non-members from participation in its operation. Within the market, transactions fall into two main categories – spot and future trading. Spot, or cash, transactions concern existing or readily available goods, on which immediate delivery can be effected, while the futures market is concerned with contracts for sale and delivery at some future, and usually specified, time.

In fact the futures contract is not a contract to buy or sell at all, but is an option to buy at an agreed price, at a stated time. From the buyer's point of view an option ensures the future availability of supplies at a fixed, maximum price. If, when the option matures, the market price is less than that negotiated, the option is not taken up, for the commodity can be obtained for less in the open market. Conversely, if the price in the market is higher, the option will be exercised and the seller will have to bear the loss. Naturally, the dealer's success depends on their being able to predict accurately the future level of supply, and setting a price which will be attractive to the potential purchaser while exposing the dealer to the minimum of risk. To achieve this the dealer must secure a continuous supply of accurate market data as the basis for forecasting future price levels. Although some dealing in futures is purely speculative, the majority of dealers depend on it for their livelihood and so base their forecasts on facts rather than hunches. In doing so they perform a valuable service, for they reduce uncertainty concerning both demand and supply in the markets in which they operate.

'Consumer' crops

Although there is a fairly clear-cut distinction between crops which comprise the raw materials of industry and those which are consumed in their natural state, it is difficult to maintain the distinction if processing is used as the delineating factor. Nowadays the distinction would seem to rest on the necessity for processing as a prerequisite of consumption, rather than the existence or absence of processing. In the case of crops which are usually classified as 'industrial', the common denominator is the fact that they must undergo some physical change before they can be consumed. This change may be relatively minor, as is the case with flour milling, or extensive – if, say, one is converting wool into a suit of clothes. By contrast 'consumer' crops may be used immediately in their natural state but, in advanced economies, an increasing proportion are now processed in some way or other prior to consumption.

Factors underlying the growth of processing

The volume of agricultural output is ultimately determined by the length of the growing season. Assuming an adequate water supply, temperature is a critical variable. Plants will not grow at or below freezing, and make very little progress until the temperature rises above 40F. Thereafter, the rate of growth doubles approximately for every 18 degree F increase in temperature, so that the farther one moves away from the equator the shorter the length of the growing season. Thus, from early times, man has been preoccupied with methods of preserving and storing food for out of-season use.

The slow growth of population until recent times is at least partly attributable to lack of success in balancing excess with famine. The growth of international trade partially alleviated the problem, but had to await the development of the steam ship and refrigeration to make any real impact. Similarly, a revolution in farming techniques has greatly increased our ability to increase crop yields and prolong the growing season, but the problems of preservation and storage still exist, and command ever-increasing attention.

Refrigeration is expensive in terms of capital installation, and suffers from the same basic disadvantage as canning and similar methods of preservation – the majority of the good stored is water. Although dehydration eliminates this diseconomy, traditional methods tended to so change the nature of the food that they were largely unacceptable. The development of freeze drying overcame most of the problems associated with satisfactory reconstitution, but the expense was too great to justify general commercial usage. However, research sponsored by the Ministry of Agriculture came up with a method of speeding up the process, and **Accelerated Freeze Drying (AFD)** was born. The improved process is less costly and has been widely adopted; for example Batchelor's Vesta range and Surprise peas, Nestle's Gold Blend instant coffee, Cadbury's Smash.

Thus we now have a situation in which the consumer is able to buy highly perishable foodstuffs at any time of the year. Not only that, as methods of preservation have improved costs have fallen, and many 'processed' foods now possess distinct advantages over 'fresh' products. Two obvious advantages are the reduction in waste and the added convenience. Canned, frozen or AFD peas are invariably of uniform quality, which is not the case with peas bought in the pod, and require the minimum of preparation.

The advantages offered by processed foods have had a marked impact on purchasing patterns, and many items traditionally associated with the fresh produce market are now sold through dry-goods outlets; that is, supermarkets and grocery shops as distinct from greengrocers. Retailing forms the subject matter of a later chapter and will not be discussed here, but a brief description of the traditional channels is called for.

The distribution of fresh produce

Essentially, fresh produce reaches the ultimate consumer either directly or via one or more intermediaries.

The functions of broker, agent and producer exchange are identical with those discussed earlier in connection with the marketing of wheat. The term wholesaler is synonymous with merchant, and is increasingly preferred to the latter designation. The most direct channel, producer–consumer, is usually only encountered on a limited and local scale, for example door-to-door sales or the stall in the local market, and most growers prefer to sell through conventional retail outlets. Sales direct to retailer fall into three categories:

1 *The producer acts as his own wholesaler* and establishes direct contact with local outlets.

2 *The producer sets up his own retail outlets* or, conversely, the retailer with a chain of outlets integrates backwards into production.

3 *The producer sells under contract to large retailers*; for example the major supermarket chains, Marks & Spencer, BHS and so on.

Few growers are able to dispose of their total output in this way, however, and most sales are made initially to the wholesaler, either direct or through the medium of a broker or agent. Most urban centres of any consequence have wholesalers who specialise in breaking down bulk supplies into small quantities for resale to the multiple or small retailers in their area. These wholesalers obtain supplies direct on a local basis, but also buy in the central markets from brokers and other wholesalers; for example Covent Garden for fruit, vegetables and flowers, Smithfield for meat, Billingsgate for fish. There can be little doubt that the degree of control exercised by some of the central markets results in diseconomies of which the producer rightly disapproves. Despite the perishability of, say, lettuce, it is difficult to account for the services which increase their value from a farm-gate price of 30p per dozen to a shop price of 40p each. Such excesses go apparently unnoticed by comparison with the criticism levelled at the promotional expenditures of the manufacturer of branded goods.

In order to ensure an adequate supply of certain basic foodstuffs the Government has seen fit to provide incentives for farmers by guaranteeing payment of a minimum price for their output. There are several methods by which this may be achieved, but the most overt and controversial method is through the establishment of a marketing board.

Agricultural marketing boards

The agricultural marketing boards operating in the United Kingdom at the present time were set up under the Agricultural Marketing Acts, 1931–58. The basic features which they have in common are:

■ They are producer-controlled.

■ They can only come into existence at the request of the majority of producers involved with the production of the commodity concerned; for example milk, hops.

■ Their declared object is to secure the best possible return for their members.

■ They are committed to improving quality, output, distribution and management within their own field of activity

Space does not permit detailed consideration of the organisation and operation of the various boards, which may be obtained from their offices on request, but in view of the fact that the boards are run by producers for producers, some comment seems called for.

In essence the constitution of marketing boards results in the creation of producer-controlled monopolies and, while it is accepted that all monopolies are not necessarily harmful, they do create supply-controlled markets which are the antithesis of the marketing concept. Either the consumer must accept what the producer is prepared to offer, or he must do without. This is tolerable if there are acceptable substitutes for the monopolist's output, for example butter/ margarine, or where the product is non-essential, but this is not the case with fresh milk, eggs, potatoes and so on.

The marketing boards pay a standard price to producers for equivalent grades of produce, irrespective of the fact that some are remote from the market and so are being subsidised by those in more economic locations. Similarly, consumers in rural areas tend to subsidise those in urban areas, particularly London, through the adoption of near-standard retail prices. It seems unlikely that maximum efficiency will be achieved so long as all farmers are treated alike and there is little incentive to concentrate on the production of those products which the consumer prefers.

At the time of writing, the following agricultural marketing boards were still operating:

- *Potato Marketing Board*
- *British Wool Marketing Board*

For information on these, readers should make direct contact.

THE DISTRIBUTION OF INDUSTRIAL GOODS

By contrast with the clearly defined patterns associated with the distribution of raw materials, it is difficult to generalise with regard to the channels of distribution associated with the three main categories of industrial goods – equipment, fabricated materials and supplies. Observation suggests that a number of different channels are used, and that selection is conditioned by a host of factors which are summarised in the following check-list:

Customer characteristics
- Number of potential users.
- Geographical distribution of potential users.
- Frequency of purchase.
- Average order size.
- Distribution of users on the basis of consumption.
- Relative importance of product to user; that is, is the product an essential input from the user's point of view, or may its purchase be postponed or delayed?
- Degree of user sophistication vis-à-vis product characteristics; that is, does the user need technical service, if so, what type?
- Credit standing.
- Preferred purchasing pattern – a single preference is unlikely to emerge owing to variations in the above factors; for example the need for after-sales service.

- Degree of associated service requirements – both before and after sale.

Middleman characteristics
- Market coverage.
- Gross margin.
- Proportion of salesmen's time available for selling product.
- Degree of technical expertise.
- Financial strength and stability.
- Stock carrying capacity.
- Servicing capability.
- Number of substitute products carried.

Company characteristics
- Size – both absolute, and relative to the industry/market of which it is a member.
- Financial strength.
- Industry position – leader or follower?
- Spatial relationship between plant(s) and major users.
- Degree of technical competence.
- Degree of specialisation.
- Breadth of product line.
- Ability to provide desired services.

Environmental and competitive characteristics
- The nature of seasonal, cyclical and secular trends in demand.
- Degree of concentration in user industry(ies).
- Nature and usage of existing distributive channels.
- Extent and nature of legal restrictions and regulations.
- The impact of taxation, for example on leasing.
- Government procurement policy.
- Consumer needs – in so far as the demand for industrial goods is derived from consumer demand, shifts in the latter will have an impact on the former.

As will be seen in a later chapter, consideration of all these factors plays an important role in determining a firm's distribution policy and results in many diverse alternatives. On the other hand, it is possible to distinguish broadly similar channels operating across the whole field of industrial goods, which suggests that the most useful approach will be to identify the basic structures and illustrate them with actual examples.

Salient features of industrial or 'business-to-business' marketing
Before proceeding to make such a review, however, it will be useful to state some of the salient features which differentiate the marketing of industrial and consumer goods implicit in the 'check-list' outlined above. These were illustrated earlier in Table 2.1.

Although the basic marketing principles described in this book are felt to be equally applicable to the marketing of all types of goods and services, there are certain differences in degree that condition their relative importance. In the case of industrial goods these differences may be summarised as:

1 *Derived demand.* The demand for industrial goods, and raw materials, is derived from the demand for consumer goods in the sense that any expansion or contraction in the latter will be reflected by a corresponding shift in the former. The more distant the manufacturer is from the production of a specific consumption good, the less direct will be the impact of a change in demand for that good.

2 *Rational buying motives dominate the industrial market.* This is frequently misinterpreted in one of two ways: (a) there is an absence of emotional motives in the industrial purchasing situation, or, (b) consumer purchasing behaviour is irrational. Neither of the above statements is correct: consumers are rational and industrial buyers are influenced by emotional factors, but there is a difference in degree; that is, the industrial buyer will emphasise objective criteria to a greater degree than the average consumer.

3 *Concentration of buyers.* The number of potential buyers for an industrial good is generally far smaller than is the case with consumer goods. Further, industrial buyers tend to be concentrated geographically, for example the cotton and woollen industries. One must be careful not to overstate the importance of this distinction for, clearly, its validity depends upon the precise nature of the product. For example the market for office supplies is both large and dispersed, whereas the market for some consumer goods may be both small and concentrated; for example speciality goods produced on a purely local basis. It is also important to remember that although a national brand may have millions of users, the producer may concentrate their direct sales and distribution efforts upon a limited number of major buyers, for example wholesalers and grocery chains.

4 *The scale of industrial purchasing is greater.* In absolute money terms this is generally, but not always, true. In a proportionate sense, that is size of purchase, vis-à-vis disposable assets, the reverse may often be true, e.g. buying a house requires the consumer to invest several years income in advance.

5 *Industrial products are technically more complex.* Again this is true absolutely but not relatively. The purchaser of a car or television set is faced with a similar degree of technical complexity as the buyer of a computer – in both instances the buyer evaluates performance rather than construction, and is dependent upon the seller for both advice and service.

6 *Industrial buying is a group process.* The same might also be said of the household as a decision-making unit for consumer purchases. It is unlikely that the latter will have formalised evaluation and decision procedures, however, both of which are common in the industrial buying context.

7 *The role of service is greater.* Again this depends upon the nature of the product and the type of service. Immediate availability is a prerequisite for sale of a convenience good – this is rarely the case with even the most common of industrial goods – and consumer durables need after-sales service just as much as many industrial goods.

8 *Leasing, renting, and the extension of credit are important.* This is increasingly true of consumer goods.

From the comments made in respect of these 'distinguishing' factors it is clear that although industrial or B2B marketing may differ in degree, there are sufficient points of similarity to permit the transfer of principles and techniques from one to the other. As such, undue emphasis of differences may be harmful if it induces practitioners in either field to neglect thought and practice in the other. In particular, it will become apparent that marketing tactics are largely a function of product and market, irrespective of whether the specific product be designated 'consumer', 'industrial', or 'business to business', so that a given mix may be equally appropriate to products in either category.

Distributive channels

As noted earlier, distributive channels tend to cut across arbitrary product/industry boundaries and attention here will be concentrated on major variations in structure.

Essentially, the same three basic alternatives are open to manufacturers of both industrial and consumer goods, namely:

1 *Direct sale to user/consumer;*
2 *Indirect sale through the medium of a third party;*
3 *A combination of both direct and indirect sale.*

Direct sale offers the greatest degree of control, but can be uneconomic where there is a large number of customers for the product in question. Under these circumstances some form of intermediary may be able to operate at a lower cost by combining the disparate, but complementary, outputs of several manufacturers for resale to small users of such products, for example building materials, office supplies. Distribution through an intermediary, or **wholesaler**, offers the manufacturer the opportunity to improve their overall profitability, albeit at the sacrifice of some measure of control, and so is frequently used to extend the coverage of the producer's own sales force.

Wholesalers vary considerably in terms of both the nature and extent of the services which they provide, and it is common to draw a broad distinction between 'full' and 'limited' service organisations. The full-service wholesaler usually employ their own sales force, holds stocks from which to make immediate delivery, provides information, advice and technical service, and is usually prepared to extend credit. As the name implies, limited-service wholesalers generally perform a restricted function, and often confine themselves solely to stockholding and delivery. In the latter case the manufacturer is responsible for stimulating demand and the provision of technical services.

For the most part, manufacturers adopt some combination of both direct and indirect sale and, as will be seen in the chapter on channel policy, the precise mix will depend upon two basic criteria – **cost** and **control**.

The distribution of steel

Although the manufacturer of steel in the UK is largely concentrated in the hands of a monopoly, which limits competition between separate production facilities, it provides a good example of the need for a complex distributive structure.

Steel is frequently thought of as an essentially homogeneous product when, in reality, it is highly complex and produced in an enormous variety of shapes and to very different specifications, to meet widely disparate end-use requirements. For example mild steel sheet, used in the fabrication of consumer durables such as cars and washing machines, is very different from electrical steels used in transformers and generators, and from high carbon steels used in the machine-tool industry. To simplify matters discussion here will be confined to flat-rolled mild steel producers. In order to meet specific end-use requirements, an order for flat-rolled mild steel may vary according to any one of the following factors:

- Hot-rolled or cold-reduced;
- Quality/ductility;
- Quantity;
- Thickness;
- Sheet or coil;
- Width (and length in the case of sheets);
- Coated or uncoated – if coated, type and thickness of coating and method of application of coating.

From the user's point of view, each of these factors is highly important and will be specified precisely to meet their exact needs. From the producer's point of view, however, such variants create diseconomies as they interrupt the smooth flow of production and reduce the mill throughput. In turn, the diseconomies created by operating the mill at less than optimum efficiency to meet customer needs are reflected in the producer's price structure. However, beyond a certain point the diseconomies involved in meeting a precise specification become so great that the producer will refuse to accept less than a minimum order quantity (MOQ). The MOQ is determined by a number of complex factors which cannot be discussed here but, over the years, increasing automation has resulted in a gradual increase in the size of the minimum acceptable order. This increase has had little impact on the large-scale user, whose minimum requirements for a given specification are normally far in excess of the MOQ, but could have been a major threat to the user with a limited demand had it not been for the existence of steel wholesalers, or 'stockholders'.

Although some stockholders are subsidiaries of the steel producers, the majority are independent organisations. Given the enormous variety of steel products, all but the largest stockholders find it necessary to specialise in some category, for example tinplate, sheet and plate, structural steels and so on. In essence, the stockholder functions by anticipating the likely needs of small users, which they combine into an acceptable mill order, normally for a 'standard' size. In fact there are no 'standard' sizes, but certain combinations of width and length have been widely adopted as they offer the maximum benefits within the mills' price structure, and so reduce the scrap loss when cutting to the exact size required. To meet the precise size requirements specified by their customers, stockholders install shearing, slitting and shaping machines and, increasingly, are ordering in coil form, which permits them to cut to any length without loss.

In addition to breaking bulk to meet small users' requirements, the stockholder also helps to even out fluctuations in supply and demand. Steel-making is a complex, multi-stage process in which an order may be 'lost' at any stage of manufacture, necessitating a 'remake'. If an order is rejected at final inspection it can take three to four weeks to replace, assuming that it can be fitted into the mill schedule immediately. Further, production of an exact quantity is a virtual impossibility, so that most orders turn out less than, or in excess of, the specified amount. Steel buyers are familiar with the technological constraints involved in steel production and adjust their buying policies accordingly.

Where a specification is known to be difficult to produce, buyers maintain sufficient stocks to cover the possibility of late or partial deliveries. However, the maintenance of stocks ties up capital, and most buyers reduce their stock levels to the minimum consistent with normal deliveries in the knowledge that temporary shortages may be made good by buying from stockholders. From the producer's point of view the stockholder performs an equally valuable service in absorbing excess supply in the short term. In addition to buying excess production against mill orders that the customer is unprepared to accept, the stockholder provides an outlet for cancelled orders and reject materials which the mill would find it uneconomic to reclaim. Thus, through specialisation and local knowledge the stockholder performs a number of valuable functions for both producer and user, at a lower cost than would be possible if they performed these functions themselves.

The factors which predispose the steel producer to adopt both a direct and indirect approach are typical of many industries with high concentration ratios. (You will recall from Chapter 5 that the **concentration ratio** is an economic concept that is widely used in comparative industry analyses in preference to the less precise distinction between perfect and imperfect competition.) Concentration ratios take into account both the size and numbers of firms in a market, and are computed by summing the percentage of total sales accounted for by a given number of firms – thus a true monopoly would have a concentration ratio of 100 per cent, while a highly oligopolistic industry might be defined as one in which the four largest firms account for more than 50 per cent of total sales. For the marketer faced with the decision of selling direct or through an intermediary, the concentration concept provides a useful rule of thumb when applied to purchases by users, as opposed to sales by producers. By ranking firms in terms of their consumption of the product concerned, it is relatively simple to arrive at a measure of concentration and decide whether direct sale is economically feasible and, if so, to what extent. Many analyses of this kind have revealed what has been termed the 'heavy half' phenomenon; that is, 50 per cent of total purchases are accounted for by a small percentage of buyers. As a generalisation, it is reasonable to state that the higher the concentration ratio the more direct sale is to be preferred, but this does not necessarily mean that the producer will attempt to make all sales direct.

Consider, for example, the supplies of the motor-car assembly industry, where a small number of buyers account for a very high percentage of total demand. Irrespective of the producer's size, or the nature of their product, they will deal direct with Ford, Toyota and so on. Over time, however, the cars produced by these companies will require replacement parts, but it is unlikely that many components manufacturers will attempt to sell them to every garage and repair shop in the United Kingdom with an uncertain demand for such parts. In consequence, the component manufacturer must decide whether to set up their own regional warehouses, to have distribution to the car manufacturer, or to use the services of motor accessory and parts wholesalers.

Similarly, the manufacturers of standardised parts such as bearings, industrial fasteners or electrical components, and the producers of general-purpose equipment such as bulldozers, fork-lift trucks or lathes will find that a high percentage of sales are accounted for by a limited number of customers. However, unless the producer has a very strong franchise with such major users, and can depend upon them consistently to absorb his output, he cannot afford to ignore the multiplicity of small users that make up the balance of the market. The more numerous and geographically segregated the latter are, the less economic direct sale becomes, so that in markets with a very low degree of concentration the producer may well find it necessary to channel their total output through an intermediary. Many operating supplies produced by small, specialised producers fall into this category; for example stationery, hand tools or cleaning materials.

Manufacturers' agents

Although attention has been focused on wholesalers as a link between producer and user, many firms prefer to employ **agents**, either in addition to, or in place of a sales force of their own.

From the manufacturer's viewpoint, the major advantage of employing agents is that they only pay commission on actual sales and so avoid the fixed costs associated with the maintenance of a sales force. Further, agents enter into a contractual agreement with their principal and so are subject to a greater degree of control than is usually possible when selling through an independent wholesaler.

Most agents handle a line of complementary but non-competing products, and operate within a clearly defined territory. The successful agent depends heavily upon their established contacts, and so offer the manufacturer a 'ready-made' salesman when introducing a new product or extending their geographical coverage. On the other hand, agents are not without disadvantage for, as noted when discussing the wheat market, the agent rarely has a complete identity of interest with their principal. This is particularly so when the agent is selling several different products, when they are likely to take the line of least resistance and sell what is in greatest demand, rather than devote time to missionary selling, that is making cold calls to stimulate demand. Also, unlike wholesalers, the agent does not take delivery of goods, and the manufacturer must maintain and finance a larger inventory than would be necessary if he sold through a wholesaler. Hence, where there are seasonal fluctuations in demand, or the manufacturer is short of working capital, the wholesaler will usually be preferred to the agent.

From the foregoing description it is clear that there is frequently a conflict between the desire for the most economic method of distribution and management's wish to retain control over the marketing of the firm's output. This conflict will be examined in greater detail in Chapter 16, but attention now must be turned to the **distribution of consumer goods**, or **retailing**. Since the publication of the last edition the importance of service industries, and especially retailing, has continued to grow – so much so that it has been decided to dedicate a separate chapter to the topic in this edition.

Summary

This rather large chapter has provided a broadly-based introduction to the subject of Channels of Distribution and has been concerned with the formal systems and structures which have developed to facilitate the movement of goods through the business system or value chain.

To begin with it was noted that in the past distribution has tended to be something of a Cinderella of marketing but, as this chapter has made clear, it now commands close attention. This importance is directly attributable to the functions of the channel which we listed as:

1 Transfer of title to the goods involved;

2 Physical movement from the point of production to the point of consumption;

3 Storage functions;

4 Communication of information concerning the availability, characteristics and price of the goods;

5 The financing of goods in transit, inventory and on purchase.

Basically, a manufacture or producer of goods or services has one or other of three basic alternatives:

■ Direct sale;

■ Sale through an intermediary;

■ A 'dual' policy combining direct sale with the use of an intermediary.

The pursuit of these options was then traced by examining in some detail the distribution of raw materials, and the distribution of industrial goods. In earlier editions we then considered the distribution of consumer goods through the retail function.

However, it is clear that the balance of power in distribution channels has shifted significantly in the second half of the last century following a revolution in retailing, to the point where this function merits separate treatment. It is this that is the focus of the next chapter.

Review questions and problems

1 Discuss the efforts of producers/users of primary commodities to stabilise markets by agreeing upon quotas, price, etc. What are the advantages/disadvantages of such agreements?

2 What factors account for the erratic short term price fluctuations in markets for agricultural products?

3 What advantages/disadvantages have processed foodstuffs over fresh produce, and how has this affected consumer purchasing patterns?

4 There are no fundamental differences between the marketing of industrial and consumer goods. Comment.

5 What basic distributive alternatives are open to the manufacturers of industrial goods? Which do you consider most appropriate to the sale of:
   ■ Basic chemicals
   ■ Computers
   ■ Electric components
   ■ Machine tools
   ■ Office supplies
   ■ Plastic pipe?
   Why?

6 Describe the economist's concept of concentration ratios. How useful is this concept to the marketer – industrial or consumer? In what way?

7 What functions add value to the product, or merely add to its final cost without adding to its value?

8 It is frequently contended that industrial buying is an essentially rational process whereas consumer purchasing is not. State your reasons for agreeing/disagreeing with this statement.

9 Does the industrial market merit special consideration or is it merely a particular application of general marketing principles?

10 Do we understand enough about how buyers and sellers interact in business-to-business markets to be able to predict buying (or selling) behaviour? If yes, discuss. If no, why not?

11 In B2B marketing there is normally a much closer link between the information-gathering and promotional sides of marketing than is found in consumer goods marketing. Discuss.

Key terms

accelerated freeze drying (AFD)
business system
business to business marketing (B2B)
channel management
channel of distribution
competitive advantage
concentration ratio
consumer goods
cost and control
direct sale
distribution
distribution of industrial goods

distributive channel
dual distribution
exclusive distribution
extractive industries
increased competition
industrial marketing
intensive distribution
intermediary
logistics
market disequilibrium
market equilibrium
marketing boards
motivation
networks

primary commodities
producer-user agreements
raw materials
relationships
retailing
selective distribution
supply chain
technological innovation
theory of comparative advantage
time based competition
value chain
wholesaler

Supplementary reading list

Christopher, Martin (1997), *Marketing Logistics*, (Oxford: Butterworth-Heinemann)

Christopher, M. G. (1992), *Logistics and supply chain management*, (London: Pearson)

Fernie, John (2003), 'Changes in the Supply Chain', Chapter 4 in *Marketing Changes*, Ed. Susan Hart, (London: Thomson)

Gattorna, John L. (Ed.) (2003) *Handbook of supply chain management*, (Aldershot: Gower Publishing)

Hill, R. W. (1973) *Marketing Technological Products to Industry* (Oxford: Pergamon).

Lancioni, Richard (2005), 'Pricing issues in industrial marketing', Editorial in *Industrial Marketing Management*, Volume 34, Number 2 February 2005

Rosenbloom, B. (1999), 'Channels of distribution'. in Baker, M.J. (ed.) *IEBM Encyclopedia of Marketing*, (London: Thomson Learning).

7

THE DISTRIBUTION OF CONSUMER GOODS - RETAILING

Learning Goals *After reading this chapter you should be able to:*

- List the main functions performed by retailers and describe their key features.

- Describe the structure of the retail trade and the main kinds of outlets.

- Explain the concept of the Wheel of Retailing.

- Summarise some of the main innovations which have taken place in recent years.

- Identify the advantages and disadvantages of various patterns of retail distribution.

- Review some current trends in retailing and their implications for the industry's future.

INTRODUCTION

As noted in the previous chapter, the demand for industrial goods is derived from the demand for consumer goods. Although this link may sometimes appear tenuous, it is clear that all other productive activities finally depend upon selling goods and services into ultimate consumption. Although several distributive options are open to the consumer-good manufacturer, almost all eventually involve a retail outlet of some type or other, and this chapter is concerned with the function and operation of such outlets.

Successful retailing depends on exactly the same factors and principles as in any other business activity – identifying customer needs and satisfying them at a profit. Since the Second World War there has been a revolution in retailing and it is now a sophisticated activity based on detailed analysis and scientific methods. But, as the recent fortunes (or misfortunes) of high street icons like Marks and Spencer, Boots, Sainsbury and W. H. Smith have made clear, insight, judgement and creativity are critical to success. It is also important to recognise that over the past 50 years or so there has been a major change in the balance of power between manufacturers and retailers in favour of the latter which has impacted significantly on the manufacturers marketing strategy.

One manifestation of this changed relationship is the growth of **category management**. Category management has been defined by the IGD as:

> *A retailer/supplier process of managing categories as strategic business units, producing enhanced business results by focusing on delivering consumer value.*

McGoldrick (2003) illustrates the implication of this change Figure 7.1:

As can be seen from this diagram, instead of all the information and formal contact being channelled through a Buyer and Account Manager or Salesman, in category management there are multiple interfaces between functions and specialists on both sides. The result is a faster exchange of more and better information to the mutual advantage of both parties. Recognition of the need for closer relationships of this kind has been a major factor in the creation of key account managers in selling organisations to deal exclusively with their major customers. Indeed, some firms like Procter & Gamble have gone so far as to set up category management teams inside the organisation of large customers like Wal-Mart.

RETAILING FUNCTIONS

Most dictionaries define retailing as 'the sale of goods in small quantities to ultimate consumers'. As such, the retail outlet constitutes the final link in the distributive chain, and is responsible for the performance of several important marketing functions, namely:

1 The physical movement and storage of goods;
2 The transfer of title to goods;
3 The provision of information concerning the nature and use of goods;
4 The standardisation, grading and final processing of goods;
5 The provision of ready availability;
6 The assumption of risk concerning the precise nature and extent of demand;
7 The financing of inventory and the extension of credit to consumers.

In many instances it is difficult to distinguish exactly where manufacturing ends and retailing begins, owing to the assumption of some of these functions by organisations that are not usually considered to be retailers or, conversely, by the assumption of functions by the retailer which are more often associated with manufacturers. Thus, in recent years there has been an increasing tendency for manufacturers to assume responsibility for the provision of information through extensive advertising and sales promotion campaigns, while many retailers have integrated backwards into wholesaling and even manufacturing activities. Essentially, the distinction must rest on the performance of those functions (1 and 2) inherent in the very nature of retailing – the physical movement of goods and arrangement of transfer of title. To a lesser extent, functions (3), (4) and (5) in the above list also serve to distinguish retailing from other forms of manufacturing and distributive activity, and an examination of these five functions follows.

Physical movement and storage

As one would expect, there is an enormous variation in the cost of transporting and storing goods depending upon the method of transport used, the length and complexity of the journey, the amount of handling and protection required and so forth. In the case of bulk cargoes for transport by sea, the cost may be as low as

Figure 7.1 Widening the retailer-supplier interface

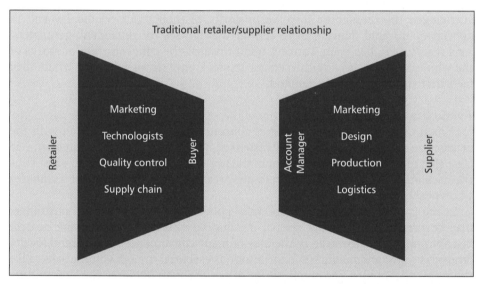

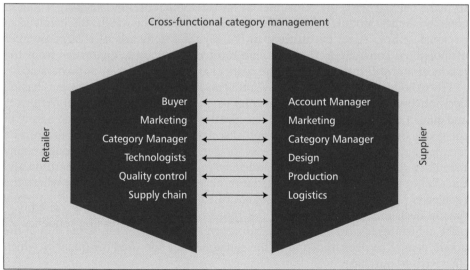

Source: McGoldrick, P. (2003), adapted from Management Horizons (1999).

£0.01 per ton mile while, at the other extreme, door-to door delivery of groceries may cost as much as £60 per ton mile. Clearly, the more homogeneous the cargo, and the larger the bulk for delivery at one point, the lower the unit cost incurred. The potential savings inherent in such economies have led in recent years to the growth of larger retail units and the virtual elimination of door-to-door delivery, although some retailers like the Co-Op do offer this. Also, with the growth of the Internet, specialised service firms like PeaPod have set up to take shopping lists from consumers and source and deliver the products to them.

Within the retail outlet, recognition of the high costs arising from counter service, both in terms of the duplication of effort in putting goods on display and then fetching them for customers on request, as well as the waste of valuable selling space, have led to almost universal adoption of self service. Competitive pressures, and the ever growing variety of goods available for sale, have also encouraged the retailer to keep the majority of their stock on display and to depend upon rapid delivery from central warehouses for replenishing supplies. As a result there has been a strong trend towards the concentration of stocks at the wholesale level, leaving the retailer to stock only those goods for which they feels there is an immediate demand.

Transfer of ownership

When one considers the degree of concentration usually associated with the production of goods and the widely dispersed nature of the consumer market, it is clear that few manufacturers will be in the position to undertake direct sale. Thus the need arises for an intermediary to perform this function and effect a **transfer of ownership**.

In the case of shopping and specialty goods, like Aga ovens, the customers may be prepared to make a special purchasing effort to seek out the nearest distribution point. However, in the case of many convenience goods brand loyalty tends to be low, and maximum distribution is essential to high volume sales. Like the steel stockholder, the retail outlet offers the manufacturer the opportunity to make contact with the consumer at an economic cost. By stocking a line of complementary products the retailer is able to spread the overheads involved in personal selling. Also, by catering to the separate demands of a large number of individual consumers, they are able to buy in economic quantities from the producer and still further reduce the costs of effecting a transfer of ownership.

From the consumer's point of view, retail outlets greatly facilitate the purchasing decision as they provide the opportunity to inspect and compare both the prices and quality of competing products. The location of retail outlets, and the nature of the goods in which they deal are readily ascertained, whereas the manufacturer's identity and location are not so easy to determine. Similarly, although many manufacturers publicise a recommended selling price, increased competition and the abolition of Resale Price Maintenance have resulted in a situation where the retailer is often the sole reliable source of this information on which so many buying decisions depend. Finally, the retailer often has to break bulk and the price, which represents the consideration given in exchange for ownership of the goods, cannot be determined until the consumer has specified the quantity which they wish to purchase.

Ready availability

Depending upon the nature of the product, consumers are prepared to go to varying lengths to obtain goods to meet their specific needs. Given the number of competing products and outlets, both retailers and manufacturers are highly sensitive to this aspect of consumer behaviour, and adjust their stockholding policies accordingly to offer the desired level of availability.

By definition, a convenience good must be immediately available as the consumer is not prepared to wait to take delivery. From the retailer's point of view the problem is less critical than it is for the manufacturer, as they will usually stock several brands which are acceptable substitutes for one another. However, although convenience goods were defined earlier as those which the consumer buys frequently and with the minimum of effort, the ultimate distinction lies not in the product itself but in the consumer's perception of it, and what may be a convenience good for some may be a specialty good for others. Thus if the customer is unable to find their preferred brand in one outlet they may well transfer all their custom to another where they can. In that the overall level of brand preference is reflected by the brand's share of the total market, most retailers will stock competing products in the same ratio to one another in the hope of maintaining store loyalty.

In the case of shopping goods, demand is neither so regular nor so predictable as is the case with convenience goods, and the retailer's stock policy, and ultimately their success are based on their judgement of the precise nature of consumer demand. Such decisions invariably create a conflict between the desire to offer a sufficiently wide selection to cater to variations in consumer preference, and the need to hold a sufficient stock of given products to meet the demand for them. A good example of this conflict, shared by both producer and retailer, is the demand for fashion goods in relation to the demand for more conservative styles. The demand for such fashion goods is frequently underestimated, and represents a lost profit opportunity of considerable dimensions. On the other hand, if the retailer overestimates likely demand they will incur additional inventory costs, and may have to sell at a loss to recover their working capital. Although such miscalculations ultimately have an effect on producers' sales, the majority of the risk is carried by the retailer.

The provision of information

Retailers supply information to both consumer and manufacturer. In the latter case, the most important information supplied by the retailer is the actual order which they place with the producer, in that it reflects future expectations concerning consumer demand by those in most direct contact with it. However, orders are subject to influence by the manufacturer's salesmen, and may represent wishful thinking rather than informed and objective opinion. Also, in the absence of information concerning stock levels, it is difficult to say whether orders are placed in anticipation of an upswing in demand, or merely to replenish stocks depleted by past demand. Even if the order does accurately reflect changing consumer preferences, it does not give the manufacturer an explanation as to the causes – to obtain such information the manufacturer will have to undertake market research.

The provision of information to consumers varies considerably in terms of both amount and quality. Often the most meaningful information provided is the opportunity to examine competing products in close juxtaposition to one another. Price is a more concrete piece of information but, as the advent of the discount house and internet shopping has proved, it is frequently a measure of the retailer's efficiency rather than the quality or value of the product.

Spoken information is still provided by retail sales assistants in many outlets, but consumers would seem to regard much of this information as emanating from a low **credibility source**; that is, they place little reliance on its accuracy or objectivity. The adoption of this attitude is unsurprising in view of the low status and pay attached to retail selling in general, which is hardly conducive to the recruitment of highly motivated personnel. Hopefully, more retailers will follow the example of pioneers like Boots and Marks & Spencer in upgrading the quality of their employees through the provision of adequate training and incentives. As things stand at present, however, manufacturers are likely to fill the information gap by the continued use of advertising and sales promotion.

Processing

The increase of pre-packed goods on display in retail outlets is an outward manifestation of the reduced importance of this traditional retailing function. In part this may be attributed to consumer preference, but it is equally due to the manufacturer's desire to make their product identifiable at the point of sale.

In general, it is more economic to pack at the factory than at the point of sale, as the volume of output permits the use of the most productive machines. However, there are a number of important exceptions to this generalisation:

1 Some products may be transported more economically in a **completely knocked-down state (CKD)**; for example beds, wardrobes, bicycles.

2 Some commodities may be preserved more easily in bulk form; for example bacon, cheese.

3 In some cases the consumer's exact requirements can only be met by processing at the point of sale; for example 'three lamb chops', 'a pint of lager'.

4 Packaging can only occur after the customer is satisfied that the goods meet his requirements; for example clothing, fresh produce.

The structure of the retail trade

At a given point in time it is impossible to derive an exact measure of the size and structure of the retail trade in Britain owing to the rapid changes which are taking place. Major changes have taken place in retailing over the last three decades, and the remainder of this chapter will discuss the nature of these developments as well as outline changes in specific sectors – for example, convenience stores.

Various social and environmental factors have affected the structure of the retail trade over recent years, affecting not only where goods are bought, but also what and how they are bought:

■ More leisure time, longer holidays;

■ More working women;

■ Increased use of large shopping outlets;

■ Less frequent shopping;

■ Access to the Internet

These factors, among others, have resulted in the growth of convenience foods and frozen foods. The growth in the consumption of convenience foods has had a major impact on the structure of modern British retailing as it led to the emergence of the supermarket which has affected all forms of retailing.

Overall, the period since the Second World War has been one of increased affluence. Britain became a society with a high demand for consumer goods. By the late 1970s this pattern had begun to change, the demand for consumer durables had slowed down, and there was a small reaction against the increased use of convenience foods with a return to 'natural' foods. Competition between sectors of the retail trade became fiercer as consumers 'tightened their belts'. Some sectors of the retail trade have fared better than others under the competitive pressure.

Some recent changes in retailing are summarised in Table 7.1, the Volume of Retail Sales 1998 – 2003. This table, and many others reproduced elsewhere, are taken from the *Marketing Pocket Book* (2005) published by The Advertising Association in association with the World Advertising Research Center (WARC), and are reproduced with their permission. One of the major problems experienced in up-dating text books of this kind is keeping factual data accurate. Given that there is a delay in publishing statistics and a further delay between completing a manuscript and its publication, data are often several years out of date. The only remedy is for the student to note the source of the tables given and then check the same source for the most recent data. In addition to the *Marketing Pocket Book* WARC publish at least ten others which provide a wealth of essential detail for marketers. An order form listing their titles, etc. together with publication details is included at the back of each book, or they can be ordered from their website at *www.warc.com*. These Pocket Books are essential source material for all serious students of marketing.

Table 7.1 Volume of retail sales, 1998-2003 (index numbers of sales per week (average 2000 prices), 2000=100

| | All retailers (3,984) | Predominantly food stores (1,712) | Predominantly non-food stores | | | | | Non-store retailers/ repair (226) |
			Total (2,045)	Non-specialised stores (361)	Textile, clothing & footwear (536)	Household goods (533)	Other stores (615)	
1998	93	96	90	92	89	86	94	93
1999	96	97	94	94	93	93	97	96
2000	100	100	100	100	100	100	100	100
2001	106	104	108	106	109	111	105	106
2002	113	108	117	111	121	121	112	113
2003	116	112	121	114	129	126	115	108

Note: Figures in brackets refer to average weekly sales in 2000 (£ million).
Source: Business Monitor SDM28, *The Marketing Pocket Book 2005*, published by WARC (*www.warc.com*)

Types of retail outlet

For descriptive purposes, British retail outlets are usually grouped into three main categories:

1 Independent retailers, including small chain stores with nine or fewer branches.

2 Multiple retailers with ten or more branches, but excluding retail co-operative societies.

3 Retail co-operative societies.

The main retail outlets excluded from this classification are department stores, gas and electricity showrooms, and mail order houses. Independent retailers have declined in recent years, both in shop numbers and in their share of retail trade. This decline is largely attributable to the aggressive price competition from supermarkets and discount houses. (See the later section on the independent grocery trade which gives a more detailed description of the decline of the independents.)

Multiple retailers have enjoyed a period of continuous expansion over a period of many years. The multiples' scale of operation enables them to employ functional specialists, to buy in bulk, and to use their extensive financial resources to acquire the best store locations. Multiple organisations may conveniently be subdivided into three groups:

1 *Food chain stores* such as Tesco and Sainsbury.

2 *Variety chain stores* such as British Home Stores, Marks & Spencer and Woolworth.

3 *Speciality chain stores* such as Boots, Halfords, IKEA and Dixons.

Co-operative retail societies collectively were formally the largest retailer in the United Kingdom and still play a major role in countries like Switzerland, Denmark and Sweden. However, in the UK the Co-op has failed to exploit fully the economies of scale open to it and has consistently lost ground to multiple and independent alike.

Department stores are another type of retail outlet which has been under increasing competitive pressure from supermarkets, multiples and superstores. Department stores are usually defined as establishments with 24 or more employees engaged in selling clothing, textiles and at least four other major commodity groups. Since 1980 department stores have been classified as mixed retail businesses making it difficult to draw direct comparisons on performance before and after this date. The number of department stores has stabilised at around 350, with new store openings matching closures. The large national store groups such as House of Fraser, Debenhams, John Lewis, have followed a policy of market repositioning hoping to attract a larger share of the 25 to 40 age group who tend to have the most disposable income. To pull this group away from the variety chain stores, these department stores have modernised and altered their emphasis to one of quality rather than price, improving store ambience and offering co-ordinated product ranges.

THE 'WHEEL OF RETAILING'

The 'wheel of retailing' is a major hypothesis concerning patterns of retail development. Advanced by Malcolm P. McNair, a professor at the Harvard Business School, the hypothesis holds that new types of retailers usually enter the market as low-status, low-margin, low-price operators, and gradually acquire more elaborate establishments and facilities involving increased investment and higher operating costs. Finally, they mature as high-cost, high-price.

Although there are a number of exceptions which suggest that the hypothesis is not universally valid, the general pattern of British retail development conforms with it remarkably closely. As a result of wartime restrictions and controls between 1939 and 1952, the normal evolution of the retail trade was brought to a virtual standstill but, with the removal of restrictions, every effort to make up for lost ground was taken. In fact the scale of innovation and the changes in retail structure which have resulted are often referred to as the **'Retail Revolution'**.

Stephen Brown (1995) summarises the dramatic structural changes in retailing as the consequence of 6 forces:

- *Concentration*
- *Rationalisation*
- *Polarisation*
- *Suburbanisation*
- *Internationalisation*
- *Information*

We have already referred to the trend towards **concentration** in retailing with the large multiples accounting for around 70 per cent of all sales. Not only have the major multiples greatly increased their market share at the expense of the independents, but mergers and acquisitions in the multiple sector have seen considerable **rationalisation** and a significant increase in the share of the largest groups. This trend is reflected in the increased size of the major outlets but has also resulted in a countervailing trend of small convenience stores (see below) which Brown terms 'polarisation'.

The development of superstores is closely linked to the trend towards **suburbanisation**. Superstores call for large sites with adequate parking – rarely available in city centres! Brown identifies four major types of development:

1 *Regional shopping centres* of 400,000 sq ft covered space with several major stores and over 100 outlets.
2 *Sub-regional shopping centres* of 200,000–400,000 sq ft of covered space, a food superstore, non-food superstore and 20–30 other outlets.
3 *Retail parks*.
4 *Stand-alone developments*.

A fifth trend of **Internationalisation** has gathered increased momentum as a result of the growth of the European Union and the opening up of the former controlled markets of eastern Europe. Some of the factors driving this trend are summarised in Table 7.2.

Finally, **information technology** has had a major impact on modern retailing and we discuss this below in the section on Automated Retailing Systems.

Some of the major changes associated with this revolution are outlined below and summarised in Figure 7.2 which illustrates the stages at which various kinds of retailing are in their life cycle.

Of all the various sectors probably the most familiar are the grocery superstores like Tesco and Asda. In the next section we summarise some of their key features before looking at some other major retailing formats.

Table 7.2 Some drivers of retailer internationalisation

Mature domestic markets	Less developed foreign markets
Stable population	Growing populations
Low to moderate economic growth	High economic growth
Regulated environment	Open environment
Intensive competition / oligopoly	Low concentration / 'free' markets

Figure 7.2 The retail life cycle

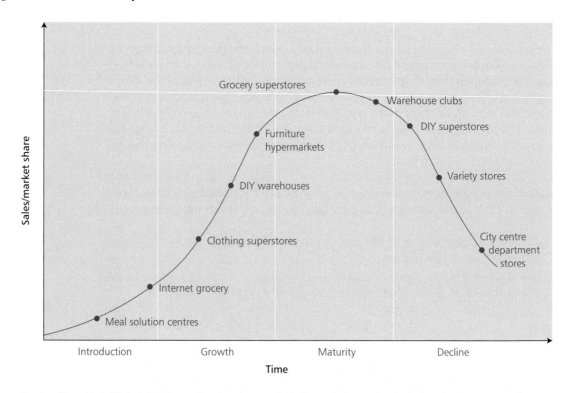

Source: Reprinted from McGoldrick, P. (2003), 'Retailing' in Baker, M.J. (ed.) *The Marketing Book*, 5th.edn (2003) with permission from Elsevier.

WHAT IS THE SIZE OF THE UK GROCERY MARKET?

The answer to this question is provided by the **IGD**. The information and illustrations used in the following section are mainly provided by the IGD, and used with their permission. For the most recent data readers are directed to their website at *www.igd.com* which publishes extensive information.

- The grocery market was worth £115.0 bn in 2003
- Groceries account for 13.4% of all household spending, making it the third largest area of expenditure, first is housing and second is transport
- Food and grocery expenditure accounts for 49p in every £1 of retail spending
- 30p in every £1 is spent in the top eight retailers (Asda, Iceland, M&S, Morrisons/Safeway, Sainsbury's, Somerfield, Tesco and Waitrose).
- In 2003, the grocery market grew by 3.3%

Figure 7.3 Size of the UK grocery market

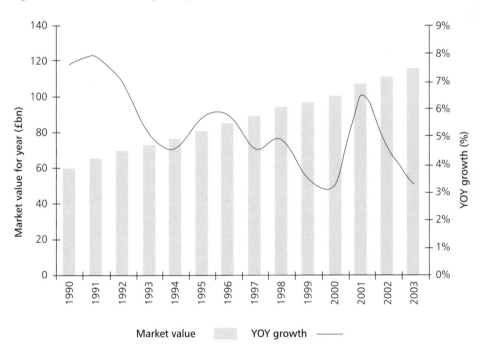

Source: IGD Research (2004)

How many grocery stores are there in the UK?
There are 104,753 grocery stores in the UK. These are split into 4 sectors, which are defined as follows.

1   *Convenience stores*: stores with sales area of less than 3,000 sq ft, open for long hours and selling products from at least 8 different grocery categories, (e.g. SPAR, Co-operative Group, Londis).

2   *Traditional retail and developing convenience stores*: sales area of less than 3,000 sq ft such as newsagents, grocers, off-licences, & some forecourts.

3   *Supermarkets & superstores*: Supermarkets-have a sales area of 3,000-25,000 sq ft selling a broad range of grocery items. Superstores-sales area above 25,000 sq ft, selling a broad range of mainly grocery items, Non-food is also sold (eg Tesco, Asda).

4   *Alternative channels*: e.g Kiosks, markets, post offices, doorstep delivery, vending, home-shopping.

How big is each sector?

The chart below shows how many stores are within each sector and how much each sector is worth.

What does the future of the grocery market look like?

Market value for 2004 is estimated at £118.1bn and it is predicted to be £133.5bn by the end of 2009. Much of this growth will be attributable to inflation however.

Figure 7.4 UK grocery market retail sectors

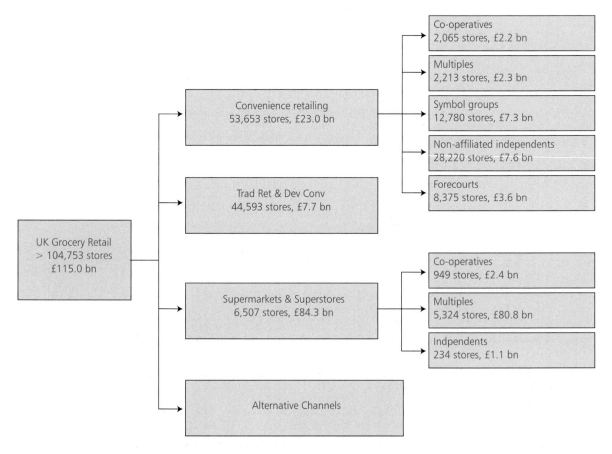

Source: IGD Research (2004)

IGD predicts that development of the UK grocery retail market will continue to be restricted by a combination of slow population growth, fierce price competition and growth in the foodservice sector as an alternative channel.

How important is non-food to Supermarkets?

It is estimated that 32% of sales going through the supermarkets is non-food. Traditional categories such as health and beauty, household, petcare, news and magazines, and tobacco, have been sold in supermarkets for some time.

More recently, supermarkets have expanded into the less-traditional non-food categories which now account for up to 10% of sales (excluding clothing) through supermarkets (IGD Research/IRI).

Which products form part of supermarket's non–food offer?

Figure 7.5 UK supermarkets non-food offerings

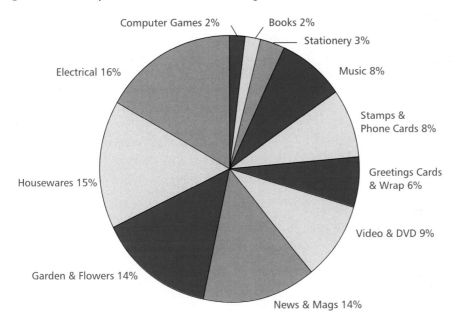

Source: IRI/IGD 2004 (Note: Excludes traditional Grocery Non-foods such as household, petcare etc)

Why are Supermarkets expanding into Non-Food?

1 Non-food lines can provide higher margins than food ranges
2 Non-food items tend to be higher priced and therefore assist total cash sales
3 Non food ranges provide customer interest and excitement, and assist in driving additional customers into the store
4 Retailers can capitalise on Christmas Trading opportunities with non-food ranges
5 Non-food categories are generally less mature and therefore more likely to benefit from technical innovation and increased customer spending

6 The overall growth in traditional grocery markets is around 3%, whereas non food areas are averaging 13% (IGD/IRI) thus providing a significant avenue for growth.

Which supermarkets are the main players in Non-Food Retailing?

Tesco's

- Aims to be as big in non-food as it is in food
- Claims a 6% share of the UK non-food market
- Non-food business amounts to £7 billion
- Includes clothing (4 brands:-Value, Tesco, Florence & Fred, Cherokee), electrical, home and leisure, toys

Grocery Wholesaling 2005

In the view of the IGD, wholesaling is fundamental to the distribution of goods within the grocery industry. Its main function is to provide a linkage between agriculture, manufacturing, retailers and caterers. Wholesale has traditionally performed four basic functions:

- Warehousing
- Transportation
- Product consolidation
- Inventory management

Wholesalers can be categorised into three different types:

1 *General Grocery Wholesalers*
Supply a wide range of food and grocery categories. Their primary customers are independent retailers and caterers. General grocery wholesalers include:
- Cash & carry depots
- Delivered wholesalers
- Mixed business providing both of the above

2 *Specialist Wholesalers*
These focus on a narrow range of often specialist categories. For example, fresh fish, fruit and vegetables, meat and poultry.

3 *Catering/Foodservice Wholesalers*
These tend to deliver to a diverse range of businesses including cafes, restaurants, fast food establishments and schools and hospitals.
IGD estimates that sales through the grocery wholesaling sector in 2003 reached £16.4 bn, representing an increase of 2.7% on 2002.

The key cash and carry operators are:
- Booker
- Makro
- Bestway
- Batleys
- Costco
- Blakemore
- Parfetts
- Dhamecha
- C.J. Lang
- TRS

The key delivered wholesale operators are:
- Palmer & Harvey
- Londis
- Key Lekkerland
- The SPAR wholesalers
- C.J. land & Son
- James Hall & Co
- A.F. Blakemore &Son
- Appleby Westward
- Capper & Co
- John Henderson

Source: IGD 2004

Asda

- Has a number of superstores which dedicate up to 40% of selling space to non-food
- Has recently launched jewellery, homeware/furniture, wellbeing zone, and prescription eyewear
- Launched its first standalone "George" clothing store in 2003

Figure 7.6   Grocery wholesaling market size and growth 1994-2003

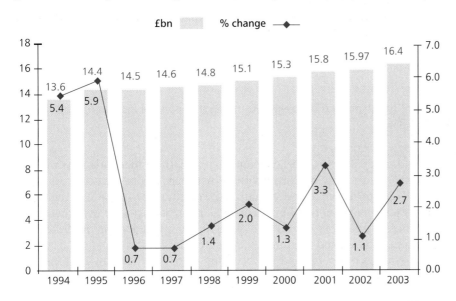

Source: IGD Research (2004)

Figure 7.7   Cash & carry vs. delivered wholesale 1994-2003

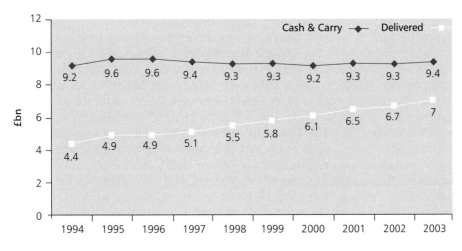

Source: IGD Research (2004)

Selling through wholesalers

The advantages of selling through a wholesaler have already been examined when discussing the distribution of industrial goods. In general, manufacturers of consumer goods will find it appropriate to make use of the wholesaler's services under the following circumstances:

1 Where a large number of small, widely dispersed outlets account for a significant share of total sales.

2 Where the manufacturer has limited working capital and is unable to bear the costs of direct selling.

3 Where the manufacturer is new to the market and seeking to gain retail acceptance.

4 Where the manufacturer has an excess supply which could be sold under a wholesaler brand, or where he has no brand of his own.

5 Where demand is irregular and/or seasonal: for example fireworks!

6 Where trade custom has resulted in channel control becoming vested in the wholesaler.

Cash-and-carry wholesaling

Cash-and-carry wholesaling developed out of the independent wholesalers and retailers' desire to remain competitive with the multiple sector. As such it represented an alternative to the formation of voluntary chains. While the setting-up of a voluntary chain resulted in formal relationship between retailer and wholesaler, cash-and-carry operations place no such restrictions on either party. As the volume of sales and the market share held by the independent grocers has fallen, cash-and carry operators have been forced to look for new customers and for new, non-grocery lines. The catering trade has become the main cash-and carry customer, taking over from the independent grocers.

Voluntary chains

The growing success of the multiple outlet rests largely on the integration of both wholesaling and retailing activities. Independent wholesalers had long realised that the growing power of the multiples would place the independent retailer at a competitive disadvantage and that it was only a matter of time before this group, which comprised their chief customers, would seek to take collective action and set up their own wholesale co-operatives. To forestall such a possibility, the more astute wholesalers took the initiative and organised **voluntary chains** of independent retailers. Essentially, such chains are based on an agreement whereby the retailer agrees to place a minimum weekly order with the wholesaler; to submit orders by a specified time, often on specially designed forms; and to accept delivery at a prescribed time. In addition many chains, or **symbol grocers** as they are often called, agree to undertake cooperative advertising campaigns, to adopt a distinctive and uniform decor or 'house style', and to carry 'own brands'. In return for these promises, the wholesaler passes on economies in storage and transportation costs in the form of lower prices, organises joint promotional activities, advises on shop layout and management, and often lends capital for store modification and improvement. Spar, Mace, VG and Londis are examples of symbol voluntary groups in the grocery trade.

While voluntary chains are most active in food retailing they are also to be found in a generally less sophisticated form in other sectors: for example, Vantage and Numark serving the needs of chemists, Interflora, as well as a number of associations in the tobacco, confectionery and hardware trades. However, as the multiples continue to expand their share of the total retail trade one may anticipate further groupings developing among the independents.

The independent grocer

When this book was first published in 1971 there were 86,000 independent grocers. Today, there are less than 55,000, a reduction of more than one third. This rate of decline was in line with that of all other outlets. However, for the multiples and co-operatives it was part of a policy of rationalisation, and for independents was the outcome of increased competitive pressure. The multiple groups have at least two advantages over the independents: first their buying power enables them to negotiate lower prices and subsequently to sell at lower prices than independents; second they have the advantage of economies of scale accruing to their large scale of operation. The independents' share of sales value and volume reflects this sector's growing difficulties. In the period 1971–81 there was a 38 per cent fall in volume, while the multiples recorded a 57 per cent increase in volume over the same period. In the face of continuing competition from multiples, the independents have had to move towards longer opening hours in order to survive, and many of them now are classed as convenience stores.

For a store to be defined as a **convenience store** it must satisfy three criteria

1 *Size and Opening hours*: The store must be under 3,000 sq ft and open for long hours every day of the week.

2 *Main Business Activity*: All stores must retail food and drink, for consumption off the premises, as their main business activity.

3 *Product Categories*: A group of fifteen products have been identified as being central to the offering of a convenience store. It must sell at least *eight* of these **core products** to qualify as a "true" convenience store. These categories are as follows:

Alcohol	Household/non-food	Health and Beauty
Confectionery	National Lottery	Packaged groceries
Food-to-go	Newspapers/magazines	Savoury snacks
Fresh	Bread/bakery products	Soft drinks
Fruit/vegetables	Milk/dairy	Tobacco

Convenience store ownership is highly fragmented, with a large number of operators present. Store operators may be divided into several types (also known as "**segments**"):

- *Co-operative* (eg United Co-operatives, The Co-operative Group)
- *Forecourts* (dealer and company-owned e.g BP, Shell, Total)
- *Multiples* (convenience specialists and some supermarket based chains) (e.g Jacksons, Tesco Express)
- *Symbols, Franchise and Fascias* (eg SPAR, Londis, Bestway)
- *Non-affiliated independents*

There are 53,653 convenience stores in the UK. Table 7.3 shows the breakdown of store numbers within each segment and the corresponding market share:

Table 7.3 UK convenience store breakdown		
	Store Numbers	Market Share
Co-operatives	2,065	3.8%
Forecourts	9,401	17.2%
Multiples	2,213	4.0%
Symbols	12,780	23.4%
Non-affiliated Independents	28,220	51.6%
Total	54,679	100.0%

Source: IGD Research 2004.

The UK convenience market was valued at £23.0 bn in 2003, a 7.3% increase on the previous year. Table 7.4 shows the market value of each segment and corresponding market share:

Table 7.4 UK convenience market: segment value and market share		
	Sales (£)	Share
Co-operatives	2,176	9.5%
Forecourts	3,630	15.8%
Multiples	2,254	9.8%
Symbols	7,316	31.8%
Non-affiliated Independents	7,647	33.2%
Total	23,023	100.0%

Source: IGD Research 2004.

The total UK grocery market was worth £115bn at the end of 2003 and convenience therefore took a 20.0% market share.

With annual growth of 7.3%, the convenience retail sector significantly outperformed the total grocery market which grew by 3.3% over the same period.

What is happening in the Convenience sector?

Consolidation:

There has been a great deal of consolidation activity in the convenience sector since 2002, resulting in fewer, larger operators. This is summarised in Table 7.5.

Co-operatives:

Co-operatives continue to move away from supermarket operations and towards convenience retailing. Expansion of co-operatives has been led by the Co-operative Group which acquired Alldays in 2002 and Balfour in July 2003.

Forecourts:

The number of forecourt stores is in decline but the quality of remaining sites is improving. Forecourt operators are now focusing on the more profitable 'shop', as profit and volume growth in fuel becomes more limited.

Convenience Multiples:

Convenience multiples perform well with high store standards continuing. Supermarket retailers are achieving significant presence within this segment and now operate 1,138 dedicated c-stores accounting for more than half the segment.

Symbol Groups:

The number of stores affiliating to a symbol group is growing rapidly as independent retailers look to display a branded fascia and have the support from a symbol operator.

Independents:

Independent store numbers are in decline. As store standards continue to improve in the c-sector, competition is intensifying resulting in a number of independents either leaving the sector or affiliating to a symbol operation.

What will the convenience market look like in the future?

IGD has made the following predictions for the convenience market in 2009:

- There will be 51,950 stores
- The market to be worth an estimated £29.0 bn

Table 7.5 Consolidation in the UK convenience sector since 2002

Business Acquired	Acquisition by	No of stores acquired
Budgens	Musgrave	235
Europa	Tesco	45
T&S Stores	Tesco	1,215
Local plus	Co-op	64
Bells Stores	Sainsbury's	54
Balfour	Co-op	111
Alldays	Co-op	603
Aberness	Somerfield	36
Jacksons	Sainsbury's	114

Source: IGD Research 2004.

Discount Stores

A 'discounter' is a retailer that offers a 'no frills' approach with the provision of low prices given priority above all other elements of the retail mix (such as

Figure 7.8   Attitudes towards discounter stores

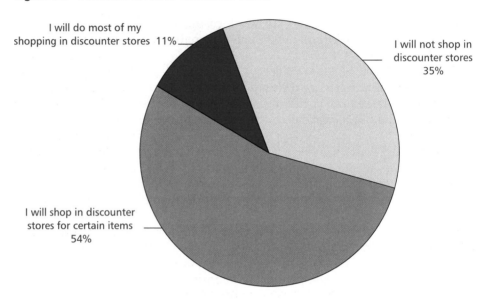

Source: IGD Research (2004)

Figure 7.9   Shoppers who will do most of their shopping in discounters

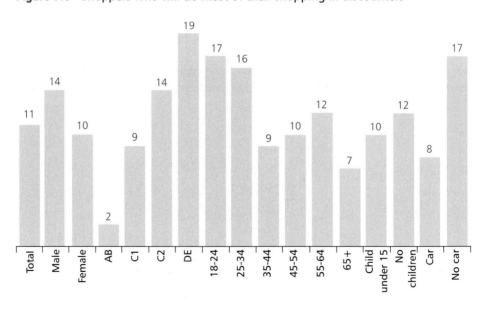

Source: IGD Research (2004)

location, customer service, range and merchandising). Discounters can be broadly divided into two types, the 'hard' or 'soft' discounter. **Hard discounters** are characterised by a limited range and very basic store interior, examples of which include the European operators Aldi, Lidl and Netto. **Soft discounters** typically have a wider range and a greater fresh offer than the hard discounters with Kwik Save the only true soft discounter now trading in the UK.

Shopping at UK Discounters

11% of shoppers are loyal to discounters doing most of their shopping in these stores. The reason that only a small percentage of shoppers claim to do most of their shopping at discounters may be attributed to the limited product offer. The more common approach to shopping in discounters is for shoppers to get a proportion of products there. Over half of respondents (54%) take this approach whilst the remaining 35% claim never to shop in discounter stores.

Shoppers who are most likely to do most of their shopping in discounters are those in social class DE and younger shoppers. High street locations may also be a determining factor for shoppers without cars in choosing discounters for their main shopping trip.

Reasons for not shopping at Discounters

IGD research indicates that the main reason for not shopping in discounters relates not to any negative perception shoppers may have of these stores but the

Figure 7.10   Reasons for not shopping at discounters

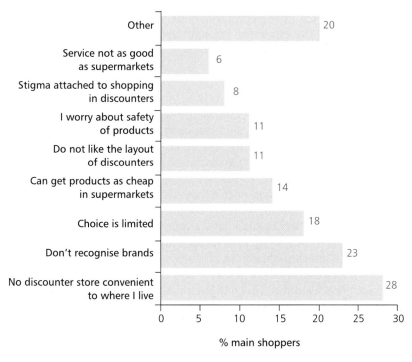

% main shoppers

Source: IGD Research (2004)

fact that there is not a store convenient to them. After the convenience factor the main barrier to shopping at discounters is the product range:

- 23% of shoppers will not shop at discounters because they don't recognise the brands
- 18% find the limited choice a barrier to shopping at discounters.

MAIL ORDER

Mail-order houses fall into two basic categories – general and specialist. The latter usually concentrate on a single product group and are particularly active in the market for seeds, bulbs, plants and small horticultural items. At the other end of the scale, mail order is dominated by the general-line firms with major sales in clothing and other household goods by firms such as Great Universal Stores (including Argos), Otto Versand (Grattan and Freemans) and Empire. Nearly half the goods sold by mail order are clothing, and another quarter is accounted for by household goods.

Between 1995 and 2002 sales grew steadily by value from £6,629 million to £8,300 million but fell back 8.2% in 2003 to £7,616 million representing 3.2% of all retail sales and down from 4.0% in 1995.

Given the extensive network of retail outlets throughout the country, the survival of mail order appears at first sight to be an enigma. In fact, it reflects the marketing skills of the operators who have consistently pursued a policy of high quality, backed by a guarantee of satisfaction that is scrupulously honoured with none of the unpleasantry found in some retail establishments. Add to this the convenience of shopping in the comfort of one's home, and generous credit and repayment terms, and the attraction remains strong.

FRANCHISING

Franchising has been a growth sector of the UK economy. It is not a new type of business organisation as its origins can be traced back two hundred years to brewers' 'tied-public house' systems. The recent growth in franchising has been encouraged by the British Franchise Association formed in 1977. The Association offers guidance to prospective franchisees and has done much to stamp out malpractice in the business. In essence a franchise agreement allows an individual to set up in an established business by adopting the name and practices of its originator; for example, McDonalds have a more or less standardised layout and menu. The franchisee usually pays a lump sum to begin with and then pays a continuing royalty to the franchisor. Franchisors exercise varying degrees of control over the operation of franchisees, and provide varying levels of support which preclude generalisation. Given the attraction of running one's own business under the protective umbrella of a franchise offering specialised retailing skills and experience normally accessible only to the large organisation, it is perhaps not surprising that only a relatively small number of UK franchises fail each year. This high success rate is probably due to the great personal motivation of the franchisees and the guidance of the franchisor. Examples of franchise operations can be found in many areas of trade – British School of Motoring, Apollo Window Blinds, Dyno-Rod Plc, Prontaprint, Pronuptia and Youngs. The best known franchise organisations are probably those in the catering and fast-food sectors – McDonalds, Burger King, and Pizza Hut – as well as car rental companies like Avis and Hertz. It should be noted that many franchisors also run their own outlets – for example, in the UK Avis runs 130 out of 190 outlets and McDonalds 1200 out of 1668.

CHANNELS OF DISTRIBUTION

In broad terms the same channels of distribution noted in respect of the manufacturer of industrial goods are also open to the consumer goods manufacturer, namely:

1 *Direct to the ultimate consumer.*
2 *Direct to the retailer for resale to the ultimate consumer*; that is, the retail outlet is regarded as the customer.
3 *Indirect sale through the medium of a wholesaler or agent.*
4 *A combination* of any or all of these alternatives.

Direct sale to ultimate consumers

Direct sale to the consumer may be achieved by the manufacturer/seller of goods and services in one of three ways:

1 *Forward integration into retailing and the establishment of one's own outlets.* (Usually it is the retailer who integrates backwards, however.)
2 *Mail order selling.*
3 *Door-to-door selling.*

The advantages and disadvantages of each of these alternatives may be summarised as:

1 *Own retail outlets*

Advantages:

(a) Complete control over the selling function: for example price setting, terms of trade, provision of services, sales training and so on.
(b) Economies of scale in storage, transportation and administration.
(c) The ability to coordinate in-store promotion with advertising and other promotional activities.
(d) Closer contact with the consumers and therefore a better understanding of their needs and preferences.

Disadvantages:

(a) Limited access to the market.
(b) The assumption of all risks.
(c) The need for extensive financial resources to cover both fixed investment and working capital needs.

Examples: Boots, British Shoe Corporation, Burtons, Singer.

2 *Mail order*

Advantages:

(*a*) Complete control.
(*b*) Economies of scale.
(*c*) Access to the whole market, including areas with insufficient population to support conventional outlets.
(*d*) Consumer convenience.

Disadvantages:

(*a*) High delivery costs.
(*b*) High promotional costs.
(*c*) High costs of building and maintaining an up-to-date mailing list.
(*d*) Costs of financing credit sales. Examples: Great Universal, John Moores, Grattan. (Note: although many of the general-line mail-order houses have their own production facilities, a large part of their merchandise represents the output of other manufacturers.)

3 *Door-to-door* - now known as **Network Marketing** (see Chapter 20).

Advantages:

(*a*) Complete control.
(*b*) Most effective method of selling certain goods and services where demonstration or complex explanation is necessary: for example vacuum cleaners, insurance policies.

Disadvantages:

(*a*) Unsolicited calls are viewed with suspicion.
(*b*) High cost – usually offset by paying low basic salary and high commission.
(*c*) Difficult to recruit and retain suitable salesmen owing to unattractive working conditions.

Examples: Avon Cosmetics, Kleen-Eze, Prudential Assurance, various publishing houses.

Table 7.6 Supermarket grocery market shares by value 2004

	Market Share
Tesco	27.3%
ASDA	16.6%
Sainsbury	15.7%
Morrison/Safeway	14.6%
Others	25.8%
Total	100.0%

Direct sale to retail outlets

In view of the high costs associated with direct sales to the consumer, most consumer-goods manufacturers prefer to sell through some form of independent retail outlet.

Given the number of retail outlets, direct sale might appear totally uneconomic at first sight. On reflection, however, it is clear that a very large percentage of sales are channelled through a very limited number of buying points and the manufacturer can gain direct access to the market through relatively few centralised purchasing agencies (Table 7.6)

As can be seen from Table 7.6 nearly three quarters of all grocery sale were made by only *four* major multiples. To access the remaining 25.8% of the market one would have to contact literally thousands of other buying points. (See Figure 7.4 for a breakdown).

As discussed in the previous chapter, the decision on whether to sell direct or not is largely an economic one and resolves itself into a policy issue concerning the relative merits of selective versus extensive distribution. The other policy issue is the degree of control exercised by the seller and we return to these issues in Chapter 16, Channel Management.

FUTURE TRENDS IN RETAILING

A major trend in recent years has been the internationalisation of retailing with major groups seeking growth through a strategy of market development. McGoldrick (2003) sees the impetus coming from three main sources:

- '*Push*' factors such as saturation or decline in the domestic market resulting in less profitable trading conditions.
- '*Pull*' factors – perceived opportunities in other national markets.
- '*Facilitating*' factors arising from the liberalisation of trade in foreign markets, exploitation of competitive advantages etc.

One or a combination of these factors may lead to a variety of entry strategies including:

1 Self start entry and organic growth
2 Acquisition
3 Franchising
4 Joint ventures
5 Concessions or 'shops in shops'.

Of course entering new markets is not without its risks and there are many examples of major retailers failing to enter foreign markets successfully for reasons we explore in more detail in Chapter 23 Marketing in Foreign Environments.

From the foregoing discussion it is quite clear that major changes have taken and continue to take place in the nature and structure of retailing. Traditionally, consideration of distribution channels, and the discussion of business systems or value chains, would give more attention and emphasis to manufacturers than to retailers as this reflected the balance of power between large manufacturers and small retailers. This position is now largely reversed and, given that the demand for industrial goods is derived from the demand for consumer goods, the emergence of large and very sophisticated retailers means that retailing has grown into a major sub-field of study in its own right. In a book of this kind we can only scratch the surface and readers are referred to the additional readings recommended at the end of the book.

To conclude we can do no better than quote Stephen Brown (op.cit.):

The upshot of these dramatic changes is that retailing is no longer the preserve of small, independent shopkeepers relying on the marketing muscle and expertise of their sophisticated suppliers. Retailing is now characterised by large, efficient and expertly managed firms with a strategic outlook and marketing orientation. Retailers dominate the channels of distribution; they are powerful brands in their own right; they engender enormous customer loyalty; and they utilise the full range of marketing mix elements in their pursuit of competitive advantage. Retailing, in short, is no longer one of the components of a manufacturer's marketing effort, but the centre of its marketing endeavours.   (p. 422)

Summary

In this chapter we have looked at the aspect of marketing with which students of marketing are likely to have the most direct experience –Retailing. Retailing is the final link in the value/supply chain through which consumer goods and services are sold into ultimate consumption, and is the ultimate determinant of the health of the whole economic system .The truth of this claim is evidenced by the fact that in early August 2005 the Bank of England announced the first cut in interest rates in two years. Why? Because stagnant retail sales were beginning to have an effect on the rest of the economy with a slowing down of overall growth, declining order books and increases in unemployment, all indicators of a possible recession.

To begin with we reviewed the main functions of retailing which include storage, availability, transfer of title, the assumption of risk about the nature and strength of demand, and the gathering of information about the needs and wants of consumers. Next we looked at the structure of the retail trade and the main kinds of retail outlets. These fall into three broad categories: independents, multiples and retail co-ops. each of which was described briefly before introducing the concept of the wheel of retailing. This concept argues that new types of retailers usually enter the market as low-status, low-margin, low-price operators and gradually move up-market until they mature as high-cost high-price outlets vulnerable to new competition and so the wheel goes round again.

Taking grocery distribution as the major example on the grounds that most households use them on a weekly, if not daily, basis we described some of the main features of this form of retailing and the nature of competition in this sector , particularly, the migration of giants like Tesco and Asda into the non-food sector. In addition we also reviewed aspects of wholesaling, cash and carry wholesalers, voluntary chains, independents, and convenience stores. Reference was also made to discount stores, mail order, and franchising.

The chapter concluded with a description of the channels of distribution open to consumer goods manufacturers which are essentially the same as those described for business-to-business markets outlined in the previous chapter.

Review questions and problems

1 There is considerable variation in the retail mark-up on a bar of soap, a household electrical appliance, a suite of furniture and a diamond ring. As all retailers perform the same basic functions why should this be so?

2 In what ways do retailers provide consumers with product information?

3 How well does McNair's concept of the 'wheel of retailing' fit changes in retail distribution in the United Kingdom?

4 What is a 'voluntary chain'? To what do they owe their existence, and what role do you expect them to play in future?

5 What basic distribution alternatives are open to the manufacturers of consumer goods, and what are the major advantages/disadvantages associated with each?

6 The last decade has witnessed an ever increasing concentration of power into the hands of a reducing number of multiple retailers. Discuss the main ways in which manufacturers have attempted to meet this challenge, indicating what degrees of success have been achieved.

7 Account for the predominance of direct manufacturers-to-user channels in the marketing of capital goods in comparison to the almost pervasive use of some type of middleman in the marketing of consumer goods. What factors determine the choice of channel in each sector?

8 Describe some of the important trends in the retailing sector, and how this might affect marketing.

9 Compare and discuss the relative advantages/disadvantages for a manufacturer of a consumer durable for the distribution of his goods through three of the four methods below:
    (a) own retail outlet;
    (b) selective distribution;
    (c) using wholesalers;
    (d) franchising.

10 What role can retail alliances play for independent retailers in maintaining competitiveness compared with retail corporate chains? Discuss the advantages and limitations of such retail alliances.

11 In many retail sectors the traditional independent operators are encountering major competition from larger multiple operators. Examine the main areas where the independent operators can compete successfully, using examples to support your answer.

12 Explain what you understand by the expression 'while manufacturers can do away with Intermediaries they cannot do away with their function'. Elaborate your answer with examples.

Key terms

buying points
cash and carry
category management
category management
completely knocked-down state
  (CKD)
concentration
convenience good
convenience multiples
convenience store
co-operatives
core products
credibility source
department stores
direct sale
discounters

door-to-door
food chain stores
forecourts
franchising
grocery retailing
independents
information
IGD
internationalisation
mail order
network marketing
non-store retailing
polarisation
provision of information
rationalisation
regional shopping centres

retail parks
retail revolution
retailing
segments
specialty chain stores
standalone developments
sub-regional shopping centres
suburbanisation
symbol grocers
symbol groups
transfer of ownership
variety chain stores
voluntary chains
wheel of retailing
wholesaling

Supplementary reading list

Gattorna, J.L. (Ed.) (2003), *Handbook of supply chain management*, (Aldershot: Gower Publishing)

McGoldrick, P. (2003), 'Retailing' in Baker, M.J. (ed.) *The Marketing Book*, 5th edn, (Oxford: Butterworth-Heinemann).

CONSUMER BEHAVIOUR

Learning Goals   *After reading this chapter you should be able to:*

- Explain and justify a simple, generalised model of the buying decision process.

- Describe the phenomenon of perception and clarify its role in determining how individuals interpret the world around them.

- Distinguish the salient characteristics and differences between the stimulus–response and cognitive explanations of learning.

- Elaborate Maslow's theory of motivation.

- Understand why personality is only one of several major influences on consumer decision-making.

- Explain the essential differences between the CAC and expectancy-value models of attitude and the nature of hierarchy of effects models of decision-making.

- Spell out the influence of culture on buyer behaviour.

- Describe the concepts of social class, reference groups, personal influence and life style and show how they can be used to help sellers devise effective marketing strategies.

- Outline a composite model of buyer behaviour.

INTRODUCTION

In *Consumer Behavior*, Blackwell, Miniard and Engel (2001) define consumer behaviour as 'those acts of individuals directly involved in obtaining and using economic goods and services, including the decision processes that precede and determine these acts'. Or, put more simply "How do people buy?" This definition enjoys a very wide measure of support in the majority of texts concerned primarily with consumer behaviour as a field of study in its own right but, in my opinion, it is important to stress that such an emphasis upon individuals tends to largely ignore an equally important area of consumption behaviour – that of organisations.

Since the first publication of this book in 1971 there has developed a major interest in organisational buying behaviour as a major sub-field of marketing. which has become known as 'business to business' marketing .This trend is particularly noticeable in the USA. In our view the terms **organisational buying behaviour (OBB)** and **business to business marketing** largely deal with the same subject matter. That said, we prefer OBB because it includes exchanges between all kinds of organisations and not just profit oriented businesses. If we were to limit discussion to the latter kind of organisation then we would exclude many **Not-for-Profit** organisations which purchase significant volumes of goods and services such as government departments, local authorities, NHS Trust Hospitals and so on. We regard the purchasing practices of all such organisations as falling within the scope of OBB and so retain this term. However, the existence of separate texts dealing with consumer and organisational buying behaviour is symptomatic of a much larger division within marketing, of which new students of the subject should be especially sensitive – namely, the dichotomisation of the subject into business marketing and consumer marketing. Ever since the first edition of this book appeared in 1971 I have argued that while there are differences between these two branches of marketing they are a matter of degree only. In essence both rest upon the same foundations, as do new sub-fields such as the marketing of services or marketing by non-profit-making organisations. Accordingly it might be more realistic to classify consumption behaviour as 'individual' or 'collective' depending upon whether such behaviour is undertaken solely in pursuit of one's own satisfaction or is engaged on in conjunction with and/or on the behalf of others. Such a classification would require one to include households in the 'collective' category and it is probably preferable to maintain the generally recognised distinction between consumer and industrial or organisational (business) behaviour which exists in the marketing literature.

In this chapter we will accept the traditional approach in which discussions of consumer behaviour are focused upon individuals or ultimate consumers and their **consumption behaviour**; that is, what they consume, how they buy, and why. In doing so it will be necessary to review a number of key concepts and ideas which have been borrowed from other behavioural sciences – notably psychology and sociology – before considering how these ideas have become incorporated in composite models of consumer behaviour. To this end we look first at contributions from psychology: namely, perception, learning, personality, motivation and attitude. Attention is then directed to social influences on consumer behaviour with specific reference to culture, social class, reference groups, role and family influence, with that section concluding with a discussion of life-style as an explanation of how and why people consume, which illustrates how the psychological and sociological foundations have been built upon by marketers. This theme is further developed by a survey of some of the major models of consumer behaviour which illustrate the main schools of thought, concluding with my own composite model of buying behaviour in which I seek to justify my earlier claim that differences between different branches of marketing are a matter of degree and not of principle.

THE BUYING DECISION PROCESS

Before looking at some of the factors which influence buying decisions it will be helpful first to consider a simple and generalised model of buying as a decision process. In broad terms this may be represented by a flow diagram containing five elements as shown in Figure 8.1.

As will become clear later in this chapter the reality is far more complex than implied by this model. As we accumulate experience and learn from past behaviour so this knowledge and the attitudes associated with it will generate feedback loops in the sequence and may short circuit the process so that one moves almost instantaneously from problem recognition to choice. For example, people shopping in a supermarket depend heavily upon the display to stimulate problem recognition – 'I'm short of instant coffee' – and immediately select a preferred brand and size which their past experience has shown to give satisfaction. (Or at least sufficient satisfaction that the opportunity cost in their time and effort to collect new information and evaluate it is not considered worthwhile.) Such behaviour does not invalidate the basic model which emphasises that the consumer purchase decision is sequential and combines both mental and physical activities.

More simply put, buying behaviour consists of a **decision process** leading to the **act of purchase** and **reflection** on how satisfactory the decision was. Depending upon the importance of the decision, and its consequences for the

Figure 8.1 The buying decision process

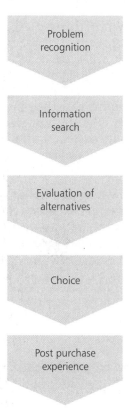

customer, buying decisions are usually classified as **high** or **low involvement** which may be extended by adding other intermediate categories.

The degree of involvement is determined by numerous factors that may may be summarised as:

- *Personal*
- *Product related*
- *Situation related.*

As might be expected, involvement is highest when the consequences of a decision are likely to affect the decision-maker personally and directly – will this enhance my self-image?, could I be sacked if I get this purchase wrong? Product related factors are associated with the risk *perceived* by the decision-maker in terms of the performance of the purchased object – does it do what it is claimed to do; might it cause physical harm or damage one's self image?

Situation related factors are closely associated with the social context in which an object is used or consumed. When buying for others, as a gift or for joint consumption, we will usually spend more time (and money) on the decision e.g. choosing a bottle of wine.

As we shall see, perception has a major influence on how we interpret the world around us, and the importance we attach to the different factors. Subjectively, we tend to perceive risk more in terms of the psychological and social consequences while, objectively, try to quantify these in terms of the physical and financial outcomes. To a greater or lesser degree (high involvement/low involvement) our perceptions will determine how long we spend coming to a decision, and the actual choice made. Faced with a new situation we are likely to engage in **extensive problem solving**. With increased experience we undertake **limited problem solving** to check out that the purchase will match our possibly revised needs. Ultimately, however, we will become so familiar with repeat purchases that our buying behaviour may be thought of as **routinised** or **habitual**. Brand loyalty reflects such behaviour and constitutes the major challenge to competitors seeking to break into a market or increase their market share.

The degree of involvement and the effort put into a purchase decision may be thought of in terms of **opportunity cost**, or the trade-off we have to make between often conflicting stimuli. Writing in *Marketing Week* in July 2004, Alan Mitchell identified six 'consumer currencies' which have to be reconciled, namely:

1 *Physical energy or work*. How long do I have to work to get the value I want from this product or service, and for what return?
2 *Emotional energy*. What are the emotional cost and benefits of this relationship or course of action? Do I mainly feel anxious, humiliated, frustrated and irritated, or do I feel 'met', recognised and reassured?
3 *Time*. How much time do I have to invest to realise this value, and for what return?
4 *Information*. How much information do I have to hand over, or acquire, to achieve my objectives?
5 *Money*
6 *Attention or mind time*. How hard do I have to think about this to get what I want? Is paying attention to it an interruption or distraction from my life, or a welcome opportunity?

Clearly, time, money and work are closely related but, nonetheless, Mitchell's conclusion that "Most value propositions represent unique mixes of benefit across these currencies" is valid.

The 'consumer' then, rather than the 'buyer', implies an active and demanding partner in the economic transaction. In response, the marketer needs to be equally active and aware, employing the tools of marketing in concert with the consumer behaviour sequence to bring together the potential buyer and the company's product.

As we shall see (for example the Hierarchy-of-effects models in Table 8.3), simple flow diagrams of the type on the previous page are capable of considerable elaboration to reflect the real complexity of most marketing problems. For example, in *The Marketing Book*, Foxall (2003) offers the expanded model shown in Figure 8.2. For the purposes of an introductory text the shorter and simpler diagrams are to be preferred.

Figure 8.2 Consumer information processing

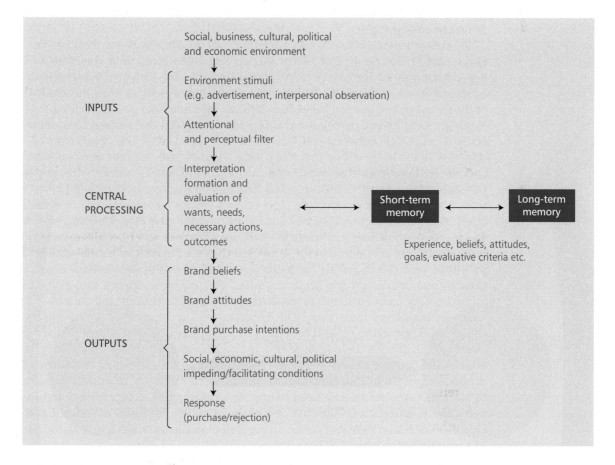

Source: Reprinted from "Consumer decision making: process, level and style', by Foxall, Gordon R., in Baker, M.J. (ed.) *The Marketing Book*, 5th.edn (2003) with permission from Elsevier.

PSYCHOLOGICAL INFLUENCES

Perception

In psychology an important and fine discrimination is made between the concepts of sensation and perception. Sensation occurs when a sense organ receives a stimulus, while perception is the interpretation of that stimulus. The distinction is particularly important for marketers, for in order to initiate an exchange process we must first establish contact through the generation of a stimulus capable of sensation by the intended recipient. For practical purposes there are five senses – seeing, hearing, touching, smelling and tasting, though experimentation has established eleven sensory mechanisms in all – and it is to one or more of the five basic senses that marketing communications stimuli are directed. However, perception is the critical factor, for this is the interpretation placed upon the stimulus and can vary widely between individuals and even within individuals over time. A frequently used example which makes this point is to compare a photograph – what the eye and the camera physically see – with a painting, which is the receiver's interpretation of that sensation. Clearly Rembrandt and Picasso perceived things rather differently and the critical question must be: 'What factors influence perception?'

In essence, if perception consists of the interpretation of a received stimulus, then, as Sperling (1967) points out, 'What we perceive at any given time, therefore, will depend not only on the nature of the actual stimulus, but also on the background or setting in which it exists – our own previous sensory experiences, our feelings of the moment, our general prejudices, desires, attitudes and goals.' Given that so many forces influence perception it is not surprising that there should frequently occur a mismatch between the interpretation intended by the originator of a stimulus (usually the seller in a marketing context) and the receiver (intended customer). It follows that those responsible for marketing stimuli should pay very careful attention to psychological findings concerning how people perceive things. A fundamental aspect of perception is that it represents the receiver's effort to organise received stimuli into a meaningful structure. In doing so two major groups of factors are involved – stimulus factors and functional factors. Stimulus factors are neutral in the sense that they are intrinsic to the stimulus and so will be received in exactly the same way by all receivers with normal sensory capabilities. On receipt the brain organises the incoming stimuli into patterns following four basic tendencies: similarity, proximity, continuity and context.

By similarity we understand the tendency of the receiver to group similar things together, while proximity results in the perception that things which are close to one another belong together. In marketing practice similarity is to be seen in the concept of segmentation, while proximity is employed in the use of prominent people to endorse particular products, in the use of generic brands like St Michael's, and so on. The need to impose a meaningful structure on stimuli is particularly noticeable in the case of continuity, which is closely associated with closure. The phenomenon of continuity is well illustrated by Sperling with the use of a simple diagram like the next one:

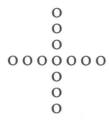

In this, one sees the dots as straight lines rather than as separate dots, and as two continuous lines rather than three or four short ones. **Closure** occurs when one completes an otherwise incomplete diagram, picture, sentence, and so on. For example, we all know what 'Beanz means'.

Finally, context, or the setting in which a stimulus is received, will have a marked effect upon perception (see any basic book for illustrations of the context influencing perception). In this sense context can have a similar 'halo' influence to proximity and is frequently used by marketers when seeking to develop an image of a product by using media or a setting which conveys the overall impression they wish to create; for example use of the Sunday colour supplements to convey a feeling of quality allied to value for money, or young people in leisure situations for Coca Cola.

As noted, stimulus factors are neutral and create sensations which are then interpreted in the light of what are generically termed functional factors. Thus individuals have an ability to screen out stimuli which they do not understand or do not wish to recognise, just as they also have an ability to modify stimuli to make them acceptable to us – a phenomenon sometimes termed 'selective perception'.

Perception is the consequence of a process in which sensory stimuli are attended to and interpreted by a person exposed to such stimuli.

Because of the enormous number and variety of sensory stimuli individuals develop coping strategies to enable them to avoid sensory overload. The essence of this strategy is selectivity in exposure, attention, and, subsequently, retention. Collectively, these comprise **selective perception**.

Selectivity operates at two levels - **conscious** and **subconscious**. Of the two, subconscious selectivity is the more effective in screening out unwanted stimuli. The reason for this is that our conscious attention/information processing ability is severely limited. As long ago as 1956 the American psychologist George Miller identified the magical number seven as the mid-point (5-9) of the capacity of our short-term memory's information processing capability for 'chunks' of information.

Short-term memory is one of the three categories distinguished in information processing. The others are sensory and long-term memory. **Sensory memory (SM)** is equivalent to the conscious recognition of a stimulus - the smell, light, movement etc-which is either discarded/stored or advanced to the short-term memory for more careful evaluation. **Long-term memory** is information that has been stored for possible future use. Thus, **short-term memory** is akin to the random access memory in your computer and controls the number of windows you can keep open simultaneously while long-term memory is equivalent to the hard disk drive and requires you to activate specific procedures to access and recover its content. In doing so you may have to close down another activity in your short-term memory/random access memory to make space for it.

Selectivity in exposure may be both conscious and subconscious. My decision to read *The Financial Times* and *The Economist* and not *The Guardian* or *New Statesman* will automatically restrict the nature of the viewpoints on business affairs that may or may not impact on my attention.

'Chunking' is a device we use to combine individual "bits" of information into more useful group's enabling us to handle large amounts of data in our working memory. For example, if I'm preparing a lecture on advertising I can easily remember the acronyms AIDA, JND, USP and DAGMAR and, having recalled these, I can unpack chunks of information to identify each of the component elements. At the same time, each of these elements may serve to trigger the recall of other related chunks. Thus, AIDA is a mnemonic for Strong's (1925) model of the stages a person goes through in making a decision to buy something - awareness, interest, desire and action. Recall of each of these components will then prompt the release of other information stored in my long-term memory concerning them as well as a related chunk that AIDA is an example of the so-called hierarchy of effects model. Now this construct was not present in my initial short-term memory but has surfaced as a result of my search for information linked or associated with AIDA and opened the new line of thinking and inquiry.

The importance of chunking was confirmed by the findings of Ognjen, Amidzic et al reported in *Nature* (2001) Writing in *The Times* (August 9th 2001) Nigel Hawkes summarised their findings as being

> ...consistent with the "chunking" theory, which maintains that expert memory relies on a database of short "chunks" of long-term memory.
> ... The scientists examined the brains of 20 (chess) players while they pitted their wits against a computer. Imaging techniques were used to observe the distribution of "gamma bursts" of electrical activity which are associated with memory.
> Measurements were taken in the five seconds after each move by the computer.
> The results showed that activity in the brains of grandmasters was centred on the frontal and parietal cortex, which are thought to be sites of remote memory storage.
> In amateurs, activity was focused on the medial temporal lobe and hippocampus, areas involved in analysing new information and relying on recent memories.

The ability of grandmasters to draw on their memory is seen as the result of many years of study and practice as a result of which they can draw on more than 100,000 patterns or memory chunks to solve problems while "Amateurs work by analysing new moves, trying to work out logically what there opponent's strategy is and how to counteract it." It would seem reasonable to assert that after many years of shopping experience individuals have exactly the same capacity to make 'instantaneous' purchase decisions when faced with the vast array of choice available in the supermarket as described earlier.

From this much simplified description it is clear that we can only attend consciously to a limited number of ideas or stimuli at any one time. Fortunately, however, our subconscious is able to screen a very large numbers of stimuli (it has been estimated at 2 million per second) and filter these to decide whether to ignore them, store them in the subconscious memory for possible future recovery, or advance them to our immediate attention or sensory memory for conscious evaluation. So, as lost in thought you step off the pavement into the path of an oncoming bus your subconscious should trigger an immediate evasive action while flooding your sensory memory to reinforce this perception.

A perception is not simply an in-built procedure governed by our autonomic nervous system. In addition to the automatic responses which have evolved with our biological systems to ensure the survival of the fittest, the dominance of humankind has been accelerated by its capacity to learn and modify behaviour. As a result human beings have developed a facility to programme their subconscious to make it much more efficient and effective in filtering and screening stimuli to determine their relevance and importance in terms of the person's beliefs and value systems. The same is even more true of our conscious behaviour where we can avoid information (**selective exposure**) or discard it because it does not meet the criteria we have developed for assessing its worth.

Thus selective perception (SP) can be seen as probably the most powerful influence over our future behaviour. At both a conscious and subconscious level it largely determines what information we will attend to and how we will interpret and process it. It is for this reason that it is seen in our model as both mediating and strongly influencing our actions or behaviour

The classic example of selective perception is that reported by Hastorf and Cantril (1954), in 'They Saw a Game: A Case History', of supporters of two American football teams Dartmouth and Princeton. The match contained a number of incidents which led to players being injured and penalties being imposed. While most uninvolved viewers felt these were the joint responsibility of both teams, supporters of the two sides were almost unanimous in their view that all the trouble was the fault of the other team.

This tendency to perceive what one wants to 'see' can be traced to several factors. First, there is our ability to screen out or ignore a very large number of stimuli and so enable us to give our full attention to those which have some particular relevance, or which strike a discordant note because of the contrast they make with other stimuli. Research has shown that we screen out the vast majority of advertisements to which we are exposed and, in fact, perceive less than 1 per cent of all those we come into contact with. Thus in order to secure our attention advertisers must use contrast, for example a colour advertisement in a black-and-white medium; loud noise (or silence) in broadcast media; luxury yacht advertisements in *The Economist*, and so forth. By the same token we possess perceptual defences which block out stimuli which are offensive, or are otherwise in conflict with our values or attitudes. The issue of relevance is also important, for clearly we will be more likely to perceive stimuli which cater to our needs, both physiological and emotional, than those which do not. On occasion physical and emotional needs may generate a conflict (termed 'cognitive dissonance') such that acquisition of a physical object to satisfy a need (a car for transportation) may generate uncertainty as to the wisdom of that choice. Under these circumstances it has been shown that purchasers of objects pay more attention to advertising or other stimuli relating to the object than do intending purchasers.

Another perceptual phenomenon of importance to the marketer is that of **preparatory set**, which, put simply, means that people tend to perceive objects in terms of their expectations (cf. closure, discussed above). A well-known marketing manifestation of the influence of preparatory set is the use of branding and price labelling. Hence, while consumers are unable to distinguish between unbranded products they have no such difficulty when brand names are given. Similarly, Gabor and Granger, Shapiro and others have clearly demonstrated that we use price as an indicator of quality and will select products with a higher price as 'better' when no differences exist with those carrying a lower price, and even when the higher-priced items are objectively inferior.

In recent years marketers have made considerable use of psychological explanations of perception in developing their communications strategies, and have developed a number of specific applications of their own. Perhaps the most sophisticated of these applications is known as **perceptual mapping**, which is founded on the premise that individuals will seek to relate to new things in terms of their relationship with or similarity to things with which they are already familiar. By collecting information from consumers of their perceptions of existing brands in a product category one can develop a two-dimensional map (usually by making use of a powerful computer program) which shows the relationships between the various brands in terms of the variables used. In Figure 8.3 it can be seen that the various brands are clustered in groups, suggesting that they are perceived as very similar. If one were to develop a new brand in this category, then this knowledge would be very valuable – either one has a product with certain characteristics and can identify the immediate opposition, or one can identify 'gaps' which it may be worth filling with a different type of product (cheap and light?). (The example shown is fictitious but it should be stressed that while Americans prefer lighter whiskies and pay a premium for them, the opposite is largely true in Britain.)

Figure 8.3 Perception of different brands of whisky in the US market

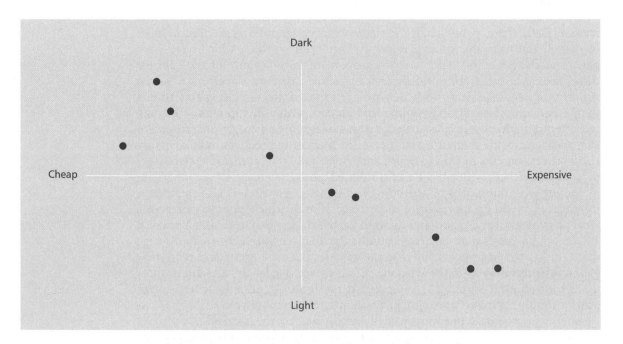

Meaning, structure and values

In the previous section we examined some of the factors that influence perception and concluded that, while there may be an objective reality, this will be interpreted both subjectively and selectively by individuals. It is these perceptions that give meaning and structure to our environment and lead to the formation of values that will further modify our perception.

In a clear and comprehensive overview of consumer behaviour, Antonides and van Raaij (1998) explain how we organise perceptions into schema that we can then use to create categories that enable us to understand the world in which we live. Schema are defined as networks of associations concerning an object – product, brand, shop etc. – based on the individuals own observations and experiences. In other words "a cluster of information held in memory" (p.112)

The importance of schema is that as we are exposed to new information we *categorise* it and then seek to classify is as part of an appropriate schema. So, when we come across a new brand or product our first action is to assign it to a category and then examine it in the context of the schema we associated it with. In the supermarket this is not a difficult task as new products are assigned to the most appropriate category – dairy foods, breakfast cereals, carbonated beverages etc. – and displayed alongside the products with which they compete most directly

Categorisation plays an important role in enabling individuals to understand and interpret their environment. Antonides and van Raaij identify *six* functions of categorisation which they distinguish as:

1 *Reduction of complexity.*

2 *Identification of objects.*

3 *Reduction of continuous learning* i.e. we draw on prior experience and memory.

4 *Ordering of categories in terms of mutual causal relationships*, e.g. alcohol and dangerous driving.

5 *Direction to behaviour* – both positive and negative.

6 *Substitution.*

While the assignment of a product or brand to a category based on its physical properties and attributes usually presents no problems, Copeland's Classification of Goods introduced in Chapter 3, makes it clear that this only the first step in assigning meaning. Depending upon our perception, and the psycho-social meaning we give a product, we may classify it as a Convenience, Shopping or Specialty good reflecting its value to us. This process is known as a **means-end chain** as illustrated in Figure 8.4.

In the market place the 'object' is more often than not a brand or corporate identity – a subject we return to in Chapter 14.

Values in the diagram refer to the specific values received by the customer which will reinforce their preference, loyalty and likelihood of repeat purchase. Depending upon the nature of the object some values will rank higher than others and the task of the marketer is to establish the customers priorities. In doing so it will be useful to to review the the listing of values developed by psychologists such as Rokeach and Kahle summarised in Table 8.1. Values are a major influence on lifestyle and we return to these when looking at Segmentation in Chapter 10.

Learning

Our discussion of perception has made it clear that in every circumstance our perception is conditioned by our prior experience, for it is this which constitutes our preparatory set or expectations and the framework into which we seek to place and organise new stimuli. In other words we have learned from our earlier experience and seek to maintain balance or consistency by relating to and interpreting new stimuli in terms of past or learned stimuli.

Learning may have a number of meanings, depending upon the context in which it is used, and Sperling (1967) comments that 'the process of learning can consist of all, or some, or one of three steps: **inventing** an original solution to a problem, or **thinking**: **committing** a solution to memory, or **memorising**: **becoming efficient** at applying the solution to a problem, or **forming a habit**'.

In essence there are two schools of thought concerning what is learned – the **stimulus–response (S–R) school**, and the **cognitive school**. Although there are some divisions within the S–R camp, the basic theory is that we learn to associate

Figure 8.4 Means end chain

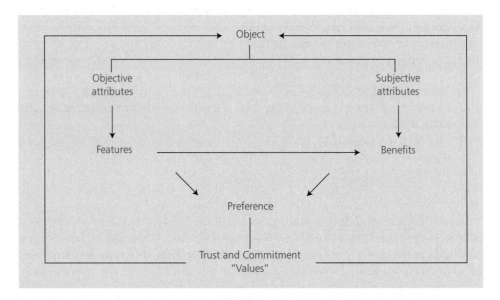

Table 8.1 Values classified by domain

Pleasure

Security

Achievement

Independence

Maturity

Conformism

Social

Source: Kahle, L.R., Beatty, S.E. and Homer, P. (1986), 'Alternative measurement approaches to consumer value: the List of Values (LOV), and Values and Lifestlyes (VALS)'. *Journal of Consumer Research*, 13, pp. 405-409, University of Chicago Press.

given responses to specific stimuli and these become habitual. One group of S–R theorists subscribe to the view that learning occurs only when there are rewards or punishments to reinforce the correct response, while others believe that learning is the result of an association between a stimulus and response occurring together, that is they are contiguous, and that reinforcement is not necessary.

In contrast to the S–R theorists the cognitive school argue that we learn cognitive structures; that is, more broadly based interpretations of the association between stimuli and alternative courses of action. For example, a mother tells her small child not to touch something because it is hot and will burn. The child, unfamiliar with the concepts of hot and burn, touches the object as soon as its mother's back is turned and howls with pain. The next time mother says something is hot or will burn the child will avoid contact, even though it is a quite different object.

In a marketing context there would seem to be support for both theories, in that some consumption behaviour is routinised and habitual (S–R school), while other purchasing decisions are subject to extensive problem-solving generalising from past experience (cognitive school).

The division of opinion about what we learn also exists in the case of how we learn. S–R theorists maintain that learning occurs through a process of trial and error – a view based on extensive experimental evidence using animals.

However, some leading members of the cognitive school (notably Wolfgang Kohler 1925) developed what is termed the **Gestalt explanation of learning** as being based on insight.

While it seems likely that the truth is a combination of both schools of thought, in which some actions are learned through direct personal experience based upon trial and error, while others are the product of reasoning, that is seeking solutions through symbolic thinking, the S–R explanations tend to dominate in consumer behaviour research in marketing.

In turn the most sophisticated statement of S–R theory which underlies much of this consumer-behaviour research is that developed by Clark Hull (1943) in *Principles of Behavior: An Introduction to Behavior Theory*, whose basic model is

$$E = D \times K \times H \times V$$

where E = behaviour and is a multiplicative function of D = drive, K = incentive potential, H = habit strength, and where V = intensity of the cue.

Drives are discussed at greater length in the section on motivation research which follows, where a distinction is made between a drive which is viewed as the initial stimulus, and a motive which is a tendency to activity. It is not felt that this distinction is important in the context of Hull's model. The remaining terms are essentially self-explanatory, and it is clear that in a marketing situation two of the variables – the incentive potential, or satisfaction offered by the product, and the intensity of the cue – are controllable to a considerable degree by the seller. It should also be noted that as the equation is multiplicative no reaction will occur if any of the variables has a zero value. At first sight this would seem to suggest that consumers would never try new products, for if they have not consumed them before, then H (or habit) would be expected to have a zero value. However, this possibility is negated by the principle of generalisation, whereby we extrapolate from past experience to a new situation. This potentiality is exploited by companies with generic brand names, where satisfactory experiences with one product group creates a favourable predisposition towards new product groups;

for example buyers of clothes from Marks & Spencer towards M & S foodstuffs. Of course, generalisation is only potential, and past experience soon teaches us that it is not always true that all the products introduced by a company will automatically yield the same level of satisfaction as the one which we originally approved of. In other words we learn to discriminate between very similar cues or stimuli.

Before leaving this brief overview of some learning-theory concepts which have been incorporated into studies of consumer behaviour it should be noted that Howard and Sheth's (1969) *Theory of Buyer Behaviour* is essentially a learning model. It should also be noted that two important areas of research in marketing draw heavily upon learning theory for their conceptual framework – namely, the study of advertising effectiveness and of brand loyalty.

Motivation

Reference was made in the last section to the distinction between a drive as an initial stimulus, and motive as a tendency to act, though the terms tend to be used interchangeably in everyday speech. However, perhaps a clearer distinction is apparent if one defines drives as physiological stimuli to action, while motives constitute the intervening variable between the stimulus and response. For example, I have a strong drive to smoke a cigarette but my doctor has told me it is bad for my health and will shorten my life. I wish to live to a ripe old age and am strongly motivated to avoid anything which prejudices that goal – result, I stop smoking and resist drive.

Drives and motives are also often called '**needs**' and one of the most enduring and widely used classification of needs is that proposed by Abraham Maslow (1943) in 'A Theory of Human Motivation' introduced in Chapter 1. According to Maslow's basic theory we possess five basic needs which can be placed in a hierarchy such that as lower-order needs are satisfied we lose interest in them and concentrate upon satisfying needs at the next higher level which have become the most pressing. The five steps in the hierarchy in ascending order are:

1 *Physiological needs;*
2 *Safety needs;*
3 *Love needs;*
4 *Esteem needs;*
5 *Self-actualisation needs.*

Physiological needs or basic drives arise mainly from internal stimuli such as hunger or thirst, though some arise from external sources which threaten the individual with pain, injury or death. It is generally believed that satisfaction of these needs is dominant and overrides all other considerations. It is significant that a marketing function as it has developed in advanced economies in the past fifty to sixty years is irrelevant in countries where basic needs are not satisfied.

Safety needs come next in importance and can themselves be ranked into a rough hierarchy – physical security; stable and routine pattern of living, that is avoid the risk of the unknown; acquisition of protection against an uncertain future (religion, insurance).

Love needs include the need for affection and the feeling of belonging to a group

MOTIVATION RESEARCH

In 1957 journalist and part-time academic Vance Packard caused a significant stir with the publication of his book *The Hidden Persuaders*. The sub-title of the book was "An introduction to the techniques of mass-persuasion through the unconscious" and its thesis was that people were being influenced and manipulated, especially by marketers in terms of our purchasing behaviour. Packard wrote: "Large-scale efforts are being made, often with impressive results, to channel our unthinking habits, our purchasing decisions, and our thought processes by the use of insights gleaned from psychiatry and the social sciences. Typically these efforts take place beneath our level of awareness; so that the appeals that move us are often, in a sense, 'hidden'."

In their defence, market researchers pointed out that in attempting to identify what motivated customer behaviour – why people behave the way they do – often this cannot be easily explained by asking the obvious question "Why did you do that?". If you do ask this question then respondents will frequently give you the answer they think you want, that is socially acceptable, or that saves them from telling you they don't know the answer. To illustrate this Packard cites research undertaken by the Color Research Institute.

"Women while waiting for a lecture had the choice of two waiting rooms. One was a functional modern chamber with gentle tones. It had been carefully designed for eye ease and to promote a relaxed feeling. The other room was a traditional room filled with period furniture, oriental rugs, expensive -looking wallpaper.

It was found that virtually all the women instinctively went into the Swedish modern room to do their waiting. Only when every chair was filled did the women start to overflow into the more ornate room. After the lecture the ladies were asked, 'Which of those two rooms do you like the better?' They looked thoughtfully at the two rooms, and then eighty-four per cent of them said the period room was the nicer room."

Similarly, when a group of people was asked if they borrowed money from personal-loan companies everyone said no. But the group had been selected from the records of a loan company! Or the sample of people who said that they didn't buy kippers because they didn't like the taste when, under direct questioning, forty per cent admitted they had never tasted a kipper. Obviously, if one wants to understand why people behave the way they do then a less direct approach is called for, and this is where motivation research comes into the picture.

According to Packard two men claimed to be the father of **motivation research – MR –** and to have started using it in the 1930s to inform merchandising and advertising decisions – Ernest Dichter, president of Motivational Research Inc. and Louis Cheskin, director of the Color Research Institute. But it was only in the early 1950s, at the end of the post-war boom, and with increased competition in the market place, that firms began to see this as a source of competitive advantage. In response, numerous others social scientists set –up in business to offer advice on how to determine what motivates customer behaviour at the subconscious level.

Most of the techniques used for probing the subconscious are derived from the practice of psychiatry. Perhaps the most common is the 'depth interview' in which the researcher engages in a dialogue with the subject and encourages them to talk about their feelings and behaviour in a non-threatening way, and through skilful probing encourage them to express thoughts that they would normally suppress. A familiar extension of this technique on a one-to-one basis is the Focus Group in which up to ten people at a time may be encouraged to talk about a topic.

In addition to interviews a variety of projective techniques, ranging from clinical tests like the Rorschach, through **TAT** or **Thematic Apperception Tests** in which subjects are asked to describe what is going on in pictures or cartoons, to sentence completion may be used. Details of these techniques will be found in more advanced texts on Market Research and Consumer Behaviour of the kind listed under Recommended Reading at the end of the chapter. But, if you can get hold of a copy of Packard's book it is well worth reading still. For example, the findings from motivation research in the 1950s into why people smoke are probably just as valid now as they were then.

– family, social group, work group, and so on. Much marketing activity seeks to cater for these needs and includes some approaches most criticised by anti-marketers, for example advertising which suggests that failure to use a product (toothpaste, shampoo, etc.) will lead to ostracism or exclusion from a group which you aspire to join.

Esteem needs include such things as recognition, status, prestige, reputation, and so forth. In affluent societies achievement of these needs is often reinforced and made public through the acquisition of physical objects which are felt to be appropriate to a person's position in life. (Consider the Sunday colour supplements for a sample of such objects.)

Self-actualisation represents the highest level of need to 'do one's own thing'. Relatively few people would seem to achieve this level and when they do they are unlikely to be much influenced by or interested in the market-place!

Maslow's hierarchy of motives constitutes a general statement of behaviour at the macro level – to understand the behaviour of the individual we need a more comprehensive classificatory scheme such as that provided by the concept of personality.

Personality

In his *Introduction to Psychology*, Ernest Hilgard (1967) defines personality as 'The configuration of individual characteristics and ways of behaving which determine an individual's unique adjustment to his environment.' While Hilgard is atypical in offering a definition, as most psychologists fail to do so, his definition reflects the consensus concept of personality as a consistent pattern of response. Because of this overall consistency in an individual's pattern of behaviour it is possible to categorise dominant traits and develop a classification of personality 'types'. In turn such classification provides a valuable working construct for marketers, as it enables them to use personality as a factor in developing marketing strategies and marketing mixes to suit them.

However, if we are to make use of personality as a basis for trying to predict human behaviour, then it follows that we must be able to agree upon what variables we need to measure, and how to measure them, as a basis for classifying individuals. Sperling (in *Psychology*) records that Gordon Allport found 4500 words which designate distinct personal forms of behaviour in the 1925 edition of the unabridged Webster's New International Dictionary, and while many of these are no doubt synonyms it underlines the problem of what traits one is to measure to arrive at a personality 'type'. As a result of this extensive range of possibilities, psychologists have devised a battery of personality tests (Allport's being one of the best known and widely used) which reflect different personality theories (Freudian, neo-Freudian, S–R learning theories) and/or the purpose for which the test has been devised. For example, if an employer is looking for persons with a particular and strongly developed personality trait, then they will prefer a test which emphasises identification and measurement of that trait.

Further, although it was stated earlier that personality is a valuable working construct for marketing practitioners, it must be recognised that the research evidence on the relationship between personality variables and consumer behaviour is conflicting. The most widely cited study is that of Franklin B. Evans (1959) 'Psychological and Objective Factors in the Prediction of Brand Choice: Ford versus Chevrolet', in which he used the Edwards Personal Preference Schedule to test for personality differences between owners of the two different makes of car, but concluded that personality is 'of little value in predicting whether an individual owns a Ford or a Chevrolet'. A number of subsequent studies would seem to confirm this conclusion, but at least as many maintain the opposite. Indeed, many writers have criticised Evans's whole approach, but Thomas S. Robertson (1970) in *Consumer Behavior*, probably makes the most useful observation when he points out that while personality data only classified correctly 63 per cent of Evans's sample, this is 'some improvement over chance'. For many marketing problems this is all we can expect, and any approach which can reduce uncertainty is to be welcomed.

However, over 40 years after Evans's study we are able to take a more balanced view of the value of personality variables as predictors of specific behaviour such as brand choice, and recognise that it is only one of several major influences upon consumer decision-making, Blackwell, Miniard and Engel (*Consumer Behavior* 2001, p214) are of the opinion that personality is unlikely to prove a useful segmentation variable, not least because a homogeneous personality profile does not necessarily imply homogeneity in other respects, and most marketing media and channels of distribution tend to be designed to match other forms of homogeneity. None the less Blackwell et al. indicate several ways in which personality theory has considerable promise for marketing applications, particularly in its role as a moderating variable (that is where a personality trait can help explain differences in the behaviour of groups which are homogeneous in other respects), or as an intervening variable where primary segmentation is based upon objective factors such as demographics, but intra-group differences can be best explained in terms of motivational attributes. However, Blackwell et al. also point out that research on personality 'has stimulated the development of broader, more behavioural concepts that are likely to be better targets for market segmentation – namely life-styles'.

In some situations individual attributes or traits may prove sufficient, but in others a more generalised statement of personality may be useful. Sperling (1967) gives a list of twelve primary dimensions of personality which is based upon extensive measurement of traits which have a very low correlation with one another but whose defining traits have a very high correlation with one another (see Table 8.2).

A more condensed statement of psychographic variables is offered by Kotler (1988) and contains the following seven items:

- *Compulsiveness*: compulsive; non-compulsive
- *Gregariousness*: extrovert; introvert
- *Autonomy*: dependent; independent
- *Conservatism*: conservative; liberal; radical
- *Authoritarianism*: authoritarian, democratic
- *Leadership*: leader; follower
- *Ambitiousness*: high achiever; low achiever

In common with most other aspects of consumer behaviour, personality has been the subject of extensive research. For example, William Wilkie reports that over 300 studies of personality and consumer behaviour have now been reported in marketing literature. (William K. Wilkie is the author of one of the many specialised texts available on the topic. His *Consumer Behavior* (1994) extended to 614 pages, contains 78 pages of notes and references, a 23-page glossary and 31 pages of index. A book such as this is essential reading for the serious student). However, Wilkie reports that the findings of these numerous studies are, to quote Harold Kassarjian, 'equivocal'. The main reason for this is that while individuals may share personality traits their behaviour is influenced by a host of other factors. It is for this reason that personality, like many other dimensions of consumer behaviour, can contribute to our understanding of why people behave the way they do but rarely provide a complete explanation.

Wilkie (op. cit.) suggests that personality research currently exhibits four distinctive trends:

1 A more holistic approach to studying patterns of behaviour rather than single decisions.

2 Focusing on consumption rather than general needs – the domain of consumer psychographics.

3 Shifting attention to related areas, for example physiological influences; the idea of a selfconcept.

4 Studying how personality affects responses to advertising.

Overall these trends have shifted attention and interest more towards the subject of consumer values and away from personality per se.

Attitude

Attitude is one of the most frequently invoked behavioural-science concepts in marketing. While its relationship to behaviour is not entirely clear, the frequent

Table 8.2 Primary dimensions of personality

1 Easy-going, generous, genial, warm *versus* cold, inflexible

2 Independent, intelligent, reliable *versus* foolish, frivolous, unreflective

3 Emotionally stable, realistic, steadfast *versus* emotionally changeable, evasive, neurotic

4 Ascendant, dominant, self-assertive *versus* self-effacing, submissive

5 Cheerful, placid, sociable, talkative *versus* agitated, depressed, reclusive, sorrowful

6 Sensitive, sympathetic, tender-hearted *versus* frank and hard-boiled, poised, unemotional

7 Cultured, aesthetic *versus* boorish, uncultured

8 Conscientious, painstaking, responsible *versus* emotionally dependent, impulsive, irresponsible

9 Adventurous, carefree, kind *versus* cautious, inhibited, reserved, withdrawn

10 Energetic, persistent, quick, vigorous *versus* daydreaming, languid, slack, tired

11 Calm, tolerant *versus* excitable, highly-strung, irritable

12 Friendly, trustful *versus* suspicious, hostile

Source: Sperling, A. D. (1967), *Psychology Made Simple* (London: W. H. Allen).

association between attitude and likely future action has resulted in extensive use of attitude surveys in the area of new-product development and in the design and execution of many promotional campaigns. Similarly, public opinion (belief or attitudes) is playing an increasing role in shaping and modifying corporate policy in areas such as consumer protection. It follows that a basic understanding of the current state of knowledge of attitude theory is vital to the student of marketing.

Just as there is no single agreed definition of marketing, so there is a multiplicity of definitions of 'attitude'. In broad terms most of these definitions fall into one of two categories which reflect two basic models in current use, which may be defined as the **cognitive–affective–conative (CAC)** and **expectancy–value (EV)**

Table 8.3 Hierarchical models of advertising effect

Model	Characteristic
Starch 1923	To be effective, an advertisement must be ... seen → read → believed → remembered → acted upon
Strong 1925	AIDA[a, b] attention → interest → desire → action
Sandage and Fryburger 1935	Interaction Model exposure → perception → integration → action
Lavidge and Steiner 1961	Hierarchy of Effects awareness → knowledge → liking → preference → conviction → purchase
Colley 1961	DAGMAR[c] unawareness → awareness → comprehension → conviction → purchase
McGuire 1969	Information Processing Model presentation → attention → comprehension → yielding → retention → behaviour
DeLozier 1976	Psychological responses to Advertising attention → perception → retention → conviction → action[d]
Peston and Thorsten 1984	Expanded Association Model[e] exposure → awareness → perception → evaluation → stimulation → search → trial → adoption

Notes:
(a) The initials of the four steps
(b) It is an interesting comment upon the intellectual condition of marketing communications practice that this model was found to be the most widely quoted of the seven in a range of current British, American and French textbooks, despite being today well past normal retirement age
(c) Colley's model is always called 'Dagmar', actually the initials of the monograph in which it was first proposed: Defining Advertising Goals for Measured Advertising Results
(d) DeLozier's model includes a final step, 'post-purchase behaviour', which is omitted here – partly for purposes of comparison and partly because it is not actually a response to advertising but a consequence of action.
(e) The Preston & Thorston model appears very different from the rest because of its many incorporated ramifications – for example, separating awareness of the advertisement from awareness of its elements from awareness of the advertised product

Source: Crosier, K. (1995), Ch. 6 in Baker M. J. (ed.), *Marketing: Theory and Practice*, 3rd edn (Basingstoke: Macmillan).

models. The cognitive–affective–conative model has been traced back to Plato's elements of the human soul – reasonable, spirited, appetitive – which in more modern terms may be defined as the realms of thought, emotions and motives, or knowing, feeling and acting. Marketers have developed a number of variants of their own of the CAC model, some of the better known of which are contained in Table 8.3 under the general heading of hierarchy-of-effects models. In all of the marketing versions, starting with Strong's AIDA (1924) and progressing through Lavidge and Steiner (1961), Rogers (1962) to Engel, Kollat and Blackwell (1968), it is assumed that one proceeds from awareness (cognitive) to preference (affective) to action (conative) – an assumption of the direction of cause and effect for which there is little empirical support. In fact it is widely recognised that frequently one or more stages occur simultaneously, for example awareness and evaluation, while impulse purchases suggest that the cognitive and affective may occur together, while the conative may, or may not, follow. Despite these deficiencies the CAC model enjoys wide support, and the effectiveness of marketing strategy is often measured in terms of its ability to move consumers up the hierarchy of effects; that is, from unawareness to awareness, from desire to action – in other words attitude is seen as a predisposition to act.

The expectancy–value model views attitude as comprising two components – beliefs and values – which are broadly equivalent to the cognitive and affective dimensions of the CAC model. It follows that the EV model is lacking a behavioural or action element and so is much more limited in its application.

The EV model is particularly associated with the work of Martin Fishbein (1975), who built upon the work of Rosenberg, which in turn was developed from Fritz Heider's consistency model. In essence Fishbein argues that an attitude comprises two components – beliefs about the attributes of an object, and the values ascribed to these beliefs. In order to maintain consistency (or balance, or congruity as it is sometimes called) consumers need to act in accordance with their beliefs and the values associated with them. Thus, while EV models do not seek to establish a link between attitude and behaviour, the association between expressed beliefs and action is strong where action occurs; that is, beliefs experienced about different brands have been found to be good predictors of actual brand preference, where the person expressing a belief about a brand actually consumes an item from that product category. However, there is a world of difference between holding a neutral or positive belief about a product and a willingness to buy it; for example, 'I believe Romeo and Juliet cigars are of the highest quality, but I would never buy them, because I do not smoke.'

This latter caveat is particularly important and explains why the EV model is theoretically more acceptable than the CAC model, which extends the link between an attitude as a predisposition to act into behaviour without specifying the catalyst which makes action necessary. From a practical point of view it is this missing link which is of crucial importance in converting the results of attitude surveys into realistic sales forecasts. In my own model of buying behaviour I term this motivation to act 'felt need', and suggest that the precise nature of this will depend very much upon specific circumstances. Clearly the implication of this is that one must seek to develop one's own check-list of causal factors in the context of one's own marketing problem. In doing so there are a number of other behavioural-science concepts which will prove helpful, including those of change agents, opinion leadership and source credibility. A review of these follows.

While we cannot prove a causal relationship between attitude and behaviour, it is clear that a favourable attitude is more likely to lead to desired action than is an unfavourable attitude. Consequently much marketing activity is devoted to creating a favourable attitude, or climate of opinion, towards an object, or to reinforcing such favourable attitudes if they already exist.

It is generally agreed that attitudes are learned initially from one's family and then from the groups to which one belongs or wishes to belong. From a marketing point of view favourable attitudes to the consumption of particular products and/or services are usually a by-product of more basic group affiliations/aspirations. For example, I wish to be accepted as a student, students wear scarves and jeans, therefore I wear a scarf and jeans. The question is, who sets the group norm which specifies scarf and jeans as the accepted dress of the group?

As in most marketing/behavioural-science issues, there is no single universally accepted answer, but the balance of evidence is that certain individuals take it upon themselves to mould and change attitudes and behaviour by setting themselves up as **opinion leaders**.

Opinion leaders achieve their satisfaction through their status as the expert adviser on some aspect of importance to a group of which he or she is a member. This status is often highly specific, for example the group expert on hi-fi systems, bargain travel, cheap places to eat, and so on, and it is unusual to find an individual who is the opinion leader on all topics of interest to a group. In other words while the existence and role of opinion leaders in influencing attitudes/ behaviour is widely accepted, using this idea operationally is restricted, due to the absence, and possibly non-existence, of a profile enabling one to identify the opinion leader.

However, to the extent that opinion leaders act as filters and amplifiers in the communication channel (see Chapter 17), their potential role as change agents is particularly significant, as is the concept of source credibility.

Source credibility refers to the confidence we place in the source of information, and has been shown to have an important influence upon the acceptability of new information as a basis for attitude change (as does the presentation of the message itself). Broadly speaking sources may be divided into two categories – personal and impersonal – and may be '**objective**' or **marketer-dominated** ('objective' only in the sense that the source is not paid for by the marketer in the same way as advertisements and salesmen are). The effectiveness of the different sources in the stages of the consumer decision process, which coincide with the stages in the CAC or EV models, has been the subject of a great deal of research.

In the *Marketing Book* (2003) Gordon Foxall explains that the conventional understanding of consumer choice needs to be modified in three ways:

1 To take account of the consumers degree of involvement in a decision.

2 To recognise that consumers vary in their decision-making style with some following an extended, deliberative approach and others buying more on impulse.

3 To give more detailed attention to the situational context in which consumer behaviour occurs.

These issues are explored in some detail and Foxall argues strongly that, while theorising about consumer behaviour is useful, more detailed research into actual buying behaviour is necessary incorporating these modifications if we are to be able to devise effective marketing mixes.

Clearly the matter is not closed and the present state of knowledge would seem to suggest that both CAC and ATR or behaviouristic models are correct under certain specific conditions

SOCIAL INFLUENCES

The preceding discussion of psychological influences has concentrated largely upon individual characteristics. In this section we are concerned primarily with people as members of groups, for, as will become clear, group membership has a profound influence upon individual behaviour. The approach followed is to start with macro concepts of culture and social class, and then refine the analysis to look at reference groups, role and family influences, and, finally, the concept of life-style.

Culture

Bennett and Kassarjian (1972), in *Consumer Behavior*, define culture as 'a set of learned beliefs, values, attitudes, habits, and forms of behaviour that are shared by a society and are transmitted from generation to generation within that society'. Bennett and Kassarjian's definition has been expanded by many more recent authors but it is still current. In the summary to his chapter on cultural influences, Wilkie (op. cit.) observes:

Culture refers to the way of life of a society. It is a very powerful force in shaping people's lives. Two major components of culture are external, material culture and internal, mental culture. Cultural norms range from fads and fashions (that may come and go very quickly), to folkways (everyday practices), to mores (moral or religious values), to laws (strict codes of behaviour). (p. 340)

The emphasis upon learned, shared and transmitted in the Bennett and Kassarjian definition is important, for it reflects attributes common to a vast multiplicity of definitions of culture. Values and beliefs are learned; they are not innate or instinctive in the way in which physiological drives are. Because they are shared they become a yardstick for behaviour, departure from which is regarded as deviancy and may be punished with considerable severity. Third, while a culture will evolve over time it possesses an enduring quality which enables it to be transmitted from generation to generation.

There are many different cultures, and Robertson suggests that a structural framework for classifying these may be developed, using three dimensions – **distributive**, **organisational** and **normative**. In his words:

The distributive dimension summarises demographic characteristics, such as income and education levels, and the distribution of the population ecologically (for example, urban, suburban, or rural) and occupationally. The organisational dimension summarises participation patterns within the culture, and the structure of cultural institutions. Social class structure and the rigidity or flexibility of this structure, as well as the nature of family relationships, are organisational topics. The normative element treats values and norms, including economic or religious philosophy.

While these three dimensions are very useful in drawing broad distinctions between, say, Eastern and Western cultures, it is obvious that they must be used with caution and as a first broad-brush basis for distinguishing between behavioural patterns. Indeed, for most marketers it is subcultures which are of more direct and immediate interest because they provide a meaningful way of segmenting a society. Sub-cultures usually develop from a basic dimension of race, religion or nationality, and it is these which tend to have most influence upon consumer behaviour. However, age and ecological sub-cultures are also distinguishable and important.

Bennett and Kassarjian (in *Consumer Behavior*) suggest that culture exerts this influence mainly upon consumption per se and media image and has greatest relevance in the sphere of international marketing. In the case of consumption differences food preferences are probably the most obvious case in point, followed by clothing and beverages (for example Muslim attitudes to alcohol). Sub-cultures have an important influence upon the acceptability of message content, particularly in terms of the cultural expectancies of the audience, e.g. technical information for men, style information for women for consumer durables, and demands careful attention by advertising strategists. (Robertson gives a number of interesting examples of 'cultural implications for marketing'.)

While it may seem obvious that culture is of most relevance to the international marketer, there is a tendency to exaggerate this. Specifically, the generalisations which are usually cited as dire warnings of the perils of ignoring the cultural differences between different international markets often serve to disguise the fact that there are probably as many different and diverse segments within the domestic market as in an overseas one. Further, given modern communications systems, it is highly likely that very similar segments for particular products may be found in most countries, despite the fact that the commonplace in the United

FAT LOSSES

The above headline appeared on a column by Ingrid Mansell that appeared in *The Times* (27/09/04) concerning the impact the Atkins diet had had on the world's biggest food companies.

While the Atkins diet was first published in the late 1960s, its revival in the early 2000s, at a time of growing publicity about the adverse effects of obesity, resulted in millions switching to high-protein, low-carbohydrate diets. This switch had a major knock-on effect on the profits of food manufacturers that had not factored this into their forecasts.

"Corporate victims include Unilever, the Anglo-Dutch consumer goods giant, whose former chairman once described Atkins as a fad. The company was forced to eat those words when it admitted that 2003 sales of its Slim-Fast products had slumped by £140 million as a result of the craze. Unilever has since conceded "We had it wrong"".

Many other manufacturers, and suppliers of their packaging, reported similar effects, highlighting the importance of monitoring trends in consumer behaviour on a continuing basis. Mansell continued:

"Companies that were slow to react to the Atkins craze are rushing to change their ways. Unilever has introduced Carb Options, carbohydrate-reduced staple foods ranging from pasta to soup to ice cream, in the UK and US. Nestlé has developed low-carbohydrate chocolate bars, while Heinz, the manufacturers of the WeightWatchers-branded ready meals, has also created a low-carb range."

Which also goes to show that most threats also offer an opportunity.

States may be a luxury in Africa or India (or the commonplace in Saudi Arabia a luxury in the United States!). Perhaps the safest policy is to be sensitive to cultural differences but act upon the existence of common sub-cultures. It is for this reason that although the EEC became a single market in 1992 in economic terms it still comprises a large number of distinct markets based upon cultural and other regional differences.

Social class

A particularly strong and pervasive, indeed universal, sub-cultural division is that of social class, whereby members of a society are stratified into a number of subdivisions. These subdivisions or classes are based upon many common characteristics, which usually include income, education, occupation and social status or prestige. These characteristics give rise to similar behavioural patterns and activities which can be differentiated from those of other social classes. This latter point is of particular importance to marketers, for the value of such a classification lies in the ability to discriminate between groupings of people and, it is hoped, to predict their behaviour under given conditions.

Many people find the concept of class offensive, because of the intrinsic implication that people can be ordered according to their worth, and argue that all people are equal. Such an argument would appear to be based largely upon an economic interpretation of equality and leads to attempts to distribute wealth more evenly through society. However, it is clear that the redistribution of wealth has relatively little to do with the value attached to the various roles filled by individuals and it is this which is the essence of social stratification. Thus in most societies teachers and priests are accorded relatively high status and prestige but earn incomes more in keeping with members of a lower class; similarly, pop singers earn more than opera singers but their earnings are probably inversely related to their prestige. So, while it is true that the status associated with given roles may change over time, it seems highly improbable that there will ever be a truly classless society.

It follows that if we wish to make use of this universal tendency for societies to 'classify' themselves, then we must identify and measure those factors or criteria upon which such a classification rests. In doing so one must not be surprised if different sets of criteria result in a different number of classes. However, most systems used in Western cultures have a close allegiance to the six-class model proposed by W. Lloyd Warner (1960) in his celebrated study of a small New England Town, *Social Class in America*:

Social class	Membership
Upper-upper	Aristocracy
Lower-upper	New rich
Upper-middle	Successful business and professional
Lower-middle	White-collar worker
Upper-lower	Blue-collar worker
Lower-lower	Unskilled

While this scheme recognises two more classes than did Centers' 1949 division into upper, middle, working and lower classes, Warner himself saw the issue as a false one in that the number of divisions is relatively arbitrary and dependent upon whose opinion you are seeking. It should also be noted that in many instances one is as much concerned with differences within classes as between them.

The most widely used system in the United Kingdom is Social Grade, developed for use by the National Readership Survey (see Table 8.4).

Table 8.4 NRS social grade definitions*

Social grade	Social status	Occupation of Chief Income Earner
A	Upper middle class	Higher managerial, administrative or professional
B	Middle class	Intermediate managerial, administrative or professional
C1	Lower middle class	Supervisory or clerical and junior managerial, administrative or professional
C2	Skilled working class	Skilled manual workers
D	Working class	Semi and unskilled manual workers
E	Those at the lowest level of subsistence	State pensioners or widows (no other earner) casual or lowest-grade workers

* These are the standard social grade classifications using definitions agreed between IPSOS-RSL and NRS Limited
Source: National Readership Survey (*www.nrs.co.uk*)

Just as the concept of culture is useful for classifying people into broadly similar groupings, so social-class concepts help refine the classification into smaller and more specific segments with greater operational potential for practitioners. Engel et al. (2001) cite a large number of studies which illustrate the application of social class in helping to interpret and predict consumer behaviour – social class has been found to be especially useful in predicting preferences for kind, quality and style of clothing, home furnishings, leisure activities, cars, consumer durables, and use of credit cards. Social class has also been shown to be associated with patterns of media usage, language patterns, source credibility and shopping behaviour. This predictive power is considerably enhanced if one is able to add to it knowledge concerning reference groups, role and family influence.

Reference groups, role and family influence

When discussing psychological influences upon behaviour the emphasis was upon the individual. But 'No man is an island', and all of us are subjected to the influence of others with whom we come into contact. This influence is particularly strong in the case of what are termed **reference groups**.

Social psychologists reserve the description 'group' for collections of two or more persons who interact with one another over time. In other words there must be some relationship between the group members which goes beyond collections of persons with common interests such as a theatre audience or passengers in an aeroplane. Bennett and Kassarjian (1972) in *Consumer Behavior* cite Krech, Crutchfield and Ballachey's (1962) definition from *Individual in Society*, namely: 'a group is (1) persons who are interdependent upon each other, such that each member's behaviour potentially influences the behaviour of each of the others,

Table 8.5 Characteristics of household population[1]

(a) Number of households in Great Britain, 2002-2003: 24,350,000

(b) Size of households, 2002-2003

	%
1 person	27
2 persons	36
3 persons	17
4 persons	13
5 persons	4
6 persons or more	1
	100
Average (mean) h/h size: 2002/3	2.40
1971	2.91

(c) Type of households, 2002

	%
1 person only	31
2 or more unrelated adults	2
Married couple	47
Cohabiting couple	8
Lone parent	10
2 or more families	1
	100

(d) Marital status by sex, 2002

	Men	Women
16 and over	%	%
Married	54	50
Cohabiting	10	9
Single	26	20
Widowed/divorced etc.	10	20
	100	100

(e) Female shoppers with/without children under 15, 2003

		%
With children (total)		31.9
0-23 months	5.9	
0-4 years	13.6	
0-15 years	31.9	
Without children		68.1
		100

(f) Working status of female main shoppers[2], 2003

	%	%
Working full time		
30+ hours per week	28.4	
Working part-time		
8-29 hours per week	18.5	
Working full or part-time		46.9
Not working and part-time		
under 8 hours per week		53.1
		100

(g) Number of economically active persons in household, 2003

	%
No persons	33
1 person	37
2 persons	31
3 or more persons	9
	100

(h) Retired/non-retired households[3], 2002-2003

	%
Retired (total)	40.2
Dependent on state pensions	16.5
Other	23.7
Non-retired	59.9
	100

(i) Static/non-static households, 2001/Q1

	%	%
Static		97.8
Non-static (total)		2.3
Newly weds households	0.4	
Movers into:		
- new homes	0.2	
- other movers	1.7	
		100

Note(s): [1] All refer to Great Britain except (g) and (h) which refer to UK
[2] According to the 'Family expenditure survey 2002-2003', 14% of households in the UK have working married women with dependent children
[3] Households consisting of one adult or one man and one woman only.
Source: *The Marketing Pocket Book 2005*, published by WARC (*www.warc.com*), citing various sources as follows:
(i) GfK NOP; (a), (b), (g), (h) 'Family expenditure survey', National Statistics © Crown Copyright 2004; (c), (d) 'General household survey', National Statistics © Crown Copyright 2004; (e), (f) National Readership Survey (NRS Ltd.), Jan 2003-Dec 2003.

and (2) the sharing of an ideology – a set of beliefs, values, and norms – which regulate their mutual conduct'.

Several different types of reference groups may be distinguished, the most basic distinction being between primary and secondary groups. A primary group is one which is small enough for all of the members to communicate with each other face to face (the family, a seminar group, the area sales team), while a secondary group is one where less continuous interaction takes place (professional societies, trade unions, companies, and so on).

When a group possesses a specified structure and specified functions then it is termed a **formal group**, but where the structure and function are unspecified, as in a circle of friends, we have an **informal group**. Both formal and informal groups have norms which prescribe the pattern of behaviour expected of members and the transmission of these norms to new members is known as socialisation. In formal groups the norms are usually much more explicit and readily identified than in informal groups, but the norms of the latter are no less demanding if one wishes to remain in membership of the group. In all cases the influence of the group is towards conformity, and the strength of this tendency will depend upon the pressure the group can bring to bear upon the individual, the importance of the group to the individual, and the number of groups to which the individual belongs.

In a marketing context perhaps the most important group of all is the family – specifically the nuclear family of husband, wife and children (the extended family includes grandparents, aunts, uncles, cousins, and so on). The nuclear family is frequently referred to as 'the household' in consumer studies, but such usage is often looser and may include any group of persons occupying the same housing unit, as does the official US Census Bureau definition.

As touched on in Chapter 3, in the past decade there has been a continuing trend away from the traditional nuclear family or household. The characteristics of the UK Household Population are set out in Table 8.5.

From this table it is clear that the number of single-person households is considerable (27 per cent) and, with an ageing population, is set to increase. It is also clear that there is a significant number of single-parent households, of working 'housewives', economically inactive persons (retired and unemployed) and so on. All of these changes are having, and will continue to have, an important impact on consumption behaviour.

Nonetheless, as a primary group the family has great influence upon motives, personality and attitudes, and acts as a mediating influence upon external influences which impinge upon it from culture, sub-culture, social class and other reference groups. Because of this mediating influence, and due to the economic inter-dependence of its members, family (household) decision-making has a profound influence upon purchasing and consumption behaviour. All of the basic disciplines upon which marketing is founded – anthropology, economics, psychology and sociology - have advanced their own explanation of household decision-making and there is no shortage of theories for the marketer to consider.

Thus, when marketers require information about household consumption, there is no shortage of theories to turn to. The problem confronting us is rather 'which one is the most useful in its application to the marketing of goods and services to families?' As we have noted elsewhere marketing is, by its very nature, a synthesising discipline, as are most professional practices, and the challenge for the marketing manager is to choose the explanation which appears most useful in any given context.

The question may well be raised as to how a greater knowledge of the decision-making processes can assist the marketing practitioner. Three obvious areas spring to mind:

1 *Product planning and design;*
2 *Developing and selecting Distribution channels;*
3 *Communication strategies.*

In terms of the design of household products (e.g. consumer durables) there may be a conflict between the technical perfection the design engineers and production techniques are capable of, and the needs of the eventual user. In the trade-off between efficiency and ease of use the marketer needs to know what are the important characteristics of the product as perceived by the product-user/decision-influencer. A good example of this was the heating and ventilation company which was seeking to develop a 23-function controller to out-perform the 21-function product of their nearest rival. It was accepted that the increased complexity would add to both the purchase price and servicing cost but it was felt this was justified in regaining their technical lead. The engineers were asked how many functions the owners of existing room controllers used. They didn't know! A small survey of consumers established that many people used the controller solely as an on-off switch (2 functions) and many more just to programme their heating to come on and off for 2 different time periods every day (4 functions). In other words, the design engineers had completely lost touch with the market reality.

A review of empirical studies of family decision-making reveals two major underlying currents:

1 *Ideological role theory;*
2 *The resource theory of power.*

The primary hypothesis in the **ideological theory of roles** is that household decision-making and activity patterns can be explained in terms of role expectations developed through the pervading culture. Each member of the family has a meaningful set of chores to perform – meaningful in the sense that such chores contribute to family survival and well-being.

The traditional and best-known exposition of family roles is the goal-orientated husband who 'gets things done', complemented by a supportive wife playing a social emotive role of 'keeping the family together'. Division of roles in this way generalises that husbands are responsible for decisions which are essentially concerned with the interface between the household and the external world, while wives take responsibility for activities within the family.

Although role theory has been useful to sociologists in understanding family survival in periods of social change, research into product decisions utilising role theory has been ambiguous and conflicting.

The alternative explanation of household power structure is **resource theory**. The main thesis is that authority and activity patterns within the family can be analysed in terms of such variables as income, education and social status. The right to make decisions influencing family welfare is related to the comparative resources brought to the marriage.

A resource in this context is defined as 'any special characteristic, skill or competence of one partner that contributes to family goal attainment' and embraces the following:

- Earning capacity (present and potential);
- Occupation (both partners);
- Education level;
- Religion;
- Life-style;
- Age.

From a practical point of view it is useful to try and classify the extent and nature of influence in the household decision-making unit and four basic role-structure categories may be distinguished:

1 *Husband dominant;*
2 *Wife dominant;*
3 *Autonomic* (an equal number of decisions is made by each partner but without consultation);
4 *Syncratic* (most decisions made jointly).

As suggested earlier, an ability to relate role structure category and purchase of specific products will be of great value in developing new products and the most effective marketing mix to promote and sell them. A very useful review of research in this area is to be found in Engel et al. (2001), p. 365ff.

Table 8.6 Family life-cycles

Age	Developmental level	Stage in the family life-cycle
18-34	*Early adulthood*	1 The bachelor stage: young, single people 2 Newly married couples: young, no children 3 The Full Nest I: young married couples with dependent children: (a) Youngest child under six (b) Youngest child over six
35-54	*Middle adulthood*	4 The Full Nest II: older married couple with dependent children
55 and older	*Later adulthood*	5 The Empty nest: older married couples with no children living with them: (a) Head in labour force (b) Head retired 6 The Solitary Survivors: the older single people (a) In labour force (b) Retired

Source: Reynolds, F.D. and Wells, W. D. (1977), *Consumer Behavior.* © The McGraw-Hill Companies Inc.

The physical or demographic composition of the family will also have a significant influence upon its consumption behaviour and the concept of the family life-cycle is a particularly useful framework for analysis. The most extensive model contains six stages (as shown in Table 8.6). For a very extensive analysis of the relationship between these stages and consumption behaviour the book by Reynolds and Wells contains five chapters dealing specifically with this topic. All major text books devote a chapter, or major part of one, to household/life cycle analysis although some now refer to the consumer life cycle (for example Wilkie 1994, Chapter 14) recognising that the traditional family is less typical than it used to be. Many research organisations have developed distinctive approaches to life cycle analysis and examples are to be found in *The Marketing Pocket Book* (2005) (See Life-style in the next section.)

Life-style

So far the discussion has focused upon major sociological concepts which have been borrowed and adapted by marketers in seeking to explain and predict consumer behaviour. We now consider a composite concept which has been developed extensively by consumer-behaviour researchers during the 1970s and early 1980s that seeks to synthesise the economic, psychological and sociological influences, namely 'lifestyle'.

In essence life-style summarises the way in which we live and is founded upon the observation that people seek consistency or balance in their lives – the old concept of homeostasis – and so organise their behaviour to try and achieve this state. We have already noticed this tendency in discussing the concepts of perception, personality and motivation, and observed how it becomes socialised in cultural traits, norms and values. Given this tendency towards consistency in behavioural response it follows that if we can identify a consumer life-style in one context, then we should be able to extrapolate from that situation and predict how they will behave in different sets of circumstances.

The measurement of life-style in the subject of an area of research known as psychographics is discussed at length in Engel et al. (1987). An excellent overview of the subject is also to be found in an article by William D. Wells (1975), 'Psychographics: A Critical Review'. In this article Wells proposes an operational definition of psychographic research as 'quantitative research intended to place consumers on psychological – as distinguished from demographic – dimensions', a definition which emphasises the distinctive features of the area – it has a quantitative rather than a qualitative orientation and goes beyond demographics. (Engel et al. point out that 'psychographics' is often used interchangeably with the mnemonic AIO standing for Activities, Interests and Opinions as a research area.) The use of life-style for segmenting consumer markets is discussed in more detail in Chapter 10.

COMPOSITE MODELS OF CONSUMER BEHAVIOUR

For many years prominent researchers in the consumer-behaviour field have attempted to develop comprehensive theories of consumer behaviour. In *Marketing: Theory and Practice* (1983), my colleague Jennifer Drayton summarised a number of the more important models – those of Nicosia, Andreasen, Engel, Kollat and Blackwell, Clawson, and Howard and Sheth – as follows:

> *These models differ in respect to their complexity and orientation but are nevertheless based upon the same strands of thought. Thus similarities are to be found in the isolation and identification of the relevant variables, and in the perspective of a dynamic decision process, with the actions of the consumer viewed as a movement towards some decision point. Although little or no attempt has been made to modify or update these models they still represent an important step in the development of our understanding of consumer behaviour.*

Basically, it is possible to identify two broad paradigms or models of consumer behaviour which may be distinguished respectively as the cognitive and behavioural explanations.

In essence the **cognitive explanation** sees consumer behaviour as the consequence of an interpersonal, cognitive, information processing activity which results in choice as the outcome of deliberation and decision-making. By contrast the **behavioural paradigm** regards choice behaviour as the consequence of prior behaviour and sees choice decisions as the consequence of determined responses to environmental stimuli (G. R. Foxall 2003).

Most major models such as those of Nicosia, Engel, Kollat and Blackwell, Howard and Sheth fall into the cognitive category and 'depict the consumer advancing along a problem-solving and decision-making sequence, the outcome of which is determined by the buyer's intellectual functioning and rational processing of information. Consumers are credited with the capacity to receive and handle quantities of information as they engage in extensive pre-purchase searches and evaluations. Further, the consumer is viewed as perceiving information critically, using decision rules and evaluative criteria to establish its personal relevance to his goals and purposes, while generally employing mental processes to reach a decision' (Shams 1989). Subscribers to cognitive explanations of consumer behaviour regard marketer initiated communications as vital cues or stimuli which make consumers aware of needs and wants and of possible solutions to these felt needs.

Thus, as Foxall (1987) has pointed out 'choice is essentially the resolution of conflict, brought about by awareness of a number of options, through cognitive evaluation of the possibilities available and a reasoned consideration of the costs and benefits which each entails'.

In her review of cognitive explanations, Shams (1989) points out that numerous authors have criticised this approach and quotes Markin and Narayana (1976) who concluded that most empirical research points to an opposite conclusion; namely, that consumers:

1 Do not seek extensive amounts of information in relation to purchase and consumption problems;

2 Do not process large amounts of information when confronted with purchase and consumption problems; and

3 Do not appear to engage in extensive problem-solving behaviour even in relation to high expenditure purchases.

– all conclusions reached by Keith Fletcher (1986) in his doctoral research 'Social Behaviour: an analysis of information and usage during the decision process'.

As a result of the criticisms of the cognitive school there has developed a renewed interest in behavioural explanations. Two main schools may be distinguished – **classical conditioning** and **operant conditioning**. Classical conditioning was referred to in the section on Learning earlier in the chapter and is usually associated with Ivan Pavlov's experiments with dogs in which he showed that a physiological response – salivation on the presentation of food – could be conditioned by the simultaneous presentation of a second stimulus – the ringing of a bell – such that a dog could be conditioned to salivate on the ringing of the bell alone. Operant conditioning is associated with the work of B. F. Skinner who argued that 'behaviour is shaped by its consequences' and so emphasises actions under the conscious control of the individual by contrast with involuntary responses of the kind studied by Pavlov. Further, operant conditioning is focused on consequences which follow behaviour while classical conditioning emphasises stimuli which precede behaviour. As noted earlier in the chapter, we learn patterns of behaviour based upon the level of satisfaction we derive. Thus satisfactory outcomes reinforce a pattern of behaviour while unsatisfactory outcomes (punishers) dissuade us from repeating such behaviour in future.

It follows that once a consumer has determined a satisfactory pattern of behaviour then s/he will continue to repeat that behaviour until it either causes dissatisfaction ('familiarity breeds contempt') or s/he becomes aware of a stimulus which suggests that a modified form of behaviour could lead to even greater satisfaction. In an attempt to accommodate both the cognitive/rational and behavioural explanations of consumer choice – both of which have clear merits and weaknesses – a composite model of buying behaviour is proposed.

Baker's composite model of buying behaviour

As noted in the introduction to this chapter there is a tendency to distinguish between individual and organisational buying behaviour by emphasising the qualitative/behavioural nature of the former and the quantitative/rational/ economic nature of the latter. In my view this distinction is largely spurious as I believe that all buying decisions are subject to the same economic and behavioural influences, and in the majority of cases follow the same basic process. This process is best observed by analysing the purchase of a product of which the user has no prior experience, for otherwise several stages may be omitted, that is the purchase of a familiar brand, or the automatic re-ordering of an industrial supply.

For a number of years now I have been developing a composite model of buying behaviour which attempts to combine both economic and behavioural factors as well as capturing the essentially sequential nature of buying decisions. The current version of the model is illustrated by Figure 8.5.

In the model:

P = a Purchase
F = a Function (unspecified)
S = a Stimulus or Stimuli
SP = Selective Perception
FN = Felt Need (Awareness)
EC = Enabling Conditions
IS = Information Search (Interest)

CBA = *Cost Benefit Analysis (Desire)*
BR = *Behavioural Response (Action)*
PPE = *Post Purchase Evaluation*

In the Pavlovian or learning model of Buyer Behaviour, reference is made to the need for some cue or stimulus to activate a drive and initiate action. In our model, this factor is placed at the very beginning of the equation on the basis that we are all constantly surrounded by external stimuli as well as being subject to our own internal stimuli. As described earlier these stimuli are screened selectively through the process of a selective perception. Those recognised and consciously attended to are defined as **FN** or **'felt need'**.

Once the need has been identified the next step is to establish whether or not there is a means of satisfying this need. This we have identified in our model

Figure 8.5 Baker's composite model of buying behaviour

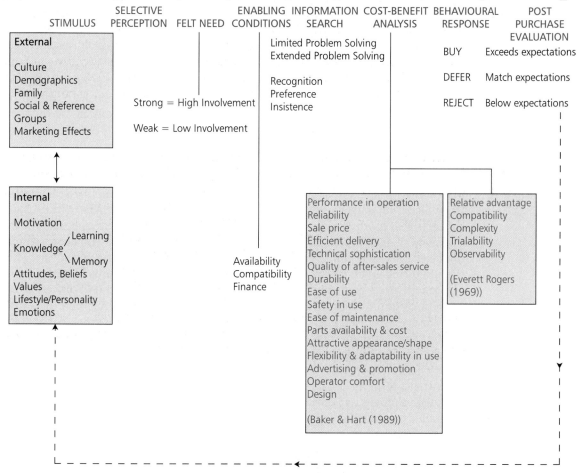

$$P = fS \ [SP \ (FN, EC, IS, CBA, BR) \ PPE]$$

as 'enabling conditions' or EC. Enabling conditions embraces all those factors which make it possible for a prospective purchaser to benefit from satisfying a felt need. The television is of no use if you have no electricity, nor a gas oven if you have no gas. Similarly, many manufacturers try to avoid mixing materials such as steel, aluminium and plastics, since each requires different skills and techniques in use and increases the investment necessary in both plant and labour. In other words, an object being considered for purchase must be compatible with the users current status and, in many cases, also with their self-image. In the absence of such enabling conditions, interest is likely to be short-lived and unlikely to proceed further to an evaluation.

Having identified the need, and establishing that this appears to be compatible with one's existing status, the next step will be to verify and validate this by collecting and evaluating further information - IS or information search in the model. Clearly, the nature and extent of this search will depend greatly upon a number of factors including the novelty of the object under consideration, the risk perceived in the decision, and the number and availability of means of satisfying the need. In the case of complex innovations with which one has no prior experience one is likely to engage in extended information gathering, especially where high prices are involved. Conversely, faced with a new brand of low cost convenience good it is unlikely one will spend much time in seeking additional information beyond that available at the point of sale.

While the next element, Cost Benefit Analysis (CBA), is placed after Information Search in the model in many cases this analysis will proceed in parallel with the gathering of information and be used to determine whether to consider or reject it. The inclusion of this factor is explicit recognition of the economic or rational school of buyer behaviour that views purchase decisions as the outcome of a careful comparison of the performance factors associated with a purchase and the price asked for any given combination of attributes.

As we have noted earlier, in the case of individual buyer behaviour decisions are frequently made *without* the extended and careful consideration implicit in the Marshallian or 'economic' model . On the other hand where more than one person is involved, or where an individual is acting on behalf of others, the evidence suggests that more attention will be given to spelling out performance factors and assessing their cost benefit. Even so, it is important to recognise that cost benefit, like selective perception, introduces significant subjectivity into the analysis. Thus the weighting given to individual performance factors or features in determining the benefit to be gained will vary from one individual to another. Further, as the concept of diminishing marginal returns makes clear, our perception of benefit will change as we acquire more of something, and also over time. It is for these reasons that no single function can capture or reflect the interaction between the variables in the model. Similarly, in order to apply the model one has to examine every decision in its own context.

In the case of an organisation considering the acquisition of a major piece of capital equipment, it is likely that considerable effort will be given to drawing up a detailed specification of the attributes or performance factors looked for. This specification will then be used to compare competitive offerings and the overall cost benefit calculated with apparently great precision. On the other hand people buy cars and houses which, proportionately, represent a much higher risk with little formal evaluation of more than a small number of key attributes that matter to them.

Initially, most people tend to think of **Performance Factors** in terms of *objective* or tangible criteria but, as the burgeoning literature on service quality shows, the term also embraces *subjective* or intangible factors too. A recent article by Woodall (2001) indicates how both dimensions are considered in purchase decisions.

Woodall cites Grönroos (1984) who, in turn, follows the suggestion of Swan and Comb that service *products* have both 'instrumental' and 'expressive' outcomes. This leads Grönroos to state that a 'satisfactory performance' in terms of the instrumental outcomes "is a prerequisite for a satisfied customer". According to Woodall, Grönroos' deconstruction of service quality led him to conclude that its principal components were technical quality, functional quality, and corporate image – the latter primarily determined by both conventional and emergent marketing techniques, but also substantially dependent upon both expectations and perceptions regarding the first two.

The penultimate variable in our model is **Behavioural Response**. At its simplest this is the action taken after completing the cost benefit analysis – to buy, defer the decision, or to reject the offer. However, our Behavioural Response may also require us to reconsider all of the preceding stages in the process. This is likely to occur when our evaluation has not identified an option that is clearly to be preferred to all others. In most competitive markets this is a common occurrence as sellers seek to ensure that their offers at least match those of the competition in terms of the price and performance factors. Indeed, choice in a competitive market means just that – the availability of more than one closely matched alternative. Of course the practices of segmentation, targeting and positioning are intended to resolve this problem by pre-identifying differences between potential customers, and then adapting the object to the specific needs of the targeted buyer. Where successful this will have influenced the perception of benefits, and the buyers response. Where unsuccessful the potential buyer will be left with a choice between two apparently identical objects, and so need to reconsider the earlier stages in order to reach a decision.

NEUROMARKETING

A study reported in the *New Scientist* in July 2005 suggests why despite the fact that in blind taste tests more people prefer Pepsi than Coke, more people drink Coke than Pepsi.

Using functional magnetic resonance imaging to scan consumers brains revealed that different areas of the brain were involved when conducting the tests. In the blind taste tests when drinking the cola they said they preferred there was more activity in a region of the brain called the ventral putamen which is associated with reward seeking mechanisms.

However, when told the identity of the cola, more activity was detected in the prefrontal cortex which is an area associated with higher thinking. This led to the conclusion that; "The results show that people make decisions based on their memories or impressions of a particular soda, as well as taste".

The findings have significant implications for marketing. To begin with they demonstrate that the assumption behind surveys, that people can accurately report reasons for their preferences, is flawed. Science shows that a great deal of what influences our preferences is unconscious. It also shows that promotion leading to brand recognition may have a significant impact on our actual purchase behaviour. Although in its infancy the new field of study termed '**neuromarketing**' has potentially major implications for marketing practice.

Finally, we have included another new variable in the current model – **Post Purchase Evaluation** or **PPE**. By doing so we acknowledge the importance of experiential learning which, in turn, will either reinforce or modify our attitudes, beliefs and values and through them our selective perception and future behaviour. In other words, as the current concern for customer relationship management makes clear, buying must be conceived of as a circular process with feedback loops. Despite this it is still believed that the linear process model provides a helpful conceptual and analytical framework to help marketers understand better how buyers choose.

Finally, however, it must always be remembered that the majority of buying decisions turn on highly specific characteristics – another reason why a general model cannot possibly accommodate all conceivable sets of circumstances.

We have already stipulated that the importance of behavioural response will depend heavily upon the objective evaluation of the available facts (albeit that these are perceived subjectively), and 'build a better product at an equivalent price or an equivalent product at a lower price' is clearly the best advice to management. But, in most competitive markets, there is often little to choose objectively between alternative offerings, and the buyer will have to make deliberate recourse to subjective value judgements to assist in distinguishing between the various items available. Because housewives do this daily when preferring Bold to Persil, Sunblest to Mother's Pride and so on and so forth, they are often characterised as choosing irrationally. Nothing could be further from the truth. The important objective decisions about a shopping basket relate to its overall mix and composition vis-à-vis the available budget the choice decision is which detergent, which bread, and so on. It would be a fatal mistake to imagine that the industrial buyer doesn't have just the same problems when deciding between Scania, Mercedes, or Leyland for his lorries or Cincinnati and/or Kearney and Trecker for his machine tools.

Summary

This chapter has ranged over a very wide area that is the subject of many substantial books in their own right. Its purpose has been to sensitise the reader to factors which influence behaviour in the market-place, but a full appreciation must depend upon extensive study of the major sources cited.

The chapter opened with a simple and generalised model of the **buying decision process** as the basis for a brief review of some of the major factors which are involved in and influence the process. Thus we looked at perception, learning, motivation, personality and attitudes as psychological factors. Next, we examined social influences on behaviour, including culture, social class, reference groups, role and family influences and the concept of life-style. This was followed by the proposal of a **composite model of buyer behaviour** designed to provide a simplified but synoptic explanation of the process.

While this is seen as helpful in an introductory textbook, it must be stressed that 'consumer behaviour' has developed into a major sub-field of marketing with many distinctive themes of its own. An overview of the subject and the evolution of consumer research is contained in a literature review published in *The Marketing Review* (Pachauri, 2002) that can be accessed on the book's website.

In the next chapter we look at buying behaviour in an organisational setting.

Review questions and problems

1 Attitudes have a central role in the development of behavioural patterns. Explain the use of attitude studies as a guide to the marketing practitioner.

2 Consider the value of the life-style concept as an approach to market segmentation.

3 The main alternative to problem-solving behaviour is habitual behaviour. Discuss the application of these patterns of behaviour to the market-place.

4 Measures of social class have been both valuable and misleading as an aid to market segmentation. Discuss the use of social class, and the possibilities offered by the addition of complementary psychographic techniques.

5 Should the marketer assume that organisational buying decisions are always based upon rational/economic considerations?

6 What do you understand by the term 'Learning'? Briefly outline any one learning theory and discuss its relevance to an understanding of consumer behaviour.

7 Maslow's theory of motivation postulates five general types of needs. Define these needs and explain with examples how their economic importance can be exploited by advertising.

8 Culture has a pervasive influence on consumption patterns. Discuss the implications of cultural factors in new product diffusion.

9 Why do groups have such a considerable influence on individual consumer behaviour? What are the implications of this for product promotion and advertising?

10 Explain how an understanding of how consumers make decisions might aid the marketer in developing a strategy.

11 Discuss the relationship between social class membership and consumption patterns.

12 Examine the view that psychological explanations of consumer behaviour may be useful theories but they are of little practical value to the marketer.

13 What are attitudes? Can they be changed? What is the relevance of attitudes to communications, advertising and marketing?

14 'The consumer is not the completely rational animal dreamed up by the classical economists and fondly termed "Economic Man" (Shanks). To what extent do you agree, and give reasons for your viewpoint.

15 In what way can a knowledge of the Behavioural Sciences (Sociology, Psychology) help the marketing/advertising executive to have a better understanding of consumer choices and purchasing behaviour?

16 Homogeneous products are for homogeneous consumers. Discuss.

17 Explain what is meant by the consumer buying decision process. Why is it important for marketers to understand the influencing factors at each stage of the process?

18 Explain how the various stages of the consumer decision-making process vary according to whether the product being chosen is classified as high involvement or low involvement.

19 Define the concept of attitudes. Describe, using a real product, strategies marketers could use to change negative attitudes which consumers may hold about their products.

20 Discuss the significance of the family in consumer behaviour.

Key terms

attitude
Baker's composite model of buying
   behaviour
behavioural paradigm
behavioural response
business to business marketing
buying decision process
chunking
classical conditioning
cognitive explanation
cognitive school
cognitive-affective-conative (CAC)
collective consumption
conscious / subconscious selectivity
consumption behaviour
cost benefit analysis (CBA)
distributive, organisation and
   normative dimensions
enabling conditions (EC)
expectancy value (EV)
extensive problem solving
family life-cycles
felt need (FN)
formal group

functional factors
gestalt explanation of learning
halo influence
homeostasis
ideological theory of roles
informal group
information search (IS)
inventing / thinking /
   memorising
lifestyle
limited problem solving
long-term memory
marketer-dominated sources
means-end chain
motivation
motivation research (MR)
needs
neuromarketing
not-for-profit
operant conditioning
opinion leaders
opportunity cost
organisational buying
   behaviour (OBB)

originator
perception
perceptual mapping
performance factors
personality
post purchase evaluation (PPE)
preparatory set
psychological influences
receiver
reference groups
resource theory
schema
selective exposure
selective perception
sensation
sensory memory (SM)
short-term memory
social class
stimulus factors
stimulus-response school
thematic apperception tests
   (TAT)

Supplementary reading list

Blackwell, R. D., Miniard, P. W., and Engel, J. F. (2001) *Consumer Behavior*, 9th edn (London: Dryden Press).,

Desmond, J. (2003), *Consumer Behaviour*, (Basingstoke: Palgrave Macmillan)

Foxall, G. R. (2005), *Understanding Consumer Choice*, (Basingstoke: Palgrave Macmillan)

Foxall G. R. (2003), 'Consumer decision-making: process, level and style, in Baker M. J. (ed.), *The Marketing Book* 5th edn., (Oxford: Butterworth-Heinemann).

ORGANISATIONAL BUYING BEHAVIOUR

Learning Goals *After reading this chapter you should be able to:*

- Explain the nature of organisational buying behaviour.

- Describe the similarities and differences between consumer buying behaviour and organisational buying behaviour.

- Make it clear why organisational buying is important.

- Outline the key concepts in organisational buying behaviour.

- Spell out the factors which influence organisational buying behaviour.

- Define what is meant by 'an interaction approach' to organisational buying behaviour.

- Describe the role of the purchasing function and explain the main reasons for its increased importance.

- Summarise some distinguishing features of business to business marketing.

INTRODUCTION

In the preceding chapter the emphasis was on individual behaviour and the influence and consequences of this in terms of buying or consumption decisions. In this chapter our attention is focused upon the way the same individuals behave when faced with the responsibility of acting on behalf of an organisation, and often as part of a **decision making unit (DMU)** or buying group.

At the outset it must be stressed that in exactly the same way that it was argued that while one can discern many differences between the marketing of consumer and industrial goods it is important not to overlook the similarities, so in the case of individual and organisational buying behaviour one must be careful not to overlook the fact that the process is the same. Thus the generalised model of buying behaviour presented at the end of

Chapter 8 is believed to be just as applicable to both individual and group buying decisions, although it is immediately acknowledged that groups may undertake a much more formal and rigorous approach than do most individuals.

In our Introduction to the preceding chapter we explained that many researchers and authors now refer to business to business marketing to emphasise differences between organisational buying and individual buying behaviour. For the reasons given we prefer to stick with **organisational buying behaviour (OBB)** as this includes a wider spectrum of organisations than businesses – a view shared by Wilkie (1994) who includes OBB as a 'special topic' in his Chapter 21. The purpose of this chapter, therefore, is to identify and describe some of the more salient features of organisational buying behaviour and point out the similarities and differences between it and individual behaviour.

To this end we shall first review the better known models which seek to describe and analyse the nature of the organisational buying process. Having established a broad framework which defines the general process, we shall then look more closely at some of the more important constituent elements beginning with the composition and activities of the buying group, together with the influence of various factors – organisational, environmental and product-related upon these activities. Next, we introduce the ideas of interaction and networks developed by the IMP Group, which are the basis of most organisational exchange behaviour, and then examine some of the reasons behind the greater importance attached to the purchasing function in recent years. Finally, we review briefly some of the characteristics of business to business marketing.

MODELS OF ORGANISATIONAL BUYING BEHAVIOUR

One of the first serious attempts to impose some structure upon the wealth of descriptive material about industrial buying behaviour was provided by Frederick Webster Jr (1965) in an article entitled 'Modelling the Industrial Buying Process'. In an effort to distinguish the important variables and the relationships between then, Webster proposed four key areas – **Problem Recognition**, the assignment of **Buying Responsibility**, the nature of the **Search Process** and the nature of the **Choice Process**, with the inference that these are sequential steps in the overall buying process.

According to Webster a buying situation is created by the recognition that there is a difference between an organisation's goals and its performance which may be remedied or solved through a purchase. In that both goal setting and problem recognition are influenced by personal and impersonal factors, both internal and external to the organisation, it follows that these have to be identified and analysed if we are to understand organisational buying decisions. In terms of the personal factors it has to be remembered that ultimately the organisational decision will be delegated to individuals, and the allocation of this responsibility will be influenced by individual, company, product, industry and market factors, so these too must be specified and understood. These same factors will also influence both the search and choice processes.

The next important contribution to the OBB literature was provided by the publication of *Industrial Buying and Creative Marketing* by P. J. Robinson, C. W. Faris and Yoram Wind (1967), which reported the results of a project sponsored by the

Marketing Science Institute. Based upon in-depth studies of three companies in the United States over a two-year period, Robinson, Faris and Wind proposed that industrial buying may be conceived of as a process consisting of eight sequential steps or buy-phases, namely:

1 *The anticipation or recognition of a problem or need*, including the realisation that a problem exists, and the awareness that a solution may be possible through a purchase of an industrial good.

2 *The determination of the quality and characteristics of the needed item.*

3 *The specific description of the item needed.*

4 *The search for, and qualification of, potential sources.*

5 *The examination of the sources*, leading to a decision concerning how the item is to be purchased.

Figure 9.1 The buygrid analytic framework for industrial buying situations

	BUY CLASSES		
	New Task	Modified Rebuy	Straight Rebuy
1 Anticipation or Recognition of a problem (Need) and a General Solution			
2. Determination of Characteristics and Quantity of Needed item			
3. Description of Characteristics and Quantity of Needed item			
4. Search for and Qualification of Potential Sources			
5. Acquisition and Analysis of Proposals			
6. Evaluation of Proposals and Selection of Supplier(s)			
7. Selection of an Order Routine			
8. Performance Feedback and Evaluation			

Source: Robinson, R. J. and Stidsen, B. (1967), *Selling in a Modern Perspective* (Boston: Allyn & Bacon).

6 *The evaluation of proposals and the selection of suppliers.*

7 *Selection of an order routine.*

8 *Performance feedback and evaluation.*

In addition, Robinson, Faris and Wind identified three distinct buy-classes, which may be defined as follows:

1 *New task* – the recognition of a purchasing problem which has not been encountered previously. The buyer will face considerable uncertainty and will seek to reduce this through the acquisition of as much information as he can obtain from both personal and impersonal sources. All the buy-phases are likely to receive careful and explicit attention.

2 *Modified rebuy* – the buyer has prior experience of the purchase problem but has reason to re-evaluate this in light of some new information or precipitative circumstance, for example a lower bid from another supplier, a change in design or specification, and so forth. Some of the buy-phases may be truncated or omitted.

3 *Straight rebuy* – the buyer is satisfied with an existing source of supply and sees no reason to change. Phases 4–7 are likely to be omitted altogether and only cursory attention given to the others; that is purchase has become habitual and routinised.

Buy-phases

While the Robinson, Faris and Wind model may appear simplistic by comparison with other, later models it possesses the particular strength that it is straightforward, robust and accords well with best practice. The model also draws attention to the sequential nature of buying decisions and invites us to consider whether the different phases are likely to involve different kinds of decisions and different members of the buying group. If so, then clearly one will need to modify one's selling tactics as the process unfolds.

As Kennedy (1983) reported, a number of empirical studies which have analysed industrial buying decisions confirm the existence of such a process which has been characterised by the various authors as follows.

In his study of over forty capital equipment purchases, T. J. Hillier (see Hill and Hillier, 1977, *Organisational Buying Behaviour*) suggested a 4-phase model:

1 *The precipitation decision stage* – when a definite course of action to solve a problem is confirmed.

2 *The product specification stage* – when broad solutions to a problem are translated into specific hardware and software requirements.

3 *The supplier selection stage* – when potential suppliers are identified and one or more selected.

4 *The commitment decision stage* – when a customer decides to what extent a supplier has fulfilled its expectation.

Such a sequence suggests that each purchase decision commenced de novo without prior experience on either side (as do the other buy-phase models). In reality, of course, buyers and sellers tend to interact and build up relationships with each other over time so that a more correct representation of the process is provided by the diagram of Figure 9.2.

Gordon T. Brand (1972) in *The Industrial Buying Decision*, proposed an 8-step model very similar to the original one of Robinson et al. (1967) namely:

1 *Problem recognition;*
2 *Determine characteristics of needed items;*
3 *Specific description;*
4 *Search for potential supplier;*
5 *Evaluate sources and products;*
6 *Select supplier;*
7 *Establish order routine;*
8 *Evaluate feedback.*

With regard to the question of who might be involved in each of these stages, this provided the focus for the *Financial Times* survey mentioned earlier in which the following questions were asked:

1 Who originates the initial decision?
2 Who surveys alternatives and determines the basic characteristics of the product required?
3 Who makes the final decision?

Figure 9.2 The cycle of industrial-buying decisions

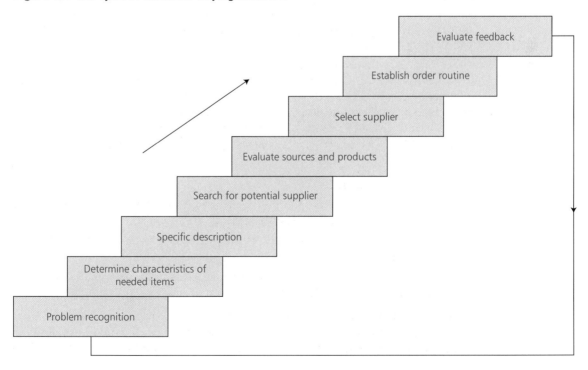

4 Who identifies the potential suppliers?

5 Who collects tenders/information from suppliers?

6 Who evaluates products offered?

7 Who authorises the purchase?

8 Who finally chooses the supplier?

9 Who monitors and evaluates the performance of both the product and the supplier?

10 Who is most likely to initiate the decisions to change supplier?

11 Who finally decides on a change in supplier and selects the new supplier?

This survey established that a wide range of participants are involved in a purchase decision. During the 1980s, an international group of researchers

Figure 9.3 Comparison of buying classes

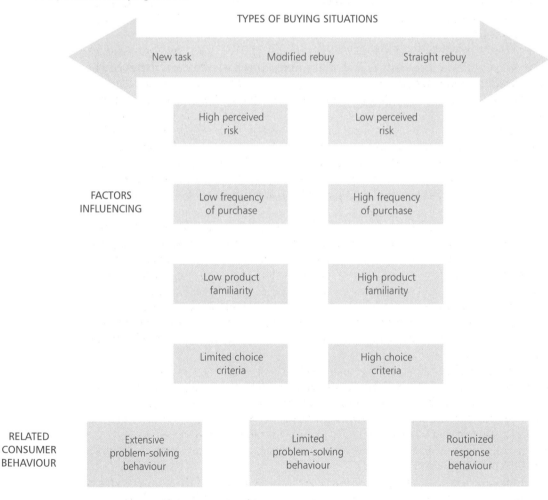

Source: Rajagopal, S. (1995), Ch. 5 in Baker, M. J. (ed.), *Marketing: Theory and Practice*, 3rd edn (London: Macmillan).

from six countries (including the author) undertook a series of in-depth case analyses of specific buying decisions in a variety of industries and settings in an attempt to determine more precisely the decision and behavioural routines in the organisational buying process. The findings of this research were published in 1986 (Parkinson and Baker, *Organisational Buying Behaviour*) and confirmed that processual interaction models best capture the organisational purchasing decision. The research also confirmed that the composite model presented in the previous chapter is equally applicable to both individual and group buying decisions.

By combining **Buy-phases** and **Buy-classes** we obtain the **Buy-grid** as depicted in Figure 9.1.

As noted, this framework may appear simplistic by comparison with the more complex and sophisticated models developed since. However, this is seen as its greatest strength, for it is relatively easy to recall, and by classifying the kind of buying decision and the stage in the process one can quickly focus attention on the key factors which apply to that location in the grid; for example, for most straight rebuys one can establish routines and procedures for automatic ordering from qualified suppliers provided that previous orders have met the predetermined requirements. In *Marketing: Theory and Practice*, Shan Rajagopal (1995) provides a useful comparison of buying classes which is reproduced as Figure 9.3.

The next important contribution to modelling OBB was that of Frederick Webster Jr and Yoram Wind (1972) who joined forces to offer 'A General Model for Understanding Organisational Buying Behaviour'. Diagrammatically this model appears as in Figure 9.4 and may be explained as follows. Organisational buying is a decision-making process carried out by individuals, in interaction with other people, in the context of a formal organisation which is subject to a variety of environmental forces. Thus the factors which impinge on and influence OBB may be classified as individual, social, organisational and environmental. In turn each of these factors may be categorised as comprising task variables, which are directly related to the specific buying problem, and non-task variables which are not.

The earlier work of the authors is readily identified in their joint model which conceives of OBB as a complex process involving many persons, multiple goals and potentially conflicting decision criteria. The process may extend over a considerable period of time, demand large amounts of information from many diverse sources and require numerous inter-organisational relationships. At the heart of the process is the buying centre which includes all members of the organisation who may be involved in the various roles of user, influencer, decider, buyer and gatekeeper (the person or persons who control the flow of information into the buying centre).

Members of the buying centre are subject to both individual and organisational goals and so their relationships encompass all the complexity of interpersonal interaction which the organisation seeks to structure, influence and control through the subsystems of tasks, structures, technology, and people. Finally, the organisation has to operate within the constraints and opportunities of the environment and the economic, technological, physical, political, legal and cultural forces which comprise it.

As Hill and Hillier (1977) point out, the main deficiency of the actual model is that it conveys a static rather than a dynamic impression, although this is partly compensated for in their description of it. Hill and Hillier also criticise the model as

Figure 9.4 The Webster & Wind model for understanding organisational buying behaviour

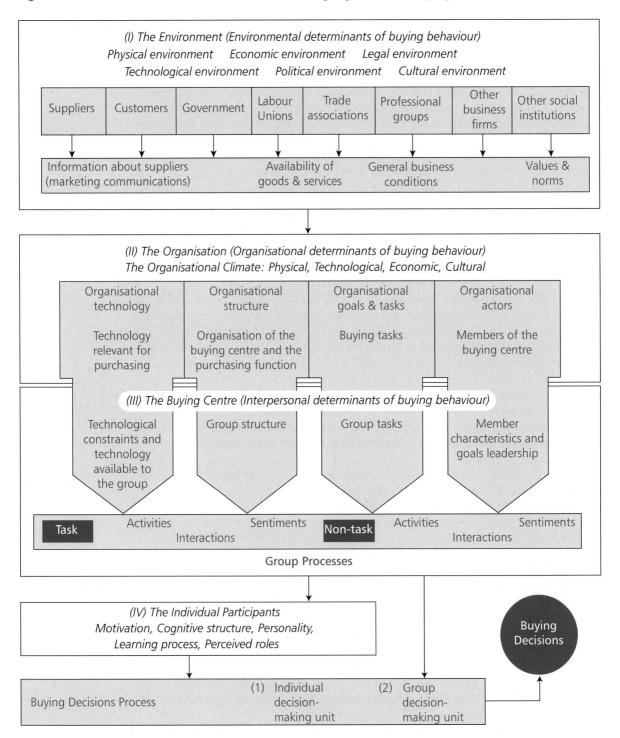

Source: American Marketing Association. Webster F. and Wind Y. (1972), 'A General Model for Understanding Organisational Buying Behaviour', *Journal of Marketing* (April), Vol. 36, 2, pp.12-14

Figure 9.5 The Sheth integrative model of industrial buying behaviour

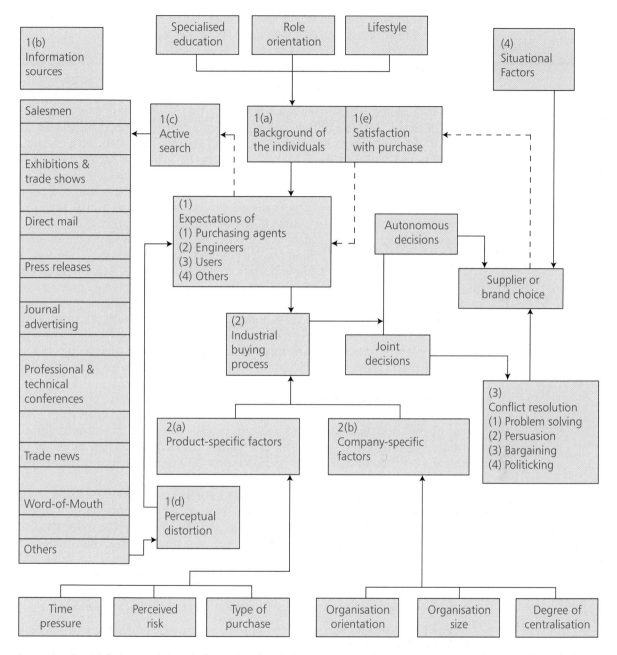

Source: American Marketing Association. Sheth, J. N. (1973), 'A Model of Industrial Buyer Behaviour', *Journal of Marketing*, October, Vol. 37, 4, pp.50-6.

'a basic skeleton of organisational buying behaviour, without any muscles or nerves', but clearly it is more complex and comprehensive than the Robinson, Faris and Wind model discussed previously. This is even more true of 'A Model of Industrial Buyer Behaviour' proposed by Jagdish N. Sheth (1973), which is summarised in Figure 9.5.

According to Sheth, OBB comprises three distinct dimensions:

1 *The psychological world of the decision-makers.*
2 *The conditions which determine joint decisions among and between these individuals.*
3 *The process of joint decision-making and conflict resolution among decision-makers.*

In terms of the first dimension it is recognised that most industrial buying decisions are made by a number of people from different backgrounds and performing different roles – Purchasing agents, Engineers, Users and Others in Box (1) of the model. The differential expectations of these individuals is seen as the result of their background (1a), information sources (1b), their active search (1c), and perceptual distortion (1d) of these sources and their satisfaction with past purchases (1e). These expectations are modified by product specific factors (2a) such as time pressure, perceived risk and the type of purchase, and company specific factors (2b) such as organisational orientation, organisational size and degree of centralisation in the course of the industrial buying process Box itself.

The third dimension and central concern of Sheth's model is how the different participants in the buying decision resolve potential conflicts between themselves arising from their different roles, expectations and perceptions. Box (3) suggests four different approaches to conflict resolution – problem solving, persuasion, bargaining, and politicking. However, in the course of arriving at their joint decision a number of ad hoc situational factors Box (4) such as temporary economic conditions, industrial relations problems, production bottlenecks and so on will play an important part. Recognition of these factors clearly injects the dynamism absent from the Webster and Wind model and so makes it more useful in an operational sense.

Since Sheth's and Webster and Wind's attempts to provide a comprehensive model of OBB the emphasis has shifted to a much more detailed analysis of how actual buying decisions are made and the precise nature of the various forces and influences involved – what Hill and Hillier characterise as 'the anatomy of a purchase', although they use this description in a narrower way than implied here.

The Hill and Hillier model is intended to analyse a purchase decision from the perspective of the buyer, and contains three major elements – usage of the purchased item, reasons for the purchase, and the purchase complexity. The intended use for the proposed purchase is seen as a vital piece of information to the seller, because it will indicate the technical content involved, the value and essentiality of the item, and therefore the degree of risk involved; the likely timing of the purchase; and whether the product is more likely to be buyer or supplier specified. Hill and Hillier then propose five main categories of use as follows:

1 For incorporation in production output, which may be to order or to stock and, in the latter case, production may be either batch or continuous;
2 For utilisation during the production processes but not incorporated in the product;
3 To provide a production facility in either manufacture, service or resale;
4 For use in maintenance operations;
5 For use in development or engineering work.

Basic reasons for purchase are summarised in the diagram and will have a significant influence upon the criteria used in arriving at a decision. This is also true of the complexity of the purchase which builds upon distinctions made by Lehmann and O'Shaughnessy (1974) who argued that 'if products could be classified on the basis of problems inherent in their adoption, such a classification might be both predictive of weightings of the relative importance of product/ supplier attributes, and predictive of buyer preferences with regard to suppliers'. Four categories are then proposed which Hill and Hillier summarise as:

1 *Routine order products* which are frequently ordered, and present no significant usage problems because everybody is familiar with them, and it is known that they can 'do the job'.
2 *Procedural-problem products*, which are known 'to do the job', but problems may arise because personnel must he taught how to use them.
3 *Performance-problem products*, where the problem concerns the technical outcome of using the products.
4 *Political-problem products*, where there is likely to be difficulty in reaching agreement among those affected if the purchase is made. This kind of problem arises when large capital outlays are involved, and more frequently when the products are an input to several departments whose needs may not be compatible.

This classification goes beyond Robinson et al.'s novelty of purchase buy-classes, and also differs in that the four categories are not seen as mutually exclusive but indeed may overlap with one another.

According to Daragh O'Reilly (1995), more recent research by Bunn (1993) has suggested that the number of basic buying situations could be increased to six.

Bunn's view was that organisational buying is affected by situational characteristics and buying activities. Situational characteristics were basically four in number:

■ *Purchase importance*: the buyer's perception of the significance of the buying decision in terms of the size of the purchase and/or the potential impact of the purchase on the functioning of the firm;
■ *Task uncertainty*: the buyer's perceived lack of information relevant to a decision situation;
■ *Extensiveness of choice set*: the buyer's perception of the breadth of alternatives available as choices in the context of a particular decision situation;
■ *Perceived buyer power*: the buyer's perception of the firm's negotiating strength in a particular buying decision situation.

Buying activities, what buyers actually do when making buying decisions, could be broken down into four principal categories:

■ *Search for information*: the buyer's effort at scanning the internal and external business environment to identify and monitor information sources relevant to the focal buying decision;
■ *Use of analysis techniques*: the extent to which the buyer makes use of formal and/or quantitative tools to objectively evaluate aspects of the buying decision;

- *Proactive focusing*: the extent to which decision-making related to the focal purchase is prospective and thus considers the strategic objectives and long-range needs of the firm;
- *Procedural control*: the extent to which the evaluation of a buying decision is guided by established policies, procedures or transaction precedents.

The research revealed six different categories of buying decision approach (situation), as follows:

- *Casual*: involves no search, no analysis, no strategic view and a lot of procedural control, low-value items – for example: an electricity supply firm buys a relay for repair purposes;
- *Routine low priority*: basically a repeat buy, checking to make sure nothing new is on the market;
- *Simple modified rebuy*: likely to involve essential items for which the buyer perceives a limited number of options available;
- *Judgemental new task*: first-time purchase of a special type of equipment;
- *Complex modified rebuy*: a structured and rational process, extensive quantitative analysis; for example a competitive bidding process;
- *Strategic new task*: focus on long-term planning, infrequent purchase, may involve different departments, can be a lengthy process.

The benefits of this research is the greater fine tuning of the buying decision approach – indeed, the use of the term 'buying decision approach' instead of 'buying situation' is an important clarifying point. So also is the definition of the key buying activities and situational characteristics separately from the situation. When combined Bunn's Taxonomy appears as in Table 9.1.

ORGANISATIONAL BUYING BEHAVIOUR AS AN INTERACTIVE PROCESS

Thus far all the models of organisational buying behaviour we have discussed have been uni-dimensional in the sense that they have looked exclusively at behaviour and processes within the customer organisation. Over the past thirty years (since the mid-1970s) the deficiencies of such an approach have been increasingly recognised, and have led to the development of much more sophisticated models and analyses in which purchasing is seen as an interactive process taking place within a network of suppliers and users. Foremost among the exponents of this approach is the **IMP Group**, which initially comprised 14 researchers drawn from five European countries (France, Germany, Italy, Sweden and the UK) and later extended to include colleagues in the USA. The major findings of the Group are reported in two major publications: *International Marketing and Purchasing*, by P. Turnbull and M. Cunningham (1980), and *International Marketing and Purchasing of Industrial Goods,* ed. Hakan Hakansson (1982). More recently another member of the Group, David Ford (1990) has edited a collection of the Group's findings in a book entitled *Understanding Business Markets: Interaction of Relationships and Networks.* The key concepts and assumptions underlying the interaction approach are described at some length in Chapter 2 of the latter book and a synopsis of these is given below.

At the outset it is important to recognise that marketing is a synthetic discipline, in the sense that it seeks to combine insights and ideas from a wide range of other disciplines in the hope that by so doing it will be able to come up with a more powerful explanation of behaviour in the real world. Thus economics,

Table 9.1 Descriptions of buying decision approaches

Variables	1 Casual	2 Routine low priority	3 Simple modified rebuy	4 Judgmental new task	5 Complex modified rebuy	6 Strategic new task
Situational Characteristics						
Purchase importance	Of minor importance	Somewhat important	Quite important	Quite important	Quite important	Extremely important
Task uncertainty	Little uncertainty	Moderately uncertain	Little uncertainty	Great amount of uncertainty	Little uncertainty	Moderately uncertain
Extensiveness of choice set	Much choice	Much choice	Narrow set of choices	Narrow set of choices	Much choice	Narrow set of choices
Buyer power	Little or no power	Moderate power	Moderate power	Moderate power	Strong power position	Strong power position
Buying Activities						
Search for information	No search made	Little effort at searching	Moderate amount of search	Moderate amount of search	High level of search	High level of search
Use of analysis techniques	No analysis performed	Moderate level of analysis	Moderate level of analysis	Moderate level of analysis	Great deal of analysis	Great deal of analysis
Proactive focus	No attention to proactive issues	Superficial consideration of proactive focus	High level of proactive focus	Moderate proactive focus	High level of proactive focus	Proactive issues dominate purchase
Procedural control	Simply transmit the order	Follow standard procedures	Follow standard procedures	Little reliance on established procedures	Follow standard procedures	Little reliance on established procedures

Source: American Marketing Association. Bunn, Michele D., (1993), 'Taxonomy of Buying Decision Approaches', *Journal of Marketing*, Vol.57, January , pp38-56

psychology, sociology, anthropology, statistics, law and so on all provide important contributions to our new discipline of marketing whose own distinctive contribution is to combine and synthesise these in new ways. In the case of the interaction approach the models of OBB described earlier provide an important input, but this has been extended by drawing upon two major theoretical models from outside the marketing literature – **Inter-organisational Theory** and **New Institutional Economic Theory**. As Hakansson notes, 'Much of the work in Inter-organisational Theory involves attempts to apply theory and concepts from intra-organisational studies to problems where several organisational units are involved. Here the focus of attention is on relationships between those organisations (hence 'relationship marketing') rather than within each individual organisation.' Three distinct approaches may be distinguished which may be identified as:

1 *Organisation based studies* in which the organisation is studied in terms of the environment within which it has to operate and interact with. The models of OBB described above fit into this category which until now has been the predominant marketing perspective and contains 'two distinct and separate approaches to the study of what occurs in industrial markets. On the one hand, there is an analysis of the manipulation of marketing variables by the seller to achieve a desired market response. On the other hand, there is a separate analysis of a single buying process and the factors which affect that process, from which lessons can be drawn for marketing.'

2 *Studies based on several organisations* which are seen as part of a network. In a marketing context this conforms with the 'distribution system perspective' in which the market is seen as 'a system of interconnected institutions performing the economic functions required to bring about exchange of goods or services'. (A supply chain perspective).

3 *Studies of the organisation in a societal context* in which 'the organisation is seen as an integrated part in a larger social system'. This approach has been little developed by the IMP Group whose work is mainly focused on approach (2) with a limited recognition of (3).

With regard to the 'New Institutional Economic Theory' the main foundation is to be found in the seminal contribution of O. E. Williamson (1975), *Markets and Hierarchies: Analysis and Antitrust Implications*. Williamson's work constitutes a criticism of perceived deficiencies within traditional micro-economic theory, particularly the view that market exchanges will maximise efficiency.

According to Williamson one must distinguish between situations where exchange efficiency will be maximised through the existence of independent units operating in a market, and those where such efficiency will be achieved through vertical integration within a single unit. Only by examining carefully the factors which influence transaction costs will one be able to determine the most effective institutional structure (including intermediary structures) and such an examination focuses attention on those variables such as bargaining relationships, organisational characteristics, information handling behaviour, and so on which are central to the study of OBB.

In the IMP Group's model, 'the marketing and purchasing of industrial goods is seen as an interaction process between two parties within a certain environment', and comprises four basic elements:

1 *The interaction process;*

2 *The participants in the interaction process;*

3 *The environment within which interactions take place;*

4 *The atmosphere affecting and affected by the interaction.*

The model is conceptualised as in Figure 9.6 and a full description of the elements is to be found in Hakansson (1982, pp. 16–23). Clearly, the approach proposed above goes a long way towards capturing the dynamic complexity of organisational buying and selling behaviour. In light of this, and not forgetting the composite model proposed in the previous chapter, it will be helpful now to look more closely at some of the constituent elements.

THE COMPOSITION OF THE BUYING GROUP

All of the models of OBB recognise that buying is a complex process in which purchasing decisions are made by a group or 'buying centre' rather than by an individual. It follows, therefore, that if one is to understand the process then one must be able to define the buying group or centre in terms of its possible composition vis-à-vis the various buying situations and phases in the buying process.

Figure 9.6 An illustration of the interaction model

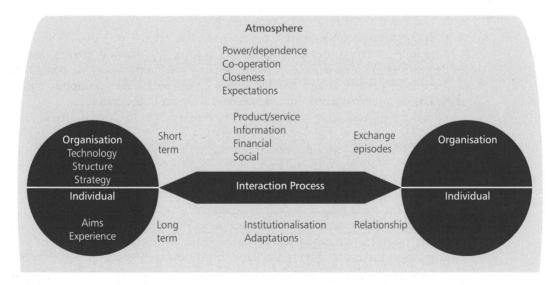

Source: IMP Group, in Hakansson, H. (ed) (1982), *International Marketing and Purchasing of Industrial Goods* © John Wiley & Sons Limited. Reproduced with permission.

As Wind (1976) has pointed out, 'the basic concept of a buying centre suggests that it is a temporary organisation unit, which may change in components and functions from one purchase to another'. This view has been supported by numerous other studies which confirm that not only do buying groups vary from decision to decision, but that their composition varies over the life of a particular purchasing decision.

With regard to who actually is involved, the *Financial Times/IMR survey*, 'How British Industry Buys' (1974), indicated a wide range of participation, including:

1	*Collective decisions*	Board Management Committee
2	*Individual (non-departmental)*	Managing Director Other Director General Manager Company Secretary
3	*Department (collective and individual)*	Department Manager Operating Manager Other Design and Engineering Production Purchasing Sales and Marketing Research & Development Finance/Accounts Other

4 *External decision*

Several studies which have analysed the composition of the buying group argue that it should be and often is a function of product-related variables. The most frequently cited such variables are:

1 The technical complexity of the product;

2 The value of the item to be purchased;

3 The frequency of purchase;

4 The product's essentiality to the production process;

5 The potential consequences of making a wrong decision;

6 The degree of inherent innovation or novelty in the product;

7 The product's overall complexity.

By analysing and rating the product on these dimensions one should be able to conclude who might be involved and the extent of their involvement in a purchasing decision.

An alternative approach to the study of the composition of buying groups has focused on the roles played by different members, which have been characterised as users, influencers, deciders and gatekeepers (Webster and Wind, see Table 9.2), or as contributors, participants, responsibles and directors (B. Klass 1961, 'What Factors Affect Industrial Buying Decisions'). Another schemata proposed by Sales Management in 1963 distinguished those who make major buying decisions, make recommendations, must approve purchases, affect the conditions of use, and conduct the buying negotiations. However, as Shan Rajagopal points out in

Chapter 5 of *Marketing: Theory and Practice* (ed. M. J. Baker, 1995), 'Operationally, conceptualisation of the buying centre by role definition is of little use to a researcher wishing to study the purchasing decision-making process. Specifically, the notion of generalised role relationships within the buying centre does not accommodate a method for ascertaining the individual membership of the buying task group, nor its decision making potential.' (This chapter on 'Organisational Buyer Behaviour' is strongly recommended for further reading on the subject.)

On the other hand, if one has a model defining the possible roles which members of a buying group may perform, then one is more likely to recognise their existence in an actual buying decision, and formulate tactics for overcoming possible resistance, while reinforcing and supporting those who are favourably disposed to a sales offer.

Another important contribution of the concept of a buying group is that it reminds us that other people in the organisation are likely to be involved in the

Table 9.2 Buying centre roles defined

Role	Description
User	As the role name implies, these are the personnel who will be using the product in question. Users may have anywhere from inconsequential to an extremely important influence on the purchase decision. In some cases, the users initiate the purchase action by requesting the product. They may even develop the product specification
Gatekeepers	Gatekeepers control information to be reviewed by other members of the buying centre. The control of information may be in terms of disseminating printed information or advertisements or through controlling which salesperson will speak to which individuals in the buying centre. To illustrate, the purchasing agent might perform this screening role by opening the gate to the buying centre for some sales personnel and closing it to others
Influencers	These individuals affect the purchasing decision by supplying information for the evaluation of alternatives or by setting buying specifications. Typically, technical personnel, such as engineers, quality control personnel and research and development personnel and individuals outside of the buying organisation can assume this role (for example an engineering consultant or an architect who writes very tight building specifications)
Deciders	Deciders are the individuals who actually make the buying decision, whether or not they have the formal authority to do so. The identity of the decider is the most difficult role to determine: buyers may have formal authority to buy, but the president of the firm may actually make the decision. A decider could be a design engineer who develops a set of specifications that only one vendor can meet
Buyers	The buyer has formal authority for selecting a supplier and implementing all procedures connected with securing the product. The power of the buyer is often usurped by more powerful members of the organisation. Often the buyer's role is assumed by the purchasing agent, who executes the clerical functions associated with a purchase order

Source: Wind, Y.; Webster, Jr., Frederick E., *Organizational Buying Behavior*, 1st edition © 1972, pp.77-79. Adapted by permission of Pearson Education Inc., Upper Saddle River, NJ.

purchase decision in addition to the designated purchasing agent or buyer. Thus, while most order inquiries are initiated by purchasing agents, and 'the buyer' is the obvious person to approach first with a selling proposition, it is important to recognise that this individual or department may have neither the discretion nor authority to make a decision. How then should one assess the purchasing function's role?

THE ROLE OF THE PURCHASING FUNCTION

In her review of industrial buying behaviour, Kennedy (1983) in *Marketing: Theory and Practice*, suggests that purchasing's involvement in buying decisions is a function of four sets of factors:

1 *The nature and status of purchasing within the organisation;*
2 *The purchasing agent's perception of their function;*
3 *Task versus non-task behaviour;*
4 *Environmental and extraneous market conditions.*

With regard to the nature and status of purchasing within an organisation it has been shown that the existence of a separate purchasing function and its size depend very much upon the overall size of the organisation as a whole. However, the size of a purchasing department does not necessarily indicate that it occupies an important place in the organisational hierarchy as it may be charged merely with an order processing-function while all the key decisions are made by R&D or manufacturing. To some extent the status of the purchasing department may be inferred from the status of its senior manager – are they a main Board director, or do they report to the Board, if at all, through a hierarchy of other more senior managers? According to Webster (1965), 'Modelling the Industrial Buying Process' the purchasing department's influence on a buying decision will tend to increase as:

- Market variables become more important in relation to product variables;
- The size of firm and spatial separation of activities increase;
- The organisation formally assigns specific responsibility to the purchasing department.

With regard to the purchasing agent's own perception of his role, most of the evidence suggests that buyers feel their contribution is undervalued. When one reflects on the contribution which efficient buying can make to the firm's overall profitability, there would seem to be some justification for this point of view. Consider, for example, a firm with the following sales and cost structure.

	Sales revenue		100
Less	Bought in materials	46	
	Labour and overheads	20	
	Cost of goods sold	68	
		32	
Less	Selling, general and administrative expense	20	
	Profit before tax		12

It is clear that any increase or decrease in the price of bought in materials will have a greater effect than a proportionately equivalent change in efficiency of any of the other business functions either separately or together. Indeed, it is paradoxical that so much attention is given to **human resource management (HRM)**, and so little to materials management, when the expenditure on the latter is usually much higher than direct labour costs in manufacturing industry!

Of course, savings on bought in materials may have nothing directly to do with the buyer but result from changes in design or specification initiated by other members of the buying group. None the less, there is good reason to believe that the purchasing agent can play a critical part in the interface between an organisation and existing and potential suppliers, and so should be accorded equal status with senior managers in the other business functions.

Recognition of the impact that professional purchasing can have on an organisation's competitiveness has resulted in a significant increase in the importance and status attached to the function in recent years. This trend is accelerating as the original industrialised economies move into a post-industrial phase in which the emphasis is on knowledge based work, and a service economy. This switch has only been possible because countries like the USA and UK have been able to **out-source** many of their needs for manufactured goods to the newly industrialising countries of South East Asia, Latin America and especially India and China.

ENVIRONMENTAL CHANGE AND THE SUPPLY SIDE

During the 1990s international competition continued to increase dramatically, as did technological change. Companies set out to become the best in their business through benchmarking of their major competitors, wider use of matrix management, decentralisation and an emphasis on the SBU as basic building block of the major multi-national firms co-ordinated through global strategies. Outsourcing of all but core activities became commonplace but raised questions of just what are the *core activities*? On the supply side Russill (1997) identified the following trends:

- The emphasis on 'providing customer response' underlined the importance of logistics
- More firms joined buying consortia to increase buying power and leverage
- Procurement's role seen as being the creation of a high-value, high performance, low-cost supply base
- The emphasis in the procurement function is the management of *relationships*
- Supply chains evolve into supply *networks* with customer influence over them extending up the suppliers own supply chains
- An increase in joint customer-supplier technology development activity
- Procurement and sourcing management perspectives become increasingly visible in the business and management debate with a corresponding increase in the development of new concepts and fashions
- Clear evidence of strategic procurement planning and action making a major contribution to achieving results breakthroughs

Moving into the 21st century procurement is increasingly seen as 'acquisition management' backed up by the formation of project teams to source suppliers and the emergence of key supplier management paralleling the growth of key account management on the supply side.

Outsourcing involves three critical decision issues identified by Wilson (op. cit.):

1 *Make-or-buy?*
2 *Single or multiple sources?*
3 *Domestic or international?*

The benefits of making oneself rather than buying-in may be summarised as:

- Control over sensitive processes.
- Costing advantages derived from marginal pricing on under-utilised assets.
- Responding to political pressures.
- Strategic flexibility, i.e. can initiate changes more quickly.
- Risk reduction/less dependency on third parties.
- Value added, i.e. to meet requirements of countries wishing to avoid pure assembly operations.
- Strategy/Image, i.e. ownership of object sold which is usually achieved by R&D, control of final quality and marketing.
- Convenience of production flow, i.e. avoid costs arising from transportation and distribution.

(Adapted from Wilson, op.cit.)

Single sourcing can offer numerous benefits in terms of economies of scope and scale, as well as simplifying relationships and reducing risk. If these are significant then vertical integration might be a better strategic option. Against this must be set the lost benefits of interacting with multiple suppliers which include greater flexibility, access to more information on technology and market developments, and the opportunity to negotiate better deals as a result of competition between suppliers. Much the same applies to confining purchases to domestic suppliers rather than international ones.

The benefits flowing from professional procurement are graphically illustrated by Russill who states that "the absence of an organised approach to procurement results in supply-side expenditure being 5 – 10 percent greater than it need be *plus* three or more of the following:

- Slow to market
- Delivery delays/lost orders
- Higher prices
- Unsophisticated/unprofessional internal procedures
- Suspect to sales pressures
- Inefficiencies
- Loss of scale economies/leverage
- Vulnerable to fraud
- Unsound legal contracts
- Absence of supplier development
- Lack of supplier control/weaker supplier performance

Clearly, the threats contained in this list are important and their avoidance potentially a source of competitive advantage.

Professional procurement is based on a number of core beliefs of which the most noteworthy are:

1 The need to access the best suppliers.

2 The need to achieve best value.

3 The need for consistency in both approach and practice.

4 The need to incorporate procurement decisions into the strategic planning process.

5 The need to recognise procurement as a strategic function in its own right.

Many firms have already accepted these beliefs and given great importance to their purchasing function. For example, IBM at Greenock in Scotland, the largest assembler of PCs in the company, buys in over 80 percent of its inputs – a much higher proportion than that suggested in our earlier example. And it is not only manufacturing firms. Government Departments, Local Government, Universities and many other organisations have come to appreciate the savings and efficiency improvements that flow from effective professional purchasing.

The basic objective of such a purchasing function is to work with suppliers which will enable the organisation to achieve the optimal cost-benefit position. In turn this involves several sub-objectives hinted at in Russill's list, namely:

- Negotiating the *best* buy in terms of price and quality
- Development of key suppliers and building strong relationships with them
- Maintaining continuity of supply – especially **just-in-time (JIT) delivery** – and consistency in the quality supplied – **Quality Assurance** – and quantity to optimise inventory control
- Identifying innovations on the supply side that may be used in improving existing products and developing new ones.

However, pending explicit recognition of the strategic importance of purchasing, purchasing agents will no doubt continue to use the tactics described by Strauss (1962) in his frequently cited study, 'Tactics of Lateral Relationships: The Purchasing Agent', for handling conflicts with other functions:

1 *Rule-oriented tactics* – the buyer works to the book. In this case a written responsibility to purchase is required.

2 *Rule-evading tactics* – the buyer revises requisitions and follows a tactic of feigned acceptance.

3 *Personal–political tactics* – the buyer projects an aura of friendship and willingly exchanges favours.

4 *Educational tactics* – the buyer attempts to persuade others to think in purchasing terms.

5 *Organisation-interaction tactics* – the buyer exhibits the willingness to communicate with other organisational departments and to participate in decision-making.

6 *Organisational change tactics* – in this case, the buyer attempts gradually to

evolve change in organisation procedures. One example of these tactics is the materials management idea.

Another factor which influences the purchasing agent's involvement in buying decisions is the emphasis upon task and non-task behaviour. In simple terms, the task elements of buying are those which may be defined and, usually, measured using objective criteria; for example supplier identification and qualification, value analysis, price, and so on. By contrast the non-task elements tend to be subjective and difficult to quantify – reputation, performance, reliability and so on. As a generalisation, it would seem that the greater the focus upon task elements and the greater the purchasing agent's perceived competence in handling these, then the greater will be the role played by the purchasing department.

A further element which seems likely to influence the importance given to purchasing is the environmental context within which the buying firm has to operate. When the external environment is dynamic and uncertain then the purchasing function is likely to assume more importance as it is called upon to help reduce the uncertainty which these conditions create. Similarly, under

OUTSOURCING INNOVATION

During the 80s and 90s many major corporations began to outsource their manufacturing to lower cost emerging economies around the world. In doing so most maintained they would still retain control over R&D and, thereby, the design and development of the future generations of new products essential to competitive success. By the middle of the first decade of the new millennium *Business Week* reports increasing signs that many firms are now outsourcing their innovation too. "Today, the likes of Dell, Motorola, and Philips are buying complete designs of some digital devices from Asian developers, Tweaking them to their own specifications, and slapping on their own brand names."

And this trend is not confined solely to the electronics sector. Boeing is working with India's HCL Technologies on software for many of the control systems on its new 7E7 Dreamliner; GlaxoSmithKline and Eli Lilly are working with Asian biotech firms to try and "cut the average $500 million cost of bringing a new drug to market" and Procter and Gamble is looking to increase the number of outsourced new products from 20% to 50% by 2010.

These trends lead BW to believe that "At a minimum, most leading Western companies are turning towards a new model of innovation, one that employs U.S. chipmakers, Taiwanese engineers, Indian software developers, and Chinese factories". Such collaboration in the supply chain is seen as offering significant improvements in the speed and efficiency of NPD – provided it works! The problem arises, as been seen with private-label brands of fmcg, when new competitors enter the market offering more competitive terms. Initially, these may centre on price but, if the established brands fail to counter-attack through innovation, dilution of brand equity seems inevitable. "The key, execs say, is to guard some sustainable competitive advantage, whether it's control over the latest technologies, the look and feel of new products, or the customer relationship".

Past history suggests this may not be as simple as it sounds. Today, Taiwanese "original design manufacturers" (ODMs), who both design and assemble products, supply 65% of the world's notebook PCs. For PDAs, ODMs account for 70% of designs, 30% of digital cameras and 20% of mobile phones. While they may currently be content to market under the brands of established leaders it would be dangerously complacent to assume this will always be the case. What does seem clear is that the customer franchise, built up through effective marketing, will have a major role to play.

conditions of recession more attention is likely to be given to the cost incurring functions, and purchasing will assume increased visibility and importance. It is under such conditions that other management functions are forced to consider the relevance of the task elements, with techniques like value analysis calling for close co-operation between purchasing and R&D, and manufacturing and inventory control calling for involvement of the finance function.

Another environmental change which is tending to increase the role of the purchasing function is the increasing concentration in many industries which is resulting in the creation of very large and professional buying groups. Indeed, in some consumer goods markets the retail buying groups are much bigger than the manufacturers that supply them but, so far inquiries in the UK by the Monopolies and Mergers Commission have not found this buying power to be harmful to the public interest.

In their book *Customer Behavior* (1999), Sheth et al. identify four forces that they believe will bring about significant changes in the importance given to purchasing in the future:

1 *The identification of procurement as a core competence.*
2 *Treating suppliers as partners.*
3 *Global sourcing and the need to take into account cross-cultural values.*
4 *A greater focus on the procurement of services.*

To these we may add, shorter product life cycles, and deregulation and open tendering.

Taken together, it seems likely that in future much greater emphasis will be given to procurement as a strategic function alongside R&D, Production, Finance and Marketing.

BUSINESS TO BUSINESS MARKETING (B2B)

Business marketing is the task of selecting, developing and managing customer relationships for the advantage of both customer and supplier, with regard to their respective skills, resources, technologies, strategies and objectives.   (Ford, 1997)

Some of the salient features of Business to Business or B2B marketing were presented in Chapter 2 in Table 2.1. Dominic Wilson (1999) summarised these under four headings:

1 *The complexity and size of organisational markets.*
2 *The nature of demand.*
3 *The smaller number of buyers.*
4 *Larger order sizes.*

These features lead to:

■ A need to adapt products
■ involving negotiation
■ with strategic implications

- involving significant perceived risk
- requiring wider participation and formal decision making procedures
- demanding professional management

In the case of a highly sophisticated and complex 'product' like an oil rig its basic performance characteristics, including its manning and operation, will need to be adapted, often significantly, to meet the customers requirements. This means that the business marketer must:

- Work with individual customers to assess their problems.
- Develop offerings that are more complex and involve adaptation to individual requirements.
- Seek to minimise the cost of adaptations while at the same time demonstrating commitment to and developing customer relationships.
- Fulfil the promises made.

(Adapted from Ford op. cit.)

In order to do this the marketing function must ensure:

1 That it has a competitive product to offer.

2 That it has undertaken appropriate research and identified potential buyers.

3 That it is known to potential buyers and included in their bid lists i.e. for direct invitation to tender.

4 That it has ensured the organisation is pre-qualified to tender according to both explicit and implicit requirements.

5 That it has established the critical success factors associated with every contract for which it is bidding.

6 That it is familiar with the competition so that it can match or better their offering and take advantage of any weaknesses they may have.

7 That it can develop a stronger value proposition embracing both objective (price, performance etc.) and subjective (quality, value etc.) elements.

8 That it is a recognised member of the network of buyers and suppliers and has established relationships with the key customers in the industry.

A moments reflection on this list of requirements suggests that precisely the same conditions apply to the successful marketing of consumer goods. In fact they are the same in kind although different in *degree*. For example, adaptation or 'mass customisation' is commonplace in consumer markets now, and the ideas of networks, interaction and relationships dominate thinking in all aspects of marketing. As we shall see in Part III, The Marketing Mix, effective marketing depends upon the clear identification of the buyers needs and the selection of the most appropriate combination of product, price, place and promotion to meet these and this is just as true for organisational buyers as it is for individuals.

An essential task in achieving this is identifying a sufficiently large potential demand to justify the effort. In all markets this involves some kind of **segmentation** and it is to this that we turn in the next chapter.

Summary

While the models discussed earlier may appear somewhat dated they are still the ones most frequently cited in specialised text books. (See, for example, Van Weele, 2005). The **Buygrid model** is still the most widely used. Although more recent research has suggested the potential for increasing the number of Buy-phases and refining the number of Buy-tasks, the basic model has the advantage that it is simple and easy to memorise. Equally, it is only a suggested framework for analysis and there is nothing to stop users modifying it to suit their particular needs. Essentially, the Buygrid model indicates that the more complex the buying decision, the greater the uncertainty attached to it, and the more important the consequences – good or bad – for the organisation, the greater the importance that will be associated with the task and the greater the likelihood that persons other than the buyer will be involved in the decision. However, the buyer will remain a key person. Often they will be responsible for coordinating the whole process even if they do not chair the DMU or project group charged with making the decision. The will also have a major influence in helping to spell out the **critical success factors (CSF)**, and qualifying suppliers, i.e. identifying sellers who can meet or better the requirements defined by the CSF.

When qualifying sellers the most important criteria used are:

- Reliability
- Cost and other financial aspect
- Technical capability
- Availability and delivery
- Quality

- Support for the buyer, e.g. training in the use of machinery, equipment etc.
- Service.

Not only is the buyer responsible for ensuring that potential suppliers can satisfy these criteria, they are usually also responsible for monitoring supplier performance to make certain that they achieve the desired performance levels in terms of the product, its pricing, delivery, and service support.

While it is important to distinguish between organisational buyer behaviour, it must also be remembered that the 'actors' who participate in organisational buying decisions are, in another capacity, the individuals whose motivations, attitudes and behaviour were looked at in Chapter 8, and it would be naive to dismiss or overlook these when analysing corporate buying behaviour. By the same token it would be equally naive to ignore the fact that if groups of people develop procedures, processes and stratagems for making buying decisions which satisfy them, then why should not individuals behave in a broadly similar manner? It is for this reason that I believe the **composite model of buying behaviour** proposed in the previous chapter is applicable in principle to all buying decisions. This is not to say that each of its elements will receive explicit and conscious attention every time a purchase is made nor that the weighting and emphasis given to the component parts will be the same from product to product, industry to industry or decision-maker to decision-maker. But it does offer a robust and workable conceptualisation or model around which to develop a more detailed analysis of specific purchase decisions.

Review questions and problems

1 'The importance of conceptual knowledge (models) of buying behaviour in understanding and predicting the possible response of the relevant market segments is widely accepted when the buyers are individuals and households: it is largely ignored, unfortunately, when the buying unit is an organisation.' (Webster and Wind, 1972). What factors do you think may have contributed to the apparent neglect of organisational buying behaviour suggested by this quotation, and what factors explain the current higher level of interest in the subject?

2 Why is the post-purchase stage included in some models of the buying process?

3 Describe, preferably with the aid of a diagram, Sheth's or any other recognised model of industrial buyer behaviour.

4 Discuss the main behavioural influences affecting organisational buying behaviour.

5 Discuss the relevance of product classification schemes to the analysis of industrial buying decisions.

6 Cabinets, Calendars, Carburettors, Carpets, Chisels and Computers are a randomly selected group of products which could be marketed both to organisations and individuals. Is there any benefit for a company serving both markets to develop separate marketing strategies for consumer and industrial markets?

7 Explain why the importance of procurement has increasingly been recognised in recent years.

8 What are the key elements of the 'interaction' approach proposed by the IMP Group?

Key terms

business to business marketing
buyclasses
buygrid
buying responsibility
buyphases
choice process
decision making unit (DMU)
extensiveness of choice set
human resource management (HRM)
IMP Group
interaction model

inter-organisational theory
just-in-time (JIT)
modified rebuy
new institutional economic theory
new task
organisational buying behaviour (OBB)
perceived buyer power
performance problem products
political problem products

problem recognition
procedural problem products
purchase importance
purchasing function
quality assurance
routine order products
search process
segmentation
straight rebuy
tactics
task uncertainty

Supplementary reading list

Baily, P. J., Farmer, D., Jessop, D. and Jones, D. (1998), *Purchasing Principles and Management*, 8th edn (Harlow: Pearson Education Ltd.).

Ford, D. Ed. (1997), *Understanding Business Markets*, (London: The Dryden Press)

Hill, R. W. and Hillier, T. J. (1977), *Organisational Buying Behaviour* (London: Macmillan).

Hutt, M. D. and Speh, T. W. (2004), *Business Marketing Management*, 8th edn (Fort Worth: Dryden Press).

Parkinson, S. T. and Baker, M. J. (1986), *Organisational Buying Behaviour* (London: Macmillan).

Van Weele, Arjan J. (2005), *Purchasing and Supply Chain Management*, 4th .Edition, (London: Thomson Learning)

Wilson, D. (1999), *Organizational Marketing*, (London: International Thomson Business Press)

See also the Journal of Purchasing and Supply Management.

MARKET SEGMENTATION

Learning Goals *After reading this chapter you should be able to:*

- Distinguish between product differentiation and market segmentation as alternative marketing strategies.

- Outline the benefits of using a segmentation approach.

- Summarise the basis for segmenting markets and describe various approaches in some detail, including:
  - geo-demographic segmentation;
  - preference segmentation;
  - benefit segmentation;
  - social character segmentation using life style and psychographics; social grading segmentation;
  - industrial segmentation;
  - international segmentation.

- Describe how to segment a market.

- Determine how to select a segmentation approach.

- Specify when it is appropriate to use market segmentation.

INTRODUCTION

From reading Chapter 1 it should be clear that while there are many definitions of marketing there is only one marketing concept. However, it is also true that many criticisms of marketing are prompted by misunderstanding and/or misapplication of this concept. Usually, the 'mistaken marketing concept' is interpreted as 'give the customer what they want' which, in many cases, is a sure road to commercial ruin. In reality the marketing concept advises that we should establish user needs and determine if, how, and to what extent it may he possible to satisfy these given one's existing and potential resources, to the mutual benefit (profit) of both parties to the exchange.

Clearly the 'real' marketing concept requires the marketer to steer a careful course between regarding every individual as a discrete marketing opportunity, and considering all customers as being the same. From the preceding chapters on Consumer and Organisational Buying Behaviour it is apparent that one can either disaggregate a population into separate groups or sub-groups, or else aggregate individuals into sub-groups, groups or populations through the use of a variety of distinctive features which must be possessed by those within the group but are absent from those excluded from it. In marketing this process is known as **market segmentation**. Thus we have progressed from **mass marketing** in which the producer offers a single, undifferentiated product to all potential customers; to **product differentiated marketing** under which the producer offers two or more different products based on their perception of differences in buying behaviour, to **target marketing** where the seller clearly defines the specific needs of particular groups of potential buyers and designs products and marketing mixes that precisely meet these needs.

In this chapter we shall look first at the concept of market segmentation and the benefits associated with the practice. Next we shall examine the basic approach to segmentation as a preliminary to a more detailed review of segmentation methods in consumer, industrial and international markets. Finally, we will consider how segmentation techniques may be applied and assess their role in marketing planning.

THE CONCEPT OF MARKET SEGMENTATION

According to Engel et al., (1972), the concept of segmentation is based upon three propositions:

1 That consumers are different;

2 That differences in consumers are related to differences in market demand;

3 That segments of consumers can be isolated within the overall market.

While these three propositions may seem eminently reasonable it has to be appreciated that, according to classical economic theory, supply and demand are homogeneous. Thus it was not until the 1930s when Chamberlin and Robinson proposed their theories of imperfect competition that explicit recognition was given to the observed reality that in the great majority of markets both supply and demand are heterogeneous. In turn it was not until the mid-1950s that a marketing writer, Wendell Smith, was to point out how recognition of diversity or heterogeneity in demand and supply suggested the existence of two quite different marketing strategies – product differentiation and market segmentation. In his seminal article 'Product Differentiation and Market Segmentation as Alternative Marketing Strategies', Smith (1956) argued that both planned and uncontrollable differences exist in the products of an industry which result in sellers making quite different appeals in support of their marketing efforts. Among the reasons for this diversity Smith proposed the following:

1 Variations in the production equipment and methods or processes used by different manufacturers of products designed for the same or similar uses.

2 Specialised or superior resources enjoyed by favourably situated manufacturers.

3 Unequal progress among competitors in design, development and improvement of products.

4 The inability of manufacturers in some industries to eliminate product variations even through the application of quality control techniques.

5 Variations in producers' estimates of the nature of market demand with reference to such matters as price sensitivity, colour, material or package size.

Five decades later it is revealing to consider the essential production orientation of Smith's analysis with its emphasis upon variations or heterogeneity on the supply side. Even point 5 seems to imply that variations exist in the suppliers' perception of demand rather than in the demand itself. However, given that such differences exist, Smith argues that marketing managers could pursue one or other of two alternative strategies. Either they could seek to bring about the convergence of individual market demands for a variety of products upon a single or limited offering to the market, which is a strategy of product differentiation usually through advertising or promotion. Or, 'In some cases, however, the marketer may determine that is better to accept divergent demand as a market characteristic and to adjust product lines and marketing strategy accordingly,' which is a strategy of marketing segmentation.

Smith summarises the differences between these two strategies admirably when he writes:

In its simplest terms product differentiation is concerned with the bending of demand to the will of supply. It is an attempt to shift or to change the slope of the demand curve for the market offering of an individual supplier . . . Segmentation is based upon developments on the demand side of the market and represents a rational and more precise adjustment of product and marketing effort to consumer or user requirements.

From this definition it is clear that segmentation is a genuine marketing concept which is intermediate between the polar extremes of the perfectly homogeneous market, which is an underlying assumption of much economic theory, and the completely heterogeneous market perspective, which constitutes the perspective of the behavioural scientist. These distinctions are illustrated in Figure 10.1 using a classification developed by Enis (1980).

Figure 10.1 A model of market segmentation

DISCIPLINE	Economics	Sociology	Psychology
CORE ASSUMPTION	Homogeneity	Groups or Clusters	Heterogeneity
APPROACH	Mass Marketing	Segmentation	Customisation
STRATEGY	Cost Leadership	Differentiation	Focus

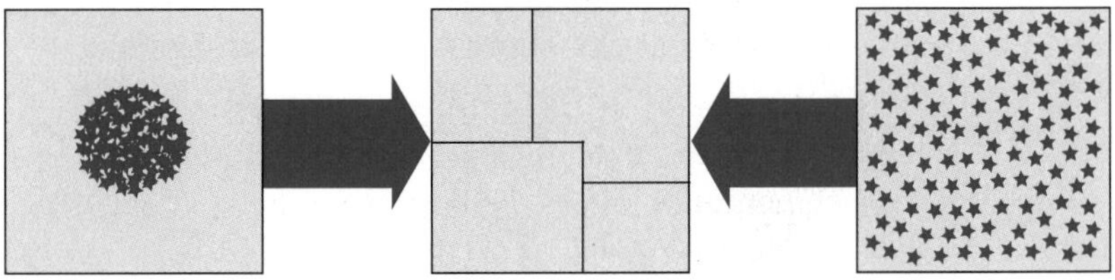

Source: Based on an idea of Enis (1980).

In the opinion of Engel et al. (1972), a segmentation approach offers the marketer the following benefits:

1 A segmentation perspective leads to a more precise definition of the market in terms of consumer needs. Segmentation thus improves management's understanding of the customer and, more importantly, why they buy.

2 Management, once it understands consumer needs, is in a much better position to direct marketing programmes that will satisfy these needs and hence parallel the demands of the market.

3 A continuous programme of market segmentation strengthens management capabilities in meeting changing market demands.

4 Management is better able to assess competitive strengths and weaknesses. Of greatest importance, it can identify those segments where competition is thoroughly entrenched. This will save company resources by forgoing a pitched battle of locked-in competition, where there is little real hope of market gain.

5 It is possible to assess a firm's strengths and weaknesses through identifying market segments. Systematic planning for future markets is thus encouraged.

6 Segmentation leads to a more efficient allocation of marketing resources. For example, product and advertising appeals can be more easily co-ordinated. Media plans can be developed to minimise waste through excess exposure. This can result in a sharper brand image, and target consumers will recognise and distinguish products and promotional appeals directed at them.

7 Segmentation leads to a more precise setting of market objectives. Targets are defined operationally, and performance can later be evaluated against these standards. Segmentation analysis generates such critical questions as these: Should we add another brand? Should we drop or modify existing products, or should we attempt to reposition a faded and obsolete brand image?

There are, however, several situations when the concept of market segmentation may not be suitable, namely:

1 Where the market is so small that sub-dividing it would not be profitable;

2 In emerging or developing markets where consumers have limited disposable income and are looking for basic products that offer functional benefits at affordable prices

3 Where heavy users account for such a high proportion of all sales that they are the only relevant target.

4 Where the brand is a dominant brand in the market, there is no need to segment as the brand is effectively a segment.

But, apart from such situations which call for an undifferentiated or mass marketing strategy, most academics and practitioners are agreed that some form of segmentation offers the best opportunity of securing a competitive advantage in the market place. This being so it will be useful to consider the various approaches to market segmentation in common use and the basis on which they have developed.

BASES FOR SEGMENTATION

According to Engel et al. (*Marketing Segmentation*), marketing managers usually divide consumers into three classes for the purpose of marketing strategy, namely:

1 *Similarity*. All consumers are basically similar. Although differences exist among consumers (for example, age, income, and so forth), these differences are not thought to be important in affecting the purchase of their specific product class. A standard product will essentially satisfy the large majority of consumers.

2 *Unique*. All consumers are unique. The differences among consumers (for example, age, income, needs, preferences, and so forth), make a standardised product or service unacceptable. Market offerings must be tailored specifically to the needs of each individual consumer.

3 *Differences/Similarities*. Consumer differences and similarities exist and are important sources of influence on market demand. Such differences can be regarded as differences in consumer needs and wants. These differences and similarities facilitate the grouping of consumers into aggregates of segments according to their needs and wants and the degree to which they are present. Marketers using a segmentation approach adapt marketing programmes to match the peculiar need combinations of each market segment.

The obvious question is 'How do marketing managers arrive at these decisions?', to which the answer is 'By examining the variables which may be used to describe consumers and their behaviour'. According to Frank et al. (1972), these variables may be classified into two broad categories:

1 *General variables* where consumers are classified by broad characteristics such as demographics, personality traits or life styles.

2 *Situation-specific variables* where consumers are grouped according to consumption patterns such as frequency of usage, brand loyalty, product benefits or perceptual maps.

In Table 10.1 we provide a summary listing of the major segmentation variables.

Clearly, many of these variables are appropriate to individual consumers rather than to organisational buyers. That said, the preceding discussion of organisational buying behaviour should have made it clear that demographic, psychographic and behavioural factors will all have some influence on the way in which organisational buyers will perceive information and their reactions to it. This being so it will be both useful and relevant to examine some of the bases for consumer segmentation in more detail before moving on to the particular case of industrial and international market segmentation.

Demographic segmentation

The first question to be answered in developing a marketing strategy is, invariably, 'Who?' That is, who is the intended customer? The most straightforward and simplest answer to this question when profiling individual customers is to use demographic factors such as **Age, Sex, Marital Status**, and so on. When profiling organisational customers then characteristics such as **Standard Industrial Classification Code (SIC)**, turnover, number of employees will be used. (SIC has now been replaced by the **NAICS North American Industry Classification System**, but several data sets still use SIC based data). The great advantage of demographic factors is that they are usually easy to establish/ identify and provide the basis for a great deal of data collection by governments, public sector bodies and marketing research agencies.

Given that so much consumption is closely correlated with demography, and that so much data is available, it is surprising that greater use is not made of demographics both for analysing current behaviour and, even more importantly, for forecasting and predicting future behaviour. For example, the consumption of basic social services such as health and education is closely age-related, yet public-sector authorities seem to be singularly inept in projecting future demand. Given the number of live births in a given year one would think it would be a simple matter to forecast the demand for post-natal care, preventive care (inoculations, and so on), nursery education, primary schooling, secondary and tertiary education and so forth. Given this information, some of which gives a lead time of 17+ years, it is difficult to understand why the necessary infrastructure is not available to meet demand. Similarly, if we know that people are living longer, and that the proportion of the population over retirement age is increasing, then it should not be difficult to predict the likely demand for sheltered housing, age-related medical care, and so on.

Commercial organisations are much more adept at using Age as a predictor variable and developing specific products targeted directly at closely defined age groupings. For example, in the USA the 46 million people in the age group 29–40 have been defined as Generation X (sometimes called Xers or baby busters by contrast to their parents, many of whom were baby boomers and now comprise the new 'grey' market). With an effective demand in excess of $125 billion this

Table 10.1 Major segmentation variables	
Demographics	Age, Sex, Education, Occupation, Income, Social Class, Family/Household status, Life-cycle stage, Religion, Nationality, Race
Location/Geography	Type of property, Urban, Suburban, Rural, Region, Country, Climatic Zone
Geodemographic	Combination of Demography and Geography
Psychographic	Personality, Perception, Motivation
Life-style	AIO (Attitudes, Interests, Opinions)
Behavioural	Benefits sought, Usage, Loyalty Preference, Perceptions, Readiness stage (unaware, aware, informed, interested, desirous, intending to buy), Marketing Factor Sensitivity (quality, price, service, advertising, sales promotion, etc.)
Organisational	Composition of DMU (decision-making unit) – Household, organisation; Loyalty, Reciprocity, etc.

age grouping represents a major market opportunity for the providers of goods and services.

Gender is another variable which is easy to establish and is closely associated with certain consumption behaviour. However, one needs to be careful not to fall into the trap of role stereotyping of yesteryear with males seen as the primary earner/breadwinner and females as household managers. Within such stereotypes products such as tyres, car batteries, power tools, home maintenance equipment and so on would be regarded as 'male' products, and clothing, food stuffs and household remedies/medicines as 'female' products. No longer! That said, one would anticipate that older men and women might still conform somewhat to these stereotypes whereas their children would not. The important point here is that in developing a marketing segment one will need to use more than one criterion to describe it precisely and accurately.

Other demographic variables which are frequently used in segmentation studies include education, occupation and income, and composite measures such as socioeconomic grouping or social class (see Chapter 8). Similarly, family/household status, life-cycle stage and so on provide a useful first set at segmenting a market and a great deal of detail on these factors is to be found in *The Marketing Pocket Book* (2005).

In recent years demographic factors have been combined with geographic/locational data to provide very powerful segmentation tools. This geo-demographic segmentation is the subject of the next section.

Geo-demographic segmentation

In his editorial to a special edition of the *Journal of the Market Research Society* (1989) on 'Geo-demographics', James Rothman traces the formal use of geo-demographics (the classification of small areas according to the characteristics of their inhabitants) to 1889 and the publication of Charles Booth's *The Life and Labour of the People in London*. Based upon his survey into the economic and social circumstances of all the families in London, Booth prepared a series of maps which depicted clearly and graphically the distribution and exact location of the eight categories or classes derived from his analysis. However the real development of geo-demographics dates from the 1960s and the publication of Claus Moser's (1961) *British Towns: a Statistical Study of their Social and Economic Differences*. Although this 'received little practical application' (Rothman, 'Geo-demographics') it preceded the seminal work of Richard Webber at the Centre for Environmental Studies which was to lay the foundation for the numerous proprietary systems such as ACORN, MOSAIC, SuperProfiles and CDMS. As Rothman points out:

> Geo-demographics is based on two simple principles. The first is that two people who live in the same neighbourhood, such as a Census Enumeration District are more likely to have similar characteristics than are two people chosen at random. The second is that neighbourhoods can be categorised in terms of the population which they contain, and that two neighbourhoods can be placed in the same category, i.e. can contain similar types of people, even though they are widely separated. These two principles used in combination, mean that demographic information about the neighbourhood in which a person lives can be used to provide information about the probability of their having certain characteristics.

This ability clearly offers an attractive opportunity for market segmentation and the development of targeted marketing strategies which has now been applied extensively in numerous areas.

ACORN AND THE ACORN FAMILY OF CONSUMER CLASSIFICATION

(The following material is taken directly from the ACORN User Guide with the permission of CACI, www.caci.co.uk)

"ACORN is the most powerful consumer targeting tool available on the market today. It combines geography with demographics and lifestyle information – places where people live with their underlying characteristics and behaviour – to create a tool for understanding the different types of people in different areas throughout the country.

It enables marketers to understand fully the kind of people buying their goods, using their services or shopping in their stores. Geodemographic targeting also helps marketers pinpoint the people who are most likely to need their products or services – and avoid those who are not.

ACORN groups the entire UK population into 5 categories, 17 groups and 56 types [*Figure 10.3*]. By analysing significant social factors and consumer behaviour, it provides precise information and an in-depth understanding of the different types of consumers in every part of the country.

Developed by CACI over 25 years ago, ACORN was the first geodemographic classification in the country. Since then we have built consumer classifications both for the UK and globally, introducing new innovative techniques for targeting consumers. ACORN remains the most respected and reliable consumer classification.

ACORN can be used to understand customers, identify profitable prospects, evaluate local markets and plan public resources.

By adding ACORN codes to a customer database, you can increase knowledge of your customers' behaviour and lifestyle. ACORN profiling will give you new insights into your customers and allow you to identify prospects who most resemble your best customers.

ACORN can be used to drive effective customer communication strategies including targeted direct mail, leaflet distribution and local newspaper advertising.

For local market planning, ACORN can be used to define and analyse the purchasing preferences and lifestyle characteristics of different areas through the UK. This results in a more effective estimation of the demand for your products and services and a more effective location planning strategy.

Once retailers and suppliers have understood the characteristics and make-up of a neighbourhood, by using ACORN they can make strategic decisions on the format of their branch or store and the range of goods carried.

- Where should I open, close or locate my next store?
- Which products will suit the area?
- How should I allocate my resources?
- What factors can influence my store performance?

As a result of this range of applications, ACORN is widely used in many sectors of business.

Financial Organisations use ACORN to understand their customers, cross-sell their product range, set branch targets, predict loyal customers, and plan their network strategy.

Retailers use ACORN to locate stores, plan product ranges, assess refurbishments, and target local marketing for stores.

Media Owners use ACORN to support advertising sales, evaluate sales potential, and develop new markets.

In *FMCG* ACORN is used to drive customer communication, in-store marketing, ranging and product distribution.

The *Public Sector* uses ACORN to target services to areas of need, and inform policy decisions.

CACI started planning the development of the new ACORN several years before the 2001 census was available. We had already successfully used a range of additional data sources, including lifestyle surveys, to update the previous version of ACORN. We now wanted to ensure we built the new ACORN using the most robust data from the best available sources [*Figure 10.3*]. In particular, we wanted to identify additional sources of data that would complement the Census.

Over 400 variables were used to build ACORN and describe the different ACORN types. Of these variables, 30% were sourced from the 2001 Census. The remainder were derived from CACI's consumer lifestyle databases, which cover all of the UK's 46 million adults and 23 million households.

Figure 10.2 ACORN data sources

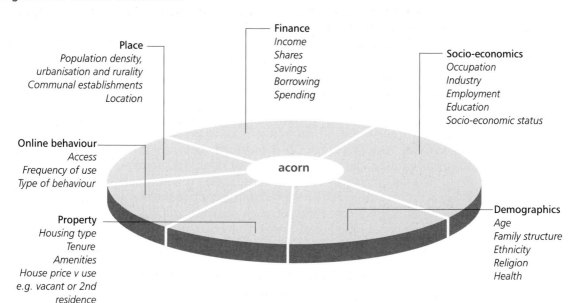

Source: ACORN user guide, CACI, *www.caci.co.uk*

Figure 10.3 ACORN consumer classification

Category	% UK Pop		Group	% UK Pop
Wealthy Achievers **1**	**26.6%**	A	Wealthy Executives	8.6
		B	Affluent Greys	7.7
		C	Flourishing Families	8.8
Urban Prosperity **2**	**10.7%**	D	Prosperous Professionals	2.2
		E	Educated Urbanites	4.6
		F	Aspiring Singles	3.9
Comfortably Off **3**	**26.6%**	G	Starting Out	2.5
		H	Secure Families	15.5
		I	Settled Suburbia	6
		J	Prudent Pensioners	2.6
Moderate Means **4**	**14.5%**	K	Asian Communities	1.6
		L	Post-Industrial Families	4.8
		M	Blue-collar Roots	8
Hard-Pressed **5**	**22.4%**	N	Struggling Families	14.1
		O	Burdened Singles	4.5
		P	High-rise Hardship	1.6
		Q	Inner City Adversity	2.1
		U	Unclassified	0.3

Source: Adapted from the ACORN user guide, CACI (2004), *www.caci.co.uk*

The unique two-stage method

CACI employed an innovative two-stage approach to creating the new ACORN. As a first stage CACI classified postcodes in the traditional manner, using a mixture of the Census and our other data sources.

The data inputs to the classification were carefully selected. This included a process of testing each variable's contribution to the power of the classification. We considered the effect of each variable individually, and their use in combination with other variables. This exhaustive testing ensured the ACORN classification was built using data that provided the greatest discrimination and targeting power.

But we didn't stop there. We then took advantage of the fact that, for the first time, the Census office attempted to publish data by geographic areas it believed contained the same kind of households.

We developed a unique second stage which selectively focused on any postcodes where ACORN might be improved. We used our substantial consumer lifestyle databases to check for subtle differences in areas which the Census office said contained the same kind of people. We then tested whether the postcodes in these areas were truly identical. When all our data sources agreed with the Census we were confident that we had the most accurate possible ACORN code.

When we identified postcodes that were not identical, we used all our additional data and a special set of decision algorithms to refine their ACORN codes.

This unique methodology produced an ACORN classification that gives better discrimination. It also allows ACORN to be updated annually more easily than even before, maintaining our picture of UK consumers' behaviour as it changes over time.

Understanding ACORN further

To help you understand ACORN further and give you in-depth and up-to-date information, CACI maintain a dedicated ACORN website. The site provides you with an extensive library of product purchasing and consumer behaviour profiles, with a pen portrait illustrating each type.

There is also a detailed explanation of the methodology behind ACORN, and, for our long-standing clients, matrices to help convert their old ACORN information into the new types.

Visit *www.caci.co.uk/ACORN*"

InSite Online

InSite is CACI's PC-based **Geographical Information System (GIS)**. This software is specifically designed for market analysis and targeting applications, by focusing on mapping capabilities. InSite is often used to compare and contrast different geographical areas; for example, store catchment areas or media geographies. Clients own customer and marketing data can be built into the system customising it for that company's specific applications. Data can be output as maps or tabular reports on screen or hard copy. InSite can also be used as a direct marketing tool – postal sector ranking can easily be carried out. Clients range from high street retailers to private health companies, building societies to market research companies.

Another well-known system developed by Richard Webber is **MOSAIC** which profiles consumers according to 58 lifestyle categories and claims to differ from competitive systems in three major respects: it analyses the country in geographical units averaging 15 households, not 150; it does not rely on Census data but uses CCN's continually updating databases to track population movements; and, finally, it incorporates information on financial behaviour at postcode level by taking advantage of CCN's position as the UK's leading credit reference agency (CCN Systems Ltd subsequently became Experian in 1997). In 1988 CCN launched MOSAIC Systems, a powerful PC-based product for identifying the unique characteristics of any given catchment area and designing the most effective marketing approach.

MOSAIC Systems is designed to bridge the gap between longer-term strategic decisions on matters such as product development, national advertising and pricing, and day-to-day tactical decisions on in-store promotion, distribution, coupon drops, branch location and other locally based activity. Being PC-based, users can test out any number of marketing tactics and have the results displayed instantly, without recourse to a bureau or to internal computing facilities. Results from the system can be either straightforward tabulation or full colour maps.

On launching the system, which is supplied as an integrated software and data-learning package, Richard Webber claimed:

> MOSAIC Systems is going to bring a hitherto unobtainable level of accuracy to local area marketing. Any one of the questions that this product addresses would have taken many hours to research. Now marketers can test out their theories in moments – quite literally at the touch of a button. It has brought the business of marketing firmly into the computer age.

MOSAIC is now one of over twenty neighbourhood classification systems offered by Experian and is available in numerous advanced economies where the Global MOSAIC classification is based on fourteen market segments common to them all.

WITH PINPOINT ACCURACY

The hidden election

The *Times* headline on Wednesday April 6, 2005 announced "The hidden election" and went on to report that the Labour and Tory parties were to spend millions of pounds on a high-tech campaign to win over some 830,000 key voters in marginal seats whose votes could determine the outcome of the overall election. The means? – **geo-demographic analysis.**

According to reporter, Tom Baldwin, "Labour is spending roughly two thirds of its £15 million campaign budget on this "ground war", rather than on billboard and newspaper advertisements. Its national communications centre in Gosforth, Newcastle upon Tyne has made 2.2 million canvassing calls in the past year. It has also posted 7 million items of mail to households since the autumn, at a rate of 1.5 million a month".

As for the Conservatives' they were to send out 3 million mailshots in the next few days, as well as 'phoning 300,000 homes with a recorded message from the Tory leader, Michael Howard.

Both parties were following the example of the Republican Party in the USA who used geo-demographic software to target key voters in swing states such as Florida and Ohio to great effect.

Faced with a hostile Westminster media, Prime Minister Blair decided to focus on direct contact with voters, with fewer press conferences and no election media 'battlebus'. Some 5000 voters in each of 60 key marginals were sent a DVD of messages from their Labour candidate and the Prime Minister with a discussion of local issues, backed up by emails to keep the voter up-to-date as the campaign developed.

Both parties used Experian's Mosaic database service with the Tories creating what they termed the 'Voter Vault' covering 165 seats in which they estimated they only need convert 830,000 of 2 million identified voters in order to win the election. To do so they used a model of each voter's propensity to vote and their propensity to support the Conservatives.

Given that both parties were using the same technology, it must be assumed that their efforts cancelled each other out to some extent. Nonetheless, by targeting specific voters on particular issues as they emerged, there can be no doubt that many traditional Labour supporters either did not vote or transferred their allegiance as the Labour Party was returned with a significantly reduced majority.

Segmentation by social grading

The use of social class as a basis for distinguishing the consumption behaviour of groups of individuals was discussed in Chapter 8. However, the validity and effectiveness of this approach has been subject to criticism and led to the establishment by the **Market Research Society** (in 1979) of a working party to examine the issues. An article by Francis Quinlan (1981), 'The Use of Social Grading in Marketing', reflected some of its conclusions and findings. Thus he wrote 'It is suggested that social grading of almost any kind is becoming of only marginal practical interest to most marketers', and cites the fact that much consumer expenditure relates to family purchasing rather than individual purchasing, with the result that household or family income/expenditure is a much better indicator of market potential than information about the individual head of household or housewife. Similar criticism has also been levelled against life-style as a basis for market segmentation.

However, while Quinlan argues that 'teachers and textbooks of marketing should not continue to refer to social grading for segmentation purposes as if it were as simple as ABC', it has to be recognised that by combining socioeconomic factors with demographic and housing characteristics even more powerful and discriminating approaches to market segmentation have been developed.

Social class and segmentation

As noted earlier, during the 1980s many marketers in the UK came to question the relevance of the traditional social class approach to market segmentation in an increasingly more egalitarian society. In order to examine the usefulness and stability of some alternative methods of measurement Granada Television commissioned the **British Market Research Bureau (BMRB)** to undertake research on the topic. The results of the research received the award of Best Paper at the 1988 Market Research Society Conference and were published as 'Can we at last say goodbye to social class?' (O'Brien and Ford, 1988).

In their paper the authors, Sarah O'Brien and Rosemary Ford, report the findings of a joint working party of the IPA, ISBA, ITCA and MRS whose report published in January 1981 concluded that:

1 Social grade provided satisfactory discriminatory powers.
2 No alternative standard classification variables were found to provide consistently better discriminatory powers.
3 No classification variables worked best across all product fields or data types.
4 There was no evidence to show a decline in the discriminatory power of social grade over the previous ten years (preceding 1979).

However, these findings appear at variance with reports such as those published by the Henley Centre and others on changing life-styles and the frequently observed fact that single earner AB households with children in private education frequently have less disposable income than C2D households with multiple earners occupying low cost public housing. Further, research by BARN indicated (1987) that in one year 32 per cent of their TV audience panel had changed social class.

Although this was seen as exceptional the fact that between 4 and 7 per cent of the panel change social class every year clearly points to a very mobile population in terms of the factors used to define social class. Against this background O'Brien and Ford felt it would be opportune to compare the usefulness of social class with some of the newer non-occupation based techniques for classifying consumers which had emerged in the 1970s and 1980s. Based upon a 50-minute interview with 1380 adult respondents the researchers were able to build up a very detailed picture of people's lives, motivations and possessions capable of being analysed by a range of non-standard demographic classifications. In the event three different variables were used – social class, lifestage and lifestyle. Social class was employed using the categories described in Figure 10.3, but collapsing A and B into a single category. Lifestage is a classification based upon a number of variables such as age, marital and working status, and presence of children. Six groups governing 83 per cent of the adult population were defined as 'power groups' reflecting their spending power in terms of disposable income, namely:

- *Granny power* (14 per cent) People aged 55–70, not in full-time employment and with no children or young dependent adults.
- *Grey power* (12 per cent) People aged 45–60 with one adult working full-time and no children or young dependent adults.
- *Older silver power* (18 per cent) Married people with older children (5–15 years) but no under fives.
- *Young silver power* (16 per cent) People who are married with children aged 0–4 years.
- *Platinum power* (7 per cent) Married people aged 40 or under but with no children.
- *Golden power* (15 per cent) Single people, with no children, aged 40 or under.

The remaining 18 per cent did not fall into any of these categories.

The Lifestyle variable was derived from a factor and cluster analysis of 54 attitudinal dimensions and yielded five clusters.

The paper by O'Brien and Ford comprises an extended and rigorous analysis of the discriminatory power of the three different classificatory systems and comes to the conclusion that social class is not dead. In fact their conclusions are very similar to those of the Working Party reported above, namely:

- Social class does discriminate;
- No alternative classification provides consistently better discriminatory powers;
- No one classification works best across all product fields.

However, the researchers also conclude that:

- Sometimes other classifications discriminate more, and frequently they are just as powerful as social class.

In other words, marketers should always consider other classifications when designing surveys and analysing data.

The second part of O'Brien and Ford's research looks at the stability and replicability of the three approaches and comes to the conclusion that life stage is superior to both lifestyle and social class on the following grounds:

- Unlike social class it can be applied consistently at an international and cross-cultural level;
- Unlike geodemographic classification it does not require a very large sample size;
- Also unlike geodemographics it is not falsely stable (that is, systems like ACORN are based on census data which can become out of date due to the period between censuses);
- Lifestyle data require only a minimal extension to standard demographic data and so can be collected quickly;
- In contrast to social class, lifestage data are less likely to be regarded as 'personal' which makes the interviewers' task easier.

These conclusions reinforce those relating to the discriminatory power of the different approaches (assuming the base data is valid and reliable), namely, social class may be an appropriate method for analysing markets but one should always consider alternative approaches which may be better given the particular context and the purposes to which the research is to be put.

Preference segmentation

While demographic factors may provide a more than adequate description of a market segment and in some cases be a major influence on consumption behaviour – for example baby products, health care products – a marketing orientation requires that we look beyond demographics to the nature of preferences, as these will permit a much better understanding of the reasons underlying differences and similarities in actual consumption behaviour. For example, using the classification developed by Enis and illustrated in Figure 10.1, we could ask consumers to evaluate a product in terms of two attributes, X and Y, e.g. texture and taste, and then plot their answers as in Figure 10.4.

In the case of homogeneous preference there are no apparent segments (at least in terms of the attributes selected), and one would expect all suppliers to

Figure 10.4 Market-preference patterns

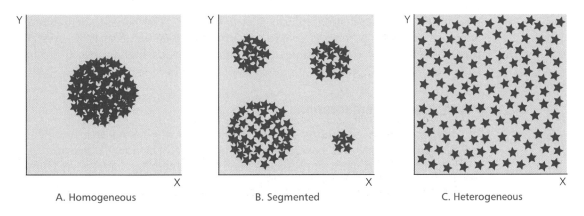

A. Homogeneous   B. Segmented   C. Heterogeneous

pursue an undifferentiated strategy, with price and availability as key elements, with advertising and promotion being used to try and develop a distinctive brand image.

Where preferences are heterogeneous, or diffused, then a brand with average attributes for X and Y would be the least unacceptable, but a more appropriate strategy might be to concentrate on one or other dimension and seek to develop a market segment and build up brand loyalty for the distinctive, brand.

Finally, where preferences are clustered, the segments are clearly identified and the producer can either concentrate on one or else develop a series of different products targeted at each of the distinct segments – a differentiated marketing strategy.

Examples of identifying new market opportunities through preference segmentation are regularly reported in the 'trade' press such as *Marketing Week* and *Campaign*. For example in the 1990s tissuemaker Scott relaunched Big Value Scotties Regular 200s Tissues as a high quality facial product made from 65 per cent recycled paper in a response to Tesco, Sainsbury's and Dixcel who had previously launched 100 per cent recycled paper brands to cater for those consumers concerned for the environment. In Scott's view 100 per cent recycled papers could not achieve the quality expectations associated with facial tissues and so saw an opportunity to plug a gap in the high quality recycled sector.

Similarly, in a report 'Going Organic', Coopers and Lybrand Deloitte cite research by Mintel which indicated that roughly one in four adults would prefer processed foods to be organically grown. Although the strongest preference (best target markets) comes from those aged 25–44, the ABs and the South West, there was surprisingly little difference between sub-groups using geo-demographic segmentation variables underlining that in this case it was expressed preferences which provided the best basis for segmenting the market.

Benefit segmentation

Another well-known approach to market segmentation is to subdivide the total market in terms of the specific benefits looked for by different consumers. This approach, pioneered by Haley, is illustrated by Table 10.2, which shows how the toothpaste market can be broken down into four distinct segments in terms of the principal benefit sought by users.

According to Gunter and Furnham (1992) an advantage of benefit segmentation is that it allows marketers to identify market segments by causal factors rather than descriptive ones like demographics. This is because "The benefit segmentation approach is based upon being able to measure consumer value systems in detail, together with what the consumer thinks about various brands in the product category of interest". (22)

Psychological segmentation

In Chapter 8 when discussing consumer behaviour we looked at a number of psychological factors that have an impact on buyer behaviour. Unsurprisingly, marketers have used many of these as a basis for segmenting markets. As Gunter and Furnham (op.cit.) comment: "Psychological classification of markets has evolved from two principal types of consumer variable: personality profiles and lifestyle profiles (psychographics)." (26) **Psychographics** evolved as a research methodology that combined the insights of motivation research, based on small samples and in-depth analysis of individuals, with the findings from personality research, usually based on large and representative samples, but with the disadvantage that it yielded poor correlations with actual buyer behaviour.

Table 10.2 Toothpaste market segment description

Segment name	The sensory segment	The sociables	The worriers	The independent segment
Principle benefit sought	Flavour, product appearance	Brightness of teeth	Decay prevention	Price
Demographic strengths	Children	Teens, young people	Large families	Men
Special behavioural characteristics	Users of mint flavoured toothpaste	Smokers	Heavy users	Heavy users
Examples of Brands disproportionately favoured	Colgate Oxygen, Macleans Freshmint	Macleans Whitening Pearl Drops	Colgate Total Crest Decay Prevention	Brands on sale
Personality characteristics	High self-involvement	High sociability	High hypochondrias	High autonomy
Life style characteristics	Hedonistic	Active	Conservative	Value oriented

Source: Adapted from Haley, R.I. (1968), 'Benefit Segmentation', *Journal of Marketing*, vol. 32, pp. 30–5. American Marketing Association.

REAL BEAUTY

In an article entitled 'On the mark', (*The Marketer*, April 2005), Lindsay Bruce gives a number of examples of how companies have successfully segmented their markets. On of the most striking examples is how Unilever developed a campaign for Dove toilet soap based on the idea of 'real beauty'.

According to the Dove website "For too long beauty has been defined by narrow, stifling stereotypes. Women have told us its time to change all that. Dove agrees. Dove's global Campaign for Real Beauty aims to change the status quo and offer in its place a broader, healthier, more democratic view of beauty".

Based on its consumer research Unilever found that the stereotype for beauty was tall, young and thin when, in reality, 'Beauty lies in the eye of the beholder' and so comes in many different forms. In fact beauty is a value based idea, not one based on demographics, which led to them using pictures of a well rounded, Reubenesque young woman and a 95 year old called Irene with the questions: "Does true beauty only squeeze into size 8?" and "Will society ever accept that 'old' can be beautiful?"

The campaign is backed up by a wide range of other initiatives (see *www.campaignforrealbeauty.co.uk*) and has enabled Unilever to target a segment not previously identified by the competition.

Psychographic analysis also incorporates demographic data and so offers a more powerful approach than any of the techniques used in isolation.

A distinguishing feature of psychographics is that it classifies consumers in terms of their values and lifestyles. Values are more broadly based than attitudes and consist of generalised beliefs about behaviour derived from experience (particularly early in one's lifetime) and mediated by families, education and religion. Values are a major determinant of lifestyle which defines the manner in which people live and their consumption patterns and behaviour. Gunter and Furnham observe: "... there is a more systematically determined concept of lifestyle built upon the social-psychological theory that people develop constructs with which to interpret, predict and control their environment. These constructs or patterns result in behaviour patterns and attitude structures maintained to minimise incompatibilities and inconsistencies in a person's life. Thus it is possible with appropriate qualitative research techniques to measure patterns among groups of people called lifestyles". (28)

Probably the best known example of this approach is the VALS™ (Values and Lifestyles) program developed by SRI International, now SRI Consulting Business Intelligence, a Californian consulting firm. The first version of VALS™ was developed in the late 1970s and has since been comprehensively revised. VALS™ places consumers into one of eight segments based on their responses to the VALS™ questionnaire. The main dimensions of the segmentation framework are primary motivation and resources, and these are described by SRI Consulting Business Intelligence as:

Primary Motivation

Consumers buy products and services and seek experiences that fulfil their characteristic preferences and give shape, substance, and satisfaction to their lives. An individual's primary motivation determines what in particular about the self or the world is the meaningful core that governs his or her activities. Consumers are inspired by one of three primary motivations: ideals, achievement, and self-expression. Consumers who are primarily motivated by ideals are guided by knowledge and principles. Consumers who are primarily motivated by achievement look for products and services that demonstrate success to their peers. Consumers who are primarily motivated by self-expression desire social or physical activity, variety, and risk.

Resources

A person's tendency to consume goods and services extends beyond age, income, and education. Energy, self-confidence, intellectualism, novelty seeking, innovativeness, impulsiveness, leadership, and vanity play a critical role. These personality traits in conjunction with key demographics determine an individual's resources. Different levels of resources enhance or constrain a person's expression of his or her primary motivation.

The relationship of these dimensions and the eight segments are illustrated in Figure 10.5, and each of the segments are defined by VALS™ in Table 10.3.

These kind of approaches to segmentation which combine life-styles and psychographics have been challenged in terms of their validity and care should be taken when using such composite methods.

Gunter and Furnham's book provides a clear and comprehensive overview of all aspects of psychographics and deal directly with issues of reliability, validity and their application to real world marketing problems. They conclude: " Psychographic research is being used more frequently in market segmentation studies for four primary reasons: (1) to identify target markets; (2) to provide better explanations of consumer behaviour (3) to improve a company's strategic marketing efforts; (4) to minimise risks for new products and business ventures". (159)

Segmentation by social character

Segmentation by social character usually involves a combination of life-style characteristics with psychographic information of the kind mentioned briefly in Chapter 8. As with the other techniques outlined already, the basic objective is to develop a profile of the intended customer in order to develop products and communication strategies that will zero-in on their specific needs and wants. By

Figure 10.5 VALS™ framework

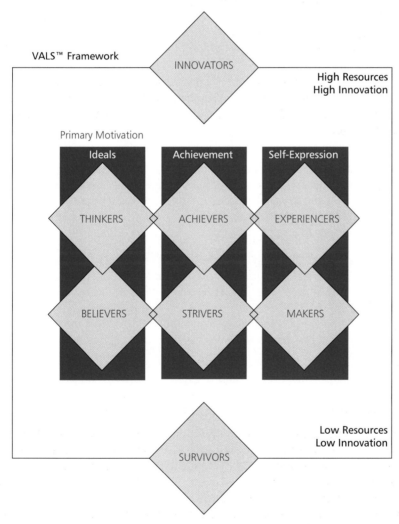

Table 10.3 Summary descriptions of the eight VALS segments

Innovators (formerly Actualizers)

Innovators are successful, sophisticated, take-charge people with high self-esteem. Because they have such abundant resources, they exhibit all three primary motivations in varying degrees. They are change leaders and are the most receptive to new ideas and technologies. Innovators are very active consumers, and their purchases reflect cultivated tastes for upscale, niche products and services.

Image is important to Innovators, not as evidence of status or power but as an expression of their taste, independence, and personality. Innovators are among the established and emerging leaders in business and government, yet they continue to seek challenges. Their lives are characterized by variety. Their possessions and recreation reflect a cultivated taste for the finer things in life.

Thinkers (formerly Fulfilleds)

Thinkers are motivated by ideals. They are mature, satisfied, comfortable , and reflective people who value order, knowledge, and responsibility. They tend to be well educated and actively seek out information in the decision-making process. They are well-informed about world and national events and are alert to opportunities to broaden their knowledge.

Thinkers have a moderate respect for the status quo institutions of authority and social decorum, but are open to consider new ideas. Although their incomes allow them many choices, Thinkers are conservative, practical consumers; they look for durability, functionality, and value in the products they buy.

Achievers

Motivated by the desire for achievement, Achievers have goal-oriented lifestyles and a deep commitment to career and family. Their social lives reflect this focus and are structured around family, their place of worship, and work. Achievers live conventional lives, are politically conservative, and respect authority and the status quo. They value consensus, predictability, and stability over risk, intimacy, and self-discovery.

With many wants and needs, Achievers are active in the consumer marketplace. Image is important to Achievers; they favour established, prestige products and services that demonstrate success to their peers. Because of their busy lives, they are often interested in a variety of time-saving devices

Experiencers

Experiencers are motivated by self-expression. As young, enthusiastic, and impulsive consumers, Experiencers quickly become enthusiastic about new possibilities but are equally quick to cool. They seek variety and excitement, savouring the new, the offbeat, and the risky. Their energy finds an outlet in exercise, sports, outdoor recreation, and social activities.

Experiencers are avid consumers and spend a comparatively high proportion of their income on fashion, entertainment, and socializing. Their purchases reflect the emphasis they place on looking good and having "cool" stuff.

Believers

Like Thinkers, Believers are motivated by ideals. They are conservative, conventional people with concrete beliefs based on traditional, established codes: family, religion, community, and the nation. Many Believers express moral codes that are deeply rooted and literally interpreted. They follow established routines, organized in large part around home, family, community, and social or religious organizations to which they belong.

As consumers, Believers are predictable; they choose familiar products and established brands. They favour American products and are generally loyal customers

Table 10.3 Summary descriptions of the eight VALS segments continued

Strivers

Strivers are trendy and fun loving. Because they are motivated by achievement, Strivers are concerned about the opinions and approval of others. Money defines success for Strivers, who don't have enough of it to meet their desires. They favour stylish products that emulate the purchases of people with greater material wealth. Many see themselves as having a job rather than a career, and a lack of skills and focus often prevents them from moving ahead.

Strivers are active consumers because shopping is both a social activity and an opportunity to demonstrate to peers their ability to buy. As consumers, they are as impulsive as their financial circumstance will allow.

Makers

Like Experiencers, Makers are motivated by self-expression. They express themselves and experience the world by working on it-building a house, raising children, fixing a car, or canning vegetables-and have enough skill and energy to carry out their projects successfully. Makers are practical people who have constructive skills and value self-sufficiency. They live within a traditional context of family, practical work, and physical recreation and have little interest in what lies outside that context.

Makers are suspicious of new ideas and large institutions such as big business. They are respectful of government authority and organized labour, but resentful of government intrusion on individual rights. They are unimpressed by material possessions other than those with a practical or functional purpose. Because they prefer value to luxury, they buy basic products.

Survivors (formerly Strugglers)

Survivors live narrowly focused lives. With few resources with which to cope, they often believe that the world is changing too quickly. They are comfortable with the familiar and are primarily concerned with safety and security. Because they must focus on meeting needs rather than fulfilling desires, Survivors do not show a strong primary motivation.

Survivors are cautious consumers. They represent a very modest market for most products and services. They are loyal to favourite brands, especially if they can purchase them at a discount.

Source: VALS™ and these definitions are © SRI Consulting Business Intelligence. *www.sric-bi.com/VALS/*

exploring the buyers attitudes, beliefs, emotions and values it is possible to build up a much more detailed picture and, as with VALS™, many organisations have come up with classifications of their own.

For example, the Canadian-based Environics Research Group has more than 20 years experience measuring, tracking and interpreting the social values/ psychographics of new car buyers in Canada, the USA, and around the world. Rather than replace their clients existing segmentation methods they seek to add depth to them by analysing the beliefs, attitudes and emotions that trigger the vehicle choices they make. From their studies they have identified up to 105 values that may be associated with the purchase of a particular brand of car and combined these to define buyers according to their shared values and outlook on life, so providing marketing managers with segments that are more actionable because they are readily identifiable in the real world. (*http://erg.environics.net/ automotive_research/*)

Psychographic profiles are usually developed from large-scale surveys (200–300 questions, 1000 plus respondents) using self-administered questionnaires covering a wide range of attitudes, opinions, and interests and Likert scales (see

Chapter 11). Responses may be analysed by simple cross-classification techniques, but given the wealth of information it is more usual to make use of the powerful multivariate techniques available in packaged computer programs such as **SPSS** (**Statistical Package for the Social Sciences**). Using techniques such as factor analysis it becomes possible to reduce the mass of data into a series of principal components which distinguish major groupings within the data

Industrial segmentation

While most segmentation studies are concerned with consumer markets the need is equally as great in many industrial markets, as was brought out by Richard Cardozo (1980) in his article 'Situational Segmentation of Industrial Markets'. Cardozo identifies four dimensions which may be used separately or in combination to classify organisational buying situations which may be regarded as 'market segments', namely:

1 *Familiarity with the buying task*; that is, Robinson et al.'s 'buyclasses'.

2 *Product type*. Here one may segment on the basis of product use in terms of components, materials and equipment (see Chapter 6 for a classification of industrial goods) which may be related to the 'degree of standardisation', namely:

   Custom – unique design for a particular customer;

   Modular – unique combination of standard available components or materials;

   Standard – combination of ingredients that has been offered previously.

3 *Importance of purchase to the buying organisation.*

4 *Type of uncertainty in the purchase situation.*

Clearly, Cardozo's approach seeks to add a behavioural and situational dimension to the more traditional Standard Industrial Classification (SIC) which is based on the nature of the product and encompasses very broad distinctions at the industry level (2 digit codes) as well as very narrow distinctions between firms (4 digit codes).

Another important dimension in both industrial and consumer markets is geography, particularly where this is a surrogate for national boundaries with all the implications these have for cultural, legal and political differences between markets.

International segmentation

Yoram Wind and Susan Douglas (1972) provided a useful schemata for segmenting international markets in an article 'International Market Segmentation'. Based upon these characteristics the authors proposed a 2-step process for segmenting international markets. First, one defines the **macro segment**, which may be one or more countries with similar market characteristics and then one sub-divides the macro segment on the basis of customer characteristics within it.

From the Wind and Douglas analysis it is clear that international segmentation, like industrial market segmentation, is a 'special case' of segmentation. By this we mean that the same factors or approaches described earlier are equally applicable to other contexts as they are to the consumer marketing environment in which they were originally developed. On the other hand, while the same principles will apply they will probably need modifying to take into account the special circumstances which enable us to identify industrial (or organisational) and international markets as being different from the general case described in most text books.

Not only will culture vary between countries, which will have a major bearing on attitudes and behaviour, but so will the institutions and infrastructure through which the marketer will seek to reach the prospective customer. Language and symbolism will also demand particular care in developing a communication strategy, all of which reinforces the point that successful segmentation is invariably based upon careful and effective marketing research. Given that marketing is a 'matching' process which seeks to ensure the seller deploys resources and skills to maximum effect in meeting customer needs, market segmentation based on sound analysis has a major role to play. We return to this theme in the final section of this chapter on 'Targeting and Positioning'

METHODS OF SEGMENTATION

In the preceding section we have looked at a number of different bases for segmenting markets without addressing the question of how one should set about the task. As is apparent from the references already cited there is a wealth of information on the subject and the discussion here can only scratch the surface. However, for a concise but comprehensive discussion of the topic one cannot better the article 'Issues and Advances in Segmentation Research' by Yoram Wind (1978). The following discussion of methods draws heavily on this source.

As Wind points out, 'Four major types of models can be used in an effort to segment a market. They include the traditional a priori and clustering-based segmentation models, and the new models of flexible and componential segmentation which are based on different sets of assumptions.' He continues:

A priori segmentation models have had as the dependent variable (the basis for segmentation) either product-specific variables (e.g. product usage, loyalty) or general customer characteristics (e.g. demographic factors). The typical research design for an a priori segmentation model involves seven stages:

1 *Selection of the (a priori) basis for segmentation.*
2 *Selection of a set of segment descriptions*
   (including hypotheses on the possible link between these descriptors and the basis for segmentation).
3 *Sample design – mostly stratified and occasionally a quota sample according to the various classes of the dependent variable.*
4 *Data collection.*
5 *Formation of the segments based on a sorting of respondents into categories.*
6 *Establishment of the (conditional) profile of the segments using multiple discriminant analysis, multiple regressional analysis, AID or some other appropriate analytical procedure.*

7 *Translation of the findings about the segments' estimated size and profile into specific marketing strategies, including the selection of target segments and the design or modification of specific marketing strategy.*

Clustering-based methods are very similar to a priori methods with the essential difference that one does not specify in advance a dependent variable but rather looks for natural clusters occurring in a data base. Needs, benefits, attitudes, lifestyle and psychographic characteristics are the most commonly used factors in establishing the existence of a cluster. This approach is also known as the post hoc method of segmentation. On occasion **a priori** and **post hoc** methods may be combined in a hybrid approach: for example, one might segment first on usage and seek to determine if there are clusters or sub-groups within these segments, using benefits, needs and so on as a basis for refining the discrimination.

As the name implies, **flexible segmentation** is a dynamic methodology which offers management "the flexibility of "building up" segments (cell or cell combination with any specific brand-switching matrix) based on the consumers' response to alternative product offerings (under various competitive and environmental conditions)' (Wind, 1978, 'Issues and Advances'). The technique depends heavily on **conjoint analysis** and computer simulations of choice behaviour and is particularly suited to concept and new product testing.

The fourth approach, which also depends upon sophisticated statistical analysis and extensive computing power, is **componential analysis**. The model, proposed by Green, differs from other segmentation models in that it seeks to predict which type of consumer will be most responsive to which product feature. The method has many similarities with flexible segmentation and is applicable to both industrial and consumer markets.

In Quinlan's opinion, flexible and componential segmentation 'has become highly academic and out of touch with real world practice', which is a view shared by Graham Hooley of the Aston Business School. In an article entitled 'Multivariate jungle – The Academic's Playground but the Manager's Minefield' (1980) he argues forcefully that the development of multivariate statistical techniques and the ready availability of massive computing power have resulted in academics presenting such methods as if they were the panacea for all ills. Such claims are regarded sceptically by practitioners and lead Hooley to propose seven commandments to govern their use, namely: 'do not be technique oriented; consider multivariate models as information for management; do not substitute multivariate methods for researcher skill and imagination; develop communication skill; avoid making statistical inferences about the parameters of multivariate models; guard against the danger of making inferences about market realities when such inferences may be due to the peculiarities of the method; exploit the complementary relationship between descriptive and predictive methods.'

Using segmentation techniques

In order to justify market segmentation most writers agree that a market segment must possess four distinct characteristics:

1 It must be *measurable*;
2 It must be sufficiently *substantial* to warrant the effort invested in it;

3 It must be *accessible* in the sense that there are channels of distribution, media and so on which permit a focused approach to it;

4 It must *respond uniquely* to the efforts directed at it.

To these four conditions defining a viable market segment Thomas, 1980 ('Market Segmentation') adds a fifth – stability – by which he means that the segment's behaviour is such that its future response may he predicted.

However, authors are less agreed upon the role which segmentation has to play in marketing strategy. Some see its role as offensive, in the sense that segmentation should be used to identify opportunities and unfilled niches in the market place which can be exploited through an aggressive strategy. Conversely, other authors see market segmentation as a means of avoiding cannibalisation of one's existing products by defining distinct segments for new products and as a defensive strategy for deterring new entrants to the market. Clearly these alternatives are not mutually exclusive for a firm with a portfolio of products, when defensive strategies will be more suited to products in the mature or decline phase of their life-cycle, while offensive strategies will be appropriate for guiding new product development and managing products in the launch phase of their life-cycle. However, it is well to heed the warning given by Resnik, Turney and Mason (1979) in 'Marketers Turn to Counter-Segmentation', who state, 'Many markets today may be characterised as **hyper-segmented**, a condition under which increasingly smaller market segments are identified and targeted.' This fragmentation may cause consumers to become confused, retail distribution difficult to maintain, and result in major diseconomies in both production and marketing. To avoid this, Resnik et al. propose that marketers will have to turn to 'counter-segmentation', involving:

1 The elimination of market segments by dropping products.

2 The fusion of segments by persuading customers to accept simpler and less-differentiated products.

On the other hand, G. Mueller-Heumann (1992, pp. 303–14) suggests that due to widespread changes, such as the shifts being experienced in demographic and psychographic population characteristics, markets will become increasingly fragmented and that 'mass customisation' of production will result. All this will have serious implications for marketing strategies in the future, challenging the 'traditional marketing thinking'.

Mueller-Heumann points to the rapid increases in **direct marketing** as a signpost for future trends. Direct marketing has become more and more influential although most current strategies still work in conjunction with a 'mass marketing focus'. The growth of direct marketing is set to increase with the rapid improvements in the use of information technology, the greater flexibility of production technology and a fragmentation of consumer demand. Future segmentation approaches, therefore, will become closer to the consumer. (Direct Marketing is dealt with in some detail in Chapter 19).

SELECTING MARKET SEGMENTS

All of the preceding discussion has been concerned with the identification of market segments. To conclude this chapter it is important to recognise that having disaggregated a market into a set of distinctive characteristics which meet the five criteria set out in the preceding section, very few organisations will wish, or be able to service them all. It follows that one must establish criteria for selecting that segment or segments that offer the greatest opportunity for the firm. This activity is frequently referred to as **targeting** and **positioning**.

In order to target a market segment Wind (1999, p. 402) suggests one must answer the following questions:

- What is the likely response to the firm's offering, including response to the positioning of the firm's products and services?
- What is the size of the segment in terms of the revenues and profits it is likely to generate?
- Can the segment be reached? (via controlled media and distribution or via a self-selection strategy)?
- What are the current and likely competitive activities directed at the target segment?
- What are the likely costs of reaching effectively the target segment?
- What is the likely impact of changes in relevant environmental conditions (for example economic conditions, life-style, legal regulations, and so on) on the potential response of the target market segment?
- Do we have the required offerings and competencies effectively to develop, reach and serve the selected segments?
- How many segments can you manage effectively?

By answering questions such as these one should be able to decide which segment(s) represent the best opportunity. This is known as **targeting**. But, selecting a target segment is only part of the problem. Rarely will a viable market segment be unoccupied so the new entrant will have to position themselves in the minds of the potential customers as being different, and better, than other competitors.

Earlier (Chapter 5) we introduced the concept of **Branding**. **Positioning** is very much concerned with branding and vice-versa. In the *Westburn Dictionary of Marketing* we find that 'Product positioning defines the location of a product or service relative to others in the same market place and then promotes it in such a way as to reinforce or change its "position" '.

According to Ries and Trout 'positioning' got started in 1972 when they wrote a series of articles entitled 'The Positioning Era' for *Advertising Age*. These ideas are fully developed in their book *Positioning: The Battle for your Mind* (1986) which is highly recommended reading. In their book, Ries and Trout claim that 'Positioning starts with a product, a piece of merchandise, a service, a company, an institution, or even a person, perhaps yourself. But positioning is what you do in the mind of a prospect. That is, you position the product in the mind of the prospect'.

To make good positioning decisions one needs to be able to answer four questions:

- What critical success factors do consumers use in choosing between competing offerings?
- How important are these relative to one another?
- How do we compare with the competition on these factors? (**Competitor analysis**)
- How do consumers use this information to make choices? (**Buyer behaviour**)

The answers to these questions may well be used to create a perceptual map as described in Chapter 8 so that one may determine how one's offering compares with the competition. Once this has been established the key issue is how does one reinforce people's perceptions if they are favourable to you, or modify them if they're not, to maintain or create a competitive advantage? Ries and Trout suggest that 'Positioning is an organised system for finding a window in the mind. It is based on the concept that communication can only take place at the right time and under the right circumstances.'

The problem faced by the marketer is that people are faced with an over-supply of information and so screen out the great majority of it. (Remember Selective Perception in the model of Buyer Behaviour in Chapter 8?). Thus, finding the window of opportunity requires a detailed understanding of the customer's needs. Ideally, one would like to find a niche which is unoccupied by anyone else. However, this is seldom possible and this makes it necessary to 'reposition the competition'. To do so one has to change consumers' existing perceptions, which is recognised as a difficult task. The most effective way is to provide 'proof' or evidence which people can readily verify for themselves. This is best achieved using objective factors which would be taken into account in a **cost–benefit analysis**. Alternatively, one can attempt to reduce the credibility or acceptability of competing products – usually by comparative advertising pointing out benefits your product has which the competition has not.

The identification and communication of intangible (service) and subjective benefits has assumed ever-increasing importance as it becomes more and more difficult to create, let alone sustain an objective competitive advantage. It is for this reason that Branding has assumed such importance in modern marketing practice. We return to this topic again in Chapter 14.

Summary

In this chapter we have looked at an analytical approach to the clear identification of consumer needs and wants as the basis for developing focused marketing strategies.

While it is true that producers have always sought to differentiate their products this strategy of **product differentiation** is quite different from one of **market segmentation**. The former tends to reflect a product orientation, in which the seller assumes that different people will have different tastes, while the latter reflects a market orientation whereby the seller finds out what people want and then sets out to create a supply of appropriate goods and services. Indeed, market segmentation is an original marketing concept, and an important theoretical underpinning of the subject of central importance.

The chapter itself has first defined the concept of market segmentation before moving on to look at some of the bases or methods available. Particular attention has been given to Demographic, Geo-demographic, Social, Psychographic and Behavioural factors. The application of these to the industrial and international context was touched on briefly before considering when and how to use segmentation techniques in order to target markets and position oneself in the chosen segment.

In the April 2005 issue of *The Marketer*, Malcolm McDonald summarised the segmentation process as comprising the following seven steps:

Phase 1: Developing Segments

1 Define the market – be clear about which 'market' you are segmenting and size it.

2 Map the market – determine how your market works and home in on the decision-makers.

3 Develop a representative sample of decision-makers, based on the differences in the features they see as key. Note who they are and size them.

4 Use the purchase behaviour of decision-makers along with who they are, to understand their real needs.

5 Group like-minded decision-makers together to form clusters; then check they qualify as segments.

Phase 2: Prioritising and selecting segments

6 Segment attractiveness – determine the potential of each segment to meet the requirements

of your company.

7 Company competitiveness – assess how well you meet the requirements of each segment compared to competitors.

In the next chapter we consider Marketing Research and the tools and techniques it uses to collect and analyse the kind of data called for in making segmentation decisions.

Review questions and problems

1 'Whenever a market for a product consists of two or more buyers then it is capable of division into meaningful buyer groups.' Discuss the validity of this statement.

2 'Without market segmentation there can be no marketing strategy.' Briefly define these terms and discuss the extent to which the statement is true.

3 Discuss the concept of reference groups as a basis for market segmentation.

4 The same market can sometimes be segmented by a number of variables. What are some of the problems that might be encountered in segmenting a market under such conditions?

5 Market segmentation is a recognition of the classification of products by consumers. Discuss.

6 Explain the problems associated with market segmentation and whether it is desirable or feasible in all situations.

7 Recommend the ways most likely to improve your marketing efforts by using a segmentation approach in each of the following markets:
(a) women's magazines;
(b) toilet soaps;
(c) computers.
Give reasons for your decision.

8 Using examples of your choice, explain how the element of social class can be used as a segmentation variable.

9 What segmentation approaches would be most appropriate for the following products: frozen vegetables, clothing, dog food, airline travel, televisions? Justify your answers.

10 Discuss how a positioning strategy might be employed in the marketing of a service such as packaged holidays.

Key terms

a priori
ACORN
branding
British Market Research Bureau (BMRB)
buyer behaviour
CACI
competitive advantage
competitor analysis
componential analysis
conjoint analysis
cost-benefit analysis
decision making unit (DMU)
direct marketing
education, occupation, income
family/household status
flexible segmentation

gender
geodemographic analysis
geodemographic segmentation
geographic information system (GIS)
grey market
hyper-segmented
life-cycle stage
lifestyle
macro segment
Market Research Society
market segmentation
mass marketing strategy
Mintel
MOSAIC
NAICS (North American

Industry Classification System)
positioning
post hoc
product differentiation
psychographics
social class
socioeconomic grouping
Standard Industrial Classification (SIC)
Statistical Package for the Social Sciences (SPSS)
target marketing
targeting
undifferentiated
VALS™ (Values and Lifestyles)
values

Supplementary reading list

Gunter, B.and Furnham, A. (1992) *Consumer Profiles. An introduction to psychographics.* London: Routledge

Hooley, G., Saunders, J. and Piercy, N. (2003) *Marketing Strategy and Competitive Positioning,* 3rd. Edition, Harlow: Pearson Education Limited *– especially Part 3.*

McDonald, M. and Dunbar, I. (2005) *Market Segmentation: How to do it, How to profit from it,* (Elsevier Butterworth Heinemann)

Wind, Y. (1999), 'Market Segmentation' in Baker, M.J. (ed.) *IEBM Encyclopedia of Marketing,* (London: Thomson Learning).

PART THREE

Managing the Marketing Mix

The notion of the **marketing mix**, conceptualised by Neil Borden as consisting of 12 distinctive activities, was introduced in Chapter 1. Subsequently, Eugene McCarthy reduced these to four principal components which he labelled Product, Price, Place and Promotion – the 4Ps – and it is these that have dominated the structure of general textbooks and introductory marketing courses for the past four decades.

Over this period the number of scholars and students of marketing has increased enormously with a corresponding increase in the amount of knowledge and information about the subject. The first edition of this book appeared in 1971 and was targeted at immediate post-Advanced level students most of whom were studying for an HNC/D in Business Studies or the Institute of Marketing's Diploma. There was only a handful of undergraduate courses, and these were to be found in the then Polytechnic sector. There were only two other British textbooks and all three contained less than 300 pages. Today, major introductory textbooks contain between 750 and 1250 pages and the section dealing with the mix elements has expanded proportionately.

And so it is with this book which has *ten* chapters covering Marketing Research, Product Policy, Packaging, Brand Management, Channel Management, Pricing and *four* chapters on different aspects of Marketing Communications. The Chapter on Branding is new to this edition, and its inclusion has become inevitable as the identity of the supplier and/or the product or service has become increasingly significant in determining the customer's choice.

The opportunity has also been taken to re-organise the material on marketing communications. To begin with, Chapter 17 reviews the process of communication and looks specifically at the **source** or origin of the message and the 'language' used, the **medium** or channel through which it is directed at an intended receiver or audience, and the **effects**, if any, on the receiver. With the growth of a new channel/medium – the **Internet** – the opportunity has been taken to distinguish more clearly between **mass communication** – essentially Advertising and Public Relations – and **personal** or **direct communication** which covers all the means used to make direct contact with customers.

As will become clear, there is an almost infinite number of combinations and permutations of the mix elements. However, as we explained earlier (Chapter 1), there is only a limited number of strategic alternatives – **cost leadership**, usually based on standardisation, mass distribution and promotion; **differentiated marketing** based on market segmentation with differentiated marketing mixes for each segment, and **niche**, **focus** or **concentrated** marketing directed towards a single, clearly defined group of customers. Accordingly, as we review each of the mix elements, we will identify which tactics are most suited to each of these strategies.

MARKETING RESEARCH*

Learning Goals — *After reading this chapter you should be able to:*

- Define marketing research.

- Explain the scope of marketing research.

- Clarify the distinction between primary and secondary data.

- Summarise the nature of desk research and list some major sources of external data.

- Describe the nature of field research and the collection of primary data.

- Explain the survey methods available to a researcher and the differences between censuses and surveys.

- Define the nature of sampling and review the types of sample in common use.

- Illustrate the various methods of making contact with respondents.

- Review some of the issues involved in the design and use of questionnaires.

- List the kinds and properties of attitude scales and their use in marketing.

- Set out the preferred structure and format of market research reports.

- Describe the role of marketing research agencies and give examples of syndicated research data.

- Discuss the issues involved in the decision to establish a market research department and the role and function of the market research manager.

* Many of the topics covered in this Chapter are discussed in much greater detail in Michael J. Baker (2003), Business and Management Research, (Helensburgh: Westburn Publishers Ltd.)

INTRODUCTION

In Parts I and II we have looked at the nature and scope of marketing, the environment in which it takes place, and the concepts and ideas which influence and control marketing practice. So, while 'Fact finding' or market research was the twelfth and final item in Neil Borden's original conceptualisation of the marketing mix (see Table 2.4), in reality it is, or should be the starting point for all marketing decisions.

The importance of marketing research should be apparent immediately when one considers the basic principles on which marketing is founded:

- The creation and maintenance of *mutually satisfying exchange relationships*.
- The *self interest of customers* who will always choose the supplier offering them the greatest value.
- The *threat of competitive substitution*.
- *Accelerating technological change*.
- *Globalisation*.

For these, and many other reasons sellers are faced with varying degrees of uncertainty about the future behaviour of customers. If we fail to research into the factors which influence this behaviour then we will be victims of what Levitt termed 'marketing myopia', the inevitable consequence of which is a loss of competitive advantage leading to decline and failure. To avoid this we should heed the message contained in a verse by Rudyard Kipling:

I had six faithful serving men,
They taught me all I knew.
Their names were Where and What and When
And Why, and How and Who.

In other words, we need constantly to ensure that we know the answers to these six questions in terms of the customers we seek to serve. The aim of market research is to provide these answers so that we may define it as:

The organised collection and analysis of information required to solve marketing problems.

In this chapter we look first at some definitions and the potential scope of marketing research. Next, we examine the nature of research and will suggest that it may be classified as **exploratory, conclusive,** or **performance monitoring.** Research may be either **continuous** or **ad hoc** and based on **secondary** or **primary sources.** Once we have decided on the type of research we wish to pursue then we must consider the most appropriate methods to use. Usually this is seen as a choice between **qualitative** and **quantitative** methods but, once we have established what this means, we will probably decide that both may be used together.

Assuming that we are unable to find the answers we are looking for from existing data (**secondary research**), it will be necessary to design a research project of our own to find out what we need to know. Here the choice will be between **observation, experimentation** and some kind of **survey (primary research).** Each of these will be described in some detail, as will a variety of the more frequently used techniques associated with them.

Following a review of the analysis and presentation of the findings from our research, we discuss the kind of research that we can buy-in from specialist marketing research agencies, and particularly **panel data**. This will be followed by a review of other issues such as **database marketing** before concluding with some thoughts on how a firm can organise for marketing research.

DEFINITIONS

It is not without significance that this chapter is entitled '**Marketing Research**' as opposed to the more familiar title '**Market Research**', although some might consider it pedantic that a distinction be drawn between the two. It is reasonable to say that most of the published literature on market research is, in fact, concerned with marketing research in that it deals with the question of research in relation to marketing on a much broader front than is implied by the former description. By definition, *market research* is concerned with measurement and analysis of markets, whereas *marketing research* is concerned with *all* those factors which impinge upon the marketing of goods and services, and so includes the study of advertising effectiveness, distributive channels, competitive products and marketing policies and the whole field of customer behaviour.

In his *Principles of Management* (second edition), E. F. L. Brech (1954) defined market research as

> *the study of all problems relating to the transfer of goods and services from producer to consumer with the aim of producing practical answers consistent with accepted theoretical principles.*

At a later point the objective of undertaking research is stated as '*to reduce the areas of uncertainty surrounding business decisions*'. Both these definitions indicate a function of much greater scope than is inherent in the more limited concept of the market and analysis of it.

An earlier definition from the American Marketing Association, namely: '*The objective gathering, recording and analysing of all facts about problems relating to the transfer and sale of goods and services from producer to consumer or user*' emphasises that marketing research is equally concerned with industrial goods – a point which is frequently overlooked in definitions which refer solely to consumers, as the latter are usually interpreted as '**ultimate**' **consumers**. It follows that marketing research is concerned with the scientific investigation of all factors which impinge upon the marketing of goods and services. Accordingly, we can see that the scope of this function is virtually limitless, and discussion here will have to be confined to those types of research most frequently undertaken in practice.

Essentially, marketing research seeks to provide answers to five basic questions: Who? What? When? Where? and How? The associated question Why? extends inquiry into the area of socio-psychology and is sometimes distinguished as a separate field known as **motivation research**. In practice, marketing research is usually concentrated on a limited number of recurrent problems, often on a continuous basis, which may be classified as follows:

Market research
The size and nature of the market in terms of the age, sex, income, occupation

and social status of consumers;

The geographical location of potential consumers;

The market shares of major competitors, that is brand-share analysis;

The structure, composition and organisation of distributive channels serving the market;

The nature of economic and other environmental trends affecting the structure of the market.

Sales research

Determination of territorial variations in sales yield;

The establishment and revision of sales territories;

Sales call planning;

Measurement of the effectiveness of salesmen;

Evaluation of sales methods and incentives;

Cost–benefit analysis of physical distribution systems;

Retail audits.

Product research

Analysis of the competitive strengths and weaknesses of existing products, i.e. both one's own and one's competitors';

Investigation of new uses for existing products;

A FAILURE OF RESEARCH

The collapse of MGRover, the UK's last remaining domestic car manufacturer in April, 2005, attracted a great deal of adverse publicity. Not only about the greed of the four directors who had bought the company for £10 and then extracted £40 million from it while accumulating massive losses running to £25 million a month when it collapsed, but also about the DTI to realise what was happening until it was too late.

When BMW divested itself of Rover in 2000 many critics already felt it was too late to revive the brand. As it was the UK Government pumped millions into the company to try and save it and set up a special department in its Department of Trade and Industry "to help the UK Automotive industry succeed".

In a scathing Editorial the *Times* Business Editor, Patience Wheatcroft, summarised the questions foremost in people's minds (April 16th 2005). She wrote:

"What on earth is the purpose of the Department of Trade and Industry?

The DTI seemed to have no idea about the financial catastrophe that was unwinding at Longbridge until the arrival of an army of administrators was inevitable. Yet it has armies of people dedicated to the automotive industry. There is even, lurking within the DTIs automotive section, a "Foresight Vehicle". Clearly, it has nothing to do with forseeing potential industrial collapses and taking prescient action."

Wheatcroft points out that in addition to a dedicated Foresight team the Automotive unit "... claims to have "Business Relationship Managers", whose job it is "to maintain regular contacts with key firms to ensure that we build and maintain a comprehensive understanding of the issues that effect their productivity and competitiveness and therefore that of the country as a whole."" In addition the DTI had a Dedicated Asia Team (what price the China option?), an Analysis Team and even an Automotive Regional Unit based in Birmingham almost next door the ailing plant.

Clearly, the DTI is aware of the theory but was singularly ineffective in putting it into practice in the case of MGRover.

Product concept testing;
Product testing;
Packaging research;
Variety reduction.

Advertising research
Copy research;
Media research;
Measurement of advertising effectiveness.

Business economics
Input–Output analysis;
Short and long-range forecasting that is based on trend analysis;
Price and profit analysis.

Export marketing research
Any or all of the above where relevant.

Motivation research

This check-list is by no means comprehensive but serves as an outline of the possible scope of research activities. Although research in most of the above areas is concerned with the recording of fact, qualitative research into the nature of attitudes and opinions is also appropriate in a number of instances, for example product concept testing.

THE PLANNING AND EXECUTION OF RESEARCH

As noted in the Introduction, marketing research may be classified as falling into one of three major categories. The first of these, **exploratory research,** is used in the early stages of most research projects when one is seeking to define the nature of a problem to be solved, what may be already known about that problem, and what additional information would be helpful in coming up with an answer. **Environmental scanning** described in Chapter 4 is a form of exploratory research – initially it is wide-ranging and loosely structured but, as the issues become clearer so does the focus. Exploratory research is also useful when generating ideas for new products or for testing attitudes and opinions. With the advent of the internet, and powerful search engines like Google, exploratory research is inexpensive and easy to initiate.

By contrast **conclusive research** is formalised and highly structured. It is based on a clear specification of a problem to be solved, precise research objectives, a carefully chosen methodology, and those techniques best suited to yield valid and reliable data.

Finally, **performance-monitoring research** is, as the name suggests, designed to compare actual with planned results so that management action may be taken if necessary. In recent years there have been increased calls for marketers to be able to quantify the consequences of specific marketing actions to the point where **marketing metrics** were cited as the most important research topic for practitioners by the Marketing Science Institute of America for the period 2000 -2004.

Marketing research activity may be of two main types – **continuous** and **ad hoc**. Marketing is an on-going process in a dynamic environment, and continuous research is essential if the firm is to remain informed of changes in the demand determinants outlined in Chapter 3 and be able to modify its policies accordingly. Much data of this type is collated by specialist organisations and government departments, but is often too generalised to meet the individual firm's specific requirements and needs to be supplemented by 'in-house' research.

However, many marketing situations are unique, for example the introduction of a new product, and demand a specific or ad hoc investigation. Such research invariably follows a clearly defined sequence which includes the following stages:

1 *Recognition* of the need for research;
2 *Analysis* of the parameters which predicate this need – problem definition;
3 *Exact statement of the objective* of the research;
4 *Formulation of an experimental or survey design* based on the analysis of Stage 2;
5 *Data collection*;
6 Tabulation and *analysis of data*;
7 *Interpretation of results* and the formulation of conclusions and recommendations;
8 Preparation and *presentation of a report* containing the findings;
9 *Evaluation of results* of action initiated on basis of research findings, that is 'feedback'.

Clearly, continuous research must follow the same procedure in the first instance, but the first four stages will be omitted subsequently.

Primary and secondary data

The data collection phase of a research investigation draws on two main sources of information, which are distinguished as primary and secondary sources. **Secondary sources** consist of existing data and should always be examined first. Frequently, however, such data have been collected for purposes peripheral to the researcher's main line of inquiry and so need to be supplemented by the collection of new, or **primary**, data. These differences in the source of data are recognised in the distinction between **Desk Research** and Original, or **Field Research**.

Desk research

Desk research into secondary data sources is a common-sense preliminary to any field research. Not only is it possible that the required information is already available, albeit in a form which requires re-tabulation, but also such research is essential to indicate the precise nature of the data to be obtained by survey or experimentation. Further, published sources are more accessible and offer savings in time and money if properly used.

Logically, desk research should begin with the firm's own records. The area in which records are usually maintained from which to compile such a database normally include:

1 *Purchasing* – stock levels, unit costs, usage rates, etc.

2 *Production* – output, material, labour, inventory, physical distribution and overhead costs, machine utilisation, etc.

3 *Personnel* – wage costs, turnover, efficiency levels, absenteeism, etc.

4 *Marketing* – promotional and administrative expenditures, market and brand data, etc.

5 *Sales* – by product volume, value, contribution to profit, order size;
    – by type of outlet/customer;
    – by area and by salesman.

6 *Finance* – all cost and accounting data.

In addition to these internal data, the researcher also has access to a large number of external sources, which may be conveniently grouped into five main categories:

1 *Government* – domestic and foreign.

2 *Universities and non-profit research organisations*; for example the Oxford Bulletin of Statistics.

3 *Trade associations*, e.g. Confederation of British Industries

4 *Academic and professional journals, the trade press.*

5 *Commercial research organisations*; for example Economist Intelligence Unit, Gallup, ACNielsen, Dun & Bradstreet, MORI etc.

The publications of government departments are far too extensive to permit full documentation here. The best place to start for UK statistics is the government website at *www.statistics.gov.uk*, and use of their 'virtual bookshelf' will help locate information such as the Annual Abstract of Statistics, Expenditure and Food Survey and General Household Survey. The Stationery Office website is another place to find useful information, at *www.tso.co.uk*.

Commonly used international sources can be located from the websites of the **United Nations** at *http://unstats.un.org* and the **International Monetary Fund**, *www.imf.org*, among others.

In the *IEBM Encyclopedia of Marketing*, Christopher West (1999,) claims that a diligent search of secondary sources can be expected to yield data on:

- Population size, structure into geo-demographic groups and growth;
- The structure of distribution and the importance of various channels;
- Total sales, imports and exports of products;
- Imports and exports by origin and destination;
- Products available and their specifications;
- New product launches;
- Sources of supply;
- New contracts and successful bidders for outstanding contracts;
- List prices;
- Advertising expenditure by product, industry sector and supplier;
- New market entrants;

- Staff movements;
- Financial performance of suppliers

As noted earlier, a search of the Internet will often yield an amazing amount of information. Indeed the main problem with the internet is not to be overwhelmed by the sheer volume of references resulting from a simple inquiry. Here the secret is the careful selection of keywords for entry into the search engine of your choice, and then combining these into strings or phrases which will eliminate material and themes that are irrelevant or peripheral to your interest. Among the better known search engines are: *www.google.com*; *www.yahoo.com*; *www.altavista.com*; *www.ask.com* (Ask Jeeves, a 'natural language' search engine), and there are also metasearch engines, which conduct multiple searches simultaneously. These include *www. dogpile.com* and *www.profusion.com*. (Web technology is constantly evolving - for the most up to date information on search engines visit *www.searchenginewatch. com*). You should also consider *www.wikipedia.org* but bear in mind that while this sources contains more entries than Encyclopedia Britannica they are posted by enthusiasts and there is no guarantee they are factually correct. (Wilson (2003) contains a very comprehensive listing of secondary sources both published and online). A very good and comprehensive guide to using the Internet as a secondary research tool is Ó Dochartaigh (2002), *The Internet Research Handbook* (London: Sage).

When using published sources it is important to ascertain the method employed in the compilation and tabulation of the data, and to avoid direct comparative analysis where this differs. Further, such data should only be used when the researcher has satisfied themself as to their validity, reliability and homogeneity.

Primary or field research

When all published sources have been evaluated, the research issue may still remain unanswered, although much more clearly defined. As noted earlier, desk research is often incapable of providing answers to highly specific problems, but it will often indicate factors which have proved important in similar situations in the past. None the less, there are a number of areas in which field research is usually necessary, and these may be summarised as:

- *Advertising research* – the effectiveness of advertisements per se; that is, copy testing, and media research – usage, coverage and so on.
- *Consumer research* – investigation of the factors underlying consumer choice and preference.
- *Distribution research* – effectiveness of alternative channel structures, methods of handling and so forth.
- *Packaging research* – colour, design, size, shape, informational content and so on.
- *Product research* – concept testing, acceptability of new product offerings, development of user and non-user profiles, and so forth.

Quantitative or qualitative?

Before deciding what kind of data one requires and how to collect it, it is necessary to consider whether one requires quantitative or qualitative data or, possibly, both.

Earlier, when considering the issues involved in defining problems and selecting possible approaches to solve them we touched on the distinction between quantitative and qualitative research. While these two approaches are often presented as if they are opposing and mutually exclusive research methodologies it was pointed out that they are in fact complementary and supportive approaches to the conduct of research.

For many years the distinction between qualitative and quantitative research was frequently presented in a polarised way as if these were alternative strategies and that quantitative and qualitative research may be regarded as polar and mutually exclusive alternatives. More recently a more balanced approach has emerged in which both kinds of researcher admit the contribution of the other. In parallel with this trend (or perhaps because of it) there has developed a growing recognition amongst the users of research that qualitative research is essential to address questions of what, how (process) and why, while quantitative research is appropriate to answer questions of whom, where, when and how (quantity).

Overall, qualitative research is best suited to areas needing a flexible approach while quantitative research is necessary to define more precisely the issues identified through qualitative methods. According to Peter Sampson (1967) the areas calling for a flexible approach may be summarised as:

1 Concept identification and exploration;
2 Identification of relevant behavioural attitudes;
3 Establishing priority among and between categories of behaviour, attitudes and so on;
4 Defining problem areas more fully and formulating hypotheses for further investigation.

In other words, and in very broad terms, one should use qualitative research:

1 To define the parameters of the market;
2 To understand the nature of the decision making process;
3 To elicit attitudinal and motivational factors which influence behaviour;
4 To help understand why people behave the way they do.

More recently, Wendy Gordon and Roy Langmaid (1988) suggested that the most important areas for qualitative research are:

- *Basic exploratory studies;*
- *New product development;*
- *Creative development;*
- *Diagnostic studies;*
- *Tactical research projects.*

Exploratory studies are usually called for when seeking to identify market opportunities for new product development, to monitor changes in consumption patterns and behaviour, to help define the parameters and characteristics of newly emerging markets or when seeking to enter established markets of which one has no prior experience. Gordon and Langmaid indicate five specific types of information which may be obtained from studies of this kind, namely:

1 *To define consumer perceptions* of the market or product field in order to help understand the competitive relationships between different types of product and/or brand in any product category – from the consumer's point of view rather than the manufacturer's.

2 *To define consumer segmentations* in relation to a product category or brand; for example psychographics and life-style segmentations.

3 *To understand the dimensions which differentiate between brands,* specifically on the basis of rational criteria and emotional beliefs. Where objective differences can be developed between products, rationality will predispose consumers to select these which conform most closely with their own preferences or criteria. Unsurprisingly, objective differences are comparatively easy to emulate with the result that emotional beliefs have come to play an increasingly important part in purchase decisions – industrial as well as consumer.

4 *To understand the purchase decision-making process and/or usage patterns.*

5 *Hypothesis generation.*

In the marketing discipline, experience has shown that qualitative research is particularly useful in a number of specific situations, which may be summarised as:

1 *Traditional preliminary exploration*

2 *Sorting and screening ideas*

3 *Exploring 'complex' behaviour*

4 *Developing explanatory models of behaviour*

5 *Enabling the decision maker to experience the world as consumers see it*

6 *To define unfilled needs and means of satisfying them.*

Most of these uses are self-explanatory and address the issue that social science research is concerned not only with facts but also with values. Through using qualitative research it becomes possible to discover what some of these underlying values are for, while one may seek to infer them from observing actual behaviour, the only real way one can establish 'why?' people behave as they do is to ask them. Even then it is not easy to get respondents to give you the real reason for we all have a tendency to rationalise behaviour (hence the emphasis upon price as an acceptable reason for not making a purchase rather than by giving offence and saying the article in question was useless, ugly or what have you). There is also the well-known human tendency to want to please and so give the researcher the answer you think the questioner is looking for.

To overcome these difficulties qualitative researchers have developed a whole battery of projective techniques so that the respondent is invited to speculate how someone else would behave in a given situation, e.g. by completing a sentence, by filling in the dialogue in a cartoon, etc. Of course, the only real basis we have for such speculation is our own knowledge and experience, attitudes and opinions, so it is hardly surprising if the projected behaviour is similar to how we would behave in the given situation. Gordon and Langmaid devote a whole chapter to Projective and Enabling Techniques, which they classify into 5 categories:

1 *Association*

2 *Completion*

3 *Construction*

4 *Expressive*

5 *Choice-ordering*

Within the **Association procedures** are to be found traditional word association tests such as "Tell me the first thing that comes to mind when I say detergent", through the classic **Rorschach ink-blot test**, to the construction of brand personalities, e.g. could you imagine Foster's Lager as a person and describe them to me. A further refinement is to provide the respondent with a pile of words and pictures and ask the respondent to choose those they associate with a brand name or product.

Completion procedures invite respondents to complete a sentence such as "People who drive Porsche motor cars are..." or the missing dialogue in a conversation between two persons. **Brand mapping**, in which respondents are invited to group like brands/products according to various criteria, is also regarded as a completion technique and enables the researcher to determine how consumers see the products competing with each other in the market place.

Construction procedures also invite respondents to construct a story from a picture (**Thematic Apperception Tests**) or in response to projective questions, through **bubble procedures** (you write in what you think the character in the drawing/cartoon is thinking) to the classification of stereotypes, e.g. you define a category of consumer and ask respondents to specify their consumption behaviour.

Expressive procedures also involve the use of drawings and the invitation to the respondent to describe their perceptions of the person and/or context. They may also include **role-playing** in which the respondent is asked to act out a particular activity, e.g. purchasing a product or playing the part of a named brand.

Finally, **choice ordering** is just that and asks respondents to rank order objects in terms of specific criteria - a technique which is very useful in determining what alternatives will be provided in multiple choice questions or for coding the answers to open-ended questions.

However, projective techniques are only one approach to qualitative research relevant mainly to marketing studies. Other qualitative methods widely used in other disciplines such as group discussions and depth interviews are dealt with later

As a broad generalisation, then, qualitative research is an essential prerequisite to most quantitative research in that it will help clarify the issues to be addressed, the parameters to be defined and measured, and the likely relationships between them

The distinction between quantitative and qualitative research and their mutual dependence, was illustrated by an article by Johannson and Nonaka (1987) entitled 'Market Research the Japanese way'. In this article, the authors report Japanese disdain for the volume of formal market research, conducted in the USA. They point out that when Sony researched the market for a lightweight portable cassette player the results indicated that consumers would only buy one with a recording facility. Akio Morita ignored this finding and the Walkman is history. Citing examples such as Matsushita and Canon the authors report how Japanese companies depend upon a combination of 'soft data' about shipments, inventory levels and retail sales. However, the authors also cite evidence of Japanese failures in American markets which they attribute to a lack of understanding of the attitudes and opinions of American consumers which could have been established by use of some of the survey techniques which they have eschewed. The conclusion is that both kinds of research are called for. Clearly with highly innovative and novel products it is unlikely that consumers could conceptualise the possibilities for a portable, personal entertainment system such as the Walkman. But, once the technological possibilities have become apparent, and markets begin to grow and mature, then the need to segment markets and position products will call for the kind of quantitative data which is unavailable when developing wholly new product concepts.

THE COLLECTION OF PRIMARY DATA

Observation

It is generally accepted that while business research is not a sufficient condition for competitive success, in the medium to long term it is certainly a necessary condition for continued survival. This conclusion may be reached by considering, for example, the explanations offered for marketing failures where a lack or absence of marketing research is most frequently cited as the primary cause. Alternatively, the reasons advanced for marketing success often cite the identification of a marketing opportunity unrecognised by competitors. Either way, keeping one's finger on the pulse of the marketplace is seen as an essential and continuing concern of the firm's management.

Observation is one of the three principal research methods – the other two being experimentation and survey. In some shape or form observation is the starting point for all research – it is an observed event or stimulus that prompts mental inquiry into its meaning and possible relevance. In the absence of understanding, and/or a satisfactory explanation, we look for additional information to help us understand and interpret the phenomenon that has come to our attention. In other words we do some research and this usually starts with further observation.

Observation may be both informal and formal. When undertaken as part of one's normal daily routine it is usually informal and loosely structured – often referred to as 'scanning' e.g. reading the *Financial Times*. Observation has a critical role to play in this activity. By contrast, observation within research is a scientific technique - indeed it is the basis of the scientific method - which is characterised by a much more structured and systematic approach than that called for in a scanning mode.

Fundamentally, the distinction between scanning and observation as a scientific technique is that scanning is only partly structured and is intended to maintain an awareness of information, actions and events which may have a bearing upon the decision makers' judgement and/or action. On the other hand, observation consists of the systematic gathering, recording and analysis of data in situations where this method is more appropriate - usually in terms of objectivity and reliability - and able to yield concrete results (e.g. the flow of persons in a shopping centre) or provide formal hypotheses about relationships which can then be tested by experimentation or survey analysis. Hence, scanning is often a precursor of observation and may result in the formulation of tentative hypotheses leading to formal observation and the development of conclusions or formal hypotheses for further testing.

Although observation may be regarded as a technique in its own right it is probably used most often as an element of one or other of the other two methods. In experimentation, observing and recording behaviour may well be the single most important technique while in survey analysis interviewers will frequently record factual information both to reduce the burden on the respondent (e.g. type of property, make of consumer durable) and to ensure accuracy where the respondent may be unsure about the correct answer (make of tyres on your car). A simple inspection will immediately provide an accurate factual answer. Similarly, a meter can record precisely what channel your TV is tuned to while questions asking you to recall this at some later date could result in considerable response error.

A major advantage and disadvantage of observation as a research method is that it is very largely a 'real-time' activity. With the advent of low cost video technology it is true that one can record events for later analysis but this is certainly not possible for participant observation where the direct involvement of the observer is an essential part of the methodology. Participant observation is particularly suited to the gathering of qualitative data where one is seeking to establish the behaviour of the subjects in a particular context (family decision making, board meeting, etc.). However, unless the observer is unknown to those they are observing, which is often difficult to achieve, there is always a danger of influencing the very behaviour one is seeking to monitor due to the control or **Hawthorne effect**.

Similarly, another danger is that by becoming a participant the observer will change their own attitudes and/or behaviour and so introduce bias into their observation. (For an extended review of the uses and problems which relate to participant observation the reader should consult Moser and Kalton (1971)). Stephen Brown provides an example of the value of an observation study in his article "Information seeking, external search and 'Shopping' behaviour" (*Journal of Marketing Management*, 1988, 4, No.1, 33-49). As the author notes in his introduction "Few topics in consumer research have generated as much discussion as pre-purchase information seeking;" but, that said, there is a clear difference between the research findings which show that consumers do not 'shop around' and the retailers belief that they do. Brown suggests that both interpretations may be correct but reflect a different perspective. Thus, retailers observe how consumers behave, while the great majority of academic researchers survey consumers and invite them to recall and reconstruct their actual behaviour. But, in doing so, most respondents focus solely upon the purchase decision and ignore or forget their antecedent behaviour when they were acquiring information and evaluating it prior to making a shopping expedition. To overcome this deficiency Brown undertook a weeklong observation study in a shopping centre and observed the behaviour of 70 groups of shoppers from their time of entry to their time of departure. While only regarded as an exploratory study Brown identified three main types of shopping behaviour, leisure shopping (17%), chore or purposeful shopping (41%), and mixed activity (42%) from which it was inferred that consumers use the occasion of shopping trips to gather information on products which they are not purchasing, presumably for future reference should it be required, i.e. 'shopping around' in the retailer's sense is incidental to the main purpose of the trip. To test this hypothesis Brown proposes a much more rigorous design incorporating both observation and face-to-face interviewing underlining the importance of using observation to help formulate hypotheses and then combining it with other approaches to test those hypotheses.

In sum, observation is usually the first step in the scientific method. Having identified a problem, observation (**successive focusing**) allows one to define those areas or issues whose detailed examination may provide a solution to the problem. However, as Bryman (2001) notes the notion of 'observation' as a research technique has been largely displaced by the more fashionable concept of 'ethnography'.

Ethnography – literally 'nation writing' – is defined as 'The scientific description of races and cultures of mankind' (*Concise Oxford Dictionary*). Under this definition the writings of Herodotus and other historians of the Classical Era would qualify as 'ethnography', as would the accounts of explorers, missionaries and colonists in more recent times.

To begin with, it is clear that observation is an integral part of all research. However, to qualify as a scientific technique Selltiz et al. (1959) state that observation must satisfy four criteria:

1 *Serve a formulated research purpose.*

2 *Be planned systematically,*

3 *Be recorded systematically* and related to more general propositions.

4 *Be subjected to checks and controls on validity and reliability.* (200)

In summary Desai (2002) lists the characteristics of ethnographic research when used in a business and management context as:

- A focus on the cultural and social content of people's actions and beliefs – looking at people as whole individuals, rather than compartmentalised consumers.

- Seeing the world from the point of view of the participants, and avoiding imposing the researchers' cultural frameworks.

- Allowing people to use their own language to describe their world.

- Looking at behaviour in the place and time at which it actually occurs – in the home, the office, the car, the supermarket.

- A long-term involvement with individuals or groups.

- The use of a range of data collection methods, including interviews, group discussions, informal conversations and observations of behaviour, and also the inclusion of cultural artefacts as part of the data – e.g. photographs, films, drawings.

A recent issue of *Marketing Business* (November/December 2002) contained a feature article entitled 'Big brother is watching you' that described the use of ethnographic techniques in marketing research. While there is obviously disagreement between practitioners as to how rigorous such studies are, with some maintaining that only trained anthropologists are adequately qualified, others take a more pragmatic view. One practitioner asserts "Ethnography is not research per se; it's looking at what we don't know we don't know... You can only find that out by living with people and going shopping with them." This 'deep hanging around' is seen as a major source of insight from which working hypotheses and more formalised data collection can be developed.

Experimentation

Because of the dynamic and complex nature of most business problems few are readily amenable to the experimental approach used so widely in the physical sciences. However, some specific problems are suited to an experimental design which, if properly controlled, will yield better and often less expensive data than can be obtained from a survey.

In an experiment the researcher usually seeks to control all the variables so that by varying one while holding the others constant they can determine the effect of the input or independent variable upon the output or dependent variable. It follows that a basic requirement for the conduct of an experiment is that one must be able to specify all the relevant variables. It is also implied that one has a theory, which can be stated as a hypothesis or hypotheses about the nature of the relationship between the variables, e.g. if two identical objects carry different prices then prospective buyers will perceive the higher priced object to be of higher quality. Alternatively, one may hypothesise that the colour of a product's packaging will influence the consumer's perception of it without any specific hypothesis about what colour will have what effect.

In a nutshell, experiments are usually undertaken to determine if there is a causal relationship between the variables under investigation. Moser and Kalton (1971) avoid a detailed philosophic discussion of the nature of **causality** but provide a useful guide to its determination. If A is a cause of the effect B then normally there would be an association between A and B. Thus, if smoking causes lung cancer one would expect that more smokers than non-smokers would contract the condition. All the statistical evidence points to this conclusion but some will seek to dismiss or ignore it on the grounds that smoking is neither a necessary nor sufficient condition for contracting lung cancer. A sufficient condition would mean that all smokers would invariably get lung cancer while a necessary condition would exist if people only got lung cancer after smoking. Clearly, neither of these conditions obtain, as there are many non-smokers who develop lung cancer. That said, the degree of association between smoking and lung cancer is so high, i.e. we can measure how many smokers and non-smokers get lung cancer and will discover that the likelihood of a smoker getting the disease is many times as great as a non-smoker, that the Government now insists that tobacco products should carry a formal health warning.

Evidence of causality is also to be found in the sequence in which events occur, it being obvious that a subsequent event cannot be the cause of an antecedent event. That said, while an antecedent event may be the cause of a subsequent event we will have to apply other tests of causality to determine whether in fact this is the case. In addition to tests of association we will also have to determine if there are any intervening variables, which may influence the apparent relationship (or even disguise it by masking the relationship or making it disappear). Moser and Kalton (1971) exemplify the problem in terms of the observed association between the income of the heads of households (I) and their conservatism (C) as measured by some suitable index. While C may increase or decrease in parallel with I (or vice versa!) and we may measure the degree of association through the calculation of the coefficient of correlation we cannot impute any causality to the relationship without also determining the time sequence - did I precede C or vice versa, and whether or not there are any intervening variables such as education, occupation, age or whatever, that might explain the relationship better. The more the possible number of intervening variables, the more complex the task of determining whether or not they have any bearing upon the relationship. It follows that in designing experiments one must have a particular concern to determine the degree of association, the sequence of events and the possible effect of intervening variables.

To address these problems 3 broad kinds of experiment are available, all of which require the establishment of a **control group** against which to compare the experimental group, namely:

1 *After-only design*
2 *Before-after design.*
3 *Before-after design with control group.*

In an after-only design the experimental group is exposed to the independent variable which it is hypothesised will cause a particular effect and their subsequent behaviour or condition is compared with that of the control group which has not been so exposed. For example, a new 'cold' remedy is administered to 100 volunteers and the progress of their cold compared with that of the 100 members of the control group who must be as closely matched as possible with the experimental group in terms of age, sex, physique, general state of health, etc. If the experimental group show a dramatic improvement then, assuming no intervening factors, we may assume there is a causal relationship between remedy and cure and express this in quantitative terms of the degree of association established.

Before-after designs are commonplace in marketing where the experimenter is seeking to determine the effect of a specific factor on people's attitudes and/or behaviour. In these cases the same people are used as both the control and experimental group. Suppose one wishes to assess the effect of a change in a marketing mix variable - price, packaging, product performance, advertising, etc. etc. - upon a group of consumers, the first step must be to establish a **benchmark** of their current attitudes/behaviour. Given the benchmark the group is then exposed to the modified **marketing mix** (always bearing in mind you can only vary one factor at a time) and their attitudes/behaviour measured again. Because of the experimental effect (see below) it would be dangerous to assume that all change detected is a direct consequence of the variation in the mix variable - that said, if change occurs it is reasonable to assume that, in part, this is due to the change in the independent variable.

The third design - before-after with control group - is generally recognised as the best of the three options in that it combines elements of both the preceding types and, most importantly, has established a benchmark for the control group before exposing the experimental group, i.e. one can quantify the similarities between control and experimental groups and not merely assume their similarity as is the case with the after-only design.

Survey research

While observation and experimentation both have an important role to play in marketing research it is the **survey** which is the best known source of primary data collection, not only in marketing but the social sciences in general. Undoubtedly this owes a great deal to their widespread use in polling opinion on political issues or other matters of current interest and concern such as health and food, or the effects of environmental pollution.

Survey method and sampling are both subjects on which a number of specialised texts have been written, and only the briefest coverage can be attempted here.

What then is a Survey?

Moser and Kalton (1971) devote over 500 pages to the subject of Survey Methods in Social Investigation but decline to offer a definition on the grounds that any "such a definition would have to be so general as to defeat its purpose, since the terms and the methods associated with it are applied to an extraordinarily wide variety of investigations, ranging from the classical poverty surveys of 100 years ago to Gallup Polls, town planning surveys, market research, as well as the innumerable investigations sponsored by research institutes, universities and government." In the *Westburn Dictionary of Marketing* Baker is less restrained and asserts that a survey is "The evaluation, analysis and description of a population based upon a sample drawn from it." In the *Marketing Handbook* (1965) Mayer adds to this attempt at a definition when he states "The essential element in the survey method is that the data are furnished by an individual in a conscious effort to answer a question." Thus Mayer sees the essence of surveys as posing questions ('the questionnaire technique') and goes on to add, "The survey method is the most widely used technique in marketing research. Some people go so far as to regard the questionnaire technique as being synonymous with marketing research. Unfortunately, the method is so universally employed in this field that many researchers use the survey technique when one of the other methods, the observational or experimental, is more appropriate."

Tull and Albaum (1973, 1993) support all three of the preceding views when they write, "Survey research is a term that is susceptible to a variety of interpretations. As most often used, it connotes a project to get information from a sample of people by use of a questionnaire. The question may be designed to obtain information that is retrospective, concurrent, or projective with regard to time. They may be asked in a personal interview, by telephone, or sent to the respondent by mail." Tull & Albaum stress that surveys are concerned with understanding or predicting behaviour and offer as their definition: "Survey research is the systematic gathering of information from (a sample of) respondents for the purpose of understanding and/or predicting some aspect of the behaviour of the population of interest."

Consideration of these definitions indicates that surveys are concerned with

- Fact finding
- By asking questions
- Of persons representative of the population of interest

- To determine attitudes and opinions; and
- To help understand and predict behaviour.

The design and execution of surveys and the methodology and techniques available is beyond the scope of an introductory text. Here we must be content with a broad overview of the survey method covering:

- The Purposes for which surveys are used
- The Advantages and Disadvantages of Survey Research
- Issues and Topics suited to surveys.

The purposes of survey research

Mayer identifies 3 kinds of survey, which he classifies as **factual**, **opinion** and **interpretive**, each of which is seen as having a distinctive purpose.

As the name implies factual surveys are concerned with securing hard, quantitative data on issues such as usage, preference and habits, e.g.

How much beer to you drink?
What is your preferred brand?
Where do you normally drink beer? etc etc.

In other words, such surveys are concerned with actual behaviour while in opinion surveys the objective is to get respondents' views upon the topic under consideration. Such opinions are almost always qualitative and may or may not be based upon actual experience. For example, a teetotaller may have quite strong perceptions about brands of beer without ever having consumed them. However, consumers' attitudes and beliefs based upon past knowledge and experience are of particular value in helping to plan future strategy, e.g. in designing a new product, developing a copy platform or selecting a distribution channel. As with factual surveys, a major purpose is to try and quantify the strength and direction of opinion as a basis for future decision-making.

By contrast interpretive surveys are used in circumstances where the respondent is asked to explain why they hold particular beliefs or behave in a particular way rather than simply state what they do, how, when and where, etc. Interpretive surveys are often the first step in primary data collection when the researcher is trying to get a feel for the topic under investigation and will often involve the use of projective techniques such as picture and cartoon tests, word and object association tests, sentence completion tests, and role playing. Depth interviewing and focused group interviews are also widely used, often to define questions to be used in a formal questionnaire for use in the factual or opinion survey.

Most market research surveys have a practical objective - to provide information on which to base decisions - while surveys of other populations are usually undertaken for theoretical reasons to enhance understanding. While such information may well be used as an input to decision making this is not its primary purpose, and this factor should be considered when using such data.

Advantages and disadvantages of survey research

In an article "The use of the survey in industrial market research" (*Journal of Marketing Management*, 1987, 3, No.l, 25-38) Susan Hart confirms that the survey is the most usual form of primary research undertaken and attributes its popularity to the following factors:

(i) The objectives of most research require factual, attitudinal and/or behavioural data. Survey research provides the researcher with the means of gathering both qualitative and quantitative data required to meet such objectives.

(ii) One of the greatest advantages of survey research is its scope: a great deal of information can be collected from a large population, economically.

(iii) Survey research conforms to the specifications of scientific research: it is logical, deterministic, general, parsimonious and specific

Alreck and Settle (1985) consider that the main advantages of surveys are that they are:

- *Comprehensive*
- *Customised*
- *Versatile*
- *Flexible*
- *Efficient*

By 'comprehensive' Alreck and Settle mean that the method is appropriate to almost all types of research (cf. Mayer's factual, opinion and interpretive categories of survey). The other four advantages are closely interrelated and boil down to the fact that one can design surveys to suit all kinds of problems and budgets. Naturally, 'dipstick' or 'quick and dirty' research where a limited budget and time pressures dictate only limited sampling using judgemental methods will lack the credibility (and validity) of the properly designed survey in which carefully designed and tested questionnaires are administered professionally to a statistically representative sample of the population. That said, virtually any research is better than none and there is considerable evidence to show that diminishing returns set in early in terms of the insights gained from research and also in terms of the confidence one can attribute to one's findings. Given then that the essence of marketing is that one should seek to determine the precise needs of prospective customers, a pragmatic approach which seeks to acquire additional information consistent with available resources is to be preferred to no research on the grounds that it lacks the rigour called for in the experimental sciences. While such rigour is attainable, the question is whether it is possible, necessary and/or worthwhile. In most student and practical projects it is not!

Of course surveys also have their disadvantages and Hart (1987) cites the following:

(i) The unwillingness of respondents to provide the desired data. The overriding concern here is of the non-response error, which can invalidate research findings.

(ii) The ability of respondents to provide data. In studying managerial decisions, it is important to target individuals in the organisation with the knowledge and experience of the subject under examination.

(iii) The influence of the questioning process on the respondents. Respondents may give the answers they think the researcher will want to hear, thus distorting the accuracy of the data.

Response errors, accidental or deliberate, may be reduced significantly through careful design and execution of the test instrument and were discussed by Webb (2000).

Issues and topics suited to surveys

From the above discussion, and particularly Table 11.1, it is clear that surveys can be used to gather data on virtually any problem which involves the attitudes and behaviour of people in either their individual capacities or as members of various kinds of social and organisational groupings. Within the domain of marketing research Alreck and Settle (1985) distinguish eight basic topic categories, namely:

- *Attitudes*
- *Images*
- *Decisions*
- *Needs*
- *Behaviour*
- *Lifestyle*

Table 11.1 Taxonomy of surveys

1 Classical Poverty Surveys (Booth, Rowntree, Bowley, Ford)
2 Regional Planning Surveys
3 Government Social Surveys
4 Market, audience and opinion research
5 Miscellaneous
- Population (Census)
- Housing
- Community studies
- Family life
- Sexual behaviour (Kinsey)
- Family expenditure
- Nutrition
- Health
- Education
- Social mobility
- Occupations and special groups
- Leisure
- Travel
- Political behaviour
- Race relations and minority groups
- Old age
- Crime and deviant behaviour

Source: Adapted from Moser, C. and Kalton, G. (1971), *Survey Methods in Social Investigation*, 2nd edn (Oxford: Heinemann Educational Books).

- *Affiliations*
- *Demographics*

Of course, these categories are neither mutually exclusive nor independent but, to the extent that they often require different treatment and measures, the classification provides a useful guide to survey planning.

Alreck and Settle subscribe to the **cognitive-affective-conative (CAC) model** of attitudes and see attitudes as a predisposition to act. They also assert that attitudes precede behaviour. In other words if you can define and measure attitudes you should be in a good position to predict behaviour. However, many researchers prefer the **expectancy-value (EV) model** developed from the work of Heider, Rosenberg and Fishbein which does not seek to establish a link between attitude and behaviour and so can accommodate problems of the kind touched on earlier when examining the purposes of survey research - namely, the teetotaller who may have strong positive attitudes towards brands of beer but with no intention of translating their attitude into behaviour. The point we are seeking to make is that one must be careful not to assume a causal relationship between attitude and behaviour albeit that the notion of consistency in both CAC and EV models indicates that if behaviour does occur it is most likely to be consistent with the pre-existing attitude - if one exists! Either way an understanding of underlying attitudes will clearly be of great value to the marketing planner.

Image is defined in the *Westburn Dictionary* as "Consumer perception of a brand, company, retail outlet, etc. Made up of two separable but interacting components, one consisting of the attributes of the object, the other consisting of the characteristics of the user." The most important word in this definition is **perception**. Objectively it is possible to list all the attributes of a product or service but the importance assigned to these attributes is likely to vary from individual to individual. It is for this reason that in personal selling the seller will invite the potential buyer to list and rank order the specific attributes they are looking for in the intended purchase so that, in turn, the seller can focus on those elements of importance to the particular buyer. But in mass markets, or when composing copy in support of personal selling, one must seek to determine the image of the object under consideration and then define clusters of attributes which correspond to worthwhile segments in the market place. Surveys offer this potential, particularly through the use of scaling devices as discussed later

Census versus sample

As will be seen, marketing researchers have access to a wide selection of survey methods and, subject to time and financial constraints, their choice will be dictated by three separate considerations:

1 Respondent selection;

2 The means of establishing contact with respondents;

3 The information required and the means of obtaining it;

Theoretically, the ideal method of collecting primary data is to undertake a **census** of the whole population possessing the attribute to be investigated. In practice such an exercise is near impossible and only practicable where the population, in the statistical sense of all units belonging to a clearly defined group, is both small and readily accessible. Thus, although one might successfully conduct a census of a narrowly defined population such as 'all students registered in the first year marketing course at X college', if one were to extend the population to all students in the college, or 'all students of marketing', it is almost certain that one would be unable to establish contact with some members of the population.

Even assuming one could complete a census of a large population, the cost would be enormous and the data so extensive that it would be out of date before it could be collated and analysed, for example the first results from the 2001 census in the UK were not released until late 2002. For these reasons most researchers content themselves with a representative sample of the population which they wish to study.

Once the marketer has precisely identified the population to be studied, for example 'the market for instant cake mixes', the researcher can set about the construction of a sample design which will yield the desired information within the everpresent time and budgetary constraints.

Sampling

Sampling is based on two fundamental principles of statistical theory which are usually termed 'The Law of Statistical Regularity', and 'The Law of Inertia of Large Numbers'. The first law holds that any group of objects taken from a larger group of such objects will tend to possess the same characteristics as the larger group. The second law holds that large groups are more stable than small groups owing to the compensating effect of deviation in opposite directions.

On the basis of these and similar principles, one can determine the size and composition of a sample which will yield a desired level of accuracy while allowing for, and eliminating, possible sources of error. In fact, a properly designed and executed sample may prove to be more accurate than a poorly conducted census.

In most instances, the researcher wants some measure of the reliability of the data he has collected, and so will select a sample design based on probability theory such that the chance that any given unit will be selected may be assigned a definite, non-zero probability. There are many types of probability-based sample design, including simple random sampling, stratified samples, cluster samples and multi-stage samples, and the interested student should consult Wilson (2003) for an up to date review.

Although some form of **probability sample** is essential if the results are to be used for predictive purposes, there is often a need for a 'quick and dirty' survey as a preliminary to such a sample, to clarify basic issues, or to provide generalised information required in a hurry. To this end three types of **non-probability sample** are sometimes used – the **convenience sample**, the **judgement sample** and the **quota sample**.

Convenience sampling consists of soliciting information from any convenient group whose views may be relevant to the subject of inquiry. Thus, one might stop passers-by on the street to ask their views on parking meters and off-street parking to get a feel for the subject, and as a basis for formulating more precise questions to be asked of a representative sample.

Judgement sampling is a slightly more refined technique in that respondents are selected on the basis of the interviewer's subjective opinion that they constitute a representative cross-section of the population to be investigated.

Quota sampling represents a distinct improvement on both these approaches in that the respondent 'type' is specified on the basis of characteristics of the population at large. Each interviewer is then assigned a quota and solicits information from people who meet the specification. Clearly, the more detailed the latter is, the more representative will be the data; for example if the quota calls for ten middle-class housewives between 20 and 35 years old, with at least one child under school age, there is a precise specification that can easily be met by visiting a residential suburb and interviewing young women pushing prams or push-chairs. In a number of cases, well-designed and well-executed quota samples have achieved results comparable to much more expensive probability samples. However, such verification can only be established in retrospect and is no basis for accurate prediction.

Sampling techniques

Table 11.2 Sampling techniques
A *Probability-based samples*
■ Random samples - unrestricted and simple
■ Stratified samples
■ Cluster samples
■ Systematic samples
■ Area
■ Multi-stage
B *Non probability-based or purposive samples*
■ Judgement
■ Quota
■ Convenience

The main sampling techniques available to the marketing researcher are summarised in Table 11.2

Planning a sample survey

The planning of a sample survey may be conveniently divided into seven steps, namely:

1 Define the *purpose and objectives* of the survey, i.e. what do you want to learn from the survey?
2 Define the *relevant population* or universe.
3 Identify the *sampling frame* and the **elementary sampling unit (ESU)**.
4 Select a *sampling procedure*.
5 Determine the *sample size*.
6 Select the *sample units*.
7 *Data collection*.

The purpose or object of the survey will usually have been defined in a research proposal when considering which of the three basic approaches – observation, experimentation, or sample survey – was the most appropriate to use. However, while the purpose should give a broad indication of the population to be surveyed it rarely defines it sufficiently precisely for the purposes of drawing a sample. An obvious requirement is that the population should comprise persons who possess the information which the survey is intended to secure, and time spent in defining precisely what this is will greatly improve the overall efficiency of the final survey. Of course, the precision with which one can define the intended respondents will depend very much upon how much one already knows about the subject under investigation. For example, if one manufactures controls for use in a process industry such as steel or pulp and paper making it is likely that one will have a complete listing of all the firms in these industries and so can easily define the universe. On the other hand if one operated a chain of international hotels almost anyone could be a potential customer and it will be necessary to specify precisely the 'product' – business traveller, conference business, tour operator, etc. - in order to begin to define the population. Even so it is unlikely that one will come up with a sufficiently comprehensive listing that one could be confident that every single firm or individual who qualifies as a sampling unit is included within it. As we have seen, **cluster sampling** is the only probabilistic approach which does not require a list of the population as the basis for drawing a random sample but all populations, e.g. business travellers, are not suited to this method. It follows that one will often breach the rules of probabilistic sampling owing to an inability to identify fully the population from which a sample is drawn, but this does not seem to occasion too much concern in the case of many surveys which claim their results are representative of the population. Within reason it should not bother the practitioner either, but it does underline the spurious accuracy which statistical analysis can confer upon dubious data.

Selection of a sampling procedure will depend upon a number of factors not least of which is the existence or otherwise of a listing of the population as discussed above. Tull and Hawkins (1987) suggest seven criteria for judging which type of survey to use, namely:

1 *Complexity*
2 *Required amount of data*
3 *Desired accuracy*
4 *Sample control*
5 *Time requirements*
6 *Acceptable level of non-response*
7 *Cost.*

Although these criteria are proposed in relation to the method of gathering data, i.e. by personal, mail, telephone or computer interview, they are equally applicable to the selection of a sampling procedure. Indeed, the selection of a sampling procedure will be influenced significantly by the preferred method of data collection and vice versa so that both will need to be considered together.

As a working generalisation the more complex a subject the more likely it is one will use personal interviewing and the less likely one will use a probabilistically based sample. With complex issues qualitative research using in-depth interviews is usually more appropriate although these may form the basis for simplified and structured questionnaires that can be administered to large samples.

Similarly, with the amount of data. The more information required the greater the likelihood that a respondent will discontinue an interview and so bias the results. Personal interviewing can help reduce this, but its cost will restrict the number of interviews compared with other methods and so may incline one to a stratified or cluster sample in preference to a simple random sample. Conversely, where one only wishes to address a limited number of fairly straightforward questions a simple random sample would be preferred because of its greater accuracy and precision.

Sample control, time and cost are also closely interrelated. Clearly the more rigorous the sampling procedure the greater the time and cost involved. From a pragmatic point of view the greater accuracy yielded by probabilistic methods may be unnecessary, particularly in a dynamic market which is changing rapidly, and so predispose the practitioner towards a purposive sample. Indeed a well-executed purposive sample may yield better and more timely data for decision making than a poorly executed random sample.

The determination of sample size is largely a technical issue concerned with the required reliability of the data to be collected, i.e. what is an acceptable level of error. Management invariably want little or no error until the budgetary implications of achieving this are spelled out. Much, therefore, will depend upon the overall importance of the decision for which the data is required. Given a budget, the sampling statistician will then use an appropriate mathematical formula to select the best design and sample size. Of course, this only applies to probability based samples; for purposive samples, judgement and experience will guide the decision.

The issue of **non-response** is one of the major problems facing researchers. Tull and Hawkins (1993) review a wide variety of sources which have addressed the topic and note that non-respondents 'have been found to differ from respondents on a variety of demographic, socio-economic, psychological, attitudinal and behavioural dimensions'. This is the crux of the issue - establishing contact and completing an interview will often yield initial response rates as low as 10 per cent (telephone surveys) 20 per cent (mail questionnaires), 30-40 per cent (online) and 60 per cent (personal interviews) but, provided the respondents are similar to non-respondents in terms of the characteristics relevant to the survey, this will not prevent the drawing of valid conclusions provided an adequate data base is collected. Various techniques have been devised to improve response rates and are described in more detail in most specialised textbooks. But, given the nature and size of the problem it is unsurprising that managers question the time and effort involved in defining a population, developing a sample frame and selecting sampling units in a random fashion when a purposive sample involving much less cost could yield virtually equivalent data.

In the final analysis, it all boils down to the risk perceptions of those responsible for taking the final decision. Personal experience suggests that senior managers who are prepared to make major investment decisions on the basis of very limited evidence will often look for unreasonable, and often spurious accuracy on issues such as market share or sales forecasts, particularly for new products. Hopefully, increased exposure to marketing research as part of their career development will encourage the next generation of senior managers to invest more research effort on strategic issues and less on tactical matters and reverse the current emphasis. In the context of research project as an element in a formal course of study it is hoped that supervisors will also adopt a pragmatic approach to these issues.

Establishing contact with respondents

Interviewing

An interview is '1. A conversation with or questioning of a person, usually conducted for television or a newspaper. 2. A formal discussion especially one in which an employer assesses a job applicant' (*Collins Concise English Dictionary*). While neither of these definitions addresses directly the nature and purpose of the interview in a research context they do establish the key elements, namely; an interview involves a personal exchange of information between an interviewer and one or more interviewees in which the interviewer seeks to obtain specific information on a topic with the co-operation of the interviewee(s).

Interviews vary considerably in their structure from highly formal exchanges in which the interviewer follows exactly a carefully designed and worded questionnaire, to highly informal exchanges in which the interviewer introduces the topic of interest and lets the discussion develop naturally by asking the respondent to expand or clarify points made. Between the former **structured interview**, which is sometimes called a formal or closed interview, and the **unstructured**, informal, non-directive or conversational interview are to be found three other kinds of interview. In the middle of the continuum is the **standardised open-ended interview** which consists entirely of formal open-ended questions in a pre-determined sequence. In turn we can distinguish two other kinds of interview intermediate between the standardised open-ended format and the ends of the continuum. First, there is the **semi-structured interview** which is a combination of both closed and open-ended questions and second, there is the **interview guide approach** where the interviewer has a checklist of topics they want to cover but interacts with the respondent and formulates ad hoc questions to get the desired information.

Clearly, unstructured and interview guide interviews are most appropriate in the early, exploratory phases of research where the researcher is seeking to gain an understanding of the topic and to formulate some preliminary working hypotheses. By the same token highly structured formal interviews ensure that each respondent is required to address exactly the same questions as all the others so that the data collected can be aggregated and analysed and regarded as representing the views of the population from which the sample respondents have been drawn.

Semi-structured interviews

These represent the halfway house between the partly and fully structured interview and comprise a combination of standardised open and closed questions in a predetermined sequence to be followed exactly by the interviewer. Such questionnaires are widely used when sampling a population to ensure that one has the necessary factual information for determining its representativeness for ensuring that quotas have been filled, etc. but when the primary purpose is to get a feel for attitudes, opinions, etc. as a preliminary to developing a fully structured interview using a carefully prepared and tested questionnaire.

Structured interviews

The major difference between the structured and the semi-structured interview is that in the former not only are the questions and structure predetermined but so also are the response categories. It should be appreciated that other than for fairly short and straightforward questionnaires very few interviews/questionnaires which are regarded as 'structured' conform exactly to the definition. Most structured questionnaires will contain 'Others' and 'Write-in' opportunities where it would be counter-productive or impossible to pre-identify and list all feasible responses, as well as the occasional open-ended question too. However, the main distinguishing feature of the structured interview is that it generates reliable data which is amenable to statistical analysis and which can be collected by trained interviewers with little or no knowledge of the research subject – something which is increasingly important the less structured the interview. That said accurate and consistent questionnaire completion is vital to ensure the data is valid and reliable

Table 11.3 summarises some of the advantages and disadvantages of different kinds of interview.

Group Discussions

Black and Champion (1976) defined the key attributes of a group discussion as being:

1 Questions are asked and responses given verbally

2 The interviewer rather than the respondent records the information elicited (Most group discussions are tape recorded for later detailed analysis).

3 The relationship between the interviewer and the respondent is structured

Table 11.3 Advantages and disadvantages of different types of interviews

	Advantages	Disadvantages
Standardised or structured interviews	Interviewer briefing and training simplified Less scope for interviewer bias Less interviewer variation Classifying, coding and analysis simpler Results comparable Higher reliability Greater opportunity for measurement	Questions must be simple and (usually) closed Data lack depth Lower validity Cannot probe Cannot obtain clarification of ambiguity Interviewers need skill and training Interviewer bias may increase
Depth focused or unstructured interviews	Question can be deep searching Data rich and full High degree of validity Probing possible Can obtain clarification of ambiguities	Greater interviewer variability Result often not comparable Reliability questionable Less scope for measurement

Source: Hart, S. J. (1987), 'The Use of the Survey in Industrial Marketing Research', *Journal of Marketing Management*.

in several specific ways, such as transitory or temporary relationship where participants are often unknown to one another, etc.

4 There is considerable flexibility in the format the interview takes.

To these attributes Sampson (1978) added the following characteristics.

1 The group varies in number but has anything between 8 to 12 individuals.

2 Individuals in the group are known to have knowledge about the topic or issues being discussed.

3 Respondents are encouraged to express their opinions and attitudes (freely) on issues being discussed.

4 The interviewer's duty is basically to guide the direction and depth of the discussions.

5 The underlying characteristic of the group situation is the need of the interviewer 'to learn about' the issues being discussed based on the respondent's own perspective.

As a methodology group discussions are adaptable to a wide range of situations amongst which Smith (1972) listed the following:

1 For research concerned with motives, attitudes and opinions where social status and acceptance are involved.

2 For bringing out ideas in the dynamic group situation which cannot be elicited by other methods.

3 For attempting to answer the question 'why' in relation to behaviour.

4 Valuable in the preliminary or exploratory stage of a research project.

5 It enables a questionnaire to be constructed for piloting and pre-testing, which should include all the possible lines of enquiry.

6 Useful for indicating the type of language people use when discussing the topic informally and ensures that in constructing a questionnaire, the wording of questions is meaningful.

Among other reasons cited in general literature Kinnear and Taylor (1987) listed the following:

1 To generate hypotheses that can be further tested quantitatively.

2 To provide overall background information on a product category.

3 To get impressions on new concepts for which there is little information available.

4 To generate ideas for new creative concepts.

5 To interpret previously obtained quantitative results.

The last application is particularly important as it emphasises that qualitative research is an essential and extricable element of the marketing research process necessary to help structure formal data collection and inform the interpretation of the data collected.

In addition to these advantages Fahad proposes ten others culled from a variety of sources as shown in Table 11.4.

Table 11.4 Advantages of group discussion

Synergism	Combined effect of the group produces a wider range of information, ideas, etc.
Snowballing	A comment by an individual often triggers a chain of responses from other respondents.
Stimulation	Respondents become more responsive after initial introduction and are more likely to express their attitudes and feelings as the general level of excitement increases.
Security	Most respondents find comfort in a group that shares their feelings and beliefs.
Spontaneity	As individuals are not required to answer specific questions, their responses are likely to be more spontaneous and less conventional.
Serendipity	The ethos of the group is likely to produce wider ideas and often when least expected.
Specialisation	Allows a more trained interviewer to be used and minimises the possibility of subjectivity.
Scientific scrutiny	Allows a closer scrutiny of the technique by allowing observers or by later playing back and analysing recording sessions.
Structure	Affords more flexibility in the topics that can be covered and in the depth in which these are treated.
Speed	Given that several individuals are being interviewed at the same time, this speeds up the process of collecting and analysing the data.

Source: Fahad P.G.A. (1986) 'Group discussions: a misunderstood technique', *Journal of Marketing Management*

Telephone interviewing

Long ago, in the 1970s, European texts felt compelled to point out that using the telephone to collect survey data was subject to considerable bias due to the fact that less than half the households had access to the technology and that such access was mainly restricted to more affluent households. Today the picture is quite different. Not only do nearly all households have access to a 'phone but, with the advent of the mobile, very large numbers of individuals may be contacted personally at almost any time. As a consequence the use of the telephone for interviewing has increased significantly from the estimate of 30% of all interviews in the 1980s. (It has always been used extensively in industrial and organisational research). In this section we examine some of the key aspects of the telephone survey method.

Telephone interviewing first took off in the USA when home ownership exceeded the 70% level. Writing in 1983, James H. Frey attributed the significant shift to the use of the telephone to the 'rising costs and declining response rates by the face-to-face survey' reinforced by improved telephone technology, research procedures and the 'nearly completely accessibility of any population via the telephone'. That said, the telephone is not appropriate to all kinds of survey and its use should be restricted to those situations where it offers significant advantages over other interviewing methods in light of the usual time and budgetary constraints. A comparison of telephone, mail, personal and online methods is shown in table 11.5.

The use of the telephone surveys has also grown in popularity with the introduction of **Computer-assisted Telephone Interviewing (CATI)**. CATI has become the generic name for a number of proprietary systems developed by commercial firms and academic institutions each of which has specialist features that makes it particularly suited for a given kind of survey problem. However, all systems share the common feature that interviewing is undertaken using a computer screen. Frey describes the process as follows:

> *The interview is actually controlled by pre-programmed machine processes. Thus, in effect, the respondent talks to the computer through the interviewer. CATI directs the flow of each interview with exactly the right question – one question at a time. Pre-programmed editing instructions work to ensure that the responses are valid and consistent with answers to previous questions. If an interviewer keys in an inappropriate response (for example, not included in response categories), an error message automatically appears on the screen and corrective measures can be implemented immediately. When the correct response is entered the computer determines which question should be asked next. The next question will not appear until the previous question has been answered with an appropriate response category. At the end of an interview, all respondents' replies are automatically and instantaneously entered into the computer memory.*

The ability to check for consistency and validity, to ensure precise and correct administration, to drop questions once sufficient data has been collected and so shorten succeeding interviews, and to create a database in one step in real time are all significant advantages of CATI. Unfortunately, the increase in telephone selling and in direct mail are resulting in respondent resistance and the problems of securing participation in surveys of all kinds are likely to become increasingly acute.

If a preliminary analysis indicates that a telephone survey is preferable to personal interviewing or mail questionnaire in terms of likely cost and speed of response then two major issues must be addressed. First, how to remove or

Table 11.5 Relative advantages and disadvantages of different survey methods

	In person	Telephone	Mail	Online
Versatility	■■■■	■	■■	■■■
Control of survey	■■	■■■	■	■■■■
Control of sample	■■■■	■■■	■■	■
Sample diversity	■	■■	■■■	■■■■
Speed of response	■■■	■■■■	■	■■
Response rate	■■■■	■■■	■	■■
Cost	■	■■■	■■	■■■■
Interviewer bias	■	■■	■■■■	■■■■
Depth of questioning	■■■■	■■■	■	■■
Sensitive questions	■■	■	■■■■	■■■
Ability to follow up	■■	■■■	■	■■■■

Key: ■■■■ =Most appropriate method ranging to ■ =Least appropriate method

reduce sources of bias and, second, what modifications are necessary to make the questionnaire suitable for administration without the use of visual cues that can be incorporated into mail and personally administered questionnaires?

Given that 'phone ownership now exceeds 90% it is likely that telephone listings provide as complete a record of the population as do Census data. It follows that one can use probability based methods of sampling and generate a random sample of the population so eliminating a major source of bias as compared with non-random samples in terms of the representitiveness of the sample. Using telephone directories one can draw a random sample by selecting a start point and then using a fixed interval based on the total number of entries to achieve a sample of the desired size. Such a sample may be stratified or unstratified. Of course some phone owners are ex-directory and will be excluded from the sample. One way of getting round this problem is to draw the numbers and then add one to them on the assumption that the first number does exist and that the new number may be either a listed or unlisted number.

Alternatively, one may already have a listing of a population of interest together with phone numbers and this may be used as sampling frame. (A detailed description of Telephone Sampling is to be found in Worcester and Downham).

Having established contact one immediately encounters the cardinal problem with all survey techniques – will the contact agree to respond? Securing collaboration may well be difficult given that many firms use the telephone for selling and the respondent may well be sceptical about your intentions and find it easier to ring off than listen to your explanation. When used as a survey technique, effective telephone interviewing calls for experienced interviewers and specially designed questionnaires. Novice researchers are unlikely to possess either! Texts such as Worcester and Downham do contain advice on questionnaire construction and administration and should be consulted by those who feel this is still the best method.

(This is quite different from recognising that the telephone is a very useful research tool for undertaking exploratory research, making contact with possible subjects for further study, checking out data collected by other means and so on).

Mail surveys

While documented evidence is hard to come by, many researchers believe that the data secured from a properly designed and executed **mail survey** is as good as that which may be obtained from face-to-face personal interviews and/or telephone surveys with the in-built checks described above.

The obvious and major advantage of the mail survey is that every firm and household in the country can be reached for the same basic cost with the result that mail surveys are estimated to cost one third as much as a personally administered questionnaire. Postal surveys also have the advantage that they are completed at the respondents' convenience so that participation may occur which would have been impossible or rejected if initiated by a personal approach or telephone call. This facility also allows the respondent to reflect on their answers, check records or consult with others if appropriate.

As with most things, however, the particular strengths of the mail survey are also regarded as weaknesses by critics of the methodology. Perhaps the strongest criticism raised is that of **respondent self-selection**, i.e. only those willing to go to the bother of completing the questionnaire will make a return. Given that in many postal surveys the return is 20 percent or less, it is understandable that one should be concerned as to whether the respondents are in fact representative of the sample which itself was designed to be representative of the target population. Users of research should probe deeply on this issue. Most published reports contain the claim that 'an examination of the respondents' characteristics revealed no significant differences from the characteristics of the sample'. Fair enough, but ask for the comparative information to satisfy yourself that this is indeed the case. Better still, ask for a sample of the non-respondents to be interviewed face-to-face or by telephone to see if their responses are in line with the 'volunteer' respondents.

Of course, the real problem is to secure better rates in the first instance and there are a number of techniques to help achieve this. Perhaps the most successful technique is the careful identification and selection of respondents in the first place. By choosing persons for whom the issues are salient and addressing the survey to them personally very high levels of response may be achieved. While there is possibly a 'halo' effect around academic institutions, which make extensive use of mail survey for reasons of economy, the author has supervised numerous surveys with response rates of 50 percent or better involving chief executives and directors of major firms. Most text books offer extensive advice on techniques for increasing response rates from the use of adhesive postage stamps (how many chief executives open up their mail?) through use of incentives to follow-up letters or telephone requests As with other technical matters the users best defence is to select a reputable and experienced practitioner and to ask them to justify the use of a particular technique or method.

Among the advantages and disadvantages of postal surveys Wilson (2003) lists the following:

Advantages
    national and international coverage
    low cost
    no interviewer bias
    respondent convenience
    piggybacking

Disadvantages
    low response rate
    biased response
    lack of control of questioning
    lack of control of respondent
    limited open-ended questions
    pre-reading of questionnaire
    response time (131)

Drop and collect surveys

While comparatively little has been written about this technique it combines the low cost of the mail or telephone survey with an element of personal involvement which encourages respondent participation. In an article in *Marketing Intelligence and Planning* (vol. 5, no. 1, 'Drop and collect Surveys: A Neglected Research Technique') Stephen Brown reviews the method and reports a simple experiment to demonstrate its effectiveness. As Brown explains:

> *The drop and collect technique involves the hand delivery and subsequent recovery of self-completion questionnaires though several other variants may exist. These include hand delivery and postal return and postal delivery and personal pick-up. By combining the strengths and avoiding the weakness of face-to-face and postal surveys, drop and collect provides a fast, cheap and reliable research tool. The speed stems from the fact that the questionnaire is completed in the respondent's own time not the interviewer's. Comparisons are obviously difficult but Walker estimates that one agent can deliver approximately 100 questionnaires per working day. This incidence of contact is not far short of that achieved in telephone surveys and, depending on the circumstances, considerably more than that attained by personal interviewing.*

A significant advantage of personal collection is that it encourages both high response rates and timely completion with up to 70 percent of questionnaires being available at the agreed collection time. Because of this high response rate it has been estimated that 'in terms of cost per completed questionnaire drop and collect surveys (are) …on average… 20-40 percent less expensive than postal surveys and around half the cost of face-to-face interviews' (Brown, 'Drop and Collect Surveys') In part the lower cost than personal interviews is because one can use relatively unskilled 'delivery agents' in place of trained interviewers and because the actual personal contact is much less. However, response rates of up to 90 percent almost match those achieved by face-to-face interviews, are equivalent to the best telephone survey returns, and are considerably in excess of the response to mail surveys.

In addition, as Brown comments, because respondents can complete the questionnaire in their own time it is possible to use longer and more detailed questionnaires than in most face-to-face or telephone surveys. Also, when collecting the completed questionnaires the collection agent can check that they have been completed correctly, clarify any points as required by the respondent as well as ask supplementary questions if desired. But, because the interaction between agent and respondent is limited the possibility of interviewer bias is greatly reduced.

A third factor in favour of the technique, cited by Brown is its reliability because of the control it gives over the sample selection process. On delivery the agent can ensure that the questionnaire is given to the intended respondent and, in the case of non-response, establish reasons for this – e.g. unable to contact, doesn't satisfy the sample criteria (e.g. non-user), unwilling etc.

As one would expect the technique also has a number of weaknesses. In common with all self-completion questionnaires there is a bias towards literate respondents, there is no guarantee that the claimed respondent actually completed the questionnaire (although personal delivery and collection helps minimise this risk), and the personal nature of the method requires one to depend on highly clustered samples compared with mail or telephone surveys (but not with face-to-face interviews).

On balance, however, the advantages outweigh the disadvantages and Brown reports the design and the implementation of an experiment to determine its effectiveness amongst retailers in Lisburn, Northern Ireland. The experiment confirmed the advantages of speed, low cost and high response rates and also showed that the nature of the covering letter, questionnaire length and sex of the delivery agent had little effect on the overall response rate.

Online survey methods

A growing survey methodology is to use the Internet, sometimes described as **CMC (computer mediated communications)**. This can be done either by using **email surveys** to conduct a survey in much the same way as the traditional mail survey, by sending the survey within the text of an email or as an attachment, or by **web surveys** in which participants visit a website to fill out an online form.

Online methods have distinct advantages in terms of speed of response; the diverse sample group available; the ability to survey large numbers at relatively low cost and the ability to conduct complex surveys in an interactive environment. Their very nature also helps considerably in collecting data ready for analysis. Conversely, disadvantages include difficulties in controlling the sample population due to **snowballing**; the potentially socio-economically restricted population; technological difficulties, including security; and the fact that the Internet has its own set of social rules (**netiquette**) which the researcher must become familiar with. **Ethics** and issues of **data protection** are also factors which researchers should consider, although this of course applies to all kinds of research, not just online.

There are several texts specialising in conducting primary research online, for example, Mann and Stewart (2000) and Hewson et al. (2003). However, the basic tenets of conducting marketing research, that is, keeping on top of current literature and considering ethical and technical implications of research strategies, apply to both offline and online methods.

QUESTIONNAIRES

Most formal **questionnaires** are **structured** so that they may be administered easily to a large number of respondents, and to simplify subsequent analysis. Conversely, **unstructured questionnaires** are of great value when one is seeking to get the feel of a problem, but they are difficult to interpret owing to the differences in emphasis and meaning which arise when respondents are allowed free choice of vocabulary. In either case, the questionnaire may conveniently be considered to consist of four basic elements.

First, all questionnaires must be identifiable and so must be given a title and a distinctive number. Further, where the questionnaire is to be administered by an interviewer, provision should be made for recording the date and time of the interview, the place where the interview took place, and the interviewer's number and signature.

Second, all questionnaires should make provision for the recording of basic respondent data as a basis for subsequent classification, and to permit comparative analysis with other surveys. These data may be obtained partly by questioning and partly by observations, and should include: age, sex, social class, occupation of head of household, marital status, family size and composition, level and type of education. Optional, but useful, data are: name and address, owner or tenant of property, type of property, ownership of consumer durables. Income is obviously a desirable piece of information, but many respondents consider such questions too much of an intrusion on their privacy and either refuse to answer or exaggerate. If personal questions of this type are to be asked, it is best to leave them until the end of the interview to avoid antagonising the respondent and possibly securing an incomplete interview.

Third, the questionnaire should contain control questions to check on respondent consistency and to ensure that it has been administered or completed in accordance with the instructions given. The form of such questions depends on the nature and subject matter of the survey.

Finally, the questionnaire must contain questions that will elicit the information required to provide answers to the problem under investigation.

Question design

Questions may be dichotomous, multiple choice or open-ended. **Dichotomous questions** require a straight yes or no answer and are easy to ask, understand, record and analyse. On the other hand a large number of questions will be necessary if detailed information is required, and the responses will not reveal possible shades of meaning. Thus, although they are useful for securing factual data, for example 'Do you have a refrigerator?', they are of limited value when seeking opinions or attitudes, when multiple choice questions are to be preferred. As the name implies, **multiple choice questions** offer the respondent a number of alternatives and so permit the collection of more detailed and accurate data, for example 'How often do you use Whizzo?'

At least once a week . . .
Once a fortnight . . .
Once a month . . .
Less than once a month . . .
Never . . .

Similarly, one can obtain a measure of the strength of opinions or attitudes, for example: 'Old age pensions should be increased.'

Strongly agree . . .
Agree . . .
Disagree . . .
Strongly disagree . . .
No opinion . . .

Some form of pilot survey is usually necessary to ensure that an adequate list of alternatives is offered, and 'All', 'None', or 'Don't know' should be included if the alternatives are not mutually exclusive. In recent years a number of sophisticated techniques, such as **multi-dimensional scaling**, have been developed to improve the quality of the data obtained through the use of multiple choice questions.

Open-ended questions give the respondent complete freedom in answering and so yield the maximum information, as well as eliminating interviewer bias. They are very useful in situations where it is impossible to formulate all possible alternatives, or shades of opinion, and reveal many facets of the respondent's attitudes and behaviour beyond the scope of dichotomous or multiple choice questions. On the other hand there are several disadvantages. The answers have to be recorded verbatim, for subsequent editing and analysis, to avoid the possibility that the interviewer is only recording what they consider significant. In addition, much of the data may be irrelevant, or become so, through the need to group it into categories for purposes of analysis.

In so far as is possible, all questions should be clear and unbiased, and phrased in terms which are meaningful to the likely respondent. To meet these requirements each question should be formulated in the light of the information which it is hoped to elicit. For example if one is investigating smoking habits there are a number of possible dimensions along which data may be secured, and it is pointless to ask a multiple dimensional question, 'What kind of cigarettes do you smoke?', which may be answered in terms of brand, price range, whether tipped or not, and so on. Similarly, the question 'Why do you smoke brand X?' may be answered in terms of quality, price or satisfaction, all of which are interrelated and so give no clear indication of the salience of such factors taken in isolation.

The sequence in which questions are asked also has an important bearing on the value of the data obtained. Most respondents are nervous or suspicious initially, and so should be asked simple questions of a non-personal nature. Conversational questions, for example. 'Have you lived here long?', and those which seek the interviewee's preference, for example 'Do you like making cakes?', often help to break the ice, as well as leading naturally into more specific questions. Sequence is also important, in that each answer inclines the respondent to make use of the same ideas in answering subsequent questions, for example, if you ask questions about price, followed by questions on reasons for brand preference, price will usually be stated as a major reason. Similarly, if you ask women questions about fashions, followed by questions on their attitude to advertising, you will get many more favourable responses than you would if you had omitted the questions on fashion.

Questionnaires should always be '**piloted**' or field tested before use to ensure that they meet the criteria outlined above.

The standard references on questionnaire design are A. N. Oppenheim (2000) *Questionnaire Design, Interviewing and Attitude Measurement*, and S. Payne (1951) *The Art of Asking Questions*.

ATTITUDE SCALES

While the precise nature of the link between **attitudes** and behaviour is subject to debate there can be no argument that attitude is one of the most important and pervasive concepts in marketing. This concept has been discussed earlier (Chapter 8) and the purpose here is to review some problems associated with the measurement of attitudes.

Many of the problems of measuring attitudes are inherent in the concept itself and in the varying interpretations of it by different theorists. However, as Gilbert A. Churchill Jr (1976) observes in *Marketing Research: Methodological Foundations*, there is substantial agreement on the following:

1 *Attitude represents a predisposition to respond to an object, and not the actual behaviour toward the object*. Attitude thus possesses the quality of readiness.

2 *Attitude is persistent over time*. It can change to be sure, but the alteration of an attitude, which is strongly held, requires substantial pressures.

3 *Attitude produces consistency in behaviour outcroppings*. Attitude is a latent variable that produces consistency in behaviour when manifested. This consistency occurs whether the manifestations are in the form of verbalisations about the object, or approach or avoidance of the object.

4 *Attitude has a directional quality*. It connotes a preference regarding the outcomes involving the object, evaluation of the object, or positive–neutral–negative affectations for the object.

Of these four clusters of attributes it is the latter which poses the strongest need for measurement through the assignment of some form of number which reflects the directional nature of an attitude. This object is achieved through **scaling** but one must be careful to determine the nature of a scale before jumping to too hasty a conclusion of the interpretation to be placed upon it.

In brief there are four types of scale, **nominal**, **ordinal**, **interval** and **ratio**, and their properties may be summarised as:

1 *Nominal scales*. This is the weakest form of scale in which the number assigned serves only to identify the objects under consideration. Library classification schemes employ nominal scales, as does the Standard Industrial Classification (SIC) such that members of the same class will be assigned the same number but each class will have a different number. By extending the number it is possible to achieve finer and finer distinctions until a unique number is assigned to a specific object, for example a telephone number.

2 *Ordinal scales* seek to impose more structure on objects by rank ordering them in terms of some property which they possess such as height or weight. As with nominal scales identical objects are given the same number but the ordinal scale has the added property that it can tell us something about the direction or relative standing of one object to another; for example 1 may represent the smallest member of a group such that we can safely say that 2 is bigger than 1, 5 is bigger than 2 and 17 is bigger than 5. However, this is all we can say (other than reversing the scale) and in order to be able to draw conclusions about differences between the numbers we must know something about the interval between the numbers.

3 *Interval scales* have this property in that they are founded on the assumption of equal intervals between numbers; that is, the space between 5 and 10 is the same as the space between 45 and 50 and in both cases this distance is five times as great as that between 1 and 2 or 11 and 12, and so on. However, it must be stressed that while we may compare the magnitude of the differences between numbers we cannot make statements about them unless the scale possesses an absolute zero, in which case we would have a ratio scale.

4 *Ratio scales*. Ratio scales are the most powerful and possess all the properties of nominal, ordinal and interval scales, while in addition they permit absolute comparisons of the objects; for example 6 feet is twice as high as 3 feet, and six times as high as 1 foot.

The above discussion is essentially descriptive – for a discussion of the mathematical properties of the various scales one should consult *Research for Marketing Decisions*, by Green, Tull and Albaum (1993).

Scaling methods in marketing

Marketing researchers have borrowed a number of different scaling techniques from the behavioural sciences, among which the most important are:

- *Thurstone's comparative judgement technique;*
- *Likert scales;*
- *Guttman Scales;*
- *The Semantic Differential;*
- *Q-sort technique.*

Thurstone scales were first introduced by L. L. Thurstone in 1928 and have been very widely used ever since. In essence a Thurstone scale is an attempt to construct an interval scale by selecting a set of statements about a subject which range from very favourable to very unfavourable expressions of attitude towards the subject, with each statement appearing to be equidistant from those on either side of it. Scales may contain eleven, nine or seven statements, which are chosen by a panel of judges from a pool so as to achieve the property of equal appearing intervals, and respondents are asked to select the statement which most accurately reflects their attitude. A score is assigned to each statement and is used, often in conjunction with scores for other sets of statements, in order to provide a summary statement of attitude towards the object of inquiry.

Likert scales differ from Thurstone scales in that respondents are presented with a series of statements and asked to indicate their degree of agreement/ disagreement with each. Respondents are usually offered five categories – Strongly Agree, Agree, Uncertain, Disagree, Strongly Disagree, though three or seven divisions are used by some researchers – and are asked to select the position corresponding most closely with their opinion. By scoring a series of statements on a given subject, for example qualities of a brand, content of an advertisement, it is possible to construct a generalised attitude towards the object with an indication of the intensity with which the attitude is held.

Guttmann scaling represents an attempt to ensure a highly desirable property of an attitude scale which is only partially achieved by the Thurstone and Likert methods – the property of unidimensionality; that is, all the statements used belong to the same dimension. The construction of Guttmann scales is more complex and laborious than for Thurstone and Likert scales, however, relatively little use is made of the method in marketing research. A useful source for the different kinds of scales is Bearden and Netemeyer (1999) *Handbook of Marketing Scales*.

In contrast the **Semantic Differential technique** developed by Osgood et al. (1952) in *Method and Theory in Experimental Psychology*, is very widely used, largely because it is much simpler to construct than any of the scales discussed so far and yet yields a very high measure of agreement with these more elaborate measures. The method consists of a series of **bipolar adjectives** (strong–weak, good–bad, etc.) separated usually by between five to nine points. The respondent is asked to check-mark the point which best indicates their attitude. Scale positions are sometimes qualified, for example:

Extremely good.
Very good.
Fairly good.
Neither good nor bad.
Fairly bad.
Very bad.
Extremely bad.

However, such qualification tends to discourage selection of the extreme positions.

Multidimensional scaling

All the scales discussed so far use a single number to represent a person's attitude – or, as Churchill (1976) puts it, '**a linear compensatory model**'. Such a model rests upon the basic assumption that attitude is **unidimensional** such that we balance negative and positive factors in arriving at a single summary statistic.

In recent years, marketing researchers have challenged this basic model and have argued that attitude is **multidimensional**. In turn this requires a concept of a multidimensional space rather than a unidimensional scale and considerable effort and ingenuity has been devoted to developing measures of this space.

The basic characteristic of multidimensional scaling is that respondents are asked to make judgements concerning the degree of similarity/ distance between pairs of stimuli using a scale which may be either metric (interval or ratio scale) or non-metric (ordinal scale). A particularly attractive feature of non-metric multi-dimensional scaling is that it converts an ordinal input into an interval scale or metric output. Thus, as long as the respondent can rank order all the stimulus pairs, it is possible to convert such 'greater than', 'less than' statements into absolute statements concerning the status of all the objects.

Multidimensional scaling is based upon sophisticated mathematical techniques, a full discussion of which is to be found in Green, Carmone and Smith (1989) *Multidimensional Scaling and Related Techniques in Marketing Analysis*. However, for normal use packaged computer programs such as M-D-SCAL are available which require only basic mathematical skills.

PRESENTATION OF FINDINGS

Space limitations preclude consideration of field interviewing procedures, and the techniques used in collating, tabulating and analysing the data collected. Once these steps have been completed, the findings, and recommendations based on them, must be presented in the form of a report.

Most research findings have to be presented to two distinct groups – general management and research specialists – and the different needs and orientation of these groups usually requires the preparation of two separate reports. The first of these consists of a fully documented technical report, while the second consists of a short but detailed account of the major findings, conclusions and recommendations abstracted from the first.

The Market Research Society has adopted the following standards as constituting the minimum acceptable content of a survey report:

1 The purpose of the survey;
2 For whom and by whom the survey was undertaken;
3 General description of the universe covered;
4 Size and nature of the sample, including a description of any weighting methods used;
5 The time when the field work was carried out;
6 The method of interviewing employed;
7 Adequate description of field staff and any control methods used;
8 A copy of the questionnaire;
9 The factual findings;
10 Bases of percentages;
11 Geographical distribution of the interviews.

In order to ensure that a technical report satisfies these minimum requirements and presents the material in a logical sequence, many organisations have adopted a formal layout on the following lines:

1 *Introduction*: Title of the report; Name of sponsor; Title of research organisation; Date of publication.
2 *Table of Contents*
3 *Preface*: Stating terms of reference, and acknowledgements where appropriate.
4 *Statement of purpose*: This generally consists of an elaboration of the terms of reference contained in the preface. It should outline the general nature of the problem to be investigated and the specific hypotheses on which the research was based.
5 *Methodology*: This section should outline the stages through which the project passed, step by step, and include a statement of the definitions adopted, the research techniques employed, the sources of data used, details of sample size and composition, a description of the methods of analysis employed, and any explanatory observations deemed necessary by the researcher.
6 *The findings*: This section consists of an abstract of those data considered relevant to the problem under investigation.
7 *Conclusions*: Those drawn from the findings.
8 *Recommendations*: Based on the conclusions.
9 *The appendices*: These should include a detailed account of the sample design and its theoretical reliability; a copy of the questionnaire and instructions to interviewers; detailed statistical tables; the bibliography and glossary of terms if appropriate; details of any tests of reliability, theoretical proofs and so forth.

In reports intended for line management as opposed to other researchers it is common to find that the conclusions and recommendations follow immediately after the statement of purpose or terms of reference, and the description of the methodology is consigned to the appendices. Reports of this nature usually also include a single-page statement of the basic purpose and findings entitled Management or **Executive Summary**.

THE ROLE OF MARKETING RESEARCH AGENCIES

It was stated earlier that many companies utilise the services of independent marketing research agencies, either to supplement their own research effort or as a substitute for a research department of their own. To provide these services, most independent agencies are capable of undertaking 'all aspects of the research process' described above, and act in both an advisory and executive capacity.

In addition to undertaking ad hoc research on behalf of client firms, some of the bigger organisations, for example Mintel and Keynote, specialise in documenting a particular area of marketing on a continuous basis. The findings from such research are usually incorporated in standardised reports which are circulated to subscribers at regular intervals, or sold to organisations on an individual report basis.

Other well known sources of continuous research data are the British Market Research Bureau's Target Group Index (*www.bmrb-tgi.co.uk*) and Taylor Nelson Sofres Superpanel (*www.tns-global.com*).

Panel data

While panel data has played a significant role in consumer marketing research for many years now, with the advent of online panels they have increased in importance as a major source of information.

The purpose of a consumer panel is to provide data about some aspect of buyer behaviour on a regular basis. To do this effectively it is essential that the members of a panel are representative of the population and/or of a particular target group. To achieve this it is important to develop an accurate profile of prospective members who are then recruited individually by the agency running the panel. Usually, all members are involved in each round of data gathering so the size tends to depend upon the degree of detail and depth of analysis called for. Accordingly, the panel size may range from as few as 100 up to 10,000.

Panels may be classified as either 'traditional' or 'access' depending upon whether they are to provide information on an on-going or an ad hoc basis respectively. Panels are best suited to the collection of objective, factual data such as who bought what, when and where as opposed to attitudinal data concerning why you did something. The data itself may be collected by means of diaries completed by panel members or by means of suitable hardware, e.g. electronic scanning of till receipts or the use of monitors on TV sets, computers etc. In the case of 'retail panels' data is gathered at the point of sale and may be merged with other panel data to give a more comprehensive overview of buyer behaviour as a basis for fine tuning marketing mix decisions.

Access panels are generally used for collecting ad hoc data for specific decisions rather than routine marketing planning of issues like product, price, place and promotion. While the pool of respondents is generally representative of the population at large, other data on lifestyle, usage of particular products etc. is used to draw sub-samples to address the specific question under investigation. When this is highly focused it may be necessary to screen potential members to ensure they satisfy the relevant criteria. Most often this is determined by the nature of the product for new product development, concept, price and advertising tests.

Online consumer access panels have grown in importance due to the decline in willingness of people to take part in telephone and personal interviews. In the absence of E-mail directories similar to telephone or postal directories random sampling is not possible, and privacy/spamming issues raise problems about using an E-mail address without the owners permission. As a result there is concern that persons who have agreed to the use of their E-mail details have an interest in the organisation and so may not be unbiased in their responses. However, as we have seen, this is not a new problem! Against these drawbacks must be offset the benefits of being able to conduct an international survey quickly and at low cost.

TNS Superpanel, running since 1991, is currently one of the UKs leading superpanels, with 15,000 households. Consumer data is recorded through palmtops and laser scanning technology, as well as with some use of code books, and collected twice weekly by an overnight polling system.

DATABASE MARKETING (DBM)

One of the most valuable assets a company possesses is its knowledge of the identity and location of actual and potential customers. Such information constitutes a database. In recent years developments in computing capacity and information technology have led to the recognition that the customer database is ideally suited to the new technology and resulted in the emergence of the new field of **database marketing**.

In his book *Marketing Management and Information Technology* Keith Fletcher (2nd edn, 1995) examines the application of IT to the whole process of marketing management and its specific application to particular marketing functions and tasks. In Chapter 10 of that volume he examines the topic of sales decisions and includes a comprehensive review of DBM. While it is stated that there is no agreed definition of DBM, that offered by Stone and Shaw (1987) captures well its essential characteristics, namely:

> *DBM is an interactive approach to marketing communications, which uses addressable communication media (such as mail, telephone and the sales force) to extend help to its target audience, to stimulate demand, and to stay close to them by recording and keeping an electronic database memory of customer, prospect and all communication and commercial contacts, to help improve future contacts.*

The key point is that the power of electronics aided and abetted by developments in telecommunications have made it possible to increase the power of the database far beyond that which was possible when depending upon a manual system. To be fully effective, however, it must be possible for the user to interact with or relate to the database (hence **relational database**) and match any variable with any other in order to develop and exploit the potential for distinctive and focused marketing efforts. It is this use of a database for marketing planning which distinguishes DBM from **direct marketing** with which it is often confused. Specifically, direct marketing embraces 'any activity which creates and profitably exploits a direct relationship between the company and the prospect (Ogilvy and Mather, 1985) and tends to focus on the communication opportunities for this such as the new electronic media, telephone selling and direct response advertising' (Fletcher, 2nd edn, 1995). From this definition it is clear that direct marketing will benefit greatly from the existence of a relational database as this will increase significantly the ability to pinpoint specific targets with unique messages but much direct marketing is developed using customer databases which do not possess this property; that is, DBM requires a more sophisticated database than is necessary for basic direct marketing.

While DBM is a suitable base for all kinds of marketing communication and effort it is particularly suited for use with the telephone. In an article entitled 'The Emergence of Marketing Databases and their Uses' Tony Coad (1990) offers the following guidelines on what he looks for in a marketing database:

Firstly, a Marketing Database contains the names and addresses of a company's customers, with as much individual characterisation as possible.

When building consumer databases for example, each responding customer can be distinguished by their demographic and lifestyle attributes.

My Company, NDL International has built over 60 consumer marketing databases for major UK companies, characterising individual customers by their individual demographic and life style qualities. Such detail – whether of individual consumers, or individual businesses – enables us to search for common characteristics among customers that relate to purchase behaviour. If we did not characterise each customer we would not be able to distinguish between them. We then could not use our database to reach people on the basis of their individuality or to help us understand the separate market segments that exist in nearly all markets.

Secondly, we need to distinguish between our customers on the basis of their purchase behaviour. This is the what, when, how much, why, where of their purchase history.

We now have all the data we need effectively to operate a marketing database. We can track purchase behaviour by the profile of that customer, so, in theory can:

- *Find out where customers for Product X live.*
- *See how customers for the standard model differ from those of the full-feature version.*
- *Find out which types of customer pay the top price for a product or service.*
- *See which sort of people buy at different outlets then vary our point of sale accordingly.*
- *Make sure that the people who are actually buying our product are those we had in mind when promoting it.*
- *Identify prospect names and addresses, and individual lifestyles as a point of contact.*

With the data, we can track purchase behaviour and profile the types of customer exhibiting that behaviour. But of course marketing databases need to present data in a form digestible to marketers, so . . .

. . . The third characteristic of a marketing database is that it should be based on relational software. This will enable any piece of data to be retrieved in any sequence and placed in any combination. Hierarchical database software does not allow this so we

cannot readily identity segments and then relate those segments to names and addresses. And we should make our consumer database address based.

Thanks to the Post Office's Postal Address File we have a means of standardising addresses – which means we can recognise duplicate entries – and can attach data from a variety of sources to the correct household with confidence.

The fourth characteristic of a marketing database is its geography. It has to be all in one place, not scattered around the company, probably on incompatible installations.

Fifthly, the output must be user friendly. Reports must be customised, friendly and rapid. Better still the output should be capable of being accepted by marketers who need not be systems analysts. PC-based output, rich in opportunities for statistical analysis, is ideal.

The sixth characteristic of a marketing database is obvious. It must belong to the marketing department and be an effective source of influence over major marketing decisions. An installation which is really part of some other function or department will never be satisfactory. The Marketing Database is now – and potentially – too important a resource to be at the wrong end of another department's priorities.

In light of the growing importance of direct marketing this is now the subject of a separate chapter (19).

THE APPLICATION OF BAYESIAN TECHNIQUES TO MARKETING RESEARCH

Traditionally, marketing research has employed a methodology based on classical statistics as exemplified by the principles stated in the section on sampling. In recent years, however, increasing attention has been given to the **Bayesian**, or **subjective**, approach to probability which incorporates the decision-maker's personal feelings regarding the likely occurrence of specified events.

The aim of marketing research is to reduce uncertainty concerning the outcome of future events or a given course of action. It is clear, however, that even the most extensive research is unlikely to result in perfect information and that even if it did, the value would not be justified by the cost. Thus, even when the results of research are available to him, the decision-maker will still be faced with some degree of uncertainty and the value of the Bayesian approach lies in its ability to quantify such uncertainties and incorporate them in an analysis of the problem. In practice, many managers make use of subjective probabilities in an informal way and always have, for example, the sales manager forecasting next year's sales adjusts the individual salesman's estimates on the basis of his own opinion of their likely accuracy; the production manager decides to use a substitute material to meet an urgent order because he feels the chances are eight out of ten it will work.

Although the Bayesian approach is rejected by many classical statisticians, it is the author's opinion that it is a valuable technique when properly applied. An example of such an application would be the assessment of a new product launch. While it is beyond the scope of this book, the student is recommended to consult one, or all, of the following:

1 Hammond, J.S. III (1967), 'Better Decisions with Preference Theory', *Harvard Business Review*, November–December, pp. 123–41.
The 'best' short introduction to the use of subjective probabilities in analysing real-world problems.

2 Chapter 6 'Research for Marketing' in Baker, M. J. (2000), *Marketing Strategy and Management*, 3rd. edn, (Basingstoke: Palgrave)

3 Congdon, P. (2001), *Bayesian Statistical Modelling*, (Chichester: John Wiley and Sons)

ORGANISING FOR MARKETING RESEARCH

In view of the frequent references to the increasingly competitive nature of the business environment one might expect that the majority of firms would have a marketing research department. Such an expectation would be reinforced by an extensive body of evidence accumulated over the past forty years or more that plainly shows that:

- Firms that undertake market research perform better than those that don't.
- The most frequently cited reason for the failure of new products is "Inadequate understanding of the market" – presumably the consequence of insufficient market research in the first place.

While recent data is hard to come by, the indications are that less than half of business firms have a formal market research department.

Several reasons may account for this of which the most obvious is that many firms are not large enough to have a dedicated marketing department, let alone a specialist marketing research function. Further, while most firms have some form of marketing information system the nature and scope of their business may not call for regular and continuous updating of market information. Added to this there is a well developed market research industry and smaller organisations may prefer to buy in market research information on an 'as required' basis. This may be in the form of subscribing to regular, syndicated research reports such as those prepared by Mintel, Keynote etc., or panel data of the kind outlined earlier. In addition, firms may commission ad hoc research projects to address particular issues without being able to justify the maintenance of a research function of their own.

The decision to set up one's own marketing research department clearly depends upon an evaluation of its potential contribution to the firm's overall operation. Such an evaluation is essentially qualitative, and will vary from firm to firm, precluding the statement of hard-and-fast rules. For our purpose it will suffice if it is assumed a decision has been made to establish such a department and attention concentrated on the factors which must be taken into account. These may be summarised as:

1 The role and function of the department;
2 Its position within the organisation structure;
3 The role and function of the department manager.

Role and function of the department

From the checklist covering the scope of marketing research it is apparent that a very large department would be necessary to cover all the areas mentioned. If a firm is undertaking research for the first time it would be well advised to draw up a list of priorities and content itself with attempting to achieve only the more important in the first instance. This does not mean that all other research must be discouraged absolutely, as too rigid lines of demarcation can only lead to an inflexible approach and the neglect of lines of inquiry complementary to the main purpose of the research.

All too often firms make the mistake of handing over responsibility for the maintenance of routine records to the newly formed marketing research department. The transfer of such records invariably creates both friction and inefficiency – it hinders the operation of the department which depends upon such records for its routine operation, for example sales, and diverts the marketing research department from its main function – research. In that much routine work involved in the compilation and maintenance of records will have preceded the setting up of a specialist research department it is best if the various divisions retain this function, making the data available as and when required. In order to avoid both duplication and fragmentation of effort, each department's responsibility should be clearly stated, and only those returns essential to the marketing research department's internal research efforts should be submitted. That said, the creation of computerised information systems greatly enhances the free flow of information within an organisation and offers the market research department almost instant access to all stored data relevant to its function.

Organisational positioning

The positioning of the marketing research department within the organisation depends very largely on the existing structure. As a generalisation, the department should have direct access to the managing director, as it is performing a staff function and, in many instances, is providing the chief executive with the raw material upon which policy, as opposed to operating decisions, will be made. In the larger organisation, with executive directors in functional appointments, the marketing director may well be delegated responsibility for directing the efforts of the research department and deciding which reports should be submitted to the chief executive. Even so there is a strong case for a 'dotted line' relationship between the managing director and the department to ensure that reports that are critical of a particular aspect of the firm's activities are given a hearing, and to avoid straining relationships between the marketing and other functional directors. Further, the managing director is concerned with the overall effectiveness of the firm and so is in a better position to see the implications of research findings without becoming subjectively involved with the possible effect on an individual department.

Some writers recommend that the manager of the marketing research department should be of equivalent status to the managers of the major operating divisions, but it is felt that this is unrealistic in view of the discrepancy in size and responsibility that usually exists. Provided the manager has access to the board of directors their status should be directly related to the importance accorded the department within the organisation as a whole.

The role and function of the marketing research manager

The job specification of the marketing research manager will vary, depending upon the size and function of the department and the degree of external control and direction. In all cases, however, the manager must be technically competent and possess personal integrity. Technical competence includes not only experience and skill in marketing and analytical techniques but also the ability to translate management problems into viable research projects capable of implementation within the constraints imposed by time, and the available budget.

Personal integrity requires that the marketing research manager interpret findings objectively in accordance with generally accepted principles of scientific inquiry. 'Lies, damned lies and statistics' can only enjoy currency so long as the unscrupulous use 'facts' to support preconceived conclusions by judicious selection, manipulation and presentation – 'massaging the data', in research jargon.

In addition to these essential requirements the manager should also possess those skills common to all managerial positions – administrative ability, an understanding of human behaviour and the ability to communicate effectively.

Make or buy?

As with most outsourcing decisions the choice between doing it oneself and sub-contracting to a third party invariably boils down to an issue of cost versus control. Because task specialisation leads to economies of scale, marketing research agencies are usually better equipped and resourced to undertake research than their clients. However, against this must be set the fact that the business usually knows its own business best and will have to bring any agent 'up to speed' before they can undertake research for them. Also there is the possibility that , even inadvertently, information about one client may leak to another and so compromise one's competitive position.

The subject of commissioning research is a topic in its own right and a useful summary is to be found in John Webb's book *Understanding and Designing Marketing Research* (2002) 2nd Edition.

Summary

This is probably the longest chapter in the book and covers a very wide range of issues. While the subject of marketing research is intrinsically no more complex or detailed than most of the other topics dealt with in other chapters, its importance in an introductory text is felt to justify a more comprehensive 'outline' than other topics. The reason for this belief is that research should underpin all aspects of marketing practice.

To begin with we defined the objective of marketing research as being "the reduction of uncertainty surrounding business decisions" – an objective admirably summarised in the aphorism "Look before you leap". While it is important that managers avoid paralysis by analysis as a result of information overload, the evidence that competitive success depends upon sound marketing intelligence is overwhelming. It follows that anyone interested in the practice of marketing should understand why this is so, as well as a knowledge of what is required to collect and evaluate relevant information about all aspects of this practice.

Information, data or 'knowledge' consists of two types. First, there are **secondary sources** which record what is already know about a subject. Obviously, to avoid the sin of re-invention, any piece of research should start with a review of what is already known about a subject. However, such a review often shows that while the existing information gives us a better understanding of our problem it does not provide us with an answer to it – the is an information 'gap'. To close this gap we need to access the **primary sources** by which is usually meant persons or organisations whose behaviour and attitudes we are interested in. Both sources were considered as was the issue of qualitative versus quantitative research.

With regard to the latter issue it was observed that, traditionally, **quantitative data** were seen as being more reliable and a better basis for decision making than **qualitative data**. After reviewing some of the reasons for this belief, it was argued that qualitative data are better at explaining why people behave the way they do , while quantitative data is better for capturing who, what where, when and how people behave. Accordingly, most research needs to combine both qualitative and quantitative elements and methods of collecting and evaluating both kinds of data were discussed in some detail.

Three principal research methods were identified and reviewed – **observation, experimentation** and **survey**. Particular attention was given to surveys as they are one of the most widely used techniques in social science research, and included consideration of sampling, sampling techniques and the planning of sample surveys. These themes led naturally to issues of establishing contact with respondents and the elicitation of information through various interviewing techniques and kinds of **survey** – Face-to-face, telephone, mail, drop and collect, and on-line.

Having established contact with those with relevant information, attention was turned to the construction of questionnaires and the use of various kinds of scale designed to obtain reliable and valid data, and the presentation of findings in a formal report.

The chapter concluded with brief overviews of several topics including the role of marketing research agencies, database marketing, Bayesian techniques and organising for marketing research. In the next chapter we look at the first of the four Ps – the Product.

Review questions and problems

1 What factors, and what sources, would you take into account in preparing a forecast of the potential market for:
   (a) A new 'snack' food?
   (b) Frozen TV dinners?
   (c) A combined refrigerator/freezer unit with a capacity of 14 cubic feet?
   (d) High bandwidth internet access?
   (e) Industrial catering equipment?
   Make whatever assumptions you like about the 'product', but state them clearly.

2 Under what circumstances would you consider a non-probability sample a useful and valid market research technique? What disadvantages do you associate with such samples?

3 Compile a short questionnaire:

(a) For sampling the opinion of industrial users on the benefits of containerisation.
(b) To elicit the opinions of consumers about freeze-dried coffee. You should stipulate how the questionnaires are to be administered and to whom.

4 Provide an explanation of the following methods of structuring samples for market research surveys:
   (a) Systematic sampling;
   (b) Cluster sampling;
   (c) Area sampling; and
   (d) Quota sampling.
   In each case, give an example of a marketing situation in which the particular method could be most effectively employed

5 Formulate the main rules to be kept in mind when designing a questionnaire. How important is question order in securing a satisfactory response?

6 Qualitative research is often criticised as producing results subject to the bias of the investigator. How far do you think this is dangerous, and what compensating advantages do you see in the qualitative approach?

7 Give a definition of an 'attitude', and discuss the difficulties of providing such a definition. Why do marketing researchers concern themselves with attitude measurements?

8 Users of a motorway service area are to be interviewed on leaving to find out, among other things, whether their decision to shop at that particular service area was dependent on their immediate need for petrol or refreshment, the distance or time since their last stop (and where that was), or on other factors. Draft a section of a face-to-face questionnaire designed to establish which of these was or were most influential, and which facilities the respondent in person has used in the current visit. Do not show any coding data or any introductory section.

9 It has been said that the art of management consists of 'taking account simultaneously of the inner workings of the firm and its interaction with external forces'. Describe the contribution of marketing research to the understanding of these external forces.

10 What are the essential stages in developing a proposal for market research? What differences would you expect to see in a proposal for industrial market research compared with a proposal for consumer market research?

11 What useful information could you hope to obtain through market research when planning to enter the market with a totally new product, based on a recent invention, about which the marketplace has no knowledge?

12 Distinguish between primary and secondary marketing research data. What are the main sources of data in each case?

13 It has been said that the initial research showed that there was no market for a dry-copying machine. However, Rank Xerox ignored the findings and proceeded to establish a successful international company based on the dry-copying concept. How would you explain this contradiction and does it invalidate the use of marketing research data as a planning tool?

14 Discuss the advantages and disadvantages of using the in-depth interview technique to undertake primary market research.

15 Describe and justify the survey methodology you would use in each of the following situations:
(a) Research on the use of under-arm deodorants to assist in the development of new product ideas.
(b) Research on consumer reactions to a new type of DVD recorder.
(c) Research to assist in the design of a petrol station forecourt.

16 Explain why and under what conditions a researcher might choose to select a qualitative rather than a quantitative approach to data collection. Use illustrations to support your line of argument.

17 Using examples, evaluate how marketing research could help in the launch of a newly packaged consumer good.

Key terms

access panels	attitude scales	bipolar adjectives
ad hoc research	Bayesian techniques	brand mapping
association procedures	bias	bubble procedures

census
choice ordering
cluster sampling
cognitive-affective-conative (CAC)
  model
completion procedures
computer mediated
  communications (CMC)
computer-assisted telephone
  interviewing (CATI)
conclusive research
conclusive research
construction procedures
continuous research
control group
convenience sample
data protection
database marketing
desk research
dichotomous questions
direct marketing
drop and collect
email survey
environmental scanning
ethics
ethnography
executive summary
expectancy-value (EV) model
experimentation
exploratory research
expressive procedures
fact finding

factual survey
field research
Guttmann scaling
Hawthorne effect
International Monetary Fund
  (IMF)
interpretive survey
interval scales
interview
interview guide approach
judgement sample
law of inertia of large
  numbers
law of statistical regularity
Likert scales
linear compensatory model
mail survey
market research
marketing metrics
marketing mix
marketing myopia
marketing research
motivation research
multidimensional scaling
multiple choice questions
netiquette
non-probability sample
observation
online consumer access
  panels
open-ended questions
opinion survey

panel data
performance monitoring
primary sources
probability sample
Q-sort technique
qualitative data
quantitative data
questionnaires
quota sampling
ratio scales
relational database
respondent self-selection
role-playing
Rorschach ink blot test
sample
scanning
secondary sources
semantic differential technique
semi-structured interview
snowballing
soft data
structured questionnaires
successive focusing
survey
thematic apperception tests
Thurstone scales
traditional panels
ultimate consumers
unidimensional scaling
United Nations (UN)
unstructured questionnaires
web survey

Supplementary reading list

Baker, M. J, (2003), *Business and Management Research*, (Helensburgh: Westburn Publishers Ltd.)

Fletcher, K. (1995) *Marketing Management and Information Technology*, 2nd edn (London: PrenticeHall).

Green, P. E., Tull, D. and Albaum, G. (1993) *Research for Marketing Decisions*, 6th edn (Englewood Cliffs, N.J.: Prentice-Hall).

Kinnear, T. C. and Taylor, J. R. (1996) *Marketing Research: An Applied Approach*, 5th edn (London: McGraw-Hill).

Parasuraman, A., Grewal, D. and Krishnan, R. (2004) *Marketing Research*, (Houghton Mifflin).

Tull, D. S. and Hawkins, D. I. (1992) *Marketing Research: Measurement and Method*, (West Drayton: Macmillan).

Wilson, A. (2003), *Marketing Research*, (Harlow: Prentice Hall)

Worcester, R. M. and Downham, J. (1988) *Consumer Market Research Handbook*, 3rd edn (London: Van Nostrand Reinhold).

12

PRODUCT* POLICY, PLANNING AND DEVELOPMENT

Learning Goals   *After reading this chapter you will be familiar with:*

- The central role of the product or service as a key element in achieving and sustaining competitive success.

- The view that change is inevitable and that progress is achieved by the continuous substitution of new and improved solutions to consumer needs such that all products and industries follow a life cycle from birth through growth to maturity and eventual decay.

- The process of new product development through which firms identify market opportunities and develop new products to exploit them.

- The procedures followed to screen ideas and translate these into successful new products.

- Some alternative organisational structures for encouraging and managing NPD.

- The need for a firm to develop a portfolio of products each at different stages of the life-cycle to ensure its survival and long-run success.

* While the emphasis here is on physical products, and a separate chapter (23) deals with the special case of services, in most instances products may be regarded as synonymous with services throughout this chapter.

INTRODUCTION

A cardinal principle of marketing is that firms should seek to determine the multidimensional nature of consumer demand, and then deploy their resources in the creation of products which will satisfy these demands. Acceptance of this principle recognises that the firm's ultimate success, whether measured by total profits, return on investment, market share or any other criterion, is largely dependent upon its product policy.

Earlier (Chapter 3, Demand and Supply), we looked briefly at the 'product' in theory and practice. In this chapter we extend this preliminary review into a consideration of the product as one, and perhaps the most important, of the 4Ps. To begin with we discuss the role of the product and its relationship to user needs and practices. Next, we examine the role of **product policy** and return to the concept of the **product life-cycle (PLC)** introduced in Chapter 2. The PLC concept underlines the inevitability of change in the market place as a result of innovation and competition. As a consequence firms must constantly seek to improve on existing products and look for new ones. Accordingly, we seek to define what constitutes a 'new' product prior to a look at the role of **new product development (NPD)** and the importance of new products. While a firm can modify or extend its product line in a number of ways, all of these are the outcome of a process with a number of distinctive stages usually distinguished an **Exploration, Screening, Business Analysis, Development, Testing** and **Commercialisation**. Each of these phases is discussed briefly and raises issues concerning the organisation of NPD activities.

To conclude the chapter we introduce the idea of **product portfolio analysis**, and the importance of having a clear policy for removing or eliminating declining products from the product line.

THE ROLE OF THE PRODUCT IN MARKETING

For many years previous to the birth of the electronic watch, a classic case study in the armoury of any business school teacher offering a course in Business Policy, General Management or Marketing Strategy was 'Hamilton Watch'. Almost without exception the first question posed on this case study was 'What is a watch?', and the answer would encompass a wide range from 'a scientific instrument for measuring time' through 'a gift' to 'a status symbol', thus allowing the instructor to make the basic point about any product, namely, that it is a bundle of attributes, and that it is the need and perception of the consumer or user which will determine which of these definitions is most apposite in any given set of circumstances. Such an insight is fundamental to the marketing concept, underlies the reason why product differentiation became the basic competitive strategy in the 1920s, and explains why market segmentation has assumed such importance in the mature and saturated markets of the advanced industrialised economies.

As we attempted to show in Chapter 8, when addressing the question of how buyers select between alternatives, choice behaviour is conditioned by both **objective** and **subjective factors**. In recent years recognition that the objective factors which are intrinsic to the product (performance and price) are relatively easy to copy has led to much greater emphasis upon the qualitative and subjective dimensions, which will become determinant when objective parity is perceived to exist. We say 'perceived' advisedly for our analysis has shown that people have difficulty in distinguishing very small differences to the extent that in business a useful working rule-of-thumb is that a difference must be at least 10 per cent between the objects which are being compared if it is to become 'noticeable'; that is, 10 per cent bigger, smaller, faster, more efficient and so on.

Two consequences flow from this:

1 Producers wrongly assume that small differentiating features will be perceived when they won't, with the result that:

2 Greater emphasis is given to creating subjective differences between competitive products through service and promotional efforts.

The net outcome of these trends is that the recent literature on marketing has tended to give little specific attention to product characteristics and product differentiation and has concentrated more upon user characteristics and market segmentation. Such a change in emphasis is believed to have gone too far, for the simple reason that objective differences are easier to develop, control and sustain than subjective differences and, if they exist, will largely eliminate the need to try and create such subjectives differences.

As H. U. Thompson (1962) observed in his book *Product Strategy*, 'You can change products: it is a comparatively simple matter of decision and cost. You can't change people – but you can influence them – but seldom if ever cheaply. It is far easier – and thus far more economical – to find out what people want and to supply it than it is to influence them to want what you make'. A sentiment echoing those of Ries and Trout on 'Positioning'.

Support for the view that too much attention has been given to market 'need' as opposed to product content is to be found in a forceful article by Bennett and Cooper. Citing the automobile industry as a microcosm of the American economy Bennett and Cooper claim that lower cost and better fuel economy are simplistic explanations of the 30 per cent market share secured by Japanese and European imports. In their view 'The Europeans and Japanese car makers have simply been better competitors; they anticipated market needs; they built a better product – one that is more reliable, has better workmanship, and is better engineered; and they did it effectively. In short, these manufacturers delivered better value to the American consumer.'

Several similar instances (TV tubes, motorcycles and so forth) are cited and lead to the conclusion that:

> *The failure to deliver product value to the customer is the prime reason for this lack of competitiveness. Twenty years of adherence to the marketing concept may have taken its toll of American enterprise. The marketing concept has diverted our attention from the product and its manufacture; instead we have focused our strategy on responses to market wants and have become preoccupied with advertising, selling, and promotion. And in the process, product value has suffered.*

This problem has become increasingly acute in recent years as a result of price competition.

With the collapse of the Soviet Bloc in the late 1980s many East European countries regained their independence and the opportunity to compete in Western Markets. While some of their products were considered to be lacking in quality and to be unsophisticated, low labour costs meant that they were attractive to customers with less disposable income. The Skoda car was such a product. While its appearance was dated, and it lacked many of the 'bells and whistles' associated with American or Japanese cars, it was well engineered, durable and reliable – in other words good value for money for someone looking for low cost basic transportation. More to the point, the features and attributes that gave the competition a competitive edge were relatively easy to replicate and were quickly adopted. Today Skoda cars, like Korean and Malaysian built cars, look very similar to those of the major manufacturers; they perform well *and* they cost less. With the rapid development of the emerging economies of Brazil, Russia, India and China – the so-called **BRIC countries** – this threat of price competition has grown rapidly and has resulted in the collapse of many manufacturing companies like MG Rover in original industrialised economies.

It is a truism to state that consumers will always prefer a better product at the same price or the same product at a lower price, but both observations underline the importance of trying to create objective product differences before resorting to the intangible and subjective elements. Satisfaction is the goal, but the product or service is the means by which it is achieved. As Lawrence Abbott (1955) has pointed out, 'what people really desire are not the products but satisfying experiences', but 'experiences are attained through activities. In order that activities may be carried out physical objects or the services of human beings are usually needed. Here lies the connecting-link between man's inner world and the outer world of economic activity. People want products because they want the experience-bringing services which they hope the products will render.'

USER NEEDS AND PRODUCT CHARACTERISTICS

Ultimately, it is probably irrelevant whether one first identifies user needs and develops product characteristics to match them or, alternatively, creates a product and then seeks out customers whose needs match these characteristics. In the final analysis the process is circular and subject to continuous adjustment. That said, there will be clear benefits if one can spell out some of the basic dimensions of user needs as this will make it that much easier to develop the appropriate product characteristics. A very helpful approach to this process is to be found in a monograph published by the Design Council by Rothwell, Gardiner and Schott (1983) which provides a framework for this section. Rothwell et al. argue that user needs can be thought of as having four dimensions which they define as follows:

- *Need elements*: An indication of the overall price and specific performance characteristics required by customers.
- *Need intensity*: A measure of the degree of importance given to each need element by potential users.
- *Need stability*: A measure of the degree to which the need remains unchanged over time.
- *Need diffusion*: A measure of how widely felt the need is. This defines the size of the potential market.

Thus 'need elements' define the properties which a product must contain and/or deliver, while 'need intensity' specifies the relative importance which consumers will attach to any given element. As we have seen when analysing how buyers choose, many properties are assumed to exist as they are intrinsic to the product, and it would not qualify for consideration at all if it didn't possess them. Further, buyers will often use a single performance or benefit criterion as a surrogate for a large number of individual product characteristics when assessing suitability or fitness for purpose; for example, few buyers of machine tools will evaluate the metallurgical analysis of the materials used, nor the precise tolerances used in constructing the tool – they will assess its suitability in terms of its output potential. By the same token the purchaser of a TV set rarely inquires into the nature of the electronic gadgetry contained in the 'box'; they are concerned with the quality of the sound and picture which these components deliver. Of course, there will always be exceptions to these generalisations, and it is for this reason that it is felt more attention should be given to spelling out the product's characteristics, for only by cataloguing them fully will we be able to establish whether our product possesses features others don't and, if so, whether these features will have appeal to a sufficient number of potential customers to constitute a viable market segment.

Table 12.1 provides a listing of product characteristics or attributes as a check list for assessing existing or proposed new products. Several sources have been used in an attempt to make the listing suitable for all categories of products.

While physical attributes are a necessary condition for purchase they are not usually sufficient, particularly where there is little to distinguish one physical product from another. In these circumstances our model of buyer behaviour shows that subjective/behavioural influences will become determinant in enabling the individual to discriminate between competitive offerings. As we noted earlier, the creation of subjective perceived differences is likely to prove more difficult and more costly than the creation of objective differences, but the likelihood of being able to achieve this will be greatly enhanced if one adopts a marketing approach and defines one's products in terms of the benefit/satisfaction it provides rather than the function it performs. Levitt first propounded this philosophy in his

Table 12.1 Product characteristics or attributes

Technical	Price	Non-Price
Performance in use	List price	Delivery
Size	Sale price	Quality of after-sales
Shape	Net price after trade-in	Service
Appearance / design	Discounts	Servicing costs
Reliability	Credit / financing arrangements	Ease of maintenance
Durability	Sale or return	Reputation (of brand)
Ease of use (complexity)	Special offers	User training
Safety in use	Cost of parts	Instructions
Flexibility / adaptability	Divisibility	Running costs
Parts availability		Depreciation
Construction materials		Operator comfort
Power source		
Power output		
Speed of operation		
Taste		
Smell		

Source: Compiled by the author from various studies. No rank order implied.

famous 'Marketing Myopia', but elaborated on it in a subsequent contribution entitled 'The Augmented Product Concept' (1983) in which he wrote:

> *One million quarter-inch drills were sold not because people wanted quarter-inch drills, but because they wanted quarter-inch holes.*

Levitt also quoted the President of Melville Shoes as saying: "People no longer buy shoes to keep their feet warm and dry. They buy them because of the way the shoes make them feel – masculine, feminine, rugged, different, sophisticated, young, glamorous, in. Buying shoes has become an emotional experience. *Our business now is selling excitement rather than shoes.*" (my emphasis) This, of course, is an extreme statement and not to be taken too seriously. Clearly, people still do buy shoes to keep their feet warm and dry, and have quite clear expectations as to the function shoes must perform. But, the point is well made that different images and associations may well encourage people to buy more shoes, to suit different moods and situations, than are required for the sole purpose of protecting one's feet. The recent advertising campaign of Clarks' shoes with the tagline 'Be your own label', is a good example of this.

In Chapter 3 we introduced a Figure representing the dimensions of a brand developed from the work of Ted Levitt. In turn, this visualisation was derived from his ideas on what he called **the augmented product** . This conceptualisation was described in his book *The Marketing Mode* published in 1969, and has been widely adopted, (although it is usually claimed by/misattributed to others). It is illustrated in Figure 12.1.

Figure 12.1 The augmented product

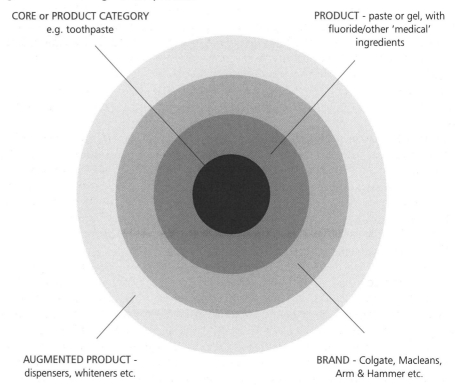

CORE or PRODUCT CATEGORY
e.g. toothpaste

PRODUCT - paste or gel, with
fluoride/other 'medical'
ingredients

AUGMENTED PRODUCT -
dispensers, whiteners etc.

BRAND - Colgate, Macleans,
Arm & Hammer etc.

Levitt wrote:

When the outputs of competing factories are essentially identical and their prices the same, the conversion of an indifferent prospect into a solid customer requires a special effort. Whether the product is cold-rolled steel or hot cross buns, whether accountancy or delicacies, competitive effectiveness increasingly demands that the successful seller offer his prospect and his customer more than the generic product itself. He must surround his generic product with a cluster of product satisfactions that differentiates his total offering from his competitors'. He must provide a total proposition , the content of which exceeds what comes out at the end of the assembly line.

At the centre of the product is the **core benefit** – the properties that will satisfy the felt need. It is this that determines the **product category** to which a good or service would be assigned for purposes of market analysis. So we would expect to find corn flakes in the breakfast cereal section of our supermarket, potato crisps in the snack food section and so on. But, as Levitt so eloquently points out, if we visit these aisles in the supermarket we will be faced with a bewildering array of offerings that are near perfect substitutes for one another. As the composite model of buyer behaviour shows we will try to act rationally by comparing attributes and features in relation to the price of the different offerings by performing a cost benefit analysis. And this is not as difficult as it sounds as the goods on the shelves display unit prices, so we can quickly compare the price of, say, 100g. of Nescafé and 100g. of Kenco. Assuming they are roughly the same how do we choose between them? Well, we look for the **augmentation** added by the seller – the packaging, the design, the brand and what it means to us, associated services, promotional offers and so on, and so on.

Many of these attributes are those that give the product what Levitt termed **excitement** – the particular appeal that captures the attention and interest of a prospective customer. But, how do you move them on to desire and action? Writing in the late 1960s Levitt wrote about **systems selling** – nowadays we would probably talk about relationship marketing, loyalty programmes, after-sales service, customer relationship management and a plethora of other techniques designed to add value for our customer. But the idea is the same – augment the product.

In augmenting the product the aim is to try and change the customer's perception of it – to increase its salience and relevance. Earlier, we introduced Copeland's classification of goods and emphasised that the essence of his classification lies in the perception of the intending buyer. We also argued that it is this perception that is a major factor influencing the elasticity of demand – if I can get you to believe that Kelloggs are superior to all other brands of breakfast cereal so that, for you, it is a specialty good, then the competition won't get a look in, and I can probably get you to pay a premium price too.

While more recent authors, e.g Saren and Tzokas, have criticised the product augmentation concept, widely popularised in Kotler's writings, like many other cases of 'out with the old, in with the new', I believe this is due to a failure to go back to the original sources and establish what they actually said, rather than the often distorted reports of what they are claimed to have said. If you read Copeland and Levitt you will find that both emphasise the need to consider the **customer-supplier context**, and not look at the product itself in isolation. But, to do this successfully, their view (and mine) is that to analyse problems it is helpful to break them down into their component parts and then see how these may be integrated into a holistic explanation. In other words, you need to think about buyer behaviour and product separately and, possibly in the abstract, before integrating and synthesising them into a view of product policy and planning.

Product policy

A firm's product policy is fundamental to the whole operation of the business. Most new companies are conceived to produce a specific product or group of products, and it is this decision which dictates the industry to which they will belong, the markets they will serve, and the nature and extent of the resources, methods and techniques they will employ. These factors often tend to be overlooked, however, for most companies are long-established members of a given industry and inextricably linked with their product line. Similarly, it is often erroneously assumed that companies are irrevocably committed to their current product mix, which ignores the fact that apart from certain highly specific capital equipment, most corporate resources may be put to other uses.

The latter assumption may be attributed to the fact that companies rarely do undertake a radical change in product policy, even when environmental changes indicate that they should – a fact which prompted Theodore Levitt (1960) to write the now classic 'Marketing Myopia'.

Levitt's thesis is that companies take too narrow a view of their market because they think in terms of their product offering, rather than in terms of the fundamental needs which these products satisfy. Thus the American railroads thought of themselves as the ultimate development in overland transportation, and failed to respond to the invention of the internal combustion engine which gave us the car, lorry and aeroplane. If the management of the railroads had thought of

PLASMA VERSUS LCD

At the beginning of 2006 the main protagonists in the battle of the flat screens – plasma and LCD - announced plans for major investments in their respective technologies.

At the present time, there is little if anything to choose between plasma and LCD at the top end of the market as their definition is better than that available from a DVD. However, by the end of the year two new disc technologies will have been launched – Sony's Blu-ray and Toshiba's HD-DVD – offering even higher definition. Such improvements are called for to enhance the quality of moving pictures in video games and could well determine which type of flat screen will be preferred by consumers.

In the immediate future, the World Cup in 2006, and the launch of three new video game consoles, are also seen as major factors in encouraging television owners to upgrade from sets using a cathode ray tube to the new digital format that is widely available in Japan and the UK As a consequence the market for flat televisions is expected to grow by 80% to around 44 million units.

If, like the battle between Betamax and VHS for the VCR standard in the 1980s, the market comes down in favour of one or other technology then Sharp and Matsushita (LCD) are likely to come into a major confrontation with Sony and LG Electronics (plasma).

(Based on reports in The Times, January 2006).

themselves as being in the 'transportation business', then doubtless they would have integrated these new methods of moving goods and people into their existing network. As it was, the expanding demand of a rapidly growing economy masked the impact of the new competition, and lulled the railroads into the complacent belief that they could look forward to continued and uninterrupted growth. Even when the threat was appreciated the railroads chose to compete head-on, failing to realise that they could not hope to duplicate the speed and convenience offered by their rivals, with the result that until recently they have appeared to be members of a dying industry. Now, however, as the result of a belated appreciation of the marketing concept, railways in many advanced economies are enjoying a new lease of life as a result of careful analysis of their comparative strengths vis-à-vis alternative forms of transportation, and a strategy of positioning based on realistic market segmentation.

The writings of Levitt and Peter Drucker, among others, have given us the concept of corporate strategy which, in essence, consists of a statement of the firm's objective, and the mix of policies to be used in the attainment of that objective. A first step in the formulation of a corporate strategy is to answer the questions

'What business are we in?' and 'What business do we want to be in?' Declining industries have invariably failed to define their business in sufficiently broad terms. Had the railroads thought of themselves as being in the 'transportation business' it is reasonable to assume that they would have been responsive to the development and introduction of new methods of transport, irrespective of whether they involved rails and locomotives.

Gulf Oil exemplifies the broad viewpoint in that it defined its role as *'servicing the travelling public'*. Although the company's past growth depended largely upon the refining and sale of petroleum products to motorists, Gulf recognised that developments in fuel cell technology and growing concern over air pollution may be sounding the death-knell of the petrol engine. The motor car represents only one stage in the evolution of personal transport, however, and it is clear that people will continue to travel even though we may not be able to predict the exact nature of the next development. While travelling, people have a need for both rest and refreshment, and to meet this continuing need Gulf developed a nation-wide network of Holiday Inns (now divested and operated as a franchise).

Hopefully, this example makes it clear that by defining the business they are in, and want to be in, Gulf did not commit themselves irrevocably to a given product mix, but will modify their product offering in the light of changes in consumer demand – this is their **product policy**.

THE CONCEPT OF THE PRODUCT LIFE-CYCLE

The above examples clearly indicate that, over time, man develops new and better ways of satisfying basic needs, with the result that as new products are introduced, established products become obsolescent and eventually pass into oblivion. In time the cycle repeats itself, and the once new product suffers the fate of the product which it originally replaced. In many ways this process resembles the human life-cycle, with its phase's of birth, growth, maturity, senility and death, and has given rise to the concept of the **product life-cycle**.

The first stage in the product life-cycle is represented by its introduction into the market. As with human beings, this is a critical stage, for the product has little to protect it from the hostile environment into which it is introduced. (Fortunately, medical science has been more successful in protecting new-born offspring than has the marketer!) Assuming survival, new products enjoy a period of increasing demand and rapid growth, but as most innovations are merely substitutes for existing products, other manufacturers will react strongly to the newcomer, and their own decline in market share, stemming the newcomer's growth. However, as the superiority of the new substitute becomes apparent many suppliers will switch to it to protect their market share, accelerating the adoption of the new product and the decline of the old. The levelling out of demand for the new product represents the onset of maturity.

In time, other new products will enter the market offering advantages over the now mature product, which will experience a decline in demand as consumers switch their allegiance. This phase has been characterised as senility or decay. Classically the product life-cycle is represented as having four basic phases as represented in Figure 12.2.

If the stylised PLC shown reflects reality then clearly the change in the inflection of the curve at A heralds rapid exponential growth, at B a levelling off of demand, at C a diminution that suggests either product rejuvenation or replacement. Although the utility of the PLC concept is occasionally challenged by sceptical practitioners their criticisms tend to reflect their own failure to understand its meaning, and to the rather naive assumption that all products will exhibit perfectly symmetrical S-shaped curves.

In fact, consideration of a number of other areas reveals that some form of **exponential function** (represented graphically by a cumulative S-shaped curve) is typical of the manner in which objects or ideas spread or **diffuse** through populations of 'adopters'. Elsewhere (Baker, 1975, in *Marketing New Industrial Products*), I have argued that the consistent and pervasive nature of the diffusion

Figure 12.2 Stage in the product life-cycle

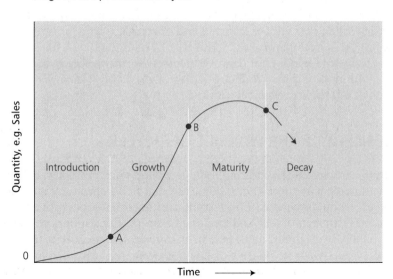

process approximates a law of nature and reflects an underlying process such that if one can initiate diffusion it will proceed to some extent automatically thereafter due to the 'bandwagon' or 'contagion' effect.

In the context of new-product marketing we find that success is usually defined in terms of achieving a predetermined sales target within a specified time period. It follows that the sooner one can achieve an initial sale the sooner diffusion will commence. In essence the logic is that proof of a sale adds conviction to the selling process, while word-of-mouth recommendation or pure visibility, for example a new car at the kerbside, will accelerate awareness of the new product's existence and so improve the probability of further purchases. Put very simply then, success or failure is highly dependent upon the speed with which we can achieve initial sales and the lesson to be learned from the concept is that effort to pre-identify 'early adopters' is essential to long-run success. In the particular, however, it is impossible to be highly specific about the particular characteristics of early adopters in different contexts and situations, as has been demonstrated by the lack of correlation between the findings of various research studies.

Such a lack of correlation does not invalidate the utility of the concept – it merely emphasises the need for persons well versed in their own product– market interface (however we define 'product' and 'market') to apply their experience and knowledge in seeing how such a basic idea can be of use to them.

Unlike the human life-cycle, however, one cannot predict the length of any of the phases of the product life-cycle – certainly there are not the equivalent of actuarial tables for new products. Further, marketers have the option to practise euthanasia and quietly dispose of products which fail to live up to expectations, or, alternatively, to prolong the life-cycle through a rejuvenation process. The analogy is a useful one, provided that one bears in mind that it is a generalisation and says nothing specific about the duration of any given phase. However, by monitoring changes in demand, one can predict the onset of growth, maturity and senility, and vary one's marketing inputs accordingly; for example, reduce the level of advertising expenditures during growth and emphasise production and physical distribution; step up the amount of sales promotion at the onset of maturity; retire the product when senility sets in. Table 12.2 provides a useful summary of how various characteristics such as cash flow and competition vary in accordance with the stages of the product life-cycle and their implications for managing the marketing mix.

WHAT IS A 'NEW' PRODUCT?

The first stage in the product life-cycle posits the introduction of a new product – the question is, 'What constitutes a new product?' There can be no hard-and-fast answer, for newness is essentially a subjective concept that depends upon one's state of knowledge or, in the case of a firm, its current range of activity. It is possible to distinguish a spectrum of newness ranging from an invention, which Mansfield (1966) has defined as 'a prescription for a new product or process that was not obvious to one skilled in the relevant art at the time the idea was generated', to a minor change in an existing, widely known product, for example the addition of a new blue whitener to a detergent.

In 1982 Booz Allen and Hamilton published a book on new product management

Table 12.2 Product life-cycle: implications for marketing

Product life-cycle	Introduction	Growth	Maturity	Decline
Characteristics				
Sales	Low	Fast growth	Slow growth	Decline
Profit	Negative	Rapid rise	Falling margins	Declining
Cash flow	Negative	Moderate	High	Moderate
Strategy				
Objective	Aggressive entry	Maximise share	Boost profits	Milk product
Focus	Non-users	New segments	Defend share	Cut costs
Customer targets	Innovators	Early adopters	Majority	Laggards
Competitor targets	Few, pre-empt	Growing number	Many Declining	
Differential advantage	Product performance	Brand image	Price and service	Price
Marketing mix				
Product	Basic	Extensions & enhancements	Differentiation, variety	Rationalise range
Price	High	Lower	Low	Stabilising
Promotion	High	High	Falling	Low
Advertising forms	Awareness	Brand performance	Loyalty	Selective
Distribution	Selective	Intensive	Intensive	Rationalise
Organisation				
Structure	Team	Market focus	Functional	Lean
Focus	Innovation	Marketing	Efficiency	Cost reduction
Culture	Freewheeling	Marketing led	Professional	Pressured

Source: Doyle, P. (1999), 'Product life-cycle management', in Baker, M.J. (ed.) *IEBM Encyclopedia of Marketing*, (London: Thomson Learning)

that is still widely cited in the literature. In this they identified *six* classes or types of new products, namely:

1 *New-to-the-world* i.e. innovations such as digital photography, GPS, 3G mobile phones etc.

2 *New product lines* i.e. the introduction of a product not previously made by the firm.

3 *Additions to existing product lines* i.e. a new model or addition to an existing range of products. Often referred to as a product line extension

4 *Improvements and revisions to existing products* i.e upgrades or modifications of existing products.

5 *Repositionings* i.e. identifying new applications for existing products e.g. Arm and Hammer's uses for its basic product baking soda.

6 *Cost reductions* While not strictly a new product lowering the price enable the firm to cater for new market segments.

For the purpose of this book a new product will be considered anything which is perceived as such by the consumer, or with which the firm has no previous experience. The former permits the inclusion of variants in existing products, and their packaging, as well as totally new products such as satellite television, body scanners or 3G mobile phones. The latter acknowledges that production of an existing product with which the firm has no previous experience raises the same marketing problems as does a totally new product. Further, it may also be perceived by consumers as a new product; for example the sale of home furnishings under the 'St Michael' brand by Marks & Spencer. The importance of product development in the firm's marketing strategy was introduced in Chapter 2 when we proposed that a firm has only a limited number of strategic alternatives which it can choose from. This view was supported by Ansoff's 'Growth Vector Matrix' which sees product development as one of only four options available to the firm. (In passing, it should be noted that research by Baker and Hart (1989) showed that the most successful firms do not regard these strategies as mutually exclusive but seek to increase market penetration while, simultaneously, developing both new products and markets.) It is for this reason that we regard new product development as being at the very heart of the organisation's strategy. It is also important to remember that the introduction of new products creates problems for buyers in that it requires them to reconsider their existing attitudes and patterns of behaviour. Many of these problems were looked at in Chapters 8 and 9 concerning consumer (individual) and organisational buyer behaviour respectively.

The role of new product development

Although it is impossible to predict the life span of a given product, there is an inevitable certainty that it will eventually be replaced by the introduction of a new substitute or even made totally obsolete as the result of technological innovation.

ACCELERATING CHANGE – COMPETITION FOR THE IPOD?

In October 2001 Apple launched its **iPod**; by 2005 it had sold more than 10 million – including 4 million in the run up to Christmas 2004. With the support of **iTunes**, the downloading service, it has quickly become the market leader, and even car manufacturers are now advertising vehicles as having iPod connections on board, for example, BMW.

In April 2005 Nokia announced the launch of its N91 mobile phone capable of storing 3000 songs and the ability to download while on the move.

It boasts a four gigabyte capacity, two megapixel camera, web browser and video technology, and a price tag of £450 (a 4Gb iPod is £140).

Other products entering the market include the Sony Playstation Portable (PSP), a gaming console which also handles movies, photos, music and acts as an internet browser and which retails at £179.

The question is whether the concept of a 'music mobile' is going to mark the beginning of the end for a dedicated media player like iPod. Motorola has already done a deal with Apple to allow their mobile handsets to be able to play iTunes downloads, and Apple has extended the capabilities of the next generation iPod to include video. Will Apple expand the capabilities of the iPod further to include telecommunications or internet access?

In Chapter 3 it was stated that branding developed in its present form as a result of the realisation that many mass markets were faced with the possibility of over-supply, such that individual manufacturers could only protect their position by distinguishing their output from that of their competitors. Many critics of advertising would argue that the claimed differences between brands are more a figment of the copywriter's imagination than a reality, and still view products such as detergents and canned peas as homogeneous. This view is admissible if one adopts a narrow definition of a product, based solely on the function that it performs in terms of objective and quantifiable criteria. However, from the arguments advanced concerning newness, it is clear that the consumer's perception is modified by subjective considerations which are not amenable to quantification. Thus a relatively minor change in a product's composition or marketing may assume major significance in the user's eyes, and result in a marked shift in demand for that product. It is argued, therefore, that branding can only succeed as a competitive strategy given the existence of perceived differences.

If this is so, it follows that a competitive market will be characterised by a continual effort to develop such differences. Clearly, the producer who succeeds in distinguishing their product from that of their competitors, through the creation of a new and desirable attribute, will enjoy an advantage which will enable them to expand sales and share of market. Such an advantage is in the nature of a monopoly, which may last for years if protected by a patent, for example the Polaroid camera and film, or be eroded overnight by imitative innovation, for example enzyme active detergents.

The role of new product development is the creation of such competitive advantages.

Over the years the American consulting firm Booz Allen Hamilton Inc. has pursued the objective of seeking to understand the management approaches that

Figure 12.3 Strategic roles for successful new products

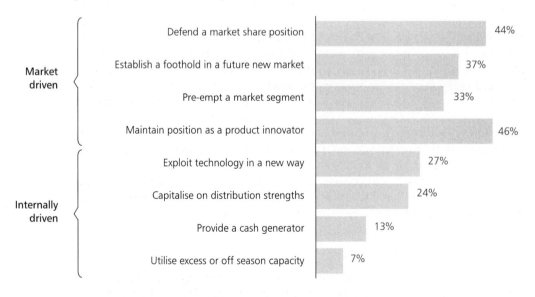

Source: Rodocanachi, P. (1983), 'The Successful Management of New Products in the 1980's'.

result in competitive advantage with a particular emphasis upon the role of new product development. In a paper given to the Esomar seminar on New Product Development (Athens, November 1983) entitled 'The Successful Management of New Products in the 1980s', Pierre Rodocanachi presented the findings of their research based upon in-depth interviews with top management of large and medium sized companies in the United States and Europe, complemented by a comprehensive mail survey of corporate executives and product managers of Fortune 1000 companies. According to this research new products play an important and diverse role in the firm's overall strategy as can be seen from Figure 12.3. These objectives are considered to be just as valid today.

The importance of new products

Any attempt to measure the contribution of new products to a firm or industry's growth and profitability is bedevilled by a lack of consensus as to what constitutes a new product. Similar difficulties also exist when one seeks to measure the failure rate of new product introductions.

Ignoring the problems of data comparability for the present, two valid generalisations may be advanced:

1 Firms are increasingly dependent upon new products for the maintenance and expansion of sales.

2 A large proportion of new product introductions are failures in the sense that they do not achieve the expected sales level, and are withdrawn from the market.

Estimates of new product failure rates vary enormously from the oft-quoted level of 80 per cent (Ross Federal Research Corporation, quoted in the *Wall Street Journal*, 5 April 1961), to an absolute low of 7 per cent (A. C. Nielsen Company, How to Strengthen Your Product Plan, 1966) if the firm makes full use of the screening and testing procedures described below. Again these estimates are very dated but they are still widely quoted today. According to *Marketing Week* magazine (8 October 1994) some analysts believe that 80 per cent of new products fail. However, this is likely to apply to minor changes in fast moving consumer goods where most of the new products launched by companies are merely extensions of those already in existence. For obvious reasons this is a cheaper and less risky alternative to a completely new product. For example by launching gravy granules Bisto were able to make use of a product improvement but still associate the product with the company's traditional reputation and image. However, the seven per cent figure is about right for more significant innovations that have been through the full new product development process described below.

In all cases the reason for failure still remains that the new product does not address a real customer need. Had the firm undertaken the kind of market research advocated in the previous chapter this likelihood would be greatly reduced.

Alternative new product strategies

Relatively few new products emanate from totally new companies, and attention here will be focused on the established firm with an existing product line. Such firms vary in their willingness to innovate and develop new products, and are usually categorised as 'leaders' and 'followers'. Many industries which are highly concentrated or oligopolistic in structure are dominated by one or a small number of firms which determine the competitive character of the market along such dimensions as price, quality, distribution policy, and innovation. These firms are the leaders. The remaining firms are thought of as followers in that they imitate the policies of the leaders and rarely possess a sufficient market share to affect industry practice through independent action.

(Although this is not the place to enter into a discussion of the evils of monopoly/oligopoly, there is a considerable body of evidence which suggests that small firms in an industry are the most innovative, and it would be wrong to assume that it is always the industry leader who stimulates innovation.)

Whether a firm is a leader or follower, there are several distinct ways in which it can add to its product line which may be summarised as:

1 *Modification of an existing product*; for example, addition of a new ingredient in a detergent, toothpaste or cake mix; increase in the cubic capacity of a car engine, adoption of disc brakes, and so on.

2 *Addition of a complementary product*; for example, a new brand of cigarette, a new flavour in a food or beverage; the development of a new model of car.

3 *Entry into an existing market new to the firm*; for example, Cadbury's entry into the cake market.

4 *Development of a new market through the introduction of a totally new product*; for example the Polaroid camera, television, computers.

These alternatives are listed in ascending order of risk. The first strategy usually entails a low level of risk, and is frequently in response to overt public demand. Thus, offering variants of their standard models improves a car maker's competitive position but requires comparatively little additional investment by the firm.

The second strategy involves a greater degree of risk, as the firm has no previous direct experience of the production and marketing of the new item. However, in so far as it is a complementary product, previous experience with similar products and markets will be almost directly relevant and reduce the risk accordingly. Entry into an existing market of which the firm has no previous experience is unlikely to be viewed favourably by the companies currently sharing that market. Thus the new entrant's inexperience is compounded by the aggressive reaction of competitors, and involves a still higher level of risk.

The fourth alternative exposes the firm to a completely unknown situation, added to which the value of fundamentally new products may take years to establish owing to the innate conservatism of the potential user. Further, it is only when a product achieves wide-scale trial that many of its limitations become apparent, which may involve the innovator in many years of adjustment and modification. At the end of this time another firm may well enter the market which the innovator has developed and deprive them of the fruits of their labours; for example IBM in the computer market. Based on three decades of research into the major reasons that new products fail Cooper (1999) summarised these as falling into *seven* major categories. In Table 12.4 he summarises the *ten* major reasons underlying new product success.

Table 12.3 Reasons for new product failure	
1	A lack of market orientation
2	Moving too quickly or too slowly – 'time to market'
3	Poor quality of execution
4	Not enough homework
5	A lack of differentiation
6	Technical problems
7	No focus, too many projects, and a lack of resources

Source: Cooper R. G. (1999), 'New product development', in Baker, M.J. (ed.) *IEBM Encyclopedia of Marketing*, (London: Thomson Learning)

Table 12.4 Reasons for new product success	
1	Product superiority
2	Strong market orientation
3	More pre-development work
4	Sharp and early new product definition
5	The right organisational structure, design and climate
6	Top management support
7	Market attractiveness and synergies
8	Well conceived and properly executed launch
9	Completeness, consistency and quality of execution
10	Adoption of a multi-stage, disciplined process

Source: Cooper R. G. (1999), 'New product development', in Baker, M.J. (ed.) *IEBM Encyclopedia of Marketing*, (London: Thomson Learning)

NEW PRODUCT DEVELOPMENT

Despite the risks involved, new product development is a competitive necessity and has prompted many companies to evolve formalised procedures for dealing with the complexities and uncertainties inherent in the process. In the survey undertaken by Booz Allen Hamilton (1982), strong support was found for a six-stage process represented diagrammatically in Figure 12.4.

It should be emphasised that the Booz Allen Hamilton process model is a greatly simplified one. While it is reproduced in most textbooks, sometimes with considerable elaboration to reflect more stages, it must be recognised that it represents the logic of the process rather than the reality. In the real world new product development frequently involves much back tracking and many feed-back loops. It would also be more accurate to show the process as circular (evolutionary) rather than linear. That said, the model has the great virtue of identifying the key stages through which every new product must pass before it reaches the customer. Further, by isolating the stages it has thrown into sharp relief the fact that costs increase rapidly as one moves from the exploratory and

Figure 12.4 Six stages of product evolution

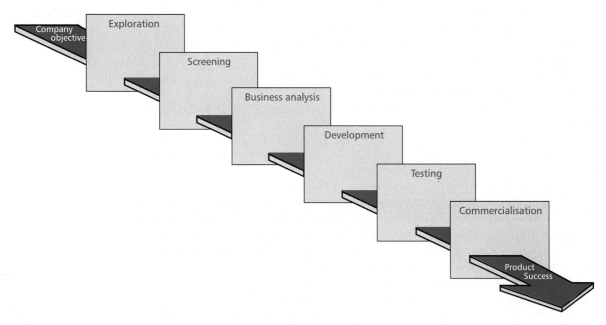

Source: Booz Allen Hamilton Inc. (1982).

creative phases into the development and marketing activities. This was reflected in the 1982 survey which indicated a significant change of emphasis from the findings of the 1968 study. Specifically:

> *Companies now conduct far more up-front analyses than in the past. Specific strategies are delineated. Ideas and concept generation are focused. Screening and evaluation are more rigorous, more attuned to strategic and performance considerations. On the whole, the up-front process receives more attention.*

While BAH do not appear to have replicated these earlier studies precisely, they continue to be a leading consultancy in the field of new product development and frequent reports can be found at their website *www.bah.com*. All these reports confirm the benefits of following a structured approach, and of concentrating attention on what has been called the 'fuzzy front end' of idea generation and concept development.

The location of new product ideas

To be effective, any search for new product ideas should be structured, in the sense that efforts should be directed towards a specific area and pursued systematically. Most firms possess some special skill or 'distinctive competence', and it is this which they should seek to exploit in developing new products. Thus, if a firm has developed a reputation for precision engineering it should seek to build on this strength, rather than branch out into mass-produced, fabricated products, Although there are cases of firms which have achieved success following a radical departure from their original product policy, we would argue that this is attributable to their developing a distinctive competence they previously lacked, or had failed to exploit.

The adoption of search criteria is essential if the firm is to avoid wasteful exploration of the multiplicity of sources open to it. Such sources may be internal or external to the firm.

Internally, every member of the company is a potential source of new product ideas, and company suggestion schemes have thrown up many more valuable suggestions than they are generally credited with. Many companies now have their own Research and Development Department, specifically charged with developing in-house projects, in addition to which Sales, Marketing and Production usually have distinct ideas of how the current product line could be improved or extended.

Externally, the firm's distributors and customers are frequently a fruitful source of ideas, as are the product offerings of one's competitors. Another major source is the published literature of the universities and professional bodies, the technical and trade press, and the various government research departments. Much of the information to be gleaned from these sources is incapable of immediate application but is sufficient to stimulate further investigation.

The major source of ideas for radical innovations is undoubtedly the private inventor, whose work may be reviewed by consulting the Patent Office files or the weekly Official Journal. (Few inventors appreciate the commercial potential of their ideas, and those that do frequently meet with a cool reception from potential manufacturers, for example Xerography and the Hovercraft, but nearly all patent their ideas.)

Screening new product ideas

In drawing up a short-list of product ideas for detailed investigation the search criteria mentioned earlier will also help reduce the need for subsequent screening, that is weeding out of marginal ideas. Such criteria usually require that:

- The product will meet a clearly defined customer need;
- The product is consistent with the firm's production and marketing policies;
- The product will utilise the firm's existing skills and resources;
- The product will contribute to the firm's long-run profitability.

Once a short-list has been compiled, the next step is to evaluate each product's potential. To ensure consistency, many firms make use of a factor-rating table similar to that reproduced in Table 12.5

A **Factor Rating Table** is a very useful device for analysing the relevance and importance of information required to solve a problem. In essence, it requires the decision maker to identify first what are the critical success factors. Table 2.2 is an example of such a listing as a basis for evaluating competitiveness. Once we have the list of factors to be considered, we then need to rank order these in terms of their importance.

Experience shows that a simple nominal scale - 1,2,3,4, etc – does not create sufficient 'distance' between the factors so it may be better to assign a percentage

Table 12.5 New product factor rating table

Factor	Ranking	Very Good	Good	Average	Poor	Very Poor
Uniqueness / Differentiation	20					
Performance / Value Added	15					
Appearance / Design	10					
Price Appeal	10					
Builds on Existing Market Strengths	8					
Builds on Existing Production Strengths	8					
Growth Market	5					
Frequency of Purchase	5					
Cyclical Demand etc.	5					
Other Specific Factors	14					

score reflecting the relative importance of the factors vis-à-vis each other.

Having formed a judgement of the contribution of each factor to the overall outcome, the next step is to rank the object under consideration in terms of how well it satisfies our requirements. Very often this will involve the use of a semantic differential scale of the kind described in Chapter 11. But, if we are inviting a number of people to complete such a scale then we may have to explain precisely what we mean by generalised descriptors like Very Good, Good etc. For examples, suppose one of our factors is the degree of control we have over the supply of inputs necessary for producing our product, then we might 'operationalise' the categories as follows:

Very Good	We own or have control of the source of supply
Good	We are a major customer (key account) of the leading supplier of the input
Average	We have good relations with the major supplier but have to source 50% of our requirements in the open market.
Poor	The company has to compete for supplies but there are several sources
Very Poor	The company has to compete for supplies from a very limited number of sources.

Our Table is included to illustrate the idea. In practice, a firm would develop a much more detailed and sophisticated set of factors, or it might employ one of the major management consultants like Booz Allen Hamilton Inc. who have extensive experience in this field.

Given the revised short-list, the next step is a detailed feasibility study based on tests of the product concept. Such tests may have been made already, but if not, it is essential that they be undertaken prior to detailed market studies and the finalisation of prototypes. In its original form the product concept represents the marketer's perception of a product which will satisfy a specific consumer want, and may differ considerably from the consumer's own perception of what is required. As it is the latter who ultimately decides whether the product will be a success, reconciliation of any discrepancy is vital. Further, outlining the broad characteristics of a new product to a potential consumer may well stimulate the latter to suggest specific attributes previously unthought of.

In some instances the product concept is too complex to be tested verbally, and some form of mock-up or prototype must be used to communicate the idea and gain consumer reaction. For example, the concept of a mobile telephone or a pick and place robot may be difficult to convey in words but eminently simple to demonstrate.

Once management is satisfied that the basic idea is indeed consistent with its policies, and within its engineering and production capabilities, it should formulate a product concept; that is, a precise statement of the need the product will fill and the form it will take. Based on this statement the marketing research department can develop a profile of the potential market and the production department can estimate unit cost at various levels of output. (The latter may necessitate the construction of a prototype(s).) Utilising these data, the marketing department can then develop its own estimate of the costs associated with varying levels of market penetration

The emphasis upon 'front-end' analysis referred to earlier has had a dramatic effect upon the mortality of new product ideas as can be seen from Figure 12.5, reproduced from Rodocanachi 'Successful Management' which compares the

Figure 12.5 Mortality of new product ideas (by stage of evolution)

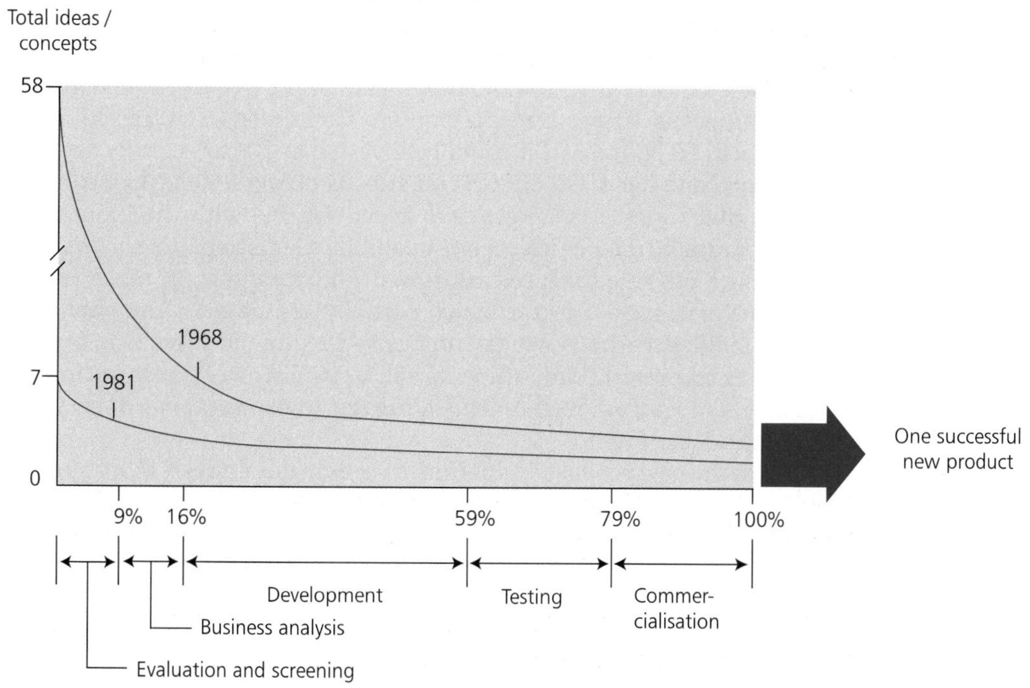

Source: Rodocanachi, P. (1983), 'The Successful Management of New Products in the 1980's'.

findings of the 1968 and 1981 Booz Allen studies.

Despite this increased emphasis upon evaluation and screening it appears that the UK and USA still lag considerably behind Japan in the attention given to this phase, which suggests that still more effort will be applied to it in future.

Business analysis

Once the firm has isolated those concepts which appear to have potential for development it needs to undertake a business analysis to test its commercial viability.

Of necessity any assessment of a new product's potential will require the firm to undertake a certain amount of research. To begin with it will need to define the market segment which it intends to target. It will then have to establish the size and potential of this segment, of any competition, the strength/performance of these competitors, and decide upon its own positioning .

Internally, it will have to prepare forecasts of the costs of developing and marketing the new product or service, and then develop various scenarios for entering the market. Based on these scenarios it will develop forecasts of sales volume/market share so that it can decide whether or not to proceed.

New product introductions represent an investment opportunity for the firm, and it is essential that such opportunities be evaluated in the light of all other possible uses of the firm's resources. In the normal course of events a company is faced with a disparate collection of investment opportunities, and so must develop a common denominator with which it may rank dissimilar projects in order of preference. The discounted cash flow (DCF) technique has been widely adopted for this purpose.

The basic principle upon which the DCF technique is based is recognition of the fact that a currently available sum of money can be invested to generate a stream of future earnings. Thus £1 invested today will be worth £1.10 a year hence if the return on investment is 10 per cent per annum. Conversely, £1 received a year hence is only worth £0.90 today if it could be invested at 10 per cent. By applying the DCF technique one can make direct comparisons of investment opportunities with very dissimilar future cash flows and select the one with the highest net present value. Naturally, the method is not infallible, as it is very dependent upon the accuracy of the predicted future cash flows. The more distant these are the less accurate they become – a factor which partially accounts for the popularity of payback and similar methods which emphasise the time in which the original investment will be recovered. Many students will be familiar with these techniques already: those that are not are recommended to refer to *An Insight into Management Accounting* by John Sizer (1989).

At this stage of the new product evaluation procedure it is unlikely that sufficient information exists to permit a detailed comparison of proposals, but even a rough computation will help reduce the list.

Product development and testing

If the business analysis indicates a profitable market opportunity then the firm will commit resources to physical development and testing. This phase of the NPD process frequently involves iterations with the preceding Business Analysis stage as more and better information about cost and performance becomes available allowing further refinement of forecasts.

In view of the high risks associated with new product introductions, field testing should logically precede firm commitment to large-scale production and marketing. **Product testing** consists of an objective appraisal of the product's performance, free of subjective associations created by other elements of the marketing mix, for example price, packaging, brand image and so on. It should not be confused with **test marketing**, which includes consideration of these factors.

The precise nature of a product test obviously depends upon the product itself but, essentially, all seek to determine how well it will perform in actual use. Certain product attributes are capable of precise measurement, for example the efficiency of an engine, the life of an electric light bulb; whereas others depend upon consumer preference and defy exact quantification, for example the taste of a food or beverage. Recognised tests exist for the measurement of most items included in the product specification and subsequently incorporated in the description of the goods as offered for sale. With the passing of the **Trade Descriptions Act 1968**, the importance of ensuring the accuracy of such quantitative statements became a matter of law rather than conscience. This Act makes it an offence to use a false trade description, which is defined as covering:

- The composition, quality, quantity, and size of goods.
- Their suitability and fitness for any particular purpose.
- Their testing or approval by any person.
- The method, origin, date of manufacture, production or processing.
- Their history and previous ownership.

Under the provisions of the Act, the use of a false description becomes a criminal offence punishable by fine and/or imprisonment, whereas previously misrepresentation was only actionable in a civil action.

As noted, however, many product qualities are a matter of individual perception and preference, the incidence of which can only be established through actual trial. In practice a number of experimental methods have been developed some of which will already be familiar to the reader as a result of their incorporation in television commercials, e.g. blind taste tests

In that the manufacturer is seeking to establish how their new offering will be perceived by the consumer, a commonly used test involves comparison with a leading competitive product. The detergent advertisement which shows two halves of a badly stained article washed in an identical manner, except for the fact that one powder is Spotto and the other Brand X, is an example of such a paired comparison. Although scientifically valid, a successful rating on a blind test in which the new product is identified solely by a code number is no guarantee of market acceptance. The purpose of such tests is to test a specific variable such as taste, texture, washing power and so forth, and thus requires that all other variables be held constant. In the real world the consumer does not normally select a product along one dimension alone, even though a single factor such as washing power may predominate. Products are bundles of attributes which are viewed collectively and which create their own associations in the mind of the potential user, so that a preference for A over B based on a single variable may be reversed when all the variables are taken into account. Thus, although a successful product test is an essential preliminary to continued development, it is not conclusive evidence of market success, and many producers will only make a final decision on the product's future after large-scale market testing.

Test marketing

Basically, **test marketing** consists of launching the product on a limited scale in a representative market, thus avoiding the costs of a full-scale launch while permitting the collection of market data which may subsequently be used for predictive purposes.

In practice the term 'test marketing' tends to be used loosely, and it is important to distinguish the original concept, as outlined above, from two associated techniques commonly confused with it.

The first of these is often referred to as **pilot marketing**, and fulfils the same function for the marketer as the pilot plant does for the production engineer, that is it tests the feasibility of the proposed course of action. In many instances companies become so involved with the development of a new product that by the time successful product tests have been completed they feel irrevocably committed, and any course of action other than full-scale marketing is unthinkable. However, companies of this type are usually aware of the critical importance of a well-designed and co-ordinated marketing plan, and so test its feasibility in practice prior to full-scale operations. Pilot marketing on a regional basis may also serve to give the firm valuable marketing experience while commissioning new plant to meet the anticipated demands of a national market.

The other practice often confused with test marketing is the **testing of mix variables**, that is measuring the effect of changes in the test variable, all other variables being held constant, for example copy testing. Such tests are often used to improve the marketing of existing products, and should not be confused with the true test market in which the collective impact of all variables is being tested simultaneously.

It is clear that if test market results are to be used to predict the likely outcome of a full-scale national launch, then the test market must constitute a representative sample of the national market. Despite the claims of various media owners it is equally clear that no such perfect microcosm exists and that test marketing is of dubious value if undertaken for predictive purposes alone. In addition to the dangers inherent in scaling up atypical test market results to derive national sales forecasts, many marketers feel that test marketing increases the risks of aggressive competitive reaction in an attempt to nip the new product in the bud. Test market validity depends heavily on the assumption that trading conditions in the market are 'normal', and it follows that any departure from such conditions will bias the results. Competitors learn quickly of test marketing operations and typically react in one of two ways. If the new product closely resembles existing brands, the manufacturers of these brands will usually step up their advertising and sales promotion in the test market to maintain existing brand loyalties and prevent the new entrant getting a foothold. These tactics also ensure the existence of 'abnormal' trading conditions during the test period. Alternatively, if the new product represents a radical departure from existing products, competitors can easily monitor its test market performance while developing their own substitutes. If the test results seem promising the imitative innovator may well enter the national market at the same time as the originator of the idea – if not before!

For these reasons many manufacturers now undertake more exhaustive tests of the mix variables and omit the test market stage altogether. This approach is strongly favoured by Japanese companies. If the new product is launched on a limited scale initially, more often than not it is in the nature of a feasibility study rather than in the hope of obtaining hard data from which to predict the outcome of a national launch.

In addition to test marketing being 'slow, expensive, and open to spying and sabotage' its demise is being hastened by the availability of alternative methods for assessing likely market response. Among these alternatives the simulated test market and scanner-based test marketing are the most popular and widely used techniques.

In a simulated test market consumers are recruited in retail outlets, asked to read an advertisement about a new product and given a free sample of it. Subsequently, the consumer is asked to rate the product (by means of a telephone interview in the USA) and these data are used to predict market response by means of a computer programme. Apparently this method is quite successful at weeding out potential failures for a modest investment ($40,000), but is less good at predicting actual potential.

A more sophisticated approach is the scanner-based test in which consumers in selected markets get an identification card which is presented at the retail check-out. Using the product codes a record is made of purchase, without the consumer or competitors knowing which product(s) are being tested, which enables prediction to be made about take-up and sales potential.

Despite the availability of less expensive and less obvious test marketing methods all the evidence suggests that many firms now skip this phase in the process. The main factor behind this is undoubtedly what is referred to as 'time-based competition' or 'time to market'. At several places we have commented on the impact of accelerating technological innovation and intensifying competition. Taken together these trends have led to shorter product life cycles and so put a premium on faster product development and early market entry. It is also believed that greater emphasis on the earlier creative and research based phases of the NPD process has done much to improve the likelihood of success without the penalties of the traditional test market.

Commercialisation

The final phase of the NPD process is commercialisation when the product is launched in the market, thus initiating its life-cycle. As can be seen from Figure 12.6, commercialisation increases the firm's financial commitment by several orders of magnitude. Capacity must be installed to cater for the anticipated demand; inventory must be built up to ensure that supplies can be made available to the distribution channel; intensive selling-in must take place to ensure widespread availability at the point of sale, or to canvass orders from prospective buyers; maintenance and servicing facilities may be necessary and a large promotional investment will be needed to create awareness of the new product's existence. Given the importance of this phase, one might reasonably expect discussions of it to dominate texts dealing with the subject, but it only requires a cursory examination to reveal that this stage rarely receives equal treatment with the

Figure 12.6 Cumulative expenditures in NPD

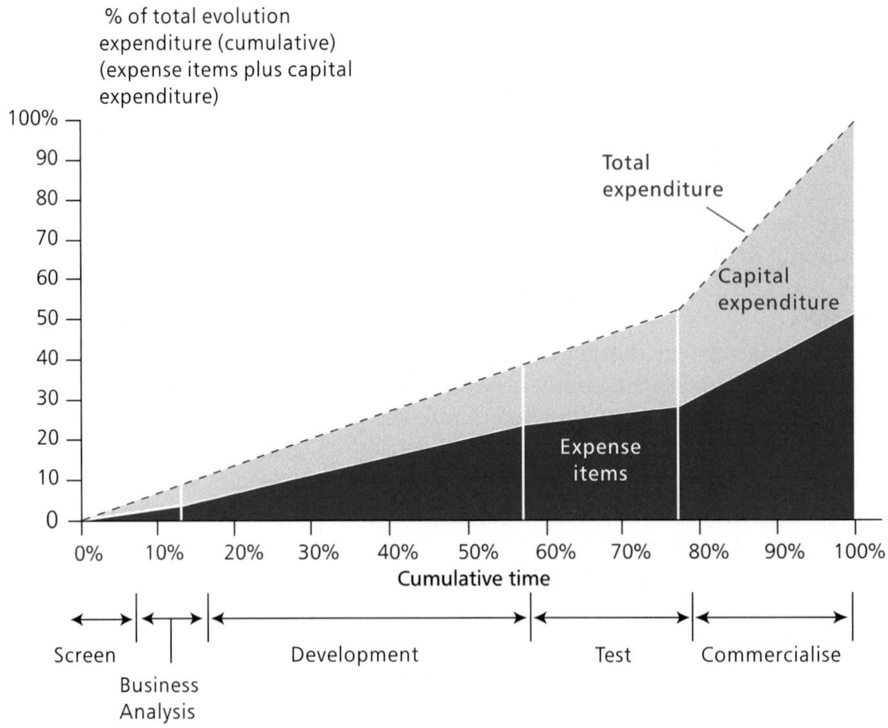

% of total evolution
expenditure (cumulative)
(expense items plus capital
expenditure)

Source: Rodocanachi, P. (1983), 'The Successful Management of New Products in the 1980's'.

preceding phases and attracts comparatively little attention.

In recent years organising for NPD has received considerable attention. Linear process models, such as the one described here, have often led to a perception that each phase is a discrete activity and the prime responsibility of different functional experts. Thus, marketing may initiate the process by identifying potential products but these get passed to R&D and Engineering to see if they're feasible technically. If they are, then Finance will be asked to test their commercial feasibility after which they will go to Production for physical development. Finally, the new product will be handed over to Marketing again for commercialisation.

This tendency to compartmentalisation leads to what has been termed a 'pass the parcel' approach with a lack of ownership and sense of urgency. Analysis of Japanese NPD suggests a quite different approach, with considerable overlap and integration of the phases, which has been likened to a rugby team rather than a relay race. To facilitate this team approach the practices of parallel processing and simultaneous engineering have been widely adopted.

In collaboration with Professor Susan Hart, the author has developed a more sophisticated model of new product development which we have called **Multiple Convergent Processing (MCP)**. The MCP model sees the Booz Allen Hamilton model as the spine of a complex set of interrelated and interdependent activities. In other words, a critical path, Developing this concept further we conceive of all the firm's functions working simultaneously and in parallel on new product development with the convergent points providing the necessary focus and integration. An example of the early stages of the MCP is shown in Figure 12.7.

Figure 12.7 An example of the early stages of the multiple convergent process

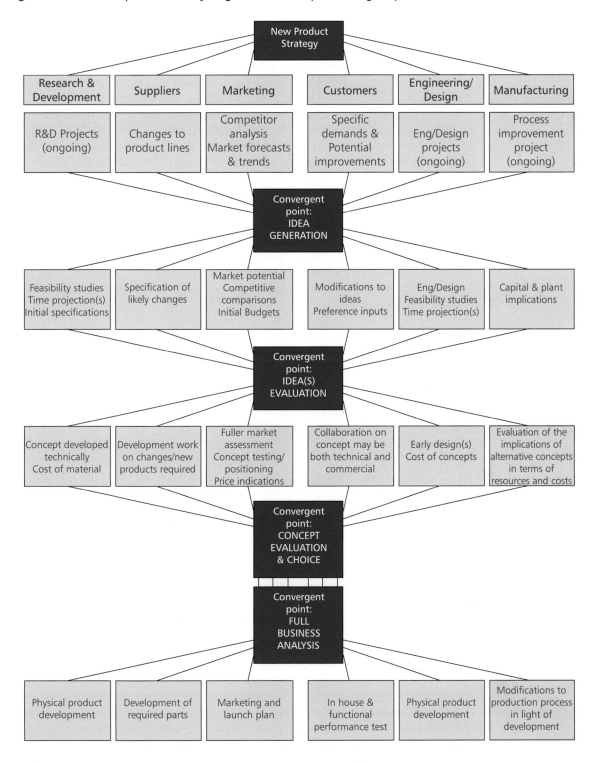

Source: Baker, M. J. and Hart, S. J. (1999), *Product Strategy and Management*, Pearson Education.

ORGANISING FOR NEW PRODUCT DEVELOPMENT

In the 1981 Booz Allen survey this issue was given considerable attention and revealed the existence of two broad approaches described as free standing and functional. As can be seen from Figure 12.8, free standing approaches, which consist of an independent team, can be sub-divided into three main types while teams based in a functional department are of four main types.

According to Rodocanachi, 'Successful companies tend to use more than one organisational concept, mixing and matching not only the approach but the types of skills and leadership elements of the team.' Based on this observation three basic organisational approaches are identified as illustrated in Figure 12.9.

These approaches are described as follows: The first is the **entrepreneurial approach**, typically used for developing new-to-the-world products. The structure requires an interdisciplinary venture team and a manager with the ability to integrate diverse functional skills. This is an autonomous new products group, usually reporting to a general manager. Success requires involvement of, and strong commitment from, top management. Typically, the process, the management structure, and the requirements for formal business planning are less rigid than other approaches. Usually, an incentive system promotes risk taking by rewarding handsomely for success.

NEW PRODUCT DEVELOPMENT

While many people associate new product development primarily with technological innovation, it is just as important in fashion retailing. In recent years, a once dominant Marks and Spencer has seen its market share eroded by competition from firms like Next. Over the period 1997-2003 Verdict Research reported an increase in Next's share of the womens-wear market from 4.1% to 6.7% while M&S recorded a fall from 16.7% to 13.5%. In an article in the *Sunday Times* (19/09/04), Richard Fletcher reports on an interview with Edward Whitefield, chairman of Management Horizons a retail strategy and operations firm;

"But Next's success over the past decade has been about more than just weak competition. Whitefield claims that the design-led culture that now dominates at Next has been the key.

"There is great commitment to design and the development of new products," he said. "There has been a huge investment in product design and fabrics."

Whitefield also cites the close relationship between Next and its manufacturers. "They are almost vertically integrated. ...The company's buyers are more like product or brand managers than traditional buyers. There's no divide between the buying and retail sides of the business.""

In an interview with Simon Wolfson, Chief Executive of Next, Fletcher reports him as saying:

"It comes down to the product. That is what customer's come for. You have got to deliver great products at great prices.If you have got the right product at the right time, customers will come. Ultimately it is the product that makes a brand. Not the brand that makes the product."

Perhaps the most important lesson is that in rapidly changing and dynamic markets, like those for fashion goods, the closest co-operation between design, manufacturing and marketing is critical to successful new product development.

Figure 12.8 New product development structures

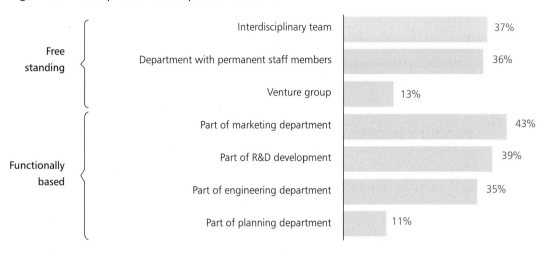

Source: Booz Allen Hamilton, in Rodocanachi, P. (1983), 'The Successful Management of New Products in the 1980's'.

Figure 12.9 New product organisation

Approach	Skill mix	Leadership
■ Entrepreneurial	■ Interdisciplinary venture team	■ Integrative manager
■ Collegial	■ New Product specialists	
	■ Marketing R&D	■ Functional manager
■ Managerial	■ Specific functions	

Source: Rodocanachi, P. (1983), 'The Successful Management of New Products in the 1980's'.

The second is the **collegial approach,** typically used to enter new businesses or add substantially different products to existing lines. This approach requires strong senior-management support and participation in decision making, a commitment to risk taking, and a formal new products process to guide the effort and ensure discipline. It also requires a clear commitment to provide whatever is necessary for success and for expediting decisions. The third is the **managerial approach.** This is the standard process used for existing business management. It involves strong planning and heavy emphasis on functional leadership to drive new products in manufacturing, distribution, marketing, or the like. It tends to be a rigid new products process involving many levels of management, quick promotion of successful new product managers, limited risk incentives, and rigorous application of financial criteria. The more successful companies match all of the elements just discussed to specific new products opportunities. The organisational approach and extent of top-management support vary, based on the specific needs of each new products opportunity. As the newness of the product increases, the entrepreneurial, integrative focus of the team increases, along with the involvement and support of top management.

Twenty years on, all three approaches are still in evidence with the multidisciplinary project team being the most popular, occurring in around 80% of companies.

PRODUCT PORTFOLIO ANALYSIS

Thus far the discussion has tended to look at products, and especially new products, as if every firm produced only a single product. In reality most firms have a range or portfolio of products each of which may be at a different stage in its life-cycle. It is recognition of this which led the Boston Consulting Group to propose a diagnostic procedure for analysing the comparative and collective performance of different products in a firm's range which has since become famous as the 'Boston Box'. While several variants of the Boston Box have been proposed they all rest on two fundamental propositions, namely that the competitive value of market share depends on the structure of competition and the stage of the product life cycle' (see G. S. Day (1977), 'Diagnosing the Product Portfolio').

The importance of taking into account the stage which a product (or industry) has reached in its life-cycle is fundamental to the whole concept and practice of marketing. As we saw in Chapter 1 when reviewing the evolution of the marketing concept, survival depends upon understanding and satisfying the needs of customers, and realisation and acceptance of the fact that over time these needs will change, often due to the action of marketers; hence, the product life-cycle. If, then, we accept the inevitability of the PLC it follows that even where we are concerned with a basic product such as steel with a life span of decades we would be unwise to assume that any particular formulation or, more important, method of manufacture is immune to competition and replacement. To guard against this possibility product differentiation has become a key competitive strategy and new product development an essential activity, so that even the overtly single product firm should have a range of products at different stages of development.

The emphasis upon market share as a surrogate for profitability has been extensively documented since the publication of the **PIMS** (**Profit Impact of Market Strategy**) analysis by the **Marketing Science Institute** based on a technique developed by General Electric. However, as Day points out, in many situations market share is a poor proxy as its use rests on the assumption that all competitors 'have the same overhead structures and experience curves, with their position on the experience curve corresponding to their market share position'. Thus market share indicates relative profitability between firms in direct competition (Ford vs General Motors) but neglects factors which affect absolute profit performance when comparing dissimilar products.

Day cites a number of other pitfalls in using portfolio analysis and the issue is discussed in considerable detail in Alan Morrison and Robin Wensley (1991), 'Boxing up or Boxed in? A Short History of the Boston Consulting Group Share/ Growth Matrix', which the student should consult for details. However, the purpose here is to introduce a conceptual approach which has secured extensive support among practicing managers for at least the three reasons cited by Day:

They [managers] are first attracted by the intuitively appealing concept that long-run corporate performance is more than the sum of the contributions of individual profit centres or product strategies. Secondly, a product portfolio analysis suggests specific marketing strategies to achieve a balanced mix of products that will produce the maximum long-run effects from scarce cash and managerial resources. Lastly the concept employs a simple matrix representation which is easy to communicate and comprehend.

A typical example of this matrix is reproduced as Figure 12.10 using market share and market growth (a proxy for stage in the PLC) as the relevant parameters. In this matrix no values are attached to market share or growth rate, although these will usually be included when assessing the comparative performance of one's own products against those of the market leader. Hence, the purpose is solely to distinguish the four basic categories of product, the desired movement of businesses over time, and the likely movement of cash between them.

Wildcat businesses (also known as problem children) represent products at the beginning of their life-cycle where hopes run high and expectations of rapid

Figure 12.10 The product portfolio

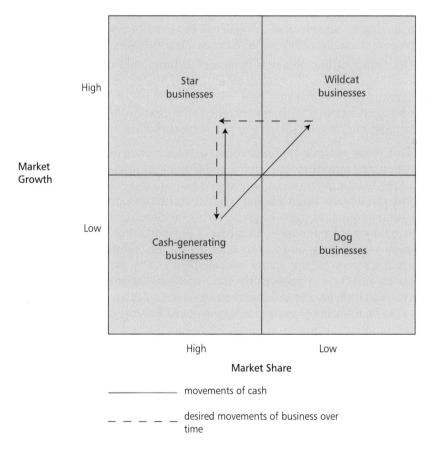

Source: The Conference Board (1974).

growth and profitability encourage the firm to invest heavily in its new product despite uncertainty as to its eventual success. Clearly, the hope is that by so doing the product or business will get on to the rapid growth curve when sales expand exponentially, and costs and overheads decline rapidly as a result of economies of scale and growing experience. At this stage of market development competition is fierce as firms jockey for position to become 'stars', and seek to secure cost and price advantages which will enable them to secure the dominant share of the new market.

To achieve this all the cash generated has to be ploughed back into the business, together with the profits from the products at the mature stage of their life-cycle represented as cash cows. Finally, while the transition from cash cow to dog is not a desired move, the PLC concept tells us that this is inevitable as the mature phase degenerates into decay and senility with declining growth and profitability.

The construction of product portfolios has significant implications for the firm's corporate planning, namely:

1 Careful and continuous watch must be kept on competitors in the star businesses, lest any of them gains leadership in market share.

2 For the corporation as a whole, the overriding objective should be to maximise the net present value of the portfolio of businesses over the planning period, subject to the constraints of financial or other corporate policies.

3 It is vital to achieve a sound balance in terms of financial and managerial resources among cash cow, wild cat and star businesses.

4 The family of businesses is dynamic. In time, wild cats will become stars – or dogs. Stars will become cows – or, if inadequately nourished – dogs. Eventually, new stars or new wild cats will be needed; hence corporate management must be ever-concerned with new products, new markets and acquisitions. It should strive to postpone corporate maturity indefinitely.

While it is not possible to pursue these issues in greater detail in an introductory text, it should be clear that Product Policy, Planning and Development is at the very heart of the marketing process. Indeed, we can safely say that the best marketing advice we can offer is 'Build a better product at the same price as your competitor or the same product at a lower price.' While achievement of this ideal will not eliminate the need for the other elements of the marketing mix – distribution and promotion – it will go a long way to ensuring success. Similarly, space limitations preclude discussion of the actual management of the product as it progresses through its life-cycle – particularly the variations in emphasis upon the mix elements both individually and together. However, an extended treatment of these issues is to be found in *Marketing Management and Strategy* (Baker, 2006).

Managing the decline phase

Given that most new products are substitutes for existing products – hence the popularity of the 'what business are we in' approach to long-term strategic planning – one should not be surprised if cumulative sales curves are reasonably symmetrical. In other words all the factors which may delay or accelerate a new product's acceptance are just as likely to work for or against it when a substitute for it is subsequently introduced to the market. However, whether or not one anticipates that the decline phase of the life-cycle will be gradual or sudden, one must have a clear policy for dealing with the ailing product.

Until recently comparatively little interest has been shown in the decline phase. 1984 there were only about five articles which dealt with the subject in any depth, and most of those were rather dated and failed to address adequately the practical problems of implementation. However, in the early 1980s George Avlonitis published a number of articles on the topic dealing with both the theoretical considerations and the practicalities, using extensive research into the UK engineering industry as an empirical foundation and launching a renewed interest in the topic.

While most writers on product elimination see it as a straight choice between phasing it out slowly – variously referred to as milking, harvesting, run-out and product petrification – and immediate withdrawal. Avlonitis (1983) identifies two further alternatives:

1 Drop from the standard range and reintroduce as a 'special'.

2 Sell out to another manufacturer ('Divert').

Avlonitis believes that the ability to reintroduce a product as a special is probably unique to the industrial market, but otherwise the strategies would seem to be equally appropriate to both consumer and industrial products. That said, such evidence as there is points to a tendency for industrial goods to be phased out gradually while consumer goods are more prone to immediate withdrawal.

Of course much will depend on whether the seller's production equipment is specific or non-specific, and the extent to which it has been depreciated. Where the production equipment can be put to other uses, or is near the end of its useful life an immediate drop decision is much more likely than a slow phase-out, and vice versa. Further, in the case of durable goods the seller will have to give careful attention to service and maintenance obligations and the provision of spare parts and components.

Once it has been decided to phase a product out then the guiding principle must be to extract the maximum benefit at the minimum cost. Luck provides an excellent set of strategic steps for accomplishing this:

1 Simplify the product line to the best selling items and, if workable, those that yield the higher gross profit margins.

2 Dress up the product with relatively inexpensive styling and feature changes that create a fresh impression.

3 Bring all marketing efforts into a narrower focus by determining which portions of the market are the heavier and more loyal users, or are best served by the existing product. Make limited resources go further in concentrated markets, including selectivity in advertising media and sharper tailoring of appeals.

4 Concentrate also on market areas and on distributors that have the best potentials. If the specific types of buyers being promoted consider the old brand as speciality in shopping behaviour, exclusive distribution agreements may obtain dealer support.

5 Offer special bonuses or other rewards for pushing of the product by distributors and their sales personnel.

6 Limit the always costly personal sales calls to only the best outlets or buyers. Substitute more telephone or mail ordering for personal calls.

7 Utilise more economical wholesale channels by shifting to agents that are shared with other products.

8 Trade down the product to lower price buyers through price reductions made possible by austerity actions.

Product elimination has been a topic of particular interest for Professor Susan Hart of Strathclyde University and three chapters on the subject are to be found in *Product Strategy and Management*.

Summary

In this chapter we have argued that the product (or service) is the raison d'etre of marketing as it is this that provides the basis for exchange between seller and buyer. We also expressed the view that the attention given to the actual product has declined in recent years due to the difficulty of maintaining a sustainable **competitive advantage** through the development of objective features and attributes. In the absence of patent or copyright protection competitors are likely to benchmark such differences and rapidly imitate them. As a result more attention has been given to adding value to the physical product through promotional efforts to build brand equity and/or the bundling of services, building of relationships etc. While all these actions are necessary to maintain competitiveness, it must be remembered that they are not a substitute for physical product development. Only if two products are seen to be near perfect substitutes for one another – Kenco and Nescafé instant coffee – will the prospective buyer seek other cues to differentiate between them. Given that objective differences are easier to identify and evaluate sellers must strive continuously to create them.

In doing so, however, we stressed the point made in Chapter 9 on individual buyer behaviour that differences exist in the buyers perception . In other words a difference must be meaningful to the intending buyer if it is to add value, so just adding more and more features will not necessarily make a product more attractive. In fact, because it adds cost, it may well make it less attractive. To avoid this a firm needs a clear product policy based on a clear understanding of the need served. It also needs to understand the implications of the product life cycle which reflects the fact that as a result of innovation and change new ways of doing things constantly replace the old. Of course, not all new ideas succeed but, if they are seen to offer additional benefits then, gradually, they will lead to the displacement of the object for which they are a substitute. While it is difficult to predict the length of the stages of a PLC, the concept is a continuing reminder of the inevitability of change and of the importance of trying to exert some control over the process.

For these reasons **new product development** is a critical element of marketing strategy with a substantial proportion of revenues being derived from new additions to the product portfolio.

The development of new products is more likely to be successful when the firm follows a structured approach to the activity which follows the sequence: Idea Generation; Concept Testing; Business Analysis: Product Development; Product Testing and Commercialisation. Each of these phases was discussed in some detail and attention drawn to the importance of managing the process effectively, especially in its earlier stages when costs are low.

The importance of product portfolio analysis was illustrated by reference to matrix analysis of the kind popularised by the Boston Consulting Group and we concluded by stressing the importance of managing the final or decline phase of the product's life.

Review questions and problems

1 Why is the firm's product policy of such central importance to its continued growth and development? Describe a declining firm or industry, and suggest how it might improve its fortunes by adopting a macro view of is markets.

2 Describe how the product life-cycle concept might be of operational use to the marketer.

3 Suggest a system for classifying 'new' products. What are the parameters on which your classification rests, and how were they selected?

4 What advantages do you perceive in being
(a) a leader, (b) a follower,
in terms of product innovations?

5 Design a rating table for evaluating new product ideas, specifying the industry in which the table is to be used.

6 How would you product test:
(a) An instant soup mix?
(b) A new plastic resin?
(c) A new model car?

7 Summarise the advantages/disadvantages of test marketing.

8 Is the fact that intuition and judgement are important factors in the development of new products a valid argument against the use of formal sequential procedures in this area?

9 Distinguish between product and market testing. Explain the contributions and limitations of each in both the consumer and the industrial goods fields.

10 Is it possible to reconcile grocery manufacturing companies' continuous introduction of new products with a supermarket policy of variety reduction?

11 Define 'product policy'. What is the role in product strategy of the product lifecycle? Under what circumstances would it be advisable to try to arrest a declining sales curve? Discuss the alternatives to attempting to arrest such decline.

12 Explain the significance and implications of the timing of a new product launch.

13 What scope is there, in your view, for the successful introduction of strict management control and evaluation procedures in the area of product planning and new product development?

14 Outline the major 'steps' in the new product evolutionary cycle, and assess the extent to which these are amenable to systematic organisation, management and control.

15 Comment on the value of a systematic approach to new product development. Can such development be planned?

16 Discuss the benefits that accrue to a company in setting up a system of regular, detailed product marketing plans.

17 Examine the limitations of test marketing exercises as a guide to full-scale product launch.

18 The rate at which new products are introduced into the marketplace has increased greatly in the last decade. This has been attributed to: (a) evidence of economic progress, OR (b) an increase in planned obsolescence. Develop an argument supporting ONE of these stands.

19 New product development may be just as important for non profit organisations as it is for business organisations. Discuss.

20 How can diffusion theory be used to improve the chances of a successful new product launch

21 Identify and evaluate the strategies a company could adopt to extend the life cycle of a product.

22 Critically appraise the usefulness of the product life-cycle concept to marketing management.

23 How is the marketing mix likely to differ between the maturity and the decline stages of the product life cycle?

24 Explain how marketers may use the Boston Box matrix in planning for marketing.

25 Assess the strengths and weaknesses of the Booz Allen Hamilton model of the new product development process. In the light of your assessment, how far do you consider that the wide acceptance and citation of this model are justified?

26 When seeking to develop and launch an innovative, high technology product on to the market, what strategic and tactical considerations should a company take into consideration?

27 Identify the stages of the New Product Development Process. Explain why it is important to have managerial support throughout the process.

28 To what extent can the risk of failure in new product development be reduced by a sound evaluation and testing process?

Key terms

augmentation
augmented product
Boston Box
BRIC countries
business analysis
collegial approach
commercialisation
competitive advantage
core benefit
customer-supplier context
development
diffuse
discounted cash flow (DCF)
entrepreneurial approach
excitement

exploration
exponential function
factor rating table
managerial approach
Marketing Science Institute (MSI)
multiple convergent processing (MCP)
new product development (NPD)
objective factors
pilot marketing
portable media players
product category
product life cycle

product policy
product portfolio
product portfolio analysis
product testing
profit impact of market strategy (PIMS)
screening
subjective factors
systems selling
test marketing
testing
testing of mix variables
time to market
Trade Descriptions Act

Supplementary reading list

Baker, M. J. (1975) *Marketing New Industrial Products*, (London: Macmillan).
Baker, M. J. (1983) *Market Development* (Harmondsworth: Penguin).
Baker, M. J. and Hart, S.J. (1999) *Product Strategy and Management*, (London: Prentice Hall)
   A revised, Second Edition of this book is due to be published by Pearson in 2006
Baker, M. J. (ed.) (2003), *The Marketing Book*, 5th Edn, (Oxford: Butterworth-Heinemann).

PACKAGING

13

Learning Goals *After reading this chapter you should be able to:*

- Describe the basic functions of packaging desired by consumers and distributors and required by law.

- Explain the use of packaging as a variable in the marketing mix.

- Review current environmental concerns and trends in packaging development.

INTRODUCTION

Surprisingly few introductory marketing texts devote much attention to the role of packaging as an element in the marketing mix. When one considers that total UK packaging industry sales amounted to over £10.9billion in 2002 it is clear that packaging costs are a major marketing expenditure and deserve fuller treatment. One reason for this may be that there is no cohesive packaging industry. There are many industries supplying packaging materials including pulp, paper and board makers; tinplate and aluminium; chemicals, polymers, pigments, colourants, adhesives etc. There are also many 'converters' that transform the materials into actual packages. These include:

- Wooden packaging – crates, pallets etc
- Paper and cardboard
- Films and foils – plastic, aluminium etc.
- Glass
- Plastic
- Steel and aluminium drums
- Metal cans and boxes
- Cushioning and shock reducing materials – foam, bubble wrap etc.

The present lack of attention is partially attributable to the tendency to classify packaging as a production cost, so that it is seldom isolated in the way that expenditures on advertising and promotion are. In part it is also attributable to the practical function which the pack performs, which tends to shield it from public scrutiny of the type directed at promotional expenditures whose practical virtues are less easily discernible. However, concerns for environmental pollution and waste in packaging have resulted in greater consumer interest in packaging in the last decade or so.

In reality packaging costs often exceed all other marketing costs and, in some instances, constitute the major element of total cost, for example cosmetics. These facts were emphasised by a cost analysis of the items in a household food basket in which it was found that while advertising only accounted for 2 per cent of the total cost, packaging materials were responsible for 22 per cent, or eleven times as much. In the same vein the chairman of Teacher's, the whisky producers, was quoted some years ago as stating 'In spite of stringent control in purchasing materials at the lowest possible cost consistent with quality, the value of the packaging material in a standard case now exceeds that of the whisky.' The same is true today.

Although more recent data are hard to come by, it is clear that the trend for packaging to comprise an increasing proportion of the total cost of convenience goods continues. Indeed it has been observed that 'We may soon reach the situation where the plastic and cardboard wrapper around four tomatoes or half a dozen nails costs more than the goods involved.' In absolute terms it is quite clear that packaging costs have increased significantly in recent years, as can be seen from Table 13.1.

Nowadays packaging is an extrinsic product attribute which is seen to have as much influence on the buyer's perceptions and behaviour as other attributes such as price, brand name and level of advertising. In an article 'Packaging for consumers', Jillian Prebble of Pira International highlighted why the role of packaging in purchasing decisions must not be underestimated. For some luxury goods the packaging may be seen as an intrinsic element of the product itself but, for the more prosaic everyday product on the supermarket shelves it can have both positive and negative impact on the customers behaviour. Prebble reports research by John West, the canned fish specialist, that revealed that 60% of men and 40% of women choose a product because of its attractive colouring and design, and that colour associations with certain products accounted for 62%

Table 13.1 UK Packaging Market 1998-2002 (£ billion)					
	1998	*1999*	*2000*	*2001*	*2002*
Paper & board	4,420	4,368	4,761	5,060	5,142
Plastic	3,085	3,225	3,385	3,510	3,609
Metals	1,336	1,352	1,270	1,320	1,094
Glass	720	832	635	660	656
Wood/Other	720	624	529	550	438
Total	10,251	10,401	10,580	11,100	10,939

Source: Calculated by the author from industry estimates.

of consumers unconscious thought processes when shopping. But the downside is that packaging is frequently the source of customer dissatisfaction. A survey by *Health Which?* in May 2000 found that 93% of the respondents reported difficulties with packaging such as safety, opening, closing and ease of use. A third reported injuries caused by packaging, and 45% said they actively avoided certain types of food and drink because of its packaging. So, given that a major supermarket may have as many as 40,000 products on its shelves, and that the customer spends only 0.4 of a second on average looking at the shelves, it is clear that attention to packaging is of critical importance to success.

Prebble cites a number of attributes that are important to the consumer in terms of product packaging, namely:

- *Portability*
- *Product protection* (before and after opening)
- *Easy opening/reclosure*
- *Product visibility*
- *Value for money*
- *Legibility*
- *Use by dating*
- *Packages that are easy to store*
- *Environmentally acceptable and waste reducing*

As with other features and attributes, the relative importance of these factors vary from consumer to consumer and over time, offering the seller many opportunities to use packaging as a competitive element in the marketing mix.

In this chapter we look first at basic packaging functions and the requirements which packaging must satisfy – distributor, consumer and legal. We then review packaging as a discrete variable in the marketing mix, and conclude with a discussion of future trends.

PACKAGING FUNCTIONS

Figure 13.1 summarises both the fundamental role of packaging – to contain, protect and identify – together with the marketing opportunities these offer for adding value and differentiating the product.

Trott (2005) uses the example of soft drinks to demonstrate the versatility of packaging materials and show how these may be used to differentiate the products and meet the needs of end-use markets. Six kinds of packaging are widely used – Glass, PET (Polyethylene terephtalate) PVC (Poly Vinyl Chloride), Aluminium, Steel/tinplate, and coated paper board e.g. Tetra Paks. The first three are resealable, the latter three are not, so all the contents must be consumed once the pack is opened. Glass and PET can be both clear and coloured. Glass communicates quality but is breakable and so less suitable for containers to be used by children. On the other hand it is widely used for water that is to be served at the table, and is often a major feature differentiating one brand from another. PET is rigid, like glass, providing a good base for graphics, and can be used for carbonated beverages. PVC is less rigid and opaque, but it can be moulded with a a handle and is widely used for milk. Cans, both aluminium and steel, are widely used for carbonated soft drinks, while TetraPak cartons are less expensive and widely used for non-carbonated fluids like fruit juices, milk etc. Corner and Paine (2002) summarise the principal functions of packaging as:

- *Containment*
- *Protection, Preservation*
- *Communication and selling*
- *Machineablility i.e. for filling*
- *Convenience and use*
- *Environmental responsibility*

Hisrich and Peters devote several pages of their book *Marketing Decisions for New and Mature Products* 2nd edn. (1991) to packaging decisions and organise the

Figure 13.1 Packaging fundamentals

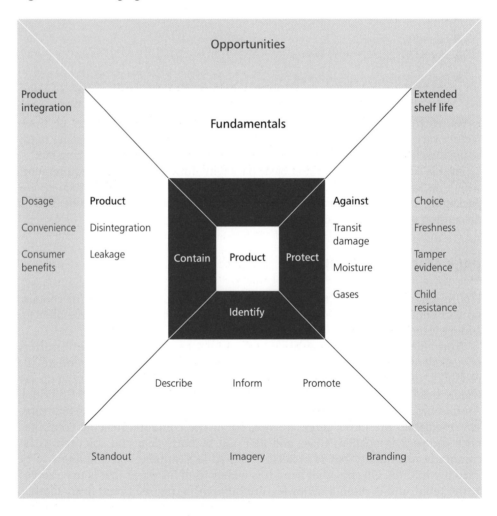

Source: PIRA International Ltd, in Stewart, B. (2004), *Packaging Design Strategies*, 2nd. edn, (Leatherhead: Pira International Ltd.).

factors to be considered under four main headings:

1 *Marketing*
2 *Product Protection*
3 *Economic Factors*
4 *Environmental Factors*

As with any classification, the actual listing tends to follow the sequence in which the author thinks it most logical to address the issues involved. Corner and Paine are primarily concerned with the physical properties of packaging materials and how they may be used, so marketing comes third in their list. Hisrich and Peters are primarily interested in product development and marketing, so marketing is placed first; but both sets of authors put environmental factors last. In reality, and as argued in Chapter 4, environmental factors control the business environment and, logically, should come first. As we shall see, numerous legal requirements prescribe and proscribe packaging decisions. It would seem sensible to outline the more important of these before addressing the other categories.

ENVIRONMENTAL REQUIREMENTS

The environmental factors influencing the packaging decision are largely set out in legislation. As this can vary considerably on a country-by-country basis it is important to check out what are the specific requirements of every national market in which one intends to sell. The principal issues to take into account are composition of the product and its labelling, and the establishment of legal rights over a product's design and packaging. In addition, it is also important to take note of green issues many of which are leading to new legislation in the more affluent economies.

Green issues

Packaging has been the subject of much criticism as a source of waste and environmental pollution. In reality the problem appears to be much greater than it is for the simple reason that we are all familiar with discarding used packaging and its unsightly appearance as litter all around us. The reality is quite different. A study by Incpen (The Industry Council for Packaging and the Environment) in 1999 estimated that used packaging amounted to 21% by weight of the average content of a dustbin. If extrapolated to all household waste this would only amount to between one and two percent of all waste. Of course this is not to say that this is not a significant amount in tonnage terms, nor that further efforts should not be made to reduce the amount if we can. However, given that nearly 80% of household waste finishes up as landfill there are clear opportunities for more recycling and re-use of packaging material.

New Zealand is a country at the forefront of the 'green' movement and has made a major effort to reduce waste and encourage recycling. A Packaging Council was set up in 1992 to involve all the parties concerned with the production and consumption of packaging with a view to taking a holistic approach to packaging waste. Today, more than 60 per cent of New Zealanders have access to recycling facilities for packaging waste and, overall, 51% of all packaging materials are collected for recycling. Further, based on its Code of Practice, the adoption of light weight materials and recycling have reduced packaging waste volumes by more than 40% over the past 12 years.

One also needs to consider that packaging reduces waste by protecting the contents and, overall, the benefits must exceed the costs or organisations would not spend money on it. The New Zealand Packaging Council cites a study that estimated that the loss of foodstuffs between grower and consumer is about 2 per cent in the developed world but that this rises to 33 percent in the developing world. The difference is largely due to packaging. Similarly, packaging enables more efficient distribution and so saves in the costs of material handling and transportation. For example, it requires only one lorry to deliver 1 million Tetrapacks for packaging milk whereas it would require many loads for the same number of glass bottles which, if recycled would have to be taken back to the bottler every time they were used. None of this is to argue against environmentally friendly packaging, merely to put it into perspective.

It is as much in the interest of the producer to save on packaging costs as it is in the customers. We should not be misled by the visibility of waste packaging to assume this is the consequence of unthinking and uncaring capitalists – their self-interest strongly reflects that of the consumer. And, if it didn't, there is legislation to make sure producers constantly seek to improve both recovery and recycling of packaging materials. Further, this legislation requires all the participants in the supply chain - converter, manufacturer, packer/filler, seller and importer - to contribute.

The UK Government publishes a 'Green Guide for Buyers' on its Sustainable Development website, and requires that environmental considerations are integrated into all public sector procurement decisions. Environmentally preferable products are defined as ones which are less harmful to human health and the environment when compared with competing products which serve the same purpose. Among other things they:

- Are fit for purpose and provide value for money;
- Are energy and resource efficient;
- Use the minimum amount of virgin materials;
- Make maximum use of post-consumer materials;
- Are non- (or less) polluting;
- Are durable, easily upgraded and repairable;
- Are reuseable, and markets and the infrastructure exist for recycling the product at the end of its life;
- Are supported by additional information to demonstrate their environmental preferability.

Dart (1999) sees an opportunity to take advantage of the demand for more environmentally friendly packaging and makes the following suggestions:

- Less bulk; simply using less material
- Removal of secondary packaging: why sell toothpaste in two containers when it is perfectly OK sold in one?

- Concentration: concentrated detergents now use less than half the the packaging material compared to before.
- Reusable: many products are now sold in a 'first time' box-tin-jar, which can then be replenished via a 'refill' pack.
- Secondary usage (especially important in developing markets): design the packaging for its original purpose and for a secondary purpose (for example a storage jar).
- Recyclable: design the material and its construction so that it can be collected back and either reused directly or reprocessed.
- Bulk or home delivery: the ultimate non-use of packaging, but not yet commonplace.

PACKAGE DESIGN

The rights to package designs are another legal aspect of packaging. In today's market where products are sold by the shape of the packaging as much as anything else, design registrations can be very valuable, especially in the areas of wine, spirits, toiletries and cosmetics packaging. Other means of securing the legal rights over a product package include the following:

- *Patent Rights* – for a new invention or application.
- *Copyright* – provided the existence and ownership can be proved this is a powerful weapon against imitators.
- *Trademarks* – may assist in distinguishing packaging from that of competitors. Directories are available in most technical libraries

To secure ownership of these legal rights you must:

1 *Identify the designer.* You must know who made the design, are they an employee or contracted labour? One person or several?
2 *Ensure that the rights have been assigned to you.* There should be a standard clause in contracts of employment concerning the ownership of copyrights. Formal assignment documents for employees and contracted workers may be advisable.
3 *Keep the original drawings.* A file should be kept with the history of the development of the packaging and signed, dated original drawings.

PROTECTION

While the basic function of any pack is to protect its contents in transit, in storage and in use, this criterion will play a major role in determining the shape, size and materials used, such practical aspects have to take full account of the marketing considerations. In most cases there will be little or no conflict between the physical characteristics considered desirable by manufacturers and distributors, and the promotional and design elements demanded by consumers.

However, it will be useful to consider the requirements of these two groups separately to emphasise the varying nature of their needs.

Distributor requirements

Protection is usually against **mechanical damage** caused by transport, handling and warehousing and calls for a knowledge of the characteristics of the product and the hazards it may encounter before it can be safely consumed. In terms of characteristics, key considerations are whether it is liquid or solid; how perishable is it; does it constitute a risk or hazard; and how complex and or durable/fragile is it?

The major sources of damage are crushing, impact and vibration. The incidence and nature of these risks can be calculated enabling the materials handling expert to prescribe the most suitable material and its characteristics. For example, the weight of a package is a major determinant of whether it will be manhandled or moved using equipment, and the likelihood of it being dropped from given heights. Once this is known suitable packaging can be designed.

The other major sources of hazard are **climatic** and include temperature, humidity and precipitation all of which may damage the container and/or its contents, eg. Corrosion of metal, water absorption by powders etc

As noted , the prime function of any pack is to protect the contents. From this it follows that pack design will depend very largely on the nature of the contents in terms of their value, physical composition and durability. In addition one must also take into account the length of the distribution channel, the amount of handling which the container will receive, and variations in climatic conditions which may he encountered between the point of manufacture and sale.

Most small items are bulk-packed in some type of outer container capable of withstanding the anticipated degree of rough handling. However, such containers can only reduce the shock of mishandling, so that the individual packs must also be capable of resisting such punishment. An example of the degree of protection necessary is provided by the findings of the Printing, Packaging and Allied Trades Research Association that containers which one man is just capable of handling are likely to be dropped from a height of three feet somewhere in transit. This distance corresponds to waist height, or the level of a lorry tailboard, and requires that containers should be able to withstand an equivalent shock. It was also found that heavier packages tended to receive more careful handing as two men were needed to lift them or else mechanical handling methods were used, for example fork-lift trucks. Such methods are widely used now, and it is in the packer's interest to determine the capacity of such equipment and take it into account in establishing bulk pack size and weight. Modifications to containers to satisfy mechanical handling requirements may well increase their intrinsic cost, but such costs are invariably more than recouped through a reduction in the amount of handling required.

Breakage in transit due to rough handling is only one aspect of protection, and equal attention must be given to spoilage from other causes. Foremost among these are moisture, fungus, insects and exposure to sunlight.

Transportation and storage costs are usually computed on the basis of weight and/or volume, and it is clearly in the manufacturer's interest to use packages which make maximum use of a given space. At the retail level the space/volume factor takes on added importance, as it directly affects the number of different items which can be put on display. Sales per square foot ,or per linear foot of shelf, are frequently used measures of retail productivity ,and it is clear that retailers will avoid packs which occupy a disproportionate amount of space in relation to their value. However, the retailer, like the manufacturer, recognises that purely physical properties must be modified in the light of consumer preferences, and so may be prepared to subordinate these in favour of packs with greater promotional appeal.

In order to offset the additional costs that may be incurred retailers have been innovative in adopting new technologies that increase efficiency.

One such process adopted in the 1970s was the **European Article Numbering system (EAN)**, used in food retailing (see *www.gs1.org*). This system started in Britain in 1977, and originated in the USA in the early 1970s under the name of the **Universal Product Code system (UPC)**. This is a system of incorporating a 13-digit item identification number, both in decimal characters and bar code form, into the product packaging. See Figure 13.2 for an example of an EAN code for a book. This code, marked on the packaging, is read by an optical scanner at the supermarket checkout desk, which retrieves the price and product description and displays this to the shopper whilst printing out this information onto the receipt.

The system has benefits in inventory control, checkout productivity and it eliminates the need for marking the price on every item in the shop. Prices are displayed near the item on the shelf. The retailer can analyse the performance of new items, advertising and the comparative performance of similar items in different supermarkets. A list of benefits suggested by the IBM Corporation is given below. Although dated 1975, all these benefits have materialised.

Front-end benefits
Improved throughput
Checker productivity
Reduced misrings
Tender reconciliation
Cash reporting
Store funds control
Check authorisation
Merchandising benefits
Point of sale movement data
Advertising analysis
Vendor analysis
New item performance analysis
Location analysis (for within and between stores)
Price management

Store operation benefits
Eliminates price marking and re-marking
Permits routine ordering
Reduces shrinkage

Figure 13.2 Example of an EAN code from a book

ISBN 0-946433-03-8

9 780946 433032

Inventory management benefits
Shelf space allocations marking
Reduced out-of-stock
Reduced backroom inventory
Warehouse and Transportation workload balancing

One weakness of the **bar code** is that it requires a 'line of sight' in order for it to be scanned. To overcome this many manufacturers and distributors have adopted **radio frequency identification (RFID)** as a means of tracking products through the supply chain. RFID uses passive electronic chips that respond to interrogation at a pre-set radio frequency which can be both read and amended as the product moves through the channels of distribution. To date, the cost of the chips make it uneconomic for low cost items so that its major use in food retailing is in tracking bulk packaging at the case level. This has major benefits for inventory control, especially for perishable goods that need to be replenished regularly at the store level from centralised distribution centres. Although at an early stage of development, this technology is set to increase in sophistication and reduce in cost, making it available for much wider use. (But see the vignette later in this chapter that raises concerns about the extension of this technology to the tagging of individual products).

CONSUMER REQUIREMENTS

Reference has already been made to the fact that the packaging of consumer goods was originally a retailing function but that competitive pressures, and the growth of branding, resulted in the manufacturer assuming responsibility for it. Through the adoption of a distinctive pack and brand name, the manufacturer is able to differentiate the product at the point of sale and to develop advertising and promotional strategies designed to create consumer preference for their output. Further, by packaging the product himself the manufacturer is able to exercise much greater control over the condition in which the ultimate consumer will receive it, and so avoid dissatisfaction arising from poor storage and packing at the retail level.

Essentially, consumers want products, and have little direct interest in their packaging per se. In many instances, however, the satisfaction to be derived from a product is dependent upon its packaging, and consumers are receptive to both technical and aesthetic improvements in pack design. Many competing products are incapable of differentiation on the basis of objective criteria, and in these instances packaging and promotion often constitute the sole distinguishing features upon which the product's success or failure depends.

A clear example of this is the United Kingdom sardine market. Some years ago a number of fish packers in Britain offered a variety of brands of sardines in competition with Scandinavian and Portuguese imports. Although sardines tend to be associated with the latter countries, the domestic product was competitively priced and secured a strong following among those who could perceive no difference in product quality – real or imagined. As a group, however, sardine eaters became increasingly frustrated by the difficulties associated with opening the conventional pack, as the tag frequently broke when the key was turned, facing them with the almost impossible task of opening the tin with an ordinary tin-opener. In part the trouble was due to the fact that few people used the key correctly, but it was also due to the lock-seamed construction of the can which required that the tag be sufficiently strong to tear open a double thickness of material at the seam. The Scandinavians overcame this problem by adopting aluminium lids, while the Portuguese soldered the lid to the body, leaving a line of weakness which opened easily. Neither course was open to the British packers – aluminium was much more expensive than in Scandinavia, and high labour costs precluded following the Portuguese practice. Consumers responded enthusiastically to the new pack and the domestic share of market sagged dismally owing to the inability of the United Kingdom packers to duplicate the improved container at a competitive price. Ease of opening is clearly a significant consumer 'plus' and many other canned products like soup and baked beans now have pull-tops eliminating the need for a tin opener.

Conventional demand curves indicate that as price falls the volume demanded will increase. In theory this relationship is continuous and we can establish the volume which will be demanded at any given price. In practice prices are discrete and should properly be represented by a 'stepped' demand curve. However, theory suggests that if the manufacturer can offer their product at a lower price they will be able to increase demand, and this is frequently achieved by offering the consumer a variety of different sizes. In addition to catering for variations in household size and usage rates, a range of pack sizes enables the manufacturer to reach consumers with limited purchasing power. As the retired population expands, less perceptive marketers will increasingly come to appreciate that lifelong consumption patterns may well have to be modified as inflation reduces the purchasing power of fixed retirement incomes. It would be naive to expect manufacturers to offer small packs at a price proportionate to the 'standard' size in view of the high proportion of fixed costs incurred irrespective of unit size. None the less, the provision of non-standard pack sizes is not only good marketing, it is a socially desirable activity.

Many products are not consumed immediately the package is opened but are used over varying periods of time. To prevent spoilage, such products must be packed in resealable containers, the most familiar of which are the screw-top bottle and jar, and the lever-lid can. Screw-top jars have long been in use for the packaging of products containing sugar, such as jam, which are susceptible to mould when exposed to the atmosphere. Lever-lid cans are widely used for packaging hygroscopic materials such as dried milk, instant coffee, cocoa and health salts, but are losing ground to plastics for certain applications. Although ease of opening and re-closure are desirable, many parents want a pack to be stable and 'child-proof', to prevent accidents to young children, and will show a preference for packs with such attributes.

Visual appeal is also an important aspect of pack design, particularly in the case of products of a luxury or semi-luxury nature where the pack itself may add to the image of product quality which the manufacturer is seeking to create. Some critics have argued that elaborate and expensive packaging is used to disguise inferior products, or to permit the seller to inflate the true worth of the product. Neither claim will sustain much examination, for poor packaging is almost always a good indicator of a poor product, and no amount of packaging can disguise a poor product for long. Similarly, few consumers are prepared to pay more for a product solely on account of its packaging unless such packaging will add to their enjoyment of the product itself – Ferrero Rocher chocolates are a classic example, and it is irrelevant if the added satisfaction is purely subjective to the consumer and incapable of objective measurement.

Finally, consumers demand packages which satisfy their information needs. Certain information is required by law, for example statement of weight and composition of product, although frequently the latter is expressed in language incomprehensible to the average consumer. In addition to this basic information, consumers favour a clearly marked price (now largely a retailer responsibility since the abolition of Resale Price Maintenance), information on how the product should or may be used, and, preferably, some view of the contents themselves.

LEGAL REQUIREMENTS

In addition to providing a distinctive and appealing means of identifying and protecting, the pack must also provide the user with information concerning its contents. Some of this information may be required by law. The production and design of packaging is influenced by the ever-increasing amount of information which must appear on it by law. In the case of food the regulations are so extensive that **The Food Standards Agency** is unable to produce large numbers of copies and Crown copyright has been waived so that anyone can download the information from their website. The *Food Law Guide* contains 13 Parts covering the Food Safety Act 1990, the Labelling and Marking of Food, with 23 specific regulations governing particular food, and a number of other topics dealing with chemical safety, genetically modified foods, marketing standards and weights and measures and runs to over 100 pages. With regard to Labelling and Marking it states:

COMPETITION IN THE UK WINE MARKET

In an article in the *Sunday Times* (April 16 2005) John Frederick explained the reasons behind the comparative failure of French wines in the UK market in competition with those from Australia. In less than a decade Australian wines have moved from a position where they were outsold 7:1 by French wines to a position where they now outperform the French in both volume and value.

Major factors behind Australia's success is the consistency, quality and value of their product sold in clearly labelled bottles naming the variety of grapes on the front and helpful , practical information on the back. By contrast "The French doggedly persisted with an entrenched and hideously complex system of wine nomenclature that only experts could hope to understand."

It is interesting to note that now the Australians have established their brands in the market they are beginning to move away from the concept of multi-regional wines e.g. South East Australia where the grapes could be sourced from any of four States, to promoting single region wines – Hunter, Yarra, Clare valleys etc.. In doing so "… the Australians are now reinventing their wine industry and, significantly, they are increasingly adopting the idea that has been the traditional basis of the French wine industry: that of terroir. This presumes that particular patches of soil, certain microclimates, fields and vineyards are best suited to particular crops, wine varieties and the production of particular sorts of wine".

The principal provisions of the regulations which apply to Great Britain are that all food which is ready for delivery to the ultimate consumer or to a catering establishment, subject to certain exceptions, be marked or labelled with:

(a) the name of the food;

(b) a list of ingredients;

(c) the appropriate durability indication, that is to say;

(i) in the case of a food other than one specified in subparagraph (ii) of this paragraph, an indication of minimum durability (a "best before" date);

(ii) in the case of food which, from the microbiological point of view is highly perishable and in consequence likely after a short period to constitute an immediate danger to health, a "use by" date;

(d) any special storage conditions or conditions of use;

(e) the name or business name and an address or registered office of the manufacturer or packer, or of a seller established within the European Community; and in certain circumstances:

(f) particulars of the place of origin of the food, if failure to give such particulars might mislead and;

(g) instructions for use if it would be difficult to make appropriate use of the food in the absence of such instructions;

(NB - There are certain exemptions and additional requirements listed in the main regulations.)

There are less onerous rules for foods which are non-pre-packed or pre-packed for direct sale.

These Regulations also attach conditions to the use of claims for foods for particular nutritional uses, reduced or low energy value claims, protein claims, vitamin or mineral claims, cholesterol claims, other nutrient claims and claims dependent on other foods; they prohibit medicinal claims. They also lay down a prescribed format for the nutritional labelling of foodstuffs.

Britain's membership of the EU has had its effect on the legal requirements for packaging – new rules were agreed for the labelling of packaged food and drink products, and these new labels appeared in British shops in 1983. The most important change was that all products had to list ingredients, including additives. The Food and Drinks Industry Council had anticipated the confusion that this might cause, and published an explanatory leaflet listing the purpose of every food additive. For example, butylated hydroxytoluene prevents oils on crisps and fried snacks going off, sodium nitrate gives bacon a long storage life and its pink colour, and monosodium glutamate is a flavour enhancer used in prepared meats and savoury foods.

We have discussed here a few of the existing and future legal requirements for packaging. It is impossible to generalise any further as there is no complete summary of legal requirements in existence at present, only partial summaries as the legal requirements will vary by type of product. Specialised advice should be sought on this from any of the trade bodies and institutions concerned.

WHAT'S IN A NAME?

In October 2005 The European Court of Justice ended a long standing dispute when it ruled that the name "Feta" could only be used to describe white cheese soaked in brine made in Greece. This ruling in based on European legislation that limits to the use of certain names to specific countries or locations such as:

- Blue Stilton and White Stilton cheeses
- Champagne
- Cornish clotted cream
- Gorgonzola cheese
- Jersey Royal potatoes
- Kalamata olives
- Newcastle Brown Ale
- Parma Ham
- Roquefort cheese
- Scotch beef

The ruling, which comes into effect in 2007 cannot be appealed despite the fact that 'feta' cheese is manufactured in large quantities in several other European countries and it is unlikely that Greece could meet the demand from these countries. Many producers in countries like Denmark, France and Germany have been making the cheese for decades and produce thousands of tons a year. In Denmark they have been making feta since the 1930s, produce 30,000 tons a year and export some of this to Greece. According to a report in *The Times* (26/10/05) the decision is particularly controversial because feta is not a place in Greece but a word derived from the Italian meaning "slice". As such it has become a generic term like 'Yorkshire Pudding' and so cannot be reserved for use by one region.

However, the judges ruled that feta has been produced in Greece for 6000 years, and uses a traditional method which requires straining without pressure. Further, Greece accounts for 85% of all feta cheese consumption in Europe and feta cheese produced in other countries "is commonly marketed with labels referring to Greek cultural traditions and civilisation".

THE RESOLUTION OF CONFLICT BETWEEN DISTRIBUTOR/USER REQUIREMENTS

Such conflict as does exist between user and distributor requirements is almost invariably resolved in favour of the user. Diseconomies in weight/volume relationships due to the use of odd-shaped containers, and losses due to breakages can often be minimised through the use of standardised outer containers. However, the manufacturer can only afford to incur such additional costs if the consumer is prepared to pay a premium for the added benefits received. Similarly, retailers are more concerned with turnover and gross margins than with the actual number of units on display. If it can be shown that although a promotional pack may occupy twice the space of a conventional container it will generate increased demand or help build store traffic, then the retailer will usually cooperate in the promotion; for example Pyrex coffee jugs filled with instant coffee. However, manufacturers are not unresponsive to retailer demands and many new packs have been developed as a result of pressure from the big food chains. Self-service has largely replaced counter service owing to the lower operating costs possible through the elimination of sales assistants. This in turn has stimulated manufacturers to develop new packaging materials to help the product sell itself and led to the elimination of many traditional practices.

In the former category may be included plastic bottles, first introduced in 1964 by ICI, aluminium foil, bubble-packs, and shrink-wrapping for prepackaged meats, and so on. In the latter category the one-trip bottle was developed to encourage supermarkets to carry carbonated beverages, which they had virtually dropped owing to the diseconomies associated with returning deposits and handling empty bottles. Innovation has not been confined to the development of new materials alone, and many improvements have been made in the use of traditional materials. Lightweight tinplate has reduced both the cost and weight of cans and closures, while increased strength has permitted the development of the aerosol, sales of which now amount to hundreds of millions every year. The difficulties described earlier in connection with sardine cans have now been overcome with the development of the Ziehfix can in which the lid is attached to the body by a rubber sealing ring and is easily stripped off. (It is doubtful if this innovation would have saved the sardine packer, for such cans cost more to manufacture than a conventional can. For a distinctive product such as John West's kipper fillets the added cost would appear to justify the convenience, however.) Similarly, the strip-top beer can has combined the advantages of two competing materials – aluminium and tinplate.

THE PACKAGE AS A MARKETING VARIABLE

In an article in the *Wall Street Journal* Alecia Swasy (1989) posed the question 'Sales lost their vim? Try repackaging', and claimed that packaging represents the last five seconds of marketing. By this she meant that the final decisions of which fast moving consumer good to buy are usually made at the point of sale when faced with an array of objectively similar packaged goods which can only be differentiated by their price, brand and packaging – the extrinsic product attributes referred to in the Introduction.

Comparatively little research has been done into 'packaging as an extrinsic product attribute' but Robert Underwood (1993) presented a paper on this subject at the AMA Winter Educators' Conference. The references cited are to be found in this paper.

Underwood quotes Schlossberg (1990) who argues that the importance of packaging as a marketing variable can be summarised by three numbers: '25 000 or the number of items in a typical grocery store; 20, or the average number of minutes a consumer spends shopping in such a store; and 80, or the percentage of shoppers who make a final decision on what they're buying while in the store'. Underwood then reviews the small number of studies which have explored the role of the package as a cue to product quality as the basis for his own research. In his view the attributes of a package such as colour, design, type of container and so on create utility for a consumer and these **'package utilities'** influence the consumer's overall perception of utility (or value) which is essentially a measure of the satisfaction of consumer wants and/or needs. Underwood proposes a conceptual model which recognises five utilities – Functional, Symbolic, Informational, Aesthetic and Structural – the first four of which are of direct importance to the consumer while the last refers to the benefits the package provides to distributors; for example ease of shipping, handling and storage. The other four utilities are defined as follows:

- *Functional package utility* is the benefit consumers derive from a product's package performing five key functions: facilitating usage, easing disbursement, providing security and protection, accommodating storage for product re-use, and allowing re-use of the actual package.
- *Symbolic package utility* is defined as internally generated feelings engendered by a product's package including self-enhancement, role position, group membership, and ego identification. Such symbolic meanings are frequently communicated by the product's package. For example, in the USA there are over 700 brands of perfume and cologne. In such a saturated market, packaging is seen as essential in communicating symbolic values or image and attracting the consumer's attention at the point of sale.
- *Informational package utility* is derived from the quantity and quality of information provided. As noted earlier, this includes factual information, often required by law, as well as the brand and imagery associated with it, advice on use, and so forth.
- *Aesthetic package utility* derived from the sensory benefit conveyed by the design, shape, colour, texture and so on of the package.

Underwood describes each of these utilities or attributes in some detail in establishing a series of propositions as to how they influence consumer perception and, possibly, behaviour. However, this is a theoretical model and, while the propositions seem eminently sensible, they still require to be operationalised and validated. Nevertheless, there are numerous case histories which lend support to the view that the package has a major influence on consumer decisions.

In recent years a number of articles have appeared describing how manufacturers have used packaging as a competitive weapon in their marketing strategy. The one-trip bottle was adopted by Schweppes in an attempt to recapture the market share lost to Beechams, who had capitalised on the supermarkets' unwillingness to handle returnable bottles by introducing the Hunt range of 'mixers' in cans. After Eight Mints' luxury image was born out of careful pack design backed up by an effective advertising campaign. Van den Bergh commissioned Rockwell glass to design a streamlined, lightweight bottle for their Tree Top line of fruit squashes to give it added appeal at the point of sale.

While the materials used are vitally important, appearance and design have a major role to play too. In an article in *Marketing Week* (March 4, 2004) Richenda Wilson cited a number of examples that confirm that a radical re-design can lead to increased sales. While all the designers interviewed agreed that customer research was important in gaining insight into consumer demands and motivations, it was also stressed that design by committee was to be avoided at all costs. It is essential that creative designers must be given latitude if they are to come up with striking ideas that will have impact at the point of sale. In doing so, however, it is important not to change things so radically that it prevents a carry-over of the established values associated with the brand, e.g. British Airways corporate redesign in the 1990s.

The contribution of packaging (reinforced by effective promotion) to the expansion of an established brand is exemplified by Paul Trott who identifies a number of brands that have maintained brand leadership since 1935 through packaging development including, Birds Custard, Cadbury's Dairy Milk Chocolate, Heinz Soups, Kelloggs Cornflakes, McVities Digestive Biscuits and Schweppes mixer drinks.

FUTURE TRENDS IN PACKAGING

Stewart (2004) devotes a chapter to a discussion of 'Intelligent packaging and smart materials' that gives a fascinating insight into current and future developments. Pointing to the benefits arising from the use of barcodes that we now take for granted, he writes:

But emerging technologies are now posed to create another revolution in consumer and supply chain benefits. At the consumer end of the spectrum, we shall see radical new materials that combine electronics and packaging to provide visual and audio displays. Modified materials will also be available with new properties, such as transparent yet waterproof paper. Our loaded trolleys will be automatically scanned in one shot, leaving us to pay by inserting our store card into a machine or directly debiting our account. It does not stop there. The future generation of intelligent packs will be able to communicate with kitchen appliances, allowing a microwaveable ready meal to specify its optimum cooking instructions directly to the oven. These developments may delight some and horrify others.

Table 13.2 summarises some of the lifestyle changes that may drive this trend towards intelligent packaging, while Table 13.3 indicates some of the new technology that may help.

In an article entitled 'Packaging – what will the 21st century require?', Jillian Prebble of Pira International recommended the use of technology road-mapping involving four key steps :

1 *Identification of key market drivers*
2 *Scenario building*
3 *Identification of technology steps*
4 *Plotting or mapping.*

Table 13.2 Consumer packaging materials

Market drivers	Significance	Technology response area	
Ageing profile	Increased home care and self-care	Monitoring	health, diet, exercise
		Prompting	drug regime
	Mobility problems	Purchasing	reordering and home delivery
		Safety	opening and closing
	Sight deterioration	Information	audio packs
	Active singles	Convenience	easy cook
Single parents	Working and caring	Social needs	communication and meeting
		Child friendly	safe cooking
		Informing	diet, allergies
		Safety	freshness indicators
	Time poor	Organisation	auto order

Source: PIRA International Ltd, in Stewart, B. (2004), *Packaging Design Strategies*, 2nd. edn, (Leatherhead: Pira International Ltd.).

Table 13.3 Non-consumer packaging materials

Market drivers	Significance	Technology response area	
Cost reductions	Production efficiency	Tracking	stock control
	Distribution efficiency	Tracking	pack movements
	Retail efficiency	Tracking	restocking
		Product ID	auto checkout
	Staffing levels	Robotics	
	Theft	Tagging	
Security concerns	Fraud	Tagging, tracking and thermochromic inks	
	Deliberate contamination	Indicators	
	Brand protection	Various	
Product integrity	Freshness and time to market	Indicators	
	Damage	Transit simulation	
Environmental obligations	Material segregation	Tagging	auto sorting
	Energy calculation	Tagging	product miles
Market share	Product innovation	Self-heating and cooling	convenience
		Electronic displays	
		Interactive	

Source: PIRA International Ltd, in Stewart, B. (2004), *Packaging Design Strategies*, 2nd. edn, (Leatherhead: Pira International Ltd.).

CARBON NEUTRAL PRODUCTS

The state of the environment has become a hot topic for consumers in recent years. One way of addressing this issue is for producers to attempt to 'nullify' the environmental impact of their products by compensatory methods.

Large companies such as BP have been taking this approach for a while, but more recently, the involvement of media personalities in such campaigns has brought them to greater public awareness.

Recent albums by Coldplay and Pink Floyd amongst others have highlighted their 'carbon-neutral' status.

Essentially this means that enough trees have ben planted to re-absorb the CO_2 created by the production, manufacture and distribution of the album.

This concept has also been expanded to include, for example, the impact of a recent Rolling Stones tour. One of the main consultancies behind this move is Future Forests (*www.futureforests.com*).

Whilst some green activists are sceptical about the whether such schemes have any beneficial impact on the environment, the concept of planting trees is seen as a tangible way of explaining to consumers the environmental soundness of products.

Table 13.4 Market factors influencing consumer packaging

Industry drivers within the retail environment	Packaging drivers within the retail environment
■ Competition	■ Environmental legislation
■ Changing retail environment	recycling
polarisation	minimisation
home shopping	■ Cost reduction
diversification of retailers	materials - reusable, cheaper, less
■ Tracking, tracing	stock levels
■ EDI, rapid ordering and supply	run lengths and speed
■ Food scares	handling - automation, ready to
■ Cost reduction	merchandise units
■ Promotions	■ Turn around, supply time
■ Consumer preferences	■ Brand enhancement
■ Organic	■ Inclusion of information
■ Fresh	tracking and traceability
■ Convenience	legislation
■ ECR	barcodes
	consumer needs, e.g. dietary information
	■ Security
	tamper evidence
	anti theft
	anti counterfeit
	■ Functionality / performance
	openability
	resalability
	New materials with enhanced properties
	e.g. thinner, stronger
	■ Shelf life
	■ On line performance

Source: Prebble, J. (2005), 'Packaging - what will the 21st century require?' Working Paper (Pira International Ltd).

The key factors thought likely to influence consumer packaging in the future are set out in Table 13.4.

Major changes in the areas of packaging systems and materials are few and far between because the problem is not only to develop a new idea, but that it should be of enough consequence to merit a change from the existing method of packaging. A change usually involves a good deal of capital expenditure, and this is the main factor which helps to maintain the status quo.

Today, however, there is a growing cost differential between the packaging currently being used and their possible substitutes. This can be shown by the amount of energy used in the creation of packaging materials.

Energy content: Glass pack   6542 kj per unit
                        Metal pack   5191 kj per unit
                        Bag in box*   3046 kj per unit
                        (* carton containing powdered or granulated products)

The actual costs will very approximately reflect these differences.

In the December 5 issue of *Marketing News* (1994) a short article emphasised many of the points made earlier about packaging's role in the marketing mix. It also pointed to the impact which retail trends were having on package design. These trends are just as important today, namely:

- *Lifestyle purchasing* As more and more consumers look for products which reflect a desired lifestyle. Packaging is being used increasingly to communicate these values.
- *Eroding brand loyalty* As private labels, generic brands and discounting have eroded traditional brand share manufacturers are redesigning their packaging to reposition their brands and emphasise their intrinsic values.
- *Shelf information overload* As the number of products increases – there are twice as many on supermarket shelves as there were 10 years ago – distinctive packaging is critical to consumer recognition/attention.
- *Line extensions* In the face of product proliferation and intensive competition many producers use their existing brands and identities when introducing new products (line extensions). Package design has a major role to play in establishing links between the old and new product.
- *Declining marketing budgets* As recessionary forces have bitten into promotional budgets the package has increased in importance as a communication variable.

Summary

In this chapter we have outlined some of the reasons why we consider that packaging deserves to be treated as a topic in its own right. To begin with it was seen that packaging performs three basic functions – to contain, protect, and identify a product. In Figure 13.1 each of these fundamental functions was elaborated on indicating how they could be extended into marketing opportunities, and a potential source of competitive advantage. Thus innovation in packaging has become a major source of adding value to products. New packaging can create new sub-categories such as pump packaging for toothpaste and liquid soap, refillable containers for detergents, and microwaveable containers.

However, packaging is not without its critics and we examined the sources and nature of some of these criticisms as well as the response of the packaging industry to them. Packaging is seen as a serious source of waste and environmental pollution. While accepting that this can be the case, the industry has responded by pointing out that packaging performs an important role in reducing waste through protecting the contents from damage and/or spoilage. Also modern packaging materials tend to be lighter, less bulky, and easier to recycle than they were. Much secondary packaging has been eliminated, e.g. a box containing a bag, while products like detergents have been concentrated and pet foods 'dehydrated' to reduce their volume. With regard to recycling, many countries have introduced legislation and regulation to encourage this but, as the example of New Zealand shows, some are more socially aware and advanced in their efforts than others. For example, the proliferation of plastic carrier bags and problems with their disposability and degradability led Irish retailers to charge customers 15 cents for each plastic bag in an effort to encourage their re-use or the use of other more permanent carrier bags.

We have also seen that packaging has an important role to play in branding and positioning. Dent (1999) offers a checklist of packaging and design features that contribute to a brand's equity:

- The shape of the container, e.g. Toilet Duck
- A distinctive opening device, e.g. Grolsch
- The packaging material, e.g. Ferrero Rocher
- The packaging material finish, e.g. Absolut Vodka
- Other distinctive physical features, e.g. the shape of the capsules in Elizabeth Arden time capsules
- The colour of the packaging, e.g. Marlboro
- The logo style, e.g. Coca Cola
- The use of a symbol, e.g. the Woolmark
- The use of a personality, e.g. Colonel Sanders

Looking to the future, it is clear that there are many exciting developments in terms of both protecting and identifying products through their packaging that will add value through reducing cost and waste as well as increasing the product's appearance and attractiveness to the customer.

Review questions and problems

1 What considerations would you take into account in selecting the basic packaging material, e.g. paper, tinplate, glass, etc., for the following items (stipulate the material to be used and the reasons for your choice in rank order of importance, i.e. cost, strength, etc.)
   - Breakfast cereal
   - Jam
   - Hand cream (a) standard quality (b) deluxe quality
   - Frozen vegetables
   - Chocolates
   - Men's shirts
   - Instant coffee
   - Salt
   - Shampoo.

2 A well-known book on packaging is entitled The Silent Salesman. Discuss.

3 Summarise: the consumer's requirements of a satisfactory pack; the retailer's requirements.

4 Select any three well-known consumer products and analyse packaging's contribution to their marketing.

5 What contribution can motivation research make to the packaging decision? Quote specific examples to illustrate your answer.

6 Account for the increased importance of packaging as an element in the marketing mix of a typical fast-moving consumer good in recent years.

7 Packaging plays a major part in the promotion of branded products. Discuss this contribution in the light of growing dissatisfaction from conservationists and consumerist interests throughout the world.

8 Write an essay on the social psychology of colour in packaging and sales promotion.

Key terms

bar code
climatic damage
copyright
European Article Numbering (EAN)
Food Standards Agency
green issues

mechanical damage
package design
package utilities
packaging
patent rights
PIRA International

radio frequency identification
  (RFID)
trademarks
Universal Product Code System
  (UPC)

Supplementary reading list

Stewart, B. (2004), *Packaging Design Strategies*, 2nd. Edition, (Leatherhead: Pira International Ltd.)
An excellent, up-to-date treatment of the subject of packaging with an emphasis on design.
Corner, E. and Paine, F. A. (2002), *Market Motivators: The Special Worlds of Packaging and Marketing*, (Cookham: CIM Publishing).
Early chapters deal with the needs and motivations of various participants in the supply chain. Later ones with design and environmental considerations.
Another useful but rather dated source is Peter Danton de Rouffignac's book *Packaging in the Marketing Mix* (1990), (Oxford: Butterworth-Heinemann). More up-to-date information may be obtained from *Pira International* which is the leading independent centre for research, consultancy, training and information services for the paper, packaging, printing and publishing industries.
Dart, P.(1999), 'Packaging and Design', in Baker, M.J. (ed.) *IEBM Encyclopedia of Marketing*, (London: Thomson Learning).
Pilditch, J. (1973), *The Silent Salesman* (London: Business Books)
Trott, P. (2005), *Innovation Management and New Product Development*, 3rd. Edition, (Harlow: Prentice-Hall)
www.piranet.com
www.packagingfedn.co.uk
www.packagingtoday.co.uk
www.landell_mills.com

BRANDING AND BRAND MANAGEMENT

14

| **Learning Goals** | *After reading this chapter you should be able to:* |

- Describe the origins and history of branding

- Explain the nature of branding and its role in modern marketing practice

- Spell out the essence and nature of brand identity

- Clarify the concept of brand equity

- Discuss the nature of brand loyalty

- Make clear the notion of customer relationship management

- Debate the importance of positioning brands against competitive offerings

INTRODUCTION

A recurring theme throughout any discussion of marketing is the importance of differentiation and the search for a sustainable competitive advantage. At the same time, however, it is recognised that accelerating technological change and global competition make this increasingly difficult to achieve – especially in an objective way. Even if you have patent protection others will copy your ideas; so the critical issue is how can sellers distinguish themselves from their direct competitors in the mind of the consumer ? In a word, the answer is through **branding**.

In this chapter we begin by tracing the history of branding and, like marketing itself, will see that the practice of branding has existed for millennia. But its nature and importance have assumed much greater significance in the last century or so. Next we look at some definitions of brands and branding and suggest eight different roles or functions they may perform. Then, we review the attributes of **brand identity** and **brand equity**, and the development of **branding strategy**. This leads to a consideration of the use of brands and branding in marketing strategy and the means of creating and sustaining loyalty. In recent years the means of achieving this has been seen to be through **customer relationship management** or **CRM**. We believe that trying to manage relationships is antithetical to the true marketing concept and suggest that what is intended is **customer satisfaction management** or **CSM**. In order to deliver satisfaction the firm must develop a thorough understanding of the customers needs, develop attributes and features that meet these, and then communicate this to their target audience through careful **positioning**.

A BRIEF HISTORY OF BRANDING

As noted in the introduction, many people think of branding as something that developed in the later twentieth century when, in reality brands have existed since the dawn of civilisation. In 1921 a Swedish archaeological expedition discovered signed ceramics in Human dating back to 4000 BC; ancient Egyptian brickmakers applied distinguishing marks to their output and, in the ruins of Pompeii similar marks were found on lead pipes, marble friezes, glassware, bronze goblets, gold and silverware and even on lava preserved loaves. So, what is a **brand**?

According to the *Oxford English Dictionary* branding is: "a name, a term, sign, symbol or design, or a combination of them, which is intended to identify the goods or services of one seller or group of sellers, and to differentiate them from those of competitors." Two key objectives are contained in this definition, namely: **identification** and **differentiation**. Historically, the emphasis was on identification so that buyers could establish who was responsible for particular goods and services and so seek redress if they were defective or, alternatively, buy from the same supplier if they were satisfied with their original purchase and wanted to buy again. Today, brands still serve these functions, but the emphasis has shifted to an ability to differentiate between large numbers of apparently identical versions of the same product.

The OED definition includes a variety of distinguishing features that might define a brand including what some authorities would consider a distinctive category, the **trademark**. Definitions of a trademark in other dictionaries are very similar to this. For example, Webster's New World Dictionary defines a trademark as: "A symbol used by business to identify goods and services by origin and manufacturers and to distinguish them from competing goods and services." What is different about a trademark is that, like a patent, it can be registered and gives the owner rights of protection against copying or counterfeiting. So a trademark is a special kind of brand but, for all other purposes we may regard them as the same as a brand.

Originally, symbols rather than words were used to identify products and you can still see evidence of this in the High Street today where different kinds of shops still use objects to signify the goods they trade in – shoes, pharmaceuticals, bakery products etc.. The reason is simple – the objects are easy to identify and may be understood by illiterate people. In advanced societies ,with high levels of literacy, words and names are equally if not more important but, in less developed countries distinctive symbols or logos are still the main basis for recognition.

According to Davis (2002) any or all of the following are appropriate definitions of a brand:

- *A brand is a tag line like "We bring good things to life"*
- *A brand is a symbol like the Nike swoosh*
- *A brand is a shape like the Coke or Absolut bottle*
- *A brand is a spokesperson like Bill Crosby for Jello*
- *A brand is a sound like Intel's familiar four notes*
- *A brand is an actual product or service - Kleenex tissue, a Xerox copier or a Sony Walkman*

In Europe branding became of particular importance in the Middle Ages due to its widespread use by the Medieval Guilds. As we saw in Chapter 1, the Guilds developed as a result of task specialisation and the emergence of distinctive trades and crafts. Guilds were responsible for the training and qualification of apprentices and the maintenance of quality. Thus branding served as a guarantee of the source and authenticity of a product, and as a legal protection against copying. It also served as a means of controlling supply in the hands of the 'authorised' producers and so retarded the growth of competition – restrictions which the Industrial Revolution and mass production were to destroy in the eighteenth century.

Another form of 'branding' that developed in the Middle Ages was the use of heraldic devices as a mark of distinction for an individual or organisation. The award of such devices was, and still is, controlled by the College of Heralds in the UK and so resembles the modern trademark that has to be registered with the controlling authority. Nowadays, an organisation can adopt virtually any name or symbol/logo that it wants, but only if it is registered as a trademark can it prevent others from copying it. Heraldry may also be seen as the pre-cursor of modern Corporate Identity programmes.

The Industrial Revolution gave birth to the Factory system and mass production. As we have seen, this was to have far reaching changes on distribution and

MODERN USE OF A HERALDIC DEVICE

During the 1980s the Thatcher Government required many public sector organisations to become more accountable and competitive, including universities. One consequence of this was recognition of the need to project a clear and consistent image to potential students and other individuals and organisations that the different institutions worked with. In common with other 'older' universities Strathclyde had adopted a heraldic device which it used in its publications, stationary, signage etc. The elements of this device were a shield, books representing knowledge, a St Andrew's Cross representing Scotland, a crown and rosettes associated with the ancient kingdom of Strathclyde. The only 'modern' element was a 'wave packet' linking the books of knowledge.

As part of a corporate identity programme the design was modified from a shield to a pentagon with the approval of the College of Arms that felt that this was both more modern and attractive. At the same time the University also adopted a phrase from the will of its Founder in 1796 in which he expressed the wish to establish "A place of useful learning" reflecting the developments in science and technology on which the Industrial Revolution was founded. These simple changes have proved to be very effective in communicating a strong and modern identity.

consumption. Perhaps the most important change was that the concentration of production led to both a physical and psychological separation between producer and consumer. Traditionally, consumers had sourced their needs from local suppliers with whom they interacted directly. Now they increasingly purchased manufactured products from 'unknown' sources with a choice of several different suppliers. In order to encourage retailers to stock their goods, and get buyers to ask for them, manufacturers branded their output. Initially, this branding served the same purpose as for the medieval craft guilds – identification of the maker, guarantee of authenticity and protection against copying.

At first, producers concentrated on making standardised products so that they could gain scale economies and offer competitive prices. But, as more and more entrepreneurs began to compete for the rapidly growing market, saturation began to occur and branding assumed greater importance as a means of differentiating the output of rival firms. One of the first producers to realise the importance of enabling consumers to identify his otherwise undifferentiated product at the point of sale was Lever who manufactured soap at his Sunlight factory in the Wirral. Like many other commodity type products, soap was sold in bulk to retailers who then cut up the block into convenient sized bars for their customers. Lever hit on the idea of supplying bars stamped with the name Sunlight and, equally important, began to advertise the superior quality of his branded product compared with the unidentifiable output of his competitors.

As more companies began to brand their output the need to protect the value of the brand – or **brand equity** – was appreciated and registration of brand names became increasingly important. In France the first brand to be registered was Societe Roquefort in 1842. In Britain it was Bass Red Triangle (1876) and in the USA one of the first trademarks was the Quaker man (Quaker Oats, 1877).

Modern branding can be seen to serve all the same purposes as medieval branding, as well as adding value in two important ways. First, in conjunction with a promotional strategy it can invest even the most prosaic product like soap with emotional dimensions. Second, a brand is like a shorthand or summary statement of a whole set of attributes, features and benefits that can easily be brought to mind when exposed to the symbol, logo, name etc.

MODERN BRANDING

"Take water and sugar: they are commodities. Process them into cola drinks and you have products. Market and promote them into Coca Cola and Pepsi: you have brands." (*Economist*, 24.11.1988) And now we know that even a commodity like water can be transformed into a powerful brand through appropriate marketing. (But see the vignette on Dasani later in this chapter).

Our review of the development of branding indicates that a brand may serve many purposes. To begin with it identifies the source of the product or service or what we may call its 'ownership'. Ownership may belong to a manufacturer and, until recently, these tended to be dominant, particularly in markets for fast moving consumer goods and consumer durables. Now, however, retailers have assumed much greater power in the channels of distribution, and so can negotiate from a position of strength, as well as introducing their 'own' brands in direct competition.

Second, a brand serves as a differentiating device – but only if it represents a meaningful differentiation to a sufficient number of customer to enable the owner to trade profitably. In other words, a name, symbol, logo etc. must be backed-up by perceived differences, albeit that they may be entirely subjective or difficult if not impossible to measure by the user. For example, Castrol has invested heavily in developing superior lubricants such as Castrol GTX which it markets as 'High Technology Engine Protection' at a premium price. In this case data may be used to support the functional difference, but few car owners have the means to verify their belief that the product is better than cheaper substitutes available to them.

Brands may be symbolic and so communicate something about themselves such as status. The use of heraldic devices communicates tradition and recognition by authority which controls their use. On the other hand, as our Strathclyde example shows, such associations may have negative overtones of stuffiness and lack of modernity – a reason why many familiar brands have been modernised over time.

Brands, and especially **umbrella brands** like Nestlé or Nike, help reduce the risk that most of us feel in buying something new for the first time. If we are familiar with the parent brand we are likely to be more confident that a new brand associated with it will live up to our expectations, and so be less risky than buying from an unknown source. Here the brand serves as the shorthand for all the qualities we associate with it and gives a halo effect to the new offering.

By contrast with an umbrella brand many organisations use **product brands** and give an unique name to every product in their portfolio. Procter and Gamble is a well known example with brands like Dreft, Tide, Daz and Fairy Snow in the

OXFORD AS A BRAND

In *The Times* (16 April 2005) the Vice-Chancellor of Oxford University, Dr. John Hood was quoted as saying:

"For over nine centuries the name Oxford University has been synonymous with excellence in teaching and learning. As guardians of this brand in the 21st century we have a duty to protect the name but equally we must consider ways to add value to the brand through the availability of carefully selected high-quality merchandise which reflect the university's history as well as its current research strengths."

Since it took out a trademark on its belted crest in 1993, Oxford has licenced this to a wide range of companies and now earns £400,000 a year from this source – a figure it hopes to increase to £5 million within the next five years. But, as reporter Patrick Foster observes, by contrast with the American Ivy League Universities that offer mainly high net value items, Oxford appears to be going distinctly down market by licensing a wide range of organisations producing everything from scientific toys and games, garden tools, baby clothes and cosmetics.

The announcement was not received with universal approval. John Williams of brand consultant Wolff Olins was quoted as saying: "Is flogging academic toys an appropriate action for an august institution of this nature? This should be one of the most exclusive brands in the world; I think this can only cheapen the brand. I think it's absolute rubbish."

Clearly, this is a quite different approach from Strathclyde which wanted to create a modern image. Oxford had a clear image; will this dilute it? Time will tell!

UMBRELLA BRANDING AT CADBURY

In July 2004 Cadbury Trebor Bassett announced "an aggressive assault on one of Nestlé Rowntree's top-selling products, Kit Kat, with the launch of Cadbury's Dairy Milk Wafer." (*Marketing Week*, 15/7/04).

The decision to badge the new wafer with the Dairy Milk logo followed a decision taken in 2003 to use this as an umbrella brand for the launch of a range of new products and variants such as Dairy Milk with mint chips. As Christine Perry commented (Marketing Week, 22/7/04): "Crucially it means that Cadbury can now support a portfolio of different products by investing in just one brand". Since the mid 1990s Cadbury has spent £10 million a year on sponsoring Coronation Street (the UKs favourite TV 'soap') with an overall focus on Dairy Milk making it the highest profile of Cadbury's brands, and a logical choice for umbrella status.

These moves were designed primarily to maintain Cadbury's hold on a stagnant chocolate market and reinforce their position against Nestlé and Masterfoods (formerly Mars) their main rivals. However, some critics see it as an example of 'brand blocking' at retail where the concentration of a wide range of variants in one location – a 'purple patch' for Dairy Milk – creates in-store impact.

detergent category. A major advantage of product brands is that the seller can offer variants of the same product in competition with each other but positioned to cater to different market segments. Also if a new product fails the failure is unlikely to have any effect on other brands in the portfolio. The main disadvantages are that each offering has to be supported by its own promotional campaign increasing costs and losing the synergy enjoyed by umbrella brands like Sony or Kodak. However, Procter and Gamble have successfully extended their product brands by using a known name on other new products, e.g Tide Coldwater, Tide with Bleach, Tide with Bleach Alternative, Tide To Go (stain remover), Tide Stainbrush etc.

Finally, registered brands confer a degree of legal protection on their owners similar to ownership of other property rights. While this may not stop counterfeiting it does ensure that the genuine owners can take action against it. For example, counterfeiting is a way of life in many South East Asian countries. In the 1980s it was commonplace in Singapore until IBM informed the Government that it would withdraw its products and services from the country unless something was done to stop copying of them. As a result legislation was not only enacted but rigorously enforced. You might still be able to buy a fake Rolex watch or Lacoste shirt there, but you will have to look very hard to do so!

BRAND IDENTITY

Discussions of branding frequently focus on the *identity* of the brand as if it has a personality. The idea of identity is closely associated with those of *image* and *personality* and is usually seen as incorporating them both. Image is regarded as the most visible aspect of identity, while personality reflects the human characteristics associated with the brand. Indeed, research into brands and their effects on buying behaviour, frequently asks consumers to describe the kind of person they think of when considering a brand. We will explore all three in this section.

Identity is one of a small number of English words which has two diametrically opposed definitions, viz.:

1. sameness, oneness, unanimity, indistinguishability, agreement accord, congruence: Identity of purpose held them together under stress.

2. personality, individuality, distinctiveness, uniqueness, particularity, singularity: Many who join the army lose their identity. (Oxford Thesaurus).

Paradoxically, it is these attributes of **sameness** and **uniqueness** which account for the growth of branding as a fundamental element of marketing strategy. Thus the brand's *uniqueness* enables you to differentiate it from closely competitive substitutes. At the same time its *sameness* is the buyers guarantee of consistency and the delivery of expected satisfactions. So, when we segment a market we are seeking to cluster prospective customers into groupings in which the members of each group or segment are very similar to one another but, and very important, different from the members of all other groups in some meaningful way. But, as we have seen, it is very difficult to establish complete ownership or a monopoly over a market segment, and we will usually find several products that are very close substitutes for one another competing for the customer's patronage. It is because customers perceive the products of different suppliers as being very similar that they become part of their **evoked set** when they experience a need for a given product category like breakfast cereals or instant coffee.

Thus, if you have a need for instant coffee it is likely that both Nescafe and Kenco will come to mind, along with several other well known brands, all of which will be displayed next to one another on the supermarket shelves. If you consider all these products to be perfect substitutes for one another then economic rationality predicts that you will select the one with the lowest price. And, if you find this difficult because of the different pack sizes, you will find that the retailer has thoughtfully provided the unit price so that you can make direct comparisons between different products and sizes. But, if you can invest your product with a distinctive identity then it will stand out from the others and may encourage the consumer to buy – or avoid – it. Clearly, creating a distinctive and positive identity for a product is a major and important aspect of effective marketing.

According to David Aaker (1996), a leading authority on brands and branding, **Brand Identity** comprises four key elements:

1 *A unique set of associations* which represent what the brand stands for and imply a promise for customers.

2 *A value proposition* involving both functional and emotional benefits.

3 *A complex bundle of dimensions* which may be organised around four perspectives – brand-as-product, brand-as-organisation, brand-as-person and brand-as-symbol.

4 *A core and extended structure.*

In Aaker's view it is important not to emphasise any one of these key elements at the expense of the others, otherwise one is likely to fall into one or other of four 'traps'.

The first of these is the **Brand Image** trap. Brand Image summarises how others perceive the brand and is based on its past and current positioning and performance. The Brand Image is usually passive in nature and is used tactically rather than strategically. By contrast the Brand Identity represents the products enduring qualities – what it is and what it stands for. So the *Identity* summarises the product's core values, beliefs, and aspirations – it looks to the future and should provide the vision for future strategy, direction and purpose.

The second trap is the **Brand Position** which Aaker defines as "the part of the brand identity and value proposition that is to be actively communicated to the target audience and that demonstrates an advantage over competing brands". Now positioning is of vital importance in enabling potential customers to distinguish one brand from another on the basis of attributes and features, benefits and values that are important to them. The problem with positioning is that it usually only confers a short-term competitive advantage because as soon as your competitors can establish what the advantage is based on they will copy it. If, therefore, one spends too much time and effort on tactical positioning one may neglect the long-term strategic development of the brand based on innovation and added value.

The third trap is what Aaker calls the 'external perspective' by which he means the customers view of the brand. Given the emphasis on establishing customer needs as the basis for effective marketing , it might appear surprising that this could be seen as a trap. Obviously it is of major importance but, in order to deliver the quality and satisfaction looked for by customers all those involved in a product's creation and supply must understand and support the Brand Identity too. So, equal attention needs to be given to the 'internal perspective' and this is achieved through internal marketing.

The fourth and final trap is termed the 'product-attribute–fixation' trap which arises when the seller believes that the product attributes are a sufficient reason for purchase. They rarely are. Product attributes are necessary because they define the customers need. But, in order to compete you must offer these attributes for otherwise you will not be part of the customer's evoked set. To give the customers what they want you have to add value through all the other dimensions that make up the brand identity. If you confine your brand's identity to its product attributes then you are likely to fail because:

- On their own they fail to differentiate one product/brand from another
- They are easy to copy
- It assumes that buyers only consider functional performance and price when selecting a product (the economists 'rational' view)
- Changing the specification may cause the buyer to reconsider the product and opt for the known and familiar specification, i.e. it limits the opportunities to 'stretch' or extend the brand and so
- It limits strategic flexibility.

It follows that to create and sustain a Brand Identity it is necessary to develop the four key elements identified earlier.

To begin with we are looking for a unique set of associations that represent what the brand stands for, and the 'promise' it offers the buyer. This must be supported by a value proposition combining both functional and emotional benefits. Taken together these may be thought of as a hierarchy with features and attributes as the foundation as they define the kind of product and the need(s) it will satisfy. Next, there are the benefits the customer may expect from consuming the product, which may be both functional and emotional. And, finally, at the top level to which all brands aspire, are the beliefs and values that customers have about the brand. As one progresses up the hierarchy a product changes from being a convenience good – any make will do – to a shopping good – the customer will actively seek a preferred make – to a specialty good when the customer's preference is so strong that they will 'accept no substitute', and would rather do without than buy an 'inferior' brand.

In order to establish the associations that customers have about brands it is necessary to conduct frequent market research to track how the brand is perceived. Brand associations can be determined by the use of indirect and projective market research techniques. These are also helpful in identifying customer motivations that can be used to position a brand against its competitors. Alternatively, one can survey consumers and ask them to compare brands on key factors used in positioning such as features, and attributes, benefits, user characteristics and use situations. Bearing in mind the point about internal marketing made earlier, it is also important to check out that those responsible for making and selling the brand have similar and consistent associations with it. Davis (2002) suggests a check list of questions that may be used for this purpose as follows:

- When I say the name of our brand what is the first thing that comes to mind? Why?
- What are the strengths and weaknesses of our brand?
- What factors have contributed to your perceptions of these strengths and weaknesses?
- What brands did you consider before you bought our brand?
- What are your perceptions of the other brands you considered? (Strengths, weaknesses, attributes).
- Why did you choose our brand?
- Has our brand met your needs and expectations?
- What benefits has our brand provided you? Does it meet your expectations?
- Describe the experience you had with our brand before you made the purchase ... as you used the product ... after you used it.
- Describe exactly what you bought when you purchased out product or service. (Benefits, hopes and the like).
- When describing our brand to another potential buyer or a friend, how would you describe it?
- Why would you recommend our brand to another person? (Or, why wouldn't you?).
- Does one brand make you feel differently about yourself (or reflect differently on you) than another?
- Describe the staff and service providers and how they interacted with you. How did they make you feel?

As well as the associations that consumers ascribe to a brand, the other component of its image is the **persona** or personality that they have. The persona may be made up of many characteristics including gender, appearance, occupation, standing or socio-economic class, education and so on. In *Building Strong Brands* David Aaker identified *five* human characteristics which he claims 93% of all brands aspire to:

- *Sincerity* (Campbell's, Hallmark, Kodak)
- *Excitement* (Porsche, Absolut)
- *Competence* (AMEX, CNN, IBM)
- *Sophistication* (Lexus, Mercedes, Revlon)
- *Ruggedness* (Levi's, Marlboro)

To determine a brand's persona one might ask respondents some or all of the following questions (adapted from Davis (2002)):

- Why do you consider Brand X to be better than others?
- What are the strengths and weaknesses of Brand X?
- If you saw someone using Brand X what would you know about him or her? (Gender, age, education, personality income etc.).
- If Brand X were a car what make would it be?
- If Brand X were a place, where would it be?
- If Brand X were a retail outlet, which would it be and why?
- What kind of animal best describes this brand?

DEVELOPING A BRAND STRATEGY

The four perspectives described above - the brand as a *product*, a *person, symbol* or *organisation* – all need to be taken into account when devising a brand strategy. While one will usually be dominant in the minds of customers, and be the differentiating factor, the others cannot be neglected or they will become a potential weakness that competitors may attack. Developing a brand strategy follows the same steps as developing an overall marketing strategy and starts with answering the question "What business are we in?" Following the advice given by Levitt in *Marketing Myopia* we must define the basic need served such as transportation as this establishes the generic market in which we are competing. However, there are many ways to satisfy a need for transportation, so we have to be much more specific in defining the segment in which we wish to compete. Once we have done this we can benchmark the attributes and features offered by firms supplying this segment. These represent the minimum specification for a product to compete in that segment. But, to be selected, we need to offer both functional and emotional benefits that appeal to the particular wants held by consumers. If we are successful in doing this, then over time we hope the customer will develop a relationship with the brand based on trust and commitment and reflected in the beliefs and values they have for it. Once this has been achieved the brand will have become a specialty product for the user for which they have strong loyalty, and will re-purchase when seeking to satisfy the need it serves.

Among the basic product related associations that a customer may consider Aaker suggested a number of dimensions. First, the **product scope** defines what it does, so a watch will record the passage of time and indicate a specific time when consulted. However, watches come in many different shapes and forms so if we are considering buying one we will first need to define the particular attributes that we are looking for. Is it to be mechanical or electronic, and if electronic, analogue or digital? What price/quality are we interested in? Most cheap electronic watches are as accurate as the most expensive mechanical chronometers so, if we are looking for low price and accuracy, Accurist, Seiko or Swatch will be preferred to Rolex. But what if we regard our watch as an esteem item? Then we are much more likely to go for the Rolex, if we can afford it, because everyone knows they are expensive and worn by celebrities in all walks of life, but especially in more up-market activities like golf and sailing, opera and classical music – definitely upper middle class interests! Finally, many products have country of origin associations. Everyone knows that fine wines and perfumes come from France, and the world's 'best' watches come from Switzerland.

It was this latter association that enabled the basic Swiss watch manufacturing industry to recover from the brink of disaster after cheap electronic watches from South East Asia flooded the world's markets in the 1970s, displacing the less expensive mechanical watch for which Switzerland was renowned (as well as similar manufacturers in many other countries like the USA and UK). What saved the Swiss watch industry was its adoption of the new technology, combined with its understanding of what buyers of watches wanted. At low prices Swatch could be an affordable fashion item to be discarded when the new model came along, while the Made in Switzerland association was a guarantee of quality and experience that could not be matched by their Asian rivals.

An important aspect of the Made in Switzerland cachet was the fact that many of the leading watch makers in the world catering to the premium price segment of the market are based there. This association with an organisation is a powerful element of Brand Identity. Indeed in many markets, and especially business-to-business markets, it is the firms name and **corporate identity** that becomes the brand. Such corporate brands are often more robust and longer-lived than individual product brands as they represent the culture, values and reputation of an organisation rather than the specific features of its current product mix. Such attributes are more difficult to copy or replicate than product attributes ,and may be used to embrace a portfolio of products that can be changed over time.

In the case of individual products then the creation of a brand **personality** may achieve the same ability to enable people to identify with it and so form a relationship which is more enduring than one based on product features alone. The formation of a brand personality is usually based on **symbolism** communicated by one or a combination of visual imagery, metaphor, or a brand heritage. Visual imagery was discussed earlier when reviewing the origins of branding as symbols recognisable by illiterate consumers – still an important consideration in many developing economies where the Coke logo, the Nike 'swoosh', and Marlboro man are known to all, and often represent an aspiration to participate in the pleasures of a more affluent Western world.

Metaphor plays an important role in communication strategy and is a major element in many brands identity. While toilet rolls are not usually a subject of everyday conversation they are a product in universal use, and a market worth many millions of Euros, Pounds or Dollars. What do the majority of users want? They want a product that is both soft and strong, and what communicates these attributes effectively? It is the little golden labrador puppy in the Andrex commercials!

As for brand heritage this is a powerful argument to tip the scales in favour of an organisation that can claim it when up against a rival that cannot. So Ford can claim "Everything we do is driven by you" while "Nobody ever got fired for buying from IBM". The mere fact that an organisation has been in business for a long time, and that its name is universally recognised, will usually tip the balance in its favour when a prospective buyer is faced with two otherwise identical product offerings.

A word of warning – being well known and familiar can easily work against you. There are numerous examples of firms and brands becoming complacent and failing to realise that they must keep pace with the competition in both product innovation and marketing if they are to retain brand loyalty as the vignette on Coca-Cola makes clear. Always remember that while the product attributes are the most basic features of the brand identity they are also the most important as they define the nature of the product and the needs served.

COCA-COLA

Competition in the global market for carbonated beverages has long been dominated by the epic struggle between giants Coke and Pepsi. For many years Pepsi has trailed Coca-Cola in terms of overall performance, largely because Coke has been more successful in selling concentrate to Soda Fountains, cafes, bars etc. In recent years however, some of the shine has gone off Coca-Cola's performance

In March 2004 Coca-Cola withdrew its Dasani brand of bottled water from the UK market following a major downturn in sales after it was revealed that the water was bottled from the public mains supply at a factory in Sidcup, Kent. While purified water dominates the market in the USA and many other global markets, in Europe and the premium segment in most other countries it is the source of supply, such as Evian, Highland Spring or Perrier that is the major differentiating factor. While tap water enjoys no cachet in the UK market Dasani was double damned when it was revealed that it contained high levels of a carcinogen called bromate.

This failure was emphasised when Coca-Cola issued a profits warning in late 2004 due to the poor performance of its new C2 brand launched in the summer. Reporting in *The Sunday Times* (November 14, 2004) Dominic Rushe wrote:

"Launched in a fizz last summer C2, Coca-Cola's low-carb, low-calorie beverage, was supposed to usher in a new era of soft drinks and hard profits at the Atlanta-based soft-drinks giant.

Backed by a $50 million (£27m) advertising campaign, C2 was viewed as the company's most exciting launch since Diet Coke in 1982.

Diet Coke created a whole new category of drinks and was an instant smash. A year after launch it was America's most popular diet drink, a position it has never relinquished.

C2, a sort of semi-skimmed Coke, was to stand between the diet and original brands. With less sugar than regular Coke but more than Diet, the drink was supposed to appeal to a middle-ground of fizzy-drink fans. If successful, a new category could have been created with C2 versions of Coke's other leading brands such as Fanta and Sprite."

Despite strong promotion, C2 was launched at a premium price when regular Coke was being heavily discounted. Sales have been flat and the outlook is poor.

Industry analysts see Coca-Cola as having a corporate culture that has become arrogant and bureaucratic at a time when their major competitors have been more innovative, both in product development and in investment in marketing. Coke's short-term reflex has been to commit an extra $400 million to marketing – by the time you read this it should be clear what effect, if any, this has had.

CORE AND EXTENDED IDENTITY

The four perspectives that go to make up the Brand Identity are seen by Aaker as comprising a **core** and an **extended identity**. The core identity is made up of those features that go to make up the essence of the brand which Aaker argues can only be identified by answering some "tough introspective questions" such as:

- What is the soul of the brand?
- What are the fundamental beliefs and values that drive the brand?
- What are the competences of the organisation behind the brand?
- What does the organisation behind the brand stand for?

As noted earlier these questions need to be asked both internally and also of the brand's most loyal and dedicated customers.

The *extended identity* comprises all those attributes that operationalise the core identity by fleshing it out and giving it detail, texture and depth. Together the core and extended identities lead to the statement of the **value proposition** which endows the brand with its unique qualities and covers the benefits that will accrue to the buyer and encourage a relationship with it. The value proposition is often expressed in a phrase or statement – a strap line – that is common to all the firm's marketing communications. Avis is known world wide because "We try harder", British Airways is "The World's favourite airline" and Coke is still "The real thing". However many brands will not aspire to global status and/or may need adapting to a local context. Where adaptation is used there is a danger of creating multiple identities and care must be taken to ensure that the core values provide a common link between them.

BRAND STRETCHING

In Chapter 2 we suggested that a firm has only a limited set of strategic alternatives to choose from. To illustrate this we described a simple 2 X 2 growth vector matrix model, and then compared this with a more complex 3 X 3 matrix. The main difference between the two is that the latter introduces an intermediate state between 'old' and 'new' and we have adopted this in Figure 14.1 to explain our understanding of the concept of **brand stretching**.

You should be warned that this is the author's own conceptualisation and will not be found in other leading textbooks. The reason for proposing the model is that, as yet, there is no common agreement about nomenclature and classification of terms used. For example, Jobber calls what Kotler defines as a **line extension** a **brand extension**; and what Kotler calls a *brand extension* Jobber calls *brand stretching*.

In our view brand stretching describes *any* strategy that uses the existing brand name as a basis for introducing modified or new products. The difference between a line and brand extension is that a line extension occurs when a firm uses the *same brand name* to introduce a variant of the basic product targeted at a new/ different segment of the market served by the product category, as well as to maintain the loyalty of existing customers. By contrast, a brand extension occurs when the firm uses its brand name to compete with a new product targeted at a

Figure 14.1 Brand stretching

Product Strategy / Brand Name	Current	Modified	New
Current	'The' Brand	Line Extension	Brand Extension
New	'Product' or Multibrands	Multibrands	New Brands

different market.

So, when Procter and Gamble introduced new detergents under its *Tide* brand these are line extensions; e.g. *Tide Coldwater* for cold water washing, or *Tide with a touch of Downey* (a fabric softener). Similarly, the introduction of new flavours and forms of packaging by Coca-Cola and Pepsi are line extensions. But when Apple Computer Inc. introduced its digital music player, the *iPod*, it stretched its name as a computer maker into a new category as a consumer electronics company – a brand extension.

The above are examples of stretching the current brand name as a result of which the firm gains knowledge of customers in new market segments. Based on this understanding it becomes possible to introduce *new brands* into these segments. In Procter and Gamble's case its understanding of the detergent market enabled it to introduce a family of brands (**multibrands**) into the same product category.

The idea of 'stretch' and 'brand elasticity' are closely related. As Mark Sherrington observed in the *Encyclopedia of Marketing* (1999):

> In principle any brand can extend into any market if one has the time, commitment and money to invest, but its inherent elasticity will tell you how long, how hard and how much it will take, and help show the steps on the way. (See Figure 14.2) The Dunhill brand moved from lighters to accessories such as pens and cufflinks, then to belts and ties, a blazer and eventually a full range of menswear. Through range extension Dunhill was able to find a higher order of brand values, such as British craftsmanship and style, on which to build its brand, rather than remain locked into smoking requisites. Lucozade was able to develop energy from a health drink to launch a new range of isotonic sports drinks. However, where a brand becomes so closely associated with the product characteristics

Figure 14.2 Brand range extension

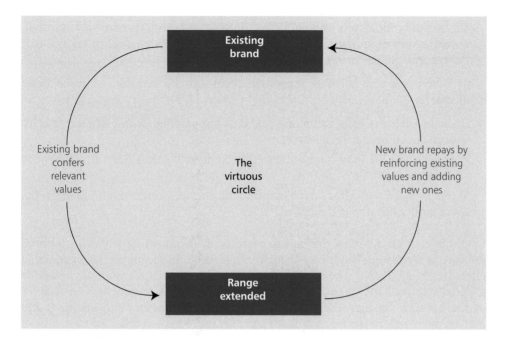

Source: Sherrington, M. (1999), 'Branding and Brand Management', in Baker, M.J. (ed.) *IEBM Encyclopedia of Marketing*, (London: Thomson Learning)

of its category its elasticity can be low. It is harder to see Ford as a range of consumer electronics than it is, for example, to see Sony as a car.

BRAND EQUITY

Traditionally, the value of a company was based on its tangible assets together with an ill-defined item termed 'Goodwill'. In many cases Goodwill was a contrived figure which enabled the firm to balance its books when reporting its assets and liabilities, and very limited effort was given to defining precisely what this 'goodwill' represented. Today, the situation is very different and the intangible assets or goodwill owned by a company have become crystallised in the notion of Brand Equity. There are numerous definitions of **Brand Equity** reflected in the following:

- The added value to the firm, the trade, or the consumer with which a given brand endows a product. (Farquhar, 1989)
- The sales and profit impact enjoyed as a result of prior years' marketing efforts versus a comparable new brand. (Brodsky, 1991)
- The set of associations and behaviour on the part of the brand's customers, channel members, and parent corporation that permits the brand to earn greater volumes or greater margins than it could without the brand name

and that gives the brand a strong, sustainable, and differentiated advantages over competitors. (Marketing Science Institute)

■ A set of brand assets and liabilities, linked to a brand, its name and symbol, that add to or subtract from the value provided by a product or service to a firm and/or that firm's customers. (Aaker, 1991)

In Feldwick's view (1996) these attributes can be reduced to three basic elements:

1 *Brand value*: the total value of a brand as a separable asset – when it is sold, or included on a balance sheet.

2 *Brand strength/loyalty*: a measure of the strength of consumers' attachment to a brand.

3 *Brand image/description*: a description of the associations and beliefs the consumer has about the brand.

Of these three the most difficult to establish without actually offering a brand for sale, or receiving a bid for its acquisition, is value. In recent years considerable effort has been given to the identification and definition of measures to establish a brand's value. One of the leading researchers on this subject is Tim Ambler of the London Business School. As a qualified accountant with senior brand management experience he recognises the dilemma between financial measures of performance – which are looked for by Boards of Directors and Financial Analysts – and non-financial measures which are frequently rejected or ignored by such decision-makers on the grounds of their subjectivity. In his view, while financial measures are *necessary* they are not *sufficient*, and other measures are needed to give a proper picture of the firm and its brands performance. These measures he terms **metrics**.

In the *Encyclopedia of Marketing* he explains:

We define a 'metric' as a measure of sufficient importance for performance assessment that it should be reviewed by the top management committee of the firm. The set of appropriate metrics will be of two types: short term costs and performance and brand equity. The word 'metric' is from music and verse and means the underlying rhythm, or measure which consistently repeats. In marketing, a metric is a measure which is used on a regular basis and which is both precise and consistent:

■ *Between marketers;*

■ *From accounting period to accounting period;*

■ *With finance and accounting measures;*

■ *With other marketing metrics, e.g. the same market is used in measuring market share and relative price;*

■ *Understood across functions, especially finance and accounting.*

In this explanation it should be noticed that Ambler makes a clear distinction between short-term measures and brand equity. This is because the brand (and firm's) equity accumulates over time and is not solely attributable to investment and activities in the periods – quarterly, bi-annually, annually – conventionally adopted for financial reporting. The problem is that, short of purchasing a brand from another organisation, it is almost impossible to place a value on the equity value of a brand. Indeed many Accounting Standards authorities do consider it impossible to put a market value on unique, intangible assets such as brands. That said, once a value has been placed on a brand this may be used strategically to measure the firm's performance by re-valuing it at the end of an accounting period in relation to the resources devoted to it during that period. To do so a combination of both financial and non-financial measures will be needed.

Ambler reviews many of these measures in the article referred to, and also summarises the main contributions to the debate to the late 1990s. More recently Davis (2002) suggested *nineteen* metrics for assessing a brand's worth, viz:

- *Positioning understanding*
- *Brand name knowledge, awareness, recognition, recall*
- *Contract fulfilment*
- *Persona recognition*
- *Association laddering*
- *Acquired customers*
- *Lost customers*
- *Market share*
- *Current customer penetration*
- *Customer loyalty*
- *Purchase frequency*
- *Community impact*
- *Brand regard*
- *Referral index*
- *Customer satisfaction*
- *Financial value*
- *Price premium*
- *Return on advertising*
- *Lifetime value of a customer*

Of all the measures suggested by various authors the most important is **loyalty**. The notion of loyalty first came to widespread public notice with the publication of a book by the Harvard Business School Press in 1996. Entitled *The Loyalty Effect* by Richard F. Reichheld, this book is based on his and his colleagues experience in the American consulting firm Bain & Company Inc. when they identified that firms that enjoyed higher profits enjoyed superior levels of customer loyalty. The corollary, obviously, is that if one can increase customer loyalty then performance and profitability should improve too. In turn this was shown to increase both employee and investor loyalty with the result that **customer relationship management (CRM)** designed to create and sustain loyalty has become one of the major aspects of marketing management in the last 10 years or so. So, to avoid the danger of being "Blinded by the flash of snapshot accounting" that measures short-term performance, CRM is focused on identifying the most profitable customers, or 'key accounts', and building strong relationships with them built on loyalty, trust and commitment. Ultimately, it is these hard to define, and even harder to measure, intangible qualities that represent brand equity.

To summarise it is much less expensive to retain a customer than it is to attract or create a new one – as a rule of thumb the ratio is 1:5 in favour of maintaining loyal customers. Second, loyal customers are much more likely to recommend preferred brands to others. Such positive **word of mouth** is equivalent to owning a force of unpaid salesmen. Third, loyal customers are much more resistant to change than dissatisfied ones. This means that when the brand is threatened by innovation and competition its owner has a breathing space in which to react to the competitive threat and counter it. Put into numbers, it has been found that (Davis):

- 72% of customers will pay a 20% premium for their preferred brand
- 50% will pay 25%
- 40% will pay 30%
- 25% say that price doesn't matter
- Over 70% use brands to guide a buying decision
- And 50% are brand driven

It is for these reasons that branding guru David Aaker argues that customer loyalty requires constant attention and management to sustain it. He recommends "Do the little things, stay close to the customer, measure satisfaction, create switching costs, provide extras and, in general, over-invest in your customer".

CUSTOMER RELATIONSHIP MANAGEMENT

In recent years **Relationship Marketing (RM)** has become one of the most fashionable management concepts. Unhappily, like the marketing mix model that preceded it, RM is regarded primarily as a tool for increasing the sellers profits through the development of so-called loyalty schemes and a variety of techniques known generically as '**customer relationship management**' or **CRM**. Given its close association with the concept of loyalty the most logical place to outline this phenomenon is in this chapter on branding.

As will become clear, my own view is that CRM runs counter to the true marketing concept and its guiding principle, that is mutual benefit and satisfaction. A major problem is that while the noun 'relationship' is itself value free most individuals interpret the word to imply a degree of intimacy of the kind experienced in interpersonal relationships. Extensive research has shown that in many everyday transactions almost the last thing the customer wants is a 'relationship' with the seller. Further, attempts to establish this may actually reduce the satisfaction experienced by the customer. It is for this reason that we propose a return to first principles and an emphasis on customer satisfaction management.

Ever since Ted Levitt (1960) published his seminal *Marketing Myopia* it has been widely accepted that the role of marketing is to help to solve the central economic problem of maximising satisfaction from the consumption of scarce resources. Three elements comprise this objective. First, there is the desire to maximise satisfaction. Second, there is the notion of 'scarce resources' and, third there is the concept of consumption.

If we are to maximise satisfaction then we need to establish whose satisfaction we are concerned with, and how we will know when we are maximising it. The answer to the first question must be 'the final consumer', and this belief underpins the very existence of free market economies. Only by allowing individuals to express their preferences through freedom of choice in a competitive market can resources be diverted and applied to maximising what constitutes 'satisfaction' for the consumer. Further, at any given point in time, aggregate consumption must reflect what consumers consider to be maximum satisfaction in terms of the assortment of goods and services available to them.

This latter qualification is of profound importance. Marketers have the ambition to exceed the objective of the economist. Their aim in life is to optimise satisfaction. Only if all consumers expressed themselves as being totally satisfied with every single item they are consuming could we claim to be optimising satisfaction. Even the most cursory inquiry would confirm that we are not. Thus the objective with marketing is to establish a dialogue with the consumer in order to add value to goods and services by tailoring them more precisely to their specific needs and wants. In other words, what distinguishes marketing from economics is a desire to look beyond the idea of homogeneous, aggregated demand and define satisfaction in terms of the individual's personal preferences.

In reality, even marketers have to recognise that it will not be possible to adapt every product to the precise needs of the potential buyer. Nonetheless, through continuous marketing research, careful segmentation, targeting and positioning effective marketers can add value for their prospective customers and, in the process, consolidate their competitive position and profitability.

Put another way true marketing begins and ends with the customer. It is their satisfaction that we are seeking to optimise so it follows that our first task must be to establish how to define this in any given situation. Clearly, considerable effort is already given to this, and many would argue that the practitioner both understands and is seeking to implement this central tenet of the marketing concept.

While this is the intention it is our belief that the reality is quite different. If we consider the curricula of marketing courses or the contents of leading textbooks such as Philip Kotler's Marketing Management: Analysis, Planning, Implementation and Control it is quite clear that their purpose is to manipulate demand to absorb the available supply. In other words what, for the past 50 years has been passed off as a 'marketing orientation' has, in reality, been a sales orientation. If it were otherwise there would be no need for regulatory legislation, or the green and consumerist movements. In our view much that is presented as 'relationship marketing' is simply an extension of the sellers desire to maintain control over buyers rather than enter into a true partnership with them. A focus on customer satisfaction would do much to achieve this and, in our view, would yield disproportionate returns for sellers adopting this approach.

It is not without significance that the current interest in and emphasis upon 'relationship marketing' occurred at a time when the practice and relevance of marketing was being widely questioned. The need for a restatement of the nature and purpose of the discipline was summarised potently in a highly influential and seminal article in the *Journal of Marketing* (1992) by Fred Webster entitled 'The Changing Face of Marketing in the Corporation'. We believe it was this article more than anything which resulted in the current enthusiasm for RM.

For many, Webster's article was seen as revolutionary and a much needed restatement of the marketing concept. Consumer marketing had lost its way and RM offered the road to redemption and a return to grace. That Webster should have been the author of such a clarion call is unsurprising given that in an earlier incarnation he had been a doyen of the less fashionable branch of marketing identified as 'industrial'. (Also now converted to the more modish 'business to business' marketing!).

Now industrial marketing had suffered a similar crisis of confidence 20 years earlier in the 1960s. While firms manufacturing consumer goods were posting record results those making industrial goods were struggling to earn an acceptable return. The essence of this crisis and its consequences are described eloquently in an article that appeared in the *Harvard Business Review* in 1970 – 'Trappings versus Substance in Industrial Marketing' by B. Charles Ames. In this article Ames' argues that industrial producers had correctly attributed the better performance of consumer goods firms to their adoption of a marketing orientation but had mistaken the 'trappings' of marketing – advertising, publicity, promotion etc. – for its 'substance' – the use of market research to establish the true nature of consumer needs and the design and development of products to satisfy these. As a result their attempts to become marketing orientated were doomed to failure.

Of course, the generalisation that, overall, consumer goods firms were performing better than those serving industrial markets disguised the reality that, in the particular, some industrial firms were performing very well. With hindsight we can see that consumer goods firms were experiencing an unprecedented boom with rapidly expanding markets, while the impact of accelerating technology and global competition was weeding out the weaker performers in the industrial sector. No amount of trappings was going to save them! In the 1990s marketing's 'mid-life crisis' was precipitated by similar problems of over capacity and increased global competition. Webster correctly diagnosed this and proposed that if consumer marketers were to recover the situation they must redefine and implement the true marketing concept.

Now, in industrial markets, relationships have always played a significant role in influencing performance and determining success and failure. It is through close relationships that sellers identify the precise needs of their customers in terms of both product specifications/prices and the ancillary services looked for by them. In the final analysis it is only the relationship that enables a buyer to discriminate between closely matched suppliers and prefer one to another. But conditions in industrial markets differ markedly from most consumer markets, if for no other reason than that there are far fewer players and that there is less variability in the objective characteristics of product offerings. In consumer markets it is not clear that it is either possible or desirable to try and develop the close interpersonal relationships that constitute the just noticeable difference in business to business markets. Nonetheless, customer relationship management has become a pre-occupation with many marketers.

A great deal of research has clearly shown that in many consumer markets the customers are NOT looking for relationships with suppliers. Indeed, if we revert to Copeland's (1923) original classification of goods as Convenience, Shopping and Specialty then we can see that the buyers wish for involvement with the seller – a 'relationship' - runs from virtually none to very close. In our view this is equally true of both business and consumer markets. Thus the 'relationship' does not provide a common thread for the design of effective marketing strategies. By contrast, 'satisfaction' is a fundamental component of all exchange and so offers a much more robust common factor around which to develop theory and practice. It is for this reason that we eschew the idea of Customer Relationship Management and propose that the focus should be on Customer Satisfaction Management - CSM

Customer relationship management is really a contradiction in terms – probably the quickest way to destroy a relationship is to try and manage it. What is meant by what we prefer to call CSM is paying careful attention to the customers needs to ensure they are receiving the satisfaction looked for so that they will automatically think of a preferred supplier and develop a loyalty for them. And it is the statistics of customer loyalty spelled out earlier in this chapter that have driven the growth of CRM/CSM.

In effect CRM/CSM means implementing the marketing concept, and what distinguishes it from earlier efforts to do this is the availability of much more and better information, and the tools to process it. Aspects of this occur at various places in the text, e.g. tracking the contents of the consumers shopping trolley at the supermarket checkout and relating these to the details held in the store's loyalty card scheme; market segmentation using geo-demographics; database management in direct marketing etc.

PRIVATE BRANDS

Increased competition at the retail level has prompted many retailers and wholesalers to develop 'own', or 'private', brands which are sold in competition

PRIVATE LABEL BRANDS

Sales of many major consumer branded goods have been declining over the past two years in Europe, including Unilever, Nescafe (including bottled waters such as Perrier and Vittel down 8.4%), Danone and L'Oreal, as a result of competition from private label brands offered by major retail chains. In the UK private-label accounted for approximately 38% of all sales of food and other fmcg, 30% in Germany, 25% in Spain, 22% in France and around 16% in the USA.

The growth of private label has been driven by the need for the longer established groups like Carrefour to meet competition from discounters such as Aldi Group (Germany) and Leader Price (France) which are almost entirely private label selling for 20% to 40% less than manufacturers brands. Given that it is widely known that firms like Nestlé, Cadbury Schweppes and Heinz already sell private-label versions of their products, many consumers are at least willing to try the lower cost alternatives. Where they find them satisfactory then the attraction of much lower prices is a strong incentive to switch.

For major manufacturers the options seem to be either to flex their muscles and discount heavily, as P&G has done with its Pampers brand of disposable diapers, or do a deal with the major discounters to get shelf space in their outlets and maintain or increase volume. Either way, given the growing power of the retailer, it seems clear that the manufacturers will have to be even more innovative and creative in their marketing if they are to resist the challenge of the growing number of specialist suppliers catering for the private-label market.

(Based on an article in *Business Week*, March 21 2005)

with the manufacturers' brands. (The latter are often termed 'national brands' as they are usually promoted on a national basis.) By avoiding the promotional expenditures necessary to maintain a national brand, private brands can be offered at a lower price, and are widely used in building store 'traffic'; that is, to induce price-conscious shoppers to come into the store in the hope that they will make other purchases.

In many instances private brands are identical with the better-known national brands and, in fact, are produced by the same manufacturers. The use of a second brand allows the manufacturer to sell off their excess production at a lower price than that asked for the major, promoted brand. Naturally, few manufacturers are willing to admit that they are practising this form of price discrimination, and the origin of such private label brands is usually a closely guarded secret. For the price conscious shopper, private brands offer considerable savings, and are perceived as of equivalent quality to the better-known national brands. However, most consumers prefer the national brands with which they are familiar, and from which they derive additional satisfactions. Whether these arise out of associations built up by advertising, or represent real differences in quality, which is often the case (for example washing-up liquids), is largely irrelevant, for the final choice rests with the consumers who will optimise their own choice criteria.

POSITIONING

The notion of positioning was introduced briefly in Chapter 10 when looking at market segmentation. As we saw, market segmentation enables one to identify groups of customers who exhibit similar buying behaviour and, at the same time, are different from other identifiable groups or segments. However, for a market segment to be attractive it must be of sufficient size to make it worthwhile to develop a product or service especially for it, and this usually means that more than one firm will wish to target that segment. So, if we are to succeed in competition with these other firms, it is essential that intending buyers can distinguish our offerings from those of other sellers and, more important, that they will perceive our offering as superior to all others. Given the difficulty of sustaining objective differences between competing products, branding – the establishment of an unique identity – has become the main basis for competition. However, to compete through branding, one must still establish a position in the customers mind that enables them to distinguish your brand from all the others.

According to Hooley et al. four conditions need to be satisfied to achieve this:

1 You must have a clear view of the target market and the characteristics of the particular customers you are aiming for.
2 The benefits on which the positioning is built must be important to the targeted customers.
3 The chosen positioning must be based on the real strengths of the company and be sustainable against attack from competitors
4 You must be able to communicate the positioning in clear and unambiguous terms to the intended audience.

Davis (2002) cites *five* principles for effective positioning:

1 *Value* - focus on the perceived benefits that customers value, as determined by your research.

2 *Uniqueness* - go where the competitors are not.

3 *Credibility* - get a credible fit between who you are and the persona of the supplier defined by your search

4 *Sustainability* - select a position which you can defend and take ownership of.

5 *Fit* - ensure the position builds on your perceived strengths

If one is to satisfy these conditions one must have a comprehensive understanding of the markets in which you wish to compete derived from marketing research of the kind considered in Chapter 11. As a minimum we need to know:

1 *What need does the product satisfy?* To begin with we may define this at the generic level as recommended by Levitt in *Marketing Myopia* e.g. transportation, energy, hunger, thirst etc. Next we need to define the product category: cars, buses, trains aeroplanes etc. and then the product form e.g. family saloon cars when we would be looking at all the models of cars meeting that definition.

2 *How do buyers choose between available alternatives?* i.e. what attributes and features do customers look for and use in comparing alternatives?

3 *How important are the different features?* To evaluate this we will need to develop a Factor Rating Table.

4 *How do the competing products compare with one another on the most important attributes?* This analysis will combine both objective factors – attributes and features – and subjective ones – the benefits customers are looking for.

5 *What would prospective buyers define as an ideal product and how do those available compare with this description?*

Once we have gathered this information the next step would be to develop a perceptual map of the kind proposed in Chapter 8 (Individual Buyer Behaviour). The limitation of such maps is that they are two dimensional and so a very simplified representation of a complex reality. Their principal advantage is that we can visualise how the competing brands compare with one another in terms of the properties or dimensions we use. Given that disposable income is a major determinant of what we can afford to pay, price is a major consideration in any buying decision and seen as an objective measure of what a product is 'worth' to us. But the concept of worth also includes our perception of value and this, as we have seen in many examples, is subjective to the intending buyer. One way of thinking about worth is in terms of quality and there is a clearly established relationship between people's perceptions of these two parameters. Some years ago I wrote an article for the Unilever in-house magazine in which I suggested how 'Baker's Box' could be used to make positioning decisions. In *Marketing Strategy and Management* (2000) this is described as follows.

Figure 14.3 Two-dimensional map

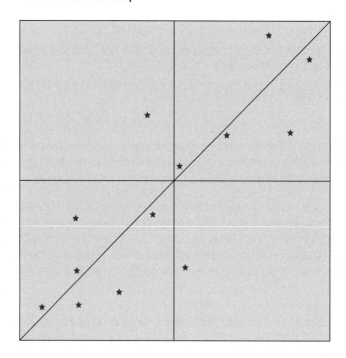

Figure 14.4 Two-dimensional perceptual map

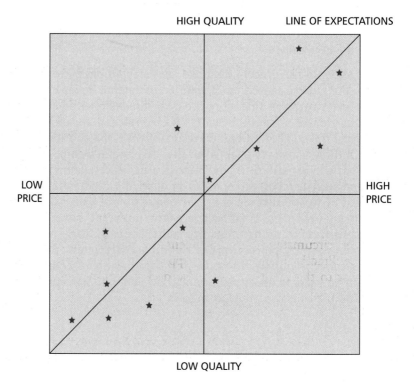

BAKER'S BOX

It is against this background that we propose Baker's Box as a diagnostic tool for capturing executive opinion on competitive positioning within a market as the basis for developing more effective marketing strategies.

In developing a competitive strategy it is vital to establish the criteria used by customers in making purchase decisions. One must also determine how the competing players seek to differentiate themselves from one another while still meeting the customer's needs. In other words, how do competitors position themselves in the market? Perceptual mapping is a method which allows one to capture both a firm's perceived performance as well as its relationship to competitive offerings. Baker's Box is based on this method.

As originally conceived perceptual mapping is a sophisticated quantitative procedure designed to overcome the problems of getting consumers to explain their evaluation and choice behaviour directly. A variety of research techniques may be used in perceptual mapping of which the most popular is multidimensional scaling (MDS). Based upon respondents' rating of the degree of similarity between alternatives 2 at a time using rating scales ranging from 'highly similar' to 'highly dissimilar' a computer based program generates a 2-dimensional map similar to that shown in Figure 14.3.

As generated there are no labels on the axes and the analyst has to infer these based on the amount of variance explained by the ratings of different parameters. Usually the 2 parameters which emerge reflect cost benefit or price quality relationships and in Figure 14.4 we have inserted these labels together with a line of best fit of the observations which we have designated 'the line of expectations'. We have also enclosed the space to create a 2x2 matrix.

The basic 'box'

On the grounds that objects (products or services) which exceed expectations have added value then those above the line will be preferred over those below the line which do not meet expectations. However, while price is essentially uni-dimensional, quality is multidimensional. It follows that in order to interpret and understand the positioning of the objects, and the basis of differentiation between them, one needs to know what factors constitute 'quality' in this market and their perceived salience. In mature markets with relatively stable market shares the identification and measurement of differentiating factors using techniques such as MDS is usually feasible – but expensive! In emerging and growth markets, where competition is more dynamic, formal measurement may not be possible or be of little value due to rapidly changing tactics.

Under the latter circumstances a judgemental approach drawing on the experience of those directly involved may be appropriate. If so then we need a basic matrix, similar to the DPM, in which the decision-makers can plot their judgement. The Basic Box illustrated in Figure 14.4 provides this. By introducing 2 further concepts of credibility and gullibility the diagnostic power may be significantly improved.

Credibility and gullibility are derivatives of knowledge, or expertise, allied to objectivity, and represent the boundaries of belief with expectations lying between

Figure 14.5 The zone of expectations

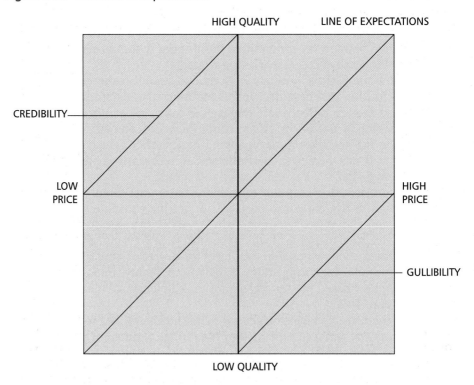

Figure 14.6 Positions and perceptions

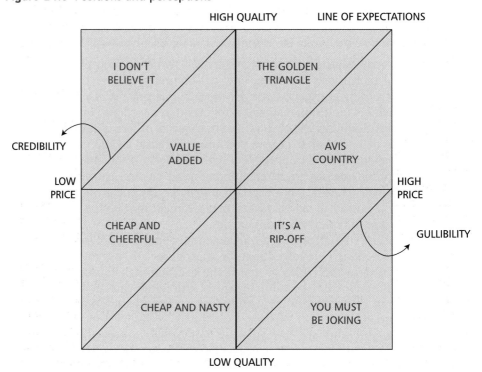

the 2 states. 'Expectation' reflects what the person with average knowledge/ expertise would regard as likely – 'You get what you pay for'. Anything which exceeds this will have added value and be preferred – but only up to a point which represents the bounds of credibility. Beyond this point potential buyers will perceive a risk which they are unwilling to take – 'There must be a catch somewhere!' Hyundai experienced this effect in 1995 when their mid-range saloon was priced at £4000–£5000 less than leading brands such as Toyota while claiming comparable quality and performance.

Persons with less than average knowledge and expertise, or who allow subjective factors to influence their judgement (I like the colour of Lada cars), exhibit a degree of gullibility. But, like credibility, there is a limit to most people's gullibility and beyond a certain point even disadvantaged consumers will refuse to buy.

In Figure 14.5 we have inserted lines parallel to expectations, representing credibility and gullibility thus creating an octet of positions.

In our experience working with executives, most people find it relatively easy to visualise where they and their principal competitors fit in such a 2-dimensional space. Following the procedure described earlier for operationalising the DPM, those responsible for developing and implementing product or brand strategy can quickly download and share their personal views. (Using transparent film and overlaying the individual plots enables one quickly to identify points of agreement and disagreement.) Once one has defined the location of the various competitive brands relative to one another, the next step is to diagnose what factors underlie or contribute to these distinctive positions, that is what are the critical success factors which combine to deliver 'quality' or 'performance'? Once the individual factors have been identified separate perceptual maps can be drawn using each of these to represent the vertical axis.

To complete the diagnosis, in Figure 14.6 we have inserted labels to describe each of the 8 possible positions. These labels are self-explanatory and may help in making initial judgements as to where to place an object as well as deciding on the strategy to be followed to either sustain or improve one's position. The implications are obvious.

First, the basic proposition must be believable otherwise you will find yourself outwith the purchase zone.

Second, if you exceed expectations you can anticipate growth and profitability and vice-versa.

Third, cheap and cheerful, value added and the golden triangle are distinct segments which reflect the logic of downward sloping demand curves in terms of salience and disposable income.

Fourth, no position is permanent. Since the end of the Second World War Japan has moved from cheap and nasty to cheap and cheerful to value added into the golden triangle. With increased price competition it may now be moving into Avis country.

In conclusion, Baker's Box is intended as a diagnostic tool to aid managerial thinking. Its objective is to help focus and structure your judgement as to where you and your competitors currently are. Once this has been established and been agreed on it is possible to decide whether one is content with the current position, and so wish to reinforce and hold it; sees advantage in attacking a new position or might want to consider withdrawal and a completely new approach. Given the strategic implications one can then concentrate resources – time and money – in a more detailed analysis of the specific issues relevant to one's chosen strategy.

To familiarise decision-makers with using the technique, and so focus on process rather than opinion (and emotion), in the first instance it might be helpful to have a trial run using a product or service outwith the firm's current range. Publications of the Economist Intelligence Unit, Keynote, and so on will provide most of the factual data needed to initiate discussion on objects – cars, instant coffee, beer – which are familiar to participants as consumers and about which they will have formed perceptions and attitudes. Once familiar with the technique, and having agreed the ground rules, a real-time analysis should yield worthwhile results.

Obviously, a diagnostic of this kind can only be as good as the basic information used to position the competing brands within the matrix. That said, constructing a perceptual map of this kind is an excellent starting point for making positioning decisions.

MICROSOFT TABLET PC

In 2002 Bill Gates of Microsoft launched their new Tablet PC with a confident prediction that sales would soon be in their millions. Two years later, in the Autumn of 2004, they were still numbered in the hundreds of thousands. Writing in *Business Week* (September 27th 2004) Stephen Wildstrom identified a number of reasons why the take –up had been slower than predicted. The most important was that it had been positioned incorrectly in the marketplace.

In his view "The Tablet's greatest potential lies in its ability to perform feats that cannot be done by typing on conventional laptops" such as entering mathematical notations or creating complex freehand drawings. However, Microsoft launched the product as a way to take notes on a screen when "Paper and pen are perfectly good for that". Not only that, the original software still required the user to tap out letters on an on-screen keyboard which rather limited its functionality as a substitute for pen and paper. While improved software has overcome this weakness it still is not seen as the best use for a product that weighs 3 pounds, gets hot and has a battery life of only four hours.

The question remains "Would the Tablet PC have chalked up more sales more quickly if it had been targeted at the right end-use market in the first place?"

Summary

In this chapter we have seen that strong brands:

1 Are easily recognised and distinguished from competing products
2 Communicate unique values
3 Encourage trust and commitment
4 Leading to loyalty and repeat purchase
5 Command premium prices and higher margins
6 Resulting in stakeholder equity and value
7 Facilitate the introduction of new products.

To begin with we looked at the history of branding and noted that the practice dates back to antiquity. We established that a brand may be a name, a term, sign, symbol, design or combination of these which enable sellers and buyers to identify and differentiate products (and services).

Originally, branding was used primarily as a guarantee of the source and the authenticity of the product. With the Industrial Revolution , and the advent of mass production, the ability of the brand to differentiate between the near homogeneous outputs of different manufacturers was added to these functions and has become the primary role of branding today.

A major advantage of a brand is that it is not as susceptible to life cycle effects in the same way that products are. Thus, over time, the producer may radically change the configuration of the product but still retain the buyer's loyalty – an effect that has given rise to the notion of brand equity. Brand equity is derived from the brand's identity which, paradoxically, reflects both sameness and uniqueness. Uniqueness which distinguishes it from competitors ,and sameness which is a guarantee of consistency and delivered satisfactions.

Different perspective of identity as a product, person, symbol or organisation were explored and related to the development of a brand strategy. This led to a discussion of issues associated with the measurement of brand equity and the need for marketing metrics and a brief look at private brands.

Finally, we re-visited the concept of positioning and the need for sellers to be able distinguish themselves from close rivals. To do so we recommended the use of perceptual mapping and illustrated this with Baker's Box, a diagnostic developed to explain the technique to brand managers in Unilever.

Review questions and problems

1 Describe the origins of branding and explain how these relate to modern practice.

2 It is said that 'identity' has two diametrically opposed meanings of 'sameness' and 'uniqueness'. How can these different attributes be reconciled in explaining the nature of Brand Identity?

3 Aaker (1996) identifies four key elements that comprise Brand Identity. What are these and what 'traps' must one avoid in developing them?

4 Outline the main factors to be taken into account when developing a brand strategy.

5 What do you understand by the term 'brand stretching'? Give examples of the practice in three product categories of your choice.

6 Develop a definition of 'Brand Equity' accounting for the different attributes and characteristics included in your definition.

7 What are marketing metrics? Identify some metrics you might use for monitoring the performance of a fast moving consumer good; a range of earth moving equipment.

8 Discuss the view that customer relationship management should really be customer satisfaction management.

9 Explain the difference between 'trappings' and 'substance' in modern marketing practice. In what sense might a brand be regarded as either one or the other?

10 What is positioning and what role do brands have to play in this practice?

Key terms

Baker's box
brand
brand equity
brand extension
brand identity
brand image
brand position
brand stretching
branding
branding strategy
core identity
corporate identity
customer relationship
    management (CRM)

customer satisfaction
    management (CSM)
differentiation
evoked set
extended identity
external perspective
goodwill
identification
identity
line extension
loyalty
metrics
multibrands
persona

personality
positioning
private brands
product brands
product scope
product-attribute-fixation
relationship marketing
sameness
symbolism
trademark
umbrella brands
uniqueness
value proposition
word of mouth

Supplementary reading list

Aaker, D. (1996), *Building Strong Brands*, (New York: The Free Press)

Aaker, D. and Joachimsthaler, E. (2000), Brand Leadership, (New York: The Free Press)

Ambler, T. and Kokkinaki, F. (1999), 'The assessment of marketing performance', in Baker, M.J. (ed.) *IEBM Encyclopedia of Marketing*, (London: Thomson Learning).

Davis, S. M. (2002), *Brand Asset Management*, (San Francisco, CA: Jossey-Bass)

Hooley, G.J., Saunders, J.A. and Piercy, N.F. (2004) *Marketing Strategy and Competitive Positioning*, 3rd. Edition (Harlow: Pearson Education Limited)

Reichheld, F. F. (1996), *The Loyalty Effect*, (Boston, MA: Harvard Business School Press)

Reichheld, F. F. (Ed.), (1996), *The Quest for Loyalty*, A Harvard Business Review Book, (Boston, MA: Harvard Business School Press)

Sherrington, M. (1999), 'Branding and Brand Management', in Baker, M.J. (ed.) *IEBM Encyclopedia of Marketing*, (London: Thomson Learning).

PRICING AND PRICE POLICY

15

Learning Goals *After reading this chapter you should be able to:*

- Explain why pricing has often been relegated to a secondary role in competitive strategy and the marketing mix.

- Identify some reasons why pricing may receive more attention in the coming decade.

- Describe and analyse the influence and impact of both internal and external factors on price determination.

- Discuss pricing objectives.

- Understand price 'formulas' or methods, and give their advantages and disadvantages.

- Explain the two main pricing alternatives, and suggest where each would be used.

- List pricing strategies used in practice and give some reasons for their use.

- Identify the influence of perception on the pricing decisions of both buyers and sellers.

- Consider and evaluate a dynamic model of pricing behaviour.

INTRODUCTION

The importance of price has been a constant, albeit implicit theme of every aspect of marketing discussed so far. Price is the basis of every transaction and at the heart of the exchange process. For the seller it determines the revenues they will receive in exchange for their goods and services. Only if these revenues exceed their costs will they survive. For buyers it reflects the expected satisfaction to be gained, which must be at least equal to that that would be gained by spending the same amount of money on any other good or service. For both parties price is an objective, quantifiable and easily understood amount, usually expressed in monetary terms. However, while sellers tend to think more of price in terms of its objective nature based on costs, buyers are more concerned with the subjective nature of value in terms of the benefits they will gain from a purchase. So, while money is a store of value for both parties, the buyer's perception of price in terms of value varies from individual to individual and over time

It is this difference that has led to major differences of opinion between academics and practitioners about the role and management of pricing. While there is a long tradition of research into the role of price, especially in economics, few of the findings appear to have been incorporated into managerial practice. In *The Marketing Book* (2003) Diamantopoulos summarises some of the reasons why this is so.

To begin with the theorists emphasise models of pricing many of which are based on complex mathematical modelling in which elegance triumphs over realism. As a consequence these models are difficult to understand and lacking in operational rules to be followed. "Second, the priorities of managers and the research interests of academics in the pricing field have not always (or even mostly) coincided." In part this may be attributed to the fact that practitioners are loathe to share their experience with academics so that the researchers lack empirical data on which to base their theories. Another reason is that the kinds of comprehensive analysis commended by the theorists call for the collection and processing of huge amounts of data. Assuming that this is possible, there is evidence to suggest that many firms do not consider it to be worth the effort and so continue to use rules of thumb based on their cost structure.

As we saw in Chapter 3 when discussing Demand and Supply, price is the mechanism which ensures that the two forces are in equilibrium. In other words, if demand exceeds supply then the price will rise to the point where the volume demanded by those willing and able to pay that price is equivalent to the volume available. Conversely, if supply exceeds demand then prices will fall until sufficient new buyers have entered the market to ensure the consumption of the available supply. Thus it is the price mechanism which determines whether firms will wish to enter or leave a given market because of the returns which may be earned on a given investment of resources. It follows that, if all markets were perfect and infinitely flexible, then the return on investment would be the same in them all.

Of course these conditions do not prevail, and the aim of the investor/entrepreneur is to get out of industries where returns are falling and into those where they are rising – usually because demand exceeds supply. But what will happen if the overall capacity to supply exceeds the overall capacity to consume? The answer is obvious – in the short run, factors of production will be surplus to requirements and become idle, as happened during the recessions in Britain in the 1980s and 1990s where over 2 million people were unemployed. During a recession, and in the short-to-medium term at the microeconomic or firm level, the emphasis is more than ever on survival and the need to ensure that revenues, which depend upon the volume sold and the price earned, exceed the costs of producing, distributing and selling that volume. Clearly, costs and prices must be primary considerations in the development of a marketing strategy.

The present propensity to produce more than we can consume is not entirely new, for as we saw in the opening chapter, it was the threat of such a situation at the beginning of the last century which led to the 'rediscovery' of the marketing concept. It also led to the emergence of product differentiation supported by promotional effort as the preferred competitive strategy. Foremost among the reasons for this change of emphasis from a concern with producing the largest volume at the lowest cost, was recognition of the fact that if products are perceived as homogeneous then consumers will prefer the lower-priced offering, and that economies of scale will invariably mean that the firm with the largest output will have the lowest costs and so be able to undercut its rivals. More correctly, it is the firm with the largest market share which will enjoy the maximum benefits of the scale and experience effects and it will use its cost advantage to maximise its returns and/or dominate its immediate competitors. In such a situation the firm with a lesser market share either has to accept the going market price, or it can seek to position its product in such a way that it will be perceived as different by a sufficient number of customers so that in effect it will have its own little monopoly and can charge a differentiated price (hence, monopolistic competition).

It is for these reasons that while price occupies a central role in economic theory, in marketing it tends to be relegated to a secondary role and much more attention is given to other elements of competitive strategy and the marketing mix. This is born out by the findings of numerous surveys. For example, during 1990 Cath Byrne of Strathclyde University undertook a survey in several European Countries on behalf of Honeywell Ltd in which she asked respondents to identify their key purchasing criteria. The results were as follows:

Key factors: Technical ability, quality.
Very important: Flexibility, reliability, delivery, scheduling, ordering convenience.
Important: Price, personal contact, service.
Quite important: Reputation, innovations, after-sales service, previous contact.
Not at all important: Image, location, payment terms, salesmen.

Similarly Ughanwa and Baker (1989, p. 84) *The Role of Design in International Competitiveness*, found price ranked third out of 16 critical success factors behind 'Performance in operation' and 'Reliability'. Results such as these may be accounted for by one or more of the following reasons:

1 Perfect competition prevails. Under these circumstances the firm cannot have a 'price policy', it must accept the market price.

2 Under conditions of imperfect competition there is a tendency towards rigid prices', and for competition to be concentrated on non-price elements such as product differentiation, advertising, service, and so on. Thus competitors prefer to avoid direct price competition, which could lead to a price war, and adopt the price level of the industry leader.

3 The construction of a demand schedule is considered impossible owing to the enormous number of interacting variables which condition consumer preference. Even if it were possible to quantify demand at various price levels the value of the information would not justify its cost, thus a trial and error approach, or acceptance of the 'going rate', is to be preferred.

4 Marketers lack an adequate understanding of the theoretical concepts and so avoid the complexities involved in developing a 'scientific' price policy.

In every field of marketing activity the suppliers emphasis upon new product development and differentiation confirms their reluctance to compete on price alone. That said it is clear that no seller can ignore the price dimension, albeit that, as the **composite model of buyer behaviour** proposed in Chapter 8 indicates, consumers will place more emphasis upon fitness for purpose in short-listing products for possible purchase. The more similar the products the more important price will be in determining the final choice, and only if both product and price are very similar indeed will the subjective association created by promotion have a significant influence on that decision. The paradox is, therefore, that while price may not be the most important element in competitive strategy, and receives comparatively little attention in the marketing literature, it can never be far from the strategists' thoughts. In other words, a competitive price is a necessary but not sufficient condition for marketing success. Further, in the short term, price may be the most effective tactical weapon, as we shall see later in this chapter and also when considering the role of sales promotion particularly in a highly competitive and/or recessionary environment.

A survey published in *Marketing News* (1986) and reproduced as Table 15.1 compares the perceived importance, or 'pressure', in various aspects of marketing compared with the findings for Europe revealed by a survey by Hermann Simon. Commenting on the data Simon suggests a number of reasons why the significance of price has increased in recent years which may be summarised as follows:

1 High inflation rates have led to higher price consciousness.
2 Stagnating or declining real incomes have induced consumers to switch to cheaper products.
3 Increased competitive pressure (and the difficulty of sustaining an advantage through differentiation) has enhanced the role of price particularly in industrial markets.
4 Aggressive pricing is a major competitive weapon in buyers' markets as suppliers seek to maintain market share.
5 New competitors use aggressive pricing strategies to break into markets and secure a foothold, for example Japan, Korea.
6 Consumerism and legislation on competition have resulted in greater market and price transparency and encouraged buyers to compare price and quality more systematically.

More recent evidence is not as detailed as that reported in the preceding studies undertaken in the 1980s. However, such evidence as there is underlines the conclusions of both Said and Simon that, under conditions of excess supply or depressed demand (**recession**), competition intensifies and price assumes increased importance as a competitive weapon. Indeed, there is much anecdotal evidence to suggest that sellers' continued use of price as a major marketing factor has resulted in a situation where consumers give it much more attention than hitherto and believe that further discounts or price cuts will always be forth-coming. In other words, current practice has led to a situation which could be characterised as 'cutting your competitor's throat and bleeding to death yourself'. The inevitable consequence (as predicted by **economic theory**) is that the least efficient and least effective producers will go to the wall.

The rapid growth of the emerging economies of South East Asia, and particularly China and India, has been largely based on their low labour costs and highly competitive prices. The result has been a declining importance in manufacturing

"THE CHINA PRICE"

According to a feature length article in *Business Week* (December 6, 2004) these "are the three scariest words in U.S. industry. In general, it means 30% to 50% less than what you can possibly make something for in the U.S. In the worst cases, it means below your cost of materials. Makers of apparel, footware, electric appliances, and plastics products, which have been shutting U.S. factories for decades, know well the futility of trying to match the China price. It has been a big factor in the loss of 2.7 million manufacturing jobs since 2000".

While the U.S. has survived waves of cheap imports from low cost countries in the past, what makes the current threat far more serious is that China is not only a low labour cost economy, it is also a high tech one. But, while the multinationals may outsource components and hardware from China or even relocate their manufacturing facilities there, the same opportunities are not available to the small to medium sized enterprises that make up more than a third of U.S. manufacturing, and it is they that are going out of business.

Among the examples quoted are moulds for manufacturing home appliances where the China price gap was 50%; crepe paper 45%; bedroom furniture 40%; LCD TV 30% and networking equipment 25%.

Given the size of its domestic market, its investment in innovation and education, and the fact 70% of its exports are from privately owned companies it seems unlikely that competition from China will go away.

Table 15.1 'Pressure' in various marketing areas as perceived by managers

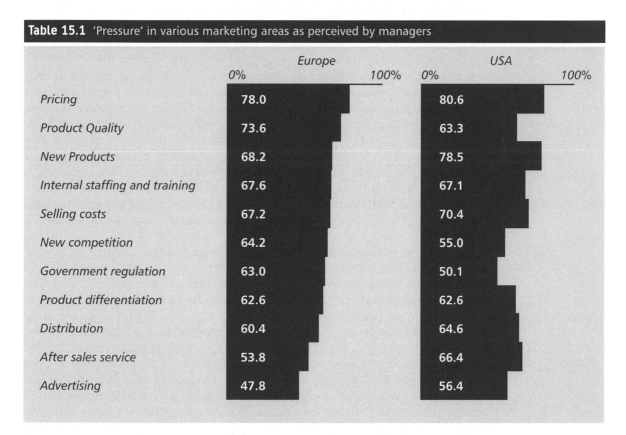

	Europe	USA
	0% — 100%	0% — 100%
Pricing	78.0	80.6
Product Quality	73.6	63.3
New Products	68.2	78.5
Internal staffing and training	67.6	67.1
Selling costs	67.2	70.4
New competition	64.2	55.0
Government regulation	63.0	50.1
Product differentiation	62.6	62.6
Distribution	60.4	64.6
After sales service	53.8	66.4
Advertising	47.8	56.4

Sources: USA, *Marketing News*, 11 June 1986, p.1; Europe, Author's study 1986

in the original industrialised economies of the West where it now accounts for less than 20% of GDP, the rest being accounted for by services. This trend has also been accelerated by the growing power of retailers, many of whom stress competitive prices as a major element of their overall strategy.

In this chapter we look first at the importance of the **pricing decision** and the **external** and **internal factors** that influence it. Next we explore the **objectives** that sellers seek to achieve through their **pricing strategy** and then contrast this with **how customers perceive price** and how it influences their **buying decisions**. Next, we consider the actual **pricing strategies** used and the **methods** employed in implementing them. Finally, we consider the role of **competitive bidding** in organisational markets and conclude with some suggestions to improve pricing decisions in practice.

EXTERNAL PRICE DETERMINANTS

A major determinant of price policy is the structure of the market in which the firm is selling its output. Many authors tend to confuse **industry structure** with **market structure**, and limit their attention to the size and number of firms engaged in creating perfect substitutes. Thus it is common to find references to monopolistic and oligopolistic industries when the total output of a given product is concentrated in the hands of one, or a few, firms. Although it is acknowledged that the true monopolist is a price-maker, and that oligopolistic industries frequently exhibit price rigidity owing to the price leadership of a dominant firm, it is felt that the industry view oversimplifies the true situation.

Conventionally, the industry approach would distinguish the manufacture of aluminium, steel, glass, paper and plastics on the basis that their output possesses different physical properties and is the result of distinctive production processes. Each would be classified as a separate industry, yet all compete with one another for the packaging market. This suggests that one must take into account not only the prices of perfect substitutes but also the prices of all goods which compete for the same market and can be used to satisfy the same basic wants. Certainly no self-respecting buyer is going to confine their attention to a single material when several acceptable alternatives are available, and the technique of **value analysis** has been developed largely to permit comparative cost analysis of competing substitutes.

If the above arguments are accepted, then it follows that the firm must look beyond the narrowly defined industry of which it considers itself a member, and should evaluate the price structure of its end market and the policies of all firms/industries operating in that market. (In the language of the economist, one must analyse the **cross-elasticity of demand**.)

The second major external price determinant is best summarised by the economist's concept of **elasticity**. As we have seen, elasticity measures the responsiveness of demand to changes in price, i.e. it is a measure of price sensitivity. Thus if a 1 per cent change in price results in a change in the amount demanded of more than 1 percent demand is said to be elastic, if less than 1 percent then demand is inelastic, and a directly proportionate change indicates unitary elasticity. Elasticity of demand is conditioned by the importance of the product in the consumer's scale of preferences, by the disposable income of existing and potential consumers, by the existence of substitutes and a number of other, lesser factors. As a summary measure it is of great value in determining the firm's basic attitude to price – if demand is elastic, pricing will be a major policy area, if inelastic it will be of secondary consequence.

Thirdly, the firm's pricing policy will be influenced by **government policy** as expressed in the extant and proposed legislation in such areas as price maintenance, monopolistic practices, minimum performance standards for products, and so on; for example the introduction of cut-price detergents by Procter & Gamble and Lever Brothers following the Monopolies Commission recommendation to this effect.

INTERNAL PRICE DETERMINANTS

The major factor conditioning the firm's price policy is its own definition of the business it is in, for this will determine the products it will produce and the nature of the markets it will seek to exploit. The **product mix** identifies the firm with an industry, while its market specifies the firms, industries and products with which it will compete, and the dimensions along which it will compete.

Traditionally, the firm's success has been measured by its **profitability**, which is simply a measure of the amount by which income exceeds expenditure. If, as implied earlier, the majority of firms accept the going market price, it is evident that profits will depend very largely on the firm's ability to minimise expenditures or costs. To this end considerable effort has been devoted to the development of sophisticated cost measurement and control systems, and management is often happier to immerse itself in the tangible realities of such systems that grapple with the complexities of price determination. Further, both shareholders and the Government require the firm to account for the way in which it spends its income, and so emphasise the need for detailed cost analyses and statements. As will be seen below, such data are widely used in the formulation of prices.

The third internal constraint on the firm's price policy is the nature and extent of its **corporate resources**, which are discussed in Chapter 21 and will not be reiterated here.

It follows from the brief outline above that the price-setter's discretion is circumscribed by a number of factors, admirably summarised by Joel Dean (1951) as:

1 The number, relative sizes and product lines of competitors who sell products to do the same job.
2 The likelihood of potential competition.
3 The stage of consumer acceptance of the product.
4 The degree of potential market segmentation and price discrimination.
5 The degree of physical difference between the seller's product and those of other companies.
6 The opportunities for variation in the product–service bundle.
7 The richness of the mixture of service and reputation in the product bundle.
   (p. 402)

PERCEPTION AND PRICING

In Chapter 8 we proposed a composite model of buying behaviour which placed considerable emphasis upon the mediating influence of selective perception in determining not only what cues or stimuli are given conscious attention, but also on the interpretation given to the information. It is the phenomenon of selective perception which modifies the strictly economic explanation of the manner in which demand will react to supply at different prices, and so may be seen to contradict the concept of 'economic rationality'. According to the latter concept buyers will always select the supplier offering the lowest price but, in reality, the market for many goods and services will contain a variety of different prices for superficially similar offerings. The explanation is, of course, that even if the offerings are objectively perfect substitutes one for another buyers may perceive them subjectively as being different. Much of the effort of competing suppliers is directed specifically at achieving such perceived differences through the creation of reputation, brand loyalty and the augmentation of the core product.

Simon (1989) devotes a chapter to the subject of 'Price Management and Psychology' and provides a comprehensive summary of the variables which influence price perception and evaluation which is reproduced as Table 15.2. From Table 15.2 it is clear that a multiplicity of factors bear upon the buyers' (both consumer and industrial) perception of price. In addition, their relative influence may well vary from one buying decision to the next as a consequence of changes in the buyers' status and/or the circumstances or context in which the decision has to be made. Thus, while there has been much research which suggests that buyers (particularly individual consumers) have poor price recall, it would be wrong to assume that this reflects price insensitivity, or lack of consideration for price in making a buying decision. Indeed, there is also a considerable body of

Table 15.2 Variables which influence price perception and evaluation

Motivational Variables	Cognitive Variables	Situation Variables

■ personal involvement
■ striving
  - social recognition
  - quality
  - cognitive consistency
  - shopping convenience
  - saving
	■ ability to compare quality
	■ ability to remember and compare prices
	■ experience
	■ trust in the supplier
	■ self-confidence
	■ application of simplified decision rules (brand loyalty, etc.)
		■ way of exhibiting price (form and quality etc.)
		■ mode of payment
		■ time pressure
		■ competitive products and prices
		■ complexity of purchasing task
		■ variability of prices
		■ price labelling
		■ product use
		■ financial situations of buyers
		■ price image of the store

Source: Simon, H. (1989), *Price Management* (Amsterdam: Elsevier Science Publishers)

research which indicates that at the time when a buyer makes a purchase decision they have a good feel for what is available in the market place so that the decision is 'rational' in terms of what the buyer is seeking to optimise at that precise time and in that specific context.

Of particular interest in terms of the psychology of pricing is the case where the price itself becomes of major importance in influencing the prospective buyer's perception of the quality of the offering. Simon provides an excellent overview of the evidence that price is used as an indicator of quality and cites Zeithman's (1988) finding that much of this is contradictory. That said, and despite the lack of much empirical support, Simon (1989) proposes 16 conditions or contexts where 'we expect the phenomenon . . .' to occur, namely:

Conditions under which quality will be inferred from the price.

1 Brand and manufacturer names do not play an important role, for example rugs, furniture.
2 Consumers have little or no experience:
   ■ Because the product is new. Note that the quality indication is effective only if the new product is not a genuine innovation which is beyond the existing reference system.
   ■ Because the purchase interval is long; that is, for infrequently purchased 'low involvement' products.
   ■ Because it is not usual for people to share their experience with the product.
3 Objective quality is difficult to evaluate:
   ■ Because of the technical complexity.
   ■ Because of the particular importance of such attributes as durability, reliability, and so forth.
4 Considerable quality differences are perceived.
5 Price itself is an important product attribute.
   ■ Prestige products (Snob, Veblen effect).
   ■ Use or display of the product are associated with social risk (wine, liquor, cosmetics, fashion products, clothing, gifts, and so on).
6 Absolute price is not too high. For very expensive products, the search for objective quality information can be rewarding. In other words, the reliance on price alone can be costly.

With respect to situational conditions, the role of price as quality indicator is the greater, thus:

7 The greater the time pressure is during the purchase.
8 The more complex the purchase task is.
9 The lower the price transparency is (for example with respect to the variation of prices for the same product).
10 The more the buyer trusts the supplier of the price information.

With respect to personal characteristics, price dependent quality evaluation should be the most important, thus:

11 The less self-confident the buyer is.

12 The less frugal the buyer is.

13 The stronger the desire is to purchase quickly and conveniently.

14 The stronger the desire is to avoid cognitive dissonance.

15 The better the economic situation of the household is.

  16 The less product-related information the buyer has.

The important point to be made here is that if these are widely held expectations (and we believe they are) then they will have an important bearing upon the way in which suppliers set their prices.

In other words, if these '**hypotheses**' reflect the pricing decision maker's perception of the situation then it is this which will govern their pricing decision. Similarly, under the conditions proposed by Simon, it would seem to make a lot of sense for the buyer to use price as an indicator of quality where the opportunity cost of getting better information is very high, together with the perceived risk of making the wrong decision. Hence, while IBM equipment is often 25 per cent more expensive than comparable competitive products there is considerable support for the view that 'Nobody ever got fired for buying IBM'. (You will recall that Baker's Box is based on the assumption that price reflects quality i.e. the 'Line of Expectations', and that customers will perceive products as being above or below that line in terms of the value they receive).

PRICING OBJECTIVES

While there is evidence to suggest that comparatively few manufacturers have clear cut, explicit and written procedures for setting prices, there can be little doubt that firms have one or other of four basic objectives identified by Robert Lanzillotti (1956) in 'Pricing Objectives in Large Companies', based on extensive field research into the subject.

Lanzillotti's findings were: 'The most typical pricing objectives cited were: (1) pricing to achieve a target return on investment; (2) stabilisation of price and margin; (3) pricing to realise a target market share; and (4) pricing to meet or prevent competition.' The main conclusions drawn from this study are considered sufficiently significant to be quoted verbatim, namely:

> The general hypothesis which emerges is that (a) the large company has a fairly well-defined pricing goal that is related to a long-range profit horizon; (b) its management seeks – especially in multi-product multi-market operations – a simultaneous decision with respect to price, cost, and product characteristics; and (c) its pricing formulas are handy devices for checking the internal consistency of the separate decisions as against the general company objective. Under this hypothesis no single theory of the firm – and certainly no single motivational hypothesis such as profit maximisation – is likely to impose an unambiguous course of action for the firm for any given situation; nor will it provide a satisfactory basis for valid and useful predictions of price behaviour
>
> (pp. 938–9).
>
> It seems reasonable to conclude that the pricing policies are in almost every case equivalent to a company policy that represents an order of priorities and choice among competing objectives rather than policies tested by any simple concept of profit maximisation
>
> (p. 939).

Another relevant aspect of the data for theoretical analysis is the conception of the market held by managements of large corporations. Individual products, markets, and pricing are not considered in isolation; the unit of decision-making is the enterprise, and pricing and marketing strategies are viewed in this global context. Because of the tremendously complex joint-cost problems and lack of knowledge of actual relationships between cost and output or sales, on the one hand, and the joint-revenue aspects of multi-product companies, on the other, pricing is frequently done for product groups with an eye to the over-all profit position of the company. This means that costing of products ends up as a result of price policy rather than the reverse. In view of the various external pressures on the company, and the nature of the strategy of the enterprise, it is doubtful if price would have any closer relationship to actual costs were detailed cost data available to management. The incentive to realise target rates of profit for the long haul better suits the objectives of management-controlled companies than any desire to profiteer or seek windfall profits (p. 940).

From these conclusions it is clear that firms do establish pricing objectives, even though they may not be stated explicitly. Frequently such objectives are implicit in the company's overall objective, in other cases they may take the form of a generalised statement such as:

'All prices must cover fully allocated costs.'
'Prices will not exceed those asked by immediate competitors.'
'Prices will be set which will discourage the entry of new firms into the market.'
'All prices must yield a return of investment not less than X per cent.'

In a study by Said, the findings summarised in Figure 15.1 do not support conventional price theory which assumes that profit is the sole and principal motivation of business firms. Indeed her evidence suggests strongly that firms are motivated by many objectives simultaneously related to profitability, security and sales. Survival is seen as the most important goal, followed by short-term profits, liquidity, medium-term profits, market share, and sales revenue, with long-run profits seen as of relatively little importance. Also of considerable interest is the fact that divisional managers and accountants placed much more stress on short-term survival/liquidity/profit goals than did managing directors and marketing managers who took a longer-term perspective and emphasised market share and long-run profitability. Experience gained from working with managers in many different industries indicates this generally to be the case.

In *Marketing: Theory and Practice* (Baker, 1995) Professor Adamantios Diamantopoulos provides an authoritative overview of the subject of pricing and summarises the findings of research into pricing objectives into a Table which is reproduced below as Table 15.3. (This chapter, and indeed all the chapters in *Marketing: Theory and Practice* are strongly recommended for reading in conjunction with this book.) In his commentary on Table 15.3, Diamantopoulos points out that firms seek to achieve multiple objectives through their pricing policies; that while some sort of profit goal enters the objective function of virtually all firms, its exact formulation can vary substantially; that sales revenue and market share dominate volume objectives; that there is little support for short-run profit maximisation but there is for long-run profit maximisation; overall, however, firms seek to earn 'satisfactory' profits.

Figure 15.1 Values of importance quoted to pricing objectives

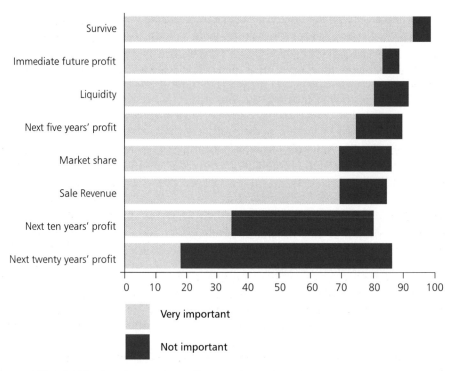

Source: Said, H. (1981), 'The Relevance of Price Theory to Price Practise'

Table 15.3 A taxonomy of pricing objectives		
Profit	*Volume*	*Financial*
■ Money profit	■ Market share	■ Cash flow
■ Gross/Net margin	■ Sales volume	■ Earnings per share
■ Contribution margin	■ Sales revenue	■ Price earnings ratio
■ Return on sales	■ Sales growth	■ Dividends
■ Return on costs	■ Capacity utilisation	
■ Return on capital employed		
■ Return on net worth		
■ Profit growth		
Competition-oriented	*Customer-oriented*	*Miscellaneous*
■ Matching/undercutting competition	■ Fair price levels	■ Projection of high quality image
■ Avoidance of price wars	■ Goodwill	■ Avoidance of government intervention
■ Limit entry	■ Value-for-money	■ Survival/security
■ Price stability	■ Full price range	
■ Money profit	■ Price maintenance in the channel	

Source: Diamantopoulos, A. (1995), 'Pricing' in Baker M. J. (ed.), *Marketing: Theory and Practice*, 3rd edn (Basingstoke: Macmillan).

PRICING FORMULAS AND METHODS

Even though the firm may not have committed itself to a formal statement of price policy, in practice its pricing behaviour is usually sufficiently consistent to permit identification and classification. Observation indicates that there are a limited number of pricing formulas, or methods, in general use, and these may be classified as:

Full-cost or cost-plus pricing

In simple terms, all this involves is the addition of a predetermined margin to the full unit cost of production and distribution, without reference to prevailing demand conditions. In practice, it is doubtful if the firm can establish its true unit cost in advance, owing to uncertainty as to the volume it can make/sell. Broadly speaking, all costs may be classified as fixed or variable. Fixed costs are incurred irrespective of the volume of output and are the result of management policy, for example the depreciation of fixed assets, the level of selling, general and administrative overheads, while variable costs fluctuate more or less directly with the volume of output, for example raw material and labour costs. In that unit cost is computed by dividing total cost by output in units, it is clear that this can only be established when the two quantities are known. The price-setter may forecast sales volume and compute unit cost on the basis of this estimate, adding the predetermined margin in order to arrive at a price. It would be purely fortuitous if demand at this price were to coincide exactly with the available supply, with the result that the seller will either be left with unsold units or else will sell his total output at a lesser profit than could have been obtained. Further, as Lanzillotti implies, the allocation of fixed costs to given products tends to be arbitrary, so that the unit cost used as the basis for a price may bear no relation to true cost at all.

Although cost plus a fixed margin may be a valid method to adopt when deciding whether to enter a new market, most sellers would be prepared to vary this price in the light of potential consumer reaction to it, implicit in current market prices. If this is so, then the price-setter's decision rule is rather different from that generally associated with full-cost pricing – cost plus a predetermined margin is not the price, it is a minimum acceptable price and the actual price adopted may be any amount greater than this. This being so, it is erroneous to contend that prices based on cost takes no account of consumer demand. However, cost-plus pricing has a number of drawbacks admirably summarised by John Winkler in Table 15.4.

Break-even analysis

Break-even analysis utilises the concepts of fixed and variable costs, and enables the price-setter to investigate the implications of any number of price–volume alternatives.

The first step in a break-even analysis is to compute the firm's total cost curve by adding the variable costs incurred at different levels of output to the fixed costs; for example, if fixed costs (FC) = £10 000, and unit variable cost (VC) = £0.25, then total cost (TC) = £10 000 + £0.25x where x = the number of units

Table 15.4 Drawbacks of cost-plus pricing

- Difficult, in advance, to determine such costs as construction, material price changes, and similar costs
- Difficult to allocate joint costs to specific products
- Not based on realistic profit goal or market share objective
- Ignores elasticity of demand
- Generally disregards competition
- Buyers are more concerned about the cost and value of product to them than about production and selling costs to supplier
- Does not distinguish between out-of-pocket and 'sunk' costs*
- Difficult to determine 'fair' return
- Ignores capital requirements and return on investment
- Many costs vary with volume, and volume depends on price charged

* Those which are spent, regardless of production level.
Source: Reprinted from 'Pricing', Winkler, J. in Baker, M. J. (ed), *The Marketing Book* 2nd Edition copyright (1999) with permission from Elsevier.

Figure 15.2 Break-even chart

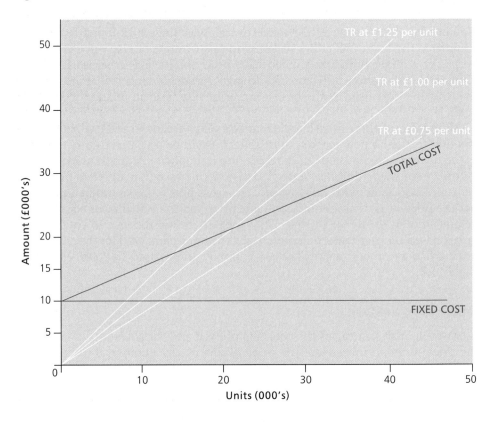

produced. The next step is to compute **total revenue** (TR) curves for the range of prices under consideration and plot these graphically as shown in Figure 15.2.

Clearly the 'break-even' point for a given price lies at the intersection of the total revenue curve for that price and the total cost curve; for example, with a price of £0.75 the firm will break even at a sales volume of 40 000 units. On its own, this information is of little value to the price-setter, unless they have some feeling for the likely volume of demand over the range of prices for which they have calculated break-even points. In reality, the price-setter will usually have at least a preliminary analysis of the potential market for the product, from which he may derive a hypothetical demand curve as shown in Figure 15.3.

By reference to the demand curve it can be seen that at a price of £0.75, 36 250 units will be demanded and the firm would incur a loss.

Closer inspection would seem to indicate that the best price is £1.00, at which 20 000 units will be sold.

Marginal costing/contribution analysis

Break-even analysis allocates fixed costs to a product at a predetermined rate in such a way that, collectively, the firm's products will absorb the firm's total fixed costs. Many price theorists contend that this conventional accounting approach can lead to incorrect decisions, and advocate the adoption of techniques based on marginal analysis as developed by economists.

In essence the marginal approach states that one should ignore fixed costs and concentrate on the relationship between variable cost and revenue, usually termed the 'contribution'. For example, if the variable cost of producing a unit is £0.25 and this unit may be sold for £0.50, then the contribution is +£0.25. It is understood that contribution means 'contribution to fixed costs, variable marketing costs, and profits', and the firm's objective in setting price should be to maximise the total contribution. If average unit cost is used as a criterion, then it is likely that the firm will reject any price less than average cost, and so forego the contribution which sale at such a price would generate. A simplified example

Figure 15.3 Hypothetical demand curve

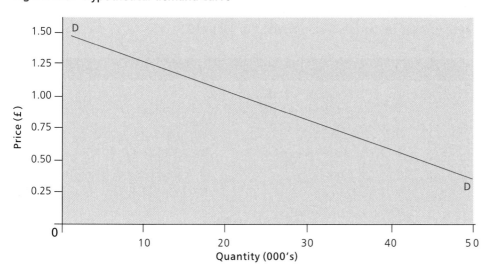

will help clarify this point.

During the day many trains in the London area carry only a few passengers, and it seems clear that the revenues earned must be less than the average cost of running a train. Ignoring the social responsibilities of a public transportation authority, such a practice seems economically suicidal. However, marginal analysis reveals that elimination of these services would lead to lower profits (bigger losses!), in that the incremental cost incurred in running a train is negligible.

The fixed investment necessary to cope with rush-hour traffic flows has already been made and is a 'sunk' cost; maintenance and engineering crews have to be paid to keep the rolling stock and track in good repair, as do railwaymen to operate the signals, drive the trains, and so on. While it is true that some of the latter may work a split shift, the majority do not, and two shifts must be employed as a minimum. Thus, running off-peak trains adds little to the fixed costs to which the transportation authority is committed if it is to provide reasonably adequate commuter services – the cost of the power used and a slight increase in maintenance and operating cost. Provided that sufficient passengers use the off-peak services to cover the cost of these variables, then a contribution will be earned towards fixed costs.

Many managers find it difficult to ignore fixed costs and so make incorrect decisions. The argument that a firm has spent £x million in developing a product, and so must continue with its production and sale in the face of unfavourable use reactions, is a classic example. The best advice in such a situation might well be 'Don't throw good money after bad'.

Contribution analysis does not simplify the problems inherent in forecasting demand and costs, but it does ensure that management does not reject projects which would improve the firm's overall profitability solely because they are not self-supporting on an average cost basis.

Other methods

The methods described above are those most frequently encountered in practice. However, they possess many faults and difficulties and numerous other approaches and techniques have been developed. Diamantopoulos (op. cit.) classifies pricing methods into three types which he calls **Cost-oriented**, **Demand-oriented** and **Competition-oriented** as summarised in Table 15.5

Table 15.5 Pricing methods

	Pricing Methods	
Cost-oriented	*Demand-oriented*	*Competition-oriented*
■ Cost-plus pricing	■ Marginal analysis	■ Product analysis pricing
■ Contribution pricing	■ Trial and error pricing	■ Value pricing
■ Target (ROI) pricing	■ Intuitive pricing	■ Price leadership/followership
■ Price-minus pricing	■ Market pricing	■ Competitive parity pricing
■ Return on costs	■ Monopsonistic pricing	

Source: Diamantopoulos, A. (1995), 'Pricing' in Baker M. J. (ed.), *Marketing: Theory and Practice*, 3rd edn (Basingstoke: Macmillan).

PENETRATION STRATEGIES

Gillette safety razors sold for 55c retail, 20c wholesale "not much more than one fifth of its manufacturing cost. But he designed it so that it could only take his patented blades. These cost him less than one cent a piece to make: he sold them for five cents. And since the blades could be used six or seven times, they delivered a shave at less than one cent a piece or at less than one-tenth the cost of a visit to a barber." (183)

A similar strategy was followed by Xerox. Rather than charge you $14,000 for a machine requiring a capital appropriation, 5 cents a copy was petty cash. The lesson is that you charge for what represents value for the customer - a shave, a copy – not on what it costs the supplier. (Based on Innovation and Entrepreneurship (1985))

Source: P. Drucker (2001).

In commenting on these methods Diamantopoulos observes that in most cases firms use more than one method. For example, for routine pricing decisions they will use cost-plus; for special situations, for example to win a large order they might well use contribution pricing.

With regard to type of pricing method, cost-oriented approaches are characterised by an emphasis on covering some combination of cost element; demand-oriented methods focus on the customer and their likely reaction to price; while competition-oriented approaches are concerned with competitive reaction.

Diamantopoulos confirms that cost-oriented methods predominate in industry with cost-plus being the most popular. Market pricing – charging what the market will bear - is the second most popular approach, with following the market leader third. The use of the other methods is limited and tends to reflect special circumstances. Elsewhere, Diamantopoulos and Mathews (1995) in *Making Pricing Decisions* have observed that:

Undoubtedly, the most important conclusion permeating the entire spectrum of findings [into price research] is that pricing behaviour is situational in nature, i.e. influenced by the specific organisational and market setting at hand. The impact of organisational factors is reflected in (a) the structure of price responsibility within the firm and (b) the kind of informational inputs and approaches utilised in price-setting. The impact of the market environment, on the other hand, is reflected in the different market and competitive conditions associated with the various product markets served by the firm which, in turn, gives rise to differences in practically all areas of price decision-making. In this context, it was demonstrated quite conclusively that the nature of the market environment impinges upon (a) the importance attached to short as well as long-run pricing objectives, (b) the suitability of alternative pricing methods, (c) the frequency and timing of price changes, (d) the effectiveness of promotional price-cutting, (e) the demand curve perceptions of decision-makers and (f) the appropriateness of different new product pricing strategies.

A summary picture in provided in Table 15.6.

Some insight into current practice was provided by project MACS (Baker and Hart, 1989) as indicated by Figure 15.4.

From these and other similar studies, the following conclusions may be drawn:

Table 15.6 Influence of the market environment on pricing behaviour

Market characteristics	Pricing objectives	Pricing methods	Price changes	Price-volume relationships	New Product pricing strategies
Market growth	■				
No. of competitors	■			■	■
Market concentration	■			■	
Product substitutability	■	■	■	■	■
Market price sensitivity	■	■	■	■	
Price competition	■	■	■	■	
Non-price competition	■	■		■	
Competitive price-cutting	■		■	■	

Source: Diamantopoulos, A. and Mathews, B. P. (1995), *Making Pricing Decisions* (Chapman and Hall).

Figure 15.4 Pricing in successful and less successful companies

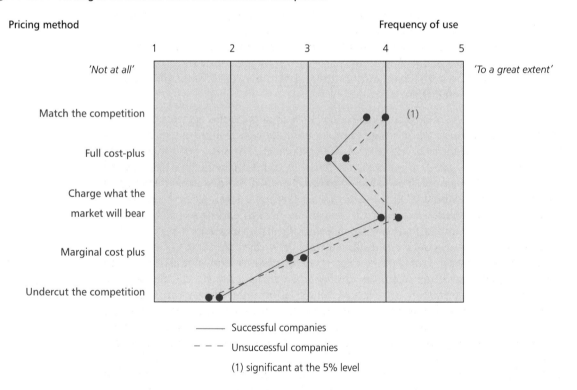

------ Successful companies

- - - Unsuccessful companies

(1) significant at the 5% level

1 Considerable attention is given to cost even when prices are not finally based on cost.

2 Full-cost methods are used much more extensively than marginal cost methods.

3 Firms are flexible in their approach to pricing with the great majority varying their profit margin to reflect market conditions.

PRICING STRATEGIES

In *Price Management*, Henry Simon (1989) confirms that while it is the product that provides value, benefit or utility, it is price which enables one to make comparative assessments between different products and it is this alone which 'determines the amount a customer must sacrifice to acquire a product'. However, in addition to its importance in establishing the **price-value** relation, Simon cites six reasons why price is an important element in the marketing mix.

1 Price elasticity is 20 times greater than advertising elasticity; that is, a 1 per cent change has a sales effect 20 times as big as a 1 per cent change in advertising expenditure.

2 The sales effect of a price change is often immediate, and so measurable, while changes in other mix variables are usually lagged and difficult to quantify.

3 Price changes are easy to effect compared with varying other mix variables.

4 Competitors react more quickly to price changes.

5 Price does not require an initially negative cash flow as do other marketing expenditures such as advertising which have a lagged effect.

6 Price and the product are the only two mix elements which feature significantly in strategic planning concepts.

So far, attention has been focused on quantitative aspects of price determination and little consideration given to the qualitative factors which shape the final pricing decision. Given the difficulties involved in constructing a demand schedule, pricing formulas can only give a broad indication of the range within which the desired sales volume might be achieved. Hence, the final price decision must depend upon a judgmental assessment of the impact of a given price strategy. In broad terms there are two alternatives open to the marketer – a high price approach aimed at 'skimming the cream' off the market, and a low price or **penetration strategy** aimed at pre-empting a significant share of the total market.

High price strategies are appropriate to mature or saturated markets, which show a degree of segmentation on the basis of quality, design features and so forth, or to the introduction of a product which differs significantly from anything currently available. In the case of existing markets, consumers in the higher income groups are often prepared to pay a premium for products which are differentiated from those appealing to the mass market; for example a Rolls-Royce or Toyota Lexus compared with a Renault or a Ford Escort. Owing to the limited demand at the higher prices, a small, high-quality producer can maintain a profitable level of sales without building up a sufficiently large market share to attract the competition of firms catering to the mass market. This does not mean that the latter type of firm will not diversify into the high price segment to make fuller use of its resources, as did Ford with its purchase of Jaguar, but the established reputation of the quality producer will provide a high degree of protection against such competition.

Skimming the market is also attractive to the firm with a new and unique product. As noted earlier, new product development invariably represents a considerable investment on the part of the innovator, and a high initial price offers the opportunity to limit the costs of launching the product into the market while earning monopoly profits. A good example of such a strategy is the launching of the Polaroid Land camera, which was originally put on the market at a price of around £100, with very limited distribution and promotion. The novelty of a camera which could produce a finished print within a matter of seconds attracted a lot of free publicity, as well as being something of a status symbol because of its price. As demand at the initial high price was exhausted, Polaroid lowered prices and 'slid down the demand curve', with the result that a basic camera is now available at around £10. It is interesting to note that in the United States, where the camera was developed and first put on sale, a rather different strategy was adopted and the camera offered originally at a relatively low price. The reasoning in this instance was that the purchase of a camera tends to be once and for all, whereas there is a continuing market for film, thus the more cameras that were sold the greater would be the demand for film. As the film was unique, and protected by patents, competition from other manufacturers such as Eastman-Kodak was precluded and offered greater long-run profitability, provided sufficient cameras could be sold.

Of course, the camera market has now changed significantly, with UK retailers such as Dixons no longer selling 35mm cameras, instead concentrating on the digital market. The adoption of reusable flash memory cards mean that film is no longer a repeat purchase product, and the emphasis has shifted to the printing of photographs, whether this is by self-service kiosks or services through retailers, or the use of home photo-printers. In the case of home photo printers a similar strategy has been adopted in that whilst initial printer purchase price is low, the cost of the repeat purchase consumables, the photo paper and ink cartridges/ toner, are relatively high.

When adopting a skimming strategy, with the intention of subsequently reducing price to appeal to a wider market, it is important not to create ill will by reducing price too quickly. This danger may be reduced by differentiating the appearance of the product and offering it as a 'stripped-down', or economy model. The use of this strategy is to be seen in the marketing of PCs as well as camcorders, mobile phones, and so on.

A low price policy recommends itself in a number of circumstances, pre-eminent among which is entering a market with a high **price-elasticity of demand**. The newcomer will have to achieve a certain level of sales in order to break even, and in the short run may only be able to wrest sales from existing products through the medium of an attractive discount on current prices. **Penetration pricing**, as this strategy is sometimes termed, usually involves the firm in accepting a loss initially, while achieving sampling of the product and the development of brand loyalty. As suggested earlier, however, few firms are willing to buy market share openly for fear of setting off a price war, and a penetration policy is usually disguised as some form of sales promotion, for example price-off labels, coupons, and so on. Where the firm possesses a cost advantage it has little to fear from a low price strategy, but it is rare that a new entrant into a market can undercut the existing brand leaders owing to the economies of scale open to them. In fact, contrary to popular belief, oligopolists often practice a low price policy to discourage the entry of new competitors into the market.

In 1954, E. R. Hawkins elaborated on these two basic strategies when he listed the pricing policies described by 'marketing specialists'. These policies may be summarised as:

1 *Odd pricing* – that is, the adoption of prices ending in odd numbers. This policy is notably prevalent in food retailing, and is also used extensively on low ticket items in general. The adoption of such prices implies the existence of a stepped or discontinuous demand curve; that is avoidance of intermediate prices ending in round numbers suggests that the price-setter believes that demand is totally inelastic at that price, for example reducing an item from 55p to 54p would not increase demand so price is reduced to 53p. One reason for using odd prices is that the customer will wait to get their change so the seller has to open the till and record the transaction. A limitation on this approach in some affluent economies is the elimination of the one cent or equivalent coin.

2 *Psychological pricing*. This differs from odd pricing in that the price need not be an odd number but merely one that has an apparent psychological significance for the buyer; for example 95p instead of £1. Prices that end in 9 also have a marked effect on people's perceptions. An article in the *Harvard Business Review* (Sept. 2003) entitled 'Mind your pricing cues' reported that raising the price of womens clothing from $34 to $39 increased demand by a third, while raising it to $44 had no effect on demand at all!

3 *Customary prices*. Such prices are fixed by custom; for example the old 5p bar of chocolate. Like the first two strategies the adoption of such prices assumes a kink in the demand curve. (The abolition of resale price maintenance and inflation seem to have seen the demise of customary prices for products like shoes and confectionery where they were formerly commonplace. However, 'psychological' prices still prevail, and 99p seems to have assumed a particular significance in this context. (However, with the disappearance of 1 cent coins in many countries this will have to change!)

4 *Pricing at the market/meeting the competition*. This strategy presumes a marked inelasticity of demand below the current market price, such that a price reduction would not be justified by increased sales revenues. This approach is frequently adopted to avoid price wars.

5 *Prestige pricing*. This strategy implies a skimming approach in which the seller gives prestige to his product by asking a price well in excess of those asked for near perfect substitutes; for example Estée Lauder cosmetics, After Eight mints.

6 *Price lining*. This policy of adopting specific prices for certain types of merchandise is common among retailers and is closely related to both psychological and customary prices; for example women's dresses, nylon stockings.

7 *Geographic pricing*. This policy is sometimes used where the marketer serves

a number of distinct regional markets and can adopt different prices in each without creating consumer or distributor ill will. Petrol is priced in this way, depending on the distance of the garage from the nearest bulk terminal.

8 *Dual pricing strategy*. The marketer sells the same product at two or more different prices. Within the same market it is necessary to use different brands, but in distinct regional markets it may be possible to justify price differentials on the grounds of varying distribution costs, cf. petrol.

The arguments for skimming and penetrating strategies are admirably summarised by Simon (1989) in Table 15.7.

In the Introduction to this chapter it was noted that pricing tends to be relegated to a secondary role in the formulation of competitive strategies. To a large degree this is due to the fact that price is highly visible and readily understood by consumers and competitors alike, whereas other elements of the marketing mix are less capable of direct and objective assessment.

However, an increasingly competitive climate has resulted in much more attention being given to the use of price as both a tactical and strategic weapon. In some cases, such as Tesco's checkout campaign, the results have been spectacular and beneficial; in others, such as Freddie Laker's Skytrain, they have been spectacular and fatal.

In his analysis Millman makes a useful distinction between price wars and price attrition and argues that the latter 'are characterised by long periods during which

Table 15.7 Arguments for skimming and penetration strategies

Skimming strategy	Penetration strategy
■ High short-run profits little affected by discounting	■ High total contribution through fast sales growth in spite of low unit contribution margins
■ Quick pay-back for real innovation during the period of monopolistic market position, reduces long-run competitive risk, quick amortisation of R&D expenses	■ Takes advantage of positive intrapersonal (consumer goods) or interpersonal (durable goods) carryover effects, builds up a strong market position (with the potential of higher prices and/or higher sales in the future)
■ High profit in early life-cycle phases, reduces the risk of obsolescence	■ Takes advantage of short-run cost reductions through (static) economies of scale
■ Allows for price reduction over time	■ Allows for fast increase of the cumulative quality by accelerating the experience curve effect. Achieves a large cost advantage that competitors will find difficult to match
■ Avoids the necessity of price increases	
■ High price implies positive prestige and quality	
■ Requires fewer financial resources	■ Reduces the risk of failure; low introductory price gives some assurance of low probability of failure
■ Requires lower capacity	■ Deters potential competitors from market entry, or delays their entry

Source: Simon, H. (1989), *Price Management* (Amsterdam: Elsevier Science Publishers).

the total price package is gradually worn down' interspersed with short bursts of high activity. By contrast a price war is 'typically the result of a battle for market share which can easily get out of hand if there is no pressure group or check mechanism with sufficient mobility and authority to restore order'.

It was Fellner who described price as 'the blunt instrument of competition'. Under the right conditions its use may bring quick and beneficial results but you are more likely to remain in good health if you can avoid being the victim of price warfare.

A STRATEGIC PRICING FRAMEWORK

Based on her extensive analysis of pricing behaviour, Said offers us a model in Figure 15.7, which she describes as follows:

As a first step, there is the decision about objectives which business firms seek to achieve through their pricing policy.

The process of price determination comprises both the firms' approach to pricing and the techniques used, which includes the following:

- *Decisions concerning the methods of pricing either cost or not cost related;*
- *Decisions concerning methods of costing for pricing purposes;*
- *Decisions concerning profit policy, the techniques used in calculating profit margins and their flexibility between products;*
- *Decisions concerning price changes in response to demand and cost fluctuations;*
- *Decisions concerning price review;*
- *Decisions concerning pricing systems to be used;*
- *Decisions concerning discount structures to be operated.*

As suggested in the model, pricing behaviour is a function of a complex of objective and subjective variables. The objective variables indicated in the model are the type of product, methods of production, methods of distribution, industry sector and size. The subjective variables are the choices made by executives responsible for pricing and the type of respondent manager. To begin with pricing objectives, the model shows a link between pricing objectives and industry sector, type of manager responsible for pricing decisions, and type of respondent manager.

Firms' approach to pricing and techniques used are functions of all these objective and subjective variables combined with pricing objectives. More specifically:

- There is an association between the pricing methods used in business firms and their pricing objectives, the type of product they produce, the methods of production and distribution they use, the industry sector they fall in, and the type of manager responsible for setting prices.

- There is an association between the costing methods used in business firms and their pricing objectives, pricing methods, the type of product, methods of production and distribution, industry sector and the type of manager responsible for pricing.

- There is an association between profit policy employed by a business firm and its pricing objectives, pricing methods, type of product, methods of production and distribution, industry sector and size.

- There is an association between price changes and pricing objectives, pricing methods, type of product, methods of production and distribution, industry sector and pricing systems.
- There is an association between firm's policy in reviewing prices and pricing objectives, pricing methods, type of product, industry sector and size.
- There is an association between pricing systems employed by firms and their pricing objectives, the type of product, methods of production and distribution, and industry sector.
- There is an association between discount structures operated by business firms and their pricing systems, type of product, methods of distribution, industry sector and size.

As shown in the model, the relationship between the different aspects of pricing behaviour is cross-sectional or one way, which indicates the case in a static analysis. However, over time these associations will show a two-way relationship, indicating a dynamic state and the adjustment of policy and practice in the light of experience. For example, a price review can result in a change in the firm's pricing objectives, which in turn will cause a change in its profit policy, pricing methods, pricing systems, price changes and so on. A change in profit policy can cause a change in pricing objectives, pricing methods, costing methods, etc. Also a change in costing methods can cause a change in pricing methods, which in turn influence profit policy, pricing objectives and consequently all the process of pricing. This model might fill an existing gap in the pricing literature on two counts:

First, it suggests a link between pricing behaviour and certain variables which play an important role in pricing, but which have received little attention previously.

Second, while recognising the interdependence and interrelationship of the various aspects of the pricing process, it considers them to be influenced significantly by the firms' overall pricing objectives, of which there may be several, and so conditioned by them.

These two points suggest the complexity of pricing decisions, which is emphasised by Livesey, Oxenfeldt, Tucker, Hague, and many others, that pricing decisions constitute a complex web, and that successful pricing requires an awareness of the many interrelationships among pricing decisions.

COMPETITIVE BIDDING

While **competitive bidding** has long been a feature of many business transactions, especially for complex projects such as constructing a building, a bridge, power station, ship etc. its use has become even more commonplace with the introduction of laws governing competition. This is especially so in the countries of the European Union where any contract worth more than a specified amount has to be advertised publicly. While such contracts are not automatically awarded to the lowest bidder, the practice has created much more interest in the principles involved.

For example, the Health and Safety Executive publishes a detailed statement of its procurement policies in which it states:

Figure 15.7 A model of pricing behaviour

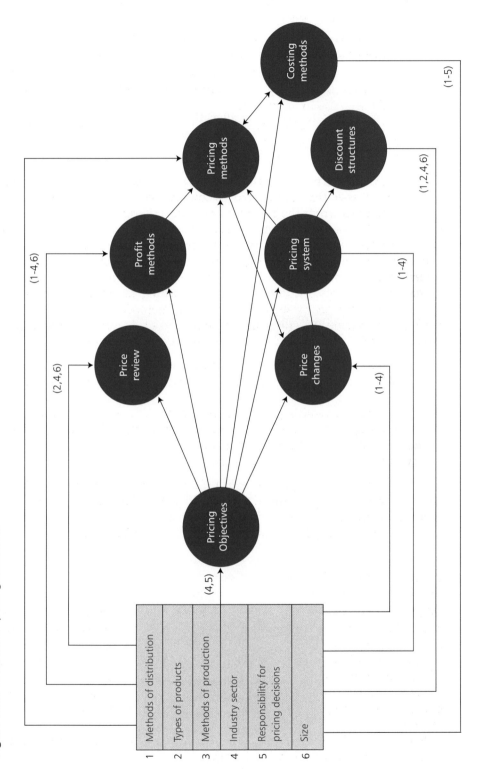

Source: Said, H. (1981), 'The Relevance of Price Theory to Price Practise'

Competitive tendering is:

- *The process of inviting a number of suppliers to make an offer for providing specified goods or services.*
- *A means of taking a defined need to the market place to find the most suitable way in which that need may be met.*
- *A way to ensure a specification is met in the most cost-effective manner, and at the same time, obtain value for money from the purchase.*

Competition helps to avoid any allegations of favouritism or collusion and discourages monopoly. The HSE encourages market interest in its work and procurement practices to ensure that more suppliers compete for the HSE's business.

The HSE places particular emphasis on the preparation of **performance driven** (output based) **specifications** that focus on the function of the product or service required – in other words the 'fitness for purpose' criteria. Quality, the duration of the contract, and delivery requirements are also stressed, and details given about the preparation, receipt and evaluation of tenders. This information is based on 'best practice' and would be expected in the majority of cases where competitive tendering is called for.

Summary

In this chapter we have examined the role of price as a key variable in the marketing mix. Traditionally, economic theory sees price as the mechanism which brings supply and demand into equilibrium. However, theories of competition designed to explain how price achieves this tend to contain a number of simplifying assumptions which clearly do not exist often in the real world. The assumption that people are homogeneous and so are willing to accept homogeneous products obviously contradicts reality. If it were true then the most efficient firms would undoubtedly dominate the market as their efficiency would enable them to offer the lowest price. With nothing to distinguish one supplier's offering from another's then buying at the lowest price is the only logical outcome and all industries would be monopolistic or oligopolistic in character.

Because user needs and wants differ there is an opportunity to escape the rigours of price competition by differentiating the product or service offering. Thus much of recent marketing thinking and practice has focused on the development of a sustainable differential advantage through non-price factors. However, in recent years characterised by recession and intensive competition many producers and sellers have turned to price as a competitive weapon in their attempts to hold or build market share. One consequence of this is that many buyers' perception of price has changed. Formerly, price was seen to be fixed. Now, it is seen as variable and negotiable – a change which has important implications for marketing managers.

However, a survey by Tack International in 2005 of B2B buyers indicated that, while price is a significant factor in selection criteria it is not always the most important, In fact their research showed only 4% of the respondents putting it in first position, 21`% second, 45% in third ,fourth or fifth place while 24% said it was not ranked at all.

Against this background we have looked at the major price determinants – internal and external – and their influence on **pricing objectives**. Following Diamantopoulos we have classified these as falling into six categories:

- Profit related;
- Volume related;
- Financially related;
- Competition-oriented;
- Customer-oriented;
- Miscellaneous.

In order to achieve their pricing objectives, organisations have access to a number of **formulas** or methods. These we reviewed in some detail paying particular attention to **cost** and **competition based approaches**. In turn, this led to a consideration of pricing strategies with **penetration** or **skimming** seen as the basic options. Next, we looked at how the buyer's **perception** of price influences their buying behaviour and particularly how price affects perceptions of quality. Finally, we proposed an alternative model of **pricing behaviour** developed from empirical research undertaken at Strathclyde University, and looked briefly at **competitive bidding**.

In the next chapter we turn our attention to the third P in the marketing mix with a discussion of the role and nature of **channel management**.

Review questions and problems

1 Summarise the major factors that should be taken into account in developing a price policy.

2 Discuss the advantages/disadvantages of each of the price 'formulas' discussed in the text.

3 Under what circumstances would you recommend
(a) a 'skimming' approach,
(b) a 'penetration' policy? Identify a current example of each and document the reasons which you believe prompted its selection.

4 Discuss the importance of price as an 'indicator of quality'.

5 What relevance have the concepts of the product life cycle and market segmentation for pricing policy?

6 Describe three ways in which product pricing policy can be used as a means of creative marketing.

7 Explain the statement that optimal pricing policies should be based upon a combination of contribution analysis techniques and a marketing-oriented view of customers.

8 Describe the uses of break-even analysis as a tool of effective marketing management.

9 Explain and comment on the view that optimal price is that price which best services the central aims of the business.

10 What have recent studies revealed about the effect of price differentials on consumers perceptions of product quality?

11 A surprisingly large number of companies relegate price policy to a secondary role in the planning of their marketing strategy. What factors might cause a company to act in this way?

12 How do contribution analysis and breakeven analysis relate to each other? What use is made of them in marketing?

13 Tooth-i-Pegs Ltd make and sell 100,000 toothbrushes per month at 40p each. The total unit cost is 38p and fixed costs amount to £10,000 per month. Market research has revealed that there would be an increase in sales to 125,000 brushes per month if the price was reduced to 38p per brush.
  Assuming that there is excess manufacturing capacity available, should Tooth-i-Pegs Ltd reduce its selling price? Prepare an advertising and marketing plan.

14 Write notes on FOUR of the following:
(i) mark-up pricing,   (ii) target pricing,
(iii) price discrimination,   (iv) loss-leaders,
(v) prestige pricing.

15 What is meant by the term 'penetration pricing?' Under what circumstances is a company most likely to use this type of pricing?

16 In determining a pricing policy, why is it important to evaluate competitors' prices? Detail the likely outcomes if a firm did not take competitors' prices into consideration, when determining the price of their product.

17 What is meant by the term price skimming? Under what circumstances might this be the most optimal pricing strategy to follow?

18 To what extent would you support the view that the British shopper has become more conscious about the value for money in recent years? Use examples to support you answer.

19 In price discounting, the principle should be that if you give something away, you've got to get something back. Discuss this proposition using examples.

Key terms

break-even analysis
buying decisions
China price
competition based approaches
competition-oriented
competitive bidding
composite model of buyer
    behaviour
contribution analysis
corporate resources
cost-oriented
cost-plus pricing
cross-elasticity of demand
customary prices
demand and supply
demand-oriented
dual pricing
economic theory
economies of scale
elasticity
elasticity of demand
equilibrium

external and internal factors
fixed costs
formulas
full cost pricing
geographic pricing
government policy
hypotheses
industry structure
marginal costing
market concept
market share
market structure
methods
models
monopolistic competition
objectives
odd pricing
penetration pricing
penetration strategy
perception
performance driven
    specifications

predetermined margin
prestige pricing
price lining
price value
pricing at the market
pricing behaviour
pricing decision
pricing objectives
pricing strategies
product differentiation
product mix
profitability
psychological pricing
quality indicator
recession
skimming
strategic pricing
sunk cost
total cost curve
total revenue
unit variable cost
value analysis

Supplementary reading list

Diamantopoulos, Adamantios, Chapters on 'Pricing' in Baker M. J. (ed.), (1996) *Marketing: Theory and Practice*, 3rd edn (Basingstoke: Macmillan), and Baker, M.J. (ed.), (2003) *The Marketing Book*, 5th. edn (Oxford: Butterworth Heinemann)

Diamantopoulos, A. and Mathews, B.P. (1995), *Making Pricing Decisions*, (London:CHapman and Hall)

Simon, H. (1989) *Price Management* (Amsterdam: Elsevier)

Winkler, J. (1986) *Pricing for Results* (London: Pan Books)

CHANNEL MANAGEMENT

16

Learning Goals   *After reading this chapter you should be able to:*

- List the five essential functions performed by a distribution channel.

- Review the advantages and disadvantages of the three basic alternatives available when selecting a distribution policy

  - direct sale;

  - sale through an intermediary;

  - a dual policy.

- Explain the channel policy decision in terms of the resolution of conflict between cost and control.

- Summarise the factors to be considered when selecting a distribution channel.

INTRODUCTION

In Chapters 6 and 7 we discussed the **supply chain** and 'Channels of Distribution' in some detail. In those chapters our intention was to describe the functions of distribution channels and then elaborate these by looking at the existing patterns for raw materials, industrial and consumer goods. In this chapter the emphasis is upon distribution as an element of the marketing mix which the marketer has to consider when developing a marketing plan.

To begin with we offer some definitions as a basis for a discussion of **channel structure**. Next, we consider some of the determinants of **channel policy** which influence the channel decision and the selection of a particular strategy. Having chosen a channel it is necessary to manage the relationship with intermediaries which raises issues of **conflict**, **control** and performance **measurement**. To conclude the chapter we summarise some current trends and look briefly at the subject of **logistics** or physical distribution.

DEFINING THE CHANNEL

Earlier (Chapter 6) we introduced the concept of the business system as the forerunner of the currently popular idea of the 'value chain'. This concept traces the flow of goods from the extraction of raw materials/growth of primary commodities through processing and fabrication into industrial or consumer goods, and their sale into ultimate consumption, along with those services necessary to facilitate consumption. In tracing this flow we identified a number of functions which have to be performed which we summarised as:

1 Transfer of title to the goods involved.
2 Physical movement from the point of production to the point of consumption.
3 Storage functions.
4 Communication of information concerning the availability, characteristics and price of the goods.
5 The financing of goods in transit, inventory, and on purchase.

The performance of these functions adds value – hence value chain – and involves the performance of a number of specialised tasks.

In *Marketing: Theory and Practice* Sean Ennis (1995) cites Bowersox and Cooper's definition of a channel as a "system of relationships among businesses that participate in the processes buying and selling products and services". From this definition it is clear that the authors conceive of channels comprising a number of members each responsible for specific tasks. As can be seen from Figure 16.1 this is usually the case, although it can also be seen that in some instances manufacturers will seek to establish direct contact with their customers.

From Figure 16.1 it is clear that channels can vary considerably in their complexity, and the basic issue is whether the manufacturer should seek to perform the functions involved or transfer/delegate these to one or other kind of specialist who will mediate (hence, intermediary) between them and the ultimate customer. We return to this issue later when discussing cost and control in distribution channels. However, the reader may wish to refer back to Chapter 6 where we summarised some of the advantages and disadvantages of direct sale and selling through intermediaries.

FACTORS INFLUENCING CHANNEL STRUCTURE

With rare exceptions most producers will find themselves faced with a number of different channels through which they might seek to reach their target market. Some understanding of the broad influences which give rise to these different channel structures will provide a useful insight when deciding which of the alternatives to use.

In reviewing various explanations of channel structure Lambert notes that there is no consensus of opinion, with some theories stressing the product life-cycle, others the characteristics of goods, and still others the size of firm. Among these theories perhaps the most detailed and best-known is that put forward by Bucklin

Figure 16.1 Channels of distribution

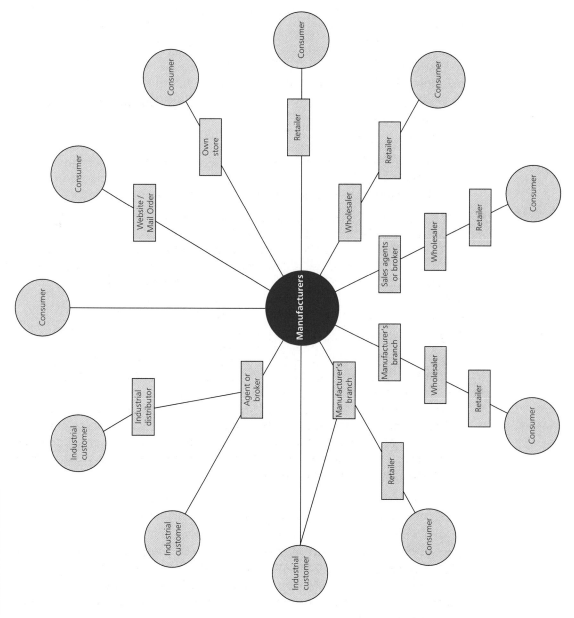

(1968) which rests upon the economic relationships between channel members and the concepts of **substitutability, postponement** and **speculation**.

According to Bucklin, marketing functions are substitutable for one another in much the same way as the basic factors of production and 'This substitutability permits the work load of one function to be shrunk and shifted to another without affecting the output of the channel'. He continues later: 'In essence, the concept of substitutability states that under competitive conditions institutions of the channel will interchange the work load among functions, not to minimise the cost of some individual function, but the total costs of the channel.'

Postponement and speculation are the converse of each other in that the principle of postponement 'states that changes in form and inventory location are to be delayed to the latest possible moment' while 'the principle of speculation holds that changes in form, and the movement of goods to forward inventories, should be made at the earliest possible time in the marketing flow in order to reduce the costs of the marketing system', for example through economies of scale. Based upon these three principles, Bucklin argues that consumer demand will determine what services are required and what value is placed upon them, and this will result in the evolution of the most efficient and cost-effective channel structure. Thus, for convenience goods ready and widespread availability is a sine qua non and we are likely to find the producer using multiple channels involving both direct and indirect sales to achieve the maximum market coverage. Conversely, for many industrial goods and consumer shopping goods the variation in consumer demand will lead to greater postponement so that precise needs can be articulated, and will frequently result in shorter channels e.g. you order furniture from the retailer who places an order direct with the manufacturer.

However, as producers and distributors jockey for position to satisfy the ultimate customer one must anticipate an ebb and flow in the competitive standing of the channel members. Lambert provides a useful synopsis of Bruce Mallen's (1977) analysis of the competitive forces which are likely to result in structural change in the channel, as follows:

1 A producer will spin-off a marketing function to a marketing intermediary(s) if the latter can perform the function more efficiently than the former.

2 If there are continual economies to be obtained within a wide range of volume changes, the middleman portion of the industry (and perhaps individual middlemen) will become bigger and bigger.

3 A producer will keep a marketing function if the producer can perform the functions at least as efficiently as the intermediary.

4 If a producer is more efficient in one market, the producer will perform the marketing function; if in another market the middleman is more efficient, then the middleman will perform the function.

5 If there are not economies of scale in a growing market, more firms may be expected to join the channel.

Of course, changes in the competitive standing of producers and distributive intermediaries will be subject to the complex interplay of the environmental forces reviewed earlier, and underlies the importance of monitoring these if one is to select the most efficient channel – a subject to which we turn next.

MAJOR DETERMINANTS OF CHANNEL POLICY

Fundamentally, the channel decision requires resolution of the often conflicting forces of **cost** and **control**.

Cost is readily understood, even if it is sometimes difficult to quantify, and several aspects of control have already been stated. However, the concept of control must be broadened to recognise the fact that a firm's ability to exercise control is a function of its competitive strength vis-à-vis other channel members. Thus it is usual to find that one member of the distributive channel dominates its practices and is regarded as the **'locus of channel control'** (see Louis P. Bucklin (1968) 'The Locus of Channel Control'). In general the dominant members are either producers or users/consumers, but there are situations where a channel intermediary may be dominant and so condition the structure and operation of the channel. The latter situation is most likely to occur where both producers and users are small and the market is geographically dispersed, and is equally true of retailer/wholesalers in the consumer goods market as it is of the industrial goods wholesaler. Overall, dominance or control is determined by a number of factors which may be summarised as:

- *Buyer/seller concentration ratios* in terms of production/consumption, and spatial relationships.
- *Technical complexity*. In the case of technically complex products, dominance will be conditioned by the relative sophistication of the producer vis-à-vis the intermediary and/or user. Thus a small firm may exercise considerable influence over much larger users or intermediaries.
- *Service requirements* – the more complex these are the more likely it is that the producer will exercise control.

In the final analysis, however, the determining factor is **economic advantage**; that is, which channel member can perform the necessary channel functions at the lowest cost consistent with the required degree of efficiency. At a given point in time the structure of a trade channel serves as a rough and ready guide as to the relative efficiency of its members, but it is clear that over time environmental changes may predicate the adoption of an alternative structure to better meet the needs of users/consumers. Similarly, lack of control may persuade a channel member to modify their policies in order to protect their position – a tendency which is implicit in Galbraith's concept of **'countervailing power'**.

Examples of competitive reaction within the distributive channel are well documented in the field of consumer goods but less so in the industrial sphere. The growth of dominant retailing institutions was noted in Chapter 9, together with the response of the independent wholesaler whose livelihood was threatened, and similar trends are to be observed in industrial markets. Among the latter may be noted the adoption of **contract purchasing**, also known as systems contracting, stockless purchasing, automatic ordering or **'Just in time'** (JIT) purchasing. Under this system, buyers negotiate contracts for the continued supply of standard requirements from a single source at a fixed price. Effectively, this reduces the actual stock of parts, supplies or components to the absolute minimum consistent with day-to-day operations, and transfers the inventory costs and risk of obsolescence to the supplier. Such contracts are invariably based upon a total cost analysis rather than on a basis of minimum price. Associated with contract purchasing there is a growing trend towards computerised ordering systems in which standardised and routine orders are placed direct with the supplier (producer or wholesaler) through the medium of electronic data processing equipment. In that these practices not only result in operating economies but also free the purchasing agent to devote more time to non-routine buying decisions, they are resulting in a fuller and more sophisticated evaluation of competitive offerings.

To counteract the growing sophistication of buyers, many sellers have switched to **systems selling**, in which they offer a complete 'package' of related products and services which would formerly have been purchased from a variety of different sources. Similarly, the appointment of market managers, as opposed to product managers, recognises the need to adapt marketing practice to the specific needs of different end-use markets.

The channel decision

Whether one accepts profit maximisation as the basic corporate objective or not, it seems reasonable to affirm that uncertainty about the future business environment, and the competitive activity of other firms, will predispose the firm to reduce costs to the minimum level consistent with achievement of its own stated objective. If this is so, then the channel decision may be viewed as a *three-stage process*. The first stage consists of a qualitative assessment of the environmental opportunity which the firm is best suited to exploit, conditioned by less tangible objectives such as 'To build the best product' or 'To provide the best after-sales service'.

A recurring theme of this book has been that goods and services may be classified as falling into one of three categories in terms of customer buying behaviour. These three categories, convenience, shopping and specialty goods, are reflected in three basic channel strategies related to what is termed the **intensity of distribution**, namely: **intensive**, **selective** and **exclusive**.

In the case of convenience goods we have seen that they are bought frequently

POTATO CRISPS

A classic example from years past was the potato crisp. Before the advent of modern foil and plastic packaging materials crisps used to be packed in greaseproof paper bags with a shelf life of around 7 to 10 days. To ensure freshness at the point of sale Smith's, the dominant supplier, had its own fleet of delivery vans and sold principally into **CTN (Confectionary, Tobacconists and Newsagent)** outlets and the licenced trade which accounted for the majority of its sales. So much so that when rival Golden Wonder adopted new packaging materials that had a shelf life of a month, and so acceptable for sale in supermarkets, Smiths were unaware that Golden Wonder had opened up a new channel of distribution and was positioning its product as a tasty snack for inclusion in children's lunch boxes. Within a year Golden Wonder was selling almost as many crisps as Smiths but, because Smiths were not monitoring sales through supermarkets they were unaware of the competitive threat.

with a minimum of effort and involvement. It follows that they must enjoy the widest possible availability for, otherwise, although one may have a preferred brand, if it is not available the customer will take the next available substitute. Under these circumstances the strategy must be to saturate the distribution channels and take advantage of all the combinations, selling direct to key accounts and through wholesalers and other intermediaries to reach as many other outlets as possible. Hence, Coca-Cola's global distribution strategy is that everyone should be within an arms-reach of their product. This is not to say that just anyone will be encouraged to stock the product as the producer is concerned that the consumer should receive it in good condition, and this may call for the provision of specialist on-site storage facilities like freezers and refrigeration equipment. That said, the emphasis will be on intensive distribution.

In the case of shopping goods the intending buyer will wish to compare what is available in terms of performance, price, appearance, after-sales service etc. and will often seek advice from resellers or retailers who specialise in the desired product. Here a strategy of **selective distribution** is called for. While the manufacturer will still wish to achieve wide distribution so that their product is within convenient reach of prospective customers, they must balance this against turning it into a commodity available everywhere. If this occurs it is unlikely that it will receive additional support at the point of sale. On the other hand, if the manufacturer restricts availability to a selection of outlets with defined catchment and trading areas they may be able to offer them preferred terms if they train their sales staff to 'push' the product . Such a strategy works particularly well where the retail outlet enjoys a strong presence in its trading area. For example, Comet, the household electrical goods retailer, stressed the training given to employees so they can advise customers on the products best suited to their needs.

Finally, in the case of **specialty goods** we know these have a particular importance for the intending buyer to the extent that they will make special efforts to secure a supply, and are unlikely to accept a substitute if offered. Thus, while many convenience goods are near perfect substitutes for one another, we have seen that brands can make them into specialty goods for some consumers. It is this knowledge that means major supermarket chains cannot afford not to stock products that enjoy this status for, if they don't, then customers are likely to switch their store preference to another where they can have access to the widest assortment. In 2004 Sainsbury, a major UK retailer, lost significant market share to rivals Tesco and Asda because of its out-of–stock position on more than five per cent of the items its customers expected to find on the shelves. They went elsewhere.

Usually, however, when we think of specialty goods we think of highly differentiated goods and services with high prices for which there is a limited demand. In these cases exclusive distribution through a very small number of outlets is part and parcel of investing the product with the up-market image that communicates exclusivity to the buyer. Rolex, Prada, Paris fashion houses all fall into this category. So, too, do things where specialist knowledge is important such as hi-fi (Bang & Olufsen), and many other high technology products.

Once the broad strategy has been determined, management must decide which mix of policies offers the optimum probability of attaining the desired result. Such decisions cannot be made in isolation, for the success of a strategy demands that the separate marketing policies in respect of price, distribution, promotion, and so forth be synthesised into a consistent and cohesive whole. When selecting a distribution strategy one variable will usually take pre-eminence over the others by virtue of the basic strategy decided upon – the **'strategic variable'**. For example, if the basic strategy is to sell mass consumption convenience goods, extensive or mass distribution may well be considered the key or strategic variable, and will condition policies adopted in respect of other mix elements. Similarly, if the basic strategy is to build a reputation for high product quality the product itself will become the strategic variable, and probably result in a high price, selective distribution policy.

In order to decide which distribution channel or combination of channels is to be preferred the marketer should then quantify the costs associated with the available alternatives. This analysis should be based initially on a check-list similar to that in Chapter 9, followed by a detailed cost breakdown for direct sale to the number of accounts thought to be necessary to achieve the desired sales volume. Such a breakdown would normally include consideration of the following:

- Number and geographical distribution of accounts;
- Number of calls per account adjusted to allow for potential order size;
- Average sales per call;
- Average time per call;
- Number of salesmen necessary to achieve the optimal call pattern;
- Salaries and commission payable;
- Travelling and administrative costs incurred;
- Costs of holding inventory;
- Costs of financing receivables;
- Costs of extending credit;
- Costs arising out of bad debts;
- Costs of providing necessary services;
- Costs of invoicing, order processing, expediting, and so forth;
- Transportation costs.

On the basis of such a cost analysis one may then compute the average selling, general and administrative costs per unit sold, and compare this with the gross margin asked by intermediaries for providing the same services and market coverage. Obviously, if the margin asked is greater than the average unit cost, direct sale will appear more attractive, and vice versa. The outcome of such an analysis is rarely clear-cut, however, and even when it does appear so it does not necessarily represent the optimal strategy. The latter may only be determined effectively on a marginal or contribution basis, which in turn will usually require the use of sophisticated software to cope with the enormous number of possible combinations and permutations.

To this point it has been assumed implicitly that the selection of distributors is made by the organisation that precedes them in the value or supply chain. At the same time we have noted at several places that in grocery retailing, and to a lesser extent other consumer goods, it is the retailer that exercises channel control with the result that it is they that choose their suppliers rather than the other way round. While it may be possible to reduce or manage the retailers power through branding, promotion, and direct selling it should be remembered that these marketing techniques evolved over a century ago when manufacturers recognised that it was the retailer who had the strongest influence on consumer choice by virtue of the stock they held, and the advice they offered to their customers. Push is direct and personal, pull is less direct and often impersonal. We will return to these issues in the next three chapters that deal with issues of marketing communications.

VERTICAL MARKETING SYSTEMS

To this point, the discussion of distribution channels has conformed with the traditional view that members of such channels are autonomous and independent organisations which are pursuing their own individual objectives. Where these objectives are not congruent there is the potential for conflict and, to try and avoid this, the channel members with the greatest leverage will seek to superimpose their goals over other members and assume control of the channel. Thus, as we have seen, conflict and control are major issues in selecting a distribution policy. Further, and implicit in the word 'superimpose', there has been the expectation that channel conflict will be resolved by competition rather than cooperation.

In many cases competition between channel members leads to inefficiencies and lost profit opportunities. To avoid this, an alternative, more co-operative form of organisation has begun to emerge in recent years and has been designated the vertical marketing system (VMS). According to the *Westburn Dictionary of Marketing and Advertising* a VMS is 'A marketing channel which has achieved some degree of vertical integration involving some central control of operational practices and programmes'. Nylen (1990) elaborates on this definition by suggesting that VMSs differ from conventional channels in four important respects:

1 VMSs use centrally prepared marketing programs.

2 Whether or not the members of a VMS are independent of each other, their activities are directed by this central program.

3 In a VMS, marketing functions are assigned to units on the basis of efficiency and effectiveness rather than on the basis of traditional roles and precedent.

4 The members in a VMS accept closer control than is usual in a conventional channel, with the result that VMSs tend to be more stable.

Following the publication of a paper by Bert C. McCammon Jr it has been customary to recognise three main types of VMS – Administered, Contractual and Corporate. The difference between three kinds of system is determined primarily by the means used to exercise control over the members. In an administered system a channel leader (sometimes termed the channel captain) has sufficient power to persuade the other members of the benefit of cooperation. In order to enjoy this power the leader will normally be the organisation which enjoys the strongest customer franchise. For most food products this now means the major multiples will set the lead although major brands like P&G, Lever Bros, Heinz and so on, will be able to moderate this power and are likely to give the lead in the channels which involve the smaller retailer chains and independents. Either way the leader of an administered VMS will be expected to spell out the terms of trade within the channel (discounts, allowances, trading areas and so forth) in order to provide the incentives necessary to keep the channel intact.

The second type of VMS is the contractual system in which the relationships between members tend to be more formalised and spelled out in official contracts. Three main kinds of contractual VMS may be distinguished – retail co-operatives, wholesale co-operatives and franchises. **Retail co-operatives** occur when independent retailers take the initiative to band together and set up their own wholesaling intermediary. Conversely **wholesaler co-operatives** occur when smaller wholesalers band together to secure the benefits of bulk buying power through pooled purchases, as well as the benefits of professional advice, joint branding and advertising, etc. commonly associated with both kinds of co-operative.

Franchises occur where the owners of products or services licence others to wholesale or retail them under the franchiser's name in exchange for the payment of a fee. Car dealerships, fast food outlets and soft drinks like Coca-Cola are probably the best known example. Franchises also depend upon a contractual relationship, but differ from retail and wholesale co-operatives which are forms of backward integration by intermediaries, whereas franchises are cases of forward integration by producers.

Finally, corporate VMSs exist where a firm integrates vertically, either backwards or forwards, and so becomes responsible for the product/service from its initial conceptualisation/production right through to its consumption and after-sales service. Nylen (1990) summarises the advantages and disadvantages of VMSs as follows:

Advantages

1   Distribution economies.
2   Marketing control.
3   Stability, reduction of uncertainty.

Disadvantages

1   Loss of incentive.
2   Investment requirements.
3   Inflexibility.

Nylen continues to suggest that the choice between VMS and conventional systems depends largely on the answers to six questions.

1 What level of power does the firm have?
2 What is the potential for economies?
3 How much marketing cooperation is needed?
4 Are appropriate channel members available?
5 Is there potential for competitive differentiation through the channel system?
6 Is there a competitive threat from integrated systems?

Clearly, the answers to these questions (like so many in marketing) will call for both formal analysis and the exercise of judgement.

Ennis (1995) describes a number of variations of Vertical Marketing Systems as follows:

- *Corporate vertical marketing system: These exist when the various channel members participating within the chain are owned by one organisation. This can occur through forward integration – where a manufacturer acquires or sets up its own wholesaling or retailing structure; or through backward integration – where a retailer or wholesaler owns its own supplier base.*

- *Contractual vertical marketing systems: The main distinguishing feature of this form of arrangement is that the relationships are formalised through a contractual agreement. This specifies the precise functions and responsibilities of each member. Typical examples of this type of structure are franchises, exclusive dealerships, and joint ventures. There is a marked absence of ownership in this situation (as compared to corporate arrangements).*

- *Alliances: Bowersox and Cooper (1992) suggest that this structure is characterised by a voluntary form of extended organisations – where two or more firms agree to develop close working relationships. At a basic level this can be described as a partnership – without necessarily producing changes or modifications in the individual way in which the parties conduct their operations. Clearly this may change over time, where parties are willing to alter their practices as they perceive individual and mutual benefits accruing. This type of structure can be described as a strategic alliance.*

- *Administered vertical marketing systems: Marketing institutions in such systems generally pursue their individual goals, and have no formal organisational structure to bind them together. The marketing programme, on the other hand, allows these organisations to collaborate informally on the goals they do share (Stern et al., 1989). While an attempt is made to inculcate a systematic approach to the planning and coordination of certain marketing activities on the part of the channel participants, the approach is to the individual rather than to the overall channel.*

CHANNEL MANAGEMENT

By now it should be clear that the selection of a distribution channel is a key issue for marketing management. Martin Christopher (1992) in *Logistics and Supply Chain Management*, cites four factors which emphasise the importance of channel management, namely:

- *The customer service explosion;*
- *Time compression;*
- *The globalisation of industry;*
- *Organisational integration.*

Clearly, the channel of distribution offers significant opportunities to add value through the creation of additional services and time and place utilities. Similarly, global competition and the creation of major trading blocs like the EU, LAFTA, NAFTA and so on, has given added emphasis to the importance of efficient and effective distribution as a source of competitive advantage. Taken together these forces call for improved coordination and integration of the firm's functions to ensure the creation and delivery of customer satisfaction. In turn, these issues throw into sharp relief the fundamental question of whether one should seek to establish direct contact with the customer, or work through an intermediary or intermediaries.

We have already noted that the growing power of retailers has done much to erode the manufacturer's franchise with the ultimate consumer (Chapter 9). To restore this loss of franchise many manufacturers have sought to integrate forward into distribution, deal direct, and/or increase their promotional effort to communicate directly with end users in order to 'pull' their products through the distribution channels. Vertical marketing systems also offer greater opportunities for integration of distributive functions. However, as we have seen in this chapter, distribution channels are all about relationships between the members and the exercise of power and control with the potential for conflict these create. (Ennis, op. cit. discusses these issues in some detail.)

Whatever the final solution, the producer will want to measure the performance of the channel and this will usually call for a combination of quantitative and qualitative measures; for example sales, inventory levels, delivery, customer satisfaction and so forth. Readers should consult one of the specialised texts for information on the selection and use of appropriate performance indicators.

PHYSICAL DISTRIBUTION

Physical distribution, or logistics as it is sometimes termed, is also a specialist topic in its own right to which only limited reference can be made in a general, introductory text of this kind.

As the term implies, physical distribution is concerned with the movement, handling, storage and delivery of raw materials, fabricated materials, components and sub-assemblies, and finished goods. All of these possess value, but they also represent capital tied up in inventory or stocks. While the appropriate level of stocks will vary according to one's position within the business system, or value chain, and the nature of the industry/market, efficiency and effectiveness will depend very much on keeping stocks to a minimum and turning them over as quickly as possible. Recognition of this underlies the current emphasis on 'just-in-time' or JIT techniques, and resulted in much closer attention being given to physical distribution.

Kotler has summarised the key decisions as:

- *Order processing* – how should orders be handled?
- *Warehousing* – where should stocks be located?
- *Inventory* – how much stock should be kept on hand?
- *Transportation* – how should goods be shipped?

Each of these functions may have an important impact on customer service and satisfaction levels and calls for careful analysis, planning and control. Suggestions for further reading are given in the appendices.

CURRENT TRENDS

Rosenbloom (1999) in the *IEBM Encyclopedia of Marketing* identifies five trends that have affected channels of distribution in recent years as:

1 More strategic emphasis by firms on channels of distribution.

2 Partnerships and strategic alliances gaining more ground.

3 Continued growth of vertical marketing systems.

4 Growing power of retailers in distribution channels.

5 Greater role for technology in channels of distribution.

With the exception of partnerships and strategic alliances, we have covered all the above issues either in this Chapter or Chapters 8 and 9. Partnerships and strategic alliances are becoming more commonplace in virtually every field of business activity and mark an important departure from the more combative and adversarial attitudes of yester-year. Undoubtedly, this trend owes much to the emphasis on relationship marketing discussed at some length in Chapter 1.

COMPETITION AND REGULATION

The trends to both concentration and collaboration in distribution channels have implications for the degree of competition that exists within them, and so is subject to scrutiny and control by regulatory authorities.

Arrangements that might be seen as in restraint of trade include selective distribution which restricts the numbers of sellers offering a product for sale; exclusive dealing agreements under which intermediaries are prohibited from carrying goods that compete directly with a supplier's own range of products; tying contracts under which a seller requires the buyer to source other goods as well; and a refusal to sell. In nearly all these cases each case will depend on its merits. For example, selective distribution may be seen as stimulating competition between different manufacturers/retailers and so be in the public interest; or a tying contract may be reasonable when a manufacturer stipulates the source of operating supplies or replacement parts. Clearly, this is a complex subject beyond the scope of an introductory textbook but it is an issue to be taken into account when deciding on a channel strategy.

Summary

While Chapters 8 and 9 were concerned primarily with describing channels of distribution as an important element in the marketing environment, this chapter has focused on distribution as an element in the marketing mix.

The chapter opened with a definition of the **marketing channel** and a reprise of the functions discussed previously. Next we reviewed the forces which influence the **structure** of marketing channels, including the often conflicting forces of **cost** and **control** which also act as major determinants of **channel policy**. A discussion of the **channel decision** followed in which we looked at the multiplicity of factors which influence the marketer's selection of a distribution channel.

The following section examined a relatively new development – the **Vertical Marketing System (VMS)** which represents greater cooperation and collaboration between members or higher levels of integration in vertically integrated organisations. Brief reviews of **channel management, physical distribution** and current trends concluded the chapter.

Review questions and problems

1 Rank the 'essential distributive functions' cited in the text in order of importance for each of the following:
   (a) Steel stockholder;
   (b) Primary commodity wholesaler –
       (i) perishable goods;
       (ii) non-perishable goods.
   (c) Packaged-food wholesaler;
   (d) 'Main' car dealer.

2 Which distribution policy do you consider most appropriate to the sale of the following products:
   ■ Car accessories;
   ■ Car tyres;
   ■ Ethical pharmaceuticals;
   ■ Household cleaning materials;
   ■ Luxury cosmetics;
   ■ Industrial robots?
   Stipulate the assumptions underlying your selection of a given policy and cite actual examples wherever possible.

3 Discuss the impact of vertical integration on the structure of traditional distribution channels.

4 Selection of a distribution policy invariably demands a compromise between cost and control. Discuss.

5 Evaluate the possible effect of mail order, automatic vending and door-to-door selling on retail distribution in the coming decade.

6 How can a manufacturer evaluate the following choices in the construction of a marketing/distribution system:
   (a) Own retail sales force and direct delivery with own transport system.
   (b) Own retail sales force and commercial warehousing/delivery service.
   (c) Wholesale salesmen and own transport system delivering to wholesalers only.
   (d) Any other combination.

7 Describe the variables which affect the design of distribution channels and comment on their relative importance.

8 What are the possible sources of innovation in distribution, describing some you are familiar with, and comment on the process of adoption or of rejection.

9 Describe the variables which affect the choice of distribution channels by a manufacturing firm.

10 Argue the case for managing the physical distribution of a company's products as an aspect of its marketing strategy.

11 What problems are inherent in producing a definition of the term 'channel of distribution'?

12 What do you understand by the total distribution cost concept? Outline the scope of the constituent centres involved and relate the importance of an understanding of the concept to the marketing manager.

13 Discuss the major considerations in designing a channel system.

14 Why is the decision about the type of channel system to be used by a manufacturer often critical to marketing success?

15 By what criteria would you judge the efficiency of a particular channel of distribution?

16 Identify and discuss some of the factors that should increase the trend towards vertical marketing systems.

17 Give reasons as to why an effective distribution strategy can give a firm a differential competitive advantage.

18 'Without purposive co-ordination, motivation and direction, channels are doomed to failure, irrespective of the way they are structured' (Stern & Ansary). Comment.

19 Discuss fully the proposition that the key concern and source of conflict in distribution channels is with the management of inventories and logistics. Use examples where possible to illustrate your answer.

Key terms

administered VMS
business system
buyer/seller concentration ratios
channel captain
channel leader
channel policy
channel structure
channels of distribution
conflict
contract purchasing
contractual VMS
control
corporate VMS
cost
countervailing power
CTN (confectionary, tobacconists

and newsagent)
customer service explosion
economic advantage
franchises
globalisation of industry
intensity of distribution
  – intensive, selective,
  exclusive
intermediary
just in time (JIT)
locus of channel control
logistics
marketing communications
measurement
organisational integration
physical distribution

postponement
retail co-operatives
selective distribution
service requirements
specialty goods
speculation
strategic variable
substitutability
superimpose
supply chain
systems selling
technical complexity
time compression
vertical marketing system
  (VMS)
wholesaler co-operatives

Supplementary reading list

Bowersox, D. J. and Closs, D. J. (1999), 'Logistics and value creation', in Baker, M.J. (ed.) *IEBM Encyclopedia of Marketing*, (London: Thomson Learning).

Christopher, M. and Payne, A. (2003), 'Integrating customer relationship management and supply chain management', in Baker, M.J. (ed.) *The Marketing Book*, 5th. Edn, (Oxford: Butterworth Heinemann).

Rosenbloom, B. (1999), 'Channel management', in Baker, M.J. (ed.) *IEBM Encyclopedia of Marketing*, (London: Thomson Learning).

MARKETING COMMUNICATIONS

- The concept of a channel of communication linking communicators with an intended audience.

- The view that effective communication is the consequence of a process similar to that described in the hierarchy of effects models; that is moving an audience from unawareness to awareness, interest and action.

- The distinction between personal and non-personal influence and their combination in the theory of the two-step flow of communication.

- The paradigm of the innovation-decision process comprising the four stages of knowledge, persuasion, decisions and confirmation and its use in planning and communication strategy.

- The nature of opinion leadership and the characteristics of opinion leaders.

- The influence of source effect.

- The concepts of consonance and dissonance.

- The relationship between message and medium.

- The role of communications as a marketing mix variable.

- The view of marketing communications as a form of information processing in which consumers play an active role.

INTRODUCTION

In Chapter 1 our very first definition of marketing stated that "The function of marketing is the establishment of contact" (Cherington, 1920). By now it will be clear that establishing contact is a necessary condition for an exchange to occur. We have seen that the concentration of production, and the development of a global market have led to a physical separation between the producers of products and their intended customers. This is also the case with many services where personal contact is no longer required, e.g. withdrawing money from your bank account via an ATM. But, for an exchange to occur, the buyer must be aware of what is on offer and these offerings must be both available and accessible. The latter requirements are met by the business system and the channels of distribution. However, the creation of awareness is the responsibility of the fourth element of the marketing mix – promotion.

Promotion is a large and complex subject covering a variety of different disciplines and activities. This is reflected by the fact that we devote three chapters to the subject and that each of these chapters is capable of further sub-division. Indeed, each of these sub-divisions is a specialist topic in its own right and the subject of individual treatment both by dedicated professional bodies and academic textbooks. It is clear that a book of this kind can only offer a brief overview.

To begin with, in this chapter we explore the nature of communication as a process that applies to all forms of communication be it advertising, direct marketing, personal selling, public relations etc. These will all be the subject of separate treatment in the next three chapters. However, in recent years there has been a significant move towards the integration of the different approaches into a coherent promotional mix. In turn this move has led to the emergence of a new school of thought known as **integrated marketing communications** or **IMC**.

Two key proponents of the IMC approach, Kitchen and Schultz (1997) point out that there are academics who question whether the integrated marketing communications (IMC) phenomenon is just another management 'fad.' In the past, effort was focused on breaking down marcom activities into definable categories, but IMC requires companies to adopt marcoms strategies that co-ordinate various different promotional elements. Further, these promotional activities need to be integrated with other marketing activities that communicate with consumers. In their study, which aimed to discover attitudes of advertising agencies in the UK toward IMC, 100% of the respondents agreed that companies should be integrated in terms of communication, advertising agency staff are spending 25% or more of their time on integrated programs, and there is a trend to more, not less, integration.

The American Association of Advertising Agencies' (AAAA) defines IMC as:

> *IMC is a concept of marketing communication planning that recognises the added value of a comprehensive plan that evaluates the strategic roles of a variety of communication disciplines—for example general advertising, direct response, sales promotion and public relations—and combines these disciplines to provide clarity, consistency and maximum communication impact*   *(Schultz 1993).*

Erdogan (1998) argued that "Factors supporting the growth of global communication and promotions such as cluttered media, advancing database technology, changing media buying practices, increasing promotional budgets at the expense of advertising, and lastly shifting market place power from manufacturers to retailers, are also effecting the integration of marketing communication activities".

Shimp (2003) reinforces the need for integration when he points out that different promotional tools are suited to the achievement of different promotional objectives. Advertising may create awareness and interest, but it might take a sales promotion or direct selling to convert these into a sale. As a result, the author proposed that IMC programmes must be designed so as to move consumers from the unawareness stage to the ultimate behaviour stage by employing appropriate communication tools. In summary, he identifies the key features of IMC as being:

1 *Start with the customer or prospect.*

2 *Use any form of relevant contact.*

3 *Achieve synergy (speak with a single voice).*

4 *Build relationships.*

5 *Affect behaviour.*

One of the best-known textbooks in the USA dealing with' promotion' as the fourth P of the marketing mix appeared in its third edition (2003) with the title *Advertising and Integrated Brand Promotion*. In the Preface to the Fourth Edition (2006) the authors (O'Guinn et al) comment:

Some people questioned that title: "Isn't it supposed to be Advertising and Integrated Marketing Communication?" We were convinced then that advertisers and agencies alike were focused on the brand and integrated brand promotion (IBP), and that integrated marketing communication (IMC) was really a thing of the past, and probably the wrong term in the first place. Our perspective proved to be correct. Advertising and promotion is all about the brand, and industry is pursuing brand awareness and competitive advantage with an ever-expanding array of advertising and promotion brand building techniques
....

Like all sellers, the authors are seeking to differentiate themselves from their competitors in suggesting that **IBP** has replaced the 'fad' for IMC. Our view is that both perspectives deserve recognition. Borden's original conceptualisation of the marketing mix included branding, personal selling, advertising, promotions and packaging, and argued for their integration so neither IMC or IBP is a novel concept. What is different is that due to the difficulty of maintaining a competitive advantage based on physical or objective factors, and the growth of service industries, emphasis on the subjective and emotional factors has grown in importance. As O'Guinn et al note, heavy users of advertising and promotion like Proctor & Gamble identify their core competitive capability as **"branding"**.

However, to create successful IMC/IBP programmes, one must first understand how each of the different promotional techniques works in isolation before considering how to combine them to best effect in a promotional strategy. Accordingly, in Chapter 18 we look at methods of mass communication; in Chapter 19 we examine direct communication methods and in Chapter 20 we deal with personal selling and sales promotion. But, in this chapter the emphasis is on theories and concepts that underpin all aspects of marketing communications.

WHAT ARE MARKETING COMMUNICATIONS?

In the *IEBM Encyclopedia of Marketing* Keith Crosier (1999) answers his own rhetorical question 'What is marketing communications?' by defining seven varieties of marketing communication as follows:

1 *Advertising* communicates via a recognisable advertisement placed in a

definable advertising medium, guaranteeing exposure to a target audience in return for a published rate for the time or space used.

2 *Publicity* communicates via a news release to definable news media in the hope of secondary exposure to a target audience in return for a published rate for the time or space used.

3 *Packaging* communicates via display, guaranteeing exposures to a potential customer at the point of sale but not normally to a wider target audience.

4 *Personal selling* communicates person to person via a sales pitch by a sales representative to a prospect, or by a sales assistant to a customer, guaranteeing exposure to a selected individual within a target market.

5 *Direct marketing* communicates person to person but through an intervening channel, such as the post (a mailshot or mailing), door-to-door delivery (a mail drop), the telephone (telemarketing) or a fax line (no specific description yet), guaranteeing exposure to a selected individual within a target market. For many years, the only form of direct marketing in use was direct mail.

6 *Sponsorship* communicates via explicit association of a product or service with an entity, event or activity, in the expectation of secondary exposure to a target audience through identification during associated media coverage.

7 *Sales promotion* communicates via a variety of promotions not encompassed by any of the definitions above, each aiming for exposure to a target audience and some furthermore offering an incentive to respond actively.

Added to these one must also consider the impact of the internet. All will be discussed in the next three chapters, with the exception of packaging which was the subject of chapter 13.

In this chapter we begin with a definition of communication and proceed to examine some of the basic models of the communication process in current circulation. References will be made to the role of attention and perception as prerequisites of action by the receiver – usually in the form of some attitudinal or behavioural change, or both – as well as to the relevance of learning theory to the propagation and understanding of marketing communication. Both these topics were introduced in Chapter 8 ('Individual Buyer Behaviour'). The chapter then looks more closely at some of the major components of any marketing communication – the source, the message and the medium – and concludes with a discussion of the role of communication in the marketing mix. Finally, we examine a suggestion by Crosier (1983) that we should abandon traditional models of the kind discussed in this chapter in favour of an alternative explanation based upon information processing theory.

COMMUNICATION DEFINED

Wilbur Schramm (1995) defined communication as 'the process of establishing a commonness or oneness of thought between a sender and a receiver'. Central to this definition is the concept that for communication to occur there must be a transfer of information from one party – the sender – which is received and understood by the other party – the receiver. In other words both receiver and sender play an active role in establishing communication – a fact which is given particular point when one considers that the average consumer is estimated to be exposed to approximately 3000 promotional messages a day but only receives nine of these messages. My colleague Keith Crosier has drawn to my attention the fact that while I assert that 'both receiver and sender play an active role' this is not clear from Schramm's model nor the pictorial representation of it in Figures 17.1 and 17.2. I agree – in fact the arrows in the figures tend to convey uni-directionality and cast the destination in a passive 'receiver' role. I do not believe Schramm intended this, and nor do I. In my composite model of consumer behaviour described in Chapter 8, the point is stressed that it is the receiver who decides whether or not to 'switch on' and thus plays an active role in the process. This point is of particular importance as much of the criticism of advertising rests on the assumption that promotional activity is something *done to* or *exercised on* passive consumers with no opportunity to control or influence the process.

Pictorially the simplest model of the communications process is shown in Figure 17.1. However, this simple model ignores the fact that it is necessary to convert ideas into a symbolic medium to enable them to be transmitted via a communication channel. To allow for this we must introduce two more elements into the model – **encoding** and **decoding** – as shown in Figure 17.2.

Figure 17.1 Simplified communication model

Source: Schramm, W. (1995), *The Process and Effects of Mass Communication* (Urbana, Ill.: University of Illinois Press).

Figure 17.2 Communication channel model

Source: Schramm, W. (1995), *The Process and Effects of Mass Communication* (Urbana, Ill.: University of Illinois Press).

As Schramm points out, this model can accommodate all types of communication so that in the case of electronic communication the encoder becomes a transmitting device – microphone, teletype, and so on – and the decoder a receiver – radio or television set, telephone, and so on. In the case of direct personal (face-to-face) communication then one person is both source and encoder, while the other is decoder and destination, and the signal is language. It follows that if an exchange of meaning is to take place, then both source and destination must be tuned in to each other and share the same language. Put another way, there must be an overlap in the field of experience of **source** and **destination** – which Schramm illustrates in Figure 17.3.

Figure 17.3 Communication channels

Source: Schramm, W. (1995), *The Process and Effects of Mass Communication* (Urbana, Ill.: University of Illinois Press).

We must also recognise that all communication is intended to have an effect and introduce the notion of feedback into our model of communication, for it is through feedback that the source learns how its signals are being interpreted. In personal communication feedback is often instantaneous through verbal acknowledgement or gesture; but in impersonal communication through the mass media it may have to be inferred from other indicators, for example audience size, circulation, readership, or monitored by sampling opinion.

The final element in Schramm's model, which is not immediately apparent from the figures, other than in the existence of arrows linking the other elements, is the channel or, more correctly channels, for messages are rarely transmitted through a single channel. Thus, in personal communications it is not merely the words which convey the message, but the intonation of our voice and the gestures which accompany them, although some might regard these as coding rather than channels. In the field of marketing communication then the channel tends to have the specific connotation of the media classes which are the subject of more extended treatment in the next chapter.

The marketer's version of Schramm's model employs slightly different terminology, but contains all of the following elements (see C. Shannon and W. Weaver, 1962, *The Mathematical Theory of Communication*):

Who . . .	*says what . . .*	*how . . .*
Communicator	Message	Channels

to whom . . .	*with what effect*
Audience	Feedback

From his model Schramm derives four basic 'conditions of success in communication . . . which must be fulfilled if the message is to arouse its intended response'. These are:

1 The message must be so designed and delivered as to gain the attention of the intended destination.

2 The message must employ signs which refer to experience common to source and destination, so as to 'get the meaning across'.

3 The message must arouse personality needs in the destination and suggest some ways to meet those needs.

4 The message must suggest a way to meet those needs which is appropriate to the group situation in which the destination finds itself at the time when they are moved to make the desired response.

Consideration of these four requirements should strike a receptive chord in the memory of the reader who is methodically working their way through the book, for they echo closely points discussed in Chapter 8 concerning hierarchy-of-effects models in consumer behaviour. In fact Schramm's four conditions are very similar to Strong's basic AIDA model – Attention, Interest, Desire and Action. It will be useful, therefore, to recapitulate on this earlier discussion, but specifically in the context of marketing communications. In doing so we will first provide a broad overview, and then pick out certain key concepts for a fuller discussion, namely diffusion theories, opinion leadership and the two-step flow of communication, source credibility and cognitive consonance and dissonance.

HOW MARKETING COMMUNICATION WORKS

One of the earliest explanations of how advertising works is based upon the **stimulus–response theory** of learning in which advertising is perceived as a stimulus, and purchasing behaviour the intended and desired response. However, it is clear that advertising, even when very intense, does not lead automatically to purchase, and it was postulated that the act of purchase is the culmination of a whole sequence of events. If this is so then it is argued that advertising's role is to move people up the steps from a state of unawareness to purchase, and a number of models of varying levels of sophistication have been put forward including Strong's *AIDA model* (Attention, Interest, Desire, Action), Lavidge and Steiner's *'Hierarchy of Effects' Model* (Awareness, Knowledge, Liking, Preference, Conviction, Purchase), and Roger's *'Innovation Adoption' Model* (Awareness, Interest, Evaluation, Trial, Adoption). The models referred to above are all old (the most recent is 1961) and relate specifically to personal communication rather than the broader field of marketing communication which is our concern here. Keith Crosier (1995) addresses this issue directly in Chapter 6 of *Marketing: Theory and Practice* and the reader is strongly advised to consult this for a much extended discussion of marketing communications in general, and the role of hierarchical models in the particular. However, all these models suggest a sequence of events which observation and experience often contradict, particularly in the case of low involvement and/or impulse purchases, and Crosier underlines the trenchant criticisms of, inter alia, Copland, Palda, Krugman, Ehrenberg and Ray. Indeed this conflict of opinion is but another manifestation of the conundrum as to whether attitude change leads to behavioural change or vice versa, there being substantial evidence for both schools of thought. However, notwithstanding this conflict of opinion, it is clear that most advertisers find the learning model intuitively appealing and often set objectives in terms of moving potential customers up the various steps from unawareness to purchase.

Two basic problems may be identified immediately: first, audiences are comprised of persons who differ from each other in many demographic and psycho-social respects; second, there is likely to be considerable variation in the levels of knowledge and awareness of different members of the audience at any given point in time. As a consequence individuals will vary in their response to the advertisers' message and the channels through which it is communicated. It follows that insight into the understanding of how such variance occurs is of vital importance in designing marketing communications.

Many communication experts subscribe to McLuhan's (1965) thesis that 'the medium is the message', and so would argue that once a target audience has been identified the primary decision is selection of the medium or channel to be used. Conversely, others point out that media planning is a complex activity only because there are so many similar media that choice between them is difficult. This being so, then it is the message which must be selected first, and this will help identify the most appropriate medium to reach the target audience. In reality, however, it seems that both approaches are used and that preference is 'situation-specific' – but, on balance, the channel seems to exercise the greater influence and will be dealt with first.

In general, channels may be divided into two major categories: personal and non-personal. As the name implies **personal channels** embrace all those situations in which a direct, face-to-face communication takes place, while **non-personal channels** comprise all media through which messages are transmitted without face-to-face communication, for example press, television, radio, posters, and so on. (It is this distinction that underlies the difference between mass communication and direct marketing covered in Chapters 18 and 19 respectively).

The available evidence suggests that both types of channel have a role to play, and it is usually held that non-personal media are most effective in establishing awareness and interest, while personal influence is necessary to move the members of an audience up the hierarchy through desire to action. Further, it has been found that personal influence is most effective in high-risk purchase situations; that is, where the consumer is expending relatively large amounts and purchases infrequently (shopping goods) or where the product/service has social connotations which link brands with social groups (speciality goods). (The obverse of this is that mass communication is most appropriate for convenience goods.)

As indicated, however, it is usual to find a combination of both personal and non-personal channels used in a given campaign. Research by Lazarsfeld (1944) showed that impersonal channels are often mediated in their effect by personal channels – the so-called 'Two-step flow of communication'. According to this model certain members of the population act as filters and amplifiers for messages and these persons have been designated **opinion leaders**. It follows that, if the two-step model applies, then the communicator should identify the opinion leaders and transmit their messages through them. Often, opinion leaders are best reached via impersonal channels and themselves become a personal channel performing the role of unpaid salesmen. Clearly, the achievement of direct face-to-face communication could be expensive and impersonal channels help reduce the cost of conveying messages to consumers. However, many messages transmitted through the mass media compete for our attention and most of these are screened out by the psychological defence mechanisms of selective perception, distortion and retention. As a result, the power of mass communication as a persuasive influence is largely discounted nowadays, and the mass media are seen primarily as leading to learning and reinforcement over time. Further, different media act in different ways and the skill of the media planner lies in selection of the medium or combination of media best suited to the audience they are seeking to reach

Reference has been made to the **message** on several occasions and its importance is obvious, for, as Kotler says, it is the means 'by which the communicator attempts to make the product meaningful and desirable to the buyer'. Perhaps the most important point about the message is that it should be designed so that it is meaningful to the recipient after the distortion which will inevitably occur on transmission through the chosen channel or channels, and its selective screening by the audience. It follows that the message is an infinitely variable element in the communication process, as it must be tailored to the differing needs and levels of knowledge/ experience of a constantly changing audience. However, two broad schools of thought exist concerning message structure and content, one favouring **consonance** (that is conforming with held beliefs, aspirations, and so forth – 'pleasant' messages), the other **dissonance** (that is contrary to held beliefs and so creating discomfort or dissonance). We return to these concepts later in the chapter.

The final element is the communicator themself. Their influence is both direct – identification of audience, selection of channel, choice of message – and indirect – the way they are perceived by the audience as the source of the message (the 'source effect'). Again, it is important to stress that the source is not necessarily the communicator but rather the origin of the message as perceived by the audience (cf. the testimonial advertisement). In turn the audience's perception of the message will be governed by its interpretation of the source credibility – a concept developed by Kelman and Hovland and seen as comprising two elements – expertness and trustworthiness. Fundamentally the precept is 'the higher the source credibility the greater the effectiveness of the communication'. However, source effect decays over time and must be reinforced through repetition. Further discussion of source effect is to be found later in this chapter.

DIFFUSION THEORIES

In discussing hierarchy-of-effects models in Chapter 8 reference was made to Everett Rogers's five-step adoption model – awareness, interest, evaluation, trial, adoption – which has been used extensively in many studies of new product marketing and marketing communications. However, Rogers' basic model has been subject to a number of criticisms. Specifically, it suggests that adoption is a consequence of the process when in fact the decision might be to reject the innovation, or even to 'wait and see', that is deferred rejection/adoption. Second, the five stages need not occur in the sequence proposed (cf. impulse purchasing) and it seems likely that evaluation is not a discrete phase, but takes place throughout the process. Further, in many instances the trial phase may be omitted. Finally, some critics have pointed out that adoption (purchase of a product) is not the final stage in the process, as post-adoption activity will occur leading to feedback which will influence subsequent behaviour.

To meet these criticisms Rogers joined forces with Floyd Shoemaker (1971) and proposed a revised 'paradigm of the innovation–decision process' containing four stages:

1 *Knowledge*: The individual is aware of the innovation and has acquired some information about it.

2 *Persuasion*: The individual forms an attitude, pro or con, towards the innovation.

3 *Decisions*: The individual performs activities which lead to an adopt-reject decision about the innovation.

4 *Confirmation*: The individual looks for reinforcement regarding their decision and may change their earlier decision if exposed to counter-reinforcing messages.

Clearly this model is more flexible and less mechanistic than the original, and permits the accommodation of the criticisms outlined earlier. Diagrammatically the model appears as shown in Figure 17.4. The reader will be familiar with the antecedent variables, for these were reviewed in Chapter 8, so attention will be focused on the process itself. However, before doing so it will be useful to introduce the concepts of adopter categories and diffusion.

Under another name (the concept of the **product life-cycle, PLC** – see Chapter 12) the diffusion process is one of the most familiar and fundamental of marketing ideas. In essence, the PLC and cumulative adoption curves are the same and show that after a slow initial start sales grow rapidly, and then begin to level off until saturation is achieved. If these sales are plotted against elapsed time from introduction of an innovation, then a normal distribution results and this has lead to attempts to analyse and classify the adoption/buying behaviour of individuals in terms of the properties of the normal distribution. Figure 17.5 illustrates this.

It follows that if we are able to identify beforehand certain individuals as being more receptive to a given innovation, then we should be able to accelerate adoption by focusing our initial marketing efforts upon them. In turn, because the diffusion process is probabilistic, this will accelerate the whole diffusion process and result in enhanced profitability.

Returning to the process of adoption, it has been determined that certain communication mixes are more appropriate than others at different stages, and this knowledge is of great value in planning a communications strategy. The knowledge stage is one of awareness and preliminary information-seeking in which impersonal sources tend to dominate. Other things being equal one could conceive of a situation in which all potential buyers of a new product were exposed to information about it simultaneously but, because of selective perception and distortion, relatively few would react to the information. **Early adopters** are those who do react quickly and they have been found to possess a number of characteristics which distinguish them from later adopters. Specifically, they make it their business to be well-informed and so make greater use of mass media and personal sources of information – both social and professional (that is sales personnel or 'change agents') – and they also tend to be better-educated, extrovert and more cosmopolitan than later adopters.

The second stage in the process is that of **persuasion**, in which the potential user moves from a state of neutral awareness to the development of an attitude towards the new object. In my model (Figure 8.5) this change is initiated by 'Felt Need' and leads to formal evaluation of possible solutions to it. In the Rogers and Shoemaker model this evaluation is based upon the perceived characteristics of the innovation – **relative advantage, compatibility, complexity, trialability** and **observability**. At this stage prospective users will seek to extend their information base and make greater use of personal sources. It is at this juncture that opinion leadership assumes great importance as the potential user will seek the advice of those they see as knowledgeable about the item under consideration.

(The innovativeness dimension, as measured by the time at which an individual adopts an innovation or innovations, is continuous. However, this variable may be partitioned into five adopter categories by laying off standard deviations from the average time of adoption.)

Relative advantage is defined as 'the degree to which an innovation is perceived as better' than an existing idea or object and it is stated that the higher the relative advantage the greater the likelihood of adoption. **Compatibility** and **complexity** are self-explanatory and tend to vary inversely with one another; that is, the more compatible an object is with one's field of experience, attitudes and value structure, and so on, the less complex it is likely to seem and vice versa. **Trialability**, or the extent to which an individual can try out an innovation before coming to a decision, is an important factor in reducing perceived risk and an

Figure 17.4 Paradigm of the innovation decision process

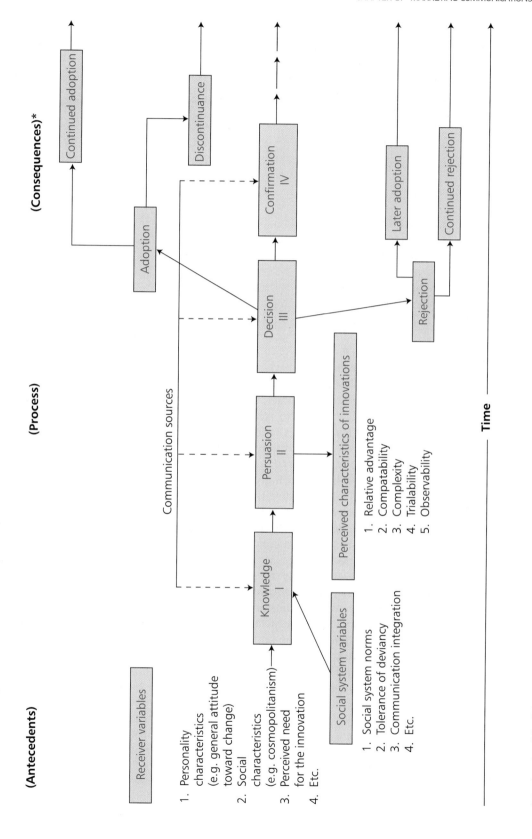

Figure 17.5 Adopter categorisation on the basis of innovativeness

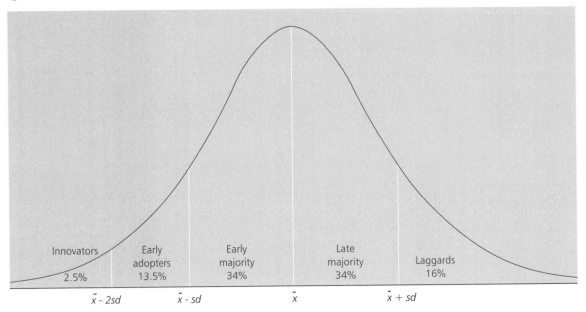

aid to speeding up decision-making (it works both ways!). Finally, **observability** refers to the visible effectiveness of the innovation.

While these perceived characteristics enjoy wide currency I am not overly fond of them myself. For example, relative advantage is really a catch-all for all the other characteristics and it is tautologous to state that the greater the perceived advantage the faster the adoption – even the clinically insane act in the manner which maximises their own perceived self-interest however misguided some people may regard it. Accordingly the reader is warned that, while the concept is appealing, one must beware that it is not meaningless due to circularity of definitions; for example, the greater the relative advantage the faster adoption but the faster the adoption the greater the perceived advantage. Certainly it is difficult to operationalise the concept, for the perception of characteristics tends to be individual-specific.

Following their evaluation the potential user will make a decision to adopt or reject which, as the model shows, is open to subsequent modification; that is, an adopter may continue in use or reject and vice versa for a rejector. Once made the decision is subject to confirmation, in which the person seeks to validate the rightness of their decision and therefore alleviate any post-decision cognitive dissonance (discussed below). This being the case it might be more accurate to show confirmation following the actual decision: 'Adoption' or 'Rejection'.

Like many marketing concepts, Rogers' diffusion model is most valuable for the insights which it gives rather than in providing direct practical applications. Thus it provides a framework for organising one's thinking about the decision process, and the stages which the individual goes through, which can be related to the specific features which distinguish a particular marketing problem.

OPINION LEADERSHIP AND THE TWO-STEP FLOW OF COMMUNICATION

Early models of communication regarded both impersonal sources (the mass media) and personal sources as establishing direct contact with an audience – the so-called 'hypodermic effect'. Belief in this model led to speculation concerning the influence of the mass media upon voting behaviour – thus the undertaking of one of the most celebrated pieces of communication research, reported in Paul F. Lazarsfeld et al.'s (1944) *The People's Choice*. Lazarsfeld and his colleagues set out to study the influence of the mass media on individual voting behaviour in the 1940 presidential election in the United States. Contrary to expectations it was found that influence did not flow directly from a medium (press, radio, and so on) to an audience but was channelled through an intermediary who was designated the 'opinion leader'. It was this finding which gave rise to the two-step model which has had a significant influence on communication research and practice ever since. However, it must be emphasised that the two step hypothesis does not exclude the possibility of a direct flow (one step) and its main contribution is in introducing the mediating effect of personal influence on impersonal communications. Thus, nowadays, the mass media are regarded primarily as **information sources**, and considerable attention is focused upon the nature and behaviour of opinion leaders – how to identify them and how to communicate effectively with them as is evident in the current enthusiasm for the so-called **viral marketing**. Engel et al. (1978) emphasise that contemporary models of social influence are built on a multi-stage interaction model in which the mass media can prompt seekers of information to approach opinion- leaders and vice versa. But, while opinion leaders do not mediate the flow of information, their potential influence as personal sources remains significant.

In simple terms an opinion leader is one to whom others turn for information and advice. However, it must be emphasised that in the usual marketing context opinion leaders are not a distinct and easily classified group in the sense in which Cabinet Ministers or Managing Directors of major companies are. More often than not opinion leaders are people just like you and me, for if they are to be effective at a personal influence level they must be accessible, which implies that they are members of reference groups with which people have contact. In fact, most reference groups develop around shared interests and some members will be seen as more influential than others in the context of that interest. But we belong to many reference groups and leader and follower roles may be reversed; for example, the captain of the football team may well seek the first reserve's opinion on the merits of different mobile phones. It is this tendency which makes identification of opinion leaders difficult but, despite this, a number of studies have been completed which permit some generalisations to be made. Writing in 1971, Thomas S. Robertson in *Innovative Behavior and Communications* offered the following:

- The *age* of opinion leaders varies by product category
- The *social status* of opinion leaders is generally the same as the advisee
- Opinion leaders exhibit high *gregariousness*

- There is limited evidence that opinion leaders are more *cosmopolitan* than advisees
- Opinion leaders generally have greater *knowledge* of the area of influence than advisees.
- Opinion leaders are more *innovative* than advisees
- There are no major distinguishing personality traits.

Research in the past three decades has done nothing to modify significantly these generalisations and Elihu Katz's summary (cited by Robertson, *Innovative Behavior*, p. 180), made in 1957, would still seem to be valid:

influence is related to (1) personification of certain values (who one is), (2) competence (what one knows), and (3) strategic social location (whom one knows). To the extent that an individual represents or personifies group values, he stands a better chance of leadership. Thus if the group emphasises an 'in' manner of dress, the person who dressed most accordingly may well be influential. Again, to the extent that an individual is highly knowledgeable, he stands a better chance of leadership. Finally, to the extent that an individual is available and active in the everyday interpersonal communication process, the better his chance of leadership.

Blackwell, Miniard and Engel (2001) state:

In general, researchers conclude that the most common characteristics of opinion leaders across categories is that they are very involved with a particular product category. They tend to read specialized publications about a specific category and actively seek information from mass media and other sources. They also possess greater self-confidences; are more outgoing and gregarious; and want to share information, talk with others, and seek their opinions. (405)

From the above summary it follows that marketers must identify the opinion leaders for their own product/service category. Certain of the generalised traits outlined above will assist in this identification, as will the trait of innovativeness. It is also clear that opinion leaders maintain their status, which gives them satisfaction, from being well-informed and so are likely to make greater use of both personal and non-personal sources of information.

SOURCE EFFECT

As the basic model of communication makes clear, all communication originates from a source and this source has a marked bearing upon the subsequent interpretation of the message. In a marketing context it is important to distinguish between the true source – the organisation which is responsible for the generation of the message and pays for its communication in promotional channels – and the perceived source, which is the consumer perception of its origin. This distinction is important because we (consumers) often identify messages with the communicator (sales agent, personality/celebrity in the television commercial) or the channel (Good Housekeeping, Reader's Digest, Radio Clyde) rather than the company 'behind' the message.

A great deal of attention has been given to source effect and extended discussions are to be found in several of the texts cited. Typical of these is DeLozier (1976) in *The Marketing Communications Process* who provides the following summary:

1 In general, a source is more persuasive when his audience perceives him as high, rather than low, in credibility.

2 A source's credibility, and thus his persuasiveness, is reduced when his audience perceives that the source has something to gain from his persuasive attempts (intention to manipulate).

3 Over time the opinion change attributed to a high-credibility source decreases, whereas the opinion change induced by a low credibility source increases, resulting in about the same level of retained opinion change for both low and high-credibility sources.

4 Reinstatement of a high-credibility source some time after his initial message presentation results in higher opinion change retention than if no reinstatement occurs; whereas reinstatement of a low-credibility source some time after his message presentation results in lower opinion change retention than if no reinstatement occurs.

5 The low-credibility source can increase his influence by arguing for a position which is against his own self-interest.

6 A communicator increases his influence if at first he expresses some views already held by his audience, followed by his intended persuasive communication.

7 A communicator increases his persuasiveness if at the beginning of his message he states that his position on the topic is the same as that of his audience, even though he may argue against that position.

8 The more similar members of an audience perceive the source to be themselves, the more persuasive the communicator will be.

9 What people think of a communicator's message affects what they think of him (his image).

10 A source is more persuasive when he holds a positive, rather than a negative, attitude towards himself, his message and his receiver.

11 The more powerful and attractive a source is perceived to be, the more influence he has on a receiver's behaviour.

As Keith Crosier has pointed out to me, one must treat such apparently authoritative statements with considerable circumspection, for much of the evidence on which they are based is derived from situations far different from those encountered in the market place (for example students' reactions to views communicated by their professors). For an extensive interpretation of marketing communications as such, students are strongly recommended to supplement this chapter with Chapter 13 of *Marketing: Theory and Practice* (1995).

Consonance and dissonance

At various places in the text reference has been made to **dissonance** and it will be useful to indicate the role this concept has to play in marketing communications.

In the discussion of perception (Chapter 8) it was indicated that we seek to organise perceived stimuli (**cognitions**) into coherent and consistent patterns which are in accord with our knowledge, beliefs and attitudes – in other words we are seeking a state of **consonance**. If two cognitions are not consonant, they may be either irrelevant, that is they have no relationship to one another, or dissonant, that is in conflict with each other. Clearly dissonant cognitions create a state of psychological tension which the individual will seek to avoid, reduce or eliminate. It is also clear that in any choice situation there is a potential for dissonance, as the recognition of choice implies alternative solutions to a perceived need. In many consumer purchasing situations these alternatives are very similar and the propensity for dissonance is correspondingly greater.

Attention was first focused upon this phenomenon by the publication of Leon A. Festinger's (1957) *A Theory of Cognitive Dissonance*, and has been the subject of much interest ever since. It is generally agreed that dissonance can arise from one of three basic causes – logical inconsistency, a conflict between attitude and behaviour or two behaviours, and when a strongly held belief is contravened or negated. Faced with a state of dissonance we tend to use a number of approaches to remove the state, and all these contain elements of **selectivity**. **Avoidance** is a clear example in which we screen out stimuli which conflict with our preferred interpretation (this can occur both before a decision and after, and may be subconscious), while in the case of rationalisation we interpret the stimuli to suit our preferred belief (cf. the example of the American football match in Chapter 8). Alternatively we can seek additional information which supports our choice – again on a selective basis or forget or suppress the inconsistent information we have. It follows that dissonance can occur at any stage of the purchase decision, though most interest has been shown in the post-purchase phase when commitment has been made to a particular choice, and is likely to be most acute in the case of major purchase decisions. In a paper given at the 1970 Market Research Society Annual Conference ('The Complementary Benefit Principle of How Advertising Works in Relation to the Product') Peter Hutchinson suggested that the existence of cognitive dissonance has two basic lessons for practitioners:

1 Perfect in manufacture those product benefits which are readily available.

2 Advertise those attributes which are not immediately observable or easily learned.

The first recommendation underlines the importance of ensuring that those dimensions on which direct comparisons can be made are highly developed in one's product, while the second emphasises the need to provide the potential user with additional reasons for preferring your alternative to all the others.

The message and the medium

Earlier in the chapter reference was made to Schramm's four basic conditions for successful communication, all of which involved the basic element of communication – the message. The message is often the subject of a separate chapter or more in specialised texts such as Shimp (2003) which should be consulted for a full discussion of the topic. Only a brief overview can be presented here.

There are three dimensions of messages which demand particular attention – **structure**, **appeal** or content, and the **symbolic code** (words, music, gesture, and so on) in which the message is couched.

The structure of a message embraces three main considerations – whether it should be a one-sided or two-sided presentation, the sequence in which information should be presented, and whether a conclusion should be offered. In fact there is no single preferred structure, for this will vary according to the audience. For example, one-sided messages are most effective with people who agree with the source, are poorly educated and unlikely to be exposed to any counter-arguments, while a two-sided message is better suited to convert persons inclining to an opposite opinion, better educated and likely to be exposed to counter-arguments Similarly, in the case of sequence some messages are more effective when they build up to a climax (high audience interest), others to an anti-climax (low audience interest), while in the case of two-sided arguments controversial material is most effective when presented first (the **primacy effect**) and bland or uninteresting information is favoured by recency, that is the material presented last is more effective. Finally, while messages are in general more effective if a conclusion is presented, this applies more to persons of low intelligence than persons of high intelligence and is less so in all cases where the source is seen as having a vested interest in the conclusion. Much of the same applies where drawing a conclusion would insult the audience's intelligence.

In the case of **message appeal**, DeLozier cites six alternative approaches – fear, distraction, participation, emotion versus rational, aggression arousal, and humour. Of these the most controversial are the use of fear appeals and distraction methods. Much criticism has been levelled against advertisements for consumer products which suggest that non-possession will lead to loss of status or social unacceptability (for example deodorants), while the use of fear is widely supported in health and safety advertising. Distraction is also criticised on the grounds that it diminishes/influences critical judgement concerning the prime subject of the communication, for example the expense account lunch or the use association in consumer advertisements. Overall the evidence regarding the efficiency of different message appeals confirms that it is situation-specific and must be varied in light of the circumstances they are expected to encounter.

Some mention has already been made of the symbolic code in which a message is couched. Here the evidence is more clear cut and indicates that while choice of words can have an important bearing upon the interpretation of a message, non-verbal communications are often more important in conveying ideas and meaning than words alone. The validity of this is readily apparent in television commercials when sound and movement can be combined to enhance the impact of the purely verbal message to be put across. The impact of 'body language' was emphasised during the 2005 General election in the UK when psychologists were employed to comment on the differences between the things politicians were saying and what their expressions and gestures revealed they were really thinking.

At this juncture no reference will be made to the advertising media through which a message is conveyed to an audience, as this is discussed at some length in the next chapter.

THE ROLE OF COMMUNICATION IN THE MARKETING MIX

As a process, marketing is firmly founded on the assumption of effective two-way communication – of consumers telling firms what they want and firms informing consumers what they have to sell. In this sense communication is central to everything the firm does, and pervades all its activities. However, when we speak of marketing communications we do so in the more restricted sense of those functional activities which are collectively known as 'promotion' – advertising, personal selling, public relations, sales promotion and so on. Each of these topics is treated at some length in the chapters which follow but before turning to these it will be useful to summarise the basic objectives of promotional strategy.

Martin Bell (1972) in *Marketing: Concepts and Strategy*, rightly observes that each item on an exhaustive list of **promotional objectives** would need a chapter to itself and contents himself by selecting seven for specific mention:

1 *Increase sales;*
2 *Maintain or improve market share;*
3 *Create or improve brand recognition, acceptance or insistence;*
4 *Create a favourable climate for future sales;*
5 *Inform and educate the market;*
6 *Create a competitive difference;*
7 *Improve promotional efficiency.*

Clearly, there is considerable overlap between these seven objectives but the distinction between them is important because emphasis upon any one will tend to lead to a different promotional mix being required. For example, creating a favourable climate for future sales is most appropriate for industrial products and consumer durables where there is a long repurchase cycle. Thus customers need to have the wisdom of their previous purchase confirmed in order to reduce post-purchase cognitive dissonance, and will also respond favourably to advice on how to get the best out of their purchase. Conversely, if one is seeking to win customers from other manufacturers, then one may be seeking to engender cognitive dissonance by suggesting the currently preferred brand is inferior to your own. To achieve these objectives it will often be necessary to use different messages and different channels – a requirement which will only be apparent if one has carefully defined the objective in advance.

Bell also cites five key conditions which favour the use of promotion in the marketing mix:

1 *A favourable trend in demand;*
2 *Strong product differentiation;*
3 *Product qualities are hidden;*
4 *Emotional buying motives exist;*
5 *Adequate funds are available.*

While a favourable trend in demand will usually result in a greater apparent return on one's promotional investment, it should not be overlooked that maintaining sales under conditions of stagnant or declining demand is equally, and sometimes more, important. Similarly, while the existence of strong product differentiation will allow clear distinctions to be drawn with competing products, it must also be remembered that the greater the departure from known and trusted concepts, the greater the intrinsic resistance to change. For these reasons it often happens that the most effective promotions are those which communicate hidden product qualities (purity, taste, durability, and so forth) which can only be recognised in use, coupled with promotions which appeal to emotional buying motives. (As noted in my model of buying behaviour in Chapter 8, faced with a need to discriminate between two objectively similar competitive brands, the subjective/emotional factors may be trivial but determinant.) Finally, it is a truism to extol the need for adequate funds but it is a factor which is often overlooked, as will be noted when discussing advertising appropriations in the next chapter.

MARKETING COMMUNICATIONS AS INFORMATION PROCESSING

In earlier editions reference was made to the eclectic nature of the foregoing review of marketing communications which was supported by a recommendation that the reader consult the named sources for a fuller treatment. At several places reference has been made to Keith Crosier who has made many helpful and cogent criticisms which I have attempted to accommodate in this revision. However, his most radical suggestion – that I completely restructure the chapter – I have chosen largely to ignore, on the grounds that he is concerned with the latest state of the art in marketing communication theory whereas my perception of an introductory text book is that it must record and analyse the received wisdom and practices which enjoy common currency. That said it is also important that the reader should be exposed to the latest thinking and this section examines Crosier's argument, referred to in the introduction to the chapter, that we abandon traditional theories in favour of one based on **information processing**.

Clues to Crosier's thinking are to be found in Chapter 13 of *Marketing: Theory and Practice* (1995, 3rd edn), but even this contribution lacks the integrative framework which becomes possible by using information processing theory. Thus his proposals are to be found in an article entitled 'Towards a Praxiology of Advertising' (Crosier, 1983), the abstract of which states:

This article argues for the need to abandon traditional models of advertising effect, if a theory is to be developed which is capable of fitting the observable reality that people use advertisements deliberately rather than being used by them. Using information processing theory as the best available organising principle, it proposes a number of candidate elements of a future, fully grounded theory of advertising.

In the opening paragraph we are told that '**Praxiology** is the study of human action. The term is used here to express the crucial idea that people voluntarily and deliberately consume and use advertisements, in contrast to the commonly implied alternative that advertising manipulates people.' Crosier then goes on to argue that:

Where advertising is concerned the prevailing grand theory is operant conditioning, expressed in the form of various hierarchical models of advertising effect all implicitly conforming to the stimulus–response – or at best stimulus–organism–response – paradigm of human behaviour. In the seventy years since Pavlov died at the age of 87, the social and cultural influences upon response to stimuli such as advertisements have of course changed considerably.

Figure 17.6 A model of advertisement-processing behaviour

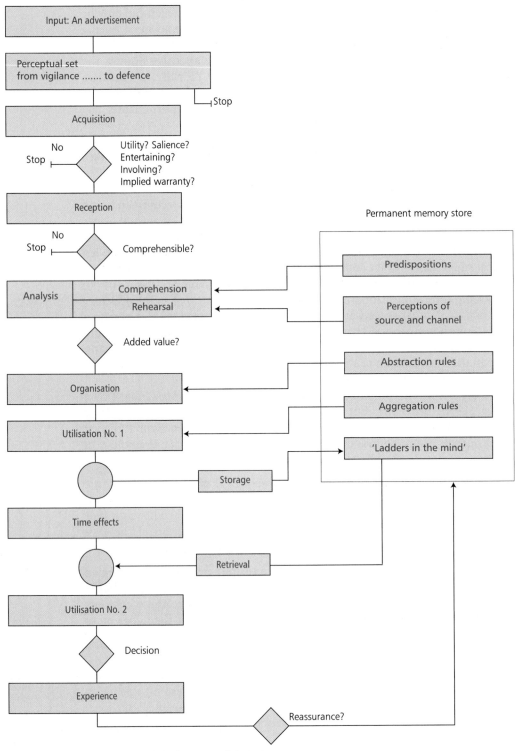

Source: Crosier, K. (1983), *International Journal of Advertising*, Vol. 2, No. 3.

Thus we need to reconsider the relevance and applicability of this model by observing how people actually behave when reacting to modern advertising.

As we have inferred earlier, 'The conversation and publications of advertising practitioners, social critics of advertising, consumerists and politicians very often hinge upon an important implicit hypothesis: that advertising is something powerful firms do to powerless (though sometime stubborn) consumers.' But this is an assumption rejected by our earlier composite model of buying behaviour and by Crosier's conceptualisation of Advertisement Processing Behaviour reproduced as Figure 17.6.

In support of his model Crosier cites Sternthal and Craig's (1982) proposal that purchase and consumption decisions are viewed in terms of how individuals acquire, organise and use information. According to this view, consumers are active seekers and users of information although they may indulge in such behaviour for purposes other than specific product purchase decisions.

(Crosier proposes six other uses in addition to 'hard' information – entertainment, added value, implied warrant, reassurance, involvement, vicarious experience.) Thus without departing entirely from the classical operant conditioning or stimulus–response process implicit in the hierarchical models, the information processing model assigns much greater important to consumers as participants rather than passive objects and so is more in keeping with the view of behaviour advanced in Chapter 8.

Shimp (2003) discusses communication as information processing in terms of two different models - the **consumer processing model (CPM)** and the **hedonic, experiential model (HEM)**. CPM perceives behaviour as being rational, cognitive, systematic and reasoned while HEM sees it as being driven by emotions in pursuit of "fun, fantasies and feelings" (Hirschman, 1982). As with so many academic models the two are polar opposites and Shimp stresses the point we have made earlier, e.g. about models of competition, "you should think of these models as bipolar perspectives that anchor a continuum of possible consumer behaviours …..Between these extremes rests the bulk of consumer behaviour,…".

Summary

This is the first of four chapters dealing with the fourth 'P' of marketing – Promotion – and has been concerned primarily with a description and analysis of communication as a **process** and its use in a marketing context.

At the outset we noted that marketing communications (marcoms) fall into two broad categories – **personal** and **non-personal**. Advertising and publicity (Public Relations) use mass communication channels, and the message is not targeted at any given individual (although, of course, it is designed to appeal to the segment or segments the seller is seeking to influence). By contrast, Personal selling and direct marketing are targeted at specific individuals and seek to establish personal contact with them, while other activities like exhibitions, sales promotion and the internet may well employ both approaches. We also noted that, while each of these activities is a specialisation in its own right, and will be discussed separately, in recent years there have been growing calls for the integration of multiple methods into what has been termed integrated **marketing communications** or **IMC** when devising a promotional strategy.

Next, we looked at the model of the communication process elaborated by Wilbur Schramm which forms the basis of most explanations of marcoms in marketing textbooks, although many neglect to attribute it to him. This model posits that communication is initiated by a source, converted into a message, and then transmitted through a suitable medium or 'channel' to a pre-identified audience whom it is assumed will be able to receive and decode the message. In that communication is a deliberate and positive action, it seems reasonable to anticipate that it will have some impact on the receiver – even if it is only to ignore or discard the communication (junk mail !) – and that this outcome will be of importance to the sender who will look for **feedback**. In other words, communication is the cue or stimulus intended to precipitate a behavioural response – the first step in our model of buyer behaviour presented in Chapter 8 and the basis of many **hierarchy of effects** models developed to explain how customers make choice decisions.

Originally, all models of communication considered that impersonal sources (the mass media) and personal sources made direct contact with the intended audience – the so-called 'hypodermic' effect. As long ago as the 1940s it was found that this was not always the case as, very often, information communicated through the mass media only came to the attention of many people through an intermediary – the **two-step flow of communication**. Such intermediaries are known as **opinion leaders**, who are seen as knowledgeable and well informed on particular topics and issues, and are accessible to others

seeking such information. Opinion leaders are very often innovators, and so play a particularly important role in promoting the adoption of new products to others. At a more generalised level, most persons who have acquired something new are keen to tell their friends and acquaintances about it and it is their contagious enthusiasm that underpins **viral marketing**.

Whether a message is received directly ,or indirectly through an intermediary, the credibility and authority given it is heavily influenced by the original source. Established brand names, corporate identities, reputable media and commentators, celebrities and others all enhance the receivers perception of a message. This was identified as the **source effect** and discussed in terms of **consonance** and **dissonance** depending upon whether actions taken by the receiver confirmed their expectations.

Finally, we looked briefly at the role of communication in the overall marketing mix and considered the proposition that it should be evaluated in terms of information processing theory. While accepting that this view provides an important elaboration of the more traditional hierarchy of effects/ stimulus response models, it was not felt that one should replace the other. Rather, both should be taken into account when seeking to answer our original question "How do marketing communications work?".

Review questions and problems

1 It has been suggested that the major thrust of consumer protection activities should be concentrated on the provision of information. Can this be justified?

2 Sandage and Fryburger's 'model' of how advertising is thought to work is based on four stages: exposure/perception/integration/action. Describe what takes place at the integration stage.

3 How might the characteristics of the 'message' itself affect the success or failure of an advertisement? Discuss with specific examples.

4 With regard to the source of a communication, what factors can provoke attitude change in the recipient? What alternatives to attitude change are open to the recipient?

5 Do we really know how advertising works? What theories have been advanced that might

help you to explain matters to a person who asks such a question?

6 Identify the main elements in a marketing communication system and say what factors are likely to limit the effectiveness of the communication.

7 Discuss the contribution of models of the hierarchy of effects to the development of advertising theory.

8 Distinguish between personal and non-personal communications and outline the marketing communications functions that each can perform.

9 What are the primary factors affecting the selection of the promotional mix components? Explain the effect each of the factors has on the final promotional mix adopted.

10 What factors may explain the widespread failure to set objectives for a marketing communications campaign before it begins?

11 The famous sage, Dr Johnson, remarked in 1759 that 'advertisements are by now so numerous that they are but negligently perused, and it is therefore become necessary to gain attention by magnificence of promise and by eloquence sometimes sublime and sometimes ridiculous.' Discuss the proposition that his view is as relevant now as it was then.

Key terms

adopter categories
adoption
AIDA (attention, interest, desire, action)
appeal
attention
avoidance
branding
channel
cognitions
cognitive consonance
compatibility
complexity
consonance
consumer processing model (CPM)
decoding
destination
diffusion
diffusion theories
dissonance

early adopters
encoding
feedback
hedonic, experiential model (HEM)
hierarchy-of-effects
hypodermic effect
information processing
information sources
integrated brand promotion
integrated marketing communications (IMC)
internet
media classes
medium
message
message appeal
non-personal channels
observability
opinion leader
perception
personal channels

persuasion
praxiology
primacy effect
product life-cycle (PLC)
promotion
promotional objectives
receiver
rejection
relative advantage
selectivity
sender
source
source credibility
source effect
stimulus-response theory
structure
symbolic code
trialability
two-step flow of communication
viral marketing

Supplementary reading list

O'Guinn, T. C., Allen, C. T., and Semenik, R. J. (2006), *Advertising and Integrated Brand Promotion*, Fourth Edition, (Mason, OH: Thomson South-Western)

Shimp, T. A. (2003), *Advertising, Promotion*, 6th. Edition, (Mason, OH: Thomson South-Western)

Van Riel, C. B. M. (1995), *The Principles of Corporate Communications* (Englewood Cliffs, N.J.: PrenticeHall).

Yeshin, T. (2006) *Advertising*, (London: Thomson)

MASS COMMUNICATION

| Learning Goals | *After reading this chapter you should be able to:* |

- Define advertising.

- List specific objectives which advertising may be used to achieve.

- Describe the historical development and evolution of advertising.

- Cite some vital statistics to help describe the size and nature of the advertising industry.

- Outline the structure of the advertising industry and distinguish the roles of the three main parties involved in the advertising process – advertisers, agents and media owners.

- Discuss the role of advertising in the marketing mix.

- Suggest how a firm might organise for advertising.

- Review the role and function of advertising agencies.

- Give advice on agency selection.

- Indicate how to evaluate different advertising media.

- Summarise some of the key features of the national press, regional press, Sunday newspapers, magazines, television, commercial radio, outdoor advertising, and the cinema

- Outline the procedure to follow when planning an advertising campaign.

- Review alternative methods for setting advertising appropriations.

- Describe methods for assessing advertising effectiveness.

- Indicate some of the economic and ethical issues associated with advertising.

- Outline the role of publicity and Public Relations in the marketing mix.

INTRODUCTION

It is important to recognise that major changes have occurred in the advertising industry in recent years the more important of which may be listed as

1 *The "Undoing" of Agency Consolidation and Globalisation.*
2 *Media Proliferation and Consolidation.*
3 *Media Clutter and Fragmentation.*
4 *Consumer control: from Blogs to TiVo.*

(O'Guinn et al. 2006)

The trend towards **agency consolidation** accelerated towards the end of the 1990s as the traditional agencies began to lose business to competition from new 'dot.com' agencies exploiting the potential of the Internet as a new channel of both communication and distribution. As in other fields of competition, economies of scope and scale promised increased market share and higher profits in an increasingly globalised market. But then the dot.com bubble burst with the realisation that the internet was a complement to, not a substitute for existing channels, reducing some of the pressure. Further, not all advertisers looked favourably on the new mega-agencies with a report in *Advertising Age* (2003) suggesting that more than half would prefer the flexibility of employing specialists for some aspects of their advertising rather than depend upon a full-service agency. Added to this, with fewer, larger agencies there were bound to be conflicts of interest with the same agency working for different companies competing with each other. And, finally, acquisitions cost money and many of the new firms are burdened with debt which is having a negative impact on their profitability. It seems likely this will encourage the selling-off of some of the acquisitions.

In terms of media, in addition to the **Internet**, **cable** and **satellite television** and new direct marketing technologies have created many new media options. So, while a more relaxed attitude to media ownership has enabled giants like News Corp to combine print and broadcast media in the same organisation, the 'clutter' created by the proliferation of media options has reduced the perceived effectiveness of mass media advertising. In turn, this has been compounded by consumers gaining greater control over the advertising messages they are exposed to. O'Guinn et al. cite Blogs and TiVo as examples. **Blogs** are web sites created by anyone with an interest in a subject on which anyone else can post their views, so making much more information available to the individual. Similarly, **TiVo** is an example of the growth of **PVRs** or **personal video recorders** that allow you to screen out broadcast advertising. As we shall see these trends have had a significant impact on the marketing communications business.

In this chapter we open with some definitions of advertising and the basic objectives it seeks to achieve, followed by a review of the evolution of advertising. This leads to a discussion of the present structure of the advertising industry supported by some key industry statistics. Next, we examine the role of advertising in the marketing mix and the advertiser's approach to managing this function. This leads naturally to a discussion of the other major participants in the industry – advertising and other specialist agencies, and the media.

After looking at some of the key issues in agency selection, each of the major **mass media** is reviewed in turn – the press, television, radio, posters, cinema, and the internet. Selecting the best combination of media in an integrated campaign plan, and setting the advertising appropriation come next, supported by a discussion of the measurement of advertising effectiveness.

Given its high visibility, advertising has been the subject of a great deal of comment on both economic and ethical grounds. A review of the main issues is offered.

Finally, we look briefly at the role of publicity in mass communication and the practice of **Public Relations**.

DEFINITIONS AND OBJECTIVES

Essentially advertising is a means of spreading information. This is too broad a description, however, to be useful as a definition, or to distinguish it from other forms of communication. The American Marketing Association has adopted the following as a definition: *Any paid form of non-personal presentation and promotion of ideas, goods or services by an identified sponsor*. This is certainly a very succinct statement and merits some elaboration. Firstly, advertising is paid for, it is a **commercial transaction**, and it is this which distinguishes it from **publicity**. It is non-personal in the sense that advertising messages, visual, spoken or written, are directed at a mass audience, and not directly at the individual as is the case in personal selling or other forms of direct marketing. Finally, advertisements are identifiable with their sponsor or originator, which is not always the case with publicity or propaganda.

The nature and role of sales promotion are dealt with in the next chapter, but it will be useful at this point to give the AMA's definition to avoid confusion with advertising per se in the meantime. **Sales promotion**: *those marketing activities, other than personal selling, advertising and publicity, that stimulate consumer purchasing and dealer effectiveness, such as displays, shows and exhibitions, demonstrations, and various non-recurrent selling efforts not in the ordinary routine.*

Shimp (2003), in his glossary, defines advertising as "a form of either mass communication or direct-to-consumer communication that is non-personal and is paid for by various business firms, non-profit organisations, and individuals who are in some way identified in the advertising message and who hope to inform or persuade members of a particular audience."

Shimp's definition includes **direct communications**, which are pinpointed to each business-to-business customer or end users. Although, the definition includes the recent phenomenon, **database marketing** or **direct advertising**, it fails to cover a more recent one, **World Wide Web advertising** (Internet advertising).

Objectives

The ultimate purpose underlying all advertising is increased awareness. Many authors would also ally this with some form of statement concerning an increase in profit, but this is anticipating an end result applicable only to trading organisations, which is also attributable to a host of other factors (clearly, advertisements sponsored by government departments concerning road safety, or the health hazards of smoking, are not designed to increase profits).

Despite the problems inherent in measuring the effectiveness of advertising, which are the subject of a later section of this chapter, it is only realistic to state that firms invest in advertising expenditures in the expectation of an improvement in profitability. If one examines the specific objectives which may motivate a particular advertising campaign, it is clear that an improvement in profit varies from a primary, to a very subsidiary motive as can be seen from Table 18.1

Table 18.1 Advertising objectives

- To communicate information
- To create awareness
- To stimulate interest
- To encourage attitudinal and behavioural change
- To build primary demand for the product
- To create, strengthen or extend brand recognition
- To increase market penetration
- To enlarge market share
- To remind, e.g. for special events, anniversaries etc.
- To prompt purchase through promotional offers
- To enhance the corporate reputation
- To encourage confidence and trust among customers and employees

The above list is by no means exhaustive, but it does indicate that the aim underlying a campaign may be directed at a short-term increase in sales volume (price deals and other promotional offers), the development of a new market, an increased share of an existing market, or the building of a favourable attitude to the company as a whole (**corporate advertising**). The latter, like an increase in retail distribution, is a long-term objective for which it would be difficult to assess the actual return on the advertising investment. Further, in both profit and not-for-profit organisations, advertising is used to encourage attitudinal and or behavioural change.

Whatever the specific objective or purpose, it is generally agreed that its statement in explicit terms is an essential prerequisite of a successful campaign. Similarly, it is also agreed that certain conditions are more favourable to successful advertising than others, for example an expanding market, or possession of a feature which differentiates the product from its competitors. This point will be returned to when discussing advertising strategy.

THE EVOLUTION OF ADVERTISING

It is often erroneously assumed that the advertising function is of recent origin, a point commented on by Henry Sampson (1874) in his *History of Advertising*, 'It is generally assumed – though the assumption has no ground for existence beyond that so common among us, that nothing exists of which we are ignorant – that advertisements are of comparatively modern origin.'

There is some evidence to suggest that the Romans practised advertising, but the earliest indication of its use in this country dates from the Middle Ages with the adoption of surnames indicative of a man's occupation, as opposed to some other distinguishing designation (Smith, Baker etc.). The producer's name is of equal importance today as a means of identifying the source of goods and services.

Signs represented the next stage in the evolution of advertising, acting as a visual expression of the tradesman's function as well as a means of locating the source of goods at a time when the numbering of houses was unknown. One can still see vestiges of the practice in the barber's pole, or the symbolic boot or glove.

The craft guilds of the Middle Ages disapproved of competition among their members, but were not averse to competition with one another in the adoption of distinctive liveries, or the sponsoring of mystery plays – an early form of institutional advertising! At the same time many guilds adopted trade marks as a means of identifying the producer, and as a guarantee of quality – the adoption of corporate symbols, as a more immediate means of recognising the firm's identity than the written word, is an interesting reversion to this practice.

Although Caxton had invented the hand press by the end of the fifteenth century, the use of the written word in advertising was limited by the low level of literacy, so confining written advertisements to the clergy. By Shakespeare's time posters had made their appearance, and the few remaining examples make it clear that advertising had assumed the function of fostering demand for new products as well as increasing demand for existing products.

Another important development at this time was the emergence of the pamphlet as an advertising medium, early examples of which disclose their sponsorship by companies bent on generating goodwill for their activities. (Later examples are more veiled as to their origin and, properly, should be considered as propaganda.) However, the seventeenth century was a period of unrest in England, resulting in government censorship which was to hinder the development of regular publications. From 1620 onwards a number of Mercuries, Gazettes, etc., made their appearance, but were mainly short-lived, and carried few advertisements.

The high cost of posters and handbills encouraged a number of publishers to experiment with the issue of free papers comprised solely of advertisements. Their success was limited, however, and posters and handbills continued as the main media until the early eighteenth century. An examination of the periodicals of the early 1700s, such as the *Tatler* and *Spectator*, reveals an increasing number of advertisements, but this growth was abruptly curtailed in 1712 by the imposition of a tax on both papers and advertisements. The first Stamp Act levied a tax of ½d per copy on publications and 12d per advertisement, supposedly to raise revenue but in fact intended to curtail a libellous and seditious press. The effect of the tax was virtually immediate – the majority of unsubsidised papers ceased publication, and the legitimate businessman severely curtailed his use of advertising. On the other hand, the quacks and charlatans, with their enormous profit margins to fall back on, continued to advertise, and it is worth noting that the generally unsavoury nature of the advertising of this time was a direct consequence of government censorship and heavy taxation. Under the circumstances neither government control nor taxation would appear to be as effective as modern critics of advertising would have one believe.

The tax on advertisements was abolished in 1853, at a time ripe for the development of mass advertising as we know it today. Mass production was a reality, and channels of distribution were being developed to cope with the physical movement of goods, creating a need for mass communication to inform consumers of the choice available to them. This need was soon recognised by the forerunner of today's advertising agent – the space salesman. Initially space salesmen located customers for the media owners, receiving commission on the space they sold. Gradually the position changed, and the agent became a space broker, or middleman, buying space wholesale from the media owner and reselling it retail, often at a profit of 25 per cent. The profits to be earned attracted competition and the agents found it necessary to offer incentives to advertisers to purchase space from them, in preference to their competitors. Thus the practice evolved of giving the advertiser free assistance in preparing his copy and later, as the number of publications increased, of selecting the media which would prove most effective in reaching the advertiser's potential customers. This system

Table 18.2 Total advertising expenditure and its relation to household expenditure and gross national income

	Total expenditure at 2000 prices[1] £m	Total expenditure at current prices £m	Expenditure as a percentage of:	
			Household expenditure at market prices	Gross national income at market prices
1989	12,040	8,641	2.77	1.68
1990	11,618	8,924	2.64	1.60
1991	10,329	8,531	2.37	1.46
1992	10,291	8,859	2.33	1.45
1993	10,354	9,139	2.27	1.42
1994	11,261	10,136	2.40	1.49
1995	11,933	11,026	2.49	1.53
1996	12,759	12,080	2.55	1.58
1997	13,841	13,340	2.65	1.65
1998	14,726	14,415	2.68	1.68
1999	15,535	15,412	2.70	1.71
2000	16,988	16,998	2.82	1.79
2001	16,338	16,537	2.60	1.66
2002	16,405	16,817	2.53	1.61
2003	16,579	17,227	2.49	1.57

Note: Internet adspend is included from 1997. [1] Deflated by the Consumer Prices Index (2,000 = 100)
Source: The Advertising Association's *Advertising Statistics Yearbook, The Marketing Pocket Book 2005*, both published by WARC (*www.warc.com*)

Table 18.3 Total advertising expenditure by medium and type

	£ million						Percentage of total					
	1998	1999	2000	2001	2002	2003	1998	1999	2000	2001	2002	2003
By medium												
National newspapers, incl. colour supplements	1,824	1,991	2,252	2,062	1,933	1,902	12.7	12.9	13.3	12.5	11.5	11.0
Regional newspapers, incl. free sheets	2,390	2,483	2,762	2,834	2,894	2,986	16.6	16.1	16.3	17.1	17.2	17.3
Consumer magazines	709	727	750	779	785	784	4.9	4.7	4.4	4.7	4.7	4.5
Business & professional magazines	1,209	1,195	1,270	1,202	1,088	1,048	8.4	7.8	7.5	7.3	6.5	6.1
Directories	780	831	868	959	990	1,029	5.4	5.4	5.1	5.8	5.9	6.0
Press production costs	620	650	702	669	643	634	4.3	4.2	4.1	4.0	3.8	3.7
Total Press	**7,531**	**7,877**	**8,604**	**8,504**	**8,333**	**8,383**	**52.2**	**51.1**	**50.6**	**51.4**	**49.6**	**48.7**
Television	4,029	4,321	4,646	4,147	4,332	4,374	28.0	28.0	27.4	25.1	25.8	25.4
of which production costs	603	648	697	622	650	656	4.2	4.2	4.1	3.8	3.9	3.8
Direct mail	1,666	1,876	2,049	2,228	2,378	2,431	11.6	12.2	12.1	13.5	14.2	14.1
Outdoor & transport, incl. prod. costs	613	649	810	788	816	901	4.3	4.2	4.8	4.8	4.9	5.2
Cinema, incl. production costs	97	123	128	164	180	180	0.7	0.8	0.8	1.0	1.1	1.0
Radio, incl. production costs	460	516	595	541	545	582	3.2	3.3	3.5	3.3	3.2	3.4
Internet[1]	19	51	155	166	233	376	0.1	0.2	0.9	1.0	1.4	2.2
Total	**14,415**	**15,412**	**16,988**	**16,537**	**16,817**	**17,227**	**100.0**	**100.0**	**100.0**	**100.0**	**100.0**	**100.0**
By type												
Display advertising												
Press[2]	4,134	4,338	4,687	4,458	4,285	4,224	28.7	28.1	27.6	27.0	25.6	24.5
Television	4,029	4,321	4,646	4,147	4,332	4,374	28.0	28.0	27.4	25.1	25.8	25.4
Other media[3]	2,855	3,215	3,738	3,886	4,152	4,470	19.8	20.9	22.0	23.5	24.5	25.9
Total display	**11,018**	**11,873**	**13,071**	**12,491**	**12,768**	**13,068**	**76.4**	**77.0**	**76.9**	**75.5**	**76.0**	**76.1**
Classified advertising[4]	3,398	3,539	3,918	4,046	4,049	4,158	23.6	23.0	23.1	24.5	24.0	24.1
Total	**14,415**	**15,412**	**16,988**	**16,537**	**16,537**	**17,227**	**100.0**	**100.0**	**100.0**	**100.0**	**100.0**	**100.0**

Note(s): [1] From 2002 internet figures include adspend on specialist recruitment websites. Internet figure for 2003 is an estimate. [2] Including financial notices and display advertising in business and professional journals, but not advertising in directories. [3] Outdoor and transport, cinema, direct mail, radio and the internet. [4] Including all directory advertising.
Source: The Advertising Association's *Advertising Statistics Yearbook*, *The Marketing Pocket Book 2005*, both published by WARC (www.warc.com)

continued until the early 1980s, with the agent looking upon the advertiser as his client, while deriving most of their income from commissions paid by the media owner. Nowadays, however, advertisers and agencies negotiate contracts for campaigns mainly on a fee basis and, in O'Guinn et al.'s view these more closely resemble a law firm's billing system, based on charging out staff time, than the usual business contract.

We return to this topic below when reviewing the **advertiser-agency relationship**.

Table 18.4 Annual expenditure by product category (press and tv)

Product category	1999	2000	2001	2002	2003
Business & industrial	435,494,813	516,181,643	158,027,757	136,562,407	111,356,922
Clothing & accessories	150,416,027	156,356,244	162,770,041	170,824,062	171,377,480
Computers	426,553,804	600,107,176	392,369,012	317,177,271	325,755,928
Cosmetics & toiletries	382,624,381	361,112,615	359,625,599	413,479,923	477,813,408
Drink	299,445,105	279,148,503	243,485,809	257,240,490	230,207,304
Electrical/electronics	0	0	21,727	20,291	6,594
Entertainment & the media	451,331,459	499,099,552	478,264,862	460,435,222	492,405,615
Finance	634,874,306	836,269,663	841,125,309	772,504,133	777,608,898
Food	614,447,295	582,058,373	524,786,225	505,413,438	479,880,257
Gardening & agriculture	18,003,478	27,465,478	22,075,576	24,826,743	27,449,486
Govt,social,political org's	156,917,516	170,141,129	201,417,964	190,492,803	213,753,091
Household appliances	60,832,447	65,223,524	68,569,137	73,376,231	61,254,824
Household equipment	182,720,256	181,574,744	246,033,143	237,797,936	250,425,479
Household stores	231,963,182	213,397,286	213,680,912	208,579,856	223,642,292
Leisure equipment	300,709,669	334,124,282	353,271,528	362,327,147	416,010,536
Mail order	288,829,422	252,787,620	230,760,946	222,618,605	204,278,686
Manufacturing	0	644	3,764	8,833	4,367
Miscellaneous	419,467	503,815	1,136,123	1,349,196	2,444,117
Motors	769,928,318	748,094,685	731,452,894	800,267,316	746,366,777
Multi advertisers	22,196,210	21,014,908	25,146,855	24,673,713	31,285,480
Office equipment & supplies	7,335,354	5,307,081	5,260,457	6,943,854	9,445,446
Online retail	23,985,462	105,695,499	40,791,176	16,007,734	13,848,118
Pharmaceutical	197,526,750	201,650,574	214,186,360	241,404,073	248,554,811
Property	34,448,651	52,940,942	43,022,840	44,655,243	47,489,995
Recruitment classified	0	4,168	38	0	2,353
Retail	637,967,240	649,901,724	587,603,913	650,553,026	684,237,287
Telecomms	-	-	383,382,061	368,564,710	449,426,394
Tobacco & accessories	19,946,549	9,722,517	11,269,156	10,735,312	2,384,234
Travel & transport	302,369,347	292,151,704	293,274,329	333,104,237	333,320,260

Source: © Nielsen Media Research (2005)

INDUSTRY STATISTICS

Before looking at the present-day practice of advertising, and the salient characteristics of the major media, it will be helpful to review some of the industry's vital statistics.

In 2003 total advertising expenditure by UK advertisers amounted to £14,415 million. The break-down of this expenditure and some comparisons with other budget headings are contained in Tables 18.2 to 18.5 inclusive. While accurate at the time of writing the sources cited should be consulted regularly for up-to-date statistics.

Table 18.5 Top 25 advertisers, 2003

| Rank | Advertiser | Total | Advertising Expenditure | | | |
			TV %	Radio %	Press %	Other %
1	Unilever UK Ltd	216,213,906	57.0%	4.3%	14.3%	24.4%
2	Procter & Gamble Ltd	202,864,792	70.6%	5.9%	12.9%	10.5%
3	COI Communications	150,424,656	50.0%	16.0%	24.0%	10.0%
4	BT Ltd	106,985,807	48.7%	5.5%	28.6%	17.3%
5	Loreal Golden Ltd	95,697,043	69.9%	0.2%	20.7%	9.2%
6	Ford Motor Company Ltd	83,597,765	45.8%	6.0%	27.5%	20.8%
7	MBNA Europe Bank Ltd	80,411,478	1.2%	0.0%	5.4%	93.3%
8	DFS Furniture PLC	77,404,141	35.6%	3.8%	36.6%	23.9%
9	Nestlé	70,947,501	68.0%	3.0%	10.0%	19.0%
10	Masterfoods	69,322,338	57.5%	2.3%	13.3%	26.9%
11	Lloyds TSB PLC	67,479,760	19.9%	0.1%	9.1%	71.0%
12	Orange PLC	65,752,902	30.0%	8.4%	19.5%	42.0%
13	Renault UK Ltd	63,883,999	45.5%	6.9%	27.3%	20.3%
14	Vauxhall Motors Ltd	61,341,239	43.0%	4.9%	39.1%	13.0%
15	Reckitt Benckiser Ltd	60,830,652	92.0%	0.9%	5.5%	1.6%
16	Capital One	59,744,662	20.5%	0.0%	2.3%	77.2%
17	Sainsbury's Supermarkets Ltd	58,696,363	44.8%	18.4%	16.0%	20.7%
18	British Sky Broadcasting Ltd	56,662,059	19.4%	3.8%	37.5%	39.3%
19	Volkswagen UK Ltd	51,155,918	47.7%	5.2%	30.4%	16.7%
20	Hutchison 3G Ltd	50,839,242	47.8%	8.5%	16.6%	27.1%
21	Halifax PLC	50,378,382	28.0%	0.4%	20.2%	51.4%
22	Toyota (GB) Ltd	49,297,335	47.8%	8.6%	27.5%	16.2%
23	Barclays Bank PLC	49,056,330	33.3%	3.0%	11.2%	52.6%
24	News Intl Newspapers Ltd	47,918,526	63.2%	13.8%	1.0%	22.0%
25	Vodafone Ltd	47,819,195	52.5%	7.2%	21.9%	18.5%

Note: Other includes Cinema, Direct Mail, Internet and Outdoor Advertising.
Source: © Nielsen Media Research (2005)

THE STRUCTURE OF ADVERTISING

The above description outlining the evolution of advertising makes it clear that at least three separate parties are involved in the advertising process:

- *The advertiser;*
- *The advertising/promotions agent;*
- *The media owner.*

To these O'Guinn et al would add '**External Facilitators**' which includes other organisations providing information or other services to the principal players.

In market terms, advertisers constitute buyers and media owners sellers, and consequently they take considerable direct interest in each other's activities. In many instances advertiser and media owner will negotiate direct with one another, but beyond a certain point the intervention of a third party becomes desirable, which accounts for the existence of advertising agents.

From the advertiser's point of view the agency constitutes a reservoir of skills which it would be difficult to duplicate in even the largest company at an economic cost – for the smaller company it would be impossible.

From the media owner's point of view, agencies act as wholesalers, bulking together a host of orders from a variety of sources, thus reducing the area of contact between buyer and seller to manageable proportions. In addition the agent is familiar with the media owner's language and method of operation, and, in a sense, acts as an interpreter between the parties. Both these factors create economies which the media owner considers justification for the payment of commission.

In addition to these three major participants at least two others have emerged in recent years – the **creative specialist** and the **media specialist**. Advertising agencies of the kind referred to above traditionally handled all aspects of their clients advertising business and so were known as **full service agencies**. However, their ability to provide the depth and quality of service across the board was questioned by some and led to the establishment of 'boutiques' or 'hot shops' specialising solely in the creative aspects of campaign planning. Not being eligible for commission on media buying, creative specialists work on a fee basis. By contrast media specialists are eligible for media commission and, because they have lower overheads, often rebate part of this as an inducement to advertisers.

Before examining the interaction of the parties in the development of an advertising campaign it will be useful to look at the role of the three major parties – advertiser, agents, and media owners – in somewhat greater detail.

THE ROLE OF ADVERTISING IN THE MARKETING MIX – THE ADVERTISER'S VIEWPOINT

As was noted earlier, the justification for advertising from the advertiser's point of view is that it increases profitability, even though it is difficult to quantify precisely to what extent. (Mail order used to be the only case where a sale could be directly credited to the publication of an advertisement, but the Internet also offers this opportunity now) Advertising is but one variable in the marketing mix, albeit an important one, and it is difficult to separate its contribution from that of the other mix elements. As was implied in the list of advertising goals in the section on 'Objectives', there are a number of ways which may increase the profitability of the firm. R. H. Colley (1961) lists 52 specific goals in *Defining Advertising Goals*, but these may be reduced into *five* major categories:

1 *To increase demand* to the point at which advertising economies of scale are achieved. The larger the fixed costs of production, the greater the unit contribution once the break-even point has been reached – 'leverage'. The advertiser may wish initially to build primary demand for the product group as a whole, anticipating that they will benefit proportionally from the overall growth of the market. Once product acceptance has been achieved, advertisers usually concentrate on building brand recognition and loyalty. Colour television is a good example of this in that early advertisements for sets tended to emphasise the benefits of colour as compared with black and white, that is selling colour rather than brand A, B or C. As the market becomes more competitive, advertisers concentrate on extolling the features of their product which differentiate it from that of other producers.

2 *The building of a 'brand image'* in a competitive, mature market has other benefits in addition to maintaining or improving the firm's competitive position. Brand recognition and brand loyalty reduce the producer's dependency on the distributive channels. This is particularly true of convenience goods, but is also applicable to shopping goods where the manufacturer can place little reliance on either the ability or interest of the retailer to sell their specific product. Only where a retailer is a sole distributor can the producer rely on an equal and corresponding interest in the sale of their product.

3 *Information gathering* invariably precedes the purchase of a product to some degree and, clearly, the ready availability of such information in the form of advertisements reduces the prospective purchaser's dependence on personal selling. Personal selling is a cost to the producer, both directly, in the payment of their sales force, and indirectly, through the margin they have to offer middlemen to perform the service on their behalf. The physical separation of producer and prospective buyer, coupled with competition, make advertising a more economic means of communication than personal contact in both the industrial and consumer selling field. Further, a good advertisement can go a long way to achieve the first two stages of the sales process – the creation of awareness and interest.

4 Most firms are subject to a *fluctuating demand* for their output, be it seasonal, cyclical or secular, and advertising can do much to minimise such fluctuations though its impact is greatest in the case of seasonal variations. Ice cream and soup are classic examples of building year-round demand for products formerly consumed during a particular season, through informing consumers of alternative uses by means of advertising.

5 Finally, it is maintained that advertising improves *profitability* in a less tangible way by creating goodwill for the firm as a whole and by improving the morale of its employees; everyone likes to work for a well-known firm.

Organisation for advertising within the firm

Recognising the enormous disparity in the size and nature of firms, it is clear that the formulation of generalisations about the nature of the advertising function within the firm is fraught with danger. At the same time, some description of the mythical 'average' firm is useful in that it provides a starting-point for an examination of actual practice in a company with which one is familiar by association, or through reading the practitioners' journals. This caveat should be continually borne in mind, however, in reading this section.

Whatever the specific objective behind the mounting of an advertising campaign, the maximum return on expenditure will only be achieved if the right information is conveyed to the right people in the right way. This is unlikely to be the case unless those responsible for the firm's advertising have a thorough understanding of:

- *The nature of the market;*
- *The nature of the product;*
- *The nature of the channels of distribution;*
- *The nature of the channels of communication – the media available, and their characteristics.*

From the discussion of the structure of advertising earlier it is clear that advertisers have four options open to them. First, they can do it for themselves 'in-house'; second, they can hand over the responsibility entirely to a full service agency; third, they can buy in creative services but handle the remainder themselves; and, fourth, they can develop their own campaigns but devolve media

Figure 18.1 Macro-relationships in advertising

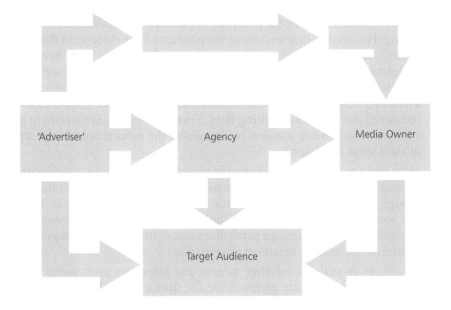

Source: Crosier, K.C. (2004), teaching materials.

buying to a specialist. In fact any combination of options could be used and this so-called 'à la carte' approach is proving increasingly popular, so that working relationships in the advertising business can be represented as in Figure 18.1.

Until the early 1980s the services of the full service agency and media specialist were 'free' in the sense that these intermediaries were paid an average 15% commission by the media owners. Obviously, it made sense for the advertiser to use these wherever possible and avoid duplication within the firm. Under these circumstances the critical factor was the ability to communicate to the agency what the firm wished to achieve, and what it has to offer the consumer which differentiates it from its competitors. Essentially, therefore, the advertising manager's role was one of liaison and interpretation (i.e. explaining management's objective to the agency and vice versa).

While this still remains the case, for the reasons set out in the Introduction, there have been significant changes in the structure of the advertising industry and in the media available. As a result the advertiser has more options available to them when deciding on the most effective combination of communication and promotional tools and make greater use of specialist facilitators rather than deal exclusively with a full service agency

In the large firm the percentage of revenue allocated to advertising may constitute a very large sum in absolute terms and necessitate the employment of a number of persons to manage it effectively. For example, General Motors

Figure 18.2 Organisation chart for the advertising department of a large, diversified company

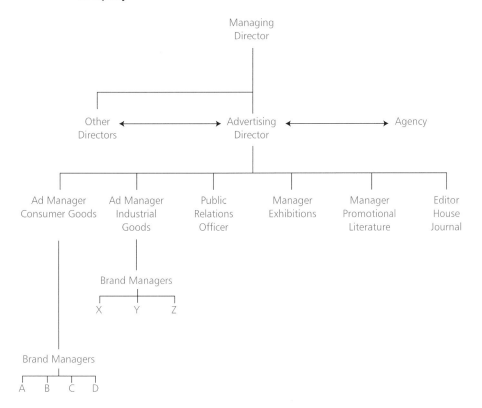

spent almost $3.5 billion on advertising in the US alone in 2003, with many other companies spending over $1 billion. In such large companies one might expect to find an organisational structure similar to that in Figure 18.2. The actual number of staff employed in each section would depend on the importance of advertising and promotion to the firm's marketing effort, and the financial resources allocated to it.

THE ADVERTISING AGENCY

The modern advertising agency of today has advanced a long way from the space salesman of a century ago, to the extent that some feel it would be more appropriate to call it a marketing agency.

With increasing competition, advertising agents have extended the range of services available to clients, the scope of which is indicated in the organisation chart for a large agency in Figure 18.3. Figure 18.4 indicates more clearly the functions and relationships within a full-service agency. Despite the apparent extent of the agency's expertise implied, it would be incorrect to assume that the agency could substitute for the firm's own marketing department. As was suggested in the preceding section, the advertiser might regard the agency as an extension of their own business, in that it would be uneconomical to duplicate its skills in terms of the creative aspects of advertising, but, at the same time, it would

Figure 18.3 Organisation chart for a large advertising agency

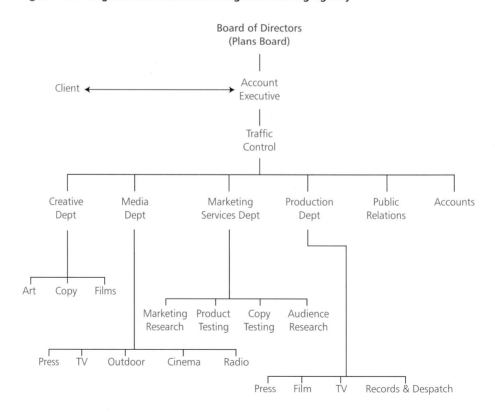

be foolish to delegate the whole marketing function to a third party specialising in only one aspect of it. Prior to the consolidation referred to earlier it was a rule of agencies not to hold competing accounts. In consequence, it was unlikely that one could secure the services of an agency with the necessary experience to handle the total marketing of a specific product. While it was also true that accounts change hands, so that one might be able to engage an agency with experience in the relevant product field, but this experience will invariably be limited to the advertising problems involved. Now the situation may be different with a mega-agency holding the accounts of firms competing head-on with one another and the question is whether the Chinese walls inside the agency are sufficient to prevent 'leakage' between account managers.

If one accepts that the agency is expert in the advertising function, it follows that it will only be able to perform effectively if it is given the full support and confidence of the advertiser. Much of the conflict which arises between advertiser and agent is the direct result of the former only giving the latter part of the information necessary to devise a successful campaign; it is the advertiser's responsibility to feed in the marketing inputs and data around which to build the campaign. While on the subject of the advertiser/agency relationship, it is appropriate to comment that there seems little evidence to suggest that agencies 'wear out', in the sense of losing their creative touch, a belief which prompts some advertisers regularly to change agencies to avoid such an occurrence. Most of the firms which are well known for the quality of their advertising have enjoyed a long and unbroken association with their agency, which suggests that mutual confidence improves over time, as does the expertise of the agent in advertising a

Figure 18.4 Micro-relationships in an advertising agency

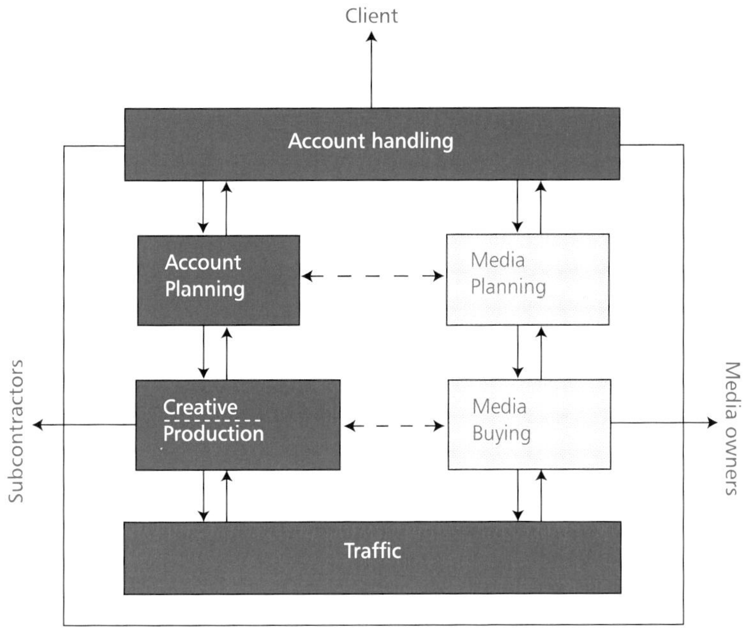

Source: Crosier, K.C. (2004), teaching materials..

particular product.

Passing reference has been made to the issue of agency remuneration and the fact that traditionally this was largely derived from a commission paid by media owners. This commission of 15% is built-in to the media rates quoted by the media owner. For the reasons set out earlier this system has changed considerably in recent years but it still alive and well in many cases. A clear explanation of the system is to be found in Chapter 17 of *The Marketing Book* (2003) and in Yeshin (2006).

Agency selection

From the above comments it is clear that the selection of an advertising agent is not to be undertaken lightly, and the following is suggested as a structured approach to the problem.

1 Prepare a short-list of agencies that you think might be suitable. Details of agencies and their existing accounts can be obtained from the *Advertiser's Annual* (published annually by Hollis PR see *www.hollis-pr.co.uk*). There is nothing to prevent you approaching an agency currently handling a competitor's account, but if they are prepared to drop the existing account to bid for yours, it is unlikely that you will achieve lasting success in this direction. Subjective information on agencies may be obtained from business acquaintances, or by asking media owners to identify the agency responsible for advertisements which you admire.

2 Construct a check-list of the factors on which you intend to base your decision and assign each a weight commensurate with the importance which you attach to each; for example:

Creativity (that is, the ability to develop a distinctive/novel approach) – 10

Previous experience in the product field – 8

Ability to undertake ad hoc research – 6, and so on . . .

3 Draw up a questionnaire to:

(a) Elicit the agency's grasp of the problems inherent in marketing your product, and its approach for dealing with them.

(b) Provide a basis around which to build a 'Presentation' – that is, an outline for a campaign.

4 Approach the agencies on the short-list and ask them if they are interested in competing for the account. (Some indication should be given of the annual appropriation to be allocated to advertising.) Once the news gets around that you are looking for an agency it is quite likely that several agencies not on the short-list will ask if they may make a presentation. One should resist the temptation to expand the field, if the initial selection was undertaken thoroughly, as it will only serve to confuse the issue, unless there is some very valid reason, for example an agency thought to be unavailable having severed its connection with a competitor.

5 Rate the completed questionnaires in line with the previously determined weights.

6 Convene a selection board from the company's executives, and rate the

presentations made as for the questionnaires. (To avoid difficulty in resolving the final outcome it is recommended that both the weights and rating scale be given a large spread, thus instead of rating from 1 to 5 use an interval of 5; Worst 5 . . . Best 25.)

Numerous surveys in practitioner magazines largely agree that when assessing an agencies performance the critical factors in order of importance are:

- *Creativity*
- *Track record/reputation for achieving results* (**'effectiveness'**)
- *Knowledge of the clients products/services/markets*
- *Good working relationships*
- *Value for money* i.e. competitive rates for services, media buying etc.

While clients emphasise the creativity of the advertising agency, their ability to deliver this will depend on the clients supplying them with the necessary information to develop a creative strategy. McDonald (1998) identifies *nine* key elements that need to be considered when developing a creative strategy statement, namely:

1 A *description of the product* – what it is, its attributes and features.
2 The *target audience* – in terms of demographics, geography, behavioural and psychological profile.
3 The *audience's problem* – what they need or want.
4 The *communication objective* – what do you want the receiver to do?
5 The *product's positioning* vis-à-vis the competition.
6 The *key benefit* offered.
7 An explanation of *how this benefit is to be obtained*.
8 The *action to be taken by the receiver*.
9 The *product/service personality*.

THE MEDIA

The third party to the advertising process is the media owners, and the aim of the following section is to review briefly the salient characteristics of the media available. Before proceeding to this review it will be helpful to outline a checklist as a basis for assessing the value of the various media. In common with most other similar lists appearing elsewhere, the outline given below is based on a checklist prepared by J W Hobson's on behalf of the IPA in 1956.

An evaluation of an advertising medium requires consideration of four major factors:

1 *The character of the medium;*
2 *The atmosphere of the medium;*
3 *The coverage of the medium;*
4 *The cost of the medium.*

Two further factors which should be taken into account are the size and position of the advertisement.

Character

The character of a medium may be largely determined on an objective and factual basis through consideration of the following:

(a) The *geographical coverage of the medium*; for example, national, regional, local.

(b) The *socioeconomic composition of the audience*.

(c) *Composition of the audience by age and sex groupings*.

(d) The *medium's physical characteristics* - visual, oral, standard of reproduction, availability of colour, possibility of movement, and so forth.

(e) *Frequency of publication*. Allied to this is the duration of interest in the medium - most daily papers are thrown away the same day, while magazines may be kept for several weeks and read by a number of people. The frequency of publication also has a direct effect on the booking of time or space, i.e. the timing of the appearance of an advertisement.

(f) The *power to reach special groups* – this is closely related to (b) and (c) above; for example the *Economist* or the *Financial Times*, *Vogue*, etc., pre-select a particular type of audience and so are especially suited to selling to this segment of the population. Further, the association of a product with a medium may give that product favourable connotations by transferring confidence in the publication to items advertised therein, for example *Good Housekeeping*.

Atmosphere

The atmosphere of a medium is difficult to define in that it is based on a subjective evaluation of its content, presentation, and so on. A broad distinction may be drawn between **acceptable** and **intrusive media**, in that the latter create impact through intrusion and irrelevance to context, for example television commercials, whereas many magazines are purchased as much for their advertisements as their other content. The concept will become clearer when related to individual media.

Coverage

The essential criterion on which coverage is judged is the actual number of persons exposed to the medium, in the sense of being made aware of its content. For example, the number of people who actually see a poster is considerably less than the number that have the opportunity to see it; on the other hand, the readership of a magazine may well exceed ten times its actual circulation.

Cost

For purposes of comparison the cost of publishing an advertisement is usually expressed in terms of '**cost per thousand**' (**CPT**), which is arrived at by dividing the cost of publication by the audience in thousands. The difficulty in ensuring comparability in the measurement of audience size in terms of coverage, as defined above, makes this a rough measure at best, and media planners are actively seeking more sophisticated measures of cost effectiveness.

Advertising expenditure by media for the years 1998 to 2003 is indicated in Table 18.2.

Size

The effect of increased size or duration of an advertisement is to increase effective coverage, but on a progressively diminishing scale. Larger advertisements enable the advertiser to make more selling points, or to create greater impact when properly used. It is also contended that 'bigness', of itself, creates confidence and prestige.

Position

Detailed studies of the positioning of advertisements within a medium have shown that certain 'slots' consistently achieve greater coverage than other positions. Further, certain positions can be very useful in isolating a particular segment of the general audience. (Timing has the same effect for broadcast messages on radio and television.)

In the following pages are given synopses of the various media available to the advertiser. While correct at the time of writing this type of information is subject to constant change and very quickly becomes dated. For detailed and up-to-date information the reader should consult **British Rate and Data** (**BRAD**, *www.brad.co.uk*). Contact with **The Advertising Association** (*www.adassoc.org.uk*) is also strongly recommended as they publish an excellent range of material including a set of 'Student Briefs' covering various aspects of advertising.

The national press

Although circulation of the national press has declined steadily since the previous edition was published – from about 13.7 million for dailies and 14.8 million for Sundays in 1997, to 11.8 million for both in 2003 – readership for both still exceeds 50% of the population. This decline has been more marked for the so-called 'quality' papers like the *Guardian* and the *Independent* than for the popular papers like the *Sun* and *Daily Mail*. In the case of the Sundays, *The Sunday Mail* has actually increased its circulation slightly, the *Sunday Times* has remained steady while the *News of the World* has suffered a loss of about 20%. Readership of the popular papers is approximately 1/3 rd ABC1 2/3rds C2DE while for the quality papers on average ABC1 readers outnumber C2DE by eight to one (88% to 11%).

Following Hobson's 'check-list', the salient characteristics of the national press may be summarised as:

Character

Newspapers are bought largely for their news value and so are singularly appropriate for announcing new products and new developments of existing products. Because of their frequency of publication they are also well suited to 'opportunity' markets; for example advertising anti-freeze during a sudden cold spell, such-and-such a race was won on X tyres, Y petrol, Z oil, and so on. Despite their short life, newspapers have a high attention value and it is estimated that an 11x3 advertisement (that is 11 inches long by 3 columns wide) is seen by one-third of the readers. Further, the advertisements in the national press are more likely to be seen by the retailer (also true of TV commercials) than are those appearing in magazines, and so have an indirect effect on the distributive channels.

In addition to their news content newspapers are also bought for the regular features they carry, and certain days have been developed to cater to specific reader interests, for example Thursday and Friday for grocery products, as the majority of grocery purchases are made on Friday and Saturday; mail order advertisements on Saturday and Sunday, to coincide with the weekend letter-writing peak, and so forth.

As their name implies, the national papers have national coverage. Their regional strength varies, however, and up-to-date data should be sought from BRAD or **NRS (National Readership Survey,** *www.nrs.co.uk*).

Atmosphere

In general terms this may be summarised as a sense of urgency and importance coupled, to a varying degree, with a certain authority. Most people read a newspaper which confirms their own view of the word and so is regarded as a high credibility source (that is the content is accepted at face value). To a certain extent, the authority of the factual content is transferred to the advertisements and may be regarded as 'assistance to selling' under the heading of 'Character'.

Quantity/Coverage

While an evaluation based solely on the number of copies bought would be an inadequate guide to the suitability of a particular paper for a particular advertisement, as noted the demographic composition of the audience for popular and quality newspapers varies significantly. Accordingly, when selecting a particular paper it is important to match its audience profile with the consumer profile of the product or service in question. (This is a useful rule-of-thumb guide to *all* media selection – that is define the **demographic characteristics** of the target consumers, and then select the medium which offers the closest match to this profile.)

Cost

Most newspaper advertising rates are based on a **charge per standard column centimetre (SCC)** – that is one column wide by one centimetre deep. The actual column width varies, as does the cost, from paper to paper. However, the cost per thousand can vary significantly from £5.69 for the *Sun* to £23.69 for the *Sunday Times* and £39.29 for the *Independent*. Once again reference should be made to BRAD for exact and up-to-date information. Charges also vary within each paper depending on the actual position of the advertisement – see 'Position' below.

Size

As a general rule, readership does not increase with the size of the advertisement in a directly proportional manner. Despite diminishing returns, the consensus of opinion favours larger advertisements because of the greater impact which they achieve and because readers 'select' advertisements to a certain extent; that is, there is a tendency to notice those of direct interest to the reader. This means that a series of small advertisements, costing the same as a single large advertisement, may be seen many times by the same people, but pass unnoticed by those with a latent demand – it is unlikely that a full-page advertisement will pass unnoted by these potential customers in the same way.

It should also be noted that there is currently a move from some of the traditional 'broadsheet' papers to produce or even change to 'tabloid' sized editions, usually referred to as 'compact' editions, for example, The *Times* and the *Independent*.

Position

The location of advertisements within the medium is at the discretion of the advertising manager, who, naturally, attempts to satisfy as many clients as possible. Owing to the demand for certain positions, however, it has been found both simpler and more lucrative to charge special rates for these favoured positions. It is clear that certain pages pre-select a particular segment of the readership owing to the nature of the features on that page, for example the women's and sports pages. It follows that if one is advertising a product which has a particular appeal to a segment of the readership, there is a greater probability of it coming to their attention if it is located on a page that caters to that interest.

The actual position within the printed media may be defined by one of the following, largely self-explanatory, terms:

- *Top, centre, bottom.*
- *Inside*, that is towards the fold, or *outside*.
- *Next matter*, that is next to editorial content.
- *Under matter*, *next and under matter*.
- *Island position*, that is matter on at least three sides.
- *Solus*, on its own, no other advertisements appearing on the same page.
- *Semi-solus*, only one other advertisement on the same page.

Research evidence on the value of such positions is inconclusive, but media planners contend that better results are obtained from some positions than others. For example it is contended that as the eye is accustomed to starting at the top of a piece of printed matter there is a greater possibility of catching the reader's attention if the advertisement is on the upper half of the page. Intuitively one is inclined to agree with observations of this type until adequate research either confirms, or infirms the hypothesis.

The regional press

At the time of writing there were 100 regional newspapers published on a regional basis in the United Kingdom. In many respects the characteristics of the regional press are similar to those of the national dailies already described, and this summary will be confined to noting certain differences, and the major advantages and disadvantages of local papers as an advertising medium.

First, local papers have the advantage that they achieve concentrated coverage of a limited area, and so are likely to achieve a greater density of readership than a national paper. Because of the 'local' content they also tend to receive closer scrutiny, but against this must be set the greater authority of the national paper.

Second, regional papers are ideally suited to developing regional markets based on local preferences – an examination of consumption patterns on a regional basis soon indicates that the British population is far from homogeneous in this respect.

Third, the limited circulation of the regional and local papers makes them a good medium for copy testing (that is, running different versions of an advertisement in order to measure their relative effectiveness as a basis for final selection). The lower circulations of these papers also makes them more economical, although the CPT rate may be comparable to, or even greater than, those of the nationals.

Fourth, and this also applies to the national papers to a lesser degree, the frequency of publication permits the development of a theme by instalments, or early repetition if desired to 'stiffen up' a campaign.

Finally, evening and weekly papers have the advantage over morning daily papers that they are taken into the home, and so are likely to be seen by more members of the household at greater leisure.

The major disadvantages associated with both regional and national papers are:

1 The poor quality newsprint does not permit a very high standard of reproduction – this may be improved by colour printing 'Inserts' on a glazed paper that will accept a smaller screen size than ordinary news-print.

2 News dates quickly, so most papers are scanned rapidly on the day of issue and discarded; that is, a newspaper advertisement is virtually a 'one-shot' attempt at attracting the public's attention, and so will usually require a number of repetitions if it is to be seen by the majority of the paper's readers.

Sunday newspapers

J. D. Hughes of Hobson, Bates and Partners wrote of this group: 'The British Sunday press is a unique phenomenon. No other country possesses anything remotely like it. It is, moreover, a phenomenon rooted deeply in the habits and behaviour of the people it serves' (*Advertiser's Weekly*, 21 Oct. 1966). When one considers that the *News of the World* alone has a readership of 27 per cent of the United Kingdom adult population, one begins to appreciate how deeply ingrained is the Sunday newspaper habit.

ARE YOU PAYING ATTENTION?

Research shows that 99.5% of viewers click through web banners on the Internet. In other words only 0.5% actually open them.

POSTAR believes that if someone looks at your poster for more than 8 seconds you are doing well.

After a 20 second radio advertisement the listener is listening to someone else, and after a 30 second television commercial (if you are watching it) it is back to the programme.

BUT research by Millward Brown discovered that a consumer spends an average of 25 minutes reading a consumer magazine. The research also discovered that 44% of consumers interact with the brand as a direct result of something they read, brand loyalty jumps by 32% and sales rise by an average of 8%

(Information published by the Association of Publishing Agencies; www.25minutes.co.uk)

Unlike daily papers, which tend to be scanned, the Sunday paper is perused at leisure and so achieves greater attention value. The actual composition of the readership varies from paper to paper, and the serious student should consult BRAD or NRS for a detailed breakdown on both a national and regional basis.

A second feature of Sunday papers which differentiates them from some of the dailies is the colour magazine, which largely overcomes the criticism of low standards of reproduction associated with newspapers in general.

Magazines

The major factor which differentiates a magazine from a newspaper is that the former pre-selects its readership through the nature of its content. A second distinguishing feature is that it is read at leisure.

Magazines, as a group, may be further subdivided into categories, and media planners have adopted the following classification:

1 *General magazines* – so designated because of their general appeal, as contrasted with:

2 *Specialist magazines*, which cater for the readership with clearly defined and specific interest – for example doctors, philatelists.

3 *The retail trade press*. This subdivision is justified because of the medium's importance in 'selling-in' a product prior to the start of a campaign aimed at the consumer.

General magazines

This category may be further subdivided into those which have a predominantly male or female readership, as compared with those which appeal to both sexes. For example *New Woman* has a predominantly female readership, *Autocar* male, *Radio Times* male and female. Overall, the characteristics of the general magazine are so diverse that one should properly attempt to rate each separately by reference to the check-list. At the same time there are a number of points which justify generalisation, namely:

Character

- Read at leisure.
- Preselect their audience by the content; for example *BBC Gardeners' World*, *Good Housekeeping*. Better standards of reproduction than newspapers.
- Longer duration of interest – for example of the ultimate readership of a woman's weekly, 60 per cent see it within two weeks of publication, 30 per cent in the next two weeks, and the remaining 10 per cent over a period of six months or longer. There are a growing number of weekly magazines such as *Hello*, *OK* and *Heat*, particularly aimed at celebrity culture.
- Readership may be ten to fifteen times circulation.
- The lower frequency of publication necessitates booking of space well in advance; that is, magazines are less flexible in this respect than newspapers.

Atmosphere

- More stable than that of the newspaper, which is affected by the news it carries.

- Higher standards of reproduction convey a greater sense of luxury than is possible with a newspaper, particularly where colour is used.

Coverage/Cost

- Difficult to estimate on a comparative basis owing to the variation in page size, on which rates are based, and of readership. Overall, the CPT is higher than that for the national or regional press, and ranges from about £7 in the mass circulation broadcasting publications, to around £25 in the glossy fashion magazines up to £72 in *Vanity Fair*. This higher cost is offset by the greater intrinsic worth of the advertisements to the reader, which ensures a higher '**page traffic**', that is number of readers per page expressed as a proportion of the total readership.

Specialist magazines

Detailed information on specialist magazines is more limited than in the case of the general magazine, largely because so few of them are included in the **National Readership Survey**. In addition to the above generalised comments, one may add that the magazines in this category are even more selective in their readership appeal. Further, the advertising content is often of equal interest to the editorial content, for example collectors' magazines listing objects for sale, technical magazines detailing new products and product improvements. With the exception of direct mail, the specialist magazine offers the greatest opportunity of reaching a highly specific audience. Advertising rates vary enormously; for example, *BBCs Gardeners World* has a CPT of £4.53, *Car* £28.09, and the *Economist* £70.83

Retail trade magazines

The need to ensure adequate distribution and availability of a product prior to the opening of a campaign directed at the ultimate consumer is advanced as the main reason for using this medium. Some media planners are sceptical as to its value, owing to the generally low level of readership – around 25 per cent – which is compounded by the sheer volume of advertisements, thus making the actual possibility of any particular advertisement being seen correspondingly small. It is also argued that the smaller retailer, at whom much of the effort is directed in the anticipation that it will reduce the amount of direct selling required, is an ordinary mortal who reads newspapers, watches TV and so on, and that advertisements in these media are more likely to be seen and carry popular authority. In the light of these arguments it is clear that each case should be considered on its merits, and that particular attention should be given to position within the medium.

Controlled circulation media

A review of print media would not be complete without some reference to controlled circulation papers and annuals and directories.

There has been a considerable growth in controlled circulation papers in recent years, particularly in the trade, technical and professional fields. Papers or magazines with a controlled circulation are not sold but are distributed free of charge to persons with a known interest in the magazine's editorial content. As with all other media, space is sold on the basis of the medium's ability to reach an audience which in this instance is closely defined. Many of these publications claim virtually total coverage of the pre-defined audience. This assertion should be treated with circumspection, but it is indisputable that some achieve spectacular results.

Annuals and directories may be subdivided into four categories:

1 *Annual special numbers* – these are published by the parent publication, usually a magazine or newspaper, as a completely separate entity; that is, they are not a 'special issue'.

2 *Annual consumer reference books*. Examples: *Whitakers Almanack, Pears Cyclopaedia.*

3 *Trade, technical and professional diaries, buyer's guides, year books*. These usually contain a mass of information which the practitioner may require at a moment's notice.

4 *Annual street directories and shopper's guides.* (Telephone directories might be considered to come within this category, especially the classified directories or '*Yellow Pages*'.)

Obviously the greatest disadvantage associated with this medium is the low flexibility that is a concomitant of annual publication. Against this may be set low cost – *AdWeekly* published a 'case history' of Automat some years ago which demonstrated how this company had concentrated its limited advertising appropriation in trade directories and, through careful positioning and repetition, achieved excellent results .

Television

Compared with the press, Television is of comparatively recent origin – it is only about 50 years since the first commercial was broadcast on British TV. As indicated in Table 18.2 TV accounts for just over 25% of all advertising expenditure, approximately the same as the Press, Classified advertising and all other media. Like the Press, however, and despite the introduction of Cable and Satellite TV, its share of advertising expenditure has been declining in recent years while that on Direct Mail and the Internet has been growing.

The importance of the medium is reflected in the publication of books devoted solely to the subject of commercial television, and the serious student should refer to these sources for a detailed description. Limitations of time and space dictate that the barest outline can be developed in this context.

Character

Above all, commercial television is a mass medium: it can be received in over 99 per cent of all British homes. On an average evening over 50 per cent of these homes will be tuned in to a commercial television station and, in the course of a day, an average of 2.9 hours of commercial transmissions will be received by the households capable of tuning in. Although, in theory, it would be possible to reach all these households simultaneously with a single advertisement, few advertisers would in fact attempt this as coverage is subdivided into 12 ITV Areas:

London	Midlands	North West
Yorkshire	Scotland	Wales and West
South and S. East	North East	East
South West	N. Ireland	Border

Thus, while national coverage is possible, most advertisers tend to advertise selectively on a regional basis. This trend is encouraged by the contractors, who on the one hand stress the purchasing behaviour which differentiates the consumers within their area from those in other areas, thus making a case for regional marketing, while on the other hand they publish statistics that demonstrate that their audience is an accurate reflection of the national audience and so suitable for a national campaign. If a note of scepticism is detected, the reader should consult some of the commercial television contractors' own publicity material to see how it is possible to substantiate essentially opposing claims from the same basic data. (This tendency is most marked in the case of those companies offering test marketing facilities, where a representative sample is a desirable prerequisite – it is difficult to accept that the inhabitants of central Scotland are identical with those of Kent and Sussex, or vice versa!)

With such a large potential audience, it follows that commercial television reaches all socioeconomic groups. As might be expected, there is a slight bias towards the lower social groups, to larger families and to housewives, but as these constitute the mass market for consumer goods, this has clear advantages for the marketers of such products.

In recent years the introduction of **Cable television** (13.5% penetration) and Direct to Home **Satellite systems** (34.8% penetration) has greatly increased the range and variety of opportunities to broadcast commercials via the television medium. (In 2005 it was estimated that viewers in the UK had access to 357 different TV channels). As noted earlier, this is a highly complex subject that is a specialist study in its own right.

The great advantage of television over all other media, with the exception of the cinema and now the internet, is its ability to combine sound, vision and movement. This combination permits the use of advertisements that demonstrate the product and its advantages, which, most would agree, is far more effective than a written or static visual representation.

Commercial television channels operate seven days a week, frequently around the clock, with the result that the composition of the audience varies according to the time segment selected: for example programmes for housewives in the afternoon, children's programmes from 4 to 6 p.m., 'family programmes' 6 to 9 p.m., adult programmes from 9 p.m. onwards. The composition of the audience also varies from day to day, and once again the student is referred to BRAD or the publications of the **Broadcaster's Audience Research Board Ltd** (BARB, *www.barb.co.uk*) for a detailed breakdown.

Television commercials themselves vary from 7-second 'spots' through multiples of 15 seconds to a normal maximum of 2 minutes. In practice, few advertisements exceed 60 seconds and most are in the 15, 30 and 60-second bracket. A readily observed feature of television commercials which is infrequently commented on is the fact that the advertisements are concentrated into a series of '**natural breaks**'. Research on the effect that this has on the viewer suggests relatively few 'viewers' attend actively to commercials and the practice of '**zapping**', or switching channels during breaks, is widespread. Some media planners have also commented adversely, however, to the effect that viewers must find it difficult to assimilate a fairly large number of advertisements within a short space of time. (An examination of peak loadings, in terms of water and electricity consumption, might lead one to believe that in fact the majority of viewers avoid the problem by attending to their toilet and making cups of tea during such breaks!)

Atmosphere

It is often claimed that a major advantage of television is that it is viewed in the home, in a relaxed atmosphere, when the audience is more receptive than is normally the case when exposed to advertising messages. Against this one must set the disadvantage that the injection of advertising into a programme is both intrusive and irrelevant. While attention may be concentrated on the programme itself, the popularity of the first and last 'spots' in the break would seem to indicate that media planners recognise that attention may wander once it is realised that a break has started, and only returns in anticipation of the commencement of the programme. With the introduction of infra-red remote controls a new phenomenon known as 'zapping' has emerged. As noted, zapping consists of switching channels during commercial breaks just to see what is going on on other channels and so reduces exposure to the advertisements being screened. 'Zipping' refers to the practice of fast-fowarding through adverts when watching back a pre-recorded programme (Yeshin 2006).

The more successful television advertisers, judged on the basis of their sales results, appear to have recognised both the intrusive and irrelevant aspects of commercials, and to have made a virtue out of necessity by issuing advertisements that superficially appear to have both these characteristics. Judging by the adverse comments directed at a margarine that gave one delusions of grandeur, one should be surprised to learn that at a time when margarine sales were in a decline the only brand showing an absolute increase in sales happened to be the one with the 'stupid' commercial.

Coverage/cost

Given the available choice, little of general use can be said.

Position

In terms of television commercials, this refers both to the time segment and the position within the segment.

Size

This is measured in terms of the duration of the commercial.

Current developments in television

A recent development are possibilities for advertisers provided by digital broadcasting - interactive digital television (iDTV) sometimes known as digital interactive television (DiTV). Adverts can invite viewers to 'press the red button' on their remote to access relevant information, and through a 'phone connection to their digital receiver (the 'return path'), consumers can request information to be sent to them, respond to polls, or enter competitions.

However, increasing use of digital technology has its downsides. One development in television viewing is the increasing use of PVRs (Personal Video Recorders) like TiVo and in the UK Sky Plus, and even plain combined hard drive and DVD recorders. These systems use hard drives to record programmes and can store many hours of programming. Their enhanced functionality allows users to record and watch programmes simultaneously, and makes it far easier to skip or edit out commercials.

There is also an increasing online audience, and broadcasters are starting to provide programmes for download - for example, some ABC programmes are available to purchase on iTunes with no adverts. Disney has recently announced a pilot where it will allow free downloads of selected shows but the advertising will be embedded in the broadcast. This is an area where there is a lot of change happening very quickly, and a good source for the latest developments in this area is the Motion Picture Association of America (*www.mpaa.org*).

Commercial radio

Until the autumn of 1973 the only commercial radio transmissions which could be received in this country were those of Radio Luxemburg. However in October 1973 Capital Radio came on the air as the first of approximately sixty local commercial radio stations authorised for the country as a whole. A second London station, London Broadcasting, came on the air shortly afterwards, while the third, Radio Clyde, started transmissions on New Year's Day 1974. Today, the average listener can tune it to 14 stations rising to over 20 in London. There are at the present 65 local radio stations and the whole ILR network has an average weekly reach of 59 per cent of the total adult population. (The advent of digital radio also allows listeners from all over the world to tune in via the Internet). Stations are allowed to include up to nine minutes of advertising in each hour of broadcasting. Time is sold on a 'spot' basis (like TV) but peak periods are different being highest in the morning and evening rush-hours (especially in-car reception). **RAJAR (Radio Joint Audience Research)** can be found at *www.rajar.co.uk.*

A great deal of information about commercial radio is to be found on the Radio Advertising Bureau's web site *www.rab.co.uk* with pages on media planning, advertisers, creativity, effectiveness, digital radio, the market place, station information, sponsorship and promotions and radio ads.

Outdoor advertising

(The 'check-list' approach will not be used for the remaining media – the student may like to formulate his/her own.) **Outdoor advertising** is often thought of as consisting solely of the poster medium. This ignores transportation advertising,

Table 18.6 Cinema, adult audience profile (percentage)

	Average audience		Average audience
Males	51	Class ABC1	64
Females	49	Class C2DE	36
Age 15-24	30		
Age 25-34	27		
Age 35+	43		

Source: Cinema Advertising Association (2005)

illuminated signs and several lesser media which properly fall into this category.

As with the press and the cinema, the advent of commercial television resulted in outdoor advertising having to reappraise its role as an advertising medium. It was realised that television had become the prime medium for the advertising of a wide range of mass consumption goods which had formerly depended far more on press, poster and cinema. There are still instances in which outdoor advertising may be used as the prime medium, but in the majority of cases outdoor advertising is sold as a complement to a television campaign on the grounds that it serves as a reminder at, or near, the actual point of sale. This fact is supplemented by a gradual increase in audience size due to increased personal mobility.

The main outdoor medium is the poster, which suffers from three main disadvantages. First, to ensure that its message is conveyed quickly and concisely it can only accommodate a short copy story. Second, posters are not seen in the context of other matter of editorial or entertainment value. Finally, production costs are relatively high, as are maintenance costs. Offsetting this are a number of advantages.

First, it has been estimated that over 90 per cent of the population goes out of doors in the course of a week and thus has an 'opportunity to see' a poster. Actual poster sighting will obviously be considerably less than this but, unlike most other media, an accurate predictive model has been developed which enables the prospective advertiser to determine in advance the type of campaign they will have to mount to reach an audience of a given size. (Current information on the poster audience can be obtained from POSTAR (Poster Audience Research) which is controlled by POSTAR Ltd. (*www.postar.co.uk*) and funded by the Outdoor Advertising Association (OAA)).

Second, poster advertising offers greater geographic flexibility than virtually any other medium; one may use a single site in a specific locality, cover all or part of a town, or all or part of the country.

Third, the cost of poster advertising is relatively low, so that an advertiser with a limited appropriation can mount both an extensive and prolonged campaign for an amount that would make little impact on television when ranged against the large budgets of the major television advertisers. (This is not to say that posters will have more impact than a television commercial as such, but rather that impact is relative such that a limited television campaign would tend to be completely dominated by that of a major advertiser on the medium.)

Fourth, posters can make full use of colour and achieve high standards of reproduction. Posters are increasingly being used with great dramatic effect and more thought is going into the use of the medium. The advertisements for 'Araldite' adhesive are a good example of this. In this poster campaign an actual motor car was attached to the poster, seemingly by Araldite, to show the great adhesive qualities of the glue.

Poster sites come in a range of sizes usually expressed in terms of the number of 'Sheets' e.g 4 sheet = 5' x 3'4". 12 sheet = 5' x 10', 48 sheet = 10' x 20' and 96 sheet = 10' x 40'. The cost of a poster site depends on its location, and it is therefore difficult to generalise. The poster industry offers advertisers various ways of mounting a poster campaign. From 'line by line' where the contractor offers individual sites to build up a specific display to suit particular marketing objectives. A free planning tool called 'Postarlite' can be found at *www.postar. co.uk*.

Transportation advertising is a familiar aspect of our everyday lives which should not be overlooked when considering media selection. For example, 1000 escalator panels on the London Underground are likely to be seen by 26% of all adults living in the London ITV region on a monthly basis including 33% of ABC1 and 38% of 15- 24 year-olds. Similarly, a National BUSADS campaign has OTS figures exceeding 80%.

The cinema

The impact of television on the cinema is readily apparent in any major town where former sites have been converted into bingo halls, warehouses or simply pulled down to make way for redevelopment. Although many may regret the passing of the local cinema, there can be no doubt that the competition of television has forced the cinema industry to undertake a massive face-lift. Cinema operators have realised that if they are to persuade customers to leave the comfort of their own fireside, and the hypnotic attraction of the 'box', they must make cinema-going an event. Despite the closure of many cinemas, many of which were themselves a mute reminder of the days of music-hall, there can be no doubt that the improvement and rebuilding programmes have greatly improved the standards of comfort offered to patrons. At the same time the film producers have concentrated on the competitive advantages which they possess, and which cannot be duplicated on the small screen – size and colour. The box office success of the James Bond films, and films like Star Wars and the Lord of the Rings Trilogy testify that the formula is a good one.

According to Pearl and Dean, who control most cinema advertising, no other medium can rival the impact of the cinema. Sitting in a darkened auditorium, the audience's full attention remains on the big screen throughout, and this captive audience produces recall that is up to five times greater than that for television commercials. The cinema audience also possesses a number of attributes that make them of particular interest to advertisers. Cinemagoers are trend setters and opinion formers who make a conscious effort to see films on the big screen rather than wait for them to be released on video or television. Cinema-going is a planned activity on which the audience expend their own time and money. It is also a shared experience with an average group size of 3 or more people and a form of escapism designed to provide enjoyment. This creates a receptive audience that has proved attractive to a wide cross-section of advertisers with the top spenders being Motors, Telecomms, Drink, Cosmetics and Toiletries, Entertainment and the Media, Food, Government, Social and Political Organisations, Household Stores, Travel and Transport and Leisure Equipment.

An examination of the composition of the cinema audience provides an interesting insight for the media planner as can be seen in Table 18.6.

Clearly, the Cinema Advertising Association's claim that it is the medium for reaching 'young adults' is justified by these statistics. This audience is of particular interest to the manufacturers of both semi-luxury goods, such as cosmetics, and consumer durables, appealing to single persons with high discretionary spending power, engaged couples and young marrieds. Television can still offer a lower cost per thousand for the same audience but lacks the high attention value of a captive audience, viewing under ideal conditions over which the advertiser, not the viewer, has control, for example sound volume, quality of picture.

Advertisements are normally of 15, 30, 60 and 120 seconds in length. Actual rates vary by cinema and may be obtained from the Cinema Advertising Association's master list of cinemas. Although the cost per 1000 of using the cinemas is greater than for television, the Cinema Advertising Association justifies this on the grounds that the cinema possesses undeniable qualitative advantages, particularly the combined impact of colour, sound, and the big-screen presentation upon a captive audience.

But, at the time of completing this revision in mid-2005, the 'breaking news' is that cinemas are once more under threat as the film makers are reducing greatly the time between the premiere of a movie, and its release in DVD format, in an effort to increase their revenues. Clearly, this loss of exclusivity could have a serious impact on cinema audiences.

MEDIA PLANNING

From the foregoing overview of the major media available to the advertiser, and the criteria to be considered when selecting them, it is clear that media selection is a complex procedure. As a topic it is outwith the scope of an introductory textbook and the reader should consult Shimp or O'Guinn for detail. An article published in the *International Journal of Advertising* (2005) proposes a model based on the Analytic Network Process (ANP) that also offers a useful tool to help solve this problem.

As the authors, Keith Coulter and Joseph Sarkis, note in their introduction "Traditional methods for media selection rely primarily on judgement and experience". Such an approach is seen to be suspect given the myriad factors that need to be considered simultaneously, and has led to the development of a number of quantitative, computer based models. However, earlier versions of such models were also suspect due to their inability to capture and incorporate the experts experience and knowledge, especially of the more qualitative dimensions like atmosphere.

This weakness was addressed successfully in the Analytic Hierarchy Process (AHP) model developed by Saaty in 1980. Coulter and Sarkis observe: "The AHP is aimed at integrating different measures, qualitative/intangible and quantitative/tangible, into a single overall score for ranking decision alternatives." This is achieved by using pairwise comparisons but was found to be unsuited to decisions involving interdependent relationships that are frequently found in media selection decisions. To overcome this problem Saaty introduced super-matrix analysis, also known as ANP, in 1996. It is this method that was used by Coulter and Sarkis in developing their media selection model, that specifically incorporates and evaluates web/internet media advertising using many of the standard media attributes (advantages/disadvantages) typically employed when comparing more traditional media.

Coulter and Sarkis' model identifies five primary categories or factors that define the attributes of advertising media and 16 sub-categories which are summarised in Table 18.7.

These were then used to evaluate six traditional media (direct mail, magazines, newspapers, outdoor, radio and television) and the new web/internet medium. Figure 18.5 describes the decision network as conceptualised by the authors comprising both interdependent and hierarchical relationships.

Although the model was only tested with three individuals who had been involved in the advertising and marketing of various products, " the comments of all three subjects would appear to validate the model". While it is expected that the results obtained will vary according to product type and life cycle stage, it was noted that all three subjects rated internet advertising as an important element in the media mix.

The methodology is fully described in the article and satisfies the authors claim that it offers a user-friendly approach to solving a complex problem, as well as enabling the incorporation of non-traditional media like the internet.

TELEVISION SPONSORSHIP

Television sponsorship is becoming increasingly prominent as a means of advertising. Using this form of advertising affords advertisers the opportunity to target viewers of particular programmes that have similar psychographic profiles

Figure 18.5   Detailed level diagrammatic representation of network decision hierarchy for managerial weights elicitation

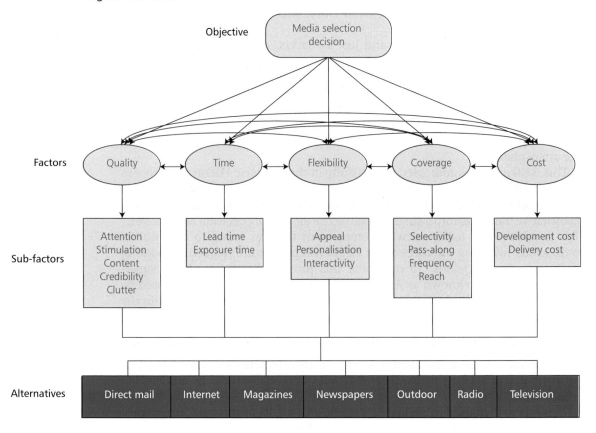

Source: Coulter, K. and Sarkis, J. (2005), *International Journal of Advertising*, Vol. 24, No. 2.

Table 18.7 Factors for media selection

Quality

1   Attention-getting capability (Attention) - ability of an ad placed in this specific media to 'grab the customer's attention' due to the nature of that media

2   Stimulating emotions (Stimulation) - ability of an ad placed in this specific media to convey emotional content and-or elicit emotional responses

3   Information content and detail (Content) - ability of an ad placed in this specific media to convey a large amount of information and/or product description

4   Credibility/prestige/image (Credibility) - ability of a specific media to lend prestige to a product through association (i.e. because that product is advertised within the media)

5   Clutter - degree to which it is difficult for a product advertised within a specific media to 'stand out' due to the large number of competitive offerings/messages

Time

1   Short lead time - degree to which an ad can be created and/or placed within a specific media in a relatively short period of time

2   Long exposure time - degree to which the communication recipient is able to examine the advertising message within a specific media for an extended period of time

Flexibility

1   Appeal to multiple senses (Appeal) - degree to which an ad placed within this specific media can communicate via sight, sound, taste, touch and/or smell concurrently

2   Personalisation - degree to which an advertising message placed within this specific media can be customised in order to target a specific individual or group of individuals

3   Interactivity - degree to which the customer can respond to information conveyed in an advertisement placed within this specific media

Coverage

1   Selectivity - degree to which an ad placed within this specific media is able to target a specific group of people

2   Pass-along audience (Pass-along) - degree to which an ad placed within this specific media is seen by those other than the original message recipient

3   Frequency/repeat exposure (Frequency) - degree to which any *single* ad placed within this specific media may be seen by any one particular individual on more than one occasion

4   Average media reach (Reach) - degree to which an ad placed within this specific media reaches a relatively wide audience

Cost

1   Development/production cost (Development cost) - relative cost of developing or producing an ad for this specific media

2   Average media delivery cost (Delivery cost) - average cost per thousand associated with this specific media

Source: Coulter, K. and Sarkis, J. (2005), *International Journal of Advertising*, Vol. 24, No. 2.

Table 18.8 Other advertising media rates

Media	Typical Rates
Aerial (Banner)	
Banner construction charge	From £70
Towing charge	From £320 per hour
Hot air balloons	
4-man	£1,000/day (banners £350-£1,200)
Balloon releases	£350/day (first two days) £295/day (thereafter)
Blimps	
Hire	£100 per day
Production of hull jackets	From £550 per set or:
Production of bespoke blimp	From £1,950
Additional tetherline banners	From £350 per banner
Bus Tickets	£2,600 per 500,000 (min) tickets (London)
In-flight print media	
American Airlines	
(American Way)	US$26,606 (ROP colour page)
Air Canada (enRoute)	US$18,500 (ROP colour page)
El Al (Atmosphere)	US$8,000 (ROP colour page)
Mobile poster vehicles	£385 per day (48 sheet)
People (promotional jackets)	£200 per day (6 hours) per person
Pizza boxes 12″	£531.25 per 1000
Takeaway containers	£37.50 per 1,000
Postcards	£35,700 per 7m per month (Cinemas)
Washroom posters	Rates £40-£157.50 per panel per 4 weeks

Source: bradgroup (*http://www.brad.co.uk*) October 2005

relevant to the type of products being advertised. Or, in the case of Tetley Tea, the product is associated with a programme that may have similar perceived values or attributes such as homeliness and warmth. Therefore, sponsorship allows products to automatically target certain segments and allows a product's attributes and image to be reinforced by the nature of the programme it sponsors e.g. the nPower Cricket Test series in 2005.

The logistics of sponsorship also make sense. Sponsorship highlights products at a time when the viewers' attention is most intense – at the beginning and end of interesting programmes. If sponsorship can work effectively with particular programmes then it allows products to reinforce its image that has already been established by other methods of advertising.

Changes adopted by the patent office have also encouraged the use of sponsorship. Since 1994 legislation has permitted slogans to be incorporated in to TV sponsorship credits. So long as the slogan is registered as part of the trade mark it may be incorporated into the credits. Now many companies are producing a much higher profile of sponsorship that interacts more closely with the relevant programme.

SOME OTHER ADVERTISING MEDIA

The list in Table 18.8 gives examples of other types of advertising media, and typical rates in 2004.

CAMPAIGN PLANNING

An excellent treatment of this subject used to be available in Olaf Ellefsen's *Campaign Planning* published by Business Publications on behalf of the IPA but, sadly, this is now out of print. However, the key factors remain much the same and are summarised in this section.

Earlier in the chapter a number of advertising objectives were stated, and it was noted that the determination of such an objective was an essential prerequisite to the formulation of a campaign plan. Assuming that management has given its advertising agency a clear statement of what it wishes to achieve, it then becomes the agency's responsibility to devise a campaign that will maximise the return on the appropriation allocated. As was inferred when discussing the agency–client relationship, the preparation of a campaign plan will require close cooperation between the parties. This will become clear if one considers the stages leading up to the introduction of a new product.

The first stage in the process is the identification of a business opportunity. Once this has been identified, the marketer will undertake marketing research as a basis for quantifying the nature and extent of this opportunity. As a result of such research a consumer profile will be drawn up stating the demographic characteristics of the potential consumer, the geographical location of the market, the frequency and method of purchase, and so on.

Armed with this profile or 'blueprint' of the intended consumer, the next stage in the process is the development of a product to satisfy the demand represented by recognition of the original opportunity. Once developed, the product will be tested. It is at this stage that the agency should be brought in. Given the consumer profile, the nature of the product and a statement of the features which differentiate it from competitors' offerings, the proposed channels of distribution and intended price bracket, the agency will be in a position to suggest an appropriate name and package. The continued growth of self-service retailing, described in Chapter 7, demands that very careful attention be paid to the latter two factors (name and package), as recognition at the point of sale is a vital stimulus to purchase. For these reasons alone the advertiser will want to feature both the brand name and pack in their advertising. If concept and product testing have been carried out the comments of the respondents should also be made available to the agency, as they invariably provide leads as to the copy platform to be adopted.

A good example of this was Johnson's Wax in the United States. When housewives were asked to list the most important properties of a floor polish, the majority gave considerable weight to the polish's ability to resist scuffing. Although 'scuffing' was not a word in common currency, the panel members had independently selected it as the most descriptive feature they were interested in. When Johnson introduced their new brand it was advertised as the 'non-scuff' polish and achieved immediate success – it was just what the customers were looking for!

A further reason for bringing in the agency at this time is to discuss the method of launching the product – test market, regional or national launch – and the timing, from selling in to the channels of distribution to the product's appearance in the retail outlet. On the basis of all this information, the agency will draw up a plan for submission to the advertiser comprising two major elements – the copy platform and the media schedule.

The copy platform is the theme around which the campaign is based, for example 'It's the real thing. Coke', while the media schedule lists the media in which the advertisements are to be published with details of size, timing, frequency and cost. The advertising literature is full of advice on the selection of USPs (unique selling points), EBTs (emotional buying triggers) and the like, but for an insight into the preparation and execution of advertising campaigns the student is strongly recommended to read one, or all, of the following books: David Ogilvy, (1965) *Confessions of an Advertising Man*, a highly readable and somewhat unconventional description of how Ogilvy became one of America's top advertising men, packed with information and advice for the aspiring advertising agent; and his more recent book (1983) *Ogilvy on Advertising*; Rosser Reeves (1970) *Reality in Advertising*, a short but highly concentrated coverage of do's and don't's in advertising, full of actual examples of advertising campaigns; Martin Mayer (1958) *Madison Avenue*, a colourful and interesting description of what goes on at the heart of the US agency business, rather dated now but still worth reading.

Setting the advertising appropriation

The decision of how much to spend on advertising and other promotional activities is one of the more difficult budgeting problems that management is called upon to make. A summary of possible approaches is outlined in Table 18.9. As will become clear in the next part of this chapter, the measurement of advertising effectiveness is, to say the least, difficult. In the absence of a directly measurable relationship between the volume of advertising and the overall profitability of the firm, the majority of managements have adopted one, or a combination, of the following 'rule-of-thumb' approaches.

Fixed percentage of sales

Under this method management allocates a percentage of either past or anticipated sales to advertising. Published data suggests there is a considerable variation in the percentage allocated to advertising, even within an industry, which, in turn, is a reflection of the different competitive strategies adopted by marketers. In this context it is noteworthy that total expenditures on advertising have remained a virtually constant percentage of the GNP in most advanced economies during the twentieth century.

Adoption of this policy may be justified on the grounds that it is rational to allocate a fixed proportion of sales revenue to advertising in the absence of a model which permits a prediction of variation in sales volume in response to variations in the volume of advertising. On the other hand, it ignores the fact that a decline in sales volume will result in a contraction of the advertising appropriation at the very time when increased advertising may be the stimulus necessary to halt the decline or reverse the trend.

In the case of companies operating in markets with an inelastic demand, the policy helps stabilise the competitive situation, always providing that it is a commonly accepted practice. Certain oligopolistic industries appear to exhibit this characteristic – the knowledge that increased advertising will not result in an increase in primary demand dissuades individual firms from attempting to improve their market share through increased advertising owing to the strong competitive response which it is bound to provoke. (This tendency was also noted with regard to the use of price reductions as a competitive weapon, unless the instigator had a clear cost advantage over their competitors.)

The 'me-too' approach

The adoption of this 'policy' was implied above, and constitutes the adoption of a level of advertising which corresponds to that of one's competitors. This is a purely defensive and negative reaction. Clearly, the firm is interested in what its competitors are doing as a guide to the policies it should adopt, but it also follows that if the firm is to improve its competitive position it must pursue policies that will enable the consumer to distinguish it from the competition and perceive it as superior.

Table 18.9 Methods of determining the promotional appropriation

Category 1: Executive judgement	AYCA: all you can afford Notional sum Arbitrary method Affordable approach
Category 2: Internal ratios	Historical parity Same as last year Inertia Fixed amount A/S ratio: advertising-to-sales A/M ratio: advertising-to-margin Per-unit allowance Case rate
Category 3: External ratios	Competitive parity Share of voice Share of market Dynamic difference
Category 4: Computer modelling	What-if models Prescriptive models Simulation Econometric analysis
Category 5: Experimentation	Experiments AMTES (Area Marketing Test Evaluation Systems)
Category 6: Objective-and-task	Task method

Source: Reprinted from 'Promotion', Crosier, K. in Baker M. J. (Ed.), *The Marketing Book* 3rd Edn. copyright (1994) with permission from Elsevier.

What we can afford

This method tends to relegate expenditures on advertising to the bottom rung of the corporate budget ladder. It implies that whatever remains after meeting operating costs, dividend payments and so on, will be spent on advertising. As with the fixed percentage of sales method, the most likely outcome is that as sales fall the unit contribution will decline to the point where no advertising can be afforded at all. Conversely, as sales rise an increasing amount will become available and the possibility of wasteful expenditures will become a reality.

The 'task' approach

In the absence of a normative model of the relationship between various levels of advertising and profitability, this method is to be preferred to any of the above practices. The first step in this method is the definition of a clear objective. Given the objective, one can prepare a campaign plan that would achieve this goal. An examination of the costs of mounting such a campaign may indicate that it is beyond the company's available resources. Within this constraint, the plan may be modified by closely evaluating each of its component parts and dispensing with the least essential. Obviously the end result will be a lesser objective than originally laid down, but it will be a realistic statement of what the firm can hope to accomplish related to current resources.

The measurement of advertising effectiveness

When discussing media selection, frequent reference was made to BRAD and

ALLOCATING THE ADVERTISING BUDGET

Writing in *The Times* (16/01/06) Amanda Andrews reported on the ways in which the emergence of new technology is causing advertisers to rethink the allocation of their budgets. "Advertisers are increasingly reluctant to spend their budgets on a single television or print advertising campaign, knowing they will not command the same audiences as once they did."

Andrews compares 1990, when 150 commercial and 27 non-commercial television programmes were watched by 15 million or more people, with 2004 in which only 3 commercial and 3 non-commercial programmes attracted such an audience.

While mass media still dominate adspend they have become increasingly fragmented, and advertisers appreciate that they need both to embrace the new technology as well as improve their understanding of consumer needs.

Dominic Proctor, chief executive of MindShare Worldwide, is quoted as saying: "To start with, it is important to tap into the needs of today's consumer. The advertising we have known in the past couple of decades has been about interruption. Adverts in the future need to be more about engagement.

Even internet advertising is still in the irritating phase of interruption. Some internet pop-up adverts [programs that pop out on to the screen unbidden when you open a page] have a negative effect and will probably be phased out. Search advertising, where Google has made its money, is very successful."

Proctor goes on to predict that the internet will become the dominant force in advertising within ten years, as it becomes more audiovisual using mobile phone technology, always provided that such advertising can engage the audience's interest. As with mass commoditisation, tailoring ads to the information needs of individual subscribers may not be too far away.

the IPA Readership Surveys as a source of information on audience composition. Head counting is a long-established practice that yields sound demographic data. A measure of audience size is of interest to the advertiser but, ultimately, the advertiser is much more concerned with the effectiveness of the advertising; that is a measure of the results of exposure to advertising. Five basic methods have been evolved to measure advertising effectiveness and these are reviewed below. (Several of the methods referred to were also discussed in Chapter 11, Marketing Research).

The measurement of awareness

Awareness is defined as 'knowledge about a company or its product without reference to the source of knowledge'. As, by definition, awareness tests do not relate knowledge to source they provide only a rough and ready guide to advertising effectiveness, and are usually undertaken as a preliminary to further tests. In the case of a new product it may be possible to isolate the source of awareness, but this is virtually impossible in the case of an established brand.

Actual measurement is obtained by asking respondents:

(a) *Straight dichotomous questions*, e.g. Have you ever heard of the XYZ company?'
    Yes . . .   No . . .

(b) *An open-ended question*; for example, 'Do you know of any companies that make a detergent with a blue whitener?'

(c) *Check-list questions with rating scales*; for example, 'How familiar are you with the XYZ company?'
    Very familiar . . . Know something about . . . Know very little about them . . .
        Never heard of . . .

Low cost and speed are cited as the major advantages of this method.

The measurement of recall

Recall – what people can remember about advertising messages – is the most frequently used measure of advertising effectiveness, on the basis that if the message has left a memorable impression it has fulfilled its communicative function. If the advertising objective is to communicate information then the method is appropriate, but in many instances the objective is to promote action, for example mail-order advertisements. Recall is also a useful measure when copy testing.

Recall studies are capable of measuring several dimensions of advertising effectiveness. At the lowest level they consist of the respondent's describing the basic theme of an advertisement, and progress through association of the correct theme with the product advertised, measures of comprehension, credibility and conviction, to significance.

Essentially, the method employed is to ask the respondent to reconstruct what he or she can remember having seen or heard advertised, either unaided – unaided recall – or with a varying degree of assistance to direct the respondent's thinking along particular lines – aided recall. Aided recall is generally preferred, as few people will spontaneously recall past events without some stimulus, in which case the researcher must guard against bias arising from too much assistance, or false answers resulting from guessing. Gallup and Robinson conduct regular surveys of recall for print media, and attempt to minimise bias by first establishing that the respondent has read the issue being tested by showing them the cover, and then asking them to establish knowledge of its content. Once the respondent has demonstrated familiarity with the test issue, they are then asked to reconstruct their memory of the advertisements without opening the magazine. The final stage is to show the respondent brand names, advertisement logotypes, and so on, and after telling them that some did not appear in the issue in question, ask them to identify those they remember. A sample of 400 is used, the interviews are recorded verbatim and, after editing, are compiled into an index of recall – the 'proved name registration'. A **PNR** is calculated for the medium as a whole, for the product group and for the specific brand. Although it is difficult to assign an absolute value to a PNR, it provides a useful guide to the advertiser in that they can measure their advertisement's performance against that of all other advertisers in the magazine and that of their immediate competitors. Further, over a period of time they can determine whether the impact of their advertising is increasing, declining or static.

A hybrid test which incorporates both aided and unaided recall is 'working along the time line'. For example you ask a respondent to describe what they did yesterday evening, anticipating that they will recall an event which involved consumption of a product in which you are interested. If the product group is mentioned, for example 'I washed, cleaned my teeth and went to bed', you might ask the name of the brand of soap or toothpaste and lead into further questions related to these products. If the product group is not mentioned then the interviewer will ask directly 'Did you clean your teeth?', and so on. Three problems are inherent in all recall studies:

1 Respondent confusion, due to either confusing the advertisement and its sponsor – Kellogg's Porridge Oats – or identifying advertisements correctly from recollections of previous campaigns.

2 Recall of advertising messages in the interview situation is not the same as recall at the point of sale (a strong argument for both poster advertising and POS display), nor does it indicate an intention to buy.

3 The ever-present danger of misinterpretation of the results.

For the two latter reasons recall investigations are often combined with:

Attitude surveys

A favourable attitude towards a company or its product nearly always precedes a decision to buy, even if this favourable predisposition is at the preconscious level, that is a consumer picks up a product on impulse without consciously identifying the motivation to purchase.

Attitude measurement may consist of a general assessment or be restricted to various dimensions of a specific brand – acceptance, preference or insistence – of either one's own or one's competitor's product. Unfortunately, it is difficult to construct a true measure of a person's attitudes, and several techniques are frequently used in combination to permit cross-checking. The more common methods are:

(a) Direct questions of the 'Do you like X?' type, followed by a request to explain why you do, or do not, like X. Direct questions suffer from their inability to distinguish between varying degrees of intensity of feeling.

Rating scales provide a partial solution and are amenable to rapid analysis, but suffer from the disadvantage that the choice of phrases which are precise, yet universally understood, is extremely difficult; that, however large, the scale may still not permit a truly accurate expression of intensity of feeling; that intermediate positions are capable of varying interpretation, for example 'What is your attitude to Widgets?'

Favourable . . . Mixed . . . Indifferent . . . Unfavourable . . .

Alternatively, one might use the scale:

Excellent, 4, 3, 2, Poor, or even a seven or ten-point scale.

(b) A second method is to ask the respondent to complete a checklist by indicating the most appropriate answer/description of those assigned to each question. By undertaking a preliminary survey it is usually possible to design questions that will cover the attributes which consumers, as opposed to advertisers, think important.

(c) A semantic differential test, in which a respondent indicates where a brand or company stands on a scale of paired opposites, either descriptive adjectives or phrases, for example reliable–unreliable.

(d) Partially structured interviews, in which the interviewer memorises the points to be covered and 'discusses' the subject with the respondent, rather than posing formal questions from a questionnaire. The lack of trained interviewers, the length of the interview and difficulties of interpretation severely limit the use of this method.

Attitude related to usage is usually considered a more significant measure of advertising effectiveness than attitude on its own, and it is usual to obtain a measure of usage as a basis for a comparison of attitudes.

Psychological measurement

The three techniques described above are designed to measure a respondent's reaction to advertising at the conscious or preconscious level. Psychological techniques are designed to probe deeper and reach to the subconscious mind. At this level the respondent is unaware of the reasons which result in certain expressed patterns of behaviour, although if asked, they will usually advance an acceptable and rational reason. As most advertising messages are directed at large audiences, the peculiarities of the individual are of little or no consequence unless they are common to a large number of individuals. It is to determine basic motivation that advertising researchers, among others, use psychological methods where direct questioning might lead to rationalisation or evasion.

Psychological techniques have limitations which require great care in their execution and interpretation, and it must be recognised that the results will be qualitative not quantitative. As noted above in regard to partially structured depth interviews, the lack of suitably qualified interviewers usually restricts the use of these techniques to small samples from which it is difficult to make acceptable projections of consumer behaviour.

The most frequently used method is the unstructured depth interview of from one to three hours, in which interviewer and respondent talk about a specific subject in the belief that if the respondent is kept talking about the same thing long enough some of their unconscious attitudes will begin to emerge.

A popular variation of the depth interview is the focused or directed group interview, in which a skilled interviewer leads a group of six to twelve people in an unstructured discussion that relates to the product and/or its advertising.

Other projective techniques used include thematic apperception tests, picture probes, narrative probes, sentence completion tests and word association tests.

Sort and count

Many advertisements contain an invitation to interested parties to write in to the advertiser for further information, free samples, and so forth. By sorting and counting the requests generated by such advertisements the advertiser can obtain much useful information at low cost.

Despite the potential bias due to respondent self-selection, this method does give valuable information in relative terms of the pulling power of different media, of different copy platforms and advertisement make-up, and of different sizes and positions within the media. The advertisements are usually keyed, that is given a coding to assist identification, either by including the code in the address, for example Dept DM7 for an edition of the *Daily Mail*, or by requiring the respondent to clip the coupon on which the information is similarly recorded.

As mentioned by Ogilvy (1965) in *Confessions of an Advertising Man*, direct mail advertisers have a continuous feedback of the pulling power of their advertisements, which supports his suggestion that those selling though more conventional channels might do well to adopt some of the former's advertising practices, for example use of long copy.

Laboratory techniques for pre-testing advertisements

A number of techniques have been developed to try and obtain an objective measure of people's response to advertisements, which interviewing methods are unable

INNOVATIVE IDEAS IN MARKETING

The growth of direct marketing has had a major impact on conventional media advertising. It is clear that if such advertising is to defend its share of the advertising budget there is a need to come up with new ideas. One such innovation is the development of programmes that act as a showcase for the sponsor's products.

Writing in the *The Times*, (13/01/06), Amanda Andrews reports on a programme called *ExtremeMakeover: Home Edition* which is being screened weekly by ABC in the United States and proving to be very popular. "Every week a team renovates the home of someone who suffered a terrible trauma, such as the death of a family member. Top designers visit a department store and deck out the newly renovated house with swanky appliances and put a new car in the drive."

However, the programme is unashamedly focused on the products of the firms of Sears, the department store, Kenmore, an appliance manufacturer, and Ford. Further, the programme is produced by a company called Endemol and Mindshare acting on behalf of the companies.

While it is doubtful if this kind of product placement will grow into a major source of revenue it should be remembered that the ever popular "soaps" were originally sponsored by the likes of Procter & Gamble and Lever Brothers on radio before migrating to television

to elicit owing to an inability to verbalise or a tendency to rationalise. The use of the instruments listed below is based on the knowledge that emotional arousal in a human being results in various responses which are under the control of the autonomic nervous system and thus largely independent of conscious control. These responses include increases in pulse and respiration rates, erection of hair follicles, changes in pupil size and electrical brain pulses, perspiration rates and so on. As each person reacts to different stimuli to a varying degree, ideally one should measure all responses simultaneously, but this is clearly impossible under normal conditions. As such it is necessary to select the method(s) which provide the most reliable results in monitoring reactions to the specific variable under test with the minimum disturbance to the subject. The most frequently used are:

1 The *psycho-galvanometer*. This instrument measures changes in the activity of the sweat glands via electrodes attached by suction to the subject's hands. Prior to exposing the subject to the test advertisements the basal level must be established for control purposes and care taken to maintain a constant temperature throughout the test. The highest reading recorded indicates maximum arousal.

2 The *eye observation camera* is used to measure pupil dilation. As light also affects the pupil, care must be taken to ensure that both control and test material are of the same luminosity. The material to be tested is back-projected into a closed box while the camera records the pupil dilation over a period of time. The greatest change occurs with the highest level of arousal. The camera may also he used to measure the subject's blink rate – the higher the rate the greater the arousal. Blinking is partly under conscious control, and is also affected by humidity, irritation and fatigue, all of which must be controlled if an accurate measure is to be obtained.

3 The *tachistoscope* is an instrument used for exposing material for controlled periods of time ranging from 1/100 of a second to several seconds. Its main use is in measuring the impact of an advertisement by determining either the point at which its features are registered (noting and legibility studies) or its visual impact (what is communicated) when exposed for only a brief period. As individual 'thresholds' vary, a norm must first be established for each subject.

4 The *eye-movement camera* tracks the movement of the eye over an advertisement by filming a point of light projected on to the eyeball. The track indicates the order and degree of attention given to the features of the advertisement.

All the above methods are subject to criticism on the grounds that they are unrealistic as a result of the laboratory situation; that only a limited number of respondents may be tested (owing to the high cost of the test and data processing equipment required), and these may not be representative; that no indication of the direction of the response is given, so that respondents have to be questioned as to their feelings, which reintroduces subjectivity into the test; that is, a marked reaction may be due to either repulsion or attraction.

In mitigation, any test is better than no test if it helps in establishing whether or not advertisements are communicating their basic point to the subject. Further, it is only through experimentation that satisfactory techniques for measuring advertising effectiveness will be evolved.

ECONOMIC AND ETHICAL ASPECTS OF ADVERTISING

The above review of advertising has concentrated on the practical aspects of the subject in so far as they affect the marketer. At the same time one must be aware that advertising is frequently the subject of criticism, and the aim of this section is to summarise the arguments both for and against. In view of the author's interest in marketing it follows that he has a favourable attitude towards advertising, and the reader is warned that this treatment is bound to be somewhat subjective.

The economic argument

Essentially the question is 'Is advertising productive in the economic sense, that is does it maximise satisfaction through the utilisation of scarce resources?' The cliche, 'It pays to advertise', is tacit recognition of the fact that advertising improves the profitability of the advertiser, but this is not to say that it necessarily makes any real contribution to the welfare of the community as a whole.

From the economist's point of view, the acid test of any economic activity is the utility of the output of that activity, which is measured by the extent to which it satisfies wants. For the economist the difficulty of accepting that advertising creates utility in this sense is both semantic and conceptual. The economist would argue that rather than satisfy existing wants the advertiser seeks to create wants for something that is already available. Advertisers would probably argue that you cannot create wants – you can only create better ways of satisfying existing wants, and that consumers derive satisfaction from advertised goods is undeniable. Similarly, to argue that advertising persuades people to consume things they do not want is to deny one of the basic assumptions of the economist – that, by and large, people are rational in their purchasing behaviour.

Many economists draw a distinction between '**informative**' and '**combative**' advertising, following the definition of Alfred Marshall (1919) in his book *Industry and Trade*. The distinction was further elaborated by Braithwaite (1928) in the *Economic Journal*, where it was claimed that advertising which contains information may be regarded as a true selling expense, whereas advertising designed to stimulate demand is non-essential and largely unproductive. In the April 1962 issue of the same journal, Samuel Courtauld was to assert 'most competitive advertising is a costly national extravagance'.

It would seem, therefore, that the critics concede the value of informative advertising as a means of making the consumer aware of the existence of goods and services and their basic properties, but that they consider combative or persuasive advertising to be a wasteful use of resources. It is difficult to see how the distinction can be maintained, since an advertisement for a new product may be justified as informative in that it makes consumers aware of the existence and characteristics of this product, but combative in that it seeks to persuade consumers to buy the new product in preference to a previously available substitute.

All advertisements contain some information, and it is a fruitless exercise to try and evaluate their individual utility in any precise manner as the informative/persuasive distinction will depend entirely on the existing state of knowledge of each individual member of the audience.

Partial recognition of this fact has diverted many economists, and other critics of advertising, to accept that '**persuasive**' advertising can be beneficial, providing that it results in lower prices. Unfortunately, this distinction ignores the fact that price stability is the same as a price reduction under conditions of inflation, and that a consistent improvement in quality may represent the equivalent of a price reduction in that it increases consumer satisfaction for the same nominal money outlay.

To summarise, the case against advertising may be stated as:

1 Advertising leads to higher prices by conditioning demand and so leads to distortion of the productive machine, for example maize may cost only £0.01 per pound, but when converted into branded cornflakes it retails at about £0.80 per pound.

2 Advertising leads to non-price competition; for example, the use of promotions. This creates diseconomies due to difficulties associated with the accurate measurement of demand, and results in a high proportion of product failures.

3 It is an unreliable guide as to value and satisfaction.

4 It leads to oligopoly and monopoly.

5 It is a waste of national resources.

Proponents of advertising would argue that:

1 Advertised goods are cheaper because:
   (a) Advertising brings about economies in 'true' selling costs, for example by reducing the need for direct selling, encouraging the development of self-service, and so forth.
   (b) It raises the scale of production, helps to stabilise output and promotes standardisation.
   (c) Competition ensures that the benefits of these economies will be passed on to the consumer.

2 Advertised goods are better goods because:
   (a) The identification of the product with the manufacturer through branding constitutes a guarantee of quality which must be maintained if the manufacturer is to secure repeat purchases from users.
   (b) To maintain market share manufacturers must constantly strive to improve their product to meet, or exceed, the claims of competing products.

3 Branded and advertised goods create a freedom of consumer choice that was unknown when the same articles were sold from bulk.

4 Advertising improves the standard of living by making new developments quickly available to the public and, by stimulating demand, creates investment, production and employment opportunities.

The ethical argument

Advertising is indicted on ethical grounds on the basis that it encourages the development of materialism. F. P. Bishop (1952), in his book The Ethics of Advertising, defines materialism as '. . . *an acquisitive ideology in which the satisfaction of material desires is held up as the sole or principal end for the individual or group*'.

In the creation of a materialistic society advertising is charged with deliberately concentrating on those motives that are least desirable in man, and of the least value to society. One can be shown innumerable advertisements that appeal to one or more of the 'seven deadly sins', or that play on the emotion most easily stimulated in the human animal – fear. Fear of being left out, of being socially unacceptable, or of being considered socially inferior in some way or other, for example dull, lifeless hair; B.O.; halitosis; X washes whiter – and it shows.

Advertising is further indicted in that it sets out to eliminate nonconformity and discourage originality in thought, word and deed. Admass leaves no room for reason, and cultivates the herd instinct.

Finally, in the words of A. S. J. Baster (1935) in *Advertising Reconsidered*, '*The major part of informative advertising is and always has been a campaign of exaggeration, half-truths, intended ambiguities, direct lies, and general deception*' (quoted by Bishop, 1952).

Most marketers would readily agree that the acquisition of material things is a means to an end and not an end in itself, but would also argue that people have free will and therefore the right to decide for themselves what level of material consumption they will seek to attain. Religion and philosophy offer us a wide range of alternatives from which to choose a set of principles that will constitute a 'good life'. Whereas mere possessions are unlikely to result in satisfaction in the total sense, it is also true that a certain level of material goods is essential to the maintenance of life. Over and above these essentials, the desired level of material possessions will depend on the society of which we are a member, our education and income.

It is also appropriate to point out that it is only in the twentieth century that the possibility of a reasonable standard of living for all members of the more affluent societies was achieved, and this, as yet, only in advanced economies. Earlier civilisations were largely based on the sweated labour of the masses and only the aristocracy could afford the luxury of philosophising about the 'good life' – only in the next world was it conceivable that all might share in the material comforts enjoyed by the few. (It is an interesting reflection on middle-class morality that the demand for labour-saving kitchen equipment only really got off the ground in this country with the demise of personal servants following the creation of alternative opportunities for female employment in the Second World War.)

Present-day 'welfare economics', designed to remove 'poverty in the midst of plenty', have grown out of the belief that we are now capable of producing sufficient to permit an adequate standard of living for all, and that the major problem is a more equitable distribution of output. At the same time, experience of a full employment policy in the post-war period has taught us that in the absence of adequate demand, production is frustrated and both human and physical resources lie idle. Many would argue that restriction of demand in recent years has mainly resulted from government policies designed to curb inflation, rather than from the inability of the productive machine to create goods in demand. It is my opinion that the inflationary trend is largely the result of a lack of demand.

In the case of the average consumer, the material possessions which constitute the good life are limited to a relatively small number of goods and services. There is a latent demand for many other goods and services, but their utility is less than the effort necessary to earn sufficient to pay for them owing to the disincentive of increasingly punitive levels of taxation. Consequently there is no incentive to work more effectively and improve productivity, an attitude which is compounded by the Government's provision of a range of social services that caters for virtually all of life's emergencies.

Despite ten years of Thatcherism in the 1980s, both government and management are still singularly ineffective in explaining the real benefits that will accrue from increased productivity, and workers resist measures to achieve this in the belief that they may be making themselves redundant. The possibility of redeploying labour into new industries creating new products to satisfy existing wants is overlooked. On the other hand if the consumer can be made to want

ADVERTISING – A FORCE FOR GOOD

While advertising is often subject to criticism, the Annual Report of the Institute of British Advertisers (ISBA) 2005 summarises succinctly why advertising has an important role to play in a free society.

In his Presidential statement John Sunderland, Chairman of Cadbury Schweppes, observed:

"According to Arts Council figures, in its first ten years from 1994 to 2004, the National Lottery spent £1.9 billion on the arts. This is a fine achievement, but in just three months between July and September 2004, British advertisers spent £3.3 billion – twice as much! That spending not only produced art and entertainment for the public but also sustained the diversity and independence of the media which displayed them.

From its earliest days, advertising has been a free source of information and education. It not only informs people about the range of choices available, but helps them to weigh one choice against another. Today, when our government wants us to behave more wisely and more sociably – whether to drive better, look after ourselves or join the armed forces or the teaching profession – to whom does it turn? The advertising industry."

While it is acknowledged that some advertising might seek to make excessive and possibly misleading claims, and that it uses emotional appeals, the industry itself monitors and regulates advertising through a number of ISBA committees and the Advertising Standards Authority. On balance,

however, it is believed that advertising promotes competition and drives up the quality of goods and services. The more extravagant the claims for a product, the more it has to live up . If it fails then consumers will look elsewhere. If its claims are true, then consumers will come to trust the brand and stay loyal to the advertiser. Surely, the essence of a free market economy?

In summary: "ISBA is clear that whilst advertising is influential it cannot persuade consumers:

- Against their will;
- To continue buying anything they do not like to do anything which offends against their common sense."

Keeping up-to-date

Inevitably, much of the factual information concerning marketing communications and the media will become dated. It follows that you should access the latest information from the many sources available.

Of particular value is *www.ofcom.org.uk* that publishes regular reports on the UK communications market. For example, in its 2005 overview it highlights the growth of digital communications and the slow decline of analogue services as a result of:

- Improved availability
- Proliferation of services
- New and enhanced consumer offerings
- Falling prices

Each of these trends is described and discussed in some detail and supported by relevant facts and figures.

Other sites to consider are:

Institute of British Advertisers *www.isba.org.uk*
Advertising Standards Authority *www.asa.org.uk*
BrandRepublic (*Campaign* and *Marketing* Magazines online) *www.brandrepublic.com*

dishwashing machines, DVDs, mobile phones, electric toothbrushes or any other similar but 'non-essential' item, this may well provide sufficient incentive to call forth the increase in productivity that has been evident in the UKs improved competitive performance in recent years.

In a sense, therefore, materialism and an acquisitive society are necessary if we are to maintain and improve the quality of life for both ourselves and those less fortunate in the developing economies. The more wealth we create domestically, the greater will be our ability to help others – an issue that was the focus of the G8 Summit meeting in Scotland in 2005.

The other argument for the retention of advertising is that it helps preserve freedom of speech and freedom of choice. Modern media are dependent upon advertising revenues for their continued existence. On their existence largely rests the continued freedom of speech for, as noted when discussing the evolution of advertising, one of the first acts of a dictatorship is to secure control of the means of mass communication.

PUBLIC RELATIONS

According to Haywood (1999) public relations barely existed as a management function, outside some Western governments and their military forces, before the 1950s. Today it is a widely established professional practice with its own professional bodies and qualifications. As a subject Public Relations is also widely taught at the undergraduate and postgraduate level in business schools around the world.

In common with other business disciplines numerous definitions are to be found. According to the UK Institute of Public Relations (1994) it is '*the planned and sustained effort to establish and maintain goodwill and mutual understanding between an organisation and its publics*'. Haywood (op. cit.) suggests that a useful working definition is '*those efforts used by management to identify and close any gap between how the organisation is seen by its key publics and how it would like to be seen*' He also emphasises that public relations is about corporate personality – what the organisation is, believes in and is seeking to achieve – rather than simply its 'image', albeit that image is an intrinsic and essential element of the corporate personality.

It is also important to emphasise that public relations involves much more than publicity. Publicity is vital in projecting an organisation's personality but is simply the visible expression of corporate policy and strategic intent. Professional public relations has an important role and contribution to make to the formulation and implementation of both policy and strategy which goes far beyond a marketing communications activity. (Corporate PR covers an organisation's relationships with all of its publics, not just its customers.) That said, PR must work closely with other marketing communications such as advertising, selling and sales promotion, and be integrated with them to achieve an efficient and effective communication strategy.

As noted, public relations seeks to project the organisation's personality and thereby establish and develop its corporate reputation with all those audiences or publics on whom it depends for its success. While customers usually come first in importance there are many other constituencies – employees, shareholders, government/politicians, the media, the general public, and so on – whose support, explicit or implicit, is vital to successful performance. Shell's handling of the Brent Spar incident in 1995 was a vivid example of how public opinion forced a major multinational corporation to revise a decision, endorsed by the British Government, with considerable loss of face for both parties. Originally, Shell proposed to sink an obsolete oil storage 'rig' in the deep Atlantic. Public concern for the possible impact of this on the environment, orchestrated by Greenpeace and other environmental organisations, resulted in a boycott of Shell products in Europe which forced the company to abandon its plans and promise to dismantle the rig onshore. In this case Greenpeace's positive PR achieved a desired outcome while Shell's ineffective PR caused considerable damage to its reputation.

In the same sense that marketing is the primary responsibility of the Chief Executive, so too is public relations. Indeed, many senior executives see acting as spokesman for their organisation as one of their major functions. By the same token the personality and image of an organisation is often inextricably linked with that of its Chairman and/ or Chief Executive. For example, the flamboyant John Harvey-Jones transformed ICI's image from that of a staid, conservative industrial company into one of a thrusting and dynamic modern corporation, undoubtedly paving the way for the re-organisation of the firm into two distinct organisations (Zeneca and ICI). Similarly, Virgin is inextricably linked to the personality of Richard Branson and 'The Apprentice' programme on UK TV has made a cult of Alan Sugar and his Amstrad organisation.

At the corporate level public relations is inextricably linked with the mission and objectives of the organisation, and it is through public relations that the values and aspirations which these represent are communicated to its various publics.

In a seminal article 'The Company is the Brand', Stephen King (1989) argued cogently that as it becomes increasingly difficult to distinguish between the products and services offered by firms, so customers use their corporate reputation or 'brand' to distinguish between them. Loyalty or goodwill towards a company is a major determinant of its asset value, as the frequently cited case of Nestle's acquisition of Rowntree Macintosh makes clear. At the time of the acquisition (1988), Rowntree Macintosh's physical asset value was under £500 million but Nestle paid £2.5 billion to secure ownership of international brands such as Kit Kat, Smarties and so on. While marketing will usually assume responsibility for individual brands such as Kit Kat, it is public relations which is responsible for promoting the corporate brand. Thus, when an organisation adopts a monolithic branding approach (all activities are transacted under a single, corporate name), or an endorsed branding strategy (all distinctive activities or 'brands' are promoted jointly with the corporate name) public relations will have a major role to play. Haywood (op. cit) suggests ten pointers to help ensure that advertising and public relations work together.

1 Involve both disciplines in the marketing planning;
2 Define complementary public relations and advertising objectives;
3 Allocate separate and firm budgets to each;
4 Agree responsibilities and planned activities;
5 Establish practical routines for coordination;
6 Have regular joint liaison sessions;

7   Get public relations/advertising to present their campaign to each other;

8   Arrange for them to make a joint presentation to the organisation's management;

9   Ensure regular exchange of all documents/ information;

10 Insist that all parties work together this year – or they might not get the chance next.

Summary

This rather long chapter has attempted to provide an overview of a large and complex subject – **advertising**. Inevitably, it has only been able to scratch the surface and the reader is strongly encouraged to refer to some of the sources cited.

Beginning with some definitions we looked next at the objectives which advertising may be used to help achieve. A discussion of the evolution of advertising followed which suggests that, while evidence of it dates back to Roman times, it is only since the abolition of taxes on advertisements in 1853 that the modern advertising industry has developed. Several tables of statistics provided some 'feel' for the size and structure of the UK advertising industry. These data were accompanied by a warning that they rapidly become dated and that one should consult the latest edition of the various sources for an accurate and up-to-date position. *The Marketing Pocket Book* is particularly useful in this context as it summarises so many other data sources.

The next section examined the structure of advertising and, specifically, the roles of advertiser,

the advertising agency and media owners. This led to a discussion of agency remuneration and selection.

An overview of the major media followed. This opened with suggestions as to how one might evaluate the available media in terms of character, atmosphere coverage and cost. Some features of and data on the major media followed – the national and regional press, magazines, television, commercial radio, outdoor advertising, the cinema and direct mail.

A short section on campaign planning reviewed some of the considerations the advertiser should take into account when planning a campaign. This was supported by advice on setting the appropriation or budget and measuring advertising effectiveness.

Next, we looked at some of the economic and ethical issues which are frequently raised about advertising but concluded that, in a free country, advertising is strongly associated with the democracy of the market place. And, finally, we looked briefly at the role and nature of public relations.

Review questions and problems

1   Your company is considering changing its advertising agency. How would you undertake the selection of a replacement?

2   Analyse the following publications, using the 'check-list' described in the text: *TV Times, Vogue, Financial Times*

3   Discuss the merits of the cinema as an advertising medium.

4   Develop an outline campaign plan for either frozen concentrated orange juice or off-peak rail travel, assuming an annual budget of £1 million.

5   What are the economic arguments for and against advertising? Which do you find more convincing? Why?

6 How would you determine the advertising budget for a new household detergent with an expected sales volume of 5 million, a recommended retail price of £1.50, and a gross margin of 25 per cent? Distinguish between above and below-the-line expenditures.

7 What problems do you associate with the derivation of a measure of advertising effectiveness?

8 Evaluate each of the following statements:
(a) Advertising costs the consumer millions of pounds every year. If advertising were eliminated, prices could be reduced and everybody would benefit.
(b) Most advertising is a social waste because it merely diverts demand from one firm to another.
(c) Advertising is of no value to the consumer because it consists of doubtful claims of small differences between similar products.

9 'We believe in advertising; it is an essential factor in the economics of modern industry.' Discuss.

10 'People in advertising are parasites. They contribute nothing to the real wealth of the community.' These sentences occur in a letter in your local newspaper. Write a reply, putting the case for advertising and advertising agencies.

11 Summarise and evaluate any five different methods by which a national advertiser can determine the annual advertising appropriation.

12 'It is not possible to make a realistic test of the effectiveness of a (television) commercial in a laboratory situation in advance of real-life exposure' (Alan Hedges). Explain.

13 What are the main print media? What are the main electronic media? List each. Take one media group from each category and describe its advantages and limitations.

14 Repetition is the key to advertising success. Evaluate the values and limitations of a repetitive campaign.

15 The Stimulus–Response Theory, as applied to advertising, stresses the importance of frequency and recency of exposure to advertisements by target audiences. Explain why this theory cannot by itself offer a satisfactory explanation of the influence of advertising on consumer buying behaviour.

16 'Personal influence is seven times more effective than magazine or newspaper advertising in the persuasion of women to switch brands of household products' (Katz and Lazarsfeld). How can this factor be employed in media planning?

16 Write a headline and 50–60 words of copy for a quarter-page ad for a teenage magazine selling a two-week desert tour of Morocco by minibus. Describe or draw the illustration if you want to use one.

17 The economist Alfred Marshall (1922) drew a distinction between 'informative' advertising and 'combative' advertising. Can such a distinction usefully be made? Discuss with examples.

Key terms

acceptable media
acquisitive society
advertiser-agency relationship
advertising agency
Advertising Association
agency consolidation
aided recall
analytic hierarchy process (AHP)
analytic network process (ANP)
blogs
blueprint
British Rate and Data (BRAD)
Broadcaster's Audience Research
  Board Ltd (BARB
broadsheets
cable television
charge per standard column
  centimetre (SCC)
cinema
Cinema Advertising Association
combative advertising
commercial transaction
conscious / preconscious level
copy platform
copy testing
corporate advertising
corporate pr
cost per thousand (CPT)
creative specialist
database marketing
demographic characteristics

digital interactive television
  (DiTV)
direct advertising
direct communications
directed group interview
emotional buying trigger
  (EBT)
external facilitators
full service agencies
informative advertising
Institute of Public Relations
interactive digital television
  (iDTV)
internet advertising
intrusive media
leverage
mass media
materialism
media
media schedule
media specialist
Napster
National Readership Survey
  (NRS)
natural breaks
newspapers
outdoor advertising
Outdoor Advertising
  Association (OAA)
page traffic
personal video recorder (PVR)

Persuasive advertising
picture probes
POSTAR (Poster Audience
  Research)
poster
press
propaganda
proved name registration (PNR)
public relations
publicity
RAJAR (Radio Joint Audience
  Research)
return path
sales promotion
satellite systems
sentence completion tests
SkyPlus
tabloids
television
television sponsorship
thematic apperception tests
TiVo
transportation advertising
unaided recall
unstructured depth interview
unique selling point (USP)
welfare economics
word association tests
world wide web advertising
zapping
zipping

Supplementary reading list

Crosier, K. (2003), 'Promotion', in Baker, M.J. (ed.) *The Marketing Book*, 5th edn., (Oxford: Butterworth Heinemann).

Haywood, R. (2005), *Corporate Reputation, The Brand and The Bottom Line* 3rd edn (Kogan Page).

O'Guinn, T. C., Allen, C. T., and Semenik, R. J. (2006), *Advertising and Integrated Brand Promotion*, Fourth Edition, (Mason, OH: Thomson South-Western)

Shimp, T. A., (2003) *Advertising, Promotion*, 6th. Edition, (Mason, OH: Thomson South-Western).

Van Riel, C. B. M. (1995) *The Principles of Corporate Communications* (Englewood Cliffs, N.J.: PrenticeHall).

Yeshin, T. (2006), *Advertising*, (London: Thomson).

DIRECT MARKETING

19

Learning Goals *After reading this chapter you should be able to:*

- Define 'direct marketing'

- Explain the nature of direct marketing and the key steps in developing a direct marketing campaign

- Summarise the main features of Telemarketing, Direct Broadcast Media and Catalogues

- Describe the essence of 'network marketing' and the situations where it may be used effectively

- Identify the potential of the Internet as a medium of communication

- Discuss the nature and impact of 'viral' marketing

INTRODUCTION

According to Keynote (*www.keynote.co.uk*) Direct Marketing is

any marketing activity aimed at individuals (either named or unnamed) as opposed to advertising aimed at mass groups. It also includes direct response advertising where such advertising is used to elicit a response from an individual (in either a business or consumer context), which includes some form of contact detail that can be added to a database for direct marketing. Therefore TV, radio, newspapers, magazines, cinema and outdoor advertising are largely excluded.

In the opinion of Patterson and O'Malley (2000) :

Direct marketing is no longer a sub-set of marketing. It is not about a set of techniques which sell products and services direct to consumers. On the contrary, it is a collage of techniques and approaches which range far beyond its initial remit. Direct marketing today is as much about customer service as it is about sales. It is as well placed for the communication of information as it is for the distribution of products. The demarcation between direct marketers and mass marketers has blurred and contemporary organisations do both.

For this reason it has been decided to devote a separate chapter to the topic in this edition.

Graeme McCorkell (2003), a former Chairman of the Institute of Direct Marketing states that: "The term '**direct marketing**' was first used in 1961. It was the brainchild of another American pioneer, Lester Wunderman. This term caught on because it was more inclusive than 'mail order'. It included a new method of ordering – by telephone – and marketing methods such as magazine subscription and continuity publishing (book and music series), that did not readily come to mind under the heading of mail order". The other American pioneer to whom McCorkell refers is Stan Rapp who, in the 1980s, referred to direct marketing as 'a method of distribution' where the exchange between buyer and seller was made direct without the intervention of any intermediary.

McCorkell continues: "Many would agree that direct distribution remains direct marketing's most important function. However, the lessons learned from direct distribution experience have enabled the principles of direct marketing to be applied to every kind of business. *To understand direct marketing, it is crucial to recognize that its beginnings were in mail order, not in direct mail.*" (*Original emphasis*)

The distinction is important because, while many confuse direct marketing with direct mail, the latter is only one of several communication channels used by direct marketers, albeit a very important one. To emphasise this distinction between direct marketing and selling through intermediaries, some practitioners use other descriptors such as database marketing and even 'relationship' marketing although the former is really a facilitating technology, and the latter term is inappropriate to describe the large number of low involvement 'transactions' that are the subject of direct marketing methods. Similarly, **e-commerce** is founded on the use of the Internet as a marketing channel, and has been the main driver of growth in direct marketing in recent years.

As was seen in Chapter 6 when discussing the Business System, the value chain, and the selection of a channel of distribution, the main attractions of dealing direct are:

- *Ownership of the relationship or customer franchise*
- *Greater control over all aspects of the transaction*
- *Lower costs*
- *Lower stocks/faster stock turn*
- *Greater efficiency*
- *Better customer feedback and market intelligence leading to*
- *Earlier identification of trends and new opportunities.*

In noting these potential advantages, it is important to stress that dealing direct is not an either/or choice. While some very successful firms like Amazon.com, Dell, easyJet, First Direct and Travelocity only sell direct, many other firms adopt a multichannel approach and sell both direct and through intermediaries. So British Airways sell through travel agents, and have some retail outlets of their own, but offer discount to customers booking online direct with *BA.com*, while GUS sells through its own chain of Argos retail outlets as well as via its catalogue and website.

The distinguishing feature of direct marketing is that it involves a **direct** interaction between seller and buyer. This characteristic is incorporated into the Direct Marketing Association's definition of it as "an interactive system of marketing that uses one or more advertising media to effect a measurable response and/or transaction at any location, with this activity stored on a database". Other important features included in this definition are 'measurable response' and 'database'.

In the past decade the marketing function has come under increasing pressure to account for the return on marketing investment, with the result that marketing metrics was identified as the most important research topic of all for the period 2000-2004, by the Marketing Science Institute of America, based on the views of practitioners in the major companies that sponsor its research programme. (See discussion in Chapter 11). But, the measurement of marketing effectiveness is notoriously difficult, forever enshrined in Lord Leverhulme's statement "Half of my advertising expenditure is wasted; the trouble is I don't know which half". Given the overall profitability of his business Leverhulme was not going to experiment with his advertising to try and find out! So a major attraction of direct marketing is that one can measure accurately the response to any given expenditure. This may be an actual purchase, the redemption of a coupon, or action upon a specific invitation to act in some way.

The other important feature of direct marketing is the creation of a database containing details of actual and potential customers. Such databases may vary enormously in terms of their degree of complexity and sophistication, ranging from a simple listing of contact details to comprehensive information about a customer, their distinguishing characteristics, past purchasing behaviour and so on. Such databases are at the very heart of customer relationship management and loyalty programmes, and play a major role in maintaining contact with customers with a view to encouraging new and repeat business. Clearly, direct marketing has been a key influence on the call for integrated marketing communications (IMC – see Chapter 17) which, according to Woodside and Rosha (1999), "...include designing and implementing a dynamic, interactive, marketer-customer system that incorporates multiple media, measured customer responses, and immediate access and use of customer databases." This ability to respond to customers individually is seen as a major source of sustainable competitive advantage (SCA).

In his book *Direct Marketing* (1998), William J McDonald describes direct marketing's distinctive contribution as follows:

> *Direct response advertising, like other forms of promotion, seeks to persuade people to buy products or services. However, there are some things that direct marketing does much better than general marketing. Virtually all of direct marketing's special competencies derive from the fact that the communications are directed at specific individuals and not at mass markets via mass media. This includes the combination of advertising and selling into a single function, the prominence of customer service, the ability to precisely target individuals, and the ability to create personalized messages that call for immediate action. Finally, the results of direct marketing campaigns can be monitored and measured.*

While the range and variety of products and services that can be, and are, sold through direct marketing is almost infinite, some are less suitable than others. This is particularly true of low value-added goods, especially those that are perishable and/or where the distribution costs are high relative to the value.

However, as McDonald points out pizzas (and many other takeaway meals) are sold successfully although burgers and fries are not.

Virtually all media can be used effectively for direct marketing campaigns, including the telephone, direct mail, television, newspapers, magazines, radio and, increasingly, the Internet. Table 18.3 summarised some statistics on the usage of these various media. In this chapter we look briefly at some of the more important applications of direct marketing – **Direct Mail**, **Telemarketing**, **Direct Response Broadcast media**, **Catalogues**, Door-to-Door or **Network Marketing**, and the Internet.

DIRECT MAIL

As noted, many people regard direct mail as being synonymous with direct marketing and it continues to account for a significant proportion of all direct contacts despite the almost universal ownership of/access to a telephone in the UK, and access to the Internet. Shimp (2003) suggests that as the internet also allows direct contact with individuals via electronic or **e-mail** the use of the post should be distinguished as '**p-mail**'. As this suggestion has yet to be widely adopted we use the term direct mail as referring to tangible (as opposed to virtual) materials sent to customers by means of the postal service.

Recent years have seen direct mail grow rapidly as a media form and it looks set to continue to grow in importance. It has become more prominent as advertisers

DIRECT MARKETING

The Federation of European Direct Marketing (FEDMA) defines it as:

"Direct Marketing is the communication by whatever means (including but not limited to mail, fax, telephone, online services, etc.) of any advertising or marketing material, which is carried out by the Direct Marketer itself or on its behalf and which is directed to particular individuals"

In 2004 DM was worth £14.99 bn, up 10.1% on 2003 probably at the expense of traditional above-the-line media. The ability to measure effectiveness of expenditure as compared with the mass media and PR is believed to be a major reason behind the switch.

E-mail marketing has been demonstrated as immediate and effective. Telemarketing on mobiles using short messaging service or 'texting' (SMS) is already in use but, with 3G MMS or media messaging services it will be possible for more information to be transmitted. The initial target is expected to be 16 – 35 year-olds. This may help account for the fact that telemarketing is still holding its own despite the fact that 70% of people find it the most intrusive kind of marketing and legislation has been enacted to restrict its use.

Direct response radio and the cinema are declining and direct mail is beginning to slow in terms of the number of items mailed as users develop more sophisticated databases and achieve better targeting of prospects.

The main developments affecting DM in recent years have been digital and satellite TV, the Internet and customer databases.

The development of CRM databases has enhanced the attractiveness of DM but low cost text messages mean that it it is cheaper to send 1000 of them and get 50 replies than to spend time seeking for better targeting using such databases.

Source: *Keynote*, June 2005

have realised their markets are less homogeneous and can no longer be simply classified into arbitrary groups like ABCD social classes.

Faced with a growing tide of 'individualism' there is a need to use an advertising vehicle that can account for a decline in market homogeneity. In the 1960s age groups such as 15–24 years old were seen as a complete market segment, now it is made up of a variety of different individualistic segments. In Europe these problems are accentuated by the advent of cross-border marketing where it will be harder to establish stereotypical consumers to target with advertising. Some clear trends can be identified transnationally such as the increasing role of working women. But the complexities outweigh these trends. For example, while Tetley tea is regarded as a standard commodity product in the UK it is more exclusive in other European countries like France.

The use of direct mail allows advertisers to get directly in touch with customers and potential customers. It is much easier to monitor in terms of responses, usage and effectiveness than other advertising media. The use of such techniques will become increasingly simple as technological advances improve databases. Data can be found by questionnaires, transactional/point-of-sale information or by telephone. The legislation that governs how such information can be collected and used will be crucial in the development of future databases.

The great advantage of direct mail, by comparison with all other media, is its selectivity. Postal delivery is possible in every part of the country – a potential which enables the advertiser to reach a small, closely identified audience with a precision that could not possibly be duplicated by any other medium until such time that everyone has access to interactive broadcast media and/or the Internet.

In the author's opinion direct mail is grossly underrated as an advertising medium, probably because of the dangers inherent in generalising from the particular. The common belief that the recipients of a direct mailing 'shot' immediately consign it to the waste-paper basket without a glance is not borne out by Table 19.1 that summarises how different social classes and age groups

Table 19.1 Treatment of last item of consumer direct mail received (percent of total)

	Opened and read	Opened only	Did not open
By social class			
AB	40	26	34
C1	40	16	44
C2	34	30	36
DE	44	12	44
By age			
16-24	50	20	30
25-34	34	17	49
35-44	39	19	42
45-54	38	25	37
55-64	38	14	47
65+	43	25	33

Source: Direct Mail Information Service (DMIS) Consumer Trends Survey 2004.

handled direct mail shots.

Direct mailing lists may be compiled by the advertiser himself from customer records, or from the same basic sources used by the direct mail house – classified telephone directories, trade directories, and so forth. Where it is intended to mount a campaign designed to increase one's market or to enter a new market, the cost would be disproportionate by comparison with the cost of 'buying' a list from a specialist direct mail house or a list broker.

The price of a direct mail shot depends upon the production costs of the items to be mailed and the size, volume, folding, inserting and labelling requirements of the mailing. In addition to the production charges, the postage must be paid and

Figure 19.1 How to plan a direct mail campaign

Planning a Direct Mail campaign is a logical step-by-step process. Whether you are using a direct mail agency or mailing house, or doing it yourself, it is important to make sure you have built these steps into your plan. . .

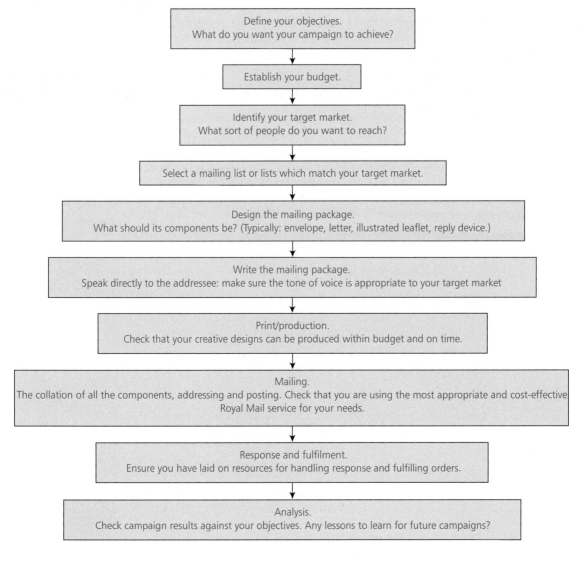

the Post Office offers discounts and incentives for direct mailers. Some statistics on direct mail advertising are given in Tables 19.2 and 19.3 and a guide to planning a direct mail campaign suggested by the Royal Mail is given in Figure 19.1 (The Royal Mail is an excellent source of advice on the whole topic.)

As with other aspects of advertising, the employment of an agency is to be recommended owing to the specialisation which they can bring to bear on the advertiser's problem. Those direct mail shots which do finish up in the waste bin most frequently do so because of either incorrect identification of a 'prospect' or poor copy and layout. A good agency will not be guilty of either of these faults.

On average a direct mailing will cost £250–£300 per thousand, which, when it is considered that three mailings is considered a desirable target to aim at, makes a campaign of any size an expensive undertaking. Against this must be set the precision with which potential customers may be reached by comparison with the lower costs of the 'buck shot' approach of the other media. A further advantage of direct mail is that its effectiveness can be measured directly, which is not the easiest of things to achieve. A summary of key areas to look for is provided by the Royal Mail's 'Planning a Direct Mail Campaign' shown in Figure 19.1.

Figure 19.1 How to plan a direct mail campaign continued.

Analysis of results can be more or less sophisticated, depending on your resources and the complexity of your campaign. The important thing is to use your defined objectives as the benchmark for measuring your success. Key areas to look at are as follows. . .

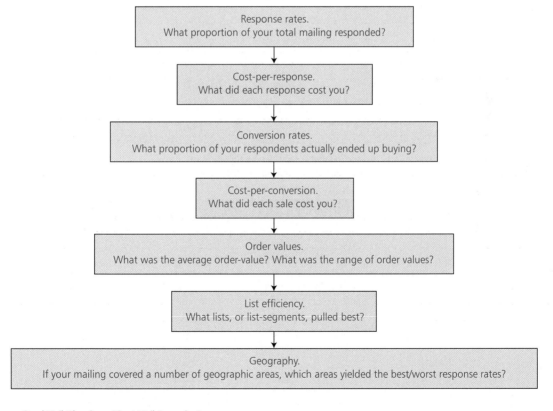

Source: Royal Mail 'Planning a Direct Mail Campaign'.

To sum up the reasons accounting for direct mail's popularity are:

- Its ability to target individuals in a highly selective way
- Its geographical 'reach' – unlike TV and radio whose reception may be confined to a given region and are unselective, with a mail campaign one can reach niche markets anywhere in the country for the same basic cost.
- The ability to personalise the communication and tailor it precisely to the recipients interests and information needs.
- Its ability to stand alone and be separated from other editorial content as occurs with the broadcast and print media
- Its cost effectiveness. While response rates may appear low (less than 11% for all campaigns in the UK) the generally low cost of a mail shot makes it very attractive compared with most other media.

An off-shoot of direct mail is door-to-door distribution of advertising material. Several companies offer this service for the distribution of samples, coupons and leaflets, utilising the services of part-time employees under the control and supervision of a full-time area supervisor, for example Vernon's Distributors. Rates vary, depending upon the nature of the material to be distributed, and the

Table 19.2 Direct mail

	Volume items (million)			Expenditure (£m)		
	Consumer items	Business items	Total items	Production costs	Postage costs	Total costs
2000	3,516	1,148	4,664	1,180	869	2,049
2001	3,706	1,233	4,939	1,308	921	2,228
2002	3,940	1,293	5,233	1,399	979	2,378
2003	4,240	1,198	5,438	1,412	1,019	2,431

Note: Direct mail refers to personally addressed advertising that is delivered through the post.
Source: The Advertising Association's *Advertising Statistics Yearbook, The Marketing Pocket Book 2005*, both published by WARC (*www.warc.com*)

Table 19.3 Senders of consumer direct mail 2003

	Percentage of total consumer volume		Percentage of total consumer volume
Bank/building society/ other financial	25.1	Utilities	5.1
		Manufacturing	3.0
Travel/charity/leisure	14.2	Government	1.6
Home shopping	13.5	Health	1.0
Insurance	9.7	Education	0.4
Retail	9.0	Not stated	2.4
Media	6.7	Other	8.1

Source: Direct Mail Information Service (DMIS).

frequency, that is every house, every tenth house, and so on. The Post Office will also deliver unaddressed mail to all 21 million UK homes.

TELEMARKETING

Telemarketing may be defined as "the systematic use of the telephone as a communications channel between a company and its customers" (*Marketing Pocket Book*, 2005). Among the applications cited are:

- *Inbound order taking*
- *Outbound selling*
- *Market research*
- *Lead generation*
- *Customer care*
- *Database building*
- *Sales support*
- *Making appointments*

The telephone and, increasingly, the Internet offer a quick and convenient means of establishing direct contact between sellers and potential customers so telephone numbers and website addresses are extensively used in conjunction with other direct marketing media.

A major decision involved in adopting telemarketing is 'in-house or bought-in'? McDonald cites a study by Fidel as listing four main advantages of using a telemarketing agency or bureau, namely:

1 *Low initial investment*
2 *Fixed operating costs*
3 *Quick start*
4 *Time flexibility (24/7 service)*

Against these advantages must be offset the lack of direct control and security; lack of employee loyalty and calibre of personnel employed, and loss of a personalised approach. These factors tend to mean that the in-house solution will be preferred for complex products and services where a high degree of technical knowledge/expertise is called for, for professional services like banking and insurance, and situations involving sensitive and/or confidential information. Otherwise, agencies and bureaux tend to be preferred.

However, there is some evidence of a backlash against out sourced telemarketing as a result of an increased volume of 'junk' telephone calls ('spam' on the Internet) and lack of local knowledge when using call centres in India for UK business. In July 2005 BT launched a new service to enable its customers to pre-identify unsolicited sales calls and so ignore them.

DIRECT RESPONSE BROADCAST MEDIA

Both television and commercial radio broadcast invitations to viewers/listeners to respond directly to offers to buy goods and services, apply for further information or take other appropriate action, e.g. attend an event, visit a retail outlet etc. As with other direct marketing approaches the major attraction of such advertising is that response can be measured accurately, including the value of direct sales, permitting precise measures of advertising effectiveness.

In the case of television, all the benefits outlined earlier can be deployed. Product attributes can be described and supported by visual evidence, demonstration, association with celebrities etc. so enhancing the impact and credibility of the message. Special offers, bargains, guarantees of satisfaction and the use of free phone numbers all increase the immediacy of the offer and encourage prompt action.

While radio lacks the ability to show and demonstrate products it has its own distinctive features that make it particularly attractive as a medium for direct marketing. Foremost among these are the ability to reach narrowly defined target segments and a much lower cost than TV. Its main drawback is that most people listen to the radio while doing something else – especially driving a car. To overcome this weakness messages need to be kept short and the follow-up action - a phone number or address – has to be repeated several times. This weakness has been significantly reduced as a result of the wider ability of mobile phones allowing a quick response while the information is fresh in people's minds. A particular advantage of radio over TV is that radio involves listeners who regularly tune in to specific programmes but, because the audiences are smaller they do not command the premium rates associated with major TV programmes like Coronation Street. Further, while spots on prime time TV usually have to be booked well in advance and call for expensively produced ads., radio has low production costs and time can usually be bought at short notice.

However, the major development in the use of broadcast media for direct marketing has been the development of interactive digital television (iDTV) sometimes known as digital interactive television (DiTV). Digital TV is accessed via a Cable, Satellite or Freeview box located near the set. All these have a 'return path' through which the viewer can interact with the broadcaster. This may involve requesting information or participating in a poll using split screen techniques.

Because most viewers sit on average 8 feet away from the screen the amount of text information that can be shown is limited, and the degree of interactivity using a remote control is much less than is possible with a keyboard and a web site, although there are remote keyboards available to use these services eg Sky Navigator. As with other innovations it is anticipated that these limitations will be quickly overcome and that more and more people will use their TVs as a main point of access to the Internet, as well as to advertisers using the broadcast media.

CATALOGUES

According to McDonald the first mail order catalogue was produced by Benjamin Franklin in 1744 and was a listing of books. However, the credit for developing the catalogue as we know it today is generally given to Montgomery Ward who started with a one-page flyer listing various textile products at below retail prices. Today catalogues are widely used in both B2B and B2C markets, and the majority are specialised and designed to prompt purchase direct from the seller.

Among the catalogues that regularly drop into my letter box are invitations from Dell to buy computers, from Viking Direct to buy office supplies, from Laithwaites to buy wines, from Cotton Traders and Hawkshead to buy clothing, and Healthspan to buy healthcare products and so on.

Research in the USA indicates that catalogue shoppers differ from traditional retail shoppers in terms of a number of important attributes. McDonald (op.cit.) states:

> They are better educated, work in professional and managerial capacities, earn more money, are more comfortable with modern technology, and own stocks and shares. They like familiar brands and prefer traditional clothing. Catalog shoppers are also do-it-yourselfers who make repairs on their homes and cars.

Clearly, one of the attractions of direct marketing is that it enables to the seller to build up their own profile of those persons most likely to repeat purchase from them, including the kinds of appeal and incentives most likely to trigger a new purchase. Through careful analysis of their database the direct marketer can regularly eliminate the infrequent purchaser and concentrate on the most profitable prospects.

PRINT MEDIA

Print media are widely used to encourage direct response by the readership. The particular advantages of newspapers and magazines in terms of both mass and highly segmented audiences were described earlier.

DOOR-TO-DOOR OR NETWORK MARKETING

(I am indebted to Mr. Riten Bhatia for providing me with this summary)

The background of **network marketing** in the UK described is a summary of a report which was prepared by MINTEL International Group Ltd. Although the report was published in 1996, not much has changed since then (except the market analysis); the framework on which **multilevel marketing (MLM)** companies operate still remains the same.

Although the border between network marketing and other types of direct selling (such as **single level marketing, SLM**) is often slightly blurred, the **DSA (Direct Selling Association)** defines multi-level marketing companies in the following way:

... those in which all sales personal personnel sell the company's products and where every individual has the additional opportunity to recruit and train new personnel, and in some cases the responsibility for local product distribution. This includes companies selling both 'High Ticket' and 'Low Ticket' products, and those who use party plan techniques.

It is a method distinct from single level marketing. Although similar selling methods are used (for example, party planning), recruitment and training is carried out by both salaried and self employed personnel who do not normally sell the companies products. This is the crucial point of difference between the two types of distribution. Some of the best known exponents of single level marketing are Tupperware and Avon.

The DSA defines party planning as something which involves selling products through explanation and demonstration of the product to a group of prospective customers by a consultant, usually in the home of a hostess (or host) who involves other people for this purpose.

Origins of Network Marketing

Network marketing began in the US about 40 years ago and arrived in the UK shortly afterwards. As a consequence of this many leading MLM operations in the UK, such as Amway, Herbalife, Mary Kay Cosmetics, Lady Remington, Reliv and Beauticontrol have US parent companies.

Direct sales have traditionally been carried out by full time representatives who market higher ticket items requiring real selling skills. However, in recent years the trend has been towards part-time direct selling which can generate sufficient income via lower ticket items without the need for true selling skills. It is against this background network marketing has grown steadily.

A network marketing company's primary function is to supply the product and give support, training and encouragement to its independent distributor base. Once the sales have been made, the products are dispatched to the distributors who organise local deliveries of orders to the end users. In order to motivate its distributor base, network marketing operations pay out particularly high levels of commission, frequently as much as 40 % of the wholesale price or, in some cases, the retail price minus VAT. Since the whole modus operandi of MLM is to consistently recruit more individuals to the network, the rewards for doing so are high. As distributors sponsor new people into the business, they become eligible for bonus and royalty payments linked to the amount of retail sales which their recruit has achieved. Retailing of product is important but recruitment is viewed as being equally important. Without recruiting an MLM company is in danger of stagnating.

Word of mouth is the most important technique involved in the network marketing process, and although free, is the most powerful form of advertising. Most networkers first spread the word within their 'warm' market which includes their immediate circle, such as family, friends and neighbours, as well as those individuals they come into contact with on a regular basis, for example their hairdressers, postman or window cleaner.

The techniques used for retailing and recruiting are broadly the same and fall mainly into three categories:

- *One to One*: meeting people and talking to people about the product and what is described as "the business opportunity".

- *Party Planning*: this involves bringing together small groups of people for the purpose of demonstrating a product or products.

- *Catalogue drop/order taking*: this is a system which is normally employed for low ticket products which need little or no explanation. Catalogues are left with potential customers and the distributor returns later to collect the order.

Other frequently used methods include leafleting, placing postcards in shops/ schools and other communal areas, cold telephone calling, door knocking, exhibitions, local press, radio advertising, viral marketing and more rarely national advertising.

Why network market?

One of the most attractive elements of network marketing is that it facilitates low cost entry to a marketplace. Companies which go this route avoid having to spend large sums of money to fund advertising and promotional support for their product in order to secure a listing in major retailing chains. When compared to traditional retailing, the biggest advantage of network marketing is that it effectively strips out retailing costs. Unlike high street retailers which face the fixed overheads of shop premises, lighting, heating, business rates and staff wages, network marketing companies are able to function with considerably lower fixed overheads as they do not require any outlets of their own. Compared with other direct selling methods such as single level marketing (SLM) operations, MLM is a way of 'kick-starting' a direct sell operation into growth, driving it via recruitment, whereas SLM can often stagnate due to lack of growth in the number of distributors/agents. With MLM, even if consultants spend a small amount of money for self consumption and do not actively retail, it reaches more people and the network grows steadily due to recruiting.

Products which lend themselves better to being network marketed tend to fall into the following categories:

- *Self- consumables*: typical examples include nutritional supplements, skincare products and cosmetics. If a distributor becomes a user before they become a seller they are likely to be enthusiastic about the product and therefore able to retail and recruit more successfully.

- *Those which can be shown or demonstrated to people reasonably easily*: smaller items such as cosmetics and jewellery are easy to carry about for demonstration purposes. Consequently, cosmetics and jewellery account for around 85% of the total products available through network marketing

- *Items which can carry fairly high profit margins*: such as jewellery and cosmetics. For this reason, many FMCG goods, such as the bulk of items sold in supermarkets, would be less suitable for network marketing.

THE INTERNET

The impact of the Internet on direct marketing has been explosive. It has led to the establishment of high profile and very successful companies like Dell and Amazon.com; it has challenged established businesses to change their methods radically, and it has led to the failure of those that have failed to adapt to the new technology. It has also resulted in massive losses on the part of investors who assumed that anything associated with the Internet was guaranteed to succeed.

Woodside and Rosha (1999) identified four important advantages of the Internet as a marketing tool:

1 *A global audience*

2 *New dynamics of consumer relationships*

3 *Convenience*

4 *The potential for massive savings*

As we have noted, the creation of the Internet means that anyone can set up a business with a global reach at virtually no cost whereas, traditionally, businesses grew gradually, and only the largest multinational corporations had a global presence. Further, as with every major innovation the early adopters tend to be a particularly attractive market opportunity. They have to be better off to buy into the new technology, and they have to be better educated to be able to understand how to use it. As a result, more and more organisations have climbed onto the internet bandwagon, leading to the rapid growth associated with the early phases of the life cycle of a successful innovation.

Statistics for countries all around the world point to a very rapid take-up to the point that in countries like the US and Europe the Internet has already entered early maturity. Between December 1999 and December 2004 the number of GB adults (15+) using the internet grew from 14.2 million to 28.1 million with the user profile looking like this:

Table 19.4 GB internet usage profile (as a percentage of GB 15+ population)

December 2004	Internet users (%)	December 2004
All Adults (15+)	**60**	*Social Grade*
Male	66	AB
Female	54	C1
		C2
Age		DE
15-17	95	
18-24	84	
25-34	82	
35-44	74	
45-54	64	
55-64	46	
65+	17	

Source: GfK NOP Internet User Profile Survey, Dec 2004.

In terms of the dynamics of consumer relationships Woodside and Rosha observed:

The information rich medium of the Internet will reduce market imperfections on which intermediaries thrive. The near perfect market conditions and consequent low switching costs have set in motion a quiet revolution – a shift in power from vendors of goods and services to the customers who buy them. Companies who understand this transfer of power and choose too capitalize on it will be richly rewarded with both peerless consumer loyalty and impressive returns. To do this companies have to learn to put the consumer in the driver's seat and treat the Internet as a personal medium.

And so it has proved to be!

As for convenience, the Internet has particular attraction for buyers of certain kinds of products; especially those where information, selection and convenience are important as with travel, insurance, financial services, books etc. Further, as with self-service in supermarkets, most of the purchase costs are incurred by the buyer who has to screen the information, make a selection, enter and confirm the details (hence less likelihood of error) and arrange payment. In light of these savings, sellers are able to offer attractive price discounts making online shopping both more convenient and more economical.

As with other direct marketing approaches, while the Internet may be used on its own it is often more effective when combined with other media and channels of communication. Thus mass communication can direct the audience to any of several possible sources of more information or means of purchasing the product or service. Where the Internet scores is that it can be accessed at any time almost anywhere. (I have stopped carrying a laptop with me when I travel as I have found Internet cafes in Pago Pago, outback Australia, indeed everywhere I go – all I need is a **flash card** to plug into the USB port). Added to this one can find both information and make direct comparisons between the offers of different suppliers and then complete the transaction in one operation. (For additional information on the impact of the Internet turn to the entry of **E-commerce** in the final chapter).

VIRAL MARKETING

(I am indebted to Mr. Riten Bhatia for providing me with this summary)

There are a lot of people out there – and they have got a whole lot to say about companies and their products and services offered. Many marketers are taking word of mouth to the next level by seeking to influence what is said by using different means of communication. The internet has made word of mouth a much more powerful and compelling tool. As a result, marketers are not only starting to use it as a vehicle for better understanding consumer sentiment, but they are also seeking ways to exert influence over that sentiment. In some instances, they're seeking to manipulate consumer opinion.(Chapell, 2004).

The question however remains how is the internet used to exert influence over individuals? **Viral marketing** describes any strategy that encourages individuals to pass on a marketing message to others. Viral marketing can be defined as making email into a form of **advocacy** or word of mouth referral endorsement from one client to other prospective clients. From a practical perspective, it is a strategy whereby people forward the message to other people on their email list or tie advertisements into or at the end of the messages. From a marketing perspective, it is the process of encouraging individuals to pass along favourable or compelling marketing information they receive in a hypermedia environment: information that is favourable or compelling either by design or by accident. (Dobele, Toleman & Beverland 2005) Off the Internet, viral marketing has been referred to as "**word-of-mouth**," "**creating a buzz**," "**leveraging the media**," "**network marketing**." But on the Internet, for better or worse, it's called "viral marketing."

With the internet and the computer being used so often for communication, 'word of mouth' translates into '**word of mouse**'. Word of mouse is good old-fashioned word of mouth, but with the ability to spread much faster because of the Internet. Another way to look at it is as advertising you don't pay for.

The original inspiration for viral marketing came from the pattern of adoption of Hotmail beginning with its launch in 1996. Tim Draper persuaded the company to include a promotional pitch for its Web-based email with a clickable URL in every outbound message sent by a Hotmail user. Therein lay one of the critical elements of viral marketing: every customer becomes an involuntary salesperson simply by using the product. This method of marketing worked wonders as it was more powerful that third-party advertising because it conveyed an implied endorsement from a friend. Experts were amazed at how quickly Hotmail spread over the global network. The rapid adoption pattern was that of a network virus. People typically sent emails to their associates and friends, both geographically close and scattered around. (Juvetson 2000)

Hotmail grew its subscriber base from zero to 12 million users in 18 months, more rapidly than any company in any media in the history of the world. Fair enough, this is the Internet after all. But it did so with an advertising budget of $50,000 - enough for some college newspaper ads and a billboard.

Is viral marketing really a new idea, or is at a flashy name for word of mouth? After all, network marketing companies such as Mary Kay Cosmetics and Amway have proven big profits can be made when people spread a company's name/product to their friends. There's a reason your email box is bombarded with get rich quick multilevel marketing pitches. Pyramid schemes and chain letters expand quite nicely today, thanks to the internet - but they are not new concepts.

Summary

Direct marketing is any form of marketing targeted at an individual as opposed to mass communication of the kind described in the previous chapter. With the ever-increasing power of the computer, and its ability to store and manipulate very large **databases**, direct marketing has grown in importance as it enables the seller to make immediate and personal contact with prospective customers. Its distinguishing characteristic is that it enables **interaction** between the sender and receiver of the communication. Formerly known as **below-the-line** promotion (with expenditure on the mass media described as **above-the-line**) the best known and most widely used medium is **direct mail**.

Direct mail is a relatively low cost medium with the capability of reaching every household in the country. While many dismiss direct mail on the grounds that much of it is consigned straight to the waste paper basket, the reality is quite different with significant numbers reading and responding to this form of promotion. Actual numbers vary by product category and reflect closely the quality of the senders mailing list. Further, even when response rates fall to as low as 2 percent for some mass mailings this is still sufficient to make the campaign worthwhile.

Telemarketing uses the telephone as a means of establishing direct contact with individuals and is widely used for direct selling. With the growth of ownership of mobile phones, and the establishment of call centres some observers predict further growth in this medium. Conversely, others see the use of the telephone as an intrusion on their privacy and are becoming resistant to the increasing number of 'cold calls' they receive. BT has seen this as an opportunity to introduce its free 'Privacy' service that allows you to identify the source of incoming calls and only accept those you wish to receive.

Direct response broadcast media are increasing in popularity as their programming enables the targeting of closely defined market segments in terms of both interests and geographical location. The use of commercial radio is now well established and understood with 365 stations available covering the whole of the UK. The innovation in broadcast media has been the introduction of **digital interactive TV (DiTV)** which allows the viewer to interact directly with the broadcaster. The impact and consequences of this new medium have still to emerge.

Catalogues were discussed briefly as was **door-to-door selling**, which is now described as **network marketing** on the grounds that it involves individuals using their networks of friends and relatives to sell a variety of products.

The **Internet** has also grown significantly as a direct marketing medium. This was only discussed briefly given that its influence and impact have been addressed in context in a number of places already, and are the subject of a closer look in the final chapter.

Review questions and problems

1 What is direct marketing? What distinguishes it from mass marketing and when might you use it as part of a promotional campaign?

2 Direct mail is often seen as a wasteful approach to promotion in that much of it is thrown away unread. If this is so why do advertisers continue to use it ?

3 Direct mail is widely used in cause related marketing e.g. by charities. What factors account for this and what suggestions have you for increasing its effectiveness.

4 Outline the steps to be followed in developing a direct mail campaign.

5 Telemarketing is an intrusion on privacy and should be banned. Discuss.

6 Under what circumstances might you use the telephone as part of a direct marketing campaign? Illustrate your answer with reference to a product or service of your choice.

7 What are direct response broadcast media? What are their advantages and disadvantages as a promotional medium?

8 Catalogues and door-to-door selling are still widely used in direct marketing. Under what circumstances might you consider using them?

9 "The impact of the Internet on direct marketing has been explosive". Explain the evidence to support this claim illustrating your answer with actual examples.

10 Viral marketing has converted word of mouth into word of mouse. Discuss.

Key terms

advocacy	e-mail	one-to-one
catalogue drop	flash card	party planning
catalogues	integrated marketing	p-mail
creating a buzz	communications (IMC	return path
database	interactive digital television	single level marketing (SLM)
digital interactive television (DiTV)	(iDTV)	spam / junk
direct mail	internet	telemarketing
direct marketing	leveraging the media	viral marketing
direct response broadcast media	measurable response	warm market
Direct Selling Association (DSA)	multi-level marketing (MLM)	word of mouse
door-to-door	network marketing	word of mouth

Supplementary reading list

McCorkell, G. (2003), 'What are direct marketing and interactive marketing?', Chapter 22 in Baker, M.J.(ed) *The Marketing Book*, 5th edn., (Oxford: Butterworth-Heinemann).

McDonald, W. J. (1998), *Direct Marketing: An Integrated Approach*, (Boston: McGraw-Hill). *A comprehensive description of all aspects of direct marketing*

Patterson, M. and O'Malley, L. (2000), 'The Evolution of the Direct Marketing Consumer', *The Marketing Review*, Volume 1, Number 1, pp.89-102

Woodside, A. G. and Rosha, R. (1999), 'Direct marketing: advancing to integrated (Internet), communications' in Baker, M.J. (ed.) *IEBM Encyclopedia of Marketing*, (London: Thomson Learning).

PERSONAL SELLING AND SALES PROMOTION

* Throughout this chapter references to the 'salesman' should be taken to apply equally to women.

INTRODUCTION

Despite the importance of advertising in disseminating information and stimulating interest in products and services, there are many circumstances where personal contact is necessary to effect a sale. Of necessity most advertising is generalised, and so cannot answer all the consumer's information needs; it cannot elaborate upon specific points perceived as significant by the individual, nor can it resolve doubts as to suitability in a particular context. Further, there can be no guarantee that the potential user's media habits will expose them to advertisements for a given product, or that if they do see the advertisement they will perceive it as relevant.

The **function of personal selling** is to provide the specific inputs which advertising, or non-personal selling, cannot offer at the individual level. It should be remembered that advertising and personal selling are complementary activities, and that their relative importance will vary depending upon the nature of the product and the buying behaviour associated with it.

Many theorists stress the nature of the product as a determinant of the appropriate promotional mix and are collectively identified as the 'Characteristics of Goods School'. Members of this school would argue that advertising will be dominant in the case of small, simple and frequently purchased items of low unit value, while personal selling is appropriate to high priced, technically complex products which are bought infrequently.

According to this view the appropriate promotional mix might be represented diagrammatically as in Figure 20.1, while the relative importance is suggested in Figure 20.2.

Figure 20.1 Selecting the promotional mix

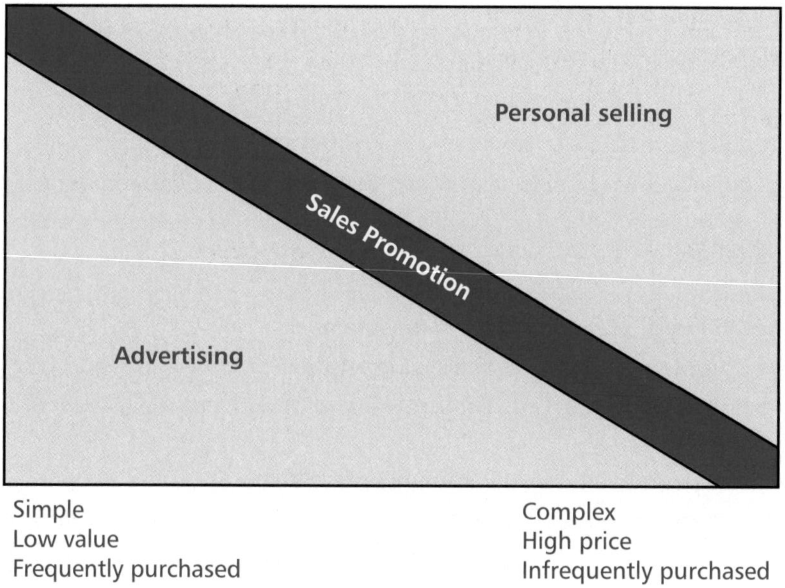

Simple	Complex
Low value	High price
Frequently purchased	Infrequently purchased

Source: Based on Robinson R. J. and Stidsen, B. (1967), *Selling in a Modern Perspective* (Boston: Allyn & Bacon).

Although useful this approach is oversimplified, for the user's perception of any given product defies classification into convenient categories. As we have seen, a 'convenience' good may be perceived as a 'shopping' good and vice versa depending upon the individual's frame of reference. The importance of allowing for the behavioural dimensions of perception is implicit in the different promotional strategies adopted by firms selling near-perfect substitutes in the economic sense, for example; Avon sells cosmetics door-to-door, Estee Lauder products are available in less than 150 outlets, Yardley and Coty are available in some 7000 department stores and chemists' shops, while Miner's brands are sold through variety chains and supermarkets. There are no hard-and-fast rules which dictate the adoption of a given promotional strategy for a product.

In recent years, however, five trends have had a major impact on the personal selling function:

1 *A concentration of buying power*, especially in the case of consumer goods.
2 *The application of information technology* and the adoption of automated buying procedures, stockless purchasing and the like.
3 *A clearer understanding of the profitability of individual customers* and an emphasis on **key account management**.
4 *An emphasis on the importance of developing strong relationships with customers to retain their loyalty*. This is reflected in the stress on relationship marketing, **customer relationship management (CRM)**, networking and so on.
5 *The development of electronic sales channels* – the Internet, Television home shopping.

In light of these trends, and the high cost of personal selling, the role and contribution of the salesman has come under close scrutiny. However, as we shall see, there are many situations where personal contact between seller and buyer are necessary and the most cost effective way of making a sale.

The second part of this chapter is concerned with **sales promotion** which are activities used to encourage purchase. Most sales promotion are of a temporary nature and are used tactically in support of other promotional efforts.

To begin with we look at some *definitions* of sales promotion and the *objectives* which sellers hope to accomplish by using it. Given that sales promotion is used in support of other promotional methods, critical decisions are the **appropriation**

Figure 20.2 Relative importance of marketing communications

Context / Activity	Industrial Goods	Convenience Goods	Shopping Goods	Speciality Goods
Personal Selling	Very High	Very Low	Average	Very High
Media Advertising	Very Low	High	Average	Very High
Sales Promotion	Low	High	Average	Very Low
Packaging	Low	Very High	Average	Very High

of the budget and the selection of a promotional method.

Following a description of the most popular forms of consumer promotion, we look at the decision to use sales promotion and the selection of the technique best suited to meet one's objectives. This is illustrated by a review of sampling as one of the most widely used methods.

THE EVOLUTION OF THE SALESMAN

Although our stereotype of a salesman probably owes more to the music-hall comedian than to reality, there can be no doubt that selling has long occupied a relatively low position in our social and economic hierarchy. Fortunately, there are signs that this state of affairs is slowly changing and that selling is increasingly regarded as a profession rather than a trade. Several factors may be distinguished as contributing to this change and the resultant increase in the flow of better qualified recruits, namely:

1 'Salesman' applies equally to all persons engaged at all levels of selling, from the retail sales clerk to the negotiator of multi-million pound contracts. As the former greatly outnumber the latter, selling tends to be identified with the functions performed by retailers rather than with manufacturer's salesman. However, increased labour costs have led to wide-scale reduction in personal selling at the retail level and have thus brought more sophisticated sales functions into sharper focus; that is, an emphasis on creative selling as opposed to mere order-taking.

2 Growing awareness of the need for personal selling in the service sector – for example banks, insurance and other professional services – has resulted in a significant improvement in both the visibility and credibility of the function.

3 The concentration of retail buying power has resulted in a clear distinction between the negotiating skills demanded in organisational buying situations, and the merchandising effort called for at the point of sale with a consequent increase in the salesman's status and importance.

4 The pressures of international competition have made it clear that the manufacturer can no longer leave their product to 'speak for itself' – effective selling and promotion are essential.

5 Increased product complexity, and more sophisticated buyers demand high-calibre salesmen. The scarcity of such personnel has boosted salary levels above those offered in many other occupations, improving selling's economic status and attracting in better-qualified recruits.

Collectively, these factors have made a career in sales more respectable, and resulted in a better understanding of the sales function.

The salesman's role

In view of the possible variations in product and market characteristics it is virtually impossible to formulate a single definition of the salesman's role. Where a user/consumer has previous experience of a product the salesman is often a passive 'order-taker' whose function is to price the product specified, take payment and effect delivery; for example 2 kg of potatoes, a packet of Whizzo, 50 tons of cold-reduced mild steel sheet. Such a situation is very different from the case where the potential buyer has no previous experience of the product and is actively seeking information; and different again from the situation where the consumer has only an ill-defined or latent demand for a product to fill a given need. In the latter situations the salesman becomes an 'order-maker' and plays an active role in the purchasing decision.

Although there is more than an element of truth in the generalisation that retailers are order-takers, whereas manufacturers' salesmen are order-makers, no such clear-cut distinction exists in reality. Many manufacturers have become sensitive to the important influence which the retail sales assistant can have on the purchasing decision, and have installed their own employees in leased departments or provided training for their customers' staff. Similarly, the high cost of personal selling has persuaded many manufacturers to adopt standardised reorder procedures and to eliminate unnecessary or uneconomic sales calls. Alternatively, less experienced personnel are assigned to perform routine functions, leaving the salesman free to devote more time to missionary and developmental selling.

Ultimately, the sales persons role is to make a sale. At several places we have cited the mnemonic **AIDA - Awareness, Interest, Desire and Action** – as summarising the stages that a buyer goes through when deciding whether or not to buy something. The salesman's job is to initiate this process and bring it to a successful conclusion.

Although emotional factors undoubtedly influence both industrial and consumer purchasing decisions at all levels, it is felt that there is a tendency to over-emphasise these and, consequently, to overstress the salesman's role as a 'persuader'. In everyday speech, 'persuasion' is often used to suggest that a person has been, or can be, induced to act against their better judgement – this is certainly the context in which Vance Packard views 'The Hidden Persuaders' of advertising. In reality it is doubted if consumers are persuaded by spurious arguments as frequently as Packard suggests, and the salesman's role might be more usefully viewed as a problem-solving activity in which facts and arguments are used to justify the selection of a given product to satisfy a specific want. The salesman's skill lies in their ability to perceive the attributes which the 'prospect' considers important, and to structure their presentation so that the product's suitability along those dimensions is adequately conveyed to the potential customer. Thus, the car salesman will emphasise performance to his male customers, and appearance and safety to his female customers – if he is a good car salesman he will also realise that the middle-aged bank clerk's concept of performance is rather different from that of the junior account executive and so on. (There is more than a grain of truth in the old adage 'Let the customer tell you what he wants and then sell it to him'; that is, given the wealth of detail which you could give the customer, concentrate on the points in which they express interest.)

While many textbooks define the first task of the salesman as prospecting this assumes that salesmen are responsible for identifying potential buyers when, in the majority of cases they are not. In reality, in most B2C markets goods and services on offer are available from designated outlets – physical and virtual – and the role of mass communication is to create awareness and encourage sufficient interest for the potential customer to make contact with the seller. Once contact is made the sales persons task is to convert interest into desire, and then close a sale. Similarly, in B2B markets established firms have a portfolio of existing customers and the primary function of the salesman is to service their needs. So, while finding new customers is important, in reality it plays a relatively minor role and it is more important to increase one's share of the customers business at the expense of your competitors.

In Chapter 1 one of the definitions of marketing we suggested was 'Marketing is selling goods that don't come back to people who do'. Given that it costs five times as much to create a customer i.e. make the first sale, as it does to keep one, repeat purchase and customer loyalty are the key to profitability. To achieve this the main function of the salesman is to ensure their customer receives the expected/promised satisfaction and all that this involves – on time delivery, fitness for purpose, performance at or above expectations, after-sales service, value for money etc. etc. It follows that maintaining contact, monitoring performance and feedback, and keeping accurate records are all key aspects of the salesman's job. Done well this gives the customer confidence, leading to trust and commitment which are at the very heart of the mutually satisfying exchange relationship that is the essence of marketing. As Donaldson (1999) observed "The role of personal selling has three interrelated functions – providing information, persuading, and creating, building and sustaining relationships".

THE ECONOMICS OF PERSONAL SELLING

A recurring theme of this book is that the well managed firm will seek to develop strategies that will enable it to achieve certain predetermined objectives. Fundamental to the firm's ability to achieve its stated aims is the need to earn profits, so that the adoption of policies, and the strategies by which they will be implemented, will revolve largely around cost/revenue considerations. This point has already been stressed at some length elsewhere but it is particularly relevant in the context of personal selling.

In absolute terms personal selling is the most expensive method whereby the producer can establish contact with the potential consumer. In 2001 the Institute of Sales and Marketing Management estimated the average cost of a salesman as £55,000. Relatively, however, it is often the least expensive method owing to the higher conversion factor achieved by direct selling vis-à-vis the use of middlemen or other promotional efforts. Whether the manufacturer should employ their own sales force, how big it should be, and how they should deploy it to maximum effect are questions which may only be resolved through a full evaluation of the alternatives. Although it is possible to quantify many of the parameters no single prescriptive formula is available, but a number of steps can be offered as the basis for structuring such an evaluation:

1 The company should state its sales target for the coming year and for the next five years or so.

2 The promotional budget should be reviewed in the light of the sales target to ascertain whether the proposed expenditures will be sufficient to generate the desired sales volume – see 'The task approach' in Chapter 18.

3 Personal and non-personal selling are complementary activities and should

not be segregated when determining the size of the promotional budget; that is, management should decide how much it is willing to spend on all promotion, before attempting to allocate it to specific promotional efforts.

4 The optimum mix of personal and non-personal promotional efforts will vary by product, firm, industry and market, and is subject to change over time, therefore the total budget should be allocated roughly in accordance with the relative importance attached to each.

5 The adequacy of the sales budget may be evaluated by reference to past sales data or, if the firm has no previous experience of direct selling, by reference to the industry/product data published by trade associations, the trade press, and so forth. A rough and ready guide is to substitute such data into the formula:

$$Sales\ budget = \frac{Sales\ budget}{Average\ cost\ per\ call} \times Average\ sales\ per\ call$$

In the absence of hard data, the firm would have to rely upon its own subjective estimates of likely events, and could easily test a large number of alternatives by running a simulation on a computer.

Once a field sales force is in existence, a continual process of adjustment is necessary to maximise its productivity. Ideally, salesmen should be used to the point where the marginal cost of making a sales call is equivalent to the marginal revenue which it generates. In practice, adoption of this principle is rarely feasible because of the high fixed costs associated with the addition of an 'incremental' salesman, unless payment is on a straight commission basis.

Deploying the field sales force

Optimum deployment of the sales force is an ever-present problem for the sales manager. Essentially this problem has three dimensions:

1 *The geographical dispersion of potential customers.*
2 *The nature of the company's product mix.*
3 *The buying needs of customers.*

The geographical dispersion of customers imposes a major constraint on sales force productivity in that time spent travelling between customers is largely wasted. The amount of travelling time will vary considerably depending upon a number of factors but, on average, it is estimated that salesmen only spend 40 per cent of their time actually in contact with customers. Clearly a major objective must be to minimise the spatial distribution of accounts, which suggests that the sales force should be organised on a territorial basis.

However, such an organisational structure may conflict with the essential requirement that salesmen know their product. For the single product company, or the company with a limited range of closely related products, this may not create any problems, but as product line diversity and/or complexity increase, so product specialisation becomes progressively more essential. In the steel industry it would be impossible for any individual to be completely familiar with all products, and specialists are required for the sale of tinplate, mild steel sheet and plate, electrical steels, billets and bars, and so on.

In turn, product knowledge must be backed by an understanding of the buying needs and practices of different customer groupings. Thus the detergent manufacturer's salesman will find it necessary to adopt a very different approach when selling to a major grocery chain as opposed the small independent outlet. Similarly, it will be necessary to use a very different strategy when selling to industrial users.

There is no simple rule which dictates that the manufacturer should organise their sales force on a territory, product or market basis and, in fact, many companies have adopted a **composite structure**. Many of the arguments examined when discussing product and market management in Chapter 12 are equally applicable in this context, but it is important to recognise that the internal organisation of the marketing department on either product or market lines does not automatically require that the sales force be organised in the same way. For obvious reasons of economy, most sales forces are organised on a territorial basis, but within these boundaries salesmen may specialise on either a product or customer needs basis. The role of the product or market manager is to supply the salesman with detailed information of the most appropriate marketing inputs, such that several product managers may brief a single salesman on the 'best' tactics to be used in respect of each of their different products. Similarly, the market manager will lay down the nature of the selling approach most suited to the particular customer grouping for which they are responsible.

At the territory level a number of techniques have been evolved in recent years to improve sales efficiency. The sales call pattern is in the nature of a 'transportation problem' in the language of management science, and is capable of at least partial solution through the use of **linear programming techniques**. In order to permit analysis it is necessary to adopt a number of simplifying assumptions, for example the relationship between time spent with a buyer and size of order, the value of new account development or 'prospecting' and so on, and it is clear that no true optimum solution is possible. None the less, the discipline of developing empirically valid generalisations is in itself worth while as it can lead to valuable insights into the more effective deployment of the field sales force.

Donaldson (1999) sees the role of **territory design** as making the most effective use of the salespersons' time and believes this will be achieved when:

- *Territories are easy to administer*
- *Sales potential is relatively easy to estimate*
- *Travel time and expense are minimised*
- *Equal sales opportunity is provided across customers and prospects*
- *Workload is equalised.*

SELLING SITUATIONS CLASSIFIED

One of the central themes of this chapter is that selling situations vary across a number of dimensions, and that one must be careful to distinguish between them. At the same time there are sufficient similarities to permit the identification of a number of situations in which a particular kind or type of selling will be appropriate. It will be useful, therefore, to outline the basis characteristics of each as a first step towards identifying the sales situation facing the company, and the necessary sales inputs to cope with it effectively.

In an investigation into sales management practice undertaken by Dr Derek Newton (1969) of the Harvard Business School, a secondary finding was that '... one can effectively isolate four basic styles of selling that cut across industry boundaries to a large degree . . .'

These four styles are characterised as:

1 *Trade selling;*

2 *Missionary selling;*

3 *Technical selling;*

4 *New business selling.*

Although there is nothing new in identifying selling styles and attaching labels to them, this classification is preferred by the author in that it offers the broadest level of categorisation consistent with utility. In summary the characteristics of the four styles are:

Trade selling

- Major aim to build sales volume by providing customers with promotional assistance, that is selling through; for example food, textiles and wholesaling.
- Personal selling subsidiary to non-personal activities.
- Low-pressure selling, with an emphasis on continuity and a thorough understanding of customer practice.

Missionary selling

- Primary aim is to build sales volume by providing direct customers with personal selling assistance; that is, to persuade ultimate users and/or consumers to buy from the company's immediate customers.
- Most typical of firms selling to distributors for resale.
- Low pressure but requires energetic, articulate persons capable of making a large number of calls in order to cover all the potential users; for example medical representatives.

Technical selling

- Primary responsibility is to increase sales to present customers through the provision of technical advice and assistance.
- Requires an ability to identify, analyse and solve customer problems, and so places a premium on technical and product knowledge.
- Continuity is an important factor in building up buyer confidence and goodwill.

New business selling

- Primary aim is to secure new customers.
- The high level of rejection of new product propositions favours the employment of mature, experienced salesmen who can take an objective view of 'failure' and have a wider range of techniques to deal with buying objections.

THE RECRUITMENT, SELECTION AND TRAINING OF SALESMEN

Attributes of the successful salesman

Given the possible variations in the role which salesmen are called upon to play in different selling situations, it would be surprising to find that potentially successful salesmen may be identified by the presence, or absence, of a stereotyped set of personality variables. On the other hand, the high costs of selection and training make it essential that wastage through salesmen turnover be minimised, and have prompted the construction of innumerable check-lists which claim to identify the attributes of a successful salesman. The majority of such lists emphasise factors such as 'intelligent, extrovert, energetic, self-confident' and so on, and a number of selection tests have been devised to measure such characteristics.

Collectively these lists, and the associated tests, presume the existence of a stereotype the validity of which is doubted by the author. This doubt would appear to be supported by the findings of Samuel N. Stevens (1958), in 'The Application of Social Science Findings to Selling and the Salesman', who has summarised 'the major conclusions which social scientists have reached in regard to social and psychological characteristics of salesmen . . .' as follows:

1 There is no significant relationship between intelligence test scores and sales success.

2 No significant relationship has been found between independent measures of personality traits and sales success.

3 No correlation exists between age and sales success.

4 There is no correlation between measurable character traits and sales success.

5 There is no significant correlation between level of education and sales success.

6 No significant correlation exists between level of sales activity and sales success among individual salesmen.

7 Each of the above factors has significance when studied in relation to all of the others in individual salesmen.

8 Such a study as that indicated in point 7 above can provide a useful tool for selection and development.

9 Salesmen are more likely to succeed when chosen with regard to the kinds of customers they will deal with than in terms of the types of products sold.

10 Salesmen differ from non-salesmen in four important ways:

   - Salesmen are persuasive rather than critical;
   - Salesmen are intuitive rather than analytical;
   - Salesmen have higher average energy levels (expressed in activity);
   - Salesmen are more strongly motivated by the desire for prestige, power, and material gain than by a service ideal or the need for security.

11 Salesmen's interests cluster around a dominantly persuasive common core.

(pp. 85–94)

Subsequent research has largely confirmed these generalisations.

Recruitment

As noted in point 7, factors 1–6 have no individual significance and their collective importance will vary depending upon the selling task to be performed – point 9. If this is so, then it follows that firms should develop their own selection procedures based on a job specification appropriate to their own sales policies and objectives. Such a job specification is vital to efficient recruitment and selection.

Most sales positions are advertised in the classified columns of the major newspapers and trade journals, and media representatives frequently quote the number of applications received by advertisers as an indication of their publication's 'pulling power'. Such statements would seem to confuse volume with quality, and usually indicate that the advertisement has failed in its function as a screening device. On occasion a loosely worded advertisement is a useful guide to the calibre of people who are actively seeking new jobs – as a means of securing applicants for a specific post it is both a wasteful and 'sloppy' approach. (A leading firm of management consultants once informed the author that they had received over 800 applications for a sales manager's post requiring previous experience with a highly specialised product. As there could not have been more than fifty people with such experience, either the consultant was 'fishing' for applicants to fill other vacancies, or he didn't know his job. In either case he was wasting his client's time and money.)

Most job advertisements require applicants to submit details of their previous experience and other evidence to indicate their potential suitability for the post. Where the job specification is fairly loose, or the employer intends to give recruits extensive training, standardised application forms greatly assist the preparation of a short-list as they ensure that all applicants supply information considered important by the prospective employer.

Selection

Once a short-list has been prepared, the final selection of candidates usually involves some combination of tests and interviews. If a job specification has been prepared the purpose of the selection procedure will be to identify the applicant who most closely matches the job profile. In the absence of a job specification selection is likely to be overly subjective.

Although many factors will be common to all sales positions, and permit the use of structured interviews, the relative importance of these factors will vary depending upon the precise nature of the selling job to be performed. To deal with this problem and permit the development of standardised selection procedures, it is recommended that some form of factor rating be employed, similar to that described in connection with the screening of new product ideas.

In recent years an increasing number of firms have adopted some form of psychological testing in addition to the traditional personal interview. Such tests are seen as a cross-check on both interviewer bias and respondent consistency, and fall into four main categories:

- *Aptitude*
- *Interest*
- *Mental ability*

■ *Personality*

Tests of this kind conform more with the American than with the British ethic and are most frequently used in companies with strong links with the United States; for example Esso, Procter & Gamble, Mars.

Criticism of psychological tests is not based solely on cultural differences, however, and a number of American marketers are equally as sceptical as their more conservative British counterparts. For example, David Mayer and Herbert Greenberg (1964) in 'What Makes a Good Salesman?', discern four reasons which appear to account for the failure of aptitude tests:

1 Tests confuse interest with ability;
2 It is possible to fake answers and give the response the interviewer is looking for;
3 Tests favour conformity not individual creativity;
4 Tests concentrate on personality traits in isolation and fail to measure the person as a whole.

In *Sales Management: Theory and Practice*, Bill Donaldson (1998) reports that an increasing number of firms are now using assessment centres which employ a variety of techniques and may appraise six to eight candidates over one to three days using a team of selection specialists.

However, psychological testing techniques are becoming increasingly sophisticated and it is anticipated that they will continue to be used.

Training

The function of the selection procedures described above is to recruit candidates who are potentially suited to the company's selling tasks. Often the firm will use previous experience as a selection criterion. But, even where the new recruit has previous experience, it is unlikely that this is directly relevant to the products, markets and administrative procedures particular to the new employer, and some training will be necessary.

The objective of training is to make the salesman more effective as judged by the firm's criteria. As is evident from the distinction drawn earlier between trade, missionary, technical and new-business selling, sales volume is only one criterion, and may be totally inappropriate in some circumstances. Although the need for training is clearly greatest in the case of new, inexperienced recruits it should be looked upon as a continuing process. Over time, products, channels and markets change, and the well-managed firm will adjust its policies accordingly – continuation training is fundamental to the effective implementation of such changes in policy.

The length, content and cost of the sales training programme varies enormously between companies, but all seek to cover two main areas – knowledge and skills. Knowledge is concerned with the acquisition of facts and will normally include coverage of:

■ *The company* – its history, structure, policies and procedures.
■ *The product(s)* – composition, manufacture, performance and usage.
■ *The market* – size, structure, composition, buying behaviour, and so on.

Skills may be subdivided into two categories – technical and behavioural. **Technical skills** cover training in techniques appropriate to various stages of the buying process such as securing interviews, opening the interview, overcoming objections and the 'close'. If the product can be demonstrated this would also be considered a technical skill.

Behavioural skills are concerned with the development of empathy between buyer and seller. They are difficult both to define and to acquire, and are usually described in texts on salesmanship under titles such as 'How to be a good listener', 'How to excite curiosity', and so forth.

According to John Lidstone (1983) in 'Putting Force Back into Sales', the modern salesman must develop his knowledge and skill in three key areas:

1 *First, he must have a fluent confidence in the financial facts upon which buying and selling are based, and in the impact of his product on his buyer's business and on his own company's costs, profits and cash flow.* In a world of constantly changing costs and prices, the salesman must be capable of ensuring not only that an order is obtained, but also that it is a profitable one.

2 *Second, he must know how to prepare, in far more detail than before, strategies for each major customer.* He must know how to ensure that all the company's resources are harnessed to achieve both short and longer-term customer satisfaction, at a profit. Such strategies, skillfully and imaginatively implemented, will do much to eliminate the 'pyrrhic sale' produced by a salesman under pressure from management, which too often has resulted in short-term gains but the long-term loss of an account.

3 *Third, he must know how to negotiate a mutually satisfactory order and long-term business, rather than just using persuasive techniques to conjure up the 'your turn next' type of order.* Many of the larger buyers have no option but to purchase from the major suppliers. But the key to success is the terms on which the contract to trade is agreed. Negotiation skills of the highest order must be developed to deal on equal terms with these major customers, many of whom have been trained to buy. So far, little more than lip service has been paid to this fact. Indeed, an uncomfortably large number of sales managers, let alone salesmen, still think that negotiation is just a smart word for selling. It is nothing of the sort.

Again, while this source may seem dated the observations are just as valid today. Indeed, the current emphasis on **customer relationship management (CRM)** and **key account management (KAM)** are based on these three key areas.

Salesman compensation

Selling is a function which lends itself to some kind of payment by results in the majority of cases. If it is borne in mind that every incentive has a corresponding disincentive, then it follows that one must determine which incentive is most appropriate to a given selling situation.

According to research undertaken by Croner Reward in conjunction with the Chartered Institute of Marketing, the average sales representative will cost the average company about £55,840 or 2½ times the base salary of £22,915 in 2006. The break down of this sum includes 10% bonus, the use of a car and business mileage, health insurance and life assurance, a full expensed mobile phone, 2 nights away a month with evening meals, a daily lunch allowance and all other reasonable expenses.

Salary only

- The salesman's income is based on their overall performance and not subject to fluctuations beyond their control, for example the impact of a credit squeeze or marked seasonality of demand.
- The method is fairest where the salesman is engaged in missionary selling or required to spend much of their time providing technical services.
- Where there are variations in territory potential it prevents friction between salesmen, and gives flexibility in sales and journey planning.
- It simplifies payment and avoids complications in the salary structure of the company as a whole.

As suggested, each of these advantages has a built-in disincentive:

- Sales effort will not be maximised when most needed.
- The quality of the services rendered will affect sales volume and so should be measured in just the same way.
- Territories should be designed so that they have the same potential to encourage salesmen to compete with one another.
- If incentives are properly designed they will ensure that all members of the company receive a reward proportionate to their contribution.

Salary and commission

This is the most frequently used method on the grounds that:

- The salary provides a basic income while the commission provides the incentive to extra effort to achieve a better standard of living.
- Variable commissions on different products ensure that salesmen give them the degree of attention desired.

Commission only

In practice this method is found very infrequently – TACK (*www.tack.co.uk*, specialist providers of sales and sales management solutions in the UK and 40 countries worldwide) reports 5.5 per cent, others nil – as it has little attraction to any but the most confident of salesmen. From the employer's point of view it has the great attraction that payment is directly related to the results achieved, but it can also create considerable friction among other employees owing to the very high earnings which can be achieved by a good salesman. However, this approach is favoured by companies like Kleeneze and Avon that sell direct through self-employed, usually part-time sales persons.

Bonus schemes

Bonuses may be paid in addition to commission, either as an individual or group incentive, as a reward for sustained effort or the achievement of a pre-designated target, or where a purely quantitative assessment would not adequately reflect performance; for example reduced sales on a falling market when such sales still represent an increase in market share.

While some salesmen receive commission it appears to be relatively small taking into account the payment of bonuses and the difference between basic and total pay, i.e. 'commission' appears to be reported as a bonus. Overall, in terms of job level between 27-40% receive some kind of bonus, and these vary between 7.9% to 14.4% (Croner Reward/CIM).

Evaluation of salesmen

In the preceding section little reference was made to the methods used in evaluating salesmen's performance, on which most remuneration schemes are based. Once again it is necessary to reiterate that the relevant criteria will depend upon the company's own sales policies and objectives but, in general, performance will be measured in both quantitative and qualitative terms. Quantitative criteria include:

- *Sales volume;*
- *Number of orders secured;*
- *Number of sales calls made;*
- *Number of service calls made;*
- *Expenses incurred;*
- *Territory contribution to profit.*

Among the qualitative criteria in common use are:

- *Degree of product knowledge;*
- *Quality of sales presentation;*
- *Rating on personality traits* such as initiative, judgement and so on;
- *Self-organisation*, that is use of time, handling of correspondence, reports and so forth;
- *Customer relationships.*

Once the relevant criteria have been selected, some basis for evaluation must be chosen.

Methods based on past performance, or involving a comparison of salesmen, suffer from the disadvantage that present conditions may differ markedly from those obtaining in the past, and that sales territories, and hence salesmen, are rarely, if ever directly comparable. To overcome these difficulties many companies prefer to measure performance against prescribed standards; for example actual sales versus forecast, number of new accounts secured versus target, expenses incurred versus budgeted expense, and so on.

Donaldson (1999) sees evaluating sales people as something of an art struggling to be a science and points to some of the problems involved in selling that underlie this:

- Salespeople have inadequate or incomplete information about their job, especially concerning the needs and preferences of customers and customer organisation.

- Salespeople usually work alone and independently without direct supervision. Although considered by many to be an advantage this independence creates problems of role clarity.
- Salespeople operate in an inter-organisational boundary position which creates role conflicts.
- The sales job is demanding in terms of the degree of innovation and creativity required. There is no one right approach.
- The job requires adaptability and sensitivity from salespeople to the needs of customers, frequently met by different degrees of antagonism, hostility and aggression.
- Sales decisions may have to be made quickly requiring decisiveness and mental alertness.
- Individual sales performance evaluation lacks direct observation of inputs – only outcomes are assessed.
- Evaluation is often inferred and subjective, people biased.
- Salespeople have little control over the conditions in which they operate.

MERCHANDISING

In the chapter on patterns of distribution reference was made to the transference of some of the 'traditional' retailing functions to the manufacturer intent upon securing greater control over the marketing of their output. Subsequently, the role of packaging and advertising were examined in the context of generating demand for particular goods and services. It now remains to consider merchandising as an extension of the selling process whereby the manufacturer seeks to ensure that the retailer sells their products as quickly and as profitably as possible.

From the manufacturer's point of view the retail outlet provides the ready availability and convenience which are so expensive to achieve by direct selling methods. Once the retailer has taken delivery of goods from the manufacturer they become their property until they can effect their resale to ultimate consumers, and it follows that until they are able to achieve this they will have neither space nor capital with which to purchase further supplies from the producer. Clearly any assistance which the manufacturer can give the retailer to stimulate demand and encourage purchase will be to their mutual advantage – this is the role of merchandising.

To maximise sales volume the sales force must ensure that its products are in the right place at the right time, in order to translate potential demand for them into effective demand. The right place means not only the outlets with the highest turnover or largest clientele but also the right place within the outlet to achieve the maximum impact on the prospective purchaser. Given the cost of a salesman's time, plus the cost of point-of-sale display material, it is obvious that merchandising efforts must be concentrated on the larger outlets which promise the greatest potential return. Within outlets, research has shown that certain locations are to be preferred. Thus in self-service outlets the best positions have been found to be:

1 *At the end of gondolas facing the main traffic flow.* (A **gondola** is a shelving unit on the main floor area which subdivides this area into a series of aisles.)

2 *At eye level on the shelves around the sides of the shop.* Impact can be further improved by siting the product immediately prior to the area normally set aside for display of the product group.

3 *In dump displays in the main traffic aisles* as these tend to cause congestion and focus attention on them.

4 *Immediately next to the checkout* – here again congestion creates a captive audience.

In shops which still retain **counter service** the preferred positions are:

1 *On the counter itself.* If this is extensive, then next to the till or scales.

2 *At eye level behind the counter.*

3 *In a dispenser placed in front of the counter.*

4 *Next to a complementary product*, for example cream next to tins of fruit.

Timing is also an important factor underlying successful merchandising. Research indicates that the majority of purchases are made at the weekend and so emphasises the need to ensure adequate display at this time. Similarly, seasonal products such as mincemeat, Easter eggs and the like must be put on display in plenty of time, as must goods which are to be the subject of heavy promotion.

ACNielsen report that in-store merchandising is becoming increasingly expensive whether it is traditional displays or **POS (point-of-sale)** materials etc. or more innovative methods like floor ads and coupon dispensers. To enable manufacturers to determine the potential pay out they offer **Controlled Store Testing** to pre-test the likely impact and return; **In-Store Observation** to provide an accurate measurement of merchandising support for the manufacturer (and their competitors), and, through their **Scantrack Aligned In-Store Observations Service**, an analysis of sales data from groups of stores with different merchandising conditions

The major pitfall to be avoided by the salesman is that of becoming a merchandiser first and a salesman second. The salesman's role is to instruct retailers in the use of proven techniques to stimulate demand at the point of sale, and it is undesirable that they should become involved in routine activities associated with stocking shelves and putting goods on display. The salesman's job is to ensure that their products are given sound merchandising and a fair share of the favoured sites, and the normal call frequency precludes them devoting much time to in-store promotion.

In view of the heavy demands on the salesman's time, many firms now employ personnel whose sole function is to assist the retailer with the creation of effective store displays. Much merchandising is purely mechanical and so can be performed by part-time or less highly paid employees than is the case when salesman are required to do their own merchandising. Numerous agencies offer merchandising services, e.g. *www.powergirls.co.uk* and *www.zoopeople.co.uk* and a Google search of 'merchandising support in-store' on 27/7/05 resulted in 91,800 hits including one for the *In-Store Marketing Institute* (*www.instoremarketer.org*)

SALES PROMOTION

The Institute of Sales Promotion defines sales promotion as follows:

> *Sales promotion is a facet of marketing which is adding value, usually of a temporary nature, to a product or service in order to persuade the end user to purchase that particular brand.*

Much advertising also satisfies this definition which accounts for the difficulties of distinguishing the precise division between above and below the line expenditure, a problem which is further compounded by the distinction between consumer and trade promotions.

In the *Marketing Book* (2003) Peattie observes that often sales promotion is defined as marketing communications activities which do not fall into the categories of advertising, selling or public relations – not a very helpful approach! Accordingly, he proposes that sales promotions are "marketing activities usually specific to a time period, place or customer group, which encourage a direct response from consumers or marketing intermediaries, through the offer of additional benefits". (458) In other words, sales promotions are non-standard, response and benefit oriented.

The basic objective underlying all promotions is an increase in sales. This aim may be further subdivided, in terms of the time dimension, by devising strategies designed at achieving either short or long-term gains. Hopefully, both aims will be achieved, but the immediate objective will condition the strategy and the promotional tools employed.

Although display advertising can be very effective in making consumers aware of the existence of a product, inertia frequently prevents consumer sampling, and some additional incentive is required to persuade non-users to try it. Promotions are designed to provide this incentive. Consumers invariably view trial of a new product as containing a risk element – perceived risk – yet without trial there is no possibility of repeat purchases. A product may be totally new, in the sense that it has never previously been offered for sale, or new in the sense that the individual has no previous experience of it. A different strategy will apply to each of these situations.

In the case of a totally new product the initial campaign will seek to obtain the widest possible trial and will employ a combination of methods, for example coupons, free samples, in-store trial, banded offers, and so forth. Where the brand is already established and has a known brand share, the promoter will adopt a more selective approach and may concentrate on those segments of the market with the lowest usage rates in combating competitors' offers and deterring loyal customers from 'switching'. A totally new offering will also merit a more prolonged campaign to encourage repurchase; this would not be justified for an established brand because of the cost of 'subsidising' users who would have bought the product without a promotion. Against this element of subsidy must be set the fact that a 'bonus' helps maintain brand loyalty in the face of one's competitors' promotions.

In highly competitive markets, where product differentiation is difficult, if not impossible, such as detergents, breakfast cereals, petrol and so on, promotions are frequently employed to secure short-term increases in sales in the knowledge that once the promotion is finished the new buyers will revert to their former brand, or a competitive brand which is running a promotion. Clearly, promotions of this type are subject to criticism on the grounds that they are combative and do nothing to increase primary demand, and it is argued that the consumer would be better served by a permanent price reduction. From an industry viewpoint there is some truth in the argument, but from the position of the individual firm there is little incentive in adopting such a policy. Faced with an inelastic demand all firms would follow suit and reduce price, but would still be faced with the need to continue promotional activity to protect their individual brand shares. If it is assumed that the manufacturer would protect their profit margin, one is drawn to the inescapable conclusion that such a price reduction would eventually lead to an overall decline in product quality.

In the case of a product like petrol, which has to conform with a technical specification, a reduction in quality of this kind is not permissible. It follows that unless a price cut or promotion can be offset against lower raw material prices then the only justification for either tactic must be the hope that the resulting increase in market share will offset the costs involved. But, as the promotional activity by the major British petrol companies has shown, petrol is essentially a commodity with convenience and price the major choice determinant. The result is that gains in market share tend to be short-lived as the suppliers to an oligopolistic market react in the way theory predicts they will.

In general, sales promotion can be used to achieve a number of marketing objectives which were summarised by C. D. Moss, P. Thorne and P. Fasey (1963) as follows:

1 *To gain customers and convert them to regular users* – particularly for new or improved products;

2 *To widen the distribution of a product;*

3 *To influence stock levels* which may be too high or too low;

4 *To reduce sales peaks and troughs and maintain economic production levels;*

5 *To cushion the effect of a price increase;*

6 *To create new interest in an established product and improve results from in-store displays.*

Finally, in the *IEBM Encyclopedia of Marketing* Ken Peattie (1999) summarises the growth in promotions as follows:

1 *Growing doubts about the cost effectiveness of advertising, in the face of rising prices and increased advertising 'clutter':* a lack of conclusive evidence to link advertising directly to consumer preference and buying behaviour, and apparent consumer hostility towards advertising has fuelled these doubts. The advent of remote controls which allow adverts to be 'zapped' has also eroded television advertisers' confidence in their ability to reach their target audience.

2 *Sales promotions have acquired new found 'respectability' through greater use by market leaders and increasing professionalism among sales promotion agencies.*

3 *Increased impulse purchasing, particularly for FMCG products:* according to the American Point of Purchase Institute, some 80 per cent of all purchase

decisions are now made in-store, and can therefore be influenced by instore promotions.

4 *Planning time horizons have been shortened, reflecting increasing market volatility and rivalry, and accelerating product life cycles.* The development of advertising campaigns which build and nurture the desired image for a brand is a slow and painstaking process. The more immediate boost offered by promotions is attractive to marketers under pressure to improve market share and sales volume in the short term.

5 *Micro-marketing approaches*: in response to fragmenting markets, promotions can provide more tailored and targeted communication than mass media.

6 *Declining brand loyalty*: caused by widening choice, narrowing perceived differences between brands and, in fmcg markets, retailers' own brands becoming increasingly credible.

7 *A 'snowball' effect* in some markets, with companies feeling obliged to match rivals' sales promotion activity, or risk losing market share and competitive position.

8 *Affordability*: national mass media have become prohibitively expensive for many companies, particularly during recessionary squeezes on marketing budgets. Promotions allow national coverage at a lower cost, cost sharing with co-promoters and can even be self-funding.

Determination of the appropriation

A distinct advantage of promotions as compared with display advertising is that the former is capable of reasonably accurate costing in terms of a desired result whereas the latter is speculative.

In setting the appropriation a two-stage approach is possible. The first stage requires the quantification of only two variables, which are reasonably accessible

IN-STORE PROMOTIONS

In the autumn of 2004 both Unilever and Colgate issued profit warnings due to the need to increase marketing expenditures to compete with arch rival Procter & Gamble. An article in *The Times* (September 21) by Carl Mortished commented: "The battle of the brands is no longer a question of billboards and two minute commercials on ITV. For the past few years advertisers have shunned the glitzy and expensive business of explaining why Persil is better than Ariel. Instead, they are offering promotional discounts and bribing retailers to place their products in the best position – at eye level and, preferably, near the checkout". With marketing experts estimating that 70% of consumer choices are made in-store manufactures are having to increase their sales promotional spend. In the USA Nielsen estimate that some 60 percent of the promotional budget is on in-store promotions with the balance spent on press and TV. But, as Mortishead points out, the dilemma is that discounting and dealer loaders erode manufacturers' margins, transfers more power to retailers like Wal-Mart and Tesco, and encourages consumers to expect even more. In his view higher investment in manufacturers brands through advertising may be the only way to reverse the trend.

to the company – sampling cost and the additional contribution arising from the sale of a marginal unit. The second stage requires the determination of three further, and less accessible, facts – the conversion rate from sampling to regular usage, frequency of purchase among regular users, number of purchases by those sampled who do not adopt the product and become regular users.

The sampling cost can usually be calculated in advance and comprises two elements – the distribution cost and the value of the sample or coupon. Where the promotion consists of a coupon redeemable on purchase of the item being promoted, the value of the unit discount must be adjusted in line with the anticipated redemption rate to arrive at a total cost – previous experience usually provides a reliable estimate of this rate.

The growth of the promotions business has resulted in the setting up of firms which specialise in all its aspects, several of which are wholly owned subsidiaries of major advertising agencies. These companies are well qualified to advise on all aspects of promotions, and will provide estimates of redemption rates with a reasonable degree of accuracy.

Once the sampling area has been defined and the nature of the offer decided, it is a relatively simple matter to calculate the redemption rate/sales volume which will ensure break-even in the short term. In order to allow for the long-term potential of a promotion an estimate must be made of the three second-stage variables referred to above. Conversion rates, like redemption rates, may be estimated with reasonable accuracy on the basis of past experience. The same is true of the percentage of those who will 'make subsequent purchases without becoming 'brand adopters'.

(Many large companies undertake continuous market research which enables them to predict at an early stage in the life of a promotion exactly how repurchase patterns will develop.) Product usage is also quite well documented, both by independent firms like Nielsen and by the larger agencies and manufacturers. Armed with this data it is possible, with a little educated guesswork to formulate an acceptable forecast of the long-term benefits.

Promotions in current usage

As every consumer is aware there is a bewildering array of promotional offers available. A comprehensive listing of these is offered by Peattie and Peattie (2003) and reproduced as Table 20.1.

Some of the distinguishing features of these promotions are:

Free samples

Of all the promotions this method offers the greatest chance of getting a consumer to actually try the product. At the same time it is the most expensive, and its usage is invariably restricted to brands with potential annual sales of several million pounds. A number of companies seek to reduce sampling cost by cooperating in a joint promotion of non-competing products on similar lines to the gift pack given to mothers of first babies.

Off-price labels

In terms of consumer acceptability the label featuring Xp off the regular price is the most popular promotion. It is also popular with retailers as it involves none

Table 20.1 Major forms of consumer promotions

Promotion	Key user sectors	Notes	Examples
Discount pricing and sales	FMCG firms, retailers	Additional volume, must compensate for lost revenue. Can spark price wars. Generally a defensive mood.	January sales. Retailer campaigns such as 'Asda Price'. Amazon offers a 40% discount on a customer's 'First Anniversary'.
Money-off coupons	FMCG grocery retailers	Redemption rates determine costs. Requires retailer co-operation. Allows some differential pricing	Mattel Inc.'s 1988 toy marketing campaign involved 582 million coupons.
Refunds	FMCG consumer durables	Avoids problems of reference price changes. Non-redemptions reduce costs compared to discounts.	To boost UK sales of its Windows XP operating system, Microsoft offered a £50 cashback deal during the first quarter of 2002.
Samples	Foods, toiletries	Expensive. Encourages trial. Effectiveness hard to measure. Can generate market research.	Agree shampoo became No. 1 in the US market within 6 months by using 31 million samples.
Payment terms	Consumer durables, retailers	Reduces real cost rather than prices. Useful for seasonal demand smoothing.	Interest-free credit offers. In 2001 brands including Compaq, Microsoft and Mitsubishi used 'Buy now, pay later' promotions.
Multipacks and multibuys	Packaged goods, retailers	Best for small, high purchase frequency items.	Kodak used a 3-for-2 offer on its Ultra film during 2001 to help boost its share of the crucial winter/festive season market.
Special features	Consumer durables	Often packaged as a 'special' or 'limited' edition.	The Citroen Xsara West Coast special edition was a major success, offering over £1,000 of extras including air conditioning and metallic paint plus a reduced price.
Quantity increases	Packaged foods, canned drinks	Relies on ability to customise packaging processes.	Canned Beers feature regular 500ml for the price of 400ml.
In-pack premiums	Packaged goods	Items placed in foodstuffs needs care regarding food safety.	During 2000 Kellogs put Sesame Street beanie toys into 25 million cereal boxes.
In-mail premiums	Packaged goods	Usually relies on handling houses for redemption.	Stonegate Egg's offer of Chicken Run movie tickets, T-shirts and egg cups helped to sell 5.2 million extra eggs during 2000.

Type	Applications	Comments	Examples
Piggy-back premiums	*Packaged goods*	Usually joint promotions, can generate complementary sales and encourage product trial.	'Free Gillette GII with Kleenex for Men' gained Gillette 100,000 trials and KFM 13% extra sales.
Competitions	Packaged foods, retailers	Good for creating interest and reinforcing ad campaigns. Needs care with legalities.	McDonald's $40 million Treasure Hunt. Heinz's 'Win a Car a Day for 100 Days' campaign.
Information	Industrial firms, consumer durables, services	Important for reducing perceived risk. Provides consumer benefits of convenience and saved time.	Product catalogues. Holiday brochures. Investment guides. CD-ROM catalogues.
Valued packaging	Retailers, FMCG firms	Packaging can be useful in itself, or can provide a game, activity, recipe or other information.	Sony's regular offer of a free case with cassette and mini-disc multipacks. The enduring Paul Masson wine carafe.
Loyalty cards	Retailers	Card applications and usage can be linked to EPOS information to create database marketing and targeted promotion opportunities. Some concerns about level of loyalty achieved.	Boots Advantage Card has over 13 million members and over 50% of its sales are card related.
Gift coupons	Petrol retailers, draught beers	Useful for non-packaged foods. Helps encourage repeat purchases.	Over 3 million users registered on-line for the Pepsi 'Stuff' merchandise collection during 2000.
Product trial	Consumer durables	Often twinned with a competition. Needs close sales support.	200,000 Apple Macs were 'home tested', 40% led to sales.
Guarantees	Consumer durables, retailers	'Pricebeat' promises often back up sales to reduce perceived risk.	Supermarket 'Refund and Replace' offers. During 2001 Vodafone and EasyJet used 'Price Promises' of refunding the difference if customers found lower prices elsewhere.
Cashback offers	Consumer durables	Costs depend upon redemption rates. Over-redemption can be insured against.	Sanyo's 1988 10-year-buyback pledge boosted TV sales by 62%.
Clubs	Airlines and hotels, children's products	Useful for generating customer loyalty.	Marriott Hotels' Rewards scheme has over 15 million members and Burger King's Kids Club has more than 5 million members worldwide.

Source: Reprinted from 'Sales Promotion', Peattie, K. in Baker, M.J. (ed.) *The Marketing Book*, 5th Edition, copyright (2003) with permission from Elsevier.

of the diseconomies associated with coupon redemption ,and also provides the opportunity to feature a price reduction in their local advertising.

The actual extent of the price reduction is an important determinant of the level of sampling, and careful thought, and preferably testing, must be given to the selection of a discount. As discussed in the chapter on pricing, some prices have the apparent effect of being perceived as less than they really are, and it is these which have the greatest impact on impulse purchases. Obviously, if sales volume can be increased sufficiently the firm may be able to both even out seasonal fluctuations and make a profit.

A price reduction is a short-term strategy, however, and the simplest for one's competitors to duplicate. For these reasons it is avoided by companies that are sensitive to a price war wherever possible. That said, the entry of major retailers like Sainsbury's into the supply of petrol has resulted in the oil majors having to make significant discounts to combat the loss of market share

Banded offers

This type of promotion takes two forms:

1 The use of an existing and well-known brand to 'carry' a free sample of another non-competing product. Both products may be produced by the same firm, for example soap and toothpaste, which has the dual advantage of increasing sales of the carrying brand while securing trial of the carried brand, or complementary products of different producers, for example instant coffee and sugar.

PRICE PROMOTIONS

Harry Potter

At midnight on Friday July 15th 2005 *Harry Potter and the Half-Blood Prince* went on sale. With a recommended sale price of £16.99 you could have pre-ordered a copy online from *tesco.com* at £8.96, from *Amazon.co.uk* at £8.99, provided you had ordered by the previous Wednesday evening, and from *whsmith.co.uk* at £9.85. Offline the prices on offer were: Asda £8.96, Woolworths £8.99, WH Smith £9.99 (pre-orders), Ottaker's £9.99 (pre-orders), and Waterstone's £11.99 including a free copy of Zizou Corder's *Lionboy*. J.K. Rowling's royalties would be based on the **RSP (recommended sale price)** so she would lose nothing, while the publisher, Bloomsbury, may well have offered some discounts for very large orders but, basically, would have been selling at between

half and two thirds of RSP and secured the margins they wanted. So, why were retailers offering the product at or near cost with the real likelihood that some might have been selling below cost so they could claim to have the lowest price on offer?

The answer is that, according to a report by Jack Malvern in *The Times* (12/7/05), it was anticipated that more than 1.7 million readers would buy the book within 24 hours of its release and 3.2 million within the first week. So, even if a bookshop only achieved a 0.6% share of these sales it would be equivalent to having a monopoly of the sales of the next largest bestseller, John Grisham, who would be expected to sell 20,000 copies in the first week. As for the supermarkets, who compete heavily on competitive prices, the high visibility of the book, and media coverage of the launch, ensures that their reputation of value for money is reinforced. Further, buying the book in a supermarket strengthens the link between a highly desired object and the outlet, as well as building store traffic and increasing the likelihood of further purchases in-store.

2 Two-for-the-price-of-one or **BOGOF – Buy One Get One Free** – or some other combination.

Electronic Point –of- Sale (EPOS) systems make it possible to combine products without having to attach them physically to one another, as used to be the case, making this a much more flexible type of promotion. It also avoids the problems of stocking non-standard sized packages on the same shelf.

Premium offers

There are three main varieties of premium offer:

1 *The free gift.* This may be contained in the package – plastic animals in breakfast cereals; attached to it – a plastic rose, tea-towels and so forth; given out at the checkout to those purchasing the item carrying the offer – bowls, china, waste-paper baskets, and so on. In some instances the offer will be the pack itself, as is the case with instant coffee packed in storage jars. A common feature of these promotions is that they encourage a collecting habit and so achieve extended trial as the consumer builds up the collection.

2 *The free, sendaway premium.* This type of promotion offers a free gift in exchange for proof of purchase of the product. This approach has greater appeal to the retailer than those promotions which require them to stock 'giveaways', especially as the promotion usually involves point of sale material that builds store traffic and stimulates impulse purchases. From the promoter's angle an added advantage is that many people buy the product intending to send off for the premium but in fact never do.

3 *Self-liquidating premiums.* These differ from the other type of premium in that the consumer has to send both money and proof of purchase to obtain the offer. The advantage to the consumer is that he secures merchandise, often carrying a leading brand name, at a significant discount on its normal retail price. The promoter benefits in that, as the name suggests, the offer pays for itself. If combined with a collecting habit, offers of this kind may run for years ensuring long-term usage, for example Kellogg's silverware offer.

Competitions

Like all other promotions these are no newcomers to the marketing scene (Lever Brothers were spending £1 million a year on promotions at the turn of the twentieth century), but they have attracted more than their usual share of attention of late as a result of tangling with the betting and gaming laws. Interest in competitions is considerable owing to the attraction of a very large prize, together with a sufficient number of consolation prizes on an area basis to encourage people to continue to try their luck.

In 2005 an ISP sponsored survey of Agencies asked which techniques had been used in the preceding 12 months. The results are summarised in Table 20.2.

From the listing of the types of promotions currently in use, it is clear that there is a wide choice of alternatives. Each of them has merits and demerits that need to be carefully evaluated before making a final selection. In the following section we reproduce, the advice given by Ogilvy, Benson & Mather on sales promotion using sampling as an example. While the company is now known as The Ogilvy Group Inc. (*www.ogilvy.com*) the advice is still relevant.

Table 20.2 Types of promotion currently in use

Type of promotion	% of Agencies using this in last 12 months (Sept. 2005)
FPD (Free Prize Draw)	90%
Instant Wins	80%
Sampling	75%
Coupons	70%
Free Gift with Pack	50%
Free Product	50%
SLP (Self-Liquidating Promotion)	40%
FMI (Free Mail-In Offer)	35%
Price Reductions	30%
BOGOF (Buy One get One Free)/Extra fill	25%
Cash Refunds	20%

Source: data provided by Incentive Today / ISP (Institute of Sales Promotion), *www.isp.org.uk*

Figure 20.3 Promotions and the marketing mix: an integrated model

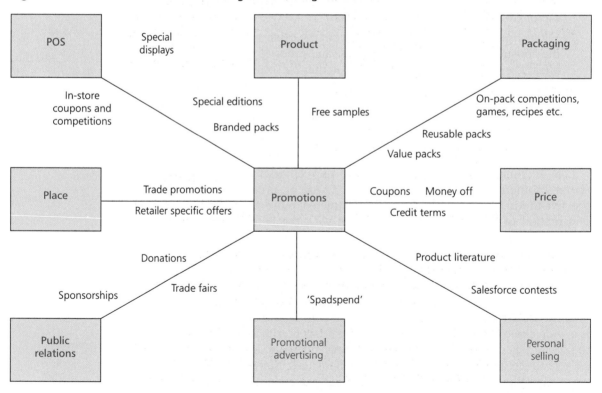

Source: Peattie, K. (1999), 'Sales Promotion', in Baker, M.J. (ed.) *IEBM Encyclopedia of Marketing*, (London: Thomson Learning)

HOW TO DECIDE WHETHER TO RUN A PROMOTION
AND WHICH PROMOTION TO CHOOSE*

* The edited extract quoted (pp.597-602) is reproduced by kind permission of The Ogilvy Group Inc. (formerly Ogilvy Benson & Mather) www.ogilvy.com. It is now dated on points of detail but the issues and approaches discussed are still valid.

Introduction

Consumer promotions are not a panacea. A belief has developed that they are the modern marketing technique. This is nonsense. Consumer promotions are just one part of the marketing mix, not a substitute for it. If a promotion is run it will normally work better as a part of the whole, fitting in with the advertising, product development, packaging, trade incentives and salesmen's incentives as a logical development of the marketing strategy. [*Indeed, as Peattie makes clear promotion is an integral part of the marketing mix. This is illustrated in Figure 20.3*]

In particular, it must be made clear that 'promotions' and 'advertising' are complementary techniques, not substitutes for each other. There is a growing body of evidence that companies who switch their marketing expenditure exclusively 'below-the-line' make temporary gains in volume at the expense of permanently undermining their brand-image and the loyalty of their most regular buyers.

A well-designed promotion can help solve certain specific marketing problems, and together with the rest of the marketing mix help to achieve a marketing objective. Therefore, before discussing whether to mount a promotion at all, and certainly before selecting the type of promotion, the marketing objectives of the brand must have been agreed, specific marketing targets set, and the problems to be overcome identified.

This assumes that the following information is available:

(a) Who is the target market for the brand?
(b) Why they use the product and how?
(c) How frequently it is bought and where?
(d) Who are its main competitors?
(e) How the consumer rates the brand compared with its competitors?

If these facts are not known, then what is needed is not a promotion but basic research into the brand to determine its problems and marketing positioning.

How to decide whether to run a promotion

(a) Determine, in order of priority, the problems facing the brand.
(b) Determine the money available to solve the problems.
(c) List and cost all the possible alternative solutions to the problems: e.g. more advertising, consumer promotions, pricing strategy, product change, etc.
(d) Estimate (or guesstimate) the effectiveness of each solution.
(e) If the answers to (c) and (d) suggest that a promotion is the most efficient answer to the brand's problem and if the answer to (b) shows there is enough money for a successful promotion then a promotion is indicated.
(f) It does not make sense to run a promotion simply because a competitor

is running one unless this has caused problems for your brand which a promotion would solve. If the problems confronting your brand, at that time, would not be solved by a promotion, then it would be a costly mistake to allow your competitor's action to stampede you into panic action. His problems or his perception of his problems may be quite different from those confronting your brand.

Which promotion to choose?

(a) The one most likely to solve the brand's problem successfully, within the available budget.

(b) You can help to decide this by looking up your problems in the chart (in the next section).

(c) Then for each promotion listed as likely to help, look up the separate section on that type of promotion.

(d) Look initially at the sub-sections on
   (i)   Advantages
   (ii)   Disadvantages
   (iii) Essentials for success
   (iv)   Points to look out for
   (v)   How much will it cost?
   [*Ogilvy Benson and Mather provided information on these for all the major types of sales promotion along the same lines as those given in the sampling example below*].

(e) Does the promotion offer an incentive to the market target, from their point of view?

(f) Consider the impact of the promotion on the image of the product. An expensive, high quality product, should have an expensive, high-quality promotion.

(g) Consider whether the consumer has any problems which the promotion could solve: e.g. if a product is messy to use, it may be worth considering a free spreader or spatula.

(h) Promotions are tactical tools. There is no formula for picking the correct one. They will usually be better if they are designed in the context of the individual brand's consumers, its market and its trade practices.

(i) Because of this need for bespoke designing it is usually better not to copy other companies' promotions but to think ideas out from scratch.

Problems and an indication of the consumer promotions most likely to help in solving them

These are suggestions, not hard and fast rules. Altering the design of a promotion may make it a suitable solution for other problems. The nature of the product, the company and the trade will also affect the best solution to any problem.

Promotions which may help

(a) To get consumer trial of new or existing product
     Free with-, in- or on-pack premium
     Money-off voucher
     Money-off offer
     Sampling
     Proprietary promotions

(b)	To obtain repeat purchasing	Any premium offer of a collectable item (free or 'self-liquidating promotion') Competition Free mail-in Free continuous mail-in (coupons) 'Money-off voucher promotion' 'Self-liquidating promotion'
(c)	To obtain long-term consumer loyalty	Continuous 'self-liquidating promotion' (coupons) Trading stamps
(d)	To increase frequency or quantity of consumer purchase in the short run	Competition Free on-, with-pack premium Free mail-in Household stock reward scheme (personality promotion) In-store self-liquidator Money-off offer (including banded packs) Shop-floor promotions Tailor-made promotions
(e)	To move high stocks out of stores	Competition Free with-pack Free mail-in Shop-floor promotions Tailor-made promotions
(f)	To get consumers to visit your premises	Free gifts Money-off voucher Shop-floor promotions Tailor-made promotions Trading stamps Proprietary promotions

(g) *To get increased distribution.* This will call for trade and salesmen's incentives primarily although a consumer promotion may be necessary to 'pull the product through'. However the choice of consumer promotion will really depend on other problems facing the brand at the time.

(h) To obtain increased stock levels/stocking in depth. As with the increased distribution this calls for trade and salesmen's incentives. The choice of a consumer promotion to 'pull the product through' will depend on other problems facing the brand at the time.

(i) To obtain information on consumer product usage. This is a research, not a promotional problem.

Sampling

The consumer is either:

(a) given some of the product free; or
(b) allowed to use the product freely during a given period.

The size of the product give-away may vary from a taste or spray to a full-sized pack.

The samples can be distributed in a number of ways:

(a) Given by a demonstrator in a store. These are usually used instantly, e.g. a tasting of food or drink, a spray of perfume.
(b) Given away with another product.
(c) Distributed in some medium, e.g. a shampoo sachet in a magazine.
(d) Delivered door-to-door.
(e) Sent on application from the consumer.
(f) Given to visitors to some specific location, e.g. hotels, exhibitions, showrooms, race tracks, etc.
(g) Where the consumer is invited to use the product freely, e.g. a car or television set, then the 'sample' is delivered, by arrangement, to the home or place of business.

Advantages

The advantage to the consumer is immediate and obvious (this does not apply if the consumer has to apply for the sample).

The consumer has to make no effort, is involved in no expense (again except in the case where he has to apply for it).

Mass sampling is by far the quickest way of obtaining widespread consumer trial.

Demonstrates to the consumer the product's qualities, and the manufacturer's faith in his product.

Creates excitement.

Disadvantages

This is very expensive.

Considerable administration is involved in distributing the samples.

The special costs of trial-sized packs can be as expensive as a normal pack.

The product needs to have an advantage, or difference, that the consumer can perceive.

It will not increase usage by existing consumers.

Essentials for success

A good product.

Efficient distribution, especially in:

(a) getting the samples to the potential market
(b) preventing samples going astray.

Where the sample is left with the consumer, it should be of sufficient size for the consumer both to appreciate the product's qualities and to form the habit of using the product. Consumers show disproportionately more gratitude for a 'full-size' sample.

Trade co-operation. This is very important. If the nature of the product makes a large sample necessary it may be necessary to persuade the trade that you are not depriving them of the profit they could have made selling the product.

A product that regular users are likely to buy frequently.

Advertising support.

Good distribution for the product so that consumers who are persuaded by the sample have the maximum opportunity to buy.

That consumers are informed where they can obtain further supplies of the product.

While not essential the conversion rate to product usage will be increased, if the consumer is given a money incentive to make the first purchase. Thus if the sample is distributed in a store the consumer's attention can be drawn to a money-off offer. If the sample is distributed away from the store or shop the sample should be accompanied by a money-off coupon or voucher.

Decisions that have to be taken:
What size sample to distribute? This will depend on:

(a)   The nature and value of the product.
(b)   Consumer usage, e.g. do not give consumers a year's supply, preferably sample the size you most want them to buy.
(c)   How apparent is the difference or advantage, e.g. can it be discerned on the first try or bite of the product?
(d)   The method of distribution to be used, e.g. you cannot put a pound pack inside a magazine; retailers prefer in-store samples to be small.
(e)   The cost of special sample packaging.
(f)   The promotional budget.

How to distribute the sample. This will depend on:

(a)   The size of the sample.
(b)   The nature of the product, e.g. is it breakable?
(c)   The market target. If it's not a mass market product there is no point in distributing door-to-door.
(d)   The possibilities for sample misuse.
(e)   The promotional budget.
(f)   The promotional objects.

How research can help
It could help to determine the most efficient sample size, e.g. how little of the product is needed to convert the consumer to the product . There could, however, be a security problem here with a new product.

Subsequently, in measuring conversion rate to the product and in planning further operations.

Points to watch/problems which may arise
In connection with any form of sampling operation. That there is adequate check on samples at all stages of distribution.

That the packaging of the sample will stand up to its method of distribution. It is advisable to check this in action. The standard pack may encounter much rougher treatment in a distributor's sack than in a standard outer moved by a forklift truck.

That any quotation received for distribution has been made with knowledge of both the weight and dimensions of the sample.

That there is no chance of the sample tainting other products or of being tainted by them.
[*See also 'Legal Clearance'*].

Sampling in stores and shops. That all details are fully discussed and agreed with the store in advance, e.g.

(a)   Dates.
(b)   Amount of space.
(c)   Location of space.
(d)   Hours the demonstrator will work. It can cause conflict if these are

markedly different from store staff.

(e)   Any necessary equipment, e.g. electrical socket.

That demonstrators are subject to adequate supervision and spot checks.

That adequate provisions are made for demonstrators to have clean overalls, etc. under all circumstances.

That if food is being sampled to eat, all food hygiene rules are strictly observed.

Samples given away with another product. That the market target for the two products is similar.

That the products are non-competitive.

Samples distributed in a Press medium. That there are no disputes between media owners and their distributors that will interfere with sample distribution.

Samples distributed door-to-door. Medicinal samples may not be distributed door-to-door.

Both the Board of Trade and CAP require manufacturers to exercise care in putting samples through letter boxes. Complaints have been made of products dangerous to children or dogs and where there is any danger of this CAP recommend personal handing over of the sample instead of distribution through the letter box.

That a sample intended to go through a letter box can go through the average letter box and that instructions cover premises with no letter boxes.

That a household sample is sufficient for a household. If it is something desired and there is not enough to go round you may cause ill-will and the market target may never even see the sample.

How much will it cost?

The following list includes some of the main costs likely to be incurred:

(a)   Cost of sample contents.
(b)   Sample packaging.
(c)   Distribution.
(d)   Advertising.
(e)   Display material.
(f)   Merchandising force.
(g)   Supporting trade and salesmen incentives.

* End of extract

LEGAL CLEARANCE

Legislation concerning promotional activity has proliferated in recent years in both the UK and European Union. This legislation is reinforced by a number of voluntary Codes of Practice, both national and international. The detail and complexity of this is beyond the scope of an introductory textbook, but the reader should be aware that any breech of such regulations is likely to attract severe penalties. Expert advice needs to be obtained and followed carefully.

It is also important to check for copyright. Similarity to a previous promotion by another company might give rise to a claim of 'passing off' or breach of copyright (apart from causing confusion among consumers and retailers!). If an outside agency is involved it should be made quite clear whether or not any work done by the agency is their copyright.

PICKING A PROMOTION

The foregoing extract from OBM's Handbook relates specifically to sampling, which is but one of many methods available. While the others are discussed in similar detail it will be helpful here to provide a summary of typical sales promotion problems and possible solutions. Table 20.3 is taken from 'Picking the Winners' by John Williams (1984) who is also the author of *The Manual of Sales Promotion*. John Williams also offers a very useful outline of the factors to be included in a promotional brief, and this is reproduced as Table 20.4 together with a check list of criteria for effective promotions – Table 20.5.

In selecting a promotion the OBM Handbook emphasises the need to conform with both statutory requirements and the various codes of practice which are published by the Committee of Advertising Practice at *www.cap.org.uk* Considerable detail on specific promotions may also be found on the Institute of Sales Promotion web site at *www.isp.org.uk*

Table 20.3 Typical problems and possible promotional solutions

Problem	Solution
1. To increase consumer awareness:	In-store raffle/display; phone-ins; sweepstakes; free draws; competitions
2. To increase penetration of new or existing products:	Free offers (with, in, or on-pack); money off coupons or offers; sampling; refund offers; multibrand schemes; banded packs, reduced price offers
3. To improve repeat purchase:	Competitions; free offers; on-pack money-off coupons; reduced price offers; refund/buy-back offers; giveaways; self-liquidating premiums; re-usable container premiums
4. To increase consumer loyalty:	Premium offers; money-off offers; personality promotions; coupons; buy one, get one free offers; twin packs; refund offers; re-usable container premiums
5. To increase purchase frequency or amount bought:	Competitions; share-outs/giveaways; free offers; personality promotions; tailor-made promotions; multibrand schemes; in-store promotions; banded packs; reduced price offers
6. To move high stocks out of stores:	In-store raffles/competitions; free offers; tailor-made promotions; in-store merchandising
7. To attract consumers to premises:	Free gifts/trials; tailor-made promotions; money-off coupons
8. Trading up to larger sizes:	Consumer choice coupons; refund offers; multibrand schemes
9. To increase distribution:	Tailor-made promotions; multibrand schemes; trade competitions; salesman's incentives; sample distribution
10. To encourage display:	On-pack premiums; banded packs; premium offers; heavy price cuts

Source: Williams, J. (1984), 'Picking the winners', *Marketing*, 26 April. Reproduced from *Marketing* magazine with the permission of the copyright owner, Haymarket Business Publications Limited.

Table 20.4 The promotional brief

Brand(s) or service(s)	Other comments/constraints in particular, space available for on-pack promotions
Pack size(s) involved	
Area(s) involved	Legal
Outlets involved (if appropriate)	Cautionary information to be included
Timing	Printing restrictions – number of colours permitted, print area, use of drawings /photographs, etc.
Budget	
Target group	Other support activity planned
Promotional objectives	Other relevant information – e.g. logo references, pack dimensions
Restrictions as to type of promotion (if applicable)	
Promotion communications, e.g. if on-pack	Confidentiality
the number of packs involved, leaflet circulation, etc.	Standard of response required – concepts, roughs, presentation layouts
Proofs of purchase required	Response from consultancy

Source: Williams, J. (1984), 'Picking the winners', *Marketing*, 26 April. Reproduced from *Marketing* magazine with the permission of the copyright owner, Haymarket Business Publications Limited.

Table 20.5 Criteria for efficient and effective promotions

1 The promotional objectives, budget and success criteria have been specified.
2 It does not attempt to do what other items in the mix can do better.
3 It is the best promotion for achieving the objectives.
4 It has maximum effect for the least cost.
5 It is consistent with the behaviour pattern of those to whom it is addressed.
6 It is consistent with brand image.
7 It gets attention and has urgency and action built into it.
8 It does not use complicated or confusing copy and is simple, clear and easy to act on and understand.
9 It uses emotional as well as rational appeals to self-interest.
10 It is legal and decent and evidently honest.
11 It sufficiently rewards all on whom its success depends.

Source: Williams, J. (1984), 'Picking the winners', *Marketing*, 26 April. Reproduced from *Marketing* magazine with the permission of the copyright owner, Haymarket Business Publications Limited.

Summary

The first part of this chapter has focused mainly on the role of personal selling. To begin with it was emphasised that personal selling is complementary to impersonal selling using other promotional methods – the precise mix depending very much upon the type of product and markets served.

Next we looked at the role of the salesman and the economics of personal selling concluding that some form of 'task' approach was best suited to determining where salespersons could be used to greatest effect. This and the deployment of the sales force were both seen as being amenable to simulation and quantification using management science techniques. Several different selling tasks were then distinguished – Trade, Missionary, Technical and New Business – which led to a review of the factors to be taken into account in the recruitment, selection and training of salespersons. Methods of compensating salespersons and evaluation of performance followed. The chapter then looked briefly at merchandising as an aspect of personal selling now largely the responsibility of a new kind of salesperson.

The second part of this chapter has been concerned with sales promotion which now accounts for the largest proportion of all promotional expenditure and is usually referred to as 'below the line'. Having defined sales promotion we then looked at its objectives and some of the reasons underlying its growth in recent years.

Next followed a discussion of some of the factors to be taken into account in determining a budget for sales promotion and an overview of the main promotions in current usage. This was supported by a discussion of when to consider running a promotion and which promotions to use. An extended analysis of sampling was then given as an example of the issues involved in deciding upon any of the major promotions.

Review questions and problems

1 Direct selling is the most expensive method of establishing contact with the potential customer. Under what circumstances is this expense justified?

2 Distinguish the essential differences between trade, missionary, technical and new-business selling. What 'type' of salesman do you consider to be best suited to each?

3 Compare and contrast the various methods of compensation discussed in the text. Which would you select in each of the following situations? Why?
   (a) Sale of capital equipment.
   (b) Sale of industrial lubricants.
   (c) Door-to-door selling of cosmetics, encyclopaedias, etc.
   (d) Sale of packaged goods to independent retail outlets.

4 Account for the importance given to merchandising.

5 What is systems selling? What advantages does it have over the traditional product specialisation approach?

6 Critically examine the alternative methods of compensating salesmen.

7 'There is something of the salesman in every good buyer. However, very few salesmen would ever make good buyers.' Discuss this view.

8 How should a sales manager determine the size of the sales force?

9 What do you think is the ideal way in which to recruit and select salesmen?

10 Show how a knowledge of interaction and influence processes in personal selling can contribute to an enhancement of sales force productivity.

11 To what extent are psychological tests of value in the selection of salesmen?

12 What are the main factors which sales managers should bear in mind when evaluating the performance of their sales forces? Give your views on the extent to which remuneration of salesmen should be related to their performance.

13 What are the most important things a salesman can do to improve their sales performance? How can management help them to do these things?

14 What factors should be taken into account when designing sales territories?

15 Write a job description for a salesman in a company manufacturing electronic component

16 'Unlike Advertising, there are no accurate national expenditure figures available for Sales Promotion, because many companies are undertaking such promotion without realising that they are doing so.' Explain this statement and outline some of the major uses of Sales Promotion.

17 From some situation in your experience, illustrate the role of 'below-the-line' sales promotion as part of the overall promotional campaign. Show how the 'below-the-line' component may be integrated with and contribute to the success of the total.

18 Define 'selling-out' and 'selling-in'. Show how a well-designed promotional campaign keeps the two elements in balance.

19 It is often suggested that the main role of 'below-the-line' expenditures for sales promotion is to encourage the marketer's and dealer's sales people. Give examples of such promotional activities, some of which would tend to support and others to refute this view.

20 In deciding on the promotional mix for a particular range of products, what circumstances would tend to favour special emphasis on:
(a) dealer incentives;
(b) sales force activity;
(c) sampling.

21 There are a wide variety of types of sales promotions – coupons, competitions, price off etc. – from which a brand manager may choose in writing annual product promotional plans. What factors should be considered in the selection/rejection process?

22 Define sales promotion and give FOUR examples of the kind of marketing objective that can be achieved by the use of sales promotion. Say which techniques you would use to achieve the objective in each case.

23 Name the major components of the promotional mix. What function does each perform and how does the marketing manager determine the amount of money to be allocated to each element in order to achieve a given communication objective?

24 Account for the boom in sports sponsorship in the last ten years.

25 How would you decide to divide available resources between direct sales representatives and other promotional activities?

Key terms

ACNielsen

AIDA (awareness, interest, desire, action)

appropriation of the budget

behavioural skills

below the line

BOGOF (buy one get one free)

bonus

brand share

Characteristics of Goods School

Committee of Advertising Practice

composite structure

controlled store testing

conversion rate

customer relationship management (CRM)

EPOS (electronic point of sale)

factor rating

forms of consumer promotion

frequency of purchase

function of personal selling

gondola

Institute of Sales Promotion

in-store observation

interviewer bias

key account management (KAM)

linear programming techniques

marginal unit

merchandising

number of purchases

order-maker

order-taker

perceived risk

personal selling

persuader

point of sale (POS)

promotional mix

prospecting

psychological testing

recruitment

respondent consistency

RSP (recommended selling price)

sales promotion

sampling

sampling cost

Scantrack Aligned In-Store Observations Service

selection of a promotional method

selection of technique

self-liquidating premiums

self-service outlets

sendaway

subsidising

switching

TACK

technical skills

territory design

Supplementary reading list

Donaldson, W. G. (1999), 'Personal selling and sales management', in Baker, M.J. (ed.) *IEBM Encyclopedia of Marketing*, (London: Thomson Learning).

Donaldson, W. G. (2003), 'Selling and Sales Management' Chapter 14 in Baker, M.J. (ed.) *The Marketing Book*, 5th edn, (Oxford: Butterworth-Heinemann).

Peattie, S. and Peattie, K. (2003), 'Sales Promotion', in Baker, M.J. (ed.) *The Marketing Book*, 5th edn, (Oxford: Butterworth-Heinemann).

Having explored the elements of the marketing mix in some detail, the purpose of this final part of the book it to look at some issues involved in putting marketing into practice.

To begin with we consider matters related to the organisation of the marketing function. Traditionally, marketing tended to be organised in a functional department like other functions such as procurement, production and finance. Under this form of organisation the major question was whether to coordinate activities around products (product/brand managers) or markets (market managers), and the advantages and disadvantages of these alternatives are weighed up. More recently, marketing has become to be seen as a company wide orientation with everyone involved in adding value and service delivery. To achieve this different structures may be necessary and there is a need for internal marketing and a view of organisations as networks rather than hierarchies.

Chapter 22 is concerned with planning and implementation/control. Several topics introduced in Chapter 2 are revisited in more detail – specifically, corporate and marketing strategy, the conduct of a marketing audit, and the preparation of a marketing plan. The second part of the chapter deals with a topic generally referred to as marketing metrics – the measures to be used in monitoring and controlling the implementation of the marketing plan – together with marketing arithmetic - techniques for calculating mark-up, discounts, stock turn etc.

The next two chapters take a look at the application of marketing in a particular context which has assumed sufficient importance to be regarded as a sub-field in its own right. First, there is the marketing of services which, in advanced economies, accounts for the major part of employment and GDP. A number of factors including intangibility, inseparability, heterogeneity, perishability and fluctuating demand are seen as calling for an extended marketing mix that includes people, process and physical evidence. While it is useful to isolate differences that call for attention, it is argued that there is a convergence between products and services as products are increasingly differentiated through the addition of services, while physical evidence is needed to reinforce the intangibility of the service promise.

Chapter 24 deals with what we term marketing in foreign environments, preferring this to the more usual international marketing for reasons set out in the text. The theories of economic development and comparative advantage are re-visited to remind us why international trade is necessary if we are to solve the problem of maximising satisfaction on a global scale. The idea of globalisation is examined and seen as being largely incorrect in its original statement of universal, undifferentiated products, and this leads to a consideration of a variety of approaches to marketing in a foreign environment.

And, finally, we look at a number of what might be called 'hot topics', i.e. those that are attracting most attention today and which are likely to continue to be of importance in the future. Obviously, this can only touch on these subjects of which the most important are seen as: marketing strategy and the Internet; E-marketing; Ethics in marketing; Green marketing; and Social marketing.

PART FOUR

THE COMPANY: ORGANISING FOR MARKETING

21

Learning Goals — *After reading this chapter you should be able to:*

- Recognise different forms of organisational structure.

- Explain the need for both differentiation and integration in the effective organisation.

- List and describe seven basic methods of organising a marketing department.

- Describe the origin, evolution and application of the product manager concept.

- Describe the market manager concept and compare and contrast it with the product manager concept.

- Discuss the relationship between the marketing concept, marketing orientation and organisational structure.

INTRODUCTION –

MARKETING ORGANISATION AND MANAGEMENT

Much of the discussion about marketing's 'mid-life crisis' prompted by a McKinsey article in 1993 and Webster's (1992) "The Changing Role of Marketing in the Corporation" came about as a result of changes in the role of marketing within the organisation. Conventionally, discussions of organisation for marketing focused upon the existence of a marketing department responsible for management of the various mix functions. However, as a result of increasing competition through the 1970s and 80s this approach changed from the manipulation of the mix functions to a view which saw marketing's role as one involving the entire organisation. Thus, Piercy & Craven's (*Encyclopedia*, 1999) observed: "Marketing organisation has become a fundamental strategic issue concerned with intra-organisational relationships and inter-organisational alliances, and the management of critical boundary spanning environmental interfaces."

611

In Webster's (1997) view this represents the fourth stage in the evolution of marketing organisation. To begin with, marketing was equated with sales and demand generation activities. In the second phase bureaucratic and hierarchical organisational forms are developed to plan and control the performance of specialists. In turn, this leads into a third phase where marketing becomes identified as a function in its own right responsible for the development of integrated marketing strategies. Nowadays, however, in response to competitive pressures, marketing competence has become integrated with other business functions in team centred organisational processes focused on the customer.

A great deal of the debate on organisational structure is reflected in the distinction between 'marketing orientation' and 'market orientation'. Superficially, this may appear a semantic quibble but the distinction is much more than this. In essence, a marketing orientation assumes the dominance of the marketing function in managing the organisation's interfaces with its markets, whereas a market orientation mirrors Drucker's (1954) original conceptualisation of the role of marketing as the need to focus all of the organisations efforts on the needs of customers and markets.

Piercy & Craven cite a number of examples to underline the speed of change in the organisation of marketing. Thus, "in 1997, IBM announced its global initiative customer relationship management in which most marketing activities are embedded. The goal is to co-ordinate customer relationships by focusing management on core business processes instead of traditional functions ..." Similarly, Procter & Gamble has adopted a "customer business development structure" while the Unilever-owned Elida Faberge "... abandoned its conventional brand management and marketing management roles by creating customer development and brand development as centres of expertise, with category management working with retailer customers as part of the sales organisation."

The debate about the most appropriate form of organisation to enable effective marketing practice continues. However, to provide some perspective, it will be useful to consider earlier approaches to this issue as many firms still have traditional structures based on hierarchical frameworks and the appointment of product, market and brand managers. Accordingly, we look first at basic organisational structures and the organisation of the marketing department. Next we discuss the product or brand manager concept and compare this with the idea of market managers. To conclude we return to a consideration of current thinking on organising for marketing as hinted at in the opening paragraph.

THE EARLY DAYS

The change from a seller's to a buyer's market in the 1950s precipitated a rash of literature promising managerial salvation through adoption of the marketing concept. With the desperation of a drowning man, corporations in every field of activity seized the straw, and marketing staff appointments proliferated. As anticipated profits failed to materialise, disillusionment set in and marketing became the scapegoat. Supporters of marketing responded by pointing out that adoption of the marketing concept requires a complete reorientation of the firm's activities which renaming the sales function was unlikely to bring about. Superficial as this description is, it serves to underline that the firm's organisational structure is critical to marketing success. In the era of excess demand, top management attention was rightly focused on increasing output, and a production orientation was both necessary and understandable. However, a firm is more than a collection of individuals, it is a social system with its own norms, status structure and system of rewards and punishments. It is unrealistic to assume that these can be changed overnight, yet many firms which originally rejected the marketing concept did so because they failed to appreciate the inherent organisational implications, or else instituted extensive changes without full consideration of the possible ramifications. Fortunately, the unhappy experiences of the disillusioned served to concentrate attention on the organisational implications associated with a marketing orientation, and considerable thought given to the issues which influence organisational structures in general and marketing departments in particular.

BASIC ORGANISATIONAL STRUCTURES

Given the possible variations in the size of firms, the products they manufacture and the markets they serve, it is clear that there can be no single organisational structure of universal applicability. Despite the infinite variations in degree, the fundamental organisational choice revolves around grouping activities by product or function. This dilemma was the subject of an article by two well-known authorities on organisation behaviour, Arthur H. Walker and Jay W. Lorsch (1968), 'Organizational choice: product vs. function', on which the following discussion is based.

Traditionally, organisational theorists have suggested that the appropriate structure should be decided on the basis of three criteria:

1 Which approach permits the maximum use of special technical knowledge?

2 Which provides the most efficient utilisation of machinery and equipment?

3 Which provides the best hope of obtaining the required control and coordination?

Walker and Lorsch felt that these traditional criteria ignored the trade-off between functional specialisation and difficulties of coordination, and product specialisation which promotes collaboration between specialists but tends to lose identification with functional goals. To make good this omission the authors proposed that three findings from the behavioural sciences should also be taken into account, namely:

1 Functional specialists tend to develop patterns of behaviour and thought that are in tune with the demands of their jobs and their prior training, and as a result these specialists (for example industrial engineers and production supervisors) have different ideas and orientation about what is important in getting the job done. This is called differentiation and is necessary for functional specialists to perform their jobs effectively.

2 Differentiation is closely related to achievement of coordination, or what behavioural scientists call integration. This means collaboration between specialised units or individuals. Recent studies have demonstrated that

there is an inverse relationship between differentiation and integration: the more two functional specialists (or their units) differ in their patterns of behaviour and thought, the more difficult it is to bring about integration between them.

3 While achievement of both differentiation and integration is possible, it can only occur when well-developed means of communication among specialists exist in the organisation, and when the specialists are effective in resolving the inevitable cross-functional conflicts.

It is suggested that these findings raise three basic questions which must be answered when choosing between a product, or functional basis of organisation:

(a) Does it permit sufficient differentiation for the effective performance of specialist tasks?

(b) Is the degree of differentiation consistent with the desired level of integration?

(c) How will the structure affect intra-firm channels of communication?

Although the appropriate structure will depend upon external factors, Walker and Lorsch suggest two useful generalisations:

1 The functional type of structure is appropriate where the firm is faced with a routine and repetitive task. Under these circumstances integration can be achieved through plans, and conflict resolved by the hierarchy.

2 Where the task involves problem-solving, that is dealing with new situations, then the product organisation is more appropriate.

However, as the authors note, most firms are faced with a combination of both routine tasks and problem-solving, e.g. the marketing of established products and new product development. As a result most firms find it necessary to adopt some form of compromise as is evident from current organisation charts. The question of the most appropriate structure for the firm as a whole will be returned to following a consideration of the organisation of the marketing department per se.

ORGANISATION OF THE MARKETING DEPARTMENT

In practice it appears that the marketing department may be organised in one of seven basic ways:

1 *Functionally oriented.*

2 *Product oriented.*

3 *Market/customer oriented.*

4 *Regionally oriented.*

5 *Functional/product orientation.*

6 *Functional/market orientation.*

7 *Functional/regional orientation.*

A marketing department organised on functional lines is illustrated in Figure

21.1. Under this structure, personnel are grouped by functional specialisation and their activities are coordinated by the marketing director or manager. Such a system enjoys the advantages of simplicity and clearly designated areas of responsibility. On the other hand such advantages are often negated by the restricted outlook which such compartmentalisation inevitably breeds. There is a tendency for each department to plough its own furrow, and efforts to coordinate the diverse interests of specialists imbued in a specific functional practice can be exceedingly wasteful of managerial time and effort. The larger the company the worse the problem becomes. Firms with broadly differentiated product lines frequently organise their marketing functions on a product or product group basis. This form of structure, depicted in Figure 21.2, is only viable where each product or product group generates sufficient sales volume to justify the inevitable duplication of effort. Consequently, this form of structure is usually found in large, decentralised companies, where each division is concerned with the manufacture of a specialised product and may be regarded as a **strategic business unit** or **SBU**.

As an alternative to a product orientation, the hypothetical firm illustrated in Figure 21.2 might prefer to organise on a market or customer basis, when its organisation chart would appear as shown in Figure 21.3.

A regional marketing organisation is most frequently found in the case of a large, decentralised company with extensive markets capable of subdivision into distinct geographical units. It is particularly appropriate to multinational firms but, in common with the product and market structure, it suffers from duplication of effort, and problems of communication and coordination.

Figure 21.1 Marketing department organised on a functional basis

Figure 21.2 Product-oriented organisation

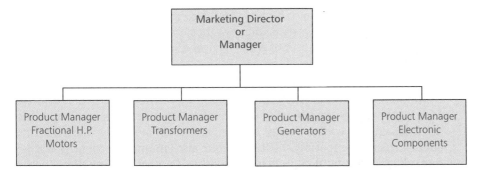

Figure 21.3 Market-oriented organisation

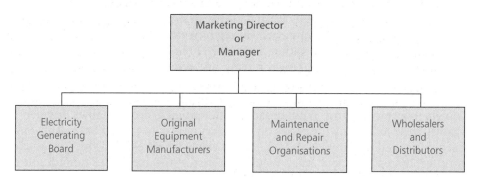

In an attempt to overcome these defects, many firms have adopted a line and staff structure which seeks to combine the benefits of functional specialisation with the varying demands of different products and markets. As there is still debate about the relative merits of organising on a product or market basis some discussion is appropriate here.

THE PRODUCT MANAGER CONCEPT

It is often implied that the **product manager concept** is of recent origin but there is evidence to suggest that General Electric had adopted such a title in the United States as early as 1894, while Libby, McNeil & Libby claim to have appointed product managers in 1919. Generally, however, the introduction of the concept is credited to its leading exponent, Procter & Gamble, who appointed a brand manager for Lava soap in 1928.

(Product manager and brand manager are interchangeable terms for the same basic function.) Essentially, the product manager's function is to coordinate all activities associated with the marketing of a given product – a function which became critical with the adoption of a product differentiation as a major dimension of competitive strategy. Opinions differ as to the precise responsibilities and authority of the product manager but, in general, it is possible to discern four major activities:

1 *Planning.* At the tactical level the product manager is usually responsible for the preparation of detailed plans for the marketing of their product, for example the preparation of budgets and determination of the precise mix of marketing inputs. At the strategic level they are responsible for anticipating change and the preparation of plans to deal effectively with this change, for example new product development.

2 *Information seeking and evaluation.* In order to anticipate change it is necessary continually to scan the environment and monitor the strength and direction of relevant trends. Specifically, this involves keeping track of competitors' activities in the widest sense; that is, one must not only keep informed about directly competing substitutes but also attempt to identify the less immediate threat implicit in new products and processes. Equally, one must

be sensitive to marketing innovations such as the development of automatic vending machines, systems selling, the Internet and so on.

3 *Coordination.* As the product 'expert', it is the product manager's responsibility to coordinate all those company functions which impinge upon the successful marketing of that product. Of all the functions, this presents the greatest challenge to the product manager as it inevitably requires him to be all things to all men. On the other hand these are the same skills required of top managers, and the product manager position can prove a valuable training and proving ground for senior appointments.

4 *Control.* This function not only incorporates the familiar price/cost and budgetary dimensions, but also includes the introduction of new products and the phasing out of old products.

No valid generalisation can be offered as to the relative importance attached to these four activities in practice as, of necessity, this will vary from firm to firm.

In an article 'Product Management versus Market Management', Michael J. Thomas (1982) looked at the role of the product manager and commented:

A long-time complaint of most product managers is that they are given responsibility without commensurate authority. But companies who have been filling product manager positions with younger, less experienced people have had to question how much responsibility should be delegated to their product managers. Responsibility often has been assigned for achievement of sales volume, market share, and sometimes profit goals but the product manager has no line authority over the functional departments that execute his plans.

Yet, we know that product or brand management works to the satisfaction of many companies. The key to understanding why is found in the expertise of the product manager. They know more about their product and the marketing plan that supports it than anyone else, and this expert power is the source of their being able to enlist the support of others. Thus the product manager is 'a recommender, a coordinator, and a watchdog who keeps an eye on his product and market place and sounds the alert when danger or opportunity arises' (Richard M. Clewett and Stanley F. Stasch, 1975, in 'Shifting Role of the Product Manager')

MARKET MANAGERS

As with any organisational innovation, the product manager system has not enjoyed unqualified success and many firms that adopted such a system during the first flush of enthusiasm in the late 1950s have since discarded it. In those instances where the product manager system has 'failed', examination usually reveals that the company was fundamentally unsuited to such an organisational structure. In a company like Procter & Gamble which is producing a group of nearly identical products from the same manufacturing facility, all of which are to be sold through the same distributive outlets, the product manager system ensures that each brand is given the individual attention it needs. On the other hand, where a company is selling the same product into a number of different end-use markets, emphasis on the product will be inappropriate. As noted earlier, the concept of market segmentation rests on the proposition that there are differences in the needs, and buying behaviour, of subgroups which collectively comprise the aggregate demand for a product. From this it follows that a different marketing strategy will be appropriate to each segment, which, in turn, predicates the appointment of market managers.

In the author's opinion the appointment of a market manager represents a better implementation of the marketing concept, for it is implicit that consumer requirements will take precedence over all other activities. It is an overt recognition that different market segments represent distinct, and often dissimilar, needs, not only in terms of precise product specification but also in terms of service requirements and buying behaviour. Further, in the case of industrial goods, it recognises that many buyers have a need for a series of related products which may usefully be combined into a 'system'; for example, National Cash Registers do not just sell business machines, they sell accounting 'systems' tailor-made to the end-user's specific requirements. Emphasis on the product may well result in the employment of salesmen specialising in given products and thus miss out on such opportunities.

As a broad generalisation it would seem that where customer buying habits are conditioned by the nature of the product and are similar across industry or user categories, then the responsibility for marketing should be vested in a product manager. Conversely, if it is possible to distinguish marked differences in the needs or buying behaviour of separate customer groups, then these should be regarded as different markets and market managers appointed.

However, as Michael Thomas (1982) points out in the article cited earlier, it would be a mistake to assume that the product-manager and market-manager approaches are mutually exclusive options. Thus:

> When companies have a variety of products channelling to a variety of markets, neither the product manager approach not the market manager approach alone is appropriate. This is a situation when a dual management approach could be utilised. If the product manager is used alone, it is very unlikely that he will be able to collect data and utilise market information for the entire market. On the other hand, if the market manager is used, he well most likely be concerned with the welfare of his own market and not care about anyone else's. He may want all the products and attention for his own market which can have a damaging effect on other markets and, in turn, on the overall effectiveness of the company.

Clearly, running product managers and market managers in tandem is a potential source of conflict, but Thomas and others regard this as a positive force which can be beneficial if managed correctly. Thomas cites B. Charles Ames (1971) who offers six rules for achieving this:

1 *Determine the need for dual management;*
2 *Define each manager's role;*
3 *Change the information and planning systems;*
4 *Select the right candidates;*
5 *Explain the concept to key functional managers;*
6 *Monitor the activities of both product and market managers.* (pp. 66–74)

Provided one can achieve and control the kind of matrix organisation which is required for such a dual management system, then 'The benefits of increased market opportunities, stronger competitive position, and, in the long run, greater profits far outweigh the added costs and conflict that will arise with its use' (Thomas, 1982). Table 21.1 summarises well the advantages and disadvantages of the kinds of marketing structures discussed this far.

Table 21.1 Comparison of marketing structures

Form	Advantages	Disadvantages	Situational Indicators
Functional	Specialisation in task activities to develop skills. Marketing tasks and responsibilities clearly defined.	Excess levels of hierarchy may reduce unity control. Direct lines of communication may be ignored. Conflicts may emerge. Integration problem for CME.	Simple marketing operations. Single primary product/market.
Product/brand	Specialisation in products/brands. More management attention to marketing requirements of different products/brands. Fast reaction to product-related changes.	Dual reporting. Too much product emphasis. More management levels and cost. Conflict.	Wide product lines sold to homogeneous groups of customers, but sharing production/marketing systems - i.e. proliferation of brands and diversified products requiring different skills/activities.
Market/customer/geographical	Specialisation in a market entity - focus on customer needs. Fast reaction to market-related changes.	Duplication of functions. Co-ordination problems. More management levels.	Limited, standardised homogeneous product line sold to customers in different industries - i.e. proliferation of markets each meriting separate efforts.
Product/market overlay	Advantages of functional product and market specialisation and integration.	Allocation of responsibilities is difficult. Duplication inefficiencies.	Multiple products and multiple markets.

Source: Piercy, N. F. (1985), *Marketing Organisation* (London: George Allen & Unwin).

THE IMPACT OF MARKETING ON ORGANISATIONAL STRUCTURE

In the organisational context, marketing may be viewed as both a **function** and a **philosophy**. All firms have marketing function, even if it only involves selecting an intermediary to sell their output, but not all firms have a marketing philosophy as embodied in the marketing concept and described in Chapter 1. Unfortunately, the distinction between the function and the philosophy is rarely stated explicitly, and has resulted in considerable misunderstanding and even acrimony.

As a function, marketing is no more, nor less, important than finance, legal, personnel, production, purchasing, research and development, or any other conceivable area of specialisation. In a given context it is only natural that more emphasis will be accorded to a specific function, which will tend to predominate over the others, but there is nothing to predicate that it will, or should, be marketing. The widely held misconception that marketers are seeking to take over other functional areas is a myth, albeit one fostered by the profession, which largely owes its existence to the high 'visibility' of marketing in the consumer goods field. Even so, firms manufacturing private brands will probably place far greater emphasis on production economies and quality control than on marketing. In the industrial goods field this tendency will be even more pronounced.

As a business philosophy, marketing requires the firm to do what it has always set out to do – combine the resources at its disposal in the manner which will best enable it to achieve its long-run profit goals. What distinguishes it from other business philosophies is that marketing perceives consumption as a **democratic process** in which consumers have the right to select preferred candidates and elect them by casting their money votes. As the political critics of marketing, and advertising in particular, should appreciate, you may delude the electorate once with spurious campaign promises but you had better not seek re-election. Further, unless you propose policies of which they approve you will have to give way to the candidate who does.

In the democratic environment of a **free enterprise economy**, success comes to the firm which sets out to discover the nature of human wants and develops products to satisfy such wants in highly specific ways. Satisfying customers can only be achieved through the concerted efforts of all members of the organisation recognising this as a common goal and working towards it. Thus, the production manager who insists on maximising productivity, in the conventional sense of maximum volume at lowest cost, by excluding non-standard items from their production schedule lacks a marketing orientation. S/he fails to see that the non-standard item might develop into a market leader, or that the fact that the salesman cannot offer it will predispose the firm's largest customer to switch to the company that can. Conversely, the production manager who balances the conventional criteria against such considerations is marketing oriented, despite their function and job title.

Acceptance of the marketing concept by individuals is insufficient in itself to make the firm marketing oriented – it must also develop an organisational structure that will permit it to translate thought into action. In today's increasingly competitive environment this demands that the firm be more creative and flexible than in the past; specifically, it requires:

- That the firm continually scan the business environment; that is, the firm must develop its own early warning system so that it is in a position not only to meet change but also to initiate it.
- That the firm utilise incoming data to formulate creative plans stating not only what it wishes to achieve, but also how and in what sequence.

- That these plans be communicated effectively to those charged with the responsibility for their implementation, and that such responsibility be backed with the necessary resources and authority
- That the firm make full use of new managerial techniques developed to assist the decision maker in arriving at an informed decision, for example management science and Bayesian decision theory.

At a given point in time, however, the firm's immediate success depends on its existing product line. If previous planning has been effective the production and sale of these products should be routine and demand a functional organisation. As noted, however, planning and new product development are problem-solving activities for which a functional structure is unsuited and some form of compromise structure is called for.

One solution is the setting up of project teams comprised of representatives from each of the functional departments (sometimes referred to as a 'matrix' organisation). Such a team may be formed on an ad hoc basis to suggest solutions to a particular problem, or to review suggestions from functional departments. Alternatively, the team may be established on a permanent basis and function as a separate department; for example, some companies have set up Long-range Planning Departments, New Product Development Departments and so on.

Another solution is evident in the trend to what has been termed 'recentralised decentralisation'. During the 1950s concepts such as the 'span of control' predisposed the management of large, diversified companies to decentralise authority on a divisional basis. Under this system each division operates virtually as a separate company, and sets up its own production and marketing organisations. In many instances, however, the benefits of specialisation were negated by diseconomies arising from duplication of effort and poor coordination, and prompted top management to recentralise certain functions at corporate headquarters. Foremost among these are purchasing and marketing. Centralised purchasing offers clear benefits due to the economics of bulk buying, while centralised marketing services permit greater specialisation and the development of a consistent marketing approach across the whole field of the firm's activities.

The protracted recession of the late 1980s and early 1990s had a considerable impact on organisational structure. As technological innovation and information technology have had their impact upon the production and manufacturing function, the numbers employed have declined significantly with a consequential increase of the numbers employed in service industries. In parallel with this switch in emphasis there has been a much wider acceptance of the marketing concept and recognition that this requires the organisation to develop relationships with its customers. To develop effective relationships firms must meet the expectations of their customers and this requires them to devote much greater effort to establishing their needs (**marketing research**), to add value by building quality into the product or service (**total quality management**) and to providing additional services to add value in consumption (**after sales service and customer care**).

The establishment and maintenance of **mutually satisfying exchange relationships** (our preferred definition of marketing) calls for a new approach to organisational structure. Two important aspects of this have been **delayering** and **empowerment**. By delayering is meant the reduction in the number of hierarchical levels to achieve flatter structures with less psychological distance between senior management and other employees. By empowerment is meant the willingness to devolve responsibility to the individual employee who, ultimately, is responsible for the quality of the firm's products and actions/ relationships.

In turn these changes have led to a reduction, or even elimination, of specialist service departments such as strategic planning. There is also evidence that some firms are greatly reducing their functional marketing departments, based on the belief that marketing is everybody's business, and giving increased attention to what has been termed 'internal marketing' in the belief that every employee is another's 'customer' and should behave accordingly.

The extent to which a firm can improve its competitive standing through organisational change is, in the final analysis, conditioned by the resources at its disposal and some reference to this dimension is called for.

CORPORATE CULTURE AND RESOURCES

In this chapter it has only been possible to look at the organisation of the marketing function in a superficial way when, as many readers will know, the topics of organisation design and development are the subject of books and courses in their own right. Before leaving the issue, however, it is vital to stress that, while organisational forms and structures may have an important part to play in determining a firm's efficiency and performance, as we saw in Chapter 2, it is the corporate culture which most often determines whether a firm will succeed or fail in the market place.

Although the concepts of climate and corporate culture have been around for several decades (indeed I used them myself in the 1960s and 1970s when researching innovativeness (see *Marketing New Industrial Products*, 1975) it was only in the 1980s and 1990s that they moved to centre stage with the recognition that it is the 'people factor' which ultimately determines the quality of a firm's performance. Given the accelerating pace of technological change and the growth in telecommunications, it is now estimated that even radical innovations will be diffused world-wide within 18 months of their first appearance. Maintaining a differential advantage in terms of the actual product or service has become increasingly difficult even in multinational corporations firmly committed to a policy of continuous new product development. Indeed, it is this very commitment which results in the rapid erosion of tangible product advantages and leads to shorter and shorter life-cycles. Under these circumstances it is the relationship between a supplier and user which is critical to user patronage and loyalty. In turn, the maintenance of the relationship depends upon the commitment and quality of the implementation by the supplier.

The validity of this claim was confirmed by the findings of numerous management books published in the 1980s based upon both anecdotal and rigorous survey based research (see, for example Peters and Waterman, 1982, *In Search of Excellence*; McBurnie and Clutterbuck, 1987, *The Marketing Edge*; and Baker and Hart, 1989, *Marketing and Competitive Success*). It was also the central theme in Stephen King's (1991) article 'Brand Building in the 1990s', in which he argued that the absence of objective differences will make consumers increasingly dependent upon the company 'brand':

It's arguable that in a competitive situation getting the company brand right is the most important job for the management. Equally, it's clear that not many companies have organised their management structures with that in mind. The companies behind the classic brands are not by any means a good model (indeed they may be increasingly wrong for their own purposes). They tend to rely too much on the traditional 'family tree' type hierarchy. That means they are too split by function to lead naturally to the innovation and imagination that any brand constantly needs. Decisions tend to be made too tactically, too low down in the organisation, with too little guidance from the top. The right organisation for a company brand implies that brand management should reside right at the top. And since inventive organisations tend to be based on small, flexible, interactive, multidisciplinary working groups, I think that our model (at a symbolic, rather than organisation chart, level) should be something like the figure ... [Figure 21.4]

The skills needed for this management working group would be those of production (the organisation and efficient running of the company's products/ services); personnel (recruitment/training/inspiring of the people who make up the corporate brand); communications (all aspects of communications, marketing and consumer/customer research); and possibly as a separate skill that of brand designer a new type of animal, concerned with design in its broadest sense (Lorenz, 1986), from R&D to adding services to products and vice versa, with a passion for the totality of the brand). The whole group to be led by the CEO – he's the real brand manager. However, such a model is translated into reality, it seems to me that many companies need to take a new look at their organisation charts, with brand-building in mind. Most authorities (e.g. Pascale and Athos, 1981; Doyle, Saunders and Wong, 1990) seem to agree that there will have to be a more flexible and less hierarchical approach, with more informal networking, in order to get the rapid response and to attract the rare skills that a successful company brand

Figure 21.4 New brand management

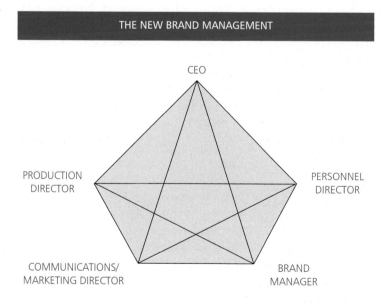

Source: King, S. (1991).'Brand Building in the 1990's', *Journal of Marketing Management*

needs. It clearly goes a lot further than organisation. What the best company brands represent is a common culture – common aims, standards, language, approaches and style. A common personality, rather than a book of rules. This may sound a little abstract and qualitative, but it is what consumers value in company brands (IBM, ICI or Marks & Spencer, for instance). That puts an enormous premium on sheer leadership from the top (Hamel and Prahalad, 1989). A company brand cannot succeed if the individuals doing the detailed work are zombies who aren't allowed to take any initiatives. Equally, it will not be a brand at all if there are no common links or if they don't know how they're expected to behave.

And so it has proved to be. Writing in 2003, (*The Marketing Book* 5th Edition), Nigel Piercy, a leading authority on marketing strategy highlights that the most significant challenge for marketing is **implementation** and so, by implication, the organisational changes necessary to achieve this.

First and foremost, Piercy emphasises the importance of internal marketing of the kind we referred to earlier. While marketing research and planning may be the primary responsibility of marketing specialist, the conversion of this into high quality products or services and the building of relationships with loyal customers are the responsibility of everyone in the organisation.

Quite recently the author was involved in helping run a one week course on marketing for a major Services organisation. At the Chief Executive's request everyone was to take exactly the same course and, because everyone could not be released at the same time, each group comprised people from all activities

In an interview with Angela Jameson of *The Times* (16/01/06), Todd Stitzer, CEO of Cadbury Schweppes since 2003, outlined his own leadership theory that he calls "The rule of ates".

""Ates" is a tool that Stitzer uses to communicate his vision for the company to his 55,000 employees around the world. "Create, communicate, motivate, evaluate, innovate and celebrate. You need to create strategy by analysing where you and your business are. When you have that strategy, you need to communicate that strategy, right to the bottom of the organisation. Then you need to motivate them to deliver on the strategy, then you need to evaluate what they have done, then you need to innovate – either to correct what didn't go well or improve what they did well. Finally, you need to celebrate."

"Of the "ates", communicates appears to be the key, Stitzer has introduced a gamut of communication initiatives. He has also made clear that he detests the thought of managers sitting in their offices and e-mailing each other." He says "I could sit at my computer and do e-mail all day, but e-mail is the antithesis of communication. I've frequently said that a smile icon doesn't do it for me. Show me your face and show me your smile."

Frequent voicemails and telephone conferences, backed up by visits, enable Stitzer to keep in touch and get his message across. While freely admitting to be in the 'treats and indulgences' business he refuses to be demonised by current campaigns against obesity. "Britain's weight problem has nothing to do with scoffing Dairy Milk instead of meals." Obesity is not a food problem, it's a whole life problem," Stitzer says. Exercise, healthy eating, home cooking – these are the antidotes to getting fat."

in the organisation. Before long it became clear that 'marketing' was despised and disliked by everyone else, and bore little if any relation to the philosophy and function we were advocating. The marketing people were seen as arrogant, condescending, and too big for their boots, with little appreciation of the extent that they depended upon everyone else from the Mail Room, Switchboard and Reception up for the implementation of their plans. Clearly, this came as a great shock to the CEO and the senior marketing personnel who perceived a marketing orientation as meaning that marketing 'ran' the organisation and that all else was subservient to this. As noted in the introduction, this interpretation of a 'marketing orientation' is at odds with Drucker's original conceptualisation of a market orientation meaning that everyone's efforts should be directed at the market and the delivery of customer satisfaction. Fortunately, the programme we were running which, essentially, was about internal marketing was able to correct the situation and resulted in more effective implementation through better co-ordination of all the human resources.

Implicit in all of this is the belief that it is the truly marketing oriented company which is most likely to have the kind of corporate culture which will ensure that its objectives match precisely those of its intended customers.

Corporate resources

The resources which a company has at its disposal are of two main types – human and physical. Such resources may be internal to the organisation, or they may be external to it in the sense that the firm can gain or exercise control over them, for example the distributive channel. Within the firm, resources, both human and physical, tend to be specific, and so limit the possible range of production and marketing activities which the firm can undertake. In the long run, however, the firm can change its 'resource mix', and the aim of planning is to determine:

- *What activities will maximise the productivity of existing resources?*
- *What markets offer the greatest potential in future?*
- *What changes need to be made in the present resource mix to enable the firm to exploit these future opportunities?*

Clearly, the answers to these questions must be based on an analysis of existing resources, which will be facilitated by the use of a check-list on the following lines:

1 *Physical resources*
- Land   – as a source of raw materials.
           – as a location for manufacturing and distributive activities.
- Buildings   – general purpose or specific, i.e. designed for light engineering, assembly, storage, etc., or for heavy manufacturing requiring special foundations, services, etc.
- Availability of and access to
           – power supplies, drainage and waste disposal
           – transportation: road, rail, canal, port facilities, etc.
- Plant equipment
           – general purpose, e.g. lathe, press
           – specific, e.g. steel rolling mill, foundry, etc.

2 *Technical resources.* Essentially these reside in the technical expertise of the firm's employees, together with the possession of patents, licences or highly specialised equipment.

3 *Financial resources.* These are comprised of the liquid assets in the firm's balance sheet, the ability to secure loans against fixed assets and the ability to raise capital in the market on the basis of past and anticipated future performance. They also comprise the skill of the firm's financial management.

4 *Purchasing resources.* Managerial expertise backed by any special advantage enjoyed by the firm by virtue of its size or connection; for example reciprocal trading agreements.

5 *Labour resources.* The skills, experience and adaptability of the work force.

6 *Marketing resources.* The degree of consumer/user acceptance or 'franchise' developed through past performance. Access to and degree of control over distribution, the specialised skills and experiences of its personnel.

The above list is by no means exhaustive but serves to indicate the factors the firm must take into account when appraising its own ability to undertake a given course of action. Clearly, the importance attached to any particular factor will depend upon the unique nature of the problem under consideration. A good example of this is provided by Samsung Electronics which set up a Global Marketing Operation (GMO) in 1999 to be responsible for the development of the Samsung brand. The GMO comprises three teams each with a different responsibility (Quelch and Harrington, 2005), namely:

1 *Marketing Strategy Team* responsible for:
   - Developing global marketing strategy
   - Controlling the GMO budget
   - Controlling the global brand campaign in coordination with Samsung's in-house agency and outside advertising agency
   - Controlling the *Samsung.com* web site and Internet-related partnerships with service providers and other corporations
   - Overseeing global customer relationship management strategies and shared marketing best practices across subsidiaries.

2 *Regional Strategy Team* responsible for:
   - Planning strategic direction for regional markets
   - Interfacing with line managers to set the market budgets by region.

3 *Product Strategy Team* responsible for:
   - Conducting market research and gathering and analysing information on competitors
   - Planning corporate marketing exhibits at trade shows
   - Conceiving and implementing strategic marketing alliances and "killer" new product concepts.

SPORTS MANAGEMENT

The success of the England teams in winning the World Cup for rugby in 2003, and the Ashes in 2005, prompted considerable interest in the management principles followed by the coaches of the successful teams. In feature articles in the Sunday Times Clive Woodward proposed a 'Top Twelve' of leadership lesson while Duncan Fletcher set out ten 'Golden Rules'. As the Table suggests while there is an overlap between the two lists, it is also clear that leaders develop their own styles of management.

Woodward's top twelve

- Good leadership is transferable across disciplines.
- Passion is all. No leader will succeed without it.
- Enjoyment is a business term.
- Only hire those who pass the '24-hour' plane journey test.
- Achieve success through setbacks, and build on success.
- Remove all 'energy sappers'.
- Establish 'teamship' rules at the outset.
- Make use of the creativity of everyone in your organisation.
- For a fresh view, go outside your industry.
- Never follow tradition for its own sake.
- Don't neglect any detail. It could make all the difference.
- Understand your team. Don't get up too close.

Fletcher's golden rules

- Joint leaders don't work.
- Never be afraid to hand responsibility to people.
- Co-opt the rebellious by awarding them management responsibility.
- Listen to what your team is telling you.
- Always be sensitive to the human balance of your team.
- If you show faith in individuals they will repay you.
- Commitment for the manager is itself a motivating force.
- Only criticise in private.
- For every action, there is a reaction - always establish the root of a problem.
- Recruit character - its very difficult to change mental make-up.

Summary

In this chapter we have looked at some of the more important factors which influence the role and positioning of marketing within an organisation. In doing so we have returned to the distinction developed initially in Chapter 1 that marketing is both a philosophy of business and a business function. Ironically, as more organisations accept the former proposition so the importance of the marketing function becomes more widely diffused through the organisation. This leads, in turn, to a lesser emphasis upon the formal marketing department. Indeed, the new organisational structures place emphasis upon organisations as networks rather than hierarchies.

An authoritative discussion of these changes and trends is to be found in the *IEBM Encyclopedia of Marketing* (Piercy and Cravens, 1999) in which the authors (Piercy and Cravens) summarise some of the most significant organisational implications of environmental and strategic change in marketing as follows:

1 *Breaking hierarchies* – speed and flexibility come from reducing organisational levels and numbers of employees, creating precise and

flexible execution of programmes (Quinn, 1992; Doyle, 1997)

2 *Reengineering* – critical organisational processes will be radically restructured to reduce cost and increase speed and flexibility (see Hamner and Champney, 1993) and to improve responsiveness to customers (Quinn, 1992).

3 *Key organisation processes* (e.g. new product planning) comprise the fundamental building blocks for new organisational designs (Porter 1996; Day 1994).

4 *Self-managing teams* – critical changes will be managed by groups with complementary skills (see Katzenbach and Smith, 1993) in the form of high-performance multi-functional teams to achieve fast precise and flexible execution of programmes possibly organised around market segments (Schultz, 1993), and possibly temporary (Doyle, 1997) – perhaps in the form of the 'collateral' or 'supplemental' organization like the task force for the major innovation (Huber, 1984).

5 *Modularity in product design and production* is changing the architecture of organisations (Baldwin and Clark 1997).

6 The *new economics of information* is altering the power structure of organisations through the widespread availability of information (Evans and Wurster 1997).

7 *Transnational organisations* – competing globally requires more complex structures and new skills (see Barlett and Ghoshal, 1989).

8 *Learning organisations* – organisations will require the continual upgrading of skills and the corporate knowledge-base (Doyle, 1997), leading to the adding of value for customers through knowledge feedback to create competitive advantage (Quinn, 1992).

9 *Customer management* – customer focus may be achieved by structural mechanisms (Schultz, 1993; Doyle, 1997).   (p.198)

Source: Piercy, N. F. and Cravens, D. W. (1999), 'Marketing organisation and management', in Baker, M.J. (ed.) *IEBM Encyclopedia of Marketing*, (London: Thomson Learning)

Subsequent developments and their implications are elaborated on further by Piercy (2003) who observes:

"More recently the organisation of marketing in Britain has been characterised by the downsizing and closure of conventional marketing departments, reinforced by the impact of category management and trade marketing strategies, and the resurgence of the power of sales departments and key account management structures in managing customer relationships in business-to-business markets".

In turn these changes have led to a perception of marketing more as process which cuts across traditional functional boundaries, a trend we anticipate will continue.

Review questions and problems

1 Distinguish the salient differences between the functional and product forms of organisational structure. Under what circumstances is each to be preferred?

2 What is the 'product manager concept'? Name five firms which have adopted this concept. (See the classified ads for clues!)

3 How does the concept of market management differ from product management? When is the former organisational structure to be preferred?

4 What distinguishes the marketing oriented firm from those which have not adopted the marketing concept?

5 Using published data, e.g. annual reports, articles in the trade press, etc., and/or personal knowledge/experience, summarise the corporate resources of a major manufacturing company. Based on your summary, what recommendations would you make to the firm's top management concerning its future strategy, i.e. on what markets/products should it concentrate its efforts?

6 Discuss the proposition that the position of the marketing department in the total organisation is particularly difficult because of the types of conflicts which tend to occur between the logic of customer satisfaction and the cost minimisation logic pursued by other departments.

7 The system of organising marketing divisions around the job of the brand manager, or product manager, has recently been widely criticised. What criticisms of this system would you expect to be valid in practice, and what opportunities does this system offer for more effective marketing management?

8 The marketing function is so central to the company's continued success that it requires to be carefully controlled by those in charge of the company. Outline a comprehensive system of such controls on marketing to ensure top management retain the responsibility with which they are charged.

9 Indicate the types of conflict which might arise in a firm employing sales, marketing and product managers and the ways in which these might be organisationally resolved.

10 Write a job description for a product manager in either:
(a) A typical company making products for industry;
(b) A typical consumer goods company.

11 In what ways would the Marketing Manager of a large company be able to do a more effective job if they were appointed to the Board as Marketing Director? How would their responsibilities change?

12 It should be possible to assess the extent of a company's commitment to marketing by looking at its organisation chart. Discuss.

13 Companies differ greatly in the organisation of their marketing functions. Discuss these differences and explain the reasons for them.

14 How does a production/sales based business organisation differ from a marketing based one?

15 Discuss the organisational implications of a company progressing from being sales oriented to being marketing oriented.

16 Consider the scope and duties of the product manager in his/her relationship with one of the following organisational functions:
(a) Research & Development;
(b) Sales Force;
(c) Manufacturing.

17 Review some of the characteristics of new organisational designs and assess their implications for marketing strategy.

18 What factors have prompted a changing view of the role of marketing in the organisation in recent years?

19 What is internal marketing? Why is it as important as external marketing?

Key terms

after sales service
communication
corporate culture
corporate resources
customer
customer care
delayering
democratic process
differentiation
empowerment
evolution of marketing
  organisation
free enterprise economy
function
functional specialisation

hierarchical frameworks
implementation
integration
internal marketing
market managers
market orientation
market oriented organisation
marketing department
marketing orientation
marketing research
matrix organisation
mutually satisfying exchange
  relationships
new brand management

people factor
philosophy
product manager concept
product or brand manager
  concept
product oriented organisation
product specialisation
product, market and brand
  managers
recentralised decentralisation
role of marketing
span of control
strategic business unit (SBU)
total quality management

Supplementary reading list

Piercy, N. F. (2003), 'Marketing implementation, organisational change and internal marketing strategy', in Baker, M.J. (ed.) *The Marketing Book*, 5th edn, (Oxford: Butterworth-Heinemann).

Piercy, N. F. (2002) *Market Led Strategic Change: A Guide to Transforming the Process of Going to Market*, 3rd. Edition, (Oxford: Butterworth-Heinemann)

Piercy, N. F. and Cravens, D. W. (1999), 'Marketing organisation and management', in Baker, M.J. (ed.) *IEBM Encyclopedia of Marketing*, (London: Thomson Learning).

Quelch, J. A., and Harrington, A. (2005), 'Samsung Electronics Company: Global Marketing Operations', *Harvard Business School*, February. *Case 9-504-051*

22

PLANNING AND IMPLEMENTING MARKETING

| Learning Goals | *After reading this chapter you will be familiar with:* |

■ The nature of corporate strategy and the key phases in the strategic process – appreciation, plan and implementation.

■ The design and execution of marketing audits.

■ The design, layout and content of a formal marketing plan.

■ The nature of 'marketing metrics'.

■ The calculation of mark-ups, discounts and stock turn.

■ The application of standard costing and budgetary control to marketing planning.

■ Ratio analysis and its use in competitive analysis.

INTRODUCTION

In the previous chapter we examined a variety of approaches to the marketing function with a view to identifying the most appropriate structure for its effective management. As we noted in the introductory chapters effective management involves four basic activities – **Analysis, Planning, Implementation** and **Control** – hence the **APIC** model, and these are the subject of this chapter. However, rather than 'analysis' we will use a term used in developing military strategies – **appreciation** by which we mean an evaluation of all the factors, both external and internal, that determine the possible courses of action open to an organisation. While evaluation of the external factors was dealt with in some detail in Chapter 4, less attention has been given to the internal factors that govern an organisation's strengths and weaknesses. Assessment of these is by means of a **marketing audit** and we describe what this involves.

Planning is a pervasive human activity by which we seek to exercise some degree of control over the future. As a process it will vary enormously depending upon a number of variables, foremost among which will be the complexity of the activity and the degree of uncertainty concerning the future situation in which the activity will take place. Fundamentally, however, all planning seeks to arrive at a present decision concerning future action – the more complex the activity and the more uncertain the future, the greater the need for formal, systematic planning procedures.

The purpose of this chapter is to provide a brief synthesis of the extended discussion of the marketing environment and the various mix elements which have been the primary focus this far to indicate how the marketer can integrate all these considerations into a marketing plan. It must be stressed that this is the briefest of introductions to a large and complex subject, which is dealt with at length in *Marketing Strategy and Management* (Baker, 2001) which was written specifically for those students who have completed an introductory course of the kind provided for by this text. Marketing planning does not figure prominently in such introductory courses, and the brief discussion provided here is intended solely to emphasise the point that the various marketing functions described earlier need to be seen as part of a coherent and integrated action plan if they are to be used effectively. However, the effectiveness of a marketing plan can only be established after it has been implemented in terms of how well it has achieved the desired objectives. To determine this we need to measure outcomes using appropriate metrics, and then use these to control the implementation. It is these topics that form the subject matter of this chapter.

THE CONCEPT OF CORPORATE STRATEGY

Several of the themes contained in this chapter have already been introduced earlier. For example in Chapter 2 we defined strategy and the importance of setting clear objectives. We also suggested that the purpose of marketing planning was to match the organisation's strengths with market opportunities while avoiding threats and eliminating any weaknesses in its competitive armoury. To do this we recommended the use of a marketing audit and SWOT analysis. Some reference was also made to the concept of corporate strategy, as, for example, when discussing new product development, but some elaboration is necessary here. Like marketing, corporate strategy is an old concept in a new and revitalised form. Probably the most important distinction between strategy as practised by earlier generations of entrepreneurs and today's professional managers is that the latter consciously and explicitly state their aims and objectives and develop plans designed to achieve them. In his book *Strategy and Structure*, Alfred D. Chandler (1962) defines corporate strategy as 'The determination of the basic long-term goals and objectives of an enterprise, and the adoption of courses of action and the allocation of resources necessary for carrying out these goals'.

This definition suggests three distinct phases in the strategic process:

- *Appreciation;*
- *Plan;*
- *Implementation.*

Each of these stages is capable of further subdivision, and we summarised these earlier as:

- *Diagnosis*: where is the company now, and why?
- *Prognosis*: where is the company headed?
- *Objectives*: where should the company be headed?
- *Strategy*: what is the best way to get there?
- *Tactics*: what specific actions should be undertaken, by whom, and when?
- *Control*: what measures should be watched to indicate whether the company is succeeding?

This sequence is very similar to the **APACS (Adaptive Planning and Control Sequence)** developed by the Marketing Science Institute (see Patrick J. Robinson and David J. Luck, 1964) described in Chapter 9, namely:

- *Step 1*   Define problem and set objectives.
- *Step 2*   Appraise overall situation.
- *Step 3*   Determine the tasks to be accomplished and identify the means to achieving these aims.
- *Step 4*   Identify alternative plans and mixes.
- *Step 5*   Estimate the expected results arising from implementation of the alternative plans.
- *Step 6*   Managerial review and decision.
- *Step 7*   Feedback of results and post audit.
- *Step 8*   Adapt programme if required.

In turn, each of these models is capable of further subdivision, but the basic three-stage model – **Appreciation, Plan, Implementation** - will serve our purposes here.

APPRECIATION: THE MARKETING AUDIT

This section builds on the ideas first introduced in Chapter 2. In 1959 the American Marketing Association published an extensive management report entitled 'Analysing and Improving Marketing Performance: Marketing Audits in Theory & Practice'. While much has been written since, this still remains the most comprehensive treatment of the subject and provides the framework for this section.

According to Edward B. Reynolds (1959):

The term 'audit' is generally understood in business usage to mean a review or appraisal of some business function or activity. As a management tool, it is traditionally used to determine the accuracy and adequacy of accounting and financial operations
. . . In the field of marketing, however, the application of the audit technique as a device for evaluating not only the operational aspects of marketing but also the philosophy and policies upon which marketing operations are based is still a far from common practice.

This is certainly not the case today in marketing where auditing is also used as a device for evaluating possible future courses of action in addition to its traditional role as a means of assessing past performance. Thus, while audits first came into use as a diagnostic device for sick and ailing companies they are now used by many organisations for a regular 'check-up'.

In his Introduction, Reynolds discerns a wide range of views on the nature and practice of the audit but identifies general agreement on four basic points:

1   A planned review is an essential requirement not only for the company in difficulty but also for the company enjoying an apparently sound marketing operation.

2   The evaluation of the marketing operation must be all inclusive, involving not only every marketing activity and every marketing practice but also the underlying marketing philosophy and policies upon which these activities and practices are based.

3   The most significant requirement for successful appraisal is the establishment of valid and realistic standards of performance.

4   The evaluation process must not confine itself to the marketing operation as it exists today but must range into the future to explore untapped marketing possibilities.

Subsequently, Abe Shuchman (1959) argued that it is important to distinguish the marketing audit from the continuous evaluations which executives make of the various marketing mix functions, on the grounds that such appraisals are far too limited in scope and are not undertaken in a planned and coherent fashion. 'They do not, within a specified interval, examine each and every facet of the total operation. There is no integrated, co-ordinated, comprehensive appraisal encompassing all marketing activities and executed systematically in accord with a planned program and schedule.' Thus he defines a marketing audit as:

a systematic, critical, and impartial review and appraisal of the total marketing operation: of the basic objectives and policies of the operation and the assumptions which underlie them as well as of the methods, procedures, personnel, and organisation employed to implement the policies and achieve the objectives.

Shuchman also emphasises that the marketing audit is a prognostic as well as a diagnostic tool:

The audit is, in addition, concerned with identifying the particular strengths of the marketing operation. It is a search for opportunities, existing and potential . . . Continued success requires continual adaptation to a constantly changing environment. It requires, therefore, continual scrutiny of the environment and of the firm's relationship to the environment, with the aim of spotting the ones which indicate both a need for modifying the firm's marketing program and the direction such modification should take. It requires an unremitting search for emerging opportunities that can and must be exploited if the marketing operation is to remain highly successful.

The need to implement a formal programme of market auditing is that otherwise marginal adjustments to facets of the mix may well result, collectively, in the operation getting out of synchronisation with its environment; that is, there is a difference between 'fine tuning' and 'tinkering'. Similarly, auditing needs to be continuous: 'in marketing as in home maintenance the time to fix the roof is when the sun is shining'.

Shuchman also identifies several problems associated with auditing:

1 Defining appropriate criteria or measures for assessing the effectiveness of the mix elements and marketing activity.

2 Selection of auditors.

3 Scheduling the audit.

4 The impact of the audit.

Alfred R. Oxenfeld in 'The Marketing Audit as a Total Evaluation Program' argues that in the absence of a formal plan of evaluation some aspects will be appraised frequently and possibly at excessive costs while some phases of the business go unappraised for very long periods – often until the company is experiencing serious difficulties. Accordingly, a marketing audit must comprise the review of objectives, policies, organisation, methods, procedures and personnel in a total evaluation programme. He then proposes five broad approaches:

1 Audits classified by *major marketing functions*;

2 Audits classified by *managerial aspects*;

3 Audits classified by *standards of appraisal*;

4 Audits classified by *frequency of evaluation*;

5 Audits classified by *sources of evaluation*.

In auditing the marketing mix it is essential to do this in an integrated way so that the contribution of the individual elements may be related to each other and not just looked at in isolation. In the latter case it is quite likely that optimising on one dimension will lead to sub-optimisation on others, and it is the maximum overall effect which is being looked for. In other words, one is seeking to achieve the optimum 'balance' between the various mix elements while, at the same time, one is monitoring them for incipient problems.

Auditing in terms of the major managerial aspects of the marketing function(s) is complementary to the auditing of the actual functions themselves, and should be executed in terms of the six dimensions (objectives and so forth) identified previously.

When auditing the objectives of a given activity one should ask the manager responsible to give you an explicit statement. Frequently such statements reveal important differences in emphasis and approach, and it is essential to ensure that such differences do not render specific objectives incompatible with each other, or with the overall purpose of the organisation.

In a recent consultancy assignment for a national non-profit organisation, it was found that Headquarter's concern with the level of subsidy required by its operational units which had led to exhortations to these units to increase their revenue generation activities, was diametrically opposed to the objective that the units give priority access to designated users at nominal charges – that is, the direct opposite of normal commercial practice whereby priority is given to those able and willing to pay the highest price, and surplus capacity is sold off at marginal rates. Clearly, until one resolves such a contradiction of scrambled objectives, operating managers will be unable to determine the appropriate policies and tactics for the management of the function or operation for which they are responsible.

As Oxenfeld notes, it is sometimes difficult to distinguish sharply between objectives and policies in practice, but in principle the difference is clear.

'Objectives represent goals and targets; policies represent broad principles which indicate how management believes these goals can best be achieved, and therefore are guides for decision and action.' Such a distinction underlines the desirability of seeking to specify objectives and policies with the greatest possible clarity in order to avoid confusion between ends and the means of achieving them.

Once the objectives and means of achieving them are clear, the auditor must seek to determine whether the remaining four elements of organisation, methods, procedures and personnel are appropriate to each sub-function, such as advertising and sales, as well as to the marketing function overall.

The third approach to classifying marketing audits suggested by Oxenfeldt is in terms of the standards of appraisal used. By definition auditing is a process of making comparisons, usually between current and past achievement, so that one can assess the rate and direction of change in the parameters being evaluated. In turn such an analysis is an essential prerequisite to the formulation of future objectives against which performance can be evaluated.

In making a comparative analysis one may use both quantitative and qualitative methods and there is a fairly vigorous debate about which is most appropriate in what circumstances. The nature of the argument is well exemplified by the comparisons which many academics and managers make between leading business schools, such that Harvard is seen as being concerned with a qualitative emphasis upon judgemental decision-making while Chicago stresses precise measurement and quantitative analysis. In turn this leads commentators to classify Harvard as a school for general (line) managers and Chicago as a school for specialist (staff) managers. Of course, what the example points out is that you can make comparisons by emphasising differences while, at the same time or for other purposes, one could easily have stressed similarities and argued that Harvard and Chicago are identical in that they are first rate business schools. As in most things the truth lies somewhere in between and an effective marketing audit will call for a judicious blend of both quantitative measurement and qualitative judgements. That said, there is much to be said for seeking to quantify subjective and judgemental appraisals through the use of Bayesian analysis as described in Chapter 11.

A further factor which has to be taken into account when devising marketing audits is the frequency of evaluation. The basic guide here must surely be the cost effectiveness of the auditing procedure, and one must beware of dissipating managerial time upon the collection of data for its own sake. Similarly one must not gravitate to the other extreme of assuming that managers are paid to make judgements and so need not dwell upon facts.

Finally, Oxenfeldt addresses the question of who should carry out the auditing function (source of evaluation). Five basic alternatives suggest themselves.

First, auditing may be considered the responsibility of the person in overall charge of an activity – 'auditing from above'. Second, one may invite a person from another functional area but at the same level in the organisation. Third, one can commission a 'task force' of individuals from various other areas in the organisation. Fourth, one can adopt a scheme of self-appraisal. And finally, one can bring in outside consultants to carry out the task. Each of these alternatives has its merits and demerits but, as a general principle, an audit is only likely to enjoy the confidence of a management group if it is actually involved in the auditing process itself to some degree. That said, most authors prefer a task force approach where this is feasible (usually restricted to large companies) followed by the use of external consultants. Where a company is attempting a marketing audit for the first time, and needs to establish both a base line (where we are today) and a procedure for implementing auditing on a continuous basis, then it is unlikely to possess the necessary expertise from within its own ranks and so will prefer to commission an experienced consultant to perform the task.

In the same manner that an overall management audit is an essential prerequisite of corporate planning, so the marketing audit is an essential prerequisite of marketing planning. In making this implied distinction, that corporate and marketing planning are different, one must be sensitive to the issue raised in Chapter 1 concerning the difference between the marketing concept and the marketing function. Following this distinction, all marketers and the great majority of successful managers would argue that in setting its corporate objectives the organisation should give priority to the needs of the market – in other words the corporate plan should be marketing orientated. However, this does not make it a marketing plan for, to be strictly accurate, such a plan is concerned with the management of the marketing function per se and its interface with the other functional areas of the business. These other functional areas will have management plans of their own (R&D, Purchasing, Production, Finance), each of which will be designed to implement the overall corporate plan. By the same token a corporate management audit will involve an evaluation of all the functional areas and go far beyond the scope of a marketing audit internally.

Externally, however, the position is very different and it is this which sometimes leads people to perceive corporate and marketing audits and plans as being the same thing.

Because it is through the market that the organisation seeks to realise its objectives, much of its external evaluation of threats and opportunities is highly consonant with the primary concerns of the marketing function. Such distinction as one would make would tend to emphasise the corporate analysis of its environment as being conducted at a macro level, while the external marketing audit is largely concerned with micro aspects. However, to conduct a micro analysis of, say, brand shares it is necessary to have some feeling of the status of the market itself and whether it is expanding, contracting or stationary vis-à-vis other competitive markets – namely, the macro position. For these reasons corporate and marketing audits of the external environment will possess a high degree of overlap although their emphasis will differ substantially

PLANNING

At this stage in the process it is important to distinguish clearly between the environmental constraints within which the firm must operate, and those activities over which it can exercise control. It is also important to recognise that in the long run all fixed constraints are variable in some degree – thus, in the short term, management must accept the existing distributive network, in the long term it can modify it through its own action, just as it can develop new markets and shape the nature of competition. However, in time the environment will change too, owing to technological innovation and competitive activity, and the firm must seek to develop objectives which are sufficiently well defined to require commitment, yet flexible enough to permit a change in emphasis and direction as the situation evolves. 'Servicing the travelling public' is a good example of an overall long-term objective which meets these criteria. In the short term, the skill lies in developing strategies which make the best use of available resources in moving the firm from where it is to where it wants to be.

The statement in the preceding paragraph reflects the reality that most planning is undertaken by existing organisations which comprise a mix of assets, resources and skills which are being deployed to service an existing market and customer base. By contrast most textbooks tend to follow the opposite assumption that the planner is in a green field or new start-up situation and so can follow the best theoretical advice of first establishing a need, and then organising resources and skills to satisfy it. This latter approach has the advantage that it allows one to spell out best practice (what is sometimes called the 'normative theory') and recommends what needs to be done in what sequence if the circumstances allow. Usually, however, this is a counsel of perfection, and most managers spend their time seeking to identify opportunities which will enable them to make optimum use of existing strengths and resources while, at the same time, seeking to adjust the future direction of the firm to ensure that it will have the necessary resources and skills to avoid future threats and exploit future opportunities.

The normative theory of strategic marketing planning is a subject in its own right and the student should consult one of the specialised texts recommended in the Supplementary Reading List for further information and advice.

The preparation of a marketing plan

If the author has segmented the textbook market correctly, many readers will be preparing for examinations, such as those set by the Chartered Institute of Marketing, which require the student to analyse a case study and prepare a written marketing plan. Hopefully, the following outline will help the student in preparing such an analysis.

Analysis of the situation: appreciation

There is little point in restating the descriptive content of a case as the objective of an appreciation is to define the central issue. This is probably best achieved by a systematic analysis of the available material in terms of:

1 What business is the company in and what are the salient features of this business?
2 What is the firm's goal, explicit or implied?
3 What resources has the company
   - Productive?
   - Technical?
   - Financial?
   - Marketing?
4 What policies, explicit or otherwise, has it adopted in respect of these resources?
5 Is there a single strategic variable which dominates all others – if so, what is it?

6 Has the firm any special skill or distinctive competence?

In analysing the case (or problem, in real life), one should seek to isolate those areas which bear directly upon both the immediate problem and the more general problem of which it is symptomatic. Once these areas have been defined they should be ranked in some rough order of importance and analysed in detail. For example, if a major issue is the nature of the product itself, one should list all the advantages and disadvantages which one can think of to permit an overall conclusion to be drawn. Similarly with all other issues. The conclusions drawn from the separate analysis of the relevant issues should then be summarised and stated as the basis upon which the plan has been based. This statement should also make explicit any assumptions which have been made, together with the reasons which support their adoption.

The marketing plan

This must be realistic in the light of the analysis described in the appreciation, and should commence by stating the overall objective or aim. If a student feels that the company's stated aims are incapable of attainment they must be able to present a very convincing argument as to why, and how, they should be changed. Thus the statement of the long-term aim must be supported by an exposition of all those factors which will affect the company's ability to achieve its objective, paying particular attention to environmental changes and changing customer needs. Following the statement of the long-term aim, the plan should state the short-term objective and the specific policies to be adopted to achieve it. In the interests of both clarity and coverage of all salient factors, some form of outline should be used similar to that given below:

SCENARIOS

Risk assessment and contingency planning usually involve the development of scenarios in which one develops visions/description of possible future states and then seeks to provide answers to the question "What if ….?"

As a technique, scenarios first came into prominence in the 1960s when Shell incorporated them as an essential part of its corporate planning activities. One scenario projected a major increase in oil prices as a result of some major event/catastrophe. When the 1973 Yom Kippur war precipitated such a crisis Shell was better prepared than most, and experienced less damage than its competitors. A compelling reason to encourage other organisations to include scenarios into their long-term planning .

Scenario planning is just as valuable for the smaller company as it is to the multinational operating on a global scale. Obviously, the scope will be more limited and focused, but the approach is much the same. To begin with one can extrapolate the likely impact of current actions and decisions under a variety of different assumptions and prepare alternative action plans to deal with events as they unfold. A more ambitious approach is to envision possible future states; select the one that has the greatest appeal and then devise plans to achieve that outcome – planning to make the future happen.

While predicting the future is notoriously difficult, there is considerable evidence that those that seek to do so in a structured way are more likely both to influence and exercise a degree of control over it.

1 *Short-term aim*, for example to increase market share by 5 per cent;

2 *Forecast of market conditions* for the period of the plan;

3 *Statement of further marketing research* to be undertaken to provide feedback on performance and to be used in the preparation of future marketing plans;

4 *Statement of product policy*;

5 *Statement of pricing policy*;

6 *Statement of packaging policy*;

7 *Statement of distribution policy*;

8 *Statement of advertising and sales promotion policy*;

9 *Statement of sales policy*;

10 *Budget statement* with explanation of how it is to be used for control purposes;

11 *Outline of how the plan is to be financed*;

12 *Timing for implementation of various policies*;

13 *Feedback and control procedures*.

Clearly, the amount of detail will vary considerably depending upon the central issue identified in the appreciation, and the data available. It should be remembered, however, that the overall marketing plan cannot be expected to go into the same detail as would be expected of, say, the media plan, but it should provide the skeleton around which such plans can be prepared by the various functional specialists. In an examination context, the main intention is to discover whether the candidate has acquired a sufficient understanding of theoretical principles, and these should always be outlined, even though case data is not available for purposes of exemplification. For example, if the case concerns a convenience good the student may consider sales promotion relevant, even though it is not specifically referred to, and so might suggest the use of a banded offer designed to increase consumer sampling, achieve increased consumer and retail inventories, and so on.

Finally, the impact of a marketing plan will be lost if it lacks clarity of expression, no matter how logical the sequence or how sophisticated the analysis. To this end, students must practise expressing themselves clearly and concisely in order to convey the maximum information in the least number of words.

IMPLEMENTATION AND CONTROL

In essence a strategy is a broad statement of the means to be employed in achieving a given objective, while the actual methods used constitute the tactics. Thus, a firm's strategy might be based on skimming the cream off the market, which suggests that the appropriate tactics would be:

- *High product quality;*
- *Distinctive design and packaging;*
- *High price;*
- *Selective distribution;*

- *Direct sale;*
- *Extensive after-sales service;*
- *Low pressure advertising, etc.*

At the risk of overstating the obvious, the success of a given strategy depends upon the coordination of the tactics into an integrated, complementary and cohesive whole. There is a finite number of alternative strategies open to the firm and, in a given market, it is usual to find several competing firms pursuing the same basic strategy simultaneously. If this is so, then observed variations in performance must arise out of the quality of the plan, or statement of tactics, and its execution. Factors such as motivation and morale have an important bearing on the execution of a plan, but also tend to be a function of the plan's quality and credibility.

The reason managers should set clear objectives is so that they have a benchmark against which they can measure the consequences of their actions, and then take such corrective moves they consider necessary. The difficulty is that objectives are based on assumptions about environmental conditions, competitive reaction, buyer behaviour etc. any or all of which may turn out to be very different from those anticipated. It follows that no strategy can be implemented slavishly without due regard for possible changes in the assumptions on which it is based. It is for this reason that management guru Henry Minzberg talks of '**emergent strategy**' by which he means the adaptation of the strategy in light of changing conditions. Such a strategy is commonplace in many situations where one has imperfect information and is acting under conditions of uncertainty; for example

As part of the combined code on corporate governance sponsored by the UK Financial Reporting Council, directors are required to identify potential risks to the organisation and prepare contingency plans for dealing with them.

In an article in *The Times* (January 13, 2006) Graham Searjeant, the Financial Editor, reported on plans drawn up by HSBC, the world's third biggest bank for dealing with a global bird flu epidemic. The impact of such an epidemic is estimated by the World Bank to result in a loss of £310 billion in advanced Western economies, with the Asian Development Bank projecting about half that amount for its region. These estimates compare with a loss of £20 billion, mainly experienced by the Hong Kong tourist trade, as a result of the 2003 SARS that killed 800 people,.

HSBC is projecting that as many as half of its employees could be affected; double the projection of the Department of Health and the World Health Organisation. In Searjeant's view this is prudent and, rather than increasing fears, raises the profile of risk assessment and contingency planning. As he comments: "Contingency planning is as old as Joseph's advice to Pharaoh on grain stocks. The richer economies become, the more we have to lose and the more sense it makes to avoid losing it. Trying to defend America from the impact of an asteroid may sound like an affectation of people with more taxpayers money than sense. All risks are not equal. The test is to assess the degree of risk against the cost of countering it."

Risk assessment and contingency planning are essential aspects of strategic planning in a volatile world environment.

sailing or gunnery.

In the case of shooting or gunnery it is generally believed that the sequence of actions is Ready, Aim, Fire when the reality is usually Ready, Fire, Aim. Now, of course, one takes aim at the target but it would be extremely surprising if the first shot were to hit it. While we might expect the wind to blow our shell off course and, in the case of gunnery will have collected all kinds of data about the weather to try and correct for it, we will consider ourselves lucky if the shell lands in the close vicinity of the target. But, once our first shell has landed we can correct our aim to allow for the conditions and, by a process of trial and error, achieve a hit. And so it is with management, a process of fine adjustments to take account of the prevailing conditions. In this sense then a strategy does 'emerge'. Unfortunately, many people mistakenly believe Minzberg is arguing for making strategy up as you go along. The real point is that, if you don't have an objective in the first place, how could you know that corrective action was called for?

In general, marketers are frequently criticised for their lack of adequate control information. By comparison with the engineer, who can measure the quality and performance of a product in very precise terms, or the accountant, who can explain to the penny where revenue is earned and what it is spent on, marketing has been poor at measuring the consequences of its actions, and using such information to make better informed decisions. A major reaction to this criticism has been the emphasis given to **marketing metrics**. Indeed this topic has been identified as the most important issue for research by the Marketing Science Institute in the USA for the period 2000 – 2004 based on the views of the practitioners who provide the funding for its research programme. Accordingly, we will look at some of the main issues associated with the subject before looking at the more prosaic, but equally important, topic of '**marketing arithmetic**'.

MARKETING METRICS

One of the leading experts on the subject of marketing metrics is Tim Ambler of the London Business School who, as qualified accountant built a formidable reputation as a marketing practitioner before 'retiring' to academe. At LBS Ambler headed up a research project sponsored by The Marketing Council and several other leading organisations into the subject of 'Marketing Metrics' which led to the publication of *Marketing and the bottom line* (2000, 2nd edition 2003). The purpose of the project was "to report best practice in marketing performance measurement" and "to pinpoint the non-financial factors that lead to business success".

In order to measure marketing performance it is necessary first to define what marketing is. As we have seen, this is not an easy task and Ambler identified at least three different approaches with which you should now be familiar. These are 'pan-company' 'functional', and 'budgetary'.

Pan-company marketing is something that an organisation has to do whether or not it recognises marketing in any explicit way "The difference lies between those who consciously espouse this customer-oriented philosophy and those who market by happenstance".

"'**Functional**' marketing is what marketing professionals do and this varies from business to business." As we saw in the previous chapter, there are numerous different organisational approaches to the practice and implementation of marketing with a trend even in large organisations to diffuse the responsibility for the function throughout the organisation.

As for 'budgetary' marketing this "sees marketing as an expenditure which means largely advertising and promotion" and when people talk about the return on marketing it is this they are usually thinking about.

In Ambler's view the first definition is the most important as every organisation has customers to satisfy, irrespective of their formal commitment to 'marketing', and so his focus is on what all the members of an organisation do to generate revenue and create wealth. In other words, "Marketing is the creation and harvesting of inward cash flow".

In order to establish what might be suitable metrics for measuring marketing performance, Ambler devotes two chapters to issues of brand equity and financial fallacies. We have already looked at the importance of brand equity as a summary statement of the value placed on an organisation beyond that attributed to its other usually physical assets, and also at some of the problems of trying to quantify this. As for 'financial fallacies' the main problem is that the modern approach is to reduce everything to single measure of Shareholder value. The problems with trying to do this are at least three.

First, while it may be possible to attach a quantified value to most aspects of a business many of these would be based on subjective judgements and so unsuited to the statement of a financial value.

Second, techniques that place a discounted present value on predicted future outcomes such as customer lifetime value (CLV) or brand values can only be assumptions that depend upon the effectiveness of current marketing which is what the organisation needs to focus on.

Third, "Shareholder value is a useful technique for determining how best to spend cash flow but it makes little contribution to understanding where it comes from." And it is the latter that is the major concern of marketing – looking ahead to identify potential threats and opportunities and devising plans to protect the organisation and ensure a healthy and prosperous future.

Having dealt with these three issues, the remainder of the book is focused on the specification and use of appropriate metrics. To begin with it is likely that the firm will have basic financial measures of costs, sales and profits but, of course, these are retrospective and do not address the detail of marketing activity. What are needed are data on market, competitor and customer behaviour and many of the measures of these such as awareness, loyalty, trust etc. are qualitative and expressed in non-financial terms. The problem tends to become one of information overload. What senior management is looking for is a limited repertoire of key performance indicators (KPI) that summarise the detail needed by the front line marketing management. It is these that comprise the 'metrics'.

Ambler is of the opinion that the selection of metrics should be delegated to the Chief Financial Officer, who is the person that will have to integrate both financial and non-financial marketing metrics for presentation to the Board, and more likely to be seen as independent and objective than if the marketers are responsible for selecting them. Further, by giving Finance the responsibility the two functions will have to work together leading to a better understanding of their respective viewpoints.

In Ambler's view metrics fall into four main categories. First, there are the standard profit and loss account metrics of sales, measured in terms of volume and value and market share when compared with the competition; marketing investment and share of voice compared with competitors; and profitability. Next there are measures of brand equity which comprise six major elements – familiarity, penetration, what customers think about the brand, what they feel about it, loyalty and availability. The other two categories are concerned with internal measures of marketing performance – innovation and employees – the importance of which have been stressed many times already.

A more broadly based discussion of the measurement of marketing effectiveness is to be found in Chapter 20 of *The Marketing Book* (2003) by Keith Ward. Like Ambler, Ward stresses the importance of shareholder value and stresses that "Shareholder value is only created when total returns are greater than required returns" i.e. exceed normal expectations given the amount of perceived risk. In other words, shareholders are concerned with future performance, and marketing has a major role to play in identifying those courses of action most likely to maintain and improve this. It follows that "many marketing activities should be evaluated and controlled as strategic investment decisions" (511) using rigorous financial evaluation procedures, albeit, as Ambler notes, these don't usually place sufficient emphasis on the marketing actions needed to generate the desired cash flows.

Ward also makes the important distinction between investment in future development and investment in maintenance to protect the value of the asset, citing the **metric of awareness (share of voice)** as one that is particularly susceptible to erosion if promotional expenditures are not kept up. He also stresses the need to monitor and vary maintenance expenditures in accordance with the product's life cycle while emphasising how the introduction of new products can transfer brand equity from a declining product to a new one.

Attention is also drawn to a major problem with expenditure on marketing activities in that it is almost invariably treated as an expense for accounting purposes and written off in the year in which it is incurred. Given this approach, the marketing budget is vulnerable to cuts to achieve short-term financial targets, which completely ignores the investment nature of many marketing activities.

Detailed study of strategic marketing planning, and the selection of relevant control measures to monitor marketing effectiveness, are subjects more suited to advanced study. In an introductory course a more germane issue is keeping track of day-to-day transactions using familiar accounting and finance techniques which we review in the next section.

MARKETING ARITHMETIC

On first acquaintance one of the more confusing aspects of marketing is the basic financial data associated with selling – mark-up, discounts, and stock-turn – and that necessary to monitor the financial health of the marketing function – standard costing, budgetary control and ratio analysis. While these factors, and the latter particularly, are more properly the province of a financial text, a brief overview is essential to underline their relevance to marketing and encourage more detailed study. (It is appreciated that many students will be pursuing a broadly based course which includes a study of accounting and finance. Such students should regard the next few pages as basic revision material.) Each of the topics identified is the subject of separate treatment in the following pages.

Mark-up

This is the amount which a firm adds to its cost of goods in order to arrive at its selling price, i.e.

$$SP = C + M$$

where SP = selling price; C = cost of goods; and M = mark-up or margin.

The mark-up, or margin as it is sometimes termed, is intended to cover selling, general and administrative expenses ('SGA' in some accounting texts and case studies) as well as a percentage for profit. The convention which frequently causes confusion is that mark-up is usually expressed as a percentage of selling price rather than cost, probably due to sellers working backwards from a going market price, as would be essential under conditions of perfect competition. That is, one accepts the market price, deducts the desired profit, assesses the SGA associated with the anticipated volume of sales and deducts this, and is left with the amount for which the product will have to be made. If this amount is less than the actual cost, one will have to accept a lower profit, or even a loss, or decide not to produce, while if it is greater an above-average profit becomes possible.

Four basic calculations are frequently called for in connection with margins and mark-ups and these are as follows:

1. Determination of selling price when costs and percentage mark-ups are given. Since the selling price always equals 100 per cent we can substitute the data given into a simple formula to arrive at the *retail price*; that is:

$$C + M = SP$$

Thus if cost = £100 and the mark-up = 25 per cent, then:

$$
\begin{aligned}
£100 \quad &= \quad SP - 25\,\% \\
&= \quad 100\,\% - 25\,\% \\
&= \quad 75\,\% \\
\therefore \ £SP &= \quad \frac{£C}{100\% - M} \\
&= \quad \frac{£100}{75\%} \\
&= \quad £133.33
\end{aligned}
$$

2 To find the *margin,* given cost and selling price, using the same figures as above, we have:

$$C + M = SP$$

$$M = SP - C$$

$$M = £133.33 - £100$$

$$M = £33.33$$

This may be expressed as a percentage of the selling price:

$$M = \frac{£33.3}{£100}$$

$$= 33.3\%$$

3 To convert a margin based on selling price to one based on *cost.* Here the formula is:

% margin on cost

$$= \frac{\% \text{ margin on selling price}}{100\% - \% \text{ margin on selling price}}$$

$$= \frac{33.3}{100 - 33.3}$$

$$= 50\%$$

4 To convert a margin based on cost to one based on selling price:

% margin on selling price

$$= \frac{\% \text{ margin on cost}}{100\% + \% \text{ margin on cost}}$$

$$= \frac{50}{100 + 50}$$

$$= 33.3\%$$

Discounts

The calculation of discounts is a constant source of confusion due to the fact that a discount is always expressed as a percentage of the *reduced* price and not the original retail selling price.

For example, a 25 per cent discount on £100 is in fact £20 and not £25; that is:

$$discount = \frac{amount\ of\ discount}{original\ price - discount}$$

$$= \frac{20}{80}\ (i.e.\ 100 - 20)$$

$$= 25\%$$

(Note: in American texts/case studies, discounts are often termed 'mark-downs'.)

Stock-turn

As the term suggests, the stock-turn is the number of times the stock 'turns over' during a given period and gives a useful indicator of how a particular type of outlet is performing. Clearly the rate of stock-turn will vary enormously according to the nature of the goods sold, being fastest in fresh foods and slowest in durables such as furniture or luxuries such as jewellery, cameras and so on. There is usually a direct relationship between the margins which manufacturers anticipate in recommending a retail selling price and the stock-turn of the average outlet. It follows that more efficient outlets (that is, those with lower operating costs) will earn higher net profits if they maintain margins and achieve average stock-turn. However, in recent years many retailers have pursued a more aggressive strategy designed to increase market share, and thereby long-term profitability, by offering discounts and increasing stock-turn.

To compute stock-turn one must divide net sales for the period by the average inventory (at selling price) for the same period. *Average inventory* is simply:

$$\frac{opening\ stock\ +\ closing\ stock}{2}$$

while net sales is total sales less any returns or allowances.

Standard costing and budgetary control

Traditionally, the accounting function concerned itself solely with recording the historical performance of an organisation. It is for this reason that many people seek to differentiate between the major business functions by characterising accounting as an orientation to the past. By the same token production is seen as being preoccupied with the present – a 'present orientation' – and marketing is conceived of as a 'future orientation', with an emphasis upon the planning and control of future activities. Nowadays such a simplistic distinction would be very far from the truth, for all business functions are conscious of the need for forward planning, and the need to control operations so as to achieve the desired outcome. Standard costing and budgetary control have been developed for just this purpose.

In his excellent introduction to the subject, *Costing: A Management Approach*, A. H. Taylor (1974) expresses the view that defining standard costs as predetermined costs or yardsticks fails adequately to 'convey the fundamental change in viewpoint of costing which occurs when a standard costing system is instituted in place of an historical costing system'. Taylor goes on to say:

> *The standard cost is what the cost of an operation or service ought to be under given conditions and subject to given conventions of costing. It is thus a notional amount which depends entirely on the conditions predicted. It is this notional amount which is treated as the value of the stock and the cost of the goods sold. The conditions associated with a standard cost are essentially a standard of efficiency and a level of activity. Using material as an example, the standard material cost of a product implies the purchase of*

the required quantity of material at an economic price and in economic lots. This in turn implies the existence of a production plan and a storing policy. All the standards inherent in the elements of cost which comprise a product cost or the cost of an operation are interdependent. To carry the argument to the extreme, it could be said that the standard costs derive from the corporate plan.

Put another way, using standard costs is very similar in principle to the economist's use of *ceteris paribus*: it enables one to predict outcomes due to the interaction between factors under consideration given no change in all the other factors which might influence that interaction. In this sense standard costs do act as yardsticks, for they enable management to ascertain whether the business is performing as planned according to the predetermined conditions necessary for that achievement – conditions which it is management's responsibility to create. Any departure or variance from the standard will immediately warn management of a difference between planned and actual which will enable it to analyse the nature of the variance, and the possibility of rectifying it. Of course, all variances are not negative, though this is most often the case in periods of inflation when costs are often rising in an unpredictable manner which cannot be accommodated when setting the standard cost. However, when positive variances do occur it is equally important that management be aware of the fact so that they may capitalise on an opportunity if such exists, for example a seasonal fall in raw material prices.

It must also be emphasised that conformity with the standard should not be accepted at face value, for it may well conceal countervailing trends – for example, a fall in cost due to greater machine efficiency counterbalanced by increased labour or material costs. Thus to use a standard costing system as one of management by exception could be dangerous. Its major benefits lie in its requirement that one should plan future operations; that is, prepare a budget, identify the conditions necessary for the successful execution of the plan, the creation of such conditions and the comparison of actual and planned performance as the basis for controlling activities (hence 'budgetary control').

To cite Taylor again:

The merits of a standard costing system may be summarized as follows:

1 *Information is provided for managerial control through the comparison of actual expenditure against standard expenditure.*
2 *The analysis of variances between actual expenditure and standard expenditure saves managerial time, because the managers need only give their attention to those operations where substantial variances occur.*
3 *Stable and presumably, sound figures of cost are provided to assist price determination.*
4 *Stable values are assigned to stock and work in progress, thus eliminating . . . anomalies . . . and assisting in the production of a true and fair view of profit and a reliable trend of profitability.*

For a discussion of the anomalies mentioned, of costing principles and their managerial use the reader should refer to the original source or consult one of the texts in the Supplementary Reading List.

Ratio analysis

In most countries, trading organisations are required to publish an annual statement of their financial affairs – most usually a **balance-sheet**, which summarises the financial position, and a **profit-and-loss account**, which is a statement of income and expenditure. The manner in which companies choose to publish these financial statements varies enormously, from the elaborate and extensive documents put out by large public companies to the minimum required by law characteristic of most private firms. However, even this minimal information can provide an analyst with a great deal of insight into the strengths and weaknesses of an organisation, and the purpose of this section is to indicate a small number of ratios which can enable such an evaluation to be made. (Such analysis is particularly important for students preparing for formal examinations using the '**case method**' as most cases contain financial statements. Only if you are able to interpret these can you decide whether or not they are relevant to the marketing problem you have been asked to solve.) The more common ratios may be grouped under four headings:

Investment measures

(a) *Return on equity*

$$= \frac{\text{Profit after tax}}{\text{Shareholders' funds}}$$

(b) *Earnings per share*

$$= \frac{\text{Profit after tax}}{\text{Number of shares issued}}$$

(c) *Price/earnings ratio*

$$= \frac{\text{Market price per share}}{\text{Earnings per share}}$$

(d) *Dividend yield*

$$= \frac{\text{Dividend per share}}{\text{Market price per share}}$$

(e) *Dividend cover*

$$= \frac{\text{Earnings per share}}{\text{Dividend per share}}$$

Measures of performance

(f) *Return on net assets*

$$= \frac{\text{Earnings before interest and tax}}{\text{Net assets}}$$

(g) *Profit margin*

$$= \frac{\text{Earnings before interest and tax}}{\text{Sales}}$$

(h) Asset turnover

$$= \frac{Sales}{Net\ assets}$$

Measures of financial status solvency

(i) Debt ratio

$$= \frac{Long\ term\ debt}{Capital\ employed}$$

(j) Interest cover

$$= \frac{Earnings\ before\ interest\ and\ tax}{Interest}$$

Liquidity

(k) Current ratio

$$= \frac{Current\ assets}{Current\ liabilities}$$

(l) Acid test

$$= \frac{Liquid\ assets}{Current\ liabilities}$$

The purpose of all the foregoing ratios is to enable an analyst to conduct a spot check on the financial health of an organisation in much the same way that a doctor takes one's pulse, temperature, blood pressure, and so forth. Diagnostically, ratios are used in combination so that a satisfactory outcome for one test is not sufficient to guarantee that all the others will yield the same result. Accordingly it is necessary to work systematically through a series of tests before a clean bill of health can be issued. Which series of tests is most appropriate will vary according to one's viewpoint, but in general all analysts will wish to consider liquidity, solvency and performance, with less importance attached to investment measures per se.

Summary

The dominant model of marketing management developed by Philip Kotler sees this as involving four major activities – **Analysis, Planning, Implementation** and **Control** – hence the APIC model. In this chapter we reviewed each of these in a fairly limited way as their detailed study is more properly the subject matter of more advanced courses. However, some overview is necessary to illustrate how the various ingredients of the mix discussed in detail in Part III need to be co-ordinated and integrated in a marketing strategy, and then put into practice by means of a detailed marketing plan.

Accordingly, we started with a brief reprise of the concept of **corporate strategy** which drives the APIC model. While 'analysis' is seen as the first stage in developing a strategy and plans for its implementation, we preferred to use the military term **appreciation** to describe this phase.

Essentially, this is because 'analysis' usually carries the connotation of 'quantitative', whereas 'appreciation' acknowledges that because strategy is concerned with the future, and usually involves guessing the intentions of the competition, a considerable amount of judgement is called. As we were to see later in the chapter when discussing metrics, judgement calls for a combination of objective (**quantifiable**) and subjective (**qualitative**) data.

The appreciation requires the decision-maker to evaluate both the external environment, which establishes the threats and opportunities facing the organisation, and the internal environment that underpins its strengths and weaknesses. As the external environment had been dealt with at length in Chapter 3 the focus was on the organisation itself by means of a **marketing audit**. Having defined the nature and objectives of the audit, consideration was given to some its advantages and disadvantages. Particular stress was given to the need for clear and unambiguous objectives to ensure the use of appropriate measures. Several different kinds of audit were identified together with ways of implementing these.

Once we have a clear appreciation of the situation and of the organisation's objectives, the next step in the process is to devise a plan for their achievement. The steps involved in preparing a plan given the kind of description contained in a case study was outlined, as was the content of the marketing plan itself.

The third phase in the process – implementation was linked with control as the two are seen to be inextricably joined together. Aspects of implementation were raised in connection with each of the elements of the mix described in Part III, so the main emphasis was on the methods to be used to measure how effective implementation is so that corrective actions may be taken if necessary. First, we considered **marketing metrics** which are all kinds of measures, both qualitative and quantitative, that are needed to evaluate overall performance in terms of creating stakeholder value. Metrics are mainly used for strategic purposes while day-to-day management control is achieved through a variety of accounting and financial techniques that were reviewed under the heading marketing arithmetic.

A recurring theme throughout the book has been that marketing planning and execution must be tailored to the situation facing an organisation. While the advice given thus far is considered to be of general application, the next two chapters deal with two 'special cases' – marketing in foreign environments and the marketing of services.

Review questions and problems

1 'Management's sensitivity to strategy should be proportionate to the instability of the environment of the firm'. Explain this statement and emphasise in your answer the major characteristics of strategic change, and the problems to be encountered by the firm committing itself to such change.

2 What would be the main headings in an annual marketing plan? Select one of these headings and show the detail with which it would be concerned, explaining how the content of your detailed section of the plan would be related to the whole.

3 'While the marketing planner is the central figure in drawing up the annual product plan, other departments in the company will make important contributions to the final plan.' Discuss.

4 Describe how a marketing audit might be conducted in a firm, and evaluate the contribution of such auditing to overall marketing control.

5 Leading businessmen have been quoted as relying to a large extent on the regular submission and analysis of financial ratios from the trading companies under their control. Why do you think they regard such measures of control as so important?

6 What is the function of a Marketing Plan and how does it relate to the Corporate Long-Range Plan of an organisation?

7 Explain the purpose and application of any six of the commonly used financial ratios relating to the operation of a business.

8 'Every major business enterprise requires a clear long-term marketing strategy in order to enable it to fulfil its obligations to its employees, shareholders and society.' Discuss.

9 Marketing planning begins with an analysis of a variety of factors including an internal audit of the firm's capabilities. What are the major factors to take into account in such an internal audit?

10 What arguments might you use to persuade a business organisation of the need to develop strategic marketing plans?

11 What are marketing metrics? What role do they play in
   (a) Controlling current performance ?
   (b) Planning future strategy ?

12 Marketing expenditure should be treated as investment. Discuss.

Key terms

adaptive planning and control sequence (APACS)
analysis, planning, implementation and control (APICS)
appreciation
appreciation, plan, implementation
auditing from above
average inventory
balance-sheet
Bayesian analysis
brand equity
budgetary marketing
case method
comparative analysis
control
corporate strategy
cost of goods
customer lifetime value (CLV)

emergent strategy
financial fallacies
frequency of evaluation
functional marketing
future orientation
implementation
key performance indicators (KPI)
margin
marketing arithmetic
marketing audit
marketing metrics
marketing plan
mark-up
metric of awareness
normative theory
objective
pan-company marketing

planning
present orientation
profit-and-loss account
qualitative
quantitative
ratio analysis
retail price
selling price
selling, general and administrative expenses (SGA)
share of voice
shareholder value
standards of appraisal
stock-turn
subjective
SWOT analysis
task force

Supplementary reading list

Ambler, T. and Kokkinaki, F. (1999), 'The assessment of marketing performance', in Baker, M.J. (ed.) *IEBM Encyclopedia of Marketing*, (London: Thomson Learning).

Ambler, Tim (2003), *Marketing and the bottom line*, 2nd edn, (London: FTPrentice Hall)

McDonald, M. (2003), 'Strategic marketing planning: theory and practice', in Baker, M.J. (ed.) *The Marketing Book*, 5th edn, (Oxford: Butterworth-Heinemann).

Sizer, J. (1989), *An Insight into Management Accounting*, 3rd edn (Harmondsworth: Penguin).

Stapleton, J. and Thomas, M. (1998), *How to Prepare a Marketing Plan*, 5th edn, (Aldershot: Gower Press)

Ward, K. (2003), 'Controlling marketing and the measurement of marketing effectiveness', in Baker, M.J. (ed.) *The Marketing Book*, 5th edn, (Oxford: Butterworth Heinemann).

Wilson, R. M. S. (1999), *Accounting for Marketing*, (London: Thomson)

THE MARKETING OF SERVICES

23

INTRODUCTION

One of the most striking features of the last three decades has been the enormous growth in the service sector within the world's advanced industrial economies. In part this growth has been due to the relentless acceleration in the pace of technological change which has resulted in significant improvements in productivity. In part it is due to the fact that the slowing down of population growth in these countries has reduced the expansion of demand for physical goods. And, in part, it is due to the flood of low cost, high quality imports from newly industrialised countries. Taken together these trends have seen a marked shift in employment from the secondary or manufacturing sector to the tertiary, services sector accompanied by a similar shift in expenditure patterns from goods to services. In this chapter we will first review the nature and extent of this growth in services before examining the factors or characteristics which are seen as differentiating services from physical products – intangibility, inseparability, heterogeneity, and perishability and fluctuating demand.

Examination of these distinguishing characteristics leads naturally into a discussion of whether the **marketing of services** is similar to or different from the **marketing of physical goods**. As one might expect two schools of thought exist – those who claim they are the same, and those who claim they are different! Our analysis will suggest a compromise and argue that, while the basic principles are equally applicable to both, the distinctive nature of services calls for an **extended marketing mix** comprising *seven elements* with **process**, **physical evidence** and **people** being added to McCarthy's familiar four Ps of **product**, **place**, **price** and **promotion**. Each of these is explored in some detail and points to the potential for applying marketing principles and ideas to the whole range of economic activity, including the service sector.

However, in the same manner that it is necessary to adjust the nature of the marketing mix to suit the nature of the product and the market which it serves, so it is with services. In the case of services this need is emphasised because as Shostack (1982) has observed:

the difference between products and services is more than semantic. Products are tangible objects that exist in both time and space; services consist solely of acts or process(es), and exist in time only.

She believes that:

the basic distinction between 'things' and 'processes' is the starting point for a focused investigation of services. Services are rendered; products are possessed. Services cannot be possessed; they can only be experienced, created or participated in.

Table 23.1 summarises some typical differences between manufacturing and service industries.

Table 23.1 Some typical differences between manufacturing industry and service industry

Manufacturing	Service
The product is generally concrete	The service is immaterial
Ownership is transferred when a purchase is made	Ownership is not generally transferred
The product can be resold	The service cannot be resold
The product can be demonstrated before purchase	The service cannot usually be effectively demonstrated (it does not exist before purchase)
The product can be stored by sellers and buyers	The product cannot be stored
Consumption is preceded by production	Production and consumption generally coincide
Production, selling and consumption are locally differentiated	Production, consumption and often even selling are spatially united
The product can be transported	The service cannot be transported (though 'producers' often can)
The seller produces	The buyer/client takes part directly in the production
Indirect contact is possible between company and client	In most cases direct contact is necessary
Can be exported	The service cannot normally be exported, but the service delivery system can

GROWTH OF SERVICES

The growth in service can be seen by the increase in employment in the service sector and the growth of services' contribution to **Gross Domestic Product (GDP)**. In 1971, services accounted for 48 per cent of GDP; in 1993, the share of employment in the service sector was 68 per cent, and by 2003 it was over 70 per cent. The reasons for the growth in services can be attributed to the following:

1 *Impact of technology* – The major technological breakthroughs achieved in recent years have been one reason for the growth in services. Technology has had a significant impact on the volume and quality of products now available, and it has been suggested (Markin, 1982) that more goods or products often lead indirectly to an increased demand for services as a result of the 'knock on' or 'multiplier' effect.

2 *Deregulation and increased competition* – In certain industries there have been changes governing the market entry requirements for firms which has resulted in greater opportunities for service companies to offer more services to customers more easily. For example, this has been a prominent feature of the financial sector in the UK, where building societies introduced cheque accounts, and created a competitive advantage over the bank by offering interest on these accounts which the banks have had to match. Likewise, banks now offer mortgages to customers and estate agents can now provide complete legal services as part of a house sale and purchase for clients.

3 *Customer sophistication* – As society becomes wealthier, and people have more time available compared with 30 to 40 years ago, the basic needs in life such as housing and food are more easily satisfied, and people begin to spend more of their income on wants, rather than needs. In this respect, they do not need more cars, refrigerators or clothing, but increasingly use their income to follow other, more leisure-based activities, such as holidays, eating out or taking up new hobbies.

Types of services

Services may be mainly **professional** or **consumer oriented**. Professional service firms may serve the business-to-business market, the private individual or may serve both market segments. Professional services are often characterised by the following: advisory and problem solving; provided by a qualified professional known for their speciality; include an assignment requested by the client; provided by a professional who is independent and not connected with other suppliers; supervised by professional associations which attempt to define the nature of the profession, to lay down requirements of competence, to control the practice of the profession and to enforce a code of ethics (Gardner, 1986). These would include services like financial advice, advertising, business and management consultancy, engineering, architectural and interior design, legal, and medical; to which may be added other agencies and brokers, such as estate agents, stock and insurance brokers and market research agencies (Yorke, 1990). Those firms which tend to be non-professional again may either be in the business-to-business market, or be consumer oriented. Those services which may be included in the former category can include office catering services, cleaning services, or offer cash transference services such as Securicor. Those service firms which may be in the latter category are the ones which the consumer is more acquainted with, such as holiday tour companies (for example Thomsons, Lunn Poly), fast food outlets (for example Burger King, McDonald's) or entertainment companies (for example Mecca, Canon).

THE NATURE AND CHARACTERISTICS OF SERVICES

The characteristics of services have been classified under four main headings, namely intangibility, inseparability, heterogeneity, perishability and fluctuating demand (Stanton, 1981).

Intangibility

Intangibility is probably the single most important factor in distinguishing services from goods. While it is possible to describe the nature and performance of physical products using objective criteria, this is only possible to a limited extent in the case of services. Intangibility has two dimensions (Bateson, 1977) – the physical inability to touch an item and the mental difficulty in accepting an idea. Although it may be possible to get opinions or attitudes from friends or colleagues about a service before purchase is made, there is no guarantee that their perceptions will match your own. These characteristics have important implications for marketing planning.

The evaluation of competition is more difficult compared with goods purchasing since the customer can touch most products to evaluate them, whereas the customer has to search for tangible clues of the service in order to evaluate it.

Another important aspect of the intangibility factor is the ease with which services can be imitated and the lack of formal patent protection – which leaves service organisations the problem of distinguishing themselves from their competitors. Shostack (1982) states that, 'while "that which is marketed" may still be a simple product or unadorned service, it is often a more complex combination of products and services'. Clearly, the tangible and objective features of some goods will dominate, while the 'physical evidence' associated with some services will be very minor and we may think of a continuum from product dominant to service dominant goods as illustrated in Figure 23.1.

However, some marketers regard the physical nature of a product as secondary in the sense that buyers are primarily concerned with the 'bundle of satisfactions' which flow from the product, rather than the product itself – for example the technical specification of a television set is rarely considered by the user, who will probably judge it on the basis of picture and sound quality as they appear to them. Further, as has been pointed out (Wickham et al., 1975), for many products tangibility does not permit physical evaluation in any meaningful way, so that such products tend to be selected on the basis of reputation, advice and experience rather than on the basis of physical examination. If this is the case, determining the benefits that consumers want or expect would be a more powerful means of developing effective marketing strategies.

Inseparability

The second differentiating factor of services is inseparability – that is to say, there is no distinction between delivery and use due to many services being produced and consumed simultaneously. Unlike manufacturing firms, the sale of the service must be made before production and consumption occurs and the customer receives the 'product' they are buying at the same time as it is being supplied. For example, you must be physically present at the dentist to receive dental treatment, or at the hairdressers to have your hair cut. In this way therefore, a retail outlet may encounter problems with unobliging staff, a restaurant may have a poor chef, or a businessman may be unhappy with the bank teller's attitude on a Monday morning.

Similarly, the service company must realise the significance of customer participation in the process. For example, customers may not have the ideal knowledge of filling out an application form for a mortgage or bank loan, completing their tax return, or even know how a self-service petrol pump works. This then breaks down the production/consumption interface because the customer is behaving in a difficult way for the firm. Therefore, service firms need to control the production side of the service as much as possible through the use of internal marketing, as customers' perceptions of the service can be badly affected by the quality of the input, as well as making the service easier to

Figure 23.1 The product-service continuum

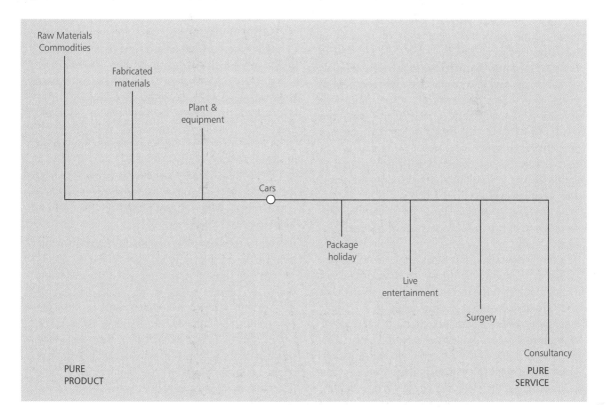

use for customers. The company must remember that some customers may not complain to the service firm directly about the poor quality service they received, but would rather show their dissatisfaction by taking their custom elsewhere, or spreading the news around their friends or colleagues about the poor treatment they received. (**Negative word-of-mouth**).

Heterogeneity

The third characteristic which distinguishes services from goods is the ability to be uniform or standard. Services are **heterogeneous**, that is, variable, while goods are usually uniform. One would usually know what to expect when one buys a car, but it is difficult to predict whether a rock band will give the same quality of performance at a concert on the opening night of their tour versus the final night performance, or for that matter, whether the same performance

THE INDUSTRIALISATION OF SERVICE

In 1976 the *Harvard Business Review* published an article with this title by Theodore Levitt. As with many of his seminal articles, Levitt was ahead of the game in identifying an important emerging trend – the growing importance of services in the advanced economies as the **NICs (Newly Industrialising Countries)** took over the supply of many manufactured products at more competitive prices than domestic producers. Using Britain as an example, Levitt argued that if the advanced economies failed to manage service delivery efficiently and effectively, then the higher labour costs generally associated with service provision would lead to a loss of international competitiveness and a decline in standards of living.

In the case of Britain he wrote: "In Britain, "to serve" remains to this day encrusted with immemorial attachments to master-servant pretensions that dull the imagination and block the path to service efficiency". Happily, we appear to have grown out of this mindset, but a recent holiday suggests it alive and well elsewhere. So, what needs to be done? Essentially, Levitt's argument is that as it is the people who cause problems with service delivery we should, as far as possible, remove them from the equation. To do so we need to "**industrialise**" services, and Levitt proposes three ways in which we may do this: via **hard technologies**, **soft technologies** and hybrid technologies.

In the case of hard technologies one substitutes "machinery, tools, or other tangible artifacts for people in the performance of service work". As examples he cites electrocardiograms, consumer credit cards, airport X-ray surveillance equipment, automatic car washes, automatic toll collectors, automatic clothes and dish washers, non-iron fabrics etc.

"Soft technologies are essentially the substitution of organised preplanned systems for individual service operatives". As examples he cites: supermarkets and other self-service establishments, fast-food restaurants like McDonald's, where portion preparation and control are highly automated, package tours, various kinds of insurance and investment schemes, and so on.

The third category, hybrid systems, combine both hard equipment and systems "to bring efficiency, order, and speed to the service process".

Levitt's argument is, essentially, that while the industrial revolution was enabled by the de-skilling of craft specialisations, this has yet to occur in many service occupations. This is most apparent in the case of the Professions where entry is restricted by qualification. Clearly, practitioners need to be knowledgeable about their subject and, hopefully, skilled in its application but, in many cases, customers might be better served by the elimination of some restrictive practices and the industrialisation of the services they offer. To do so calls for management.

would be appropriate for their fans anyway. This problem of expecting people to perform in an identical way each time is hampered due to the high level of contact between 'producer' and consumer – for example, how would you feel if a customer is aggressive towards you, or if a sales assistant is too impatient to answer your queries? Therefore it is difficult to forecast and ensure provision of the same quality of a service over time when the quality itself can be affected by both the performance of the provider of the service, at the time at which it is provided, as well as the behaviour of the consumer. Due to this inseparability it therefore is difficult, if not impossible, for the service organisation to standardise output and gain economies of scale in much the same way as a manufacturing organisation.

Perishability and fluctuating demand

The fourth major dimension which distinguishes between services and goods is that services cannot be stored or inventoried in the same way as physical goods. This inability to store services means that unused service capacity and revenue is lost forever. For example, empty seats in theatres, unsold air tickets, and unbooked rooms in hotels illustrate the risk inherent in **service perishability**. This problem is overcome, usually, in certain service industries such as tourism and communications where service firms encourage the ordinary consumer to take a weekend break at a quiet time of year or to use the telephone at off-peak times, in order to get people to use these services so ensuring the service organisation will not suffer from too great a fluctuation in demand. **Demand management** in services is far more subtle than it is for products, and it would be much more constructive to think in terms of capacity availability; that is, one can only consume what is available, yet this point is frequently ignored in developing marketing strategies for services.

MANAGING SERVICES MARKETING – THE SEVEN PS

Many marketing scholars have been preoccupied with discussing whether the marketing of services is similar to or different from the marketing of physical goods. There are two different schools of thought with regard to the applicability of product marketing concepts and techniques to services marketing – that is **product-based** versus **service-based** approaches. One school of thought believes that services are not different from physical goods, and that therefore the same concepts and techniques used in goods marketing can be directly translated to services marketing. Most of the arguments suggested by the adopters of this view centre round the following two points:

1 *The claimed differences between goods and services are exaggerated and provide little insight to understanding either of them.* In addition the preoccupation with such a simple service–product classification is myopic and likely to be unsuitable. Instead more multidimensional classifications are needed in which the marketing strategy of the firm is a function of offer characteristics, market characteristics and characteristics of the exchange process (Wickham et al., 1975; Goodfellow, 1983).

2 *The most important criterion to be considered when marketing any product (including physical goods, services, ideas and so forth) is the buyer's expectations.* Many commentators argue that consumers are not buying goods or services, but the value satisfaction of the offering. So it is suggested that the process of marketing strategy formulation should start with a product concept which recognises the bundle of benefits, often including both tangible and intangible aspects as it is perceived by the potential buyer (Levitt, 1974; Donnelly and George, 1981).

Dissatisfaction with this approach leads many authors to take their thinking to the other extreme and call for a **theory for marketing services**. According to the service-based approach, it is argued that services possess certain distinguishing features which make them fundamentally different from physical goods. Therefore the suggestion advanced is that service marketers must develop a unique process of marketing strategy formulation for services which differs from the traditional one.

The development of a service marketing theory as a frame of reference which guides the marketer's thinking deals with either the service area (that is, its organisational aspects (Blois, 1982), consumer behaviour (Blois, 1982), marketing mix activities (Shostack, 1984; Donnelly, 1976)) or a specific aspect of it, for example, professional services (Gummesson, 1979).

According to this approach, it is argued that the marketing of services is much more complex than the marketing of goods due to fundamental difference in the end products, and the simultaneous production and consumption processes. As such it is suggested that service marketers need new tools, strategies and organisation structures to carry out the process of marketing services effectively.

While these opposed schools of thought still exist, and are useful in highlighting polarised views on the subject, in recent years many service providers have recognised both the need to 'industrialise' services, and to address the differentiating factors, by adopting practices used by the sellers of physical goods. In parallel, the goods producer has recognised that service enhancement is an important source of differentiation. As a result there has been what Adrian Palmer sees as a **convergence** between the two sectors which is illustrated in Table 23.2

This convergence reflects an appreciation that the conventional marketing mix needs to be modified. In 1982 Booms and Bitner suggested that McCarthy's concept of four Ps for product marketing be extended to seven Ps, by the addition of three new factors - process, physical evidence and people. In the case of product marketing the physical evidence already existed but, as we have seen repeatedly, objective factors are seldom sufficient to differentiate one competitor from another. So, in marketing physical goods the process and people factors have assumed increasing importance.

From a services marketing point of view the seven Ps may be described as follows:

Product

From Chapter 12 it can be clearly seen that the marketer of physical goods has a variety of strategic options open to them when determining their product range. In the same way, the service marketer is faced with similar decisions in developing their **product mix**. The product mix should take into account that services are made up of two parts – the '**core service**' and the '**auxiliary service**' (Grönroos, 1980). The core service is similar to what Levitt (1980) termed the '**generic product**'; that is, it is the basic service which is offered, for example, dry cleaning. The 'auxiliary' service is similar to Levitt's (1980) '**augmented product**'; that is to say, the added benefits which differentiate the service from competitors. In the case of dry cleaning, this could be same day delivery service to your home or office so that you do not have the hassle of picking the garment up at the end of the day. The quality of the service can be divided into two types – **technical quality**, that is the actual cleaning of the garment, and the **functional quality**, that is how the service is actually presented or delivered (Grönroos, 1982). This aspect of the service is important with respect to 'physical evidence', as the customer will evaluate anything which is tangible about the service, such as the care with which the garment is packed or the uniform of the delivery boy, so it is necessary to ensure all aspect of the service, be it core or auxiliary, are of a high standard.

Process

The **process** element of the service marketing mix is concerned with the way in which the service is delivered to the customer. This has two points of interest to the service marketer. First, the inseparability characteristic of services has an important implication for how the service company's personnel deliver the service to the customer and how the customer participates in the service delivery process. Secondly, the 'auxiliary' aspect of the service, that is the added value of the service, becomes an important competitive weapon in differentiating the

Table 23.2 Points of convergence between the goods and services sectors

Intangibility	Services are increasingly augmented with tangible evidence (e.g. brochures, staff uniforms).
	Goods are increasingly augmented with tangible evidence (e.g. after-sales warranties).
Inseparability	Service consumption is increasingly separated from production (e.g. telephone banking).
	Goods are increasingly produced in the presence of customers (e.g. while you wait bespoke tailoring).
Perishability	Services are becoming better at storing tangible components of a service offer and in managing the pattern of demand (e.g. restaurants).
	Goods are now more likely to be supplied using 'just-in-time' principles (e.g. automotive car components).
Variability	Industrialisation of services allows levels of reliability to be achieved that matches those of goods.
Lack of ownership	Addition of tangibles allows customers to 'own' evidence of service (e.g. a telephone 'calling card').
	Goods manufacturers increasingly sell the services which a good provides, rather than passing on ownership (e.g. car leasing arrangements).

Source: Reprinted from 'The marketing of services', Palmer, A. in Baker, M.J. (ed.) *The Marketing Book*, 5th Edition, copyright (2003) with permission from Elsevier.

service from competitors when the service is experienced by customers. One example of how process can be used to competitive advantage is through the marketing of financial services. The basic need for a bank is to store money in a safe place until we need access to it. This access has been improved considerably over the last few years by banks when they introduced services such as **ATMs (Automated Teller Machines)**, charge cards, online banking etc.. However, when ATMs were first introduced, although advances in technology did increase the availability of the service, customers did not know how to use them, and they were then left to work it out for themselves. Therefore, the overall effectiveness of the service process fundamentally depends on how the customers use the service. Lowe (1988) reinforces this point that services have been defined as 'acts rather than things' and this casts some light on the concept of 'process'. Many benefits from services occur not so much as a result of what is offered, as in the way in which it is offered.

Price

Pricing a service is generally believed to be more difficult than the pricing of manufactured goods as discussed in Chapter 15. Cowell (1995) has produced a useful table highlighting the variety of prices for selected services.

From Table 23.3, it is clear that services range from those supplied by the private company, to public utilities and professional service groups. It is also fair to assume that there are many different factors which influence price, one of which can be the service's role in society. For example, the pricing for public transport such as buses or trains will often be determined by **public regulation** in order to make the service attractive, and within reach of the majority of people. Pricing in professional services such as solicitors' and stockbrokers' fees are largely governed by professional bodies, whereas services such as hairdressing or car hire charges are largely governed by **market demand**. This classification by Rathmell (1974) has proved useful in clarifying how prices in the service sector can be set, but it leaves a great deal to be desired when setting price at the tactical level and using price as a marketing weapon.

Wilson (1972) believes 'Outside the areas of fixed, standard or customary prices, the use of pricing in the marketing mix remains primitive and awaits only intelligent application for substantial rewards to be reaped'. This is echoed by Cowell who believes 'pricing has not yet received the attention it deserves' with regards to service marketing, and that 'As with other marketing mix elements, the price of a service should be related to the achievement of marketing and organisational goals and should be appropriate for the service organisation's marketing programme'. The difficulty, it is said, lies in the diverse nature and characteristics of services which leads to sweeping generalisations.

Cowell discusses how the characteristics of services can influence the service price, although he emphasises that these should be considered in addition to the traditional forces which influence price, these being costs, competition and demand. There are five categories which he considers:

1 *Service perishability* – since services cannot be inventoried like manufactured goods, service companies have to be prepared for fluctuations in demand at certain times of the year. Cowell cites the example of the holiday tour market,

where price discounts can be made at the last minute, in order to sell unused holidays. However, he warns against increasing 'customer sophistication' where buyers almost expect these bargains to be made available at certain times of the year, and therefore hold back until the cheaper holidays are advertised, since they know the tour operator will he more keen to sell at a cheaper price than to have unsold holidays. However, in order to offset this trend and encourage potential customers, some companies have offered discounts of several hundred pounds off summer holidays to those customers who book early.

2 Competition between service companies increases in certain industries when customers can afford the luxury of postponing the use of the service and be able to 'shop around' for the best deal by telling the interested parties how little other companies have offered, for example van removals.

3 *Intangibility* – since customers using the service for the first time may not know how to evaluate what they are receiving for their money exactly, they may evaluate the service on the basis of the tangible features of the service that they receive. Taking you back to Shostack's (1977) tangibility/intangibility continuum (Figure 23.1), most goods have a degree of the service element attached to them, and likewise, most services have a degree of tangibility as well. 'The higher the material content, the more will prices set tend to be

Table 23.3 Price terminology for selected services

Terminology	Typical services
Admission	Theatre entry
Charge	Hairdressing
Commission	Stockbroking service
Dues	Union membership
Fare	Transport
Fee	Legal service
Honorarium	Guest speaker
Interest	Use of money
Premium	Insurance
Rate	Municipal services
Rent	Property usage
Retainer	Consultant's services
Salary	Employee services
Subscription	Membership
Tariff	Utilities
Toll	Road use
Tuition	Education
Wage	Employee services

Source: Reprinted from *The Marketing of Services*, Cowell, D. copyright (1984) with permission from Elsevier.

based on costs, and the greater the tendency towards more standard prices. The smaller the material content the more customer orientated and the less standard will prices be' (Cowell).

Service companies can use this to their advantage when, if a customer negotiates a lower price for the use of the service, the company has at its disposal the ability to vary the quality of the service according to what it perceives the customer is getting for their money. For example, Ryanair restrict the baggage allowance to 15 kg, 5kg less than other airlines, while on other airlines, flying Business Class will get you 10kg more than Economy class.

4 When services are more or less standardised with regards to their use (for example laundrettes), prices are usually very competitive. Alternatively, companies may be subject to regulations regarding the minimum price they may charge, or they may have the freedom to sell at whatever price the market will bear.

5 *Inseparability* – The degree of price competition in the market will to a large extent be influenced by the number of competing firms within that area. Customers may be limited to a small geographic area in order to experience the service, or only be able to use the service at particular times, which will influence the price service companies can charge.

The price of services is influenced by a number of factors namely: the **planned market position** for the service product; the **stage of the life-cycle** of the service product; **elasticity of demand**; the **competitive situation**; and the **strategic role of price**. Gabor (1980) identified two methods for pricing services:

1 *Cost-based pricing* – either a profit-oriented method, where price setting is done by professional associations, or government controlled.

2 *Market-oriented pricing* – the company is either setting prices for competitive reasons or because the firm is customer oriented.

Cowell feels that 'many of the tactical price techniques used to sell tangibles can be used to sell intangibles', citing such tactics as **differential** or **flexible pricing**; **discrete pricing**; **discount pricing**; **diversionary pricing**; **guarantee pricing**; **high price maintenance pricing**; **loss leader pricing**; **offset pricing**; and **price lining** which can be suitable for setting prices in services. He also outlines three additional aspects of service pricing which are inherent to services:

1 *Price negotiation* – many services' prices can be negotiated before the client receives the service, such as interest payments on loans, or advertising agency fees.

2 *Competitive bidding* – this is more prominent in organisational markets when the client can shop around for the best deal, and is required in the EU for public sector contracts above a certain minimum value.

3 *Price awareness* – similar to the pricing of goods, this is when the service company can set its pricing strategy according to how the market perceives the nature of pricing in that particular service industry. When the customer is relatively unsure of the price, the service company can use this to its advantage, as they tend to perceive price as an indicator of quality, due to the lack of evidence available (Eiglier and Langeard, 1977).

Current practice supports Cowell's belief that the pricing of services 'still remains largely a combination of good management, experience, trial and error, intuition and good luck'.

Place

This is the environment in which the service is assembled and where the firm and customer interact, and any tangible commodities which facilitate performance or communication of the service.

Place has a number of aspects of concern to the service marketer – the actual location of the premises, the look of the premises, and the channels of distribution used. All of these aspects vary in importance of course, depending on the service offered, and the preferred channel(s) of distribution of the service marketer.

First, the inseparability characteristic of services means that the distribution channels are far shorter than for a goods manufacturer – the customer almost always has to visit the **'manufacturer'** in order to receive the service. Therefore the location of the premises is important. The location of a dentist will vary according to whether they would like to be based in a local community where the customers' main requirements would be to visit somewhere nearby for treatment, or whether they should set their surgery in the middle of a large town, where it would be convenient for commuters to visit during the day without too much disruption to their working day, thereby saving them the inconvenience of taking a day off work to visit the dentist. This means that in order to expand, service firms have to either build more outlets (unlike goods manufacturers who expand production facilities, or make them more efficient). This has an important drawback in that it is a very capital intensive process. Alternatives for service firms may be to franchise the operation or to use agents to promote the service. However, although this may solve the expansion problem, the service company is faced with losing control over the quality of the service since it will not be their own staff they are training, and who will be providing the service.

As far as the look of the premises is concerned, the client will be searching for physical clues in assessing the success of the company. For example, the client would not have a great deal of confidence in a solicitor if the solicitor's office was poorly furnished. This would imply that the solicitor either did not care about their job, and therefore the client's problems, or that they were not successful enough even to afford to pay a few hundred pounds to have the office decorated, in which case, there may be something wrong with the solicitor's services or reputation.

The channels of distribution available to a number of service marketers have improved considerably over recent years due to improvements in telecommunications. This is especially the case in banking, where transactions can be made using either electronic systems or ATMs.

Promotion

From Chapters 18 and 19 the uses and benefits of promotional techniques such as advertising, sales promotion, and public relations became clear for physical products, but how appropriate are these same techniques for the **promotion** of services?

Few service firms are national or international in size and scope, but tend to be local firms servicing the local community. There are of course exceptions to this, especially with regards to franchise operations such as the Body Shop and Tie Rack and the international professional service firms, such as advertising agencies, management consultancies and accountancy firms. However, many service firms are based locally. By implication, therefore, this would mean that most service firms undertake promotion only at the local level.

The effectiveness of promotional campaigns has been disputed regarding the advertising of services. Rathmell (1974) has stated that the intangibility feature of services means that the service cannot be viewed physically, and so cannot be advertised or shown in the same way as physical goods, but needs to be presented as an idea. The difficulty is made even more acute in trying to use sales promotion techniques such as demonstrations, money off coupons, and posting samples of the service around the areas you would like to target because of the intangibility feature. Unwin (1975) echoed this difficulty in saying: service advertising is difficult. It offers no tangible rewards, no immediate sensations. The service advertiser has to deal in abstractions like prudence, safety and peace of mind. They are often left with describing the invisible, articulating the imaginary and defining the indistinct. It is difficult to know what to highlight and where to draw the line. And how many service customers really know what they want, or even if they want it?

In order to minimise the problems associated with advertising a service, Shostack (1977) recommended neutralising the intangibility of the service by associating some form of tangible evidence to the service in the promotional material. Berry (1980) also feels that this would make the service more 'palpable' (that is, understandable) for the consumer. Other strategies could be through seeking professional endorsements by trade associations or using popular personalities in order to create or improve customer confidence. Lowe (1988) has found that **word-of-mouth promotion** is perhaps the best for service companies as the intangible nature of services means that people find it difficult to make a judgement on relatively objective grounds, so they rely on the experience of those who actually used the service to a greater degree than might be the case if a tangible product were involved.

Despite these caveats, many services are marketed effectively using the mass media - for example, the Norwich Union 'Quote me happy' TV campaign.

Physical evidence

Since a service is inherently intangible, it is important for the client to search for tangible or physical clues which enable them to evaluate the service. 'Service firms must be aware that every aspect of the company with which the consumer comes into contact will be used as a measure of the level of service that he can expect from the organisation' (Lowe, 1988). **Physical evidence** are those tangible clues which the consumer may receive during the process of receiving the service, which 'verify either the existence or the completion of a service' (Shostack, 1982). She further classifies physical evidence into two categories – **peripheral evidence** and **essential evidence**.

■ *Peripheral evidence* – is usually 'possessed as part of the purchase of a service, but it has little or no independent value'. She cites the example of a cheque book which is not of any use without the funds transfer and storage service that it represents.

- *Essential evidence* – is 'unlike peripheral evidence . . . [as it] cannot be possessed by the consumer'. However, Shostack believes that essential evidence may be 'so dominant in its impact on service purchase and use that it must be considered virtually an element in its own right' For example, the age and configuration of the aircraft used by an airline.

However, one important point should be made about the management of physical evidence. Research should be conducted in order to assess the expectations of the target market's perceptions of the service environment – what may represent the standard of physical evidence expected from a particular service organisation may seem like an expensive luxury which will be passed on to the client in the form of higher prices or fees. An example of this would be having a doorman in splendid livery outside a restaurant.

People

Of all the controllable variables marketing executives have at their disposal, the people factor in the services marketing mix is perhaps the least they can rely on in getting their marketing mix 'right', and the most important one they have to get right. The problem lies in inseparability of the production/consumption interface, and therefore, the satisfaction of not only the recipient of the service, that is the customer, but also the providers of the service, that is the company's own personnel become extremely important.

Service personnel are present at two levels within the organisation – contact personnel and support personnel. Contact personnel are those individuals whom the customers see – such as waiters or receptionists – and on whom the customers judge the service when they search for tangible clues as to the quality of the service. The value they attribute to the service relies a great deal on the conduct of the contact personnel.

It is very rare for customers to meet the chefs who prepare the meals or the cleaning staff who prepare guests' bedrooms. Imagine being served by a waiter who has an unkempt appearance when you are visiting a restaurant, or being told by a member of the cabin crew that the only difference between paying for a first class air ticket and club class is that you have spent £200 more than the other passengers. This type of behaviour is hardly conducive to developing customer loyalty in the medium-to-long term, and yet both are real examples of the behaviour of service personnel. Had the individuals been happy with their jobs, this type of ill-mannered and off-putting behaviour could have been avoided and customer satisfaction maintained. How can a company ensure that its personnel at both levels will provide a quality service leaving a favourable impression on customers?

The answer lies in 'internal marketing' (Grönroos, 1982), the purpose of which is to have 'motivated and customer-conscious employees'. Employees, who are seen as internal customers, and jobs as internal products, should work in an organisation that 'creates an internal environment which supports customer consciousness and sales-mindedness among their personnel' (Grönroos).

Employees need to become 'ambassadors for the organisation' (Lewis, 1989) as the 'quality of the service and the quality of the service providers are inseparable' (Chase, 1978). The more competent the customer contact personnel, the better the service–business–client relationship will be, which will culminate in the service organisation receiving a positive reference. This relationship has been termed '**positive circles**' (Normann, 1985).

So how should the service company attract and maintain the type of desirable personnel who will leave a positive impression on customers? Lowe (1988) proposes the use of good communications within the organisation since 'customer contact personnel cannot be expected to perform well if they are not fully informed about what the company is doing, and why'. In addition, it has been recommended (Berry, 1980) that a service employer apply traditional marketing tools such as market research and market segmentation in order that '(1) the best possible people can be employed and retained and, (2) they will do the best possible work' by identifying and satisfying employees needs, wants and aspirations.

Considerations an employer needs to make regarding the company guidelines and practices would be working conditions, shift work, flexible working hours, day-to-day benefits, either financial or in-kind (for example tips, taxi fares home or free meals at the end of the shift), holiday entitlement, training, career development opportunities, promotion prospects, career evaluations, pensions and life assurance. By identifying what one is able to afford to give personnel, and the minimum standard of benefits personnel are prepared to take, one is partially on the way to satisfying the personnel one would like to hire.

The marketing executive can also apply **market segmentation** techniques when it comes to identifying the ideal personnel to hire. 'Market segmentation is relevant as people are as different as employees as they are as consumers' (Lewis). The aim of internal marketing is to 'increase job satisfaction, increase productivity and decrease absenteeism . . . and to train personnel to enhance their skills and to encourage a customer orientation; and to supervise and evaluate their performance' (Lewis).

However, internal marketing has been viewed as insufficient, and it is believed that internal marketing should be viewed as a managerial philosophy that has strategic as well as tactical implications throughout the company and its various business functions. In other words, it should permeate the whole of the service company.

If service organisations care about both employees and customers, the pay-off will be in terms of increased motivations and satisfaction; a high level of service quality as compared to the quality expected by customers, and therefore customer satisfaction; and in turn, hopefully, customer loyalty and increased level of business activity.

In the same manner, two other functions to be performed in a service firm have been suggested (Grönroos, 1989), namely the **interactive marketing function** in order to manage all the resources involved in the buyer-seller interface (that is, the physical/technical environment, the contact personnel, and the customers), and the **internal marketing function** which is concerned with satisfying the employees as the first market of the service firm.

The proposition is of a '**relationship definition of marketing**' which states 'marketing is to establish, maintain, enhance and commercialise customer relationships (often, but not necessarily long-term relationships) so that the objectives of the parties involved are met. This is done by a mutual exchange and fulfilment of promises' (Grönroos). The relationship and the transaction definitions of marketing would be enhanced by developing a service culture amongst most if not all employees, and treating each customer as an individual, rather than a one-off single financial transaction. Relationship-building skills have been classified into such categories as joint problem definition, and to 'listen, be patient and modest' (Kubr, 1976), but these have been taken further (McGivern, 1983) with the need for high levels of interaction between parties, the need for trust, and the contingency of the methods used being advocated.

However, this basic marketing mix has been criticised (Grönroos) with the emphasis being put on continuously adapting the supplier's operations to meet customer's needs and, more particularly, to match customers' expected and perceived needs. This continuous adaptation (Yorke, 1990) will involve many people at different levels within the organisation, but the overall objective would still be to protect the existing customer base resulting in continuing exchanges and lower marketing costs per customer.

It is concluded (Yorke) that at least in professional service firms:

organisations should adopt a more client-centred or market-oriented approach to their planned growth. The organisation should not focus entirely on production efficiency, current service offerings or sales, but on meeting the needs of particular clients, recognising, in addition, that client needs are rarely static but continue to evolve as the nature of their business changes.

This would suggest that this 'strategy demands new thinking on the part of professional organisations, not only in continually appraising client needs, but also in developing a flexibility of operation involving changes in organisation structure and the continuing education of partners and employees in dealing with client problems'.

Summary

The importance of services to the British economy has been growing both in terms of employment and in relation to GDP. This growth can be attributed to the impact of technology, deregulation and increased competition and increasing customer sophistication. Services may be professional or consumer oriented, and there is a great deal of crossover between the two categories. Services also have characteristics which differentiate them from goods and which make marketing planning more difficult – namely, intangibility, inseparability, heterogeneity, and perishability and fluctuating demand. The service marketing mix has since been extended to seven Ps, which may be listed as product, price, process, promotion, place, physical evidence and people.

While the marketing of services has established itself as a distinct sub-field of marketing, there has been a growing tendency towards a transfer between it and mainstream marketing. While service marketers increasingly recognise the importance of physical evidence, so the sellers of tangible goods have accepted that it is necessary to bundle services with their products to help differentiate them from the competition. It has also been accepted that quality and delivery depend heavily on the people involved placing an emphasis on process and the importance of internal marketing. As a result of this convergence marketing has become everybody's business in all kinds of organisation.

Review questions and problems

1 Describe and evaluate the marketing techniques used to match supply and demand in one of the following:
   (a) The package holiday industry;
   (b) Fast-food restaurants.

2 Why are product positioning and differentiation such difficult concepts to operationalise in many service industries?

3 'In most cases the everyday contact with customers is a more important part of marketing activities than advertising and mass communication' (Grönroos, 1984, p. 42). Provide a reasoned explanation of why 94.1 per cent of a randomly selected group of 219 service companies agreed with the above contention.

4 Describe why marketing activities in service companies are different from those carried out in manufacturing companies.

5 Evaluate the use of information technology (IT) in improving the service provision in ONE of the following services:
   (a) A major high-street retailer of upmarket clothing and interior design;
   (b) A national distribution company;
   (c) An international airline.

6 'Managing supply and demand is the key task of the service manager' (Sasser, 1976). Discuss this statement, and explain ways in which a marketing specialist could help service managers achieve this objective.

7 Describe and evaluate the marketing channels and delivery systems used by ONE of the following organisations:

(a) A trans-Atlantic charter airline business;
(b) An international firm of chartered accountants;
(c) A UK-based package holiday company catering to the needs of young people.

8 What is meant by the "industrialisation of service"? Illustrate your answer with examples of services that have benefited from industrialisation.

9 'The internal marketing concept is the key to service marketing' (Grönroos, 1981). Evaluate this concept and choose a service which might especially benefit from this approach, and indicate why.

10 How, and why, does the need to manage demand affect the marketing of services? Illustrate your answer as extensively as possible.

11 'Deregulation and increased competition is changing the marketing environment of financial services.' Discuss this contention.

12 Evaluate the usefulness of having a different approach to marketing personal services from that used in marketing manufactured goods.

13 Describe how either a national clearing bank or large firm of management consultants could benefit from an awareness of service marketing theory.

14 In the last few years, customer care has been receiving increased attention from both academics and practitioners. Is this a passing fad or a real, substantive change in the way a business operates? Discuss.

Key terms

7ps (product, place, price,
promotion + process, physical
evidence, people)
augmented product
automated teller machines (ATM)
auxiliary service
bundle of satisfactions
competitive situation
consumer oriented
contact personnel
convergence
core service
customer sophistication
demand management
differential / flexible pricing
discount pricing
discrete pricing
diversionary pricing
elasticity of demand
essential evidence
evaluation of competition
extended marketing mix
fluctuating demand
functional quality
generic product
gross domestic product (GDP)

growth in services
guarantee pricing
hard technologies
heterogeneous
high price maintenance
pricing
hybrid technologies
inseparability
intangibility
interactive marketing function
internal marketing function
knock-on effect
loss leader pricing
manufacturer
market demand
market segmentation
marketing of physical goods
marketing of services
mental difficulty
multiplier effect
negative word-of-mouth
NICs (newly industrialising
countries)
offset pricing
people factor
peripheral evidence

perishability
physical evidence
physical inability
place
planned market position
price positioning
process
product mix
product-based approach
production/consumption
interface
professional oriented
promotion
public regulation
relationship definition of
marketing
service perishability
service-based approach
soft technologies
stage of the life-cycle
strategic role of price
support personnel
technical quality
theory for marketing services
word-of-mouth promotion

Supplementary reading list

Bateson, J. E. G. (1992), *Managing Services Marketing*, 2nd edn (London: Dryden Press).
Cowell, D. (1995), *The Marketing of Services*, 2nd edn (London: Heinemann).
Grönroos, C. (1985), *Strategic Marketing: Marketing in Service Industries* (Oxford: Chartwell-Bratt).
Gabbott, M. and Hogg, G., Editors (1997), *Contemporary Services Marketing Management A Reader*, (London: The Dryden Press)
(25 *seminal papers charting the development of the services marketing school of thought up to 1997*)

MARKETING IN A
FOREIGN ENVIRONMENT

24

Learning Goals *After reading this chapter you will be familiar with:*

- Rostow's concept of the stages of economic growth and development.

- The reasons why the marketing function adds value and improves productivity even in countries with endemic supply deficiencies.

- Ricardo's Theory of Comparative Advantage and the benefits which flow from specialisation and international trade.

- The factors which encourage firms to enter foreign markets.

- Sources of information and methods for establishing the existence of foreign market opportunities.

- The differences between a globalised or undifferentiated marketing strategy compared with the use of a segmentation (differentiated or concentrated) approach.

- The alternative approaches to marketing in foreign environments.

- The implications of regional trading blocs for international competition.

- The effects of environmental change on international marketing practices.

INTRODUCTION

Earlier editions of this book included a chapter called Marketing in a Foreign Environment in which we offered a synoptic and greatly simplified introduction to three questions.

1 To what extent are the principles and practices discussed in this book relevant to other countries at different stages of economic

development?

2 For what reasons might countries wish to engage in international trade?

3 What alternatives are open to firms wishing to sell in another country?

But, while I still believe it important to describe the stages through which countries pass in order to become advanced economies, and the foundations on which international trade is based, it is clear that more attention must be given to the emergence of a global market and its implications for marketing management.

Thus the intention of this chapter is to provide the reader with an introduction to some of the issues associated with marketing in a global marketplace. It cannot and does not pretend to be an exposition of the important sub-field of marketing known as International Marketing which is the subject of text books and courses in its own right.

A recurring theme throughout this book has been the perceived challenge of the emerging economies with a particular emphasis on the BRIC countries – Brazil, Russia, India and China - which are seen as rapidly catching up with the affluent post-industrialised countries of the world. In January 2005 the author was invited to give a keynote address at a conference held at India's leading business school – the Institute of Management at Ahmedabad - on the theme of *Emerging Economies*. Rather than adopting the approach taken by most speakers, which was to look directly at the perceived challenges to be addressed by managers in India, I chose to remind the audience that this was not a new problem and that all the worlds advanced economies had already gone through this stage. This being so, the best place to begin is with a review of the experience of those countries rather than re-inventing the hard won lessons of the past. While this would seem to be a common sense attitude the problem with common sense is that there doesn't seem to be much of it about! We already have a powerful description and analysis of the stages of economic growth yet few textbooks make any explicit reference to it, nor to the theory of comparative advantage which spells out the benefits of international trade and accounts for the present pre-occupation with globalisation. We will not be guilty of this omission and look at all three of these subjects.

Having established the reasons why firms wish to enter foreign markets we discuss the location of market opportunity and the choice between global and segmented strategies. Finally, having decided on a strategy and targeted the market we review the methods of market entry available.

STAGES OF ECONOMIC DEVELOPMENT

In Chapter 1 we introduced the reader to Walt Rostow's model (1962) of 'The Stages of Economic Growth'. It will be recalled that Rostow proposes that in achieving the status of an advanced, modern economy all economies must pass through a series of evolutionary phases identified as:

1 *The traditional society.*

2 *The pre-conditions for take-off.*

3 *The take-off.*

4 *The drive to maturity.*

5 *The age of high mass consumption.*

6 *Beyond the age of high mass consumption –the search for quality.*

Elsewhere (*The Marketing Book*, Baker, 1994), we have pointed out that Rostow's stages of economic development correspond quite closely to Maslow's need hierarchy such that traditional societies are concerned very much with survival while the modern, advanced and affluent economies are moving from the esteem/high mass consumption phase into one dominated by self-actualisation and the search for quality.

The evolutionary and sequential nature of Rostow's 'stages' demonstrates close parallels with our now familiar concept of the **product life-cycle (PLC)**, albeit that it is not clear whether stage 5 represents a decline into decadence and senility, and stage 6 a new PLC or a rejuvenation of the existing life-cycle/progression. Nonetheless, the concept does possess the advantages which have led us to advocate the PLC – it describes a process, and it distinguishes a number of discrete phases which can be used both as a basis for classification and for prognosis. Thus as our discussion of 'The Evolution of an Economic Theory of Consumption' in Chapter 1 shows, we can both diagnose the stage of development which an economy has reached, and propose strategies and policies for reaping the maximum advantage from its existing status, as well as suggesting how it might best move to a more advanced stage if this is desired and possible.

The question as to whether economic growth and development are desirable objectives may seem a naive one, but it is important to recognise that much of the criticism levelled against marketing arises from its close association with the stage of high mass consumption. Indeed marketing is often seen as both the agent and engine of mass high consumption which is criticised for its emphasis on excessive materialism (Galbraith, 1957), its wasteful use of resources (q.v. *The Waste Makers* by Vance Packard, 1961, or *Limits to Growth*, Meadows et al., 1972) and its destruction of our environment. If these things are bad, and most would agree that they are, then it is all too easy to see marketing as guilty by association. At least two points deserve to be made in this context.

First, while marketing as we know it appears to be a consequence of an ability to create an excess supply of particular goods and services, which only exists to a significant degree in mature high consumption economies, this is not the same as proving that its concept and practice are only relevant to this phase of economic development. Second, the most vocal adversaries of economic growth are those who directly and indirectly are enjoying its benefits to the full and so have both the leisure and the means to proselytise their views. Things doubtless look different to a subsistence farmer with an annual income measured in hundreds rather than thousands of dollars.

In a book called *In Defence of Economic Growth*, Wilfred Beckerman (1974) sums up the basic issue succinctly when he observes that:

The growth problem is a problem of how resources should be allocated over time. Economists, and we hope politicians too, are concerned primarily with maximising welfare, which may be seen as comprising two elements – the level of consumption and the equality of its distribution. In addressing the problem of how to maximise welfare it is of the utmost importance that we consider the time dimension, for it is apparent that future consumption is highly dependent upon present consumption, in the sense that investment in new plant and equipment, in research and development, in education, etc.

requires us to accept a lower level of current consumption in order to reap greater benefits (or welfare) in the future.

It follows, as Beckerman pointed out, that 'the essential point is that it is consumption over some relevant time period which should be maximised, not the growth rate'.

To be correct we should recognise that what we are seeking is **optimum growth**, which we can define as the growth rate at which the sacrifice of present consumption necessary to promote future growth is just balanced by the extra future consumption this will generate.

In assessing what is an optimum growth rate we are again faced with the intractable problem identified earlier – namely, that 'optimum' is a subjective concept and will be perceived differently by different pressure groups. Thus, influential critics like Galbraith have suggested that mankind keeps on raising the definition of optimum instead of being satisfied with what it has got. If we regard the United States as the pacemaker, in that its citizens enjoy the highest standard of living in the world, we can see immediately that standards there have increased significantly in the past decade – for the rest of us trying to catch up it appears we are faced with an ever-receding frontier. And so we come to the crux of the controversy, for it is marketing which is cast in the role of villain in the piece. In *The Affluent Society*, Galbraith (1974) comments:

> *As a society becomes increasingly affluent, wants are increasingly created by the process by which they are satisfied. This may operate passively. Increases in consumption, the counterpart of increases in production, act by suggestion or emulation to create wants. Or producers may proceed actively to create wants through advertising and salesmanship. Wants then come to depend on output.*

In the same vein Professor Harry Johnson (1961) of Chicago made the following observation in his *Money, Trade and Economic Growth*: 'The fact that wants are created and not original with the individual, raises a fundamental philosophical problem, whether the satisfaction of wants created by those who satisfy them can be regarded as social gain.' It would appear, then, that while growth is essential to ensure an improved standard of living, for most of us the marketing function is in some way responsible for exaggerating consumption needs to the point where the level of growth necessary to sustain such consumption is beyond the optimum and becomes wasteful.

Lest you view these as more examples of outdated thinking we would remind you that these were precisely the issues discussed at the **G8** conference of the world's wealthiest economies at Gleneagles in Scotland in June 2005.

MARKETING AND ECONOMIC GROWTH

From the foregoing discussion it seems reasonable to conclude that while one may have some reservations about both the nature and extent of consumption in affluent and mature economies, the achievement of such a state is desirable and one to be pursued by economies at lower levels of development. That said it seems reasonable to inquire into the relevance which marketing has both in advanced economies, where it has been accused of creating conspicuous consumption, and in developing countries, which by definition are foreign environments when compared with the UK and where many point to the scarcity of basic commodities as evidence that it is production not marketing which is needed.

Let me deal first with the advanced economies. While marketing is often identified with materialism it is important to recognise that this is not the same as proving that marketing is a materialistic business philosophy. It is probably nearer the truth to assert that, as a business philosophy, marketing is neutral and that overtones of materialism merely mirror society's preoccupation with improving the standard of living. In turn, this laudable objective became embroiled with a perceived need to maintain a high level of employment; and employment results in increased production of goods. Obviously, if such increased supplies are not consumed, the process becomes sterile so we get into a vicious circle of stimulating consumption to increase demand and maintain employment opportunities. If we are not careful we lose sight of our real objective of improving human welfare and begin to confuse the means (growth) with the end (a better standard of living). The standard of living is concerned primarily with the quality of life and, while an increase in the quantity of goods and services may be an essential part of that quality, the two are not synonymous. In fact in advanced countries it would seem that beyond a certain point the consumption of physical goods is subject to diminishing returns and may reduce the quality of life due to environmental pollution, creation of stress, loss of leisure and recreational opportunities, and so on.

It seems to me both ironical and paradoxical, assuming that marketing is so powerful in persuading people to consume more against their own interests, that few suggest that these same skills and techniques cannot be used in the interest of conservation and moderation. In fact they can, and I predict that this will increasingly be the case. Thus in post-industrial society marketing will have a crucial role to play in identifying the satisfactions which people are seeking, for, as we have seen, the central economic problem is that of maximising satisfaction from the consumption of scarce resources. Where marketers tend to differ from economists is in the emphasis they give to measuring individual consumer preferences as the basis for resource allocation – in other words they give greater attention to the subjective and qualitative dimensions of demand than is common with economists.

As has been pointed out to me on numerous occasions on visits to developing economies, their problem is seen very differently. Supply deficiency or scarcity is seen as the fundamental problem and marketing is regarded as superfluous when there is such an obvious imbalance between supply and demand. Such a viewpoint is perfectly valid if you think marketing is a sort of sophisticated selling, and concerned solely with demand stimulation by means of advertising, promotion and packaging.

To recapitulate, economies are concerned with maximising the satisfaction gained from the consumption of scarce resources. It is the satisfaction of individual consumers we are concerned with, and it would be paternalistic, not to say presumptuous, to assume that any single person is able to specify just what gives people the greatest satisfaction without asking them. To point to the fact that the available supply is consumed is not to prove that we are maximising satisfaction – it only goes to prove that something is better than nothing. My need for shoes is stronger than my need for brown shoes. If you only produce black shoes which I do not particularly like, they are still preferable to no shoes at all, but you are not maximising my satisfaction. Certainly you are not going to motivate me to work harder to own two pairs of shoes I do not like. (In passing it should be mentioned that one of the reasons why marketing is now practised in what used to be Soviet countries is that they had an awful lot of black shoes no one would buy!)

At this point it is important to stress that in the world today there economies at all the different stages of development from traditional society through to post-industrial knowledge based service economies. Currently, most attention is focused on the so-called BRIC countries (Brazil, Russia, India and China) that have achieved take-off and are growing rapidly. So much so that by 2020 India and China will be approaching the size of the United States' economy and, by 2050 will be significantly bigger.

The BRIC countries are usually described as 'emergent' and are in hot pursuit of the **newly industrialised economies (NICs)** like South Korea, Taiwan and Singapore which achieved take-off some 30-40 years ago. Trailing behind are the **less developed countries (LDCs)** many of which possess a number of characteristics that distinguish them from more developed countries. Among these characteristics may be cited:

- *Distinctive social divisions* based on wealth, religion and, often, tribal affiliations.
- *Few democratic institutions* –power is concentrated in the hands of a ruling elite.
- *Poorly administered.*
- *Heavy expenditure on security* – military and police.
- *Wealth concentrated in the hands of the ruling elite* – the vast majority live at or below the poverty line.
- *Limited competition* – production and distribution dominated by monopolies and oligopolies.
- *Poor infrastructure.*
- *Vulnerable exports* – mainly primary products/commodities with a very narrow base, e.g. oil, tea, coffee, cotton etc.
- *Rural de-population, massive urbanisation.*

All of these represent barriers to economic growth which require the establishment of free markets, competition and professional management to stimulate development. Marketing should play an increasingly significant role', an assertion which echoes the sentiments of such well-known authors as Galbraith, Drucker and McCarthy.

Consider what Drucker had to say as far back as 1958 in 'Marketing and Economic Development':

> *My thesis is very briefly as follows, Marketing occupies a critical role in respect to the development of such 'growth' [i.e. underdeveloped] areas. Indeed, marketing is the most important 'multiplier' of such development. It is in itself in every one of these areas the least developed, the most backward part of the economic system. Its development, above all others, makes possible economic integration and the fullest utilisation of whatever assets and productive capacity an economy already possesses. It mobilises latent economic energy.* (pp. 252–9)

In the first instance most would agree with Kindleberger (1958) in *Economic Development*, that whether markets stimulate development or vice versa, distribution systems tend to be neglected and are the source of considerable inefficiency. It follows that improvements in physical distribution are likely to have a high pay-off and help break the vicious circle so typical of the developing economy, where surpluses are small or non-existent, leaving little or nothing for investment to provide the necessary stimulus to growth. Allied with developments in physical distribution it is also clear that efficient retail practice has a significant contribution to make in optimising the satisfaction derived from the available supply. Austen cites a study by Slater which showed that ten years after supermarkets were introduced into Puerto Rico they accounted for 40 per cent of all food sales in San Juan and offered lower prices than traditional small outlets. In a similar vein several studies in Latin America have claimed that mass retailing methods used by Sears, Roebuck have been an important contributor to economic growth.

However, marketing can perhaps make the greatest impact by ensuring that scarce resources are channelled into those products which offer the greatest consumer satisfaction. Unfortunately in economies where scarcity is endemic it is often difficult to persuade managers that an ability to sell everything they can make is not necessarily the same as maximising satisfaction. A simple case history will help make the point.

In Nigeria soft drinks such as coke, lemonade and orangeade are extremely popular and often difficult to obtain. A survey by marketing students at the University of Nigeria in Enugu showed that although the major bottling company was able to sell all its output, customers were not entirely satisfied with the product mix, which emphasised coke and contained relatively small proportions of orange and lemon flavours. It appeared that consumers had a very strong preference for orange and deliveries were consumed immediately; lemon ranked second, but it was only after both orange and lemon were sold out that coke became acceptable as third best, but still preferable to no soft drink at all. Because demand exceeded supply, the manager assumed that all was well and paid little attention to new firms being set up concentrating mainly on orange and lemon flavours. In ignoring this potential competition he clearly had forgotten that some years previously coke had built up its sales in preference to beer, which had now lost its dominant place in the beverage market.

The moral is as clear in developing economies as it is in developed ones – an understanding of consumer needs is fundamental to long-run business success, and therefore to optimising the allocation of scarce resources. In turn it is clear that the scarcer resources are, the greater the need to optimise the return from them, so that even where growth is restrained voluntarily marketing practices and techniques have a major role to play in ensuring the greatest possible return in terms of consumer satisfaction.

By improving the efficiency of the marketing function we improve profitability, and increased profitability means a larger surplus to invest in expanding production facilities. In other words **marketing productivity** is an essential contributor to reducing and solving the scarcity problem.

To conclude, it seems to me that the marketing concept is universal to all stages of economic development and to ignore it is to slow down the optimum rate of growth as I have defined it – put another way, neglect of the marketing concept wastes scarce resources. When it comes to application of the concept then it is clear that different marketing functions are more relevant in some situations than in others. In developing countries one needs market research as an essential input to planning future development; one needs greatly improved distribution to ensure that the limited goods available are put into consumption in the most efficient manner possible; one needs greater control over distribution to eliminate distortion of the price mechanism through diversion into a black-market operation. One has proportionately a much lesser need for promotional and selling activities than is the case in advanced economies, where supply and demand are much closer to equilibrium. However, these differences do not deny the relevance of marketing, merely a better understanding of its application.

It follows, therefore, that in principle the concepts and practices discussed in this book are of relevance to all countries whatever their stage of economic development. However, in seeking to apply the ideas in this book one should be mindful of Robert Bartels' (1968) conclusions when addressing the question 'Are Domestic and International Marketing Dissimilar?', namely:

1 Marketing is a process of twofold character: technical and social.

2 Marketing technology, i.e. '... the application of principles, rules, or knowledge relating to the non-human elements of marketing', has universal validity and potentially universal applicability.

3 'The applicability of marketing technology is dependent upon circumstances of the environments in which it is applied'; that is, cultural and societal factors condition the technical factors.

4 There are wide differences in cultural and societal factors between countries and, therefore, in marketing practice. Despite these differences the relationships between marketing practice and environment are susceptible to generalisations in analysis termed 'comparative marketing'. Thus, although the marketer may expect both differences and similarities between foreign and domestic markets, 'both are embraced within a consistent body of marketing theory'.

Having read this section you may well be struck by the fact that many (indeed most) of the references are 20 or more years old. Unfortunately, this does not reflect inadequate revision by the author. It reflects the sad fact that comparatively little has occurred to improve the lot of the under-developed economies in the second half of the twentieth century. The rich continue to get richer and the poor, poorer.

So much for marketing within countries at different stages of economic development. What about trade between them?

INTERNATIONAL TRADE

While trade between nations is of almost equal antiquity as exchange between individuals, the theoretical explanation for it had to await the statement of David Ricardo's 'Theory of Comparative Advantage' in the early nineteenth century. To demonstrate the application of his theory and the benefits which would flow from specialisation by nations, Ricardo used the following example (see *Dictionary of Modern Economics*, ed. David W. Pearce, Macmillan, 1981):

	Labour hours required to produce	
	1 gallon wine	1 yard cloth
Portugal	80	90
England	120	100

Portugal has an absolute advantage in the production of both commodities since the input requirements are less than those for England. Portugal's **comparative cost advantage** for wine is 80:120 which is less than the rate of 90:100 for cloth. If Portugal specialises in accordance with her comparative cost advantage then for every yard of cloth she ceases to produce she can have 1⅛ gallons of wine, for each embodies 90 labour hours. If, as Ricardo postulates, the exchange rate after trade between cloth and wine is 1:1, then Portugal can exchange her 1⅛ gallons of wine to obtain 1⅛ yards of cloth. In other words, Portugal can obtain 1⅛ yards of cloth for the 90 labour hours which would only have yielded 1 yard of cloth produced domestically. However, England gains too, for despite her absolute inferiority she can translate the 120 hours required to produce a gallon of wine into the production of 1⅕ yards of cloth which by international exchange can be converted into 1⅕ gallons of wine.

Nowadays, modern theory has established that the only necessary condition for the possibility of gains from trade is that **price ratios** should differ between countries, but the essential concept remains the same – that by specialisation and through trade countries improve their overall standard of living. The strict application of this doctrine was challenged by Bruce Scott (1984) in an article 'National Strategy for Stronger US Competitiveness'.

According to Scott one must reject the static theory of comparative advantage in favour of a **dynamic approach** founded on a national strategy towards long-run competitiveness. Thus:

Japan's remarkable post-war economic growth is based, in considerable measure, on the Japanese government's rejection of static, conventional economic theories. Japanese leaders recognised that Japan could create competitive advantages by mobilising technology, capital, and skilled labour to attack problems or identify opportunities in selected sectors. They created a strategy of dynamic comparative advantage at the national level that parallels the strategy of a diversified company as it shifts resources from less to more promising areas. As a high level MITI official explained in a 1970 OECD publication:

'Should Japan have entrusted its future, according to the theory of comparative advantage, to these industries characterised by intensive use of labour? [With a population of 100 million] had [Japan] chosen to specialise in this kind of industry, it would almost permanently have been unable to break away from the Asian pattern of stagnation and poverty . . .'

The Ministry of International Trade and Industry decided to establish industries which require intensive employment of capital and technology, such as steel, oil refining, petrochemicals, automobiles, aircraft, industrial machinery of all sorts, and later electronics, including electronic computers. From a short-run, static viewpoint, encouragement of such industries would seem to conflict with economic rationalism. But, from a long-range point of view, these are precisely the industries where income elasticity of demand is high, technological progress is rapid, and labour productivity rises fast. It was clear that without these industries it would be difficult to raise [our] standard of living to that of Europe and America; whether right or wrong, Japan had to have these heavy and chemical industries.

As Scott points out, Portugal should have chosen to specialise in the growth industry of the day (cloth) and forsaken the production of port wine! (In *The Comparative Advantages of Nations*, Michael Porter, 1990, dismisses Ricardo's theory as inadequate and incomplete and proposes that the only lasting, sustainable advantage is a country's people. This book is essential reading for those seeking a modern and detailed analysis). However, both Scott and Porter miss the point. Ricardo's example took 'labour' (i.e. people) as the factor of production most appropriate to the analysis of eighteenth century agricultural economies. Today, knowledge (people) and technology are more relevant factors of production - but this does not invalidate Ricardo's *conceptualisation* of the issue.

However, Japan's success in penetrating world markets with its modern products confirms the necessity for international trade, for without imports it would be impossible to produce these and exports are essential to pay for them.

Of necessity, Britain has long been involved in foreign trade in order to make good her limited endowment of land and raw materials. During the middle of the last century she had a virtual monopoly of international trade, but since that time her share has declined continuously. In large degree this decline has been due to the enormous expansion in international trade, for in absolute terms her total trade today is many times greater than it was during the last century. Several factors may be distinguished as having contributed to this growth, including:

- Nationalistic policies, emphasising self-sufficiency, have yielded to the logic of the theory of comparative advantage; that is, that countries will maximise their growth by specialising in those activities with the greatest marginal product, and exchanging excess supplies for the surplus output of other specialised economies. The creation of international trading communities is an implicit recognition of this, for example EU, EFTA, LAFTA (Latin America Free Trade Association), NAFTA, and so on.

- Politically, it has been realised that the removal of trade barriers will not only stimulate the growth of economies but will also lead to cultural exchange and the easing of international tension.

- The 'population explosion' has created new mass markets and expanded the demand for all types of goods and services.

- Developments in communications and transportation have opened up hitherto inaccessible markets.

- The removal of trade barriers has intensified competition in formerly protected markets, and encouraged domestic manufacturers to develop new products and to look farther afield for markets in which to sell them.

Factors which predispose the firm to enter international markets

Fundamentally, entry into any new market, domestic or foreign, is undertaken to increase overall profitability. In turn, the decision to enter the international market may arise from any combination of a number of factors, among which may be distinguished:

1 *Loss of domestic market share due to increased competition.* Whereas a price reduction in the home market might be suicidal, the firm using a contribution approach may be able to increase total profits by selling at a lower price in foreign markets. (This strategy is often precluded by the existence of antidumping agreements.)

2 *Loss of domestic market share due to product obsolescence.* In many cases products made obsolete by the introduction of more sophisticated substitutes are still appropriate to less advanced countries, for example oil lamps.

3 *Saturation of the domestic markets precluding the attainment of scale economies.* Unlike the previous points, which presume the existence of excess capacity, this situation suggests that an increase in market size will permit the firm to expand its production and reduce average cost. In turn, this will permit the firm to expand its domestic market, as well as compete more effectively overseas.

4 *The provision of incentives.* Incentives to enter international markets are of both the 'push' and 'pull' variety, and invariably originate at government level. International agreements such as GATT (General Agreement on Tariffs and Trade) frequently exclude the provision of direct subsidies to exporters, but there are a number of ways in which a government can provide indirect support.

In addition to the information and promotional support represented by these expenditures, the exporter can also call upon other departments such as the DTI (Department of Trade and Industry) for specialised help, can insure against loss through the Export Credits Guarantee Department, and receive preferential tax treatment for expenses incurred.

'Pull' incentives are those offered by foreign governments to encourage entry into their national market. Originally, such incentives included import licences and tax relief on profits, but these are less common now. Most developing economies wish to develop domestic industry, in order to create employment opportunities, as well as wishing to conserve foreign exchange. Consequently, pull incentives are now largely designed to attract foreign firms to establish subsidiaries, rather than to attract the importation of finished goods. Probably the strongest incentive of all, however, is the existence of potential demand backed by purchasing power. Essentially, such market opportunities are of three types:

- *Type 1:* One can offer an equivalent product at a lower price.
- *Type 2:* One can offer a better product at a competitive price.
- *Type 3:* One can offer a product which is not available in the foreign market.

In view of the high labour costs/low productivity of many of our industries, few type 1 markets are open to British exporters and attention is largely concentrated on type 2 and type 3 situations.

Over the years many traditional British exports have built up a reputation for quality, soundly based on product superiority, for example woollens, speciality cotton textiles, china, machine tools, and so forth. Unfortunately, complacency and poor marketing have allowed competitors to pre-empt many type 2 markets.

Type 3 markets offer the greatest profit opportunity of all, but are the least common. Further, the small size of the domestic market, and insular thinking, frequently delay the development of technological innovations, allowing other countries to overtake us, for example the Hovercraft, body scanners.

The location of market opportunity

In general, the identification of foreign market opportunities will result from systematic marketing research of the type described in Chapter 11. In the particular, however, it is usually necessary to modify this approach for a number of reasons:

1 Most companies are seeking a market for an existing product with which they have had considerable domestic experience; that is, one is seeking to match needs with a product, rather than develop a product to satisfy identified but unfilled needs.

2 Few companies or executives have any 'feel' for foreign markets, which tend to be totally unknown quantities in a way which the home market can never be. Some might argue that this is an advantage in that it demands a fuller and more scientific analysis, with less dependence on subjective, judgemental opinions.

3 Few countries possess the wealth of published data available for use in domestic desk research, making precise quantification difficult.

4 Field research using survey methods is frequently precluded because of language difficulties, the non-availability of trained personnel, cost, and so on.

5 There are literally dozens of countries which might represent a potential market, and some form of screening procedure is essential to reduce the list to manageable proportions.

In the latter context the development of comparative marketing as an area of study offers considerable hope in that it is concerned with 'The identification and analysis of common factors and differences in marketing concepts, systems and techniques among various societies, including nations' (David Carson, 1967, in 'Comparative Marketing – A New-Old Aid'). As the title of Carson's article suggests, comparative analysis is a long-established technique, but it is only in the 1970s that it became the subject of formal study in the marketing context. As a result of these studies a number of formal classificatory systems have been, or are in the course of being, developed which take into account economic, geographic and human factors. Although none of these systems has yet been accepted as definitive, reference to any or all of them should permit early elimination of countries which are clearly unsuited as potential markets for a given product or service. Similarly, a study of the differences and common factors between countries should sensitise the marketer to their relative importance when formulating a marketing strategy.

Sources of information

In the nature of things, the classificatory systems being developed by marketing theorists are based largely on generalisations, and should be regarded as a screening device. Once a short-list of potential markets has been decided upon, the researcher must seek out more detailed data. A number of sources are available to assist them in this task, some of which have already been quoted in Chapter 11. These may be supplemented by reference to:

- The Department of Trade and Industry;
- Chambers of Commerce;
- Commercial Officers of the Diplomatic Service;
- Export Councils;
- Institute of Directors;
- Chartered Institute of Marketing;
- Trade Associations;
- The Foreign Departments of the major banks, and so on.

(The DTI publishes a wide selection of publications - visit *www.dti.gov.uk*)

Many of the sources quoted can provide first hand information on specific opportunities, as well as advising on the procedure to be followed, and the pitfalls to be avoided, when entering specific markets.

Field research

Although it is generally true that few countries have market research organisations capable of undertaking field research, this certainly does not apply to the advanced, affluent economies which represent the best potential markets for British goods. On the other hand few companies are prepared to make a large-scale entry into a foreign market, and so baulk at the expenditure that an extensive survey would involve. Consequently, many would-be exporters confine their field research to a 'fact-finding' tour in which they solicit the opinions of informed sources, the quality of which varies enormously. Owing to the uncertainties associated with entry into a foreign market, as opposed to risks which are quantifiable, many marketers prefer to enlist the support of a third party in the country concerned, that is an indirect approach, which is usually regarded as a substitute for field research.

GLOBALISATION VERSUS SEGMENTATION

Since the publication of 'Marketing Myopia' in 1960 Ted Levitt has been recognised as one of the foremost marketing thinkers of our time with the added advantage that he can and does communicate his ideas clearly and vigorously. This is certainly the case with his article which appeared in the May–June 1983 issue of the *Harvard Business Review* – 'The Globalisation of Markets' – which opens with the following sentences:

A powerful force now drives the world toward a single converging commonality, and that force is technology. It has proletarianised communication, transport, and travel, making them easily and cheaply accessible to the world's most isolated places and impoverished multitudes. Suddenly no place and nobody is insulated from the alluring attractions of modernity. Almost everybody everywhere wants all the things they have heard about, seen or experienced via the new technological facilitators that drive their wants and wishes. And it drives these increasingly into global commonality, thus homogenising markets everywhere.

The result is a new commercial reality – the explosive emergence of **global markets** for globally standardised products, gigantic world scale markets of previously unimagined magnitudes.

The article, which is reprinted in his book *The Marketing Imagination* (1983), develops this theme at some length, and argues that countries (Japan) and firms (Coca-Cola) which have appreciated this trend enjoy enormous economies of scale in production, distribution and marketing, and by using price as a competitive weapon are able to devastate the competition. This trend is accelerated by the newly industrialising countries' (NICs') desire for modernity, as a result of which they have run up enormous external debts, and made the old patterns of international trade obsolete. As a consequence the multinational corporations which have dominated the scene for so long are giving way to the global corporation, and:

The multinational and the global corporation are not the same. The multinational corporation operates in a number of countries, where in each case it adjusts with accommodating care and therefore high relative costs to the presumptive special conditions of the particular country. In contrast, the global corporation operates with resolute constancy and therefore at low relative costs as if the entire world (or major regions of it) were a single, largely identical entity; it does and sells the same things in the same single way everywhere.

My own view is that this thesis will be seen as being as overstated as 'Marketing Myopia' was. The weakness in Levitt's argument is that he is overlooking a basic concept of marketing, which is that one can pursue three quite different strategies, distinguishable as **undifferentiated**, **differentiated** and **concentrated**. Global corporations pursue an undifferentiated strategy, while multinationals follow a differentiated and sometimes concentrated approach; that is, they adjust the product or service to what they perceive as the particular needs of different groups of customers or '**market segments**'. Of course Levitt has to recognise the existence of such segments which, if nothing else, will continue to exist because of the unequal distribution of income, and has to admit that the global corporation will appeal only to those who don't mind an undifferentiated product.

Now under certain circumstances an undifferentiated product will be preferable to no product at all, as we saw in the example of coke in Nigeria cited earlier, but, as I have pointed out elsewhere ('Maxims for Marketing in the Eighties', Baker, 1980–81), one of the marketing's maxims is that 'The act of consumption changes the consumer.' In other words, the Model T at $500 was much preferable to no car at all, but once you had come to appreciate its basic benefits you also became aware of its basic faults, including that 'you can have any colour you like so long as it's black', and so come to want a product which is differentiated in some way or other. General Motors recognised this fact when Ford would not accept it and displaced him as market leader.

Experience suggests that while one can pursue an undifferentiated (global?) strategy successfully for some of the time, ultimately you will have to change it – at least to a different undifferentiated strategy, but probably to a differentiated or concentrated strategy. As such this argument is inconsistent and contradictory

– a fact which is emphasised with some irony by Chapter 4 of Levitt's *Marketing Imagination* which is entitled "Differentiation – of Anything'!

This view would certainly seem to be shared by Alvin Toffler (1984) in his book *Previews and Promises*, when he observed:

> *Take mass production. Nothing was more characteristic of the industrial era. Yet we're already moving from a mass production, mass consumption economy to what I've called a 'de-massified' economy.*
>
> *In traditional mass manufacturing, factories pour out a stream of identical objects, by the million. In the Third Wave sector, mass production is replaced by its opposite: de-massified production – short runs, even customized, one-by-one production, based on computers and numerical controls. Even where we turn out millions of identical components, they are frequently configured into more and more customized end products.*
>
> *The significance of this can't be overestimated. It's not simply that products are now more varied. The processes of production are themselves transformed. The smokestack – that symbol of the industrial, assembly-line society – is becoming a relic.*
>
> *We still think of ourselves as a mass production society, yet in the advanced sectors of the economy, mass production is already an outmoded technique. And the idea that we can keep our old mass manufacturing industries competitive indefinitely is based on ignorance of what is actually happening on the factory floor.*
>
> *The new technologies make diversity as cheap as uniformity. In fact, in many industries, it's customize or die. This is exactly the opposite of what was required in the Second Wave economy.*
>
> *In fact, it is almost a dialectical return to preindustrial, one-of-a-kind production, but now on a high technology basis.*
>
> *And exactly the same trends are visible in the distribution system, too, where we see more and more market segmentation, direct mail targeting, specialty stores, and even individualized delivery systems based on home computers and teleshopping. People are increasingly diverse, and, as a result, the mass market is breaking into small, continually changing sectors.*

Perhaps the most telling indictment against the globalisation argument is that it is production orientated in the sense that it seeks to 'drive' the wants and wishes of potential users toward commonality rather than modify the supply to match a varying demand. As we shall see in the next sections, which look at different approaches to marketing in foreign environments, such an approach is reasonable when one is entering foreign markets for the first time or has only a limited interest in selling to such markets and wishes to minimise the risk. Otherwise, given the diversity of behaviour discussed in Chapters 8, 9 and 10 (Consumer Behaviour, Organisational Buyer Behaviour and Market Segmentation), it would be surprising, to say the least, if extending the geographical scope of one's marketing did not increase this diversity.

Notwithstanding the above comments, more and more products are being perceived and launched as global brands. National borders are becoming less significant to many major corporations in the promotion of their key products. Companies like Coca-Cola, Mars and Ford are trying to have a more homogeneous strategy and product that promotes their products to a large market. According to *Marketing Week* marketing research has shown that the variations in consumers' attitudes and tastes may not be as great as would be expected. These trends are often attributed to cheaper travel and the globalisation of the media. The convergence of consumers' tastes and attitudes means it is becoming easier to globalise brands, especially commodities like soft drinks, cosmetics and confectionery.

A key date in the globalisation of brands was the change that one of the leading confectionery brands underwent in 1990 when Mars' Marathon bar attempted globalisation of the product. When globalising brands there is a need to search out common factors to name and position the product effectively in a cross-section of markets. This can lead to a watering-down effect. In order to avoid this problem local variations will often be needed, for example in terms of naming or packaging. Different cultures will have sensitivities to certain colours, names or advertising campaigns for example, and it may be necessary to account for these. Only when a brand develops a stereotype that can transcend cultures do these problems diminish, as is the case with products like Coca-Cola and Marlboro cigarettes.

However, the opportunity to develop truly global brands has been moderated by the recognition that many will sell better if adapted to local conditions. For example, the Chinese eat more chicken than beef so the emphasis in South East Asia is on the former. This process of adaptation has been termed **glocalisation** and is based on a marketing orientation that starts with the customers needs and wants and tailors the product to meet these through a differentiated or concentrated marketing strategy

CHARACTERISTICS OF THE GLOBAL MARKET

The above comments on globalisation indicate that, in our opinion, Levitt's original conceptualisation of globalisation, which is still widely subscribed to, is flawed and is antithetical to the marketing concept. It is a production and selling orientation that seeks to impose the will of the seller on the buyer rather than starting with the buyers needs and working back from these in deciding what the firm should produce to satisfy them. However this criticism does not invalidate the fact that in the past 30 years or so a truly global market has developed.

Many of the factors leading to the development of this global market were summarised in the earlier quotation from Levitt's 1983 article on globalisation. Driven by technology, advances in communication and transportation have made even the most remote communities aware of the attractions of modern products and mass consumption that offers a better quality of life and higher standard of living. Of course, technological innovation is not a new phenomenon but, as we pointed out in Chapter 1, it is one that is accelerating as each new breakthrough paves the way for many other related developments.

In 1903 the first manned flight covered a distance of 120 feet. In 2005 a new generation of super-jumbo jet was launched by Airbus with a fuselage longer than that first flight. In the past 25 years the impact of technological change has probably been as great as in the preceding 75 years. As an enabling technology the microchip has underpinned an enormous expansion on the management of information and made possible the solution of unbelievably complex problems such as those involved in telecommunications, space exploration, bio technology, genetic engineering and so forth.

According to Moore's Law, computing capacity doubles every 18 months and is accompanied by massive economies of scale and reductions in cost. By the

1990s personal computers were readily available at competitive prices allowing direct access to the world wide web and the Internet, creating a new 'virtual' marketplace in which even small organisations could compete on a level basis with giant multinational corporations (MNCs). Indeed, it is this phenomenon which accounts for the emergence of a truly global market.

In parallel with these developments, a major shift began to occur as manufacturing moved to countries with low labour costs, especially in South East Asia. As the original industrialised countries outsourced much of their production and operations to these countries so a new knowledge and service based economy began to take their place. Perhaps one of the most surprising decisions of early 2005 was IBMs decision to divest itself of it PC business which it sold to a Chinese company. This sale was prompted by a major shift in IBMs strategy to become an integrated solutions supplier.

Lee and Carter (2005) summarise the forces driving this kind of change under seven headings:

- The emergence of a *global service economy*.
- The emergence of *new economic powerhouses*.
- New directions in *global engagement*.
- *Growing transparency* in global practices.
- Advent of *new technologies*.
- Changing nature of *competition*.
- Changing *consumer demographics and expectations*.

Even in less developed countries services account for 40% of **Gross Domestic Product (GDP)**, while in Hong Kong it is 90%. Services also absorb more labour but add more value per capita – nearly 50% on average – and comprise a significant proportion of the total value of manufactured goods. Further, while international sales of services is less than a quarter of physical goods it is growing annually at more than twice the pace, and accelerating as the advanced economies outsource more and more of their production.

Reference has already been made to the BRIC countries that are posting record growth rates and rapidly catching up with the original industrial economies of Western Europe and the United States as the 'workshop of the world'.

Globalisation itself is a natural consequence of Ricardo's theory of comparative advantage based on specialisation, the division of labour and free trade. However, unless and until greater control can be achieved over the business cycle of inflation and recession, it is clear that the self-interest of the more affluent countries will be greatly exaggerated in the boom or bust conditions experienced by the developing economies that do business with them. Unbridled free trade of the kind described as 'Anglo-Saxon' capitalism in Chapter 1, needs to be mediated by regulation and international agreement. It is this that calls for what Lee and Carter term 'a new direction in global engagement' and was the theme of the G8 summit of the world's wealthiest nations held at Gleneagles in Scotland in the summer of 2005.

Changes in demographics and their implications for consumption have already been commented on, as have changes in competition, and the impact of new technology. All reinforce the need for a constant monitoring of the environment along the lines advocated in Chapter 4.

Finally, satellite technology and telecommunications mean that news spreads instantaneously – the effects of the tsunami on Indonesia were seen in Eastern Africa before the wave hit their coast. It is this that is motivating the pressure for greater transparency in both government and corporate behaviour. Social responsibility and ethical practices are now high on the corporate agenda.

Taken together it is these new 'megatrends' that Lee and Carter argue call for a new appreciation of and approach to global marketing management. Their book of this title is strongly recommended as an exposition of how the broadly based general theory explained in books like this needs to be adapted and modified to compete successfully in this new environment.

INTERNATIONAL MARKETING STRATEGY –
AN EMERGING ECONOMY VIEW

From time to time we have felt it necessary to remind the reader that textbooks such as this are written from the point of view of the large organisation, as it these that have the major influence on market structure and competition. At the same time it is also necessary to remember that the great majority of organisations are small to medium sized enterprises (SMEs) so that much of the advice may not be directly relevant to them. This caveat is especially true of the practice of globalisation as few small companies have the resources required to operate effectively in another country, let alone in many.

Of course, this does not prevent SMEs exporting to other countries, and the Internet has made it possible for even the smallest company to have a global presence. However, for the SME the real implication of globalisation is not so much the opportunity to sell in other countries but the likely impact of foreign companies competing with them in their own regional or national market. In this sense globalisation is potentially a major threat to the small firm with a regional market. Reference has already been made to the threat of competition from emerging economies, e.g. 'the China price'. In this section we report the findings of recent research in India – another emerging economy – which documents the approach being taken by Indian firms as they seek to move into other countries national markets.

Research by Oburai and Baker (*Vikalpa*, 2005) investigates the international marketing strategies adopted in twelve different business sectors in India in an attempt to explore and explain the similarities and differences found in a varied set of industries. The business sectors examined were Automobiles, CDs, Cement, Paints, Pharmaceuticals, Socks, Software, Syringes, Tea exports, Textiles, Two-wheeler tyres, and Watch components. The examples span the old economy industries such as the assembly and manufacturing enterprises that are both skill and capital intensive, and also the new economy sectors that are information intensive

Short descriptions of four of the industries studied follow to give a 'flavour' of both the more traditional and new industries where Indian firms play an increasingly important role in international trade.

Tea Exports

India produces almost one third of all the tea produced in the world. In 1999, the world production was almost three billion kilograms. However, India exports less than 200 million kg. India is also a big tea consuming nation Increasing unit value realisation from exports is a key challenge facing Indian firms. The main areas which have room for improvement are blending (processing), packing (tea bags), branding and marketing of tea. Moving up the value chain from being an agricultural commodity producer to being a marketer of life style and luxury products is a big challenge. Tata Tea acquired the Tetley brand from its UK owners and is making sustained efforts at becoming a high value life style marketer. While this upgrade is being attempted, India will need to continue to make efforts at holding on to its world market share in tea exports, and market shares in important markets. Government has a crucial role in organising the large number of tea farms and in helping tea boards and other institutions in charting out a strategy for the future.

Paints Industry

Asian Paints has embarked on an aggressive acquisition strategy to gain market leadership in several emerging markets. International business today accounts for 20% of the firm's revenues, and the company has presence in 22 countries. Asian Paints has a clear strategy with an objective of becoming a *leader in the emerging markets*. This strategy has several operational and strategic aspects.

First, the company acquired a few loss making businesses with a view to improve their performance by rationalising products, brands, and distribution outlets. Their focus on emerging markets is driven by the idea of leveraging the experience the company has gained in India over the last several decades. The sourcing of raw material (e.g. titanium dioxide), production and storing of finished goods and transport are managed using modern management techniques in a cost efficient manner. Shipping costs are very high in this industry with freight charges of around Rs 40 a litre (almost $1 per litre).

Acquiring market leaders in small markets requires limited resources as opposed to acquiring leading brands and firms in developed markets. Of the emerging markets, the company chooses the ones with high growth prospects (above 6% per annum). Asian Paints may have only limited resources, but recognises its limitation and operates within the resource constraints. While resources provide the initial momentum, its *ability to streamline processes* is what gives the company an extraordinary advantage over its competition.

CDs (Compact Discs)

Moser Baer India (MBI) is the third largest manufacturer of optical storage media in the world. MBI is one of the lowest cost manufacturers of CD-Rs globally. The company's production costs are lower than that of its Taiwanese counterparts by almost 62 per cent'. MBI has also invested heavily in increasing its CD and DVD (recordable, writable and pre-recorded) formats manufacturing capacities. About 80% of its revenues of Rs.1600 crore a year come from export and 60-70% of its revenues are earned by sales to OEM companies. Most of the world's leading brands source products from Moser Baer. MBI has increased manufacturing capacity to two billion units per year. 'The optical storage media industry has a 15 billion unit capacity, of which 70% of manufacturing is confined to Taiwan and Japan. MBI has started putting up a manufacturing facility in East Germany, and also has plans to firm up its strategy for the US in the near future. It is in talks with Imation Corp. of the US.

MBI has manufacturing scale built using less capital than it would take to build similar capacities elsewhere in the world, process skills to reduce material cost, lower manpower costs, and strong distribution channels for servicing its global OEM clients. Its capacities are currently concentrated in the factories located in Delhi.

Syringes and needles

Hindustan Syringes and Medical Devices (HMD) is a closely held company and derives about 25% of its revenues from exports to the US and Europe. In the Indian disposable Syringes market, which is nearly 1 Billion units p.a., HMD enjoys over 65% market share. Imports constitute 10% of this market . In the disposable needle market , HMD has a 70% market share, followed by imported brands with a 25% market share. The size of the disposable needles market is 1.5 billion units per annum. DISPOVAN is the dominant brand in the Indian market and has been able to maintain and increase its market share in face of stiff competition from major multinationals and domestic challengers'.

HMD has seven manufacturing facilities in India and had plans to increase its turnover to Rs. 250 crore by 2004. The World Health Organisation estimated the annual global demand of needles and syringes at 25-30 billion Disposable syringes account for a major proportion of the firm's turnover. HMD has been an OEM supplier for nearly 15 years. HMD is among the global top five manufacturers in the insulin syringe market. In 2002 the company started manufacturing auto disposable syringes in collaboration with Star Syringes of the UK. 'Manufacturing of products requires critical imports, and the company imports 95% of consumables and disposables'.

HMD has global scale facilities and relies on *high volumes to gain low cost and high quality advantages*. The company continues to expand its manufacturing capacities and distribution network.

Analysis of international marketing strategies

In order to analyse the strategies of the 12 case companies the researchers employed a mix of case research (Yin 1994) and grounded theoretic methodology (Glaser and Strauss 1967). Twelve variables were extracted from the sector case studies and case summaries and these are summarised in Table 24.1. The columns define the twelve key variables and our assessment of the degree of importance (measured on a Likert scale of 1-5) for each of the 10 variables for each of the 12 chosen industries.

The twelve variables in Table 1 above may be categorised into three broad categories namely Business/sector characteristics, product characteristics and market/transaction characteristics.

- *Business/sector characteristics:* Capital requirement, Technology requirement, Process skill requirement, Value addition prospects, Need for supplier network, and Export volumes.

    A number of the businesses studied require high capital and technology

Table 24.1 International marketing in India - a comparison of twelve industries / business sectors

No	Industry	Business Characteristics						Product Characteristics			Market & Transaction Characteristics		
		Capital Require ment	Tech. Require ment	Process Skill	Value Addition Prospects	Need for Supplier Network	Export Volume	Unit Value	Dura- bility	Freight Cost	Market Sophist- ication	Direct Contact with Customer	Competition
1	Automobiles	High	High	Med	High	High	Med	High	High	High	High	High	High
2	CDs	High	High	Med	Med	Low	High	Low	Med	Low	High	Low	High
3	Cement	High	Low	Low	Low	Med	High	Low	High	High	Low	Low	High
4	Paints	Med	Med	Med	med	Med	High	Low	Med	High	Med	Med	High
5	Pharmaceutical	High	High	High	High	Low	High	Low	Low	Low	High	Low	High
6	Socks Manuf.	Low	Low	Low	Low	Low	High	Low	Low	Low	Low	Low	High
7	Software	Low	High	Med	High	Low	Low	High	Med	Low	High	High	Med
8	Syringes	Med	Med	Low	Low	Low	High	Low	Low	Low	High	Low	Med
9	Tea Exports	Low	Low	Low	Low	Low	High	Med	Low	Low	Med	Low	Med
10	Textiles Sector	Med	Med	Med	Med	Med	High	Med	Med	Low	Med	Low	High
11	Two-Wheeler Tyres	Med	High	Med	Med	Low	Med	High	Med	Med	High	Med	Med
12	Watch parts	Med	High	High	Med	Low	Med	Med	Med	Low	High	Med	Low

Source: Oburai, P. and Baker, M. J. (2005), Reproduced with permission from the article titled 'International Marketing Strategies in India: An Application of Mixed Method Investigation', published in *Vikalpa: The Journal for Decision Makers*, a quarterly publication of the Indian Institute of Management, Ahmedabad, India.

investments. Process skill requirements are also very high in pharmaceutical and watch components making. Several of the industries (e.g. cars) need strong and extensive supplier networks. Value addition prospects in cars, software, and pharmaceuticals businesses may be more substantial than in a few other sectors such as socks and cement. Export volumes need to be high in several of the sectors examined. Software sector is an exception, as is the automobile business.

■ *Product characteristics:* Unit value, Durability and Freight cost.

Cars have high unit value, as do customised software solutions. Both cars and software programs are durable with medium to long life cycles. Most services are considered to be highly perishable. However, this is not the case with software or with many products that use embedded software. For example, cars and other durables including washing machines, TVs and mobile phones increasingly use electronic chips. However, products have a transferability issue to deal with. Cars incur fairly high shipping freight, as does a cement bag or paint can. Software and other services do not have this transport problem.

■ *Market/Transaction characteristics:* Market sophistication, Direct contact with customers and competition.

Competition in several sectors is high, and markets for a few products such as cars and watch parts can be very sophisticated. Contact with customers is crucial in many ways and managing customer relationships and nurturing these can be argued to be a crucial competence. In a number of international business situations, exporters may only be in contact with OEMs and hence may not have a direct contact with the end consumer.

The degree of importance that appears in the table is a *subjective assessment* on the part of the researchers and appears in the table as High (5), Medium (3) or Low (1) representing the variables nature and strength. This measurement is relative to the set of the chosen industries.

This study may also provide some prognosis for Indian businesses. The businesses that may have bright international prospects for the future will be from both manufacturing and service sectors. From the service sectors, insurance, banking firms may have the best prospects of all. The education sector can see a bright future if it can make calculated moves and bear associated risks. On the manufacturing front, motorcycle firms from India can take on a significant global role. Here Indian firms will have to focus on the small fuel efficient size engine motorcycle segment. Performance bikes and other high end segments may not be in their reach for some time to come given that an Indian consumer market for this segment is virtually non-existent at the moment. This prescription, however, does not preclude the internationalisation possibilities for parts and component suppliers. One can say that in the course of natural evolution, supplier firms (e.g. automotive batteries, tyres, and components) to all of the above twelve sectors that we examined should be able to increase their international presence.

Internationalisation is an imperative. That a large number of Indian organisations that do not internationalise may perish is not a dire prediction, but appears to be an inevitable outcome of the one-market world thesis. There will continue to be markets that will have strong and dominant local aspects attached to them. These markets will be fewer, and the local aspect a diminishing one. Competition will be more severe in these markets, and value addition possibilities transient and the technology element will be conspicuous by its absence. Strategies woven around commodities cannot be sources of sustainable competitive advantage. Many businesses will need to focus on serving the needs of sophisticated markets and consumers no matter where they are, irrespective of their location or country of residence. This top-end segment focus is necessary for both growth and constant renewal of competences. However, this does not preclude alternative strategies that aim to serve other segments. Our analysis that identified twelve key dimensions/ variables that go into the making of international marketing strategies shows that *direct contact with end customers* is an important element, but is only one among the set of variables identified. Several Indian firms are looking at acquisitions abroad, buying capacities (production facilities) or setting up offices (software firms). Some caution may be in order before such irretrievable and large investments are made. Firms from India and elsewhere would do well to also avoid being export myopic (Baker 1979). International marketing requires a multi-faceted strategic approach, and flexibility is as important as commitment. Market commitment is not synonymous with making fixed investments. Continuous value creation and delivery should be the focus of strategies. The twelve variables identified should be examined to look for harmonious balance and their ability to continue to provide a competitive edge. Most sectors and businesses may require strategies tailored for their specific needs and situations (Baker 1985). This means that those firms that have vast advantages, say in logistics or in managing customer contact, may think of enlarging their product portfolios, or the number of markets that they serve. *Thinking in terms of the twelve dimensions* individually and collectively while formulating and implementing international marketing strategies can help managers uncover the similarities and differences across business sectors. This is just a way of moving away from having focus solely on products, markets or business requirements.

The main point that emerges from this analysis of a number of Indian firms/ industries is that it is already accepted that if they are to survive in a global economy they must enhance their skills and competences to defend their domestic markets. More important, to prosper they must pursue market opportunities beyond the boundaries of these domestic markets and develop appropriate international marketing strategies.

APPROACHES TO MARKETING IN FOREIGN ENVIRONMENTS

As we have seen, there are numerous threats and opportunities which might predispose the firm to consider selling in foreign markets – the question is, 'How does one set about it?' In ascending order of commitment the alternatives available may be summarised as:

- *Exporting;*
- *Licensing;*
- *Contract manufacturing;*
- *Management contracting;*
- *Joint Venture;*
- *Establishment of subsidiaries.*

Direct exporting is essentially direct selling in a foreign market, and thus requires the firm to take full responsibility for establishing contact with potential customers. **Indirect exporting** occurs when the exporter employs the services of middlemen to look after the distribution, and often the complete marketing, of the product. **Channel policy** is a technical aspect of marketing, and the general principles discussed in Chapter 6 and elsewhere are equally applicable to foreign and domestic markets. Thus, the same considerations of cost versus control should be evaluated in the context of direct versus indirect exporting. The decision to export direct will almost always necessitate the establishment of sales offices and the appointment of full-time employees to staff them, although other functions, such as physical distribution and advertising, may be delegated to agents. Supporters of the direct approach argue that the setting up of branch offices and the employment of salesmen are reassuring to potential buyers as they represent a definite commitment to the market, as well as giving the marketer direct control over elements such as price, credit policy, after-sales service, and so forth.

In the case of technically complex industrial goods, with a small, clearly defined potential market, the direct approach is probably to be preferred. However, where the product is simple, largely undifferentiated and aimed at a mass market, most manufacturers prefer to use middlemen and test the market before committing themselves to an extensive sales and distribution network. As in the home market, middlemen fall into two main categories – merchants or whole-salers who purchase goods outright for resale, and agents who act on the manufacturer's behalf in return for a fee or commission on sales. The same problems of control discussed earlier have to be discounted against the economics of using middlemen, although it is probably true to say that the middleman's contacts in a foreign country are more valuable to the manufacturer than they are in a domestic market

OTHER ALTERNATIVES

Broadly speaking, three other alternatives are open to the firm which wishes to operate on an international scale:

1 It can **license** a foreign company to manufacture to its specification, for example Pilkington licensed Corning Glass to manufacture float glass in the United States.
2 It can undertake a **joint venture** with another company; for example Gerber's alliance with Corn Products.
3 It can set up a **subsidiary** company.

Licensing has several factors to recommend it:

■ It avoids the risk of expropriation of assets by the 'host' country, already familiar to many British companies with subsidiaries overseas.
■ It avoids direct competition with the licensee on their home ground. (Obviously, the licensee must have the same skills and resources as the licensor or there would be no point in taking up the license.)
■ It allows the capital resources that would be tied up in increased capacity, at home or abroad, to be deployed in other profitable opportunities. In the

absence of the necessary capital resources, it permits the earning of increased profits which would otherwise be unattainable.

■ It enables the product to be produced at a competitive price, which might not be possible if it were to be exported as a finished good; for example float glass is both bulky and fragile and transportation costs would probably price it out of every foreign market where it is currently produced under licence.

■ Licensing avoids import tariffs and restrictions, and minimises the possibility of loss due to a change in trade policy.

■ It avoids the risks of product failure.

The major disadvantage to licensing is that the royalties are invariably less than the normal profits which would be earned if the product were manufactured and sold by the licensor.

Joint ventures require a greater commitment by the firm than is necessary in the case of licensing but, if successful, offer greater rewards for the risks assumed. An alliance with a well established foreign distributor or manufacturer smooths the exporter's entry into the market, but can lead to bitter conflict over policy and practice.

The establishment of a foreign subsidiary exposes one to all the risks which licensing minimises. Tax incentives are often offset by requirements that nationals of the foreign country hold a majority of the shares in the subsidiary, in which case it becomes a joint venture. It is also probably true to say that such incentives are directly proportionate to the risks.

In politically stable countries, however, the wholly owned subsidiary frequently offers the greatest potential – a factor which tends to be overlooked by restrictions on overseas investment. Economies of local production can be reinforced by the parent's technical, financial and marketing expertise and resources. Past experience would seem to suggest that the parent should avoid keeping too tight a rein on its subsidiary, and should be prepared to appoint foreign managers and delegate authority for all but major policy decisions to them. Long established European companies active in international markets would appear to have accepted this principle, but American firms have only lately begun to come round to this point of view, after some fairly costly attempts to retain full control at 'head office'.

Space limitations preclude fuller analysis of international marketing, for which the reader must refer to specialised texts on the subject. It is worth reiterating, however, that such texts rest on the same marketing principles as have been discussed in this book, so that their major contribution lies in the descriptive content rather than in their treatment of marketing technology.

Summary

In this chapter we have attempted a broadly based and wide-ranging review of the scope and nature of marketing in a foreign environment. We have deliberately avoided using the more commonplace term 'International Marketing' for two reasons. First, this is an introductory text book concerned with general principles. In our view the general principles of marketing are universally applicable so that the material contained in earlier chapters is just as relevant to foreign markets as domestic ones. Despite this, our second reason for not using the more usual and more fashionable 'international marketing' is because this constitutes a distinctive sub-field of the subject which deserves specialised treatment and it is not possible to achieve this in an introductory text. For these reasons we have chosen to emphasise how marketing is a vital element in economic growth wherever it occurs.

To begin with, we pointed out that many observers appear to see the challenge of the emerging BRIC economies as a new one whereas, in our opinion, knowledge of Rostow's model of the stages of economic growth points clearly to the challenges and possible solutions associated with with this phase of economic development. Similarly, given that economies are associated with nation states, then the advantages and disadvantages of competition and exchange between them is an issue of major importance and the theory of comparative advantage provides important insights into the benefits of international trade.

As a result of accelerating technological change Levitt (1983) articulated the view that globalisation was occurring and resulting in "the explosive emergence of global markets for globally standardised products". While globalisation has come about it has not followed the path suggested by Levitt which we characterised as being flawed in that it represented an undifferentiated marketing strategy which, in turn, reflects a production orientation. While it is true that there are global brands their marketing has frequently been adapted to reflect local conditions – glocalisation – which is a differentiated strategy based on a marketing orientation. In truth, the main impact of technological change, reinforced by the development of the Internet, has been the creation of an ability to access markets anywhere in the world which is the real meaning of global markets.

Recognising the opportunity offered by marketing in foreign environments the chapter concluded with a review of the different marketing approaches available.

Review questions and problems

1 Every advanced economy was once an emerging economy. Discuss.

2 Describe Rostow's model of stages of economic growth. In what ways might it be used in informing policy in a developing country?

3 Explain Ricardo's theory of comparative advantage. Of what relevance is it today?

4 Outline Levitt's views on globalisation. Why might these be described as 'production oriented'?

5 What is 'glocalisation'? Explain its application to a global brand of your choice in terms of two different countries.

6 Planning for international market entry and development involves a process of matching company capabilities and objectives with the requirements and characteristics of selected country markets. Discuss with reference to company and country examples.

7 Using company examples to illustrate your answer, evaluate the major trends currently taking place in the global competitive strategies of MNEs.

8 'Global marketing is not just standardisation of the marketing mix.' Evaluate this statement with particular reference to the product and promotion elements of the mix.

Key terms

BRIC countries	gross domestic product (GDP)	NAFTA
channel policy	incentives	newly industrialised economies
comparative cost advantage	indirect exporting	(NICs)
concentrated strategy	international marketing	optimum growth
Department of Trade and Industry	international trading	price ratios
(DTI)	communities	product life-cycle (PLC)
differentiated strategy	joint venture	pull incentives
direct exporting	LAFTA	quality of life
dynamic approach	less developed countries	scale economies
EFTA	(LDCs)	segmentation
emergent economies	license	standard of living
EU	market segments	subsidiary
global market	marketing productivity	theory of comparative
global service economy	materialism	advantage
globalisation	megatrends	undifferentiated strategy
glocalisation	multinational corporations	virtual marketplace
	(MNCs)	

Supplementary reading list

Bennett, R. and Blythe, J. (2002), *International Marketing: Strategy, Planning, Market Entry and Implementation* 3rd edn, (London: Kogan Page).

Bradley, F. (2004), *International Marketing Strategy*, 5th edn (FT Prentice-Hall)

Czinkota, M. and Ronkainen, I. K. (2003), *International Marketing*, 7th edn (South Western College Publishing).

Douglas, S. P. and Craig, C. S. (1995), *Global Marketing Strategies* (New York: McGraw-Hill).

Jain, S. C. (1993), *International Marketing Management*, 4th edn (Wadsworth).

Jeannet, J. P. and Hennessey, H. D. (2004), *Global Marketing Strategies*, 6th edn (Boston: Houghton Mifflin).

Lee, K. and Carter, S. (2005), *Global Marketing Management*, (Oxford: Oxford University Press)

Paliwoda, S. J. (1995), *International Marketing*, 2nd edn (London: Heinemann).

Usunier, J. C. and Lee, J. (2005), *Marketing Across Cultures* 4th edn (Upper Saddle River, NJ.: Prentice Hall).

Yip, G. S. (2003), *Total Global Strategy II* (Upper Saddle River, NJ.: Prentice Hall).

Young, S., Hamill, J. and Wheeler, C. (1989), *International Market Entry and Development: Strategy and Management* (Brighton: Wheatsheaf).

CURRENT ISSUES AND FUTURE TRENDS

25

Learning Goals

■ After reading this chapter you will be familiar with some of the current and future issues that need to be addressed by marketers.

INTRODUCTION

In the ten years that have elapsed since the last major revision of this book numerous changes have occurred in marketing practice, many of which were anticipated in the equivalent chapter in that edition. The nature and consequences of these changes have been incorporated in the main body of the text, but it still remains to highlight some current issues that are likely to have a significant impact in the future. Before doing so, however, it is important to underline a constant theme throughout the book – *there are very few genuinely new problems.* Most of the issues which pre-occupy us today have also exercised the minds of previous generations. It follows that we should first consider what we already know before wasting time and effort in re-inventing hard-won knowledge. It is for this reason that we have stressed the insights and seminal contributions of some of the earlier researchers in marketing as well as our indebtedness to scholars in other disciplines like economics, psychology and sociology.

Consider, for example, the 'future strategic imperatives and priorities for marketing' identified by Peter Doyle in the Second Edition of his book *Marketing Management and Strategy* (1997):

- *Speed* – in reducing design and delivery cycle times;
- *Customisation* – to meet customer needs in increasingly fragmented markets;
- *Quality* – as a basic prerequisite for competitiveness;
- *Information* – as a source of competitive advantage;
- *Core focus* – on real corporate capabilities;

- *Globalisation* – to spread risks and costs internationally;
- *Software differentiation* – augmenting products with service and the like;
- *Partnerships* – with customers and distributors;
- *Innovation* – for constant new products and processes, and;
- *Recognising multiple stakeholders* in the firm.

Nearly ten years on these remain the priorities today and their implications have been explored in the main body of the text. Accordingly, for this chapter, we will confine our attention to six topics that we think will dominate the marketing scene over the next few years:

1 *The implications of the Internet for marketing strategy*
2 *E-marketing*
3 *Ethics in marketing*
4 *Environmental issues and the importance of 'Green Marketing'*
5 *Social marketing*
6 *A new model of marketing*

MARKETING STRATEGY AND THE INTERNET

Writing in the *Harvard Business Review* in 2001, Michael Porter made an important point that is still frequently overlooked – the Internet is an **enabling technology** the impact of which has been greatest in industries "constrained by high costs for communicating, gathering information, or accomplishing transactions". While **E-commerce** has permeated large organisations, and spawned a generation of **dot.com organisations**, proportionately its impact has been greatest on small to medium sized firms. This is because in a global market the economies of scale in manufacturing that gave rise to the multinational corporation have been largely eroded due to advances in other technologies, the widespread availability of cheap labour in emerging economies like the South East Asian 'tigers' and, more recently, countries like India and China. As a result economies of scale are now mainly to be found in marketing expenditure on selling, promotion and distribution.

As we have seen, for an effective demand to exist a customer must be aware of the existence of a good or service that might meet their need, and be able to get access to it – consumption is a function of availability. With the advent of the Internet and the worldwide web even the smallest organisation can make itself known to a world market at negligible cost. This ability greatly increases the scope of competition through a **levelling effect**, that significantly reduces the potential for sustaining a competitive advantage, with a marked impact on industry structure. As we saw in Chapter 4, structure, conduct and performance are inextricably linked to one another from which it follows that all organisations must be sensitive to the potential effects of the Internet on their strategy.

Indeed, it was this issue that prompted Porter, one of the world's leading authorities on competitive strategy, to explore the Internet's implications for strategy. While written some years ago on a topic notorious for the rapidity of change, many of his observations have either come about or remain valid. Most importantly, Porter argues that the Internet has not made strategy obsolete but needs to be incorporated into one's strategy to complement existing ways of doing things. As with any innovation its introduction encourages experimentation which can lead to mixed, and sometimes misleading messages from the marketplace. Accordingly, one should not rush to conclusions but should monitor trends to detect those which are likely to survive.

Thus, during the launch phase many firms used, and continue to use price as a competitive weapon. As has been evident in numerous failures, it is questionable how long individual firms can sustain this, especially as many of the start-up costs have been subsidised or set off against stock. While competitive prices are attractive when the buyer knows the precise specification of the desired product or service, backed up by a reputable brand, economic rationality would predict that you would buy from the lowest cost supplier – the *DaVinci Code* or the latest *Harry Potter* are the same everywhere. On the other hand, if you are not quite sure what you would like to read, browsing a bookshop adds value and so can command a higher price. Indeed, with most shopping goods, and all specialty goods, the shopping experience is an integral part of the exchange. So while the price conscious segment may grow, higher premiums may be obtained from less price-sensitive customers seeking additional services and experiences.

Porter observes:

Indeed the Internet has given rise to an array of new performance metrics that have only a loose relationship to economic value, such as pro forma measures of income that remove "nonrecurring" costs like acquisitions. The dubious connection between reported metrics and actual profitability has served only to amplify the confusing signals about what has been happening in the marketplace.

As a consequence the inflated stock prices of the dot.com bubble did not reflect real economic value which Porter observes is "nothing more than the gap between price and costs, and is reliably measured only by sustained profitability". This is the acid test, and the two drivers that determine profitability are industry structure and sustainable competitive advantage. As has become apparent, in many cases the Internet did not alter existing structures, and/or was unable to confer a sustainable advantage in that its benefits were available to all that adopted it.

This outcome confirms Porter's prediction that his model of the five competitive forces would still prevail, and that one would still need to review these on an individual industry/company basis in order to determine the likely impact of the Internet on competition. He perceived the potential positive impacts as consisting of a dampening of the bargaining power of channels, reduced barriers to entry and increased operating efficiencies. However, potential negative impacts were increased bargaining power, lower barriers to entry, a more open system reducing proprietary advantages, increased competition from a larger market, and reduced variable costs, e.g. on promotion, which would emphasise the importance of fixed costs and prompt price competition. Ebay is an example of the potential of the positive impacts while competition in auto retailing illustrated the negative impacts.

The rush into the Internet was based, according to Porter, on the assumption that its use would increase switching costs and create strong network effects with important first-mover advantages for strong new economy brands. These assumptions were flawed. Other new technologies have made switching much simpler and network effects only create a barrier to entry if they are proprietary to one company. Few can achieve this and it has also been difficult to establish strong internet brands.

While most of the attention on the impact of the Internet has been focused on the **B2C** market its use was pioneered in **B2B** markets where it has had major effects on procurement and the use of outsourcing.. While supply partnerships are often promoted as offering a 'win-win' outcome for both parties, it is clear that this is not always the case. Dominant sellers/buyers will still seek to obtain concessions from their 'partners' leading to instability in the supply chain and opportunities for new competitors. Similarly, while outsourcing can reduce costs in the short term and increase flexibility, in the long term it can lead to homogeneous inputs, a lack of distinctiveness, and increased price competition. In a word "**commoditisation**".

The **digital marketplace** creates the opportunity to automate corporate procurement and offers buyers "low transaction costs, easier access to price and product information, convenient purchase of associated services, and, sometimes, the ability to pool volume. The benefits to suppliers include lower selling costs, lower transaction costs, access to wider markets and the avoidance of powerful channels". (Porter, op.cit.). However, the nature and extent of these potential benefits will vary in terms of the existing industry structure and the products involved emphasising the importance of the structure/conduct/performance model introduced in Chapter 4. It must also be remembered that it is in the nature of competition that successful firms may be expected to develop new strategies to cope with the changing competitive environment. It follows that an innovation like the Internet represents a major opportunity but only if it is integrated effectively into the firm's operations.

Porter reiterates that the only sure way to achieve a sustainable competitive advantage is by operating at a lower cost or commanding a premium price. These may be obtained in two ways – **operational effectiveness** and **strategic positioning**. He sees the Internet as "arguably the most powerful tool available today for enhancing operational effectiveness. By easing and speeding the exchange of real time information, it enables improvements throughout the entire value chain, across almost every company and industry". But these benefits are available to all and are easily copied. In consequence, it is more difficult to maintain an operational advantage so, if anything, strategic positioning and flexible implementation have become even more important.

Porter comments: "Strategy goes far beyond the pursuit of best practices. It involves the configuration of a tailored value chain – the series of activities required to produce and deliver a product or service – that enables a company to offer unique value. To be defensible, moreover, the value chain must be highly integrated". As we saw in Chapter 4, when it is, competitors need to be able to replicate it all to compete directly.

In Porter's opinion, confirmed by events, many Internet pioneers have "competed in ways that violate nearly every precept of good strategy. Rather than focus on profits, they have sought to maximise revenues and market share at all costs, pursuing customers indiscriminately through discounting, giveaways, promotions, channel incentives, and heavy advertising". This is a destructive **zero-sum** form of competition and a 'race to the bottom'.

Much of Porter's diagnosis has been confirmed by events. While the Internet has created opportunities for new kinds of companies to develop, comparatively few have been 'successful' and profitable on a large scale. The major beneficiaries have been small to medium sized firms that can now access a global market without incurring the huge promotional costs that previously precluded this. As an enabling technology it has the potential to confer significant benefits but these are available to all. Failure to integrate the potential of the Internet into one's ongoing strategy and operations can only result in a loss of competitiveness.

In 2000 research by the *Institute of Customer Service* led by Chris Voss of London Business School identified seven factors that make eCommerce qualitatively unlike anything that has preceded it (Johns, 2002). These are identified as:

1 *It challenges traditional business models.* Lower costs, new distribution routes, new partnerships, and new approaches to customer segmentation all create opportunities for imaginative entrepreneurs.

2 *It exploits the new economics of information.*

3 *It can create new networks of communication.* Organisations can now promote and sell their goods and services through many websites.

4 *It takes out some intermediaries and generates opportunities for others.*

5 *It generates high velocity – of information, logistics and money.*

6 *It promotes transparency, especially for pricing.*

7 *It significantly enhances customer power.*

Johns argues that in order to exploit these changes it is essential to take a customer focused view of the business. In his view conventional marketing, proselytised by the 'marketing management' school, is mechanical due to its emphasis on manipulation of the 4Ps in terms of what is considered important to the organisation.

> Rarely is what is important to the organisation, of equal importance to the customer. Remember that what a company sells is never what the customer buys.
> The company sells cold, dead fish; the customer buys sushi.

In other words, the customer is seeking to satisfy what have been termed the **4Cs** of **Convenience, Consumer needs/wants, Cost** and **Communication.** Clearly, goods and services must be available; they must deliver the satisfactions looked for by customers and meet their expectations; they must add value, and the supplier must be trusted by the customer, leading to a relationship between them. Even in the case of low involvement goods and services, the brand, and all that it signifies for the customer, can convert a basic transaction into a relationship with that brand.

Where much eCommerce has failed it is because it has failed to encourage a relationship with the customer. Johns cites research that shows that visit-to-buy conversion rates are very low – less that 2% in the majority of cases; that 41% of online shoppers are more likely to buy if they have human contact with the supplier, e.g. by telephone contact, and that 50% say that email response is unsatisfactory. However, many online organisations also use automated telephone answering systems which are a source of irritation and frustration to callers, and so compound the communication failings.

The answer to these problems is to improve the service levels and Johns makes a number of suggestions to achieve this classified into three groups that he terms foundation factors, potential differentiators, and exciters.

Foundation factors cover four elements:

1 *Website responsiveness*

2 *Ease of navigation*

3 *Website effectiveness*

4 *Fulfilment and delivery*

Potential differentiators include creating trust, providing information and feedback, and enabling the buyer to customise the product or service to their particular need, e.g. Dell with computers.

As for 'exciters' these are mainly comprised of proactive and value added services. **Proactive services** are of the kind where you ask the supplier to notify you when something occurs in which you are interested, e.g. special offers, while value added services are those that exceed the customers expectations of what they will receive.

While we do not see the Internet as replacing traditional channels of communication and distribution, it is clear that it offers benefits that cannot be ignored and need to be incorporated into the organisation's marketing strategy. This will remain a major challenge for management in the coming years with those firms that do it well prospering, while others that do not will lose market share. For example, Reed Elsevier, Europe's largest media group, reported in 2005 that its online sales had increased to 29% of turnover compared with nothing five years previously. Further, rather than seeing Google as a threat, Elsevier had formed an alliance with them – Google looking after delivery and Elsevier looking after content – so optimising their respective strengths.

E-MARKETING

In the decade that has passed since the last major revision of this book perhaps the most important single development has been the growth of the Internet and the emergence of what has come to be known as **e-marketing**. Despite a number of teething troubles, including the bursting of the dot.com bubble,

THE INTERNET AS CHANNEL OF COMMUNICATION/DISTRIBUTION

In 2001 George Shaheen resigned as CEO of Andersen Consulting (now Accenture) to take over online grocer Webvan which collapsed soon after with losses of nearly $1 billion. When asked why it failed he stated "The basic mistake was it was built for scale. It was conceived under the belief that if you build it, they will come. There weren't enough loyal customers for repeat shopping, and the reason is a huge behavioural science problem". (Business Week, June 27, 2005).

The message is clear – the Internet is a new and additional channel of communication / distribution. It is not a substitute for old ones, but is complementary to them and the same principles of effective marketing apply just as much to it as any other channels.

reminiscent of the famous seventeenth century collapse of the South Sea Bubble, also precipitated by extravagant get-rich-quick speculation, electronic media have had a major impact on the practice of marketing. The ability to process huge volumes of data have led to the creation of powerful databases like ACORN, to JIT and stockless purchasing, to **customer relationship management (CRM)**, to new channels of communication and distribution. As we have seen, however, electronic technology offers an opportunity to innovate in marketing practice; it is not a universal panacea capable of solving all marketing problems, and certainly not a substitute for the more traditional techniques and approaches with which this book is mainly concerned.

One of the leading UK authorities on e-marketing is David Chaffey, the author of a leading textbook on the subject and the contributor of an authoritative overview in *The Marketing Book* 5th Edition (2003). To begin with Chaffey identifies a number of very similar descriptors – **electronic commerce, electronic business,** and **electronic marketing.** The latter is probably the most broadly defined as "the use of electronic communications technology to achieve marketing objectives". Chaffey then defines what he means by 'electronic communications technology' as follows:

1 *The use of Internet-based (TCP/IP) network technology for communications within an organisation using an intranet, beyond the organisation to partners such as suppliers, distributors and key account customers using password-based access to extranets and the open Internet, where information is accessible to all with Internet access.*

2 *The use of webservers or websites to enable informational or financial exchanges as e-commerce transactions.*

3 *The use of other digital access platforms, such as interactive digital TV, wireless or mobile phones and games consoles.*

4 *The use of electronic mail for managing enquiries (in-bound e-mail) and for promotion (outbound e-mail).*

5 *Integration of the digital access platforms and e-mail with other information systems, such as customer databases and applications for customer relationship management and supply chain management.*

In an article which appeared in the *Journal of Customer Behaviour* in 2005, Constantinides draws attention to the spectacular growth of the Internet, its economic importance and potential as a present and future commercial environment. "During ten years of commercial presence, more than nine hundred million web users worldwide (ClickZ Statistics, 2004) have gained access to a vast virtual high street displaying a wide assortment of products, services, information, entertainment, education offered for browsing or sale on an ubiquitous, global basis. Having broken all previous adoption rates records of technological innovations, the Internet and more specifically its multimedia hypertext component better know as the Web, is widely considered as the motor behind the extraordinary high-tech boom and bust of the 1990s".

Citing numerous examples, Constantinides focuses on the on-line customers behaviour and the implications this has for the marketer, particularly in terms of those factors that are under the marketers control, and those that are not. While factors such as the environment and the personal characteristics of the customer are outwith the marketers control for both traditional and virtual customers, there are some essential differences when examining the controllable elements. Constantinides observes: "Regarding controllable marketing tools it can be argued that the decision-making process of online consumers can be influenced not only by online but also by physical marketing in the form of mass advertising, sales promotions, publicity or direct marketing". But, in his opinion, these are not likely to play a significant role in acquiring and retaining online customers. In part this is because of the diminishing effectiveness of mass marketing, the changing nature of the virtual consumer, and the more limited geographical reach of traditional methods in a global market. Indeed, he likens surfing the Internet to the experience of a traditional shopper walking through a shopping mall who may stop in front of a store they have never seen before and decide whether or not to enter it and, possibly, buy something. In other words it is the 'shopping experience' that prompts action and in the same way that the store appearance, display, layout etc. may attract custom so may the organisations web site.

The website is seen as the focus for most e-marketing. Not only is it the major source of information about the organisation, but it a shop window for the goods and services it has on offer. As noted, some parts of the website will be open to allcomers while other can only be accessed by registering (so providing the owner with useful information on who is interested in it), and still others only available to persons who are members, e.g. CIMs 'knowledgehub', or otherwise authorised to use it, e.g customers.

Constantinides notes: "The positive impact of a Web shop on the potential customer – and mainly the first-time visitor – must be powerful and immediate in order to be effective. Web sites failing to capture the attention of the virtual potential customer in a very short time could risk losing substantial online business. According to a recent report of *doubleClick.com* while the average number of web pages viewed per session is up by 12% in 2004 against 2003, the average consumer now spends 29 seconds per page down from 32.5 last year". It follows that design, and the viewers web experience, are critical success factors and Constantinides reports the findings of his extensive research into the subject.

ADOPTION OF COMMUNICATIONS TECHNOLOGY IN THE UK

In its Annual review of the communications market published in July 2005 **Ofcom**, the communications regulator, reported that broadband internet connections had overtaken the number of dial-up connections. Since its launch in 2001 broadband connections had reached 8.1 million by June 2005 taking only four years to become ubiquitous – something that took television 30 years to accomplish!

This large-scale adoption has created a digital mass market making it possible to download music, listen to the radio, play network computer games or watch television online.

Other details from the review showed that 62 per cent of households are now connected to some form of digital television and that in 2004 mobile telecom revenues of £12.3 billion surpassed those of fixed lines at £10.5 billion. Overall, the spend on communications is now £19.78 up from £14.45 in 2000, a growth rate of nearly 4 per cent per year.

(Source: *The Times*, 14/7/2005)

Thus, most studies point to the fact that 'usability' is the most important factor followed by 'trust building'.

In his analysis Chaffey (2003) identifies *six* key changes involved in using both traditional and digital media which he summarises as:

1 From *push to pull.*

2 From *monologue to dialogue.*

3 From *one-to-many to one-to-some and one-to-one.*

4 From *one-to-many to many-to-many communications.*

5 From *'lean-back' to 'lean-forward'.*

6 *Integrated.*

In other words digital media have different properties from traditional media but these are largely complementary and need to be integrated.

E-TAILING

Without doubt the Internet, and especially its multimedia hypertext component known as the Web, has had a revolutionary impact on communication and led to the emergence of completely new patterns of buyer behaviour variously known as *e-commerce* and *e-tailing*. In 2004 it is estimated that over 60 percent of adult internet users in the USA were active online buyers and made 134 million purchases, while in Europe more than 30 per cent of internet users bought online. The trend is accelerating and Forrester Research predicts that online sales could reach 12% of general merchandise sales in the US by 2010.

As would be expected, the scope and nature of these changes has attracted huge attention from academics and practitioners alike, and resulted in numerous studies and reports on the effect e-marketing has had. In general, most researchers agree that virtual consumers behave in much the same way as traditional consumers buying from physical outlets. However, given that e-commerce is in its infancy, one should not assume that this will always be the case and it is quite possible that with increased experience new generations of shoppers may develop new patterns of behaviour.

For example, it could be that an increasing volume of convenience goods will be bought without the physical hassle of sourcing them in retail outlets (bricks and mortar). By contrast, shopping as a social and leisure experience for shopping and specialty goods may take on an even greater role in our lives. Either way, the consumers experience of the physical or virtual environment will have a major effect on behaviour and it is already apparent that there are important differences between the two. Constantinides (2004) in a wide ranging review of the customers web experience, argues that there are some essential differences when buying online in terms of the ways in which the seller can control factors that influence the buyer's decision making process.

In his view, traditional marketing activities like mass advertising, sales promotion, publicity and direct marketing are less likely to play a significant role in attracting and retaining online customers.. In part this is due to the diminishing effectiveness of mass marketing; in part to the changing nature of the virtual consumer; and in part to the fact that traditional marketing tools do not have the same potential to reach a dispersed global market at a low cost in the way that the web can. But, to exploit this opportunity, it is vital that web sites attract and hold the surfers attention, and enable them to interact easily with the site so as to move them from interest to desire and action. Web design and the web

Basically, marketers can use the Internet as a communication channel, a distribution channel, a direct sales channel or a combination of these. As with any other marketing decision the acid test is which approach is likely to prove most effective in terms of achieving the organisation's objectives. Issues of cost versus control are critical in any distribution channel decision (see Chapter 16) but, as we saw when reviewing the business system in Chapter 5, the existing channels tend to have evolved as the most efficient means of moving goods and services along the supply or value chain. In this sense they represent part of the marketing environment within which both existing and new firms must work. What distinguishes the Internet as a distribution channel is that it offers an opportunity to even the smallest start-up company to reach a global market with a minimal investment and significant benefits arising from what is called disintermediation.

Essentially, disintermediation means by-passing intermediaries such as agents, wholesalers, retailers etc. and going direct to the customer. The prime advantages of doing this are that through direct interaction with potential customers one can save on distribution costs, improve on service delivery and build up a customer franchise of one's own, rather than depending on the reseller. As noted a critical thing to consider is the design of the website and making sure that it is readily identified by the major search engines like Google that direct new users to potential suppliers. Another thing to remember is that, as with the traditional channels, the Internet is accessible to all so that if you decide to establish a web presence you need to monitor carefully all the others who have chosen the same option.

It is also important to recognise that the impact of the Internet has been different in B2B as compared with B2C situations. Apart from monopolists, sellers generally have less power than their customers with the result that B2B buyers have adopted electronic methods as a means of improving their performance and competitiveness. Reference has already been made to stockless purchasing where the buyer's database identifies stock movements and automatically re-orders from its suppliers when necessary, reducing administrative costs for both parties and generally improving efficiency, control and performance. E-procurement also enables greater use of competitive bidding and price comparisons leading to economies for the buyer and a lower, more competitive cost base.

ETHICS IN MARKETING

While ethical issues have always existed in the domain of marketing, it is only in recent years that they have begun to attract explicit attention in mainstream marketing textbooks. Indeed the contemporary interest in ethics would seem to be closely related to the emergence of relationship marketing as the dominant paradigm in place of the marketing management model with its focus on the transaction which preceded it. Under the latter representation the transaction has often been seen as an adversarial model in which business seeks to 'win' at the expense of the consumer. It was this perception which gave rise to the consumerist movement of the 1950s and 60s, epitomised by books such as Vance Packard's *Hidden Persuaders*.

Nowadays, it is widely accepted that marketing is all about mutually satisfying exchange relationships in which both parties gain the satisfaction and benefits they are seeking. It is also accepted that 'relationship' implies a long-term and continuing association whereas 'transaction' refers to a one-off, or single exchange, albeit that a sequence of transactions may lead to a relationship. For a relationship to succeed there is an assumption that certain principles of behaviour will be accepted and observed and it is these which constitute the ethical dimension of the association.

According to N. Craig Smith in the *IEBM Encyclopedia of Marketing* (1999):

> *Marketing ethics can be defined as both the study of the moral evaluation of marketing and the standards applied in the judgement of marketing decisions, behaviours and institutions as morally right or wrong. It refers to a discipline and the subject matter of that discipline, the 'rules' governing the appropriateness of marketing conduct. It is a subset of business ethics, which in turn is a subset of ethics or moral philosophy. More simply, marketing ethics is about the moral problems of marketing managers. It includes, for example, the ethical considerations concerned with product safety, truth in advertising, and fairness in pricing. It is an integral part of marketing decision-making.*

Questions of what is right and wrong in business relationships have been discussed and debated for centuries, and Smith cites the Roman philosopher Cicero who examined the moral duties of merchants in his *De Officiis* as an early example. These questions found expression in the concept of social responsibility as an issue for corporate decision makers, and in classes with titles such as 'Business and Society', during the 1960s and 70s. Within the subject of marketing, ethical issues were most often identified with specific topics, with truth in advertising being one of the earliest and widely discussed themes. Product safety also attracted considerable attention, particularly after Ralph Nader's *Unsafe at any Speed* drew widespread attention to product defects in GM cars during the mid-1960s. Similarly, an increasing concern for the environment and the birth of the 'Green' movement focused concern on products and processes damaging to the environment such as the use of CFC as a propellant in aerosol products.

The latter is an excellent example of the need for both improved consumer education and regulation of business practice. Traditionally buyers and sellers have been regarded as being on an equal footing with the onus resting on the buyer to ensure that they received what they bargained for. Thus the Common Law concept of **caveat emptor** (let the buyer beware) assumes that if goods are openly available for sale then it is the buyer's responsibility to decide whether or not they wish to buy. With the increased availability of manufactured goods following the Industrial Revolution, and the insertion of intermediaries in channels of distribution between producer and consumer, **legislation** [the Sale of Goods Act 1892] was enacted to give greater protection to consumers and ensure that goods were fit for the purpose for which they were sold.

During the twentieth century the growing complexity of goods and services required a significant expansion in legislation to provide consumers with protection in terms of their basic rights as spelled out by President Kennedy in his first consumer address to Congress in 1962 namely:

1 *The right to safety* – to be protected against the marketing of goods which are hazardous to health or life.

2 *The right to be informed* – to be protected against fraudulent, deceitful or grossly misleading information, advertising, labelling or other practices, and

to be given the facts needed to make an informed choice.

3 *The right to choose* – to be assured, wherever possible, access to a variety of products and services at competitive prices and in those industries in which government regulations are substituted, an assurance of satisfactory quality and service at fair prices.

4 *The right to be heard* – to be assured that consumer interests will receive full and sympathetic consideration in the formulation of government policy and fair expeditious treatment in its administrative tribunals.

While the emergence of consumerism and the need for legislation to protect consumers have been designated 'the shame of marketing' on the grounds that a business discipline founded on the concept of mutual satisfaction should have no need for imposed regulations, most reasonable people would agree that in the real world of rapid technological innovation and change the market is too imperfect a mechanism to ensure producers will always act ethically to protect their long-term interests. Equally, in a competitive market-place the formulation of rules and regulations, through legislation and industry codes of practice, provides a baseline for minimum standards of performance common to all.

Clearly, if legislation exists breaches are illegal and can be dealt with by legal processes. That said, there will always be controversy about marginal cases and grey areas where interpretation will differ according to the individual's point of view. The nature and extent of these grey areas will become even more difficult where clear guidelines don't exist as is often the case with legislation. In a survey of marketing practitioners to determine what constitutes the most difficult ethical problem, Chonko and Hunt (1985) identified the following *10* issues in rank order of frequency of citation:

1 *Bribery* (most frequently cited; includes gifts from outside vendors, 'money under the table', payment of questionable commissions)

2 *Fairness* (manipulation of others, corporate interests in conflict with family interests, inducing customers to use services not needed)

3 *Honesty* (misrepresenting services and capabilities, lying to customers to obtain orders)

4 *Price* (differential pricing, meeting competitive prices, charging higher prices than firms with similar products while claiming superiority)

5 *Product* (products that do not benefit consumers, product and brand copyright infringements, product safety, exaggerated performance claims)

6 *Personnel* (hiring, firing, employee evaluation)

7 *Confidentiality* (temptation to use or obtain classified, secret or competitive information)

8 *Advertising* (misleading customers, crossing the line between puffery and misleading)

9 *Manipulation of data* (distortion, falsifying figures or misusing statistics or information)

10 *Purchasing* (reciprocity in supplier selection).

As Smith (op. cit.) observes many of these issues are not unique to marketing and apply to all managers. That said, as issues in the domain of business generally, they all impinge and impact upon the marketing function itself. In his chapter in the *IEBM Encyclopedia of Marketing*, however, Smith concentrates on those issues which he considers specific to marketing, namely:

- *Marketing research*
- *Target marketing*
- *Product policy*
- *Pricing*
- *Distribution*
- *Personal selling and salesforce management*
- *Advertising and sales promotion.*

Some of the key topics/issues which he identifies are as follows:

Marketing research: Research integrity – the potential conflict between scientific/ professional objectivity and business/commercial obligations. The rights of respondents – to choose, to safety and privacy (anonymity), to be informed (lack of deception) and to respect.

Target marketing: As this involves the selection of particular individuals this can give rise to problems of inclusion – intrusion of privacy, stereotyping, exploitation of vulnerable persons – and exclusion such as the withholding of products or services from disadvantaged sub-groups.

Product policy: The major ethical issues in product policy are:

- Product safety
- 'Questionable' products, that are harmful, in bad taste, or not considered socially beneficial
- 'Me-too' products and product counterfeiting
- Environmental impacts of products and packaging
- Deceptive practices in packaging or product quality specifications
- Planned obsolescence
- Arbitrary product elimination
- Service product delivery

Pricing: Like product issues, pricing is subject to extensive regulation on issues such as price fixing, price discrimination, predatory pricing and deceptive pricing.

Distribution: Most issues in distribution relate to the exercise of channel power whereby the larger and more powerful members in a channel use this power to exact an unfair advantage from their suppliers and/or customers. A particular topic of concern here is the power of multiple retailers. Franchising has also been cited as an area subject to abuse.

Personal selling: Smith suggests that conflicts can arise in 3 distinct areas or interfaces: between sales person and customer, sales person and company, and competitors. These are summarised as:

Sales person: customers

1   The use of gifts and entertainment
2   Questionable/psychological sales techniques
3   Over-selling
4   Misrepresentation
5   Account discrimination/favouritism
6   Conflicts of interest.

Sales person: company

1   Equity in evaluation and compensation
2   Use of company assets
3   Falsifying expense accounts and sales reports
4   Salesperson compliance with company policy.

Sales person: competitor

1   Disparagement
2   Tampering with a competitor's product
3   Spying
4   Exclusionary behaviour
5   Discussing prices.
(These activities are generally illegal.)

Advertising and sales promotion: The basic issue here is truth in advertising. This may involve a deliberate intention to deceive (**deception**) or unintentional (**misleading**). In most countries the advertising profession has sought to retain responsibility for self-regulation preferring this to excessive regulation through legislation. To this end regulating bodies, such as the Advertising Standards Authority in the UK, publish detailed codes of practice and have formal procedures for receiving and dealing with complaints

The above summary clearly identifies specific areas of particular concern to marketers. The key problem in handling ethical issues is that there are often no hard and fast rules concerning individual or corporate behaviour. Where society has a clear view on what is acceptable/unacceptable these views are enshrined in legislation which is enforceable through the process of law. Where the interpretation of **moral values**, such as those contained in various religions, is left to the individual then it is not surprising if the boundaries between right and wrong become blurred or fuzzy. Offering a client a cup of tea would hardly be regarded as bribery, or occasionally using office stationery as theft. On the other hand a weekend in the Ritz claimed on expenses, or hiring out your company car to someone else would probably be regarded as wrong.

As the concern for ethical behaviour in marketing grows it may be expected that philosophical issues such as these will receive more formal attention. As to whether this increased attention will permeate the treatment of the various sub-fields as identified above or become focused in specific courses on marketing ethics remains to be seen. To conclude, however, Smith proposed the following maxims for determining whether or not your marketing is ethical:

- *The golden rule*: Do unto others as you would have them do unto you.
- *The media test*: Would I be embarrassed in front of colleagues/family/friends, if my decision was publicised in the media?

IS IT ETHICAL?

An article in *The Times* (28 April 2005) presented a foretaste of changes in retailing practices that are likely to have a major impact on shopping behaviour in the not-too-distant future. Entitled 'Big Brother: the spy in your shopping trolley', the author, Steve Boggan, looked at some of the implications of the adoption of radio frequency identification (RFID) technology and posed the question "Useful tool for shoppers, or an unacceptable invasion of privacy?"

Ever since the adoption of bar codes as a means of identifying and tracking stock units, retailers have looked for increasingly sophisticated means of profiling shopper behaviour. RFID offers this potential.

RFID is not a new technology – it has been used in defence systems for some time to identify friend from foe – but it is the capability to use very small microchips to store large amounts of information that have opened up the opportunity to use it in more prosaic, everyday activities like shopping. Where it differs from bar codes is that it can identify precisely each stock unit and not just the type – Heinz Baked Beans, Nescafe, etc. – and it does not need to be scanned with a laser. Instead RFID communicates with radio signals when interrogated by an RFID reader.

While RFID tags in supermarkets are unlikely, at least at first, to contain the kind of detailed information that is going to be included in the new British biometric passports, the potential is there. Currently their main use is in identifying and tracking bulk packages through the supply chain and greatly enhancing efficiency in the process. Boggan writes: "It has been predicted that vast supermarket chains such as Wal-Mart in the US could save up to $7.6 billion (£3 billion, *sic*) a year by knowing exactly where every item is along its supply chain if its suppliers could attach tags to each product. At the moment, they can't: at around 15-20p the tags are too expensive. But the price is falling and once they reach 3p or less, individual tagging will be possible".

Once this happens retailers will begin to use the technology to monitor buyer behaviour. Boggan reports of the trialling of its use in the Extra Future Store in Germany by Metro in conjunction with "...a host of partners including Intel, IBM, Cisco Systems. Coca-Cola, Kraft, Johnson & Johnson, Procter & Gamble, Microsoft and Nestlé,...." Currently, the information is being used only to ensure shelves are constantly re-stocked, but it is the potential to incorporate it in conjunction with a loyalty card that is causing concern about privacy issues. These concerns become even more acute when it is suggested that when used in conjunction with a credit card it would be possible simply to pass through a scanner and have the whole transaction recorded instantaneously rather than having to record each item at a check out. The big question is whether the tags will then be de-activated or will they remain active? Leaving them active means that, for example, a smart microwave could read the instructions on the tagged micro-wavable meal, or your washing machine could decide on the best cycle for your clothes. But, if they are left active they could be read by readers in all kinds of other places too.

Overall the benefits from RFID are considerable. In addition to increased efficiency in the supply chain of the kind described earlier, tagging will help prevent fraud by counterfeiters of all kinds, identify patients in hospitals to ensure they get the right medication and treatment, and to identify buried pipes and cables saving time in making repairs not to mention accidentally damaging such installations. As for everyday purchases, so long as the safeguards on Data Protection are enforced, then it would seem to be down to the individual to decide whether the benefits outweigh the disadvantages.

- *The invoice test*: Are payments being requested that could not be fully disclosed within company accounts?
- *Good ethics is good business*: The belief that good ethics is in the long-term best interests of the firm.
- *The professional ethic*: Would the action be viewed as proper by an objective panel of professional colleagues?
- *When in doubt, don't.*

As an increasing number of high profile cases in Europe and the USA have demonstrated, many senior executives have failed to observe these principles and have been found guilty in legal proceedings against them and sentenced to periods of imprisonment.

GREEN MARKETING

Ecological concerns now represent a significant factor to be taken into account in **environmental planning**. Further, they are now of global concern as the number of natural disasters attributable to climatic change appears to grow every year, for example droughts and floods attributed to El Niño, atmospheric pollution associated with burning of the Indonesian forests, and so on. The global nature of the causes of these problems has ensured that they have been the subject of a series of environmental summits at which both the developed and developing nations seek to agree limits to pollution, deforestation, and so on which have resulted in ozone depletion and the greenhouse effect.

Unfortunately, while there is widespread public support for more environmentally friendly behaviour, individual consumers are less inclined to modify their own consumption behaviour to achieve this end. In the absence of regulation, which resulted in the withdrawal of CFC propellants in aerosol sprays, decisions about the suitability of 'green' products rests very much with the individual. Nonetheless, the number of individuals who are prepared to modify consumption behaviour and express a preference for green products is sufficiently large to constitute an important market segment. According to Georges Haour it is difficult to define precisely what is a green product because:

> Depending on the region, the culture and the time, criteria for green-ness indeed differ. They may include 'organically grown' fruits and vegetables, no preservatives, lower ecological impact in use of materials, or upon processing and usage (that is lower energy consumption, no toxic substance used), long-life products, as well as returnable or minimum packaging.

It follows that the range of products promoted on a green platform varies widely. Haour cites the case of the Canadian supermarket chain Loblaws that has introduced a 'green line' which now counts for well over 100 products, including things such as phosphate free detergents, energy efficient light bulbs, unbleached coffee filters, reusable cloth nappies in place of disposable diapers and so on.

As discussed in Chapter 13 packaging materials have been a major area of interest on the basis that the most ecological packaging is no packaging at all. But, as Haour points out, one needs to make a full evaluation of materials and energy content, as well as transport, storage, and preservation requirements of a given package in terms of the total product package system before it is possible to determine whether disposable packaging is preferable to recyclable packaging or vice versa. In addition, as he points out:

Analyses of the same system will yield different results depending on local conditions such

GREEN AND ETHICAL CONSUMER

A detailed Report of this title was Published by Keynote in 2005. among the salient points made were:

Green and ethical products only account for a small percentage of total consumer expenditure but represent significant niche markets.

Keynote found that "For the majority of consumers, price overrides ethical considerations as a key factor in their decision-making". Consequently, E & G concerns are more strongly expressed by the affluent.

Fair trades have been growing rapidly and consumer pressure groups, boycotts and legislation are having an impact e.g. the introduction of a Congestion Charge in central London has reduced traffic by 25%. In general, however, the Government has taken a *laissez-faire* approach. On the other hand more companies now have corporate social responsibility (CSR) policies which cover G & E issues.

For 2002 the Co-operative Bank estimated expenditures of £1,170m on food; £1,473m on green household goods; £3,309m on charitable donations; £187m on personal goods including cosmetics not tested on animals; £2,582m on ethical boycotts; £1,568m on local shopping; £3,386m on ethical banking; £3,510m on ethical investment etc. giving a grand total of just under £20 billion.

A survey in 2004 indicated that 55% of females and 42% of males would recycle and are concerned about G & E issues. Overall, however, consumer attitudes are "ambivalent".

A major factor appears to be availability, for example the stocking of Fair trade goods like coffee and bananas in supermarkets which have led to considerable growth. More publicity, books and reports are also helping to increase awareness of the issues.

For example, a report by the National Consumer Council (NCC) *Rating Retailers for Health* examined each of the supermarkets influence on a healthy diet based on factors like the salt content in own-label processed foods, quality of nutrition labelling and advice, and emphasis given to junk foods vis-à-vis healthy foods. The main finding was that supermarket's policy had a major impact, e.g. Morrison's have 25% more salt in sliced bread and sausages than do the Co-op; Tesco give three times as much shelf space to junk foods and snacks like crisps, biscuits and sweets compared with fresh fruit while in Marks & Spencer equal space is given to the two categories. Marked out of 10 the results were:

Waitrose	6.5
Sainsbury	5.5
Co-op	5.0
Tesco	3.5
ASDA	3.0
Morrisons	2.0

The growth of sales of organic foods has slowed significantly in recent years but has still grown from £110 million in 1995 to £1,120 million in 2004 with about 10% of the population claiming to buy on a regular basis.

The Keynote Report concludes:

"Incorporating eco-friendly aspects such as community development and pollution-free activity and establishing a longer-term approach to profit and development, will become increasingly attractive as market assets for companies either genuinely interested in seeking more ethical production or a more market-orientated 'green rinse'".

as availability and price of materials, energy and transport. All these vary substantially from country to country.

Variety and choice are also seen as a contributory factor. Thus a reduction in the number of brands available in the supermarket would significantly reduce the storage and display space and the energy required particularly for refrigeration. Other savings might also arrive through more efficient logistics management and a more effective use of transportation.

Haour concludes that 'Reconciling ecology with economy makes complete ethical and business sense. Indeed, ecological solutions favour optimal use of energy and materials, minimising waste, transport and storage costs'. From this point of view then, green marketing represents a significant opportunity – always provided that it isn't used against you!

SOCIAL MARKETING

The notion of 'social marketing' emerged soon after Kotler and Levy's seminal 1969 articles on 'Broadening the Marketing Concept' and 'Beyond Marketing: The Furthering Concept', both of which explored how marketing techniques and practices might be applied in a non-commercial context. At the time of writing (Summer 2005) it has been given a particular prominence in light of the growing concern about obesity in affluent societies, especially among young persons. Fortuitously, some of the leading researchers on the subject presented a paper on the subject at the UK Academy of Marketing's Annual Conference held in Dublin in July 2005. The paper by Laura McDermott, Martine Stead and Gerard Hastings entitled 'What is and What is Not Social Marketing' represents the most up-to-date evaluation of the definition of the topic and forms the basis for the following summary.

In 1971 Kotler and Zaltman, based on research undertaken during the 1960s, first defined social marketing as "the application of marketing to the solution of social and health problems". Since then it has evolved to become "a strategic planning framework comprising consumer research, segmentation and targeting, objective setting and the manipulation of the marketing mix" (MacFadyen et al. 2003). However, social marketing has often been confused with closely related concepts such as societal marketing, socially responsible marketing and non-profit marketing, leading Alan Andreasen (2002) to argue that it is its emphasis on voluntary behaviour change that makes it unique.

In an article published in the *Journal of Public Policy and Marketing* ('Marketing Social Marketing in the Social Change Marketing Place', Vol. 21, Spring 2002, 3-13), Andreasen suggests a number of benchmarks for identifying an approach that could be legitimately called 'social marketing'. In summary these benchmarks are:

- the use of behaviour change to design and evaluate interventions
- projects consistently use audience research
- careful segmentation of target audiences is used to ensure efficient and effective use of scarce resources

- creating attractive and motivational exchanges are central to any influence strategy
- the strategy makes use of all the traditional elements of the marketing mix
- careful attention is paid to the competition faced by the desired behaviour

These benchmarks were used by McDermott et al. as the starting point for their review. Using a variety of databases and a combination of keywords, a systematic search of the literature was undertaken. The titles and abstracts generated were then assessed to determine whether:

1 The programme was self-defined as social marketing.

2 The programme provided evidence of at least two of Andreasen's social marketing criteria.

This evaluation yielded twenty papers describing sixteen studies of which about half described North American research and the other half research from developing countries. However, analysis of the papers suggested that relying on the authors self-definition of social marketing resulted in a limited evidence base, and disappointingly narrow interpretations of social marketing. Given that McDermott et al. were concerned with whether social marketing ideas worked rather than whether social marketing labels work, they decided to develop their own set of criteria. These are based on Andreasen's original six criteria and are reproduced as Table 25.2. Applying the criteria and the interpretations/explanations listed, the

Table 25.2 Revised relevance criteria and scoring procedure		
	Benchmark	*Explanation*
1	*Behaviour change*	Intervention seeks to change behaviour and has specific measurable behavioural objectives.
2	*Audience research*	Formative research is conducted to identify target consumer characteristics and needs. Intervention elements are pre-tested with the target group.
3	*Segmentation*	Different segmentation variables are considered when selecting the intervention target group. Intervention strategy is tailored for the selected segment/s.
4	*Exchange*	Intervention considers what will motivate people to engage voluntarily with the intervention and offers them something beneficial in return. The offered benefit may be intangible (eg. personal satisfaction) or tangible (eg. incentives for participating in the programme and making behavioural changes).
5	*Marketing mix*	Intervention consists of promotion (communications) plus at least one other marketing 'P' ('product', 'price', 'place'). Other Ps might include 'policy change' or 'people' (eg. training is provided to intervention delivery agents).
6	*Competition*	Intervention considers the appeal of competing behaviours (including current behaviour). Intervention uses strategies that seek to minimise the competition.

Source: McDermott, L., Stead, M. and Hastings, G. (2005), 'What Is and What Is Not Social Marketing: The Challenge of Reviewing the Evidence', *Journal of Marketing Management*

review team assessed over 200 studies and identified 27 that satisfied them. Of these, four were labelled 'social marketing' and had been included in the original review, but the majority would have been omitted.

This analysis points to a recurrent problem in marketing and in the conduct of literature searches – the absence of clear and agreed definitions. That said, the revised set of criteria provide a useful basis for the identification of social marketing interventions in future. Health is obviously an area of major public concern and it is anticipated that significantly increased resource will be directed to the determination of how marketing practices may be adapted and deployed to influence attitudes and behaviour. In parallel it is expected that research in social marketing will have important implications in cognate fields such as **cause related marketing, marketing for non profit organisations (NPOs), sport marketing** and the like.

A NEW MODEL OF MARKETING?

As noted in Chapter 1, a recent article in the *Journal of Marketing* has prompted extensive debate about the need for a new model, or paradigm, of the domain of marketing. At the Australia and New Zealand Marketing Academy (ANZMAC) conference held in Freemantle, WA, in December 2005 a special session lasting half a day was given to arguments for and against the adoption of this new model. In the absence of agreement on the subject, it is clear that it would be premature to argue for or against the model when documenting the evolution of the accepted wisdom about marketing. On the other hand, when discussing Current Trends and Future Issues, an overview of the arguments is clearly important for those new to the subject of marketing.

The article that precipitated the debate is entitled "Evolving to a New Dominant Logic of Marketing" by Stephen L. Vargo and Robert F. Lusch (Vol. 68, No. 1, 2004). In the abstract the authors write:

> The purpose of this article is to illuminate the evolution of **marketing** thought toward a new dominant logic. …Briefly, **marketing**, has moved from a goods-dominant view, in which tangible output and discrete transactions were central, to a service-dominant view, in which intangibility, exchange processes, and relationships are central.

The authors then stress that their interpretation of 'service-centred' should not be equated with current conceptualisations of services as a residual, i.e. not a tangible good; something to add value to a good – value-added services; or service 'industries like health care and education. They state:

> Rather, we define services as the application of specialised competences (knowledge and skills) through deeds, processes, and performances to the benefit of another entity or the entity itself……. Thus, the service-centred dominant logic represents a reoriented philosophy that is applicable to all **marketing** offerings, including those that involve tangible output (goods) in the process of service provision.

In order to justify and sustain the case for a new model or paradigm of marketing involves a closely argued case running to 17 pages of text, and supported by 4 pages of references. Given the numerous warnings elsewhere in this textbook concerning selectivity and bias, the reader is warned that the following summary of what I consider to be the important issues is a personal one and that, if you find them interesting or provocative, you should read the original yourself and form your own judgement.

To begin with Vargo and Lusch's analysis starts with a summary of the evolution of marketing thought that reflects the overview provided in Chapter 1. As the latter mirrors that to be found in most standard marketing textbooks, then we are agreed on the point of departure, and know "where we are". The need for a new 'worldview' or dominant logic is predicated on the proposition that "Marketing inherited a model of exchange from economics, which had a dominant logic based on the exchange of "goods", which usually are manufactured output. The dominant logic focused on tangible resources, embedded value and transactions." However, this view is not seen as appropriate today.

Over the past 50 years or so the focus on resources as "stuff" that is to be acquired and used by humans – what we would normally think of as natural and physical resources – has changed to a view that incorporates intangible and dynamic functions calling for human ingenuity and appraisal. "Everything is neutral (or perhaps even a resistance) until humankind learns what to do with it (Zimmerman 1951). Essentially, resources are not; they become."

To explain this distinction the authors intoduce the distinction between *operand* and *operant resources* (my emphasis). **Operand resources** are those on which some act or operation has to be performed to produce an effect while, **operant resources** are those that produce effects. Increased interest in operant resources "began to shift in the late twentieth century as humans began to realise that skills and knowledge were the most important types of resources." Although prior reference had been made to the work of Malthus (1798), and his conclusion that the continued growth of population would result in the exhaustion of natural resources, no explicit link is made by the authors to numerous forecasts in the 1960s of the inevitable truth of this prediction, unless humankind could make them go further. Thus it was publications such as the Club of Rome's *Limits to Growth* that precipitated the recognition of the primacy of operant over operand resources.

The logic and importance of this is manifest in Vargo and Lusch's statement that:

> *Operant resources are often invisible and intangible; often they are core competences or organisational processes. They are likely to be dynamic and infinite (sic) and not static and finite, as is usually the case with operand resources. Because operant resources produce effects, they enable humans both to multiply the value of natural resources and to create additional operant skills.*

If, then, this primacy is the defining characteristic of the new 'service-centred logic' few would challenge it; whether they would describe it as a service-centred logic is another matter. Vargo and Lusch believe that this perceived shift (hint: they perceive it; I'm not sure yet) has important implications for marketing and they start with an examination of the 'Goods versus Services' schools of thought.

Traditional marketing is seen as focusing on operand resources, is goods centered and concerned with the notion of utility(ies). Service-centered marketing is seen as comprising four elements which are summarised as:

1 *Identify or develop core competences, the fundamental knowledge and skills of an*

economic entity that represent potential competitive advantage.

2 *Identify other entities (potential customers) that could benefit from these competences.*

3 *Cultivate relationships that involve the customers in developing customised, competitively compelling value propositions to meet specific needs.*

4 *Gauge marketplace feedback by analysing financial performance from exchange to learn how to improve the firm's offering to customers and improve firm performance.*

This view is grounded in and largely consistent with resource advantage theory.

It is customer centric and market driven.

Vargo and Lusch then proceed to compare the two views and identify six differences between them, all centered on the operand/operant distinction. These attributes are then analysed in the context of eight foundational premises (FPs). These premises are:

1 The application of specialised skills and knowledge is the fundamental unit of exchange.

2 Indirect exchange masks the fundamental unit of exchange.

3 Goods are distribution mechanisms for service provision.

4 Knowledge is the fundamental source of competitive advantage.

5 All economies are service economies.

6 The customer is always a coproducer.

7 The enterprise can only make value propositions.

8 The service-centered view is customer oriented and relational.

Each of these premises is discussed and evaluated in some detail.

FP1 recognises the importance of task specialisation and the division of labour (discussed by us in Chapter 1) as depending on exchange for their existence. The principle issue debated is the narrow focus on tangible output with exchange value, and the role and contribution of service activities in creating and enhancing that value. In my view the arguments deployed pay insufficient attention to the reasons for the original emphasis on the 'product', and the present emphasis on the 'service'. As a result it presents a polarised, 'black-and-white' explanation that is inconsistent with a wider knowledge/understanding of economics which is presented as a monolithic and internally consistent discipline devoid of schisms and alternative explanations.

FP2 addresses the issue of the physical and psychological separation that developed as a consequence of the Industrial Revolution and led to the the development of complex marketing systems to link the factory with the customer. The existence of these systems is seen as masking the fundamental nature of the exchange process which, according to Vargo and Lusch is that: "People still exchange their services for other services. Money, goods, organisations, and vertical marketing systems are only the exchange vehicles." But, ask yourself, in most low involvement transactions have you the slightest interest in who, precisely, was responsible for the creation of the good for which you are paying money ?

FP3 follows automatically from FP2 which depended on this premise that

"Goods are distribution mechanisms for service provision". It is claimed that: "Goods are not the common denominator of exchange; the common denominator is the application of specialised knowledge, mental skills, and, to a lesser extent, physical labour (skills)." This is truly an heroic premise, and while the authors may cite a handful of distinguished academics as their authority, I am not convinced that the man on the Clapham omnibus quite sees it that way.

FP4 that "Knowledge is the fundamental source of competitive advantage" is superficially uncontentious but the premise omits specific reference to the qualification contained in their quotation from Day (1994) that such advantage will only accrue if you can "make it work". Otherwise, as my old boss used to say, knowledge is just so-much luggage that has to be carted about – you can buy books full of knowledge by the container load and finish up only with a headache of where to store them.

FP5 that "All economies are service economies" might be true if you accept the authors earlier premises. But, a more balanced and less controversial claim might be appropriate if one considers the relative proportions of effort expended on products and services in different national economies. Ultimately, of course, if you take the view that natural resources have no value until they are "serviced" by humans then the premise is tautological or true by definition.

Much the same arguments apply to *FP6* that "The customer is always a coproducer" for without consumption there is no exchange – a fact recognised by Adam Smith when he stated that "The sole end and purpose of production is consumption". This fact was self evident to him at the time when he emphasised the need to increase the output of physical goods if the operants were not to fall victim to the Malthusian controls of disease, famine, and war, all of which would have eliminated surplus operants while stabilising the operands.

FP7 is uncontentious. Value, like beauty, lies in the eye of the beholder. Truly, "The firm can only make value propositions" – it is the customer that will determine if value actually exists.

Finally, *FP8* states "A service-centered view is customer oriented and relational". But, if you revisit Chapter 1 and the discussion of the 'Three Eras' explanation of the evolution of modern marketing, and substitute "Production" for "goods-centered", then the next step is marketing. You may also recall my own 1973 definition of marketing as "The creation and maintenance of mutually satisfying exchange relationships" – no mention of goods or services, or of the mix of goods and services that give rise to satisfaction, nor to the obvious corollary, that satisfaction implies perceived value. The problem, as I have argued at length elsewhere, is that the marketing concept was high-jacked by the marketing management school of thought in the USA, who then promoted marketing as something to do *to* customers rather than *for* customers. Only when it was realised that this didn't work were the true intentions of the marketing concept – customer oriented and relational – implemented.

In sum, I believe that the logic of the service-centered approach reflects the logic and intentions of the marketing era as distinguished from the production era that preceded it. Where I have difficulty with Vargo and Lusch's proposal is that in order to recognise the importance of services/operant activities they seem to think it is necessary to deny the role of physical resources and technology in creating physical objects that are necessary to realise the value of those service activities. In other words, without operand or physical resources to work with we would soon all die of starvation.

In their *discussion* the first issue appears to concern the degree of customisation incorporated into physical goods. I have to confess to having some difficulty in following their argument, especially in terms of their definition of 'normative qualities'. According to Vargo and Lusch "The goods-centered view implies that the qualities of manufactured goods (e.g. tangibility), the separation of production and consumption, standardisation, and nonperishability are normative qualities (Zeithaml, Parasuraman and Berry 1985)." As a consequence, "From what we argue the marketing perspective should be, the qualities are often neither valid nor desirable."

I have great difficulty in accepting this claim, which is almost as bad as the academic economist's view that to purchase on the basis of emotional beliefs, rather than giving precedence to price, is 'irrational'. In the great majority of purchase decisions our survival does not depend on buying anything – we can always take it or leave it. Furthermore, the existence of producers attempting to satisfy picky customers has led to greater choice and variety than has ever existed before. What the authors see as the service-centerd view of exchange is what, since 1987, has been known as 'mass customisation' in which producers like Dell involve customers directly in specifying the attributes and features that they desire in their computer. Now, with a complex product such as this, if I know precisely what I want then I can become a co-producer but what if I can't? Or what about my motor car when I only wish to order a limited number of 'extras' because otherwise the standard model meets virtually all of my needs? Or what about canned vegetables? The activities involved in getting these to my preferred retail outlet are extensive, complex and expensive. There is a huge variety on offer, and keen competition between suppliers of the same product category. And, if you are dissatisfied with the manufacturers attempt to satisfy your need you can always go to the Farmer's Market and buy 'the real thing' for a much higher price. Or, better still why not become a producer yourself and find out if the time involved improves your overall standard of living?

To be fair, many of the attributes of the service-centered view recognise that marketing should be about 'mutually satisfying exchange relationships' in which both producer and consumer have a role to play and in which, as we argued in Chapter 1, supply should be determined by demand. In my opinion, these are the distinguishing features of the marketing concept and a marketing orientation, which has taken rather longer to put into practice than one would have liked. On the other hand those organisations that have bought into the concept and are marketing oriented are more successful. Ultimately, natural selection and the 'invisible hand' will prevail. In this sense Vargo and Lusch may be seen as seeking to accelerate the process and, as they say, they are looking for 'reorientation rather than reinvention' (p.14).

To achieve this re-orientation they argue for:

*A service-centered college curriculum would be grounded by a course in principles of **marketing**, which would subordinate goods to service provision, emphasising the former as distribution mechanisms for the latter.*

Clearly, this would call for a radical restructuring of textbooks like this, which will become imperative if the service-centered view advocated by Vargo and Lusch does indeed become the dominant paradigm. By now you should have gathered that I doubt if it will.

As with any debate, the proponents have to exaggerate their case to make their point. So we would agree that the marketing management concept has paid insufficient attention to the wants of consumers. On the other hand it has done very well in catering to their needs. What is called for is more fine tuning to ensure that the goods and services created cost effectively by producers/sellers match ever more closely the needs of buyers/consumers. As we have said, mass customisation has recognised the benefits of doing this, as has the emphasis on customer relationship management and getting closer to the customer. But producers have an important role to play too. Giving the customer what they (think) they want is not necessarily the way to ensure the optimum utilisation of scarce physical resources. In solving the basic economic problem of maximising satisfaction through the use of scarce resources both producer and consumer have an equal role to play. Handing over 'dominance' to users does not appear to be the best way to achieve this.

So much for my views. In the same issue of the *Journal of Marketing* there are also invited commentaries from some much better known marketing scholars. You should read these too if you intend to study marketing in greater detail. For the time being, however, the jury is out.

Summary

In this chapter we have looked at six issues that we think will have a significant influence on marketing thinking and practice in the future. No doubt many others could be cited but, in general, we consider it likely that there will be few if any revolutionary breakthroughs. So that the continuing challenge will be to determine how to adapt our current knowledge and understanding to solving the fundamental problem with which we started - maximising satisfaction from the consumption of scarce resources . It is hoped that the study of this text will have helped provide at least some of the possible answers.

Review questions and problems

1 What are the major implications of the Internet for marketing strategy? How, specifically, might it impact on advertising and retailing practice?

2 The Internet is a complement to not a substitute for existing channels of communication and distribution. Discuss.

3 What is e-commerce? How do you see it evolving in the future?

4 Some people might consider 'ethical marketing' to be an oxymoron. What factors might account for this view and how would you rebut them?

5 Draw up a check list for establishing whether an organisation's marketing is ethical or not.

6 "Consumerism is the shame of marketing". Explain the meaning of this statement.

7 Identify the main concerns that have led to the emergence of a 'Green' movement. In what ways can marketing respond to these?

8 What is 'social marketing' and why is it likely to be of increased importance in the future?

9 The concept and principles of marketing are relevant to all kinds of organisation that are seeking to establish a relationship with an individual. Do you agree? If so 'why'? If not 'why not'?

Key terms

4Cs (convenience, consumer needs/wants, cost and communication)
B2B
B2C
cause related marketing
caveat emptor
commoditisation
communication channel
customer relationship management (CRM)
deception
digital marketplace
direct sales channel
disintermediation
distribution channel
dot.com organisation

Ebay
ecological concerns
e-commerce
electronic business
electronic commerce
electronic communications technology
electronic marketing
e-marketing
enabling technology
environmental planning
e-procurement
ethics
exciters
foundation factors
green marketing
legislation
levelling effect

marketing for non-profit organisations
misleading
moral values
mutually satisfying exchange relationship
non-profit marketing
operational effectiveness
potential differentiators
proactive services
shopping experience
social marketing
socially responsible marketing
sport marketing
strategic positioning
transaction
website
zero-sum

Supplementary reading list

Current issues and future trends are best tracked by regular access to newspapers, the business press, and current affairs programmes on the broadcast media.

Hart, S. (ed) (2003), *Marketing Changes*, (London: Thomson)

GLOSSARY

This is intended as a short guide - for the full description of each item readers should consult the main text.

4Cs (convenience, consumer needs/wants, cost and communication).

4Ps (product, price, place, promotion) introduced by Eugene McCarthy in the 1960s the 4Ps are considered the four major elements of the 'marketing mix'.

7Ps (product, place, price, promotion, process, physical evidence, people) extension of McCarthy's '4Ps' with process, physical evidence, people, proposed by Booms and Bitner (1981)to extend the concept to embrace services.

a priori extrapolating from a general principle to predict the outcome of a specific case.

absolute income hypothesis one of three theories which have evolved in an attempt to explain variations in aggregate consumption functions. This theory holds that expenditure/savings are a function of income.

accelerated freeze drying (AFD) a process to preserve foods through a process of rapid dehydration, for example, instant coffee, 'Smash' potatoes.

acceptable media communications which are intrinsic to the media they are present in, for example adverts in magazines.

access panels see panels.

ACORN a geodemographic analysis system which categorises the population into specific sub-groups, developed by CACI.

acquisitive society a society which wishes to acquire either knowledge or material possessions.

ad hoc research research for a specific purpose.

adaptive planning and control sequence (APACS) an eight-step model to create a marketing strategy developed by the Marketing Science Institute (Robinson and Luck 1964).

adoption the decision to buy and become a regular user of a product or service.

advertising paid for promotion of a firm or product, this can be 'informative', 'combative' (Marshall 1919), or 'persuasive'.

advocacy communications addressing controversial subjects and expressing a particular point of view about them.

age of high mass consumption an aim of an economically developed society.

AIDA (awareness/attention, interest, desire, action) a hierarchy of effects model dating from Strong (1924).

aided recall see recall.

analysis, planning, implementation and control (APICS) the four basic activities of effective management.

analytic hierarchy process (AHP) a process for making decisions about resource allocation in terms of the organisation's objectives, sub-objectives and strategies.

analytic network process (ANP) a model proposed by Coulter and Sarkis (2005) to guide media selection by combining analysis of a number of known factors with expert knowledge.

Anglo-Saxon interpretation of capitalism characterised by free competition, ad hoc transactions and short term profit seeking.

appreciation an evaluation of all factors, both external and internal, that determine the possible courses of action open to an organisation.

appropriation of the budget setting aside a proportion of finance for a specific task.

association procedures a research technique using procedures such as word association or picture tests, for example, Rorschach's ink-blot test to establish a subject's opinions on a topic.

assumptions an assumption is a 'best guess' about a future state of affairs that has to be made when making decisions without complete information.

attention conscious recognition of a stimulus.

attitude a behavioural state which enables marketers to predict future actions.

attitude scales a scale of statements used to determine the attitude of the respondent .

augmentation the attributes of a core product added by the seller, for example, packaging, design and brand.

augmented product Levitt (1980), the combination of the core product and added attributes.

auxiliary service   the benefits which differentiate the service from competitors, similar to the 'augmented product'.

avoidance   when stimuli are screened out which conflict with our preferred interpretation of a message.

Baker's box   a diagnostic tool to aid managerial thinking, consisting of a perceptual map using multi-dimensional scaling. Its objective is to help focus and structure management's judgement as to where they and their competitors currently are.

Baker's composite model of buying behaviour   a model which seeks to synthesise/integrate different interpretations of buyer behaviour developed in different social sciences   economics, sociology, psychology etc.

balance-sheet   the financial state of a company represented by a comparison of its assets and its liabilities.

barcode   a series of vertical lines which can be read by an optical scanner, representing the nature, provenance and in some cases the price of a product. See also **European Article Numbering**.

Bayesian analysis   A name applied generically to statistical decision theory, normally consisting of a subjective approach to probability which incorporates the decision-maker's personal feelings regarding the likely occurrence of specified events.

behaviour   physical acts performed or undertaken by individuals as opposed to attitudes, beliefs or opinions which constitute a state of mind towards a conceptor object, and may not lead to physical action.

below the line   when advertising agencies are not paid commission for purchasing space from various media.

bias   in research terms when a researchers expectations shape the nature of the results.

bipolar adjectives   two words which represent opposite ends of a scale, for example, hot, cold; strongly agree, strongly disagree. .

blogs   online personal log or diary, usually about a particular subject.

blueprint   a basic plan which sets out how to perform a function.

BOGOF (buy one get one free)   a kind of promotional activity in which the purchase of one product entitles the customer to another of the same product for free.

bonus   a promotion which offers an extra percentage of a product as an incentive, for example, 33% extra free.

Boston Box   a technique developed by the Boston Consulting Group to analyse the comparative and collective performance of different products in a firm's range by looking at the structure of competition and the stage of the product life cycle.

brand   in simple terms, a brand is something (e.g. a name, a logo) which both identifies a product and differentiates it from its competition.

brand equity   The value given to a brand which recognises its worth as an asset. This value reflects the market share held by the brand, the degree of loyalty and recognition it enjoys, its perceived quality and any other attributes which distinguish it positively from competitive offerings e.g. patent protection, trademark etc.

brand extension   using an established brand to launch new products which can be related to it, normally when the firm uses its brand name to compete with a new product targeted at a different market. See also 'line extension'.

brand identity   generally used to describe the image and personality (human characteristics) of the brand.

brand image   how others perceive the brand based on its past and current positioning and importance.

brand mapping   a research technique whereby subjects are invited to group brands/products according to various criteria.

brand position   the aspect of brand identity which enables a product to differentiate itself in the marketplace from its competitors.

brand share   the proportion of all sales for a given product category held by a given brand.

brand stretching   any strategy that uses the existing brand name as a basis for introducing modified or new products.

branding   the practice of giving a distinctive name and identity to a product to enable potential buyers to distinguish it from closely competing alternatives.

break-even analysis   a technique for estimating the point at which revenues will cover costs based on estimates of price, market size etc.

BRIC countries   Brazil, Russia, India and China.

broadsheets   the larger of the two sizes of newspaper, see **tabloid**.

bubble procedures   a projective research technique which invites respondents to fill in the 'bubble' containing the thoughts of the person in a particular situation.

budgetary marketing   marketing as an expenditure, mainly in terms of advertising and promotion (Ambler 2000).

bundle of satisfactions   the collective perceived benefits from a particular product.

business analysis   an important element of micro-environmental analysis used to establish the attractiveness or otherwise of exploiting a market opportunity.

business to business marketing (B2B)   marketing activities between businesses.

business to consumer (B2C)   marketing activities between a business and its consumers.

buy classes   - a classification system developed by Robinson, Faris and Wind to describe the purchase decision facing a buyer. For example, a situation not encountered before (new task); a change in price or specification (modified rebuy) or a simple routine re-purchase of the same product (straight rebuy).

buyer behaviour   how consumers use the information available to them to make purchase choices.

buygrid   an analytic framework for buying decisions created from an analysis of buy classes and buy phases.

buying decision process   the sequence of issues/facts taken into account by a prospective buyer when considering a potential purchase .

buyphases   the steps a consumer goes through in order to purchase a product.

CACI   Consolidated Analysis Centers Inc. an organisation specialising in techniques for the geo-demographic analysis of markets.

case method   an analytical approach based on the study of detailed descriptions (cases) of organisations, industries, markets etc.

cash and carry   a wholesaling concern which keeps costs, and subsequently prices down by expecting customers to pay for and immediately remove goods they have purchased, rather than offering credit and delivery service. Membership of these concerns is generally restricted to retailers.

catalogue drop   a form of selling where a catalogue is left with a customer and a salesperson calls back at another time to take the order.

category management   where the firm manages categories 'as strategic business units, producing enhanced business results by focusing on delivering customer value' (IGD).

causality   the relationship between cause and effect.

cause related marketing   the application of marketing techniques and practices developed in a commercial context to promote good causes like the Red Cross or Salvation Army.

caveat emptor   literally 'let the buyer beware' indicating that it is the buyer's responsibility to ensure that they are getting what they bargain for.

census   a survey of every member of a relevant population.

channel   see channel of distribution.

channel captain   the member of the channel with the greatest influence enabling them to dictate the terms of trade in the channel.

channel leader   see channel captain.

channel management   the management of the tasks involved in progressing the transfer of goods and services between seller and buyer.

channel of distribution   a channel consists of all those steps through which a product must pass between its point of production and consumption.

channel policy   the seller's decision of which channel(s) to use to make the goods or service available to potential buyers, e.g. direct sale, via retailers, online, etc.

channel structure   the alternatives available within the channel of distribution, e.g the existence of intermediaries such as wholesalers, retailers etc.

channels of communication   the various media through which sellers can make contact with potential customers, e.g. print, broadcast, cinema, the Internet etc.

channel of distribution   the network or system that supports all the exchanges a product must go through between its point of production, and consumption.

Characteristics of Goods School   a school of thought which argues that advertising is appropriate for selling small, simple, frequently purchased goods, but that personal selling is more appropriate to high priced, technologically complex products which are purchased infrequently.

China price   a term used to describe the highly competitive prices asked for goods made in China which is often less than the manufactured cost in many advanced economies.

choice   the availability of products or services that are very close substitutes for one another in the perception of the intending buyer.

choice ordering   a qualitative research method where researchers can project behaviour from the responses subjects give to requests to rank order objects in response to specified criteria.

choice process   see buying decision process.

chunking   this is a process used to aid memory, by linking information in an easily recalled way, for example by the use of acronyms such as AIDA (awareness, interest, desire, action).

classical conditioning   the method used by Pavlov

linking two stimuli until an association between them was 'learned' so that behaviour would be triggered even when one of the stimuli was removed e.g. ringing a bell when presenting food to a dog causing it to salivate. Eventually, ringing the bell alone was enough to cause salivation.

climatic damage   damage to products caused by climate for example temperature, humidity or precipitation.

cluster sampling   The process of sampling on the basis of clearly defined groups or units within a population.

cognition   an individual's understanding of an object or concept derived from their perception, attitudes, beliefs, learned behaviour and needs.

cognitive consonance   the attempt to maintain consistency between perceptions, attitudes, values and behaviour.

cognitive-affective-conative (CAC) model   the cognitive-affective-conative model has been traced back to Plato's elements of the human soul - reasonable, spirited, appetitive - which in more modern terms may be defined as the realms of thought, emotions and motives, or knowing, feeling and acting. AIDA is one such example.

collegial approach   an approach to NPD typically used to enter new businesses or add substantially different products to existing lines.

combative advertising   making direct comparisons with the performance of a competitor's offering suggesting it is not as good as the one being advertised.

commercial transaction   any exchange where there is a transfer of value between buyer and seller.

commercialisation   the act of introducing a new product into the market for the first time.

commoditisation   the elimination of differences between competing products.

communication channel   see channels of communication.

comparative analysis   analysing the performance of two products by comparing certain factors.

comparative cost advantage   the difference in cost between two methods of production.

compatibility   the extent to which a new product is compatible with an existing production system or way of doing things.

competence   knowledge/skill learned or acquired by an individual or organisation that enables efficient and effective performance of specific tasks.

competition and market structure   a theoretical approach developed by industrial economists that holds that the structure of an industry will govern both the conduct and performance of firms in that industry.

competition-oriented pricing   pricing based on competitor pricing.

competitive advantage   a source of differentiation between a firm and its competitors which confers an advantage on it.

competitive bidding   when a number of firms tender (submit a specification and quotation) to win a project or sale.

competitive strategy   the decision by an organisation as to the basis on which it will compete in a market, i.e. cost leadership, differentiation, focus.

competitive variables   those factors which firms competing within a market emphasise in seeking to develop a competitive advantage.

competitor analysis   comparing critical success factors of a company and its competitors.

complete monopoly   when one firm has total control of the market for a particular product.

completely knocked-down state (CKD)   commonly known at the consumer stage as 'flat-pack', this refers to when items such as beds are packaged in their constituent parts to ease transportation and packaging.

completion procedures   a qualitative research method where researchers can project behaviour from the responses subjects give to complete given statements or dialogue.

componential analysis   using statistical analysis to predict which type of consumer will be most responsive to which product feature.

composite model of buyer behaviour   see Baker's model.

composite   composed of several different parts.

computer mediated communications (CMC)   in modern terms, using the Internet as a communications device, for example, email, web surveys etc.

computer-assisted telephone interviewing (CATI)   when an interviewer using the telephone is guided by software which records and reacts to each response as it is given, for example, by modifying the next question to be asked depending on the response to the previous question.

concentrated strategy   when a producer deliberately selects one of the major market segments and concentrates all their efforts upon it.

concentration   the extent to which the market is concentrated by a monopoly or oligopoly.

concentration ratio   a numerical calculation of the degree of concentration of a market.

conclusive research   a highly structured form of

research with a clear specification of the problem to be solved and a precise methodology.

confidence factor   the amount of confidence a manager has in their data when making a major decision.

conjoint analysis   a scaling technique used to determine the 'best fit' value between two approaches to take into account the information available.

consonance   The achievement of a consistent self-image. Self-image is the way we see ourselves and consonance represents our effort to behave in a manner consistent with this perception of ourself.

construction procedures   a qualitative research method where researchers can project behaviour from the stories subjects tell in response to picture cues or to their reaction to stereotypes.

consumer behaviour   the actions of the individual or organisation which lead to the attainment of goods and services.

consumer goods   goods destined for use by the ultimate household consumer and in such form that they can be used without further commercial processing.

consumer processing model (CPM)   a communication as information processing model (Shimp 2003) which perceives behaviour as being rational, cognitive, systematic and reasoned.

consumer services   services provided to consumers, see 'professional services' as a comparison.

consumption behaviour   see consumer behaviour.

continuous research   regularly repeated research to track changes in behaviour.

contract purchasing   when a firm agrees to purchase a product at a price, amount and time specified at the outset of the agreement.

contribution analysis   a financial technique used to determine the amount contributed to cover fixed costs after the deduction of direct/variable costs. Any surplus over fixed costs is profit.

control group   in experimental design, a group of subjects who are monitored but do not experience the full experimental conditions in order to give a comparison or 'base line' against which the experimental group(s) can be compared. .

controlled store testing   testing of in-store merchandising to assess potential return.

convenience goods   consumer goods which the customer usually purchases frequently, immediately and with the minimum of effort.

convenience multiples   chains of small convenience stores established by major retailers such as Tesco.

convenience sample   soliciting information from any convenient group whose views may be relevant to the subject of inquiry.

convenience store   a store of under 3,000 square feet, open for long hours each day of the week, retailing food and drink for consumption off the premises as their main business, and selling at least 8 of the 15 'core products'.

convergence   when two elements come together.

conversion rate   the rate at which one thing changes to another, for example, the number of people who try a product once, to the number of people who become regular purchasers.

co-operatives   a form of organisation in which suppliers or buyers agree to join forces to increase their bargaining power.

copy platform   the theme around which the advertising campaign is to be based.

copy testing   running different versions of an advert in order to measure their relative effectiveness as a basis for final selection.

copyright   exclusive right to control and reproduce original material.

core benefit   the properties of a product that will satisfy the felt need.

core identity   the features that make up the essence of the brand.

core products   a group of 15 products central to the concept of the 'convenience store' ranging from alcohol and confectionary to soft drinks and tobacco.

core service   the basic service offered, similar to the 'generic product'.

corporate advertising   advertising designed to promote a whole organisation.

corporate culture   the shared values, beliefs, norms and traditions within an organisation which influence and shape the behaviour of the individuals comprising it.

corporate identity   the collection of symbols which organisations use to represent how they wish to be perceived.

corporate PR   the relationship of an organisation with all of its contacts, including suppliers and customers.

corporate resources   the tangible and intangible assets available to an organisation.

corporate strategy   the decisions made and the activities undertaken by an organisation to achieve its broad long-term goals.

cost benefit analysis (CBA)   the objective analysis of benefits of a product versus cost.

cost leadership strategy   where the company seeks increased sales for its products in its present markets through more aggressive pricing.

cost of goods   the total or net cost of the products

or services sold by the firm.

cost-oriented pricing   pricing determined on the basic costs of production.

cost-plus pricing   the practice of adding to an estimated product cost an amount of money to arrive at a selling price.

costs   the expenses of a business which can consist of fixed and variable costs, so, the 'total cost curve' is calculated by adding fixed costs to (unit variable costs multiplied by the number of units).

countervailing power   a state proposed by Galbraith (1956), in which the market power of buyers and sellers cancel each other out, and so encourages an equitable equilibrium within the market.

creative specialist   an advertising agency member responsible for developing the advertising concept from the initial brief.

critical success factors (CSF)   those factors considered critical to success in a competitive market.

cross impact matrix   a matrix which allows key issues to be analysed in the context of other key issues.

cross-elasticity of demand   Cross-elasticity of demand measures one of the most important demand relationships - namely the closeness of substitutes or the degree of complementarity of demand. A high cross-elasticity means that the commodities are close substitutes for each other, while a zero cross-elasticity means that they are independent of each other in the market. Finally a negative cross-elasticity means that the goods are complementary in the market in that one stimulates the sales of another.

CTN (confectionary, tobacconists and newsagent).

customary prices   prices fixed by custom, for example, 'penny' sweets.

Customer   the actual or intended purchaser of goods and/or services.

customer analysis   the compilation and analysis of information pertaining to customers.

customer care   activities performed on behalf of the customer to add value and encourage loyalty.

customer lifetime value (CLV)   a measure of the total value to be earned from a customer over the lifetime of the relationship.

customer relationship management (CRM)   an aspect of marketing management particularly concerned with creating and sustaining customer loyalty by 'managing' the relationship with the customer.

customer satisfaction management

(CSM)   paying attention to the customers needs to ensure they are receiving the satisfaction looked for so that they will automatically think of a preferred supplier and develop a loyalty to them.

customer service explosion   the increased emphasis give to customer services as it becomes more difficult to create a competitive advantage based on product differences.

customer sophistication   when the customer base has knowledge about the product and market which shapes their expectations.

customer-supplier context   the environment in which a transaction takes place.

data protection   the principles and regulations which govern the use of data on individuals (for the UK see www.dataprotection.gov.uk).

database marketing   this combines data on the location and contact details of customers with their purchase records, enquiries and other pertinent information available to form an electronic record of the customer base which can be searched and categorised on any number of criteria, allowing detailed and focused marketing.

decentralisation   the spreading of responsibility for a function across different departments.

deception   activities intended to confuse or deceive customers.

decision making unit (DMU)   a group of people or sub-groups involved in the decision making process.

decoding   in communication terms, the step between the signal and the destination, for example television, as opposed to 'encoding'.

degree of competition   a measure of the number of firms actively competing in a market; see concentration.

delayering   a reduction in the number of hierarchical levels to achieve flatter structures with less psychological distance between senior management and other employees.

demand   an expression of the relationship between price and the amount which will be purchased/ consumed.

demand elasticity   a measure of the sensitivity of sales to changes in the price asked.

demand management   influencing demand to suit supply - for example, promoting weekend hotel breaks at a quiet time of year.

demand curve   the graphical representation of the demand schedule.

demand schedules   information which shows the existence and nature of market opportunities.

demand-enhancing marketing   increasing the

potential market through increasing demand, for example through advertising.

demand-oriented pricing based on expected customer reaction to price.

democratic process in marketing terms, when consumers have an element of choice as to what they purchase, and the right to make any choice they wish.

demographics the study of the size, composition, behaviour and distribution of populations.

department stores large, general stores on multi-levels, selling a wide variety of merchandise including clothing and soft furnishings and with a minimum of 25 staff.

desk research the first stage of research usually conducted using secondary sources.

dichotomous questions questions which require a straight yes or no answer.

differentiated strategy a differentiated strategy exists where the supplier seeks to supply a modified version of the basic product to each of the major subgroups which comprise the basic markets.

differentiation distinguishing a product from competitors by introducing different attributes.

diffusion the process of initial slow sales, followed by rapid sales growth until saturation, also known as the 'product life cycle'.

digital interactive television (DiTV) digital television which usually has a 'return path' which allows the viewer to interact with the broadcaster.

digital marketplace virtual markets made possible by the Internet and the development of e-commerce.

direct advertising advertising aimed at the end consumer.

direct communications direct communication between two parties, either 'B2B' or 'B2C'.

direct exporting sales to customers in foreign markets without making use of an intermediary.

direct mail the use of mail communications to promote involvement in the subject of the communication.

direct marketing marketing and selling products directly to and interactively with an individual, through channels such as mail, internet and telephone.

direct response broadcast media radio and television promotion designed to prompt action by the listener/viewer.

direct sale when the producer sells directly to the consumer with no intermediary.

directed group interview in which a group of respondents, led by an interviewer, has a discussion about the topic under research.

discipline a subject of study or instruction.

discounted cash flow (DCF) a financial technique used to calculate the 'present value' of future earnings allowing for the effects of inflation on those earnings.

discounters retail stores which sacrifice elements of the retail mix such as range of products to keep prices low. For example in grocery terms, these can be 'hard discounters' who have a very limited range and store interior, e.g. Aldi, and 'soft discounters' which have a wider range and more fresh produce available, e.g. Kwik Save.

disintermediation the elimination of intermediaries in the supply chain.

disposable income that proportion of an individual's income available for consumption or investment after meeting prior charges such as income tax.

dissonance the opposite of consonance, when stimuli are in conflict which causes a state of psychological tension which individuals seek to avoid, reduce or eliminate.

distinctive competence any factor at which a firm is uniquely good by comparison with its main competitors (Selznick 1957).

distribution channel see channels.

diversification The process of introducing new products (which may or may not be related to the company's present products) into existing or new markets.

division of labour the breakdown of the production process into individual steps which can be performed by different groups of people as opposed to one person completing the whole manufacturing process, thereby increasing overall productivity.

domain used to define the scope, nature and boundaries of a subject.

door-to-door a form of direct selling where the seller or their agent physically visits the potential customer in their home.

drive to maturity defined by Rostow as 'when a society has effectively applied the range of [then] modern technology to the bulk of its resources'.

drop and collect a kind of survey methodology where a questionnaire is left with a respondent for self-completion and then collected/returned at a later time.

dual distribution when the manufacturer sells part of the output direct but entrusts the balance of their sales to an intermediary.

dual pricing when the same product is sold at different prices, for example, in the one country the same product may be sold under different brands at different prices.

early adopters customers who tend to be the first to purchase a new product.

ecological concerns concern about the possible impact of consumption upon the natural environment.

e-commerce using electronic technology to conduct business.

economic theory the body of knowledge concerned with the maximisation of satisfaction based on the consumption of scarce resources.

economies of scale where a firm with large output will have lower costs per unit and can therefore undercut smaller competitors.

economy the efficient and effective use of resources as related to an organisation or geographic region.

EDLP (every day low price).

effective demand demand backed up by purchasing power.

elasticity of demand an increase or decrease in the asking price will result in a proportionate change in the quantity demanded.

electronic commerce see e-commerce.

electronic marketing see e-marketing.

elementary sampling unit (ESU) the basic sample from which the final respondents are selected.

e-mail a form of electronic communication.

email survey using email to send out a questionnaire to potential respondents. This can be in the text of the email or as an attachment.

e-marketing using electronic technology to implement marketing strategies.

emergent economies nations like India and China which have begun to industrialise and are growing rapidly.

emergent strategy a term coined by Mintzberg to describe how managers develop strategies as a reaction to events as they occur.

emotional buying trigger (EBT) a stimulus in a marketing communication that prompts an emotional response.

empowerment the willingness to devolve responsibility to an individual employee who, ultimately, is responsible for the quality of the firm's products and actions/relationships.

enabling conditions (EC) those conditions necessary for a desired action to be taken.

enabling technology the technology necessary to achieve a desired outcome.

encoding in communication terms, encoding is the step that links the source and the signal, for example a transmission device like a microphone,

as opposed to a 'decoder'.

entrepreneurial approach an approach to NPD typically used for developing new-to-the-world products.

environmental analysis the compilation and examination of data related to the environment in order to identify key trends and developments as a basis for anticipating their likely effect on an organisation. The major factors are political, economic, social and technological hence PEST analysis.

environmental factors the factors incorporated in an environmental analysis.

environmental scanning a term developed by Francis Aguilar of the Harvard Business School (1967) to describe the activities of managers in monitoring their external environment.

EPOS (electronic point of sale) a scanning system used to read bar codes.

e-procurement online purchasing.

equilibrium a state in which supply and demand are in balance.

equipment Those industrial goods which do not become part of the physical product and which are exhausted only after repeated use, such as major installations or installations equipment, and auxiliary accessories or auxiliary equipment.

essential evidence see evidence.

esteem needs recognition of personal status, often through acquisition of material possessions.

ethics acceptable moral standards.

ethnography the scientific study of human society and our environment.

EU European Union, formerly the EEC or European Economic Community or 'Common Market'.

European Article Numbering (EAN) a system developed in the 1970s from the Universal Product Code System in the USA, which uses a 13 digit numeric and 'barcode' on packaging to identify a product and provide related information.

evaluation of competition using attributes of products of services to compare them.

evidence physical evidence is the tangible outcome of receiving a service or product, and this can be further subdivided in service terms into peripheral evidence (a part of the service with no independent value) or essential (a part of the product or service which can not be owned by the customer) (Shostack 1982).

evoked set the set of products triggered in the mind of a customer by a particular need, for example, instant coffee might trigger Nescafé, Maxwell House and Kenco.

evolution of marketing organisation proposed

as a four phase process in which marketing has moved from sales and demand generation to an integrated part of the business function (Webster 1997).

excess supply   created when supply outstrips demand.

exclusive distribution   see 'intensity of distribution'.

excitement   in marketing terms (Levitt) this is the particular appeal that captures the attention and interest of a prospective customer.

executive summary   a single-page statement of the basic purpose and findings of a report.

expectancy-value (EV) model   the EV model is particularly associated with the work of Martin Fishbein (based on Rosenberg and Heider), who argues that an attitude comprises two components - beliefs about the attributes of an object and the values ascribed to these beliefs. In order to maintain consistency (or balance, or congruity, as it is sometimes called) consumers need to act in accordance with their beliefs and the values associated with them.

exploratory research   research undertaken in the early stages of a project to define the nature of the problem to be solved, and reviewing what is already known about the problem.

exponential growth   the rate at which something multiplies itself, for example, xy where y is the exponent.

exponential function   in marketing this is often represented by an s-shaped curve representing low initial sales, through a period of rapid growth, to a slow down when market saturation is reached.

expressive procedures   a qualitative research method where researchers can project behaviour from subjects 'expressions' of behaviour for example, through the use of drawings or role playing.

extended identity   the aspect of a brand which extends and represents the product attributes.

extended marketing mix   an elaboration of the original 4Ps model of Product, Price, Place and Promotion to include Process, People and Physical Evidence which are considered important for the marketing of services.

external and internal factors   those factors that need to be considered in a marketing audit and /or SWOT analysis.

external facilitators   third party organisations who provide information or services to a company.

external perspective   evaluating the organisation and its actions from the customer's point of view.

extractive industries   industries which provide raw materials, for example mining, drilling for oil etc.

extrapolative techniques   projective techniques based on past performance and environmental conditions.

fabricated materials   Those industrial goods which become a part of the finished product and which have undergone processing beyond that required for raw materials but not so much as finished parts.

fact finding   more commonly known as market research.

factor rating table   this is a device for analysing the relevance and importance of information required to solve a problem, usually by identifying and rank ordering critical success factors.

family life-cycles   a sociological concept developed in the early 1930s which posits that families change over time and that these changes are accompanied by significant changes in their consumption behaviour.

fast moving consumer goods (FMCG)   see convenience goods.

feedback   in communication terms, information which is generated from the destination of a signal which is returned to the source and impacts on future signals.

felt need (FN)   a consciously experienced, unsatisfied state.

field research   the collection of original or primary data.

financial fallacies   financially incorrect assumptions, often based on incorrect data.

fixed costs   those costs that cannot be altered in the short or medium term and which exist irrespective of the volume of output.

focus strategy   the same as a concentrated strategy.

franchising   when one company grants to another the right to use any tangible or intangible possession it owns, such as a trademark, business method or recipe for the purpose of trade, in return for benefits such as expansion for a very low investment, and the receipt of fees, royalties, or profits.

free enterprise economy   a marketplace in which both the manufacturer and the consumer have freedom to produce and consume with no regulatory interference.

free sample   a promotional method which involves giving potential customers a free trial of the product.

freedom of entry   the ease or otherwise of entering a new market determined by the legal, economic, political and other 'barriers' that may limit access.

frequency of evaluation   how often a marketing analysis or audit is carried out.

frequency of purchase   the elapsed time between repeat purchases of the same product/service.

full cost pricing   an approach which includes all costs, fixed and variable, to which is then added the required profit margin.

full service agencies   organisations such as advertising agencies that provide a complete range of services to their clients.

function of personal selling   to provide information on an individual basis which advertising is unable to cover.

functional factors   the activities associated with the performance of a specified function such as finance, R&D, production etc.

functional marketing   the practice of marketing professionals (Ambler 2000).

functional quality   see quality.

functional specialisation   when each aspect of a marketing strategy is assigned to a specialist team.

future orientation   see orientation.

G8   a group of the 8 leading economic powers in the world.

gatekeepers, amplifiers and filters (GAFs)   people who are expert in the sector of the environment in which the organisation is scanning for information. In order to accomplish their task they must be positioned on the boundary between the organisation and its circumscribing environment. GAFs are at the forefront of expertise and are defined as gatekeepers because it is through them that the organisation is able to look out into the surrounding environment. They are amplifiers because they are closest to the source of weak signals, and filters because it is through their expertise that they are able to distinguish the signal and screen out the 'noise' surrounding it.

generic product   describing a class of product not a specific brand, similar to the 'core service'.

geo-demographic segmentation   the division of people into groups according to where they live and information about that location.

geographic information system (GIS)   a software mapping system (for example InSite) which enables companies to analyse and compare different geographical districts, for example, store catchment areas.

geographic pricing   different prices for different geographical regions, for example, petrol.

Germanic-Alpine interpretation of capitalism   based on controlled competition, long term development and relationships and strong social involvement.

gestalt psychology   the branch of psychology that holds that individuals are conscious of a perceptual field as a whole rather than the individual perceptual stimuli the comprise it; i.e. we perceive what we expect to perceive.

globalisation   the marketing of products and services worldwide using the same marketing mix in every country or region.

glocalisation   the adaptation of elements of the marketing mix to suit the conditions prevailing in a given market.

gondola   a free-standing shelving unit in a supermarket that customers can walk round.

goodwill   an intangible company asset. In marketing terms, see also brand equity.

green issues   issues of concern to persons concerned with the impact of consumption on the environment.

green marketing   the marketing of goods which are seen to be environmentally 'friendly' e.g. recycled packaging.

grey market   a group of consumers characterised as being aged over 40. Can also be used to describe a situation where products are sold (legally) to end users by an intermediary not directly authorised by the producer.

gross domestic product (GDP)   the value of all the goods and services produced by a single nation during a year.

Guttmann scaling   a scale where all the statements used belong to the same dimension, for example agreement only, rather than agreement/disagreement as with Thurstone or Likert scales.

halo influence   the perceived transfer of positive attributes to other products/activities of an organisation.

hard technologies   see technology.

Hawthorne effect   the danger of an observer influencing the behaviour they are there to observe by their very presence.

hedonic, experiential model (HEM)   a communication as information processing model (Shimp 2003) which perceives behaviour as being driven by emotions in pursuit of happiness.

heterogeneous   variable, or of multiple different elements.

hierarchical frameworks   a concept that identifies linkages between a sequence of events or activities and anticipated outcomes.

hierarchy-of-effects   a proposition that advertisements or other marketing stimuli exert influence on an audience through a progression or sequence of events; e.g. a sale is the consequence of the sequence AIDA - Awareness, Interest, Desire, Action.

homeostasis   a state of balance achieved when psychological needs are satisfied.

homogeneity   a state in which the objects under consideration are seen as identical.

human motivation   the inner state that activates or moves people towards goals, resulting in purposive means/ends behaviour.

human resource management (HRM)   the management of personnel within an organisation.

hybrid technologies   see **technology**.

hyper-segmented   when a market is divided into increasingly smaller segments .

hypodermic effect   a communication model depicting a one step communication process where impersonal (e.g. mass media) or personal sources make direct contact with an audience.

hypothesis   a statement which may be accepted or rejected based on subsequent findings.

IMP Group   a group of mainly European scholars who have developed theories of interaction and networking in industrial or B2B markets.

implementation   the act of translating plans into action.

incentives   an inducement to act in a way beneficial to the offeror e.g. a discount to encourage purchase.

income   payment in money or kind in exchange for goods or services rendered with a defined period of time.

indirect exporting   sale to a domestic customer who then re-sells in a foreign market.

industrial concentration   see **concentration**.

industrial goods   goods which are destined for use in producing other goods or rendering services, as contrasted with goods destined to be sold to ultimate consumers.

industrial marketing   the activities involved in the sale of industrial goods, nowadays commonly referred to as B2B or 'business or business' marketing.

industrial revolution   a period of major breakthroughs in economic development during the nineteenth century.

industry   the collection of firms that are engaged in producing goods or services which are close substitutes for one another, e.g. the motor car industry.

inelastic demand   where changes in price have little or no effect on the quantity demanded.

infinitely elastic   a marginal reduction in price will result in everyone with a demand for that good buying from the supplier offering this price.

informal group   a group such as a circle of friends that has no specified structure.

information processing   The acquisition, storage and interpretation of information usually with respect to making decisions on specific issues or topics.

information search (IS)   the stage following awareness and interest at which the individual or organisation actively looks for more information on the object of interest.

information sources   for example the mass media.

informative advertising   advertising with a high information content designed to explain the features of a product or service and stimulate primary demand for it.

inseparability   when you can not differentiate between two things, for example, in services, there is often no distinction between delivery and use as many services are produced and consumed simultaneously.

in-store observation   a method to check in-store merchandising support for different manufacturers and their competitors.

intangible   something which is not measurable or possible to quantify.

integrated brand promotion (IBP)   a promotional strategy based specifically on the brand image.

integrated marketing communications (IMC)   a marketing communications strategy which requires that a company adopts strategies that co-ordinate different promotional elements and that these promotional activities are integrated with other marketing activities that communicate with customers.

integration   the co-ordination of different units into a cohesive strategy.

intensity of distribution   intensive (through as wide a range of retailers as possible), selective (through a limited number of potential retailers in order to maximise profits whilst minimising costs), exclusive (through a limited number of outlets thereby conferring a degree of exclusivity on those outlets.).

interactive digital television (iDTV)   see **DiTV**.

interactive marketing function   the management of all the factors in the buyer-seller relationship (as opposed to 'internal marketing') (Gronroos 1989).

intermediary   a person or organisation that buys and re-sells without changing the form of the product.

internal marketing   where every employee in a

firm is seen as another employee's 'customer' and all parties behave accordingly (as opposed to interactive marketing) (Gronroos 1989).

international marketing the sale of goods and services in more than one country.

international trading communities associations of countries with agreed terms of trade within the community and between the community and non-members; e.g. LAFTA Latin American Free Trade Association.

internationalisation the process of establishing trade relationships with other countries initially via exporting and then through the development of operations, independently or through joint ventures, in the countries concerned.

internet the global network of computers which hosts the world wide web.

inter-organisational theory the use and application between (inter) organisations of theories from intra-organisational approaches .

interval scales see scales.

interview this involves a personal exchange of information between an interviewer and one or more interviewees, in which the interviewer seeks to obtain specific information on a topic with the co-operation of the interviewee(s). These can range from being formal ('structured', or 'closed', in which the interviewer follows a carefully worded questionnaire with a limited set of responses to choose from), through 'open-ended' (open ended questions in a pre-determined sequence), to 'semi-structured' (which is a combination of closed and open ended questions) and the 'interview guide approach' (when an interviewer has a checklist of topics to cover but freedom to interact with the respondent and create questions as the need arises).

interviewer bias see bias.

intrusive media communications which interrupt the medium they are present in, for example, television commercials.

joint venture the formation of a business partnership by two or more individuals or organisations.

judgement sample when respondents are selected on the basis of the interviewer's subjective opinion that they constitute a representative cross-section of the population to be investigated.

just in time (JIT) when supply is co-ordinated with demand so that there is no need to keep stock of a product and it is manufactured and delivered as it is needed.

key accounts the most profitable customers of a firm.

key account management (KAM) the management of the relationship with the most profitable customers of a firm.

key performance indicators (KPI) a limited set of variables that summarise the details of performance needed by marketing managers.

knock-on effect when one event causes other events.

latent demand A demand which the consumer is unable to satisfy, usually for lack of purchasing power.

Law of inertia of large numbers large groups are more stable than small groups owing to the compensating effect of deviation in opposite directions.

Law of statistical regularity any group of objects taken from a larger group of such objects will tend to possess the same characteristics as the larger group.

less developed countries (LDCs) largely discarded in favour of the less perjorative 'newly industrialising' or 'developing' countries.

leverage an additional benefit that accrues to an individual or organisation by virtue of their power or relationship, e.g. ownership of a material in short supply, entitlement to landing time at an international airport etc.

licence authorise another to make use of one's intellectual property in return for an agreed payment.

life-cycle stage see product life cycle.

lifestyle the manner in which people live and their consumption patterns and behaviour.

Likert scales a form of scale where respondents are presented with a series of statements and asked to indicate their degree of agreement/disagreement with each, on a scale of usually five to seven options.

line extension when a firm uses the same brand name to introduce a variant of the basic product targeted at a new/different segment of the market served by the product category, as well as to maintain the loyalty of existing customers. See also **brand extension**.

linear compensatory model when a scale is used to represent a person's attitude by assuming that we balance positive and negative factors to come to a single summary position, which can be represented by a single number. See for comparison **multidimensional scaling**.

linear programming technique developed

by Danzig (1949), a mathematical model of relationships between conditions to find the best solution to a problem.

locus of channel control   A function of the firm's competitive strength vis-à-vis other members of a 'channel of distribution'.

logistics   the strategic management of the movement and storage of material into production and eventually as finished goods into the distribution channels to the final purchaser.

long-term memory   this is information which is stored for possible future recall and use.

love needs   need for affection and feeling of belonging to a social group.

loyalty   the tendency of a customer to repeat purchase a particular product.

macro environmental analysis   defines the threats and opportunities facing the firm, and their competitors, both presently and in the future.

macro level concentration   at the national level, the proportion of total industry output accounted for by some predetermined percentage of all firms.

macro segment   the basic area to be segmented into sub-groups.

mail order   the purchase of goods or services through the medium of mail services.

mail survey   the administration of a questionnaire by means of the mail service.

managerial school   a view of marketing as a problem solving and decision making process drawing on economics, psychology, sociology and statistics, developed in the 1950s and 60s by authors such as McCarthy (1960) and Kotler (1967). This was the dominant approach until the 1990s.

managerial approach   an approach to NPD and the standard process used for existing business management.

manufacturer   an individual or organisation that makes products through the use of machinery.

margin   the amount of profit gained from a sale once all costs have been deducted.

marginal cost   the rate of change of the total cost of production depending on output.

marginal unit   each item which has a known profit margin.

market   originally a physical location where sellers and buyers could establish contact with one another. Nowadays includes any situation where buyers and sellers can establish communication with one another.

market demand   the demand of the potential consumer base for a service or product, which can often be used to formulate strategy for example pricing.

market development   a strategy where the company seeks increased sales by expanding into a new geographical market.

market manager   when the marketing strategy of a product is overseen by a market manager based on the fact that different markets may have different needs from the same product.

market opportunity   potential markets.

market orientation   a business orientation where the primary focus is on the market place, customers, competitors and distributors.

market oriented organisation   an organisation with a market orientation.

market penetration   where the company seeks increased sales for its present products in its present markets through more aggressive pricing, promotion and distribution.

market research   the measurement and analysis of markets; see **marketing research**.

market segmentation   when a market is divided into sub-groups through the use of distinctive features which are common to those within the group and absent from those excluded from it.

market segments   a group of buyers who have broadly similar needs and wants that differ in some relevant way from those of other customers in the same market.

market share   the percentage of the total market accounted for by a single product or firm.

market structure   the definition of a market in terms of its salient characteristics - number of firms, degree of concentration, size, value, etc.

marketing   the preferred definition of Baker is 'mutually satisfying exchange relationships'.

marketing arithmetic   the actual formulae associated with defining specific financial data.

marketing as a concept   school of thought from 1930s onwards with increased emphasis on the consumer, but main emphasis on stimulation of demand through advertising and personal selling.

marketing as a process   school of thought in late nineteenth century through to 1930. Strongly associated with business to business marketing.

marketing audit   a comprehensive analysis of the business and its aims to develop a marketing plan.

marketing boards   organisations established to promote and regulate the marketing of goods and services.

marketing communications mix   a sub group of the 'marketing mix' which includes aspects such as advertising, publicity, sales promotion and packaging.

marketing concept consists essentially of three basic elements: a customer orientation that places them at the centre of all the organisation's thinking and activities; an orientation that seeks to coordinate and integrate all the organisation's efforts towards common goals; a profit orientation based on maximising customer satisfaction.

marketing department a department within an organisation responsible for the management of the marketing function.

marketing function what marketing managers actually do.

marketing leverage a situation unique to the firm which can give them an advantage, for example the patent over a particular process.

marketing management the management of activities involved in setting marketing objectives, formulating and implementing action plans, and the measurement of outcomes.

marketing management school in which marketing is the dominant managerial function of the firm, and the focus is on the market and customers.

marketing metrics the ability to statistically quantify marketing research and performance.

marketing mix the marketing mix refers to the apportionment of effort, the combination, the design, and the integration of the elements of marketing into a programme or mix which, on the basis of appraisal of the market forces, will best achieve the objectives of an enterprise at a given time. The idea of the mix of functions was conceived by Neil Borden in 1965, and the best known model is that of the 4Ps.

marketing myopia a term made famous by Ted Levitt (1960), which describes what happens when companies become too product oriented (and thereby focused on manufacture and distribution), so that they lose sight of the basic need which the product satisfies, and their business strategy suffers as a result.

marketing of services essentially the same process as that used for the marketing of physical products which involves manipulation of the elements of the marketing mix. It is suggested that services call for consideration of Process, People and Physical Evidence in addition to the 'usual' 4Ps.

marketing orientation a company determining what the customer wants, then making what it can sell.

marketing plan the overall structure into which a marketer integrates elements of the marketing mix.

marketing research as opposed to 'market research', marketing research concerns using scientific methods to collect information about all those factors which impinge upon the marketing of goods and services, and so including the measurement and analysis of markets, the study of advertising effectiveness, distributive channels, competitive products and marketing policies, and the whole field of consumer behaviour.

mark-up the amount added to the cost of goods to establish a selling price.

Maslow's hierarchy of human needs a 5 level hierarchy of basic needs, often represented as a pyramid, developed by Abraham Maslow in 1943, ranging from the most basic physiological needs, through safety, love and esteem needs to self-actualisation at the apex.

mass marketing when the producer offers a single undifferentiated product to all potential customers.

mass media communication which reaches a large proportion of the public, for example, press, television, radio, posters, cinema and the internet.

materialism a desire for material goods and possessions such as money over emotional fulfilment.

matrix organisation project teams made up of representatives from each of the functional departments.

means-end chain a procedure for analysing a consumer's knowledge of a product by relating its attributes to the desired benefits and the values associated with them.

mechanical damage damage to products caused by handling, for example transportation.

mechanical revolution generally attributed to the harnessing of steam power.

media in the marketing context this means advertising media rather than news or mass media.

media classes the major sub-divisions of advertising media newspapers, magazines, radio, TV etc.

media schedule a formal plan/document spelling out the media to be used, when and where in the execution of an advertising campaign.

media specialist an advertising expert responsible for selecting the appropriate media for a campaign.

medium singular form of media.

megatrends large scale changes in the business landscape, after the book by Naisbitt (1982) of the same name.

merchandising the arrangement of in-store displays to ensure effective exposure of the product.

message   in communication terms the message should be meaningful to the recipient, even after distortion through its mode of transmission.

message appeal   there are six alternative approaches (DeLozier 1976): fear, distraction, participation, emotion versus rational, aggression arousal and humour, and the use of some of these can be controversial and must be carefully considered.

metasearch   in internet terms, software which conducts multiple searches simultaneously and compiles the results.

metric of awareness   how aware customers are of the product. Can also be called 'share of voice'.

metrics   consistent measures used to analyse a firm and its brands performance.

micro level of concentration   at the industry level, the percentage share of total sales of that industry accounted for by a predetermined percentage of all firms in the industry.

micro-economic paradigm   maximising profit from the nature of the transaction between buyer and seller.

micro-environmental analysis   analysis of the immediate environment within which the firm competes defined by the industry, markets, channels, customers and competitors with which it interacts.

modified rebuy   a situation in which some change has occurred that calls for re-evaluation of the normal purchasing procedure (straight rebuy).

monopolistic competition   the theory of monopolistic competition developed by Edwin Chamberlin to describe the type of market structure (Theory of Monopolistic Competition, 1933), which combines the characteristics of both perfect competition and monopoly. Can be used to describe when a firm differentiates its product sufficiently to create its own market without any direct competition.

monopoly   the case of a single seller, enjoying absence of competition of any kind, with complete control over the supply of the product, including control over entry into the industry.

moral values   those values that define an individual's perception of morally acceptable behaviour.

MOSAIC   a specific geodemographic database used since 1988 and based on information from a credit reference agency (CCN, now Experian).

motivation   an inner state, or need, that drives people towards goals, resulting in a behaviour; 'why' consumers act as they do.

motivation research (MR)   research intended to establish why consumers act as they do.

multibrands   a family of brands in the same product category.

multidimensional scaling   The basic characteristic of multidimensional scaling is that respondents are asked to make judgements concerning the degree of similarity/distance between pairs of stimuli using a scale which may be either metric (interval or ratio scale) or non-metric (ordinal scale). (See 'scales'). These judgements, for example, 'greater than x, less than y' combine the dimensions of x and y as opposed to unidimensional scaling, which only measures one dimension, for example, I agree or disagree with x.

multidisciplinary   consisting of more than one discipline.

multi-level marketing (MLM)   see **network marketing**.

multinational corporations (MNCs)   a firm that operates on a large scale in numerous different countries.

multiple choice questions   questions which offer the respondent a number of alternative answers.

multiple convergent processing (MCP)   a model of new product development developed by Baker and Hart (1999).

multivariate analysis   An approach widely used in marketing research due to the complexity of most marketing problems, where several factors are operating together, when one wishes to estimate the influence of each of the variables on the end result.

mutually satisfying exchange relationships   the essence of marketing.

NAICS (North American Industry Classification System)   a method for classifying economic activities, and a replacement of the Standard Industrial Classification (SIC) code.

natural breaks   regular breaks in television programming designed to fit in with the flow of the programme.

needs, wants and choice   a need is something fundamental to the maintenance of life, such as food, drink, shelter and clothing. Needs are largely physiological in the sense that they are basic and instinctive drives with which we are born. It is clear, however, that a need may be satisfied by any one of a large number of alternatives, for example thirst may be assuaged by water, tea, coffee, beer, wine, and so on. The availability of alternative means of satisfying a need constitutes choice, provision of which is central to the practice of marketing. In the absence of substitute, or alternative goods, there can be no choice and needs and wants become synonymous. Where there is more than one way of satisfying a basic need, physiological drives will be modified by economic, sociological and psychological factors. Variations in these factors will predispose individuals to prefer a specific alternative and this preference constitutes a want.

negative word-of-mouth   see word of mouth.

netiquette   the unwritten code of behaviour for users of the Internet.

network marketing   when a company uses a number of independent distributors to sell its products, normally working on a commission basis, and these distributors are also responsible for recruiting new distributors to expand the sales force. Can also be called 'multi-level marketing'.

new international business realities   factors facing businesses in recent years.

new product development (NPD)   The development of a new product is seen as a sequential process normally containing six distinct phases: exploration, screening, business analysis, development, testing, commercialisation. (Booz Allen Hamilton 1982).

new task   the situation faced by a potential buyer when they develop a need for a product for which they have no prior knowledge or experience requiring consideration of all the buyphases.

newspapers   a major print medium published daily or weekly on a national or regional basis.

niche strategy   A market niche strategy coincides with a concentrated marketing strategy in that the firm realises that it lacks the resources to compete directly with bigger firms in the industry and so seeks to identify a particular niche or segment of the market upon which it can concentrate all its energies.

NICs   newly industrialising countries.

No-frills   a way of keeping prices low through economising on other aspects of the retail mix such as location and range of products. Such stores are also known as 'discounters'.

non-personal channels   all media through which messages are transmitted without face-to-face communications, for example, press, TV, posters etc.

non-probability sampling   a selective procedure for choosing a sample as opposed to 'probability sampling'.

non-profit marketing   the application of procedures and techniques developed in a commercial context to the activities of not-for-profit and cause related marketing.

non-store retailing   any form of retailing e.g. direct mail, the Internet, where the buyer purchases without having to visit a store.

normative theory   the basic structures and parameters of a subject, or the recognised 'best practice'.

not-for-profit   organisations that seek to deliver benefits to their stakeholders but of a non-monetary nature e.g. RNLI, The National Trust.

objective   a desired outcome which is established to measure the effectiveness of a course of action intended to achieve some purpose or goal. Objectives should be quantifiable and capable of measurement so as to provide a benchmark against which to compare actual performance.

objective factors   these are factors that are intrinsic to the product, for example, performance and price.

observability   how visibly effective a product innovation is.

observation   one of the 3 main experimental techniques along with experimentation and survey, which may be either 'informal' for example everyday observations, (also called 'scanning'), or 'formal' observation, a scientific technique which consists of the systematic gathering recording and analysis of data.

odd pricing   pricing a product with a figure ending in an odd number.

oligopoly   oligopolistic markets exist when there are so few sellers of a particular product or service that the market activities of the seller have an important effect on the other sellers.

open-ended questions   these give the respondent complete freedom in answering so giving maximum information and limiting interviewer bias.

operant conditioning   seeking to change behaviour by altering the consequences of that behaviour, e.g. giving an unpleasant taste to harmful substances.

opinion leader   members of the population who act as filters and amplifiers for messages, and provide a step in the communication process between sources and the audience.

opportunity cost   the trade off required between two conflicting stimuli, for example, time and money.

optimum growth   the growth rate at which the sacrifice of present consumption necessary to promote future growth is just balanced by the extra future consumption this will generate.

organisational buying behaviour (OBB)   the

process followed when buying on behalf of an organisation.

organisational culture   the set of beliefs and values that influence behaviour within an organisation; "the way we do things around here".

organisational revolution   when the factory system superseded the cottage industry system.

orientation   in business function, production is seen as a 'present orientation' whereas marketing is seen as a 'future orientation'.

outdoor advertising   the oldest of the five major advertising media involving the use of poster sites and transport advertising.

package utilities   generally divided into five groups (Underwood 1993) these include functional, symbolic, information, aesthetic and structural utilities of packaging which influence the customers perception of the value of the product.

packaging   materials designed to enable a product to be protected, stored and used. Other factors to consider include appearance, cost and disposability/ recyclability. .

page traffic   a measure of the number of persons actually reading a page in a newspaper or magazine.

pan-company marketing   marketing across an organisation, not necessarily as a defined function (Ambler 2000).

panels   groups of consumers monitored to provide data about some aspect of buyer behaviour. These can be traditional (on-going and collecting general data for strategy decisions) or access (ad-hoc, and usually to collect data for a specific decision).

parameter theory   developed in the 1930s by the Copenhagen School and the forerunner of the modern concept of relationship marketing.

patent rights   an exclusive right granted to an inventor for a period of 17 years to produce and sell the product, process or material described in the patent.

penetration pricing   launching a new product at a low price (or even at a loss) to gain customers from existing products.

people factor   the impact of the personal relationship between buyer and seller which determine's the quality of a firm's performance within the marketplace.

perceived risk   the customer's fear of trying a new product.

perception   is the interpretation of sensations received, or 'stimuli'.

perceptual mapping   the creation of a plot or 'map' representing how consumers perceive comparative products along certain dimensions or attributes derived by non-metric multidimensional scaling.

perfect substitutes   when consumers perceive all the competitive offerings as being identical.

performance driven specifications   these focus on the function of the product or service required   in other words the 'fitness for purpose' criteria.

performance factors   those features and attributes taken into account when selecting products and services for purchase/consumption.

performance monitoring research   compares actual performance with planned results to help guide management strategy.

peripheral evidence   see evidence.

perishability   how long a product may be stored before it becomes unsuitable for use. Also one of the factors used to distinguish services from physical goods. Unlike physical products services cannot be stored for later sale so that a failure to sell at the time of creation results in a complete loss of the service e.g. seats at the theatre, in transport, or hotel rooms.

permanent income hypothesis   this holds that expenditures are based on average income expectations over time. The hypothesis recognises that consumption patterns are relatively stable over time, which suggests that consumers average out their expenditures, i.e. under inflation they anticipate that they will make good current dissaving, due to price increases, out of future wage increases.

persona   the human qualities of a brand, categorised by Aaker (1996) as sincerity, excitement, competence, sophistication and ruggedness.

personal channels   situations in which a direct face-to-face communication takes place.

personal selling   oral presentation in a conversation with one or more prospective buyers for the purpose of making a sale.

personal video recorder (PVR)   a video recording device such as TiVo or SkyPlus which gives the user a great deal of control over what they record and how they replay it.

personality   a personal and unique way of responding to the environment; those characteristics that account for differences among people and that are predictive of their behaviour.

personnel   in services, personnel can be contact (those who the customers interact with) or 'support' (people who provide part of the overall service without direct interaction with the consumer).

persuader   the role of a salesman, using 'persuasion' to effect a sale.

persuasion   when a potential user moves from a state of neutral awareness about a product to the development of an attitude towards that object.

persuasive advertising   advertising designed to elicit an attitude towards something.

PEST (political, economic, sociological, technological)   an analysis based on the four major categories of the macro-environment.

philosophy   a particular school of thought. In business terms, the marketing philosophy is that the firm needs to combine the resources at its disposal in the manner which will enable it to achieve its long term profit goals, whilst remembering that consumption is a 'democratic process'.

physical distribution   see logistics.

physical evidence   see evidence.

physiological needs   basic needs essential to survival, for example, thirst or hunger.

pilot marketing   tests the feasibility of the proposed marketing plan for a product.

place   one of the 4Ps, 'place' takes into account all those activities involved in making products available to customers.

planned market position   where the firm envisages the product or service in the market.

planning   the method by which we seek to exercise some degree of control over the future.

p-mail   postal contact (Shimp 2003) as opposed to e-mail.

point of sale (POS)   materials or goods displayed next to the sales point to act as a reminder to the customer (can also be called point-of-service). Point-of-purchase are promotional materials placed in the shop near to the shelves stocking the product, for example advertising special offers.

polarisation   when items move towards two opposing extremes, for example, in terms of retailing, small convenience stores are the 'polar opposite' of superstores.

population   not only the numbers of people in a group, but also attributes such as age, sex and geographical distribution, and family size.

portable media players   handheld devices allowing access different to digital media.

portfolio   a collection of related items as in the 'product portfolio'.

positioning   establishing a unique place in the competitive market for a product so that a sub-group of consumers perceive the product to be different in an important way from its competitors.

positive circles   (Normann 1985) in which the good performance of the 'contact personnel' gives a positive reflection on the whole service business.

post hoc   after the fact, for example collecting data then defining the method of analysis depending on the data gathered.

post industrial information era   an age characterised by customisation, decentralisation, self-help, communication, networks and information overload.

post purchase evaluation (PPE)   the final stage in the composite model of buying behaviour in which the consumer compares actual performance/satisfaction with that expected.

poster   the medium used in outdoor advertising.

postponement   delaying a decision.

potential demand   where a consumer possesses purchasing power but is not currently buying.

praxiology   'the study of human action' (Crosier 1983).

pre-conditions for take off   necessary stages for a society to develop economically. In Western Europe these were the evolution of modern science and the widening of the market.

predetermined margin   an amount added to the costs of producing a product which gives a set level of profit.

preparatory set   perceptual phenomenon by which people tend to perceive objects in terms of their expectations.

present orientation   see orientation.

Press   print media including national and regional newspapers, consumer magazines, business and professional magazines, and directories.

prestige pricing   when the high price of a product implies prestige compared to lower priced competitors.

price elasticity of demand   elasticity is the ratio of the relative change in the dependent variable (demand) to the relative change in an independent variable (price, consumer income). Thus, demand is said to be elastic when the relative change in the independent factor is greater than the relative change in the quantity demanded, and inelastic when it is less than the relative change in the quantity demanded.

price positioning   the use of price to influence the buyer's perception of a product vis-à-vis competing products.

pricing at the market   when a price reduction would not be justified by increased sales due to a perceived market price for a product.

pricing objectives   the outcomes anticipated from the adoption of a given price strategy.

pricing/pricing strategies   there are many approaches to setting a price for a product or service, including differential/flexible pricing; discrete pricing; discount pricing; diversionary pricing; guarantee pricing; high price maintenance pricing; loss leader pricing; offset pricing and price lining (adopting specific prices for specific categories of product).

primacy effect when information which is presented first is more effective, for example, in two-sided arguments controversial material is most effective when presented first.

primary commodities materials in their natural state.

primary data new data collected for the purpose of research.

primary sector this is concerned with the production of raw materials and includes industries such as agriculture, forestry and fishing.

primary sources raw data and documents in their original state.

private brands own brands of retailers which are sold in competition with manufacturer brands, often at a lower price, for example, Tesco Value products.

probability probability reflects the likelihood of an event expressed on a scale which runs from certain to impossible, to which, by convention, have been assigned the values 1.0 and 0.0 respectively. Intermediate points are assigned values which reflect the frequency with which they are expected to occur and the critical issue is the basis upon which the expectation is founded.

probability sampling when a sample is selected objectively, in that there is a known or calculable probability of being selected for every member of the population under research.

problem recognition the first step in the decision-making process.

problem solving can be 'extensive' often used in a new situation using the largest amount of information we can obtain, or 'limited', often used when we have experience of a particular subject and only need to assimilate a small amount of new information to make a decision.

process in services, this is the way in which a service is delivered to the customer.

product a combination of objective (tangible) and subjective (intangible) properties designed to provide need-satisfying experiences to consumers.

product brands brands which are given to each product family within a company portfolio, for example, Tide and Daz.

product category this is assigned depending on the core benefit of the product, for example, crisps are assigned to the snack food section of the supermarket.

product development where the company seeks increased sales by developing the existing product.

product differentiated marketing when a producer offers two or more different products based on their perception of differences in buying behaviour.

product life-cycle (PLC) the conventional PLC is seen as comprising four basic stages when sales are plotted against elapsed time from introduction. First, there is a period of very slow growth when the new product or idea is introduced to prospective users. This phase is terminated by a transition to a period of very rapid growth which eventually levels off into a period of maturity followed by a decline culminating in termination of the life cycle. The PLC should be seen as a generalised model of the stage through which all successful products will ultimately pass. It is not a predictive or forecasting tool.

product manager concept when it is the role of the product manager to coordinate all activities associated with the marketing of a given product, including planning, information seeking and evaluation, coordination and control.

product mix the nature of the different products of a firm.

product oriented organisation an organisation in which the primary focus is on technology and what it can make rather than customers and their needs.

product policy the strategy chosen for a particular product, for example, modifying the product offering in the light of changes in consumer demand.

product portfolio the collection of products offered for sale by an organisation.

product portfolio analysis a technique developed by the Boston Consulting Group for analysing individual products at different stages in their life cycle.

product scope the range of uses of a product.

product testing an objective appraisal of the product's performance, free of subjective associations created by other elements of the marketing mix, for example, price or brand image. See also **test marketing**.

product-attribute-fixation a focus on the attributes, features and functions of the product rather than the values and benefits looked for by customers.

production orientation an emphasis on increasing supply and reducing costs.

production/consumption interface the point at

which the producer and the consumer interact.

profession   a practice which is regulated by its practitioners. This regulation consists of restricting admission to persons who have demonstrated mastery of a defined body of knowledge.

professional services   services which require the provider to be qualified and often governed by a professional association which sets down standards of service and regulates the providers.

Profit Impact of Market Strategy (PIMS)   a major study undertaken by the Marketing Science Institute to analyse the profit performance of businesses under varying conditions.

profitability   an excess of income or revenues over expenditure; maximising profitability is seen as the primary objective of commercial organisations.

profit-and-loss account   a financial statement of income and expenditure.

promotion   promotion includes all activities involved in bringing the product to the attention of the intended customer and persuading them to buy it.

promotional mix   see the marketing communications mix.

promotional objectives   the objectives which determine a firm's promotional strategy, for example, increasing sales or improving brand recognition may require a different promotional mix.

propaganda   publicly communicating an opinion for or against a specific topic .

prospecting   identifying a potential market for a product.

proved name registration (PNR)   a method to measure aided recall of advertising.

psychographic analysis   a method of segmentation combining personality and demographic profiles.

psychological influences   non-physiological drives learned through the process of socialisation which impacts on consumer behaviour.

psychological pricing   using a price which has a psychological significance for the buyer, for example, 9.99 as opposed to 10.00.

public regulation   government rules about the provision of services or product, for example, public transport pricing.

public relations (PR)   strategy/ies to successfully manage the relationship between a firm and the public.

publicity   unpaid promotion of a firm or product, as opposed to 'advertising' which is paid for. .

pull incentives   incentives offered to ultimate consumers to create a demand for a product and 'pull' it through the channels of distribution.

purchasing function   the person or persons within an organisation who are responsible for buying goods and services required by the organisation. With specialisation and the growth of outsourcing purchasing or procurement has come to be seen as a strategic function.

pure monopoly   when a firm is the sole supplier of a particular product or service, so much so that the firm and industry are synonymous.

Q-sort technique   a methodology for collecting and processing data whereby the subjects sort statements into different categories.

qualitative data   data that reflects attitudes and opinions collected by unstructured or semi-structured methods to gain insight into buyer behaviour. The insights gained may then be tested/validated by means of quantitative research using a representative sample of the population of interest.

quality   in services, quality can be either technical (the service itself) or functional (the way the service is delivered) (Gronroos 1982).

quality assurance   a guarantee of quality.

quality indicator   any cue or stimulus used by the prospective buyer to assess quality. Price is frequently used as such an indicator.

quality of life   personal satisfaction with one's 'standard of living'.

quantitative   a method of analysis which provides data, normally numerical, for statistical analysis .

quantitative data   data which can be statistically analysed.

QUEST (quick environmental scanning technique)   is a 'future research process' (Nanus 1982) to allow a comprehensive first approximation of environmental trends and events critical to strategic decisions.

questionnaires   a form of survey using questions which can be either open-ended, or have a choice of pre-set answers.

quota sampling   when a respondent 'type' is specified on the basis of characteristics of the population at large.

radio frequency identification (RFID)   uses passive electronic chips that are read by radio frequencies to track products through channels of distribution.

ratio analysis   a methodology for analysing financial information to monitor performance against objectives and over time; e.g. current assets related to current liabilities.

ratio scales   the most powerful of scales which permit absolute comparison of the objects e.g. 6 metres is twice as high as 3 metres and six times as high as 1 metre.

rationalisation   generally any action designed to improve efficiency. Specifically, it is a form of ego-defence in which unattainable goals are discarded as undesirable while attainable goals are seen as being more desirable.

raw materials   those industrial materials which in part or in whole become a portion of the physical product but which have undergone no more processing than is required for convenience, protection, economy in storage, transportation or handling. Materials in their natural state can also be termed primary commodities.

recall   what people can remember of a message. It can be 'aided' (prompted by a stimulus) or 'unaided' (no prompting).

receiver   in communication terms, someone who receives and understands information transferred by a 'sender'.

recentralised decentralisation   when functions which have been devolved to different groups within an organisation are brought back under close control of a core group.

recession   a period of depressed demand due to external economic factors.

reference groups   comprise associations of people who are interdependent, so that their behaviour can affect each other, who share an ideology comprising beliefs, values and norms that regulates their mutual conduct.

regional shopping centres   large, purpose built collection of retail outlets sharing a common site with access to major transportation links, and offering extensive parking facilities which attracts customers from an extensive geographical catchment area.

rejection   one of three possible outcomes of the buying decision process; the others are adoption or purchase, and deferral - the postponement of a decision for the time being.

relationship marketing   the dominant paradigm of marketing from the early 1990s when it took over from the managerial school. It has its basis in Europe in the 1930s but became dominant after a seminal article in the Journal of Marketing by Fred Webster Jr in 1992. Relationship marketing emphasises that both buyers and sellers benefit more if they enter into a continuing relationship within which the seller makes a special effort to determine the buyers needs and meet them, while the buyer rewards the seller with their continuing patronage. This approach is felt to reflect the true meaning of the marketing concept by contrast with approaches which emphasise the transaction as the basis of exchange relationships.

relative advantage   the degree to which a product is perceived as better than an existing product - the higher the relative advantage, the higher the likelihood of adoption.

relative income hypothesis   holds that expenditures/saving patterns depend upon the relative position of the spending unit on the income scale, and not on the absolute income earned. This hypothesis recognises the 'keeping up with the Joneses' phenomenon.

resource theory   a view that sees strategy as the matching of an organisation's resources, or 'strengths', with market opportunities.

respondent consistency   a tendency to avoid making contradictory statements when responding to questioning.

respondent self-selection   a view that persons who agree to be interviewed have a particular interest in a subject and so may give biased answers.

retail co-operatives   voluntary association of retailers who agree to collaborate with one another for purposes of sourcing goods (economies of scale), promotional purposes etc.

retail parks   see regional shopping centres.

retail price   the final price asked of the consumer.

retail revolution   the scale of innovation and changes in retail structure during the later part of the twentieth century, following the restrictions from the World Wars which lasted until 1952, and which had stagnated the normal evolution of the retail trade.

retailing   all those activities necessary to sell goods into final consumption.

return path   in DiTV terms this is a means for an end user to interact with the broadcaster normally via a telephone line connected to their digibox, using their remote control.

Rorschach ink blot test   a test where respondents are asked to look at pictures of 'ink blots' and describe the associations that come to mind.

RSP (recommended selling price)   also known as recommended retail price (RRP) this is the price the manufacturer assigns to a product for sale to the end consumer.

safety needs   physical and lifestyle security often achieved through group membership.

sales orientation   a company selling what it can produce.

sales promotion   promoting a firm or product

through methods other than advertising, such as by displays or demonstrations.

sample   a subset of a population.

sampling   the process of selecting a subgroup of a population of interest for the collection of information that may then be generalised to the whole population. Samples may be probability or non-probability based and vary significantly in terms of cost and reliability.

scale economies   savings in costs accruing from operating on a larger scale. While these are important in manufacturing, technological innovation has reduced their importance and scale in marketing has become more important.

scales   these can be nominal scales (where the number assigned only serves to identify the objects under consideration), ordinal scales (these scales seek to impose more structure on objects by rank ordering them in terms of some property which they possess such as height or weight), Interval scales (founded on the assumption of equal intervals between numbers, i.e. the space between 5 and 10 is the same as the space between 45 and 50 and in both cases this distance is five times as great as that between 1 and 2 or 11 and 12 etc.), and ratio scales (these are the most powerful and possess all the properties of nominal, ordinal and interval scales, while in addition they have an absolute zero point, so they permit absolute comparisons of the objects e.g. 6 metres is twice as high as 3 metres and six times as high as 1 metre).

scientific management   the development of management as a discipline, dating from the early twentieth century.

screening   the evaluation of an object, e.g. ideas and concepts in new product development, to assess their suitability.

search domain   the definition of the firm's environment.

secondary sector   firms which change the nature and form of raw materials through some form of manufacturing process to the point where they are suitable for consumption either by industrial users or ultimate consumers.

secondary sources   existing research and data usually consulted as the first stage in a research project.

segmentation   the act of disaggregating market demand into a number of discrete sub-markets for the purpose of developing specific marketing mixes for some or all of them.

selective distribution   see 'intensity of distribution'.

selective exposure   the avoidance of stimuli that may not be congruent with the intended receiver's self-perception, values or beliefs.

selective perception   when individuals screen out stimuli which they do not understand or do not wish to recognise. This can be conscious or subconscious.

self-actualisation   the highest level of Maslow's 'hierarchy of needs', representing the personal need to 'do one's own thing'.

self-analysis   that part of the marketing audit designed to identify the organisation's strengths and weaknesses.

self-liquidating premiums   a sales promotion, the costs of which are covered by payments from those tasking up the offer.

self-service outlets   outlets where the customer selects the merchandise themself.

self-sufficiency   the second of three stages of economic development.

selling, general and administrative expenses (SGA)   usually covered, along with profit, by the 'margin'.

semantic differential technique   a five to nine point scale between two polar opposites, for example, strong/weak, good/bad.

semi-structured interview   see 'interview'.

sendaway   a sales promotion in which the person taking up the offer has to apply, or 'sendaway', for it.

sender   in communication terms, the part which initiates a transfer of information to a 'receiver'.

sensation   sensation occurs when a sense organ receives a stimulus.

sensory memory (SM)   this is equivalent to conscious recognition of a stimulus.

sentence completion tests   a projective technique in which the respondent completes a sentence on the premise that by imputting the thought to a third person they are more likely to reveal their true beliefs which they might suppress if asked a direct question.

service perishability   see 'perishability'.

service-based approach   the use of a marketing mix where service elements are emphasised more than objective attributes and features.

services   any activity or benefit performed by individuals and/or organisations where the object of marketing is an intangible, aimed at satisfying the needs and wants of customers and/or industrial users without any acquisition of physical goods arising from the exchange transaction.

share of voice   see 'metric of awareness'.

shareholder value   the value of the equity in an organisation if it were to be sold. This is reflected in the share price but, given the value of intangible value of assets like brands, it can only be determined accurately by a sale of the business.

shopping goods   consumer goods which the customer in the process of selection and purchase characteristically compares on bases such as suitability, quality, price and style.

short-term memory   the first stage of the memory process, able to hold around 7 pieces of information simultaneously (Miller 1956).

single level marketing (SLM)   an operation which employs direct selling methods   see multi level marketing as a contrast.

skimming   also known as 'skimming the market', this is charging the highest price customers are prepared to pay so restricting sales to those for whom it has the greatest salience and the necessary purchasing power. This is often followed by the introduction of an 'economy' version of the product at a lower price for wider consumption.

snowballing   when something increases in size in an out of control manner.

social class   the stratification of a society into a number of sub-divisions based upon common characteristics such as income, education, occupation, and social status or prestige.

social marketing   an alternative interpretation of marketing as a purely business orientated activity which proposes that its philosophical base and justification rests in meeting the needs of society.

socially responsible marketing   marketing practices that are seen to be socially responsible, e.g. not promoting alcohol to teenagers.

socioeconomic grouping   the social class to which an individual belongs.

soft data   qualitative data that has not been quantified.

soft technologies   see technology.

source   the origination of a stimulus.

source credibility   the audience's perception of the expertness and trustworthiness of the source.

source effect   when the audience's reaction to a message is shaped by their perception of the source.

spam/junk   in internet terms spam is unsolicited contact, normally by email, and junk is the telephone equivalent.

span of control   the manpower of a specific level of an organisation.

specialisation   the third and final stage of a society's economic development.

specialty chain stores   multiple retailers offering a narrow selection of product lines but in great depth, e.g. Office Works.

specialty goods   consumer goods on which a significant group of buyers characteristically insist and for which they are willing to make a special purchasing effort.

speculation   predicting a course of action which will create maximum profit.

standard of living   the level of subsistence or material wealth of a society.

standards of appraisal   the predefined standards by which performance can be measured.

Statistical Package for the Social Sciences (SPSS)   a software package containing several multivariate analysis techniques.

stimulus   any kind or form of change that acts on a sense organ - vision, bearing, taste, smell, touch which includes pressure, pain, cold and warmth, balance, muscle coordination or kinaesthetic sense, and the visceral senses. The stimulus may be chemical, mechanical or physical in nature.

stimulus factors   are neutral in the sense that they are intrinsic to the stimulus and so will be received in exactly the same way by all receivers with normal sensory capabilities. When received by the brain they are organised into patterns following tendencies of similarity, proximity, continuity and context.

stimulus-response theory   one of the earliest explanations for how advertising works, based upon the idea that advertising is perceived as the stimulus, and purchasing behaviour is the intended and desired response.

stock-turn   the number of times stock 'turns over' (is sold) in a given period.

straight rebuy   a purchase made without any re-evaluation of the price or properties of the good or service.

strategic/key issues   issues which may have a significant impact upon the organisation's performance.

strategic alternatives   possible strategies for the firm to pursue.

strategic business unit (SBU)   a self contained unit within a corporation able to operate as a business in its own right.

strategic marketing planning (SMP)   SMP is concerned with establishing the goal or purpose of an organisation and the means chosen for achieving that goal.

strategic variable   the variable which takes precedence in a product strategy.

strategy   the objectives, purposes or goals to be pursued by an organisation and the plans for their achievement.

structured questionnaires   questionnaires in which the possible answers have been predetermined.

subjective factors   perceived as opposed to actual differences between products.

subsidise   to give help by providing financial support.

substitutability   when one function can replace another without changing the outcome.

suburbanisation   a move towards the suburbs and away from city centres, characterised in retailing by the rise of retail parks in suburban locations.

successive focusing   a series of steps performed by managers starting with undirected viewing narrowing down through using more formal information sources to reach a decision.

sunk cost   a fixed initial expenditure.

super-corporation   from Galbraith (1974); when one firm has such control over supplies of essential goods and services that it may excise undue influence over the operation of the state.

superimpose   the attempt of one party to exercise their will over others.

supplies   those industrial goods which do not become a part of the physical product or which are continually exhausted in facilitating the operation of an enterprise.

supply   technically, a projection of the volume of goods or services which would be made available at any given price. In ordinary usage, the total volume offered for sale in a market.

supply chain   all those individuals and organisations involved in the creation and distribution of goods and services to make them available for consumption.

survey   the evaluation, analysis and description of a population based upon a sample drawn from it. There are three main kinds, factual (designed to collect quantitative data), opinion (designed to collect qualitative opinions from subjects) and interpretive (when respondents are asked to explain why they hold particular beliefs or behave in a certain way).

survival   the most basic stage of economic development.

switching   changing from purchasing one brand to another.

SWOT analysis (strengths, weaknesses, opportunities and threats)   a popular shorthand for the environmental analysis and marketing audit which comprises an essential part of formal strategic marketing planning. Specifically, strengths and weaknesses relate to the present and expected future status of the company and are determined through the marketing audit while opportunities and threats exist in the present and future environment in which the organisation is to operate.

symbol grocers   members of a voluntary chain who agree to adopt a house style and carry 'own brands' from the wholesaler and in return can benefit from joint promotional strategies and capital for store improvements. Spar is an example of this practice.

symbol groups   other associations of retailers who trade under a shared identity.

symbolic code   representation of a message in terms of words, music, gestures etc.

symbolism   the representation of a product or related concepts in symbolic form.

synthetic discipline   a synthetic discipline is one that seeks to 'synthesise' (incorporate) knowledge and ideas derived from other disciplines into an integrated and systematic way of thinking.

systems selling   adding value to a product with a broader set of benefits, for example after sales service.

tabloids   a kind of daily newspaper.

tactics   specific, short-term actions taken to implement a chosen strategy.

take off   the take off of the market comes through achieving rapid growth in a limited group of sectors. It is defined as occurring when society is able to sustain an annual rate of net investment of around 10%.

target marketing   where the seller defines the needs of groups of potential buyers and designs products specifically to meet these needs.

targeting   using a series of questions to select a market segment on which to concentrate.

task force   a group of individuals put together to perform a specific function.

task specialisation   as individuals are freed by society's economic development to specialise in their specific fields of interest they become more skilled, and individual productivity is increased.

task uncertainty   the risk perceived in taking a course of action due to lack of information about the possible outcome.

technical complexity   the degree to which an object is perceived as difficult to use or understand due to its technical properties.

technical quality   see quality.

technological innovation   a major source of economic growth and a condition of overall competitiveness.

technology   in services, after Levitt (1976) can be

categorised as 'hard' (when machinery provides a service for example a dishwasher), 'soft' (when pre-planned systems provide a service for example, package holidays) or 'hybrid' (a combination of hard equipment and soft systems).

telemarketing   selling using the telephone as the channel of communication.

television   one of the 'big five' advertising media.

television sponsorship   where a firm or product sponsors a specific programme or series of programmes and at the beginning and end of each episode and commercial break this link is highlighted. This is becoming increasingly common in the UK market.

territory design   organising sales territories to maximise opportunities and potential and minimise costs, for example, travel and time.

tertiary sector   all organisations which provide services such as retailing, banking etc.

test marketing   test marketing consists of launching the product on a limited scale in a representative market, thus avoiding the costs of a full-scale launch while permitting the collection of market data which may subsequently be used for predictive purposes, and includes factors such as price, packaging and brand image as well as the product itself.

testing of mix variables   this is when only one attribute of the marketing mix, for example packaging, is tested as opposed to test marketing which looks at the collective impact of all variables simultaneously.

thematic apperception tests (TAT)   a projective technique used in motivation research.

theories of competition   the essence of competition is rivalry between business units to get customer patronage, thereby increasing sales and consequently security, growth and profits.

theory for marketing services   this approach argues that the marketing of services is more complex than the marketing of goods due to the difference in the end product and the simultaneous production and consumption process.

theory of comparative advantage   originated by Ricardo in the early 19thC, the essential concept is that by specialisation and through trade, countries improve their overall standard of living.

three era's conceptualisation   production, sales and marketing   identified by Robert Keith in the US in the 1950s, the process of a company through a production orientation and a sales orientation to a marketing orientation.

Thurstone scales   an attempt to construct an interval scale by selecting a set of statements about a subject which range from very unfavourable to very favourable expressions of attitude about the subject. Each statement has an associated score.

time to market   the time to develop a product and get it on to the market.

total cost curve   see costs.

total quality management   adding value to a product or service by increasing the intrinsic quality.

total revenue   total amount of income generated by a product before costs are deducted.

Trade Descriptions Act   a UK Government Act regulating the accuracy of quantitative statements about a product.

Trademark   a special kind of brand, or symbol, which can be registered and gives the owner rights of protection against copying or counterfeiting.

traditional panels   see 'panels'.

traditional societies   societies characterised by a lack of technology in which approximately 75% of all activity is focussed on food production.

transactions   an exchange between a buyer and seller.

transfer of ownership   when an intermediary acts between the producer and the consumer to effect a sale.

transportation advertising   advertising on the transportation system, for example adverts on the London Underground or at bus shelters.

trialability   the extent to which an individual is able to try out an innovation before coming to a decision.

umbrella brands   brands which encompass several products from the same manufacturer, for example, Nestlé, Nike.

unaided recall   see 'recall'.

undifferentiated strategy   an undifferentiated strategy exists when the supplier offers the same or undifferentiated product to all persons or organisations believed to have a demand for a product of that type. When the emphasis is on price as the only differentiating factor, this is known as a cost-leadership strategy.

unidimensional scaling   see multidimensional scaling.

unique selling point (USP)   a concept developed by Rosser Reeves that proposed that effective advertising required the identification of a differentiating factor that was unique to it.

uniqueness   the differentiating factor that enable potential buyers to distinguish between products that are close substitutes for one another. Increasingly this is the Brand as opposed to some physical aspect of the product.

unit variable cost the costs incurred in producing an additional unit of output.

Universal Product Code System (UPC) a system of product identification using numbers to identify an object for sale. See **barcode**.

unstructured questionnaires or interviews which do not follow a set pattern, as opposed to 'directed' methods.

VALS™ (Values and Lifestyles) a specific process of segmentation developed by SRI Consulting Business Intelligence, which uses dimensions of motivation and resources and categorises consumers into one of eight segments.

value analysis the systematic evaluation of the individual elements of a manufactured product to determine the optimum combination to satisfy the users needs at minimum cost.

value chain a concept that recognises that there is a continuous link or chain right the way through from the extraction of raw materials to the provision of post-purchase service. Value is added at each stage and a major strategic consideration is where and how value is added as this is a source of competitive advantage.

value chain analysis analysis to identify where value is added.

value proposition this endows the brand with its unique qualities and benefits that will accrue to the buyer and encourage a relationship with it.

values generalised beliefs about behaviour derived from personal experience and mediated by environment.

variety chain stores multiple retailers offering a wide range of merchandise, e.g. Marks and Spencer.

vertical integration when a firm takes over a different level in the distributive channel, for example, a firm which has become dominant in the extraction or production of a basic raw material may integrate forward into the processing of that raw material into a finished product. Conversely, a manufacturing concern may decide to integrate backwards into primary production in order to achieve control over essential factor inputs. Similarly, firms engaged in primary or secondary industries may perceive advantages through integrating forward into the tertiary sector and achieving control of the distributive function.

vertical marketing system (VMS) a marketing channel which is vertically integrated, either administered (led by one 'channel leader'), contractual (officially organised by a prearranged contract) or corporate (when one firm expands through integration to take on other parts of the system).

viral marketing a process whereby marketing communications are aimed at opinion leaders and then these opinion leaders will spread the message through electronic means.

virtual marketplace a market that has no physical location but exists in cyberspace.

VOIP (Voice Over Internet Protocol) allows voice transmissions over the internet as well as data.

voluntary chains these are groups of independent retailers who agree to use one wholesaler and place minimum regular orders through an agreed system with that wholesaler. In return, the retailer gains from economies on storage and transportation.

warm market in network marketing, the immediate circle of contacts of a distributor.

weak signal management an aspect of environmental analysis that seeks to identify early indications of potential changes so that the organisation can prepare contingency plans for dealing with such changes if they materialise.

web survey a kind of survey method where respondents visit a website and fill out a questionnaire online.

website a collection of 'pages' of information, which can be graphical (including video), textual and aural, and which are available on the Internet to be visited.

wheel of retailing a hypothesis developed by McNair (1958) where new retailers enter the market as low margin, low price operators, then gradually develop into more elaborate companies finally maturing as high cost, high price established businesses.

wholesaler an intermediary in the supply chain that buys in bulk for resale to others.

widening of the market a wider market brings not only increased trading opportunities but also international influence in terms of finance and incentives.

wi-max a development which allows broadband to expand its interconnectivity to a range of 30 miles.

word association tests a projective technique used in motivation research in which the respondent is asked to write down the first thing that comes into their minds when presented with a particular word.

word of mouse word of mouth in the electronic environment, for example, a satisfied customer posting a review of a product on a website.

word of mouth the recommendation of a product to a potential customer by an existing customer. 'Negative' word of mouth is when an existing customer actively discourages a potential customer from purchasing a product.

world wide web information stored on the **internet**

zapping the practice of switching through several channels using a remote control during advertising breaks in programming.

zipping fast forwarding through a pre-recorded broadcast to avoid the commercials.

BIBLIOGRAPHY

Sources cited are usually the original ones. Many texts, e.g. Aaker, de Chernatony and McDonald, Kotler, McDonald etc. have been published in numerous subsequent editions.

Aaker, D.A. (1991) *Managing Brand Equity: Capitalising on the Value of a Brand Name* (New York: The Free Press).

Aaker, D. (1996), *Building Strong Brands*, New York: The Free Press.

Aaker, D. and Joachimsthaler, E. (2000), *Brand Leadership*, (New York: The Free Press).

Abbas, M. (1995), 'Relationship Marketing', unpublished working paper, University of Strathclyde.

Abbott, L. (1955), *Quality and Competition* (New York: Columbia University Press).

Advertising Association, The in Association with WARC, (2005), *The Marketing Pocketbook* (London: WARC).

Aguilar, F. (1967), *Scanning the Business Environment* (New York: Macmillan).

Allen, G.C. (1970), *The Structure of Industry in Britain* (London: Longmans).

AMA (1959), Analysing and Improving Marketing Performance: Marketing Audits.

Ambler, T. (2003), *Marketing and the bottom line*, 2nd edn, (London: FTPrentice Hall).

Ambler, T. and Kokkinaki, F. (1999), 'The assessment of marketing performance', in Baker, M.J. (ed.) *IEBM Encyclopedia of Marketing*, (London: Thomson Learning).

American Management Association (1959), 'The Marketing Audit: its nature, purposes and problems', *Analysing and Improving Market Performance*, Report 32.

Ames, B. C. (1970), 'Trappings Versus Substance in Industrial Marketing', *Harvard Business Review*, July–August.

Ames, B. C. (1971), 'Dilemma of Product/Market Management', *Harvard Business Review*, March–April.

Anderson, J. E. (1956), 'How to Price for Maximum Profits', *Management Methods*, November.

Andreasen, A. R. (1965), 'Attitudes and Customer Behaviour: A Decision Model', in Preston, L. E. (ed.), *New Research in Marketing* (Berkeley: University of California Press).

Andreasen, A. R. (2002), 'Marketing social marketing in the social change marketplace'. *Journal of Public Policy and Marketing*, 21(1), pp.3-13.

Ansoff, H. I. (1968), *Corporate Strategy* (Harmondsworth: Pelican).

Ansoff, H. I. (1988), *New Corporate Strategy* (New York: John Wiley and Sons).

Antonides, G. and van Raaij, W.F. (1998) *Consumer Behaviour, A European Perspective* (England: John Wiley & Sons Ltd.).

Arndt, J. (1984), 'The Anthropology of Marketing Systems: Symbols, Shared Meanings, and Ways of Life in Interorganizational Networks', Paper given at the Proceedings International Research Seminar on Industrial Marketing, Stockholm School of Economics.

Austen, F. (1978), 'The Relevance of Marketing to Developing Countries', Paper to the Marketing Education Group of the United Kingdom, North Region Workshop.

Avlonitis, G. A. (1983), 'The Product-Elimination Decision and Strategies', *Industrial Marketing Management*, 12, pp. 31–43.

Baily, P. J. Farmer, D., Jessop, D. and Jones, D. (1998), *Purchasing Principles and Management*, 8th edn (Harlow: Pearson Education Ltd.).

Baker, M. J. (1975), *Marketing New Industrial Products*, (London: Macmillan).

Baker, M. J. (1980), 'Maxims for Marketing in the Eighties', *Advertising*, 66, Winter.

Baker, M. J. (1983), *Market Development* (Harmondsworth: Penguin).

Baker, M. J. (1991), *Research For Marketing* (London: Macmillan).

Baker, M. J. (1992), *Marketing Strategy and Management*, 2nd edn (Basingstoke: Macmillan).

Baker, M. J. (1994), *The Marketing Book*, 3rd edn (Oxford: Butterworth-Heinemann).

Baker, M. J. (ed.), (1995a), *Companion Encyclopedia of Marketing* (London: Routledge).

Baker, M. J. (ed.), (1995b), *Marketing: Theory and Practice*, 3rd edn (London: Macmillan).

Baker, M. J. (2000), *Marketing Strategy and Management*, 3rd. edn, (Basingstoke: Palgrave). (A new 4th Edition is to be published in 2006).

Baker, M. J. (2003), *Business and Management Research*, (Helensburgh: Westburn Publishers Ltd.).

Baker, M. J. (ed.) (2003), *The Marketing Book*, 5th Edn, (Oxford: Butterworth-Heinemann).

Baker, M. J. and Hart, S. J. (1989), *Marketing and Competitive Success* (London: Philip Allan).

Baker, M. J and Hart, S. J. (1999), *Product Strategy and Management*, (London: Prentice Hall), A revised, Second Edition of this book is due to be published by Pearson in 2006.

Baldwin, Carliss Y. and Clark, Kim B. 'Managing in an age of modularity', Harvard Business Review, Sept/Oct 1997, 75(5): 84-93.

Barlett, C. A. and Ghoshal, S. (1989). *Managing accross borders: The transnational solution*.(Boston: Harvard Business School Press).

Bartels, R. (1968a), 'Are Domestic and International Marketing Dissimilar?', *Journal of Marketing*, July.

Bartels, R. B. (1968b), 'The General Theory of Marketing', *Journal of Marketing*, XXXII, January, pp. 29–30.

Bartels, R. B. (1988), *The History of Marketing Thought*, 3rd edn (Columbus, Ohio: Publishing Horizons Inc.).

Baster, A. J. (1935), *Advertising Reconsidered*.

Bates, J. P. and Parkinson, J. R. (1969), *Business Economics*.

Bateson, J. E. G. (1977), 'Do we need service marketing?', in Eigler, P. (ed.), *Marketing Consumer Services*, (Boston, Mass.: Marketing Science Institute).

Bateson, J. E. G. (1992), *Managing Services Marketing*, 2nd edn (London: Dryden Press).

Bearden, W.O. and Netemeyer, R.G. (1999), *Handbook of Marketing Scales* (Sage Publications Inc.).

Beckerman, W. (1974), *In Defence of Economic Growth* (London: Cape).

Bell, M. (1972), *Marketing: Concepts and Strategy*, 2nd edn (Boston, Mass.: Houghton Mifflin).

Bennett, P. D. and Kasserjian, H.J. (1972), *Consumer Behavior* (Englewood Cliffs, N.J.: Prentice-Hall).

Bennett, R. (1995), *International Marketing: Strategy, Planning, Market Entry and Implementation* (London: Kogan Page).

Bennett, R. and Blythe, J. (2002) *International Marketing: Strategy, Planning, Market Entry and Implementation* 3rd edn, (London: Kogan Page).

Bennett, R. C. and Cooper, R. G. (1982), 'The misuse of Marketing: An American tragedy', *McKinsey Quarterly*, Autumn .

Bernard, K. (1995), in Baker M. J. (ed.), *Marketing: Theory and Practice*, 3rd edn (Basingstoke: Macmillan).

Berry, L. L. (1980), 'Services Marketing is Different', *Business*, May–June, pp. 24–9.

Berry, L. L. (1981), 'The Employee as Customer', *Journal of Retail Marketing*, March.

Berry, L. L. (1983), 'Relationship Marketing' in Berry, L. L., Shostack, G. Lyn and Upatis, G. D. (eds), *Emerging Perspectives on Services Marketing* (Chicago: American Marketing Association).

Berry, L. L., Zeithamil, V. A. and Parasuraman, P. (1985), 'Quality Counts in Services Too', *Business Horizons*, May–June, pp. 44–52.

BIM (1964), *Survey of Manufacturers Marketing Costs* (Information Summary no. 111).

BIM (1966), *Methods of Selecting and Training Salesmen* (Information Summary 87).

BIM (1970), *Marketing Organisation in British Industry* .

Bishop, F. P. (1952), The Ethics of Advertising, cited in Turner, E. S. (1952), *The Shocking History of Advertising* (London: Michael Joseph).

Blackwell, R. D., Miniard, P. W., and Engel, J. F., (2001), *Consumer Behaviour*, 9th edn (London: Dryden Press).

Blois, K. (1982), 'Organisational Structure and Marketing Policies in Service Firms', Paper presented at the 11th Annual Conference of the European Academy for Advanced Research in Marketing, April.

Booms, B. H. and Bitner, M.J. (1981), 'Marketing strategies and Organisation Structures for Service Firms', in *Marketing of Services* (Chicago: American Marketing Association, pp.47-51.

Booth, C. (1889), *The Life and Labour of People in London* (London and New York: Macmillan).

Booz Allen Hamilton (1982), *New Products Management for the 1980s* (New York: Booz Allen Hamilton Inc.).

Borden, N. (1964), 'The Concept of the Marketing Mix', *Journal of Advertising Research*, vol. 4, June, pp. 2-7.

Bowersox, D. J. (1969), 'Physical Distribution Development, Current Status and Potential', *Journal of Marketing*, XXXIII, January, pp. 63–70.

Bowersox, D. J. and Closs, D. J. (1999), 'Logistics and value creation', in Baker, M.J. (ed.) *IEBM Encyclopedia of Marketing*, (London: Thomson Learning).

Bowersox, D. J. and Cooper, M. B. (1992), *Strategic Marketing Channel Management* (New York: McGraw-Hill).

Bradley, F. (2004) *International Marketing Strategy*, 5th edn (FT Prentice-Hall).

Braithwaite, D. (1928), 'The economic effects of advertisement', *Economic Journal*, March, vol. 38, pp. 16–37.

Brand, G. T. (1972), *The Industrial Buying Decision* (London: Cassell Associated Business Programmes).

Brech, E. F. L. (1954), *Principles of Management*, 2nd edn (London: Longman).

British Rate and Data (BRAD).

Brown, R. and Cook, D. (1990), 'Strategy and Performance in British Exporters', *Quarterly Review of Marketing*, Spring.

Brown, S. (1995), 'Retailing', Ch. 24 in *Gower Handbook of Marketing*, 4th edn.

Brownlie, D. (1994), in Baker, M. J. (ed.) *The Marketing Book*, 3rd edn (Oxford: Butterworth Heinemann).

Brownlie, D. (1999a), 'Environmental Analysis', in Baker, M.J. (ed.) *IEBM Encyclopedia of Marketing*, (London: Thomson Learning).

Brownlie, D. (1999b), 'Environmental Scanning' in Baker, M.J. (ed.) *The Marketing Book*, 4th.edn (Oxford: Butterworth-Heinemann).

BS4778:1987 (1987).

Bucklin, L. P. (1968), 'The Locus of Channel Control', *Proceedings of the Fall, 1968, Conference of the AMA*, pp. 142–7.

Bunn, Michele D., (1993), 'Taxonomy of Buying Decision Approaches', *Journal of Marketing*, Vol.57, January , pp38-56.

Cannon, H. and Morgan, F. (1990), 'A Strategic Pricing Framework', *Journal of Consumer Marketing*, vol 17, no. 3, pp. 57–68.

Cardozo, R. (1980), 'Situational Segmentation of Industrial Markets', *European Journal of Marketing*, vol. 14, no. 516.

Carf, C. and Navasky, V. (1984), *The Experts Speak*, New York: Pantheon Books.

Carson, D. (1967), 'Comparative Marketing – A New Old Aid', *Harvard Business Review*, May–June.

Carson, D. (1995) 'Customer care and satisfaction', Ch. 43 in Baker, M. J. (ed), Companion Encyclopedia of Marketing (London: Routledge) .

Carson, D. and Gilmore, A. (1989–90), 'Customer Care: the neglected domain', I*rish Marketing Review*, 4(3), pp. 49–61.

Carson, D. and Gilmore, A. (1993–4), 'Enhancing Service Quality: A Case Study', *Irish Marketing Review*, 6, pp. 64–73.

Cass, T. (1968), 'Making Decisions in Marketing', *Marketing Forum*, May–June, pp. 15–24.

Caves, R. (1972), *American Industry: Structure, Conduct and Performance*, 3rd edn (Englewood Cliffs, N.J.: Prentice-Hall).

Chamberlin, E. J. (1933), *The Theory of Monopolistic Competition* (Cambridge, Mass.: Harvard University Press).

Chamberlin, E. J. (1957), *Towards a More General Theory of Value* (New York: Oxford University Press).

Chan, K. C. and McDermott, M. C. (1995), 'Beyond Relationship Marketing: Flexible and Intelligent Relationship Management Strategy (FIRMS), Ch. 21 in Baker M. J. (ed.), *Marketing: Theory and Practice*, 3rd edn (Basingstoke: Macmillan).

Chandler, A. D. (1962), *Strategy and Structure* (Cambridge, Mass.: MIT Press).

Chapell, Alan (2004), The Good Word on Word of Mouth [WWW] http://www.imediaconnection. com/content/4677.asp (Accessed on 9th June, 2005).

Chase, R. B. (1978), 'Where Does the Consumer Fit in a Service Operation?', *Harvard Business Review*, vol. 56, November–December, pp. 137–42.

Cherington, P. T. (1920), *The Elements of Marketing* (London: Macmillan).

Chisnall, P. M. (1992), *Marketing Research*, 4th edn (New York: McGraw-Hill). (7th edn 2004).

Chonke, L. B. and Hunt, S. D. (1985), 'Ethics and Marketing Management: An Empirical Investigation', *Journal of Business Research*, 13.

Chote, R. (1995), 'Decay of the Dismal Science', *Financial Times*, 28 March.

Christopher, M. (1992), *Logistics and Supply Chain Management* (London: Pitman).

Christopher, M. (1997), *Marketing Logistics*, (Oxford: Butterworth-Heinemann).

Christopher, M. and Payne, A. (2003), 'Integrating customer relationship management and supply chain management', in Baker, M.J. (ed.) *The Marketing Book*, 5th. Edn, (Oxford: Butterworth Heinemann).

Christopher, M. G., Kennedy, S. H., McDonald, M. M. and Wills, G. S. C. (1980), *Effective Marketing Management* (Aldershot: Gower).

Chung, E. K. and Heeler, R. M. (1995), 'The Economic Basis of Marketing' in Baker M. J. (ed.), *Companion Encyclopedia of Marketing* (London: Routledge).

Churchill, G. A. Jr (1976), *Marketing Research: Methodological Foundations* (Fort Worth: Holt-Saunders/ Dryden Press), pp. 206–7.

Clark, J. M. (1961), *Competition as a Dynamic Process* (Washington D.C.: Brookings Institution).

Clarke, R. (1993), 'Trends in Concentration in UK Manufacturing, 1980–89', Ch. 7 in Casson, M. and Creedy, J. (eds), *Industrial Concentration and Economic Inequality* (Aldershot: Edward Elgar Publishing Ltd).

Clawson, J. (1950), 'Lewin's Psychology and Motives in Marketing', in Cox, R. and Alderson, W. (eds), Theory in Marketing (Glencoe, Ill.: Irwin).

Clewett, R. J. and Stasch, S. F. (1975), 'Shifting Role of the Product Manager', Harvard Business Review, January–February.

Club of Rome (1972), *Report* (The Limits to Growth).

Coad, T. (1990), 'The Emergence of Marketing Databases and their Uses', *Direct Marketing Handbook* (Telephone Marketing Services, British Telecom).

Coad, T. (1993), *Marketing Business Magazine*, October.

Cole, H. S. D. et al. (1973), *Thinking About the Future* (London: Chatto & Windus for Sussex University Press).

Colley, R. H. (1961), *Defining Advertising Goals* (New York: Association of National Advertisers).

Collins, M. (1986), 'Sampling' in Worcester, R. and Downham, J., *Consumer Market Research Handbook*, 3rd edn (ESOMAR).

Conference Board, The (1974), 'Why Products Fail'.

Congdon, P. (2001), *Bayesian Statistical Modelling*, (Chichester: John Wiley and Sons).

Constantinides C (2005), 'The Impact Of Web Experience on Virtual Buying Behaviour: An empirical study', *Journal of Customer Behaviour* Vol4, No. 3.

Converse, P. D. H., Huegy, H. W. M. and Mitchell, R. V. (1965), *Elements of Marketing*, 7th edn (Englewood Cliffs, N.J.: Prentice-Hall).

Cooper R. G. (1999), 'New product development', in Baker, M.J. (ed.) *IEBM Encyclopedia of Marketing*, (London: Thomson Learning).

Cooper R. G. (2005), *Product Leadership: pathways to profitable innovation*, 2nd edn (New York: Basic Books).

Copeland, M. T. (1923), 'Relation of Consumers' Buying Habits to Marketing Methods', *Harvard Business Review*, April.

Corner, E. and Paine, F. A (2002), *Market Motivators: The Special Worlds of Packaging and Marketing*, (Cookham: CIM Publishing).

Coulter, K. and Sarkis, J. (2005), 'Development of a media selection model', *International Journal of Advertising*, Vol. 24, No. 2, pp. 193-215.

Courtauld, S. (1962), *Economic Journal*, April.

Cowell, D. (1984), *The Marketing of Services* (Oxford: Heinemann).

Cowell, D. (1995), *The Marketing of Services*, 2nd edn (London: Heinemann).

Cox, O. and Enis, B. (1973), *Experimentation for Marketing Decisions* (London: Intext).

Cravens, D. W. (1988), 'Gaining Strategic Marketing Advantage', *Business Horizons*, September–October, pp. 44–54.

Crosby, P. B. (1979), Quality is Free (New York: McGraw-Hill).

Crosier, K. (1975), 'What Exactly is Marketing?' *Quarterly Review of Marketing*, Winter.

Crosier, K. (1983), 'Toward a praxiology of advertising', *International Journal of Advertising*, Vol. 2, No. 3, (July-Sept).

Crosier, K. (1994), 'Promotion' in Baker, M.J. (ed.) *The Marketing Book*, 3rd edn. (London: Butterworth-Heinemann).

Crosier, K. (1995a),'Marketing communications', Ch. 37 in Baker, M. J. (ed), *Companion Encyclopedia of Marketing* (London: Routledge).

Crosier, K. (1995b) 'Marketing Communications', Ch. 13 in Baker, M. J. (ed), *Marketing: Theory and Practice*, 3rd ed .

Crosier, K. (2003), 'Promotion', in Baker, M.J. (ed.) *The Marketing Book*, 5th edn., (Oxford: Butterworth Heinemann).

Czinkota, M. and Ronkainen, I. K. (2003) *International Marketing*, 7th edn (South Western College Publishing).

Dalton, G. (1974), *Economic Systems and Society* (Harmondsworth: Penguin).

Dart, P.(1999), 'Packaging and Design', in Baker, M.J. (ed.) *IEBM Encyclopedia of Marketing*, (London: Thomson Learning).

Davidson, H. (1981), 'How and Why Shoppers Buy', *Marketing*, 28 October.

Davis, Scott M. (2002), *Brand Asset Management*, San Francisco: CA: Jossey-Bass.

Day, G. S. (1977), 'Diagnosing the Product Portfolio', *Journal of Marketing*, April.

Day, G. S. and Wensley, R. (1988), 'Assessing Advantage: A Framework for Diagnosing Competitive Superiority', *Journal of Marketing*, Vol 52, April, pp.1-20.

de Chernatony, L. and McDonald, M. H. B. (1992), *Creating Powerful Brands* (Oxford: ButterworthHeinemann).

de Rouffignac, P. D. (1990), *Packaging in the Marketing Mix* (Oxford: Butterworth-Heinemann).

Deal, T. E. and Kennedy, A. A. (1982), *Corporate Cultures* (Reading, Mass.: Addison Wesley).

Dean, J. (1951), *Managerial Economics* (New York: Prentice-Hall).

DeLozier, M. W. (1976), *The Marketing Communications Process* (New York: McGraw-Hill).

Deming, W. E. (1982), *Out of the Crisis* (Cambridge, Mass: MIT Press).

Desmond, J. (2002), *Consuming Behaviour*, (Basingstoke: Palgrave Macmillan).

Diamantopoulos, A. (1995), 'Pricing' in Baker M. J. (ed.), *Marketing: Theory and Practice*, 3rd edn (Basingstoke: Macmillan).

Diamantopoulos, A., (2003), 'Pricing' in Baker M.J. (ed.), *The Marketing Book*, 5th. edn, (Oxford: Butterworth Heinemann).

Diamontopoulos, A. and Mathews, B. (1995), *Making Pricing Decisions* (London: Chapman and Hall).

Dibb, S., Simpkin, L., Pride, W. M. and Ferrell, O. C. (1994), *Marketing Concepts and Strategies*, 2nd European edition (London: Houghton Mifflin).

Dobele, Angela, Toleman, David and Beverland, Michael (2005), 'Controlled infection! Spreading the brand message through viral marketing'. *Business Horizons*. Greenwich: Mar/Apr 2005. Vol. 48, Iss. 2; p. 143.

Donaldson, W. G. (1990), 'Sales Management' in Baker, M.J. (ed.), *Marketing: Theory and Practice*, 3rd edn (London: Macmillan).

Donaldson, W.G. (1998), *Sales Management* 2nd edn (Basingstoke:Macmillan).

Donaldson, W. G. (1999), 'Personal selling and sales management', in Baker, M.J. (ed.) *IEBM Encyclopedia of Marketing*, (London: Thomson Learning).

Donaldson, W. G. (2003), 'Selling and Sales Management' Chapter 14 in Baker, M.J. (ed.) *The Marketing Book*, 5th. edn, (Oxford: Butterworth-Heinemann).

Donnelly, J. H. Jr (1976), 'Marketing Intermediaries in Channels of Distribution of Services', *Journal of Marketing*, vol. 40(1), January, pp. 55–7.

Donnelly, J. H. Jr and George, W. R. (eds), (1981), *Marketing of Services* (Chicago: American Marketing Association).

Douglas, S. P. and Craig, C. S. (1995), *Global Marketing Strategies* (New York: McGraw-Hill).

Dowling, G. (1994), 'Searching for a New Advertising Agency: A Client Perspective', *International Journal of Advertising*, 13, pp. 229–42.

Doyle, P. (1999), 'Product life-cycle management', in Baker, M.J. (ed.) *IEBM Encyclopedia of Marketing*, (London: Thomson Learning).

Drakeford, J. F. and Farbridge, V. (1986), 'Interviewing and Field Control', Ch. 6 in Worcester, R. and Downham, J. *Consumer Market Research Handbook*, 3rd edn (ESOMAR).

Drucker, P. F. (1954), *The Practice of Management* (New York: Harper & Row).

Drucker, P. F. (1958), 'Marketing and Economic Development', *Journal of Marketing*, January, pp. 252–9.

Drucker, Peter F. (2001), *The Essential Drucker*, (New York, NY: Harper Collins Publishers Inc.).

Dudley, J. (1992), *Strategies for the Single Market* (London: Kogan Page).

Duke, R. (1991), 'Post-Saturation Competition in UK Grocery Retailing', *Journal of Marketing Management*, vol. 7(1).

Dussart, C. (1994), in Baker, M. J., *Perspectives on Marketing Management* (Chichester: John Wiley).

Easton, G. (1992), *Learning From Case Studies*, 2nd edn (Englewood Cliffs, N.J.: Prentice-Hall).

Ehrenberg, A. S. C and Goodhart, G. J. (1980), 'How Advertising Works', in *Understanding Buyer Behaviour* (New York: J. Walter Thompson/Market Research Corporation of America).

Eiglier, P. and Langeard, E. (1977), 'A New Approach to Service Marketing'. in *Marketing Consumer Services: New Insights Report* (Boston: Marketing Science Institute), pp. 77–115.

Elliot, D. (1974), 'Concentration in UK Manufacturing Industry', *Trade and Industry*, 1st August.

Engel, J. F. et al. (1972), *Marketing Segmentation* (New York: Holt, Rinehart & Winston).

Engel, J. F., Blackwell, R. D. and Miniard, P. W. (1995), *Consumer Behavior*, 8th edn (Fort Worth: The Dryden Press).

Engel, J. F., Kollat, D. T. and Blackwell, R. D. (1978), *Consumer Behavior* (New York: Holt, Rinehart & Winston).

Enis, B. (1980), *Marketing Principles* 3rd edn. (Santa Moncia, CA: Goodyear).

Enis, B. and Roaring, K. (1981), 'Service Marketing: Different Product, Similar Strategy', in Donnelly, J. H. Jr and George, W. R. (eds), *Marketing of Services* (Chicago: American Marketing Association).

Ennis, S. (1995), 'Channel Management', Chap 12 in Baker, M. J. (ed), *Marketing: Theory and Practice*, 3rd ed (London: Macmillan).

Erdogan, Z. (1998), personal communication.

Evans, F. B. (1959), 'Psychological and Objective Factors in the Prediction of Brand Choice: Ford vs. Chevrolet', *Journal of Business*, vol. 32, October.

Evans and Worster (1997) 'Strategy and the new economics of information', *Harvard Business Review*, September-October.

Fahad, P.G.A. (1986)'Group discussions: a misunderstood technique', *Journal of Marketing Management*, Vol 1. No. 3, pp.315-27.

Feigenbaum, A. V. (1991), *Total Quality Control*, 3rd edn (New York: McGraw-Hill).

Feldwick (1996) 'What is brand equity anyway, and how do you measure it?', *Journal of Market Research Society*, 38 (2), 85-104.

Ferber, R. and Verdoorn, P. J. (1962), *Research Methods in Economics and Business* (New York: Collier-Macmillan).

Ferguson, P. (1988), *Industrial Economics: Issues and Perspectives* (Basingstoke: Macmillan).

Fernie, J. (2003), 'Changes in the Supply Chain', Chapter 4 in *Marketing Changes*, Ed. Susan Hart, (London: Thomson).

Festinger, L. A. (1957), *A Theory of Cognitive Dissonance* (New York: Row and Peterson).

Financial Times/IMR (1974), 'How British Industry Buys', *Financial Times*.

Fishbein, M. and Ajzen, I. (1975), *Belief, Attitude, Intention and Behaviour* (Reading, Mass.: AddisonWesley).

Fletcher, K. (1986), 'Social Behaviour: an analysis of information and usage during the decision process', unpublished PhD, University of Stathclyde.

Fletcher, K. (1995), *Marketing Management and Information Technology*, 2nd edn (London: PrenticeHall).

Ford, D. (ed.) (1997), *Understanding Business Markets*, (London: The Dryden Press).

Ford, D. (ed.), (1990), *Understanding Business Markets: Interaction of Relationships and Networks* (London: Academic Press).

Foster, P. (2005), *The Times*, 16th April.

Foster, P. and Davis, J. (1994), *Mastering Marketing*, 3rd edn (Basingstoke: Macmillan).

Foxall, G. R. (1983), *Consumer Choice* (London: Macmillan).

Foxall, G. R. (1987), 'Radical Behaviourism and Consumer Research: Theoretical Promise and Empirical Problems', *International Journal of Research in Marketing*, vol. 4, pp. 111–29.

Foxall G. R. (2003), 'Consumer decision-making: process, level and style, in Baker M. J. (ed.), *The Marketing Book* 5th edn., (Oxford: Butterworth-Heinemann).

Foxall, G. R. (2005), *Understanding Consumer Choice*, (Basingstoke: Palgrave Macmillan).

Frank, R., Massy, W. and Wind, J. (1972), *Market Segmentation* (Englewood Cliffs, N.J.: Prentice-Hall).

Frederick, J. (2005), 'Australia Trounces France', *The Sunday Times*, 16th April.

Fullerton, R. A. (1988), 'How Modern is Modern Marketing?', *Journal of Marketing*, Vol.52 No. 1, January, pp. 108-25.

Gabbott, M. and Hogg, G. (eds) (1997), *Contemporary Services Marketing Management A Reader*, (London: The Dryden Press).

Gabor, A. (1980), *Pricing Principles and Practice* (London: Heinemann), Ch. 10, pp. 168–76.

Galbraith, J. K. (1958), *American Capitalism: The Concept of Countervailing Power* (Boston: Houghton Mifflin).

Galbraith, J. K. (1958), *The Affluent Society* (Harmondsworth: Penguin).

Galbraith, J. K. (1974), *The New Industrial State* (London: Penguin).

Gallagher, W. J. (1969), *Report Writing for Management* (Reading, Mass.: Addison-Wesley).

Gardner, C. A. (1986), 'Dissertation Proposal' (Washington DC: George Washington University).

Gattorna, J. L. (Ed.), (2003), *Handbook of supply chain management*, (Aldershot: Gower Publishing).

Gilbert, D. and Bailey, N. (1990), 'The Development of Marketing – A Compendium of Historical Approaches', *Quarterly Review of Marketing*, Winter.

Gofton, K. (1984), 'What Moves the Client?' *Marketing*, 27 September.

Goodfellow, J. H. (1983), 'The Marketing of Goods of Services as a Multidimensional Concept', *The Quarterly Review of Marketing*, Spring, pp. 19–27.

Gordon, W. and Langmaid, R. (1988), *Qualitative Market Research* (Aldershot: Gower).

Green, P. E. and Carmone, F. J. (1970), *Multidimensional Scaling and Related Techniques in Marketing Analysis* (Boston: Allyn & Bacon).

Green, P. E. and Tull, D. S. (1978), *Research for Marketing Decisions*, 4th edn (Englewood Cliffs, N.J.: Prentice-Hall).

Green, P.E., Tull, D. S. and Albaum, G. (1988), *Research for Marketing Decisions*, 5th edn. (Englewood Cliffs, N.J.: Prentice Hall).

Green, P. E., Tull, D. and Albaum, G. (1993), *Research for Marketing Decisions*, 6th edn (Englewood Cliffs, N.J.: Prentice-Hall).

Grönroos, C. (1980), 'Designing a Long Range Marketing Strategy for Services', *Long Range Planning*, vol. 13(2), pp. 36–42.

Grönroos, C. (1981), 'Internal Marketing – an Integral Part of Marketing theory', in Donnelly, J. H. Jr and George, W. R. (eds), *Marketing of Services* (Chicago: American Marketing Association), pp. 236–8.

Grönroos, C. (1982), *Strategic Management and Marketing in the Service Sector* (Helsinki: Swedish School of Economics and Business Administration).

Grönroos, C. (1984), 'A Service Quality Model', *European Journal of Marketing*, vol. 18(4).

Grönroos, C. (1985), *Strategic Marketing: Marketing in Service Industries* (Oxford: Chartwell-Bratt).

Grönroos, C. (1989), 'A Relationship Approach to Marketing of Services: Some Implications', *Proceedings from the 18th Annual Conference of the European Marketing Academy* (Greece: Athens School of Economics and Business Science).

Gummesson, E. (1979), 'The Marketing of Professional Services: An Organisational Dilemma', *European Journal of Marketing*, vol. 13(5), pp. 308–18.

Gunter, B. and Furnham, A.(1992), *Consumer Profiles. An introduction to psychographics.* (London: Routledge).

Hakansson, H. (ed) (1982), *International Marketing and Purchasing of Industrial Goods* (New York: John Wiley).

Halbert, M. (1965), *The Meaning and Sources of Marketing Theory* (New York: McGraw-Hill).

Haley, R.I. (1968), 'Benefit Segmentation', *Journal of Marketing*, vol. 32, pp. 30–5.

Halfpenny P. (1979), 'The Analysis of Qualitative Data', *Sociological Review*, 27 April.

Hammond, J.S. III (1967), 'Better Decisions with Preference Theory', *Harvard Business Review*, November–December, pp. 123–41.

Hamner and Champney (1993), *Corporate Reputation, the Brand and the Bottom Line* (Kogan Page).

Hart, S. J. (1987), 'The Use of the Survey in Industrial Marketing Research', *Journal of Marketing Management*, 3 (Summer).

Hart, S. J. (ed.) (2003), *Marketing Changes*, (London: Thomson).

Hastorf, A. H. and Cantril, H. (1954), 'They Saw a Game: A Case History', *Journal of Abnormal and Social Psychology*, vol. 49, pp. 129–34.

Hawkins, E. R. (1954), 'Price Policies and Theories', *Journal of Marketing*, XVIII, January, pp. 233–40.

Haynes, W. W. (1962), *Pricing Decisions in Small Business* (Lexington: University of Kentucky Press).

Haywood, R. (1995), 'Public relations', Ch. 41 in Baker, M. J. (ed) *Companion Encyclopedia of Marketing* (London: Routledge).

Haywood, R. (2005), *Corporate Reputation, The Brand and The Bottom Line* 3rd edn (Kogan Page).

Heeler, R. M., and Chung, E. K. (1999), 'The economics basis of marketing', in Baker, M.J. (ed.) *IEBM Encyclopedia of Marketing*, (London: Thomson Learning).

Hewson, C., Yule, P. Laurent, D. and Vogel, C. (2003), *Internet Research Methods: a practical guide for the social and behavioural sciences*, (London: Sage).

Hilgard, E. (1967), *Introduction to Psychology* (Harcourt Brace).

Hill, R. W. (1973), *Marketing Technological Products to Industry* (Oxford: Pergamon).

Hill, R. W. and Hillier, T. J. (1977), *Organisational Buying Behaviour* (London: Macmillan).

Hill, T. and Westwood, R. (1997),'SWOT Analysis: it's time for a product recall', *Long Range Planning*, vol.30 no. 1, February, pp.46-52.

Hisrich and Peters (1991) *Marketing Decisions for New and Mature Products* 2nd edn.

Hisrich, R.D. Peters M.P. and Shepherd, D.A. (2004), *Entrepreneurship* (McGrawHill Education).

Hobson (1956), *Selection of Advertising Media* Business Publications on Behalf of the IPA

Holmes, C. (1986), 'Multivariate Analysis of Market Research Data', Ch. 13 in Worcester, R. and Downham, J., *Consumer Market Research Handbook*, 3rd edn (ESOMAR).

Hooley, G. J. (1980), 'Multivariate Jungle – The Academics' Playground but the Managers' Minefield', *European Journal of Marketing*, 14, pp.379–448.

Hooley, G., Saunders, J. and Piercy, N. (2003), *Marketing Strategy and Competitive Positioning*, 3rd. edn, (Harlow: Pearson Education Limited).

Hooley, G. J., West, C. J. and Lynch, J. E. (1983), *Marketing in the UK: A Survey of Current Practice and Performance* (Institute of Marketing)

Howard J. A. and Sheth, J. N. (1969), *Theory of Buyer Behaviour* (Wiley).

Huber, G. P. (1984), 'The Nature and Design of Post-Industrial Organizations', *Management Science*, Vol. 30, No. 8, August, 1984, pp. 928- 951.

Hull, C. (1943), *Principles of Behaviour: An Introduction to Behaviour Theory* (New York: Appleton Century Crofts).

Hutchinson, P. (1970), 'The Complementary Benefit Principle of How Advertising Works in Relation to the Product', Paper given at the Market Research Society Annual Conference.

Hutt, M. D. and Speh, T. W. (2004), *Business Marketing Management*, 8th edn (Fort Worth: Dryden Press).

Institute of Management (1999), *Business Checklists: Marketing and Strategy*, (Hodder and Stoughton).

Jain, S. C. (1993), *International Marketing Management*, 4th edn (Wadsworth).

Jeannet, J. P. and Hennessey, H. D. (2004) Global *Marketing Strategies*, 6th edn (Boston: Houghton Mifflin).

Johansson, J. K. and Nonaka, I. (1987), 'Market Research the Japanese Way', *Harvard Business Review*, vol. 65, May–June.

Johns, T. (2002), 'eService Strategy', *Marketing Insights*, October –December 2002.

Johnson, H. (1961), *Money, Trade and Economic Growth*, 2nd edn (London: Allen and Unwin), .

Johnson, M. (1984), 'Supermarket Scientists', *Marketing*, 13 September.

Johnson, S. C. and Jones, C. (1957), 'How to Organise for New Products', *Harvard Business Review*, vol. 35, May–June.

Juran. J. M. (ed.), (1988), *Quality Control Handbook* (New York: McGraw-Hill).

Jurvetson, S. (2000), 'What is Viral Marketing?' [WWW] http://www.dfj.com/cgi-bin/artman/publish/steve_may00.shtml (Accessed on 9th June, 2005).

Kahle, L.R., Beatty, S.E. and Homer, P. (1986), 'Alternative measurement approaches to consumer value: the List of Values (LOV), and Values and Lifestlyes (VALS)'. *Journal of Consumer Research*, 13, pp. 405-409.

Katz, E. (1957), in Robertson, T. S., *Innovative Behaviour and Communications* (New York: Holt, Rinehart & Winston), p. 180.

Kast, F.E. and Rosenzweig, J.E. (1974), *Organisation and Management: A System Approach*, 2nd edn (Maidenhead: McGraw-Hill).

Katzenbach, J.R. and Smith, D.K. (1993). *The wisdom of teams: Creating the high-performance organization*, (Boston: Harvard Business School).

Kennedy, A. (1983) 'Buyer Behaviour' Chap 5 in Baker, M. J. (ed), *Marketing: Theory and Practice* 2nd edn(Basingstoke: Macmillan).

Key Note Publications Ltd (1989), *Sales Promotion*, London.

Keynotes (1992), *Meat and Meat Products*.

Keynote (2005), *Green and Ethical Consumer* February 2005, Keynote.

Kindleberger, C. (1958), Economic Development (New York: McGraw-Hill).

King, S. (1991), 'Brand Building in the 1990's', *Journal of Marketing Management*, vol. 7(1).

Kinnear, T. C. and Taylor, J. R. (1996), *Marketing Research: An Applied Approach*, 5th edn (London: McGraw-Hill).

Klass, B. (1961), 'What Factors Affect Industrial Buying Decisions?', *Industrial Marketing*.

Kohler, W. (1925), *The Mentality of Apes* (New York: Harcourt, Brace and World).

Kotler, P. (1988), *Marketing Management: Analysis, Planning, Implementation and Control*, 6th edn (Englewood Cliffs, N.J.: Prentice-Hall).

Kotler, P. and Andreasen, A. R. (1991), *Strategic Marketing for Non-profit Organisations*, 4th edn (Englewood Cliffs, N.J.: Prentice-Hall).

Kotler, P. and Andreasen, A. R. (1995), 'Strategic Marketing for Non-Profit Organisations', Ch. 53 in Baker, M. J. (ed.), *Companion Encyclopedia of Marketing* (London: Routledge).

Kotler, P. and Armstrong, G. (1993), *Marketing: an Introduction*, 3rd edn (Englewood Cliffs, N.J.: Prentice-Hall).

Kotler, P. and Bloom, P. N. (1984), *Marketing Professional Services* (Englewood Cliffs, N.J.: Prentice-Hall).

Kotler, P. and Levy, S. (1969a), 'Broadening the Concept of Marketing', *Journal of Marketing*, vol. 33, January.

Kotler, P. and Levy, S. (1969b), 'Beyond Marketing: The Furthering Concept', *California Management Review*, Winter, vol. XII, no. 2.

Kotler, P., Gregor, W. and Rodgers, W. (1977), 'The Marketing Audit Comes of Age', *Sloan Management Review*, Winter, Vol 18, No. 2 pp. 25-43.

Krech, D., Crutchfield, R. and Ballachey, E. (1962), *Individual in Society* (New York: McGraw-Hill).

Kubr, M. (ed.), (1976), *Management Consulting: A Guide to the Profession* (Geneva: ILO).

Lambert D. M. (1978), *The Distribution Channels Decision* (New York: The Society of Management Accountants and National Society of Accountants).

Lancioni, R. (2000). 'New developments in supply chain management for. the millennium'. *Industrial Marketing Management*, 29, 1–6.

Lancioni, R.(2005), 'Pricing issues in industrial marketing', Editorial in *Industrial Marketing Management*, Volume 34, Number 2 February 2005.

Lanzillotti, R. (1956), 'Pricing Objectives in Large Companies', *American Economic Review*, XLVIII, December, pp. 921–40.

Lawson, R. W. (1988), 'The Family Life Cycle: A Demographic Analysis', *Journal of Marketing Management*, Summer.

Lazarsfeld, P. F. (1944), *The People's Choice* (Sloan and Pearce).

Lee, K.and Carter, S. (2005), *Global Marketing Management*, (Oxford: Oxford University Press).

Lehmann, O. R. and O'Shaughnessy, G. (1974), 'Difference in Attribute Importance for Different Industrial Products', *Journal of Marketing*, April.

Levitt, T. (1960), 'Marketing Myopia', *Harvard Business Review*, July–August.

Levitt, T. (1974), *Marketing for Business Growth* (New York: McGraw-Hill).

Levitt, T. (1976), 'Industrialisation of Service', *Harvard Business Review*, September–October, pp. 63–74.

Levitt, T. (1983), *The Augmented Product Concept*.

Levitt, T. (1983), 'The Globalisation of Markets', *Harvard Business Review*, May–June.

Levitt, T. (1983), *The Marketing Imagination* (New York: Free Press).

Lewis, B. R. (1989), 'Customer Care in Service Organisations', *Marketing Intelligence and Planning*, vol. 7(5/6), pp. 18–22.

Lidstone, L. (1983), 'Putting Force Back Into Sales', *Marketing*, 22 September.

Lowe, A. (1988), 'The Marketing of Services', Unit 19, University of Strathclyde MCom in Marketing for Industrialising Countries by Distance Learning (Glasgow: University of Strathclyde).

Lucey, J. (1987), *Management Information Systems*, 5th edn (Eastleigh: DP Publications).

McBurnie, T. and Clutterbuck, D. (1987), *The Marketing Edge* (Harmondsworth: Pengiun).

McCarthy, E. J. (1966), *Basic Marketing* (Homewood, Ill.: Irwin).

McCarthy, E. J. and Perreault, W. D. Jnr. (1994), *Basic Marketing*, 8th edn (Homewood, Ill.: Irwin).

McClelland, W. G. (1966), *Costs and Competition in Retailing* (London: Macmillan).

McConkey, D. D. (1988), 'Planning in a Changing Environment', *Business Horizons*, September–October.

McCorkell, G. (2003), 'What are direct marketing and interactive marketing?', Chapter 22 in Baker, M.J.(ed) *The Marketing Book*, 5th edn., (Oxford: Butterworth-Heinemann).

McDermott, L., Stead, M. and Hastings, G. (2005), 'What Is and What Is Not Social Marketing: The Challenge of Reviewing the Evidence', *Journal of Marketing Management* 21, pp.545-553.

McDonald, E. H. and Stromberger, T. L. (1969), 'Cost Control for the Professional Service Firm', *Harvard Business Review*, January–February, pp. 109–21.

McDonald, M. (1999), 'Developing and implementing a marketing plan', in Baker, M.J. (ed.) *IEBM Encyclopedia of Marketing*, (London: Thomson Learning).

McDonald, M. (2003), 'Strategic marketing planning: theory and practice', in Baker, M.J. (ed.) *The Marketing Book*, 5th edn, (Oxford: Butterworth-Heinemann).

McDonald, M.and Dunbar, I. (2005), *Market Segmentation: How to do it, How to profit from it*, (Elsevier Butterworth Heinemann).

McDonald, W. J. (1998), *Direct Marketing: An Integrated Approach*, (Boston: McGraw-Hill).

MacFadyen, L., Stead, M., and Hastings, G. B. (2003), 'Social marketing' in Baker, M. J. (ed.), *The Marketing Book*, 5th edn. (Oxford: Butterworth Heinemann).

McFarlane-Smith, J. (1972), *Interviewing in Market and Social Research* (London: Routledge and Kegan Paul).

McGivern, C. (1983), 'Some Facets of the Relationship Between Consultants and Clients in Organisations', *Journal of Managment Studies*, vol. 20(3), pp. 367–86.

McGoldrick, P. (2003), 'Retailing' in Baker, M.J. (ed.) *The Marketing Book*, 5th edn, (Oxford: Butterworth-Heinemann).

McKitterick, J. B. (1957), 'What is the Marketing Management Concept?', in Frank M. Bass (ed.), *The Frontiers of Marketing Thought and Science*, (Chicago; American Marketing Association), pp. 71-81.

McLuhan, M. (1965), Understanding Media: the Extensions of Man (London: McGraw-Hill).

Magnuson, W. G. (1972), 'Consumerism and the Emerging Goals of a New Society', in Gaedeke, R. M. and Etcheson, W. W. (eds), *Consumerism* (San Fransisco: Canfield Press).

Mann, C. and Stewart, F. (2000), *Internet Communication and Qualitative Research: a handbook for researching online*, (London: Sage).

Mansfield, E. (1966), *The Economics of Technological Change* (New York: W. W. Norton).

Marketing Week (1995), 'Media Speak', *Marketing Week*, 26 January, p. 90.

Markin, R. (1982), *Marketing Strategy and Management* (New York: John Wiley).

Markin, R. and Narayana (1976), 'Behaviour Control: Are Consumers Beyond Freedom and Dignity', *Advances in Consumer Research*, vol. 2, pp. 222–8.

Marshall, A. (1919), *Industry and Trade* (London).

Maslow, A. (1943), 'A Theory of Human Motivation', *Psychological Review*, 50.

Matthews, J. B., Buzzell, R., Levitt, T. and Frank, N. (1964), *Marketing: An Introductory Analysis* (New York: McGraw-Hill).

Mayer, D. and Greenberg, H. (1964), 'What Makes a Good Salesman?', *Harvard Business Review*, XLII, July–August, pp. 119–25.

Mayer, M. (1958), *Madison Avenue* (Harmondsworth: Penguin).

Meadows, D. et al. (1972), *Limits to Growth* (London: Earth Island).

Meffert, H. and Kirchgeog, M. (1995), 'Green Marketing', in Baker, M. J. (ed.), *Companion Encyclopedia of Marketing* (London: Routledge).

Miles, I. (1990), 'Teleshopping: Just Around the Corner?', *RSA Journal*, February.

Millar, R. (1993), *Marketing Business Magazine*, June.

Millman, F. (1983), 'Price Wars', *Quarterly Review of Marketing*, January.

Mitchell, J. (1974), *How to Write Reports* (London: Fontana).

Möller, K. and Wilson, D. (1999), 'Business Marketing', in Baker, M.J. (ed.) *IEBM Encyclopedia of Marketing*, (London: Thomson Learning).

Morgan, A. (1976), *A Guide to Consumer Promotions*, 2nd edn (Ogilvy Benson and Mather).

Moroney, M. J. (1956), *Facts From Figures* (London: Pelican).

Morrison, A. and Wensley, R. (1991), 'Boxing Up or Boxed In? A Short History of the Boston Consulting Group Share/Growth Matrix', *Journal of Marketing Management*, vol. 7(2).

Mortishead, C. (2004), The Times, 21st September.

Morton-Williams, J. (1986), 'Questionnaire Design', Ch. 5 in Worcester, R. and Downham, J. *Consumer Market Research Handbook*, 3rd edn (ESOMAR).

Moser, C. (1961), *British Towns: A Statistical Study of their Social and Economic Differences* (London: Oliver and Boyd).

Moser, C. and Kalton, G. (1971), *Survey Methods in Social Investigation*, 2nd edn (Oxford: Heinemann Educational Books).

Moss, C. D., Thorne, P. and Fasey, P. (1963), 'The Distribution of Coupons', *Quarterly Review of Marketing*, January.

Mueller-Heumann, G. (1992), 'Market Fragmentation and Mass Customisation', *Journal of Marketing Management*, vol. 8, pp. 303–14.

Murphy, C. (1994), 'Own Goal', *Marketing Week*, 19 August, p. 28.

Nader, R. (1965), *Unsafe at any Speed* (New York: Grossman).

Naisbitt, J. (1982), *Megatrends: Ten new directions transforming our lives*, (New York: Warner Books, Inc.).

Nanus, B. (1982), 'QUEST – Quick Environment Scanning Technique', in *Long Range Planning*, vol. 15, no. 2, pp. 39–45.

National Readership Survey.

Newton, D. (1969), 'Get the Most Out of Your Field Sales Force', *Harvard Business Review*, September–October, pp. 130–43.

Nicosia, F. M. (1966), *Consumer Decision Processes* (Englewood Cliffs, N.J.: Prentice-Hall).

Normann, R (1985), *Service Management: Strategy and Leadership in Service Businesses* (London: John Wiley).

Nylen, D.W. (1990) *Marketing decision-making handbook*, (New Jersey: Prentice-Hall Inc).

Ó Dochartaigh, N. (2002), *The Internet Research Handbook*, (London: Sage).

O'Brien, S. and Ford, R. (1988), 'Can We at Last Say Goodbye to Social Class', *Journal of the Market Research Society*, vol. 30, no. 3, July.

O'Guinn, T. C., Allen, C. T., and Semenik, R. J. (2006), *Advertising and Integrated Brand Promotion*, Fourth edn, (Mason, OH: Thomson South-Western).

O'Reilly, D. (1995), 'Unit 3: The Buying Situation', University of Strathclyde, MSc in Procurement Management, Organisational Buying Behaviour.

Oakland, J. (1995), in Baker, M. J. (ed.), *Companion Encyclopedia of Marketing* (London: Routledge), pp. 957–8.

Oburai, P. and Baker, M. J. (2005), 'International Marketing Strategies in India: An Application of Mixed Method Investigation', *Vikalpa: The Journal for Decision Makers*, Vol. 30, 4, October-December, pp.11-23.

Office of Fair Trading (1985), *Competition in Retailing*, June.

Ogilvy, D. (1965), *Confessions of an Advertising Man* (New York: Dell).

Ogilvy, D. (1983), *Ogilvy on Advertising*, London: Pan Book) .

Ogilvy, Benson and Mather (1985), *A Guide to Consumer Promotions*, 2nd edn (A. Morgan).

Ohmae, K. (1982), *The Mind of the Strategist* (Harmondsworth: Penguin).

Oppenheim, A. N. (2000), *Questionnaire Design, Interviewing and Attitude Measurement*, (New York: Continuum International Publishing Group).

Osgood, C. et al. (1952), *Method and Theory in Experimental Psychology* (New York: Oxford University Press).

Oxenfeld, A. R. (1975), 'The Marketing Audit as a Total Evaluation Programme'. *Pricing Strategies* (New York: AMACOM).

Packard, V. (1957), *Hidden Persuaders* (London: Longmans Green).

Packard, V. (1961), *The Waste Makers* (London: Longmans Green).

Paliwoda, S. J. (1995), *International Marketing*, 2nd edn (London: Heinemann).

Paliwoda, S. and Ryans, J. K. Jr (1993), *International Marketing Reader* (London: Routledge).

Palmer, A. (2000), *Principles of Marketing*, (USA: Oxford University Press) .

Palmer, A. (2003). 'The marketing of services', in Baker, M.J. (ed.) *The Marketing Book*, 5th edn, (Oxford: Butterworth-Heinemann).

Parasuraman, A., Grewal, D. and Krishnan, R. (2004), *Marketing Research*, (Houghton Mifflin).

Parkinson, S. T. and Baker, M. J. (1986), *Organisational Buying Behaviour* (London: Macmillan).

Patterson, M. and O'Malley, L. (2000), 'The Evolution of the Direct Marketing Consumer', *The Marketing Review*, Volume 1, Number 1, pp.89-102.

Payne, S. L. (1951), *The Art of Asking Questions* (Princeton University Press).

Pearce, D. W. (ed.), (1981), *Dictionary of Modern Economics* (London: Macmillan).

Peattie, K. (1999), 'Sales Promotion', in Baker, M.J. (ed.) *IEBM Encyclopedia of Marketing*, (London: Thomson Learning).

Peattie, K. and Charter, M. (1994), 'Green Marketing', in Baker, M. J. (1994), *The Marketing Book*, 3rd edn (Oxford: Butterworth-Heinemann).

Peattie, S. and Peattie, K. (2003), 'Sales Promotion', in Baker, M.J. (ed.) *The Marketing Book*, 5th edn, (Oxford: Butterworth-Heinemann).

Perry, C. (2005), *Marketing Week*, 22nd July.

Peters, T. and Waterman, R. (1982), *In Search of Excellence* (New York: Harper and Row).

Peterson, C. (1984), 'Cinderella in the Limelight', *Marketing*, November.

Piercy, N. F. (1985), *Marketing Organisation* (London: George Allen & Unwin).

Piercy, N. F. (2002), *Market Led Strategic Change: A Guide to Transforming the Process of Going to Market*, 3rd. edn, (Oxford: Butterworth-Heinemann).

Piercy, N. F. (2003), 'Marketing implementation, organisational change and internal marketing strategy', in Baker, M.J. (ed.) *The Marketing Book*, 5th edn, (Oxford: Butterworth-Heinemann).

Piercy, N. F. and Cravens, D. W. (1995), in Baker, M. J. (ed.), *Companion Encyclopedia of Marketing* (London: Routledge).

Piercy, N. F. and Cravens, D. W. (1999), 'Marketing organisation and management', in Baker, M.J. (ed.) *IEBM Encyclopedia of Marketing*, (London: Thomson Learning).

Pilditch, J. (1973), *The Silent Salesman* (London: Business Books).

Pinxt, L. (1984), 'A Nation of Importers', *Marketing*, 4 October.

Porter, M. (1980), *Competitive Strategy: Techniques for Analyzing Industries and Competitors* (New York: Free Press).

Porter, M. E. (1985), *Competitive Advantage* (New York: Free Press).

Porter, M. E. (1990), *The Competitive Advantage of Nations* (London: Macmillan).

Porter, M. (1996), 'What is Strategy?', *Harvard Business Review*, Nov/Dec.

Prebble, J. (2005), 'Packaging - what will the 21st century require?' Working Paper (Pira International Ltd).

Price, Christopher (2005), 'Top Ten Technology Trends for 2005', *The Sunday Times*, 2nd January.

Quelch, J. A., Buzzell, R. D. and Salama, E. R. (1990), *The Marketing Challenge of 1992* (Reading, Mass.: Addison-Wesley).

Quelch, J. A., and Harrington, A. (2005), 'Samsung Electronics Company: Global Marketing Operations', Harvard Business School, February. Case 9-504-051.

Quinlan, F. (1981), 'The Use of Social Grading in Marketing', *Quarterly Review of Marketing*, Autumn.

Rajagopal, S. (1995), Ch. 5 in Baker, M. J. (ed.), *Marketing: Theory and Practice*, 3rd edn (London: Macmillan).

Rathmell, J. M. (1974), *Marketing in the Service Sector* (London: Winthrop).

Reeves, R. (1970), 'Reality in Advertising', in O. Klepner and I. Settell (eds), *Exploring Advertising* (Englewood Cliffs, N.J.: Prentice-Hall).

Reichheld, Frederick F., (1996), *The Loyalty Effect*, (Boston, MA: Harvard Business School Press).

Reichheld, Frederick F., (Ed.), (1996), *The Quest for Loyalty*, A Harvard Business Review Book, (Boston, MA: Harvard Business School Press).

Reid, W. and Myddelton, D. R. (1971), *The Meaning of Company Accounts* (Aldershot: Gower Press).

Resnik, A. H., Turney, P. B. B. and Mason, J. B. (1979), 'Marketers Turn to Counter-Segmentation', *Harvard Business Review*, September/October.

Reynolds, F.D. and Wells, W. D. (1977), *Consumer Behavior* (McGraw-Hill).

Ries, A. and Trout, J. (1972), 'The Positioning Era', *Advertising Age*.

Ries, A. and Trout, J. (1986), *Positioning: The Battle For Your Mind* (New York: McGraw-Hill).

Robertson, T. S. (1970), *Consumer Behaviour* (Glenview, Ill.: Scott Foresman).

Robertson, T. S. (1971), *Innovative Behaviour and Communications* (New York: Holt, Rinehart & Winston).

Robinson R. J. and Stidsen, B. (1967), *Selling in a Modern Perspective* (Boston: Allyn & Bacon).

Robinson, J. (1933), *The Economics of Imperfect Competition* (London: Macmillan).

Robinson, P. J. and Luck, D. J. (1964), *Promotional Decision Making Practice and Theory*, Marketing Science Institute series (New York: McGraw-Hill).

Robinson, P. J., Faris, C. W. and Wind, Y (1967), *Industrial Buying and Creative Marketing* (Boston: Allyn & Bacon).

Rodger, L. W. (1971), *Marketing in a Competitive Economy*, 3rd edn (London: Cassell).

Rodocanachi, P. (1983), 'The Successful Management of New Products in the 1980's', Paper given at ESOMAR seminar on New Product Development, (Athens, November 1983).

Rogers, E.M. (2003) *Diffusion of Innovations*, 5th edn (The Free Press).

Rosenbloom, B. (1995), 'Channels of Distribution', in Baker, M. J. (ed.), *Companion Encyclopedia of Marketing* (London: Routledge), pp. 137–54.

Rosenbloom, B. (1999), 'Channel management', in Baker, M.J. (ed.) *IEBM Encyclopedia of Marketing*, (London: Thomson Learning).

Rosenbloom, B. (1999), 'Channels of distribution'. in Baker, M.J. (ed.) *IEBM Encyclopedia of Marketing*, (London: Thomson Learning).

Rostow, W. W. (1962), *The Process of Economic Growth*, 2nd edn (New York: McGraw-Hill).

Rothman, J. (1986), 'Experimental Designs and Models', Ch. 3 in Worcester, R. and Downham, J. *Consumer Market Research Handbook*, 3rd edn (ESOMAR).

Rothman, J. (1989), 'Editorial', *Journal of the Market Research Society*, vol. 31, no. 1, January.

Rothwell, R., Gardiner, P. and Schott, K (1983), *Design and the Economy* (London: The Design Council).

Rushe, D. (2004), *The Sunday Times*, 14th November.

Said, H. (1981), 'The Relevance of Price Theory to Price Practise', unpublished PhD Dissertation, University of Strathclyde, Scotland.

Sampson, P. (1967), 'Commonsense in Qualitative Research', *Commentary*, vol. 9, no. 1, January.

Sampson, H. (1874), *History of Advertising*.

Samuelson, P. (1989), *Economics: An Introductory Analysis*, 13th edn (New York: McGraw-Hill),

Sasser, W. E. (1976), 'Matching Supply and Demand in Service Industries', *Harvard Business Review*, November–December, pp. 133–40.

Scherer, F. M. and Ross, D. (1990), *Industrial Market Structure and Economic Performance*, 3rd edn (Boston: Houghton-Mifflin).

Schiffman, L. and Kanuk, L. (1994), *Consumer Behaviour*, 5th edn (Englewood Cliffs, N.J.: PrenticeHall).

Schlaifer, R. (1969), *Analysis of Decisions Under Uncertainty* (New York: McGraw-Hill).

Schramm, W. (1995), *The Process and Effects of Mass Communication* (Urbana, Ill.: University of Illinois Press).

Schuchman, A (1959) 'The Marketing Audit: Its nature, purposes, and problems', *Analyzing and Improving Marketing Performance*, Report No. 32 (New York: American Management Association).

Schultz, D. E. and Kitchen, P. J., 'Integrated Marketing Communications in U.S. Advertising Agencies: An Exploratory Study', *Journal of Advertising Research*, 37 (5), (September-October): 7-18.

Scott, B. (1984), 'National Strategy for Stronger US Competitiveness', *Harvard Business Review*, March– April.

Servan-Schreiber, J. J. (1967), *The American Challenge* (London: Hamish Hamilton).

Seymour, B (1984), 'Centres of Attraction', *Marketing*, 6 September.

Shams, H. (1989), 'Incremental Consumption and the Purchase of Experiential Products', Unpublished PhD Dissertation, University of Surrey, England.

Shannon, C. and Weaver, W. (1962), *The Mathematical Theory of Communication* (Urbana, Ill.: University of Illinois Press).

Sherrington, M. (1999), 'Branding and Brand Management', in Baker, M.J. (ed.) *IEBM Encyclopedia of Marketing*, (London: Thomson Learning).

Sheth, J. N. (1973), 'A Model of Industrial Buyer Behaviour', *Journal of Marketing*, October Vol. 37, 4, pp.50-6.

Sheth, J., N., Mittal, B., and Newman, B. I., (1999), *Customer Behavior*, (Orlando: The Dryden Press).

Shimp, T. A., (2003), *Advertising, Promotion*, 6th. edn, (Mason, OH: Thomson South-Western).

Shoemaker, F. (1971), *Communications of Innovations*, 2nd edn (New York: Free Press).

Shostack, G. L. (1977), 'Breaking Free From Product Marketing', *Journal of Marketing*, vol. 41(2), pp. 73–80.

Shostack, G. L. (1982), 'How to Design a Service', *European Journal of Marketing*, vol. 16(1), pp. 49–63.

Shostack, G. L. (1984), 'Designing Services that Deliver', *Harvard Business Review*, January– February, pp. 133–9.

Simon, H. (1989), *Price Management* (Amsterdam: Elsevier Science Publishers).

Sizer, J. (1989), *An Insight into Management Accounting*, 3rd edn (Harmondsworth: Penguin).

Skinner, A. (ed.), (1970), *The Wealth of Nations* by Adam Smith (Harmondsworth: Pelican Books).

Smith, A. [1776] *The Wealth of Nations*.

Smith, N. C. (1995), 'Marketing ethics' Ch. 52 in Baker, M. J. (ed), *Companion Encyclopedia of Marketing* (London: Routledge).

Smith, W. (1956), 'Product Differentiation and Market Segmentation as Alternative Marketing Strategies', *Journal of Marketing*, July.

Sperling, A. D. (1967), *Psychology Made Simple* (London: W. H. Allen).

Stanton, N. J. (1981), *Fundamentals of Marketing* (New York: McGraw-Hill).

Stapleton, Jo. and Thomas, M.(1998), *How to Prepare a Marketing Plan*, 5th. edn, (Aldershot: Gower Press).

Stephenson, C. P. (1968), 'What is a Product?', British Agents Review, reprinted in *Marketing Forum*, March/April.

Stern, L. I. et al. (1989), *Management of the Marketing Channel* (Englewood Cliffs, N.J.: Prentice-Hall).

Sternthal, B. and Craig, C. S. (1982), *Consumer Behaviour: An Information Processing Perspective* (Englewood Cliffs, N.J.: Prentice-Hall).

Stevens, S. N. (1958), 'The Application of Social Science Findings to Selling and the Salesman', Aspects of Modern Marketing, *AMA Management Report no. 15* (New York: AMA).

Stewart, Bill (2004), *Packaging Design Strategies*, 2nd. edn, (Leatherhead: Pira International Ltd.).

Strauss, G. (1962), 'Tactics of Lateral Relationships: The Purchasing Agent', *Administrative Science Quarterly*, 7 September.

Swasy, A. (1989), 'Sales lost their Vim? Try Repackaging', *Wall Street Journal*, 11 October.

Tarver, J.L. (1987), 'In Search of a Competitive Edge in Banking: A Personnel Approach', *International Bank Marketing*, vol. 5(1), pp. 61–8.

Taylor, A. H. (1974), *Costing: A Management Approach, Pan Management Series* (London: Pan).

Technology Foresight Programme (1995), *Progress Through Partnership* (Office of Science and Technology).

Tedlow, R. S. and Jones, G. (eds), (1993), 'The Fourth Phase of Marketing', in Tedlow, R. S. and Jones, G. (eds) *The Rise and Fall of Mass Marketing* (London: Routledge).

Tedlow, R. S. and Jones, G. (eds), (1993), *The Rise and Fall of Mass Marketing* (London: Routledge).

Thomas, M. (1980), 'Market Segmentation', *Quarterly Review of Marketing*, vol. 6, no. 1.

Thomas, M. (1981), 'Customer Care: The Ultimate Marketing Tool', in Wensley, R. (ed.), *Reviewing Effective Research and Good Practise in Marketing* (Warwick: Marketing Education Group), pp. 283–94.

Thomas, M. J. (1982), 'Product Management vs. Market Management', *Quarterly Review of Marketing*, Summer 1982, pp. 22–5.

Thomas, M. J. (1989), *The Marketing Handbook*, 3rd edn (Aldershot: Gower).

Thompson, H. U. (1962), *Product Strategy*.

Toffler, A. (1971), *Future Shock*, (London: Pan).

Toffler, A. (1984), *Previews and Promises* (London: Pan).

Torgerson, W. (1958), *Theory and Methods of Scaling* (Wiley).

Tracy, E. (1984), 'Testing Time for Test Marketing', *Fortune*, 29 October.

Treadgold, A. and Davies, R. L. (1988), *The Internationalization of Retailing* (Harlow: Longman).

Trott, P. (2005), *Innovation Management and New Product Development*, 3rd. edn, (Harlow: Prentice-Hall).

Tull, D.S. and Hawkins, D. I. (1993), *Marketing Research: Measurement and Method*, 6th edn, (New York: Macmillan) .

Tull, D. S. and Hawkins, D. I. (1992), *Marketing Research: Measurement and Method*, (West Drayton: Macmillan).

Turnbull, P. and Cunningham, M. (1980), *International Marketing and Purchasing* (London: Macmillan).

Ughanwa, D. O. and Baker, M. J. (1989), *The Role of Design in International Competitiveness* (London: Routledge).

UK Institute of Public Relations (1994).

Underwood, R. (1993), Paper at the AMA Winter Educators' Conference, Proceedings, pp. 212–17.

Unwin, S. (1975), 'Customised Communications: A Concept for Service Advertising', *Advertising Quarterly*, vol. 44, Summer, pp. 18–30.

Usunier, J. C. (1993), *International Marketing: A Cultural Approach* (Englewood Cliffs, N.J.: PrenticeHall).

Usunier, J. C. and Lee, J. (2005), *Marketing Across Cultures* 4th edn (Upper Saddle River, NJ.: Prentice Hall).

Van Riel, C. B. M. (1995), *The Principles of Corporate Communications* (Englewood Cliffs, N.J.: PrenticeHall).

Van Weele, A. J, (2005), *Purchasing and Supply Chain Management*, 4th edn, (London: Thomson Learning.

Vargo, Stephen L. and Lusch, Robert F. (2004) 'Evolving to a New Dominant Logic of Marketing, *Journal of Marketing*, Vol 68, No. 1.

Walker, A. H. and Lorsch, J. W. (1968), 'Organizational Choice: Product vs. Function', *Harvard Business Review*, XLIV, vi, November–December, pp. 129–38.

Ward, K. (2003), 'Controlling marketing and the measurement of marketing effectiveness', in Baker, M.J. (ed.) *The Marketing Book*, 5th edn, (Oxford: Butterworth Heinemann).

Warner, W. L. (1960), *Social Class in America* (New York: Harper & Row).

Waterson, M. (1993), 'Are Industrial Economists Still Interested in Concentration?', in Casson, M. and Creedy, J. (eds), *Industrial Concentration and Economic Inequality* (Aldershot: Edward Elgar).

Watts, B. K. R. (1978), *Business and Financial Management*, 3rd edn (M and E Handbooks), ch. 10. Webster, F. Jr (1965), 'Modelling the Industrial Buying Process', *Journal of Marketing Research*, November.

Webb, J. (2002), *Understanding and Designing Marketing Research* 2nd edn. (London: International Thomson).

Webster, F. Jr (1992), 'The Changing Role of Marketing in the Corporation', *Journal of Marketing*, Vol.56, October, pp. 1-17.

Webster, F. Jr and Wind, Y. (1972), 'A General Model for Understanding Organisational Buying Behaviour', *Journal of Marketing*, April, Vol. 36, 2, pp.12-14.

Webster, F. E. and Wind, Y. (1972), *Organisational Buying Behavior*, (Englewood Cliffs, NJ: Prentice-Hall).

Wells, W. D. (1975), 'Psychographics: A Critical Review', *Journal of Marketing Research*, vol. XII, May, pp. 196–213.

West, C (1999), 'Marketing research' in Baker, M. J. (ed), *IEBM Encyclopedia of Marketing*, (London: Thomson Learning).

Wheatcroft, Patience (2005), Editorial (Business), *The Times*, 16th April.

Wickham, R. G., Fitzroy, P. T. and Mandry, G. D. (1975), 'Marketing of Services: An Evaluation of the Theory', *European Journal of Marketing*, vol. 9(1), pp. 59–67.

Wilkie, W. K. (1994), *Consumer Behaviour*, 3rd edn, (John Wiley).

Williams, J. (1984), 'Picking the winners', *Marketing*, 26 April.

Williamson, O. E. (1975), *Markets and Hierarchies: Analysis and Antitrust Implications* (New York: Free Press).

Wilson, A. (1972), *The Marketing of Professional Services* (London: McGraw-Hill).

Wilson, A. (2003), *Marketing Research: an integrated approach*, (Harlow: Pearson Education Limited).

Wilson, D. (1999), *Organizational Marketing*, (London: International Thomson Business Press).

Wilson, R. (2004), *Marketing Week*, 4th March.

Wilson, R. M S.(1999), *Accounting for Marketing*, (London: Thomson).

Wind, Y. (1976), 'Organisational Buying Centres: A Research Agenda' in Zaltman, G. and Bonoma, T. V. (eds), *Organisational Buying Behaviour* (AMA).

Wind, Y. (1978), 'Issues and Advances in Segmentation Research', *Journal of Marketing Research*, August.

Wind, Y. (1995), 'Market Segmentation', in Baker, M. J. (ed.), *Companion Encyclopedia of Marketing* (London: Routledge).

Wind, Y. (1999), 'Market Segmentation' in Baker, M.J. (ed.) *IEBM Encyclopedia of Marketing*, (London: Thomson Learning).

Wind, Y. and Douglas, S. (1972), 'International Market Segmentation', *European Journal of Marketing*, vol. 5, no. 1.

Winkler, J. (1986), *Pricing for Results* (London: Pan Books).

Winkler, J. (1991), 'Pricing', Ch. 16 in Baker, M.J. (ed), *The Marketing Book* 2nd edn (London: Heinemann).

Woodside, A. G. and Rosha, R. (1999), ' Direct marketing: advancing to integrated (Internet), communications' in Baker, M.J. (ed.) *IEBM Encyclopedia of Marketing*, (London: Thomson Learning).

Worcester, R. M. and Downham, J. (1988), *Consumer Market Research Handbook*, 3rd edn (London: Van Nostrand Reinhold).

Yasumuro, K. (1993), 'Conceptualising an Adaptable Marketing System', pp. 205–35 in Tedlow, R. S. and Jones, G. (eds), *The Rise and Fall Of Mass Marketing*, (London: Routledge).

Yeshin, T. (2006), *Advertising*, (London: Thomson).

Yip, G. S. (1992), *Total Global Strategy: Managing for Worldwide Competitive Advantage* (Englewood Cliffs, N.J.: Prentice-Hall).

Yip, G. S. (2003) *Total Global Strategy II* (Upper Saddle River, NJ.: Prentice Hall).

Yorke, D. A. (1990), 'Interactive Perceptions of Suppliers and Corporate Clients in the Marketing of Professional Services: A Comparison of Accounting and Legal Services in the UK, Canada and Sweden', *Journal of Marketing Management*, vol. 5(3), pp. 307–23.

Young, S., Hamill, J. and Wheeler, C. (1989), *International Market Entry and Development: Strategy and Management* (Brighton: Wheatsheaf).